MIPS Reference Data

CORE INSTRUCTION SET

NAME, MNEMONIC	FORMAT	OPERATION (in Verilog)	OPCODE / FUNCT (Hex)
Add	add	R	$R[rd] = R[rs] + R[rt]$ (1)	$0 / 20_{hex}$
Add Immediate	addi	I	$R[rt] = R[rs] + SignExtImm$ (1,2)	8_{hex}
Add Imm. Unsigned	addiu	I	$R[rt] = R[rs] + SignExtImm$ (2)	9_{hex}
Add Unsigned	addu	R	$R[rd] = R[rs] + R[rt]$	$0 / 21_{hex}$
And	and	R	$R[rd] = R[rs] \& R[rt]$	$0 / 24_{hex}$
And Immediate	andi	I	$R[rt] = R[rs] \& ZeroExtImm$ (3)	c_{hex}
Branch On Equal	beq	I	if($R[rs]==R[rt]$) PC=PC+4+BranchAddr (4)	4_{hex}
Branch On Not Equal	bne	I	if($R[rs]!=R[rt]$) PC=PC+4+BranchAddr (4)	5_{hex}
Jump	j	J	PC=JumpAddr (5)	2_{hex}
Jump And Link	jal	J	$R[31]$=PC+8;PC=JumpAddr (5)	3_{hex}
Jump Register	jr	R	PC=R[rs]	$0 / 08_{hex}$
Load Byte Unsigned	lbu	I	$R[rt]=\{24'b0,M[R[rs]+SignExtImm](7:0)\}$ (2)	24_{hex}
Load Halfword Unsigned	lhu	I	$R[rt]=\{16'b0,M[R[rs]+SignExtImm](15:0)\}$ (2)	25_{hex}
Load Linked	ll	I	$R[rt] = M[R[rs]+SignExtImm]$ (2,7)	30_{hex}
Load Upper Imm.	lui	I	$R[rt] = \{imm, 16'b0\}$	f_{hex}
Load Word	lw	I	$R[rt] = M[R[rs]+SignExtImm]$ (2)	23_{hex}
Nor	nor	R	$R[rd] = \sim (R[rs] \mid R[rt])$	$0 / 27_{hex}$
Or	or	R	$R[rd] = R[rs] \mid R[rt]$	$0 / 25_{hex}$
Or Immediate	ori	I	$R[rt] = R[rs] \mid ZeroExtImm$ (3)	d_{hex}
Set Less Than	slt	R	$R[rd] = (R[rs] < R[rt]) ? 1 : 0$	$0 / 2a_{hex}$
Set Less Than Imm.	slti	I	$R[rt] = (R[rs] < SignExtImm) ? 1 : 0$ (2)	a_{hex}
Set Less Than Imm. Unsigned	sltiu	I	$R[rt] = (R[rs] < SignExtImm) ? 1 : 0$ (2,6)	b_{hex}
Set Less Than Unsig.	sltu	R	$R[rd] = (R[rs] < R[rt]) ? 1 : 0$ (6)	$0 / 2b_{hex}$
Shift Left Logical	sll	R	$R[rd] = R[rt] << shamt$	$0 / 00_{hex}$
Shift Right Logical	srl	R	$R[rd] = R[rt] >>> shamt$	$0 / 02_{hex}$
Store Byte	sb	I	$M[R[rs]+SignExtImm](7:0) = R[rt](7:0)$ (2)	28_{hex}
Store Conditional	sc	I	$M[R[rs]+SignExtImm] = R[rt]$; $R[rt] = (atomic) ? 1 : 0$ (2,7)	38_{hex}
Store Halfword	sh	I	$M[R[rs]+SignExtImm](15:0) = R[rt](15:0)$ (2)	29_{hex}
Store Word	sw	I	$M[R[rs]+SignExtImm] = R[rt]$ (2)	$2b_{hex}$
Subtract	sub	R	$R[rd] = R[rs] - R[rt]$ (1)	$0 / 22_{hex}$
Subtract Unsigned	subu	R	$R[rd] = R[rs] - R[rt]$	$0 / 23_{hex}$

(1) May cause overflow exception
(2) SignExtImm = { 16{immediate[15]}, immediate }
(3) ZeroExtImm = { 16{1b'0}, immediate }
(4) BranchAddr = { 14{immediate[15]}, immediate, 2'b0 }
(5) JumpAddr = { PC+4[31:28], address, 2'b0 }
(6) Operands considered unsigned numbers (vs. 2's comp.)
(7) Atomic test&set pair; R[rt] = 1 if pair atomic, 0 if not atomic

BASIC INSTRUCTION FORMATS

R	opcode	rs	rt	rd	shamt	funct
	31 26	25 21	20 16	15 11	10 6	5 0

I	opcode	rs	rt	immediate
	31 26	25 21	20 16	15 0

J	opcode	address
	31 26	25 0

NAME, MNEMONIC	FORMAT	OPERATION	/ FUNCT (Hex)
Branch On FP True	bc1t	FI	if(FPcond)PC=PC+4+BranchAddr (4)	11/8/1/--
Branch On FP False	bc1f	FI	if(! FPcond)PC=PC+4+BranchAddr (4)	11/8/0/--
Divide	div	R	Lo=R[rs]/R[rt]; Hi=R[rs]%R[rt]	0/--/--/1a
Divide Unsigned	divu	R	Lo=R[rs]/R[rt]; Hi=R[rs]%R[rt] (6)	0/--/--/1b
FP Add Single	add.s	FR	$F[fd]= F[fs] + F[ft]$	11/10/--/0
FP Add Double	add.d	FR	$\{F[fd],F[fd+1]\} = \{F[fs],F[fs+1]\} + \{F[ft],F[ft+1]\}$	11/11/--/0
FP Compare Single	c.x.s*	FR	$FPcond = (F[fs]\ op\ F[ft]) ? 1 : 0$	11/10/--/y
FP Compare Double	c.x.d*	FR	$FPcond = (\{F[fs],F[fs+1]\}\ op\ \{F[ft],F[ft+1]\}) ? 1 : 0$	11/11/--/y
* (x is eq, lt, or le) (op is ==, <, or <=) (y is 32, 3c, or 3e)				
FP Divide Single	div.s	FR	$F[fd] = F[fs] / F[ft]$	11/10/--/3
FP Divide Double	div.d	FR	$\{F[fd],F[fd+1]\} = \{F[fs],F[fs+1]\}/ \{F[ft],F[ft+1]\}$	11/11/--/3
FP Multiply Single	mul.s	FR	$F[fd] = F[fs] * F[ft]$	11/10/--/2
FP Multiply Double	mul.d	FR	$\{F[fd],F[fd+1]\} = \{F[fs],F[fs+1]\} * \{F[ft],F[ft+1]\}$	11/11/--/2
FP Subtract Single	sub.s	FR	$F[fd]=F[fs] - F[ft]$	11/10/--/1
FP Subtract Double	sub.d	FR	$\{F[fd],F[fd+1]\} = \{F[fs],F[fs+1]\} - \{F[ft],F[ft+1]\}$	11/11/--/1
Load FP Single	lwc1	I	$F[rt]=M[R[rs]+SignExtImm]$ (2)	31/--/--/--
Load FP Double	ldc1	I	$F[rt]=M[R[rs]+SignExtImm]$; $F[rt+1]=M[R[rs]+SignExtImm+4]$ (2)	35/--/--/--
Move From Hi	mfhi	R	$R[rd] = Hi$	0/--/--/10
Move From Lo	mflo	R	$R[rd] = Lo$	0/--/--/12
Move From Control	mfc0	R	$R[rd] = CR[rs]$	10/0/--/0
Multiply	mult	R	$\{Hi,Lo\} = R[rs] * R[rt]$	0/--/--/18
Multiply Unsigned	multu	R	$\{Hi,Lo\} = R[rs] * R[rt]$ (6)	0/--/--/19
Shift Right Arith.	sra	R	$R[rd] = R[rt] >> shamt$	0/--/--/3
Store FP Single	swc1	I	$M[R[rs]+SignExtImm] = F[rt]$ (2)	39/--/--/--
Store FP Double	sdc1	I	$M[R[rs]+SignExtImm] = F[rt]$; $M[R[rs]+SignExtImm+4] = F[rt+1]$ (2)	3d/--/--/--

FLOATING-POINT INSTRUCTION FORMATS

FR	opcode	fmt	ft	fs	fd	funct
	31 26	25 21	20 16	15 11	10 6	5 0

FI	opcode	fmt	ft	immediate
	31 26	25 21	20 16	15 0

PSEUDOINSTRUCTION SET

NAME	MNEMONIC	OPERATION
Branch Less Than	blt	if($R[rs]<R[rt]$) PC = Label
Branch Greater Than	bgt	if($R[rs]>R[rt]$) PC = Label
Branch Less Than or Equal	ble	if($R[rs]<=R[rt]$) PC = Label
Branch Greater Than or Equal	bge	if($R[rs]>=R[rt]$) PC = Label
Load Immediate	li	$R[rd] = immediate$
Move	move	$R[rd] = R[rs]$

REGISTER NAME, NUMBER, USE, CALL CONVENTION

NAME	NUMBER	USE	PRESERVED ACROSS A CALL?
$zero	0	The Constant Value 0	N.A.
$at	1	Assembler Temporary	No
$v0-$v1	2-3	Values for Function Results and Expression Evaluation	No
$a0-$a3	4-7	Arguments	No
$t0-$t7	8-15	Temporaries	No
$s0-$s7	16-23	Saved Temporaries	Yes
$t8-$t9	24-25	Temporaries	No
$k0-$k1	26-27	Reserved for OS Kernel	No
$gp	28	Global Pointer	Yes
$sp	29	Stack Pointer	Yes
$fp	30	Frame Pointer	Yes
$ra	31	Return Address	Yes

OPCODES, BASE CONVERSION, ASCII SYMBOLS ③

MIPS opcode (31:26)	(1) MIPS funct (5:0)	(2) MIPS funct (5:0)	Binary	Decimal	Hexadecimal	ASCII Character	Decimal	Hexadecimal	ASCII Character
(1)	sll	add.f	00 0000	0	0	NUL	64	40	@
		sub.f	00 0001	1	1	SOH	65	41	A
j	srl	mul.f	00 0010	2	2	STX	66	42	B
jal	sra	div.f	00 0011	3	3	ETX	67	43	C
beq	sllv	sqrt.f	00 0100	4	4	EOT	68	44	D
bne		abs.f	00 0101	5	5	ENQ	69	45	E
blez	srlv	mov.f	00 0110	6	6	ACK	70	46	F
bgtz	srav	neg.f	00 0111	7	7	BEL	71	47	G
addi	jr		00 1000	8	8	BS	72	48	H
addiu	jalr		00 1001	9	9	HT	73	49	I
siti	movz		00 1010	10	a	LF	74	4a	J
sltiu	movn		00 1011	11	b	VT	75	4b	K
andi	syscall	round.w.f	00 1100	12	c	FF	76	4c	L
ori	break	trunc.w.f	00 1101	13	d	CR	77	4d	M
xori		ceil.w.f	00 1110	14	e	SO	78	4e	N
lui	sync	floor.w.f	00 1111	15	f	SI	79	4f	O
	mfhi		01 0000	16	10	DLE	80	50	P
(2)	mthi		01 0001	17	11	DC1	81	51	Q
	mflo	movz.f	01 0010	18	12	DC2	82	52	R
	mtlo	movn.f	01 0011	19	13	DC3	83	53	S
			01 0100	20	14	DC4	84	54	T
			01 0101	21	15	NAK	85	55	U
			01 0110	22	16	SYN	86	56	V
			01 0111	23	17	ETB	87	57	W
	mult		01 1000	24	18	CAN	88	58	X
	multu		01 1001	25	19	EM	89	59	Y
	div		01 1010	26	1a	SUB	90	5a	Z
	divu		01 1011	27	1b	ESC	91	5b	[
			01 1100	28	1c	FS	92	5c	\
			01 1101	29	1d	GS	93	5d	]
			01 1110	30	1e	RS	94	5e	^
			01 1111	31	1f	US	95	5f	_
lb	add	cvt.s.f	10 0000	32	20	Space	96	60	`
lh	addu	cvt.d.f	10 0001	33	21	!	97	61	a
lwl	sub		10 0010	34	22	"	98	62	b
lw	subu		10 0011	35	23	#	99	63	c
lbu	and	cvt.w.f	10 0100	36	24	$	100	64	d
lhu	or		10 0101	37	25	%	101	65	e
lwr	xor		10 0110	38	26	&	102	66	f
	nor		10 0111	39	27	'	103	67	g
sb			10 1000	40	28	(	104	68	h
sh			10 1001	41	29	)	105	69	i
swl	slt		10 1010	42	2a	*	106	6a	j
sw	sltu		10 1011	43	2b	+	107	6b	k
			10 1100	44	2c	,	108	6c	l
			10 1101	45	2d	-	109	6d	m
swr			10 1110	46	2e	.	110	6e	n
cache			10 1111	47	2f	/	111	6f	o
ll	tge	c.f.f	11 0000	48	30	0	112	70	P
lwcl	tgeu	c.un.f	11 0001	49	31	1	113	71	q
lwc2	tlt	c.eq.f	11 0010	50	32	2	114	72	r
pref	tltu	c.ueq.f	11 0011	51	33	3	115	73	s
	teq	c.olt.f	11 0100	52	34	4	116	74	t
idc1		c.ult.f	11 0101	53	35	5	117	75	u
ldc2	tne	c.ole.f	11 0110	54	36	6	118	76	v
		c.ule.f	11 0111	55	37	7	119	77	w
sc		c.sf.f	11 1000	56	38	8	120	78	x
swc1		c.ngle.f	11 1001	57	39	9	121	79	y
swc2		c.seq.f	11 1010	58	3a	:	122	7a	z
		c.ngl.f	11 1011	59	3b	;	123	7b	{
		c.lt.f	11 1100	60	3c	<	124	7c		
sdcl		c.nge.f	11 1101	61	3d	=	125	7d	}
sdc2		c.le.f	11 1110	62	3e	>	126	7e	~
		c.ngt.f	11 1111	63	3f	?	127	7f	DEL

(1) opcode) 31:26) == 0

(2) opcode(31:26) == 17_{ten} (11_{hex}); if fmt(25:21)==16_{ten} (10_{hex}) $f = $ s (single);
if fmt(25:21)==17_{ten} (11_{hex}) $f = $ d (double)

IEEE 754 FLOATING-POINT STANDARD ④

$$(-1)^S \times (1 + \text{Fraction}) \times 2^{(\text{Exponent - Bias})}$$

where Single Precision Bias = 127,
Double Precision Bias = 1023

IEEE 754 Symbols

Exponent	Fraction	Object
0	0	± 0
0	$\neq 0$	$\pm$ Denorm
1 to MAX - 1	anything	$\pm$ Fl. Pt. Num.
MAX	0	$\pm \infty$
MAX	$\neq 0$	NaN

S.P. MAX = 255, D.P. MAX = 2047

IEEE Single Precision and Double Precision Formats:

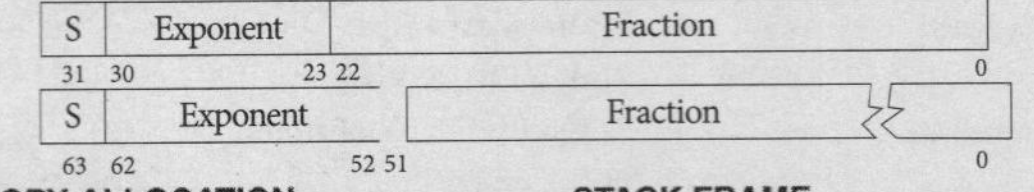

MEMORY ALLOCATION / STACK FRAME

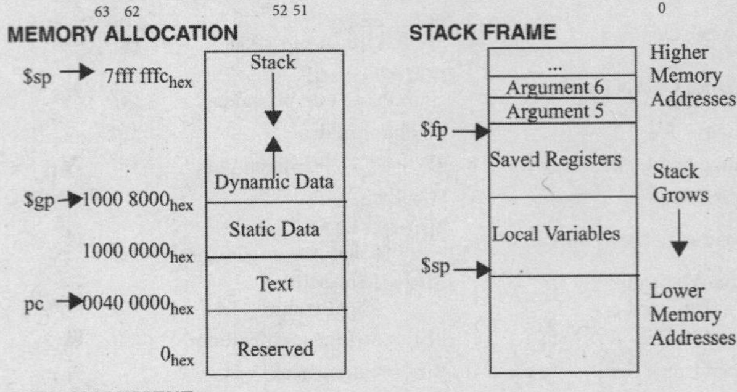

DATA ALIGNMENT

Double Word							
Word				Word			
Halfword		Halfword		Halfword		Halfword	
Byte	Byte	Byte	Byte	Byte	Byte	Byte	Byte
0	1	2	3	4	5	6	7

Value of three least significant bits of byte address (Big Endian)

EXCEPTION CONTROL REGISTERS: CAUSE AND STATUS

BD	Interrupt Mask	Exception Code

31   15   8   6   2

Pending Interrupt	UM	EL	IE

15   8   4   1   0

BD = Branch Delay, UM = User Mode, EL = Exception Level, IE = Interrupt Enable

EXCEPTION CODES

Number	Name	Cause of Exception	Number	Name	Cause of Exception
0	Int	Interrupt (hardware)	9	Bp	Breakpoint Exception
4	AdEL	Address Error Exception (load or instruction fetch)	10	RI	Reserved Instruction Exception
5	AdES	Address Error Exception (store)	11	CpU	Coprocessor Unimplemented
6	IBE	Bus Error on Instruction Fetch	12	Ov	Arithmetic Overflow Exception
7	DBE	Bus Error on Load or Store	13	Tr	Trap
8	Sys	Syscall Exception	15	FPE	Floating Point Exception

SIZE PREFIXES

SIZE	PREFIX	SYMBOL	SIZE	PREFIX	SYMBOL	SIZE	PREFIX	SYMBOL	SIZE	PREFIX	SYMBOL
1000^1	Kilo-	K	2^{10}	Kibi-	Ki	1000^6	Exa-	E	2^{60}	Exbi-	Ei
1000^2	Mega-	M	2^{20}	Mebi-	Mi	1000^7	Zetta-	Z	2^{70}	Zebi-	Zi
1000^3	Giga-	G	2^{30}	Gibi-	Gi	1000^8	Yotta-	Y	2^{80}	Yobi-	Yi
1000^4	Tera-	T	2^{40}	Tebi-	Ti	1000^9	Ronna-	R	2^{90}	Robi-	Ri
1000^5	Peta-	P	2^{50}	Pebi-	Pi	1000^{10}	Quecca-	Q	2^{100}	Quebi-	Qi

In Praise of *Computer Organization and Design: The Hardware/ Software Interface,* Sixth Edition

"With general purpose and specialized processors present in many aspects of everyday life, it is now more important than ever, that the next generation of computer engineers understand how computers compute and also the many tradeoffs and optimizations necessary to build fast energy-efficient machines. For several generations of students, *Computer Organization and Design* by Patterson and Hennesey has served as the gateway into the complex world of hardware/ software interfaces; the memory hierarchy; and the benefits and hazards of pipelining (pun intended)."

—Mark Hempstead, *Tufts University*

"*Computer Organization and Design* is the computer architecture book for your (virtual) bookshelf. The book is both timeless and new, as it complements venerable principles—Moore's Law, abstraction, common case fast, redundancy, memory hierarchies, parallelism, and pipelining—with emerging trends from good (e.g., architectures targeting deep learning) to bad (processor core cyberattacks)."

—Mark D. Hill, *University of Wisconsin-Madison*

"The new edition of *Computer Organization and Design* keeps pace with advances in emerging processor architectures and applications, where AI, security and virtualization will be supported on open instruction set architectures (e.g., RISC-V). This text acknowledges these changes, but continues to provide a rich foundation of the fundamentals in *Computer Organization and Design* which will be needed for the designers of hardware and software that will power next generation secure, performant and efficient systems."

—Dave Kaeli, *Northeastern University*

"There are timeless principles in computer system design, which are essential to understand the organization and performance of any computer architecture. Based on these principles and using a unique pedagogical approach, Patterson and Hennessy present the evolution of computer architecture from uniprocessors to the latest innovations on domain-specific architectures. The inclusion of the Google TPU supercomputer as an example of DNN-DSA in this new edition, heralds the rise of a new generation of computer architects."

—Euripides Montagne, *University of Central Florida*

"*Computer Organization and Design* is the ultimate classic textbook that is still current and applicable. It is very readable, and provides valuable insight into the hardware/ software interface, which is useful both for future hardware engineers and for software developers interested in improving performance and energy-efficiency. The MIPS architecture is ideal for teaching computer organization. It is straightforward, yet closely resembles both ARM and RISC-V."

—Tali Moreshet, *Boston University*

S I X T H   E D I T I O N

Computer Organization and Design

THE HARDWARE/SOFTWARE INTERFACE

David A. Patterson has been teaching computer architecture at the University of California, Berkeley, since joining the faculty in 1977, where he held the Pardee Chair of Computer Science. His teaching has been honored by the Distinguished Teaching Award from the University of California, the Karlstrom Award from ACM, and the Mulligan Education Medal and Undergraduate Teaching Award from IEEE. Patterson received the IEEE Technical Achievement Award and the ACM Eckert-Mauchly Award for contributions to RISC, and he shared the IEEE Johnson Information Storage Award for contributions to RAID. He also shared the IEEE John von Neumann Medal and the C & C Prize with John Hennessy. Like his co-author, Patterson is a Fellow of both AAAS organizaitons, the Computer History Museum, ACM, and IEEE, and he was elected to the National Academy of Engineering, the National Academy of Sciences, and the Silicon Valley Engineering Hall of Fame. He served as chair of the CS division in the Berkeley EECS department, as chair of the Computing Research Association, and as President of ACM. This record led to Distinguished Service Awards from ACM and CRA. He received the Tapia Achievement Award for Civic Science and Diversifying Computing and shared the 2017 ACM A.M. Turing Award with Hennessy.

At Berkeley, Patterson led the design and implementation of RISC I, likely the first VLSI reduced instruction set computer, and the foundation of the commercial SPARC architecture. He was a leader of the Redundant Arrays of Inexpensive Disks (RAID) project, which led to dependable storage systems from many companies. He was also involved in the Network of Workstations (NOW) project, which led to cluster technology used by Internet companies and later to cloud computing. These projects earned three dissertation awards from ACM. In 2016 he became Professor Emeritus at Berkeley and a Distinguished Engineer at Google, where he works on domain specific architectures for machine learning. He is also the Vice Chair of RISC-V International and the Director of the RISC-V International Open Source Laboratory.

John L. Hennessy was the tenth president of Stanford University, where he has been a member of the faculty since 1977 in the departments of electrical engineering and computer science. Hennessy is a Fellow of the IEEE and ACM; a member of the National Academy of Engineering, the National Academy of Science, and the American Philosophical Society; and a Fellow of the American Academy of Arts and Sciences. Among his many awards are the 2001 Eckert-Mauchly Award for his contributions to RISC technology, the 2001 Seymour Cray Computer Engineering Award, and the 2000 John von Neumann Award, which he shared with David Patterson. In 2017 they shared the ACM A.M. Turing Award. He has also received seven honorary doctorates.

In 1981, he started the MIPS project at Stanford with a handful of graduate students. After completing the project in 1984, he took a leave from the university to cofound MIPS Computer Systems (now MIPS Technologies), which developed one of the first commercial RISC microprocessors. As of 2006, over 2 billion MIPS microprocessors have been shipped in devices ranging from video games and palmtop computers to laser printers and network switches. Hennessy subsequently led the DASH (Director Architecture for Shared Memory) project, which prototyped the first scalable cache coherent multiprocessor; many of the key ideas have been adopted in modern multiprocessors. In addition to his technical activities and university responsibilities, he has continued to work with numerous start-ups both as an early-stage advisor and an investor.

He is currently director of Knight-Hennessy Scholars and serves as non-executive chairman of Alphabet.

SIXTH EDITION

Computer Organization and Design

THE HARDWARE/SOFTWARE INTERFACE

David A. Patterson
University of California, Berkeley
Google, Inc.

John L. Hennessy
Stanford University

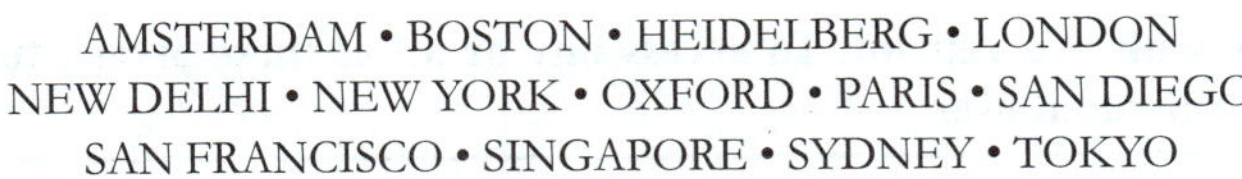

ELSEVIER

RELX India Pvt. Ltd.
Registered Office: 818, 8th Floor, Indraprakash Building, 21, Barakhamba Road, New Delhi-110 001
Corporate Office: 14th Floor, Building No. 10B, DLF Cyber City, Phase II, Gurgaon -122 002, Haryana, India

---

Computer Organization and Design: The Hardware/ Software Interface, 6/e MIPS Edition, David A. Patterson and John L. Hennessy

Copyright © 2021 by Elsevier, Inc.

All rights reserved.

ISBN: 978-0-12-820109-1

This reprint of Computer Organization and Design: The Hardware/ Software Interface, 6/e MIPS Edition by David A. Patterson and John L. Hennessy was undertaken by RELX India Private Limited and is published by arrangement with Elsevier Inc.

Copyright © 2022 by RELX India Pvt. Ltd.

Indian Reprint ISBN: 978-93-5107-396-3

First Printed in India 2021
Reprinted 2022 (thrice)

Notices

Practitioners and researchers must always rely on their own experience and knowledge in evaluating and using any information, methods, compounds or experiments described herein. Because of rapid advances in the medical sciences, in particular, independent verification of diagnoses and drug dosages should be made. To the fullest extent of the law, no responsibility is assumed by Elsevier, authors, editors or contributors for any injury and/or damage to persons or property as a matter of products liability, negligence or otherwise, or from any use or operation of any methods, products, instructions, or ideas contained in the material herein.

This publication is licensed for sale in India, Bangladesh, Bhutan, Maldives, Nepal, Pakistan and Sri Lanka only. Circulation of this version outside these territories is unauthorized and illegal.

Online resources are not available with this reprint. To access any or all of these assets, the original edition must be purchased by the individual user

---

Printed and bound in India at Rajkamal Electric Press, Kundli (Haryana).

*To Linda,
who has been, is, and always will be the love of my life*

Contents

5   Large and Fast: Exploiting Memory Hierarchy   390

6   Parallel Processors from Client to Cloud   524

APPENDICES

A   Assemblers, Linkers, and the SPIM Simulator   A-610

B   The Basics of Logic Design   B-692

O N L I N E   C O N T E N T

Graphics and Computing GPUs   C-2

Mapping Control to Hardware   D-2

Survey of Instruction Set Architectures

Preface

The most beautiful thing we can experience is the mysterious. It is the source of all true art and science.

Albert Einstein, *What I Believe*, 1930

About This Book

We believe that learning in computer science and engineering should reflect the current state of the field, as well as introduce the principles that are shaping computing. We also feel that readers in every specialty of computing need to appreciate the organizational paradigms that determine the capabilities, performance, energy, and, ultimately, the success of computer systems.

Modern computer technology requires professionals of every computing specialty to understand both hardware and software. The interaction between hardware and software at a variety of levels also offers a framework for understanding the fundamentals of computing. Whether your primary interest is hardware or software, computer science or electrical engineering, the central ideas in computer organization and design are the same. Thus, our emphasis in this book is to show the relationship between hardware and software and to focus on the concepts that are the basis for current computers.

The switch from uniprocessor to multicore microprocessors and the recent emphasis on domain specific architectures confirmed the soundness of this perspective, given since the first edition. While programmers could ignore the advice and rely on computer architects, compiler writers, and silicon engineers to make their programs run faster or be more energy-efficient without change, that era is over. Our view is that for at least the next decade, most programmers are going to have to understand the hardware/software interface if they want programs to run efficiently on modern computers.

The audience for this book includes those with little experience in assembly language or logic design who need to understand basic computer organization as well as readers with backgrounds in assembly language and/or logic design who want to learn how to design a computer or understand how a system works and why it performs as it does.

About the Other Book

Some readers may be familiar with *Computer Architecture: A Quantitative Approach*, popularly known as Hennessy and Patterson. (This book in turn is often called Patterson and Hennessy.) Our motivation in writing the earlier book was to describe the principles of computer architecture using solid engineering fundamentals and quantitative cost/performance tradeoffs. We used an approach that combined examples and measurements, based on commercial systems, to create realistic design experiences. Our goal was to demonstrate that computer architecture could be learned using quantitative methodologies instead of a descriptive approach. It was intended for the serious computing professional who wanted a detailed understanding of computers.

A majority of the readers for this book do not plan to become computer architects. The performance and energy efficiency of future software systems will be dramatically affected, however, by how well software designers understand the basic hardware techniques at work in a system. Thus, compiler writers, operating system designers, database programmers, and most other software engineers need a firm grounding in the principles presented in this book. Similarly, hardware designers must understand clearly the effects of their work on software applications.

Thus, we knew that this book had to be much more than a subset of the material in *Computer Architecture*, and the material was extensively revised to match the different audience. We were so happy with the result that the subsequent editions of *Computer Architecture* were revised to remove most of the introductory material; hence, there is much less overlap today than with the first editions of both books.

Changes for the Sixth Edition

There is arguably been more change in the technology and business of computer architecture since the fifth edition than there were for the first five:

- *The slowing of Moore's Law.* After 50 years of biannual doubling of the number of transistors per chip, Gordon Moore's prediction no longer holds. Semiconductor technology will still improve, but more slowly and less predictably than in the past.

- *The rise of Domain Specific Architectures (DSA).* In part due to the slowing of Moore's Law and in part due to the end of Dennard Scaling, general purpose processors are only improving a few percent per year. Moreover, Amdahl's Law limits the practical benefit of increasing the number of processors per chip. In 2020, it is widely believed that the most promising path forward is DSA. It doesn't try to run everything well like general purpose processors, but focuses on running programs of one domain much better than conventional CPUs.

- *Microarchitecture as a security attack surface.* Spectre demonstrated that speculative out-of-order execution and hardware multithreading make

Chapter or Appendix	Sections	Software focus	Hardware focus
1. Computer Abstractions and Technology	1.1 to 1.12	Read carefully	Read carefully
	(web) 1.13 (History)	Read for culture	Read for culture
2. Instructions: Language of the Computer	2.1 to 2.14	Read carefully	Review or read
	(web) 2.15 (Compilers & Java)	Read if have time	
	2.16 to 2.22	Read carefully	Review or read
	(web) 2.23 (History)	Read for culture	Read for culture
E. RISC Instruction-Set Architectures	(web) E.1 to E.6	Read if have time	
3. Arithmetic for Computers	3.1 to 3.5	Read carefully	Read carefully
	3.6 to 3.8 (Subword Parallelism)	Read carefully	Read carefully
	3.9 to 3.10 (Fallacies)	Review or read	Review or read
	(web) 3.11 (History)	Read for culture	Read for culture
B. The Basics of Logic Design	B.1 to B.13		Reference
4. The Processor	4.1 (Overview)	Read carefully	Read carefully
	4.2 (Logic Conventions)		Read carefully
	4.3 to 4.4 (Simple Implementation)	Review or read	Read carefully
	4.5 (Multicycle Implementation)		Read if have time
	4.6 (Pipelining Overview)	Review or read	Read carefully
	4.7 (Pipelined Datapath)	Review or read	Read carefully
	4.8 to 4.10 (Hazards, Exceptions)		Read carefully
	4.11 to 4.13 (Parallel, Real Stuff)	Read carefully	Read carefully
	(web) 4.14 (Verilog Pipeline Control)		Read if have time
	4.15 to 4.16 (Fallacies)	Read carefully	Read carefully
	(web) 4.17 (History)	Read for culture	Read for culture
D. Mapping Control to Hardware	(web) D.1 to D.6		Read if have time
5. Large and Fast: Exploiting Memory Hierarchy	5.1 to 5.10	Read carefully	Read carefully
	(web) 5.11 (Redundant Arrays of Inexpensive Disks)	Read if have time	Read if have time
	(web) 5.12 (Verilog Cache Controller)		Reference
	5.13 to 5.16	Read carefully	Read carefully
	(web) 5.17 (History)	Read for culture	Read for culture
6. Parallel Process from Client to Cloud	6.1 to 6.9	Read carefully	Read carefully
	(web) 6.10 (Clusters)	Read if have time	Read if have time
	6.11 to 6.15	Read carefully	Read carefully
	(web) 6.16 (History)	Read for culture	Read for culture
A. Assemblers, Linkers, and the SPIM Simulator	A.1 to A.11	Reference	Reference
C. Graphics Processor Units	(web) C.1 to C.11	Reference	Reference

Read carefully    Read if have time    Reference 

Review or read   Read for culture

timing based side-channel attacks practical. Moreover, these are not due to bugs that can be fixed, but a fundamental challenge to this style of processor design.

■ *Open instruction sets and open source implementations.* The opportunities and impact of open source software have come to computer architecture. Open instruction sets like RISC-V enables organizations to build their own processors without first negotiating a license, which has enabled open-source implementations that are shared to freely download and use as well as proprietary implementations of RISC-V. Open source software and hardware are a boon to academic research and instruction, allowing students to see and enhance industrial strength technology.

■ *The re-virticalization of the information technology industry.* Cloud computing has led to no more than a half-dozen companies that provide computing infrastructure for everyone to use. Much like IBM in the 1960s and 1970s, these companies determine both the software stack and the hardware that they deploy. The changes above have led to some of these "hyperscalers" developing their own DSA and RISC-V chips for deployment in their clouds.

The sixth edition of COD reflects these recent changes, updates all the examples and figures, responds to requests of instructors, plus adds a pedagogic improvement inspired by textbooks I used to help my grandchildren with their math classes.

■ The Going Faster section is now in every chapter. It starts with a Python version in Chapter 1, whose poor performance inspires learning C and then rewriting matrix multiply in C in Chapter 2. The remaining chapters accelerate matrix multiply by leveraging data level parallelism, instruction level parallelism, thread level parallelism, and by adjusting memory accesses to match the memory hierarchy of a modern server. This computer has 512-bit SIMD operations, speculative out-of-order execution, three levels of caches, and 48 cores. All four optimizations add only 21 lines of C code yet speedup matrix multiply by almost 50,000, cutting it from nearly 6 hours in Python to less than 1 second in optimized C. If I were a student again, this running example would inspire me to use C and learn the underlying hardware concepts of this book.

■ With this edition, every chapter has a Self Study section that asks thought provoking questions and supplies the answers afterwards to help you evaluate if you follow the material on your own.

■ Besides explaining that Moore's Law and Dennard Scaling no longer hold, we've de-emphasized Moore's Law as a change agent that was prominent in the fifth edition.

■ Chapter 2 has more material to emphasize that binary data has no inherent meaning—the program determines the data type—not an easy concept for beginners to grasp.

- Chapter 2 also includes a short description of the RISC-V as a contrasting instruction set to MIPS alongside ARMv7, ARMv8, and x86. (There is also a companion version of this book based on RISC-V instead of MIPS, and we're updating that with the other changes as well.)

- The benchmark example of Chapter 2 is upgraded to SPEC2017 from SPEC2006.

- At instructors' request, we have restored the multi-cycle implementation of MIPS as an online section in Chapter 4 between the single-cycle implementation and the pipelined implementation. Some instructors find these three steps an easier path to teach pipelining.

- The Putting It All Together examples of Chapters 4 and 5 were updated to the recent ARM A53 microarchitecture and the Intel i7 6700 Skyelake microarchitecture.

- The Fallacies and Pitfalls Sections of Chapters 5 and 6 added pitfalls around hardware security attacks of Row Hammer and Spectre.

- Chapter 6 has a new section introducing DSAs using Google's Tensor Processing Unit (TPU) version 1. Chapter 6's Putting it All Together section is updated to compare Google's TPUv3 DSA supercomputer to a cluster of NVIDIA Volta GPUs.

Finally, we updated all the exercises in the book.

While some elements changed, we have preserved useful book elements from prior editions. To make the book work better as a reference, we still place definitions of new terms in the margins at their first occurrence. The book element called "Understanding Program Performance" sections helps readers understand the performance of their programs and how to improve it, just as the "Hardware/ Software Interface" book element helped readers understand the tradeoffs at this interface. "The Big Picture" section remains so that the reader sees the forest despite all the trees. "Check Yourself" sections help readers to confirm their comprehension of the material on the first time through with answers provided at the end of each chapter. This edition still includes the green MIPS reference card, which was inspired by the "Green Card" of the IBM System/360. This card should be a handy reference when writing MIPS assembly language programs.

Instructor Support

We have collected a great deal of material to help instructors teach courses using this book. Solutions to exercises, figures from the book, lecture slides, and other materials are available to adopters from the publisher. Check the publisher's Web site for more information:

https://textbooks.elsevier.com/web/manuals.aspx?isbn=9780128201091

Concluding Remarks

If you read the following acknowledgments section, you will see that we went to great lengths to correct mistakes. Since a book goes through many printings, we have the opportunity to make even more corrections. If you uncover any remaining, resilient bugs, please contact the publisher.

This edition is the third break in the long-standing collaboration between Hennessy and Patterson, which started in 1989. The demands of running one of the world's great universities meant that President Hennessy could no longer make the substantial commitment to create a new edition. The remaining author felt once again like a tightrope walker without a safety net. Hence, the people in the acknowledgments and Berkeley colleagues played an even larger role in shaping the contents of this book. Nevertheless, this time around there is only one author to blame for the new material in what you are about to read.

Acknowledgments for the Sixth Edition

With every edition of this book, we are very fortunate to receive help from many readers, reviewers, and contributors. Each of these people has helped to make this book better.

Special thanks goes to Dr. Rimas Avizenis, who developed the various versions of matrix multiply and supplied the performance numbers as well. I deeply appreciate his continued help after he has graduated from UC Berkeley. As I worked with his father while I was a graduate student at UCLA, it was a nice symmetry to work with Rimas when he was a graduate student at UC Berkeley.

I also wish to thank my longtime collaborator **Randy Katz** of UC Berkeley, who helped develop the concept of great ideas in computer architecture as part of the extensive revision of an undergraduate class that we did together.

I'd like to thank **David Kirk**, **John Nickolls**, and their colleagues at NVIDIA (Michael Garland, John Montrym, Doug Voorhies, Lars Nyland, Erik Lindholm, Paulius Micikevicius, Massimiliano Fatica, Stuart Oberman, and Vasily Volkov) for writing the first in-depth appendix on GPUs. I'd like to express again my appreciation to **Jim Larus**, recently named Dean of the School of Computer and Communications Science at EPFL, for his willingness in contributing his expertise on assembly language programming, as well as for welcoming readers of this book with regard to using the simulator he developed and maintains.

I am also very grateful to **Jason Bakos** of the University of South Carolina, who updated and created new exercises agian for this edition. The originals were prepared for the fourth edition by **Perry Alexander** (The University of Kansas); **Javier Bruguera** (Universidade de Santiago de Compostela); **Matthew Farrens** (University of California, Davis); **David Kaeli** (Northeastern University); **Nicole Kaiyan** (University of Adelaide); **John Oliver** (Cal Poly, San Luis Obispo); **Milos Prvulovic** (Georgia Tech); and **Jichuan Chang**, **Jacob Leverich**, **Kevin Lim**, and **Partha Ranganathan** (all from Hewlett-Packard). Thanks also to **Peter J. Ashenden** (Ashenden Design Pty Ltd) for his involvement in previous editions.

Additional thanks goes to **Jason Bakos** for developing the new lecture slides.

I am grateful to the many instructors who have answered the publisher's surveys, reviewed our proposals, and attended focus groups to analyze and respond to our plans for this and previous editions. They include the following individuals: Focus Groups in 2012: Bruce Barton (Suffolk County Community College), Jeff Braun (Montana Tech), Ed Gehringer (North Carolina State), Michael Goldweber (Xavier University), Ed Harcourt (St. Lawrence University), Mark Hill (University of Wisconsin, Madison), Patrick Homer (University of Arizona), Norm Jouppi (HP Labs), Dave Kaeli (Northeastern University), Christos Kozyrakis (Stanford University), Zachary Kurmas (Grand Valley State University), Jae C. Oh (Syracuse University), Lu Peng (LSU), Milos Prvulovic (Georgia Tech), Partha Ranganathan (HP Labs), David Wood (University of Wisconsin), Craig Zilles (University of Illinois at Urbana-Champaign). Surveys and Reviews: Mahmoud Abou-Nasr (Wayne State University), Perry Alexander (The University of Kansas), Hakan Aydin (George Mason University), Hussein Badr (State University of New York at Stony Brook), Mac Baker (Virginia Military Institute), Ron Barnes (George Mason University), Douglas Blough (Georgia Institute of Technology), Kevin Bolding (Seattle Pacific University), Miodrag Bolic (University of Ottawa), John Bonomo (Westminster College), Jeff Braun (Montana Tech), Tom Briggs (Shippensburg University), Scott Burgess (Humboldt State University), Fazli Can (Bilkent University), Warren R. Carithers (Rochester Institute of Technology), Bruce Carlton (Mesa Community College), Nicholas Carter (University of Illinois at Urbana-Champaign), Anthony Cocchi (The City University of New York), Don Cooley (Utah State University), Robert D. Cupper (Allegheny College), Edward W. Davis (North Carolina State University), Nathaniel J. Davis (Air Force Institute of Technology), Molisa Derk (Oklahoma City University), Nathan B. Dodge (The University of Texas at Dallas), Derek Eager (University of Saskatchewan), Ernest Ferguson (Northwest Missouri State University), Rhonda Kay Gaede (The University of Alabama), Etienne M. Gagnon (UQAM), Costa Gerousis (Christopher Newport University), Paul Gillard (Memorial University of Newfoundland), Michael Goldweber (Xavier University), Georgia Grant (College of San Mateo), Merrill Hall (The Master's College), Tyson Hall (Southern Adventist University), Ed Harcourt (St. Lawrence University), Justin E. Harlow (University of South Florida), Paul F. Hemler (Hampden-Sydney College), Martin Herbordt (Boston University), Steve J. Hodges (Cabrillo College), Kenneth Hopkinson (Cornell University), Dalton Hunkins (St. Bonaventure University), Baback Izadi (State University of New York—New Paltz), Reza Jafari, Robert W. Johnson (Colorado Technical University), Bharat Joshi (University of North Carolina, Charlotte), Nagarajan Kandasamy (Drexel University), Rajiv Kapadia, Ryan Kastner (University of California, Santa Barbara), E.J. Kim (Texas A&M University), Jihong Kim (Seoul National University), Jim Kirk (Union University), Geoffrey S. Knauth (Lycoming College), Manish M. Kochhal (Wayne State), Suzan Koknar-Tezel (Saint Joseph's University), Angkul Kongmunvattana (Columbus State University), April Kontostathis (Ursinus College), Christos Kozyrakis (Stanford University), Danny Krizanc (Wesleyan University), Ashok Kumar, S. Kumar (The University of Texas), Zachary Kurmas (Grand Valley State University), Robert N. Lea (University of Houston), Baoxin Li (Arizona State

University), Li Liao (University of Delaware), Gary Livingston (University of Massachusetts), Michael Lyle, Douglas W. Lynn (Oregon Institute of Technology), Yashwant K Malaiya (Colorado State University), Bill Mark (University of Texas at Austin), Ananda Mondal (Claflin University), Euripides Montagne (University of Central Florida), Tali Moreshet (Boston University), Alvin Moser (Seattle University), Walid Najjar (University of California, Riverside), Danial J. Neebel (Loras College), John Nestor (Lafayette College), Jae C. Oh (Syracuse University), Joe Oldham (Centre College), Timour Paltashev, James Parkerson (University of Arkansas), Shaunak Pawagi (SUNY at Stony Brook), Steve Pearce, Ted Pedersen (University of Minnesota), Lu Peng (Louisiana State University), Gregory D Peterson (The University of Tennessee), Milos Prvulovic (Georgia Tech), Partha Ranganathan (HP Labs), Dejan Raskovic (University of Alaska, Fairbanks) Brad Richards (University of Puget Sound), Roman Rozanov, Louis Rubinfield (Villanova University), Md Abdus Salam (Southern University), Augustine Samba (Kent State University), Robert Schaefer (Daniel Webster College), Carolyn J. C. Schauble (Colorado State University), Keith Schubert (CSU San Bernardino), William L. Schultz, Kelly Shaw (University of Richmond), Shahram Shirani (McMaster University), Scott Sigman (Drury University), Bruce Smith, David Smith, Jeff W. Smith (University of Georgia, Athens), Mark Smotherman (Clemson University), Philip Snyder (Johns Hopkins University), Alex Sprintson (Texas A&M), Timothy D. Stanley (Brigham Young University), Dean Stevens (Morningside College), Nozar Tabrizi (Kettering University), Yuval Tamir (UCLA), Alexander Taubin (Boston University), Will Thacker (Winthrop University), Mithuna Thottethodi (Purdue University), Manghui Tu (Southern Utah University), Dean Tullsen (UC San Diego), Rama Viswanathan (Beloit College), Ken Vollmar (Missouri State University), Guoping Wang (Indiana-Purdue University), Patricia Wenner (Bucknell University), Kent Wilken (University of California, Davis), David Wolfe (Gustavus Adolphus College), David Wood (University of Wisconsin, Madison), Ki Hwan Yum (University of Texas, San Antonio), Mohamed Zahran (City College of New York), Amr Zaky (Santa Clara University), Gerald D. Zarnett (Ryerson University), Nian Zhang (South Dakota School of Mines & Technology), Xiaoyu Zhang (California State University San Marcos), Jiling Zhong (Troy University), Huiyang Zhou (The University of Central Florida), Weiyu Zhu (Illinois Wesleyan University).

A special thanks also goes to **Mark Smotherman** for making multiple passes to find technical and writing glitches that significantly improved the quality of this edition.

We wish to thank the extended Morgan Kaufmann family for agreeing to publish this book again under the able leadership of **Steve Merken** and **Beth LoGiudice**: I certainly couldn't have completed the book without them. We also want to extend thanks to **Beula Christopher**, who managed the book production process, and **Patrick Ferguson**, who did the cover design.

The contributions of the nearly 150 people we mentioned here have helped make this sixth edition what I hope will be our best book yet. Enjoy!

David A. Patterson

1

Computer Abstractions and Technology

Civilization advances by extending the number of important operations which we can perform without thinking about them.

Alfred North Whitehead,
An Introduction to Mathematics, 1911

1.1   Introduction

Welcome to this book! We're delighted to have this opportunity to convey the excitement of the world of computer systems. This is not a dry and dreary field, where progress is glacial and where new ideas atrophy from neglect. No! Computers are the product of the incredibly vibrant information technology industry, all aspects of which are responsible for almost 10% of the gross national product of the United States, and whose economy has become dependent in part on the rapid improvements in information technology. This unusual industry embraces innovation at a breathtaking rate. In the last 40 years, there have been a number of new computers whose introduction appeared to revolutionize the computing industry; these revolutions were cut short only because someone else built an even better computer.

This race to innovate has led to unprecedented progress since the inception of electronic computing in the late 1940s. Had the transportation industry kept pace with the computer industry, for example, today we could travel from New York to London in a second for a penny. Take just a moment to contemplate how such an improvement would change society—living in Tahiti while working in San Francisco, going to Moscow for an evening at the Bolshoi Ballet—and you can appreciate the implications of such a change.

Computers have led to a third revolution for civilization, with the information revolution taking its place alongside the agricultural and the industrial revolutions. The resulting multiplication of humankind's intellectual strength and reach naturally has affected our everyday lives profoundly and changed the ways in which the search for new knowledge is carried out. There is now a new vein of scientific investigation, with computational scientists joining theoretical and experimental scientists in the exploration of new frontiers in astronomy, biology, chemistry, and physics, among others.

The computer revolution continues. Each time the cost of computing improves by another factor of 10, the opportunities for computers multiply. Applications that were economically infeasible suddenly become practical. In the recent past, the following applications were "computer science fiction."

- *Computers in automobiles:* Until microprocessors improved dramatically in price and performance in the early 1980s, computer control of cars was ludicrous. Today, computers reduce pollution, improve fuel efficiency via engine controls, and increase safety through nearly automated driving and air bag inflation to protect occupants in a crash.

- *Cell phones:* Who would have dreamed that advances in computer systems would lead to more than half of the planet having mobile phones, allowing person-to-person communication to almost anyone anywhere in the world?

- *Human genome project:* The cost of computer equipment to map and analyze human DNA sequences was hundreds of millions of dollars. It's unlikely that anyone would have considered this project had the computer costs been 10 to 100 times higher, as they would have been 15 to 25 years earlier. Moreover, costs continue to drop; you will soon be able to acquire your own genome, allowing medical care to be tailored to you.

- *World Wide Web:* Not in existence at the time of the first edition of this book, the web has transformed our society. For many, the web has replaced libraries and newspapers.

- *Search engines:* As the content of the web grew in size and in value, finding relevant information became increasingly important. Today, many people rely on search engines for such a large part of their lives that it would be a hardship to go without them.

Clearly, advances in this technology now affect almost every aspect of our society. Hardware advances have allowed programmers to create wonderfully useful software, which explains why computers are omnipresent. Today's science fiction suggests tomorrow's killer applications: already on their way are glasses that augment reality, the cashless society, and cars that can drive themselves.

Classes of Computing Applications and Their Characteristics

Although a common set of hardware technologies (see Sections 1.4 and 1.5) is used in computers ranging from smart home appliances to cell phones to the largest supercomputers, these different applications have different design requirements and employ the core hardware technologies in different ways. Broadly speaking, computers are used in three different classes of applications.

Personal computers (PCs) in the form of laptops are possibly the best known form of computing, which readers of this book have likely used extensively. Personal computers emphasize delivery of good performance to single users at low cost and usually execute third-party software. This class of computing drove the evolution of many computing technologies, which is only about 40 years old!

Servers are the modern form of what were once much larger computers, and are usually accessed only via a network. Servers are oriented to carrying large workloads, which may consist of either single complex applications—usually a scientific or engineering application—or handling many small jobs, such as would occur in building a large web server. These applications are usually based on software from another source (such as a database or simulation system), but are often modified or customized for a particular function. Servers are built from the same basic technology as desktop computers, but provide for greater computing, storage, and input/output capacity. In general, servers also place a greater emphasis on dependability, since a crash is usually more costly than it would be on a single-user PC.

Servers span the widest range in cost and capability. At the low end, a server may be little more than a desktop computer without a screen or keyboard and cost a thousand dollars. These low-end servers are typically used for file storage, small business applications, or simple web serving (see Section 6.11). At the other extreme are **supercomputers**, which at the present consist of hundreds of thousands of processors and many **terabytes** of memory, and cost tens to hundreds of millions of dollars. Supercomputers are usually used for high-end scientific and engineering calculations, such as weather forecasting, oil exploration, protein structure determination, and other large-scale problems. Although such supercomputers represent the peak of computing capability, they represent a relatively small fraction of the servers and a relatively small fraction of the overall computer market in terms of total revenue.

Embedded computers are the largest class of computers and span the widest range of applications and performance. Embedded computers include the microprocessors found in your car, the computers in a television set, and the networks of processors that control a modern airplane or cargo ship. A popular term today is Internet of Things (IoT), which suggests many small devices that all communicate wirelessly over the Internet. Embedded computing systems are designed to run one application or one set of related applications that are normally integrated with the hardware and delivered as a single system; thus, despite the large number of embedded computers, most users never really see that they are using a computer!

personal computer (PC) A computer designed for use by an individual, usually incorporating a graphics display, a keyboard, and a mouse.

server A computer used for running larger programs for multiple users, often simultaneously, and typically accessed only via a network.

supercomputer A class of computers with the highest performance and cost; they are configured as servers and typically cost tens to hundreds of millions of dollars.

terabyte (TB) Originally 1,099,511,627,776 (2^{40}) bytes, although communications and secondary storage systems developers started using the term to mean 1,000,000,000,000 (10^{12}) bytes. To reduce confusion, we now use the term **tebibyte (TiB)** for 2^{40} bytes, defining *terabyte* (TB) to mean 10^{12} bytes. Figure 1.1 shows the full range of decimal and binary values and names.

embedded computer A computer inside another device used for running one predetermined application or collection of software.

Decimal term	Abbreviation	Value	Binary term	Abbreviation	Value	% Larger
kilobyte	KB	1000^1	kibibyte	KiB	2^{10}	2%
megabyte	MB	1000^2	mebibyte	MiB	2^{20}	5%
gigabyte	GB	1000^3	gibibyte	GiB	2^{30}	7%
terabyte	TB	1000^4	tebibyte	TiB	2^{40}	10%
petabyte	PB	1000^5	pebibyte	PiB	2^{50}	13%
exabyte	EB	1000^6	exbibyte	EiB	2^{60}	15%
zettabyte	ZB	1000^7	zebibyte	ZiB	2^{70}	18%
yottabyte	YB	1000^8	yobibyte	YiB	2^{80}	21%
ronnabyte	RB	1000^9	robibyte	RiB	2^{90}	24%
queccabyte	QB	1000^{10}	quebibyte	QiB	2^{100}	27%

FIGURE 1.1   The 2^X vs. 10^Y bytes ambiguity was resolved by adding a binary notation for all the common size terms. In the last column we note how much larger the binary term is than its corresponding decimal term, which is compounded as we head down the chart. These prefixes work for bits as well as bytes, so *gigabit* (Gb) is 10^9 bits while *gibibits* (Gib) is 2^{30} bits. The society that runs the metric system created the decimal prefixes, with the last two proposed only in 2019 in anticipation of the global capacity of storage systems. All the names are derived from the entymology in Latin of the powers of 1000 that they represent.

Embedded applications often have unique application requirements that combine a minimum performance with stringent limitations on cost or power. For example, consider a music player: the processor need only be as fast as necessary to handle its limited function, and beyond that, minimizing cost and power are the most important objectives. Despite their low cost, embedded computers often have lower tolerance for failure, since the results can vary from upsetting (when your new television crashes) to devastating (such as might occur when the computer in a plane or cargo ship crashes). In consumer-oriented embedded applications, such as a digital home appliance, dependability is achieved primarily through simplicity—the emphasis is on doing one function as perfectly as possible. In large embedded systems, techniques of redundancy from the server world are often employed. Although this book focuses on general-purpose computers, most concepts apply directly, or with slight modifications, to embedded computers.

Elaboration: *Elaborations* are short sections used throughout the text to provide more detail on a particular subject that may be of interest. Disinterested readers may skip over an *Elaboration*, since the subsequent material will never depend on the contents of the *Elaboration*.

Many embedded processors are designed using *processor cores*, a version of a processor written in a hardware description language, such as Verilog or VHDL (see Chapter 4). The core allows a designer to integrate other application-specific hardware with the processor core for fabrication on a single chip.

Welcome to the PostPC Era

The continuing march of technology brings about generational changes in computer hardware that shake up the entire information technology industry. Since the fourth edition of the book we have undergone such a change, as significant in the

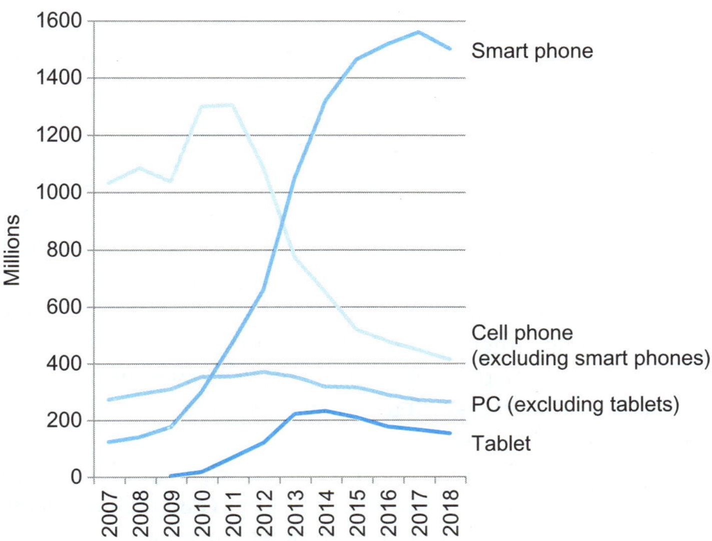

FIGURE 1.2   The number manufactured per year of tablets and smart phones, which reflect the PostPC era, versus personal computers and traditional cell phones. Smart phones represent the recent growth in the cell phone industry, and they passed PCs in 2011. PCs, tablets, and traditional cell phone categories are declining. The peak volume years text are 2011 for cell phones, 2013 for PCs, and 2014 for tablets. PCs fell from 20% of total units shipped in 2007 to 10% in 2018.

past as the switch starting 40 years ago to personal computers. Replacing the PC is the **personal mobile device (PMD)**. PMDs are battery operated with wireless connectivity to the Internet and typically cost hundreds of dollars, and, like PCs, users can download software ("apps") to run on them. Unlike PCs, they no longer have a keyboard and mouse, and are more likely to rely on a touch-sensitive screen or even speech input. Today's PMD is a smart phone or a tablet computer, but tomorrow it may include electronic glasses. Figure 1.2 shows the rapid growth time of tablets and smart phones versus that of PCs and traditional cell phones.

Taking over from the traditional server is **Cloud Computing**, which relies upon giant datacenters that are now known as *Warehouse Scale Computers* (WSCs). Companies like Amazon and Google build these WSCs containing 50,000 servers and then let companies rent portions of them so that they can provide software services to PMDs without having to build WSCs of their own. Indeed, **Software as a Service (SaaS)** deployed via the cloud is revolutionizing the software industry just as PMDs and WSCs are revolutionizing the hardware industry. Today's software developers will often have a portion of their application that runs on the PMD and a portion that runs in the Cloud.

What You Can Learn in This Book

Successful programmers have always been concerned about the performance of their programs, because getting results to the user quickly is critical in creating

Personal mobile devices (PMDs) are small wireless devices to connect to the Internet; they rely on batteries for power, and software is installed by downloading apps. Conventional examples are smart phones and tablets.

Cloud Computing refers to large collections of servers that provide services over the Internet; some providers rent dynamically varying numbers of servers as a utility.

Software as a Service (SaaS) delivers software and data as a service over the Internet, usually via a thin program such as a browser that runs on local client devices, instead of binary code that must be installed, and runs wholly on that device. Examples include web search and social networking.

successful software. In the 1960s and 1970s, a primary constraint on computer performance was the size of the computer's memory. Thus, programmers often followed a simple credo: minimize memory space to make programs fast. In the last two decades, advances in computer design and memory technology have greatly reduced the importance of small memory size in most applications other than those in embedded computing systems.

Programmers interested in performance now need to understand the issues that have replaced the simple memory model of the 1960s: the parallel nature of processors and the hierarchical nature of memories. Moreover, as we explain in Section 1.7, today's programmers need to worry about energy efficiency of their programs running either on the PMD or in the Cloud, which also requires understanding what is below your code. Programmers who seek to build competitive versions of software will therefore need to increase their knowledge of computer organization.

We are honored to have the opportunity to explain what's inside this revolutionary machine, unraveling the software below your program and the hardware under the covers of your computer. By the time you complete this book, we believe you will be able to answer the following questions:

- How are programs written in a high-level language, such as C or Java, translated into the language of the hardware, and how does the hardware execute the resulting program? Comprehending these concepts forms the basis of understanding the aspects of both the hardware and software that affect program performance.

- What is the interface between the software and the hardware, and how does software instruct the hardware to perform needed functions? These concepts are vital to understanding how to write many kinds of software.

- What determines the performance of a program, and how can a programmer improve the performance? As we will see, this depends on the original program, the software translation of that program into the computer's language, and the effectiveness of the hardware in executing the program.

- What techniques can be used by hardware designers to improve performance? This book will introduce the basic concepts of modern computer design. The interested reader will find much more material on this topic in our advanced book, *Computer Architecture: A Quantitative Approach*.

- What techniques can be used by hardware designers to improve energy efficiency? What can the programmer do to help or hinder energy efficiency?

multicore microprocessor *A microprocessor containing multiple processors ("cores") in a single integrated circuit.*

- What are the reasons for and the consequences of the switch from sequential processing to parallel processing? This book gives the motivation, describes the current hardware mechanisms to support parallelism, and surveys the new generation of "multicore" microprocessors (see Chapter 6).

- Since the first commercial computer in 1951, what great ideas did computer architects come up with that lay the foundation of modern computing?

Without understanding the answers to these questions, improving the performance of your program on a modern computer or evaluating what features might make one computer better than another for a particular application will be a complex process of trial and error, rather than a scientific procedure driven by insight and analysis.

This first chapter lays the foundation for the rest of the book. It introduces the basic ideas and definitions, places the major components of software and hardware in perspective, shows how to evaluate performance and energy, introduces integrated circuits (the technology that fuels the computer revolution), and explains the shift to multicores.

In this chapter and later ones, you will likely see many new words, or words that you may have heard but are not sure what they mean. Don't panic! Yes, there is a lot of special terminology used in describing modern computers, but the terminology actually helps, since it enables us to describe precisely a function or capability. In addition, computer designers (including your authors) *love* using **acronyms**, which are *easy* to understand once you know what the letters stand for! To help you remember and locate terms, we have included a **highlighted** definition of every term in the margins the first time it appears in the text. After a short time of working with the terminology, you will be fluent, and your friends will be impressed as you correctly use acronyms such as BIOS, CPU, DIMM, DRAM, PCIe, SATA, and many others.

To reinforce how the software and hardware systems used to run a program will affect performance, we use a special section, *Understanding Program Performance*, throughout the book to summarize important insights into program performance. The first one appears below.

acronym A word constructed by taking the initial letters of a string of words. For example: **RAM** is an acronym for Random Access Memory, and **CPU** is an acronym for Central Processing Unit.

Understanding Program Performance

The performance of a program depends on a combination of the effectiveness of the algorithms used in the program, the software systems used to create and translate the program into machine instructions, and the effectiveness of the computer in executing those instructions, which may include input/output (I/O) operations. This table summarizes how the hardware and software affect performance.

Hardware or software component	How this component affects performance	Where is this topic covered?
Algorithm	Determines both the number of source-level statements and the number of I/O operations executed	Other books!
Programming language, compiler, and architecture	Determines the number of computer instructions for each source-level statement	Chapters 2 and 3
Processor and memory system	Determines how fast instructions can be executed	Chapters 4, 5, and 6
I/O system (hardware and operating system)	Determines how fast I/O operations may be executed	Chapters 4, 5, and 6

Check Yourself sections are designed to help readers assess whether they comprehend the major concepts introduced in a chapter and understand the implications of those concepts. Some *Check Yourself* questions have simple answers; others are for discussion among a group. Answers to the specific questions can be found at the end of the chapter. *Check Yourself* questions appear only at the end of a section, making it easy to skip them if you are sure you understand the material.

1. The number of embedded processors sold every year greatly outnumbers the number of PC and even PostPC processors. Can you confirm or deny this insight based on your own experience? Try to count the number of embedded processors in your home. How does it compare with the number of conventional computers in your home?

2. As mentioned earlier, both the software and hardware affect the performance of a program. Can you think of examples where each of the following is the right place to look for a performance bottleneck?

   ■ The algorithm chosen
   ■ The programming language or compiler
   ■ The operating system
   ■ The processor
   ■ The I/O system and devices

1.2 Seven Great Ideas in Computer Architecture

We now introduce seven great ideas that computer architects have been invented in the last 60 years of computer design. These ideas are so powerful they have lasted long after the first computer that used them, with newer architects demonstrating their admiration by imitating their predecessors. These great ideas are themes that we will weave through this and subsequent chapters as examples arise. To point out their influence, in this section we introduce icons and highlighted terms that represent the great ideas and we use them to identify the nearly 100 sections of the book that feature use of the great ideas.

Use Abstraction to Simplify Design

Both computer architects and programmers had to invent techniques to make themselves more productive, for otherwise design time would lengthen as dramatically as resources grew. A major productivity technique for hardware and software is to use **abstractions** to represent the design at different levels of

representation; lower-level details are hidden to offer a simpler model at higher levels. We'll use the abstract painting icon to represent this second great idea.

Make the Common Case Fast

Making the **common case fast** will tend to enhance performance better than optimizing the rare case. Ironically, the common case is often simpler than the rare case and hence is often easier to enhance. This common sense advice implies that you know what the common case is, which is only possible with careful experimentation and measurement (see Section 1.6). We use a sports car as the icon for making the common case fast, as the most common trip has one or two passengers, and it's surely easier to make a fast sports car than a fast minivan!

Performance via Parallelism

Since the dawn of computing, computer architects have offered designs that get more performance by performing operations in parallel. We'll see many examples of parallelism in this book. We use multiple jet engines of a plane as our icon for **parallel performance**.

Performance via Pipelining

A particular pattern of parallelism is so prevalent in computer architecture that it merits its own name: **pipelining**. For example, before fire engines, a "bucket brigade" would respond to a fire, which many cowboy movies show in response to a dastardly act by the villain. The townsfolk form a human chain to carry a water source to fire, as they could much more quickly move buckets up the chain instead of individuals running back and forth. Our pipeline icon is a sequence of pipes, with each section representing one stage of the pipeline.

Performance via Prediction

Following the saying that it can be better to ask for forgiveness than to ask for permission, the next great idea is **prediction**. In some cases it can be faster on average to guess and start working rather than wait until you know for sure, assuming that the mechanism to recover from a misprediction is not too expensive and your prediction is relatively accurate. We use the fortune-teller's crystal ball as our prediction icon.

Hierarchy of Memories

Programmers want memory to be fast, large, and cheap, as memory speed often shapes performance, capacity limits the size of problems that can be solved, and the cost of memory today is often the majority of computer cost. Architects have found that they can address these conflicting demands with a **hierarchy of memories**, with

the fastest, smallest, and most expensive memory per bit at the top of the hierarchy and the slowest, largest, and cheapest per bit at the bottom. As we shall see in Chapter 5, caches give the programmer the illusion that main memory is nearly as fast as the top of the hierarchy and nearly as big and cheap as the bottom of the hierarchy. We use a layered triangle icon to represent the memory hierarchy. The shape indicates speed, cost, and size: the closer to the top, the faster and more expensive per bit the memory; the wider the base of the layer, the bigger the memory.

Dependability via Redundancy

Computers not only need to be fast; they need to be dependable. Since any physical device can fail, we make systems **dependable** by including redundant components that can take over when a failure occurs *and* to help detect failures. We use the tractor-trailer as our icon, since the dual tires on each side of its rear axles allow the truck to continue driving even when one tire fails. (Presumably, the truck driver heads immediately to a repair facility so the flat tire can be fixed, thereby restoring redundancy!)

In the prior edition, we listed an eighth great idea, which was "Designing for Moore's Law." Gordon Moore, one of the founders of Intel, made a remarkable prediction in 1965: integrated circuit resources would double every year. A decade later he amended his prediction to doubling every 2 years.

His prediction was accurate, and for 50 years, Moore's Law shaped computer architecture. As computer designs can take years, the resources available per chip ("transistors"; see page 24) could easily double or triple between the start and finish of the project. Like a skeet shooter, computer architects had to anticipate where the technology would be when the design finishes rather than design for when it starts.

Alas, no exponential growth can last forever, and Moore's Law is no longer accurate. The slowing of Moore's Law is shocking for computer designers who have long leveraged it. Some do not want to believe it is over, despite the substantial evidence to the contrary. Part of the reason is confusion between saying that Moore's prediction of the biannual doubling rate is now incorrect and claiming that semiconductors will no longer improve. Semiconductor technology *will* continue to improve, but more slowly than in the past. Starting with this edition, we will discuss the implications of the slowing of Moore's Law, especially in Chapter 6.

Elaboration: During the heydays of Moore's Law, the cost per chip resource would drop with each new technology generation. In the latest technologies, the cost per resource may be flat or even *rising* with each new generation, due to the cost of the new equipment, the elaborate processes invented to make chips work at these finer feature sizes, and the reduction of the *number* of companies who are investing in these new technologies to push the state-of-the-art. Less competition naturally leads to higher prices.

1.3 Below Your Program

A typical application, such as a word processor or a large database system, may consist of millions of lines of code and rely on sophisticated software libraries that implement complex functions in support of the application. As we will see, the hardware in a computer can only execute extremely simple low-level instructions. To go from a complex application to the simple instructions involves several layers of software that interpret or translate high-level operations into simple computer instructions, an example of the great idea of **abstraction**.

Figure 1.3 shows that these layers of software are organized primarily in a hierarchical fashion, with applications being the outermost ring and a variety of **systems software** sitting between the hardware and applications software.

There are many types of systems software, but two types of systems software are central to every computer system today: an operating system and a compiler. An **operating system** interfaces between a user's program and the hardware and provides a variety of services and supervisory functions. Among the most important functions are:

- Handling basic input and output operations

- Allocating storage and memory

- Providing for protected sharing of the computer among multiple applications using it simultaneously.

Examples of operating systems in use today are Linux, iOS, Android, and Windows.

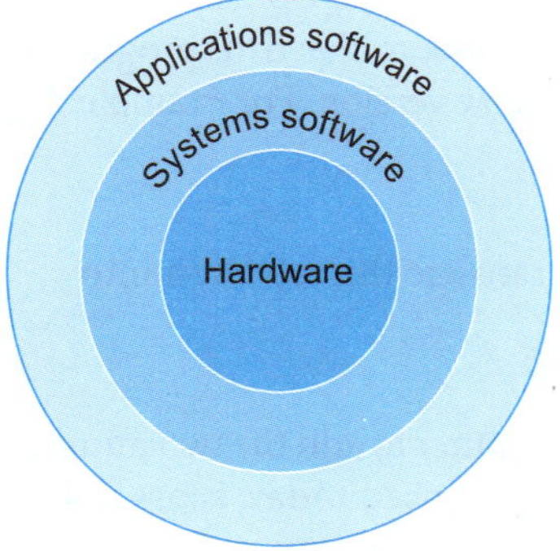

FIGURE 1.3   A simplified view of hardware and software as hierarchical layers, shown as concentric circles with hardware in the center and applications software outermost. In complex applications, there are often multiple layers of application software as well. For example, a database system may run on top of the systems software hosting an application, which in turn runs on top of the database.

In Paris they simply stared when I spoke to them in French; I never did succeed in making those idiots understand their own language.

Mark Twain, *The Innocents Abroad*, 1869

ABSTRACTION

systems software Software that provides services that are commonly useful, including operating systems, compilers, loaders, and assemblers.

operating system Supervising program that manages the resources of a computer for the benefit of the programs that run on that computer.

compiler A program that translates high-level language statements into assembly language statements.

Compilers perform another vital function: the translation of a program written in a high-level language, such as C, C++, Java, or Visual Basic into instructions that the hardware can execute. Given the sophistication of modern programming languages and the simplicity of the instructions executed by the hardware, the translation from a high-level language program to hardware instructions is complex. We give a brief overview of the process here and then go into more depth in Chapter 2 and in Appendix A.

From a High-Level Language to the Language of Hardware

To actually speak to electronic hardware, you need to send electrical signals. The easiest signals for computers to understand are *on* and *off*, and so the computer alphabet is just two letters. Just as the 26 letters of the English alphabet do not limit how much can be written, the two letters of the computer alphabet do not limit what computers can do. The two symbols for these two letters are the numbers 0 and 1, and we commonly think of the computer language as numbers in base 2, or *binary numbers*. We refer to each "letter" as a **binary digit** or **bit**. Computers are slaves to our commands, which are called **instructions**. Instructions, which are just collections of bits that the computer understands and obeys, can be thought of as numbers. For example, the bits

binary digit Also called a **bit**. One of the two numbers in base 2 (0 or 1) that are the components of information.

instruction A command that computer hardware understands and obeys.

```
1000110010100000
```

tell one computer to add two numbers. Chapter 2 explains why we use numbers for instructions *and* data; we don't want to steal that chapter's thunder, but using numbers for both instructions and data is a foundation of computing.

The first programmers communicated to computers in binary numbers, but this was so tedious that they quickly invented new notations that were closer to the way humans think. At first, these notations were translated to binary by hand, but this process was still tiresome. Using the computer to help program the computer, the pioneers invented programs to translate from symbolic notation to binary. The first of these programs was named an **assembler**. This program translates a symbolic version of an instruction into the binary version. For example, the programmer would write

assembler A program that translates a symbolic version of instructions into the binary version.

```
add A,B
```

and the assembler would translate this notation into

```
1000110010100000
```

This instruction tells the computer to add the two numbers A and B. The name coined for this symbolic language, still used today, is **assembly language**. In contrast, the binary language that the machine understands is the **machine language**.

assembly language A symbolic representation of machine instructions.

machine language A binary representation of machine instructions.

Although a tremendous improvement, assembly language is still far from the notations a scientist might like to use to simulate fluid flow or that an accountant might use to balance the books. Assembly language requires the programmer to write one line for every instruction that the computer will follow, forcing the programmer to think like the computer.

The recognition that a program could be written to translate a more powerful language into computer instructions was one of the great breakthroughs in the early days of computing. Programmers today owe their productivity—and their sanity—to the creation of **high-level programming languages** and compilers that translate programs in such languages into instructions. Figure 1.4 shows the relationships among these programs and languages, which are more examples of the power of **abstraction**.

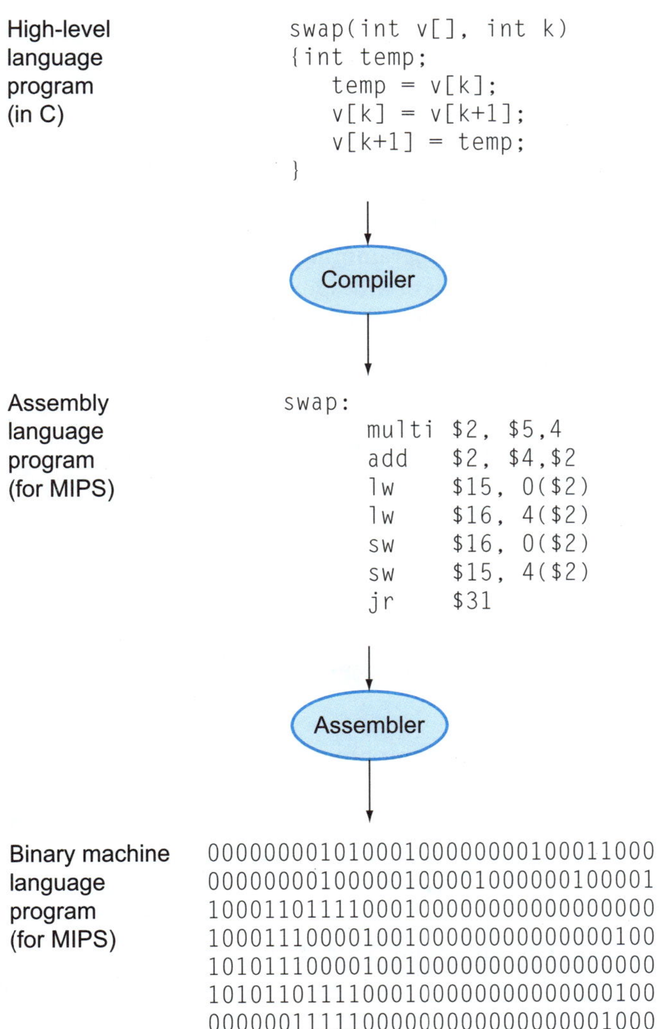

ABSTRACTION

high-level programming language A portable language such as C, C++, Java, or Visual Basic that is composed of words and algebraic notation that can be translated by a compiler into assembly language.

FIGURE 1.4   C program compiled into assembly language and then assembled into binary machine language. Although the translation from high-level language to binary machine language is shown in two steps, some compilers cut out the middleman and produce binary machine language directly. These languages and this program are examined in more detail in Chapter 2.

A compiler enables a programmer to write this high-level language expression:

```
A + B
```

The compiler would compile it into this assembly language statement:

```
add A,B
```

As shown above, the assembler would translate this statement into the binary instructions that tell the computer to add the two numbers A and B.

High-level programming languages offer several important benefits. First, they allow the programmer to think in a more natural language, using English words and algebraic notation, resulting in programs that look much more like text than like tables of cryptic symbols (see Figure 1.4). Moreover, they allow languages to be designed according to their intended use. Hence, Fortran was designed for scientific computation, Cobol for business data processing, Lisp for symbol manipulation, and so on. There are also domain-specific languages for even narrower groups of users, such as those interested in machine learning, for example.

The second advantage of programming languages is improved programmer productivity. One of the few areas of widespread agreement in software development is that it takes less time to develop programs when they are written in languages that require fewer lines to express an idea. Conciseness is a clear advantage of high-level languages over assembly language.

The final advantage is that programming languages allow programs to be independent of the computer on which they were developed, since compilers and assemblers can translate high-level language programs to the binary instructions of any computer. These three advantages are so strong that today little programming is done in assembly language.

1.4   Under the Covers

Now that we have looked below your program to uncover the underlying software, let's open the covers of your computer to learn about the underlying hardware. The underlying hardware in any computer performs the same basic functions: inputting data, outputting data, processing data, and storing data. How these functions are performed is the primary topic of this book, and subsequent chapters deal with different parts of these four tasks.

When we come to an important point in this book, a point so important that we hope you will remember it forever, we emphasize it by identifying it as a *Big Picture* item. We have about a dozen Big Pictures in this book, the first being the five components of a computer that perform the tasks of inputting, outputting, processing, and storing data.

Two key components of computers are **input devices**, such as the microphone, and **output devices**, such as the speaker. As the names suggest, input feeds the

input device
A mechanism through which the computer is fed information, such as a keyboard.

output device
A mechanism that conveys the result of a computation to a user, such as a display, or to another computer.

computer, and output is the result of computation sent to the user. Some devices, such as wireless networks, provide both input and output to the computer.

Chapters 5 and 6 describe input/output (I/O) devices in more detail, but let's take an introductory tour through the computer hardware, starting with the external I/O devices.

The five classic components of a computer are input, output, memory, datapath, and control, with the last two sometimes combined and called the processor. Figure 1.5 shows the standard organization of a computer. This organization is independent of hardware technology: you can place every piece of every computer, past and present, into one of these five categories. To help you keep all this in perspective, the five components of a computer are shown on the front page of each of the following chapters, with the portion of interest to that chapter highlighted.

The **BIG** Picture

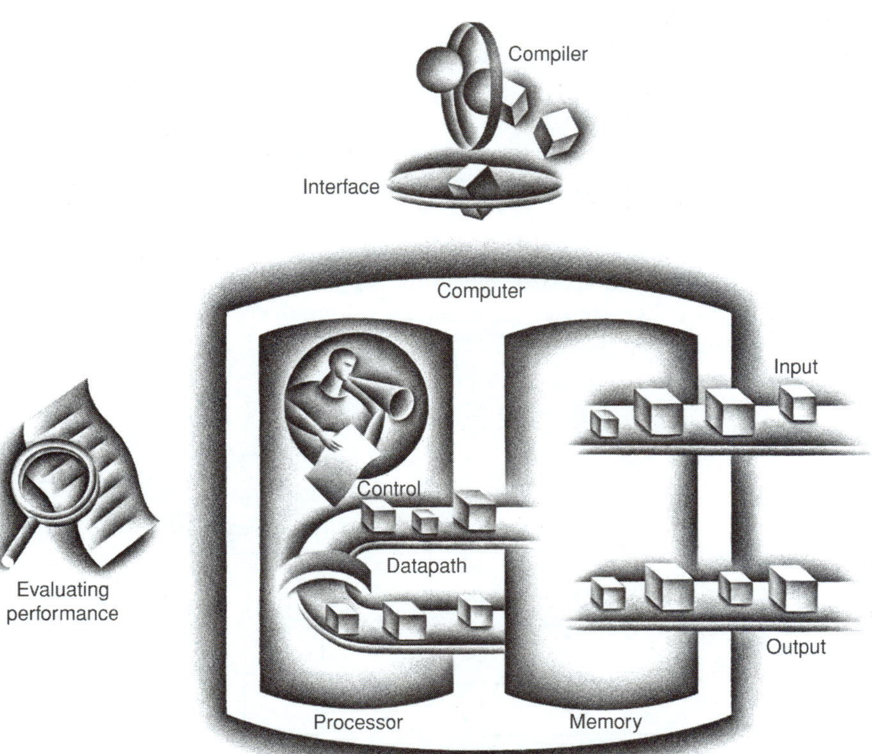

FIGURE 1.5 The organization of a computer, showing the five classic components. The processor gets instructions and data from memory. Input writes data to memory, and output reads data from memory. Control sends the signals that determine the operations of the datapath, memory, input, and output.

Through the Looking Glass

The most fascinating I/O device is probably the graphics display. Most personal mobile devices use **liquid crystal displays (LCDs)** to get a thin, low-power display. The LCD is not the source of light; instead, it controls the transmission of light. A typical LCD includes rod-shaped molecules in a liquid that form a twisting helix that bends light entering the display, from either a light source behind the display or less often from reflected light. The rods straighten out when a current is applied and no longer bend the light. Since the liquid crystal material is between two screens polarized at 90 degrees, the light cannot pass through unless it is bent. Today, most LCD displays use an **active matrix** that has a tiny transistor switch at each pixel to precisely control current and make sharper images. A red-green-blue mask associated with each dot on the display determines the intensity of the three-color components in the final image; in a color active matrix LCD, there are three transistor switches at each point.

The image is composed of a matrix of picture elements, or **pixels**, which can be represented as a matrix of bits, called a *bit map*. Depending on the size of the screen and the resolution, the display matrix in a typical tablet ranges in size from 1024 X 768 to 2048 X 1536. A color display might use 8 bits for each of the three colors (red, blue, and green), for 24 bits per pixel, permitting millions of different colors to be displayed.

The computer hardware support for graphics consists mainly of a *raster refresh buffer*, or *frame buffer*, to store the bit map. The image to be represented onscreen is stored in the frame buffer, and the bit pattern per pixel is read out to the graphics display at the refresh rate. Figure 1.6 shows a frame buffer with a simplified design of just 4 bits per pixel.

The goal of the bit map is to faithfully represent what is on the screen. The challenges in graphics systems arise because the human eye is very good at detecting even subtle changes on the screen.

liquid crystal display A display technology using a thin layer of liquid polymers that can be used to transmit or block light according to whether a charge is applied.

active matrix display A liquid crystal display using a transistor to control the transmission of light at each individual pixel.

pixel The smallest individual picture element. Screens are composed of hundreds of thousands to millions of pixels, organized in a matrix.

Through computer displays I have landed an airplane on the deck of a moving carrier, observed a nuclear particle hit a potential well, flown in a rocket at nearly the speed of light and watched a computer reveal its innermost workings.

Ivan Sutherland, the "father" of computer graphics, *Scientific American*, 1984

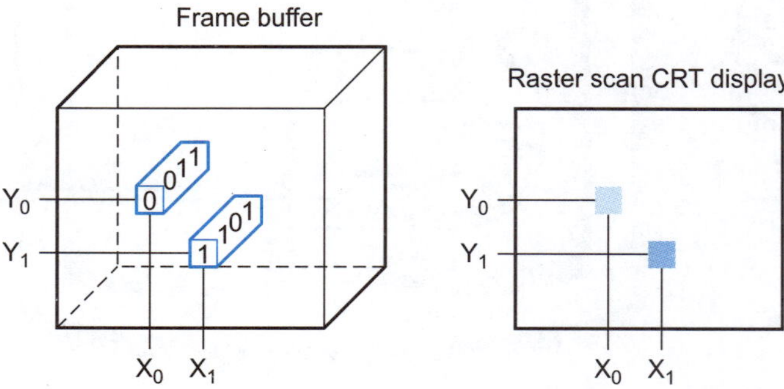

FIGURE 1.6   Each coordinate in the frame buffer on the left determines the shade of the corresponding coordinate for the raster scan CRT display on the right. Pixel (X_0, Y_0) contains the bit pattern 0011, which is a lighter shade on the screen than the bit pattern 1101 in pixel (X_1, Y_1).

Touchscreen

While PCs also use LCD displays, the tablets and smartphones of the PostPC era have replaced the keyboard and mouse with touch sensitive displays, which has the wonderful user interface advantage of users pointing directly what they are interested in rather than indirectly with a mouse.

While there are a variety of ways to implement a touch screen, many tablets today use capacitive sensing. Since people are electrical conductors, if an insulator like glass is covered with a transparent conductor, touching distorts the electrostatic field of the screen, which results in a change in capacitance. This technology can allow multiple touches simultaneously, which allows gestures that can lead to attractive user interfaces.

Opening the Box

Figure 1.7 shows the contents of the Apple iPhone Xs Max smart phone. Unsurprisingly, of the five classic components of the computer, I/O dominates this device. The list of I/O devices includes a capacitive multitouch LCD display, front-facing camera, rear-facing camera, microphone, headphone jack, speakers, accelerometer, gyroscope, Wi-Fi network, and Bluetooth network. The datapath, control, and memory are a tiny portion of the components.

The small rectangles in Figure 1.8 contain the devices that drive our advancing technology, called **integrated circuits** and nicknamed **chips**. The A12 package seen in the middle of in Figure 1.8 contains two large ARM processors and four little ARM processors that operate with a clock rate of 2.5 GHz. The *processor* is the active part of the computer, following the instructions of a program to the letter. It adds numbers, tests numbers, signals I/O devices to activate, and so on. Occasionally, people call the processor the **CPU**, for the more bureaucratic-sounding **central processor unit**.

Descending even lower into the hardware, Figure 1.9 reveals details of a microprocessor. The processor logically comprises two main components: datapath and control, the respective brawn and brain of the processor. The **datapath** performs the arithmetic operations, and **control** tells the datapath, memory, and I/O devices what to do according to the wishes of the instructions of the program. Chapter 4 explains the datapath and control for a higher performance design.

The iPhone Xs Max package in Figure 1.8 also includes a memory chip with 32 gibibits or 2 GiB of capacity. The **memory** is where the programs are kept when they are running; it also contains the data needed by the running programs. The memory is a DRAM chip. *DRAM* stands for **dynamic random access memory**. DRAMs are used together to contain the instructions and data of a program. In contrast to sequential access memories, such as magnetic tapes, the *RAM* portion of the term *DRAM* means that memory accesses take basically the same amount of time no matter what portion of the memory is read.

integrated circuit Also called a chip. A device combining dozens to millions of transistors.

central processor unit (CPU) Also called processor. The active part of the computer, which contains the datapath and control and which adds numbers, tests numbers, signals I/O devices to activate, and so on.

datapath The component of the processor that performs arithmetic operations

control The component of the processor that commands the datapath, memory, and I/O devices according to the instructions of the program.

memory The storage area in which programs are kept when they are running and that contains the data needed by the running programs.

dynamic random access memory (DRAM) Memory built as an integrated circuit; it provides random access to any location. Access times are 50 nanoseconds and cost per gigabyte in 2020 was $3 to $6.

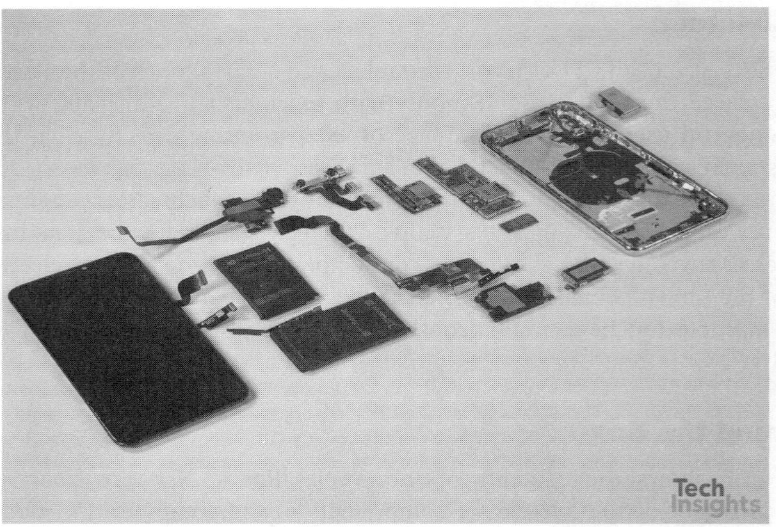

FIGURE 1.7   Components of the Apple iPhone Xs Max cell phone. At the left is the capacitive multitouch screen and LCD display. Next to it is the battery. To the far right is the metal frame that attaches the LCD to the back of the iPhone. The small components surrounding in the center are what we think of as the computer; they are not simple rectangles to fit compactly inside the case next to the battery. Figure 1.8 shows a close-up of the board to the left of the metal case, which is the logic printed circuit board that contains the processor and the memory (Courtesy TechInsights, www.techIngishts.com).

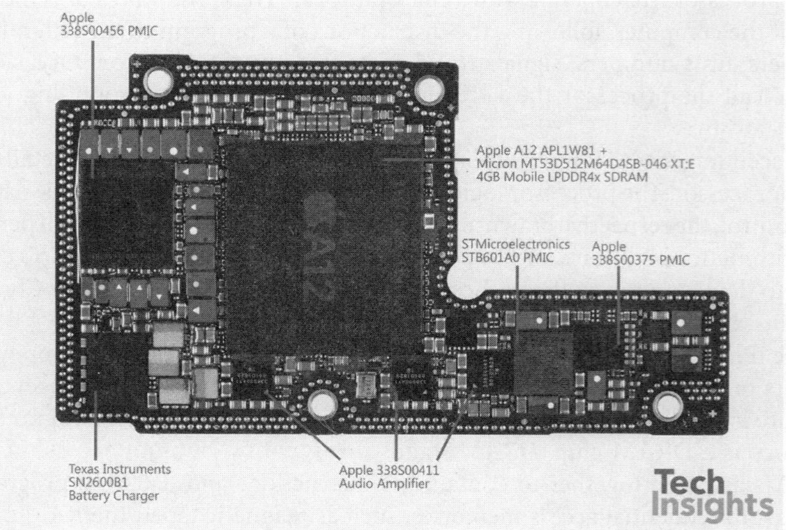

FIGURE 1.8   The logic board of Apple iPhone Xs Max in Figure 1.7. The large integrated circuit in the middle is the Apple A12 chip, which contains two large ARM processor cores and four little ARM processor cores that run at 2.5 GHz, as well as 2 GiB of main memory inside the package. Figure 1.9 shows a photograph of the processor chip inside the A12 package. A similar-sized chip on a symmetric board attached to the back is the 64 GiB flash memory chip for nonvolatile storage. The other chips on the board include power management integrated controller and audio amplifier chips (Courtesy TechInsights, www.techIngishts.com).

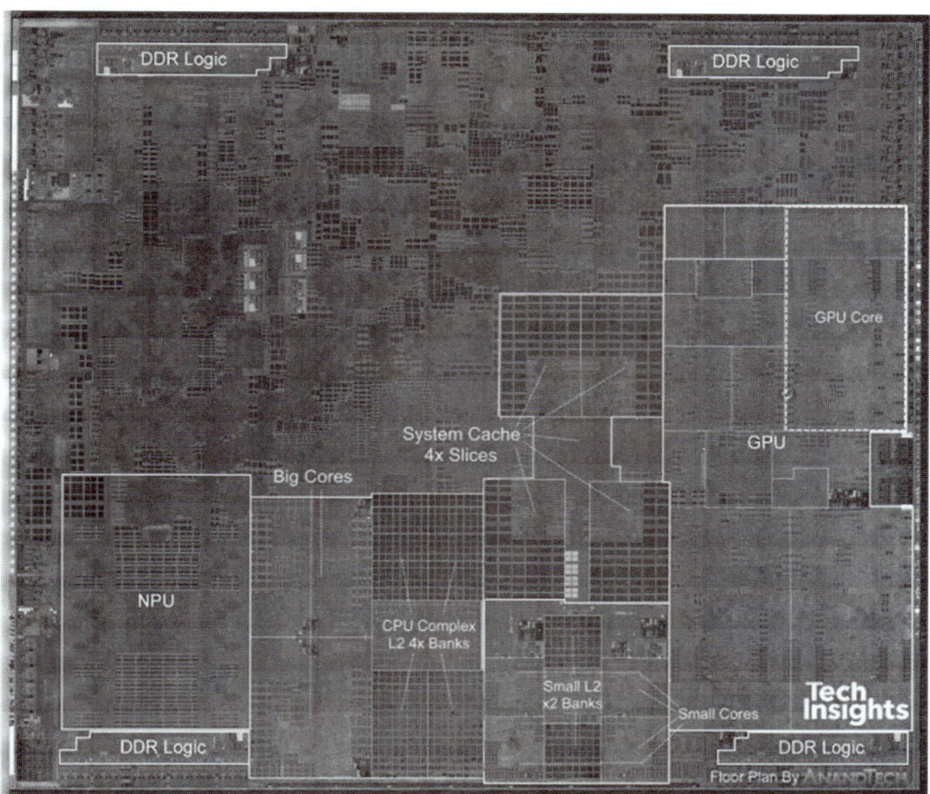

FIGURE 1.9   The processor integrated circuit inside the A12 package. The size of chip is 8.4 by 9.91 mm, and it was manufactured originally in a 7-nm process (see Section 1.5). It has two identical ARM big processors or cores in the lower middle of the chip, four small cores on the lower right of the chip, a graphical processor unit (GPU) on the far right (see Section 6.6), and a domain-specific accelerator for neural networks (see Section 6.7), called the NPU, on the far left. In the middle are second-level cache memories (L2) for the big and small cores (see Chapter 5). At the top and bottom of the chip are interfaces to main memory (DDR DRAM) (Courtesy TechInsights, www.techinsights.com, and AnandTech, www.anandtech.com).

Descending into the depths of any component of the hardware reveals insights into the computer. Inside the processor is another type of memory—cache memory. **Cache memory** consists of a small, fast memory that acts as a buffer for the DRAM memory. (The nontechnical definition of *cache* is a safe place for hiding things.) Cache is built using a different memory technology, **static random access memory (SRAM)**. SRAM is faster but less dense, and hence more expensive, than DRAM (see Chapter 5). SRAM and DRAM are two layers of the **memory hierarchy**.

cache memory A small, fast memory that acts as a buffer for a slower, larger memory.

static random access memory (SRAM) Also memory built as an integrated circuit, but faster and less dense than DRAM.

instruction set architecture Also called **architecture**. An abstract interface between the hardware and the lowest-level software that encompasses all the information necessary to write a machine language program that will run correctly, including instructions, registers, memory access, I/O, and so on.

application binary interface (ABI) The user portion of the instruction set plus the operating system interfaces used by application programmers. It defines a standard for binary portability across computers.

The **BIG** Picture

implementation Hardware that obeys the architecture abstraction.

volatile memory Storage, such as DRAM, that retains data only if it is receiving power.

nonvolatile memory A form of memory that retains data even in the absence of a power source and that is used to store programs between runs. A DVD disk is nonvolatile.

As mentioned above, one of the great ideas to improve design is abstraction. One of the most important **abstractions** is the interface between the hardware and the lowest-level software. Software communicates to hardware via a vocabulary. The words of the vocabulary are called instructions, and the vocabulary itself is called the **instruction set architecture**, or simply **architecture**, of a computer. The instruction set architecture includes anything programmers need to know to make a binary machine language program work correctly, including instructions, I/O devices, and so on. Typically, the operating system will encapsulate the details of doing I/O, allocating memory, and other low-level system functions so that application programmers do not need to worry about such details. The combination of the basic instruction set and the operating system interface provided for application programmers is called the **application binary interface (ABI)**.

An instruction set architecture allows computer designers to talk about functions independently from the hardware that performs them. For example, we can talk about the functions of a digital clock (keeping time, displaying the time, setting the alarm) independently from the clock hardware (quartz crystal, LED displays, plastic buttons). Computer designers distinguish architecture from an **implementation** of an architecture along the same lines: an implementation is hardware that obeys the architecture abstraction. These ideas bring us to another Big Picture.

> Both hardware and software consist of hierarchical layers using abstraction, with each lower layer hiding details from the level above. One key interface between the levels of abstraction is the *instruction set architecture*—the interface between the hardware and low-level software. This abstract interface enables many *implementations* of varying cost and performance to run identical software.

A Safe Place for Data

Thus far, we have seen how to input data, compute using the data, and display data. If we were to lose power to the computer, however, everything would be lost because the memory inside the computer is **volatile**—that is, when it loses power, it forgets. In contrast, a DVD disk doesn't forget the movie when you turn off the power to the DVD player, and is thus a **nonvolatile memory** technology.

To distinguish between the volatile memory used to hold data and programs while they are running and this nonvolatile memory used to store data and programs between runs, the term **main memory** or **primary memory** is used for the former, and **secondary memory** for the latter. Secondary memory forms the next lower layer of the **memory hierarchy**. DRAMs have dominated main memory since 1975, but **magnetic disks** dominated secondary memory starting even earlier. Because of their size and form factor, personal Mobile Devices use **flash memory**, a nonvolatile semiconductor memory, instead of disks. Figure 1.8 shows the chip containing the 64 GiB flash memory of the iPhone Xs. While slower than DRAM, it is much cheaper than DRAM in addition to being nonvolatile. Although costing more per bit than disks, it is smaller, it comes in much smaller capacities, it is more rugged, and it is more power efficient than disks. Hence, flash memory is the standard secondary memory for PMDs. Alas, unlike disks and DRAM, flash memory bits wear out after 100,000 to 1,000,000 writes. Thus, file systems must keep track of the number of writes and have a strategy to avoid wearing out storage, such as by moving popular data. Chapter 5 describes disks and flash memory in more detail.

Communicating with Other Computers

We've explained how we can input, compute, display, and save data, but there is still one missing item found in today's computers: computer networks. Just as the processor shown in Figure 1.5 is connected to memory and I/O devices, networks interconnect whole computers, allowing computer users to extend the power of computing by including communication. Networks have become so popular that they are the backbone of current computer systems; a new personal mobile device or server without a network interface would be ridiculed. Networked computers have several major advantages:

- *Communication*: Information is exchanged between computers at high speeds.

- *Resource sharing*: Rather than each computer having its own I/O devices, computers on the network can share I/O devices.

- *Nonlocal access*: By connecting computers over long distances, users need not be near the computer they are using.

Networks vary in length and performance, with the cost of communication increasing according to both the speed of communication and the distance that information travels. Perhaps the most popular type of network is *Ethernet*. It can be up to a kilometer long and transfer at up to 100 gigabits per second. Its length and speed make Ethernet useful to connect computers on the same floor of a building; hence, it is an example of what is generically called a **local area network**. Local area networks are interconnected with switches that can also provide routing services and security. **Wide area networks** cross continents and are the backbone of the Internet, which supports the web. They are typically based on optical fibers and are leased from telecommunication companies.

Networks have changed the face of computing in the last 40 years, both by becoming much more ubiquitous and by making dramatic increases in performance.

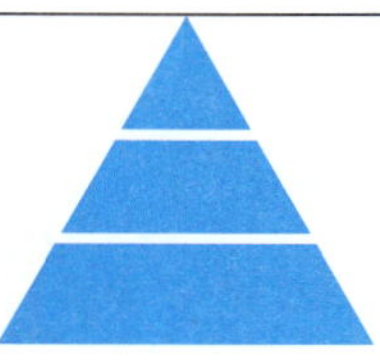

main memory Also called **primary memory**. Memory used to hold programs while they are running; typically consists of DRAM in today's computers.

secondary memory Nonvolatile memory used to store programs and data between runs; typically consists of flash memory in PMDs and magnetic disks in servers.

magnetic disk Also called **hard disk**. A form of nonvolatile secondary memory composed of rotating platters coated with a magnetic recording material. Because they are rotating mechanical devices, access times are about 5 to 20 milliseconds and cost per gigabyte in 2020 was $0.01 to $0.02.

flash memory A nonvolatile semiconductor memory. It is cheaper and slower than DRAM but more expensive per bit and faster than magnetic disks. Access times are about 5 to 50 microseconds and cost per gigabyte in 2020 was $0.06 to $0.12.

local area network (LAN) A network designed to carry data within a geographically confined area, typically within a single building.

wide area network (WAN) A network extended over hundreds of kilometers that can span a continent.

In the 1970s, very few individuals had access to electronic mail, the Internet and web did not exist, and physically mailing magnetic tapes was the primary way to transfer large amounts of data between two locations. Local area networks were almost nonexistent, and the few existing wide area networks had limited capacity and restricted access.

As networking technology improved, it became much cheaper and had a much higher capacity. For example, the first standardized local area network technology, developed about 40 years ago, was a version of Ethernet that had a maximum capacity (also called bandwidth) of 10 million bits per second, typically shared by tens of, if not a hundred, computers. Today, local area network technology offers a capacity of from 1 to 100 gigabits per second, usually shared by at most a few computers. Optical communications technology has allowed similar growth in the capacity of wide area networks, from hundreds of kilobits to gigabits and from hundreds of computers connected to a worldwide network to millions of computers connected. This combination of dramatic rise in deployment of networking combined with increases in capacity have made network technology central to the information revolution of the last 30 years.

For the last 15 years another innovation in networking is reshaping the way computers communicate. Wireless technology is widespread, which enabled the PostPC Era. The ability to make a radio in the same low-cost semiconductor technology (CMOS) used for memory and microprocessors enabled a significant improvement in price, leading to an explosion in deployment. Currently available wireless technologies, called by the IEEE standard name 802.11ac, allow for transmission rates from 1 to 1300 million bits per second. Wireless technology is quite a bit different from wire-based networks, since all users in an immediate area share the airwaves.

Check Yourself

- Semiconductor DRAM memory, flash memory, and disk storage differ significantly. For each technology, list its volatility, approximate relative access time, and approximate relative cost compared to DRAM.

1.5 Technologies for Building Processors and Memory

Processors and memory have improved at an incredible rate, because computer designers have long embraced the latest in electronic technology to try to win the race to design a better computer. Figure 1.10 shows the technologies that have been used over time, with an estimate of the relative performance per unit cost for each technology. Since this technology shapes what computers will be able to do and how quickly they will evolve, we believe all computer professionals should be familiar with the basics of integrated circuits.

transistor An on/off switch controlled by an electric signal.

A **transistor** is simply an on/off switch controlled by electricity. The *integrated circuit* (IC) combined dozens to hundreds of transistors into a single chip. When Gordon Moore predicted the continuous doubling of resources, he was predicting

Year	Technology used in computers	Relative performance/unit cost
1951	Vacuum tube	1
1965	Transistor	35
1975	Integrated circuit	900
1995	Very large-scale integrated circuit	2,400,000
2020	Ultra large-scale integrated circuit	500,000,000,000

FIGURE 1.10   Relative performance per unit cost of technologies used in computers over time. Source: Computer Museum, Boston, with 2020 extrapolated by the authors. See 🌐 Section 1.13.

the growth rate of the number of transistors per chip. To describe the tremendous increase in the number of transistors from hundreds to millions, the adjective *very large scale* is added to the term, creating the abbreviation *VLSI*, for **very large-scale integrated circuit**.

This rate of increasing integration has been remarkably stable. Figure 1.11 shows the growth in DRAM capacity since 1977. For decades, the industry has consistently quadrupled capacity every 3 years, resulting in an increase in excess of 16,000 times! Figure 1.11 also shows the slowdown due to the slowing of Moore's Law; quadrupuling capacity has taken 6 years recently.

To understand how manufacture integrated circuits, we start at the beginning. The manufacture of a chip begins with **silicon**, a substance found in sand. Because silicon does not conduct electricity well, it is called a **semiconductor**. With a special chemical process, it is possible to add materials to silicon that allow tiny areas to transform into one of three devices:

- Excellent conductors of electricity (using either microscopic copper or aluminum wire)

- Excellent insulators from electricity (like plastic sheathing or glass)

- Areas that can conduct or insulate under special conditions (as a switch)

very large-scale integrated (VLSI) circuit A device containing hundreds of thousands to millions of transistors.

silicon A natural element that is a semiconductor.

semiconductor A substance that does not conduct electricity well.

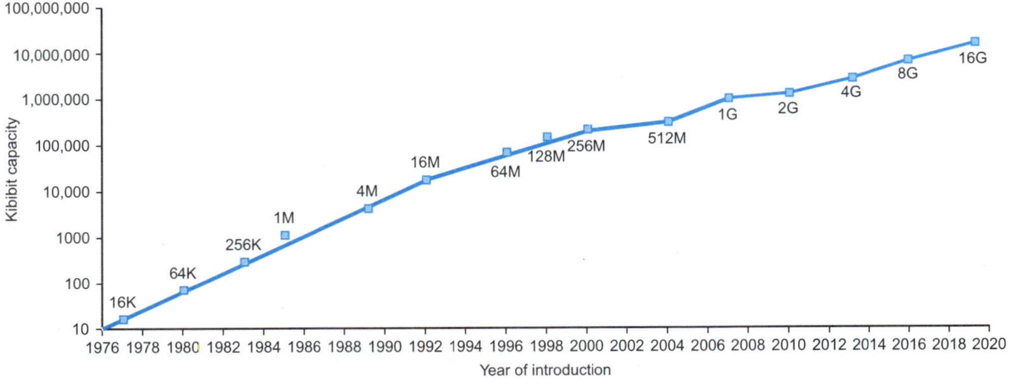

FIGURE 1.11   Growth of capacity per DRAM chip over time. The *y*-axis is measured in kibibits (2^{10} bits). The DRAM industry quadrupled capacity almost every three years, a 60% increase per year, for 20 years. In recent years, the rate has slowed down and is somewhat closer to doubling every three years. With the slowing of Moore's Law and difficulties in reliable manufacturing of smaller DRAM cells given the challenging aspect ratios of their three-dimensional structure.

Transistors fall in the last category. A VLSI circuit, then, is just billions of combinations of conductors, insulators, and switches manufactured in a single small package.

The manufacturing process for integrated circuits is critical to the cost of the chips and hence important to computer designers. Figure 1.12 shows that process. The process starts with a **silicon crystal ingot**, which looks like a giant sausage. Today, ingots are 8–12 inches in diameter and about 12–24 inches long. An ingot is finely sliced into **wafers** no more than 0.1 inches thick. These wafers then go through a series of processing steps, during which patterns of chemicals are placed on each wafer, creating the transistors, conductors, and insulators discussed earlier. Today's integrated circuits contain only one layer of transistors but may have from two to eight levels of metal conductor, separated by layers of insulators.

silicon crystal ingot
A rod composed of a silicon crystal that is between 8 and 12 inches in diameter and about 12 to 24 inches long.

wafer A slice from a silicon ingot no more than 0.1 inches thick, used to create chips.

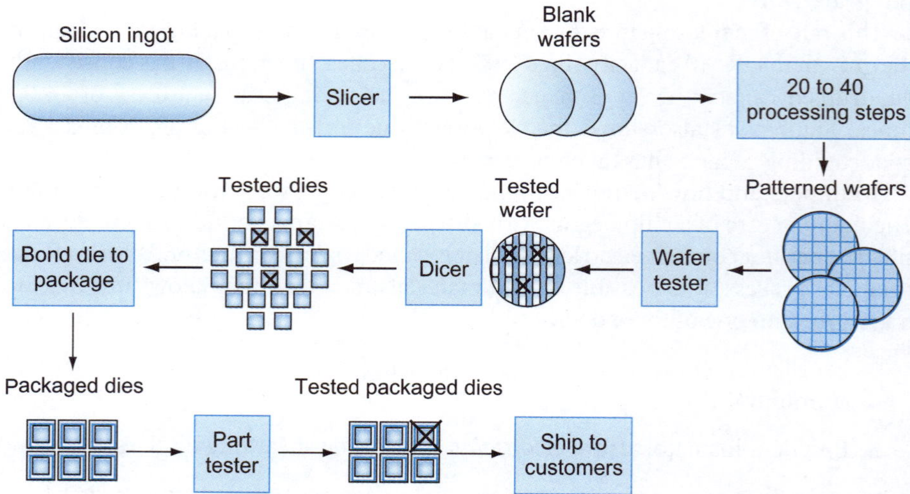

FIGURE 1.12   The chip manufacturing process. After being sliced from the silicon ingot, blank wafers are put through 20 to 40 steps to create patterned wafers (see Figure 1.13). These patterned wafers are then tested with a wafer tester, and a map of the good parts is made. Then, the wafers are diced into dies (see Figure 1.9). In this figure, one wafer produced 20 dies, of which 17 passed testing. (X means the die is bad.) The yield of good dies in this case was 17/20, or 85%. These good dies are then bonded into packages and tested one more time before shipping the packaged parts to customers. One bad packaged part was found in this final test.

defect A microscopic flaw in a wafer or in patterning steps that can result in the failure of the die containing that defect.

die The individual rectangular sections that are cut from a wafer, more informally known as **chips**.

A single microscopic flaw in the wafer itself or in one of the dozens of patterning steps can result in that area of the wafer failing. These **defects**, as they are called, make it virtually impossible to manufacture a perfect wafer. The simplest way to cope with imperfection is to place many independent components on a single wafer. The patterned wafer is then chopped up, or *diced*, into these components, called **dies** and more informally known as **chips**. Figure 1.13 shows a photograph of a wafer containing microprocessors before they have been diced; earlier, Figure 1.9 shows an individual microprocessor die.

Dicing enables you to discard only those dies that were unlucky enough to contain the flaws, rather than the whole wafer. This concept is quantified by the

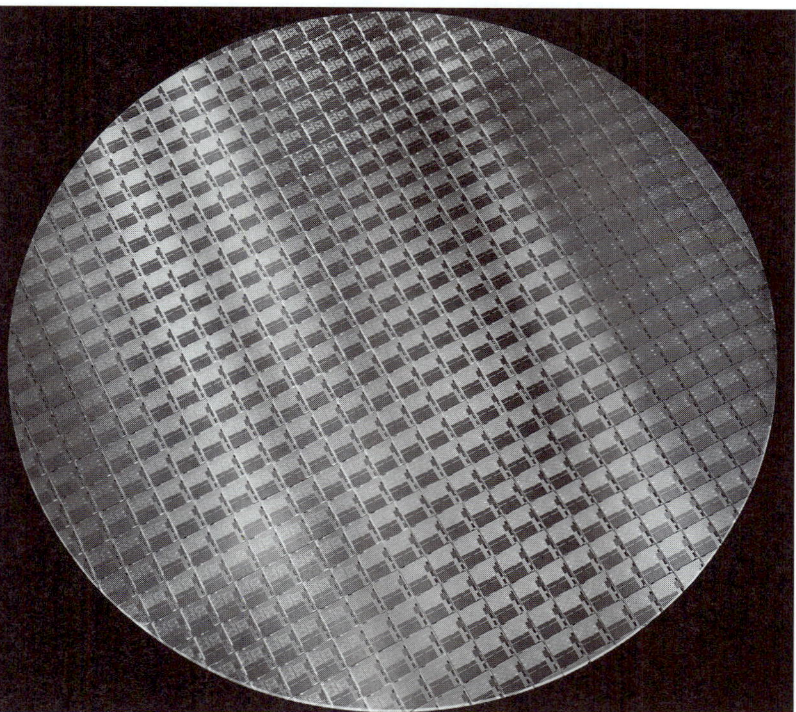

FIGURE 1.13   A 12-inch (300-mm) wafer this 10nm wafer contains 10th Gen Intel® Core™ processors, code-named "Ice Lake" (Courtesy Intel). The number of dies on this 300-mm (12-inch) wafer at 100% yield is 506. According to AnandTech,[1] each Ice Lake die is 11.4 by 10.7 mm. The several dozen partially rounded chips at the boundaries of the wafer are useless; they are included because it is easier to create the masks used to pattern the silicon. This die uses a 10-nm technology, which means that the smallest features are approximately 10 nm in size, although they are typically somewhat smaller than the actual feature size, which refers to the size of the transistors as "drawn" versus the final manufactured size.

yield of a process, which is defined as the percentage of good dies from the total number of dies on the wafer.

The cost of an integrated circuit rises quickly as the die size increases, due both to the lower yield and the smaller number of dies that fit on a wafer. To reduce the cost, using the next generation process shrinks a large die as it uses smaller sizes for both transistors and wires. This improves the yield and the die count per wafer. A 7-nanometer (nm) process was state-of-the-art in 2020, which means essentially that the smallest feature size on the die is 7 nm.

Once you've found good dies, they are connected to the input/output pins of a package, using a process called *bonding*. These packaged parts are tested a final time, since mistakes can occur in packaging, and then they are shipped to customers.

While we have talked about the cost of chips, there is a difference between cost and price. Companies charge as much as the market will bear to maximize the

yield The percentage of good dies from the total number of dies on the wafer.

---

[1]Ian Cutress, "I Ran Off with Intel's Tiger Lake Wafer. Who Wants a Die Shot?" January 13, 2020, https://www.anandtech.com/show/15380/i-ran-off-with-intels-tiger-lake-wafer-who-wants-a-die-shot

return on their investment, which must cover costs like a company's research and development (R&D), marketing, sales, manufacturing equipment maintenance, building rental, cost of financing, pretax profits, and taxes. Margins can be higher on unique chips that come from only one company, like microprocessors, versus chips that are commodities supplied by several companies, like DRAMs. The price fluctuates based on the ratio of supply and demand, and it is easy for multiple companies to build more chips than the market demands.

Elaboration: The cost of an integrated circuit can be expressed in three simple equations:

$$\text{Cost per die} = \frac{\text{Cost per wafer}}{\text{Dies per wafer} \times \text{yield}}$$

$$\text{Dies per wafer} \approx \frac{\text{Wafer area}}{\text{Die area}}$$

$$\text{Yield} = \frac{1}{(1 + (\text{Defects per area} \times \text{Die area}))^n}$$

The first equation is straightforward to derive. The second is an approximation, since it does not subtract the area near the border of the round wafer that cannot accommodate the rectangular dies (see Figure 1.13). The final equation is based on empirical observations of yields at integrated circuit factories, with the exponent related to the number of critical processing steps.

Hence, depending on the defect rate and the size of the die and wafer, costs are generally not linear in the die area.

Check Yourself

A key factor in determining the cost of an integrated circuit is volume. Which of the following are reasons why a chip made in high volume should cost less?

1. With high volumes, the manufacturing process can be tuned to a particular design, increasing the yield.

2. It is less work to design a high-volume part than a low-volume part.

3. The masks used to make the chip are expensive, so the cost per chip is lower for higher volumes.

4. Engineering development costs are high and largely independent of volume; thus, the development cost per die is lower with high-volume parts.

5. High-volume parts usually have smaller die sizes than low-volume parts and therefore have higher yield per wafer.

1.6   Performance

Assessing the performance of computers can be quite challenging. The scale and intricacy of modern software systems, together with the wide range of performance improvement techniques employed by hardware designers, have made performance assessment much more difficult.

When trying to choose among different computers, performance is an important attribute. Accurately measuring and comparing different computers is critical to purchasers and therefore to designers. The people selling computers know this as well. Often, salespeople would like you to see their computer in the best possible light, whether or not this light accurately reflects the needs of the purchaser's application. Hence, understanding how best to measure performance and the limitations of performance measurements is important in selecting a computer.

The rest of this section describes different ways in which performance can be determined; then, we describe the metrics for measuring performance from the viewpoint of both a computer user and a designer. We also look at how these metrics are related and present the classical processor performance equation, which we will use throughout the text.

Defining Performance

When we say one computer has better performance than another, what do we mean? Although this question might seem simple, an analogy with passenger airplanes shows how subtle the question of performance can be. Figure 1.14 lists some typical passenger airplanes, together with their cruising speed, range, and capacity. If we wanted to know which of the planes in this table had the best performance, we would first need to define performance. For example, considering different measures of performance, we see that the plane with the highest cruising speed was the Concorde (retired from service in 2003), the plane with the longest range is the Boeing 777-200LR, and the plane with the largest capacity is the Airbus A380-800.

Airplane	Passenger capacity	Cruising range (miles)	Cruising speed (m.p.h.)	Passenger throughput (passengers × m.p.h.)
Boeing 737	240	3000	564	135,360
BAC/Sud Concorde	132	4000	1350	178,200
Boeing 777-200LR	301	9395	554	166,761
Airbus A380-800	853	8477	587	500,711

FIGURE 1.14 The capacity, range, and speed for a number of commercial airplanes. The last column shows the rate at which the airplane transports passengers, which is the capacity times the cruising speed (ignoring range and takeoff and landing times).

Let's suppose we define performance in terms of speed. This still leaves two possible definitions. You could define the fastest plane as the one with the highest cruising speed, taking a single passenger from one point to another in the least time. If you were interested in transporting 500 passengers from one point to another, however, the Airbus A380-800 would clearly be the fastest, as the last column of the figure shows. Similarly, we can define computer performance in several different ways.

If you were running a program on two different desktop computers, you'd say that the faster one is the desktop computer that gets the job done first. If you were running a datacenter that had several servers running jobs submitted by many users, you'd say that the faster computer was the one that completed the most

response time Also called **execution time**. The total time required for the computer to complete a task, including disk accesses, memory accesses, I/O activities, operating system overhead, CPU execution time, and so on.

jobs during a day. As an individual computer user, you are interested in reducing **response time**—the time between the start and completion of a task—also referred to as **execution time**. Datacenter managers are often interested in increasing **throughput** or **bandwidth**—the total amount of work done in a given time. Hence, in most cases, we will need different performance metrics as well as different sets of applications to benchmark personal mobile devices, which are more focused on response time, versus servers, which are more focused on throughput.

throughput Also called **bandwidth**. Another measure of performance, it is the number of tasks completed per unit time.

Throughput and Response Time

EXAMPLE

Do the following changes to a computer system increase throughput, decrease response time, or both?

1. Replacing the processor in a computer with a faster version

2. Adding additional processors to a system that uses multiple processors for separate tasks—for example, searching the web

ANSWER

Decreasing response time almost always improves throughput. Hence, in case 1, both response time and throughput are improved. In case 2, no one task gets work done faster, so only throughput increases.

If, however, the demand for processing in the second case was almost as large as the throughput, the system might force requests to queue up. In this case, increasing the throughput could also improve response time, since it would reduce the waiting time in the queue. Thus, in many real computer systems, changing either execution time or throughput often affects the other.

In discussing the performance of computers, we will be primarily concerned with response time for the first few chapters. To maximize performance, we want to minimize response time or execution time for some task. Thus, we can relate performance and execution time for a computer X:

$$\text{Performance}_X = \frac{1}{\text{Execution time}_X}$$

This means that for two computers X and Y, if the performance of X is greater than the performance of Y, we have

$$\text{Performance}_X > \text{Performance}_Y$$

$$\frac{1}{\text{Execution time}_X} > \frac{1}{\text{Execution time}_Y}$$

$$\text{Execution time}_Y > \text{Execution time}_X$$

That is, the execution time on Y is longer than that on X, if X is faster than Y.

In discussing a computer design, we often want to relate the performance of two different computers quantitatively. We will use the phrase "X is n times faster than Y"—or equivalently "X is n times as fast as Y"—to mean

$$\frac{\text{Performance}_X}{\text{Performance}_Y} = n$$

If X is n times as fast as Y, then the execution time on Y is n times as long as it is on X:

$$\frac{\text{Performance}_X}{\text{Performance}_Y} = \frac{\text{Execution time}_Y}{\text{Execution time}_X} = n$$

Relative Performance

If computer A runs a program in 10 seconds and computer B runs the same program in 15 seconds, how much faster is A than B?

EXAMPLE

We know that A is n times as fast as B if

$$\frac{\text{Performance}_A}{\text{Performance}_B} = \frac{\text{Execution time}_B}{\text{Execution time}_A} = n$$

ANSWER

Thus the performance ratio is

$$\frac{15}{10} = 1.5$$

and A is therefore 1.5 times as fast as B.

In the above example, we could also say that computer B is 1.5 times *slower than* computer A, since

$$\frac{\text{Performance}_A}{\text{Performance}_B} = 1.5$$

means that

$$\frac{\text{Performance}_A}{1.5} = \text{Performance}_B$$

For simplicity, we will normally use the terminology *as fast as* when we try to compare computers quantitatively. Because performance and execution time are reciprocals, increasing performance requires decreasing execution time. To avoid the potential confusion between the terms *increasing* and *decreasing*, we usually say "improve performance" or "improve execution time" when we mean "increase performance" and "decrease execution time."

Measuring Performance

Time is the measure of computer performance: the computer that performs the same amount of work in the least time is the fastest. Program *execution time* is measured in seconds per program. However, time can be defined in different ways, depending on what we count. The most straightforward definition of time is called *wall clock time*, *response time*, or *elapsed time*. These terms mean the total time to complete a task, including disk accesses, memory accesses, *input/output* (I/O) activities, operating system overhead—everything.

Computers are often shared, however, and a processor may work on several programs simultaneously. In such cases, the system may try to optimize throughput rather than attempt to minimize the elapsed time for one program. Hence, we might want to distinguish between the elapsed time and the time over which the processor is working on our behalf. **CPU execution time** or simply **CPU time**, which recognizes this distinction, is the time the CPU spends computing for this task and does not include time spent waiting for I/O or running other programs. (Remember, though, that the response time experienced by the user will be the elapsed time of the program, not the CPU time.) CPU time can be further divided into the CPU time spent in the program, called **user CPU time**, and the CPU time spent in the operating system performing tasks on behalf of the program, called **system CPU time**. Differentiating between system and user CPU time is difficult to do accurately, because it is often hard to assign responsibility for operating system activities to one user program rather than another and because of the functionality differences among operating systems.

For consistency, we maintain a distinction between performance based on elapsed time and that based on CPU execution time. We will use the term *system performance* to refer to elapsed time on an unloaded system and *CPU performance* to refer to user CPU time. We will focus on CPU performance in this chapter, although our discussions of how to summarize performance can be applied to either elapsed time or CPU time measurements.

CPU execution time Also called **CPU time**. The actual time the CPU spends computing for a specific task.

user CPU time The CPU time spent in a program itself.

system CPU time The CPU time spent in the operating system performing tasks on behalf of the program.

Understanding Program Performance

Different applications are sensitive to different aspects of the performance of a computer system. Many applications, especially those running on servers, depend as much on I/O performance, which, in turn, relies on both hardware and software. Total elapsed time measured by a wall clock is the measurement of interest. In some application environments, the user may care about throughput, response time, or a complex combination of the two (e.g., maximum throughput with a worst-case response time). To improve the performance of a program, one must have a clear definition of what performance metric matters and then proceed to look for performance bottlenecks by measuring program execution and looking for the likely bottlenecks. In the following chapters, we will describe how to search for bottlenecks and improve performance in various parts of the system.

Although as computer users we care about time, when we examine the details of a computer it's convenient to think about performance in other metrics. In particular, computer designers may want to think about a computer by using a measure that relates to how fast the hardware can perform basic functions. Almost all computers are constructed using a clock that determines when events take place in the hardware. These discrete time intervals are called **clock cycles** (or **ticks, clock ticks, clock periods, clocks, cycles**). Designers refer to the length of a **clock period** both as the time for a complete *clock cycle* (e.g., 250 picoseconds, or 250 ps) and as the *clock rate* (e.g., 4 gigahertz, or 4 GHz), which is the inverse of the clock period. In the next subsection, we will formalize the relationship between the clock cycles of the hardware designer and the seconds of the computer user.

clock cycle Also called **tick, clock tick, clock period, clock,** or **cycle.** The time for one clock period, usually of the processor clock, which runs at a constant rate.

clock period The length of each clock cycle.

1. Suppose we know that an application that uses both personal mobile devices and the Cloud is limited by network performance. For the following changes, state whether only the throughput improves, both response time and throughput improve, or neither improves.

   a. An extra network channel is added between the PMD and the Cloud, increasing the total network throughput and reducing the delay to obtain network access (since there are now two channels).

   b. The networking software is improved, thereby reducing the network communication delay, but not increasing throughput.

   c. More memory is added to the computer.

2. Computer C's performance is 4 times as fast as the performance of computer B, which runs a given application in 28 seconds. How long will computer C take to run that application?

Check Yourself

CPU Performance and Its Factors

Users and designers often examine performance using different metrics. If we could relate these different metrics, we could determine the effect of a design change on the performance as experienced by the user. Since we are confining ourselves to CPU performance at this point, the bottom-line performance measure is CPU execution time. A simple formula relates the most basic metrics (clock cycles and clock cycle time) to CPU time:

$$\text{CPU execution time for a program} = \text{CPU clock cycles for a program} \times \text{Clock cycle time}$$

Alternatively, because clock rate and clock cycle time are inverses,

$$\text{CPU execution time for a program} = \frac{\text{CPU clock cycles for a program}}{\text{Clock rate}}$$

This formula makes it clear that the hardware designer can improve performance by reducing the number of clock cycles required for a program or the length of the clock cycle. As we will see in later chapters, the designer often faces a trade-off between the number of clock cycles needed for a program and the length of each cycle. Many techniques that decrease the number of clock cycles may also increase the clock cycle time.

EXAMPLE

Improving Performance

Our favorite program runs in 10 seconds on computer A, which has a 2 GHz clock. We are trying to help a computer designer build a computer, B, which will run this program in 6 seconds. The designer has determined that a substantial increase in the clock rate is possible, but this increase will affect the rest of the CPU design, causing computer B to require 1.2 times as many clock cycles as computer A for this program. What clock rate should we tell the designer to target?

ANSWER

Let's first find the number of clock cycles required for the program on A:

$$\text{CPU time}_A = \frac{\text{CPU clock cycles}_A}{\text{Clock rate}_A}$$

$$10 \text{ seconds} = \frac{\text{CPU clock cycles}_A}{2 \times 10^9 \dfrac{\text{cycles}}{\text{second}}}$$

$$\text{CPU clock cycles}_A = 10 \text{ seconds} \times 2 \times 10^9 \frac{\text{cycles}}{\text{second}} = 20 \times 10^9 \text{ cycles}$$

CPU time for B can be found using this equation:

$$\text{CPU time}_B = \frac{1.2 \times \text{CPU clock cycles}_A}{\text{Clock rate}_B}$$

$$6 \text{ seconds} = \frac{1.2 \times 20 \times 10^9 \text{ cycles}}{\text{Clock rate}_B}$$

$$\text{Clock rate}_B = \frac{1.2 \times 20 \times 10^9 \text{ cycles}}{6 \text{ seconds}} = \frac{0.2 \times 20 \times 10^9 \text{ cycles}}{\text{second}} = \frac{4 \times 10^9 \text{ cycles}}{\text{second}} = 4\,\text{GHz}$$

To run the program in 6 seconds, B must have twice the clock rate of A.

Instruction Performance

The performance equations above did not include any reference to the number of instructions needed for the program. However, since the compiler clearly generated instructions to execute, and the computer had to execute the instructions to run the program, the execution time must depend on the number of instructions in a program. One way to think about execution time is that it equals the number of instructions executed multiplied by the average time per instruction. Therefore, the number of clock cycles required for a program can be written as

$$\text{CPU clock cycles} = \text{Instructions for a program} \times \frac{\text{Average clock cycles}}{\text{per instruction}}$$

The term **clock cycles per instruction**, which is the average number of clock cycles each instruction takes to execute, is often abbreviated as **CPI**. Since different instructions may take different amounts of time depending on what they do, CPI is an average of all the instructions executed in the program. CPI provides one way of comparing two different implementations of the same instruction set architecture, since the number of instructions executed for a program will, of course, be the same.

clock cycles per instruction (CPI) Average number of clock cycles per instruction for a program or program fragment.

Using the Performance Equation

Suppose we have two implementations of the same instruction set architecture. Computer A has a clock cycle time of 250 ps and a CPI of 2.0 for some program, and computer B has a clock cycle time of 500 ps and a CPI of 1.2 for the same program. Which computer is faster for this program and by how much?

EXAMPLE

ANSWER

We know that each computer executes the same number of instructions for the program; let's call this number I. First, find the number of processor clock cycles for each computer:

$$\text{CPU clock cycles}_A = I \times 2.0$$

$$\text{CPU clock cycles}_B = I \times 1.2$$

Now we can compute the CPU time for each computer:

$$\text{CPU time}_A = \text{CPU clock cycles}_A \times \text{Clock cycle time}$$

$$= I \times 2.0 \times 250 \text{ ps} = 500 \times I \text{ ps}$$

Likewise, for B:

$$\text{CPU time}_B = I \times 1.2 \times 500 \text{ ps} = 600 \times I \text{ ps}$$

Clearly, computer A is faster. The amount faster is given by the ratio of the execution times:

$$\frac{\text{CPU performance}_A}{\text{CPU performance}_B} = \frac{\text{Execution time}_B}{\text{Execution time}_A} = \frac{600 \times I \text{ ps}}{500 \times I \text{ ps}} = 1.2$$

We can conclude that computer A is 1.2 times as fast as computer B for this program.

The Classic CPU Performance Equation

instruction count The number of instructions executed by the program.

We can now write this basic performance equation in terms of **instruction count** (the number of instructions executed by the program), CPI, and clock cycle time:

$$\text{CPU times} = \text{Instruction count} \times \text{CPI} \times \text{Clock cycle time}$$

or, since the clock rate is the inverse of clock cycle time:

$$\text{CPU times} = \frac{\text{Instruction count} \times \text{CPI}}{\text{Clock rate}}$$

These formulas are particularly useful because they separate the three key factors that affect performance. We can use these formulas to compare two different implementations or to evaluate a design alternative if we know its impact on these three parameters.

Comparing Code Segments

A compiler designer is trying to decide between two code sequences for a particular computer. The hardware designers have supplied the following facts:

EXAMPLE

	CPI for each instruction class		
	A	B	C
CPI	1	2	3

For a particular high-level language statement, the compiler writer is considering two code sequences that require the following instruction counts:

	Instruction counts for each instruction class		
Code sequence	A	B	C
1	2	1	2
2	4	1	1

Which code sequence executes the most instructions? Which will be faster? What is the CPI for each sequence?

ANSWER

Sequence 1 executes $2 + 1 + 2 = 5$ instructions. Sequence 2 executes $4 + 1 + 1 = 6$ instructions. Therefore, sequence 1 executes fewer instructions.

We can use the equation for CPU clock cycles based on instruction count and CPI to find the total number of clock cycles for each sequence:

$$\text{CPU clock cycles} = \sum_{i=1}^{n} (\text{CPI}_i \times \text{C}_i)$$

This yields

$$\text{CPU clock cycles}_1 = (2 \times 1) + (1 \times 2) + (2 \times 3) = 2 + 2 + 6 = 10 \text{ cycles}$$

$$\text{CPU clock cycles}_2 = (4 \times 1) + (1 \times 2) + (1 \times 3) = 4 + 2 + 3 = 9 \text{ cycles}$$

So code sequence 2 is faster, even though it executes one extra instruction. Since code sequence 2 takes fewer overall clock cycles but has more instructions, it must have a lower CPI. The CPI values can be computed by

$$\text{CPI} = \frac{\text{CPU clock cycles}}{\text{Instruction count}}$$

$$\text{CPI}_1 = \frac{\text{CPU clock cycles}_1}{\text{Instruction count}_1} = \frac{10}{5} = 2.0$$

$$\text{CPI}_2 = \frac{\text{CPU clock cycles}_2}{\text{Instruction count}_2} = \frac{9}{6} = 1.5$$

Figure 1.15 shows the basic measurements at different levels in the computer and what is being measured in each case. We can see how these factors are combined to yield execution time measured in seconds per program:

$$\text{Time} = \text{Seconds/Program} = \frac{\text{Instructions}}{\text{Program}} \times \frac{\text{Clock cycles}}{\text{Instruction}} \times \frac{\text{Seconds}}{\text{Clock cycle}}$$

Always bear in mind that the only complete and reliable measure of computer performance is time. For example, changing the instruction set to lower the instruction count may lead to an organization with a slower clock cycle time or higher CPI that offsets the improvement in instruction count. Similarly, because CPI depends on type of instructions executed, the code that executes the fewest number of instructions may not be the fastest.

The **BIG** Picture

Components of performance	Units of measure
CPU execution time for a program	Seconds for the program
Instruction count	Instructions executed for the program
Clock cycles per instruction (CPI)	Average number of clock cycles per instruction
Clock cycle time	Seconds per clock cycle

FIGURE 1.15   The basic components of performance and how each is measured.

How can we determine the value of these factors in the performance equation? We can measure the CPU execution time by running the program, and the clock cycle time is usually published as part of the documentation for a computer. The instruction count and CPI can be more difficult to obtain. Of course, if we know the clock rate and CPU execution time, we need only one of the instruction count or the CPI to determine the other.

We can measure the instruction count by using software tools that profile the execution or by using a simulator of the architecture. Alternatively, we can use hardware counters, which are included in most processors, to record a variety of measurements, including the number of instructions executed, the average CPI, and often, the sources of performance loss. Since the instruction count depends on the architecture, but not on the exact implementation, we can measure the instruction count without knowing all the details of the implementation. The CPI, however, depends on a wide variety of design details in the computer, including both the memory system and the processor structure (as we will see in Chapter 4 and Chapter 5), as well as on the mix of instruction types executed in an application. Thus, CPI varies by application, as well as among implementations with the same instruction set.

The above example shows the danger of using only one factor (instruction count) to assess performance. When comparing two computers, you must look at all three components, which combine to form execution time. If some of the factors are identical, like the clock rate in the above example, performance can be determined by comparing all the nonidentical factors. Since CPI varies by instruction mix, both instruction count and CPI must be compared, even if clock rates are identical. Several exercises at the end of this chapter ask you to evaluate a series of computer and compiler enhancements that affect clock rate, CPI, and instruction count. In Section 1.13, we'll examine a common performance measurement that does not incorporate all the terms and can thus be misleading.

instruction mix
A measure of the dynamic frequency of instructions across one or many programs.

Understanding Program Performance

The performance of a program depends on the algorithm, the language, the compiler, the architecture, and the actual hardware. The following table summarizes how these components affect the factors in the CPU performance equation.

Hardware or software component	Affects what?	How?
Algorithm	Instruction count, possibly CPI	The algorithm determines the number of source program instructions executed and hence the number of processor instructions executed. The algorithm may also affect the CPI, by favoring slower or faster instructions. For example, if the algorithm uses more divides, it will tend to have a higher CPI.
Programming language	Instruction count, CPI	The programming language certainly affects the instruction count, since statements in the language are translated to processor instructions, which determine instruction count. The language may also affect the CPI because of its features; for example, a language with heavy support for data abstraction (e.g., Java) will require indirect calls, which will use higher CPI instructions.
Compiler	Instruction count, CPI	The efficiency of the compiler affects both the instruction count and average cycles per instruction, since the compiler determines the translation of the source language instructions into computer instructions. The compiler's role can be very complex and affect the CPI in complicated ways.
Instruction set architecture	Instruction count, clock rate, CPI	The instruction set architecture affects all three aspects of CPU performance, since it affects the instructions needed for a function, the cost in cycles of each instruction, and the overall clock rate of the processor.

Elaboration: Although you might expect that the minimum CPI is 1.0, as we'll see in Chapter 4, some processors fetch and execute multiple instructions per clock cycle. To reflect that approach, some designers invert CPI to talk about *IPC*, or *instructions per clock cycle*. If a processor executes on average 2 instructions per clock cycle, then it has an IPC of 2 and hence a CPI of 0.5.

Elaboration: Although clock cycle time has traditionally been fixed, to save energy or temporarily boost performance, today's processors can vary their clock rates, so we would need to use the *average* clock rate for a program. For example, the Intel Core i7 will temporarily increase clock rate by about 10% until the chip gets too warm. Intel calls this *Turbo mode*.

Check Yourself

A given application written in Java runs 15 seconds on a desktop processor. A new Java compiler is released that requires only 0.6 as many instructions as the old compiler. Unfortunately, it increases the CPI by 1.1. How fast can we expect the application to run using this new compiler? Pick the right answer from the three choices below:

a. $\dfrac{15 \times 0.6}{1.1} = 8.2 \text{ sec}$

b. $15 \times 0.6 \times 1.1 = 9.9 \text{ sec}$

c. $\dfrac{1.5 \times 1.1}{0.6} = 27.5 \text{ sec}$

1.7 The Power Wall

Figure 1.16 shows the increase in clock rate and power of nine generations of Intel microprocessors over 36 years. Both clock rate and power increased rapidly for decades, and then flattened or dropped off recently. The reason they grew together is that they are correlated, and the reason for their recent slowing is that we have run into the practical power limit for cooling commodity microprocessors.

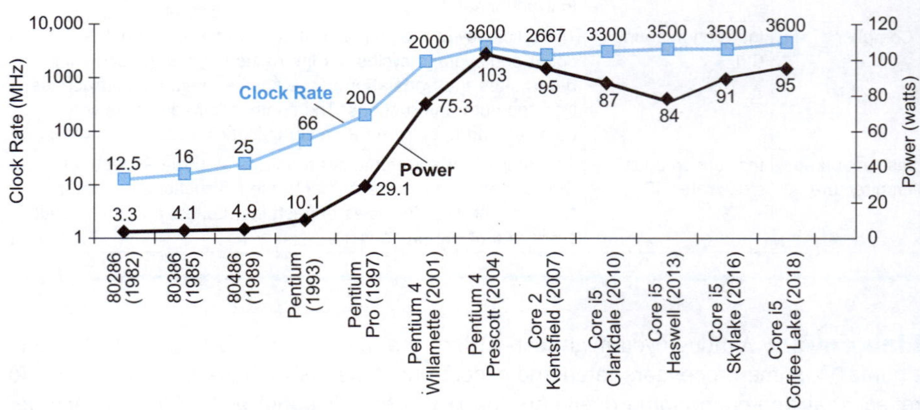

FIGURE 1.16   Clock rate and Power for Intel x86 microprocessors over nine generations and 36 years. The Pentium 4 made a dramatic jump in clock rate and power but less so in performance. The Prescott thermal problems led to the abandonment of the Pentium 4 line. The Core 2 line reverts to a simpler pipeline with lower clock rates and multiple processors per chip. The Core i5 pipelines follow in its footsteps.

Although power provides a limit to what we can cool, in the PostPC Era the really critical resource is energy. Battery life can trump performance in the personal mobile device, and the architects of warehouse scale computers try to reduce the costs of powering and cooling 50,000 servers as the costs are high at this scale. Just as measuring time in seconds is a safer measure of program performance than a rate like MIPS (see Section 1.11), the energy metric joules is a better measure than a power rate like watts, which is just joules/second.

The dominant technology for integrated circuits is called CMOS (complementary metal oxide semiconductor). For CMOS, the primary source of energy consumption is so-called dynamic energy—that is, energy that is consumed when transistors switch states from 0 to 1 and vice versa. The dynamic energy depends on the capacitive loading of each transistor and the voltage applied:

$$Energy \propto Capacitive\ load \times Voltage^2$$

This equation is the energy of a pulse during the logic transition of $0 \rightarrow 1 \rightarrow 0$ or $1 \rightarrow 0 \rightarrow 1$. The energy of a single transition is then

$$Energy \propto 1/2 \times Capacitive\ load \times Voltage^2$$

The power required per transistor is just the product of energy of a transition and the frequency of transitions:

$$Power \propto 1/2 \times Capacitive\ load \times Voltage^2 \times Frequency\ switched$$

Frequency switched is a function of the clock rate. The capacitive load per transistor is a function of both the number of transistors connected to an output (called the *fanout*) and the technology, which determines the capacitance of both wires and transistors.

With regard to Figure 1.16, how could clock rates grow by a factor of 1000 while power grew by only a factor of 30? Energy and thus power can be reduced by lowering the voltage, which occurred with each new generation of technology, and power is a function of the voltage squared. Typically, the voltage was reduced about 15% per generation. In 20 years, voltages have gone from 5 V to 1 V, which is why the increase in power is only 30 times.

Relative Power

Suppose we developed a new, simpler processor that has 85% of the capacitive load of the more complex older processor. Further, assume that it has adjustable voltage so that it can reduce voltage 15% compared to processor B, which results in a 15% shrink in frequency. What is the impact on dynamic power?

EXAMPLE

ANSWER

$$\frac{\text{Power}_{new}}{\text{Power}_{old}} = \frac{\langle\text{Capacitive load} \times 0.85\rangle \times \langle\text{Voltage} \times 0.85\rangle^2 \times \langle\text{Frequency switched} \times 0.85\rangle}{\text{Capacitive load} \times \text{Voltage}^2 \times \text{Frequency switched}}$$

Thus the power ratio is

$$0.85^4 = 0.52$$

Hence, the new processor uses about half the power of the old processor.

The problem today is that further lowering of the voltage appears to make the transistors too leaky, like water faucets that cannot be completely shut off. Even today about 40% of the power consumption in server chips is due to leakage. If transistors started leaking more, the whole process could become unwieldy.

To try to address the power problem, designers have already attached large devices to increase cooling, and they turn off parts of the chip that are not used in a given clock cycle. Although there are many more expensive ways to cool chips and thereby raise their power to, say, 300 watts, these techniques are generally too expensive for personal computers and even servers, not to mention personal mobile devices.

Since computer designers slammed into a power wall, they needed a new way forward. They chose a different path from the way they designed microprocessors for their first 30 years.

Elaboration: Although dynamic energy is the primary source of energy consumption in CMOS, static energy consumption occurs because of leakage current that flows even when a transistor is off. In servers, leakage is typically responsible for 40% of the energy consumption. Thus, increasing the number of transistors increases power dissipation, even if the transistors are always off. A variety of design techniques and technology innovations are being deployed to control leakage, but it's hard to lower voltage further.

Elaboration: Power is a challenge for integrated circuits for two reasons. First, power must be brought in and distributed around the chip; modern microprocessors use hundreds of pins just for power and ground! Similarly, multiple levels of chip interconnect are used solely for power and ground distribution to portions of the chip. Second, power is dissipated as heat and must be removed. Server chips can burn more than 100 watts, and cooling the chip and the surrounding system is a major expense in Warehouse Scale Computers (see Chapter 6).

1.8   The Sea Change: The Switch from Uniprocessors to Multiprocessors

The power limit has forced a dramatic change in the design of microprocessors. Figure 1.17 shows the improvement in response time of programs for desktop microprocessors over time. Since 2002, the rate has slowed from a factor of 1.5 per year to a factor of only 1.03 per year.

Rather than continuing to decrease the response time of a single program running on the single processor, as of 2006 all desktop and server companies are shipping microprocessors with multiple processors per chip, where the benefit is often more on throughput than on response time. To reduce confusion between the words processor and microprocessor, companies refer to processors as "cores," and such microprocessors are generically called multicore microprocessors. Hence, a "quadcore" microprocessor is a chip that contains four processors or four cores.

In the past, programmers could rely on innovations in hardware, architecture, and compilers to double performance of their programs every 18 months without having to change a line of code. Today, for programmers to get significant improvement in response time, they need to rewrite their programs to take advantage of multiple processors. Moreover, to get the historic benefit of running faster on new microprocessors, programmers will have to continue to improve performance of their code as the number of cores increases.

To reinforce how the software and hardware systems work hand in hand, we use a special section, *Hardware/Software Interface*, throughout the book, with the first one appearing below. These elements summarize important insights at this critical interface.

Up to now, most software has been like music written for a solo performer; with the current generation of chips we're getting a little experience with duets and quartets and other small ensembles; but scoring a work for large orchestra and chorus is a different kind of challenge.

Brian Hayes, *Computing in a Parallel Universe,* 2007.

PARALLELISM

Parallelism has always been critical to performance in computing, but it was often hidden. Chapter 4 will explain **pipelining**, an elegant technique that runs programs faster by overlapping the execution of instructions. Pipelining is one example of *instruction-level parallelism*, where the parallel nature of the hardware is abstracted away so the programmer and compiler can think of the hardware as executing instructions sequentially.

Forcing programmers to be aware of the parallel hardware and to explicitly rewrite their programs to be parallel had been the "third rail" of computer architecture, for companies in the past that depended on such a change in behavior failed (see Section 6.16). From this historical perspective, it's startling that the whole IT industry bet its future that programmers will successfully switch to explicitly parallel programming.

Hardware/ Software Interface

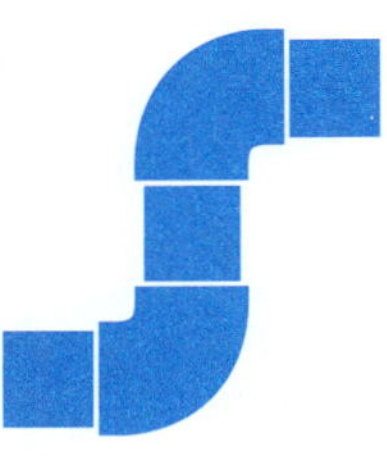

PIPELINING

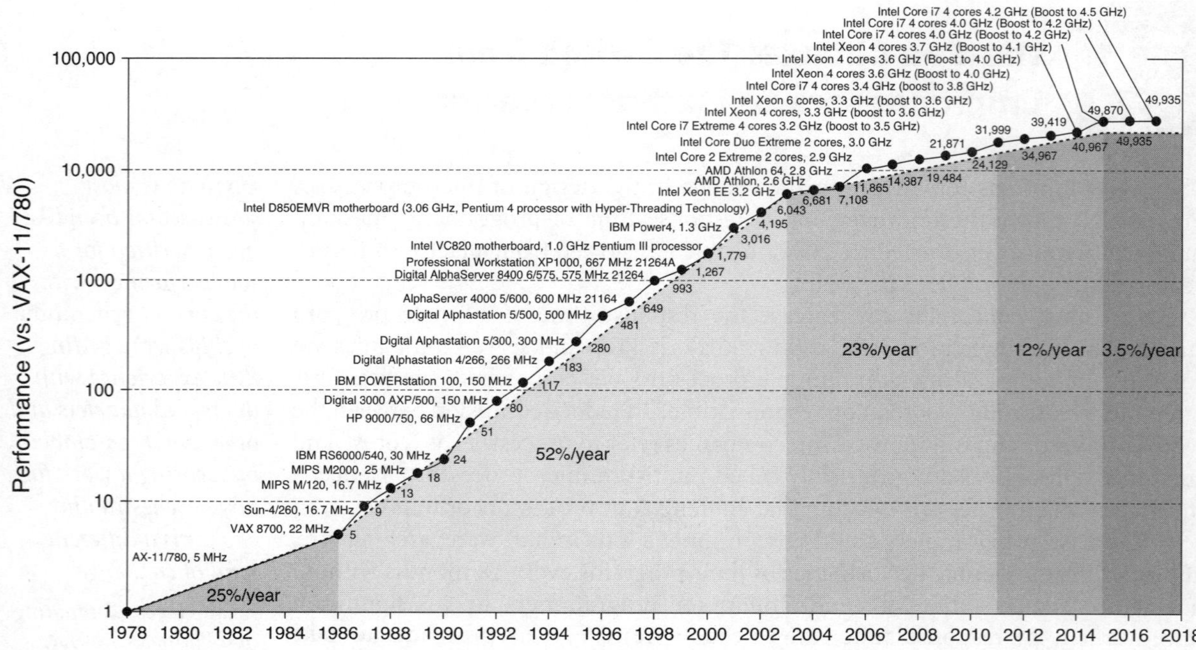

FIGURE 1.17 Growth in processor performance since the mid-1980s. This chart plots performance relative to the VAX 11/780 as measured by the SPECint benchmarks (see Section 1.11). Prior to the mid-1980s, processor performance growth was largely technology-driven and averaged about 25% per year. The increase in growth to about 52% since then is attributable to more advanced architectural and organizational ideas. The higher annual performance improvement of 52% since the mid-1980s meant performance was about a factor of seven higher in 2002 than it would have been had it stayed at 25%. Since 2002, the limits of power, available instruction-level parallelism, and long memory latency have slowed uniprocessor performance recently, to about 3.5% per year. (From Hennssey JL, Patterson DA. Computer Architecture: A Qualitative Approach, ed 6. Waltham, MA: Elsevier, 2017.)

Why has it been so hard for programmers to write explicitly parallel programs? The first reason is that parallel programming is by definition performance programming, which increases the difficulty of programming. Not only does the program need to be correct, solve an important problem, and provide a useful interface to the people or other programs that invoke it, the program must also be fast. Otherwise, if you don't need performance, just write a sequential program.

The second reason is that fast for parallel hardware means that the programmer must divide an application so that each processor has roughly the same amount to do at the same time, and that the overhead of scheduling and coordination doesn't fritter away the potential performance benefits of parallelism.

As an analogy, suppose the task was to write a newspaper story. Eight reporters working on the same story could potentially write a story eight times faster. To achieve this increased speed, one would need to break up the task so that each reporter had something to do at the same time. Thus, we must *schedule* the sub-tasks. If anything went wrong and just one reporter took longer than the seven others did, then the benefits of having eight writers would be diminished. Thus, we must *balance the load* evenly to get the desired speedup. Another danger would be if reporters had to spend a lot of time talking to each other to write their sections. You would also fall short if one part of the story, such as the conclusion, couldn't be written until all of the other parts were completed. Thus, care must be taken to *reduce communication and synchronization overhead*. For both this analogy and parallel programming, the challenges include scheduling, load balancing, time for synchronization, and overhead for communication between the parties. As you might guess, the challenge is stiffer with more reporters for a newspaper story and more processors for parallel programming.

To reflect this sea change in the industry, the next five chapters in this edition of the book each have a section on the implications of the parallel revolution to that chapter:

- *Chapter 2, Section 2.11: Parallelism and Instructions: Synchronization.* Usually independent parallel tasks need to coordinate at times, such as to say when they have completed their work. This chapter explains the instructions used by multicore processors to synchronize tasks.

- *Chapter 3, Section 3.6: Parallelism and Computer Arithmetic: Subword Parallelism.* Perhaps the simplest form of parallelism to build involves computing on elements in parallel, such as when multiplying two vectors. Subword parallelism relies on wider arithmetic units that can operate on many operands simultaneously.

- *Chapter 4, Section 4.11: Parallelism via Instructions.* Given the difficulty of explicitly parallel programming, tremendous effort was invested in the 1990s in having the hardware and the compiler uncover implicit parallelism, initially via **pipelining**. This chapter describes some of these aggressive techniques, including fetching and executing multiple instructions simultaneously and guessing on the outcomes of decisions, and executing instructions speculatively using **prediction**.

- *Chapter 5, Section 5.10: Parallelism and Memory Hierarchies: Cache Coherence.* One way to lower the cost of communication is to have all processors use the same address space, so that any processor can read or write any data. Given that all processors today use caches to keep a temporary copy of the data in faster memory near the processor, it's easy to imagine that parallel programming would be even more difficult if the caches associated with each processor had inconsistent values of the shared data. This chapter describes the mechanisms that keep the data in all caches consistent.

- *Chapter 5, Section 5.11: Parallelism and Memory Hierarchy: Redundant Arrays of Inexpensive Disks.* This section describes how using many disks in conjunction can offer much higher throughput, which was the original inspiration of *Redundant Arrays of Inexpensive Disks* (RAID). The real popularity of RAID proved to be to the much greater dependability offered by including a modest number of redundant disks. The section explains the differences in performance, cost, and dependability between the different RAID levels.

I thought [computers] would be a universally applicable idea, like a book is. But I didn't think it would develop as fast as it did, because I didn't envision we'd be able to get as many parts on a chip as we finally got. The transistor came along unexpectedly. It all happened much faster than we expected.

J. Presper Eckert, coinventor of ENIAC, speaking in 1991

workload A set of programs run on a computer that is either the actual collection of applications run by a user or constructed from real programs to approximate such a mix. A typical workload specifies both the programs and the relative frequencies.

benchmark A program selected for use in comparing computer performance.

In addition to these sections, there is a full chapter on parallel processing. Chapter 6 goes into more detail on the challenges of parallel programming; presents the two contrasting approaches to communication of shared addressing and explicit message passing; describes a restricted model of parallelism that is easier to program; discusses the difficulty of benchmarking parallel processors; introduces a new simple performance model for multicore microprocessors; and, finally, describes and evaluates four examples of multicore microprocessors using this model.

As mentioned above, Chapters 3 to 6 use matrix vector multiply as a running example to show how each type of parallelism can significantly increase performance.

Appendix C describes an increasingly popular hardware component that is included with desktop computers, the *graphics processing unit* (GPU). Invented to accelerate graphics, GPUs are becoming programming platforms in their own right. As you might expect, given these times, GPUs rely on **parallelism.**

Appendix C describes the NVIDIA GPU and highlights parts of its parallel programming environment.

1.9 Real Stuff: Benchmarking the Intel Core i7

Each chapter has a section entitled "Real Stuff" that ties the concepts in the book with a computer you may use every day. These sections cover the technology underlying modern computers. For this first "Real Stuff" section, we look at how integrated circuits are manufactured and how performance and power are measured, with the Intel Core i7 as the example.

SPEC CPU Benchmark

A computer user who runs the same programs day in and day out would be the perfect candidate to evaluate a new computer. The set of programs run would form a **workload**. To evaluate two computer systems, a user would simply compare the execution time of the workload on the two computers. Most users, however, are not in this situation. Instead, they must rely on other methods that measure the performance of a candidate computer, hoping that the methods will reflect how well the computer will perform with the user's workload. This alternative is usually followed by evaluating the computer using a set of **benchmarks**—programs specifically chosen to measure performance. The benchmarks form a workload that the user hopes will predict the performance of the actual workload. As we noted above, to make the **common case fast**, you first need to know accurately which case is common, so benchmarks play a critical role in computer architecture.

SPEC (*System Performance Evaluation Cooperative*) is an effort funded and supported by a number of computer vendors to create standard sets of benchmarks for modern computer systems. In 1989, SPEC originally created a benchmark set

Description	Name	Instruction Count x 10⁹	CPI	Clock cycle time (seconds x 10⁻⁹)	Execution Time (seconds)	Reference Time (seconds)	SPECratio
Perl interpreter	perlbench	2684	0.42	0.556	627	1774	2.83
GNU C compiler	gcc	2322	0.67	0.556	863	3976	4.61
Route planning	mcf	1786	1.22	0.556	1215	4721	3.89
Discrete Event simulation - computer network	omnetpp	1107	0.82	0.556	507	1630	3.21
XML to HTML conversion via XSLT	xalancbmk	1314	0.75	0.556	549	1417	2.58
Video compression	x264	4488	0.32	0.556	813	1763	2.17
Artificial Intelligence: alpha-beta tree search (Chess)	deepsjeng	2216	0.57	0.556	698	1432	2.05
Artificial Intelligence: Monte Carlo tree search (Go)	leela	2236	0.79	0.556	987	1703	1.73
Artificial Intelligence: recursive solution generator (Sudoku)	exchange2	6683	0.46	0.556	1718	2939	1.71
General data compression	xz	8533	1.32	0.556	6290	6182	0.98
Geometric mean							2.36

FIGURE 1.18   SPECspeed 2017 Integer benchmarks running on a 1.8 GHz Intel Xeon E5-2650L. As the equation on page 35 explains, execution time is the product of the three factors in this table: instruction count in billions, clocks per instruction (CPI), and clock cycle time in nanoseconds. SPECratio is simply the reference time, which is supplied by SPEC, divided by the measured execution time. The single number quoted as SPECspeed 2017 Integer is the geometric mean of the SPECratios. SPECspeed 2017 has multiple input files for perlbench, gcc, x264, and xz. For this figure, execution time and total clock cycles are the sum running times of these programs for all inputs.

focusing on processor performance (now called SPEC89), which has evolved through five generations. The latest is SPEC CPU2017, which consists of a set of 10 integer benchmarks (SPECspeed 2017 Integer) and 13 floating-point benchmarks (SPECspeed 2017 Floating Point). The integer benchmarks vary from part of a C compiler to a chess program to a quantum computer simulation. The floating-point benchmarks include structured grid codes for finite element modeling, particle method codes for molecular dynamics, and sparse linear algebra codes for fluid dynamics.

Figure 1.18 describes the SPEC integer benchmarks and their execution time on the Intel Core i7 and shows the factors that explain execution time: instruction count, CPI, and clock cycle time. Note that CPI varies by more than a factor of 4.

To simplify the marketing of computers, SPEC decided to report a single number to summarize all 10 integer benchmarks. Dividing the execution time of a reference processor by the execution time of the measured computer normalizes the execution time measurements; this normalization yields a measure, called the *SPECratio*, which has the advantage that bigger numeric results indicate faster performance. That is, the SPECratio is the inverse of execution time. A SPECspeed 2017 summary measurement is obtained by taking the geometric mean of the SPECratios.

Elaboration: When comparing two computers using SPECratios, use the geometric mean so that it gives the same relative answer no matter what computer is used to normalize the results. If we averaged the normalized execution time values with an arithmetic mean, the results would vary depending on the computer we choose as the reference.

The formula for the geometric mean is

$$\sqrt[n]{\prod_{i=1}^{n} \text{Execution time ratio}_i}$$

where Execution time ratio$_i$ is the execution time, normalized to the reference computer, for the ith program of a total of n in the workload, and

$$\prod_{i=1}^{n} a_i \text{ means the product } a_1 \times a_2 \times \ldots \times a_n$$

SPEC Power Benchmark

Given the increasing importance of energy and power, SPEC added a benchmark to measure power. It reports power consumption of servers at different workload levels, divided into 10% increments, over a period of time. Figure 1.19 shows the results for a server using Intel Nehalem processors similar to the above.

Target Load %	Performance (ssj_ops)	Average Power (watts)
100%	4,864,136	347
90%	4,389,196	312
80%	3,905,724	278
70%	3,418,737	241
60%	2,925,811	212
50%	2,439,017	183
40%	1,951,394	160
30%	1,461,411	141
20%	974,045	128
10%	485,973	115
0%	0	48
Overall Sum	26,815,444	2,165
Σssj_ops / Σpower =		12,385

FIGURE 1.19   SPECpower_ssj2008 running on a dual socket 2.2 GHz Intel Xeon Platinum 8276L with 192 GiB of DRAM and one 80 GB SSD disk.

SPECpower started with another SPEC benchmark for Java business applications (SPECJBB2005), which exercises the processors, caches, and main memory as well as the Java virtual machine, compiler, garbage collector, and pieces of the operating system. Performance is measured in throughput, and the units are business operations per second. Once again, to simplify the marketing of computers, SPEC boils these numbers down to a single number, called "overall ssj_ops per watt." The formula for this single summarizing metric is

$$\text{overall ssj\_ops per watt} = \left(\sum_{i=0}^{10} \text{ssj\_ops}_i \right) \Big/ \left(\sum_{i=0}^{10} \text{power}_i \right)$$

where ssj_ops_i is performance at each 10% increment and power_i is power consumed at each performance level.

 ## Going Faster: Matrix Multiply in Python

To demonstrate the impact of the ideas in this book, every chapter has a "Going Faster" section that improves the performance of a program that multiplies a matrix times a vector. We start with this Python program:

```python
for i in xrange(n):
    for j in xrange(n):
        for k in xrange(n):
            C[i][j] += A[i][k] * B[k][j]
```

We are using the n1-standard-96 server in Google Cloud Engine, which has two Intel Skylake Xeon chips, and each chip has 24 processors or cores and running Python version 3.1. If the matrices are 960 X 960, it takes about 5 minutes to run using Python 2.7. Since floating point computations go up with the cube of the matrix dimension, it would take almost 6 hours to run if the matrices were 4096 X 4096. While it is quick to write the matrix multiply in Python, who wants to wait that long to get the answer?

In Chapter 2, we are converting the Python version of matrix multiply to a C version, which increases performance by a factor of 200. The C programming abstraction is much closer to the hardware than Python is, which is why we use it as the programming example in this book. Closing the abstraction gap also makes it much faster than Python [Leiserson, 2020].

- In the category of data level parallelism, in Chapter 3, we use subword parallelism via C intrinsics to increase performance by a factor of about 8.

- In the category of instruction level parallelism, in Chapter 4, we use loop unrolling to exploit multiple instruction issue and out-of-order execution hardware to increase performance by another factor of about 2.

- In the category of memory hierarchy optimization, in Chapter 5, we use cache blocking to increase performance on large matrices by another factor of about 1.5.

- In the category of thread level parallelism, in Chapter 6, we use parallel for loops in OpenMP to exploit multicore hardware to increase performance by another factor of 12–17.

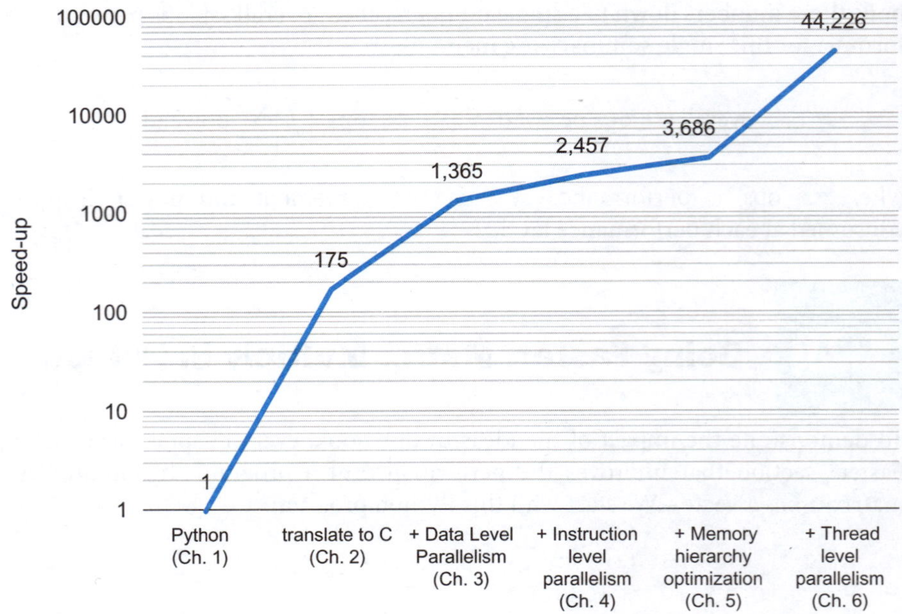

FIGURE 1.20   Optimizations of matrix multiply program in Python in the next five chapters of this book.

The last four steps leverage understanding of how the underlying hardware really works in a modern microprocessor, and collectively only require 21 lines of C code. Figure 1.20 shows speedup on a log scale of factor of nearly 50,000 over the original Python version. Instead of waiting almost 6 hours, it would take less than a second!

Elaboration: To accelerate Python, programmers commonly call highly optimized libraries instead of writing the code in Python itself. Since we are trying to show the inherent speed of Python versus C, we show the matrix multiply speed in Python itself. If we used the NumPy library instead, a 960 X 960 matrix multiply would take much less than 1 second instead of 5 minutes.

1.11   Fallacies and Pitfalls

The purpose of a section on fallacies and pitfalls, which will be found in every chapter, is to explain some commonly held misconceptions that you might encounter. We call them *fallacies*. When discussing a fallacy, we try to give a counterexample. We also discuss *pitfalls*, or easily made mistakes. Often pitfalls are generalizations of principles that are only true in a limited context. The purpose of these sections is to help you avoid making these mistakes in the computers you may design or use. Cost/performance fallacies and pitfalls have ensnared many a computer architect, including us. Accordingly, this section suffers no shortage of relevant examples. We start with a pitfall that traps many designers and reveals an important relationship in computer design.

Pitfall: Expecting the improvement of one aspect of a computer to increase overall performance by an amount proportional to the size of the improvement.

The great idea of making the **common case fast** has a demoralizing corollary that has plagued designers of both hardware and software. It reminds us that the opportunity for improvement is affected by how much time the event consumes.

A simple design problem illustrates it well. Suppose a program runs in 100 seconds on a computer, with multiply operations responsible for 80 seconds of this time. How much do I have to improve the speed of multiplication if I want my program to run five times faster?

The execution time of the program after making the improvement is given by the following simple equation known as **Amdahl's Law**:

Amdahl's Law A rule stating that the performance enhancement possible with a given improvement is limited by the amount that the improved feature is used. It is a quantitative version of the law of diminishing returns.

$$\text{Execution time after improvement}$$

$$= \frac{\text{Execution time affected by improvement}}{\text{Amount of improvement}} + \text{Execution time unaffected}$$

For this problem:

$$\text{Execution time after improvement} = \frac{80 \text{ seconds}}{n} + (100 - 80 \text{ seconds})$$

Since we want the performance to be five times faster, the new execution time should be 20 seconds, giving

$$20 \text{ seconds} = \frac{80 \text{ seconds}}{n} + 20 \text{ seconds}$$

$$0 = \frac{80 \text{ seconds}}{n}$$

That is, there is *no amount* by which we can enhance-multiply to achieve a fivefold increase in performance, if multiply accounts for only 80% of the workload. The performance enhancement possible with a given improvement is limited by the amount that the improved feature is used. In everyday life this concept also yields what we call the law of diminishing returns.

We can use Amdahl's Law to estimate performance improvements when we know the time consumed for some function and its potential speedup. Amdahl's Law, together with the CPU performance equation, is a handy tool for evaluating potential enhancements. Amdahl's Law is explored in more detail in the exercises.

Amdahl's Law is also used to argue for practical limits to the number of parallel processors. We examine this argument in the Fallacies and Pitfalls section of Chapter 6.

Fallacy: Computers at low utilization use little power.

Power efficiency matters at low utilizations because server workloads vary. Utilization of servers in Google's warehouse scale computer, for example, is between 10% and 50% most of the time and at 100% less than 1% of the time. Even given five years to learn how to run the SPECpower benchmark well, the specially configured computer with the best results in 2020 still uses 33% of the peak power at 10% of the load the same as in 2012 for the last edition. Systems in the field that are not configured for the SPECpower benchmark are surely worse.

Since servers' workloads vary but use a large fraction of peak power, Luiz Barroso and Urs Hölzle [2007] argue that we should redesign hardware to achieve "energy-proportional computing." If future servers used, say, 10% of peak power at 10% workload, we could reduce the electricity bill of datacenters and become good corporate citizens in an era of increasing concern about CO_2 emissions.

Fallacy: Designing for performance and designing for energy efficiency are unrelated goals.

Since energy is power over time, it is often the case that hardware or software optimizations that take less time save energy overall even if the optimization takes a bit more energy when it is used. One reason is that all of the rest of the computer is consuming energy while the program is running, so even if the optimized portion uses a little more energy, the reduced time can save the energy of the whole system.

Pitfall: Using a subset of the performance equation as a performance metric.

We have already warned about the danger of predicting performance based on simply one of clock rate, instruction count, or CPI. Another common mistake is to use only two of the three factors to compare performance. Although using two of the three factors may be valid in a limited context, the concept is also easily misused. Indeed, nearly all proposed alternatives to the use of time as the performance metric have led eventually to misleading claims, distorted results, or incorrect interpretations.

million instructions per second (MIPS) A measurement of program execution speed based on the number of millions of instructions. MIPS is computed as the instruction count divided by the product of the execution time and 10^6.

One alternative to time is **MIPS (million instructions per second)**. For a given program, MIPS is simply

$$\text{MIPS} = \frac{\text{Instruction count}}{\text{Execution time} \times 10^6}$$

Since MIPS is an instruction execution rate, MIPS specifies performance inversely to execution time; faster computers have a higher MIPS rating. The good news about MIPS is that it is easy to understand, and faster computers mean bigger MIPS, which matches intuition.

There are three problems with using MIPS as a measure for comparing computers. First, MIPS specifies the instruction execution rate but does not take into account the capabilities of the instructions. We cannot compare computers with different instruction sets using MIPS, since the instruction counts will certainly differ. Second, MIPS varies between programs on the same computer; thus, a computer cannot have a single MIPS rating. For example, by substituting for execution time, we see the relationship between MIPS, clock rate, and CPI:

$$\text{MIPS} = \frac{\text{Instruction count}}{\dfrac{\text{Instruction count} \times \text{CPI}}{\text{Clock rate}} \times 10^6} = \frac{\text{Clock rate}}{\text{CPI} \times 10^6}$$

The CPI varied by a factor of 4 for SPECspeed 2017 Integer on an Intel Xeon computer in Figure 1.18, so MIPS does as well. Finally, and most importantly, if a new program executes more instructions but each instruction is faster, MIPS can vary independently from performance!

Consider the following performance measurements for a program:

Check Yourself

Measurement	Computer A	Computer B
Instruction count	10 billion	8 billion
Clock rate	4 GHz	4 GHz
CPI	1.0	1.1

  a. Which computer has the higher MIPS rating?

  b. Which computer is faster?

1.12 Concluding Remarks

Although it is difficult to predict exactly what level of cost/performance computers will have in the future, it's a safe bet that they will be much better than they are today. To participate in these advances, computer designers and programmers must understand a wider variety of issues.

Both hardware and software designers construct computer systems in hierarchical layers, with each lower layer hiding details from the level above. This great idea of **abstraction** is fundamental to understanding today's computer systems, but it does not mean that designers can limit themselves to knowing a single abstraction. Perhaps the most important example of abstraction is the interface between hardware and low-level software, called the *instruction set architecture*. Maintaining the instruction set architecture as a constant enables many implementations of that architecture—presumably varying in cost and performance—to run identical software. On the downside, the architecture may preclude introducing innovations that require the interface to change.

Where … the ENIAC is equipped with 18,000 vacuum tubes and weighs 30 tons, computers in the future may have 1,000 vacuum tubes and perhaps weigh just 1½ tons.

Popular Mechanics, March 1949

There is a reliable method of determining and reporting performance by using the execution time of real programs as the metric. This execution time is related to other important measurements we can make by the following equation:

$$\frac{\text{Seconds}}{\text{Program}} = \frac{\text{Instructions}}{\text{Program}} \times \frac{\text{Clock cycles}}{\text{Instruction}} \times \frac{\text{Seconds}}{\text{Clock cycle}}$$

We will use this equation and its constituent factors many times. Remember, though, that individually the factors do not determine performance: only the product, which equals execution time, is a reliable measure of performance.

The **BIG** Picture

Execution time is the only valid and unimpeachable measure of performance. Many other metrics have been proposed and found wanting. Sometimes these metrics are flawed from the start by not reflecting execution time; other times a metric that is valid in a limited context is extended and used beyond that context or without the additional clarification needed to make it valid.

The key hardware technology for modern processors is silicon. While silicon fuels the advance of hardware, new ideas in the organization of computers have improved price/performance. Two of the key ideas are exploiting parallelism in the program, typically today via multiple processors, and exploiting locality of accesses to a **memory hierarchy**, typically via caches.

Energy efficiency has replaced die area as the most critical resource of microprocessor design. Conserving power while trying to increase performance has forced the hardware industry to switch to multicore microprocessors, thereby forcing the software industry to switch to programming parallel hardware. **Parallelism** is now required for performance.

Computer designs have always been measured by cost and performance, as well as other important factors such as energy, dependability, cost of ownership, and scalability. Although this chapter has focused on cost, performance, and energy, the best designs will strike the appropriate balance for a given market among all the factors.

Road Map for This Book

At the bottom of these abstractions are the five classic components of a computer: datapath, control, memory, input, and output (refer to Figure 1.5). These five components also serve as the framework for the rest of the chapters in this book:

- *Datapath:* Chapter 3, Chapter 4, Chapter 6, and Appendix C
- *Control:* Chapter 4, Chapter 6, and Appendix C

- *Memory*: Chapter 5

- *Input*: Chapters 5 and 6

- *Output*: Chapters 5 and 6

As mentioned above, Chapter 4 describes how processors exploit implicit parallelism, Chapter 6 describes the explicitly parallel multicore microprocessors that are at the heart of the parallel revolution, and  **Appendix C** describes the highly parallel graphics processor chip. Chapter 5 describes how a memory hierarchy exploits locality. Chapter 2 describes instruction sets—the interface between compilers and the computer—and emphasizes the role of compilers and programming languages in using the features of the instruction set. Appendix A provides a reference for the instruction set of Chapter 2. Chapter 3 describes how computers handle arithmetic data. Appendix B introduces logic design.

1.13 Historical Perspective and Further Reading

For each chapter in the text, a section devoted to a historical perspective can be found online on a site that accompanies this book. We may trace the development of an idea through a series of computers or describe some important projects, and we provide references in case you are interested in probing further.

The historical perspective for this chapter provides a background for some of the key ideas presented in this opening chapter. Its purpose is to give you the human story behind the technological advances and to place achievements in their historical context. By understanding the past, you may be better able to understand the forces that will shape computing in the future. Each Historical Perspective section online ends with suggestions for further reading, which are also collected separately online under the section "**Further Reading**." The rest of **Section 1.13** is found online.

> *An active field of science is like an immense anthill; the individual almost vanishes into the mass of minds tumbling over each other, carrying information from place to place, passing it around at the speed of light.*
>
> Lewis Thomas, "Natural Science," in *The Lives of a Cell*, 1974

1.14 Self-Study

Starting with the sixth edition, we are adding a section in every chapter with some hopefully thought-provoking exercises along with their solutions to help readers check to see if they're following the material.

Mapping great ideas in architecture to the real world. Find the best match of the seven great ideas from computer architecture to these real-world examples:

1. Reducing time to do laundry by washing the next load while drying the last load

2. Hiding a spare key in case you lose your front door key

3. Checking the weather forecast for cities you would drive through when deciding which route to take on a long winter trip

4. Express checkout lanes in grocery stores for 10 items or less

5. The local branch of a large city library system

6. Automobile powered by an electric motor on all four wheels

7. Optional self-driving automobile mode that requires purchase of self-parking and navigation options

How do you measure fastest? Consider three different processors P1, P2, and P3 executing the same instruction set. P1 has a clock cycle time of 0.33 ns and a CPI of 1.5; P2 has a clock cycle time of 0.40 ns and a CPI of 1.0; P3 has clock cycle time of 0.25 ns and a CPI of 2.2.

1. Which has the highest clock rate? What is it?

2. Which is the fastest computer? If answer is different from above, explain why. Which is the slowest?

3. How do the answers to (1) and (2) reflect the importance of benchmarks?

Amdahl's Law and brotherhood. Amdahl's Law is basically the Law of Diminishing Returns, which applies to investments as well as computer architecture. Here is an example that helps explain the law—Your brother has joined a start-up and is trying to convince you to invest some of your savings, since, he claims, "it's a sure thing!"

1. You decide to invest 10% of your savings. What must be the return on your investment in the start-up to double your overall wealth, assuming the start-up was your only investment?

2. Assuming the start-up investment delivers the return you calculated in (1), how much of your savings would you have to invest to realize 90% of start-up's increase? How about 95%?

3. How do the results relate to Amdahl's observation about computers? What does it say about brotherhood?

DRAM price versus cost. Figure 1.21 plots the price of DRAM chips from 1975 to 2020, while Figure 1.11 shows capacity per DRAM chip over the same period. They show a 1,000,000-fold increase in capacity (16 Kbit to 16 Gbit) and a 25,000,000-fold reduction in price per gigabyte ($100 million to $4). Note that the price per GiB fluctuates up and down over time, while capacity per chip has a smooth growth curve.

1. Can you see evidence of the slowing of Moore's Law in Figure 1.21?

2. Why might price improve by a factor of 25 higher than the improvement in capacity per chip? What might be other reasons than the increasing chip capacity?

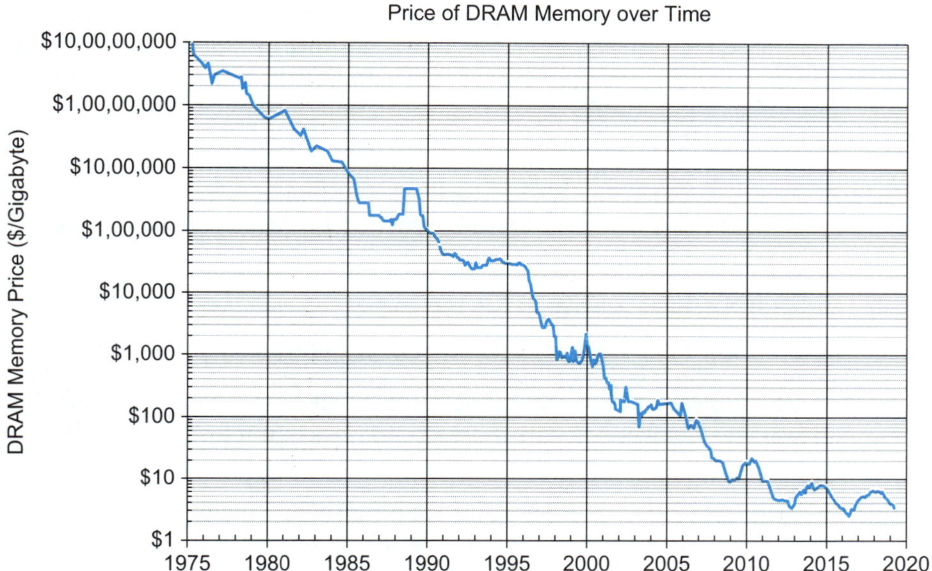

FIGURE 1.21   Price of memory per gigabyte between 1975 and 2020. (Source: https://jcmit. net/memoryprice.htm)

3. Why do you think price per gigabyte fluctuates over 3- to 5-year periods? Is it be related to the chip cost formulas on page 28 or to other forces in the marketplace?

Answers to Self-Study

Mapping great ideas in architecture to the real world:

1. Performance via pipelining

2. Dependability via redundancy (although you could argue it is also a use of performance via parallelism)

3. Performance via prediction

4. Make the common case fast

5. Hierarchy of memories

6. Performance via parallelism (although you could argue it is also a use of dependability via redundancy)

7. Use abstraction to simplify design

Fastest Computer

1. The clock rates are the inverse of the clock cycle time. P1 = $1/(0.33 \times 10^{-9}$ seconds) = 3 GHz; P2 = $1/(0.40 \times 10^{-9}$ seconds) = 2.5 GHz; P3 = $1/(0.25 \times 10^{-9}$ seconds) = 4 GHz. P3 has the highest clock rate.

2. Since they all have the same instruction set architecture, their programs all have the same instruction count, so we can measure performance as the product of average clock cycles per instruction (CPI) times clock cycle time, which is also the average time of an instruction:

   a. P1 = 1.5 X 0.33 ns = 0.495 ns.

   (You could also calculate average instruction time using CPI/clock rate, or 1.5/3.0 GHz = 0.495 ns)

   b. P2 = 1.0 X 0.40 ns = 0.400 ns (or 1.0/2.5 GHz = 0.400 ns)

   c. P3 = 2.2 X 0.25 ns = 0.550 ns (or 1.0/4.0 GHz = 0.550 ns)

   P2 is the fastest and P3 is the slowest. Despite having the highest clock rate, on average, P3 takes so many more clock cycles that it loses the benefit of a higher clock rate.

3. The CPI calculation was based on running some benchmarks. If they are representative of real workloads, these answers to these questions are correct. If the benchmarks are unrealistic, they may not. The difference between things easy to advertise, like clock rate versus actual performance, highlights the importance of developing good benchmarks.

Brotherhood and Amdahl's Law

1. 11X return on investment to double your savings: 90% X 1 + 10% X 11 = 2.0.

2. You must invest 89% of your wealth to get 90% of the full return.

    90% of 11X = 9.9X and 11% X 1 + 89% X 11 = 9.9.

    You must invest 94.5% of wealth to get 95% return.

    95% of 11X = 10.45X and 5.5% X 1 + 94.5% X 11 = 10.45.

3. Just as the part you do not invest limits the return on investment even for high returns for a successful start-up, the part of the computer that you do not accelerate limits the benefits of acceleration, no matter how much faster you make that improved piece. The amount you invest will be influenced by your faith in your brother's judgment, especially since 90% of all start-ups do not succeed!

Price Versus Cost of Memory

1. Although the prices fluctuate, it does look like pricing is flattening out since 2013, which is consistent with the slowing of Moore's Law. For example, DRAM was $4/GB in 2013 and 2016 as well as in 2019. There is no other such long period as flat in the past.

2. Neither figure mentions the volume of DRAM chips, which can explain why price improves more than capacity per chip. There are typically manufacturing learning curves where every factor-of-10 increase in volume

can result in, say, a factor-of-2 reduction in cost. There were also innovations in packaging of the chips that can lower costs and thus prices over this long time period.

3. DRAMs are commodity parts, as there are multiple companies manufacturing similar products, and thus they are subject to market pressures and fluctuating prices. Prices go up when demand exceeds supply and they fall when vice versa. The industry has a history of periods when DRAMs are very profitable, so they build more manufacturing lines, until there is an oversupply and prices drop, and so they cut back new manufacturing lines.

1.15 Exercises

The relative time ratings of exercises are shown in square brackets after each exercise number. On average, an exercise rated [10] will take you twice as long as one rated [5]. Sections of the text that should be read before attempting an exercise will be given in angled brackets; for example, <§1.4> means you should have read Section 1.4, Under the Covers, to help you solve this exercise.

1.1 [2] <§1.1> List and describe three types of computers.

1.2 [5] <§1.2> The seven great ideas in computer architecture are similar to ideas from other fields. Match the seven ideas from computer architecture, "Use Abstraction to Simplify Design", "Make the Common Case Fast", "Performance via Parallelism", "Performance via Pipelining", "Performance via Prediction" "Hierarchy of Memories", and "Dependability via Redundancy" to the following ideas from other fields:

a. Assembly lines in automobile manufacturing

b. Suspension bridge cables

c. Aircraft and marine navigation systems that incorporate wind information

d. Express elevators in buildings

e. Library reserve desk

f. Increasing the gate area on a CMOS transistor to decrease its switching time

g. Building self-driving cars whose control systems partially rely on existing sensor systems already installed into the base vehicle, such as lane departure systems and smart cruise control systems

1.3 [2] <§1.3> Describe the steps that transform a program written in a high-level language such as C into a representation that is directly executed by a computer processor.

1.4 [2] <$1.4> Assume a color display using 8 bits for each of the primary colors (red, green, blue) per pixel and a frame size of 1280 X 1024.

a. What is the minimum size in bytes of the frame buffer to store a frame?

b. How long would it take, at a minimum, for the frame to be sent over a 100 Mbit/s network?

1.5 [4] <$1.6> Consider three different processors P1, P2, and P3 executing the same instruction set. P1 has a 3 GHz clock rate and a CPI of 1.5. P2 has a 2.5 GHz clock rate and a CPI of 1.0. P3 has a 4.0 GHz clock rate and has a CPI of 2.2.

a. Which processor has the highest performance expressed in instructions per second?

b. If the processors each execute a program in 10 seconds, find the number of cycles and the number of instructions.

c. We are trying to reduce the execution time by 30% but this leads to an increase of 20% in the CPI. What clock rate should we have to get this time reduction?

1.6 [5] Consider the table given next, which tracks several performance indicators for Intel desktop processors since 2010.

The "Tech" column shows the minimum feature size of each processor's fabrication process. Assume that the die size has remained relatively constant and the number of transistors that comprise each processor scales at $(1/t)^2$, where $t =$ the minimum feature size.

For each performance indicator, calculate the average rate of improvement from 2010 to 2019, as well as the number of years required to double each at that corresponding rate.

Desktop processor	Year	Tech	Max. clock speed (GHz)	Integer IPC/ core	Cores	Max. DRAM Bandwidth (GB/s)	SP floating point (Gflop/s)	L3 cache (MiB)
Westmere i7-620	2010	32	3.33	4	2	17.1	107	4
Ivy Bridge i7-3770K	2013	22	3.90	6	4	25.6	250	8
Broadwell i7-6700K	2015	14	4.20	8	4	34.1	269	8
Kaby Lake i7-7700K	2017	14	4.50	8	4	38.4	288	8
Coffee Lake i7-9700K	2019	14	4.90	8	8	42.7	627	12
Imp./year			__%	__%	__%	__%	__%	__%	__%
Doubles every			__years	__years	__years	__years	__years	__years	__years

1.7 [20] <§1.6> Consider two different implementations of the same instruction set architecture. The instructions can be divided into four classes according to their CPI (class A, B, C, and D). P1 with a clock rate of 2.5 GHz and CPIs of 1, 2, 3, and 3, and P2 with a clock rate of 3 GHz and CPIs of 2, 2, 2, and 2.

Given a program with a dynamic instruction count of 1.0E6 instructions divided into classes as follows: 10% class A, 20% class B, 50% class C, and 20% class D, which is faster: P1 or P2?

a. What is the global CPI for each implementation?

b. Find the clock cycles required in both cases.

1.8 [15] <§1.6> Compilers can have a profound impact on the performance of an application. Assume that for a program, compiler A results in a dynamic instruction count of 1.0E9 and has an execution time of 1.1 s, while compiler B results in a dynamic instruction count of 1.2E9 and an execution time of 1.5 s.

a. Find the average CPI for each program given that the processor has a clock cycle time of 1 ns.

b. Assume the compiled programs run on two different processors. If the execution times on the two processors are the same, how much faster is the clock of the processor running compiler A's code versus the clock of the processor running compiler B's code?

c. A new compiler is developed that uses only 6.0E8 instructions and has an average CPI of 1.1. What is the speedup of using this new compiler versus using compiler A or B on the original processor?

1.9 The Pentium 4 Prescott processor, released in 2004, had a clock rate of 3.6 GHz and voltage of 1.25 V. Assume that, on average, it consumed 10 W of static power and 90 W of dynamic power.

The Core i5 Ivy Bridge, released in 2012, had a clock rate of 3.4 GHz and voltage of 0.9 V. Assume that, on average, it consumed 30 W of static power and 40 W of dynamic power.

1.9.1 [5] <§1.7> For each processor find the average capacitive loads.

1.9.2 [5] <§1.7> Find the percentage of the total dissipated power comprised by static power and the ratio of static power to dynamic power for each technology.

1.9.3 [15] <§1.7> If the total dissipated power is to be reduced by 10%, how much should the voltage be reduced to maintain the same leakage current? Note: power is defined as the product of voltage and current.

1.10 Assume for arithmetic, load/store, and branch instructions, a processor has CPIs of 1, 12, and 5, respectively. Also assume that on a single processor a program requires the execution of 2.56E9 arithmetic instructions, 1.28E9 load/store instructions, and 256 million branch instructions. Assume that each processor has a 2 GHz clock frequency.

Assume that, as the program is parallelized to run over multiple cores, the number of arithmetic and load/store instructions per processor is divided by 0.7 x p (where p is the number of processors) but the number of branch instructions per processor remains the same.

1.10.1 [5] <§1.7> Find the total execution time for this program on 1, 2, 4, and 8 processors, and show the relative speedup of the 2, 4, and 8 processor result relative to the single processor result.

1.10.2 [10] <§§1.6, 1.8> If the CPI of the arithmetic instructions was doubled, what would the impact be on the execution time of the program on 1, 2, 4, or 8 processors?

1.10.3 [10] <§§1.6, 1.8> To what should the CPI of load/store instructions be reduced in order for a single processor to match the performance of four processors using the original CPI values?

1.11 Assume a 15 cm diameter wafer has a cost of 12, contains 84 dies, and has 0.020 defects/cm². Assume a 20 cm diameter wafer has a cost of 15, contains 100 dies, and has 0.031 defects/cm².

1.11.1 [10] <§1.5> Find the yield for both wafers.

1.11.2 [5] <§1.5> Find the cost per die for both wafers.

1.11.3 [5] <§1.5> If the number of dies per wafer is increased by 10% and the defects per area unit increases by 15%, find the die area and yield.

1.11.4 [5] <§1.5> Assume a fabrication process improves the yield from 0.92 to 0.95. Find the defects per area unit for each version of the technology given a die area of 200 mm².

1.12 The results of the SPEC CPU2006 bzip2 benchmark running on an AMD Barcelona has an instruction count of 2.389E12, an execution time of 750 s, and a reference time of 9650 s.

1.12.1 [5] <§§1.6, 1.9> Find the CPI if the clock cycle time is 0.333 ns.

1.12.2 [5] <§1.9> Find the SPECratio.

1.12.3 [5] <§§1.6, 1.9> Find the increase in CPU time if the number of instructions of the benchmark is increased by 10% without affecting the CPI.

1.12.4 [5] <§§1.6, 1.9> Find the increase in CPU time if the number of instructions of the benchmark is increased by 10% and the CPI is increased by 5%.

1.12.5 [5] <§§1.6, 1.9> Find the change in the SPECratio for this change.

1.12.6 [10] <§1.6> Suppose that we are developing a new version of the AMD Barcelona processor with a 4 GHz clock rate. We have added some additional instructions to the instruction set in such a way that the number of instructions has been reduced by 15%. The execution time is reduced to 700 s and the new SPECratio is 13.7. Find the new CPI.

1.12.7 [10] <§1.6> This CPI value is larger than obtained in 1.11.1 as the clock rate was increased from 3 GHz to 4 GHz. Determine whether the increase in the CPI is similar to that of the clock rate. If they are dissimilar, why?

1.12.8 [5] <§1.6> By how much has the CPU time been reduced?

1.12.9 [10] <§1.6> For a second benchmark, libquantum, assume an execution time of 960 ns, CPI of 1.61, and clock rate of 3 GHz. If the execution time is reduced by an additional 10% without affecting to the CPI and with a clock rate of 4 GHz, determine the number of instructions.

1.12.10 [10] <§1.6> Determine the clock rate required to give a further 10% reduction in CPU time while maintaining the number of instructions and with the CPI unchanged.

1.12.11 [10] <§1.6> Determine the clock rate if the CPI is reduced by 15% and the CPU time by 20% while the number of instructions is unchanged.

1.13 Section 1.11 cites as a pitfall the utilization of a subset of the performance equation as a performance metric. To illustrate this, consider the following two processors. P1 has a clock rate of 4 GHz, average CPI of 0.9, and requires the execution of 5.0E9 instructions. P2 has a clock rate of 3 GHz, an average CPI of 0.75, and requires the execution of 1.0E9 instructions.

1.13.1 [5] <§§1.6, 1.11> One usual fallacy is to consider the computer with the largest clock rate as having the largest performance. Check if this is true for P1 and P2.

1.13.2 [10] <§§1.6, 1.11> Another fallacy is to consider that the processor executing the largest number of instructions will need a larger CPU time. Considering that processor P1 is executing a sequence of 1.0E9 instructions and that the CPI of processors P1 and P2 do not change, determine the number of instructions that P2 can execute in the same time that P1 needs to execute 1.0E9 instructions.

1.13.3 [10] <§§1.6, 1.11> A common fallacy is to use MIPS (millions of instructions per second) to compare the performance of two different processors, and consider that the processor with the largest MIPS has the largest performance. Check if this is true for P1 and P2.

1.13.4 [10] <§1.11> Another common performance figure is MFLOPS (millions of floating-point operations per second), defined as

MFLOPS = No. FP operations / (execution time $\times$ 1E6)

but this figure has the same problems as MIPS. Assume that 40% of the instructions executed on both P1 and P2 are floating-point instructions. Find the MFLOPS figures for the processors.

1.14 Another pitfall cited in Section 1.11 is expecting to improve the overall performance of a computer by improving only one aspect of the computer. Consider a computer running a program that requires 250 s, with 70 s spent executing FP instructions, 85 s executed L/S instructions, and 40 s spent executing branch instructions.

1.14.1 [5] <§1.11> By how much is the total time reduced if the time for FP operations is reduced by 20%?

1.14.2 [5] <§1.11> By how much is the time for INT operations reduced if the total time is reduced by 20%?

1.14.3 [5] <§1.11> Can the total time can be reduced by 20% by reducing only the time for branch instructions?

1.15 Assume a program requires the execution of 50×10^6 FP instructions, 110×10^6 INT instructions, 80×10^6 L/S instructions, and 16×10^6 branch instructions. The CPI for each type of instruction is 1, 1, 4, and 2, respectively. Assume that the processor has a 2 GHz clock rate.

1.15.1 [10] <§1.11> By how much must we improve the CPI of FP instructions if we want the program to run two times faster?

1.15.2 [10] <§1.11> By how much must we improve the CPI of L/S instructions if we want the program to run two times faster?

1.15.3 [5] <§1.11> By how much is the execution time of the program improved if the CPI of INT and FP instructions is reduced by 40% and the CPI of L/S and Branch is reduced by 30%?

1.16 [5] <§1.8> When a program is adapted to run on multiple processors in a multiprocessor system, the execution time on each processor is comprised of computing time and the overhead time required for locked critical sections and/or to send data from one processor to another.

Assume a program requires t = 100 s of execution time on one processor. When run p processors, each processor requires t/p s, as well as an additional 4 s of overhead, irrespective of the number of processors. Compute the per-processor execution time for 2, 4, 8, 16, 32, 64, and 128 processors. For each case, list the corresponding speedup relative to a single processor and the ratio between actual speedup versus ideal speedup (speedup if there was no overhead).

§1.1, page 10: Discussion questions: many answers are acceptable.

§1.4, page 24: DRAM memory: volatile, short access time of 50 to 70 nanoseconds, and cost per GB is $5 to $10. Disk memory: nonvolatile, access times are 100,000 to 400,000 times slower than DRAM, and cost per GB is 100 times cheaper than DRAM. Flash memory: nonvolatile, access times are 100 to 1000 times slower than DRAM, and cost per GB is 7 to 10 times cheaper than DRAM.

§1.5, page 28: 1, 3, and 4 are valid reasons. Answer 5 can be generally true because high volume can make the extra investment to reduce die size by, say, 10% a good economic decision, but it doesn't have to be true.

§1.6, page 33: 1. a: both, b: latency, c: neither. 7 seconds.

§1.6, page 40: b.

§1.11, page 53: a. Computer A has the higher MIPS rating. b. Computer B is faster.

Answers to Check Yourself

Instructions: Language of the Computer

I speak Spanish
to God, Italian to
women, French to
men, and German to
my horse.

Charles V, Holy Roman Emperor
(1500–1558)

The Five Classic Components of a Computer

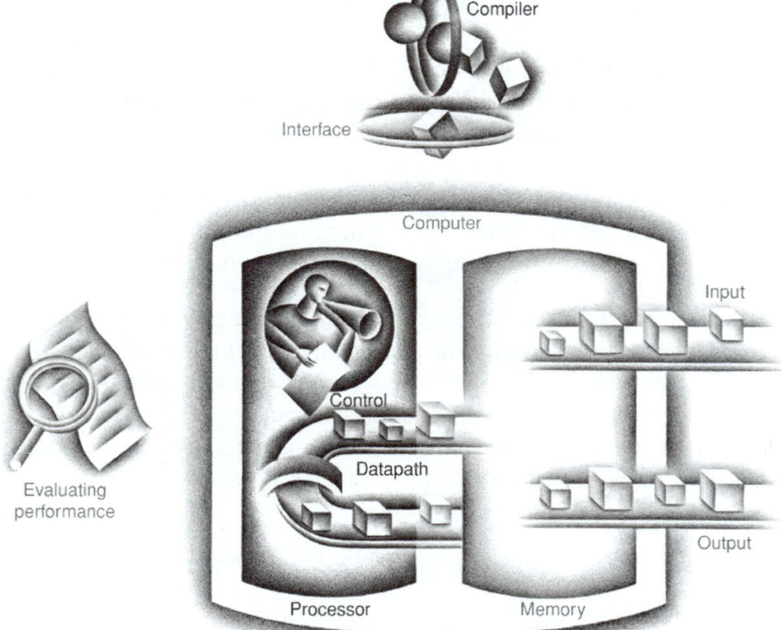

2.1   Introduction

instruction set The
vocabulary of commands
understood by a given
architecture.

To command a computer's hardware, you must speak its language. The words of a computer's language are called *instructions*, and its vocabulary is called an **instruction set**. In this chapter, you will see the instruction set of a real computer, both in the form written by people and in the form read by the computer. We introduce instructions in a top-down fashion. Starting from a notation that looks like a restricted programming language, we refine it step-by-step until you see the real language of a real computer. Chapter 3 continues our downward descent, unveiling the hardware for arithmetic and the representation of floating-point numbers.

You might think that the languages of computers would be as diverse as those of people, but in reality computer languages are quite similar, more like regional dialects than like independent languages. Hence, once you learn one, it is easy to pick up others.

The chosen instruction set comes from MIPS Technologies, and is an elegant example of the instruction sets designed since the 1980s. To demostrate how easy it is to pick up other instruction sets, we will take a quick look at three other popular instruction sets.

1. ARMv7 is similar to MIPS. More than 100 billion chips with ARM processors will be manufactured between 2017 and 2020, making it the most popular instruction set in the world.

2. The second example is the Intel x86, which powers both the PC and the cloud of the PostPC Era.

3. The third example is ARMv8, which extends the address size of the ARMv7 from 32 bits to 64 bits. Ironically, as we shall see, this 2013 instruction set is closer to MIPS than it is to ARMv7.

This similarity of instruction sets occurs because all computers are constructed from hardware technologies based on similar underlying principles and because there are a few basic operations that all computers must provide. Moreover, computer designers have a common goal: to find a language that makes it easy to build the hardware and the compiler while maximizing performance and minimizing cost and energy. This goal is time honored; the following quote was written before you could buy a computer, and it is as true today as it was in 1946:

> *It is easy to see by formal-logical methods that there exist certain [instruction sets] that are in abstract adequate to control and cause the execution of any sequence of operations. ... The really decisive considerations from the present point of view, in selecting an [instruction set], are more of a practical nature: simplicity of the equipment demanded by the [instruction set], and the clarity of its application to the actually important problems together with the speed of its handling of those problems.*

> Burks, Goldstine, and von Neumann, 1946

The "simplicity of the equipment" is as valuable a consideration for today's computers as it was for those of the 1940s. The goal of this chapter is to teach an instruction set that follows this advice, showing both how it is represented in hardware and the relationship between high-level programming languages and this more primitive one. Our examples are in the C programming language; ⊕ **Section 2.15** shows how these would change for an object-oriented language like Java.

By learning how to represent instructions, you will also discover the secret of computing: the **stored-program concept**. Moreover, you will exercise your "foreign language" skills by writing programs in the language of the computer and running them on the simulator that comes with this book. You will also see the impact of programming languages and compiler optimization on performance. We conclude with a look at the historical evolution of instruction sets and an overview of other computer dialects.

We reveal our first instruction set a piece at a time, giving the rationale along with the computer structures. This top-down, step-by-step tutorial weaves the components with their explanations, making the computer's language more palatable. Figure 2.1 gives a sneak preview of the instruction set covered in this chapter.

stored-program concept The idea that instructions and data of many types can be stored in memory as numbers, leading to the stored program computer.

2.2   Operations of the Computer Hardware

Every computer must be able to perform arithmetic. The MIPS assembly language notation

```
add a, b, c
```

instructs a computer to add the two variables b and c and to put their sum in a.

This notation is rigid in that each MIPS arithmetic instruction performs only one operation and must always have exactly three variables. For example, suppose we want to place the sum of four variables b, c, d, and e into variable a. (In this section we are being deliberately vague about what a "variable" is; in the next section we'll explain in detail.)

The following sequence of instructions adds the four variables:

```
add a, b, c    # The sum of b and c is placed in a
add a, a, d    # The sum of b, c, and d is now in a
add a, a, e    # The sum of b, c, d, and e is now in a
```

Thus, it takes three instructions to sum the four variables.

The words to the right of the sharp symbol (#) on each line above are *comments* for the human reader, and the computer ignores them. Note that unlike other programming languages, each line of this language can contain at most one

There must certainly be instructions for performing the fundamental arithmetic operations.

Burks, Goldstine, and von Neumann, 1946

MIPS operands

Name	Example	Comments
32 registers	`$s0-$s7, $t0-$t9, $zero, $a0-$a3, $v0-$v1, $gp, $fp, $sp, $ra, $at`	Fast locations for data. In MIPS, data must be in registers to perform arithmetic, register `$zero` always equals 0, and register `$at` is reserved by the assembler to handle large constants.
2^{30} memory words	`Memory[0], Memory[4], . . . , Memory[4294967292]`	Accessed only by data transfer instructions. MIPS uses byte addresses, so sequential word addresses differ by 4. Memory holds data structures, arrays, and spilled registers.

MIPS assembly language

Category	Instruction	Example	Meaning	Comments
Arithmetic	add	`add $s1,$s2,$s3`	$s1 = $s2 + $s3	Three register operands
	subtract	`sub $s1,$s2,$s3`	$s1 = $s2 – $s3	Three register operands
	add immediate	`addi $s1,$s2,20`	$s1 = $s2 + 20	Used to add constants
Data transfer	load word	`lw $s1,20($s2)`	$s1 = Memory[$s2 + 20]	Word from memory to register
	store word	`sw $s1,20($s2)`	Memory[$s2 + 20] = $s1	Word from register to memory
	load half	`lh $s1,20($s2)`	$s1 = Memory[$s2 + 20]	Halfword memory to register
	load half unsigned	`lhu $s1,20($s2)`	$s1 = Memory[$s2 + 20]	Halfword memory to register
	store half	`sh $s1,20($s2)`	Memory[$s2 + 20] = $s1	Halfword register to memory
	load byte	`lb $s1,20($s2)`	$s1 = Memory[$s2 + 20]	Byte from memory to register
	load byte unsigned	`lbu $s1,20($s2)`	$s1 = Memory[$s2 + 20]	Byte from memory to register
	store byte	`sb $s1,20($s2)`	Memory[$s2 + 20] = $s1	Byte from register to memory
	load linked word	`ll $s1,20($s2)`	$s1 = Memory[$s2 + 20]	Load word as 1st half of atomic swap
	store condition. word	`sc $s1,20($s2)`	Memory[$s2+20]=$s1;$s1=0 or 1	Store word as 2nd half of atomic swap
	load upper immed.	`lui $s1,20`	$s1 = 20 * 2^{16}	Loads constant in upper 16 bits
Logical	and	`and $s1,$s2,$s3`	$s1 = $s2 & $s3	Three reg. operands; bit-by-bit AND
	or	`or $s1,$s2,$s3`	$s1 = $s2 | $s3	Three reg. operands; bit-by-bit OR
	nor	`nor $s1,$s2,$s3`	$s1 = ~ ($s2 | $s3)	Three reg. operands; bit-by-bit NOR
	and immediate	`andi $s1,$s2,20`	$s1 = $s2 & 20	Bit-by-bit AND reg with constant
	or immediate	`ori $s1,$s2,20`	$s1 = $s2 | 20	Bit-by-bit OR reg with constant
	shift left logical	`sll $s1,$s2,10`	$s1 = $s2 << 10	Shift left by constant
	shift right logical	`srl $s1,$s2,10`	$s1 = $s2 >> 10	Shift right by constant
Conditional branch	branch on equal	`beq $s1,$s2,25`	if ($s1 == $s2) go to PC + 4 + 100	Equal test; PC-relative branch
	branch on not equal	`bne $s1,$s2,25`	if ($s1!= $s2) go to PC + 4 + 100	Not equal test; PC-relative
	set on less than	`slt $s1,$s2,$s3`	if ($s2 < $s3) $s1 = 1; else $s1 = 0	Compare less than; for `beq, bne`
	set on less than unsigned	`sltu $s1,$s2,$s3`	if ($s2 < $s3) $s1 = 1; else $s1 = 0	Compare less than unsigned
	set less than immediate	`slti $s1,$s2,20`	if ($s2 < 20) $s1 = 1; else $s1 = 0	Compare less than constant
	set less than immediate unsigned	`sltiu $s1,$s2,20`	if ($s2 < 20) $s1 = 1; else $s1 = 0	Compare less than constant unsigned
Unconditional jump	jump	`j 2500`	go to 10000	Jump to target address
	jump register	`jr $ra`	go to $ra	For switch, procedure return
	jump and link	`jal 2500`	$ra = PC + 4; go to 10000	For procedure call

FIGURE 2.1 MIPS assembly language revealed in this chapter. This information is also found in Column 1 of the MIPS Reference Data Card at the front of this book.

instruction. Another difference from C is that comments always terminate at the end of a line.

The natural number of operands for an operation like addition is three: the two numbers being added together and a place to put the sum. Requiring every instruction to have exactly three operands, no more and no less, conforms to the philosophy of keeping the hardware simple: hardware for a variable number of operands is more complicated than hardware for a fixed number. This situation illustrates the first of three underlying principles of hardware design:

Design Principle 1: Simplicity favors regularity.

We can now show, in the two examples that follow, the relationship of programs written in higher-level programming languages to programs in this more primitive notation.

Compiling Two C Assignment Statements into MIPS

This segment of a C program contains the five variables a, b, c, d, and e. Since Java evolved from C, this example and the next few work for either high-level programming language:

EXAMPLE

```
a = b + c;
d = a - e;
```

The translation from C to MIPS assembly language instructions is performed by the *compiler*. Show the MIPS code produced by a compiler.

A MIPS instruction operates on two source operands and places the result in one destination operand. Hence, the two simple statements above compile directly into these two MIPS assembly language instructions:

ANSWER

```
add a, b, c
sub d, a, e
```

Compiling a Complex C Assignment into MIPS

EXAMPLE

A somewhat complex statement contains the five variables f, g, h, i, and j:

```
f = (g + h) - (i + j);
```

What might a C compiler produce?

The compiler must break this statement into several assembly instructions, since only one operation is performed per MIPS instruction. The first MIPS instruction calculates the sum of g and h. We must place the result somewhere, so the compiler creates a temporary variable, called t0:

```
add t0,g,h # temporary variable t0 contains g + h
```

Although the next operation is subtract, we need to calculate the sum of i and j before we can subtract. Thus, the second instruction places the sum of i and j in another temporary variable created by the compiler, called t1:

```
add t1,i,j # temporary variable t1 contains i + j
```

Finally, the subtract instruction subtracts the second sum from the first and places the difference in the variable f, completing the compiled code:

```
sub f,t0,t1 # f gets t0 - t1, which is (g + h) - (i + j)
```

Check Yourself

For a given function, which programming language likely takes the most lines of code? Put the three representations below in order.

1. Java

2. C

3. MIPS assembly language

Elaboration: To increase portability, Java was originally envisioned as relying on a software interpreter. The instruction set of this interpreter is called *Java bytecodes* (see Section 2.15), which is quite different from the MIPS instruction set. To get performance close to the equivalent C program, Java systems today typically compile Java bytecodes into the native instruction sets like MIPS. Because this compilation is normally done much later than for C programs, such Java compilers are often called *Just In Time* (JIT) compilers. Section 2.12 shows how JITs are used later than C compilers in the start-up process, and Section 2.13 shows the performance consequences of compiling versus interpreting Java programs.

2.3   Operands of the Computer Hardware

Unlike programs in high-level languages, the operands of arithmetic instructions are restricted; they must be from a limited number of special locations built directly in hardware called *registers*. Registers are primitives used in hardware design that are also visible to the programmer when the computer is completed, so you can think of registers as the bricks of computer construction. The size of a register in the MIPS architecture is 32 bits; groups of 32 bits occur so frequently that they are given the name **word** in the MIPS architecture.

word The natural unit of access in a computer, usually a group of 32 bits; corresponds to the size of a register in the MIPS architecture.

One major difference between the variables of a programming language and registers is the limited number of registers, typically 32 on current computers, like MIPS. (See ⊕ **Section 2.23** for the history of the number of registers.) Thus, continuing in our top-down, stepwise evolution of the symbolic representation of the MIPS language, in this section we have added the restriction that the three operands of MIPS arithmetic instructions must each be chosen from one of the 32 32-bit registers.

The reason for the limit of 32 registers may be found in the second of our three underlying design principles of hardware technology:

Design Principle 2: Smaller is faster.

A very large number of registers may increase the clock cycle time simply because it takes electronic signals longer when they must travel farther.

Guidelines such as "smaller is faster" are not absolutes; 31 registers may not be faster than 32. Yet, the truth behind such observations causes computer designers to take them seriously. In this case, the designer must balance the craving of programs for more registers with the designer's desire to keep the clock cycle fast. Another reason for not using more than 32 is the number of bits it would take in the instruction format, as Section 2.5 demonstrates.

Chapter 4 shows the central role that registers play in hardware construction; as we shall see in this chapter, effective use of registers is critical to program performance.

Although we could simply write instructions using numbers for registers, from 0 to 31, the MIPS convention is to use two-character names following a dollar sign to represent a register. Section 2.8 will explain the reasons behind these names. For now, we will use $s0, $s1, ... for registers that correspond to variables in C and Java programs and $t0, $t1, ... for temporary registers needed to compile the program into MIPS instructions.

Compiling a C Assignment Using Registers

It is the compiler's job to associate program variables with registers. Take, for instance, the assignment statement from our earlier example:

```
f=(g + h) - (i + j);
```

The variables f, g, h, i, and j are assigned to the registers $s0, $s1, $s2, $s3, and $s4, respectively. What is the compiled MIPS code?

EXAMPLE

ANSWER

The compiled program is very similar to the prior example, except we replace the variables with the register names mentioned above plus two temporary registers, $t0 and $t1, which correspond to the temporary variables above:

```
add $t0,$s1,$s2 # register $t0 contains g + h
add $t1,$s3,$s4 # register $t1 contains i + j
sub $s0,$t0,$t1 # f gets $t0 - $t1, which is (g + h)-(i + j)
```

Memory Operands

Programming languages have simple variables that contain single data elements, as in these examples, but they also have more complex data structures—arrays and structures. These complex data structures can contain many more data elements than there are registers in a computer. How can a computer represent and access such large structures?

Recall the five components of a computer introduced in Chapter 1 and repeated on page 67. The processor can keep only a small amount of data in registers, but computer memory contains billions of data elements. Hence, data structures (arrays and structures) are kept in memory.

As explained above, arithmetic operations occur only on registers in MIPS instructions; thus, MIPS must include instructions that transfer data between memory and registers. Such instructions are called **data transfer instructions**. To access a word in memory, the instruction must supply the memory **address**. Memory is just a large, single-dimensional array, with the address acting as the index to that array, starting at 0. For example, in Figure 2.2, the address of the third data element is 2, and the value of Memory[2] is 10.

data transfer instruction A command that moves data between memory and registers.

address A value used to delineate the location of a specific data element within a memory array.

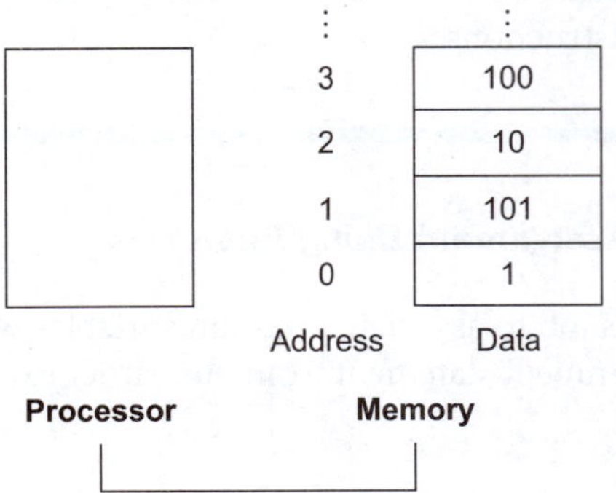

FIGURE 2.2 Memory addresses and contents of memory at those locations. If these elements were words, these addresses would be incorrect, since MIPS actually uses byte addressing, with each word representing four bytes. Figure 2.3 shows the memory addressing for sequential word addresses.

The data transfer instruction that copies data from memory to a register is traditionally called *load*. The format of the load instruction is the name of the operation followed by the register to be loaded, then a constant and register used to access memory. The sum of the constant portion of the instruction and the contents of the second register forms the memory address. The actual MIPS name for this instruction is lw, standing for *load word*.

Compiling an Assignment When an Operand Is in Memory

Let's assume that A is an array of 100 words and that the compiler has associated the variables g and h with the registers $s1 and $s2 as before. Let's also assume that the starting address, or *base address,* of the array is in $s3. Compile this C assignment statement:

```
g = h + A[8];
```

Although there is a single operation in this assignment statement, one of the operands is in memory, so we must first transfer A[8] to a register. The address of this array element is the sum of the base of the array A, found in register $s3, plus the number to select element 8. The data should be placed in a temporary register for use in the next instruction. Based on Figure 2.2, the first compiled instruction is


```
lw      $t0,8($s3)  # Temporary reg $t0 gets A[8]
```

(On the next page we'll make a slight adjustment to this instruction, but we'll use this simplified version for now.) The following instruction can operate on the value in $t0 (which equals A[8]) since it is in a register. The instruction must add h (contained in ($2) to A[8] (contained in $t0) and put the sum in the register corresponding to g (associated with $s1):

```
add     $s1,$s2,$t0 # g = h + A[8]
```

The constant in a data transfer instruction (8) is called the *offset,* and the register added to form the address ($s3) is called the *base register.*

In addition to associating variables with registers, the compiler allocates data structures like arrays and structures to locations in memory. The compiler can then place the proper starting address into the data transfer instructions.

Hardware/ Software Interface

Since 8-bit *bytes* are useful in many programs, virtually all architectures today address individual bytes. Therefore, the address of a word matches the address of one of the 4 bytes within the word, and addresses of sequential words differ by 4. For example, Figure 2.3 shows the actual MIPS addresses for the words in Figure 2.2; the byte address of the third word is 8.

In MIPS, words must start at addresses that are multiples of 4. This requirement is called an **alignment restriction**, and many architectures have it. (Chapter 4 suggests why alignment leads to faster data transfers.)

alignment restriction
A requirement that data be aligned in memory on natural boundaries.

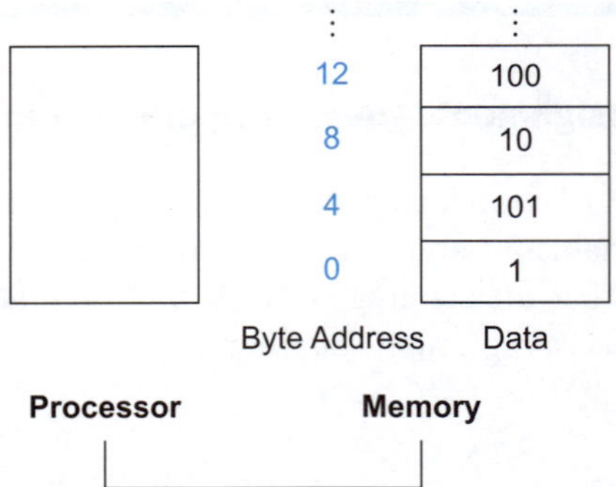

FIGURE 2.3 Actual MIPS memory addresses and contents of memory for those words. The changed addresses are highlighted to contrast with Figure 2.2. Since MIPS addresses each byte, word addresses are multiples of 4: there are 4 bytes in a word.

Computers divide into those that use the address of the leftmost or "big end" byte as the word address versus those that use the rightmost or "little end" byte. MIPS is in the *big-endian* camp. Since the order matters only if you access the identical data both as a word and as four bytes, few need to be aware of the endianess. (Appendix A shows the two options to number bytes in a word.)

Byte addressing also affects the array index. To get the proper byte address in the code above, *the offset to be added to the base register $s3 must be 4 × 8, or 32,* so that the load address will select A[8] and not A[8/4]. (See the related pitfall on page 168 of Section 2.21.)

The instruction complementary to load is traditionally called *store*; it copies data from a register to memory. The format of a store is similar to that of a load: the name of the operation, followed by the register to be stored, then offset to select the array element, and finally the base register. Once again, the MIPS address is specified in part by a constant and in part by the contents of a register. The actual MIPS name is sw, standing for *store word*.

Hardware/ Software Interface

As the addresses in loads and stores are binary numbers, we can see why the DRAM for main memory comes in binary sizes rather than in decimal sizes. That is, in gebibytes (2^{30}) or tebibytes (2^{40}), not in gigabytes (10^9) or terabytes (10^{12}); see Figure 1.1.

Compiling Using Load and Store

Assume variable h is associated with register $s2 and the base address of the array A is in $s3. What is the MIPS assembly code for the C assignment statement below?

```
A[12] = h + A[8];
```

Although there is a single operation in the C statement, now two of the operands are in memory, so we need even more MIPS instructions. The first two instructions are the same as the prior example, except this time we use the proper offset of 32 for byte addressing in the load word instruction to select A[8], and the add instruction places the sum in $t0:


```
lw    $t0,32($s3)  # Temporary reg $t0 gets A[8]
add   $t0,$s2,$t0  # Temporary reg $t0 gets h + A[8]
```

The final instruction stores the sum into A[12], using 48 (4 × 12) as the offset and register $s3 as the base register.

```
sw    $t0,48($s3)  # Stores h + A[8] back into A[12]
```

Load word and store word are the instructions that copy words between memory and registers in the MIPS architecture. Other brands of computers use other instructions along with load and store to transfer data. An architecture with such alternatives is the Intel x86, described in Section 2.19.

Hardware/ Software Interface

Many programs have more variables than computers have registers. Consequently, the compiler tries to keep the most frequently used variables in registers and places the rest in memory, using loads and stores to move variables between registers and memory. The process of putting less commonly used variables (or those needed later) into memory is called *spilling* registers.

The hardware principle relating size and speed suggests that memory must be slower than registers, since there are fewer registers. This is indeed the case; data accesses are faster if data is in registers instead of memory.

Moreover, data is more useful when in a register. A MIPS arithmetic instruction can read two registers, operate on them, and write the result. A MIPS data transfer instruction only reads one operand or writes one operand, without operating on it.

Thus, registers take less time to access *and* have higher throughput than memory, making data in registers both faster to access and simpler to use. Accessing registers also uses less energy than accessing memory. To achieve highest performance and conserve energy, an instruction set architecture must have a sufficient number of registers, and compilers must use registers efficiently.

Constant or Immediate Operands

Many times a program will use a constant in an operation—for example, incrementing an index to point to the next element of an array. In fact, more than half of the MIPS arithmetic instructions have a constant as an operand when running the SPEC CPU2006 benchmarks.

Using only the instructions we have seen so far, we would have to load a constant from memory to use one. (The constants would have been placed in memory when the program was loaded.) For example, to add the constant 4 to register $s3, we could use the code

```
lw $t0, AddrConstant4($s1)   # $t0 = constant 4
add $s3,$s3,$t0              # $s3 = $s3 + $t0 ($t0 == 4)
```

assuming that `$s1 + AddrConstant4` is the memory address of the constant 4.

An alternative that avoids the load instruction is to offer versions of the arithmetic instructions in which one operand is a constant. This quick add instruction with one constant operand is called *add immediate* or `addi`. To add 4 to register $s3, we just write

```
addi    $s3,$s3,4           # $s3 = $s3 + 4
```

Constant operands occur frequently, and by including constants inside arithmetic instructions, operations are much faster and use less energy than if constants were loaded from memory.

The constant zero has another role, which is to simplify the instruction set by offering useful variations. For example, the move operation is just an add instruction where one operand is zero. Hence, MIPS dedicates a register $zero to be hard-wired to the value zero. (As you might expect, it is register number 0.) Using frequency to justify the inclusions of constants is another example of the great idea of making the **common case fast**.

Check Yourself

Given the importance of registers, what is the rate of increase in the number of registers in a chip over time?

1. Very fast: They increased as fast as Moore's law, which predicted doubling the number of transistors on a chip every 24 months.

2. Very slow: Since programs are usually distributed in the language of the computer, there is inertia in instruction set architecture, and so the number of registers increases only as fast as new instruction sets become viable.

Elaboration: Although the MIPS registers in this book are 32 bits wide, there is a 64-bit version of the MIPS instruction set with 32 64-bit registers. To keep them straight, they are officially called MIPS-32 and MIPS-64. In this chapter, we use a subset of MIPS-32. 🌐 **Appendix E** shows the differences between MIPS-32 and MIPS-64. Sections 2.16 and 2.17 show the much more dramatic difference between the 32-bit address ARMv7 and its 64-bit successor, ARMv8.

Elaboration: The MIPS offset plus base register addressing is an excellent match to structures as well as arrays, since the register can point to the beginning of the structure and the offset can select the desired element. We'll see such an example in Section 2.13.

Elaboration: The register in the data transfer instructions was originally invented to hold an index of an array with the offset used for the starting address of an array. Thus, the base register is also called the *index register*. Today's memories are much larger and the software model of data allocation is more sophisticated, so the base address of the array is normally passed in a register since it won't fit in the offset, as we shall see.

Elaboration: Since MIPS supports negative constants, there is no need for subtract immediate in MIPS.

2.4 Signed and Unsigned Numbers

First, let's quickly review how a computer represents numbers. Because people have 10 fingers, we are taught to think in base 10, but numbers may be represented in any base. For example, 123 base 10 = 1111011 base 2.

Numbers are kept in computer hardware as a series of high and low electronic signals, and so they are considered base 2 numbers. (Just as base 10 numbers are called *decimal* numbers, base 2 numbers are called *binary* numbers.)

A single digit of a binary number is thus the "atom" of computing, since all information is composed of **binary digits** or *bits*. This fundamental building block can be one of two values, which can be thought of as several alternatives: high or low, on or off, true or false, or 1 or 0.

Generalizing the point, in any number base, the value of *i*th digit *d* is

$$d \times \text{Base}^i$$

where *i* starts at 0 and increases from right to left. This representation leads to an obvious way to number the bits in the word: simply use the power of the base for that bit. We subscript decimal numbers with *ten* and binary numbers with *two*. For example,

$$1011_{two}$$

represents

$$
\begin{aligned}
&(1 \times 2^3) + (0 \times 2^2) + (1 \times 2^1) + (1 \times 2^0)_{ten} \\
= &(1 \times 8) + (0 \times 4) + (1 \times 2) + (1 \times 1)_{ten} \\
= &\quad 8 \quad + \quad 0 \quad + \quad 2 \quad + \quad 1_{ten} \\
= &\ 11_{ten}
\end{aligned}
$$

binary digit Also called **binary bit**. One of the two numbers in base 2, 0 or 1, that are the components of information.

We number the bits 0, 1, 2, 3, . . . from *right to left* in a word. The drawing below shows the numbering of bits within a MIPS word and the placement of the number 1011_{two}:

31 30 29 28	27 26 25 24	23 22 21 20	19 18 17 16	15 14 13 12	11 10 9 8	7 6 5 4	3 2 1 0
0 0 0 0	0 0 0 0	0 0 0 0	0 0 0 0	0 0 0 0	0 0 0 0	0 0 0 0	1 0 1 1

(32 bits wide)

least significant bit The rightmost bit in a MIPS word.

Since words are drawn vertically as well as horizontally, leftmost and rightmost may be unclear. Hence, the phrase **least significant bit** is used to refer to the rightmost bit (bit 0 above) and **most significant bit** to the leftmost bit (bit 31).

most significant bit The leftmost bit in a MIPS word.

The MIPS word is 32 bits long, so it can represent 2^{32} different 32-bit patterns. It is natural to let these combinations represent the numbers from 0 to $2^{32} -1$ ($4{,}294{,}967{,}295_{ten}$):

$$0000\ 0000\ 0000\ 0000\ 0000\ 0000\ 0000\ 0000_{two} = 0_{ten}$$
$$0000\ 0000\ 0000\ 0000\ 0000\ 0000\ 0000\ 0001_{two} = 1_{ten}$$
$$0000\ 0000\ 0000\ 0000\ 0000\ 0000\ 0000\ 0010_{two} = 2_{ten}$$
$$. . . \qquad\qquad . . .$$
$$1111\ 1111\ 1111\ 1111\ 1111\ 1111\ 1111\ 1101_{two} = 4{,}294{,}967{,}293_{ten}$$
$$1111\ 1111\ 1111\ 1111\ 1111\ 1111\ 1111\ 1110_{two} = 4{,}294{,}967{,}294_{ten}$$
$$1111\ 1111\ 1111\ 1111\ 1111\ 1111\ 1111\ 1111_{two} = 4{,}294{,}967{,}295_{ten}$$

That is, 32-bit binary numbers can be represented in terms of the bit value times a power of 2 (here *xi* means the *i*th bit of *x*):

$$(x31 \times 2^{31}) + (x30 \times 2^{30}) + (x29 \times 2^{29}) + \ldots + (x1 \times 2^{1}) + (x0 \times 2^{0})$$

For reasons we will shortly see, these positive numbers are called unsigned numbers.

Hardware/ Software Interface

Base 2 is not natural to human beings; we have 10 fingers and so find base 10 natural. Why didn't computers use decimal? In fact, the first commercial computer *did* offer decimal arithmetic. The problem was that the computer still used on and off signals, so a decimal digit was simply represented by several binary digits. Decimal proved so inefficient that subsequent computers reverted to all binary, converting to base 10 only for the relatively infrequent input/output events.

Overflow When the results of an operation are larger than can be represented in a register.

Keep in mind that the binary bit patterns above are simply *representatives* of numbers. Numbers really have an infinite number of digits, with almost all being 0 except for a few of the rightmost digits. We just don't normally show leading 0s.

Hardware can be designed to add, subtract, multiply, and divide these binary bit patterns. If the number that is the proper result of such operations cannot be represented by these rightmost hardware bits, *overflow* is said to have occurred.

It's up to the programming language, the operating system, and the program to determine what to do if overflow occurs.

Computer programs calculate both positive and negative numbers, so we need a representation that distinguishes the positive from the negative. The most obvious solution is to add a separate sign, which conveniently can be represented in a single bit; the name for this representation is *sign and magnitude*.

Alas, sign and magnitude representation has several shortcomings. First, it's not obvious where to put the sign bit. To the right? To the left? Early computers tried both. Second, adders for sign and magnitude may need an extra step to set the sign because we can't know in advance what the proper sign will be. Finally, a separate sign bit means that sign and magnitude has both a positive and a negative zero, which can lead to problems for inattentive programmers. As a result of these shortcomings, sign and magnitude representation was soon abandoned.

In the search for a more attractive alternative, the question arose as to what would be the result for unsigned numbers if we tried to subtract a large number from a small one. The answer is that it would try to borrow from a string of leading 0s, so the result would have a string of leading 1s.

Given that there was no obvious better alternative, the final solution was to pick the representation that made the hardware simple: leading 0s mean positive, and leading 1s mean negative. This convention for representing signed binary numbers is called *two's complement* representation (an *Elaboration* on page 85 explains this unusual name):

$$
\begin{array}{rcl}
0000\ 0000\ 0000\ 0000\ 0000\ 0000\ 0000\ 0000_{two} &=& 0_{ten} \\
0000\ 0000\ 0000\ 0000\ 0000\ 0000\ 0000\ 0001_{two} &=& 1_{ten} \\
0000\ 0000\ 0000\ 0000\ 0000\ 0000\ 0000\ 0010_{two} &=& 2_{ten} \\
\cdots & & \cdots \\
0111\ 1111\ 1111\ 1111\ 1111\ 1111\ 1111\ 1101_{two} &=& 2{,}147{,}483{,}645_{ten} \\
0111\ 1111\ 1111\ 1111\ 1111\ 1111\ 1111\ 1110_{two} &=& 2{,}147{,}483{,}646_{ten} \\
0111\ 1111\ 1111\ 1111\ 1111\ 1111\ 1111\ 1111_{two} &=& 2{,}147{,}483{,}647_{ten} \\
1000\ 0000\ 0000\ 0000\ 0000\ 0000\ 0000\ 0000_{two} &=& -2{,}147{,}483{,}648_{ten} \\
1000\ 0000\ 0000\ 0000\ 0000\ 0000\ 0000\ 0001_{two} &=& -2{,}147{,}483{,}647_{ten} \\
1000\ 0000\ 0000\ 0000\ 0000\ 0000\ 0000\ 0010_{two} &=& -2{,}147{,}483{,}646_{ten} \\
\cdots & & \cdots \\
1111\ 1111\ 1111\ 1111\ 1111\ 1111\ 1111\ 1101_{two} &=& -3_{ten} \\
1111\ 1111\ 1111\ 1111\ 1111\ 1111\ 1111\ 1110_{two} &=& -2_{ten} \\
1111\ 1111\ 1111\ 1111\ 1111\ 1111\ 1111\ 1111_{two} &=& -1_{ten}
\end{array}
$$

The positive half of the numbers, from 0 to $2{,}147{,}483{,}647_{ten}$ ($2^{31}-1$), use the same representation as before. The following bit pattern ($1000 \ldots 0000_{two}$) represents the most negative number $-2{,}147{,}483{,}648_{ten}$ (-2^{31}). It is followed by a declining set of negative numbers: $-2{,}147{,}483{,}647_{ten}$ ($1000 \ldots 0001_{two}$) down to -1_{ten} ($1111 \ldots 1111_{two}$).

Two's complement does have one negative number, $-2{,}147{,}483{,}648_{ten}$, that has no corresponding positive number. Such imbalance was also a worry to the inattentive programmer, but sign and magnitude had problems for both the programmer *and* the hardware designer. Consequently, every computer today uses two's complement binary representations for signed numbers.

Two's complement representation has the advantage that all negative numbers have a 1 in the most significant bit. Hardware needs to test only this bit to see if a number is positive or negative (with the number 0 considered positive). This bit is often called the *sign bit*. By recognizing the role of the sign bit, we can represent positive and negative 32-bit numbers in terms of the bit value times a power of 2:

$$(x31 \times -2^{31}) + (x30 \times 2^{30}) + (x29 \times 2^{29}) + \ldots + (x1 \times 2^{1}) + (x0 \times 2^{0})$$

The sign bit is multiplied by -2^{31}, and the rest of the bits are then multiplied by positive versions of their respective base values.

EXAMPLE

Binary to Decimal Conversion

What is the decimal value of this 32-bit two's complement number?

$$1111 \quad 1111 \quad 1111 \quad 1111 \quad 1111 \quad 1111 \quad 1111 \quad 1100_{two}$$

Substituting the number's bit values into the formula above:

ANSWER

$$(1 \times -2^{31}) + (1 \times 2^{30}) + (1 \times 2^{29}) + \ldots + (1 \times 2^{2}) + (0 \times 2^{1}) + (0 \times 2^{0})$$
$$= -2^{31} + 2^{30} + 2^{29} + \ldots + 2^{2} + 0 + 0$$
$$= -2{,}147{,}483{,}648_{ten} + 2{,}147{,}483{,}644_{ten}$$
$$= -4_{ten}$$

We'll see a shortcut to simplify conversion from negative to positive soon.

Just as an operation on unsigned numbers can overflow the capacity of hardware to represent the result, so can an operation on two's complement numbers. Overflow occurs when the leftmost retained bit of the binary bit pattern is not the same as the infinite number of digits to the left (the sign bit is incorrect): a 0 on the left of the bit pattern when the number is negative or a 1 when the number is positive.

Hardware/ Software Interface

Signed versus unsigned applies to loads as well as to arithmetic. The *function* of a signed load is to copy the sign repeatedly to fill the rest of the register—called *sign extension*—but its *purpose* is to place a correct representation of the number within that register. Unsigned loads simply fill with 0s to the left of the data, since the number represented by the bit pattern is unsigned.

When loading a 32-bit word into a 32-bit register, the point is moot; signed and unsigned loads are identical. MIPS does offer two flavors of byte loads: *load byte* (`lb`) treats the byte as a signed number and thus sign-extends to fill the 24 left-most bits of the register, while *load byte unsigned* (`lbu`) works with unsigned integers. Since C programs almost always use bytes to represent characters rather than consider bytes as very short signed integers, `lbu` is used practically exclusively for byte loads.

Unlike the numbers discussed above, memory addresses naturally start at 0 and continue to the largest address. Put another way, negative addresses make no sense. Thus, programs want to deal sometimes with numbers that can be positive or negative and sometimes with numbers that can be only positive. Some programming languages reflect this distinction. C, for example, names the former *integers* (declared as `int` in the program) and the latter *unsigned integers* (`unsigned int`). Some C style guides even recommend declaring the former as `signed int` to keep the distinction clear.

Hardware/ Software Interface

Let's examine two useful shortcuts when working with two's complement numbers. The first shortcut is a quick way to negate a two's complement binary number. Simply invert every 0 to 1 and every 1 to 0, then add one to the result. This shortcut is based on the observation that the sum of a number and its inverted representation must be $111 \ldots 111_{two}$, which represents -1. Since $x + \bar{x} = -1$, therefore $x + \bar{x} + 1 = 0$ or $\bar{x} + 1 = -x$ (We use the notation $\bar{x}$ to mean invert every bit in x from 0 to 1 and vice versa.)

Negation Shortcut

EXAMPLE

Negate 2_{ten}, and then check the result by negating -2_{ten}.

ANSWER

$$2_{ten} = 0000\ 0000\ 0000\ 0000\ 0000\ 0000\ 0000\ 0010_{two}$$

Negating this number by inverting the bits and adding one,

$$
\begin{aligned}
&\ \ 1111\ 1111\ 1111\ 1111\ 1111\ 1111\ 1111\ 1101_{two} \\
+&\ \hspace{26em} 1_{two} \\
\hline
=&\ \ 1111\ 1111\ 1111\ 1111\ 1111\ 1111\ 1111\ 1110_{two} \\
=&\ -2_{ten}
\end{aligned}
$$

Going the other direction,

$$1111\ 1111\ 1111\ 1111\ 1111\ 1111\ 1111\ 1110_{two}$$

is first inverted and then incremented:

$$
\begin{aligned}
&\ \ 0000\ 0000\ 0000\ 0000\ 0000\ 0000\ 0000\ 0001_{two} \\
+&\ \hspace{26em} 1_{two} \\
\hline
=&\ \ 0000\ 0000\ 0000\ 0000\ 0000\ 0000\ 0000\ 0010_{two} \\
=&\ \ 2_{ten}
\end{aligned}
$$

Our next shortcut tells us how to convert a binary number represented in n bits to a number represented with more than n bits. For example, the immediate field in the load, store, branch, add, and set on less than instructions contains a two's complement 16-bit number, representing $-32{,}768_{ten}$ (-2^{15}) to $32{,}767_{ten}$ ($2^{15}-1$). To add the immediate field to a 32-bit register, the computer must convert that 16-bit number to its 32-bit equivalent. The shortcut is to take the most significant bit from the smaller quantity—the sign bit—and replicate it to fill the new bits of the larger quantity. The old nonsign bits are simply copied into the right portion of the new word. This shortcut is called *sign extension*.

EXAMPLE

Sign Extension Shortcut

Convert 16-bit binary versions of 2_{ten} and -2_{ten} to 32-bit binary numbers.

ANSWER

The 16-bit binary version of the number 2 is

$$0000\ 0000\ 0000\ 0010_{two} = 2_{ten}$$

It is converted to a 32-bit number by making 16 copies of the value in the most significant bit (0) and placing that in the left-hand half of the word. The right half gets the old value:

$$0000\ 0000\ 0000\ 0000\ 0000\ 0000\ 0000\ 0010_{two} = 2_{ten}$$

Let's negate the 16-bit version of 2 using the earlier shortcut. Thus,

$$0000\ 0000\ 0000\ 0010_{two}$$

becomes

$$
\begin{aligned}
&1111\ 1111\ 1111\ 1101_{two}\\
+\ &\underline{\hspace{6em}1_{two}}\\
=\ &1111\ 1111\ 1111\ 1110_{two}
\end{aligned}
$$

Creating a 32-bit version of the negative number means copying the sign bit 16 times and placing it on the left:

$$1111\ 1111\ 1111\ 1111\ 1111\ 1111\ 1111\ 1110_{two} = -2_{ten}$$

This trick works because positive two's complement numbers really have an infinite number of 0s on the left and negative two's complement numbers have an infinite number of 1s. The binary bit pattern representing a number hides leading bits to fit the width of the hardware; sign extension simply restores some of them.

Summary

The main point of this section is that we need to represent both positive and negative integers within a computer word, and although there are pros and cons to any option, the unanimous choice since 1965 has been two's complement.

Elaboration: For signed decimal numbers, we used "−" to represent negative because there are no limits to the size of a decimal number. Given a fixed word size, binary and hexadecimal (see Figure 2.4) bit strings can encode the sign; hence we do not normally use "+" or "−" with binary or hexadecimal notation.

What is the decimal value of this 64-bit two's complement number?

$$1111\ 1111\ 1111\ 1111\ 1111\ 1111\ 1111\ 1111\ 1111\ 1111\ 1111\ 1111\ 1111\ 1111\ 1111\ 1000_{two}$$

Check Yourself

1) -4_{ten}

2) -8_{ten}

3) -16_{ten}

4) $18,446,744,073,709,551,608_{ten}$

What is the decimal value if it is instead a 64-bit unsigned number?

Elaboration: Two's complement gets its name from the rule that the unsigned sum of an n-bit number and its n-bit negative is 2^n; hence, the negation or complement of a number x is $2^n - x$, or its "two's complement."

A third alternative representation to two's complement and sign and magnitude is called one's complement. The negative of a one's complement is found by inverting each bit, from 0 to 1 and from 1 to 0, or $\overline{x}$. This relation helps explain its name since the complement of x is $2^n - x - 1$. It was also an attempt to be a better solution than sign and magnitude, and several early scientific computers did use the notation. This representation is similar to two's complement except that it also has two 0s: $00\ldots00_{two}$ is positive 0 and $11\ldots11_{two}$ is negative 0. The most negative number, $10\ldots000_{two}$, represents $-2,147,483,647_{ten}$, and so the positives and negatives are balanced. One's complement adders did need an extra step to subtract a number, and hence two's complement dominates today.

A final notation, which we will look at when we discuss floating point in Chapter 3, is to represent the most negative value by $00\ldots000_{two}$ and the most positive value by $11\ldots11_{two}$, with 0 typically having the value $10\ldots00_{two}$. This is called a biased notation, since it biases the number such that the number plus the bias has a non-negative representation.

one's complement A notation that represents the most negative value by $10\ldots000_{two}$ and the most positive value by $01\ldots11_{two}$, leaving an equal number of negatives and positives but ending up with two zeros, one positive ($00\ldots00_{two}$) and one negative ($11\ldots11_{two}$). The term is also used to mean the inversion of every bit in a pattern: 0 to 1 and 1 to 0.

biased notation A notation that represents the most negative value by $00\ldots000_{two}$ and the most positive value by $11\ldots11_{two}$, with 0 typically having the value $10\ldots00_{two}$, thereby biasing the number such that the number plus the bias has a nonnegative representation.

2.5   Representing Instructions in the Computer

We are now ready to explain the difference between the way humans instruct computers and the way computers see instructions.

Instructions are kept in the computer as a series of high and low electronic signals and may be represented as numbers. In fact, each piece of an instruction can be considered as an individual number, and placing these numbers side by side forms the instruction.

Since registers are referred to by almost all instructions, there must be a convention to map register names into numbers. In MIPS assembly language, registers $s0 to $s7 map onto registers 16 to 23, and registers $t0 to $t7 map onto registers 8 to 15. Hence, $s0 means register 16, $s1 means register 17, $s2 means register 18,..., $t0 means register 8, $t1 means register 9, and so on. We'll describe the convention for the rest of the 32 registers in the following sections.

EXAMPLE

Translating a MIPS Assembly Instruction into a Machine Instruction

Let's do the next step in the refinement of the MIPS language as an example. We'll show the real MIPS language version of the instruction represented symbolically as

```
add $t0,$s1,$s2
```

first as a combination of decimal numbers and then of binary numbers.

ANSWER

The decimal representation is

0	17	18	8	0	32

Each of these segments of an instruction is called a *field*. The first and last fields (containing 0 and 32 in this case) in combination tell the MIPS computer that this instruction performs addition. The second field gives the number of the register that is the first source operand of the addition operation (17=$s1), and the third field gives the other source operand for the addition (18=$s2). The fourth field contains the number of the register that is to receive the sum (8=$t0). The fifth field is unused in this instruction, so it is set to 0. Thus, this instruction adds register $s1 to register $s2 and places the sum in register $t0.

This instruction can also be represented as fields of binary numbers as opposed to decimal:

000000	10001	10010	01000	00000	100000
6 bits	5 bits	5 bits	5 bits	5 bits	6 bits

This layout of the instruction is called the **instruction format**. As you can see from counting the number of bits, this MIPS instruction takes exactly 32 bits—the same size as a data word. In keeping with our design principle that simplicity favors regularity, all MIPS instructions are 32 bits long.

To distinguish it from assembly language, we call the numeric version of instructions **machine language** and a sequence of such instructions *machine code*.

It would appear that you would now be reading and writing long, tedious strings of binary numbers. We avoid that tedium by using a higher base than binary that converts easily into binary. Since almost all computer data sizes are multiples of 4, **hexadecimal** (base 16) numbers are popular. Since base 16 is a power of 2, we can trivially convert by replacing each group of four binary digits by a single hexadecimal digit, and vice versa. Figure 2.4 converts between hexadecimal and binary.

instruction format
A form of representation of an instruction composed of fields of binary numbers.

machine language Binary representation used for communication within a computer system.

hexadecimal Numbers in base 16.

Hexadecimal	Binary	Hexadecimal	Binary	Hexadecimal	Binary	Hexadecimal	Binary
0_{hex}	0000_{two}	4_{hex}	0100_{two}	8_{hex}	1000_{two}	c_{hex}	1100_{two}
1_{hex}	0001_{two}	5_{hex}	0101_{two}	9_{hex}	1001_{two}	d_{hex}	1101_{two}
2_{hex}	0010_{two}	6_{hex}	0110_{two}	a_{hex}	1010_{two}	e_{hex}	1110_{two}
3_{hex}	0011_{two}	7_{hex}	0111_{two}	b_{hex}	1011_{two}	f_{hex}	1111_{two}

FIGURE 2.4 The hexadecimal-binary conversion table. Just replace one hexadecimal digit by the corresponding four binary digits, and vice versa. If the length of the binary number is not a multiple of 4, go from right to left.

Because we frequently deal with different number bases, to avoid confusion we will subscript decimal numbers with *ten*, binary numbers with *two*, and hexadecimal numbers with *hex*. (If there is no subscript, the default is base 10.) By the way, C and Java use the notation 0x*nnnn* for hexadecimal numbers.

Binary to Hexadecimal and Back

EXAMPLE

Convert the following hexadecimal and binary numbers into the other base:

eca8 6420_{hex}

0001 0011 0101 0111 1001 1011 1101 1111_{two}

ANSWER

Using Figure 2.4, the answer is just a table lookup one way:

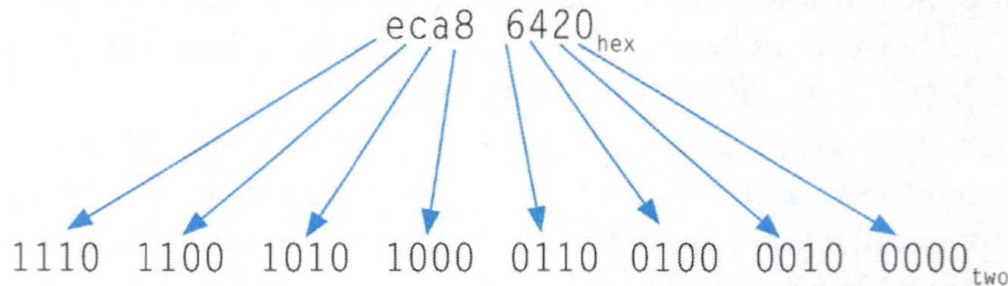

And then the other direction:

MIPS Fields

MIPS fields are given names to make them easier to discuss:

op	rs	rt	rd	shamt	funct
6 bits	5 bits	5 bits	5 bits	5 bits	6 bits

Here is the meaning of each name of the fields in MIPS instructions:

- *op*: Basic operation of the instruction, traditionally called the **opcode**.

- *rs*: The first register source operand.

- *rt*: The second register source operand.

- *rd*: The register destination operand. It gets the result of the operation.

- *shamt*: Shift amount. (Section 2.6 explains shift instructions and this term; it will not be used until then, and hence the field contains zero in this section.)

- *funct*: Function. This field, often called the *function code,* selects the specific variant of the operation in the op field.

opcode The field that denotes the operation and format of an instruction.

A problem occurs when an instruction needs longer fields than those shown above. For example, the load word instruction must specify two registers and a constant. If the address were to use one of the 5-bit fields in the format above, the constant within the load word instruction would be limited to only 2^5 or 32. This constant is used to select elements from arrays or data structures, and it often needs to be much larger than 32. This 5-bit field is too small to be useful.

Hence, we have a conflict between the desire to keep all instructions the same length and the desire to have a single instruction format. This leads us to the final hardware design principle:

Design Principle 3: Good design demands good compromises.

The compromise chosen by the MIPS designers is to keep all instructions the same length, thereby requiring different kinds of instruction formats for different kinds of instructions. For example, the format above is called *R-type* (for register) or *R-format*. A second type of instruction format is called *I-type* (for immediate) or *I-format* and is used by the immediate and data transfer instructions. The fields of I-format are

op	rs	rt	constant or address
6 bits	5 bits	5 bits	16 bits

The 16-bit address means a load word instruction can load any word within a region of $\pm 2^{15}$ or 32,768 bytes ($\pm 2^{13}$ or 8192 words) of the address in the base register rs. Similarly, add immediate is limited to constants no larger than $\pm 2^{15}$. We see that more than 32 registers would be difficult in this format, as the rs and rt fields would each need another bit, making it harder to fit everything in one word.

Let's look at the load word instruction from page 77:

```
lw    $t0,32($s3)    # Temporary reg $t0 gets A[8]
```

Here, 19 (for $s3) is placed in the rs field, 8 (for $t0) is placed in the rt field, and 32 is placed in the address field. Note that the meaning of the rt field has changed for this instruction: in a load word instruction, the rt field specifies the *destination* register, which receives the result of the load.

Although multiple formats complicate the hardware, we can reduce the complexity by keeping the formats similar. For example, the first three fields of the R-type and I-type formats are the same size and have the same names; the length of the fourth field in I-type is equal to the sum of the lengths of the last three fields of R-type.

In case you were wondering, the formats are distinguished by the values in the first field: each format is assigned a distinct set of values in the first field (op) so that the hardware knows whether to treat the last half of the instruction as three fields (R-type) or as a single field (I-type). Figure 2.5 shows the numbers used in each field for the MIPS instructions covered so far.

Instruction	Format	op	rs	rt	rd	shamt	funct	address
add	R	0	reg	reg	reg	0	32_{ten}	n.a.
sub (subtract)	R	0	reg	reg	reg	0	34_{ten}	n.a.
add immediate	I	8_{ten}	reg	reg	n.a.	n.a.	n.a.	constant
lw (load word)	I	35_{ten}	reg	reg	n.a.	n.a.	n.a.	address
sw (store word)	I	43_{ten}	reg	reg	n.a.	n.a.	n.a.	address

FIGURE 2.5 MIPS instruction encoding. In the table above, "reg" means a register number between 0 and 31, "address" means a 16-bit address, and "n.a." (not applicable) means this field does not appear in this format. Note that add and sub instructions have the same value in the op field; the hardware uses the funct field to decide the variant of the operation: add (32) or subtract (34).

EXAMPLE

Translating MIPS Assembly Language into Machine Language

We can now take an example all the way from what the programmer writes to what the computer executes. If $t1 has the base of the array A and $s2 corresponds to h, the assignment statement

```
A[300] = h + A[300];
```

is compiled into

```
lw    $t0,1200($t1) # Temporary reg $t0 gets A[300]
add   $t0,$s2,$t0   # Temporary reg $t0 gets h + A[300]
sw    $t0,1200($t1) # Stores h + A[300] back into A[300]
```

What is the MIPS machine language code for these three instructions?

ANSWER

For convenience, let's first represent the machine language instructions using decimal numbers. From Figure 2.5, we can determine the three machine language instructions:

Op	rs	rt	rd	address/ shamt	funct
35	9	8		1200	
0	18	8	8	0	32
43	9	8		1200	

The lw instruction is identified by 35 (see Figure 2.5) in the first field (op). The base register 9 ($t1) is specified in the second field (rs), and the destination register 8 ($t0) is specified in the third field (rt). The offset to select A[300] (1200 = 300 × 4) is found in the final field (address).

The add instruction that follows is specified with 0 in the first field (op) and 32 in the last field (funct). The three register operands (18, 8, and 8) are found in the second, third, and fourth fields and correspond to $s2, $t0, and $t0.

The sw instruction is identified with 43 in the first field. The rest of this final instruction is identical to the lw instruction.

Since $1200_{ten} = 0000\ 0100\ 1011\ 0000_{two}$, the binary equivalent to the decimal form is:

100011	01001	01000	0000 0100 1011 0000		
000000	10010	01000	01000	00000	100000
101011	01001	01000	0000 0100 1011 0000		

Note the similarity of the binary representations of the first and last instructions. The only difference is in the third bit from the left, which is highlighted here.

The desire to keep all instructions the same size is in conflict with the desire to have as many registers as possible. Any increase in the number of registers uses up at least one more bit in every register field of the instruction format. Given these constraints and the design princple that smaller is faster, most instruction sets today have 16 or 32 general purpose registers.

Hardware/ Software Interface

Figure 2.6 summarizes the portions of MIPS machine language described in this section. As we shall see in Chapter 4, the similarity of the binary representations of related instructions simplifies hardware design. These similarities are another example of regularity in the MIPS architecture.

MIPS machine language

Name	Format	Example						Comments
add	R	0	18	19	17	0	32	add $s1,$s2,$s3
sub	R	0	18	19	17	0	34	sub $s1,$s2,$s3
addi	I	8	18	17		100		addi $s1,$s2,100
lw	I	35	18	17		100		lw $s1,100($s2)
sw	I	43	18	17		100		sw $s1,100($s2)
Field size		6 bits	5 bits	5 bits	5 bits	5 bits	6 bits	All MIPS instructions are 32 bits long
R-format	R	op	rs	rt	rd	shamt	funct	Arithmetic instruction format
I-format	I	op	rs	rt		address		Data transfer format

FIGURE 2.6 MIPS architecture revealed through Section 2.5. The two MIPS instruction formats so far are R and I. The first 16 bits are the same: both contain an *op* field, giving the base operation; an *rs* field, giving one of the sources; and the *rt* field, which specifies the other source operand, except for load word, where it specifies the destination register. R-format divides the last 16 bits into an *rd* field, specifying the destination register; the *shamt* field, which Section 2.6 explains; and the *funct* field, which specifies the specific operation of R-format instructions. I-format combines the last 16 bits into a single *address* field.

The BIG Picture

Today's computers are built on two key principles:

1. Instructions are represented as numbers.

2. Programs are stored in memory to be read or written, just like numbers.

These principles lead to the *stored-program* concept; its invention let the computing genie out of its bottle. Figure 2.7 shows the power of the concept; specifically, memory can contain the source code for an editor program, the corresponding compiled machine code, the text that the compiled program is using, and even the compiler that generated the machine code.

One consequence of instructions as numbers is that programs are often shipped as files of binary numbers. The commercial implication is that computers can inherit ready-made software provided they are compatible with an existing instruction set. Such "binary compatibility" often leads industry to align around a small number of instruction set architectures.

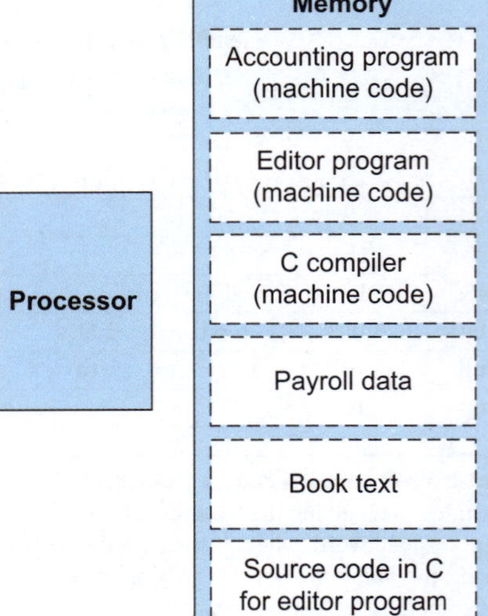

FIGURE 2.7 The stored-program concept. Stored programs allow a computer that performs accounting to become, in the blink of an eye, a computer that helps an author write a book. The switch happens simply by loading memory with programs and data and then telling the computer to begin executing at a given location in memory. Treating instructions in the same way as data greatly simplifies both the memory hardware and the software of computer systems. Specifically, the memory technology needed for data can also be used for programs, and programs like compilers, for instance, can translate code written in a notation far more convenient for humans into code that the computer can understand.

What MIPS instruction does this represent? Choose from one of the four options below.

op	rs	rt	rd	shamt	funct
0	8	9	10	0	34

1. `sub $t0, $t1, $t2`

2. `add $t2, $t0, $t1`

3. `sub $t2, $t1, $t0`

4. `sub $t2, $t0, $t1`

If a person is age 40_{ten}, what is their age in hexidecimal?

"Contrariwise,"
continued Tweedledee,
"if it was so, it might
be; and if it were so,
it would be; but as it
isn't, it ain't. That's
logic."

Lewis Carroll,
Alice's Adventures in
Wonderland, 1865

2.6 Logical Operations

Although the first computers operated on full words, it soon became clear that it was useful to operate on fields of bits within a word or even on individual bits. Examining characters within a word, each of which is stored as 8 bits, is one example of such an operation (see Section 2.9). It follows that operations were added to programming languages and instruction set architectures to simplify, among other things, the packing and unpacking of bits into words. These instructions are called logical operations. Figure 2.8 shows logical operations in C, Java, and MIPS.

Logical operations	C operators	Java operators	MIPS instructions
Shift left	`<<`	`<<`	`sll`
Shift right	`>>`	`>>>`	`srl`
Bit-by-bit AND	`&`	`&`	`and, andi`
Bit-by-bit OR	`|`	`|`	`or, ori`
Bit-by-bit NOT	`~`	`~`	`nor`

FIGURE 2.8 C and Java logical operators and their corresponding MIPS instructions. MIPS implements NOT using a NOR with one operand being zero.

The first class of such operations is called *shifts*. They move all the bits in a word to the left or right, filling the emptied bits with 0s. For example, if register `$s0` contained

$$0000\ 0000\ 0000\ 0000\ 0000\ 0000\ 0000\ 1001_{two} = 9_{ten}$$

and the instruction to shift left by 4 was executed, the new value would be:

$$0000\ 0000\ 0000\ 0000\ 0000\ 0000\ 1001\ 0000_{two} = 144_{ten}$$

The dual of a shift left is a shift right. The actual name of the two MIPS shift instructions are called *shift left logical* (sll) and *shift right logical* (srl). The following instruction performs the operation above, assuming that the original value was in register $s0 and the result should go in register $t2:

```
sll  $t2,$s0,4  # reg $t2 = reg $s0 << 4 bits
```

We delayed explaining the *shamt* field in the R-format. Used in shift instructions, it stands for *shift amount*. Hence, the machine language version of the instruction above is

op	rs	rt	rd	shamt	funct
0	0	16	10	4	0

The encoding of sll is 0 in both the op and funct fields, rd contains 10 (register $t2), rt contains 16 (register $s0), and shamt contains 4. The rs field is unused and thus is set to 0.

Shift left logical provides a bonus benefit. Shifting left by i bits gives the same result as multiplying by $2i$, just as shifting a decimal number by i digits is equivalent to multiplying by $10i$. For example, the above sll shifts by 4, which gives the same result as multiplying by 2^4 or 16. The first bit pattern above represents 9, and $9 \times 16 = 144$, the value of the second bit pattern.

Another useful operation that isolates fields is **AND**. (We capitalize the word to avoid confusion between the operation and the English conjunction.) AND is a bit-by-bit operation that leaves a 1 in the result only if both bits of the operands are 1. For example, if register $t2 contains

> **AND** A logical bit-by-bit operation with two operands that calculates a 1 only if there is a 1 in *both* operands.

$$0000 \quad 0000 \quad 0000 \quad 0000 \quad 0000 \quad 1101 \quad 1100 \quad 0000_{two}$$

and register $t1 contains

$$0000 \quad 0000 \quad 0000 \quad 0000 \quad 0011 \quad 1100 \quad 0000 \quad 0000_{two}$$

then, after executing the MIPS instruction

```
and $t0,$t1,$t2     # reg $t0 = reg $t1 & reg $t2
```

the value of register $t0 would be

$$0000 \quad 0000 \quad 0000 \quad 0000 \quad 0000 \quad 1100 \quad 0000 \quad 0000_{two}$$

As you can see, AND can apply a bit pattern to a set of bits to force 0s where there is a 0 in the bit pattern. Such a bit pattern in conjunction with AND is traditionally called a *mask*, since the mask "conceals" some bits.

To place a value into one of these seas of 0s, there is the dual to AND, called OR. It is a bit-by-bit operation that places a 1 in the result if *either* operand bit is a 1. To elaborate, if the registers $t1 and $t2 are unchanged from the preceding example, the result of the MIPS instruction

```
or $t0,$t1,$t2 # reg $t0 = reg $t1 | reg $t2
```

is this value in register $t0:

$$0000\ 0000\ 0000\ 0000\ 0011\ 1101\ 1100\ 0000_{two}$$

The final logical operation is a contrarian. NOT takes one operand and places a 1 in the result if one operand bit is a 0, and vice versa. Using our prior notation, it calculates $\bar{x}$.

In keeping with the three-operand format, the designers of MIPS decided to include the instruction NOR (NOT OR) instead of NOT. If one operand is zero, then it is equivalent to NOT: A NOR 0 = NOT (A OR 0)=NOT (A).

If the register $t1 is unchanged from the preceding example and register $t3 has the value 0, the result of the MIPS instruction

```
nor $t0,$t1,$t3 # reg $t0 = ~ (reg $t1 | reg $t3)
```

is this value in register $t0:

$$1111\ 1111\ 1111\ 1111\ 1100\ 0011\ 1111\ 1111_{two}$$

Figure 2.8 above shows the relationship between the C and Java operators and the MIPS instructions. Constants are useful in AND and OR logical operations as well as in arithmetic operations, so MIPS also provides the instructions *and immediate* (andi) and *or immediate* (ori). Constants are rare for NOR, since its main use is to invert the bits of a single operand; thus, the MIPS instruction set architecture has no immediate version.

> **OR** A logical bit-by-bit operation with two operands that calculates a 1 if there is a 1 in *either* operand.

> **NOT** A logical bit-by-bit operation with one operand that inverts the bits; that is, it replaces every 1 with a 0, and every 0 with a 1.

> **NOR** A logical bit-by-bit operation with two operands that calculates the NOT of the OR of the two operands. That is, it calculates a 1 only if there is a 0 in *both* operands.

Elaboration: The full MIPS instruction set also includes exclusive or (XOR), which sets the bit to 1 when two corresponding bits differ, and to 0 when they are the same. C allows *bit fields* or *fields* to be defined within words, both allowing objects to be packed within a word and to match an externally enforced interface such as an I/O device. All fields must fit within a single word. Fields are unsigned integers that can be as short as 1 bit. C compilers insert and extract fields using logical instructions in MIPS: and, or, sll, and srl.

Elaboration: Logical AND immediate and logical OR immediate put 0s into the upper 16 bits to form a 32-bit constant, unlike add immediate, which does sign extension.

Which operations can isolate a field in a word?

1. AND

2. A shift left followed by a shift right

2.7   Instructions for Making Decisions

What distinguishes a computer from a simple calculator is its ability to make decisions. Based on the input data and the values created during computation, different instructions execute. Decision making is commonly represented in programming languages using the *if* statement, sometimes combined with *go to* statements and labels. MIPS assembly language includes two decision-making instructions, similar to an *if* statement with a *go to*. The first instruction is

```
beq register1, register2, L1
```

This instruction means go to the statement labeled L1 if the value in register1 equals the value in register2. The mnemonic beq stands for *branch if equal*. The second instruction is

```
bne register1, register2, L1
```

It means go to the statement labeled L1 if the value in register1 does *not* equal the value in register2. The mnemonic bne stands for *branch if not equal*. These two instructions are traditionally called **conditional branches**.

EXAMPLE

Compiling *if-then-else* into Conditional Branches

In the following code segment, f, g, h, i, and j are variables. If the five variables f through j correspond to the five registers $s0 through $s4, what is the compiled MIPS code for this C *if* statement?

```
if (i == j) f = g + h; else f = g -h;
```

ANSWER

Figure 2.9 is a flowchart of what the MIPS code should do. The first expression compares for equality, so it would seem that we would want the branch if registers are equal instruction (beq). In general, the code will be more efficient if we test for the opposite condition to branch over the code that performs the subsequent *then* part of the *if* (the label Else is defined below) and so we use the branch if registers are *not* equal instruction (bne):

```
bne $s3,$s4,Else    # go to Else if i ≠ j
```

The next assignment statement performs a single operation, and if all the operands are allocated to registers, it is just one instruction:

```
add $s0,$s1,$s2      # f = g + h (skipped if i ≠ j)
```

We now need to go to the end of the *if* statement. This example introduces another kind of branch, often called an *unconditional branch*. This instruction says that the processor always follows the branch. To distinguish between conditional and unconditional branches, the MIPS name for this type of instruction is *jump*, abbreviated as j (the label Exit is defined below).

```
j Exit        # go to Exit
```

The assignment statement in the *else* portion of the *if* statement can again be compiled into a single instruction. We just need to append the label Else to this instruction. We also show the label Exit that is after this instruction, showing the end of the *if-then-else* compiled code:

```
Else:sub $s0,$s1,$s2 # f = g - h (skipped if i = j)
Exit:
```

Notice that the assembler relieves the compiler and the assembly language programmer from the tedium of calculating addresses for branches, just as it does for calculating data addresses for loads and stores (see Section 2.12).

conditional branch An instruction that requires the comparison of two values and that allows for a subsequent transfer of control to a new address in the program based on the outcome of the comparison.

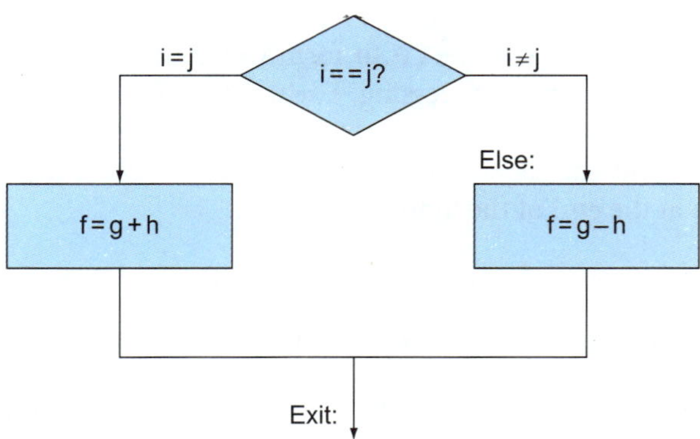

FIGURE 2.9 Illustration of the options in the if statement above. The left box corresponds to the *then* part of the *if* statement, and the right box corresponds to the *else* part.

Hardware/ Software Interface

Compilers frequently create branches and labels where they do not appear in the programming language. Avoiding the burden of writing explicit labels and branches is one benefit of writing in high-level programming languages and is a reason coding is faster at that level.

Loops

Decisions are important both for choosing between two alternatives—found in *if* statements—and for iterating a computation—found in loops. The same assembly instructions are the building blocks for both cases.

EXAMPLE

Compiling a *while* Loop in C

Here is a traditional loop in C:

```
while (save[i] == k)
        i += 1;
```

Assume that i and k correspond to registers $s3 and $s5 and the base of the array save is in $s6. What is the MIPS assembly code corresponding to this C segment?

ANSWER

AU3

The first step is to load save[i] into a temporary register. Before we can load save[i] into a temporary register, we need to have its address. Before we can add i to the base of array save to form the address, we must multiply the index i by 4 due to byte addressing. Fortunately, we can use shift left logical, since shifting left by 2 bits multiplies by 2^2 or 4 (see page 94 in the prior section). We need to add the label Loop to it so that we can branch back to that instruction at the end of the loop:

```
Loop: sll  $t1,$s3,2   # Temp reg $t1 = i * 4
```

To get the address of save[i], we need to add $t1 and the base of save in $s6:

```
add $t1,$t1,$s6     # $t1 = address of save[i]
```

Now we can use that address to load save[i] into a temporary register:

```
lw $t0,0($t1)       # Temp reg $t0 = save[i]
```

The next instruction performs the loop test, exiting if save[i] ≠ k:

```
bne $t0,$s5, Exit   # go to Exit if save[i] ≠ k
```

The next instruction adds 1 to i:

```
addi  $s3,$s3,1          # i = i + 1
```

The end of the loop branches back to the *while* test at the top of the loop. We just add the Exit label after it, and we're done:

```
    j       Loop                # go to Loop
Exit:
```

(See the exercises for an optimization of this sequence.)

Hardware/ Software Interface

Such sequences of instructions that end in a branch are so fundamental to compiling that they are given their own buzzword: a **basic block** is a sequence of instructions without branches, except possibly at the end, and without branch targets or branch labels, except possibly at the beginning. One of the first early phases of compilation is breaking the program into basic blocks.

basic block A sequence of instructions without branches (except possibly at the end) and without branch targets or branch labels (except possibly at the beginning).

The test for equality or inequality is probably the most popular test, but sometimes it is useful to see if a variable is less than another variable. For example, a *for* loop may want to test to see if the index variable is less than 0. Such comparisons are accomplished in MIPS assembly language with an instruction that compares two registers and sets a third register to 1 if the first is less than the second; otherwise, it is set to 0. The MIPS instruction is called *set on less than,* or slt. For example,

```
slt    $t0, $s3, $s4    # $t0 = 1 if $s3 < $s4
```

means that register $t0 is set to 1 if the value in register $s3 is less than the value in register $s4; otherwise, register $t0 is set to 0.

Constant operands are popular in comparisons, so there is an immediate version of the set on less than instruction. To test if register $s2 is less than the constant 10, we can just write

```
slti   $t0,$s2,10       # $t0 = 1 if $s2 < 10
```

Hardware/ Software Interface

MIPS compilers use the slt, slti, beq, bne, and the fixed value of 0 (always available by reading register $zero) to create all relative conditions: equal, not equal, less than, less than or equal, greater than, greater than or equal.

Heeding von Neumann et al.'s warning about the simplicity of the "equipment," the MIPS architecture doesn't include branch on less than because it is too complicated; either it would stretch the clock cycle time or it would take extra clock cycles per instruction. Two faster instructions are more useful.

Hardware/ Software Interface

Comparison instructions must deal with the dichotomy between signed and unsigned numbers. Sometimes a bit pattern with a 1 in the most significant bit represents a negative number and, of course, is less than any positive number, which must have a 0 in the most significant bit. With unsigned integers, on the other hand, a 1 in the most significant bit represents a number that is *larger* than any that begins with a 0. (We'll soon take advantage of this dual meaning of the most significant bit to reduce the cost of the array bounds checking.)

MIPS offers two versions of the set on less than comparison to handle these alternatives. *Set on less than* (slt) and *set on less than immediate* (slti) work with signed integers. Unsigned integers are compared using *set on less than unsigned* (sltu) and *set on less than immediate unsigned* (sltiu).

EXAMPLE

Signed versus Unsigned Comparison

Suppose register $s0 has the binary number

1111 1111 1111 1111 1111 1111 1111 1111$_{\text{two}}$

and that register $s1 has the binary number

0000 0000 0000 0000 0000 0000 0000 0001$_{\text{two}}$

What are the values of registers $t0 and $t1 after these two instructions?

```
slt        $t0, $s0, $s1 # signed comparison
sltu       $t1, $s0, $s1 # unsigned comparison
```

ANSWER

The value in register $s0 represents -1_{ten} if it is an integer and $4{,}294{,}967{,}295_{\text{ten}}$ if it is an unsigned integer. The value in register $s1 represents 1_{ten} in either case. Then register $t0 has the value 1, since $-1_{\text{ten}} < 1_{\text{ten}}$, and register $t1 has the value 0, because $4{,}294{,}967{,}295_{\text{ten}} > 1_{\text{ten}}$.

Treating signed numbers as if they were unsigned gives us a low cost way of checking if $0 \leq x < y$, which matches the index out-of-bounds check for arrays. The key is that negative integers in two's complement notation look like large numbers in unsigned notation; that is, the most significant bit is a sign bit in the former notation but a large part of the number in the latter. Thus, an unsigned comparison of $x < y$ also checks if x is negative as well as if x is less than y.

Bounds Check Shortcut

EXAMPLE

Use this shortcut to reduce an index-out-of-bounds check: jump to `IndexOutOfBounds` if $\$s1 \geq \$t2$ or if $\$s1$ is negative.

ANSWER

The checking code just uses `sltu` to do both checks:

```
sltu $t0,$s1,$t2 # $t0 = 0 if $s1>=length or $s1<0
beq $t0,$zero,IndexOutOfBounds #if bad, goto Error
```

Case/Switch Statement

Most programming languages have a *case* or *switch* statement that allows the programmer to select one of many alternatives depending on a single value. The simplest way to implement *switch* is via a sequence of conditional tests, turning the *switch* statement into a chain of *if-then-else* statements.

Sometimes the alternatives may be more efficiently encoded as a table of addresses of alternative instruction sequences, called a **jump address table** or **jump table**, and the program needs only to index into the table and then jump to the appropriate sequence. The jump table is then just an array of words containing addresses that correspond to labels in the code. The program loads the appropriate entry from the jump table into a register. It then needs to jump using the address in the register. To support such situations, computers like MIPS include a *jump register* instruction (`jr`), meaning an unconditional jump to the address specified in a register. Then it jumps to the proper address using this instruction. We'll see an even more popular use of `jr` in the next section.

jump address table Also called **jump table**. A table of addresses of alternative instruction sequences.

Hardware/ Software Interface

Although there are many statements for decisions and loops in programming languages like C and Java, the bedrock statement that implements them at the instruction set level is the conditional branch.

Elaboration: If you have heard about *delayed branches*, covered in Chapter 4, don't worry: the MIPS assembler makes them invisible to the assembly language programmer.

Check Yourself

I.   C has many statements for decisions and loops, while MIPS has few. Which of the following do or do not explain this imbalance? Why?

  1. More decision statements make code easier to read and understand.
  2. Fewer decision statements simplify the task of the underlying layer that is responsible for execution.
  3. More decision statements mean fewer lines of code, which generally reduces coding time.
  4. More decision statements mean fewer lines of code, which generally results in the execution of fewer operations.

II. Why does C provide two sets of operators for AND (& and &&) and two sets of operators for OR (| and ||), while MIPS doesn't?

  1. Logical operations AND and OR implement & and |, while conditional branches implement && and ||.
  2. The previous statement has it backwards: && and || correspond to logical operations, while & and | map to conditional branches.
  3. They are redundant and mean the same thing: && and || are simply inherited from the programming language B, the predecessor of C.

ABSTRACTION

procedure A stored subroutine that performs a specific task based on the parameters with which it is provided.

2.8   Supporting Procedures in Computer Hardware

A **procedure** or function is one tool programmers use to structure programs, both to make them easier to understand and to allow code to be reused. Procedures allow the programmer to concentrate on just one portion of the task at a time; parameters act as an interface between the procedure and the rest of the program and data, since they can pass values and return results. We describe the equivalent to procedures in Java in **Section 2.15**, but Java needs everything from a computer that C needs. Procedures are one way to implement **abstraction** in software.

You can think of a procedure like a spy who leaves with a secret plan, acquires resources, performs the task, covers his or her tracks, and then returns to the point of origin with the desired result. Nothing else should be perturbed once the mission is complete. Moreover, a spy operates on only a "need to know" basis, so the spy can't make assumptions about his employer.

Similarly, in the execution of a procedure, the program must follow these six steps:

1. Put parameters in a place where the procedure can access them.

2. Transfer control to the procedure.

3. Acquire the storage resources needed for the procedure.

4. Perform the desired task.

5. Put the result value in a place where the calling program can access it.

6. Return control to the point of origin, since a procedure can be called from several points in a program.

As mentioned above, registers are the fastest place to hold data in a computer, so we want to use them as much as possible. MIPS software follows the following convention for procedure calling in allocating its 32 registers:

- $a0-$a3: four argument registers in which to pass parameters

- $v0-$v1: two value registers in which to return values

- $ra: one return address register to return to the point of origin

In addition to allocating these registers, MIPS assembly language includes an instruction just for the procedures: it jumps to an address and simultaneously saves the address of the following instruction in register $ra. The **jump-and-link instruction** (jal) is simply written

```
jal ProcedureAddress
```

The *link* portion of the name means that an address or link is formed that points to the calling site to allow the procedure to return to the proper address. This "link," stored in register $ra (register 31), is called the **return address**. The return address is needed because the same procedure could be called from several parts of the program.

To support such situations, computers like MIPS use *jump register* instruction (jr), introduced above to help with case statements, meaning an unconditional jump to the address specified in a register:

```
jr    $ra
```

jump-and-link instruction An instruction that jumps to an address and simultaneously saves the address of the following instruction in a register ($ra in MIPS).

return address A link to the calling site that allows a procedure to return to the proper address; in MIPS it is stored in register $ra.

caller The program that instigates a procedure and provides the necessary parameter values.

callee A procedure that executes a series of stored instructions based on parameters provided by the caller and then returns control to the caller.

program counter (PC) The register containing the address of the instruction in the program being executed.

stack A data structure for spilling registers organized as a last-in-first-out queue.

stack pointer A value denoting the most recently allocated address in a stack that shows where registers should be spilled or where old register values can be found. In MIPS, it is register $sp.

push Add element to stack.

pop Remove element from stack.

The jump register instruction jumps to the address stored in register $ra—which is just what we want. Thus, the calling program, or **caller**, puts the parameter values in $a0–$a3 and uses jal X to jump to procedure X (sometimes named the **callee**). The callee then performs the calculations, places the results in $v0 and $v1, and returns control to the caller using jr $ra.

Implicit in the stored-program idea is the need to have a register to hold the address of the current instruction being executed. For historical reasons, this register is almost always called the **program counter**, abbreviated *PC* in the MIPS architecture, although a more sensible name would have been *instruction address register*. The jal instruction actually saves PC + 4 in register $ra to link to the following instruction to set up the procedure return.

Using More Registers

Suppose a compiler needs more registers for a procedure than the four argument and two return value registers. Since we must cover our tracks after our mission is complete, any registers needed by the caller must be restored to the values that they contained *before* the procedure was invoked. This situation is an example in which we need to spill registers to memory, as mentioned in the *Hardware/Software Interface* section above.

The ideal data structure for spilling registers is a **stack**—a last-in-first-out queue. A stack needs a pointer to the most recently allocated address in the stack to show where the next procedure should place the registers to be spilled or where old register values are found. The **stack pointer** is adjusted by one word for each register that is saved or restored. MIPS software reserves register 29 for the stack pointer, giving it the obvious name $sp. Stacks are so popular that they have their own buzzwords for transferring data to and from the stack: placing data onto the stack is called a **push**, and removing data from the stack is called a **pop**.

By historical precedent, stacks "grow" from higher addresses to lower addresses. This convention means that you push values onto the stack by subtracting from the stack pointer. Adding to the stack pointer shrinks the stack, thereby popping values off the stack.

EXAMPLE

Compiling a C Procedure That Doesn't Call Another Procedure

Let's turn the example on page 73 from Section 2.2 into a C procedure:

```c
int leaf_example (int g, int h, int i, int j)
{
    int f;

    f = (g + h) - (i + j);
    return f;
}
```

What is the compiled MIPS assembly code?

The parameter variables g, h, i, and j correspond to the argument registers $a0, $a1, $a2, and $a3, and f corresponds to $s0. The compiled program starts with the label of the procedure:


```
leaf_example:
```

The next step is to save the registers used by the procedure. The C assignment statement in the procedure body is identical to the example on page 74, which uses two temporary registers. Thus, we need to save three registers: $s0, $t0, and $t1. We "push" the old values onto the stack by creating space for three words (12 bytes) on the stack and then store them:

```
addi $sp, $sp, -12  # adjust stack to make room for 3 items
sw   $t1, 8($sp)    # save register $t1 for use afterwards
sw   $t0, 4($sp)    # save register $t0 for use afterwards
sw   $s0, 0($sp)    # save register $s0 for use afterwards
```

Figure 2.10 shows the stack before, during, and after the procedure call.

The next three statements correspond to the body of the procedure, which follows the example on page 74:

```
add $t0,$a0,$a1 # register  $t0 contains g + h
add $t1,$a2,$a3 # register  $t1 contains i + j
sub $s0,$t0,$t1 # f = $t0 - $t1, which is (g + h)-(i + j)
```

To return the value of f, we copy it into a return value register:

```
add $v0,$s0,$zero # returns f ($v0 = $s0 + 0)
```

Before returning, we restore the three old values of the registers we saved by "popping" them from the stack:

```
lw $s0, 0($sp)  # restore register $s0 for caller
lw $t0, 4($sp)  # restore register $t0 for caller
lw $t1, 8($sp)  # restore register $t1 for caller
addi $sp,$sp,12 # adjust stack to delete 3 items
```

The procedure ends with a jump register using the return address:

```
jr $ra  # jump back to calling routine
```

In the previous example, we used temporary registers and assumed their old values must be saved and restored. To avoid saving and restoring a register whose value is never used, which might happen with a temporary register, MIPS software separates 18 of the registers into two groups:

- $t0-$t9: temporary registers that are *not* preserved by the callee (called procedure) on a procedure call

- $s0-$s7: saved registers that must be preserved on a procedure call (if used, the callee saves and restores them)

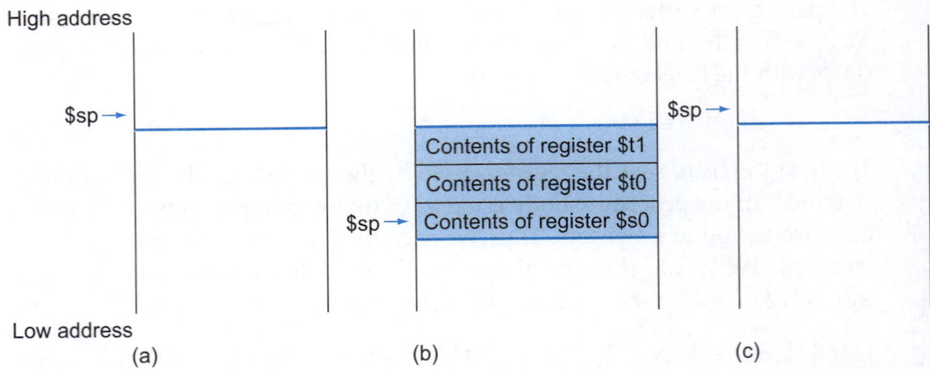

FIGURE 2.10 The values of the stack pointer and the stack (a) before, (b) during, and (c) after the procedure call. The stack pointer always points to the "top" of the stack, or the last word in the stack in this drawing.

This simple convention reduces register spilling. In the example above, since the caller does not expect registers $t0 and $t1 to be preserved across a procedure call, we can drop two stores and two loads from the code. We still must save and restore $s0, since the callee must assume that the caller needs its value.

Nested Procedures

Procedures that do not call others are called *leaf* procedures. Life would be simple if all procedures were leaf procedures, but they aren't. Just as a spy might employ other spies as part of a mission, who in turn might use even more spies, so do procedures invoke other procedures. Moreover, recursive procedures even invoke "clones" of themselves. Just as we need to be careful when using registers in procedures, more care must also be taken when invoking nonleaf procedures.

For example, suppose that the main program calls procedure A with an argument of 3, by placing the value 3 into register $a0 and then using jal A. Then suppose that procedure A calls procedure B via jal B with an argument of 7, also placed in $a0. Since A hasn't finished its task yet, there is a conflict over the use of register $a0. Similarly, there is a conflict over the return address in register $ra, since it now has the return address for B. Unless we take steps to prevent the problem, this conflict will eliminate procedure A's ability to return to its caller.

One solution is to push all the other registers that must be preserved onto the stack, just as we did with the saved registers. The caller pushes any argument registers ($a0–$a3) or temporary registers ($t0–$t9) that are needed after the call. The callee pushes the return address register $ra and any saved registers ($s0–$s7) used by the callee. The stack pointer $sp is adjusted to account for the number of registers placed on the stack. Upon the return, the registers are restored from memory and the stack pointer is readjusted.

Compiling a Recursive C Procedure, Showing Nested Procedure Linking

Let's tackle a recursive procedure that calculates factorial:

```
int fact (int n)
{
    if (n < 1) return (1);
        else return (n * fact(n - 1));
}
```

What is the MIPS assembly code?

The parameter variable n corresponds to the argument register $a0. The compiled program starts with the label of the procedure and then saves two registers on the stack, the return address and $a0:


```
fact:
    addi   $sp, $sp, -8 # adjust stack for 2 items
    sw     $ra, 4($sp)  # save the return address
    sw     $a0, 0($sp)  # save the argument n
```

The first time fact is called, sw saves an address in the program that called fact. The next two instructions test whether n is less than 1, going to L1 if n ≥ 1.

```
slti $t0,$a0,1     # test for n<1
beq  $t0,$zero,L1  # if n >= 1, go to L1
```

If n is less than 1, fact returns 1 by putting 1 into a value register: it adds 1 to 0 and places that sum in $v0. It then pops the two saved values off the stack and jumps to the return address:

```
addi   $v0,$zero,1 # return 1
addi   $sp,$sp,8   # pop 2 items off stack
jr     $ra         # return to caller
```

Before popping two items off the stack, we could have loaded $a0 and $ra. Since $a0 and $ra don't change when n is less than 1, we skip those instructions.

If n is not less than 1, the argument n is decremented and then fact is called again with the decremented value:

```
L1: addi $a0,$a0,-1   # n >= 1: argument gets (n - 1)
    jal fact          # call fact with (n - 1)
```

The next instruction is where `fact` returns. Now the old return address and old argument are restored, along with the stack pointer:

```
lw   $a0, 0($sp)   # return from jal: restore argument n
lw   $ra, 4($sp)   # restore the return address
addi $sp, $sp, 8   # adjust stack pointer to pop 2 items
```

Next, the value register $v0 gets the product of old argument $a0 and the current value of the value register. We assume a multiply instruction is available, even though it is not covered until Chapter 3:

```
mul  $v0,$a0,$v0    # return n * fact (n - 1)
```

Finally, `fact` jumps again to the return address:

```
jr   $ra            # return to the caller
```

Hardware/ Software Interface

A C variable is generally a location in storage, and its interpretation depends both on its *type* and *storage class*. Examples include integers and characters (see Section 2.9). C has two storage classes: *automatic* and *static*. Automatic variables are local to a procedure and are discarded when the procedure exits. Static variables exist across exits from and entries to procedures. C variables declared outside all procedures are considered static, as are any variables declared using the keyword *static*. The rest are automatic. To simplify access to static data, MIPS software reserves another register, called the **global pointer**, or $gp.

global pointer The register that is reserved to point to the static area.

Figure 2.11 summarizes what is preserved across a procedure call. Note that several schemes preserve the stack, guaranteeing that the caller will get the same data back on a load from the stack as it stored onto the stack. The stack above $sp is preserved simply by making sure the callee does not write above $sp; $sp is

Preserved	Not preserved
Saved registers: $s0–$s7	Temporary registers: $t0–$t9
Stack pointer register: $sp	Argument registers: $a0–$a3
Return address register: $ra	Return value registers: $v0–$v1
Stack above the stack pointer	Stack below the stack pointer

FIGURE 2.11 What is and what is not preserved across a procedure call. If the software relies on the frame pointer register or on the global pointer register, discussed in the following subsections, they are also preserved.

itself preserved by the callee adding exactly the same amount that was subtracted from it; and the other registers are preserved by saving them on the stack (if they are used) and restoring them from there.

Allocating Space for New Data on the Stack

The final complexity is that the stack is also used to store variables that are local to the procedure but do not fit in registers, such as local arrays or structures. The segment of the stack containing a procedure's saved registers and local variables is called a **procedure frame** or **activation record**. Figure 2.12 shows the state of the stack before, during, and after the procedure call.

Some MIPS software uses a **frame pointer** ($fp) to point to the first word of the frame of a procedure. A stack pointer might change during the procedure, and so references to a local variable in memory might have different offsets depending on where they are in the procedure, making the procedure harder to understand. Alternatively, a frame pointer offers a stable base register within a procedure for local memory-references. Note that an activation record appears on the stack whether or not an explicit frame pointer is used. We've been avoiding using $fp by avoiding changes to $sp within a procedure: in our examples, the stack is adjusted only on entry and exit of the procedure.

procedure frame Also called **activation record**. The segment of the stack containing a procedure's saved registers and local variables.

frame pointer A value denoting the location of the saved registers and local variables for a given procedure.

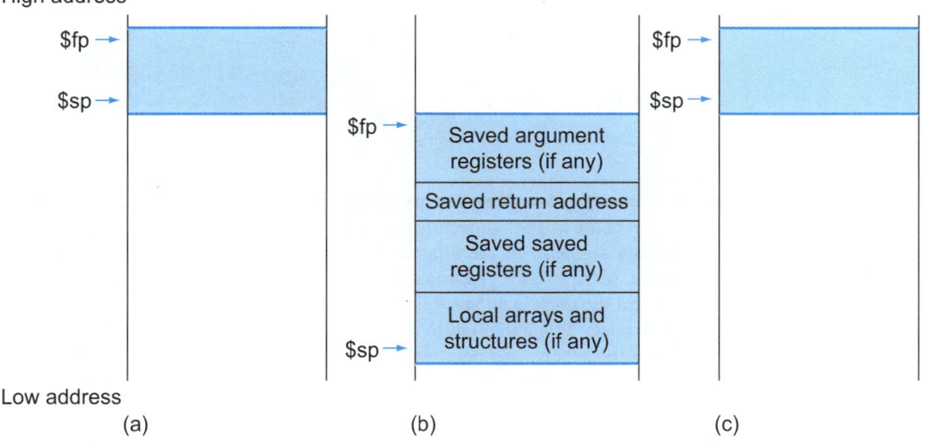

FIGURE 2.12 Illustration of the stack allocation (a) before, (b) during, and (c) after the procedure call. The frame pointer ($fp) points to the first word of the frame, often a saved argument register, and the stack pointer ($sp) points to the top of the stack. The stack is adjusted to make room for all the saved registers and any memory-resident local variables. Since the stack pointer may change during program execution, it's easier for programmers to reference variables via the stable frame pointer, although it could be done just with the stack pointer and a little address arithmetic. If there are no local variables on the stack within a procedure, the compiler will save time by *not* setting and restoring the frame pointer. When a frame pointer is used, it is initialized using the address in $sp on a call, and $sp is restored using $fp. This information is also found in Column 4 of the MIPS Reference Data Card at the front of this book.

Allocating Space for New Data on the Heap

text segment The segment of a UNIX object file that contains the machine language code for routines in the source file.

In addition to automatic variables that are local to procedures, C programmers need space in memory for static variables and for dynamic data structures. Figure 2.13 shows the MIPS convention for allocation of memory. The stack starts in the high end of memory and grows down. The first part of the low end of memory is reserved, followed by the home of the MIPS machine code, traditionally called the **text segment**. Above the code is the *static data segment*, which is the place for constants and other static variables. Although arrays tend to be a fixed length and thus are a good match to the static data segment, data structures like linked lists tend to grow and shrink during their lifetimes. The segment for such data structures is traditionally called the *heap*, and it is placed next in memory. Note that this allocation allows the stack and heap to grow toward each other, thereby allowing the efficient use of memory as the two segments wax and wane.

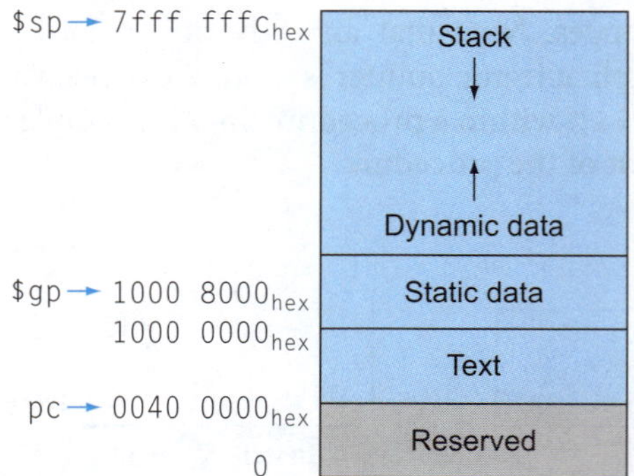

FIGURE 2.13 The MIPS memory allocation for program and data. These addresses are only a software convention, and not part of the MIPS architecture. The stack pointer is initialized to $7fff\ fffc_{hex}$ and grows down toward the data segment. At the other end, the program code ("text") starts at $0040\ 0000_{hex}$. The static data starts at $1000\ 0000_{hex}$. Dynamic data, allocated by `malloc` in C and by `new` in Java, is next. It grows up toward the stack in an area called the heap. The global pointer, $gp, is set to an address to make it easy to access data. It is initialized to $1000\ 8000_{hex}$ so that it can access from $1000\ 0000_{hex}$ to $1000\ ffff_{hex}$ using the positive and negative 16-bit offsets from $gp. This information is also found in Column 4 of the MIPS Reference Data Card at the front of this book.

C allocates and frees space on the heap with explicit functions. `malloc()` allocates space on the heap and returns a pointer to it, and `free()` releases space on the heap to which the pointer points. Memory allocation is controlled by programs in C, and it is the source of many common and difficult bugs. Forgetting to free space leads to a "memory leak," which eventually uses up so much memory that the operating system may crash. Freeing space too early leads to "dangling pointers," which can cause pointers to point to things that the program never intended. Java uses automatic memory allocation and garbage collection primarily to avoid such bugs.

Figure 2.14 summarizes the register conventions for the MIPS assembly language. This convention is another example of making the **common case fast**: most procedures can be satisfied with up to 4 arguments, 2 registers for a return value, 8 saved registers and 10 temporary registers without ever going to memory.

Name	Register number	Usage	Preserved on call?
$zero	0	The constant value 0	n.a.
$v0–$v1	2–3	Values for results and expression evaluation	no
$a0–$a3	4–7	Arguments	no
$t0–$t7	8–15	Temporaries	no
$s0–$s7	16–23	Saved	yes
$t8–$t9	24–25	More temporaries	no
$gp	28	Global pointer	yes
$sp	29	Stack pointer	yes
$fp	30	Frame pointer	yes
$ra	31	Return address	yes

FIGURE 2.14 MIPS register conventions. Register 1, called $at, is reserved for the assembler (see Section 2.12), and registers 26–27, called $k0-$k1, are reserved for the operating system. This information is also found in Column 2 of the MIPS Reference Data Card at the front of this book.

Elaboration: What if there are more than four parameters? The MIPS convention is to place the extra parameters on the stack just above the frame pointer. The procedure then expects the first four parameters to be in registers $a0 through $a3 and the rest in memory, addressable via the frame pointer.

As mentioned in the caption of Figure 2.12, the frame pointer is convenient because all references to variables in the stack within a procedure will have the same offset. The frame pointer is not necessary, however. The GNU MIPS C compiler uses a frame pointer, but the C compiler from MIPS does not; it treats register 30 as another save register ($s8).

Elaboration: Some recursive procedures can be implemented iteratively without using recursion. Iteration can significantly improve performance by removing the overhead associated with procedure calls. For example, consider a procedure used to accumulate a sum:

```c
int sum (int n, int acc) {
  if (n >0)
      return sum(n - 1, acc + n);
  else
      return acc;
}
```

Consider the procedure call sum(3,0). This will result in recursive calls to sum(2,3), sum(1,5), and sum(0,6), and then the result 6 will be returned four times. This recursive call of sum is referred to as a *tail call*, and this example use of tail recursion can be implemented very efficiently (assume $a0 = n and $a1 = acc):

```
sum: slti $t0, $a0, 1          # test if n <= 0
     bne $t0, $zero, sum_exit   # go to sum_exit if n <= 0
     add$a1, $a1, $a0           # add n to acc
     addi$a0, $a0, -1           # subtract 1 from n
     j sum                      # go to sum
sum_exit:
     add$v0, $a1, $zero         # return value acc
     jr $ra                     # return to caller
```

Check Yourself

Which of the following statements about C and Java are generally true?

1. C programmers manage data explicitly, while it's automatic in Java.

2. C leads to more pointer bugs and memory leak bugs than does Java.

!(@ | = > (wow open tab at bar is great)

Fourth line of the keyboard poem "Hatless Atlas," 1991 (some give names to ASCII characters: "!" is "wow," "(" is open, "|" is bar, and so on).

2.9 Communicating with People

Computers were invented to crunch numbers, but as soon as they became commercially viable they were used to process text. Most computers today offer 8-bit bytes to represent characters, with the *American Standard Code for Information Interchange* (ASCII) being the representation that nearly everyone follows. Figure 2.15 summarizes ASCII.

ASCII value	Character	ASCII value	Character	ASCII value	Character	ASCII value	Character	ASCII value	Character	ASCII value	Character
32	space	48	0	64	@	80	P	96	`	112	p
33	!	49	1	65	A	81	Q	97	a	113	q
34	"	50	2	66	B	82	R	98	b	114	r
35	#	51	3	67	C	83	S	99	c	115	s
36	$	52	4	68	D	84	T	100	d	116	t
37	%	53	5	69	E	85	U	101	e	117	u
38	&	54	6	70	F	86	V	102	f	118	v
39	'	55	7	71	G	87	W	103	g	119	w
40	(	56	8	72	H	88	X	104	h	120	x
41	)	57	9	73	I	89	Y	105	i	121	y
42	*	58	:	74	J	90	Z	106	j	122	z
43	+	59	;	75	K	91	[	107	k	123	{
44	,	60	<	76	L	92	\	108	l	124		
45	-	61	=	77	M	93	]	109	m	125	}
46	.	62	>	78	N	94	^	110	n	126	~
47	/	63	?	79	O	95	_	111	o	127	DEL

FIGURE 2.15 ASCII representation of characters. Note that upper- and lowercase letters differ by exactly 32; this observation can lead to shortcuts in checking or changing upper- and lowercase. Values not shown include formatting characters. For example, 8 represents a backspace, 9 represents a tab character, and 13 a carriage return. Another useful value is 0 for null, the value the programming language C uses to mark the end of a string. This information is also found in Column 3 of the MIPS Reference Data Card at the front of this book.

ASCII versus Binary Numbers

We could represent numbers as strings of ASCII digits instead of as integers. How much does storage increase if the number 1 billion is represented in ASCII versus a 32-bit integer?

One billion is 1,000,000,000, so it would take 10 ASCII digits, each 8 bits long. Thus the storage expansion would be $(10 \times 8)/32$ or 2.5. Beyond the expansion in storage, the hardware to add, subtract, multiply, and divide such decimal numbers is difficult and would consume more energy. Such difficulties explain why computing professionals are raised to believe that binary is natural and that the occasional decimal computer is bizarre.

A series of instructions can extract a byte from a word, so load word and store word are sufficient for transferring bytes as well as words. Because of the popularity of text in some programs, however, MIPS provides instructions to move bytes. *Load byte* (`lb`) loads a byte from memory, placing it in the rightmost 8 bits of a register. *Store byte* (`sb`) takes a byte from the rightmost 8 bits of a register and writes it to memory. Thus, we copy a byte with the sequence

```
lb $t0,0($sp)      # Read byte from source
sb $t0,0($gp)      # Write byte to destination
```

Characters are normally combined into strings, which have a variable number of characters. There are three choices for representing a string: (1) the first position of the string is reserved to give the length of a string, (2) an accompanying variable has the length of the string (as in a structure), or (3) the last position of a string is indicated by a character used to mark the end of a string. C uses the third choice, terminating a string with a byte whose value is 0 (named null in ASCII). Thus, the string "Cal" is represented in C by the following 4 bytes, shown as decimal numbers: 67, 97, 108, 0. (As we shall see, Java uses the first option.)

Compiling a String Copy Procedure, Showing How to Use C Strings

The procedure `strcpy` copies string y to string x using the null byte termination convention of C:

```
void strcpy (char x[], char y[])
{
    int i;

    i = 0;
    while ((x[i] = y[i]) != '\0') /* copy & test byte */
    i += 1;
}
```

What is the MIPS assembly code?

ANSWER

Below is the basic MIPS assembly code segment. Assume that base addresses for arrays x and y are found in $a0 and $a1, while i is in $s0. strcpy adjusts the stack pointer and then saves the saved register $s0 on the stack.

To initialize i to 0, the next instruction sets $s0 to 0 by adding 0 to 0 and placing that sum in $s0:

```
        add     $s0,$zero,$zero # i = 0 + 0
```

This is the beginning of the loop. The address of y[i] is first formed by adding i to y[]:

```
    L1: add     $t1,$s0,$a1  # address of y[i] in $t1
```

Note that we don't have to multiply i by 4 since y is an array of *bytes* and not of words, as in prior examples.

Load byte (lb) sign extends the byte while load byte unsigned (lbu) zero extends it.

To load the character in y[i], we use lbu, which puts the character into $t2:

```
        lbu     $t2, 0($t1)  # $t2 = y[i]

    strcpy:
        addi    $sp,$sp,-4   # adjust stack for 1 more item
        sw      $s0, 0($sp)  # save $s0
```

A similar address calculation puts the address of x[i] in $t3, and then the character in $t2 is stored at that address.

```
        add     $t3,$s0,$a0  # address of x[i] in $t3
        sb      $t2, 0($t3)  # x[i] = y[i]
```

Next, we exit the loop if the character was 0. That is, we exit if it is the last character of the string:

```
        beq     $t2,$zero,L2 # if y[i] == 0, go to L2
```

If not, we increment i and loop back:

```
        addi    $s0, $s0,1   # i = i + 1
        j       L1           # go to L1
```

If we don't loop back, it was the last character of the string; we restore $s0 and the stack pointer, and then return.

```
L2: lw      $s0, 0($sp)  # y[i] == 0: end of string.
                         # Restore old $s0
    addi    $sp,$sp,4    # pop 1 word off stack
    jr      $ra          # return
```

String copies usually use pointers instead of arrays in C to avoid the operations on i in the code above. See Section 2.14 for an explanation of arrays versus pointers.

Since the procedure strcpy above is a leaf procedure, the compiler could allocate i to a temporary register and avoid saving and restoring $s0. Hence, instead of thinking of the $t registers as being just for temporaries, we can think of them as registers that the callee should use whenever convenient. When a compiler finds a leaf procedure, it exhausts all temporary registers before using registers it must save.

Characters and Strings in Java

Unicode is a universal encoding of the alphabets of most human languages. Figure 2.16 gives a list of Unicode alphabets; there are almost as many *alphabets* in Unicode as there are useful *symbols* in ASCII. To be more inclusive, Java uses Unicode for characters. By default, it uses 16 bits to represent a character.

The MIPS instruction set has explicit instructions to load and store such 16-bit quantities, called *halfwords*. Load half (lh) loads a halfword from memory, placing it in the rightmost 16 bits of a register. Like load byte, *load half* (lh) treats the halfword as a signed number and thus sign-extends to fill the 16 leftmost bits of the register, while *load halfword unsigned* (lhu) works with unsigned integers. Thus, lhu is the more popular of the two just as lbu is more popular than lb. Store half (sh) takes a halfword from the rightmost 16 bits of a register and writes it to memory. We copy a halfword with the sequence

```
lhu $t0,0($sp) # Read halfword (16 bits) from source
sh  $t0,0($gp) # Write halfword (16 bits) to destination
```

Strings are a standard Java class with special built-in support and predefined methods for concatenation, comparison, and conversion. Unlike C, Java includes a word that gives the length of the string, similar to Java arrays.

Elaboration: MIPS software tries to keep the stack aligned to word addresses, allowing the program to always use lw and sw (which must be aligned) to access the stack. This convention means that a char variable allocated on the stack occupies 4 bytes, even though it needs less. However, a C string variable or an array of bytes *will* pack 4 bytes per word, and a Java string variable or array of shorts packs 2 halfwords per word.

Latin	Malayalam	Tagbanwa	General Punctuation
Greek	Sinhala	Khmer	Spacing Modifier Letters
Cyrillic	Thai	Mongolian	Currency Symbols
Armenian	Lao	Limbu	Combining Diacritical Marks
Hebrew	Tibetan	Tai Le	Combining Marks for Symbols
Arabic	Myanmar	Kangxi Radicals	Superscripts and Subscripts
Syriac	Georgian	Hiragana	Number Forms
Thaana	Hangul Jamo	Katakana	Mathematical Operators
Devanagari	Ethiopic	Bopomofo	Mathematical Alphanumeric Symbols
Bengali	Cherokee	Kanbun	Braille Patterns
Gurmukhi	Unified Canadian Aboriginal Syllabic	Shavian	Optical Character Recognition
Gujarati	Ogham	Osmanya	Byzantine Musical Symbols
Oriya	Runic	Cypriot Syllabary	Musical Symbols
Tamil	Tagalog	Tai Xuan Jing Symbols	Arrows
Telugu	Hanunoo	Yijing Hexagram Symbols	Box Drawing
Kannada	Buhid	Aegean Numbers	Geometric Shapes

FIGURE 2.16 Example alphabets in Unicode. Unicode version 4.0 has more than 160 "blocks," which is their name for a collection of symbols. Each block is a multiple of 16. For example, Greek starts at 0370_{hex}, and Cyrillic at 0400_{hex}. The first three columns show 48 blocks that correspond to human languages in roughly Unicode numerical order. The last column has 16 blocks that are multilingual and are not in order. A 16-bit encoding, called UTF-16, is the default. A variable-length encoding, called UTF-8, keeps the ASCII subset as eight bits and uses 16 or 32 bits for the other characters. UTF-32 uses 32 bits per character. New Unicode versions are released every June, with version 13.0 in 2020. Versions 9.0 to 13.0 added various Emojis, while earlier versions added new language blocks and hieroglyphs. The total is almost 150,000 characters. To learn more, see *www.unicode.org*.

Elaboration: Reflecting the international nature of the web, most web pages today use Unicode instead of ASCII.

Check Yourself

I. Which of the following statements about characters and strings in C and Java are true?

1. A string in C takes about half the memory as the same string in Java.

2. Strings are just an informal name for single-dimension arrays of characters in C and Java.

3. Strings in C and Java use null (0) to mark the end of a string.

4. Operations on strings, like length, are faster in C than in Java.

II. Which type of variable that can contain $1,000,000,000_{ten}$ takes the most memory space?

1. `int` in C

2. `string` in C

3. `string` in Java

Newcomers to computing are surprised that the type of the data is not encoded inside the data, but instead in the *program* that operates on that data.

To illustrate, we give an example from natural languages. What does the word "won" mean? You cannot answer that question without knowing the context, specifically the language that it is supposed to be in. Here are four alternatives:

1.   In English, it is the verb that is the past tense of win.

2.   In Korean, it is a noun that is the monetary unit of South Korea.

3.   In Polish, it is an adjective that means nice smelling.

4.   In Russian, it is an adjective that means stinks.

A binary number can also represent several types of data. For example, the 32-bit pattern

```
01100010 01100001 01010000 00000000
```

could represent the following:

1.   1,650,544,640 if the program treats it as an unsigned integer.

2.   +1,650,544,640 if the program treats it as a signed integer.

3.   "baP" if the program treats it as a null-terminated ASCII string.

4.   The color dark blue if the program treats the bit pattern as a mixture of the four base colors cyan, magenta, yellow, and black of the Pantone color-matching system.

The Big Picture on page 92 reminds us that instructions are also represented as numbers, so the bit pattern could represent the MIPS machine language instruction

```
011000    10011    00001    01010    00000    000000
```

which corresponds to the assembly language instruction multiply (see Chapter 3):

```
mult $t2, $s3, $at
```

If you accidentally give a word-processing program an image, it will try to interpret it as text, and you will see bizarre images on the screen; you will run into similar issues if you give text data to a graphics display program. This unrestricted behavior of a stored program computer is why file systems have a naming convention of the suffix giving the type of the file (for example, .jpg, .pdf, .txt) to enable the program check for mismatches by file name to reduce such embarrassing scenarios.

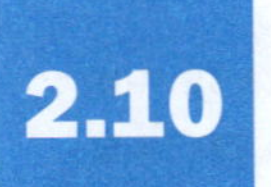 2.10   MIPS Addressing for 32-bit Immediates and Addresses

Although keeping all MIPS instructions 32 bits long simplifies the hardware, there are times where it would be convenient to have a 32-bit constant or 32-bit address. This section starts with the general solution for large constants, and then shows the optimizations for instruction addresses used in branches and jumps.

32-Bit Immediate Operands

Although constants are frequently short and fit into the 16-bit field, sometimes they are bigger. The MIPS instruction set includes the instruction *load upper immediate* (lui) specifically to set the upper 16 bits of a constant in a register, allowing a subsequent instruction to specify the lower 16 bits of the constant. Figure 2.17 shows the operation of lui.

EXAMPLE

Loading a 32-Bit Constant

What is the MIPS assembly code to load this 32-bit constant into register $s0?

```
0000  0000  0011  1101  0000  1001  0000  0000
```

ANSWER

First, we would load the upper 16 bits, which is 61 in decimal, using lui:

```
lui $s0, 61   # 61 decimal = 0000  0000  0011  1101  binary
```

The value of register $s0 afterward is

```
0000  0000  0011  1101  0000  0000  0000  0000
```

The next step is to insert the lower 16 bits, whose decimal value is 2304:

```
ori $s0, $s0, 2304 # 2304 decimal = 0000 1001 0000 0000
```

The final value in register $s0 is the desired value:

```
0000  0000  0011  1101  0000  1001  0000  0000
```

The machine language version of lui $t0, 255   # $t0 is register 8:

001111	00000	01000	0000 0000 1111 1111

Contents of register $t0 after executing lui $t0, 255:

0000 0000 1111 1111	0000 0000 0000 0000

FIGURE 2.17 The effect of the lui **instruction.** The instruction lui transfers the 16-bit immediate constant field value into the leftmost 16 bits of the register, filling the lower 16 bits with 0s.

Either the compiler or the assembler must break large constants into pieces and then reassemble them into a register. As you might expect, the immediate field's size restriction may be a problem for memory addresses in loads and stores as well as for constants in immediate instructions. If this job falls to the assembler, as it does for MIPS software, then the assembler must have a temporary register available in which to create the long values. This need is a reason for the register $at, (assembler temporary), which is reserved for the assembler.

Hence, the symbolic representation of the MIPS machine language is no longer limited by the hardware, but by whatever the creator of an assembler chooses to include (see Section 2.12). We stick close to the hardware to explain the architecture of the computer, noting when we use the enhanced language of the assembler that is not found in the processor.

Hardware/ Software Interface

Elaboration: Creating 32-bit constants needs care. The instruction `addi` copies the left-most bit of the 16-bit immediate field of the instruction into the upper 16 bits of a word. *Logical or immediate* from Section 2.6 loads 0s into the upper 16 bits and hence is used by the assembler in conjunction with `lui` to create 32-bit constants.

Addressing in Branches and Jumps

The MIPS jump instructions have the simplest addressing. They use the final MIPS instruction format, called the *J-type*, which consists of 6 bits for the operation field and the rest of the bits for the address field. Thus,

```
j    10000    # go to location 10000
```

could be assembled into this format (it's actually a bit more complicated, as we will see):

2	10000
6 bits	26 bits

where the value of the jump opcode is 2 and the jump address is 10000.

Unlike the jump instruction, the conditional branch instruction must specify two operands in addition to the branch address. Thus,

```
bne  $s0,$s1,Exit  # go to Exit if $s0 ≠ $s1
```

is assembled into this instruction, leaving only 16 bits for the branch address:

5	16	17	Exit
6 bits	5 bits	5 bits	16 bits

If addresses of the program had to fit in this 16-bit field, it would mean that no program could be bigger than 2^{16}, which is far too small to be a realistic option today. An alternative would be to specify a register that would always be added to the branch address, so that a branch instruction would calculate the following:

$$\text{Program counter} = \text{Register} + \text{Branch address}$$

This sum allows the program to be as large as 2^{32} and still be able to use conditional branches, solving the branch address size problem. Then the question is, which register?

The answer comes from seeing how conditional branches are used. Conditional branches are found in loops and in *if* statements, so they tend to branch to a nearby instruction. For example, about half of all conditional branches in SPEC benchmarks go to locations less than 16 instructions away. Since the *program counter* (PC) contains the address of the current instruction, we can branch within $\pm 2^{15}$ words of the current instruction if we use the PC as the register to be added to the address. Almost all loops and *if* statements are much smaller than 2^{16} words, so the PC is the ideal choice.

This form of branch addressing is called **PC-relative addressing**. As we shall see in Chapter 4, it is convenient for the hardware to increment the PC early to point to the next instruction. Hence, the MIPS address is actually relative to the address of the following instruction (PC + 4) as opposed to the current instruction (PC). It is yet another example of making the **common case fast**, which in this case is addressing nearby instructions.

Like most recent computers, MIPS uses PC-relative addressing for all conditional branches, because the destination of these instructions is likely to be close to the branch. On the other hand, jump-and-link instructions invoke procedures that have no reason to be near the call, so they normally use other forms of addressing. Hence, the MIPS architecture offers long addresses for procedure calls by using the J-type format for both jump and jump-and-link instructions.

Since all MIPS instructions are 4 bytes long, MIPS stretches the distance of the branch by having PC-relative addressing refer to the number of *words* to the next instruction instead of the number of bytes. Thus, the 16-bit field can branch four times as far by interpreting the field as a relative word address rather than as a relative byte address. Similarly, the 26-bit field in jump instructions is also a word address, meaning that it represents a 28-bit byte address.

PC-relative addressing An addressing regime in which the address is the sum of the *program counter* (PC) and a constant in the instruction.

Elaboration: Since the PC is 32 bits, 4 bits must come from somewhere else for jumps. The MIPS jump instruction replaces only the lower 28 bits of the PC, leaving the upper 4 bits of the PC unchanged. The loader and linker (Section 2.12) must be careful to avoid placing a program across an address boundary of 256 MB (64 million instructions); otherwise, a jump must be replaced by a jump register instruction preceded by other instructions to load the full 32-bit address into a register.

Showing Branch Offset in Machine Language

The *while* loop on pages 98–99 was compiled into this MIPS assembler code:

```
Loop:sll $t1,$s3,2      # Temp reg $t1 = 4 * i
     add  $t1,$t1,$s6    # $t1 = address of save[i]
     lw   $t0,0($t1)     # Temp reg $t0 = save[i]
     bne  $t0,$s5, Exit  # go to Exit if save[i] ≠ k
     addi $s3,$s3,1      # i = i + 1
     j    Loop           # go to Loop
Exit:
```

If we assume we place the loop starting at location 80000 in memory, what is the MIPS machine code for this loop?

The assembled instructions and their addresses are:

80000	0	0	19	9	2	0
80004	0	9	22	9	0	32
80008	35	9	8		0	
80012	5	8	21		2	
80016	8	19	19		1	
80020	2	20000				
80024	. . .					

Remember that MIPS instructions have byte addresses, so addresses of sequential words differ by 4, the number of bytes in a word. The bne instruction on the fourth line adds 2 words or 8 bytes to the address of the *following* instruction (80016), specifying the branch destination relative to that following instruction (8 + 80016) instead of relative to the branch instruction (12 + 80012) or using the full destination address (80024). The jump instruction on the last line does use the full address (20000 × 4 = 80000), corresponding to the label Loop.

Hardware/ Software Interface

Most conditional branches are to a nearby location, but occasionally they branch far away, farther than can be represented in the 16 bits of the conditional branch instruction. The assembler comes to the rescue just as it did with large addresses or constants: it inserts an unconditional jump to the branch target, and inverts the condition so that the branch decides whether to skip the jump.

EXAMPLE

Branching Far Away

Given a branch on register $s0 being equal to register $s1,

```
beq   $s0, $s1, L1
```

replace it by a pair of instructions that offers a much greater branching distance.

ANSWER

These instructions replace the short-address conditional branch:

```
      bne    $s0, $s1, L2
      j      L1
L2:
```

MIPS Addressing Mode Summary

addressing mode One of several addressing regimes delimited by their varied use of operands and/or addresses.

Multiple forms of addressing are generically called **addressing modes**. Figure 2.18 shows how operands are identified for each addressing mode. The MIPS addressing modes are the following:

1. *Immediate addressing,* where the operand is a constant within the instruction itself

2. *Register addressing,* where the operand is a register

3. *Base* or *displacement addressing,* where the operand is at the memory location whose address is the sum of a register and a constant in the instruction

4. *PC-relative addressing,* where the branch address is the sum of the PC and a constant in the instruction

5. *Pseudodirect addressing,* where the jump address is the 26 bits of the instruction concatenated with the upper bits of the PC

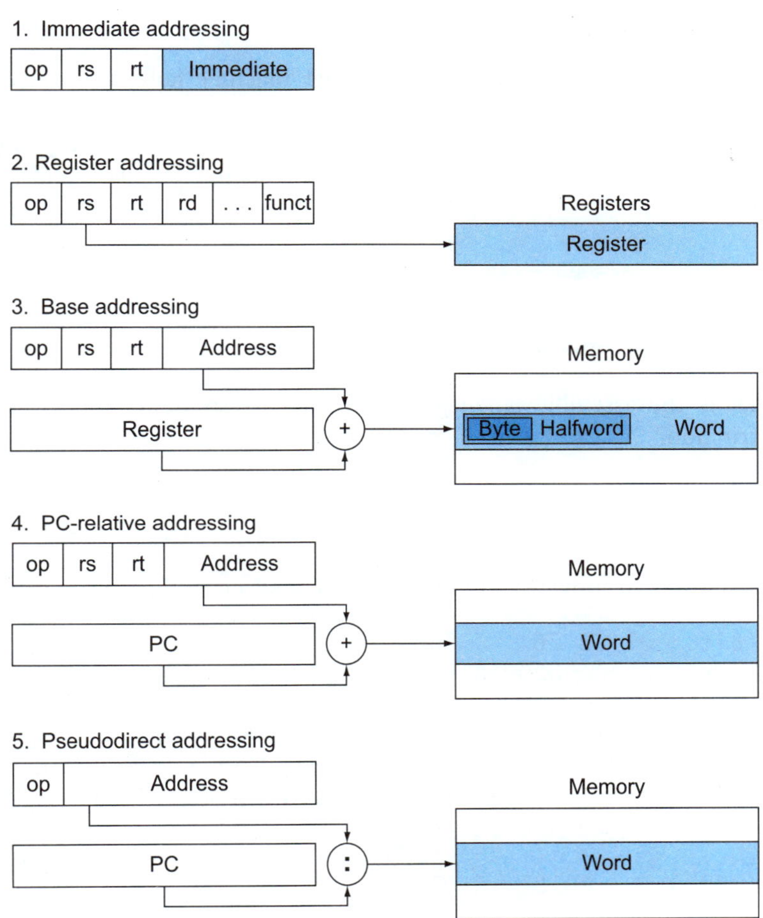

FIGURE 2.18 Illustration of the five MIPS addressing modes. The operands are shaded in color. The operand of mode 3 is in memory, whereas the operand for mode 2 is a register. Note that versions of load and store access bytes, halfwords, or words. For mode 1, the operand is 16 bits of the instruction itself. Modes 4 and 5 address instructions in memory, with mode 4 adding a 16-bit address shifted left 2 bits to the PC and mode 5 concatenating a 26-bit address shifted left 2 bits with the 4 upper bits of the PC. Note that a single operation can use more than one addressing mode. Add, for example, uses both immediate (`addi`) and register (`add`) addressing.

Although we show MIPS as having 32-bit addresses, nearly all microprocessors (including MIPS) have 64-bit address extensions (see ⊕ **Appendix E**). These extensions were in response to the needs of software for larger programs. The process of instruction set extension allows architectures to expand in such a way that is able to move software compatibly upward to the next generation of architecture.

Hardware/ Software Interface

Decoding Machine Language

Sometimes you are forced to reverse-engineer machine language to create the original assembly language. One example is when looking at "core dump." Figure 2.19 shows the MIPS encoding of the fields for the MIPS machine language. This figure helps when translating by hand between assembly language and machine language.

EXAMPLE

Decoding Machine Code

What is the assembly language statement corresponding to this machine instruction?

```
00af8020hex
```

ANSWER

The first step in converting hexadecimal to binary is to find the op fields:

```
(Bits: 31 28 26                                   5    2 0)
       0000 0000 1010 1111 1000 0000 0010 0000
```

We look at the op field to determine the operation. Referring to Figure 2.19, when bits 31–29 are 000 and bits 28–26 are 000, it is an R-format instruction. Let's reformat the binary instruction into R-format fields, listed in Figure 2.20:

```
op           rs        rt        rd        shamt     funct
000000       00101     01111     10000     00000     100000
```

The bottom portion of Figure 2.19 determines the operation of an R-format instruction. In this case, bits 5–3 are 100 and bits 2–0 are 000, which means this binary pattern represents an add instruction.

We decode the rest of the instruction by looking at the field values. The decimal values are 5 for the rs field, 15 for rt, and 16 for rd (shamt is unused). Figure 2.14 shows that these numbers represent registers $a1, $t7, and $s0. Now we can reveal the assembly instruction:

```
add $s0,$a1,$t7
```

op(31:26)								
28–26 / 31–29	0(000)	1(001)	2(010)	3(011)	4(100)	5(101)	6(110)	7(111)
0(000)	R-format	Bltz/gez	jump	jump & link	branch eq	branch ne	blez	bgtz
1(001)	add immediate	addiu	set less than imm.	set less than imm. unsigned	andi	ori	xori	load upper immediate
2(010)	TLB	FlPt						
3(011)								
4(100)	load byte	load half	lwl	load word	load byte unsigned	load half unsigned	lwr	
5(101)	store byte	store half	swl	store word			swr	
6(110)	load linked word	lwcl						
7(111)	store cond. word	swcl						

op(31:26)=010000 (TLB), rs(25:21)								
23–21 / 25–24	0(000)	1(001)	2(010)	3(011)	4(100)	5(101)	6(110)	7(111)
0(00)	mfc0		cfc0		mtc0		ctc0	
1(01)								
2(10)								
3(11)								

op(31:26)=000000 (R-format), funct(5:0)								
2–0 / 5–3	0(000)	1(001)	2(010)	3(011)	4(100)	5(101)	6(110)	7(111)
0(000)	shift left logical		shift right logical	sra	sllv		srlv	srav
1(001)	jump register	jalr			syscall	break		
2(010)	mfhi	mthi	mflo	mtlo				
3(011)	mult	multu	div	divu				
4(100)	add	addu	subtract	subu	and	or	xor	not or (nor)
5(101)			set l.t.	set l.t. unsigned				
6(110)								
7(111)								

FIGURE 2.19 MIPS instruction encoding. This notation gives the value of a field by row and by column. For example, the top portion of the figure shows **load word** in row number 4 (100_{two} for bits 31–29 of the instruction) and column number 3 (011_{two} for bits 28–26 of the instruction), so the corresponding value of the op field (bits 31–26) is 100011_{two}. An underlined name means the field is used elsewhere. For example, R-format in row 0 and column 0 (op = 000000_{two}) is defined in the bottom part of the figure. Hence, subtract in row 4 and column 2 of the bottom section means that the funct field (bits 5–0) of the instruction is 100010_{two} and the op field (bits 31–26) is 000000_{two}. The floating point value in row 2, column 1 is defined in Figure 3.18 in Chapter 3. Bltz/gez is the opcode for four instructions found in Appendix A: bltz, bgez, bltzal, and bgezal. This chapter describes instructions given in full name using color, while Chapter 3 describes instructions given in mnemonics using color. Appendix A covers all instructions.

Name	Fields						Comments
Field size	6 bits	5 bits	5 bits	5 bits	5 bits	6 bits	All MIPS instructions are 32 bits long
R-format	op	rs	rt	rd	shamt	funct	Arithmetic instruction format
I-format	op	rs	rt	address/immediate			Transfer, branch, imm. format
J-format	op	target address					Jump instruction format

FIGURE 2.20 MIPS instruction formats.

Figure 2.20 shows all the MIPS instruction formats. Figure 2.1 on page 70 shows the MIPS assembly language revealed in this chapter. The remaining hidden portion of MIPS instructions deals mainly with arithmetic and real numbers, which are covered in the next chapter.

Check Yourself

I. What is the range of addresses for conditional branches in MIPS ($K = 1024$)?

   1. Addresses between 0 and $64\,K - 1$

   2. Addresses between 0 and $256\,K - 1$

   3. Addresses up to about 32 K before the branch to about 32 K after

   4. Addresses up to about 128 K before the branch to about 128 K after

II. What is the range of addresses for jump and jump and link in MIPS ($M = 1024\,K$)?

   1. Addresses between 0 and $64\,M - 1$

   2. Addresses between 0 and $256\,M - 1$

   3. Addresses up to about 32 M before the branch to about 32 M after

   4. Addresses up to about 128 M before the branch to about 128 M after

   5. Anywhere within a block of 64 M addresses where the PC supplies the upper 6 bits

   6. Anywhere within a block of 256 M addresses where the PC supplies the upper 4 bits

III. What is the MIPS assembly language instruction corresponding to the machine instruction with the value $0000\ 0000_{hex}$?

   1. j

   2. R-format

   3. addi

   4. sll

   5. mfc0

   6. Undefined opcode: there is no legal instruction that corresponds to 0

2.11 Parallelism and Instructions: Synchronization

Parallel execution is easier when tasks are independent, but often they need to cooperate. Cooperation usually means some tasks are writing new values that others must read. To know when a task is finished writing so that it is safe for another to read, the tasks need to synchronize. If they don't synchronize, there is a danger of a **data race**, where the results of the program can change depending on how events happen to occur.

For example, recall the analogy of the eight reporters writing a story on page 44 of Chapter 1. Suppose one reporter needs to read all the prior sections before writing a conclusion. Hence, he or she must know when the other reporters have finished their sections, so that there is no danger of sections being changed afterwards. That is, they had better synchronize the writing and reading of each section so that the conclusion will be consistent with what is printed in the prior sections.

In computing, synchronization mechanisms are typically built with user-level software routines that rely on hardware-supplied synchronization instructions. In this section, we focus on the implementation of *lock* and *unlock* synchronization operations. Lock and unlock can be used straightforwardly to create regions where only a single processor can operate, called a *mutual exclusion*, as well as to implement more complex synchronization mechanisms.

The critical ability we require to implement synchronization in a multiprocessor is a set of hardware primitives with the ability to *atomically* read and modify a memory location. That is, nothing else can interpose itself between the read and the write of the memory location. Without such a capability, the cost of building basic synchronization primitives will be high and will increase unreasonably as the processor count increases.

There are a number of alternative formulations of the basic hardware primitives, all of which provide the ability to atomically read and modify a location, together with some way to tell if the read and write were performed atomically. In general, architects do not expect users to employ the basic hardware primitives, but instead expect that the primitives will be used by system programmers to build a synchronization library, a process that is often complex and tricky.

Let's start with one such hardware primitive and show how it can be used to build a basic synchronization primitive. One typical operation for building synchronization operations is the *atomic exchange* or *atomic swap*, which interchanges a value in a register for a value in memory.

To see how to use this to build a basic synchronization primitive, assume that we want to build a simple lock where the value 0 is used to indicate that the lock is free and 1 is used to indicate that the lock is unavailable. A processor tries to set the lock by doing an exchange of 1, which is in a register, with the memory address corresponding to the lock. The value returned from the exchange instruction is 1 (unavailable) if some other processor had already claimed access, and 0 (free)

data race Two memory accesses form a data race if they are from different threads to same location, at least one is a write, and they occur one after another.

otherwise. In the latter case, the value is also changed to 1 (unavailable), preventing any competing exchange in another processor from also retrieving a 0 (free).

For example, consider two processors that each try to do the exchange simultaneously: this race is broken, since exactly one of the processors will perform the exchange first, returning 0 (free), and the second processor will return 1 (unavailable) when it does the exchange. The key to using the exchange primitive to implement synchronization is that the operation is atomic: the exchange is indivisible, and two simultaneous exchanges will be ordered by the hardware. It is impossible for two processors trying to set the synchronization variable in this manner to both think they have simultaneously set the variable.

Implementing a single atomic memory operation introduces some challenges in the design of the processor, since it requires both a memory read and a write in a single, uninterruptible instruction.

An alternative is to have a pair of instructions in which the second instruction returns a value showing whether the pair of instructions was executed as if the pair were atomic. The pair of instructions is effectively atomic if it appears as if all other operations executed by any processor occurred before or after the pair. Thus, when an instruction pair is effectively atomic, no other processor can change the value between the instruction pair.

In MIPS this pair of instructions includes a special load called a *load linked* and a special store called a *store conditional*. These instructions are used in sequence: if the contents of the memory location specified by the load linked are changed before the store conditional to the same address occurs, then the store conditional fails. The store conditional is defined to both store the value of a (presumably different) register in memory *and* to change the value of that register to a 1 if it succeeds and to a 0 if it fails. Since the load linked returns the initial value, and the store conditional returns 1 only if it succeeds, the following sequence implements an atomic exchange on the memory location specified by the contents of $s1:

```
again:  addi   $t0,$zero,1        #copy locked value
        ll     $t1,0($s1)         #load linked
        sc     $t0,0($s1)         #store conditional
        beq    $t0,$zero,again    #branch if store fails(0)
        add    $s4,$zero,$t1      #put load value in $s4
```

Any time a processor intervenes and modifies the value in memory between the `ll` and `sc` instructions, the `sc` returns 0 in $t0, causing the code sequence to try again. At the end of this sequence, the contents of $s4 and the memory location specified by $s1 have been atomically exchanged.

Elaboration: Although it was presented for multiprocessor synchronization, atomic exchange is also useful for the operating system in dealing with multiple processes in a single processor. To make sure nothing interferes in a single processor, the store conditional also fails if the processor does a context switch between the two instructions (see Chapter 5).

Elaboration: An advantage of the load linked/store conditional mechanism is that it can be used to build other synchronization primitives, such as *atomic compare and swap* or *atomic fetch-and-increment*, which are used in some parallel programming models. These involve more instructions between the `ll` and the `sc`, but not too many.

Since the store conditional will fail after either another attempted store to the load linked address or any exception, care must be taken in choosing which instructions are inserted between the two instructions. In particular, only register-register instructions can safely be permitted; otherwise, it is possible to create deadlock situations where the processor can never complete the `sc` because of repeated page faults. In addition, the number of instructions between the load linked and the store conditional should be small to minimize the probability that either an unrelated event or a competing processor causes the store conditional to fail frequently.

When do you use primitives like load linked and store conditional?

1. When cooperating threads of a parallel program need to synchronize to get proper behavior for reading and writing shared data

2. When cooperating processes on a uniprocessor need to synchronize for reading and writing shared data

Check Yourself

2.12

Translating and Starting a Program

This section describes the four steps in transforming a C program in a file in nonvolatile storage into a program running on a computer. Figure 2.21 shows the translation hierarchy. Some systems combine these steps to reduce translation time, but these are the logical four phases that programs go through. This section follows this translation hierarchy.

Compiler

The compiler transforms the C program into an *assembly language program*, a symbolic form of what the machine understands. High-level language programs take many fewer lines of code than assembly language, so programmer productivity is much higher.

In 1975, many operating systems and assemblers were written in **assembly language** because memories were small and compilers were inefficient. The million-fold increase in memory capacity per single DRAM chip has reduced program size concerns, and optimizing compilers today can produce assembly language programs nearly as good as an assembly language expert, and sometimes even better for large programs.

assembly language
A symbolic language that can be translated into binary machine language.

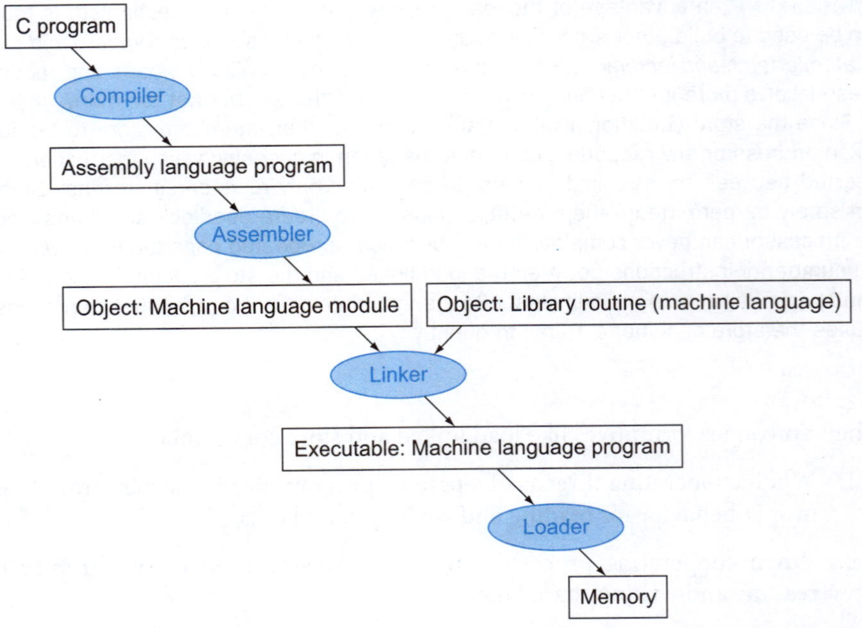

FIGURE 2.21 A translation hierarchy for C. A high-level language program is first compiled into an assembly language program and then assembled into an object module in machine language. The linker combines multiple modules with library routines to resolve all references. The loader then places the machine code into the proper memory locations for execution by the processor. To speed up the translation process, some steps are skipped or combined. Some compilers produce object modules directly, and some systems use linking loaders that perform the last two steps. To identify the type of file, UNIX follows a suffix convention for files: C source files are named `X.C`, assembly files are `X.S`, object files are named `X.O`, statically linked library routines are `X.a`, dynamically linked library routes are `X.SO`, and executable files by default are called `a.out`. MS-DOS uses the suffixes `.C`, `.ASM`, `.OBJ`, `.LIB`, `.DLL`, and `.EXE` to the same effect.

Assembler

Since assembly language is an interface to higher-level software, the assembler can also treat common variations of machine language instructions as if they were instructions in their own right. The hardware need not implement these instructions; however, their appearance in assembly language simplifies translation and programming. Such instructions are called **pseudoinstructions**.

pseudoinstruction
A common variation
of assembly language
instructions often treated
as if it were an instruction
in its own right.

As mentioned above, the MIPS hardware makes sure that register $zero always has the value 0. That is, whenever register $zero is used, it supplies a 0, and the programmer cannot change the value of register $zero. Register $zero is used to create the assembly language instruction that copies the contents of one register to another. Thus the MIPS assembler accepts this instruction even though it is not found in the MIPS architecture:

```
move $t0,$t1       # register $t0 gets register $t1
```

The assembler converts this assembly language instruction into the machine language equivalent of the following instruction:

```
add $t0,$zero,$t1 # register $t0 gets 0 + register $t1
```

The MIPS assembler also converts blt (branch on less than) into the two instructions slt and bne mentioned in the example on page 101. Other examples include bgt, bge, and ble. It also converts branches to faraway locations into a branch and jump. As mentioned above, the MIPS assembler allows 32-bit constants to be loaded into a register despite the 16-bit limit of the immediate instructions.

In summary, pseudoinstructions give MIPS a richer set of assembly language instructions than those implemented by the hardware. The only cost is reserving one register, $at, for use by the assembler. If you are going to write assembly programs, use pseudoinstructions to simplify your task. To understand the MIPS architecture and be sure to get best performance, however, study the real MIPS instructions found in Figures 2.1 and 2.19.

Assemblers will also accept numbers in a variety of bases. In addition to binary and decimal, they usually accept a base that is more succinct than binary yet converts easily to a bit pattern. MIPS assemblers use hexadecimal.

Such features are convenient, but the primary task of an assembler is assembly into machine code. The assembler turns the assembly language program into an *object file*, which is a combination of machine language instructions, data, and information needed to place instructions properly in memory.

To produce the binary version of each instruction in the assembly language program, the assembler must determine the addresses corresponding to all labels. Assemblers keep track of labels used in branches and data transfer instructions in a **symbol table**. As you might expect, the table contains pairs of symbols and addresses.

symbol table A table that matches names of labels to the addresses of the memory words that instructions occupy.

The object file for UNIX systems typically contains six distinct pieces:

- The *object file header* describes the size and position of the other pieces of the object file.

- The *text segment* contains the machine language code.

- The *static data segment* contains data allocated for the life of the program. (UNIX allows programs to use both *static data,* which is allocated throughout the program, and *dynamic data,* which can grow or shrink as needed by the program. See Figure 2.13.)

- The *relocation information* identifies instructions and data words that depend on absolute addresses when the program is loaded into memory.

- The *symbol table* contains the remaining labels that are not defined, such as external references.

■ The *debugging information* contains a concise description of how the modules were compiled so that a debugger can associate machine instructions with C source files and make data structures readable.

The next subsection shows how to attach such routines that have already been assembled, such as library routines.

Linker

What we have presented so far suggests that a single change to one line of one procedure requires compiling and assembling the whole program. Complete retranslation is a terrible waste of computing resources. This repetition is particularly wasteful for standard library routines, because programmers would be compiling and assembling routines that by definition almost never change. An alternative is to compile and assemble each procedure independently, so that a change to one line would require compiling and assembling only one procedure. This alternative requires a new systems program, called a **link editor** or **linker**, which takes all the independently assembled machine language programs and "stitches" them together.

There are three steps for the linker:

1. Place code and data modules symbolically in memory.

2. Determine the addresses of data and instruction labels.

3. Patch both the internal and external references.

The linker uses the relocation information and symbol table in each object module to resolve all undefined labels. Such references occur in branch instructions, jump instructions, and data addresses, so the job of this program is much like that of an editor: it finds the old addresses and replaces them with the new addresses. Editing is the origin of the name "link editor," or linker for short. The reason a linker is useful is that it is much faster to patch code than it is to recompile and reassemble.

If all external references are resolved, the linker next determines the memory locations each module will occupy. Recall that Figure 2.13 on page 110 shows the MIPS convention for allocation of program and data to memory. Since the files were assembled in isolation, the assembler could not know where a module's instructions and data would be placed relative to other modules. When the linker places a module in memory, all *absolute* references—that is, memory addresses that are not relative to a register—must be *relocated* to reflect its true location.

The linker produces an **executable file** that can be run on a computer. Typically, this file has the same format as an object file, except that it contains no unresolved references. It is possible to have partially linked files, such as library routines, that still have unresolved addresses and hence result in object files.

---

linker Also called **link editor**. A systems program that combines independently assembled machine language programs and resolves all undefined labels into an executable file.

executable file A functional program in the format of an object file that contains no unresolved references. It can contain symbol tables and debugging information. A "stripped executable" does not contain that information. Relocation information may be included for the loader.

Linking Object Files

Link the two object files below. Show updated addresses of the first few instructions of the completed executable file. We show the instructions in assembly language just to make the example understandable; in reality, the instructions would be numbers.

Note that in the object files we have highlighted the addresses and symbols that must be updated in the link process: the instructions that refer to the addresses of procedures A and B and the instructions that refer to the addresses of data words X and Y.

Object file header			
	Name	Procedure A	
	Text size	100_{hex}	
	Data size	20_{hex}	
Text segment	Address	Instruction	
	0	lw $a0, 0($gp)	
	4	jal 0	
	...	...	
Data segment	0	(X)	
	...	...	
Relocation information	Address	Instruction type	Dependency
	0	lw	X
	4	jal	B
Symbol table	Label	Address	
	X	–	
	B	–	
Object file header			
	Name	Procedure B	
	Text size	200_{hex}	
	Data size	30_{hex}	
Text segment	Address	Instruction	
	0	sw $a1, 0($gp)	
	4	jal 0	
	...	...	
Data segment	0	(Y)	
	...	...	
Relocation information	Address	Instruction type	Dependency
	0	sw	Y
	4	jal	A
Symbol table	Label	Address	
	Y	–	
	A	–	

ANSWER

Procedure A needs to find the address for the variable labeled X to put in the load instruction and to find the address of procedure B to place in the jal instruction. Procedure B needs the address of the variable labeled Y for the store instruction and the address of procedure A for its jal instruction.

From Figure 2.13 on page 110, we know that the text segment starts at address $40\ 0000_{hex}$ and the data segment at $1000\ 0000_{hex}$. The text of procedure A is placed at the first address and its data at the second. The object file header for procedure A says that its text is 100_{hex} bytes and its data is 20_{hex} bytes, so the starting address for procedure B text is $40\ 0100_{hex}$, and its data starts at $1000\ 0020_{hex}$.

Executable file header		
	Text size	300_{hex}
	Data size	50_{hex}
Text segment	Address	Instruction
	$0040\ 0000_{hex}$	lw $a0, 8000_{hex}($gp)
	$0040\ 0004_{hex}$	jal $40\ 0100_{hex}$
	...	...
	$0040\ 0100_{hex}$	sw $a1, 8020_{hex}($gp)
	$0040\ 0104_{hex}$	jal $40\ 0000_{hex}$
	...	...
Data segment	Address	
	$1000\ 0000_{hex}$	(X)
	...	...
	$1000\ 0020_{hex}$	(Y)
	...	...

Now the linker updates the address fields of the instructions. It uses the instruction type field to know the format of the address to be edited. We have two types here:

1. The jals are easy because they use pseudodirect addressing. The jal at address $40\ 0004_{hex}$ gets $40\ 0100_{hex}$ (the address of procedure B) in its address field, and the jal at $40\ 0104_{hex}$ gets $40\ 0000_{hex}$ (the address of procedure A) in its address field.

2. The load and store addresses are harder because they are relative to a base register. This example uses the global pointer as the base register. Figure 2.13 shows that $gp is initialized to $1000\ 8000_{hex}$. To get the address $1000\ 0000_{hex}$ (the address of word X), we place 8000_{hex} in the address field of lw at address $40\ 0000_{hex}$. The address field of lw is sign extended, so 8000_{hex} becomes $FFFF\ 8000_{hex}$, or -32768_{two}. Similarly, we place 7980_{hex} in the address field of sw at address $40\ 0100_{hex}$ to get the address $1000\ 0020_{hex}$ (the address of word Y).

Elaboration: Recall that MIPS instructions are word aligned, so `jal` drops the right two bits to increase the instruction's address range. Thus, it use 26 bits to create a 28-bit byte address. Hence, the actual address in the lower 26 bits of the `jal` instructions in this example are $10\ 0000_{hex}$ rather than $40\ 0000_{hex}$ and $10\ 0040_{hex}$, versus $40\ 0100_{hex}$.

Loader

Now that the executable file is on disk, the operating system reads it to memory and starts it. The **loader** follows these steps in UNIX systems:

1. Reads the executable file header to determine size of the text and data segments.

2. Creates an address space large enough for the text and data.

3. Copies the instructions and data from the executable file into memory.

4. Copies the parameters (if any) to the main program onto the stack.

5. Initializes the machine registers and sets the stack pointer to the first free location.

6. Jumps to a start-up routine that copies the parameters into the argument registers and calls the main routine of the program. When the main routine returns, the start-up routine terminates the program with an `exit` system call.

Section A.3 and A.4 in Appendix B describe linkers and loaders in more detail.

loader A systems program that places an object program in main memory so that it is ready to execute.

Dynamically Linked Libraries

The first part of this section describes the traditional approach to linking libraries before the program is run. Although this static approach is the fastest way to call library routines, it has a few disadvantages:

- The library routines become part of the executable code. If a new version of the library is released that fixes bugs or supports new hardware devices, the statically linked program keeps using the old version.

- It loads all routines in the library that are called anywhere in the executable, even if those calls are not executed. The library can be large relative to the program; for example, the standard C library is 2.5 MB.

These disadvantages lead to **dynamically linked libraries (DLLs)**, where the library routines are not linked and loaded until the program is run. Both the program and library routines keep extra information on the location of nonlocal procedures and their names. In the initial version of DLLs, the loader ran a dynamic linker, using the extra information in the file to find the appropriate libraries and to update all external references.

"Virtually every problem in computer science can be solved by another level of indirection."

David Wheeler

dynamically linked libraries (DLLs) Library routines that are linked to a program during execution.

The downside of the initial version of DLLs was that it still linked all routines of the library that might be called, versus only those that are called during the running of the program. This observation led to the lazy procedure linkage version of DLLs, where each routine is linked only *after* it is called.

Like many innovations in our field, this trick relies on a level of indirection. Figure 2.22 shows the technique. It starts with the nonlocal routines calling a set of dummy routines at the end of the program, with one entry per nonlocal routine. These dummy entries each contain an indirect jump.

The first time the library routine is called, the program calls the dummy entry and follows the indirect jump. It points to code that puts a number in a register to

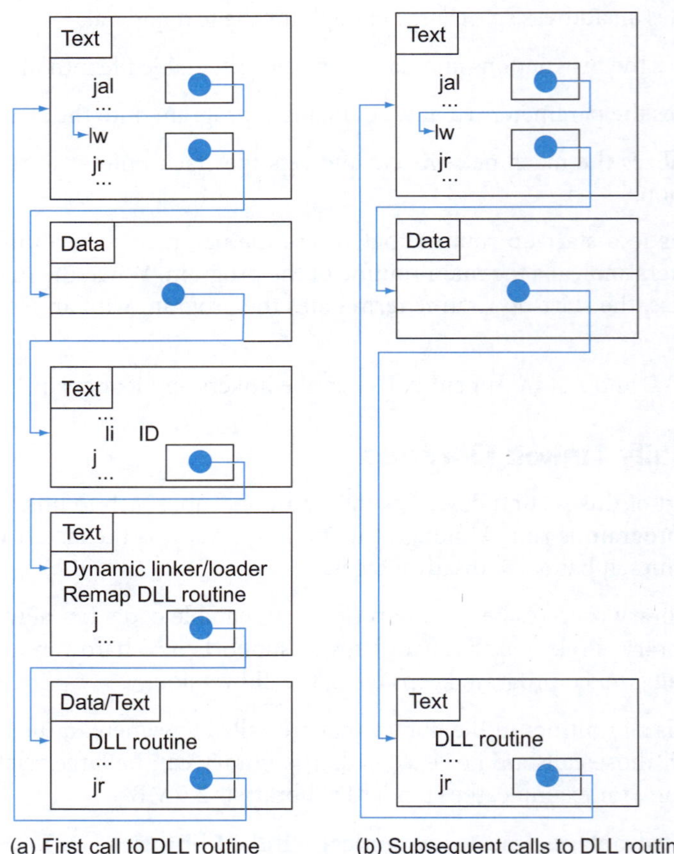

(a) First call to DLL routine   (b) Subsequent calls to DLL routine

FIGURE 2.22 Dynamically linked library via lazy procedure linkage. (a) Steps for the first time a call is made to the DLL routine. (b) The steps to find the routine, remap it, and link it are skipped on subsequent calls. As we will see in Chapter 5, the operating system may avoid copying the desired routine by remapping it using virtual memory management.

identify the desired library routine and then jumps to the dynamic linker/loader. The linker/loader finds the desired routine, remaps it, and changes the address in the indirect jump location to point to that routine. It then jumps to it. When the routine completes, it returns to the original calling site. Thereafter, the call to the library routine jumps indirectly to the routine without the extra hops.

In summary, DLLs require extra space for the information needed for dynamic linking, but do not require that whole libraries be copied or linked. They pay a good deal of overhead the first time a routine is called, but only a single indirect jump thereafter. Note that the return from the library pays no extra overhead. Microsoft's Windows relies extensively on dynamically linked libraries, and it is also the default when executing programs on UNIX systems today.

Starting a Java Program

The discussion above captures the traditional model of executing a program, where the emphasis is on fast execution time for a program targeted to a specific instruction set architecture, or even a specific implementation of that architecture. Indeed, it is possible to execute Java programs just like C. Java was invented with a different set of goals, however. One was to run safely on any computer, even if it might slow execution time.

Figure 2.23 shows the typical translation and execution steps for Java. Rather than compile to the assembly language of a target computer, Java is compiled first to instructions that are easy to interpret: the **Java bytecode** instruction set (see Section 2.15). This instruction set is designed to be close to the Java language so that this compilation step is trivial. Virtually no optimizations are performed. Like the C compiler, the Java compiler checks the types of data and produces the proper operation for each type. Java programs are distributed in the binary version of these bytecodes.

A software interpreter, called a **Java Virtual Machine (JVM)**, can execute Java bytecodes. An interpreter is a program that simulates an instruction set architecture.

Java bytecode
Instruction from an instruction set designed to interpret Java programs.

Java Virtual Machine (JVM) The program that interprets Java bytecodes.

Java program

Compiler

Class files (Java bytecodes)   Java library routines (machine language)

Just In Time compiler   Java Virtual Machine

Compiled Java methods (machine language)

FIGURE 2.23 A translation hierarchy for Java. A Java program is first compiled into a binary version of Java bytecodes, with all addresses defined by the compiler. The Java program is now ready to run on the interpreter, called the *Java Virtual Machine* (JVM). The JVM links to desired methods in the Java library while the program is running. To achieve greater performance, the JVM can invoke the JIT compiler, which selectively compiles methods into the native machine language of the machine on which it is running.

For example, the MIPS simulator used with this book is an interpreter. There is no need for a separate assembly step since either the translation is so simple that the compiler fills in the addresses or JVM finds them at runtime.

The upside of interpretation is portability. The availability of software Java virtual machines meant that most people could write and run Java programs shortly after Java was announced. Today, Java virtual machines are found in hundreds of millions of devices, in everything from cell phones to Internet browsers.

The downside of interpretation is lower performance. The incredible advances in performance of the 1980s and 1990s made interpretation viable for many important applications, but the factor of 10 slowdown when compared to traditionally compiled C programs made Java unattractive for some applications.

To preserve portability and improve execution speed, the next phase of Java development was compilers that translated *while* the program was running. Such **Just In Time compilers (JIT)** typically profile the running program to find where the "hot" methods are and then compile them into the native instruction set on which the virtual machine is running. The compiled portion is saved for the next time the program is run, so that it can run faster each time it is run. This balance of interpretation and compilation evolves over time, so that frequently run Java programs suffer little of the overhead of interpretation.

As computers get faster so that compilers can do more, and as researchers invent betters ways to compile Java on the fly, the performance gap between Java and C or C++ is closing. 🌐 **Section 2.15** online goes into much greater depth on the implementation of Java, Java bytecodes, JVM, and JIT compilers.

Just In Time compiler (JIT) The name commonly given to a compiler that operates at runtime, translating the interpreted code segments into the native code of the computer.

Check Yourself

Which of the advantages of an interpreter over a translator do you think was most important for the designers of Java?

1. Ease of writing an interpreter

2. Better error messages

3. Smaller object code

4. Machine independence

2.13   A C Sort Example to Put It All Together

One danger of showing assembly language code in snippets is that you will have no idea what a full assembly language program looks like. In this section, we derive the MIPS code from two procedures written in C: one to swap array elements and one to sort them.

```
void swap(int v[], int k)
  {
    int temp;
    temp = v[k];
    v[k] = v[k+1];
    v[k+1] = temp;
  }
```

FIGURE 2.24 A C procedure that swaps two locations in memory. This subsection uses this procedure in a sorting example.

The Procedure swap

Let's start with the code for the procedure swap in Figure 2.24. This procedure simply swaps two locations in memory. When translating from C to assembly language by hand, we follow these general steps:

1.   Allocate registers to program variables.

2.   Produce code for the body of the procedure.

3.   Preserve registers across the procedure invocation.

This section describes the swap procedure in these three pieces, concluding by putting all the pieces together.

Register Allocation for swap

As mentioned on page 103, the MIPS convention on parameter passing is to use registers $a0, $a1, $a2, and $a3. Since swap has just two parameters, v and k, they will be found in registers $a0 and $a1. The only other variable is temp, which we associate with register $t0 since swap is a leaf procedure (see page 106). This register allocation corresponds to the variable declarations in the first part of the swap procedure in Figure 2.24.

Code for the Body of the Procedure swap

The remaining lines of C code in swap are

```
temp = v[k];
v[k] = v[k+1];
v[k+1] = temp;
```

Recall that the memory address for MIPS refers to the *byte* address, and so words are really 4 bytes apart. Hence we need to multiply the index k by 4 before adding it to the address. *Forgetting that sequential word addresses differ by 4 instead of by 1 is a common mistake in assembly language programming.* Hence the first step is to get the address of v[k] by multiplying k by 4 via a shift left by 2:

```
sll   $t1, $a1,2      # reg $t1 = k * 4
add   $t1, $a0,$t1    # reg $t1 = v + (k * 4)
                      # reg $t1 has the address of v[k]
```

Now we load v[k] using $t1, and then v[k+1] by adding 4 to $t1:

```
lw    $t0, 0($t1)     # reg $t0 (temp) = v[k]
lw    $t2, 4($t1)     # reg $t2 = v[k + 1]
                      # refers to next element of v
```

Next we store $t0 and $t2 to the swapped addresses:

```
sw    $t2, 0($t1)     # v[k] = reg $t2
sw    $t0, 4($t1)     # v[k + 1] = reg $t0 (temp)
```

Now we have allocated registers and written the code to perform the operations of the procedure. What is missing is the code for preserving the saved registers used within swap. Since we are not using saved registers in this leaf procedure, there is nothing to preserve.

The Full swap Procedure

We are now ready for the whole routine, which includes the procedure label and the return jump. To make it easier to follow, we identify in Figure 2.25 each block of code with its purpose in the procedure.

Procedure body		

```
swap: sll   $t1, $a1, 2      # reg $t1 = k * 4
      add   $t1, $a0, $t1    # reg $t1 = v + (k * 4)
                             # reg $t1 has the address of v[k]
      lw    $t0, 0($t1)      # reg $t0 (temp) = v[k]
      lw    $t2, 4($t1)      # reg $t2 = v[k + 1]
                             # refers to next element of v
      sw    $t2, 0($t1)      # v[k] = reg $t2
      sw    $t0, 4($t1)      # v[k+1] = reg $t0 (temp)
```

Procedure return		

```
      jr    $ra             # return to calling routine
```

FIGURE 2.25 MIPS assembly code of the procedure *swap* **in Figure 2.24.**

The Procedure sort

To ensure that you appreciate the rigor of programming in assembly language, we'll try a second, longer example. In this case, we'll build a routine that calls the swap procedure. This program sorts an array of integers, using bubble or exchange sort, which is one of the simplest if not the fastest sorts. Figure 2.26 shows the C version of the program. Once again, we present this procedure in several steps, concluding with the full procedure.

```
void sort (int v[], int n)
{
    int i, j;
    for (i = 0; i < n; i += 1) {
        for (j = i - 1; j >= 0 && v[j] > v[j + 1]; j+=1) {
            swap(v,j);
        }
    }
}
```

FIGURE 2.26 A C procedure that performs a sort on the array v.

Register Allocation for sort

The two parameters of the procedure sort, v and n, are in the parameter registers $a0 and $a1, and we assign register $s0 to i and register $s1 to j.

Code for the Body of the Procedure sort

The procedure body consists of two nested *for* loops and a call to swap that includes parameters. Let's unwrap the code from the outside to the middle.

The first translation step is the first *for* loop:

```
for (i = 0; i <n; i += 1) {
```

Recall that the C *for* statement has three parts: initialization, loop test, and iteration increment. It takes just one instruction to initialize i to 0, the first part of the *for* statement:

```
move    $s0, $zero    # i = 0
```

(Remember that move is a pseudoinstruction provided by the assembler for the convenience of the assembly language programmer; see page 130.) It also takes just one instruction to increment i, the last part of the *for* statement:

```
addi    $s0, $s0,    1 # i += 1
```

The loop should be exited if i $<$ n is *not* true or, said another way, should be exited if i $\geq$ n. The set on less than instruction sets register $t0 to 1 if $s0 $<$ $a1 and to 0 otherwise. Since we want to test if $s0 $\geq$ $a1, we branch if register $t0 is 0. This test takes two instructions:

```
for1tst:slt $t0, $s0, $a1       # reg $t0 = 0 if $s0 ≥ $a1 (i≥n)
        beq $t0, $zero,exit1    # go to exit1 if $s0 ≥ $a1 (i≥n)
```

The bottom of the loop just jumps back to the loop test:

```
        j for1tst               # jump to test of outer loop
exit1:
```

The skeleton code of the first *for* loop is then

```
        move    $s0, $zero     # i = 0
for1tst:slt $t0, $s0, $a1 # reg $t0 = 0 if $s0 ≥ $a1 (i≥n)
        beq     $t0, $zero,exit1 # go to exit1 if $s0 ≥ $a1 (i≥n)
                . . .
                (body of first for loop)
                . . .
        addi    $s0, $s0, 1 # i += 1
        j       for1tst        # jump to test of outer loop
exit1:
```

Voila! (The exercises explore writing faster code for similar loops.)
The second *for* loop looks like this in C:

```
for (j = i -1; j >= 0 && v[j]>v[j + 1]; j -= 1) {
```

The initialization portion of this loop is again one instruction:

```
addi        $s1, $s0, -1 # j = i - 1
```

The decrement of j at the end of the loop is also one instruction:

```
addi        $s1, $s1, -1 # j -= 1
```

The loop test has two parts. We exit the loop if either condition fails, so the first test must exit the loop if it fails (*j*<0):

```
for2tst: slti $t0, $s1, 0 # reg $t0 = 1 if $s1 < 0 (j < 0)
        bne $t0, $zero, exit2 # go to exit2 if $s1 < 0 (j < 0)
```

This branch will skip over the second condition test. If it doesn't skip, j $\geq$ 0.

The second test exits if v[j] >v[j + 1] is *not* true, or exits if v[j] ≤ v[j + 1]. First we create the address by multiplying j by 4 (since we need a byte address) and add it to the base address of v:

```
sll    $t1, $s1, 2    # reg $t1 = j * 4
add    $t2, $a0, $t1 # reg $t2 = v + (j * 4)
```

Now we load v[j]:

```
lw     $t3, 0($t2)    # reg $t3 = v[j]
```

Since we know that the second element is just the following word, we add 4 to the address in register $t2 to get v[j + 1]:

```
lw     $t4, 4($t2)    # reg $t4 = v[j + 1]
```

The test of v[j] ≤ v[j + 1] is the same as v[j + 1] ≥ v[j], so the two instructions of the exit test are

```
slt    $t0, $t4, $t3      # reg $t0 = 0 if $t4 ≥ $t3
beq    $t0, $zero, exit2 # go to exit2 if $t4 ≥ $t3
```

The bottom of the loop jumps back to the inner loop test:

```
j    for2tst    # jump to test of inner loop
```

Combining the pieces, the skeleton of the second *for* loop looks like this:

```
        addi $s1, $s0, -1       # j = i - 1
for2tst:slti $t0, $s1, 0        # reg $t0 = 1 if $s1 < 0 (j < 0)
        bne $t0, $zero, exit2 # go to exit2 if $s1 < 0 (j < 0)
        sll $t1, $s1, 2         # reg $t1 = j * 4
        add $t2, $a0, $t1       # reg $t2 = v + (j * 4)
        lw  $t3, 0($t2)         # reg $t3 = v[j]
        lw  $t4, 4($t2)         # reg $t4 = v[j + 1]
        slt $t0, $t4, $t3       # reg $t0 = 0 if $t4 ≥ $t3
        beq $t0, $zero, exit2 # go to exit2 if $t4 ≥ $t3
           . . .
        (body of second for loop)
           . . .
        addi $s1, $s1, -1       # j -= 1
        j  for2tst              # jump to test of inner loop
exit2:
```

The Procedure Call in sort

The next step is the body of the second *for* loop:

```
swap(v,j);
```

Calling swap is easy enough:

```
jal    swap
```

Passing Parameters in sort

The problem comes when we want to pass parameters because the sort procedure needs the values in registers $a0 and $a1, yet the swap procedure needs to have its parameters placed in those same registers. One solution is to copy the parameters for sort into other registers earlier in the procedure, making registers $a0 and $a1 available for the call of swap. (This copy is faster than saving and restoring on the stack.) We first copy $a0 and $a1 into $s2 and $s3 during the procedure:

```
move    $s2, $a0      # copy parameter $a0 into $s2
move    $s3, $a1      # copy parameter $a1 into $s3
```

Then we pass the parameters to swap with these two instructions:

```
move    $a0, $s2      # first swap parameter is v
move    $a1, $s1      # second swap parameter is j
```

Preserving Registers in sort

The only remaining code is the saving and restoring of registers. Clearly, we must save the return address in register $ra, since sort is a procedure and is called itself. The sort procedure also uses the saved registers $s0, $s1, $s2, and $s3, so they must be saved. The prologue of the sort procedure is then

```
addi    $sp,$sp,-20   # make room on stack for 5 registers
sw      $ra,16($sp)   # save $ra on stack
sw      $s3,12($sp)   # save $s3 on stack
sw      $s2, 8($sp)   # save $s2 on stack
sw      $s1, 4($sp)   # save $s1 on stack
sw      $s0, 0($sp)   # save $s0 on stack
```

The tail of the procedure simply reverses all these instructions, then adds a jr to return.

The Full Procedure sort

Now we put all the pieces together in Figure 2.27, being careful to replace references to registers $a0 and $a1 in the *for* loops with references to registers $s2 and $s3. Once again, to make the code easier to follow, we identify each block of code with its purpose in the procedure. In this example, nine lines of the sort procedure in C became 35 lines in the MIPS assembly language.

Elaboration: One optimization that works with this example is *procedure inlining*. Instead of passing arguments in parameters and invoking the code with a jal instruction, the compiler would copy the code from the body of the swap procedure where the call to swap appears in the code. Inlining would avoid four instructions in this example. The downside of the inlining optimization is that the compiled code would be bigger if the inlined procedure is called from several locations. Such a code expansion might turn into *lower* performance if it increased the cache miss rate; see Chapter 5.

Saving registers			
sort:	addi	$sp,$sp, -20	# make room on stack for 5 registers
	sw	$ra, 16($sp)	# save $ra on stack
	sw	$s3,12($sp)	# save $s3 on stack
	sw	$s2, 8($sp)	# save $s2 on stack
	sw	$s1, 4($sp)	# save $s1 on stack
	sw	$s0, 0($sp)	# save $s0 on stack

Procedure body				
Move parameters		move	$s2, $a0	# copy parameter $a0 into $s2 (save $a0)
		move	$s3, $a1	# copy parameter $a1 into $s3 (save $a1)
Outer loop		move	$s0, $zero	# i = 0
	for1tst:slt		$t0, $s0,$s3	# reg$t0=0if$s0Š$s3(iŠn)
		beq	$t0, $zero, exit1	# go to exit1 if $s0 Š $s3 (i Š n)
Inner loop		addi	$s1, $s0, -1	# j = i - 1
	for2tst:slti		$t0, $s1,0	# reg$t0=1if$s1<0(j<0)
		bne	$t0, $zero, exit2	# go to exit2 if $s1 < 0 (j < 0)
		sll	$t1, $s1, 2	# reg $t1 = j * 4
		add	$t2, $s2, $t1	# reg $t2 = v + (j * 4)
		lw	$t3, 0($t2)	# reg $t3 = v[j]
		lw	$t4, 4($t2)	# reg $t4 = v[j + 1]
		slt	$t0, $t4, $t3	# reg $t0 = 0 if $t4 Š $t3
		beq	$t0, $zero, exit2	# go to exit2 if $t4 Š $t3
Pass parameters and call		move	$a0, $s2	# 1st parameter of swap is v (old $a0)
		move	$a1, $s1	# 2nd parameter of swap is j
		jal	swap	# swap code shown in Figure 2.25
Inner loop		addi	$s1, $s1, -1	# j -= 1
		j	for2tst	# jump to test of inner loop
Outer loop	exit2:	addi	$s0, $s0, 1	# i += 1
		j	for1tst	# jump to test of outer loop

Restoring registers			
exit1:	lw	$s0, 0($sp)	# restore $s0 from stack
	lw	$s1, 4($sp)	# restore $s1 from stack
	lw	$s2, 8($sp)	# restore $s2 from stack
	lw	$s3,12($sp)	# restore $s3 from stack
	lw	$ra,16($sp)	# restore $ra from stack
	addi	$sp,$sp, 20	# restore stack pointer

Procedure return		
jr	$ra	# return to calling routine

FIGURE 2.27 MIPS assembly version of procedure sort **in Figure 2.26.**

Understanding Program Performance

Figure 2.28 shows the impact of compiler optimization on sort program performance, compile time, clock cycles, instruction count, and CPI. Note that unoptimized code has the best CPI, and O1 optimization has the lowest instruction count, but O3 is the fastest, reminding us that time is the only accurate measure of program performance.

Figure 2.29 compares the impact of programming languages, compilation versus interpretation, and algorithms on performance of sorts. The fourth column shows that the unoptimized C program is 8.3 times faster than the interpreted Java code for Bubble Sort. Using the JIT compiler makes Java 2.1 times *faster* than the unoptimized C and within a factor of 1.13 of the highest optimized C code. (🌐 Section 2.15 gives more details on interpretation versus compilation of Java and the Java and MIPS code for Bubble Sort.) The ratios aren't as close for Quicksort in Column 5, presumably because it is harder to amortize the cost of runtime compilation over the shorter execution time. The last column demonstrates the impact of a better algorithm, offering three orders of magnitude a performance increases by when sorting 100,000 items. Even comparing interpreted Java in Column 5 to the C compiler at highest optimization in Column 4, Quicksort beats Bubble Sort by a factor of 50 (0.05 × 2468, or 123 times faster than the unoptimized C code versus 2.41 times faster).

Elaboration: The MIPS compilers always save room on the stack for the arguments in case they need to be stored, so in reality they always decrement $sp by 16 to make room for all four argument registers (16 bytes). One reason is that C provides a vararg option that allows a pointer to pick, say, the third argument to a procedure. When the compiler encounters the rare vararg, it copies the four argument registers onto the stack into the four reserved locations.

gcc optimization	Relative performance	Clock cycles (millions)	Instruction count (millions)	CPI
None	1.00	158,615	114,938	1.38
01 (medium)	2.37	66,990	37,470	1.79
02 (full)	2.38	66,521	39,993	1.66
03 (procedure integration)	2.41	65,747	44,993	1.46

FIGURE 2.28 Comparing performance, instruction count, and CPI using compiler optimization for Bubble Sort. The programs sorted 100,000 words with the array initialized to random values. These programs were run on a Pentium 4 with a clock rate of 3.06 GHz and a 533 MHz system bus with 2 GB of PC2100 DDR SDRAM. It used Linux version 2.4.20.

Language	Execution method	Optimization	Bubble Sort relative performance	Quicksort relative performance	Speedup Quicksort vs. Bubble Sort
C	Compiler	None	1.00	1.00	2468
	Compiler	O1	2.37	1.50	1562
	Compiler	O2	2.38	1.50	1555
	Compiler	O3	2.41	1.91	1955
Java	Interpreter	–	0.12	0.05	1050
	JIT compiler	–	2.13	0.29	338

FIGURE 2.29 Performance of two sort algorithms in C and Java using interpretation and optimizing compilers relative to unoptimized C version. The last column shows the advantage in performance of Quicksort over Bubble Sort for each language and execution option. These programs were run on the same system as Figure 2.28. The JVM is Sun version 1.3.1, and the JIT is Sun Hotspot version 1.3.1.

2.14   Arrays versus Pointers

A challenge for any new C programmer is understanding pointers. Comparing assembly code that uses arrays and array indices to the assembly code that uses pointers offers insights about pointers. This section shows C and MIPS assembly versions of two procedures to clear a sequence of words in memory: one using array indices and one using pointers. Figure 2.30 shows the two C procedures.

The purpose of this section is to show how pointers map into MIPS instructions, and not to endorse a dated programming style. We'll see the impact of modern compiler optimization on these two procedures at the end of the section.

Array Version of Clear

Let's start with the array version, clear1, focusing on the body of the loop and ignoring the procedure linkage code. We assume that the two parameters array and size are found in the registers $a0 and $a1, and that i is allocated to register $t0.

The initialization of i, the first part of the *for* loop, is straightforward:

```
        move    $t0,$zero    # i = 0 (register $t0 = 0)
```

To set array[i] to 0 we must first get its address. Start by multiplying i by 4 to get the byte address:

```
loop1:  sll    $t1,$t0,2    # $t1 = i * 4
```

Since the starting address of the array is in a register, we must add it to the index to get the address of array[i] using an add instruction:

```
        add    $t2,$a0,$t1  # $t2 = address of array[i]
```

```
clear1(int array[], int size)
{
    int i;
    for (i = 0; i < size; i += 1)
        array[i] = 0;
}
clear2(int *array, int size)
{
    int *p;
    for (p = &array[0]; p < &array[size]; p = p + 1)
        *p = 0;
}
```

FIGURE 2.30 Two C procedures for setting an array to all zeros. Clear1 uses indices, while clear2 uses pointers. The second procedure needs some explanation for those unfamiliar with C. The address of a variable is indicated by &, and the object pointed to by a pointer is indicated by *. The declarations declare that array and p are pointers to integers. The first part of the *for* loop in clear2 assigns the address of the first element of array to the pointer p. The second part of the *for* loop tests to see if the pointer is pointing beyond the last element of array. Incrementing a pointer by one, in the last part of the *for* loop, means moving the pointer to the next sequential object of its declared size. Since p is a pointer to integers, the compiler will generate MIPS instructions to increment p by four, the number of bytes in a MIPS integer. The assignment in the loop places 0 in the object pointed to by p.

Finally, we can store 0 in that address:

```
sw   $zero, 0($t2)      # array[i] = 0
```

This instruction is the end of the body of the loop, so the next step is to increment i:

```
addi $t0,$t0,1          # i = i + 1
```

The loop test checks if i is less than size:

```
slt  $t3,$t0,$a1        # $t3 = (i < size)
bne  $t3,$zero,loop1    # if (i < size) go to loop1
```

We have now seen all the pieces of the procedure. Here is the MIPS code for clearing an array using indices:

```
        move  $t0,$zero      # i = 0
loop1:  sll   $t1,$t0,2      # $t1 = i * 4
        add   $t2,$a0,$t1    # $t2 = address of array[i]
        sw    $zero, 0($t2)  # array[i] = 0
        addi  $t0,$t0,1      # i = i + 1
        slt   $t3,$t0,$a1    # $t3 = (i < size)
        bne   $t3,$zero,loop1 # if (i < size) go to loop1
```

(This code works as long as size is greater than 0; ANSI C requires a test of size before the loop, but we'll skip that legality here.)

Pointer Version of Clear

The second procedure that uses pointers allocates the two parameters array and size to the registers $a0 and $a1 and allocates p to register $t0. The code for the second procedure starts with assigning the pointer p to the address of the first element of the array:

```
move    $t0,$a0         # p = address of array[0]
```

The next code is the body of the *for* loop, which simply stores 0 into p:

```
loop2:  sw   $zero,0($t0)  # Memory[p] = 0
```

This instruction implements the body of the loop, so the next code is the iteration increment, which changes p to point to the next word:

```
addi    $t0,$t0,4       # p = p + 4
```

Incrementing a pointer by 1 means moving the pointer to the next sequential object in C. Since p is a pointer to integers, each of which uses 4 bytes, the compiler increments p by 4.

The loop test is next. The first step is calculating the address of the last element of array. Start with multiplying size by 4 to get its byte address:

```
sll     $t1,$a1,2       # $t1 = size * 4
```

and then we add the product to the starting address of the array to get the address of the first word *after* the array:

```
add  $t2,$a0,$t1        # $t2 = address of array[size]
```

The loop test is simply to see if p is less than the last element of array:

```
slt  $t3,$t0,$t2        # $t3 = (p<&array[size])
bne  $t3,$zero,loop2    # if (p<&array[size]) go to loop2
```

With all the pieces completed, we can show a pointer version of the code to zero an array:

```
        move $t0,$a0            # p = address of array[0]
loop2:  sw$zero,0($t0)          # Memory[p] = 0
        addi $t0,$t0,4          # p = p + 4
        sll  $t1,$a1,2          # $t1 = size * 4
        add  $t2,$a0,$t1        # $t2 = address of array[size]
        slt  $t3,$t0,$t2        # $t3 = (p<&array[size])
        bne  $t3,$zero,loop2 # if (p<&array[size]) go to loop2
```

As in the first example, this code assumes size is greater than 0.

Note that this program calculates the address of the end of the array in every iteration of the loop, even though it does not change. A faster version of the code moves this calculation outside the loop:

```
        move  $t0,$a0         # p = address of array[0]
        sll   $t1,$a1,2       # $t1 = size * 4
        add   $t2,$a0,$t1     # $t2 = address of array[size]
loop2:  sw$zero,0($t0)        # Memory[p] = 0
        addi  $t0,$t0,4       # p = p + 4
        slt   $t3,$t0,$t2     # $t3 = (p<&array[size])
        bne   $t3,$zero,loop2 # if (p<&array[size]) go to loop2
```

Comparing the Two Versions of Clear

Comparing the two code sequences side by side illustrates the difference between array indices and pointers (the changes introduced by the pointer version are highlighted):

```
      move $t0,$zero     # i = 0                 move $t0,$a0      # p = & array[0]
loop1:sll  $t1,$t0,2     # $t1 = i * 4           sll  $t1,$a1,2    # $t1 = size * 4
      add  $t2,$a0,$t1   # $t2 = &array[i]       add  $t2,$a0,$t1  # $t2 = &array[size]
      sw   $zero, 0($t2) # array[i] = 0    loop2:sw   $zero,0($t0) # Memory[p] = 0
      addi $t0,$t0,1     # i = i + 1             addi $t0,$t0,4    # p = p + 4
      slt  $t3,$t0,$a1   # $t3 = (i < size)      slt  $t3,$t0,$t2  # $t3=(p<&array[size])
      bne  $t3,$zero,loop1# if () go to loop1    bne  $t3,$zero,loop2# if () go to loop2
```

The version on the left must have the "multiply" and add inside the loop because i is incremented and each address must be recalculated from the new index. The memory pointer version on the right increments the pointer p directly. The pointer version moves the scaling shift and the array bound addition outside the loop, thereby reducing the instructions executed per iteration from 6 to 4. This manual optimization corresponds to the compiler optimization of strength reduction (shift instead of multiply) and induction variable elimination (eliminating array address calculations within loops). Section 2.15 describes these two and many other optimizations.

Elaboration: As mentioned ealier, a C compiler would add a test to be sure that size is greater than 0. One way would be to add a jump just before the first instruction of the loop to the slt instruction.

People used to be taught to use pointers in C to get greater efficiency than that available with arrays: "Use pointers, even if you can't understand the code." Modern optimizing compilers can produce code for the array version that is just as good. Most programmers today prefer that the compiler do the heavy lifting.

Advanced Material: Compiling C and Interpreting Java

This section gives a brief overview of how the C compiler works and how Java is executed. Because the compiler will significantly affect the performance of a computer, understanding compiler technology today is critical to understanding performance. Keep in mind that the subject of compiler construction is usually taught in a one- or two-semester course, so our introduction will necessarily only touch on the basics.

The second part of this section is for readers interested in seeing how an **objected oriented language** like Java executes on a MIPS architecture. It shows the Java byte-codes used for interpretation and the MIPS code for the Java version of some of the C segments in prior sections, including Bubble Sort. It covers both the Java Virtual Machine and JIT compilers.

The rest of ⊕ **Section 2.15** can be found online.

object oriented language A programming language that is oriented around objects rather than actions, or data versus logic.

2.16 Real Stuff: ARMv7 (32-bit) Instructions

ARM is the most popular instruction set architecture for embedded devices, with more than 100 billion devices through 2016. Standing originally for the Acorn RISC Machine, later changed to Advanced RISC Machine, ARM came out the same year as MIPS and followed similar philosophies. Figure 2.31 lists the similarities. The principle difference is that MIPS has more registers and ARM has more addressing modes.

There is a similar core of instruction sets for arithmetic-logical and data transfer instructions for MIPS and ARM, as Figure 2.32 shows.

Addressing Modes

Figure 2.33 shows the data addressing modes supported by ARM. Unlike MIPS, ARM does not reserve a register to contain 0. Although MIPS has just three simple data addressing modes (see Figure 2.18), ARM has nine, including fairly complex calculations. For example, ARM has an addressing mode that can shift one register by any amount, add it to the other registers to form the address, and then update one register with this new address.

	ARM	MIPS
Date announced	1985	1985
Instruction size (bits)	32	32
Address space (size, model)	32 bits, flat	32 bits, flat
Data alignment	Aligned	Aligned
Data addressing modes	9	3
Integer registers (number, model, size)	15 GPR × 32 bits	31 GPR × 32 bits
I/O	Memory mapped	Memory mapped

FIGURE 2.31 Similarities in ARM and MIPS instruction sets.

	Instruction name	ARM	MIPS
Register-register	Add	add	addu, addiu
	Add (trap if overflow)	adds; swivs	add
	Subtract	sub	subu
	Subtract (trap if overflow)	subs; swivs	sub
	Multiply	mul	mult, multu
	Divide	—	div, divu
	And	and	and
	Or	orr	or
	Xor	eor	xor
	Load high part register	—	lui
	Shift left logical	lsl[1]	sllv, sll
	Shift right logical	lsr[1]	srlv, srl
	Shift right arithmetic	asr[1]	srav, sra
	Compare	cmp, cmn, tst, teq	slt/i,slt/iu
Data transfer	Load byte signed	ldrsb	lb
	Load byte unsigned	ldrb	lbu
	Load halfword signed	ldrsh	lh
	Load halfword unsigned	ldrh	lhu
	Load word	ldr	lw
	Store byte	strb	sb
	Store halfword	strh	sh
	Store word	str	sw
	Read, write special registers	mrs, msr	move
	Atomic Exchange	swp, swpb	ll;sc

FIGURE 2.32 ARM register-register and data transfer instructions equivalent to MIPS core. Dashes mean the operation is not available in that architecture or not synthesized in a few instructions. If there are several choices of instructions equivalent to the MIPS core, they are separated by commas. ARM includes shifts as part of every data operation instruction, so the shifts with superscript 1 are just a variation of a move instruction, such as lsr[1]. Note that ARM has no divide instruction.

Addressing mode	ARM	MIPS
Register operand	X	X
Immediate operand	X	X
Register + offset (displacement or based)	X	X
Register + register (indexed)	X	—
Register + scaled register (scaled)	X	—
Register + offset and update register	X	—
Register + register and update register	X	—
Autoincrement, autodecrement	X	—
PC-relative data	X	—

FIGURE 2.33 Summary of data addressing modes. ARM has separate register indirect and register + offset addressing modes, rather than just putting 0 in the offset of the latter mode. To get greater addressing range, ARM shifts the offset left 1 or 2 bits if the data size is halfword or word.

Compare and Conditional Branch

MIPS uses the contents of registers to evaluate conditional branches. ARM uses the traditional four condition code bits stored in the program status word: *negative, zero, carry,* and *overflow*. They can be set on any arithmetic or logical instruction; unlike earlier architectures, this setting is optional on each instruction. An explicit option leads to fewer problems in a pipelined implementation (see Chapter 4). ARM uses conditional branches to test condition codes to determine all possible unsigned and signed relations.

CMP subtracts one operand from the other and the difference sets the condition codes. Compare negative (CMN) *adds* one operand to the other, and the sum sets the condition codes. TST performs logical AND on the two operands to set all condition codes but overflow, while TEQ uses exclusive OR to set the first three condition codes.

One unusual feature of ARM is that every instruction has the option of executing conditionally, depending on the condition codes. Every instruction starts with a 4-bit field that determines whether it will act as a no operation instruction (nop) or as a real instruction, depending on the condition codes. Hence, conditional branches are properly considered as conditionally executing the unconditional branch instruction. Conditional execution allows avoiding a branch to jump over a single instruction. It takes less code space and time to simply conditionally execute one instruction.

Figure 2.34 shows the instruction formats for ARM and MIPS. The principal differences are the 4-bit conditional execution field in every instruction and the smaller register field, because ARM has half the number of registers.

Unique Features of ARM

Figure 2.35 shows a few arithmetic-logical instructions not found in MIPS. Since it does not have a dedicated register for 0, it has separate opcodes to perform

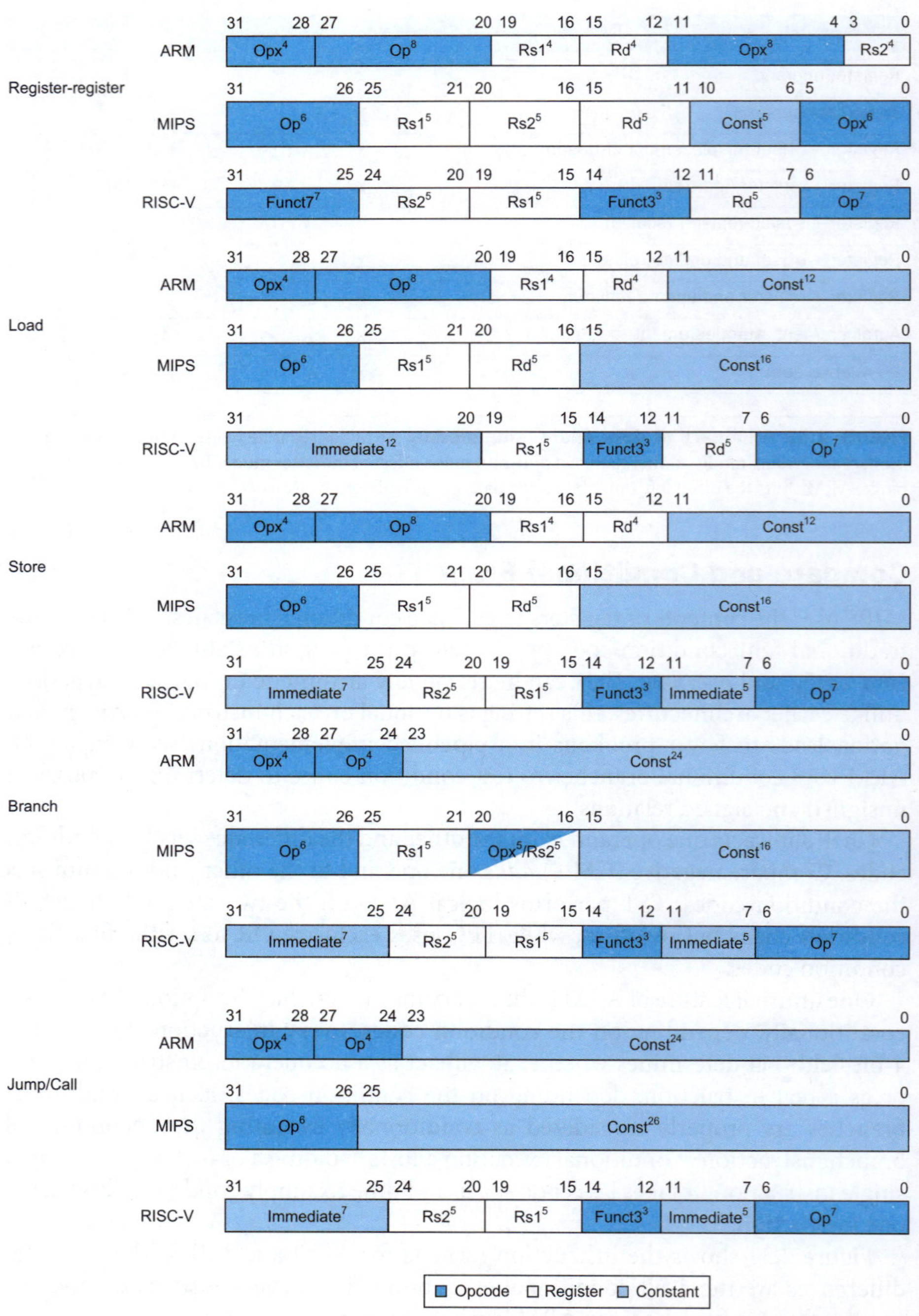

FIGURE 2.34 Instruction formats for ARM, MIPS, and RISC-V. The differences result from whether the architecture has 16 registers like ARM or 32 registers like MIPS and RISC-V.

Name	Definition	ARM	MIPS
Load immediate	Rd = Imm	mov	addi $0,
Not	Rd = ~(Rs1)	mvn	nor $0,
Move	Rd = Rs1	mov	or $0,
Rotate right	Rd = Rs i >> i $Rd_{0...i-1} = Rs_{31-i...31}$	ror	
And not	Rd = Rs1 & ~(Rs2)	bic	
Reverse subtract	Rd = Rs2 − Rs1	rsb, rsc	
Support for multiword integer add	CarryOut, Rd = Rd + Rs1 + OldCarryOut	adcs	—
Support for multiword integer sub	CarryOut, Rd = Rd − Rs1 + OldCarryOut	sbcs	—

FIGURE 2.35 ARM arithmetic/logical instructions not found in MIPS.

some operations that MIPS can do with $zero. In addition, ARM has support for multiword arithmetic.

ARM's 12-bit immediate field has a novel interpretation. The eight least-significant bits are zero-extended to a 32-bit value, then rotated right the number of bits specified in the first four bits of the field multiplied by two. One advantage is that this scheme can represent all powers of two in a 32-bit word. Whether this split actually catches more immediates than a simple 12-bit field would be an interesting study.

Operand shifting is not limited to immediates. The second register of all arithmetic and logical processing operations has the option of being shifted before being operated on. The shift options are shift left logical, shift right logical, shift right arithmetic, and rotate right.

ARM also has instructions to save groups of registers, called *block loads and stores*. Under control of a 16-bit mask within the instructions, any of the 16 registers can be loaded or stored into memory in a single instruction. These instructions can save and restore registers on procedure entry and return. These instructions can also be used for block memory copy, and they also reduce code size on procedure entry and exit.

2.17 Real Stuff: ARMv8 (64-bit) Instructions

Of the many potential problems in an instruction set, the one that is almost impossible to overcome is having too small a memory address. While the x86 was successfully extended first to 32-bit addresses and then later to 64-bit addresses, many of its brethren were left behind. For example, the 16-bit address MOStek 6502 powered the Apple II, but even given this headstart with the first commercially successful personal computer, its lack of address bits condemned it to the dustbin of history.

ARM architects could see the writing on the wall of their 32-bit address computer, and began design of the 64-bit address version of ARM in 2007. It was revealed in 2013. Rather than some minor cosmetic changes to make all the registers 64 bits wide, which is basically what happened to the x86, ARM did a complete overhaul. The good news is that if you know MIPS it will be easier to pick up ARMv8, as the 64-bit version is called.

First, as compared to MIPS, ARM dropped virtually all of the unusual features of the prior ARM architecture, referred to as ARM v7:

- There is no conditional execution field, as there was in nearly every instruction in v7.

- The immediate field is simply a 12 bit constant, rather than essentially an input to a function that produces a constant as in v7.

- They dropped Load Multiple and Store Multiple instructions.

- The PC is no longer one of the registers, which resulted in unexpected branches if you wrote to it.

Second, ARM added missing features that are useful in MIPS

- V8 has 32 general-purpose registers, which compiler writers surely love. Like MIPS, one register is hardwired to 0, although in load and store instructions it instead refers to the stack pointer.

- Its addressing modes work for all word sizes in ARMv8, which was not the case in ARMv7.

- It includes a divide instruction, which was omitted from ARMv7.

- It adds the equivalent of MIPS branch if equal and branch if not equal.

As the philosophy of the v8 instruction set is much closer to MIPS than it is to v7, our conclusion is that the main similarity between ARMv7 and ARMv8 is the name.

 Real Stuff: RISC-V Instructions

The instruction set most similar to MIPS also originated in academia. The good news is that if you know MIPS, it will be very easy to pick up RISC-V. However, RISC-V is an open architecture that is controlled by RISC-V International and not a proprietary architecture that is owned by a company like ARM, MIPS, or x86. MIPS and RISC-V share the same design philosophy, despite MIPS being 25 years more senior than RISC-V. Both also have 32-bit address versions and 64-bit address versions. To show their similarity, Figure 2.34 compares instruction formats for ARM, MIPS, and RISC-V. Here are the common features between RISC-V and MIPS:

- All instructions are 32 bit wide for both architectures.

- Both have 32 general-purpose registers, with one register being hardwired to 0.

- The only way to access memory is via load and store instructions on both architectures.

- Unlike some architectures, there are no instructions that can load or store many registers in MIPS or RISC-V.

- Both have instructions that branch if a register is equal to zero and branch if a register is not equal to zero.

- Both sets of addressing modes work for all data sizes.

One of the main differences between MIPS and RISC-V is for conditional branches other than equal or not equal. Although RISC-V simply provides branch instructions to compare two registers, MIPS relies on a comparison instruction that sets a register to 0 or 1 depending on whether the comparison is true. Programmers then follow that comparison instruction with a branch on equal to or not equal to zero depending on the desired outcome of the comparison. Keeping with its minimalist philosophy, MIPS only performs less than comparisons, leaving it up to the programmer to switch order of operands or to switch the condition being tested by the branch to get all the desired outcomes.

2.19 Real Stuff: x86 Instructions

Designers of instruction sets sometimes provide more powerful operations than those found in ARM, MIPS, and RISC-V. The goal is generally to reduce the number of instructions executed by a program. The danger is that this reduction can occur at the cost of simplicity, increasing the time a program takes to execute because the instructions are slower. This slowness may be the result of a slower clock cycle time or of requiring more clock cycles than a simpler sequence.

The path toward operation complexity is thus fraught with peril. Section 2.21 demonstrates the pitfalls of complexity.

Beauty is altogether in the eye of the beholder.

Margaret Wolfe Hungerford, *Molly Bawn, 1877*

Evolution of the Intel x86

ARM and MIPS were the vision of single small groups in 1985; the pieces of these architectures fit nicely together, and the whole architecture can be described succinctly. Such is not the case for the x86; it is the product of several independent groups who evolved the architecture over 40 years, adding new features to the original instruction set as someone might add clothing to a packed bag. Here are important x86 milestones.

- **1978**: The Intel 8086 architecture was announced as an assembly language–compatible extension of the then successful Intel 8080, an 8-bit microprocessor. The 8086 is a 16-bit architecture, with all internal registers 16 bits wide. Unlike MIPS, the registers have dedicated uses, and hence the 8086 is not considered a **general-purpose register** architecture.

general-purpose register (GPR) A register that can be used for addresses or for data with virtually any instruction.

- **1980**: The Intel 8087 floating-point coprocessor is announced. This architecture extends the 8086 with about 60 floating-point instructions. Instead of using registers, it relies on a stack (see 🌐 **Section 2.23** and **Section 3.7**).

- **1982**: The 80286 extended the 8086 architecture by increasing the address space to 24 bits, by creating an elaborate memory-mapping and protection model (see Chapter 5), and by adding a few instructions to round out the instruction set and to manipulate the protection model.

- **1985**: The 80386 extended the 80286 architecture to 32 bits. In addition to a 32-bit architecture with 32-bit registers and a 32-bit address space, the 80386 added new addressing modes and additional operations. The added instructions make the 80386 nearly a general-purpose register machine. The 80386 also added paging support in addition to segmented addressing (see Chapter 5). Like the 80286, the 80386 has a mode to execute 8086 programs without change.

- **1989–95**: The subsequent 80486 in 1989, Pentium in 1992, and Pentium Pro in 1995 were aimed at higher performance, with only four instructions added to the user-visible instruction set: three to help with multiprocessing (Chapter 6) and a conditional move instruction.

- **1997**: After the Pentium and Pentium Pro were shipping, Intel announced that it would expand the Pentium and the Pentium Pro architectures with MMX (Multi Media Extensions). This new set of 57 instructions uses the floating-point stack to accelerate multimedia and communication applications. MMX instructions typically operate on multiple short data elements at a time, in the tradition of *single instruction, multiple data* (SIMD) architectures (see Chapter 6). Pentium II did not introduce any new instructions.

- **1999**: Intel added another 70 instructions, labeled SSE (*Streaming SIMD Extensions*) as part of Pentium III. The primary changes were to add eight separate registers, double their width to 128 bits, and add a single precision floating-point data type. Hence, four 32-bit floating-point operations can be performed in parallel. To improve memory performance, SSE includes cache prefetch instructions plus streaming store instructions that bypass the caches and write directly to memory (see Chapter 5).

- **2001**: Intel added yet another 144 instructions, this time labeled SSE2. The new data type is double precision arithmetic, which allows pairs of 64-bit floating-point operations in parallel. Almost all of these 144 instructions are versions of existing MMX and SSE instructions that operate on 64 bits of data in parallel. Not only does this change enable more multimedia operations, it gives the compiler a different target for floating-point operations than the unique stack architecture. Compilers can choose to use the eight SSE registers as floating-point registers like those found in other computers. This change boosted the floating-point performance of the Pentium 4, the first microprocessor to include SSE2 instructions.

- **2003**: A company other than Intel enhanced the x86 architecture this time. AMD announced a set of architectural extensions to increase the address space from 32 to 64 bits. Similar to the transition from a 16- to 32-bit address space in 1985 with the 80386, AMD64 widens all registers to 64 bits. It also increases the number of registers to 16 and increases the number of 128-bit SSE registers to 16. The primary ISA change comes from adding a new mode called *long mode* that redefines the execution of all x86 instructions with 64-bit addresses and data. To address the larger number of registers, it adds a new prefix to instructions. Depending how you count, long mode also adds four to ten new instructions and drops 27 old ones. PC-relative data addressing is another extension. AMD64 still has a mode that is identical to x86 (*legacy mode*) plus a mode that restricts user programs to x86 but allows operating systems to use AMD64 (*compatibility mode*). These modes allowed a more graceful transition to 64-bit addressing than the HP/Intel IA-64 architecture.

- **2004**: Intel capitulates and embraces AMD64, relabeling it *Extended Memory 64 Technology* (EM64T). The major difference is that Intel added a 128-bit atomic compare and swap instruction, which probably should have been included in AMD64. At the same time, Intel announced another generation of media extensions. SSE3 adds 13 instructions to support complex arithmetic, graphics operations on arrays of structures, video encoding, floating-point conversion, and thread synchronization (see Section 2.11). AMD added SSE3 in subsequent chips and the missing atomic swap instruction to AMD64 to maintain binary compatibility with Intel.

- **2006**: Intel announces 54 new instructions as part of the SSE4 instruction set extensions. These extensions perform tweaks like sum of absolute differences, dot products for arrays of structures, sign or zero extension of narrow data to wider sizes, population count, and so on. They also added support for virtual machines (see Chapter 5).

- **2007**: AMD announces 170 instructions as part of SSE5, including 46 instructions of the base instruction set that adds three operand instructions like MIPS.

- **2011**: Intel ships the Advanced Vector Extension that expands the SSE register width from 128 to 256 bits, thereby redefining about 250 instructions and adding 128 new instructions.

- **2015**: Intel ships AVX-512, which widens the registers and operations from 256 to 512 bits, and once again redefines hundreds of instructions as well as adds many more.

This history illustrates the impact of the "golden handcuffs" of compatibility on the x86, as the existing software base at each step was too important to jeopardize with significant architectural changes.

Whatever the artistic failures of the x86, keep in mind that this instruction set largely drove the PC generation of computers and still dominates the cloud portion of the PostPC Era. Manufacturing 250M x86 chips per year may seem small compared to billions of ARMv7 chips, but many companies would love to control such a market since the chips are much more expensive. Nevertheless, this checkered ancestry has led to an architecture that is difficult to explain and impossible to love.

Brace yourself for what you are about to see! Do *not* try to read this section with the care you would need to write x86 programs; the goal instead is to give you familiarity with the strengths and weaknesses of the world's most popular desktop architecture.

Rather than show the entire 16-bit, 32-bit, and 64-bit instruction set, in this section we concentrate on the 32-bit subset that originated with the 80386. We start our explanation with the registers and addressing modes, move on to the integer operations, and conclude with an examination of instruction encoding.

x86 Registers and Data Addressing Modes

The registers of the 80386 show the evolution of the instruction set (Figure 2.36). The 80386 extended all 16-bit registers (except the segment registers) to 32 bits, prefixing an *E* to their name to indicate the 32-bit version. We'll refer to them generically as GPRs (*general-purpose registers*). The 80386 contains only eight GPRs. This means MIPS programs can use four times as many and ARMv7 twice as many.

Figure 2.37 shows the arithmetic, logical, and data transfer instructions are two-operand instructions. There are two important differences here. The x86 arithmetic and logical instructions must have one operand act as both a source and a destination; ARMv7 and MIPS allow separate registers for source and destination. This restriction puts more pressure on the limited registers, since one source register must be modified. The second important difference is that one of the operands can be in memory. Thus, virtually any instruction may have one operand in memory, unlike ARMv7 and MIPS.

Data memory-addressing modes, described in detail below, offer two sizes of addresses within the instruction. These so-called *displacements* can be 8 bits or 32 bits.

Although a memory operand can use any addressing mode, there are restrictions on which *registers* can be used in a mode. Figure 2.38 shows the x86 addressing modes and which GPRs cannot be used with each mode, as well as how to get the same effect using MIPS instructions.

x86 Integer Operations

The 8086 provides support for both 8-bit (*byte*) and 16-bit (*word*) data types. The 80386 adds 32-bit addresses and data (*double words*) in the x86. (AMD64 adds 64-bit addresses and data, called *quad words*; we'll stick to the 80386 in this section.) The data type distinctions apply to register operations as well as memory accesses.

Almost every operation works on both 8-bit data and on one longer data size. That size is determined by the mode and is either 16 bits or 32 bits.

Clearly, some programs want to operate on data of all three sizes, so the 80386 architects provided a convenient way to specify each version without expanding code size significantly. They decided that either 16-bit or 32-bit data dominates most programs, and so it made sense to be able to set a default large size. This default data size is set by a bit in the code segment register. To override the default data size, an 8-bit *prefix* is attached to the instruction to tell the machine to use the other large size for this instruction.

The prefix solution was borrowed from the 8086, which allows multiple prefixes to modify instruction behavior. The three original prefixes override the default

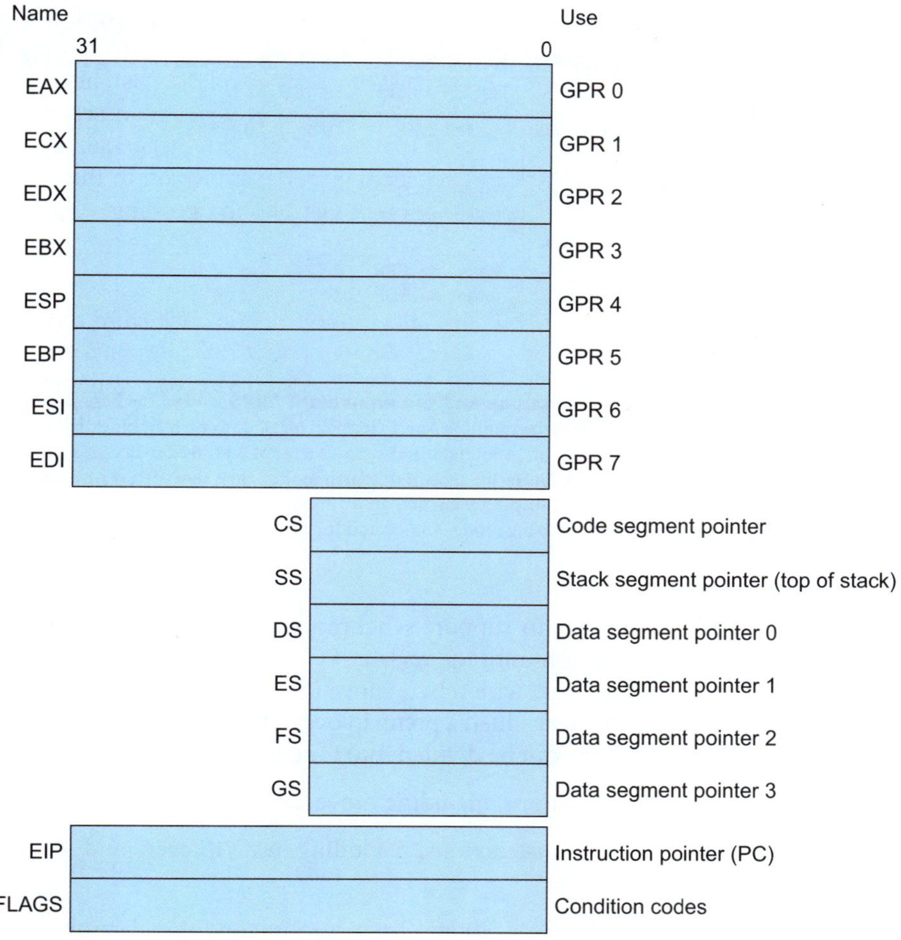

FIGURE 2.36 The 80386 register set. Starting with the 80386, the top eight registers were extended to 32 bits and could also be used as general-purpose registers.

Source/destination operand type	Second source operand
Register	Register
Register	Immediate
Register	Memory
Memory	Register
Memory	Immediate

FIGURE 2.37 Instruction types for the arithmetic, logical, and data transfer instructions. The x86 allows the combinations shown. The only restriction is the absence of a memory-memory mode. Immediates may be 8, 16, or 32 bits in length; a register is any one of the 14 major registers in Figure 2.36 (not EIP or EFLAGS).

Mode	Description	Register restrictions	MIPS equivalent
Register indirect	Address is in a register.	Not ESP or EBP	`lw $s0,0($s1)`
Based mode with 8- or 32-bit displacement	Address is contents of base register plus displacement.	Not ESP	`lw $s0,100($s1) # <= 16-bit` `                # displacement`

Base plus scaled index	The address is
	Base + (2^{Scale} x Index)
	where Scale has the value 0, 1, 2, or 3.
		Base: any GPR
		Index: not ESP
			`mul  $t0,$s2,4`
			`add  $t0,$t0,$s1`
			`lw   $s0,0($t0)`

Base plus scaled index with 8- or 32-bit displacement	The address is
	Base + (2^{Scale} x Index) + displacement
	where Scale has the value 0, 1, 2, or 3.
		Base: any GPR
		Index: not ESP
			`mul  $t0,$s2,4`
			`add  $t0,$t0,$s1`
			`lw   $s0,100($t0) #<=16-bit`
			`                  # displacement`

FIGURE 2.38 x86 32-bit addressing modes with register restrictions and the equivalent MIPS code. The Base plus Scaled Index addressing mode, not found in ARM or MIPS, is included to avoid the multiplies by 4 (scale factor of 2) to turn an index in a register into a byte address (see Figures 2.25 and 2.27). A scale factor of 1 is used for 16-bit data, and a scale factor of 3 for 64-bit data. A scale factor of 0 means the address is not scaled. If the displacement is longer than 16 bits in the second or fourth modes, then the MIPS equivalent mode would need two more instructions: a `lui` to load the upper 16 bits of the displacement and an `add` to sum the upper address with the base register `$s1`. (Intel gives two different names to what is called Based addressing mode—Based and Indexed—but they are essentially identical and we combine them here.)

segment register, lock the bus to support synchronization (see Section 2.11), or repeat the following instruction until the register ECX counts down to 0. This last prefix was intended to be paired with a byte move instruction to move a variable number of bytes. The 80386 also added a prefix to override the default address size.

The x86 integer operations can be divided into four major classes:

1. Data movement instructions, including move, push, and pop

2. Arithmetic and logic instructions, including test, integer, and decimal arithmetic operations

3. Control flow, including conditional branches, unconditional jumps, calls, and returns

4. String instructions, including string move and string compare

The first two categories are unremarkable, except that the arithmetic and logic instruction operations allow the destination to be either a register or a memory location. Figure 2.39 shows some typical x86 instructions and their functions.

Conditional branches on the x86 are based on *condition codes* or *flags*, like ARMv7. Condition codes are set as a side effect of an operation; most are used to compare the value of a result to 0. Branches then test the condition codes. PC-relative branch addresses must be specified in the number of bytes, since unlike ARMv7 and MIPS, 80386 instructions are not all 4 bytes in length.

String instructions are part of the 8080 ancestry of the x86 and are not commonly executed in most programs. They are often slower than equivalent software routines (see the fallacy on page 167).

Figure 2.40 lists some of the integer x86 instructions. Many of the instructions are available in both byte and word formats.

Instruction	Function
`je name`	`if equal(condition code) {EIP=name};` `EIP-128 <= name < EIP+128`
`jmp name`	`EIP=name`
`call name`	`SP=SP-4; M[SP]=EIP+5; EIP=name;`
`movw EBX,[EDI+45]`	`EBX=M[EDI+45]`
`push ESI`	`SP=SP-4; M[SP]=ESI`
`pop EDI`	`EDI=M[SP]; SP=SP+4`
`add EAX,#6765`	`EAX= EAX+6765`
`test EDX,#42`	Set condition code (flags) with EDX and 42
`movsl`	`M[EDI]=M[ESI];` `EDI=EDI+4; ESI=ESI+4`

FIGURE 2.39 Some typical x86 instructions and their functions. A list of frequent operations appears in Figure 2.40. The CALL saves the EIP of the next instruction on the stack. (EIP is the Intel PC.)

Instruction	Meaning
Control	**Conditional and unconditional branches**
`jnz, jz`	Jump if condition to EIP + 8-bit offset; `JNE` (for `JNZ`), `JE` (for `JZ`) are alternative names
`jmp`	Unconditional jump—8-bit or 16-bit offset
`call`	Subroutine call—16-bit offset; return address pushed onto stack
`ret`	Pops return address from stack and jumps to it
`loop`	Loop branch—decrement ECX; jump to EIP + 8-bit displacement if ECX $\neq 0$
Data transfer	**Move data between registers or between register and memory**
`move`	Move between two registers or between register and memory
`push, pop`	Push source operand on stack; pop operand from stack top to a register
`les`	Load ES and one of the GPRs from memory
Arithmetic, logical	**Arithmetic and logical operations using the data registers and memory**
`add, sub`	Add source to destination; subtract source from destination; register-memory format
`cmp`	Compare source and destination; register-memory format
`shl, shr, rcr`	Shift left; shift logical right; rotate right with carry condition code as fill
`cbw`	Convert byte in eight rightmost bits of EAX to 16-bit word in right of EAX
`test`	Logical AND of source and destination sets condition codes
`inc, dec`	Increment destination, decrement destination
`or, xor`	Logical OR; exclusive OR; register-memory format
String	**Move between string operands; length given by a repeat prefix**
`movs`	Copies from string source to destination by incrementing ESI and EDI; may be repeated
`lods`	Loads a byte, word, or doubleword of a string into the EAX register

FIGURE 2.40 Some typical operations on the x86. Many operations use register-memory format, where either the source or the destination may be memory and the other may be a register or immediate operand.

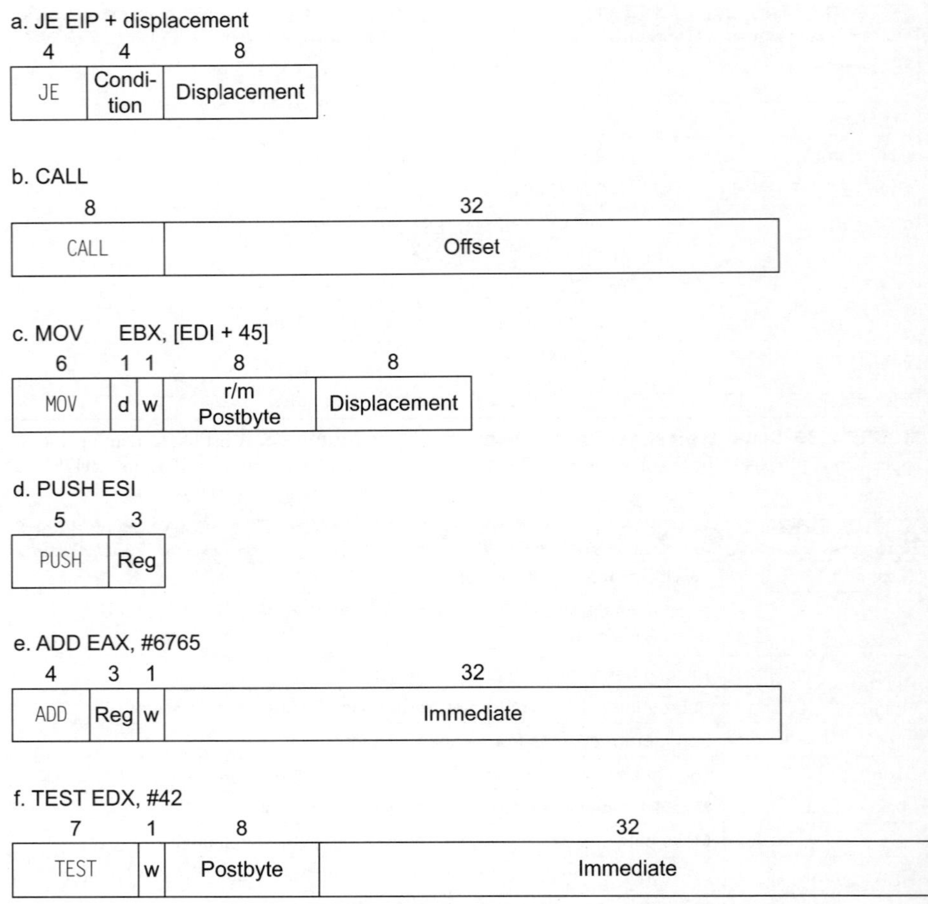

FIGURE 2.41 Typical x86 instruction formats. Figure 2.42 shows the encoding of the postbyte. Many instructions contain the 1-bit field w, which says whether the operation is a byte or a double word. The d field in MOV is used in instructions that may move to or from memory and shows the direction of the move. The ADD instruction requires 32 bits for the immediate field, because in 32-bit mode, the immediates are either 8 bits or 32 bits. The immediate field in the TEST is 32 bits long because there is no 8-bit immediate for test in 32-bit mode. Overall, instructions may vary from 1 to 15 bytes in length. The long length comes from extra 1-byte prefixes, having both a 4-byte immediate and a 4-byte displacement address, using an opcode of 2 bytes, and using the scaled index mode specifier, which adds another byte.

x86 Instruction Encoding

Saving the worst for last, the encoding of instructions in the 80386 is complex, with many different instruction formats. Instructions for the 80386 may vary from 1 byte, when there are no operands, up to 15 bytes.

Figure 2.41 shows the instruction format for several of the example instructions in Figure 2.39. The opcode byte usually contains a bit saying whether the operand is 8 bits or 32 bits. For some instructions, the opcode may include the addressing mode and the register; this is true in many instructions that have the form "register = register op

reg	w = 0	w = 1 16b	w = 1 32b	r/m	mod = 0 16b	mod = 0 32b	mod = 1 16b	mod = 1 32b	mod = 2 16b	mod = 2 32b	mod = 3
0	AL	AX	EAX	0	addr=BX+SI	=EAX	same	same	same	same	same
1	CL	CX	ECX	1	addr=BX+DI	=ECX	addr as	addr as	addr as	addr as	as
2	DL	DX	EDX	2	addr=BP+SI	=EDX	mod=0	mod=0	mod=0	mod=0	reg
3	BL	BX	EBX	3	addr=BP+SI	=EBX	+ disp8	+ disp8	+ disp16	+ disp32	field
4	AH	SP	ESP	4	addr=SI	=(sib)	SI+disp8	(sib)+disp8	SI+disp16	(sib)+disp32	"
5	CH	BP	EBP	5	addr=DI	=disp32	DI+disp8	EBP+disp8	DI+disp16	EBP+disp32	"
6	DH	SI	ESI	6	addr=disp16	=ESI	BP+disp8	ESI+disp8	BP+disp16	ESI+disp32	"
7	BH	DI	EDI	7	addr=BX	=EDI	BX+disp8	EDI+disp8	BX+disp16	EDI+disp32	"

FIGURE 2.42 The encoding of the first address specifier of the x86: mod, reg, r/m. The first four columns show the encoding of the 3-bit reg field, which depends on the w bit from the opcode and whether the machine is in 16-bit mode (8086) or 32-bit mode (80386). The remaining columns explain the mod and r/m fields. The meaning of the 3-bit r/m field depends on the value in the 2-bit mod field and the address size. Basically, the registers used in the address calculation are listed in the sixth and seventh columns, under mod = 0, with mod = 1 adding an 8-bit displacement and mod = 2 adding a 16-bit or 32-bit displacement, depending on the address mode. The exceptions are 1) r/m = 6 when mod = 1 or mod = 2 in 16-bit mode selects BP plus the displacement; 2) r/m = 5 when mod = 1 or mod = 2 in 32-bit mode selects EBP plus displacement; and 3) r/m = 4 in 32-bit mode when mod does not equal 3, where (sib) means use the scaled index mode shown in Figure 2.38. When mod = 3, the r/m field indicates a register, using the same encoding as the reg field combined with the w bit.

immediate." Other instructions use a "postbyte" or extra opcode byte, labeled "mod, reg, r/m," which contains the addressing mode information. This postbyte is used for many of the instructions that address memory. The base plus scaled index mode uses a second postbyte, labeled "sc, index, base."

Figure 2.42 shows the encoding of the two postbyte address specifiers for both 16-bit and 32-bit mode. Unfortunately, to understand fully which registers and which addressing modes are available, you need to see the encoding of all addressing modes and sometimes even the encoding of the instructions.

x86 Conclusion

Intel had a 16-bit microprocessor two years before its competitors' more elegant architectures, such as the Motorola 68000, and this head start led to the selection of the 8086 as the CPU for the IBM PC. Intel engineers generally acknowledge that the x86 is more difficult to build than computers like ARMv7 and MIPS, but the large market meant in the PC Era that AMD and Intel could afford more resources to help overcome the added complexity. What the x86 lacks in style, it made up for in market size, making it beautiful from the right perspective.

Its saving grace is that the most frequently used x86 architectural components are not too difficult to implement, as AMD and Intel have demonstrated by rapidly improving performance of integer programs since 1978. To get that performance, compilers must avoid the portions of the architecture that are hard to implement fast.

In the PostPC Era, however, despite considerable architectural and manufacturing expertise, x86 has not yet been competitive in the personal mobile device.

2.20   Going Faster: Matrix Multiply in C

We start by rewriting the Python program from Section 1.10. Figure 2.43 shows a version of a matrix–matrix multiply written in C. This program is commonly called *DGEMM*, which stands for Double precision GEneral Matrix Multiply. Because we are passing the matrix dimension as the parameter n, this version of DGEMM uses single dimensional versions of matrices C, A, and B and address arithmetic to get better performance instead of using the more intuitive two-dimensional arrays that we saw in Python. The comments in the figure remind us of this more intuitive notation. Figure 2.44 shows the x86 assembly language output for the inner loop of Figure 2.43. The five floating-point instructions start with a v and include sd in the name, which stands for scalar double precision.

Figure 2.45 shows the performance of the C program as were vary the optimization parameter as compared to the Python program. Even the unoptimized C program is dramatically faster. As we increase optimization levels, it gets even faster; the cost is longer compile time. The reasons for the speed-up are fundamentally using a compiler instead of an interpreter and because the type declarations of C allow the compiler to produce much more efficient code.

```
1.  void dgemm (int n, double* A, double* B, double* C)
2.  {
3.    for (int i = 0; i < n; ++i)
4.      for (int j = 0; j < n; ++j)
5.      {
6.        double cij = C[i+j*n]; /* cij = C[i][j] */
7.        for( int k = 0; k < n; k++ )
8.          cij += A[i+k*n] * B[k+j*n]; /* cij += A[i][k]*B[k][j] */
9.        C[i+j*n] = cij; /* C[i][j] = cij */
10.     }
11. }
```

FIGURE 2.43 C version of a double precision matrix multiply, widely known as DGEMM for Double-precision GEneral Matrix Multiply (GEMM).

```
 1.  vmovsd (%r10),%xmm0            # Load 1 element of C into %xmm0
 2.  mov    %rsi,%rcx               # register %rcx = %rsi
 3.  xor    %eax,%eax               # register %eax = 0
 4.  vmovsd (%rcx),%xmm1            # Load 1 element of B into %xmm1
 5.  add    %r9,%rcx                # register %rcx = %rcx + %r9
 6.  vmulsd (%r8,%rax,8),%xmm1,%xmm1 # Multiply %xmm1, element of A
 7.  add    $0x1,%rax               # register %rax = %rax + 1
 8.  cmp    %eax,%edi               # compare %eax to %edi
 9.  vaddsd %xmm1,%xmm0,%xmm0       # Add %xmm1, %xmm0
10.  jg     30 <dgemm+0x30>         # jump if %eax > %edi
11.  add    $0x1,%r11               # register %r11 = %r11 + 1
12.  vmovsd %xmm0,(%r10)            # Store %xmm0 into C element
```

FIGURE 2.44 The x86 assembly language for the body of the nested loops generated by compiling the unoptimized C code in Figure 2.43 using gcc with −O3 optimization flags.

−O0 (fastest compile time)	−O1	−O2	−O3 (fastest run time)
77	208	212	212

FIGURE 2.45 Performance over the Python program on page 49 for the C program in Figure 2.43 as we increase the level of optimization of the GCC C compiler, with −O0 doing no code size or performance optimization, thereby improving compile time and −O3 being most aggressive for run time and code size. In this case, −O2 and −O3 produce the same x86 code. Most programmers use −O2 as the default compiler flag. GCC also offers a −Os optimization option, which aims at smallest code size.

2.21　Fallacies and Pitfalls

Fallacy: More powerful instructions mean higher performance.

Part of the power of the Intel x86 is the prefixes that can modify the execution of the following instruction. One prefix can repeat the following instruction until a counter counts down to 0. Thus, to move data in memory, it would seem that the natural instruction sequence is to use move with the repeat prefix to perform 32-bit memory-to-memory moves.

An alternative method, which uses the standard instructions found in all computers, is to load the data into the registers and then store the registers back to memory. This second version of this program, with the code replicated to reduce loop overhead, copies at about 1.5 times faster. A third version, which uses the larger floating-point registers instead of the integer registers of the x86, copies at about 2.0 times faster than the complex move instruction.

Fallacy: Write in assembly language to obtain the highest performance.

At one time compilers for programming languages produced naïve instruction sequences; the increasing sophistication of compilers means the gap between compiled code and code produced by hand is closing fast. In fact, to compete with current compilers, the assembly language programmer needs to understand the concepts in Chapters 4 and 5 thoroughly (processor pipelining and memory hierarchy).

This battle between compilers and assembly language coders is one situation in which humans are losing ground. For example, C offers the programmer a chance to give a hint to the compiler about which variables to keep in registers versus spilled to memory. When compilers were poor at register allocation, such hints were vital to performance. In fact, some old C text-books spent a fair amount of time giving examples that effectively use register hints. Today's C compilers generally ignore such hints, because the compiler does a better job at allocation than the programmer does.

Even *if* writing by hand resulted in faster code, the dangers of writing in assembly language are the longer time spent coding and debugging, the loss in portability, and the difficulty of maintaining such code. One of the few widely accepted axioms of software engineering is that coding takes longer if you write more lines, and it clearly takes many more lines to write a program in assembly language than in C or Java. Moreover, once it is coded, the next danger is that it will become a popular program. Such programs always live longer than expected, meaning that someone will have to update the code over several years and make it work with new releases of operating systems and new models of machines. Writing in higher-level language instead of assembly language not only allows future compilers to tailor the code to future machines, it also makes the software easier to maintain and allows the program to run on more instruction set architectures.

Fallacy: The importance of commercial binary compatibility means successful instruction sets don't change.

While backwards binary compatibility is sacrosanct, Figure 2.46 shows that the x86 architecture has grown dramatically. The average is more than one instruction per month over its 40-year lifetime!

Pitfall: Forgetting that sequential word addresses in machines with byte addressing do not differ by one.

Many an assembly language programmer has toiled over errors made by assuming that the address of the next word can be found by incrementing the address in a register by one instead of by the word size in bytes. Forewarned is forearmed!

Pitfall: Using a pointer to an automatic variable outside its defining procedure.

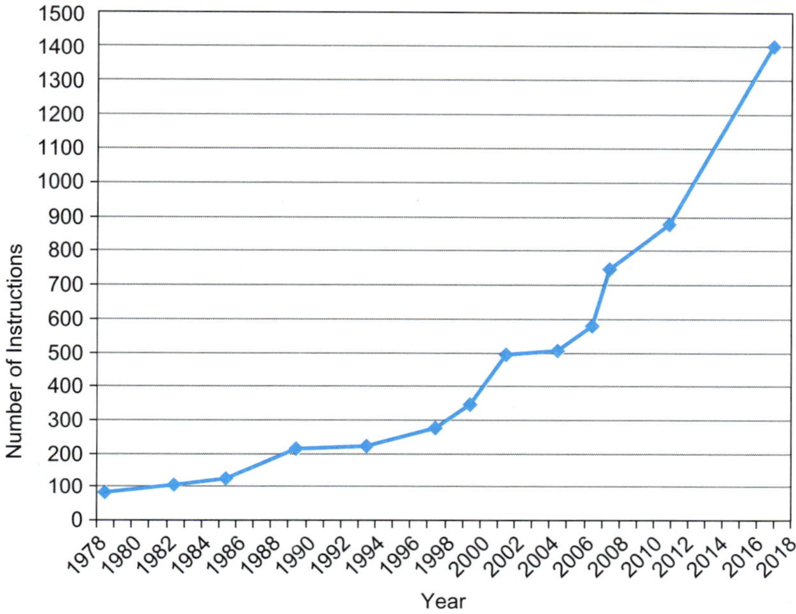

FIGURE 2.46 Growth of x86 instruction set over time. While there is clear technical value to some of these extensions, this rapid change also increases the difficulty for other companies to try to build compatible processors.

A common mistake in dealing with pointers is to pass a result from a procedure that includes a pointer to an array that is local to that procedure. Following the stack discipline in Figure 2.12, the memory that contains the local array will be reused as soon as the procedure returns. Pointers to automatic variables can lead to chaos.

2.22 Concluding Remarks

The two principles of the *stored-program* computer are the use of instructions that are indistinguishable from numbers and the use of alterable memory for programs. These principles allow a single machine to aid environmental scientists, financial advisers, and novelists in their specialties. The selection of a set of instructions that the machine can understand demands a delicate balance among the number of instructions needed to execute a program, the number of clock cycles needed by an instruction, and the speed of the clock. As illustrated in this chapter, three design principles guide the authors of instruction sets in making that delicate balance:

Less is more.

Robert Browning,
Andrea del Sarto, 1855

1. *Simplicity favors regularity.* Regularity motivates many features of the MIPS instruction set: keeping all instructions a single size, always requiring three register operands in arithmetic instructions, and keeping the register fields in the same place in each instruction format.

2. *Smaller is faster.* The desire for speed is the reason that MIPS has 32 registers rather than many more.

3. *Good design demands good compromises.* One MIPS example was the compromise between providing for larger addresses and constants in instructions and keeping all instructions the same length.

Another big idea in this chapter is that numbers have no inherent type. A given bit pattern can represent an integer number, or a string, or a color, or even an instruction. It is the program that determines the type of the data.

COMMON CASE FAST

We also saw the great idea of **making the common case fast** applied to instruction sets as well as computer architecture. Examples of making the common MIPS case fast include PC-relative addressing for conditional branches and immediate addressing for larger constant operands.

Above this machine level is assembly language, a language that humans can read. The assembler translates it into the binary numbers that machines can understand, and it even "extends" the instruction set by creating symbolic instructions that aren't in the hardware. For instance, constants or addresses that are too big are broken into properly sized pieces, common variations of instructions are given their own name, and so on. Figure 2.47 lists the MIPS instructions we have covered so far, both real and pseudoinstructions. Hiding details from the higher level is another example of the great idea of **abstraction**.

ABSTRACTION

Each category of MIPS instructions is associated with constructs that appear in programming languages:

- Arithmetic instructions correspond to the operations found in assignment statements.

- Transfer instructions are most likely to occur when dealing with data structures like arrays or structures.

- Conditional branches are used in *if* statements and in loops.

- Unconditional jumps are used in procedure calls and returns and for *case/ switch* statements.

These instructions are not born equal; the popularity of the few dominates the many. For example, Figure 2.48 shows the popularity of each class of instructions for SPEC CPU2006. The varying popularity of instructions plays an important role in the chapters about datapath, control, and pipelining.

After we explain computer arithmetic in Chapter 3, we reveal the rest of the MIPS instruction set architecture.

MIPS instructions	Name	Format	Pseudo MIPS	Name	Format
add	add	R	move	move	R
subtract	sub	R	multiply	mult	R
add immediate	addi	I	multiply immediate	multi	I
load word	lw	I	load immediate	li	I
store word	sw	I	branch less than	blt	I
load half	lh	I	branch less than or equal	ble	I
load half unsigned	lhu	I			
store half	sh	I	branch greater than	bgt	I
load byte	lb	I	branch greater than or equal	bge	I
load byte unsigned	lbu	I			
store byte	sb	I			
load linked	ll	I			
store conditional	sc	I			
load upper immediate	lui	I			
and	and	R			
or	or	R			
nor	nor	R			
and immediate	andi	I			
or immediate	ori	I			
shift left logical	sll	R			
shift right logical	srl	R			
branch on equal	beq	I			
branch on not equal	bne	I			
set less than	slt	R			
set less than immediate	slti	I			
set less than immediate unsigned	sltiu	I			
jump	j	J			
jump register	jr	R			
jump and link	jal	J			

FIGURE 2.47 The MIPS instruction set covered so far, with the real MIPS instructions on the left and the pseudoinstructions on the right. Appendix A (Section A.10) describes the full MIPS architecture. Figure 2.1 shows more details of the MIPS architecture revealed in this chapter. The information given here is also found in Columns 1 and 2 of the MIPS Reference Data Card at the front of the book.

Instruction class	MIPS examples	HLL correspondence	Frequency	
			Integer	Ft. pt.
Arithmetic	add, sub, addi	Operations in assignment statements	16%	48%
Data transfer	lw, sw, lb, lbu, lh, lhu, sb, lui	References to data structures, such as arrays	35%	36%
Logical	and, or, nor, andi, ori, sll, srl	Operations in assignment statements	12%	4%
Conditional branch	beq, bne, slt, slti, sltiu	*If* statements and loops	34%	8%
Jump	j, jr, jal	Procedure calls, r eturns, and *case/switch* statements	2%	0%

FIGURE 2.48 MIPS instruction classes, examples, correspondence to high-level program language constructs, and percentage of MIPS instructions executed by category for the average integer and floating point SPEC CPU2006 benchmarks. Figure 3.24 in Chapter 3 shows average percentage of the individual MIPS instructions executed.

2.23   Historical Perspective and Further Reading

This section surveys the history of *instruction set architectures* (ISAs) over time, and we give a short history of programming languages and compilers. ISAs include accumulator architectures, general-purpose register architectures, stack architectures, and a brief history of ARM and the x86. We also review the controversial subjects of high-level-language computer architectures and reduced instruction set computer (RISC) architectures. The history of programming languages includes Fortran, Lisp, Algol, C, Cobol, Pascal, Simula, Smalltalk, C++, and Java, and the history of compilers includes the key milestones and the pioneers who achieved them. The rest of  **Section 2.23** is found online.

2.24   Self-Study

Instructions as Numbers. Given this binary number:

00000001010010110100100000100000$_{\text{two}}$

What is it in hexadecimal format?
Assuming it is an unsigned number, what is it in decimal?
Does the value change if it is considered a signed number?
What assembly language program does it represent?

Instructions as Numbers and Insecurity. Although programs are just numbers in memory, Chapter 5 shows how to tell the computer how to protect the program from being modified by labeling a portion of the address space as read-only. Clever attackers exploit bugs in C programs to nevertheless insert their own code during program execution despite that program being protected.

Here is a simple string copy program that copies what the user types into a local variable on the stack.

```c
#include <string.h>
void copyinput (char *input)
{
   char copy[10];
   strcpy(copy, input); // no bounds checking in strcpy
}
int main (int argc, char **argv)
{
   copyinput(argv[1]);
   return 0;
}
```

What happens if the user writes much more than 10 characters as input? What could be the consequence to program execution? How could this let an attacker take over program execution?

While being faster. Here is the MIPS code for the C while loop from pages 98–99:

```
Loop: sll  $t1,$s3,2      # Temp reg $t1 = i * 4
      add  $t1,$t1,$s6    # $t1 = address of save[i]
      lw   $t0,0($t1)     # Temp reg $t0 = save[i]
      bne  $t0,$s5, Exit  # go to Exit if save[i] ≠ k
      addi $s3,$s3,1      # i = i + 1
      j    Loop           # go to Loop
Exit:
```

Assume the loop typically executes 10 times. Make the loop faster by executing on average one branch instruction per loop rather than both one jump instruction and one branch instruction.

The Anti-Compiler. Here is a portion of MIPS assembly language with comments for the first five instructions.

```
sll $t0, $s0, 2      # $t0 = f * 4
add $t0, $s6, $t0    # $t0 = &A[f]
sll $t1, $s1, 2      # $t1 = g * 4
add $t1, $s7, $t1    # $t1 = &B[g]
lw $s0, 0($t0)       # f = A[f]
addi $t2, $t0, 4     #
lw $t0, 0($t2)       #
add $t0, $t0, $s0    #
sw $t0, 0($t1)       #
```

Assume that the variables f, g, h, i, and j are assigned to registers $s0, $s1, $s2, $s3, and $s4, respectively. Assume that the base address of the arrays A and B are in registers $s6 and $s7, respectively. Complete the comments for the last four instructions.

Self-Study Answers

Instructions as Numbers.

Binary: **00000001010010110100100000100000**$_{two}$

Hexadecimal: **014B4820**$_{hex}$

Decimal: **21710880**$_{ten}$
Since the leading bit is a 0, it is the same decimal value whether signed or unsigned integer.

Assembly language:

```
add t1, t2, t3
```

Machine language:

31 2625	2120	1615	1110	65	0
SPECIAL 000000	t2 01010	t3 01011	t1 01001	0 00000	ADD 100000
6	5	5	5	5	6

Instructions as Numbers and Insecurity.
The local variable copy can safely copy user input up to nine characters followed by the null character that terminates a string. Anything longer will overwrite other values on the stack. As the stack grows down, the values below the stack include stack frames from earlier procedure calls, which include return addresses. A careful attacker can not only insert code onto the stack but can overwrite return addresses in the stack so that the program could eventually use the attacker's return address to start executing code placed on the stack after some procedures returned.

While being faster. The trick is to invert the conditional branch and have it jump to the top of the loop rather than having it skip the jump at the bottom of the loop. To match the semantics of the while loop, the code must first check to see if save[i] == k before incrementing i.

```
      sll $t1,$s3,2       # Temp reg $t1 = i * 4
      add $t1,$t1,$s6     # $t1 = address of save[i]
      lw $t0,0($t1)       # Temp reg $t0 = save[i]
      bne $t0,$s5, Exit   # go to Exit if save[i] ≠ k
Loop: addi $s3,$s3,1      # i = i + 1
      sll $t1,$s3,2       # Temp reg $t1 = i * 4
      add $t1,$t1,$s6     # $t1 = address of save[i]
      lw $t0,0($t1)       # Temp reg $t0 = save[i]
      beq $t0,$s5, Loop   # go to Loop if save[i] = k
Exit:
```

The Anti-Compiler.

```
sll $t0, $s0, 2      # $t0 = f * 4
add $t0, $s6, $t0    # $t0 = &A[f]
sll $t1, $s1, 2      # $t1 = g * 4
add $t1, $s7, $t1    # $t1 = &B[g]
lw $s0, 0($t0)       # f = A[f]
addi $t2, $t0, 4     # $t2=$t0+4 => $t2 points to A[f+1] now
lw $t0, 0($t2)       # $t0 = A[f+1]
add $t0, $t0, $s0    # $t0 = $t0 + $s0=> $t0 is now A[f]+A[f+1]
sw $t0, 0($t1)       # store the result into B[g]
```

2.25   Exercises

Appendix A describes the MIPS simulator, which is helpful for these exercises. Although the simulator accepts pseudoinstructions, try not to use pseudoinstructions for any exercises that ask you to produce MIPS code. Your goal should be to learn the real MIPS instruction set, and if you are asked to count instructions, your count should reflect the actual instructions that will be executed and not the pseudoinstructions.

There are some cases where pseudoinstructions must be used (for example, the la instruction when an actual value is not known at assembly time). In many cases, they are quite convenient and result in more readable code (for example, the li and move instructions). If you choose to use pseudoinstructions for these reasons, please add a sentence or two to your solution stating which pseudoinstructions you have used and why.

2.1 [5] <§2.2> For the following C statement, what is the corresponding MIPS assembly code? Assume that the C variables f, g, and h, have already been placed in registers $s0, $s1, and $s2, respectively. Use a minimal number of MIPS assembly instructions.

```
f = g + (h - 5);
```

2.2 [5] <§2.2> Write a single C statement that corresponds to the two MIPS assembly instructions below.

```
add f, g, h
add f, i, f
```

2.3 [5] <§§2.2, 2.3> For the following C statement, write the corresponding MIPS assembly code. Assume that the variables f, g, h, i, and j are assigned to registers $s0, $s1, $s2, $s3, and $s4, respectively. Assume that the base address of the arrays A and B are in registers $s6 and $s7, respectively.

```
B[8] = A[i-j];
```

2.4 [5] <§§2.2, 2.3> For the MIPS assembly instructions above, what is the corresponding C statement? Assume that the variables f, g, h, i, and j are assigned to registers $s0, $s1, $s2, $s3, and $s4, respectively. Assume that the base address of the arrays A and B are in registers $s6 and $s7, respectively.

```
sll   $t0, $s0, 2      # $t0 = f * 4
add   $t0, $s6, $t0    # $t0 = &A[f]
sll   $t1, $s1, 2      # $t1 = g * 4
add   $t1, $s7, $t1    # $t1 = &B[g]
lw    $s0, 0($t0)      # f = A[f]
addi  $t2, $t0, 4
lw    $t0, 0($t2)
add   $t0, $t0, $s0
sw    $t0, 0($t1)
```

2.5 [5] <§2.3> Show how the value 0xabcdef12 would be arranged in memory of a little-endian and a big-endian machine. Assume the data are stored starting at address 0 and that the word size is 4 bytes.

2.6 [5] <§2.4> Translate 0xabcdef12 into decimal.

2.7 [5] <§§2.2, 2.3> Translate the following C code to MIPS. Assume that the variables f, g, h, i, and j are assigned to registers $s0, $s1, $s2, $s3, and $s4, respectively. Assume that the base address of the arrays A and B are in registers $s6 and $s7, respectively. Assume that the elements of the arrays A and B are 8-byte words:

```
B[8] = A[i] + A[j];
```

2.8 [10] <§§2.2, 2.3> Translate the following MIPS code to C. Assume that the variables f, g, h, i, and j are assigned to registers $s0, $s1, $s2, $s3, and $s4, respectively. Assume that the base address of the arrays A and B are in registers $s6 and $s7, respectively.

```
addi  $t0, $s6, 4
add   $t1, $s6, $0
sw    $t1, 0($t0)
lw    $t0, 0($t0)
add   $s0, $t1, $t0
```

2.9 [20] <§§2.3, 2.5> For each MIPS instruction in Exercise 2.8, show the value of the opcode (op), source register (rs) and funct field, and destination register (rd) fields. For the I-type instructions, show the value of the immediate field, and for the R-type instructions, show the value of the second source register (rt).

2.10 Assume that registers $s0 and $s1 hold the values 0x8000000000000000 and 0xD000000000000000, respectively.

2.10.1 [5] <§2.4> What is the value of $t0 for the following assembly code?

```
add $t0, $s0, $s1
```

2.10.2 [5] <§2.4> Is the result in $t0 the desired result, or has there been overflow?

2.10.3 [5] <§2.4> For the contents of registers $s0 and $s1 as specified above, what is the value of $t0 for the following assembly code?

```
sub $t0, $s0, $s1
```

2.10.4 [5] <§2.4>Is the result in $t0 the desired result, or has there been overflow?

2.10.5 [5] <§2.4> For the contents of registers $s0 and $s1 as specified above, what is the value of $t0 for the following assembly code?

```
add $t0, $s0, $s1
add $t0, $t0, $s0
```

2.10.6 [5] <§2.4> Is the result in $t0 the desired result, or has there been overflow?

2.11 Assume that $s0 holds the value 128_{ten}.

2.11.1 [5] <§2.4> For the instruction add $t0, $s0, $s1, what is the range(s) of values for $s1 that would result in overflow?

2.11.2 [5] <§2.4> For the instruction `sub $t0, $s0, $s1`, what is the range(s) of values for $s1 that would result in overflow?

2.11.3 [5] <§2.4> For the instruction `sub $t0, $s1, $s0`, what is the range(s) of values for $s1 that would result in overflow?

2.12 [5] <§§2.4, 2.5>

Provide the type and assembly language instruction for the following binary value: `0000 0010 0001 0000 1000 0000 0010 0000`$_{two}$. Hint: Figure 2.20 may be helpful.

2.13 [5] <§§2.4, 2.5> Provide the type and hexadecimal representation of following instruction: `sw $t1, 32($t2)`

2.14 [5] <§2.5> Provide the type, assembly language instruction, and binary representation of instruction described by the following MIPS fields:

```
op=0, rs=3, rt=2, rd=3, shamt=0, funct=34
```

2.15 [5] <§2.5> Provide the type, assembly language instruction, and binary representation of instruction described by the following MIPS fields:

```
op=0x23, rs=1, rt=2, const=0x4
```

2.16 [5] <§2.5> Assume that we would like to expand the MIPS register file to 128 registers and expand the instruction set to contain four times as many instructions.

2.16.1 [5] <§2.5> How would this affect the size of each of the bit fields in the R-type instructions?

2.16.2 [5] <§2.5> How would this affect the size of each of the bit fields in the I-type instructions?

2.16.3 [5] <§§2.5, 2.10> How could each of two propose changes decrease the size of an MIPS assembly program? On the other hand, how could the proposed change increase the size of an MIPS assembly program?

2.17 Assume the following register contents:

```
$t0=0xAAAAAAAA, $t1=0x12345678
```

2.17.1 [5] <§2.6> For the register values shown above, what is the value of $t2 for the following sequence of instructions?

```
sll $t2, $t0, 44
or $t2, $t2, $t1
```

2.17.2 [5] <§2.6> For the register values shown above, what is the value of $t2 for the following sequence of instructions?

```
sll $t2, $t0, 4
andi $t2, $t2, -1
```

2.17.3 [5] <§2.6> For the register values shown above, what is the value of $t2 for the following sequence of instructions?

```
srl $t2, $t0, 3
andi $t2, $t2, 0xFFEF
```

2.18 [10] <§2.6> Find the shortest sequence of MIPS instructions that extracts bits 16 down to 11 from register $t0 and uses the value of this field to replace bits 31 down to 26 in register $t1 without changing the other bits of registers $t0 and $t1 (Be sure to test your code using $t0 = 0 and $t1 = 0xffffffffffffffff. Doing so may reveal a common oversight.).

2.19 [5] <§2.6> Provide a minimal set of MIPS instructions that may be used to implement the following pseudoinstruction:

```
not $t1, $t2        // bit-wise invert
```

2.20 [5] <§2.6> For the following C statement, write a minimal sequence of MIPS assembly instructions that does the identical operation. Assume $t0 = A and $s0 is the base address of C.

```
A = C[0] << 4;
```

2.21 [5] <§2.7> Assume $t0 holds the value 0x010100000. What is the value of $t2 after the following instructions?

```
        slt $t2, $0, $t0
        bne $t2, $0, ELSE
        j DONE
ELSE: addi $t2, $t2, 2
DONE:
```

2.22 Suppose the *program counter* (PC) is set to 0×20000000.

2.22.1 [5] <§2.10> What range of addresses can be reached using the MIPS *jump-and-link* (`jai`) instruction? (In other words, what is the set of possible values for the PC after the jump instruction executes?)

2.22.2 [5] <§2.10> What range of addresses can be reached using the MIPS *branch if equal* (`beq`) instruction? (In other words, what is the set of possible values for the PC after the branch instruction executes?)

2.23 Consider a proposed new instruction named `rpt`. This instruction combines a loop's condition check and counter decrement into a single instruction. For example, `rpt $s0, loop` would do the following:

```
if (x29 > 0) {
        x29 = x29 - 1;
        goto loop
}
```

2.23.1 [5] <§2.7, 2.10> If this instruction were to be implemented in the MIPS instruction set, what is the most appropriate instruction format?

2.23.2 [5] <§2.7> What is the shortest sequence of MIPS instructions that performs the same operation?

2.24 Consider the following MIPS loop:

```
LOOP: slt  $t2, $0,  $t1
      beq  $t2, $0,  DONE
      subi $t1, $t1, 1
      addi $s2, $s2, 2
      j    LOOP
DONE:
```

2.24.1 [5] <§2.7> Assume that the register `$t1` is initialized to the value 10. What is the value in register `$s0` assuming the `$s0` is initially zero?

2.24.2 [5] <§2.7> For each of the loops above, write the equivalent C code routine. Assume that the registers `$s1`, `$s2`, `$t1`, and `$t2` are integers A, B, i, and `temp`, respectively.

2.24.3 [5] <§2.7> For the loops written in MIPS assembly above, assume that the register `$t1` is initialized to the value N. How many MIPS instructions are executed?

2.25 [10] <§2.7> Translate the following C code to MIPS assembly code. Use a minimum number of instructions. Assume that the values of a, b, i, and j are in registers $s0, $s1, $t0, and $t1, respectively. Also, assume that register $s2 holds the base address of the array D.

```
for(i=0; i<a; i++)
    for(j=0; j<b; j++)
        D[4*j] = i + j;
```

2.26 [5] <§2.7> How many MIPS instructions does it take to implement the C code from Exercise 2.25? If the variables a and b are initialized to 10 and 1 and all elements of D are initially 0, what is the total number of MIPS instructions that is executed to complete the loop?

2.27 [5] <§2.7> Translate the following loop into C. Assume that the C-level integer i is held in register $t1, $s2 holds the C-level integer called result, and $s0 holds the base address of the integer MemArray.

```
            addi $t1, $0, 0
    LOOP:   lw   $s1, 0($s0)
            add  $s2, $s2, $s1
            addi $s0, $s0, 4
            addi $t1, $t1, 1
            slti $t2, $t1, 100
            bne  $t2, $s0, LOOP
```

2.28 [10] <§2.7> Rewrite the loop from Exercise 2.27 reduce the number of MIPS instructions executed. Hint: Notice that variable i is used only for loop control.

2.29 [30] <§2.8> Implement the following C code in MIPS assembly. Hint: Remember that the stack pointer must remain aligned on a multiple of 16.

```
int fib(int n){
    if (n==0)
        return 0;
    else if (n == 1)
        return 1;
    else
        return fib(n-1) + fib(n-2);
}
```

2.30 [20] <§2.8> For each function call, show the contents of the stack after the function call is made. Assume the stack pointer is originally at address 0x7ffffffc, and follow the register conventions as specified in Figure 2.11.

2.31 [20] <§2.8> Translate function f into MIPS assembly language. If you need to use registers $t0 through $t7, use the lower-numbered registers first. Assume the function declaration for func is "int f(int a, int b);". The code for function f is as follows:

```
int f(int a, int b, int c, int d){
  return func(func(a,b),c + d);
}
```

2.32 [5] <§2.8> Can we use the tail-call optimization in this function? If no, explain why not. If yes, what is the difference in the number of executed instructions in f with and without the optimization?

2.33 [5] <§2.8> Right before your function f from Exercise 2.31 returns, what do we know about contents of registers $t5, $s3, $ra, and $sp? Keep in mind that we know what the entire function f looks like, but for function func we only know its declaration.

2.34 [30] <§2.9> Write a program in MIPS assembly language to convert an ASCII number string containing positive and negative integer decimal strings, to an integer. Your program should expect register $a0 to hold the address of a null-terminated string containing some combination of the digits 0 through 9. Your program should compute the integer value equivalent to this string of digits, then place the number in register $v0. If a non-digit character appears anywhere in the string, your program should stop with the value −1 in register $v0. For example, if register $t0 points to a sequence of three bytes 50_{ten}, 52_{ten}, 0_{ten} (the null-terminated string "24"), then when the program stops, register $v0 should contain the value 24_{ten}. The RISC-V mul instruction takes two registers as input. There is no "muli" instruction. Thus, just store the constant 10 in a register.

2.35 [5] <§2.9> For the following code:

```
lbu $t0, 0($t1)
sw  $t0, 0($t2)
```

Assume that the register $t1 contains the address 0x10000000 and the data at address is 0x11223344.

2.35.1 [5] <§2.3, 2.9> What value is stored in 0x10000004 on a big-endian machine?

2.35.2 [5] <§2.3, 2.9> What value is stored in 0x10000004 on a little-endian machine?

2.36 [5] <§2.10> Write the MIPS assembly code that creates the 32-bit constant ll/sc and stores that value to register $t1.

2.37 [10] <§2.11> Write the MIPS assembly code to implement the following C code as an atomic "set max" operation using the lI/sc instructions. Here, the argument shvar contains the address of a shared variable, which should be replaced by x if x is greater than the value it points to:

```
void setmax(int* shvar, int x) {
  // Begin critical section
  if (x > *shvar)
     *shvar = x;
  // End critical section}
}
```

2.38 [5] <§2.11> Using your code from Exercise 2.37 as an example, explain what happens when two processors begin to execute this critical section at the same time, assuming that each processor executes exactly one instruction per cycle.

2.39 Assume for a given processor the CPI of arithmetic instructions is 1, the CPI of load/store instructions is 10, and the CPI of branch instructions is 3. Assume a program has the following instruction breakdowns: 500 million arithmetic instructions, 300 million load/store instructions, 100 million branch instructions.

2.39.1 [5] <§§1.6, 2.13> Suppose that new, more powerful arithmetic instructions are added to the instruction set. On average, through the use of these more powerful arithmetic instructions, we can reduce the number of arithmetic instructions needed to execute a program by 25%, and the cost of increasing the clock cycle time by only 10%. Is this a good design choice? Why?

2.39.2 [5] <§§1.6, 2.13> Suppose that we find a way to double the performance of arithmetic instructions. What is the overall speedup of our machine? What if we find a way to improve the performance of arithmetic instructions by 10 times?

2.40 Assume that for a given program 70% of the executed instructions are arithmetic, 10% are load/store, and 20% are branch.

2.40.1 [5] <§2.21> Given the instruction mix and the assumption that an arithmetic instruction requires 2 cycles, a load/store instruction takes 6 cycles, and a branch instruction takes 3 cycles, find the average CPI.

2.40.2 [5] <§§1.6, 2.13> For a 25% improvement in performance, how many cycles, on average, may an arithmetic instruction take if load/store and branch instructions are not improved at all?

2.40.3 [5] <§§1.6, 2.13> For a 50% improvement in performance, how many cycles, on average, may an arithmetic instruction take if load/store and branch instructions are not improved at all?

2.41 [10] <§2.21> Suppose the MIPS ISA included a scaled offset addressing mode similar to the ×86 one described in Section 2.19 (Figure 2.35). Describe how you would use scaled offset loads to further reduce the number of assembly instructions needed to carry out the function given in Exercise 2.4.

2.42 [10] <§2.21> Suppose the MIPS ISA included a scaled offset addressing mode similar to the ×86 one described in Section 2.19 (Figure 2.35). Describe how you would use scaled offset loads to further reduce the number of assembly instructions needed to implement the C code given in Exercise 2.7.

Answers to Check Yourself

§2.2, page 72: MIPS, C, Java

§2.3, page 78: 2) Very slow

§2.4, page 85: First question: 2) -8_{ten}. Second question: 4) $18,446,744,073,709,551,608_{ten}$.

§2.5, page 93: First question: 4) sub $t2, $t0, $t1. Second question: 28_{hex}.

§2.6, page 95: Both. AND with a mask pattern of 1 s will leaves 0 s everywhere but the desired field. Shifting left by the right amount removes the bits from the left of the field. Shifting right by the appropriate amount puts the field into the right-most bits of the word, with 0 s in the rest of the word. Note that AND leaves the field where it was originally, and the shift pair moves the field into the rightmost part of the word.

§2.7, page 102: I. All are true. II. 1).

§2.8, page 112: Both are true.

§2.9, page 116: I. 1) II. 3)

§2.10, page 126: I. 4) +−128 K. II. 6) a block of 256 M. III. 4) sll

§2.11, page 129: Both are true.

§2.12, page 138: 4) Machine independence.

Arithmetic for Computers

Numerical precision is the very soul of science.

Sir D'arcy Wentworth Thompson
On Growth and Form, 1917

The Five Classic Components of a Computer

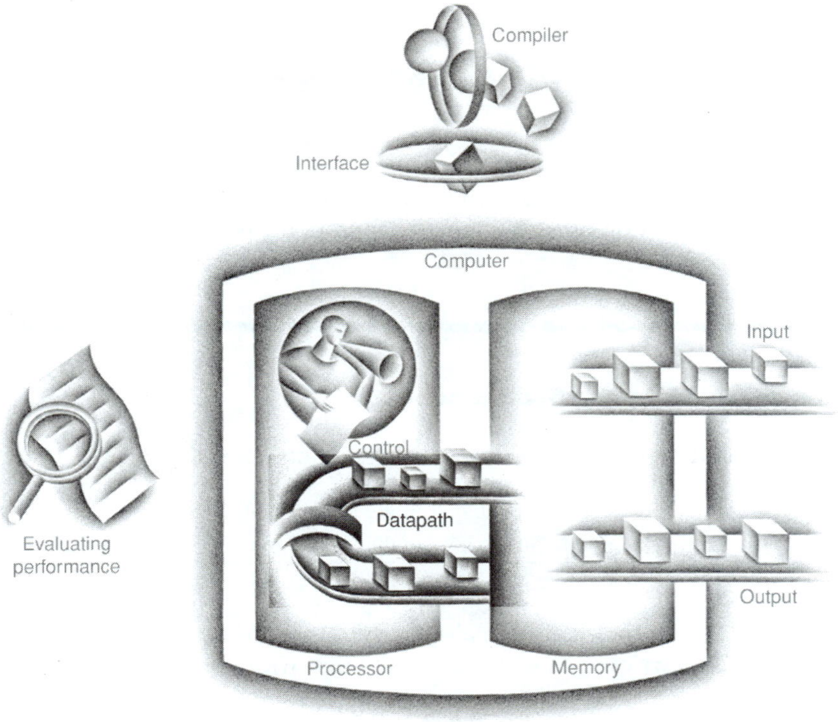

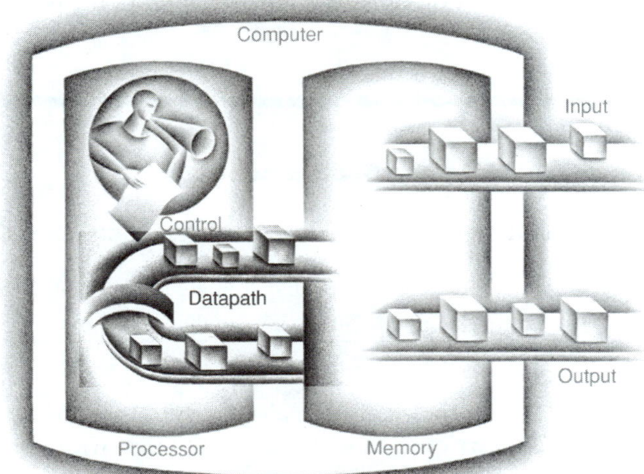

3.1   Introduction

Computer words are composed of bits; thus, words can be represented as binary numbers. Chapter 2 shows that integers can be represented either in decimal or binary form, but what about the other numbers that commonly occur? For example:

- What about fractions and other real numbers?

- What happens if an operation creates a number bigger than can be represented?

- And underlying these questions is a mystery: How does hardware really multiply or divide numbers?

The goal of this chapter is to unravel these mysteries including representation of real numbers, arithmetic algorithms, hardware that follows these algorithms, and the implications of all this for instruction sets. These insights may explain quirks that you have already encountered with computers. Moreover, we show how to use this knowledge to make arithmetic-intensive programs go much faster.

3.2   Addition and Subtraction

Subtraction: Addition's Tricky Pal

No. 10, Top Ten Courses for Athletes at a Football Factory, David Letterman et al., *Book of Top Ten Lists,* 1990

Addition is just what you would expect in computers. Digits are added bit by bit from right to left, with carries passed to the next digit to the left, just as you would do by hand. Subtraction uses addition: the appropriate operand is simply negated before being added.

Binary Addition and Subtraction

EXAMPLE

Let's try adding 6_{ten} to 7_{ten} in binary and then subtracting 6_{ten} from 7_{ten} in binary.

$$
\begin{array}{rll}
  & 0000\ 0000\ 0000\ 0000\ 0000\ 0000\ 0000\ 0111_{two} & = 7_{ten} \\
+ & 0000\ 0000\ 0000\ 0000\ 0000\ 0000\ 0000\ 0110_{two} & = 6_{ten} \\
\hline
= & 0000\ 0000\ 0000\ 0000\ 0000\ 0000\ 0000\ 1101_{two} & = 13_{ten}
\end{array}
$$

The 4 bits to the right have all the action; Figure 3.1 shows the sums and carries. The carries are shown in parentheses, with the arrows showing how they are passed.

ANSWER

Subtracting 6_{ten} from 7_{ten} can be done directly:

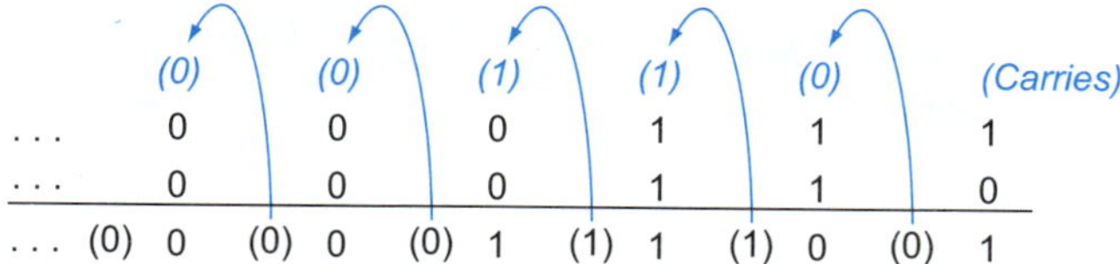

FIGURE 3.1 **Binary addition, showing carries from right to left.** The rightmost bit adds 1 to 0, resulting in the sum of this bit being 1 and the carry out from this bit being 0. Hence, the operation for the second digit to the right is $0 + 1 + 1$. This generates a 0 for this sum bit and a carry out of 1. The third digit is the sum of $1 + 1 + 1$, resulting in a carry out of 1 and a sum bit of 1. The fourth bit is $1 + 0 + 0$, yielding a 1 sum and no carry.

$$
\begin{aligned}
&\quad\ 0000\ 0000\ 0000\ 0000\ 0000\ 0000\ 0000\ 0111_{two} = 7_{ten}\\
-\ &\quad\ 0000\ 0000\ 0000\ 0000\ 0000\ 0000\ 0000\ 0110_{two} = 6_{ten}\\
=\ &\quad\ 0000\ 0000\ 0000\ 0000\ 0000\ 0000\ 0000\ 0001_{two} = 1_{ten}
\end{aligned}
$$

or via addition using the two's complement representation of -6:

$$
\begin{aligned}
&\quad\ 0000\ 0000\ 0000\ 0000\ 0000\ 0000\ 0000\ 0111_{two} = 7_{ten}\\
+\ &\quad\ 1111\ 1111\ 1111\ 1111\ 1111\ 1111\ 1111\ 1010_{two} = -6_{ten}\\
=\ &\quad\ 0000\ 0000\ 0000\ 0000\ 0000\ 0000\ 0000\ 0001_{two} = 1_{ten}
\end{aligned}
$$

Recall that overflow occurs when the result from an operation cannot be represented with the available hardware, in this case a 32-bit word. When can overflow occur in addition? When adding operands with different signs, overflow cannot occur. The reason is the sum must be no larger than one of the operands. For example, $-10 + 4 = -6$. Since the operands fit in 32 bits and the sum is no larger than an operand, the sum must fit in 32 bits as well. Therefore, no overflow can occur when adding positive and negative operands.

There are similar restrictions to the occurrence of overflow during subtract, but it's just the opposite principle: when the signs of the operands are the *same*, overflow cannot occur. To see this, remember that $c - a = c + (-a)$ because we subtract by negating the second operand and then add. Therefore, when we subtract operands of the same sign we end up by *adding* operands of *different* signs. From the prior paragraph, we know that overflow cannot occur in this case either.

Knowing when overflow cannot occur in addition and subtraction is all well and good, but how do we detect it when it *does* occur? Clearly, adding or subtracting two 32-bit numbers can yield a result that needs 33 bits to be fully expressed.

The lack of a 33rd bit means that when overflow occurs, the sign bit is set with the *value* of the result instead of the proper sign of the result. Since we need just one extra bit, only the sign bit can be wrong. Hence, overflow occurs when adding two positive numbers and the sum is negative, or vice versa. This spurious sum means a carry out occurred into the sign bit.

Overflow occurs in subtraction when we subtract a negative number from a positive number and get a negative result, or when we subtract a positive number from a negative number and get a positive result. Such a ridiculous result means a borrow occurred from the sign bit. Figure 3.2 shows the combination of operations, operands, and results that indicate an overflow.

Operation	Operand A	Operand B	Result indicating overflow
$A + B$	≥ 0	≥ 0	< 0
$A + B$	< 0	< 0	≥ 0
$A - B$	≥ 0	< 0	< 0
$A - B$	< 0	≥ 0	≥ 0

FIGURE 3.2   Overflow conditions for addition and subtraction.

We have just seen how to detect overflow for two's complement numbers in a computer. What about overflow with unsigned integers? Unsigned integers are commonly used for memory addresses where overflows are ignored.

The computer designer must therefore provide a way to ignore overflow in some cases and to recognize it in others. The MIPS solution is to have two kinds of arithmetic instructions to recognize the two choices:

- Add (`add`), add immediate (`addi`), and subtract (`sub`) cause exceptions on overflow.

- Add unsigned (`addu`), add immediate unsigned (`addiu`), and subtract unsigned (`subu`) do *not* cause exceptions on overflow.

Because C ignores overflows, the MIPS C compilers will always generate the unsigned versions of the arithmetic instructions `addu`, `addiu`, and `subu`, no matter what the type of the variables. The MIPS Fortran compilers, however, pick the appropriate arithmetic instructions, depending on the type of the operands.

⊕ **Appendix B** describes the hardware that performs addition and subtraction, which is called an **Arithmetic Logic Unit** or **ALU**.

Arithmetic Logic Unit (ALU) Hardware that performs addition, subtraction, and usually logical operations such as AND and OR.

Elaboration: A constant source of confusion for `addiu` is its name and what happens to its immediate field. The u stands for unsigned, which means addition cannot cause an overflow exception. However, the 16-bit immediate field is sign extended to 32 bits, just like `addi`, `slti`, and `sltiu`. Thus, the immediate field is signed, even if the operation is "unsigned."

Hardware/ Software Interface

The computer designer must decide how to handle arithmetic overflows. Although some languages like C and Java ignore integer overflow, languages like Ada and Fortran require that the program be notified. The programmer or the programming environment must then decide what to do when overflow occurs.

MIPS detects overflow with an **exception**, also called an **interrupt** on many computers. An exception or interrupt is essentially an unscheduled procedure call. The address of the instruction that overflowed is saved in a register, and the computer jumps to a predefined address to invoke the appropriate routine for that exception. The interrupted address is saved so that in some situations the program can continue after corrective code is executed. (Section 4.10 covers exceptions in

exception Also called **interrupt** on many computers. An unscheduled event that disrupts program execution; used to detect overflow, for example.

more detail; Chapter 5 describes other situations where exceptions and interrupts occur.) MIPS calls an exception that comes from outside the processor an **interrupt**.

MIPS includes a register called the *exception program counter* (EPC) to contain the address of the instruction that caused the exception. The instruction *move from system control* (`mfc0`) is used to copy EPC into a general-purpose register so that MIPS software has the option of returning to the offending instruction via a jump register instruction after the execution of the corrective code.

interrupt An exception that comes from outside of the processor. (Some architectures use the term *interrupt* for all exceptions.)

Summary

A major point of this section is that, independent of the representation, the finite word size of computers means that arithmetic operations can create results that are too large to fit in this fixed word size. It's easy to detect overflow in unsigned numbers, although these are almost always ignored because programs don't want to detect overflow for address arithmetic, the most common use of natural numbers. Two's complement presents a greater challenge, yet some software systems require detection of overflow, so today all computers have a way to detect it.

Some programming languages allow two's complement integer arithmetic on variables declared byte and half, whereas MIPS only has integer arithmetic operations on full words. As we recall from Chapter 2, MIPS does have data transfer operations for bytes and halfwords. What MIPS instructions should be generated for byte and halfword arithmetic operations?

Check Yourself

1. Load with `lbu`, `lhu`; arithmetic with `add`, `sub`, `mult`, `div`; then store using `sb`, `sh`.

2. Load with `lb`, `lh`; arithmetic with `add`, `sub`, `mult`, `div`; then store using `sb`, `sh`.

3. Load with `lb`, `lh`; arithmetic with `add`, `sub`, `mult`, `div`, using AND to mask result to 8 or 16 bits after each operation; then store using `sb`, `sh`.

Elaboration: One feature not generally found in general-purpose microprocessors is *saturating* operations. Saturation means that when a calculation overflows, the result is set to the largest positive number or most negative number, rather than a modulo calculation as in two's complement arithmetic. Saturation is likely what you want for media operations. For example, the volume knob on a radio set would be frustrating if, as you turned it, the volume would get continuously louder for a while and then immediately very soft. A knob with saturation would stop at the highest volume no matter how far you turned it. Multimedia extensions to standard instruction sets often offer saturating arithmetic.

Elaboration: MIPS can trap on overflow, but unlike many other computers, there is no conditional branch to test overflow. A sequence of MIPS instructions can discover overflow. For signed addition, the sequence is the following (see the *Elaboration* on page 95 in Chapter 2 for a description of the `xor` instruction):

```
addu $t0, $t1, $t2 # $t0 = sum, but don't trap
xor  $t3, $t1, $t2 # Check if signs differ
slt  $t3, $t3, $zero # $t3 = 1 if signs differ
bne  $t3, $zero, No_overflow # $t1, $t2 signs ≠,
                             # so no overflow
xor $t3, $t0, $t1 # signs =; sign of sum match too?
                  # $t3 negative if sum sign different
slt $t3, $t3, $zero # $t3 = 1 if sum sign different
bne $t3, $zero, Overflow # All 3 signs ≠; goto overflow
```

For unsigned addition ($t0 = $t1 + $t2), the test is

```
addu $t0, $t1, $t2      # $t0 = sum
nor $t3, $t1, $zero     # $t3 = NOT $t1
                        # (2's comp - 1: 2³² - $t1 - 1)
sltu $t3, $t3, $t2      # (2³² - $t1 - 1) < $t2
                        # ⇒ 2³² - 1 < $t1 + $t2
bne $t3,$zero,Overflow  # if(2³²-1<$t1+$t2) goto overflow
```

Elaboration: In the preceding text, we said that you copy EPC into a register via `mfc0` and then return to the interrupted code via jump register. This directive leads to an interesting question: since you must first transfer EPC to a register to use with jump register, how can jump register return to the interrupted code *and* restore the original values of *all* registers? Either you restore the old registers first, thereby destroying your return address from EPC, which you placed in a register for use in jump register, or you restore all registers but the one with the return address so that you can jump—meaning an exception would result in changing that one register at any time during program execution! Neither option is satisfactory.

To rescue the hardware from this dilemma, MIPS programmers agreed to reserve registers $k0 and $k1 for the operating system; these registers are *not* restored on exceptions. Just as the MIPS compilers avoid using register $at so that the assembler can use it as a temporary register (see *Hardware/Software Interface* in Section 2.10), compilers also abstain from using registers $k0 and $k1 to make them available for the operating system. Exception routines place the return address in one of these registers and then use jump register to restore the instruction address.

Elaboration: The speed of addition is increased by determining the carry in to the high-order bits sooner. There are a variety of schemes to anticipate the carry so that the worst-case scenario is a function of the $\log_2$ of the number of bits in the adder instead of the full number of adder bits. These anticipatory signals are faster because they go through fewer gates in sequence, but it takes many more gates to anticipate the proper carry. The most popular is *carry lookahead*, which Section B.6 in 🌐 **Appendix B** describes.

3.3 Multiplication

Now that we have completed the explanation of addition and subtraction, we are ready to build the more vexing operation of multiplication.

First, let's review the multiplication of decimal numbers in longhand to remind ourselves of the steps of multiplication and the names of the operands. For reasons that will become clear shortly, we limit this decimal example to using only the digits 0 and 1. Multiplying 1000_{ten} by 1001_{ten}:

```
Multiplicand            1000 ten
Multiplier      x  1001       ten
                   ─────────
                   1000
                  0000
                 0000
                1000
                ─────────
Product         1001000 ten
```

The first operand is called the *multiplicand* and the second the *multiplier*. The final result is called the *product*. As you may recall, the algorithm learned in grammar school is to take the digits of the multiplier one at a time from right to left, multiplying the multiplicand by the single digit of the multiplier, and shifting the intermediate product one digit to the left of the earlier intermediate products.

The first observation is that the number of digits in the product is considerably larger than the number in either the multiplicand or the multiplier. In fact, if we ignore the sign bits, the length of the multiplication of an n-bit multiplicand and an m-bit multiplier is a product that is $n + m$ bits long. That is, $n + m$ bits are required to represent all possible products. Hence, like add, multiply must cope with overflow because we frequently want a 32-bit product as the result of multiplying two 32-bit numbers.

In this example, we restricted the decimal digits to 0 and 1. With only two choices, each step of the multiplication is simple:

1. Just place a copy of the multiplicand ($1 \times$ multiplicand) in the proper place if the multiplier digit is a 1, or

2. Place 0 ($0 \times$ multiplicand) in the proper place if the digit is 0.

Although the decimal example above happens to use only 0 and 1, multiplication of binary numbers must always use 0 and 1, and thus always offers only these two choices.

Now that we have reviewed the basics of multiplication, the traditional next step is to provide the highly optimized multiply hardware. We break with tradition in the belief that you will gain a better understanding by seeing the evolution of the multiply hardware and algorithm through multiple generations. For now, let's assume that we are multiplying only positive numbers.

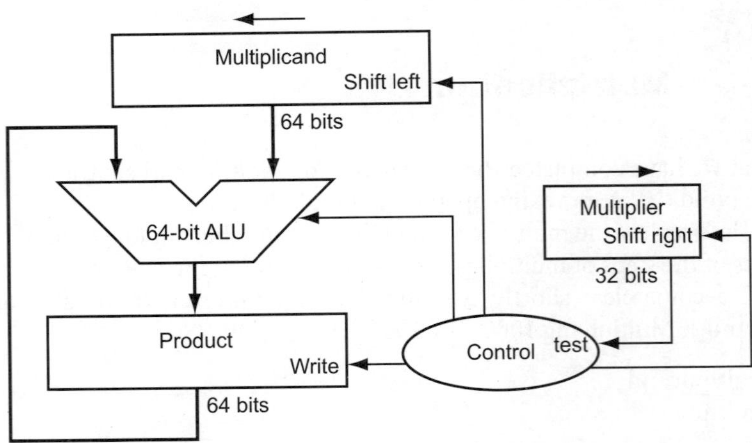

FIGURE 3.3   First version of the multiplication hardware. The Multiplicand register, ALU, and Product register are all 64 bits wide, with only the Multiplier register containing 32 bits. (Appendix B describes ALUs.) The 32-bit multiplicand starts in the right half of the Multiplicand register and is shifted left 1 bit on each step. The multiplier is shifted in the opposite direction at each step. The algorithm starts with the product initialized to 0. Control decides when to shift the Multiplicand and Multiplier registers and when to write new values into the Product register.

Sequential Version of the Multiplication Algorithm and Hardware

This design mimics the algorithm we learned in grammar school; Figure 3.3 shows the hardware. We have drawn the hardware so that data flows from top to bottom to resemble more closely the paper-and-pencil method.

Let's assume that the multiplier is in the 32-bit Multiplier register and that the 64-bit Product register is initialized to 0. From the paper-and-pencil example above, it's clear that we will need to move the multiplicand left one digit each step, as it may be added to the intermediate products. Over 32 steps, a 32-bit multiplicand would move 32 bits to the left. Hence, we need a 64-bit Multiplicand register, initialized with the 32-bit multiplicand in the right half and zero in the left half. This register is then shifted left 1 bit each step to align the multiplicand with the sum being accumulated in the 64-bit Product register.

Figure 3.4 shows the three basic steps needed for each bit. The least significant bit of the multiplier (Multiplier0) determines whether the multiplicand is added to the Product register. The left shift in step 2 has the effect of moving the intermediate operands to the left, just as when multiplying with paper and pencil. The shift right in step 3 gives us the next bit of the multiplier to examine in the following iteration. These three steps are repeated 32 times to obtain the product. If each step took one clock cycle, this algorithm would require almost 100 clock cycles to multiply two 32-bit numbers. The relative importance of arithmetic operations like multiply varies with the program, but addition and subtraction may be anywhere from 5 to 100 times more popular than multiply. Accordingly, in many applications, multiply can take multiple clock cycles without significantly affecting performance. Yet Amdahl's Law (see Section 1.11) reminds us that even a moderate frequency for a slow operation can limit performance.

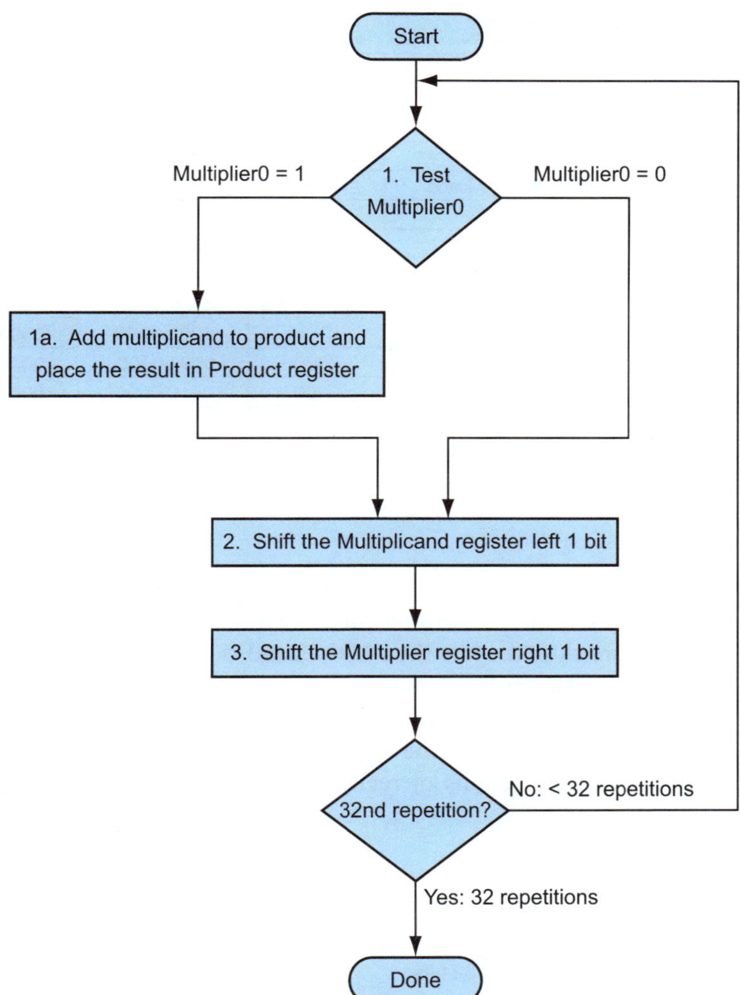

FIGURE 3.4   The first multiplication algorithm, using the hardware shown in Figure 3.3. If the least significant bit of the multiplier is 1, add the multiplicand to the product. If not, go to the next step. Shift the multiplicand left and the multiplier right in the next two steps. These three steps are repeated 32 times.

A Multiply Algorithm

EXAMPLE

Using 4-bit numbers to save space, multiply $2_{ten} \times 3_{ten}$, or $0010_{two} \times 0011_{two}$.

ANSWER

Figure 3.5 shows the value of each register for each of the steps labeled according to Figure 3.4, with the final value of $0000\ 0110_{two}$ or 6_{ten}. Color is used to indicate the register values that change on that step, and the bit circled is the one examined to determine the operation of the next step.

Iteration	Step	Multiplier	Multiplicand	Product
0	Initial values	0001①	0000 0010	0000 0000
1	1a: 1 $\Rightarrow$ Prod = Prod + Mcand	0011	0000 0010	0000 0010
	2: Shift left Multiplicand	0011	0000 0100	0000 0010
	3: Shift right Multiplier	000①	0000 0100	0000 0010
2	1a: 1 $\Rightarrow$ Prod = Prod + Mcand	0001	0000 0100	0000 0110
	2: Shift left Multiplicand	0001	0000 1000	0000 0110
	3: Shift right Multiplier	000⓪	0000 1000	0000 0110
3	1: 0 $\Rightarrow$ No operation	0000	0000 1000	0000 0110
	2: Shift left Multiplicand	0000	0001 0000	0000 0110
	3: Shift right Multiplier	000⓪	0001 0000	0000 0110
4	1: 0 $\Rightarrow$ No operation	0000	0001 0000	0000 0110
	2: Shift left Multiplicand	0000	0010 0000	0000 0110
	3: Shift right Multiplier	0000	0010 0000	0000 0110

FIGURE 3.5 Multiply example using algorithm in Figure 3.4. The bit examined to determine the next step is circled in color.

This algorithm and hardware are easily refined to take 1 clock cycle per step. The speed-up comes from performing the operations in parallel: the multiplier and multiplicand are shifted while the multiplicand is added to the product if the multiplier bit is a 1. The hardware only has to ensure that it tests the right bit of the multiplier and gets the preshifted version of the multiplicand. The hardware is usually further optimized to halve the width of the adder and registers by noticing where there are unused portions of registers and adders. Figure 3.6 shows the revised hardware.

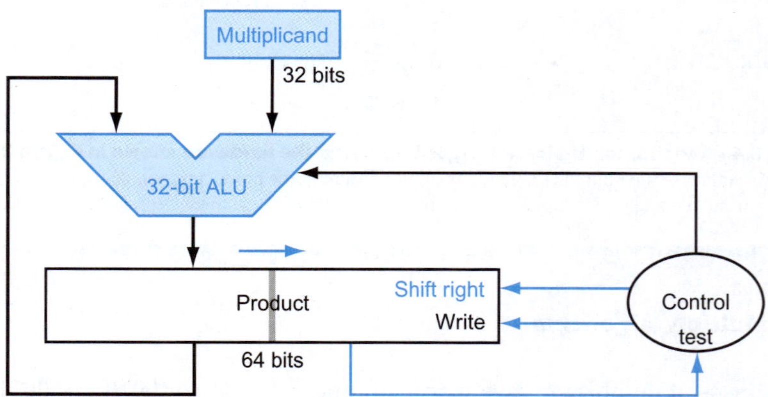

FIGURE 3.6   Refined version of the multiplication hardware. Compare with the first version in Figure 3.3. The Multiplicand register, ALU, and Multiplier register are all 32 bits wide, with only the Product register left at 64 bits. Now the product is shifted right. The separate Multiplier register also disappeared. The multiplier is placed instead in the right half of the Product register. These changes are highlighted in color. (The Product register should really be 65 bits to hold the carry out of the adder, but it's shown here as 64 bits to highlight the evolution from Figure 3.3.)

Replacing arithmetic by shifts can also occur when multiplying by constants. Some compilers replace multiplies by short constants with a series of shifts and adds. Because one bit to the left represents a number twice as large in base 2, shifting the bits left has the same effect as multiplying by a power of 2. As mentioned in Chapter 2, almost every compiler will perform the strength reduction optimization of substituting a left shift for a multiply by a power of 2.

Hardware/
Software
Interface

Signed Multiplication

So far, we have dealt with positive numbers. The easiest way to understand how to deal with signed numbers is to first convert the multiplier and multiplicand to positive numbers and then remember the original signs. The algorithms should then be run for 31 iterations, leaving the signs out of the calculation. As we learned in grammar school, we need negate the product only if the original signs disagree.

It turns out that the last algorithm will work for signed numbers, provided that we remember that we are dealing with numbers that have infinite digits, and we are only representing them with 32 bits. Hence, the shifting steps would need to extend the sign of the product for signed numbers. When the algorithm completes, the lower word would have the 32-bit product.

Faster Multiplication

Moore's Law provided so much more in resources that hardware designers could build much faster multiplication hardware. Whether the multiplicand is to be added or not is known at the beginning of the multiplication by looking at each of the 32 multiplier bits. Faster multiplications are possible by essentially providing one 32-bit adder for each bit of the multiplier: one input is the multiplicand ANDed with a multiplier bit, and the other is the output of a prior adder.

A straightforward approach would be to connect the outputs of adders on the right to the inputs of adders on the left, making a stack of adders 32 high. An alternative way to organize these 32 additions is in a parallel tree, as Figure 3.7 shows. Instead of waiting for 32 add times, we wait just the $\log_2 (32)$ or five 32-bit add times.

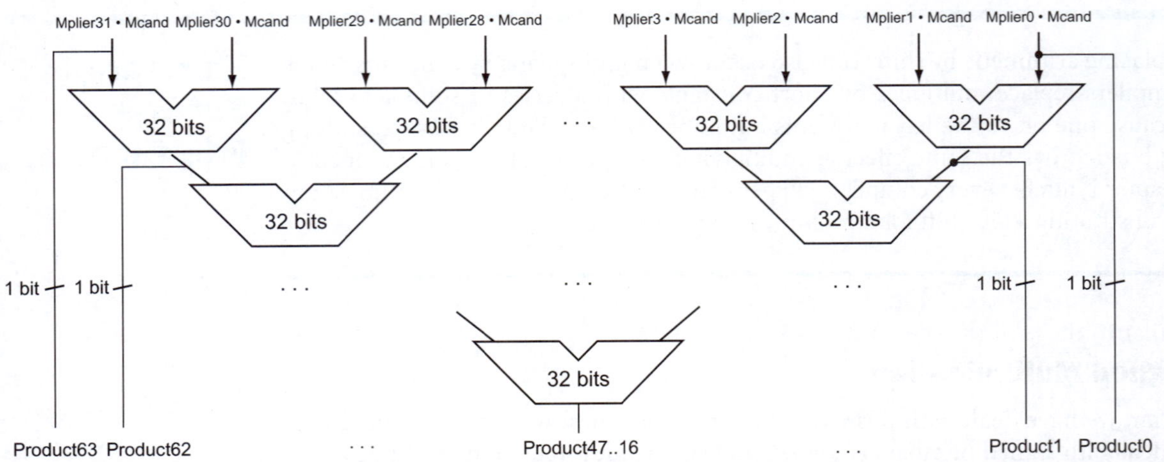

FIGURE 3.7   Fast multiplication hardware. Rather than use a single 32-bit adder 31 times, this hardware "unrolls the loop" to use 31 adders and then organizes them to minimize delay.

PIPELINING

In fact, multiply can go even faster than five add times because of the use of *carry save adders* (see Section B.6 in 🌐 **Appendix B**) and because it is easy to **pipeline** such a design to be able to support many multiplies simultaneously (see Chapter 4).

Multiply in MIPS

MIPS provides a separate pair of 32-bit registers to contain the 64-bit product, called *Hi* and *Lo*. To produce a properly signed or unsigned product, MIPS has two instructions: multiply (`mult`) and multiply unsigned (`multu`). To fetch the integer 32-bit product, the programmer uses *move from lo* (`mflo`). The MIPS assembler generates a pseudoinstruction for multiply that specifies three general-purpose registers, generating `mflo` and `mfhi` instructions to place the product into registers.

PARALLELISM

Summary

Multiplication hardware simply shifts and adds, as derived from the paper-and-pencil method learned in grammar school. Compilers even use shift instructions for multiplications by powers of 2. With much more hardware we can do the adds in **parallel**, and do them much faster.

Hardware/ Software Interface

Both MIPS multiply instructions ignore overflow, so it is up to the software to check to see if the product is too big to fit in 32 bits. There is no overflow if Hi is 0 for `multu` or the replicated sign of Lo for `mult`. The instruction *move from hi* (`mfhi`) can be used to transfer Hi to a general-purpose register to test for overflow.

3.4 Division

The reciprocal operation of multiply is divide, an operation that is even less frequent and even more quirky. It even offers the opportunity to perform a mathematically invalid operation: dividing by 0.

Let's start with an example of long division using decimal numbers to recall the names of the operands and the grammar school division algorithm. For reasons similar to those in the previous section, we limit the decimal digits to just 0 or 1. The example is dividing $1{,}001{,}010_{ten}$ by 1000_{ten}:

$$
\begin{array}{r}
1001_{ten} \quad \text{Quotient}\\
\text{Divisor } 1000_{ten} \overline{)\,1001010_{ten}} \quad \text{Dividend}\\
-1000\\
\overline{10}\\
101\\
1010\\
-1000\\
\overline{10_{ten}} \quad \text{Remainder}
\end{array}
$$

Divide's two operands, called the **dividend** and **divisor**, and the result, called the **quotient**, are accompanied by a second result, called the **remainder**. Here is another way to express the relationship between the components:

$$\text{Dividend} = \text{Quotient} \times \text{Divisor} + \text{Remainder}$$

where the remainder is smaller than the divisor. Occasionally, programs use the divide instruction simply to get the remainder, ignoring the quotient.

The basic grammar school division algorithm tries to see how big a number can be subtracted, creating a digit of the quotient on each attempt. Our carefully selected decimal example uses only the numbers 0 and 1, so it's easy to figure out how many times the divisor goes into the portion of the dividend: it's either 0 times or 1 time. Binary numbers contain only 0 or 1, so binary division is restricted to these two choices, thereby simplifying binary division.

Let's assume that both the dividend and the divisor are positive and hence the quotient and the remainder are nonnegative. The division operands and both results are 32-bit values, and we will ignore the sign for now.

A Division Algorithm and Hardware

Figure 3.8 shows hardware to mimic our grammar school algorithm. We start with the 32-bit Quotient register set to 0. Each iteration of the algorithm needs to move the divisor to the right one digit, so we start with the divisor placed in the left half of the 64-bit Divisor register and shift it right 1 bit each step to align it with the dividend. The Remainder register is initialized with the dividend.

Divide et impera.

Latin for "Divide and rule," ancient political maxim cited by Machiavelli, 1532

dividend A number being divided.

divisor A number that the dividend is divided by.

quotient The primary result of a division; a number that when multiplied by the divisor and added to the remainder produces the dividend.

remainder The secondary result of a division; a number that when added to the product of the quotient and the divisor produces the dividend.

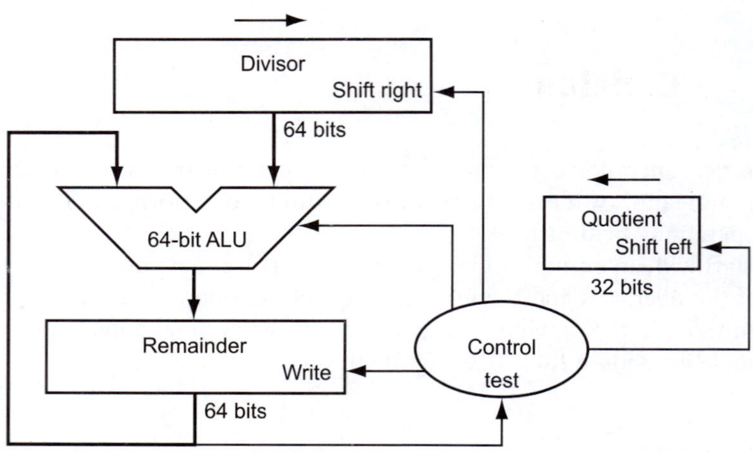

FIGURE 3.8   First version of the division hardware. The Divisor register, ALU, and Remainder register are all 64 bits wide, with only the Quotient register being 32 bits. The 32-bit divisor starts in the left half of the Divisor register and is shifted right 1 bit each iteration. The remainder is initialized with the dividend. Control decides when to shift the Divisor and Quotient registers and when to write the new value into the Remainder register.

Figure 3.9 shows three steps of the first division algorithm. Unlike a human, the computer isn't smart enough to know in advance whether the divisor is smaller than the dividend. It must first subtract the divisor in step 1; remember that this is how we performed the comparison in the set on less than instruction. If the result is positive, the divisor was smaller or equal to the dividend, so we generate a 1 in the quotient (step 2a). If the result is negative, the next step is to restore the original value by adding the divisor back to the remainder and generate a 0 in the quotient (step 2b). The divisor is shifted right and then we iterate again. The remainder and quotient will be found in their namesake registers after the iterations are complete.

<table><tr><td>

EXAMPLE

</td><td>

A Divide Algorithm

Using a 4-bit version of the algorithm to save pages, let's try dividing 7_{ten} by 2_{ten}, or $0000\ 0111_{two}$ by 0010_{two}.

</td></tr><tr><td>

ANSWER

</td><td>

Figure 3.10 shows the value of each register for each of the steps, with the quotient being 3_{ten} and the remainder 1_{ten}. Notice that the test in step 2 of whether the remainder is positive or negative simply tests whether the sign bit of the Remainder register is a 0 or 1. The surprising requirement of this algorithm is that it takes $n + 1$ steps to get the proper quotient and remainder.

</td></tr></table>

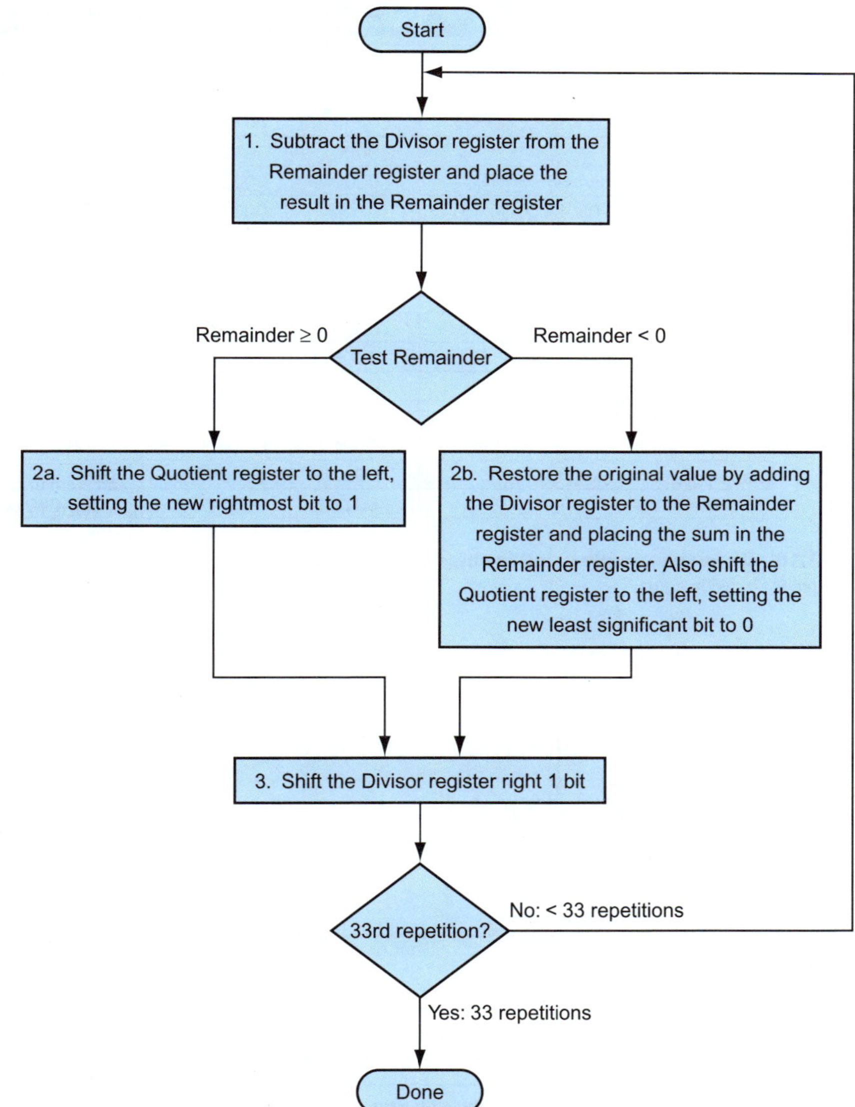

FIGURE 3.9   A division algorithm, using the hardware in Figure 3.8. If the remainder is positive, the divisor did go into the dividend, so step 2a generates a 1 in the quotient. A negative remainder after step 1 means that the divisor did not go into the dividend, so step 2b generates a 0 in the quotient and adds the divisor to the remainder, thereby reversing the subtraction of step 1. The final shift, in step 3, aligns the divisor properly, relative to the dividend for the next iteration. These steps are repeated 33 times.

This algorithm and hardware can be refined to be faster and cheaper. The speed-up comes from shifting the operands and the quotient simultaneously with the subtraction. This refinement halves the width of the adder and registers by noticing where there are unused portions of registers and adders. Figure 3.11 shows the revised hardware.

Iteration	Step	Quotient	Divisor	Remainder
0	Initial values	0000	0010 0000	0000 0111
1	1: Rem = Rem – Div	0000	0010 0000	①110 0111
	2b: Rem < 0 ⟹ +Div, sll Q, Q0 = 0	0000	0010 0000	0000 0111
	3: Shift Div right	0000	0001 0000	0000 0111
2	1: Rem = Rem – Div	0000	0001 0000	①111 0111
	2b: Rem < 0 ⟹ +Div, sll Q, Q0 = 0	0000	0001 0000	0000 0111
	3: Shift Div right	0000	0000 1000	0000 0111
3	1: Rem = Rem – Div	0000	0000 1000	①111 1111
	2b: Rem < 0 ⟹ +Div, sll Q, Q0 = 0	0000	0000 1000	0000 0111
	3: Shift Div right	0000	0000 0100	0000 0111
4	1: Rem = Rem – Div	0000	0000 0100	⓪000 0011
	2a: Rem ≥ 0 ⟹ sll Q, Q0 = 1	0001	0000 0100	0000 0011
	3: Shift Div right	0001	0000 0010	0000 0011
5	1: Rem = Rem – Div	0001	0000 0010	⓪000 0001
	2a: Rem ≥ 0 ⟹ sll Q, Q0 = 1	0011	0000 0010	0000 0001
	3: Shift Div right	0011	0000 0001	0000 0001

FIGURE 3.10   Division example using the algorithm in Figure 3.9. The bit examined to determine the next step is circled in color.

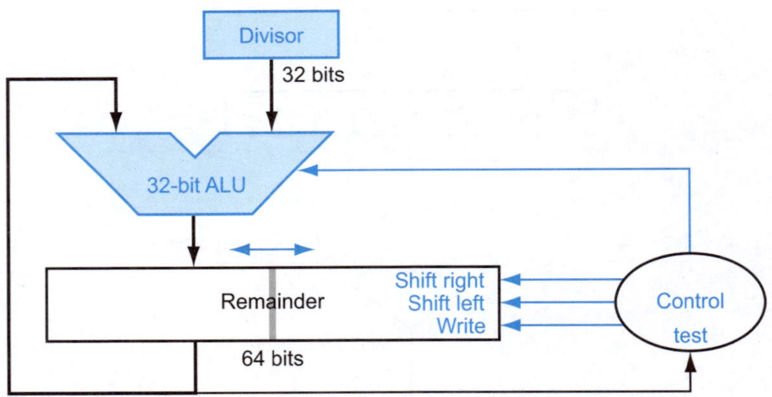

FIGURE 3.11   An improved version of the division hardware. The Divisor register, ALU, and Quotient register are all 32 bits wide, with only the Remainder register left at 64 bits. Compared to Figure 3.8, the ALU and Divisor registers are halved and the remainder is shifted left. This version also combines the Quotient register with the right half of the Remainder register. (As in Figure 3.6, the Remainder register should really be 65 bits to make sure the carry out of the adder is not lost.)

Signed Division

So far, we have ignored signed numbers in division. The simplest solution is to remember the signs of the divisor and dividend and then negate the quotient if the signs disagree.

Elaboration: The one complication of signed division is that we must also set the sign of the remainder. Remember that the following equation must always hold:

$$\text{Dividend} = \text{Quotient} \times \text{Divisor} + \text{Remainder}$$

To understand how to set the sign of the remainder, let's look at the example of dividing all the combinations of $\pm 7_{ten}$ by $\pm 2_{ten}$. The first case is easy:

$$+7 \div +2: \text{Quotient} = +3, + \text{Remainder} = +1$$

Checking the results:

$$+7 = 3 \times 2 + (+1) = 6 + 1$$

If we change the sign of the dividend, the quotient must change as well:

$$-7 \div +2: \text{Quotient} = -3$$

Rewriting our basic formula to calculate the remainder:

$$\text{Remainder} = (\text{Dividend} - \text{Quotient} \times \text{Divisor}) = -7 - (-3x + 2)$$
$$= -7 - (-6) = -1$$

So,

$$-7 \div +2: \text{Quotient} = -3, \text{Remainder} = -1$$

Checking the results again:

$$-7 = -3 \times 2 + (-1) = -6 - 1$$

The reason the answer isn't a quotient of -4 and a remainder of $+1$, which would also fit this formula, is that the absolute value of the quotient would then change depending on the sign of the dividend and the divisor! Clearly, if

$$-(x \div y) \neq (-x) \div y$$

programming would be an even greater challenge. This anomalous behavior is avoided by following the rule that the dividend and remainder must have the same signs, no matter what the signs of the divisor and quotient.

We calculate the other combinations by following the same rule:

$$+7 \div -2: \text{Quotient} = -3, \text{Remainder} = +1$$
$$-7 \div -2: \text{Quotient} = +3, \text{Remainder} = -1$$

Thus the correctly signed division algorithm negates the quotient if the signs of the operands are opposite and makes the sign of the nonzero remainder match the dividend.

Faster Division

Moore's Law applies to division hardware as well as multiplication, so we would like to be able to speed up division by throwing hardware at it. We used many adders to speed up multiply, but we cannot do the same trick for divide. The reason is that we need to know the sign of the difference before we can perform the next step of the algorithm, whereas with multiply we could calculate the 32 partial products immediately.

There are techniques to produce more than one bit of the quotient per step. The *SRT division* technique tries to **predict** several quotient bits per step, using a table lookup based on the upper bits of the dividend and remainder. It relies on subsequent steps to correct wrong predictions. A typical value today is 4 bits. The key is guessing the value to subtract. With binary division, there is only a single choice. These algorithms use 6 bits from the remainder and 4 bits from the divisor to index a table that determines the guess for each step.

The accuracy of this fast method depends on having proper values in the lookup table. The fallacy on page 239 in Section 3.9 shows what can happen if the table is incorrect.

Divide in MIPS

You may have already observed that the same sequential hardware can be used for both multiply and divide in Figures 3.6 and 3.11. The only requirement is a 64-bit register that can shift left or right and a 32-bit ALU that adds or subtracts. Hence, MIPS uses the 32-bit Hi and 32-bit Lo registers for both multiply and divide.

As we might expect from the algorithm above, Hi contains the remainder, and Lo contains the quotient after the divide instruction completes.

To handle both signed integers and unsigned integers, MIPS has two instructions: *divide* (`div`) and *divide unsigned* (`divu`). The MIPS assembler allows divide instructions to specify three registers, generating the `mflo` or `mfhi` instructions to place the desired result into a general-purpose register.

Summary

The common hardware support for multiply and divide allows MIPS to provide a single pair of 32-bit registers that are used both for multiply and divide. We accelerate division by predicting multliple quotient bits and then correcting mispredictions later. Figure 3.12 summarizes the enhancements to the MIPS instruction set for the last two sections.

MIPS assembly language

Category	Instruction	Example		Meaning	Comments
Arithmetic	add	add	$s1,$s2,$s3	$s1 = $s2 + $s3	Three operands; overflow detected
	subtract	sub	$s1,$s2,$s3	$s1 = $s2 − $s3	Three operands; overflow detected
	add immediate	addi	$s1,$s2,100	$s1 = $s2 + 100	+ constant; overflow detected
	add unsigned	addu	$s1,$s2,$s3	$s1 = $s2 + $s3	Three operands; overflow undetected
	subtract unsigned	subu	$s1,$s2,$s3	$s1 = $s2 − $s3	Three operands; overflow undetected
	add immediate unsigned	addiu	$s1,$s2,100	$s1 = $s2 + 100	+ constant; overflow undetected
	move from coprocessor register	mfc0	$s1,$epc	$s1 = $epc	Copy Exception PC + special regs
	multiply	mult	$s2,$s3	Hi, Lo = $s2 × $s3	64-bit signed product in Hi, Lo
	multiply unsigned	multu	$s2,$s3	Hi, Lo = $s2 × $s3	64-bit unsigned product in Hi, Lo
	divide	div	$s2,$s3	Lo = $s2 / $s3, Hi = $s2 mod $s3	Lo = quotient, Hi = remainder
	divide unsigned	divu	$s2,$s3	Lo = $s2 / $s3, Hi = $s2 mod $s3	Unsigned quotient and remainder
	move from Hi	mfhi	$s1	$s1 = Hi	Used to get copy of Hi
	move from Lo	mflo	$s1	$s1 = Lo	Used to get copy of Lo
Data transfer	load word	lw	$s1,20($s2)	$s1 = Memory[$s2 + 20]	Word from memory to register
	store word	sw	$s1,20($s2)	Memory[$s2 + 20] = $s1	Word from register to memory
	load half unsigned	lhu	$s1,20($s2)	$s1 = Memory[$s2 + 20]	Halfword memory to register
	store half	sh	$s1,20($s2)	Memory[$s2 + 20] = $s1	Halfword register to memory
	load byte unsigned	lbu	$s1,20($s2)	$s1 = Memory[$s2 + 20]	Byte from memory to register
	store byte	sb	$s1,20($s2)	Memory[$s2 + 20] = $s1	Byte from register to memory
	load linked word	ll	$s1,20($s2)	$s1 = Memory[$s2 + 20]	Load word as 1st half of atomic swap
	store conditional word	sc	$s1,20($s2)	Memory[$s2+20]=$s1;$s1=0 or 1	Store word as 2nd half atomic swap
	load upper immediate	lui	$s1,100	$s1 = 100 * 2^{16}	Loads constant in upper 16 bits
Logical	AND	AND	$s1,$s2,$s3	$s1 = $s2 & $s3	Three reg. operands; bit-by-bit AND
	OR	OR	$s1,$s2,$s3	$s1 = $s2 | $s3	Three reg. operands; bit-by-bit OR
	NOR	NOR	$s1,$s2,$s3	$s1 = ~ ($s2 |$s3)	Three reg. operands; bit-by-bit NOR
	AND immediate	ANDi	$s1,$s2,100	$s1 = $s2 & 100	Bit-by-bit AND with constant
	OR immediate	ORi	$s1,$s2,100	$s1 = $s2 | 100	Bit-by-bit OR with constant
	shift left logical	sll	$s1,$s2,10	$s1 = $s2 << 10	Shift left by constant
	shift right logical	srl	$s1,$s2,10	$s1 = $s2 >> 10	Shift right by constant
Conditional branch	branch on equal	beq	$s1,$s2,25	if ($s1 == $s2) go to PC + 4 + 100	Equal test; PC-relative branch
	branch on not equal	bne	$s1,$s2,25	if ($s1 != $s2) go to PC + 4 + 100	Not equal test; PC-relative
	set on less than	slt	$s1,$s2,$s3	if ($s2 < $s3) $s1 = 1; else $s1 = 0	Compare less than; two's complement
	set less than immediate	slti	$s1,$s2,100	if ($s2 < 100) $s1 = 1; else $s1=0	Compare < constant; two's complement
	set less than unsigned	sltu	$s1,$s2,$s3	if ($s2 < $s3) $s1 = 1; else $s1=0	Compare less than; natural numbers
	set less than immediate unsigned	sltiu	$s1,$s2,100	if ($s2 < 100) $s1 = 1; else $s1 = 0	Compare < constant; natural numbers
Unconditional jump	jump	j	2500	go to 10000	Jump to target address
	jump register	jr	$ra	go to $ra	For switch, procedure return
	jump and link	jal	2500	$ra = PC + 4; go to 10000	For procedure call

FIGURE 3.12 MIPS core architecture. The memory and registers of the MIPS architecture are not included for space reasons, but this section added the Hi and Lo registers to support multiply and divide. MIPS machine language is listed in the MIPS Reference Data Card at the front of this book.

MIPS divide instructions ignore overflow, so software must determine whether the quotient is too large. In addition to overflow, division can also result in an improper calculation: division by 0. Some computers distinguish these two anomalous events. MIPS software must check the divisor to discover division by 0 as well as overflow.

Elaboration: An even faster algorithm than Figure 3.9 does not immediately add the divisor back if the remainder is negative. It simply *adds* the dividend to the shifted remainder in the following step, since $(r + d) \times 2 - d = r \times 2 + d \times 2 - d = r \times 2 + d$. This *nonrestoring* division algorithm, which takes 1 clock cycle per step, is explored further in the exercises; the algorithm in Figure 3.9 is called *restoring* division. A third algorithm that doesn't save the result of the subtract if it's negative is called a *nonperforming* division algorithm. It averages one-third fewer arithmetic operations.

3.5   Floating Point

*Speed gets you
nowhere if you're
headed the wrong way.*

American proverb

Going beyond signed and unsigned integers, programming languages support numbers with fractions, which are called *reals* in mathematics. Here are some examples of reals:

$$3.14159265\ldots_{\text{ten}}\ (\text{pi})$$

$$2.71828\ldots_{\text{ten}}\ (e)$$

$$0.000000001_{\text{ten}}\ \text{or}\ 1.0_{\text{ten}} \times 10^{-9}\ (\text{seconds in a nanosecond})$$

$$3{,}155{,}760{,}000_{\text{ten}}\ \text{or}\ 3.15576_{\text{ten}} \times 10^{9}\ (\text{seconds in a typical century})$$

scientific notation
A notation that renders numbers with a single digit to the left of the decimal point.

Notice that in the last case, the number didn't represent a small fraction, but it was bigger than we could represent with a 32-bit signed integer. The alternative notation for the last two numbers is called **scientific notation**, which has a single digit to the left of the decimal point. A number in scientific notation that has no leading 0s is called a **normalized** number, which is the usual way to write it. For example, $1.0_{\text{ten}} \times 10^{-9}$ is in normalized scientific notation, but $0.1_{\text{ten}} \times 10^{-8}$ and $10.0_{\text{ten}} \times 10^{-10}$ are not.

normalized A number in floating-point notation that has no leading 0s.

Just as we can show decimal numbers in scientific notation, we can also show binary numbers in scientific notation:

$$1.0_{\text{two}} \times 2^{-1}$$

To keep a binary number in normalized form, we need a base that we can increase or decrease by exactly the number of bits the number must be shifted to have one nonzero digit to the left of the decimal point. Only a base of 2 fulfills our need. Since the base is not 10, we also need a new name for decimal point; *binary point* will do fine.

Computer arithmetic that supports such numbers is called **floating point** because it represents numbers in which the binary point is not fixed, as it is for integers. The programming language C uses the name *float* for such numbers. Just as in scientific notation, numbers are represented as a single nonzero digit to the left of the binary point. In binary, the form is

$$1.xxxxxxxxx_{\text{two}} \times 2^{yyyy}$$

(Although the computer represents the exponent in base 2 as well as the rest of the number, to simplify the notation we show the exponent in decimal.)

A standard scientific notation for reals in normalized form offers three advantages. It simplifies exchange of data that includes floating-point numbers; it simplifies the floating-point arithmetic algorithms to know that numbers will always be in this form; and it increases the accuracy of the numbers that can be stored in a word, since the unnecessary leading 0s are replaced by real digits to the right of the binary point.

Floating-Point Representation

A designer of a floating-point representation must find a compromise between the size of the **fraction** and the size of the **exponent**, because a fixed word size means you must take a bit from one to give a bit to the other. This tradeoff is between *precision* and *range*: increasing the size of the fraction enhances the precision of the fraction, while increasing the size of the exponent increases the range of numbers that can be represented. As our design guideline from Chapter 2 reminds us, good design demands good compromise.

Floating-point numbers are usually a multiple of the size of a word. The representation of a MIPS floating-point number is shown below, where *s* is the sign of the floating-point number (1 meaning negative), *exponent* is the value of the 8-bit exponent field (including the sign of the exponent), and *fraction* is the 23-bit number. As we recall from Chapter 2, this representation is *sign and magnitude*, since the sign is a separate bit from the rest of the number.

31	30	29	28	27	26	25	24	23	22	21	20	19	18	17	16	15	14	13	12	11	10	9	8	7	6	5	4	3	2	1	0
s	exponent								fraction																						

1 bit   8 bits   23 bits

In general, floating-point numbers are of the form

$$(-1)^{S} \times F \times 2^{E}$$

F involves the value in the fraction field and E involves the value in the exponent field; the exact relationship to these fields will be spelled out soon. (We will shortly see that MIPS does something slightly more sophisticated.)

floating point
Computer arithmetic that represents numbers in which the binary point is not fixed.

fraction The value, generally between 0 and 1, placed in the fraction field. The fraction is also called the *mantissa*.

exponent In the numerical representation system of floating-point arithmetic, the value that is placed in the exponent field.

These chosen sizes of exponent and fraction give MIPS computer arithmetic an extraordinary range. Fractions almost as small as $2.0_{ten} \times 10^{-38}$ and numbers almost as large as $2.0_{ten} \times 10^{38}$ can be represented in a computer. Alas, extraordinary differs from infinite, so it is still possible for numbers to be too large. Thus, overflow exceptions can occur in floating-point arithmetic as well as in integer arithmetic. Notice that **overflow** here means that the exponent is too large to be represented in the exponent field.

Floating point offers a new kind of exceptional event as well. Just as programmers will want to know when they have calculated a number that is too large to be represented, they will want to know if the nonzero fraction they are calculating has become so small that it cannot be represented; either event could result in a program giving incorrect answers. To distinguish it from overflow, we call this event **underflow**. This situation occurs when the negative exponent is too large to fit in the exponent field.

One way to reduce chances of underflow or overflow is to offer another format that has a larger exponent. In C this number is called *double*, and operations on doubles are called **double precision** floating-point arithmetic; **single precision** floating point is the name of the earlier format.

The representation of a double precision floating-point number takes two MIPS words, as shown below, where s is still the sign of the number, *exponent* is the value of the 11-bit exponent field, and *fraction* is the 52-bit number in the fraction field.

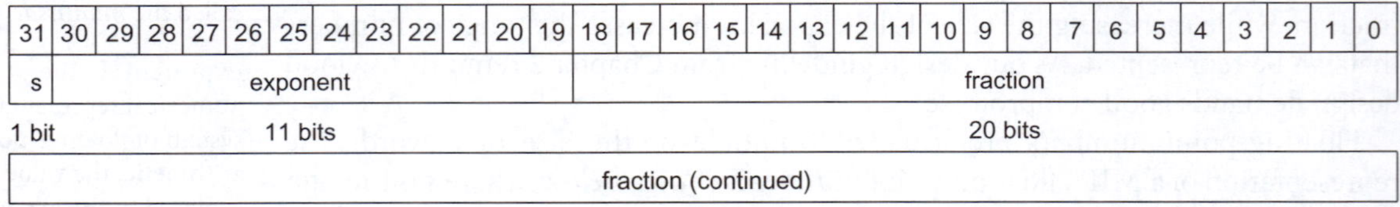

MIPS double precision allows numbers almost as small as $2.0_{ten} \times 10^{-308}$ and almost as large as $2.0_{ten} \times 10^{308}$. Although double precision does increase the exponent range, its primary advantage is its greater precision because of the much larger fraction.

These formats go beyond MIPS. They are part of the *IEEE 754 floating-point standard*, found in virtually every computer invented since 1980. This standard has greatly improved both the ease of porting floating-point programs and the quality of computer arithmetic.

To pack even more bits into the significand, IEEE 754 makes the leading 1-bit of normalized binary numbers implicit. Hence, the number is actually 24 bits long in single precision (implied 1 and a 23-bit fraction), and 53 bits long in double precision (1 + 52). To be precise, we use the term *significand* to represent the 24- or 53-bit number that is 1 plus the fraction, and *fraction* when we mean the 23- or 52-bit number. Since 0 has no leading 1, it is given the reserved exponent value 0 so that the hardware won't attach a leading 1 to it.

Single precision		Double precision		Object represented
Exponent	Fraction	Exponent	Fraction	
0	0	0	0	0
0	Nonzero	0	Nonzero	± denormalized number
1–254	Anything	1–2046	Anything	± floating-point number
255	0	2047	0	± infinity
255	Nonzero	2047	Nonzero	NaN (Not a Number)

FIGURE 3.13 EEE 754 encoding of floating-point numbers. A separate sign bit determines the sign. Denormalized numbers are described in the *Elaboration* on page 232. This information is also found in Column 4 of the MIPS Reference Data Card at the front of this book.

Thus $00 \ldots 00_{two}$ represents 0; the representation of the rest of the numbers uses the form from before with the hidden 1 added:

$$(-1)^S \times (1 + \text{Fraction}) \times 2^E$$

where the bits of the fraction represent a number between 0 and 1 and E specifies the value in the exponent field, to be given in detail shortly. If we number the bits of the fraction from *left to right* $s1, s2, s3, \ldots$, then the value is

$$(-1)^S \times (1 + (s1 \times 2^{-1}) + (s2 \times 2^{-2}) + (s3 \times 2^{-3}) + (s4 \times 2^{-4}) + \ldots) \times 2^E$$

Figure 3.13 shows the encodings of IEEE 754 floating-point numbers. Other features of IEEE 754 are special symbols to represent unusual events. For example, instead of interrupting on a divide by 0, software can set the result to a bit pattern representing $+\infty$ or $-\infty$; the largest exponent is reserved for these special symbols. When the programmer prints the results, the program will print an infinity symbol. (For the mathematically trained, the purpose of infinity is to form topological closure of the reals.)

IEEE 754 even has a symbol for the result of invalid operations, such as 0/0 or subtracting infinity from infinity. This symbol is *NaN*, for *Not a Number*. The purpose of NaNs is to allow programmers to postpone some tests and decisions to a later time in the program when they are convenient.

The designers of IEEE 754 also wanted a floating-point representation that could be easily processed by integer comparisons, especially for sorting. This desire is why the sign is in the most significant bit, allowing a quick test of less than, greater than, or equal to 0. (It's a little more complicated than a simple integer sort, since this notation is essentially sign and magnitude rather than two's complement.)

Placing the exponent before the significand also simplifies the sorting of floating-point numbers using integer comparison instructions, since numbers with bigger exponents look larger than numbers with smaller exponents, as long as both exponents have the same sign.

Negative exponents pose a challenge to simplified sorting. If we use two's complement or any other notation in which negative exponents have a 1 in the most significant bit of the exponent field, a negative exponent will look like a big number. For example, $1.0_{two} \times 2^{-1}$ would be represented as

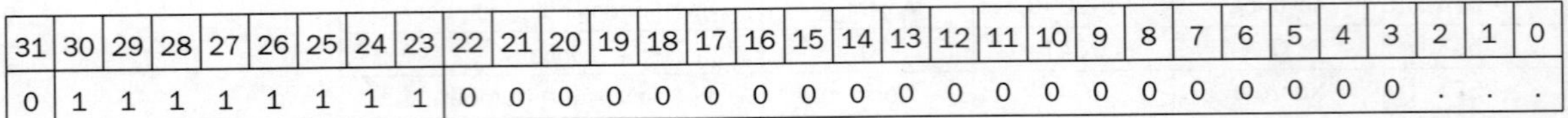

(Remember that the leading 1 is implicit in the significand.) The value $1.0_{two} \times 2^{+1}$ would look like the smaller binary number

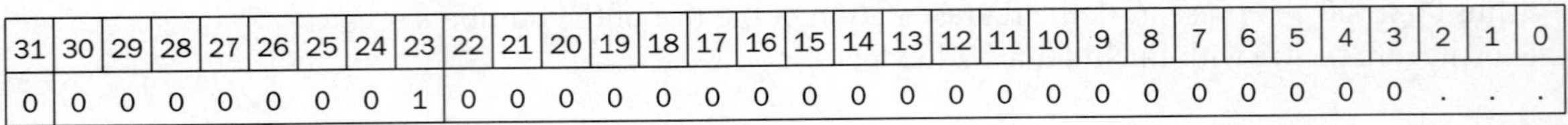

The desirable notation must therefore represent the most negative exponent as $00 \ldots 00_{two}$ and the most positive as $11 \ldots 11_{two}$. This convention is called *biased notation*, with the bias being the number subtracted from the normal, unsigned representation to determine the real value.

IEEE 754 uses a bias of 127 for single precision, so an exponent of -1 is represented by the bit pattern of the value $-1 + 127_{ten}$, or $126_{ten} = 0111\ 1110_{two}$, and $+1$ is represented by $1 + 127$, or $128_{ten} = 1000\ 0000_{two}$. The exponent bias for double precision is 1023. Biased exponent means that the value represented by a floating-point number is really

$$(-1)^S \times (1 + \text{Fraction}) \times 2^{(\text{Exponent} - \text{Bias})}$$

The range of single precision numbers is then from as small as

$$\pm 1.00000000000000000000000_{two} \times 2^{-126}$$

to as large as

$$\pm 1.11111111111111111111111_{two} \times 2^{+127}.$$

Let's demonstrate.

Floating-Point Representation

Show the IEEE 754 binary representation of the number -0.75_{ten} in single and double precision.

The number -0.75_{ten} is also

$$-3/4_{\text{ten}} \quad \text{or} \quad -3/2^2_{\text{ten}}$$

It is also represented by the binary fraction

$$-11_{\text{two}}/2^2_{\text{ten}} \quad \text{or} \quad -0.11_{\text{two}}$$

In scientific notation, the value is

$$-0.11_{\text{two}} \times 2^0$$

and in normalized scientific notation, it is

$$-1.1_{\text{two}} \times 2^{-1}$$

The general representation for a single precision number is

$$(-1)^S \times (1 + \text{Fraction}) \times 2^{(\text{Exponent}-127)}$$

Subtracting the bias 127 from the exponent of $-1.1_{\text{two}} \times 2^{-1}$ yields

$$(-1)^1 \times (1 + .1000\ 0000\ 0000\ 0000\ 0000\ 000_{\text{two}}) \times 2^{(126-127)}$$

The single precision binary representation of -0.75_{ten} is then

31	30	29	28	27	26	25	24	23	22	21	20	19	18	17	16	15	14	13	12	11	10	9	8	7	6	5	4	3	2	1	0
1	0	1	1	1	1	1	0	1	0	0	0	0	0	0	0	0	0	0	0	0	0	0	0	0	0	0	0	0	0	0	0

1 bit   8 bits   23 bits

The double precision representation is

$$(-1)^1 \times (1 + .1000\ 0000\ 0000\ 0000\ 0000\ 0000\ 0000\ 0000\ 0000\ 0000\ 0000\ 0000\ 0000_{\text{two}}) \times 2^{(1022-1023)}$$

31	30	29	28	27	26	25	24	23	22	21	20	19	18	17	16	15	14	13	12	11	10	9	8	7	6	5	4	3	2	1	0
1	0	1	1	1	1	1	1	1	1	1	0	1	0	0	0	0	0	0	0	0	0	0	0	0	0	0	0	0	0	0	0

1 bit   11 bits   20 bits

0	0	0	0	0	0	0	0	0	0	0	0	0	0	0	0	0	0	0	0	0	0	0	0	0	0	0	0	0	0	0	0

32 bits

Now let's try going the other direction.

EXAMPLE

Converting Binary to Decimal Floating Point

What decimal number is represented by this single precision float?

31	30	29	28	27	26	25	24	23	22	21	20	19	18	17	16	15	14	13	12	11	10	9	8	7	6	5	4	3	2	1	0
1	1	0	0	0	0	0	0	1	0	1	0	0	0	0	0	0	0	0	0	0	0	0	0	0	0	0	0	0	0	0	0

ANSWER

The sign bit is 1, the exponent field contains 129, and the fraction field contains $1 \times 2^{-2} = 1/4$, or 0.25. Using the basic equation,

$$\begin{aligned}
(-1)^S \times (1 + \text{Fraction}) \times 2^{(\text{Exponent} - \text{Bias})} &= (-1)^1 \times (1 + 0.25) \times 2^{(129 - 127)} \\
&= -1 \times 1.25 \times 2^2 \\
&= -1.25 \times 4 \\
&= -5.0
\end{aligned}$$

In the next few subsections, we will give the algorithms for floating-point addition and multiplication. At their core, they use the corresponding integer operations on the significands, but extra bookkeeping is necessary to handle the exponents and normalize the result. We first give an intuitive derivation of the algorithms in decimal and then give a more detailed, binary version in the figures.

Following IEEE guidelines, the IEEE 754 committee was reformed 20 years after the standard to see what changes, if any, should be made. The revised standard IEEE 754-2008 includes nearly all the IEEE 754-1985 and adds a 16-bit format ("half precision") and a 128-bit format ("quadruple precision"). Half precision has a 1-bit sign, 5-bit exponent (with a bias of 15), and a 10-bit fraction. Quadruple precision has a 1-bit sign, 15-bit exponent (with a bias of 262143), and a 112-bit fraction. No hardware has yet been built that supports quadruple precision, but it will surely come. The revised standard also add decimal floating point arithmetic, which IBM mainframes have implemented.

Elaboration: In an attempt to increase range without removing bits from the significand, some computers before the IEEE 754 standard used a base other than 2. For example, the IBM 360 and 370 mainframe computers used base 16. Since changing the IBM exponent by one means shifting the significand by 4 bits, "normalized" base 16 numbers can have up to 3 leading bits of 0s! Hence, hexadecimal digits mean that up to 3 bits must be dropped from the significand, which leads to surprising problems in the accuracy of floating-point arithmetic. IBM mainframes now support IEEE 754 as well as the hex format.

Floating-Point Addition

Let's add numbers in scientific notation by hand to illustrate the problems in floating-point addition: $9.999_{ten} \times 10^1 + 1.610_{ten} \times 10^{-1}$. Assume that we can store only four decimal digits of the significand and two decimal digits of the exponent.

Step 1. To be able to add these numbers properly, we must align the decimal point of the number that has the smaller exponent. Hence, we need a form of the smaller number, $1.610_{ten} \times 10^{-1}$, that matches the larger exponent. We obtain this by observing that there are multiple representations of an unnormalized floating-point number in scientific notation:

$$1.610_{ten} \times 10^{-1} = 0.1610_{ten} \times 10^0 = 0.01610_{ten} \times 10^1$$

The number on the right is the version we desire, since its exponent matches the exponent of the larger number, $9.999_{ten} \times 10^1$. Thus, the first step shifts the significand of the smaller number to the right until its corrected exponent matches that of the larger number. But we can represent only four decimal digits so, after shifting, the number is really

$$0.016_{ten} \times 10^1$$

Step 2. Next comes the addition of the significands:

$$
\begin{array}{r}
9.999_{ten} \\
+ \quad 0.016_{ten} \\
\hline
10.015_{ten}
\end{array}
$$

The sum is $10.015_{ten} \times 10^1$.

Step 3. This sum is not in normalized scientific notation, so we need to adjust it:

$$10.015_{ten} \times 10^1 = 1.0015_{ten} = 10^2$$

After the addition we may have to shift the sum to put it into normalized form, adjusting the exponent appropriately. This example shows shifting to the right, but if one number were positive and the other were negative, it would be possible for the sum to have many leading 0s, requiring left shifts. Whenever the exponent is increased or decreased, we must check for overflow or underflow—that is, we must make sure that the exponent still fits in its field.

Step 4. Since we assumed that the significand can be only four digits long (excluding the sign), we must round the number. In our grammar school algorithm, the rules truncate the number if the digit to the right of the desired point is between 0 and 4 and add 1 to the digit if the number to the right is between 5 and 9. The number

$$1.0015_{ten} \times 10^2$$

is rounded to four digits in the significand to

$$1.002_{ten} \times 10^2$$

since the fourth digit to the right of the decimal point was between 5 and 9. Notice that if we have bad luck on rounding, such as adding 1 to a string of 9s, the sum may no longer be normalized and we would need to perform step 3 again.

Figure 3.14 shows the algorithm for binary floating-point addition that follows this decimal example. Steps 1 and 2 are similar to the example just discussed: adjust the significand of the number with the smaller exponent and then add the two significands. Step 3 normalizes the results, forcing a check for overflow or underflow. The test for overflow and underflow in step 3 depends on the precision of the operands. Recall that the pattern of all 0 bits in the exponent is reserved and used for the floating-point representation of zero. Moreover, the pattern of all 1 bits in the exponent is reserved for indicating values and situations outside the scope of normal floating-point numbers (see the *Elaboration* on page 232). For the example below, remember that for single precision, the maximum exponent is 127, and the minimum exponent is -126.

EXAMPLE

Binary Floating-Point Addition

Try adding the numbers 0.5_{ten} and -0.4375_{ten} in binary using the algorithm in Figure 3.14.

ANSWER

Let's first look at the binary version of the two numbers in normalized scientific notation, assuming that we keep 4 bits of precision:

$$
\begin{aligned}
0.5_{ten} &= 1/2_{ten} & &= 1/2^1_{ten} \\
&= 0.1_{two} & &= 0.1_{two} \times 2^0 & &= 1.000_{two} \times 2^{-1} \\
-0.4375_{ten} &= -7/16_{ten} & &= -7/2^4_{ten} \\
& & &= -0.0111_{two} = -0.0111_{two} \times 2^0 = -1.110_{two} \times 2^{-2}
\end{aligned}
$$

Now we follow the algorithm:

Step 1. The significand of the number with the lesser exponent ($-1.11_{two} \times 2^{-2}$) is shifted right until its exponent matches the larger number:

$$-1.110_{two} \times 2^{-2} = -0.111_{two} \times 2^{-1}$$

Step 2. Add the significands:

$$1.000_{two} \times 2^{-1} + (-0.111_{two} \times 2^{-1}) = 0.001_{two} \times 2^{-1}$$

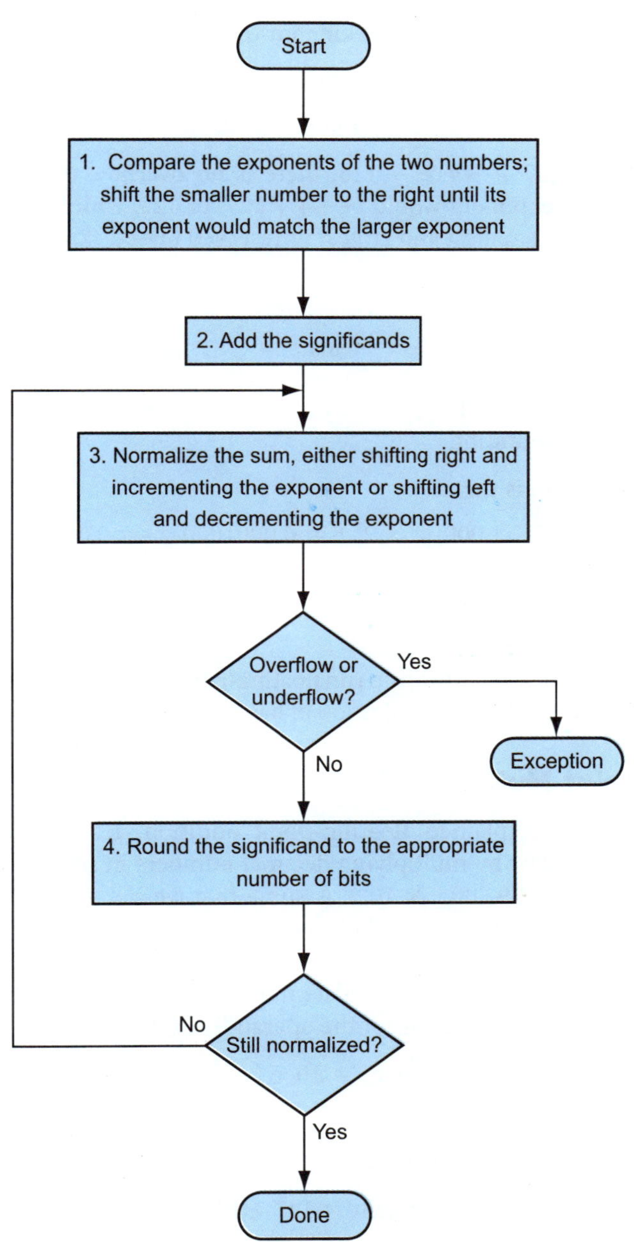

FIGURE 3.14 Floating-point addition. The normal path is to execute steps 3 and 4 once, but if rounding causes the sum to be unnormalized, we must repeat step 3.

Step 3.   Normalize the sum, checking for overflow or underflow:

$$0.001_{two} \times 2^{-1} = 0.010_{two} \times 2^{-2} = 0.100_{two} \times 2^{-3}$$
$$= 1.000_{two} \times 2^{-4}$$

Since $127 \geq -4 \geq -126$, there is no overflow or underflow. (The biased exponent would be $-4 + 127$, or 123, which is between 1 and 254, the smallest and largest unreserved biased exponents.)

Step 4.   Round the sum:

$$1.000_{two} \times 2^{-4}$$

The sum already fits exactly in 4 bits, so there is no change to the bits due to rounding.

This sum is then

$$1.000_{two} \times 2^{-4} = 0.0001000_{two} = 0.0001_{two}$$
$$= 1/2^4_{\ ten} \qquad = 1/16_{ten} \qquad = 0.0625_{ten}$$

This sum is what we would expect from adding 0.5_{ten} to -0.4375_{ten}.

Many computers dedicate hardware to run floating-point operations as fast as possible. Figure 3.15 sketches the basic organization of hardware for floating-point addition.

Floating-Point Multiplication

Now that we have explained floating-point addition, let's try floating-point multiplication. We start by multiplying decimal numbers in scientific notation by hand: $1.110_{ten} \times 10^{10} \times 9.200_{ten} \times 10^{-5}$. Assume that we can store only four digits of the significand and two digits of the exponent.

Step 1.   Unlike addition, we calculate the exponent of the product by simply adding the exponents of the operands together:

$$\text{New exponent} = 10 + (-5) = 5$$

Let's do this with the biased exponents as well to make sure we obtain the same result: $10 + 127 = 137$, and $-5 + 127 = 122$, so

$$\text{New exponent} = 137 + 122 = 259$$

This result is too large for the 8-bit exponent field, so something is amiss! The problem is with the bias because we are adding the biases as well as the exponents:

$$\text{New exponent} = (10 + 127) + (-5 + 127) = (5 + 2 \times 127) = 259$$

Accordingly, to get the correct biased sum when we add biased numbers, we must subtract the bias from the sum:

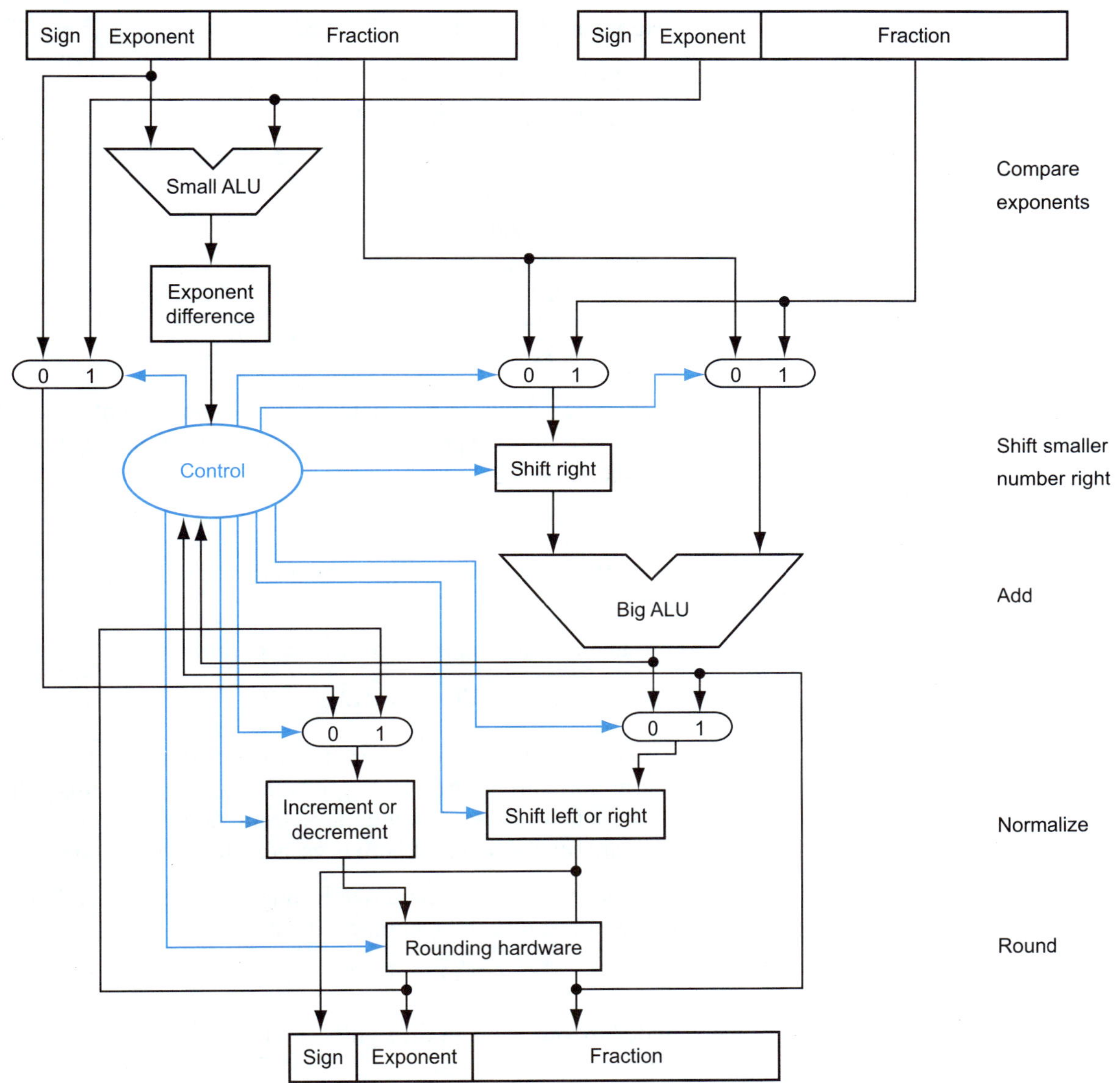

FIGURE 3.15 Block diagram of an arithmetic unit dedicated to floating-point addition. The steps of Figure 3.14 correspond to each block, from top to bottom. First, the exponent of one operand is subtracted from the other using the small ALU to determine which is larger and by how much. This difference controls the three multiplexors; from left to right, they select the larger exponent, the significand of the smaller number, and the significand of the larger number. The smaller significand is shifted right, and then the significands are added together using the big ALU. The normalization step then shifts the sum left or right and increments or decrements the exponent. Rounding then creates the final result, which may require normalizing again to produce the actual final result.

New exponent $= 137 + 122 - 127 = 259 - 127 = 132 = (5 + 127)$

and 5 is indeed the exponent we calculated initially.

Step 2.   Next comes the multiplication of the significands:

$$
\begin{array}{r}
1.110_{\text{ten}} \\
\times\ \ 9.200_{\text{ten}} \\
\hline
0000 \\
0000\ \ \\
2220\ \ \ \ \\
9990\ \ \ \ \ \ \\
\hline
10212000_{\text{ten}}
\end{array}
$$

There are three digits to the right of the decimal point for each operand, so the decimal point is placed six digits from the right in the product significand:

$$10.212000_{\text{ten}}$$

Assuming that we can keep only three digits to the right of the decimal point, the product is 10.212×10^5.

Step 3.   This product is unnormalized, so we need to normalize it:

$$10.212_{\text{ten}} \times 10^5 = 1.0212_{\text{ten}} \times 10^6$$

Thus, after the multiplication, the product can be shifted right one digit to put it in normalized form, adding 1 to the exponent. At this point, we can check for overflow and underflow. Underflow may occur if both operands are small—that is, if both have large negative exponents.

Step 4.   We assumed that the significand is only four digits long (excluding the sign), so we must round the number. The number

$$1.0212_{\text{ten}} \times 10^6$$

is rounded to four digits in the significand to

$$1.021_{\text{ten}} \times 10^6$$

Step 5.   The sign of the product depends on the signs of the original operands. If they are both the same, the sign is positive; otherwise, it's negative. Hence, the product is

$$+1.021_{\text{ten}} \times 10^6$$

The sign of the sum in the addition algorithm was determined by addition of the significands, but in multiplication, the sign of the product is determined by the signs of the operands.

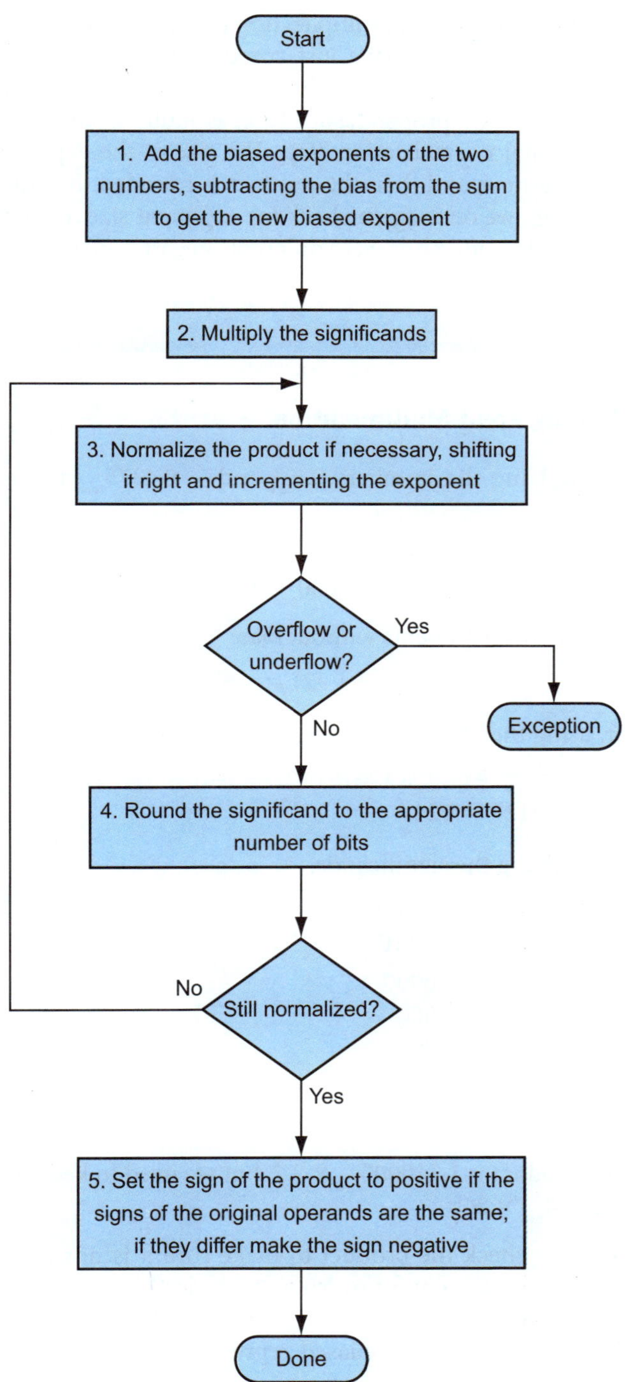

FIGURE 3.16 Floating-point multiplication. The normal path is to execute steps 3 and 4 once, but if rounding causes the sum to be unnormalized, we must repeat step 3.

Once again, as Figure 3.16 shows, multiplication of binary floating-point numbers is quite similar to the steps we have just completed. We start with calculating the new exponent of the product by adding the biased exponents, being sure to subtract one bias to get the proper result. Next is multiplication of significands, followed by an optional normalization step. The size of the exponent is checked for overflow or underflow, and then the product is rounded. If rounding leads to further normalization, we once again check for exponent size. Finally, set the sign bit to 1 if the signs of the operands were different (negative product) or to 0 if they were the same (positive product).

EXAMPLE

ANSWER

Binary Floating-Point Multiplication

Let's try multiplying the numbers 0.5_{ten} and -0.4375_{ten}, using the steps in Figure 3.16.

In binary, the task is multiplying $1.000_{two} \times 2^{-1}$ by $-1.110_{two} \times 2^{-2}$.

Step 1. Adding the exponents without bias:

$$-1 + (-2) = -3$$

or, using the biased representation:

$$(-1 + 127) + (-2 + 127) - 127 = (-1 - 2) + (127 + 127 - 127)$$
$$= -3 + 127 = 124$$

Step 2. Multiplying the significands:

$$
\begin{array}{r}
1.000_{two} \\
\times \quad 1.110_{two} \\
\hline
0000 \\
1000 \\
1000 \\
1000 \\
\hline
1110000_{two}
\end{array}
$$

The product is $1.110000_{two} \times 2^{-3}$, but we need to keep it to 4 bits, so it is $1.110_{two} \times 2^{-3}$.

Step 3. Now we check the product to make sure it is normalized, and then check the exponent for overflow or underflow. The product is already normalized and, since $127 \geq -3 \geq -126$, there is no overflow or underflow. (Using the biased representation, $254 \geq 124 \geq 1$, so the exponent fits.)

Step 4. Rounding the product makes no change:

$$1.110_{two} \times 2^{-3}$$

Step 5.   Since the signs of the original operands differ, make the sign of the product negative. Hence, the product is

$$-1.110_{two} \times 2^{-3}$$

Converting to decimal to check our results:

$$-1.110_{two} \times 2^{-3} = -0.001110_{two} = -0.00111_{two}$$
$$= -7/2^5{}_{ten} = -7/32_{ten} = -0.21875_{ten}$$

The product of 0.5_{ten} and -0.4375_{ten} is indeed -0.21875_{ten}.

Floating-Point Instructions in MIPS

MIPS supports the IEEE 754 single precision and double precision formats with these instructions:

- Floating-point *addition, single* (`add.s`) and *addition, double* (`add.d`)

- Floating-point *subtraction, single* (`sub.s`) and *subtraction, double* (`sub.d`)

- Floating-point *multiplication, single* (`mul.s`) and *multiplication, double* (`mul.d`)

- Floating-point *division, single* (`div.s`) and *division, double* (`div.d`)

- Floating-point *comparison, single* (`c.x.s`) and *comparison, double* (`c.x.d`), where x may be *equal* (`eq`), *not equal* (`neq`), *less than* (`lt`), *less than or equal* (`le`), *greater than* (`gt`), or *greater than or equal* (`ge`)

- Floating-point *branch, true* (`bclt`) and *branch, false* (`bclf`)

Floating-point comparison sets a bit to true or false, depending on the comparison condition, and a floating-point branch then decides whether or not to branch, depending on the condition.

The MIPS designers decided to add separate floating-point registers—called $f0, $f1, $f2, ...—used either for single precision or double precision. Hence, they included separate loads and stores for floating-point registers: `lwc1` and `swc1`. The base registers for floating-point data transfers which are used for addresses remain integer registers. The MIPS code to load two single precision numbers from memory, add them, and then store the sum might look like this:

```
lwc1      $f4,c($sp)    # Load 32-bit F.P. number into F4
lwc1      $f6,a($sp)    # Load 32-bit F.P. number into F6
add.s     $f2,$f4,$f6   # F2 = F4 + F6 single precision
swc1      $f2,b($sp)    # Store 32-bit F.P. number from F2
```

A double precision register is really an even-odd pair of single precision registers, using the even register number as its name. Thus, the pair of single precision registers $f2 and $f3 also form the double precision register named $f2.

Figure 3.17 summarizes the floating-point portion of the MIPS architecture revealed in this chapter, with the additions to support floating point shown in color. Similar to Figure 2.19 in Chapter 2, Figure 3.18 shows the encoding of these instructions.

MIPS floating-point operands

Name	Example	Comments
32 floating-point registers	`$f0, $f1, $f2, . . . , $f31`	MIPS floating-point registers are used in pairs for double precision numbers.
2^{30} memory words	Memory[0], Memory[4], . . . , Memory[4294967292]	Accessed only by data transfer instructions. MIPS uses byte addresses, so sequential word addresses differ by 4. Memory holds data structures, such as arrays, and spilled registers, such as those saved on procedure calls.

MIPS floating-point assembly language

Category	Instruction	Example	Meaning	Comments
Arithmetic	FP add single	`add.s   $f2,$f4,$f6`	$f2 = $f4 + $f6	FP add (single precision)
	FP subtract single	`sub.s   $f2,$f4,$f6`	$f2 = $f4 − $f6	FP sub (single precision)
	FP multiply single	`mul.s   $f2,$f4,$f6`	$f2 = $f4 × $f6	FP multiply (single precision)
	FP divide single	`div.s   $f2,$f4,$f6`	$f2 = $f4 / $f6	FP divide (single precision)
	FP add double	`add.d   $f2,$f4,$f6`	$f2 = $f4 + $f6	FP add (double precision)
	FP subtract double	`sub.d   $f2,$f4,$f6`	$f2 = $f4 − $f6	FP sub (double precision)
	FP multiply double	`mul.d   $f2,$f4,$f6`	$f2 = $f4 × $f6	FP multiply (double precision)
	FP divide double	`div.d   $f2,$f4,$f6`	$f2 = $f4 / $f6	FP divide (double precision)
Data transfer	load word copr. 1	`lwc1   $f1,100($s2)`	$f1 = Memory[$s2 + 100]	32-bit data to FP register
	store word copr. 1	`swc1   $f1,100($s2)`	Memory[$s2 + 100] = $f1	32-bit data to memory
Conditional branch	branch on FP true	`bc1t   25`	if (cond == 1) go to PC + 4 + 100	PC-relative branch if FP cond.
	branch on FP false	`bc1f   25`	if (cond == 0) go to PC + 4 + 100	PC-relative branch if not cond.
	FP compare single (eq,ne,lt,le,gt,ge)	`c.lt.s $f2,$f4`	if ($f2 < $f4) cond = 1; else cond = 0	FP compare less than single precision
	FP compare double (eq,ne,lt,le,gt,ge)	`c.lt.d $f2,$f4`	if ($f2 < $f4) cond = 1; else cond = 0	FP compare less than double precision

MIPS floating-point machine language

Name	Format	Example						Comments
`add.s`	R	17	16	6	4	2	0	`add.s   $f2,$f4,$f6`
`sub.s`	R	17	16	6	4	2	1	`sub.s   $f2,$f4,$f6`
`mul.s`	R	17	16	6	4	2	2	`mul.s   $f2,$f4,$f6`
`div.s`	R	17	16	6	4	2	3	`div.s   $f2,$f4,$f6`
`add.d`	R	17	17	6	4	2	0	`add.d   $f2,$f4,$f6`
`sub.d`	R	17	17	6	4	2	1	`sub.d   $f2,$f4,$f6`
`mul.d`	R	17	17	6	4	2	2	`mul.d   $f2,$f4,$f6`
`div.d`	R	17	17	6	4	2	3	`div.d   $f2,$f4,$f6`
`lwc1`	I	49	20	2	100			`lwc1   $f2,100($s4)`
`swc1`	I	57	20	2	100			`swc1   $f2,100($s4)`
`bc1t`	I	17	8	1	25			`bc1t   25`
`bc1f`	I	17	8	0	25			`bc1f   25`
`c.lt.s`	R	17	16	4	2	0	60	`c.lt.s $f2,$f4`
`c.lt.d`	R	17	17	4	2	0	60	`c.lt.d $f2,$f4`
Field size		6 bits	5 bits	5 bits	5 bits	5 bits	6 bits	All MIPS instructions 32 bits

FIGURE 3.17   MIPS floating-point architecture revealed thus far. See Appendix A, Section A.10, for more detail. This information is also found in column 2 of the MIPS Reference Data Card at the front of this book.

op(31:26):								
28–26 / 31–29	0(000)	1(001)	2(010)	3(011)	4(100)	5(101)	6(110)	7(111)
0(000)	Rfmt	Bltz/gez	j	jal	beq	bne	blez	bgtz
1(001)	addi	addiu	slti	sltiu	ANDi	ORi	xORi	lui
2(010)	TLB	FlPt						
3(011)								
4(100)	lb	lh	lwl	lw	lbu	lhu	lwr	
5(101)	sb	sh	swl	sw			swr	
6(110)	lwc0	lwc1						
7(111)	swc0	swc1						

op(31:26) = 010001 (FlPt), (rt(16:16) = 0 => c = f, rt(16:16) = 1 => c = t), rs(25:21):								
23–21 / 25–24	0(000)	1(001)	2(010)	3(011)	4(100)	5(101)	6(110)	7(111)
0(00)	mfc1		cfc1		mtc1		ctc1	
1(01)	bc1.c							
2(10)	f = single	f = double						
3(11)								

op(31:26) = 010001 (FlPt), (f above: 10000 => f = s, 10001 => f = d), funct(5:0):								
2–0 / 5–3	0(000)	1(001)	2(010)	3(011)	4(100)	5(101)	6(110)	7(111)
0(000)	add.f	sub.f	mul.f	div.f		abs.f	mov.f	neg.f
1(001)								
2(010)								
3(011)								
4(100)	cvt.s.f	cvt.d.f			cvt.w.f			
5(101)								
6(110)	c.f.f	c.un.f	c.eq.f	c.ueq.f	c.olt.f	c.ult.f	c.ole.f	c.ule.f
7(111)	c.sf.f	c.ngle.f	c.seq.f	c.ngl.f	c.lt.f	c.nge.f	c.le.f	c.ngt.f

FIGURE 3.18   MIPS floating-point instruction encoding. This notation gives the value of a field by row and by column. For example, in the top portion of the figure, lw is found in row number 4 (100_{two} for bits 31–29 of the instruction) and column number 3 (011_{two} for bits 28–26 of the instruction), so the corresponding value of the op field (bits 31–26) is 100011_{two}. Underlined text means the field is used elsewhere. For example, FlPt in row 2 and column 1 (op = 010001_{two}) is defined in the bottom part of the figure. Hence sub.f in row 0 and column 1 of the bottom section means that the funct field (bits 5–0) of the instruction is 000001_{two} and the op field (bits 31–26) is 010001_{two}. Note that the 5-bit rs field, specified in the middle portion of the figure, determines whether the operation is single precision (f = s, so rs = 10000) or double precision (f = d, so rs = 10001). Similarly, bit 16 of the instruction determines if the bc1.c instruction tests for true (bit 16 = 1=> bc1.t) or false (bit 16 = 0=> bc1.f). This information is also found in column 2 of the MIPS Reference Data Card at the front of this book.

One issue that architects face in supporting floating-point arithmetic is whether to use the same registers used by the integer instructions or to add a special set for floating point. Because programs normally perform integer operations and floating-point operations on different data, separating the registers will only slightly increase the number of instructions needed to execute a program. The major impact is to create a separate set of data transfer instructions to move data between floating-point registers and memory.

The benefits of separate floating-point registers are having twice as many registers without using up more bits in the instruction format, having twice the register bandwidth by having separate integer and floating-point register sets, and being able to customize registers to floating point; for example, some computers convert all sized operands in registers into a single internal format.

EXAMPLE

Compiling a Floating-Point C Program into MIPS Assembly Code

Let's convert a temperature in Fahrenheit to Celsius:

```
float f2c (float fahr)
        {
                return ((5.0/9.0) *(fahr - 32.0));
        }
```

Assume that the floating-point argument `fahr` is passed in `$f12` and the result should go in `$f0`. (Unlike integer registers, floating-point register 0 can contain a number.) What is the MIPS assembly code?

ANSWER

We assume that the compiler places the three floating-point constants in memory within easy reach of the global pointer `$gp`. The first two instructions load the constants 5.0 and 9.0 into floating-point registers:

```
f2c:
     lwc1 $f16,const5($gp) # $f16 = 5.0 (5.0 in memory)
     lwc1 $f18,const9($gp) # $f18 = 9.0 (9.0 in memory)
```

They are then divided to get the fraction 5.0/9.0:

```
     div.s $f16, $f16, $f18 # $f16 = 5.0 / 9.0
```

(Many compilers would divide 5.0 by 9.0 at compile time and save the single constant 5.0/9.0 in memory, thereby avoiding the divide at runtime.) Next, we load the constant 32.0 and then subtract it from fahr ($f12):

```
lwc1 $f18, const32($gp)# $f18 = 32.0
sub.s $f18, $f12, $f18 # $f18 = fahr - 32.0
```

Finally, we multiply the two intermediate results, placing the product in $f0 as the return result, and then return

```
mul.s $f0, $f16, $f18  # $f0 = (5/9)*(fahr - 32.0)
jr $ra                 # return
```

Now let's perform floating-point operations on matrices, code commonly found in scientific programs.

Compiling Floating-Point C Procedure with Two-Dimensional Matrices into MIPS

EXAMPLE

Most floating-point calculations are performed in double precision. Let's per–form matrix multiply of C = C + A * B. This code is a simplified version of the DGEMM program in Figure 2.43 on page 166. Let's assume C, A, and B are all square matrices with 32 elements in each dimension.

```
void mm (double c[][], double a[][], double b[][])
{
        int i, j, k;
        for (i = 0; i != 32; i = i + 1)
        for (j = 0; j != 32; j = j + 1)
        for (k = 0; k != 32; k = k + 1)
          c[i][j] = c[i][j] + a[i][k] *b[k][j];
}
```

The array starting addresses are parameters, so they are in $a0, $a1, and $a2. Assume that the integer variables are in $s0, $s1, and $s2, respectively. What is the MIPS assembly code for the body of the procedure?

ANSWER

Note that c[i][j] is used in the innermost loop above. Since the loop index is k, the index does not affect c[i][j], so we can avoid loading and storing c[i][j] each iteration. Instead, the compiler loads c[i][j] into a register outside the loop, accumulates the sum of the products of a[i][k] and b[k][j] in that same register, and then stores the sum into c[i][j] upon termination of the innermost loop.

We keep the code simpler by using the assembly language pseudoinstructions li (which loads a constant into a register), and l.d and s.d (which the assembler turns into a pair of data transfer instructions, lwc1 or swc1, to a pair of floating-point registers).

The body of the procedure starts with saving the loop termination value of 32 in a temporary register and then initializing the three *for* loop variables:

```
    mm: . . .
        li      $t1, 32  # $t1 = 32 (row size/loop end)
        li      $s0, 0   # i = 0; initialize 1st for loop
 L1:    li      $s1, 0   # j = 0; restart 2nd for loop
 L2:    li      $s2, 0   # k = 0; restart 3rd for loop
```

To calculate the address of c[i][j], we need to know how a 32 × 32, two-dimensional array is stored in memory. As you might expect, its layout is the same as if there were 32 single-dimension arrays, each with 32 elements. So the first step is to skip over the i "single-dimensional arrays," or rows, to get the one we want. Thus, we multiply the index in the first dimension by the size of the row, 32. Since 32 is a power of 2, we can use a shift instead:

```
    sll $t2, $s0, 5        # $t2 = i * 2⁵ (size of row of c)
```

Now we add the second index to select the jth element of the desired row:

```
    addu $t2, $t2, $s1   # $t2 = i * size(row) + j
```

To turn this sum into a byte index, we multiply it by the size of a matrix element in bytes. Since each element is 8 bytes for double precision, we can instead shift left by 3 since 8 is a power of 2:

```
    sll $t2, $t2, 3        # $t2 = byte offset of [i][j]
```

Next we add this sum to the base address of c, giving the address of c[i][j], and then load the double precision number c[i][j] into $f4:

```
    addu $t2, $a0, $t2  # $t2 = byte address of c[i][j]
    l.d  $f4, 0($t2)     # $f4 = 8 bytes of c[i][j]
```

The following five instructions are virtually identical to the last five: calculate the address and then load the double precision number b[k][j].

```
 L3: sll $t0, $s2, 5     # $t0 = k * 2⁵ (size of row of b)
     addu $t0, $t0, $s1 # $t0 = k * size(row) + j
     sll $t0, $t0, 3     # $t0 = byte offset of [k][j]
     addu $t0, $a2, $t0 # $t0 = byte address of b[k][j]
     l.d $f16, 0($t0)    # $f16 = 8 bytes of b[k][j]
```

Similarly, the next five instructions are like the last five: calculate the address and then load the double precision number a[i][k].

```
sll     $t0, $s0, 5     # $t0 = i * 2^5 (size of row of a)
addu    $t0, $t0, $s2   # $t0 = i * size(row) + k
sll     $t0, $t0, 3     # $t0 = byte offset of [i][k]
addu    $t0, $a1, $t0   # $t0 = byte address of a[i][k]
l.d     $f18, 0($t0)    # $f18 = 8 bytes of a[i][k]
```

Now that we have loaded all the data, we are finally ready to do some floating-point operations! We multiply elements of a and b located in registers $f18 and $f16, and then accumulate the sum in $f4.

```
mul.d $f16, $f18, $f16 # $f16 = a[i][k] * b[k][j]
add.d $f4, $f4, $f16   # f4 = c[i][j] + a[i][k] * b[k][j]
```

The final block increments the index k and loops back if the index is not 32. If it is 32, and thus the end of the innermost loop, we need to store the sum accumulated in $f4 into c[i][j].

```
addiu  $s2, $s2, 1     # $k = k + 1
bne    $s2, $t1, L3    # if (k ! = 32) go to L3
s.d    $f4, 0($t2)     # c[i][j] = $f4
```

Similarly, these final four instructions increment the index variable of the middle and outermost loops, looping back if the index is not 32 and exiting if the index is 32.

```
addiu  $s1, $s1, 1     # $j = j + 1
bne    $s1, $t1, L2    # if (j != 32) go to L2
addiu  $s0, $s0, 1     # $i = i + 1
bne    $s0, $t1, L1    # if (i != 32) go to L1

...
```

Figure 3.22 below shows the x86 assembly language code for a slightly different version of DGEMM in Figure 3.21.

Elaboration: The array layout discussed in the example, called *row-major order*, is used by C and many other programming languages. Fortran instead uses *column-major order*, whereby the array is stored column by column.

Elaboration: Only 16 of the 32 MIPS floating-point registers could originally be used for double precision operations: $f0, $f2, $f4, …, $f30. Double precision is computed using pairs of these single precision registers. The odd-numbered floating-point registers were used only to load and store the right half of 64-bit floating-point numbers. MIPS-32 added l.d and s.d to the instruction set. MIPS-32 also added "paired single" versions of all floating-point instructions, where a single instruction results in two parallel floating-point operations on two 32-bit operands inside 64-bit registers (see Section 3.6). For example, add.ps $f0, $f2, $f4 is equivalent to add.s $f0, $f2, $f4 followed by add.s $f1, $f3, $f5.

Elaboration: Another reason for separate integers and floating-point registers is that microprocessors in the 1980s didn't have enough transistors to put the floating-point unit on the same chip as the integer unit. Hence, the floating-point unit, including the floating-point registers, was optionally available as a second chip. Such optional accelerator chips are called *coprocessors*, and explain the acronym for floating-point loads in MIPS: `lwc1` means load word to coprocessor 1, the floating-point unit. (Coprocessor 0 deals with virtual memory, described in Chapter 5.) Since the early 1990s, microprocessors have integrated floating point (and just about everything else) on chip.

Elaboration: As mentioned in Section 3.4, accelerating division is more challenging than multiplication. In addition to SRT, another technique to leverage a fast multiplier is *Newton's iteration*, where division is recast as finding the zero of a function to find the reciprocal $1/c$, which is then multiplied by the other operand. Iteration techniques *cannot* be rounded properly without calculating many extra bits. A TI chip solved this problem by calculating an extra-precise reciprocal.

Elaboration: Java embraces IEEE 754 by name in its definition of Java floating-point data types and operations. Thus, the code in the first example could have well been generated for a class method that converted Fahrenheit to Celsius.

The second example above uses multiple dimensional arrays, which are not explicitly supported in Java. Java allows arrays of arrays, but each array may have its own length, unlike multiple dimensional arrays in C. Like the examples in Chapter 2, a Java version of this second example would require a good deal of checking code for array bounds, including a new length calculation at the end of row access. It would also need to check that the object reference is not null.

Accurate Arithmetic

guard The first of two extra bits kept on the right during intermediate calculations of floating-point numbers; used to improve rounding accuracy.

round Method to make the intermediate floating-point result fit the floating-point format; the goal is typically to find the nearest number that can be represented in the format.

Unlike integers, which can represent exactly every number between the smallest and largest number, floating-point numbers are normally approximations for a number they can't really represent. The reason is that an infinite variety of real numbers exists between, say, 0 and 1, but no more than 2^{53} can be represented exactly in double precision floating point. The best we can do is getting the floating-point representation close to the actual number. Thus, IEEE 754 offers several modes of rounding to let the programmer pick the desired approximation.

Rounding sounds simple enough, but to round accurately requires the hardware to include extra bits in the calculation. In the preceding examples, we were vague on the number of bits that an intermediate representation can occupy, but clearly, if every intermediate result had to be truncated to the exact number of digits, there would be no opportunity to round. IEEE 754, therefore, always keeps two extra bits on the right during intermediate additions, called **guard** and **round**, respectively. Let's do a decimal example to illustrate their value.

Rounding with Guard Digits

EXAMPLE

Add $2.56_{ten} \times 10^0$ to $2.34_{ten} \times 10^2$, assuming that we have three significant decimal digits. Round to the nearest decimal number with three significant decimal digits, first with guard and round digits, and then without them.

ANSWER

First we must shift the smaller number to the right to align the exponents, so $2.56_{ten} \times 10^0$ becomes $0.0256_{ten} \times 10^2$. Since we have guard and round digits, we are able to represent the two least significant digits when we align exponents. The guard digit holds 5 and the round digit holds 6. The sum is

$$\begin{array}{r} 2.3400_{ten} \\ + \; 0.0256_{ten} \\ \hline 2.3656_{ten} \end{array}$$

Thus the sum is $2.3656_{ten} \times 10^2$. Since we have two digits to round, we want values 0 to 49 to round down and 51 to 99 to round up, with 50 being the tiebreaker. Rounding the sum up with three significant digits yields $2.37_{ten} \times 10^2$.

Doing this *without* guard and round digits drops two digits from the calculation. The new sum is then

$$\begin{array}{r} 2.34_{ten} \\ + \; 0.02_{ten} \\ \hline 2.36_{ten} \end{array}$$

The answer is $2.36_{ten} \times 10^2$, off by 1 in the last digit from the sum above.

Since the worst case for rounding would be when the actual number is halfway between two floating-point representations, accuracy in floating point is normally measured in terms of the number of bits in error in the least significant bits of the significand; the measure is called the number of **units in the last place**, or **ulp**. If a number were off by 2 in the least significant bits, it would be called off by 2 ulps. Provided there is no overflow, underflow, or invalid operation exceptions, IEEE 754 guarantees that the computer uses the number that is within one-half ulp.

units in the last place (ulp) The number of bits in error in the least significant bits of the significand between the actual number and the number that can be represented.

Elaboration: Although the example above really needed just one extra digit, multiply can need two. A binary product may have one leading 0 bit; hence, the normalizing step must shift the product one bit left. This shifts the guard digit into the least significant bit of the product, leaving the round bit to help accurately round the product.

IEEE 754 has four rounding modes: always round up (toward $+ \infty$), always round down (toward $- \infty$), truncate, and round to nearest even. The final mode determines what to do if the number is exactly halfway in between. The U.S. *Internal Revenue Service* (IRS) always rounds 0.50 dollars up, possibly to the benefit of the IRS. A more equitable way would be to round up this case half the time and round down the other half. IEEE 754 says that if the least significant bit retained in a halfway case would be odd, add one;

if it's even, truncate. This method always creates a 0 in the least significant bit in the tie-breaking case, giving the rounding mode its name. This mode is the most commonly used, and the only one that Java supports.

The goal of the extra rounding bits is to allow the computer to get the same results as if the intermediate results were calculated to infinite precision and then rounded. To support this goal and round to the nearest even, the standard has a third bit in addition to guard and round; it is set whenever there are nonzero bits to the right of the round bit. This **sticky bit** allows the computer to see the difference between $0.50 \ldots 00_{ten}$ and $0.50 \ldots 01_{ten}$ when rounding.

sticky bit: A bit used in rounding in addition to guard and round that is set whenever there are nonzero bits to the right of the round bit.

The sticky bit may be set, for example, during addition, when the smaller number is shifted to the right. Suppose we added $5.01_{ten} \times 10^{-1}$ to $2.34_{ten} \times 10^2$ in the example above. Even with guard and round, we would be adding 0.0050 to 2.34, with a sum of 2.3450. The sticky bit would be set, since there are nonzero bits to the right. Without the sticky bit to remember whether any 1s were shifted off, we would assume the number is equal to 2.345000 … 00 and round to the nearest even of 2.34. With the sticky bit to remember that the number is larger than 2.345000 … 00, we round instead to 2.35.

fused multiply add A floating-point instruction that performs both a multiply and an add, but rounds only once after the add.

Elaboration: PowerPC, AMD SSE5, and Intel AVX architectures provide a single instruction that does a multiply and add on three registers: $a = a + (b \times c)$. Obviously, this instruction allows potentially higher floating-point performance for this common operation. Equally important is that instead of performing two roundings—after the multiply and then after the add—which would happen with separate instructions, the multiply add instruction can perform a single rounding after the add. A single rounding step increases the precision of multiply add. Such operations with a single rounding are called **fused multiply add**. It was added to the IEEE 754-2008 standard (see  Section 3.11).

Summary

The *Big Picture* that follows reinforces the stored-program concept from Chapter 2; the meaning of the information cannot be determined just by looking at the bits, for the same bits can represent a variety of objects. This section shows that computer arithmetic is finite and thus can disagree with natural arithmetic. For example, the IEEE 754 standard floating-point representation

$$(-1)^5 \times (1 + \text{Fraction}) \times 2^{(\text{Exponent} - \text{Bias})}$$

is almost always an approximation of the real number. Computer systems must take care to minimize this gap between computer arithmetic and arithmetic in the real world, and programmers at times need to be aware of the implications of this approximation.

The BIG Picture

Bit patterns have no inherent meaning. They may represent signed integers, unsigned integers, floating-point numbers, instructions, and so on. What is represented depends on the instruction that operates on the bits in the word.

The major difference between computer numbers and numbers in the real world is that computer numbers have limited size and hence limited precision; it's possible to calculate a number too big or too small to be represented in a word. Programmers must remember these limits and write programs accordingly.

C type	Java type	Data transfers	Operations
int	int	lw, sw, lui	addu, addiu, subu, mult, div, AND, ANDi, OR, ORi, NOR, slt, slti
unsigned int	—	lw, sw, lui	addu, addiu, subu, multu, divu, AND, ANDi, OR, ORi, NOR, sltu, sltiu
char	—	lb, sb, lui	add, addi, sub, mult, div AND, ANDi, OR, ORi, NOR, slt, slti
—	char	lh, sh, lui	addu, addiu, subu, multu, divu, AND, ANDi, OR, ORi, NOR, sltu, sltiu
float	float	lwc1, swc1	add.s, sub.s, mult.s, div.s, c.eq.s, c.lt.s, c.le.s
double	double	l.d, s.d	add.d, sub.d, mult.d, div.d, c.eq.d, c.lt.d, c.le.d

Hardware/ Software Interface

In the last chapter, we presented the storage classes of the programming language C (see the *Hardware/Software Interface* section in Section 2.7). The table above shows some of the C and Java data types, the MIPS data transfer instructions, and instructions that operate on those types that appear in Chapter 2 and this chapter. Note that Java omits unsigned integers.

Check Yourself

The revised IEEE 754-2008 standard added a 16-bit floating-point format with five exponent bits. What do you think is the likely range of numbers it could represent?

1. $1.0000\ 00 \times 2^0$ to $1.1111\ 1111\ 11 \times 2^{31}, 0$

2. $\pm 1.0000\ 0000\ 0 \times 2^{-14}$ to $\pm 1.1111\ 1111\ 1 \times 2^{15}, \pm 0, \pm \infty, \text{NaN}$

3. $\pm 1.0000\ 0000\ 00 \times 2^{-14}$ to $\pm 1.1111\ 1111\ 11 \times 2^{15}, \pm 0, \pm \infty, \text{NaN}$

4. $\pm 1.0000\ 0000\ 00 \times 2^{-15}$ to $\pm 1.1111\ 1111\ 11 \times 2^{14}, \pm 0, \pm \infty, \text{NaN}$

Elaboration: To accommodate comparisons that may include NaNs, the standard includes *ordered and unordered* as options for compares. Hence, the full MIPS instruction set has many flavors of compares to support NaNs. (Java does not support unordered compares.)

In an attempt to squeeze every last bit of precision from a floating-point operation, the standard allows some numbers to be represented in unnormalized form. Rather than having a gap between 0 and the smallest normalized number, IEEE allows *denormalized numbers* (also known as *denorms* or *subnormals*). They have the same exponent as zero but a nonzero fraction. They allow a number to degrade in significance until it becomes 0, called *gradual underflow*. For example, the smallest positive single precision normalized number is

$$1.0000\ 0000\ 0000\ 0000\ 0000\ 000_{two} \times 2^{-126}$$

but the smallest single precision denormalized number is

$$0.0000\ 0000\ 0000\ 0000\ 0000\ 001_{two} \times 2^{-126},\ or\ 1.0_{two} \times 2^{-149}$$

For double precision, the denorm gap goes from 1.0×2^{-1022} to 1.0×2^{-1074}.

The possibility of an occasional unnormalized operand has given headaches to floating-point designers who are trying to build fast floating-point units. Hence, many computers cause an exception if an operand is denormalized, letting software complete the operation. Although software implementations are perfectly valid, their lower performance has lessened the popularity of denorms in portable floating-point software. Moreover, if programmers do not expect denorms, their programs may surprise them.

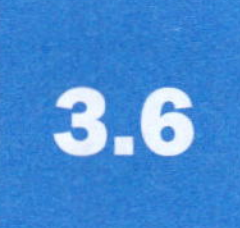

3.6 Parallelism and Computer Arithmetic: Subword Parallelism

Since every desktop microprocessor and smart phone by definition has its own graphical display, as transistor budgets increased it was inevitable that support would be added for graphics operations.

Many graphics systems originally used 8 bits to represent each of the three primary colors plus 8 bits for a location of a pixel. The addition of speakers and microphones for teleconferencing and video games suggested support of sound as well. Audio samples need more than 8 bits of precision, but 16 bits are sufficient.

Every microprocessor has special support so that bytes and halfwords take up less space when stored in memory (see Section 2.9), but due to the infrequency of arithmetic operations on these data sizes in typical integer programs, there was little support beyond data transfers. Architects recognized that many graphics and audio applications would perform the same operation on vectors of this data. By partitioning the carry chains within a 128-bit adder, a processor could use **parallelism** to perform simultaneous operations on short vectors of sixteen 8-bit operands, eight 16-bit operands, four 32-bit operands, or two 64-bit operands. The cost of such partitioned adders was small.

Given that the parallelism occurs within a wide word, the extensions are classified as *subword parallelism*. It is also classified under the more general name of *data level parallelism*. They have been also called vector or SIMD, for single instruction, multiple data (see Section 6.6). The rising popularity of multimedia

applications led to arithmetic instructions that support narrower operations that can easily operate in parallel.

For example, ARM added more than 100 instructions in the NEON multimedia instruction extension to support subword parallelism, which can be used either with ARMv7 or ARMv8. It added 256 bytes of new registers for NEON that can be viewed as 32 registers 8 bytes wide or 16 registers 16 bytes wide. NEON supports all the subword data types you can imagine *except* 64-bit floating point numbers:

- 8-bit, 16-bit, 32-bit, and 64-bit signed and unsigned integers

- 32-bit floating point numbers

Figure 3.19 gives a summary of the basic NEON instructions.

Data transfer	Arithmetic	Logical/Compare
VLDR.F32	VADD.F32, VADD{L,W}{S8,U8,S16,U16,S32,U32}	VAND.64, VAND.128
VSTR.F32	VSUB.F32, VSUB{L,W}{S8,U8,S16,U16,S32,U32}	VORR.64, VORR.128
VLD{1,2,3,4}.{I8,I16,I32}	VMUL.F32, VMULL{S8,U8,S16,U16,S32,U32}	VEOR.64, VEOR.128
VST{1,2,3,4}.{I8,I16,I32}	VMLA.F32, VMLAL{S8,U8,S16,U16,S32,U32}	VBIC.64, VBIC.128
VMOV.{I8,I16,I32,F32}, #imm	VMLS.F32, VMLSL{S8,U8,S16,U16,S32,U32}	VORN.64, VORN.128
VMVN.{I8,I16,I32,F32}, #imm	VMAX.{S8,U8,S16,U16,S32,U32,F32}	VCEQ.{I8,I16,I32,F32}
VMOV.{I64,I128}	VMIN.{S8,U8,S16,U16,S32,U32,F32}	VCGE.{S8,U8,S16,U16,S32,U32,F32}
VMVN.{I64,I128}	VABS.{S8,S16,S32,F32}	VCGT.{S8,U8,S16,U16,S32,U32,F32}
	VNEG.{S8,S16,S32,F32}	VCLE.{S8,U8,S16,U16,S32,U32,F32}
	VSHL.{S8,U8,S16,U16,S32,S64,U64}	VCLT.{S8,U8,S16,U16,S32,U32,F32}
	VSHR.{S8,U8,S16,U16,S32,S64,U64}	VTST.{I8,I16,I32}

FIGURE 3.19   Summary of ARM NEON instructions for subword parallelism. We use the curly brackets {} to show optional variations of the basic operations: {S8,U8,8} stand for signed and unsigned 8-bit integers or 8-bit data where type doesn't matter, of which 16 fit in a 128-bit register; {S16,U16,16} stand for signed and unsigned 16-bit integers or 16-bit type-less data, of which 8 fit in a 128-bit register; {S32,U32,32} stand for signed and unsigned 32-bit integers or 32-bit type-less data, of which 4 fit in a 128-bit register; {S64,U64,64} stand for signed and unsigned 64-bit integers or type-less 64-bit data, of which 2 fit in a 128-bit register; {F32} stand for signed and unsigned 32-bit floating point numbers, of which 4 fit in a 128-bit register. Vector Load reads one n-element structure from memory into 1, 2, 3, or 4 NEON registers. It loads a single n-element structure to one lane (See Section 6.6), and elements of the register that are not loaded are unchanged. Vector Store writes one n-element structure into memory from 1, 2, 3, or 4 NEON registers.

Elaboration: In addition to signed and unsigned integers, ARM includes "fixed-point" format of four sizes called I8, I16, I32, and I64, of which 16, 8, 4, and 2 fit in a 128-bit register, respectively. A portion of the fixed point is for the fraction (to the right of the binary point) and the rest of the data is the integer portion (to the left of the binary point). The location of the binary point is up to the software. Many ARM processors do not have floating point hardware and thus floating point operations must be performed by library routines. Fixed point arithmetic can be significantly faster than software floating point routines, but more work for the programmer.

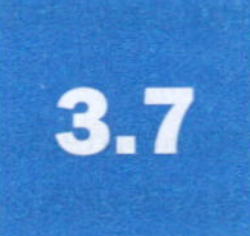

3.7   Real Stuff: Streaming SIMD Extensions and Advanced Vector Extensions in x86

The original MMX (*MultiMedia eXtension*) and SSE (*Streaming SIMD Extension*) instructions for the x86 included similar operations to those found in ARM NEON. Chapter 2 notes that in 2001 Intel added 144 instructions to its architecture as part of SSE2, including double precision floating-point registers and operations. It includes eight 64-bit registers that can be used for floating-point operands. AMD expanded the number to 16 registers, called XMM, as part of AMD64, which Intel relabeled EM64T for its use. Figure 3.20 summarizes the SSE and SSE2 instructions.

In addition to holding a single precision or double precision number in a register, Intel allows multiple floating-point operands to be packed into a single 128-bit SSE2 register: four single precision or two double precision. Thus, the 16 floating-point registers for SSE2 are actually 128 bits wide. If the operands can be arranged in memory as 128-bit aligned data, then 128-bit data transfers can load and store multiple operands per instruction. This packed floating-point format is supported by arithmetic operations that can operate simultaneously on four singles (PS) or two doubles (PD).

In 2011 Intel doubled the width of the registers again, now called YMM, with *Advanced Vector Extensions (AVX)*. Thus, a single operation can now specify eight 32-bit floating-point operations or four 64-bit floating-point operations. The legacy SSE and SSE2 instructions now operate on the lower 128 bits of the YMM registers. Thus, to go from 128-bit and 256-bit operations, you prepend the letter "v" (for vector) in front of the SSE2 assembly language operations and then use the

Data transfer	Arithmetic	Compare
`MOV{A/U}{SS/PS/SD/PD} xmm, mem/xmm`	`ADD{SS/PS/SD/PD} xmm,mem/xmm`	`CMP{SS/PS/SD/PD}`
	`SUB{SS/PS/SD/PD} xmm,mem/xmm`	
`MOV {H/L} {PS/PD} xmm, mem/xmm`	`MUL{SS/PS/SD/PD} xmm,mem/xmm`	
	`DIV{SS/PS/SD/PD} xmm,mem/xmm`	
	`SQRT{SS/PS/SD/PD} mem/xmm`	
	`MAX {SS/PS/SD/PD} mem/xmm`	
	`MIN{SS/PS/SD/PD} mem/xmm`	

FIGURE 3.20   The SSE/SSE2 floating-point instructions of the x86. xmm means one operand is a 128-bit SSE2 register, and mem/xmm means the other operand is either in memory or it is an SSE2 register. We use the curly brackets {} to show optional variations of the basic operations: {SS} stands for *Scalar Single* precision floating point, or one 32-bit operand in a 128-bit register; {PS} stands for *Packed Single* precision floating point, or four 32-bit operands in a 128-bit register; {SD} stands for Scalar Double precision floating point, or one 64-bit operand in a 128-bit register; {PD} stands for *Packed Double* precision floating point, or two 64-bit operands in a 128-bit register; {A} means the 128-bit operand is aligned in memory; {U} means the 128-bit operand is unaligned in memory; {H} means move the high half of the 128-bit operand; and {L} means move the low half of the 128-bit operand.

YMM register names instead of the XMM register name. For example, the SSE2 instruction to perform two 64-bit floating-point additions

```
addpd %xmm0, %xmm4
```

It becomes

```
vaddpd %ymm0, %ymm4
```

which now produces four 64-bit floating-point multiplies.

In 2015, Intel doubled the registers again to 512 bits, now called ZMM, with AVX512 in some of its microprocessors.

Elaboration: AVX also added three address instructions to x86. For example, `vaddpd` can now specify

```
vaddpd %ymm0, %ymm1, %ymm4 # %ymm4 = %ymm0 + %ymm1
```

instead of the standard two address version

```
addpd %xmm0, %xmm4 # %xmm4 = %xmm4 + %xmm0
```

(Unlike MIPS, the destination is on the right in x86.) Three addresses can reduce the number of registers and instructions needed for a computation.

Going Faster: Subword Parallelism and Matrix Multiply

Recall that Figure 2.43 on page 166 shows an unoptimized version of DGEMM in C. To demonstrate the performance impact of subword parallelism, we rerun the code using AVX. While compiler writers may eventually be able to routinely produce high-quality code that uses the AVX instructions of the x86, for now we must "cheat" by using C intrinsics that more or less tell the compiler exactly how to produce good code. Figure 3.21 shows the enhanced version of Figure 2.43.

The declaration on line 7 of Figure 3.21 uses the `__m512d` data type, which tells the compiler the variable will hold 8 double-precision floating-point values (8 × 64 bits = 512 bits). The intrinsic `_mm512_load_pd()` also on line 7 uses AVX instructions to load 8 double-precision floating-point numbers in parallel (`_pd`) from the matrix C into c0. The address calculation C+i+j*n represents element C[i+j*n]. Symmetrically, the final step on line 13 uses the intrinsic `_mm256_store_pd()` to store 8 double-precision floating-point numbers from c0 into the matrix C. As we are going through 8 elements each iteration, the outer *for* loop on line 4 increments i by 8 instead of by 1 as on line 3 of Figure 2.43.

Inside the loops, on line 10 we first load 8 elements of A again using `_mm512_load_pd()`. To multiply these elements by one element of B, we first use the intrinsic `_mm512_broadcast_sd()`, which makes eight identical copies of the scalar double precision number—in this case an element of B—in one of the ZMM registers.

We then use _mm512_fmadd_pd on line 11 to multiply the 8 double-precision results in parallel and then add the 8 products to the 8 sums in c0.

Figure 3.22 shows resulting x86 code for the body of the inner loops produced by the compiler. You can see the four AVX512 instructions—they all start with v and use pd for parallel double precision—that correspond to the C intrinsics mentioned previously. The code is very similar to that in Figure 2.44 the integer instructions are nearly identical (but different registers), and the floating-point instruction differences are generally just going from *scalar double* (sd) using XMM registers to *parallel double* (pd) with ZMM registers. One exception is line 4 of Figure 3.22. Every element of A must be multiplied by one element of B. One solution is to place eight identical copies of the 64-bit B element side-by-side into the 512-bit ZMM register, which is just what the instruction vbroadcastsd does. The other difference is that the original program has separate multiply and add floating point operations, whereas the AVX512 version using a single floating-point operation in line 6 that performs multiply and add.

The AVX version is 7.5 times as fast, which is very close to the factor of 8.0 increase that you might hope for from performing 8 times as many operations at a time by using **subword parallelism**. Chapters 3, 4, 5, and 6 will further improve DGEMM performance using the ideas that each chapter introduces.

```
1.    #include <x86intrin.h>
2.    void dgemm (int n, double* A, double* B, double* C)
3.    {
4.    for (int i = 0; i < n; i+=8)
5.      for (int j = 0; j < n; ++j)
6.        {
7.          __m512d c0 = _mm512_load_pd(C+i+j*n); // c0 = C[i][j]
8.          for( int k = 0; k < n; k++ )
9.            {  // c0 += A[i][k]*B[k][j]
10.              __m512d bb = _mm512_broadcastsd_pd(_mm_load_sd(B+j*n+k));
11.              c0 = _mm512_fmadd_pd(_mm512_load_pd(A+n*k+i), bb, c0);
12.            }
13.        _mm512_store_pd(C+i+j*n, c0); // C[i][j] = c0
14.        }
15. }
```

FIGURE 3.21 Optimized version of DGEMM using C intrinsics to generate the AVX512 subword-parallel instructions for the x86. Figure 3.22 shows the assembly language produced by the compiler for the inner loop.

```
1.   vmovapd (%r11),%zmm1              # Load 8 elements of C into %zmm1
2.   mov       %rbx,%rcx               # register %rcx = %rbx
3.   xor       %eax,%eax               # register %eax = 0
4.   vbroadcastsd (%rax,%r8,8),%zmm0   # Make 8 copies of B element in %zmm0
5.   add       $0x8,%rax               # register %rax = %rax + 8
6.   vfmadd231pd    (%rcx),%zmm0,%zmm1 # Parallel mul & add %zmm0, %zmm1
7.   add       %r9,%rcx                # register %rcx = %rcx
8.   cmp       %r10,%rax               # compare %r10 to %rax
9.   jne       50 <dgemm+0x50>         # jump if not %r10 != %rax
10.  add       $0x1, %esi              # register % esi = % esi + 1
11.  vmovapd %zmm1, (%r11)             # Store %zmm1 into 8 C elements
```

FIGURE 3.22 The x86 assembly language for the body of the nested loops generated by compiling the optimized C code in Figure 3.21. Note the similarities to Figure 2.44 on page 167, of Chapter 2, with the primary difference being that the original floating-point operations are now using ZMM registers and using the pd versions of the instructions for parallel double precision instead of the sd version for scalar double precision, and it is performing a single multiply–add instruction instead of a separate multiply instruction and a separate add instruction.

3.9 Fallacies and Pitfalls

Arithmetic fallacies and pitfalls generally stem from the difference between the limited precision of computer arithmetic and the unlimited precision of natural arithmetic.

Fallacy: Just as a left shift instruction can replace an integer multiply by a power of 2, a right shift is the same as an integer division by a power of 2.

Recall that a binary number x, where x^i means the ith bit, represents the number

$$\ldots + (x^3 \times 2^3) + (x^2 \times 2^2) + (x^1 \times 2^1) + (x0 \times 2^0)$$

Shifting the bits of c right by n bits would seem to be the same as dividing by $2n$. And this *is* true for unsigned integers. The problem is with signed integers. For example, suppose we want to divide -5_{ten} by 4_{ten}; the quotient should be -1_{ten}. The two's complement representation of -5_{ten} is

$$1111\ 1111\ 1111\ 1111\ 1111\ 1111\ 1111\ 1111_{two}$$

Thus mathematics may be defined as the subject in which we never know what we are talking about, nor whether what we are saying is true.

Bertrand Russell, *Recent Words on the Principles of Mathematics*, 1901

According to this fallacy, shifting right by two should divide by 4_{ten} (2^2):

$$0011\ 1111\ 1111\ 1111\ 1111\ 1111\ 1111\ 1110_{two}$$

With a 0 in the sign bit, this result is clearly wrong. The value created by the shift right is actually $1{,}073{,}741{,}822_{ten}$ instead of -1_{ten}.

A solution would be to have an *arithmetic right shift* that extends the sign bit instead of shifting in 0s. A 2-bit arithmetic shift right of -5_{ten} produces

$$1111\ 1111\ 1111\ 1111\ 1111\ 1111\ 1111\ 1110_{two}$$

The result is -2_{ten} instead of -1_{ten}; close, but no cigar.

Pitfall: Floating-point addition is not associative.

Associativity holds for a sequence of two's complement integer additions, even if the computation overflows. Alas, because floating-point numbers are approximations of real numbers and because computer arithmetic has limited precision, it does not hold for floating-point numbers. Given the great range of numbers that can be represented in floating point, problems occur when adding two large numbers of opposite signs plus a small number. For example, let's see if $c + (a + b) = (c + a) + b$. Assume $c = -1.5_{ten} \times 10^{38}$, $a = 1.5_{ten} \times 10^{38}$, and $b = 1.0$, and that these are all single precision numbers.

$$
\begin{aligned}
c + (a + b) &= -1.5_{ten} \times 10^{38} + (1.5_{ten} \times 10^{38} + 1.0) \\
&= -1.5_{ten} \times 10^{38} + (1.5_{ten} \times 10^{38}) \\
&= 0.0 \\
(c + a) + b &= (-1.5_{ten} \times 10^{38} + 1.5_{ten} \times 10^{38}) + 1.0 \\
&= (0.0_{ten}) + 1.0 \\
&= 1.0
\end{aligned}
$$

Since floating-point numbers have limited precision and result in approximations of real results, $1.5_{ten} \times 10^{38}$ is so much larger than 1.0_{ten} that $1.5_{ten} \times 10^{38} + 1.0$ is still $1.5_{ten} \times 10^{38}$. That is why the sum of c, a, and b is 0.0 or 1.0, depending on the order of the floating-point additions, so $c + (a + b) \neq (c + a) + b$. Therefore, floating-point addition is not associative.

Fallacy: Parallel execution strategies that work for integer data types also work for floating-point data types.

Programs have typically been written first to run sequentially before being rewritten to run concurrently, so a natural question is, "Do the two versions get the same answer?" If the answer is no, you presume there is a bug in the parallel version that you need to track down.

This approach assumes that computer arithmetic does not affect the results when going from sequential to parallel. That is, if you were to add a million numbers together, you would get the same results whether you used 1 processor or 1000 processors. This assumption holds for two's complement integers, since integer addition is associative. Alas, since floating-point addition is not associative, the assumption does not hold.

A more vexing version of this fallacy occurs on a parallel computer where the operating system scheduler may use a different number of processors depending on what other programs are running on a parallel computer. As the varying number of processors from each run would cause the floating-point sums to be calculated in different orders, getting slightly different answers each time despite running identical code with identical input may flummox unaware parallel programmers.

Given this quandary, programmers who write parallel code with floating-point numbers need to verify whether the results are credible even if they don't give the same exact answer as the sequential code. The field that deals with such issues is called numerical analysis, which is the subject of textbooks in its own right. Such concerns are one reason for the popularity of numerical libraries such as LAPACK and SCALAPAK, which have been validated in both their sequential and parallel forms.

Pitfall: The MIPS instruction add immediate unsigned (`addiu`) *sign-extends its 16-bit immediate field.*

Despite its name, add immediate unsigned (`addiu`) is used to add constants to signed integers when we don't care about overflow. MIPS has no subtract immediate instruction, and negative numbers need sign extension, so the MIPS architects decided to sign-extend the immediate field.

Fallacy: Only theoretical mathematicians care about floating-point accuracy.

Newspaper headlines of November 1994 prove this statement is a fallacy (see Figure 3.23). The following is the inside story behind the headlines.

The Pentium used a standard floating-point divide algorithm that generates multiple quotient bits per step, using the most significant bits of divisor and dividend to guess the next 2 bits of the quotient. The guess is taken from a lookup table containing -2, -1, 0, $+1$, or $+2$. The guess is multiplied by the divisor and subtracted from the remainder to generate a new remainder. Like nonrestoring division, if a previous guess gets too large a remainder, the partial remainder is adjusted in a subsequent pass.

Evidently, there were five elements of the table from the 80486 that Intel engineers thought could never be accessed, and they optimized the logic to return 0 instead of 2 in these situations on the Pentium. Intel was wrong: while the first 11 bits were always correct, errors would show up occasionally in bits 12 to 52, or the 4th to 15th decimal digits.

A math professor at Lynchburg College in Virginia, Thomas Nicely, discovered the bug in September 1994. After calling Intel technical support and getting no official reaction, he posted his discovery on the Internet. This post led to a story in a trade magazine, which in turn caused Intel to issue a press release. It called the bug a glitch that would affect only theoretical mathematicians, with the average spreadsheet

FIGURE 3.23 A sampling of newspaper and magazine articles from November 1994, including the *New York Times*, *San Jose Mercury News*, *San Francisco Chronicle*, and *Infoworld*. The Pentium floating-point divide bug even made the "Top 10 List" of the *David Letterman Late Show* on television. Intel eventually took a $500 million write-off to replace the buggy chips.

user seeing an error every 27,000 years. IBM Research soon counterclaimed that the average spreadsheet user would see an error every 24 days. Intel soon threw in the towel by making the following announcement on December 21:

> *"We at Intel wish to sincerely apologize for our handling of the recently publicized Pentium processor flaw. The Intel Inside symbol means that your computer has a microprocessor second to none in quality and performance. Thousands of Intel employees work very hard to ensure that this is true. But no microprocessor is ever perfect. What Intel continues to believe is technically an extremely minor problem has taken on a life of its own. Although Intel firmly stands behind the quality of the current version of the Pentium processor, we recognize that many users have concerns. We want to resolve these concerns. Intel will exchange the current version of the Pentium processor for an updated version, in which this floating-point divide flaw is corrected, for any owner who requests it, free of charge anytime during the life of their computer."*

Analysts estimate that this recall cost Intel $500 million, and Intel engineers did not get a Christmas bonus that year.

This story brings up a few points for everyone to ponder. How much cheaper would it have been to fix the bug in July 1994? What was the cost to repair the damage to Intel's reputation? And what is the corporate responsibility in disclosing bugs in a product so widely used and relied upon as a microprocessor?

3.10 Concluding Remarks

Over the decades, computer arithmetic has become largely standardized, greatly enhancing the portability of programs. Two's complement binary integer arithmetic is found in every computer sold today, and if it includes floating point support, it offers the IEEE 754 binary floating-point arithmetic.

Computer arithmetic is distinguished from paper-and-pencil arithmetic by the constraints of limited precision. This limit may result in invalid operations through calculating numbers larger or smaller than the predefined limits. Such anomalies, called "overflow" or "underflow," may result in exceptions or interrupts, emergency events similar to unplanned subroutine calls. Chapters 4 and 5 discuss exceptions in more detail.

Floating-point arithmetic has the added challenge of being an approximation of real numbers, and care needs to be taken to ensure that the computer number selected is the representation closest to the actual number. The challenges of imprecision and limited representation of floating point are part of the inspiration for the field of numerical analysis. The recent switch to **parallelism** shines the searchlight on numerical analysis again, as solutions that were long considered safe on sequential computers must be reconsidered when trying to find the fastest algorithm for parallel computers that still achieves a correct result.

Data-level parallelism, specifically subword parallelism, offers a simple path to higher performance for programs that are intensive in arithmetic operations for either integer or floating-point data. We showed that we could speed up matrix multiply nearly eightfold by using instructions that could execute eight floating-point operations at a time.

With the explanation of computer arithmetic in this chapter comes a description of much more of the MIPS instruction set. One point of confusion is the instructions covered in these chapters versus instructions executed by MIPS chips versus the instructions accepted by MIPS assemblers. Two figures try to clarify.

Figure 3.24 lists the MIPS instructions covered in this chapter and Chapter 2. We call the set of instructions on the left-hand side of the figure the *MIPS core*. The instructions on the right we call the *MIPS arithmetic core*. On the left of Figure 3.25 are the instructions the MIPS processor executes that are not found in Figure 3.24. We call the full set of hardware instructions *MIPS-32*. On the right of Figure 3.25 are the instructions accepted by the assembler that are not part of MIPS-32. We call this set of instructions *Pseudo MIPS*.

Figure 3.26 gives the popularity of the MIPS instructions for SPEC CPU2006 integer and floating-point benchmarks. All instructions are listed that were responsible for at least 0.2% of the instructions executed.

MIPS core instructions	Name	Format	MIPS arithmetic core	Name	Format
add	add	R	multiply	mult	R
add immediate	addi	I	multiply unsigned	multu	R
add unsigned	addu	R	divide	div	R
add immediate unsigned	addiu	I	divide unsigned	divu	R
subtract	sub	R	move from Hi	mfhi	R
subtract unsigned	subu	R	move from Lo	mflo	R
AND	AND	R	move from system control (EPC)	mfc0	R
AND immediate	ANDi	I	floating-point add single	add.s	R
OR	OR	R	floating-point add double	add.d	R
OR immediate	ORi	I	floating-point subtract single	sub.s	R
NOR	NOR	R	floating-point subtract double	sub.d	R
shift left logical	sll	R	floating-point multiply single	mul.s	R
shift right logical	srl	R	floating-point multiply double	mul.d	R
load upper immediate	lui	I	floating-point divide single	div.s	R
load word	lw	I	floating-point divide double	div.d	R
store word	sw	I	load word to floating-point single	lwc1	I
load halfword unsigned	lhu	I	store word to floating-point single	swc1	I
store halfword	sh	I	load word to floating-point double	ldc1	I
load byte unsigned	lbu	I	store word to floating-point double	sdc1	I
store byte	sb	I	branch on floating-point true	bc1t	I
load linked (*atomic update*)	ll	I	branch on floating-point false	bc1f	I
store cond. (*atomic update*)	sc	I	floating-point compare single	c.x.s	R
branch on equal	beq	I	(x = eq, neq, lt, le, gt, ge)		
branch on not equal	bne	I	floating-point compare double	c.x.d	R
jump	j	J	(x = eq, neq, lt, le, gt, ge)		
jump and link	jal	J			
jump register	jr	R			
set less than	slt	R			
set less than immediate	slti	I			
set less than unsigned	sltu	R			
set less than immediate unsigned	sltiu	I			

FIGURE 3.24   The MIPS instruction set. This book concentrates on the instructions in the left column. This information is also found in columns 1 and 2 of the MIPS Reference Data Card at the front of this book.

Note that although programmers and compiler writers may use MIPS-32 to have a richer menu of options, MIPS core instructions dominate integer SPEC CPU2006 execution, and the integer core plus arithmetic core dominate SPEC CPU2006 floating point, as the table below shows.

Instruction subset	Integer	Fl. pt.
MIPS core	98%	31%
MIPS arithmetic core	2%	66%
Remaining MIPS-32	0%	3%

Remaining MIPS-32	Name	Format	Pseudo MIPS	Name	Format
exclusive or (rs ⊕ rt)	xor	R	absolute value	abs	rd,rs
exclusive or immediate	xori	I	negate (*signed or unsigned*)	neg*s*	rd,rs
shift right arithmetic	sra	R	rotate left	rol	rd,rs,rt
shift left logical variable	sllv	R	rotate right	ror	rd,rs,rt
shift right logical variable	srlv	R	multiply and don't check oflw (*signed or uns.*)	mul*s*	rd,rs,rt
shift right arithmetic variable	srav	R	multiply and check oflw (*signed or uns.*)	mulo*s*	rd,rs,rt
move to Hi	mthi	R	divide and check overflow	div	rd,rs,rt
move to Lo	mtlo	R	divide and don't check overflow	divu	rd,rs,rt
load halfword	lh	I	remainder (*signed or unsigned*)	rem*s*	rd,rs,rt
load byte	lb	I	load immediate	li	rd,imm
load word left (*unaligned*)	lwl	I	load address	la	rd,addr
load word right (*unaligned*)	lwr	I	load double	ld	rd,addr
store word left (*unaligned*)	swl	I	store double	sd	rd,addr
store word right (*unaligned*)	swr	I	unaligned load word	ulw	rd,addr
load linked (*atomic update*)	ll	I	unaligned store word	usw	rd,addr
store cond. (*atomic update*)	sc	I	unaligned load halfword (*signed or uns.*)	ulh*s*	rd,addr
move if zero	movz	R	unaligned store halfword	ush	rd,addr
move if not zero	movn	R	branch	b	Label
multiply and add (S or *uns.*)	madd*s*	R	branch on equal zero	beqz	rs,L
multiply and subtract (S or *uns.*)	msub*s*	I	branch on compare (*signed or unsigned*)	bx*s*	rs,rt,L
branch on ≥ zero and link	bgezal	I	(x = lt, le, gt, ge)		
branch on < zero and link	bltzal	I	set equal	seq	rd,rs,rt
jump and link register	jalr	R	set not equal	sne	rd,rs,rt
branch compare to zero	bxz	I	set on compare (*signed or unsigned*)	sx*s*	rd,rs,rt
branch compare to zero likely	bxzl	I	(x = lt, le, gt, ge)		
(x = lt, le, gt, ge)			load to floating point (*s or d*)	l.*f*	rd,addr
branch compare reg likely	bxl	I	store from floating point (*s or d*)	s.*f*	rd,addr
trap if compare reg	tx	R			
trap if compare immediate	txi	I			
(x = eq, neq, lt, le, gt, ge)					
return from exception	rfe	R			
system call	syscall	I			
break (*cause exception*)	break	I			
move from FP to integer	mfc1	R			
move to FP from integer	mtc1	R			
FP move (*s or d*)	mov.*f*	R			
FP move if zero (*s or d*)	movz.*f*	R			
FP move if not zero (*s or d*)	movn.*f*	R			
FP square root (*s or d*)	sqrt.*f*	R			
FP absolute value (*s or d*)	abs.*f*	R			
FP negate (*s or d*)	neg.*f*	R			
FP convert (*w, s, or d*)	cvt.*f.f*	R			
FP compare un (*s or d*)	c.xn.*f*	R			

FIGURE 3.25 Remaining MIPS-32 and Pseudo MIPS instruction sets. *f* means single (S) or double (d) precision floating-point instructions, and *s* means signed and unsigned (U) versions. MIPS-32 also has FP instructions for multiply and add/sub (madd.*f*/ msub.*f*), ceiling (ceil.*f*), truncate (trunc.*f*), round (round.*f*), and reciprocal (recip.*f*). The underscore represents the letter to include to represent that datatype.

Core MIPS	Name	Integer	Fl. pt.	Arithmetic core + MIPS-32	Name	Integer	Fl. pt.
add	add	0.0%	0.0%	FP add double	add.d	0.0%	10.6%
add immediate	addi	0.0%	0.0%	FP subtract double	sub.d	0.0%	4.9%
add unsigned	addu	5.2%	3.5%	FP multiply double	mul.d	0.0%	15.0%
add immediate unsigned	addiu	9.0%	7.2%	FP divide double	div.d	0.0%	0.2%
subtract unsigned	subu	2.2%	0.6%	FP add single	add.s	0.0%	1.5%
AND	AND	0.2%	0.1%	FP subtract single	sub.s	0.0%	1.8%
AND immediate	ANDi	0.7%	0.2%	FP multiply single	mul.s	0.0%	2.4%
OR	OR	4.0%	1.2%	FP divide single	div.s	0.0%	0.2%
OR immediate	ORi	1.0%	0.2%	load word to FP double	l.d	0.0%	17.5%
NOR	NOR	0.4%	0.2%	store word to FP double	s.d	0.0%	4.9%
shift left logical	sll	4.4%	1.9%	load word to FP single	l.s	0.0%	4.2%
shift right logical	srl	1.1%	0.5%	store word to FP single	s.s	0.0%	1.1%
load upper immediate	lui	3.3%	0.5%	branch on floating-point true	bc1t	0.0%	0.2%
load word	lw	18.6%	5.8%	branch on floating-point false	bc1f	0.0%	0.2%
store word	sw	7.6%	2.0%	floating-point compare double	c.x.d	0.0%	0.6%
load byte	lbu	3.7%	0.1%	multiply	mul	0.0%	0.2%
store byte	sb	0.6%	0.0%	shift right arithmetic	sra	0.5%	0.3%
branch on equal (zero)	beq	8.6%	2.2%	load half	lhu	1.3%	0.0%
branch on not equal (zero)	bne	8.4%	1.4%	store half	sh	0.1%	0.0%
jump and link	jal	0.7%	0.2%				
jump register	jr	1.1%	0.2%				
set less than	slt	9.9%	2.3%				
set less than immediate	slti	3.1%	0.3%				
set less than unsigned	sltu	3.4%	0.8%				
set less than imm. uns.	sltiu	1.1%	0.1%				

FIGURE 3.26   The frequency of the MIPS instructions for SPEC CPU2006 integer and floating point. All instructions that accounted for at least 0.2% of the instructions are included in the table. Pseudoinstructions are converted into MIPS-32 before execution, and hence do not appear here.

For the rest of the book, we concentrate on the MIPS core instructions—the integer instruction set excluding multiply and divide—to make the explanation of computer design easier. As you can see, the MIPS core includes the most popular MIPS instructions; be assured that understanding a computer that runs the MIPS core will give you sufficient background to understand even more ambitious computers. No matter what the instruction set or its size—MIPS, RISC-V, ARM, x86—never forget that bit patterns have no inherent meaning. The same bit pattern may represent a signed integer, unsigned integer, floating-point number, string, instruction, and so on. In stored program computers, it is the operation on the bit pattern that determines its meaning.

Historical Perspective and Further Reading

This section surveys the history of the floating point going back to von Neumann, including the surprisingly controversial IEEE standards effort, plus the rationale for the 80-bit stack architecture for floating point in the x86. See the rest of 🌐 **Section 3.11** online.

Gresham's Law ("Bad money drives out Good") for computers would say, "The Fast drives out the Slow even if the Fast is wrong."

W. Kahan, *1992*

3.12 Self-Study

Data can be anything. In the Self-Study section at the end of Chapter 2, we saw the binary bit pattern **00000001010010110100100000100000**$_{two}$ in hexadecimal, decimal, and as a MIPS assembly language instruction. What IEEE 754 Floating Point number does it represent?

Big numbers. What is the largest, positive two's complement 32-bit integer? Can you represent it exactly in IEEE 754 single precision floating point? If not, how close can you get? What about IEEE 754 half-precision floating point?

Brainy Arithmetic. Machine learning is starting to work so well that it is revolutionizing many industries (see Section 6.7 of Chapter 6). It uses floating point numbers to learn, but unlike scientific programming, it does not need lots of precision. Double precision floating point, the standard-bearer of scientific programming, is overkill, as 32 bits is sufficient. Ideally it could use half-precision (16 bits), since that is much more efficient in computation and memory. However, machine learning training often deals with very small numbers, so the range is important.

These observations about the needs of machine learning led to a new format that is not part of the IEEE standard called *Brain Float 16* (named after Google's Brain division, which invented the format). Figure 3.27 shows the three formats.

Assume Brain Float 16 follows the same conventions as IEEE 754, just with different sizes of fields. What is the smallest nonzero, positive number that you can represent in the three formats? How much smaller is that number for Brain Float 16 than for IEEE fp32? Than fp16?(If you know about subnormals or denorms, ignore them for this question.)

Brainy Area and Energy. A common operation in machine learning is to multiply and accumulate like we see in DGEMM, with the multiply occupying most of the silicon area and using most of the energy. If we have fast multipliers like in Figure 3.7, they are primarily a function of the square of size of the inputs. What are the correct ratios of area/energy of the three formats for multiplies?

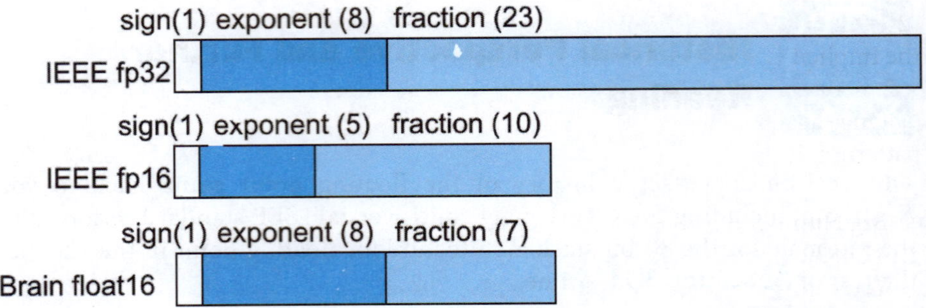

FIGURE 3.27   Floating-point format for IEEE 754 single precision (fp32), IEEE 754 half-precision (fp16), and Brain Float 16. Google's TPUv3 hardware uses Brain Float 16 (see Section 6.11).

1. 32^2 versus 16^2 versus 16^2 for fp32, fp16, and Brain float, respectively

2. 8^2 versus 5^2 versus 8^2

3. 23^2 versus 10^2 versus 7^2

4. 24^2 versus 11^2 versus 8^2

Brainy Programming. Can you think of software benefits of IEEE fp32 and Brain Float 16 having the same-sized exponents?

Brainy Choices. For the domain for machine learning, which of the following are true about Brain Float 16 arithmetic versus IEEE 754 half-precision floating point?

1. Brain Float 16 multipliers take much less hardware than IEEE 754 half-precision.

2. Brain Float 16 multiplies take much less energy than IEEE 754 half-precision.

3. Brain Float 16 is easier for software than IEEE 754 half-precision when converting from IEEE 754 full-precision software.

4. All of the above.

Self Study Answers

Data car. be anything. Mapping the binary number into the IEEE 754 floating-point format:

Sign (1)	Exponent (8)	Fraction (23)
0	00000010_{two}	$10010110100100000100000_{two}$
+	2_{ten}	$4{,}933{,}664_{ten}$

Since the exponent bias for single precision floating point is 127, the exponent is actually $2 - 127$ or -125. The fraction can be thought of as $4{,}933{,}664_{ten}/$

$(2^{23} - 1) = 4{,}933{,}664_{ten}/8{,}388{,}607_{ten} = 0.58813865043_{ten}$. The actual significand adds the implicit 1, so the real number the binary pattern represents is $1.58813865043_{ten} \times 2^{-125}$ or about $3.7336959_{ten} \times 10^{-38}$.

Once again, this exercise demonstrates that there is no inherent meaning in a bit pattern; it depends solely on how software interprets it.

Big Numbers. The largest, positive two's complement 32-bit integer is $2^{31} - 1 = 2{,}147{,}483{,}647$

You cannot represent it exactly in IEEE 754 single precision floating point.

Sign (1)	Exponent (8)	Fraction (23)
0	00000010_{two}	$00000000000000000000000_{two}$
+	158_{ten}	0_{ten}

$= 1.0 \times 2^{(158 - 127)} = 1.0 \times 2^{31} = 2{,}147{,}483{,}648$, so off by 1 from $2^{31} - 1$.

The largest number you can represent in IEEE 754 half precision is

Sign (1)	Exponent (5)	Fraction (10)
0	11110_{two}	1111111111_{two}
+	30_{ten}	1023_{ten}

$= (1 + 1023/1024) \times 2^{(30 - 15)} = 1.999 \times 2^{15} = 65{,}504$, so it is off by many orders of magnitude.

Converting integers to IEEE half-precision float can cause overflow. (The 5-bit exponent 11111_{two} is reserved for infinites and NaNs in half-precision, like the exponent 11111111_{two} is reserved for single precision.)

Brainy Arithmetic. Smallest nonzero positive numbers per format:
IEEE fp32 1.0×2^{-126}
IEEE fp16 1.0×2^{-14}
Brain float16 1.0×2^{-126}
Since IEEE fp32 and Brain Float 16 have the same-sized exponents, they can represent the same smallest nonzero positive number. The smallest number they can represent is 2^{112} times smaller than that of IEEE fp16, or about 5×10^{33}.

Brainy Area and Energy. The exponent and sign fields are not involved in the multiplications, so the answer is a function of the size of significands. As there is an implicit 1 followed by the fraction in these formats, the correct answer is number 4: 24^2 versus 11^2 versus 8^2. That makes IEEE fp16 multiplier about twice (121/64) the size or energy of Brain Float 16 and IEEE fp32 about nine (576/64) times larger.

Brainy Programming. Since the exponents are the same, that means software will have the same behavior for underflows and overflows, Not a Numbers (NaNs), infinities, and so on, which means software using Brain Float 16 to replace IEEE fp32 in some calculations will likely have fewer compatibility problems than switching to IEEE fp16.

Brainy Choices. The answer is 4, all of the above. Remarkably, for machine learning applications, Brain Float 16 is easier for both hardware designers and software programmers. Not surprisingly, Brain Float 16 is very popular for machine learning, and Google's TPUv2 and TPUv3 were the first processors to implement it (see Section 6.11)

Never give in, never give in, never, never, never—in nothing, great or small, large or petty—never give in.

Winston Churchill, address at Harrow School, 1941

3.13   Exercises

3.1 [5] <§3.2> What is 5ED4 2 07A4 when these values represent unsigned 16-bit hexadecimal numbers? The result should be written in hexadecimal. Show your work.

3.2 [5] <§3.2> What is 5ED4 2 07A4 when these values represent signed 16-bit hexadecimal numbers stored in sign-magnitude format? The result should be written in hexadecimal. Show your work.

3.3 [10] <§3.2> Convert 5ED4 into a binary number. What makes base 16 (hexadecimal) an attractive numbering system for representing values in computers?

3.4 [5] <§3.2> What is 4365 − 3412 when these values represent unsigned 12-bit octal numbers? The result should be written in octal. Show your work.

3.5 [5] <§3.2> What is 4365 − 3412 when these values represent signed 12-bit octal numbers stored in sign-magnitude format? The result should be written in octal. Show your work.

3.6 [5] <§3.2> Assume 185 and 122 are unsigned 8-bit decimal integers. Calculate 185 − 122. Is there overflow, underflow, or neither?

3.7 [5] <§3.2> Assume 185 and 122 are signed 8-bit decimal integers stored in sign-magnitude format. Calculate 185 + 122. Is there overflow, underflow, or neither?

3.8 [5] <§3.2> Assume 185 and 122 are signed 8-bit decimal integers stored in sign-magnitude format. Calculate 185 2 122. Is there overflow, underflow, or neither?

3.9 [10] <§3.2> Assume 151 and 214 are signed 8-bit decimal integers stored in two's complement format. Calculate 151 + 214 using saturating arithmetic. The result should be written in decimal. Show your work.

3.10 [10] <§3.2> Assume 151 and 214 are signed 8-bit decimal integers stored in two's complement format. Calculate 151 2 214 using saturating arithmetic. The result should be written in decimal. Show your work.

3.11 [10] <§3.2> Assume 151 and 214 are unsigned 8-bit integers. Calculate 151 + 214 using saturating arithmetic. The result should be written in decimal. Show your work.

3.12 [20] <§3.3> Using a table similar to that shown in Figure 3.6, calculate the product of the octal unsigned 6-bit integers 62 and 12 using the hardware described in Figure 3.3. You should show the contents of each register on each step.

3.13 [20] <§3.3> Using a table similar to that shown in Figure 3.6, calculate the product of the octal unsigned 8-bit integers 62 and 12 using the hardware described in Figure 3.5. You should show the contents of each register on each step.

3.14 [10] <§3.3> Calculate the time necessary to perform a multiply using the approach given in Figures 3.3 and 3.5 if an integer is 8 bits wide and each step of the operation takes 4 time units. Assume that in step 1a an addition is always performed—either the multiplicand will be added, or a zero will be. Also assume that the registers have already been initialized (you are just counting how long it takes to do the multiplication loop itself). If this is being done in hardware, the shifts of the multiplicand and multiplier can be done simultaneously. If this is being done in software, they will have to be done one after the other. Solve for each case.

3.15 [10] <§3.3> Calculate the time necessary to perform a multiply using the approach described in the text (31 adders stacked vertically) if an integer is 8 bits wide and an adder takes 4 time units.

3.16 [20] <§3.3> Calculate the time necessary to perform a multiply using the approach given in Figure 3.7 if an integer is 8 bits wide and an adder takes 4 time units.

3.17 [20] <§3.3> As discussed in the text, one possible performance enhancement is to do a shift and add instead of an actual multiplication. Since 9×6, for example, can be written $(2 \times 2 \times 2 + 1) \times 6$, we can calculate 9×6 by shifting 6 to the left 3 times and then adding 6 to that result. Show the best way to calculate $0 \times 33 \times 0 \times 55$ using shifts and adds/subtracts. Assume both inputs are 8-bit unsigned integers.

3.18 [20] <§3.4> Using a table similar to that shown in Figure 3.10, calculate 74 divided by 21 using the hardware described in Figure 3.8. You should show the contents of each register on each step. Assume both inputs are unsigned 6-bit integers.

3.19 [30] <§3.4> Using a table similar to that shown in Figure 3.10, calculate 74 divided by 21 using the hardware described in Figure 3.11. You should show the contents of each register on each step. Assume A and B are unsigned 6-bit integers. This algorithm requires a slightly different approach than that shown in Figure 3.9. You will want to think hard about this, do an experiment or two, or else go to the web to figure out how to make this work correctly. (Hint: one possible solution involves using the fact that Figure 3.11 implies the remainder register can be shifted either direction.)

3.20 [5] <§3.5> What decimal number does the bit pattern 0×0C000000 represent if it is a two's complement integer? An unsigned integer?

3.21 [10] <§3.5> If the bit pattern 0×0C000000 is placed into the Instruction Register, what MIPS instruction will be executed?

3.22 [10] <§3.5> What decimal number does the bit pattern $\texttt{0×0C000000}$ represent if it is a floating point number? Use the IEEE 754 standard.

3.23 [10] <§3.5> Write down the binary representation of the decimal number 63.25 assuming the IEEE 754 single precision format.

3.24 [10] <§3.5> Write down the binary representation of the decimal number 63.25 assuming the IEEE 754 double precision format.

3.25 [10] <§3.5> Write down the binary representation of the decimal number 63.25 assuming it was stored using the single precision IBM format (base 16, instead of base 2, with 7 bits of exponent).

3.26 [20] <§3.5> Write down the binary bit pattern to represent -1.5625×10^{-1} assuming a format similar to that employed by the DEC PDP-8 (the leftmost 12 bits are the exponent stored as a two's complement number, and the rightmost 24 bits are the fraction stored as a two's complement number). No hidden 1 is used. Comment on how the range and accuracy of this 36-bit pattern compares to the single and double precision IEEE 754 standards.

3.27 [20] <§3.5> IEEE 754-2008 contains a half precision that is only 16 bits wide. The leftmost bit is still the sign bit, the exponent is 5 bits wide and has a bias of 15, and the mantissa is 10 bits long. A hidden 1 is assumed. Write down the bit pattern to represent -1.5625×10^{-1} assuming a version of this format, which uses an excess-16 format to store the exponent. Comment on how the range and accuracy of this 16-bit floating point format compares to the single precision IEEE 754 standard.

3.28 [20] <§3.5> The Hewlett-Packard 2114, 2115, and 2116 used a format with the leftmost 16 bits being the fraction stored in two's complement format, followed by another 16-bit field which had the leftmost 8 bits as an extension of the fraction (making the fraction 24 bits long), and the rightmost 8 bits representing the exponent. However, in an interesting twist, the exponent was stored in sign-magnitude format with the sign bit on the far right! Write down the bit pattern to represent -1.5625×10^{-1} assuming this format. No hidden 1 is used. Comment on how the range and accuracy of this 32-bit pattern compares to the single precision IEEE 754 standard.

3.29 [20] <§3.5> Calculate the sum of 2.6125×10^{1} and $4.150390625 \times 10^{-1}$ by hand, assuming A and B are stored in the 16-bit half precision described in Exercise 3.27. Assume 1 guard, 1 round bit, and 1 sticky bit, and round to the nearest even. Show all the steps.

3.30 [30] <§3.5> Calculate the product of -8.0546875×10^{0} and $-1.79931640625 \times 10^{-1}$ by hand, assuming A and B are stored in the 16-bit half precision format described in Exercise 3.27. Assume 1 guard, 1 round bit, and 1 sticky bit, and round to the nearest even. Show all the steps; however, as is done in the example in the text, you can do the multiplication in human-readable format instead of using the techniques described in Exercises 3.12 through 3.14. Indicate if there is overflow or underflow. Write your answer in both the 16-bit floating point format described in Exercise 3.27 and also as a decimal number. How accurate is your result? How does it compare to the number you get if you do the multiplication on a calculator?

3.31 [30] <§3.5> Calculate by hand 8.625×10^1 divided by -4.875×10^0. Show all the steps necessary to achieve your answer. Assume there is a guard, a round bit, and a sticky bit, and use them if necessary. Write the final answer in both the 16-bit floating point format described in Exercise 27 and in decimal and compare the decimal result to that which you get if you use a calculator.

3.32 [20] <§3.9> Calculate $(3.984375 \times 10^{-1} + 3.4375 \times 10^{-1}) + 1.771 \times 10^3$ by hand, assuming each of the values are stored in the 16-bit half precision format described in Exercise 3.27 (and also described in the text). Assume 1 guard, 1 round bit, and 1 sticky bit, and round to the nearest even. Show all the steps, and write your answer in both the 16-bit floating point format and in decimal.

3.33 [20] <§3.9> Calculate $3.984375 \times 10^{-1} + (3.4375 \times 10^{-1} + 1.771 \times 10^3)$ by hand, assuming each of the values are stored in the 16-bit half precision format described in Exercise 3.27 (and also described in the text). Assume 1 guard, 1 round bit, and 1 sticky bit, and round to the nearest even. Show all the steps, and write your answer in both the 16-bit floating point format and in decimal.

3.34 [10] <§3.9> Based on your answers to 3.32 and 3.33, does $(3.984375 \times 10^{-1} + 3.4375 \times 10^{-1}) + 1.771 \times 10^3 = 3.984375 \times 10^{-1} + (3.4375 \times 10^{-1} + 1.771 \times 10^3)$?

3.35 [30] <§3.9> Calculate $(3.41796875 \times 10^{-3} \times 6.34765625 \times 10^{-3}) \times 1.05625 \times 10^2$ by hand, assuming each of the values are stored in the 16-bit half precision format described in Exercise 3.27 (and also described in the text). Assume 1 guard, 1 round bit, and 1 sticky bit, and round to the nearest even. Show all the steps, and write your answer in both the 16-bit floating point format and in decimal.

3.36 [30] <§3.9> Calculate $3.41796875 \times 10^{-3} \times (6.34765625 \times 10^{-3} \times 1.05625 \times 10^2)$ by hand, assuming each of the values are stored in the 16-bit half precision format described in Exercise 3.27 (and also described in the text). Assume 1 guard, 1 round bit, and 1 sticky bit, and round to the nearest even. Show all the steps, and write your answer in both the 16-bit floating point format and in decimal.

3.37 [10] <§3.9> Based on your answers to 3.35 and 3.36, does $(3.41796875 \times 10^{-3} \times 6.34765625 \times 10^{-3}) \times 1.05625 \times 10^2 = 3.41796875 \times 10^{-3} \times (6.34765625 \times 10^{-3} \times 1.05625 \times 10^2)$?

3.38 [30] <§3.9> Calculate $1.666015625 \times 10^0 \times (1.9760 \times 10^4 + -1.9744 \times 10^4)$ by hand, assuming each of the values are stored in the 16-bit half precision format described in Exercise 3.27 (and also described in the text). Assume 1 guard, 1 round bit, and 1 sticky bit, and round to the nearest even. Show all the steps, and write your answer in both the 16-bit floating point format and in decimal.

3.39 [30] <§3.9> Calculate $(1.666015625 \times 10^0 \times 1.9760 \times 10^4) + (1.666015625 \times 10^0 \times -1.9744 \times 10^4)$ by hand, assuming each of the values are stored in the 16-bit half precision format described in Exercise 3.27 (and also described in the text). Assume 1 guard, 1 round bit, and 1 sticky bit, and round to the nearest even.

Show all the steps, and write your answer in both the 16-bit floating point format and in decimal.

3.40 [10] <§3.9> Based on your answers to 3.38 and 3.39, does $(1.666015625 \times 10^0 \times 1.9760 \times 10^4) + (1.666015625 \times 10^0 \times -1.9744 \times 10^4) = 1.666015625 \times 10^0 \times (1.9760 \times 10^4 + -1.9744 \times 10^4)$?

3.41 [10] <§3.5> Using the IEEE 754 floating point format, write down the bit pattern that would represent $-1/4$. Can you represent $-1/4$ exactly?

3.42 [10] <§3.5> What do you get if you add $-1/4$ to itself 4 times? What is $-1/4 \times 4$? Are they the same? What should they be?

3.43 [10] <§3.5> Write down the bit pattern in the fraction of value 1/3 assuming a floating point format that uses binary numbers in the fraction. Assume there are 24 bits, and you do not need to normalize. Is this representation exact?

3.44 [10] <§3.5> Write down the bit pattern in the fraction of value 1/3 assuming a floating point format that uses Binary Coded Decimal (base 10) numbers in the fraction instead of base 2. Assume there are 24 bits, and you do not need to normalize. Is this representation exact?

3.45 [10] <§3.5> Write down the bit pattern assuming that we are using base 15 numbers in the fraction of value 1/3 instead of base 2. (Base 16 numbers use the symbols 0–9 and A–F. Base 15 numbers would use 0–9 and A–E.) Assume there are 24 bits, and you do not need to normalize. Is this representation exact?

3.46 [20] <§3.5> Write down the bit pattern assuming that we are using base 30 numbers in the fraction of value 1/3 instead of base 2. (Base 16 numbers use the symbols 0–9 and A–F. Base 30 numbers would use 0–9 and A–T.) Assume there are 20 bits, and you do not need to normalize. Is this representation exact?

3.47 [45] <§§3.6, 3.7> The following C code implements a four-tap FIR filter on input array sig_in. Assume that all arrays are 16-bit fixed-point values.

```
for (i = 3;i < 128;i + +)
sig_out[i] = sig_in[i-3] * f[0] + sig_in[i-2] * f[1]
  + sig_in[i-1] * f[2] + sig_in[i] * f[3];
```

Assume you are to write an optimized implementation of this code in assembly language on a processor that has SIMD instructions and 128-bit registers. Without knowing the details of the instruction set, briefly describe how you would implement this code, maximizing the use of sub-word operations and minimizing the amount of data that is transferred between registers and memory. State all your assumptions about the instructions you use.

4

The Processor

In a major matter, no details are small.

French Proverb

Five Classic Components of a Computer

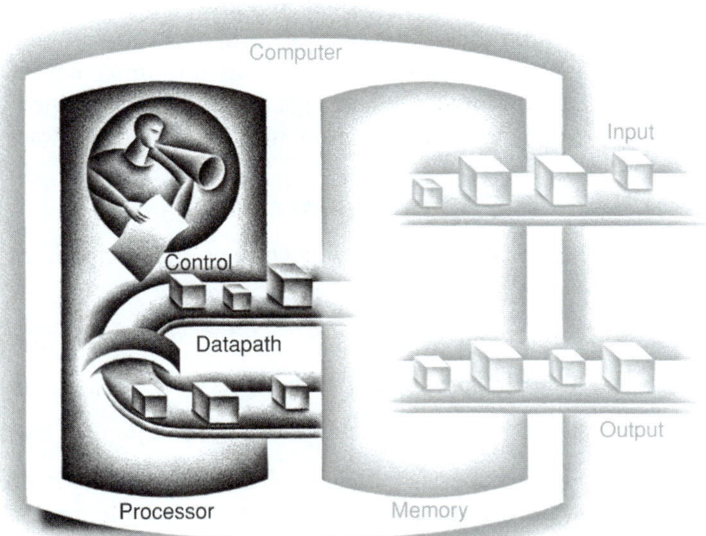

4.1   Introduction

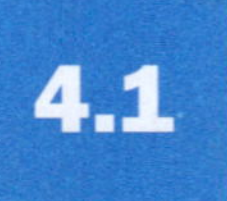

Chapter 1 explains that the performance of a computer is determined by three key factors: instruction count, clock cycle time, and *clock cycles per instruction* (CPI). Chapter 2 explains that the compiler and the instruction set architecture determine the instruction count required for a given program. However, the implementation of the processor determines both the clock cycle time and the number of clock cycles per instruction. In this chapter, we construct the datapath and control unit for two different implementations of the MIPS instruction set.

This chapter contains an explanation of the principles and techniques used in implementing a processor, starting with a highly abstract and simplified overview in this section. It is followed by a section that builds up a datapath and constructs a simple version of a processor sufficient to implement an instruction set like MIPS. The bulk of the chapter covers a more realistic **pipelined** MIPS implementation, followed by a section that develops the concepts necessary to implement more complex instruction sets, like the x86.

For the reader interested in understanding the high-level interpretation of instructions and its impact on program performance, this initial section and Section 4.6 present the basic concepts of pipelining. Recent trends are covered in Section 4.11, and Section 4.12 describes the recent Intel Core i7 and ARM Cortex-A8 architectures. Section 4.13 shows how to use instruction-level parallelism to more than double the performance of the matrix multiply from Section 3.8. These sections provide enough background to understand the pipeline concepts at a high level.

For the reader interested in understanding the processor and its performance in more depth, Sections 4.3, 4.4, and 4.7 will be useful. Those interested in learning how to build a processor should also cover 4.2, 4.8, 4.9, and 4.10. For readers with an interest in modern hardware design, 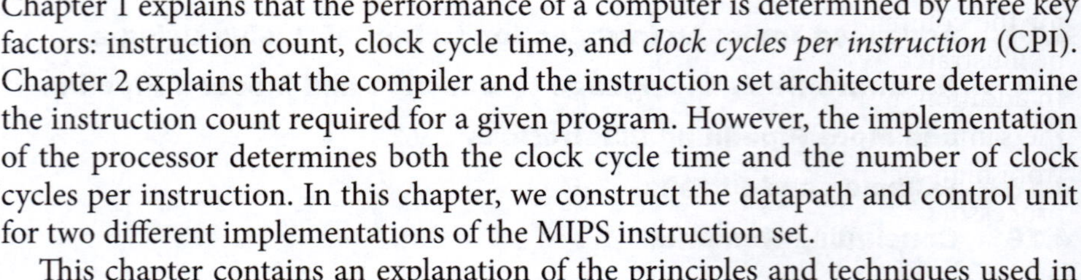 **Section 4.14** describes how hardware design languages and CAD tools are used to implement hardware, and then how to use a hardware design language to describe a pipelined implementation. It also gives several more illustrations of how pipelining hardware executes.

A Basic MIPS Implementation

We will be examining an implementation that includes a subset of the core MIPS instruction set:

- The memory-reference instructions *load word* (`lw`) and *store word* (`sw`)

- The arithmetic-logical instructions `add`, `sub`, `AND`, `OR`, and `slt`

- The instructions *branch equal* (`beq`) and *jump* (`j`), which we add last

This subset does not include all the integer instructions (for example, shift, multiply, and divide are missing), nor does it include any floating-point instructions.

However, it illustrates the key principles used in creating a datapath and designing the control. The implementation of the remaining instructions is similar.

In examining the implementation, we will have the opportunity to see how the instruction set architecture determines many aspects of the implementation, and how the choice of various implementation strategies affects the clock rate and CPI for the computer. Many of the key design principles introduced in Chapter 1 can be illustrated by looking at the implementation, such as *Simplicity favors regularity*. In addition, most concepts used to implement the MIPS subset in this chapter are the same basic ideas that are used to construct a broad spectrum of computers, from high-performance servers to general-purpose microprocessors to embedded processors.

An Overview of the Implementation

In Chapter 2, we looked at the core MIPS instructions, including the integer arithmetic-logical instructions, the memory-reference instructions, and the branch instructions. Much of what needs to be done to implement these instructions is the same, independent of the exact class of instruction. For every instruction, the first two steps are identical:

1. Send the *program counter* (PC) to the memory that contains the code and fetch the instruction from that memory.

2. Read one or two registers, using fields of the instruction to select the registers to read. For the load word instruction, we need to read only one register, but most other instructions require reading two registers.

After these two steps, the actions required to complete the instruction depend on the instruction class. Fortunately, for each of the three instruction classes (memory-reference, arithmetic-logical, and branches), the actions are largely the same, independent of the exact instruction. The simplicity and regularity of the MIPS instruction set simplifies the implementation by making the execution of many of the instruction classes similar.

For example, all instruction classes, except jump, use the arithmetic-logical unit (ALU) after reading the registers. The memory-reference instructions use the ALU for an address calculation, the arithmetic-logical instructions for the operation execution, and branches for comparison. After using the ALU, the actions required to complete various instruction classes differ. A memory-reference instruction will need to access the memory either to read data for a load or write data for a store. An arithmetic-logical or load instruction must write the data from the ALU or memory back into a register. Lastly, for a branch instruction, we may need to change the next instruction address based on the comparison; otherwise, the PC should be incremented by 4 to get the address of the next instruction.

Figure 4.1 shows the high-level view of a MIPS implementation, focusing on the various functional units and their interconnection. Although this figure shows most of the flow of data through the processor, it omits two important aspects of instruction execution.

First, in several places, Figure 4.1 shows data going to a particular unit as coming from two different sources. For example, the value written into the PC can come from one of two adders, the data written into the register file can come from either the ALU or the data memory, and the second input to the ALU can come from a register or the immediate field of the instruction. In practice, these data lines cannot simply be wired together; we must add a logic element that chooses from among the multiple sources and steers one of those sources to its destination. This selection is commonly done with a device called a *multiplexor*, although this device might better be called a *data selector*. Appendix B describes the multiplexor, which selects from among several inputs based on the setting of its control lines. The control lines are set based primarily on information taken from the instruction being executed.

The second omission in Figure 4.1 is that several of the units must be controlled depending on the type of instruction. For example, the data memory must read

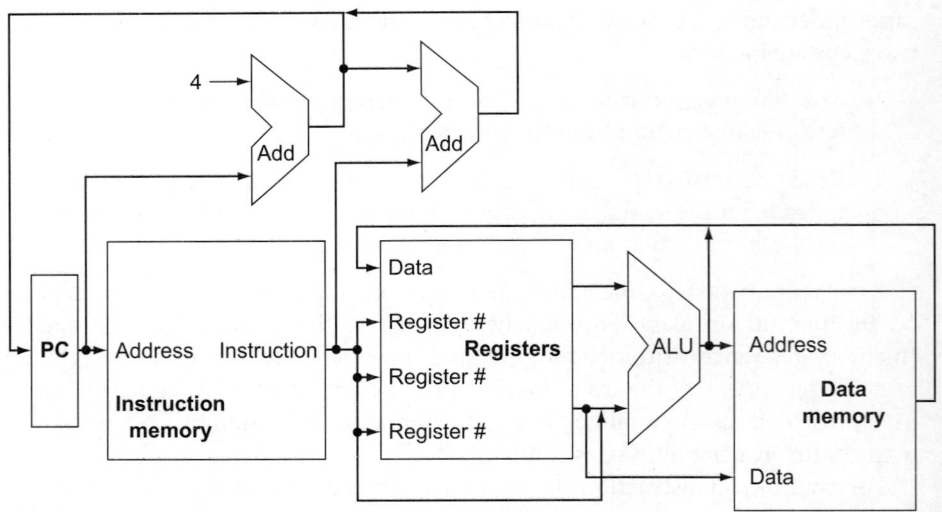

FIGURE 4.1 An abstract view of the implementation of the MIPS subset showing the major functional units and the major connections between them. All instructions start by using the program counter to supply the instruction address to the instruction memory. After the instruction is fetched, the register operands used by an instruction are specified by fields of that instruction. Once the register operands have been fetched, they can be operated on to compute a memory address (for a load or store), to compute an arithmetic result (for an integer arithmetic-logical instruction), or a compare (for a branch). If the instruction is an arithmetic-logical instruction, the result from the ALU must be written to a register. If the operation is a load or store, the ALU result is used as an address to either load a value from memory into the registers or store a value from the registers. The result from the ALU or memory is written back into the register file. Branches require the use of the ALU output to determine the next instruction address, which comes either from the ALU (where the PC and branch offset are summed) or from an adder that increments the current PC by 4. The thick lines interconnecting the functional units represent buses, which consist of multiple signals. The arrows are used to guide the reader in knowing how information flows. Since signal lines may cross, we explicitly show when crossing lines are connected by the presence of a dot where the lines cross.

on a load and write on a store. The register file must be written only on a load or on an arithmetic-logical instruction. And, of course, the ALU must perform one of several operations. (Appendix B describes the detailed design of the ALU.) Like the multiplexors, control lines are set on the basis of various fields in the instruction to direct these operations.

Figure 4.2 shows the datapath of Figure 4.1 with the three required multiplexors added, as well as control lines for the major functional units. A *control unit*, which has the instruction as an input, is used to determine how to set the control lines for the functional units and two of the multiplexors. The third multiplexor,

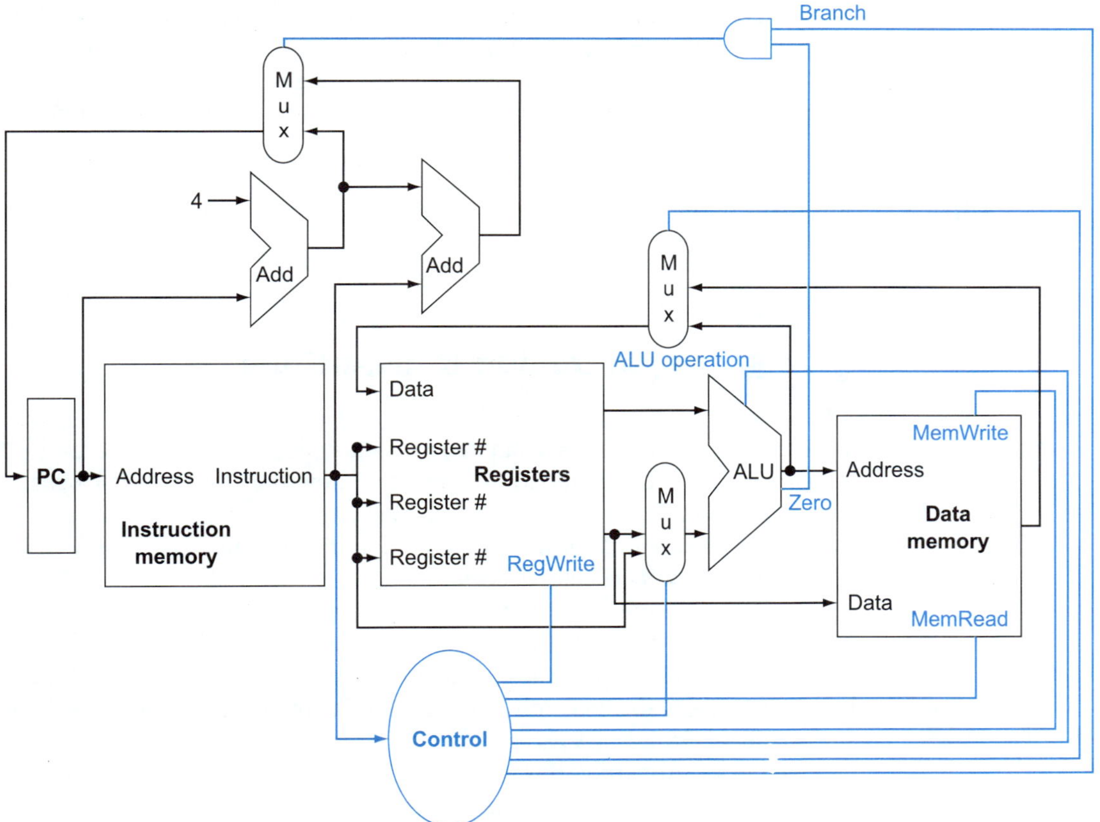

FIGURE 4.2 The basic implementation of the MIPS subset, including the necessary multiplexors and control lines. The top multiplexor ("Mux") controls what value replaces the PC (PC + 4 or the branch destination address); the multiplexor is controlled by the gate that "ANDs" together the Zero output of the ALU and a control signal that indicates that the instruction is a branch. The middle multiplexor, whose output returns to the register file, is used to steer the output of the ALU (in the case of an arithmetic-logical instruction) or the output of the data memory (in the case of a load) for writing into the register file. Finally, the bottommost multiplexor is used to determine whether the second ALU input is from the registers (for an arithmetic-logical instruction or a branch) or from the offset field of the instruction (for a load or store). The added control lines are straightforward and determine the operation performed at the ALU, whether the data memory should read or write, and whether the registers should perform a write operation. The control lines are shown in color to make them easier to see.

which determines whether PC + 4 or the branch destination address is written into the PC, is set based on the Zero output of the ALU, which is used to perform the comparison of a beq instruction. The regularity and simplicity of the MIPS instruction set means that a simple decoding process can be used to determine how to set the control lines.

In the remainder of the chapter, we refine this view to fill in the details, which requires that we add further functional units, increase the number of connections between units, and, of course, enhance a control unit to control what actions are taken for different instruction classes. Sections 4.3 and 4.4 describe a simple implementation that uses a single long clock cycle for every instruction and follows the general form of Figures 4.1 and 4.2. In this first design, every instruction begins execution on one clock edge and completes execution on the next clock edge.

While easier to understand, this approach is not practical, since the clock cycle must be severely stretched to accommodate the longest instruction. After designing the control for this simple computer, we will look at faster implementations with all their complexities, including exceptions.

Check Yourself

How many of the five classic components of a computer—shown on page 255—do Figures 4.1 and 4.2 include?

4.2 Logic Design Conventions

To discuss the design of a computer, we must decide how the hardware logic implementing the computer will operate and how the computer is clocked. This section reviews a few key ideas in digital logic that we will use extensively in this chapter. If you have little or no background in digital logic, you will find it helpful to read 🌐 **Appendix B** before continuing.

The datapath elements in the MIPS implementation consist of two different types of logic elements: elements that operate on data values and elements that contain state. The elements that operate on data values are all **combinational**, which means that their outputs depend only on the current inputs. Given the same input, a combinational element always produces the same output. The ALU in Figure 4.1 and discussed in 🌐 **Appendix B** is an example of a combinational element. Given a set of inputs, it always produces the same output because it has no internal storage.

combinational element An operational element, such as an AND gate or an ALU.

Other elements in the design are not combinational, but instead contain *state*. An element contains state if it has some internal storage. We call these elements **state elements** because, if we pulled the power plug on the computer, we could restart it accurately by loading the state elements with the values they contained before we pulled the plug. Furthermore, if we saved and restored the state elements, it would be as if the computer had never lost power. Thus, these state elements completely characterize the computer. In Figure 4.1, the instruction and data memories, as well as the registers, are all examples of state elements.

state element A memory element, such as a register or a memory.

A state element has at least two inputs and one output. The required inputs are the data value to be written into the element and the clock, which determines when the data value is written. The output from a state element provides the value that was written in an earlier clock cycle. For example, one of the logically simplest state elements is a D-type flip-flop (see ⊕ Appendix B), which has exactly these two inputs (a value and a clock) and one output. In addition to flip-flops, our MIPS implementation uses two other types of state elements: memories and registers, both of which appear in Figure 4.1. The clock is used to determine when the state element should be written; a state element can be read at any time.

Logic components that contain state are also called *sequential*, because their outputs depend on both their inputs and the contents of the internal state. For example, the output from the functional unit representing the registers depends both on the register numbers supplied and on what was written into the registers previously. The operation of both the combinational and sequential elements and their construction are discussed in more detail in ⊕ Appendix B.

Clocking Methodology

A **clocking methodology** defines when signals can be read and when they can be written. It is important to specify the timing of reads and writes, because if a signal is written at the same time it is read, the value of the read could correspond to the old value, the newly written value, or even some mix of the two! Computer designs cannot tolerate such unpredictability. A clocking methodology is designed to make hardware predictable.

For simplicity, we will assume an **edge-triggered clocking** methodology. An edge-triggered clocking methodology means that any values stored in a sequential logic element are updated only on a clock edge, which is a quick transition from low to high or *vice versa* (see Figure 4.3). Because only state elements can store a data value, any collection of combinational logic must have its inputs come from a set of state elements and its outputs written into a set of state elements. The inputs are values that were written in a previous clock cycle, while the outputs are values that can be used in a following clock cycle.

clocking methodology The approach used to determine when data is valid and stable relative to the clock.

edge-triggered clocking A clocking scheme in which all state changes occur on a clock edge.

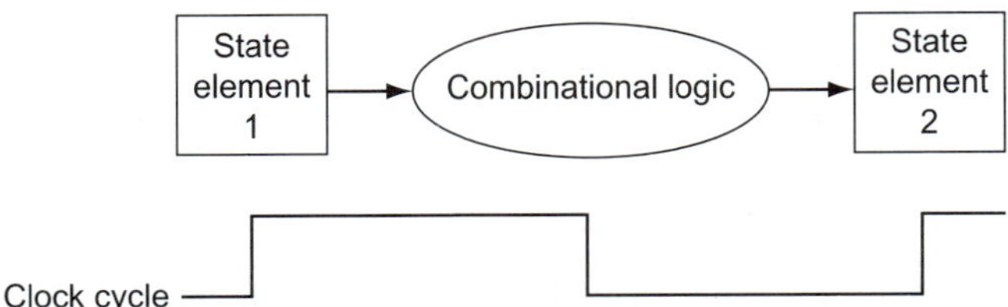

FIGURE 4.3 Combinational logic, state elements, and the clock are closely related. In a synchronous digital system, the clock determines when elements with state will write values into internal storage. Any inputs to a state element must reach a stable value (that is, have reached a value from which they will not change until after the clock edge) before the active clock edge causes the state to be updated. All state elements in this chapter, including memory, are assumed to be positive edge-triggered; that is, they change on the rising clock edge.

Figure 4.3 shows the two state elements surrounding a block of combinational logic, which operates in a single clock cycle: all signals must propagate from state element 1, through the combinational logic, and to state element 2 in the time of one clock cycle. The time necessary for the signals to reach state element 2 defines the length of the clock cycle.

control signal A signal used for multiplexor selection or for directing the operation of a functional unit; contrasts with a *data signal*, which contains information that is operated on by a functional unit.

For simplicity, we do not show a write **control signal** when a state element is written on every active clock edge. In contrast, if a state element is not updated on every clock, then an explicit write control signal is required. Both the clock signal and the write control signal are inputs, and the state element is changed only when the write control signal is asserted and a clock edge occurs.

asserted The signal is logically high or true.

We will use the word **asserted** to indicate a signal that is logically high and *assert* to specify that a signal should be driven logically high, and *deassert* or **deasserted** to represent logically low. We use the terms assert and deassert because when we implement hardware, at times 1 represents logically high and at times it can represent logically low.

deasserted The signal is logically low or false.

An edge-triggered methodology allows us to read the contents of a register, send the value through some combinational logic, and write that register in the same clock cycle. Figure 4.4 gives a generic example. It doesn't matter whether we assume that all writes take place on the rising clock edge (from low to high) or on the falling clock edge (from high to low), since the inputs to the combinational logic block cannot change except on the chosen clock edge. In this book we use the rising clock edge. With an edge-triggered timing methodology, there is *no* feedback within a single clock cycle, and the logic in Figure 4.4 works correctly. In 🌐 **Appendix B**, we briefly discuss additional timing constraints (such as setup and hold times) as well as other timing methodologies.

For the 32-bit MIPS architecture, nearly all of these state and logic elements will have inputs and outputs that are 32 bits wide, since that is the width of most of the data handled by the processor. We will make it clear whenever a unit has an input or output that is other than 32 bits in width. The figures will indicate *buses*, which are signals wider than 1 bit, with thicker lines. At times, we will want to combine several buses to form a wider bus; for example, we may want to obtain a 32-bit bus by combining two 16-bit buses. In such cases, labels on the bus lines will make it

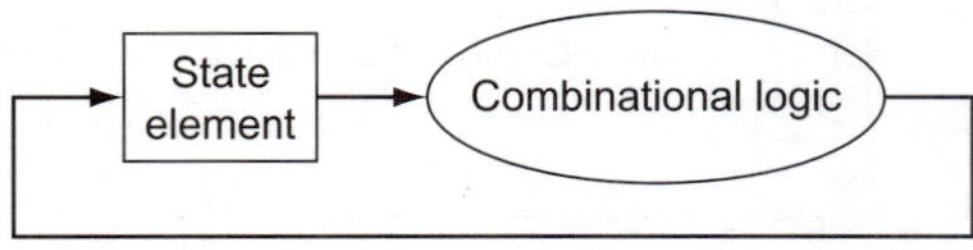

FIGURE 4.4 An edge-triggered methodology allows a state element to be read and written in the same clock cycle without creating a race that could lead to indeterminate data values. Of course, the clock cycle still must be long enough so that the input values are stable when the active clock edge occurs. Feedback cannot occur within one clock cycle because of the edge-triggered update of the state element. If feedback were possible, this design could not work properly. Our designs in this chapter and the next rely on the edge-triggered timing methodology and on structures like the one shown in this figure.

clear that we are concatenating buses to form a wider bus. Arrows are also added to help clarify the direction of the flow of data between elements. Finally, **color** indicates a control signal as opposed to a signal that carries data; this distinction will become clearer as we proceed through this chapter.

True or false: Because the register file is both read and written on the same clock cycle, any MIPS datapath using edge-triggered writes must have more than one copy of the register file.

Elaboration: There is also a 64-bit version of the MIPS architecture, and, naturally enough, most paths in its implementation would be 64 bits wide.

4.3   Building a Datapath

A reasonable way to start a datapath design is to examine the major components required to execute each class of MIPS instructions. Let's start at the top by looking at which **datapath elements** each instruction needs, and then work our way down through the levels of **abstraction**. When we show the datapath elements, we will also show their control signals. We use abstraction in this explanation, starting from the bottom up.

Figure 4.5a shows the first element we need: a memory unit to store the instructions of a program and supply instructions given an address. Figure 4.5b also shows the **program counter (PC)**, which as we saw in Chapter 2 is a register that holds the address of the current instruction. Lastly, we will need an adder to increment the PC to the address of the next instruction. This adder, which is combinational, can be built from the ALU described in detail in 🌐 **Appendix B** simply by wiring the control lines so that the control always specifies an add operation. We will draw such an ALU with the label *Add*, as in Figure 4.5, to indicate that it has been permanently made an adder and cannot perform the other ALU functions.

To execute any instruction, we must start by fetching the instruction from memory. To prepare for executing the next instruction, we must also increment the program counter so that it points at the next instruction, 4 bytes later. Figure 4.6 shows how to combine the three elements from Figure 4.5 to form the portion of a datapath that fetches instructions and increments the PC to obtain the address of the next sequential instruction.

Now let's consider the R-format instructions (see Figure 2.20 on page 126). They all read two registers, perform an ALU operation on the contents of the registers, and write the result to a register. We call these instructions either *R-type instructions* or *arithmetic-logical instructions* (since they perform arithmetic or logical operations). This instruction class includes add, sub, AND, OR, and slt,

A B S T R A C T I O N

datapath element
A unit used to operate on or hold data within a processor. In the MIPS implementation, the datapath elements include the instruction and data memories, the register file, the ALU, and adders.

program counter (PC) The register containing the address of the instruction in the program being executed.

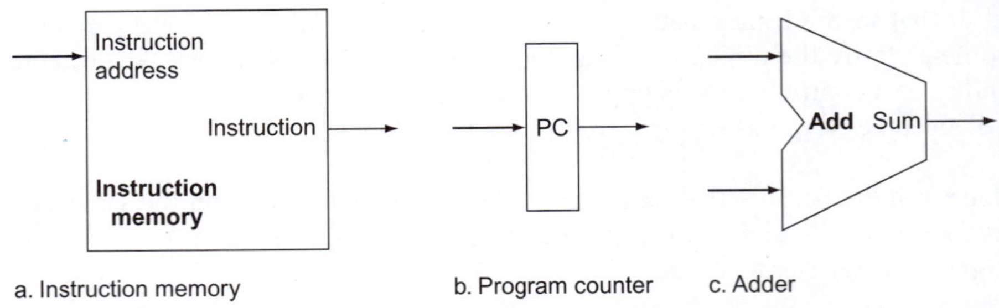

FIGURE 4.5 Two state elements are needed to store and access instructions, and an adder is needed to compute the next instruction address. The state elements are the instruction memory and the program counter. The instruction memory need only provide read access because the datapath does not write instructions. Since the instruction memory only reads, we treat it as combinational logic: the output at any time reflects the contents of the location specified by the address input, and no read control signal is needed. (We will need to write the instruction memory when we load the program; this is not hard to add, and we ignore it for simplicity.) The program counter is a 32-bit register that is written at the end of every clock cycle and thus does not need a write control signal. The adder is an ALU wired to always add its two 32-bit inputs and place the sum on its output.

which were introduced in Chapter 2. Recall that a typical instance of such an instruction is add $t1,$t2,$t3, which reads $t2 and $t3 and writes $t1.

The processor's 32 general-purpose registers are stored in a structure called a **register file**. A register file is a collection of registers in which any register can be read or written by specifying the number of the register in the file. The register file contains the register state of the computer. In addition, we will need an ALU to operate on the values read from the registers.

R-format instructions have three register operands, so we will need to read two data words from the register file and write one data word into the register file for each instruction. For each data word to be read from the registers, we need an input to the register file that specifies the *register number* to be read and an output from the register file that will carry the value that has been read from the registers. To write a data word, we will need two inputs: one to specify the register number to be written and one to supply the *data* to be written into the register. The register file always outputs the contents of whatever register numbers are on the Read register inputs. Writes, however, are controlled by the write control signal, which must be asserted for a write to occur at the clock edge. Figure 4.7a shows the result; we need a total of four inputs (three for register numbers and one for data) and two outputs (both for data). The register number inputs are 5 bits wide to specify one of 32 registers ($32 = 2^5$), whereas the data input and two data output buses are each 32 bits wide.

Figure 4.7b shows the ALU, which takes two 32-bit inputs and produces a 32-bit result, as well as a 1-bit signal if the result is 0. The 4-bit control signal of the ALU is described in detail in ⊕ **Appendix B**; we will review the ALU control shortly when we need to know how to set it.

register file A state element that consists of a set of registers that can be read and written by supplying a register number to be accessed.

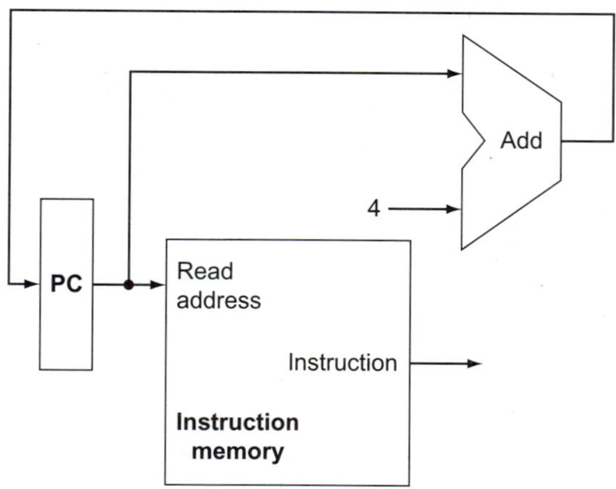

FIGURE 4.6 A portion of the datapath used for fetching instructions and incrementing the program counter. The fetched instruction is used by other parts of the datapath.

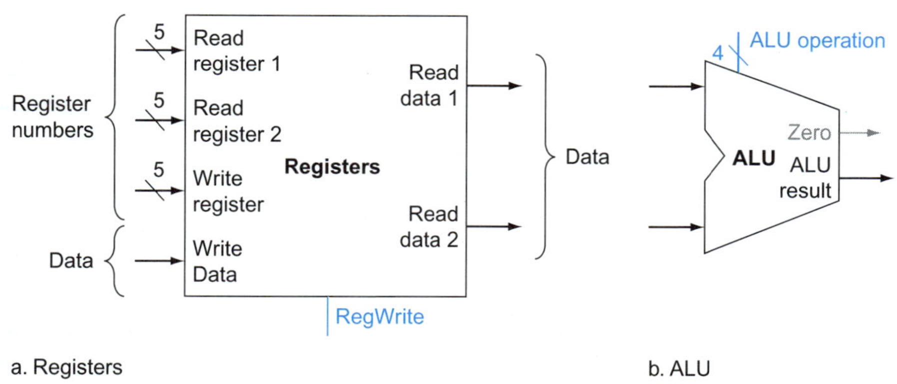

a. Registers   b. ALU

FIGURE 4.7 The two elements needed to implement R-format ALU operations are the register file and the ALU. The register file contains all the registers and has two read ports and one write port. The design of multiported register files is discussed in Section B.8 of ⊕ **Appendix B**. The register file always outputs the contents of the registers corresponding to the Read register inputs on the outputs; no other control inputs are needed. In contrast, a register write must be explicitly indicated by asserting the write control signal. Remember that writes are edge-triggered, so that all the write inputs (i.e., the value to be written, the register number, and the write control signal) must be valid at the clock edge. Since writes to the register file are edge-triggered, our design can legally read and write the same register within a clock cycle: the read will get the value written in an earlier clock cycle, while the value written will be available to a read in a subsequent clock cycle. The inputs carrying the register number to the register file are all 5 bits wide, whereas the lines carrying data values are 32 bits wide. The operation to be performed by the ALU is controlled with the ALU operation signal, which will be 4 bits wide, using the ALU designed in ⊕ **Appendix B**. We will use the Zero detection output of the ALU shortly to implement branches. The overflow output will not be needed until Section 4.10, when we discuss exceptions; we omit it until then.

Next, consider the MIPS load word and store word instructions, which have the general form `lw  $t1,offset_value($t2)` or `sw  $t1,offset_value($t2)`. These instructions compute a memory address by adding the base register, which is `$t2`, to the 16-bit signed offset field contained in the instruction. If the instruction is a store, the value to be stored must also be read from the register file where it resides in `$t1`. If the instruction is a load, the value read from memory must be written into the register file in the specified register, which is `$t1`. Thus, we will need both the register file and the ALU from Figure 4.7.

Furthermore, we will need a unit to **sign-extend** the 16-bit offset field in the instruction to a 32-bit signed value, and a data memory unit to read from or write to. The data memory must be written on store instructions; hence, data memory has read and write control signals, an address input, and an input for the data to be written into memory. Figure 4.8 shows these two elements.

The `beq` instruction has three operands, two registers that are compared for equality, and a 16-bit offset used to compute the **branch target address** relative to the branch instruction address. Its form is `beq  $t1,$t2,offset`. To implement this instruction, we must compute the branch target address by adding the sign-extended offset field of the instruction to the PC. There are two details in the definition of branch instructions (see Chapter 2) to which we must pay attention:

- The instruction set architecture specifies that the base for the branch address calculation is the address of the instruction *following* the branch. Since we compute PC + 4 (the address of the next instruction) in the instruction fetch datapath, it is easy to use this value as the base for computing the branch target address.

- The architecture also states that the offset field is shifted left 2 bits so that it is a word offset; this shift increases the effective range of the offset field by a factor of 4.

To deal with the latter complication, we will need to shift the offset field by 2.

As well as computing the branch target address, we must also determine whether the next instruction is the instruction that follows sequentially or the instruction at the branch target address. When the condition is true (i.e., the operands are equal), the branch target address becomes the new PC, and we say that the **branch** is **taken**. If the operands are not equal, the incremented PC should replace the current PC (just as for any other normal instruction); in this case, we say that the **branch** is **not taken**.

Thus, the branch datapath must do two operations: compute the branch target address and compare the register contents. (Branches also affect the instruction fetch portion of the datapath, as we will deal with shortly.) Figure 4.9 shows the structure of the datapath segment that handles branches. To compute the branch target address, the branch datapath includes a sign extension unit, from Figure 4.8 and an adder. To perform the compare, we need to use the register file shown in Figure 4.7a to supply the two register operands (although we will not need to write into the register file). In addition, the comparison can be done using the ALU we

---

sign-extend To increase the size of a data item by replicating the high-order sign bit of the original data item in the high-order bits of the larger, destination data item.

branch target address The address specified in a branch, which becomes the new program counter (PC) if the branch is taken. In the MIPS architecture the branch target is given by the sum of the offset field of the instruction and the address of the instruction following the branch.

branch taken A branch where the branch condition is satisfied and the program counter (PC) becomes the branch target. All unconditional jumps are taken branches.

branch not taken or (untaken branch) A branch where the branch condition is false and the program counter (PC) becomes the address of the instruction that sequentially follows the branch.

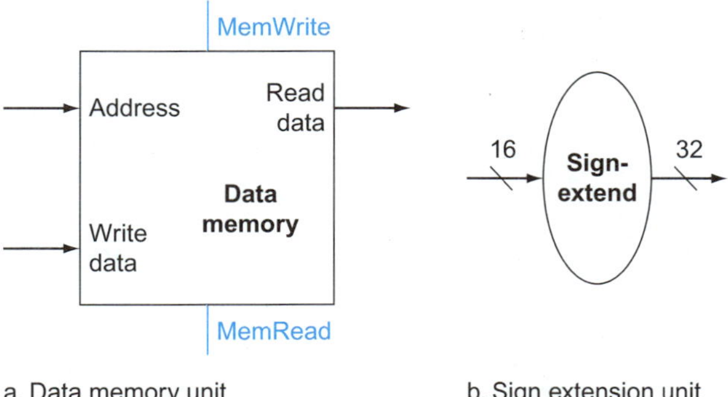

a. Data memory unit   b. Sign extension unit

FIGURE 4.8 The two units needed to implement loads and stores, in addition to the register file and ALU of Figure 4.7, are the data memory unit and the sign extension unit. The memory unit is a state element with inputs for the address and the write data, and a single output for the read result. There are separate read and write controls, although only one of these may be asserted on any given clock. The memory unit needs a read signal, since, unlike the register file, reading the value of an invalid address can cause problems, as we will see in Chapter 5. The sign extension unit has a 16-bit input that is sign-extended into a 32-bit result appearing on the output (see Chapter 2). We assume the data memory is edge-triggered for writes. Standard memory chips actually have a write enable signal that is used for writes. Although the write enable is not edge-triggered, our edge-triggered design could easily be adapted to work with real memory chips. See Section B.8 of **Appendix B** for further discussion of how real memory chips work.

designed in **Appendix B**. Since that ALU provides an output signal that indicates whether the result was 0, we can send the two register operands to the ALU with the control set to do a subtract. If the Zero signal out of the ALU unit is asserted, we know that the two values are equal. Although the Zero output always signals if the result is 0, we will be using it only to implement the equal test of branches. Later, we will show exactly how to connect the control signals of the ALU for use in the datapath.

The jump instruction operates by replacing the lower 28 bits of the PC with the lower 26 bits of the instruction shifted left by 2 bits. Simply concatenating 00 to the jump offset accomplishes this shift, as described in Chapter 2.

Elaboration: In the MIPS instruction set, **branches are delayed**, meaning that the instruction immediately following the branch is always executed, *independent* of whether the branch condition is true or false. When the condition is false, the execution looks like a normal branch. When the condition is true, a delayed branch first executes the instruction immediately following the branch in sequential instruction order before jumping to the specified branch target address. The motivation for delayed branches arises from how pipelining affects branches (see Section 4.9). For simplicity, we generally ignore delayed branches in this chapter and implement a nondelayed beq instruction.

delayed branch A type of branch where the instruction immediately following the branch is always executed, independent of whether the branch condition is true or false.

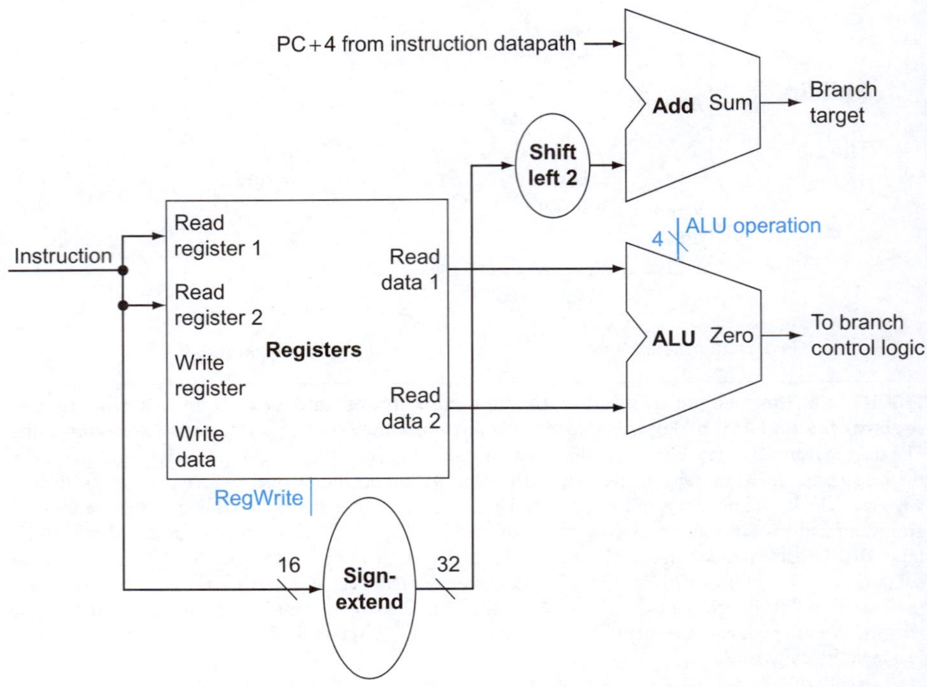

FIGURE 4.9 The portion of a datapath for a branch uses the ALU to evaluate the branch condition and a separate adder to compute the branch target as the sum of the incremented PC and the sign-extended, lower 16 bits of the instruction (the branch displacement), shifted left 2 bits. The unit labeled *Shift left 2* is simply a routing of the signals between input and output that adds 00_{two} to the low-order end of the sign-extended offset field; no actual shift hardware is needed, since the amount of the "shift" is constant. Since we know that the offset was sign-extended from 16 bits, the shift will throw away only "sign bits." Control logic is used to decide whether the incremented PC or branch target should replace the PC, based on the Zero output of the ALU.

Creating a Single Datapath

Now that we have examined the datapath components needed for the individual instruction classes, we can combine them into a single datapath and add the control to complete the implementation. This simplest datapath will attempt to execute all instructions in one clock cycle. Thus, no datapath resource can be used more than once per instruction, so any element needed more than once must be duplicated. We therefore need a memory for instructions separate from one for data. Although some of the functional units will need to be duplicated, many of the elements can be shared by different instruction flows.

To share a datapath element between two different instruction classes, we may need to allow multiple connections to the input of an element, using a multiplexor and control signal to select among the multiple inputs.

Building a Datapath

The operations of arithmetic-logical (or R-type) instructions and the memory instructions datapath are quite similar. The key differences are the following:

- The arithmetic-logical instructions use the ALU, with the inputs coming from the two registers. The memory instructions can also use the ALU to do the address calculation, although the second input is the sign-extended 16-bit offset field from the instruction.

- The value stored into a destination register comes from the ALU (for an R-type instruction) or the memory (for a load).

Show how to build a datapath for the operational portion of the memory-reference and arithmetic-logical instructions that uses a single register file and a single ALU to handle both types of instructions, adding any necessary multiplexors.

To create a datapath with only a single register file and a single ALU, we must support two different sources for the second ALU input, as well as two different sources for the data stored into the register file. Thus, one multiplexor is placed at the ALU input and another at the data input to the register file. Figure 4.10 shows the operational portion of the combined datapath.

Now we can combine all the pieces to make a simple datapath for the core MIPS architecture by adding the datapath for instruction fetch (Figure 4.6), the datapath from R-type and memory instructions (Figure 4.10), and the datapath for branches (Figure 4.9). Figure 4.11 shows the datapath we obtain by composing the separate pieces. The branch instruction uses the main ALU for comparison of the register operands, so we must keep the adder from Figure 4.9 for computing the branch target address. An additional multiplexor is required to select either the sequentially following instruction address (PC + 4) or the branch target address to be written into the PC.

Now that we have completed this simple datapath, we can add the control unit. The control unit must be able to take inputs and generate a write signal for each state element, the selector control for each multiplexor, and the ALU control. The ALU control is different in a number of ways, and it will be useful to design it first before we design the rest of the control unit.

I. Which of the following is correct for a load instruction? Refer to Figure 4.10.

   a. MemtoReg should be set to cause the data from memory to be sent to the register file.

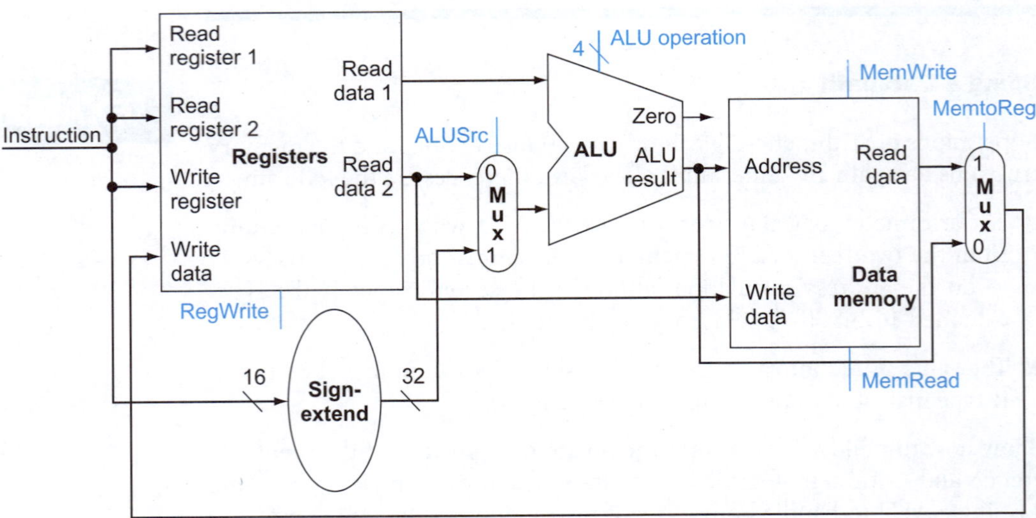

FIGURE 4.10 The datapath for the memory instructions and the R-type instructions. This example shows how a single datapath can be assembled from the pieces in Figures 4.7 and 4.8 by adding multiplexors. Two multiplexors are needed, as described in the example.

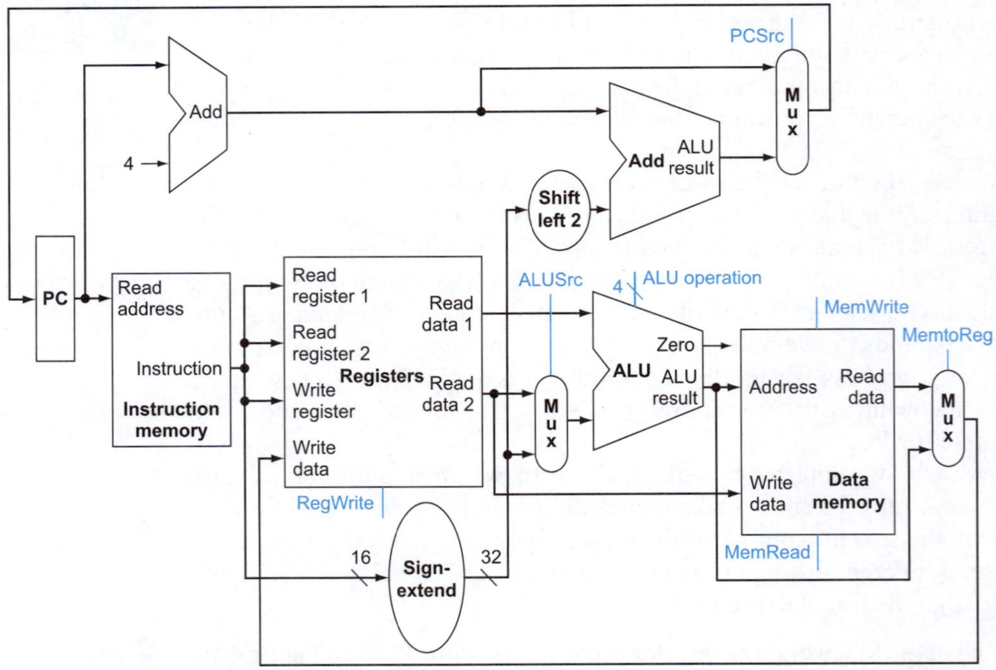

FIGURE 4.11 The simple datapath for the core MIPS architecture combines the elements required by different instruction classes. The components come from Figures 4.6, 4.9, and 4.10. This datapath can execute the basic instructions (load-store word, ALU operations, and branches) in a single clock cycle. Just one additional multiplexor is needed to integrate branches. The support for jumps will be added later.

   b. MemtoReg should be set to cause the correct register destination to be sent to the register file.

   c. We do not care about the setting of MemtoReg for loads.

II. The single-cycle datapath conceptually described in this section *must* have separate instruction and data memories, because

   a. the formats of data and instructions are different in MIPS, and hence different memories are needed.

   b. having separate memories is less expensive.

   c. the processor operates in one clock cycle and cannot use a single-ported memory for two different accesses within that clock cycle.

4.4 A Simple Implementation Scheme

In this section, we look at what might be thought of as the simplest possible implementation of our MIPS subset. We build this simple implementation using the datapath of the last section and adding a simple control function. This simple implementation covers *load word* (`lw`), *store word* (`sw`), *branch equal* (`beq`), and the arithmetic-logical instructions `add`, `sub`, `AND`, `OR`, and `set on less than`. We will later enhance the design to include a jump instruction (`j`).

The ALU Control

The MIPS ALU in 🌐 **Appendix B** defines the 6 following combinations of four control inputs:

ALU control lines	Function
0000	AND
0001	OR
0010	add
0110	subtract
0111	set on less than
1100	NOR

Depending on the instruction class, the ALU will need to perform one of these first five functions. (NOR is needed for other parts of the MIPS instruction set not found in the subset we are implementing.) For load word and store word instructions, we use the ALU to compute the memory address by addition. For the R-type instructions, the ALU needs to perform one of the five actions (AND, OR, subtract, add, or set on less than), depending on the value of the 6-bit funct (or function) field in the low-order bits of the instruction (see Chapter 2). For branch equal, the ALU must perform a subtraction.

We can generate the 4-bit ALU control input using a small control unit that has as inputs the function field of the instruction and a 2-bit control field, which we call ALUOp. ALUOp indicates whether the operation to be performed should be add (00) for loads and stores, subtract (01) for `beq`, or determined by the operation encoded in the funct field (10). The output of the ALU control unit is a 4-bit signal that directly controls the ALU by generating one of the 4-bit combinations shown previously.

In Figure 4.12, we show how to set the ALU control inputs based on the 2-bit ALUOp control and the 6-bit function code. Later in this chapter we will see how the ALUOp bits are generated from the main control unit.

This style of using multiple levels of decoding—that is, the main control unit generates the ALUOp bits, which then are used as input to the ALU control that generates the actual signals to control the ALU unit—is a common implementation technique. Using multiple levels of control can reduce the size of the main control unit. Using several smaller control units may also potentially increase the speed of the control unit. Such optimizations are important, since the speed of the control unit is often critical to clock cycle time.

There are several different ways to implement the mapping from the 2-bit ALUOp field and the 6-bit funct field to the four ALU operation control bits. Because only a small number of the 64 possible values of the function field are of interest and the function field is used only when the ALUOp bits equal 10, we can use a small piece of logic that recognizes the subset of possible values and causes the correct setting of the ALU control bits.

As a step in designing this logic, it is useful to create a *truth table* for the interesting combinations of the function code field and the ALUOp bits, as we've

Instruction opcode	ALUOp	Instruction operation	Funct field	Desired ALU action	ALU control input
LW	00	load word	XXXXXX	add	0010
SW	00	store word	XXXXXX	add	0010
Branch equal	01	branch equal	XXXXXX	subtract	0110
R-type	10	add	100000	add	0010
R-type	10	subtract	100010	subtract	0110
R-type	10	AND	100100	AND	0000
R-type	10	OR	100101	OR	0001
R-type	10	set on less than	101010	set on less than	0111

FIGURE 4.12 How the ALU control bits are set depends on the ALUOp control bits and the different function codes for the R-type instruction. The opcode, listed in the first column, determines the setting of the ALUOp bits. All the encodings are shown in binary. Notice that when the ALUOp code is 00 or 01, the desired ALU action does not depend on the function code field; in this case, we say that we "don't care" about the value of the function code, and the funct field is shown as XXXXXX. When the ALUOp value is 10, then the function code is used to set the ALU control input. See Appendix B.

done in Figure 4.13; this **truth table** shows how the 4-bit ALU control is set depending on these two input fields. Since the full truth table is very large ($2^8 = 256$ entries) and we don't care about the value of the ALU control for many of these input combinations, we show only the truth table entries for which the ALU control must have a specific value. Throughout this chapter, we will use this practice of showing only the truth table entries for outputs that must be asserted and not showing those that are all deasserted or don't care. (This practice has a disadvantage, which we discuss in Section D.2 of 🌐 **Appendix D**.)

Because in many instances we do not care about the values of some of the inputs, and because we wish to keep the tables compact, we also include **don't-care terms**. A don't-care term in this truth table (represented by an X in an input column) indicates that the output does not depend on the value of the input corresponding to that column. For example, when the ALUOp bits are 00, as in the first row of Figure 4.13, we always set the ALU control to 0010, independent of the function code. In this case, then, the function code inputs will be don't cares in this line of the truth table. Later, we will see examples of another type of don't-care term. If you are unfamiliar with the concept of don't-care terms, see 🌐 **Appendix B** for more information.

Once the truth table has been constructed, it can be optimized and then turned into gates. This process is completely mechanical. Thus, rather than show the final steps here, we describe the process and the result in Section D.2 of 🌐 **Appendix D**.

truth table From logic, a representation of a logical operation by listing all the values of the inputs and then in each case showing what the resulting outputs should be.

don't-care term An element of a logical function in which the output does not depend on the values of all the inputs. Don't-care terms may be specified in different ways.

Designing the Main Control Unit

Now that we have described how to design an ALU that uses the function code and a 2-bit signal as its control inputs, we can return to looking at the rest of the control. To start this process, let's identify the fields of an instruction and the control lines that are needed for the datapath we constructed in Figure 4.11. To understand how to connect the fields of an instruction to the datapath, it is useful to review

ALUOp		Funct field						
ALUOp1	ALUOp0	F5	F4	F3	F2	F1	F0	Operation
0	0	X	X	X	X	X	X	0010
X	1	X	X	X	X	X	X	0110
1	X	X	X	0	0	0	0	0010
1	X	X	X	0	0	1	0	0110
1	X	X	X	0	1	0	0	0000
1	X	X	X	0	1	0	1	0001
1	X	X	X	1	0	1	0	0111

FIGURE 4.13 The truth table for the 4 ALU control bits (called Operation). The inputs are the ALUOp and function code field. Only the entries for which the ALU control is asserted are shown. Some don't-care entries have been added. For example, the ALUOp does not use the encoding 11, so the truth table can contain entries 1X and X1, rather than 10 and 01. Note that when the function field is used, the first 2 bits (F5 and F4) of these instructions are always 10, so they are don't-care terms and are replaced with XX in the truth table.

Field	0	rs	rt	rd	shamt	funct
Bit positions	31:26	25:21	20:16	15:11	10:6	5:0

a. R-type instruction

Field	35 or 43	rs	rt	address	
Bit positions	31:26	25:21	20:16	15:0	

b. Load or store instruction

Field	4	rs	rt	address	
Bit positions	31:26	25:21	20:16	15:0	

c. Branch instruction

FIGURE 4.14 The three instruction classes (R-type, load and store, and branch) use two different instruction formats. The jump instructions use another format, which we will discuss shortly. (a) Instruction format for R-format instructions, which all have an opcode of 0. These instructions have three register operands: rs, rt, and rd. Fields rs and rt are sources, and rd is the destination. The ALU function is in the funct field and is decoded by the ALU control design in the previous section. The R-type instructions that we implement are add, sub, AND, OR, and slt. The shamt field is used only for shifts; we will ignore it in this chapter. (b) Instruction format for load (opcode = 35_{ten}) and store (opcode = 43_{ten}) instructions. The register rs is the base register that is added to the 16-bit address field to form the memory address. For loads, rt is the destination register for the loaded value. For stores, rt is the source register whose value should be stored into memory. (c) Instruction format for branch equal (opcode = 4). The registers rs and rt are the source registers that are compared for equality. The 16-bit address field is sign-extended, shifted, and added to the PC + 4 to compute the branch target address.

the formats of the three instruction classes: the R-type, branch, and load-store instructions. Figure 4.14 shows these formats.

There are several major observations about this instruction format that we will rely on:

opcode The field that denotes the operation and format of an instruction.

- The op field, which as we saw in Chapter 2 is called the **opcode**, is always contained in bits 31:26. We will refer to this field as Op[5:0].

- The two registers to be read are always specified by the rs and rt fields, at positions 25:21 and 20:16. This is true for the R-type instructions, branch equal, and store.

- The base register for load and store instructions is always in bit positions 25:21 (rs).

- The 16-bit offset for branch equal, load, and store is always in positions 15:0.

- The destination register is in one of two places. For a load it is in bit positions 20:16 (rt), while for an R-type instruction it is in bit positions 15:11 (rd). Thus, we will need to add a multiplexor to select which field of the instruction is used to indicate the register number to be written.

The first design principle from Chapter 2—*simplicity favors regularity*—pays off here in specifying control.

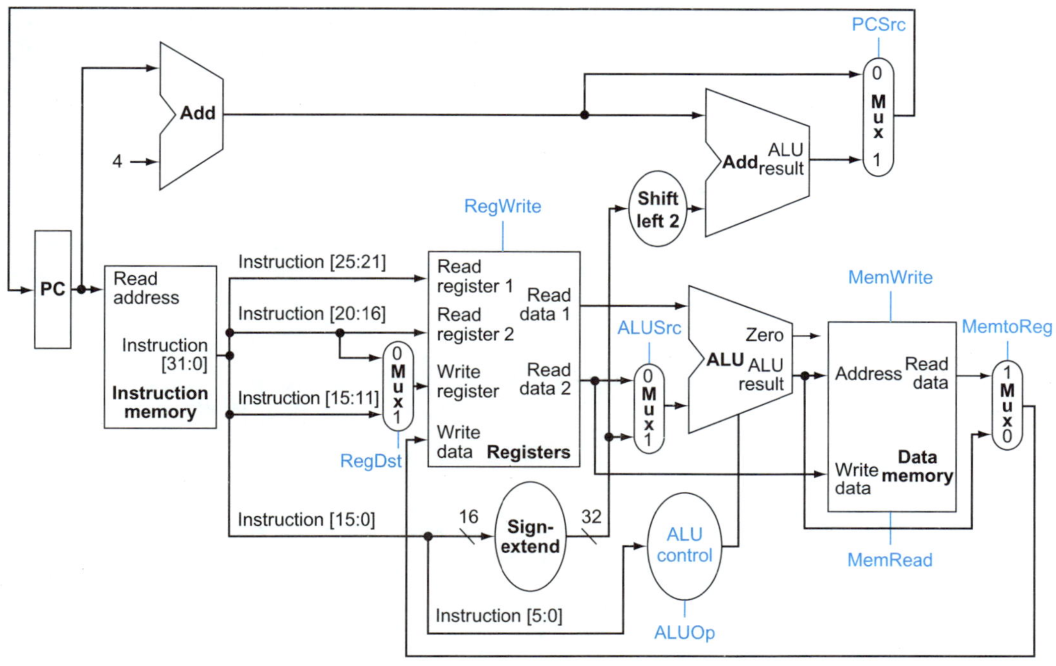

FIGURE 4.15 The datapath of Figure 4.11 with all necessary multiplexors and all control lines identified. The control lines are shown in color. The ALU control block has also been added. The PC does not require a write control, since it is written once at the end of every clock cycle; the branch control logic determines whether it is written with the incremented PC or the branch target address.

Using this information, we can add the instruction labels and extra multiplexor (for the Write register number input of the register file) to the simple datapath. Figure 4.15 shows these additions plus the ALU control block, the write signals for state elements, the read signal for the data memory, and the control signals for the multiplexors. Since all the multiplexors have two inputs, they each require a single control line.

Figure 4.15 shows seven single-bit control lines plus the 2-bit ALUOp control signal. We have already defined how the ALUOp control signal works, and it is useful to define what the seven other control signals do informally before we determine how to set these control signals during instruction execution. Figure 4.16 describes the function of these seven control lines.

Now that we have looked at the function of each of the control signals, we can look at how to set them. The control unit can set all but one of the control signals based solely on the opcode field of the instruction. The PCSrc control line is the exception. That control line should be asserted if the instruction is branch on equal (a decision that the control unit can make) *and* the Zero output of the ALU, which is used for equality comparison, is asserted. To generate the PCSrc signal, we will need to AND together a signal from the control unit, which we call *Branch*, with the Zero signal out of the ALU.

Signal name	Effect when deasserted	Effect when asserted
RegDst	The register destination number for the Write register comes from the rt field (bits 20:16).	The register destination number for the Write register comes from the rd field (bits 15:11).
RegWrite	None.	The register on the Write register input is written with the value on the Write data input.
ALUSrc	The second ALU operand comes from the second register file output (Read data 2).	The second ALU operand is the sign-extended, lower 16 bits of the instruction.
PCSrc	The PC is replaced by the output of the adder that computes the value of PC + 4.	The PC is replaced by the output of the adder that computes the branch target.
MemRead	None.	Data memory contents designated by the address input are put on the Read data output.
MemWrite	None.	Data memory contents designated by the address input are replaced by the value on the Write data input.
MemtoReg	The value fed to the register Write data input comes from the ALU.	The value fed to the register Write data input comes from the data memory.

FIGURE 4.16 The effect of each of the seven control signals. When the 1-bit control to a two-way multiplexor is asserted, the multiplexor selects the input corresponding to 1. Otherwise, if the control is deasserted, the multiplexor selects the 0 input. Remember that the state elements all have the clock as an implicit input and that the clock is used in controlling writes. Gating the clock externally to a state element can create timing problems. (See **Appendix B** for further discussion of this problem.)

These nine control signals (seven from Figure 4.16 and two for ALUOp) can now be set on the basis of six input signals to the control unit, which are the opcode bits 31 to 26. Figure 4.17 shows the datapath with the control unit and the control signals.

Before we try to write a set of equations or a truth table for the control unit, it will be useful to try to define the control function informally. Because the setting of the control lines depends only on the opcode, we define whether each control signal should be 0, 1, or don't care (X) for each of the opcode values. Figure 4.18 defines how the control signals should be set for each opcode; this information follows directly from Figures 4.12, 4.16, and 4.17.

Operation of the Datapath

With the information contained in Figures 4.16 and 4.18, we can design the control unit logic, but before we do that, let's look at how each instruction uses the datapath. In the next few figures, we show the flow of three different instruction classes through the datapath. The asserted control signals and active datapath elements are highlighted in each of these. Note that a multiplexor whose control is 0 has a definite action, even if its control line is not highlighted. Multiple-bit control signals are highlighted if any constituent signal is asserted.

Figure 4.19 shows the operation of the datapath for an R-type instruction, such as `add $t1,$t2,$t3`. Although everything occurs in one clock cycle, we can

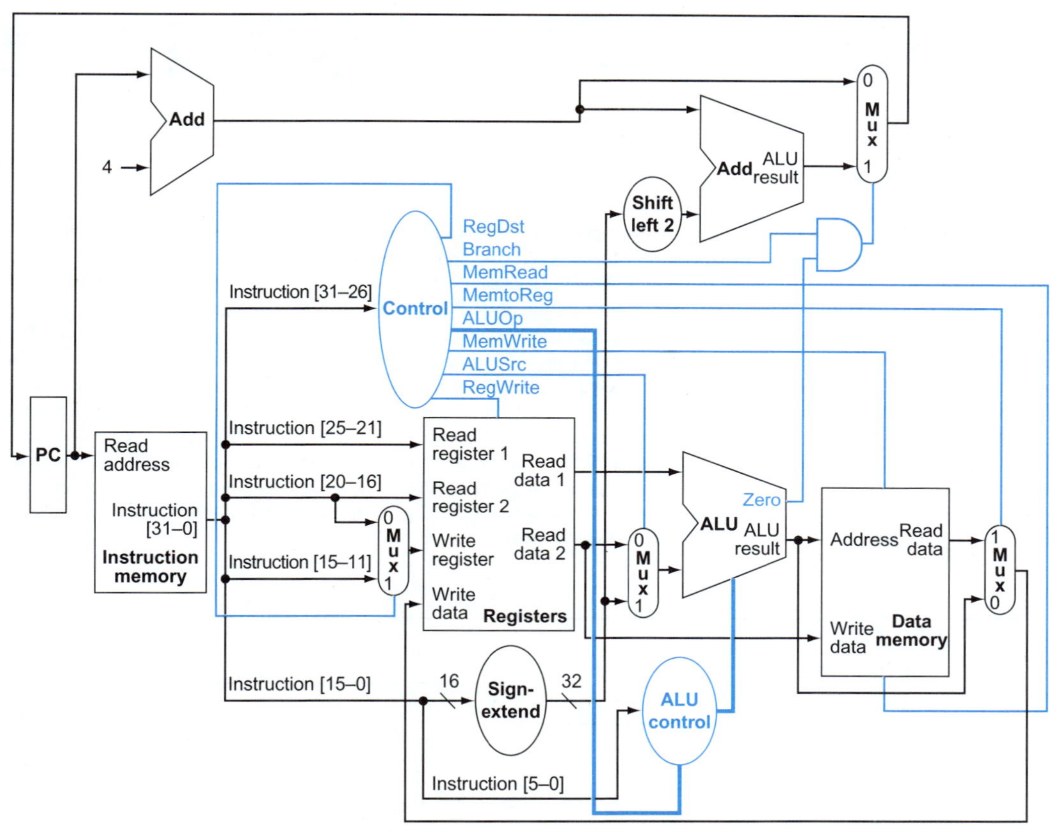

FIGURE 4.17 The simple datapath with the control unit. The input to the control unit is the 6-bit opcode field from the instruction. The outputs of the control unit consist of three 1-bit signals that are used to control multiplexors (RegDst, ALUSrc, and MemtoReg), three signals for controlling reads and writes in the register file and data memory (RegWrite, MemRead, and MemWrite), a 1-bit signal used in determining whether to possibly branch (Branch), and a 2-bit control signal for the ALU (ALUOp). An AND gate is used to combine the branch control signal and the Zero output from the ALU; the AND gate output controls the selection of the next PC. Notice that PCSrc is now a derived signal, rather than one coming directly from the control unit. Thus, we drop the signal name in subsequent figures.

think of four steps to execute the instruction; these steps are ordered by the flow of information:

1. The instruction is fetched, and the PC is incremented.

2. Two registers, $t2 and $t3, are read from the register file; also, the main control unit computes the setting of the control lines during this step.

3. The ALU operates on the data read from the register file, using the function code (bits 5:0, which is the funct field, of the instruction) to generate the ALU function.

Instruction	RegDst	ALUSrc	Memto-Reg	Reg-Write	Mem-Read	Mem-Write	Branch	ALUOp1	ALUOp0
R-format	1	0	0	1	0	0	0	1	0
lw	0	1	1	1	1	0	0	0	0
sw	X	1	X	0	0	1	0	0	0
beq	X	0	X	0	0	0	1	0	1

FIGURE 4.18 The setting of the control lines is completely determined by the opcode fields of the instruction. The first row of the table corresponds to the R-format instructions (add, sub, AND, OR, and slt). For all these instructions, the source register fields are rs and rt, and the destination register field is rd; this defines how the signals ALUSrc and RegDst are set. Furthermore, an R-type instruction writes a register (Reg-Write = 1), but neither reads nor writes data memory. When the Branch control signal is 0, the PC is unconditionally replaced with PC + 4; otherwise, the PC is replaced by the branch target if the Zero output of the ALU is also high. The ALUOp field for R-type instructions is set to 10 to indicate that the ALU control should be generated from the funct field. The second and third rows of this table give the control signal settings for lw and sw. These ALUSrc and ALUOp fields are set to perform the address calculation. The MemRead and MemWrite are set to perform the memory access. Finally, RegDst and RegWrite are set for a load to cause the result to be stored into the rt register. The branch instruction is similar to an R-format operation, since it sends the rs and rt registers to the ALU. The ALUOp field for branch is set for a subtract (ALU control = 01), which is used to test for equality. Notice that the MemtoReg field is irrelevant when the RegWrite signal is 0: since the register is not being written, the value of the data on the register data write port is not used. Thus, the entry MemtoReg in the last two rows of the table is replaced with X for don't care. Don't cares can also be added to RegDst when RegWrite is 0. This type of don't care must be added by the designer, since it depends on knowledge of how the datapath works.

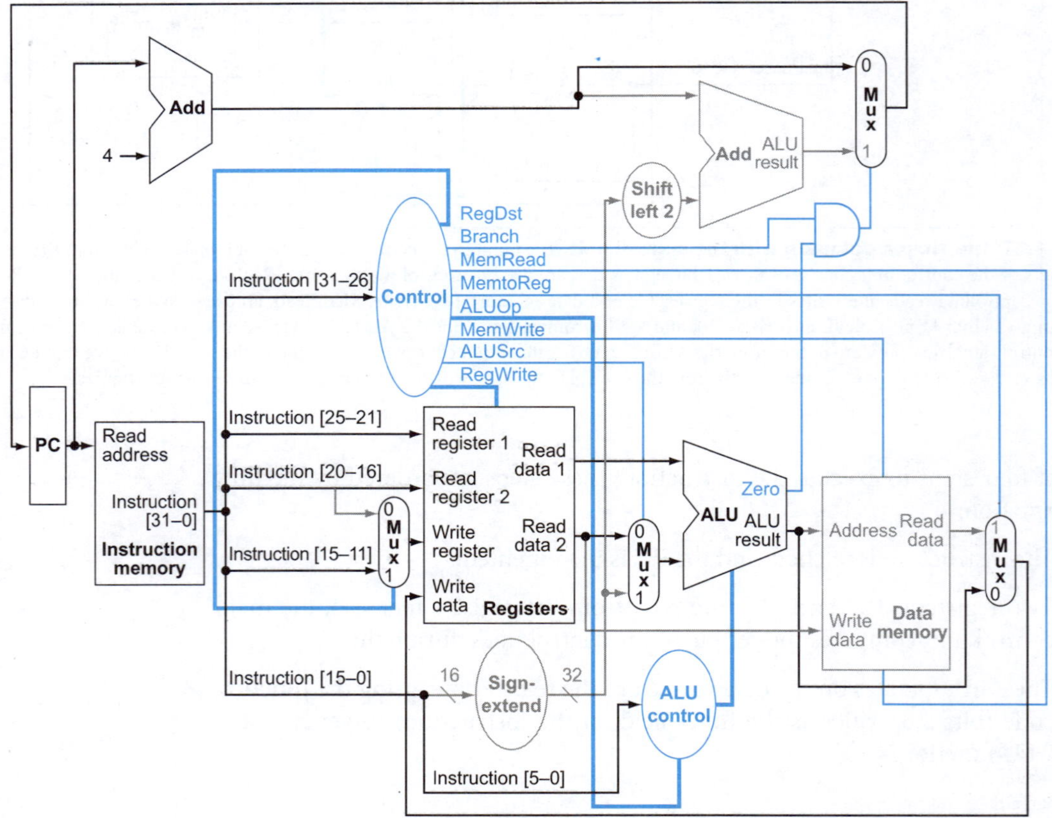

FIGURE 4.19 The datapath in operation for an R-type instruction, such as add $t1, $t2, $t3**.** The control lines, datapath units, and connections that are active are highlighted.

4. The result from the ALU is written into the register file using bits 15:11 of the instruction to select the destination register ($t1).

Similarly, we can illustrate the execution of a load word, such as

```
lw $t1, offset($t2)
```

in a style similar to Figure 4.19. Figure 4.20 shows the active functional units and asserted control lines for a load. We can think of a load instruction as operating in five steps (similar to how the R-type executed in four):

1. An instruction is fetched from the instruction memory, and the PC is incremented.

2. A register ($t2) value is read from the register file.

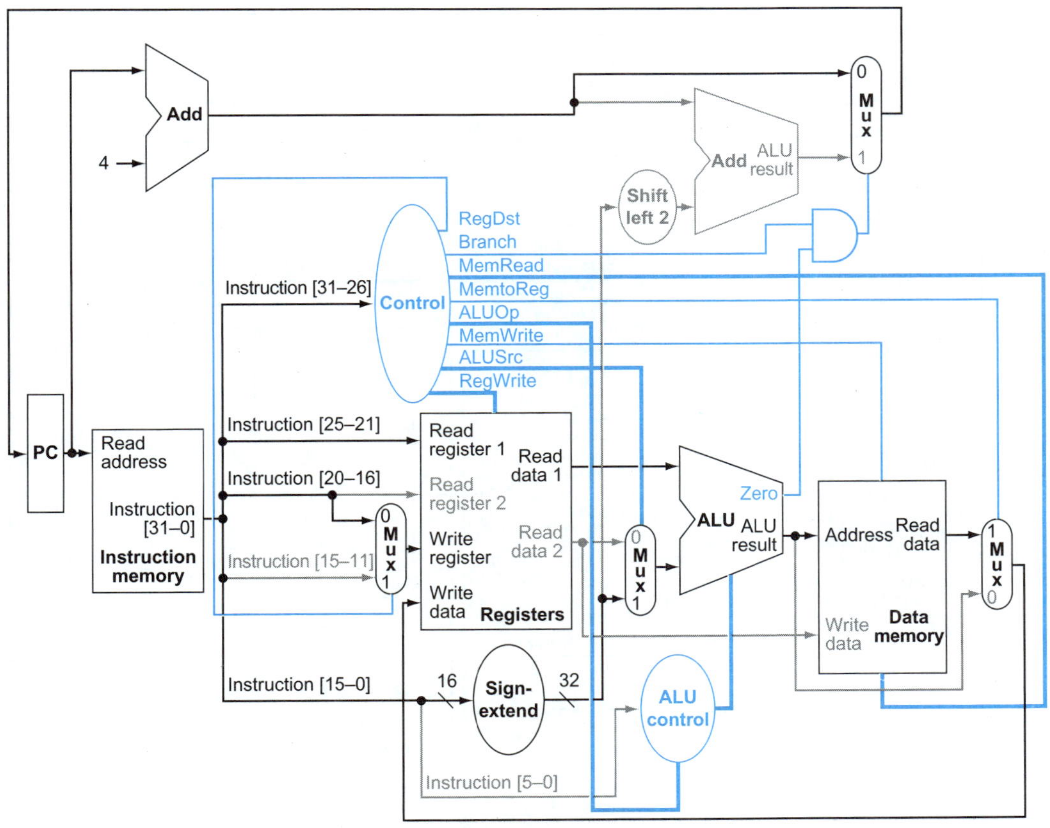

FIGURE 4.20 The datapath in operation for a load instruction. The control lines, datapath units, and connections that are active are highlighted. A store instruction would operate very similarly. The main difference would be that the memory control would indicate a write rather than a read, the second register value read would be used for the data to store, and the operation of writing the data memory value to the register file would not occur.

3. The ALU computes the sum of the value read from the register file and the sign-extended, lower 16 bits of the instruction (offset).

4. The sum from the ALU is used as the address for the data memory.

5. The data from the memory unit is written into the register file; the register destination is given by bits 20:16 of the instruction ($t1).

Finally, we can show the operation of the branch-on-equal instruction, such as beq $t1, $t2, offset, in the same fashion. It operates much like an R-format instruction, but the ALU output is used to determine whether the PC is written with PC + 4 or the branch target address. Figure 4.21 shows the four steps in execution:

1. An instruction is fetched from the instruction memory, and the PC is incremented.

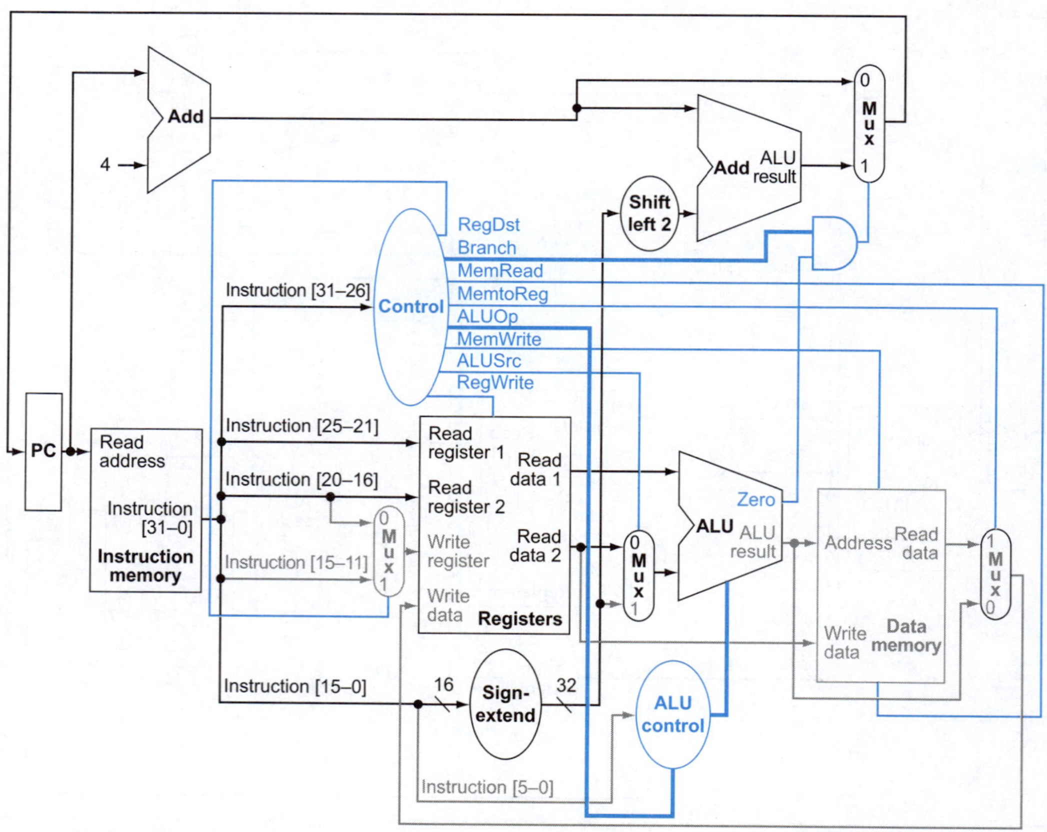

FIGURE 4.21 The datapath in operation for a branch-on-equal instruction. The control lines, datapath units, and connections that are active are highlighted. After using the register file and ALU to perform the compare, the Zero output is used to select the next program counter from between the two candidates.

2. Two registers, $t1 and $t2, are read from the register file.

3. The ALU performs a subtract on the data values read from the register file. The value of PC + 4 is added to the sign-extended, lower 16 bits of the instruction (offset) shifted left by two; the result is the branch target address.

4. The Zero result from the ALU is used to decide which adder result to store into the PC.

Finalizing Control

Now that we have seen how the instructions operate in steps, let's continue with the control implementation. The control function can be precisely defined using the contents of Figure 4.18. The outputs are the control lines, and the input is the 6-bit opcode field, Op [5:0]. Thus, we can create a truth table for each of the outputs based on the binary encoding of the opcodes.

Figure 4.22 shows the logic in the control unit as one large truth table that combines all the outputs and that uses the opcode bits as inputs. It completely specifies the control function, and we can implement it directly in gates in an automated fashion. We show this final step in Section D.2 in ⊕ **Appendix D**.

Input or output	Signal name	R-format	lw	sw	beq
Inputs	Op5	0	1	1	0
	Op4	0	0	0	0
	Op3	0	0	1	0
	Op2	0	0	0	1
	Op1	0	1	1	0
	Op0	0	1	1	0
Outputs	RegDst	1	0	X	X
	ALUSrc	0	1	1	0
	MemtoReg	0	1	X	X
	RegWrite	1	1	0	0
	MemRead	0	1	0	0
	MemWrite	0	0	1	0
	Branch	0	0	0	1
	ALUOp1	1	0	0	0
	ALUOp0	0	0	0	1

FIGURE 4.22 The control function for the simple single-cycle implementation is completely specified by this truth table. The top six rows of the table gives the combinations of input signals that correspond to the four opcodes, one per column, that determine the control output settings. (Remember that Op [5:0] corresponds to bits 31:26 of the instruction, which is the op field.) The bottom portion of the table gives the outputs for each of the four opcodes. Thus, the output RegWrite is asserted for two different combinations of the inputs. If we consider only the four opcodes shown in this table, then we can simplify the truth table by using don't cares in the input portion. For example, we can detect an R-format instruction with the expression $\overline{Op5} \cdot \overline{Op2}$, since this is sufficient to distinguish the R-format instructions from lw, sw, and beq. We do not take advantage of this simplification, since the rest of the MIPS opcodes are used in a full implementation.

single-cycle implementation Also called single clock cycle implementation. An implementation in which all instructions are executed in one clock cycle. While easy to understand, it is too slow to be practical.

EXAMPLE

ANSWER

Now that we have a **single-cycle implementation** of most of the MIPS core instruction set, let's add the jump instruction to show how the basic datapath and control can be extended to handle other instructions in the instruction set.

Implementing Jumps

Figure 4.17 shows the implementation of many of the instructions we looked at in Chapter 2. One class of instructions missing is that of the jump instruction. Extend the datapath and control of Figure 4.17 to include the jump instruction. Describe how to set any new control lines.

The jump instruction, shown in Figure 4.23, looks somewhat like a branch instruction but computes the target PC differently and is not conditional. Like a branch, the low-order 2 bits of a jump address are always 00_{two}. The next lower 26 bits of this 32-bit address come from the 26-bit immediate field in the instruction. The upper 4 bits of the address that should replace the PC come from the PC of the jump instruction plus 4. Thus, we can implement a jump by storing into the PC the concatenation of

- the upper 4 bits of the current PC + 4 (these are bits 31:28 of the sequentially following instruction address)

- the 26-bit immediate field of the jump instruction

- the bits 00_{two}

Figure 4.24 shows the addition of the control for jump added to Figure 4.17. An additional multiplexor is used to select the source for the new PC value, which is either the incremented PC (PC + 4), the branch target PC, or the jump target PC. One additional control signal is needed for the additional multiplexor. This control signal, called *Jump*, is asserted only when the instruction is a jump—that is, when the opcode is 2.

Field	000010	address
Bit positions	31:26	25:0

FIGURE 4.23 Instruction format for the jump instruction (opcode = 2). The destination address for a jump instruction is formed by concatenating the upper 4 bits of the current PC + 4 to the 26-bit address field in the jump instruction and adding 00 as the 2 low-order bits.

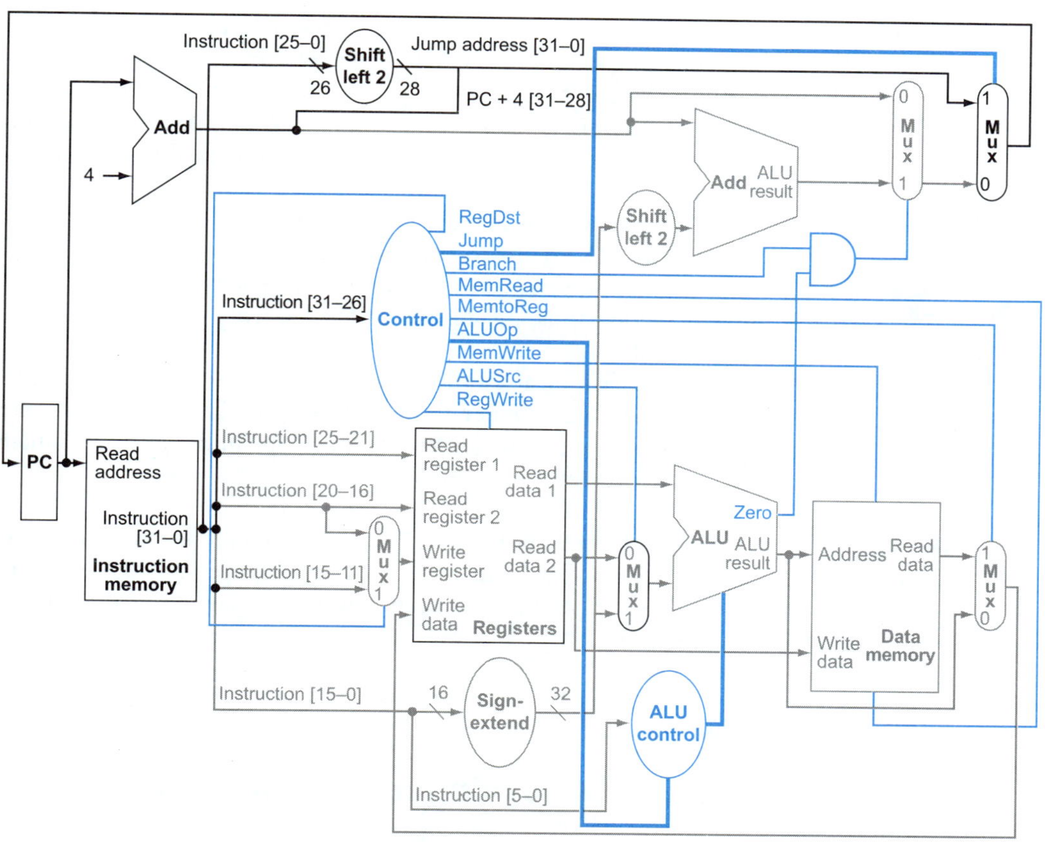

FIGURE 4.24 The simple control and datapath are extended to handle the jump instruction. An additional multiplexor (at the upper right) is used to choose between the jump target and either the branch target or the sequential instruction following this one. This multiplexor is controlled by the jump control signal. The jump target address is obtained by shifting the lower 26 bits of the jump instruction left 2 bits, effectively adding 00 as the low-order bits, and then concatenating the upper 4 bits of PC + 4 as the high-order bits, thus yielding a 32-bit address.

Why a Single-Cycle Implementation Is Not Used Today

Although the single-cycle design will work correctly, it would not be used in modern designs because it is inefficient. To see why this is so, notice that the clock cycle must have the same length for every instruction in this single-cycle design. Of course, the longest possible path in the processor determines the clock cycle. This path is almost certainly a load instruction, which uses five functional units in series: the instruction memory, the register file, the ALU, the data memory, and the register file. Although the CPI is 1 (see Chapter 1), the overall performance of a single-cycle implementation is likely to be poor, since the clock cycle is too long.

The penalty for using the single-cycle design with a fixed clock cycle is significant, but might be considered acceptable for this small instruction set. Historically, early computers with very simple instruction sets did use this implementation technique. However, if we tried to implement the floating-point unit or an instruction set with more complex instructions, this single-cycle design wouldn't work well at all.

Because we must assume that the clock cycle is equal to the worst-case delay for all instructions, it's useless to try implementation techniques that reduce the delay of the common case but do not improve the worst-case cycle time. A single-cycle implementation thus violates the great idea from Chapter 1 of making the **common case fast**.

In section 4.6, we'll look at another implementation technique, called pipelining, that uses a datapath very similar to the single-cycle datapath but is much more efficient by having a much higher throughput. Pipelining improves efficiency by executing multiple instructions simultaneously.

Check Yourself

Look at the control signals in Figure 4.22. Can you combine any together? Can any control signal output in the figure be replaced by the inverse of another? (Hint: take into account the don't cares.) If so, can you use one signal for the other without adding an inverter?

4.5   A Multicycle Implementation

In the prior section, we broke each instruction into a series of steps corresponding to the functional unit operations that were needed. We can use these steps to create a **multicycle implementation**. In a multicycle implementation, each *step* in the execution will take 1 clock cycle. The multicycle implementation allows a functional unit to be used more than once per instruction, as long as it is used on different clock cycles. This sharing can help reduce the amount of hardware required. The ability to allow instructions to take different numbers of clock cycles and the ability to share functional units within the execution of a single instruction are the major advantages of a multicycle design. This online section describes the multicycle implementation of MIPS.

Although it could reduce hardware costs, almost all chips today use pipelining instead to increase performance over a single cycle implementation, so some readers may want to skip multicycle and go directly to pipelining. However, some instructors see pedagogic advantages to explaining multicycle implementation before pipelining, so we offer this implementation option online.

4.6 An Overview of Pipelining

Pipelining is an implementation technique in which multiple instructions are overlapped in execution. Today, **pipelining** is nearly universal.

This section relies heavily on one analogy to give an overview of the pipelining terms and issues. If you are interested in just the big picture, you should concentrate on this section and then skip to Sections 4.11 and 4.12 to see an introduction to the advanced pipelining techniques used in recent processors such as the Intel Core i7 and ARM Cortex-A8. If you are interested in exploring the anatomy of a pipelined computer, this section is a good introduction to Sections 4.7 through 4.10.

Anyone who has done a lot of laundry has intuitively used pipelining. The *non-pipelined* approach to laundry would be as follows:

1. Place one dirty load of clothes in the washer.

2. When the washer is finished, place the wet load in the dryer.

3. When the dryer is finished, place the dry load on a table and fold.

4. When folding is finished, ask your roommate to put the clothes away.

When this load is done, start over with the next dirty load.

The *pipelined* approach takes much less time, as Figure 4.25 shows. As soon as the washer is finished with the first load and placed in the dryer, you load the washer with the second dirty load. When the first load is dry, you place it on the table to start folding, move the wet load to the dryer, and put the next dirty load into the washer. Next you have your roommate put the first load away, you start folding the second load, the dryer has the third load, and you put the fourth load into the washer. At this point all steps—called *stages* in pipelining—are operating concurrently. As long as we have separate resources for each stage, we can pipeline the tasks.

The pipelining paradox is that the time from placing a single dirty sock in the washer until it is dried, folded, and put away is not shorter for pipelining; the reason pipelining is faster for many loads is that everything is working in parallel, so more loads are finished per hour. Pipelining improves throughput of our laundry system. Hence, pipelining would not decrease the time to complete one load of laundry, but when we have many loads of laundry to do, the improvement in throughput decreases the total time to complete the work.

If all the stages take about the same amount of time and there is enough work to do, then the speed-up due to pipelining is equal to the number of stages in the pipeline, in this case four: washing, drying, folding, and putting away. Therefore, pipelined laundry is potentially four times faster than nonpipelined: 20 loads would take about 5 times as long as 1 load, while 20 loads of sequential laundry takes 20

Never waste time.
American proverb

pipelining An implementation technique in which multiple instructions are overlapped in execution, much like an assembly line.

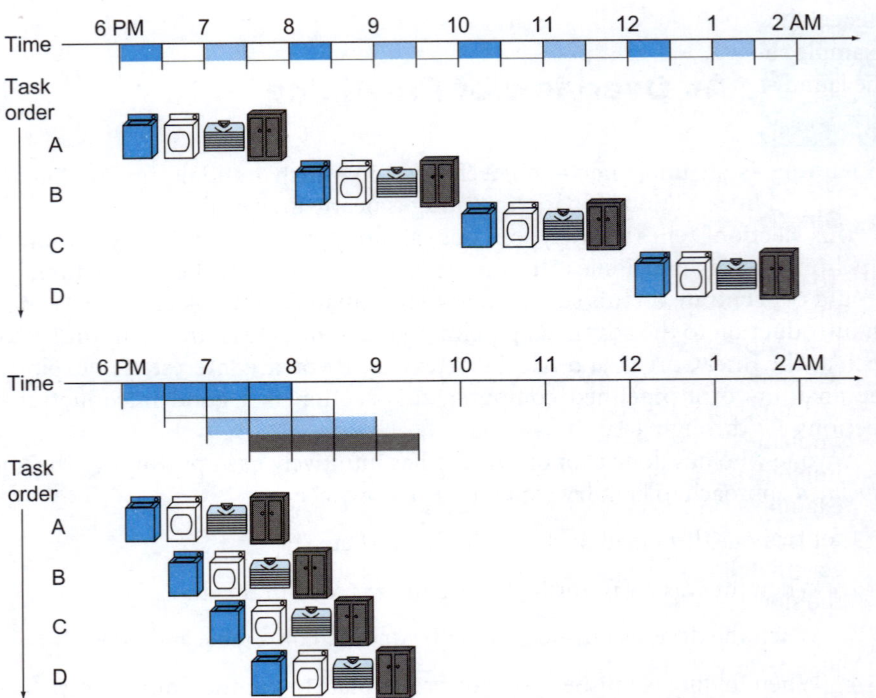

FIGURE 4.25 The laundry analogy for pipelining. Ann, Brian, Cathy, and Don each have dirty clothes to be washed, dried, folded, and put away. The washer, dryer, "folder," and "storer" each take 30 minutes for their task. Sequential laundry takes 8 hours for 4 loads of wash, while pipelined laundry takes just 3.5 hours. We show the pipeline stage of different loads over time by showing copies of the four resources on this two-dimensional time line, but we really have just one of each resource.

times as long as 1 load. It's only 2.3 times faster in Figure 4.25, because we only show 4 loads. Notice that at the beginning and end of the workload in the pipelined version in Figure 4.25, the pipeline is not completely full; this start-up and wind-down affects performance when the number of tasks is not large compared to the number of stages in the pipeline. If the number of loads is much larger than 4, then the stages will be full most of the time and the increase in throughput will be very close to 4.

The same principles apply to processors where we pipeline instruction-execution. MIPS instructions classically take five steps:

1. Fetch instruction from memory.

2. Read registers while decoding the instruction. The regular format of MIPS instructions allows reading and decoding to occur simultaneously.

3. Execute the operation or calculate an address.

4. Access an operand in data memory.

5. Write the result into a register.

Hence, the MIPS pipeline we explore in this chapter has five stages. The following example shows that pipelining speeds up instruction execution just as it speeds up the laundry.

Single-Cycle versus Pipelined Performance

To make this discussion concrete, let's create a pipeline. In this example, and in the rest of this chapter, we limit our attention to eight instructions: load word (lw), store word (sw), add (add), subtract (sub), AND (and), OR (or), set less than (slt), and branch on equal (beq).

Compare the average time between instructions of a single-cycle implementation, in which all instructions take one clock cycle, to a pipelined implementation. The operation times for the major functional units in this example are 200 ps for memory access, 200 ps for ALU operation, and 100 ps for register file read or write. In the single-cycle model, every instruction takes exactly one clock cycle, so the clock cycle must be stretched to accommodate the slowest instruction.

Figure 4.26 shows the time required for each of the eight instructions. The single-cycle design must allow for the slowest instruction—in Figure 4.26 it is lw—so the time required for every instruction is 800 ps. Similarly to Figure 4.25, Figure 4.27 compares nonpipelined and pipelined execution of three load word instructions. Thus, the time between the first and fourth instructions in the nonpipelined design is 3 × 800 ns or 2400 ps.

All the pipeline stages take a single clock cycle, so the clock cycle must be long enough to accommodate the slowest operation. Just as the single-cycle design must take the worst-case clock cycle of 800 ps, even though some instructions can be as fast as 500 ps, the pipelined execution clock cycle must have the worst-case clock cycle of 200 ps, even though some stages take only 100 ps. Pipelining still offers a fourfold performance improvement: the time between the first and fourth instructions is 3 × 200 ps or 600 ps.

We can turn the pipelining speed-up discussion above into a formula. If the stages are perfectly balanced, then the time between instructions on the pipelined processor—assuming ideal conditions—is equal to

$$\text{Time between instructions}_{\text{pipelined}} = \frac{\text{Time between instruction}_{\text{nonpipelined}}}{\text{Number of pipe stages}}$$

Instruction class	Instruction fetch	Register read	ALU operation	Data access	Register write	Total time
Load word (lw)	200 ps	100 ps	200 ps	200 ps	100 ps	800 ps
Store word (sw)	200 ps	100 ps	200 ps	200 ps		700 ps
R-format (add, sub, AND, OR, slt)	200 ps	100 ps	200 ps		100 ps	600 ps
Branch (beq)	200 ps	100 ps	200 ps			500 ps

FIGURE 4.26 Total time for each instruction calculated from the time for each component. This calculation assumes that the multiplexors, control unit, PC accesses, and sign extension unit have no delay.

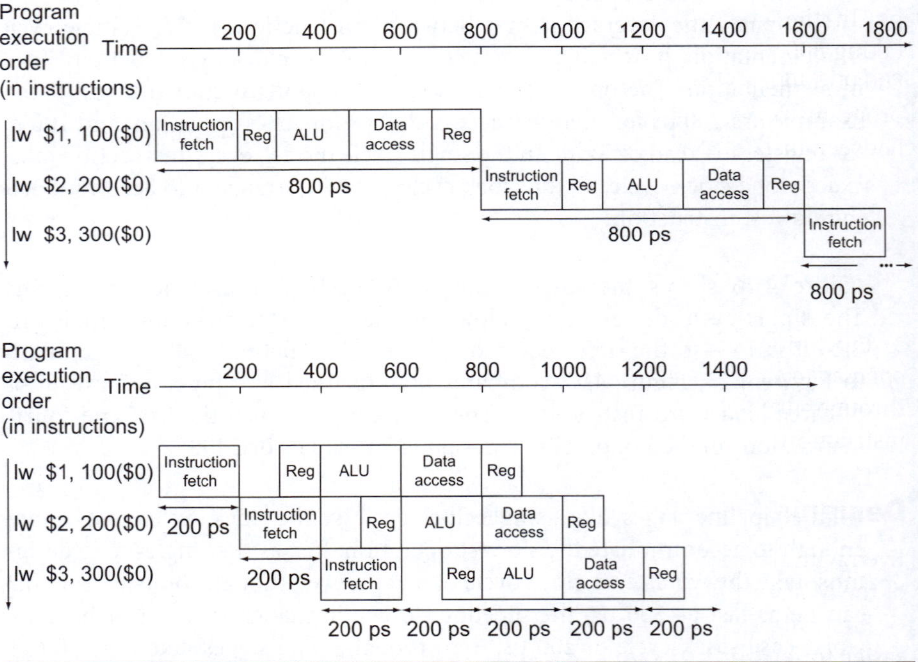

FIGURE 4.27 Single-cycle, nonpipelined execution in top versus pipelined execution in bottom. Both use the same hardware components, whose time is listed in Figure 4.26. In this case, we see a fourfold speed-up on average time between instructions, from 800 ps down to 200 ps. Compare this figure to Figure 4.25. For the laundry, we assumed all stages were equal. If the dryer were slowest, then the dryer stage would set the stage time. The pipeline stage times of a computer are also limited by the slowest resource, either the ALU operation or the memory access. We assume the write to the register file occurs in the first half of the clock cycle and the read from the register file occurs in the second half. We use this assumption throughout this chapter.

Under ideal conditions and with a large number of instructions, the speed-up from pipelining is approximately equal to the number of pipe stages; a five-stage pipeline is nearly five times faster.

The formula suggests that a five-stage pipeline should offer nearly a fivefold improvement over the 800 ps nonpipelined time, or a 160 ps clock cycle.

The example shows, however, that the stages may be imperfectly balanced. Moreover, pipelining involves some overhead, the source of which will be clearer shortly. Thus, the time per instruction in the pipelined processor will exceed the minimum possible, and speed-up will be less than the number of pipeline stages.

Moreover, even our claim of fourfold improvement for our example is not reflected in the total execution time for the three instructions: it's 1400 ps versus 2400 ps. Of course, this is because the number of instructions is not large. What would happen if we increased the number of instructions? We could extend the previous figures to 1,000,003 instructions. We would add 1,000,000 instructions in the pipelined example; each instruction adds 200 ps to the total execution time. The total execution time would be 1,000,000 × 200 ps + 1400 ps, or 200,001,400 ps. In the nonpipelined example, we would add 1,000,000 instructions, each taking 800 ps, so total execution time would be 1,000,000 × 800 ps + 2400 ps, or 800,002,400 ps. Under these conditions, the ratio of total execution times for real programs on nonpipelined to pipelined processors is close to the ratio of times between instructions:

$$\frac{800,002,400\,ps}{200,001,400\,ps} = \frac{800\,ps}{200\,ps} \simeq 4.00$$

Pipelining improves performance by *increasing instruction throughput, as opposed to decreasing the execution time of an individual instruction*, but instruction throughput is the important metric because real programs execute billions of instructions.

Designing Instruction Sets for Pipelining

Even with this simple explanation of pipelining, we can get insight into the design of the MIPS instruction set, which was designed for pipelined execution.

First, all MIPS instructions are the same length. This restriction makes it much easier to fetch instructions in the first pipeline stage and to decode them in the second stage. In an instruction set like the x86, where instructions vary from 1 byte to 15 bytes, pipelining is considerably more challenging. Modern implementations of the x86 architecture actually translate x86 instructions into simple operations that look like MIPS instructions and then pipeline the simple operations rather than the native x86 instructions! (See Section 4.11.)

Second, MIPS has only a few instruction formats, with the source register fields being located in the same place in each instruction. This symmetry means that the second stage can begin reading the register file at the same time that the hardware is determining what type of instruction was fetched. If MIPS instruction formats were not symmetric, we would need to split stage 2, resulting in six pipeline stages. We will shortly see the downside of longer pipelines.

Third, memory operands only appear in loads or stores in MIPS. This restriction means we can use the execute stage to calculate the memory address and then access memory in the following stage. If we could operate on the operands in memory, as in the x86, stages 3 and 4 would expand to an address stage, memory stage, and then execute stage.

Fourth, as discussed in Chapter 2, operands must be aligned in memory. Hence, we need not worry about a single data transfer instruction requiring two data memory accesses; the requested data can be transferred between processor and memory in a single pipeline stage.

Pipeline Hazards

There are situations in pipelining when the next instruction cannot execute in the following clock cycle. These events are called *hazards*, and there are three different types.

Structural Hazard

structural hazard When a planned instruction cannot execute in the proper clock cycle because the hardware does not support the combination of instructions that are set to execute.

The first hazard is called a **structural hazard**. It means that the hardware cannot support the combination of instructions that we want to execute in the same clock cycle. A structural hazard in the laundry room would occur if we used a washer-dryer combination instead of a separate washer and dryer, or if our roommate was busy doing something else and wouldn't put clothes away. Our carefully scheduled pipeline plans would then be foiled.

As we said above, the MIPS instruction set was designed to be pipelined, making it fairly easy for designers to avoid structural hazards when designing a pipeline. Suppose, however, that we had a single memory instead of two memories. If the pipeline in Figure 4.27 had a fourth instruction, we would see that in the same clock cycle the first instruction is accessing data from memory while the fourth instruction is fetching an instruction from that same memory. Without two memories, our pipeline could have a structural hazard.

Data Hazards

data hazard Also called a **pipeline data hazard**. When a planned instruction cannot execute in the proper clock cycle because data that is needed to execute the instruction is not yet available.

Data hazards occur when the pipeline must be stalled because one step must wait for another to complete. Suppose you found a sock at the folding station for which no match existed. One possible strategy is to run down to your room and search through your clothes bureau to see if you can find the match. Obviously, while you are doing the search, loads must wait that have completed drying and are ready to fold as well as those that have finished washing and are ready to dry.

In a computer pipeline, data hazards arise from the dependence of one instruction on an earlier one that is still in the pipeline (a relationship that does not really exist when doing laundry). For example, suppose we have an add instruction followed immediately by a subtract instruction that uses the sum ($s0):

```
add   $s0, $t0, $t1
sub   $t2, $s0, $t3
```

Without intervention, a data hazard could severely stall the pipeline. The add instruction doesn't write its result until the fifth stage, meaning that we would have to waste three clock cycles in the pipeline.

Although we could try to rely on compilers to remove all such hazards, the results would not be satisfactory. These dependences happen just too often and the delay is just too long to expect the compiler to rescue us from this dilemma.

The primary solution is based on the observation that we don't need to wait for the instruction to complete before trying to resolve the data hazard. For the code sequence above, as soon as the ALU creates the sum for the add, we can supply it as an input for the subtract. Adding extra hardware to retrieve the missing item early from the internal resources is called **forwarding** or **bypassing**.

> **forwarding** Also called **bypassing**. A method of resolving a data hazard by retrieving the missing data element from internal buffers rather than waiting for it to arrive from programmer-visible registers or memory.

Forwarding with Two Instructions

For the two instructions above, show what pipeline stages would be connected by forwarding. Use the drawing in Figure 4.28 to represent the datapath during the five stages of the pipeline. Align a copy of the datapath for each instruction, similar to the laundry pipeline in Figure 4.25.

Figure 4.29 shows the connection to forward the value in $s0 after the execution stage of the add instruction as input to the execution stage of the sub instruction.

EXAMPLE

ANSWER

In this graphical representation of events, forwarding paths are valid only if the destination stage is later in time than the source stage. For example, there cannot be a valid forwarding path from the output of the memory access stage in the first

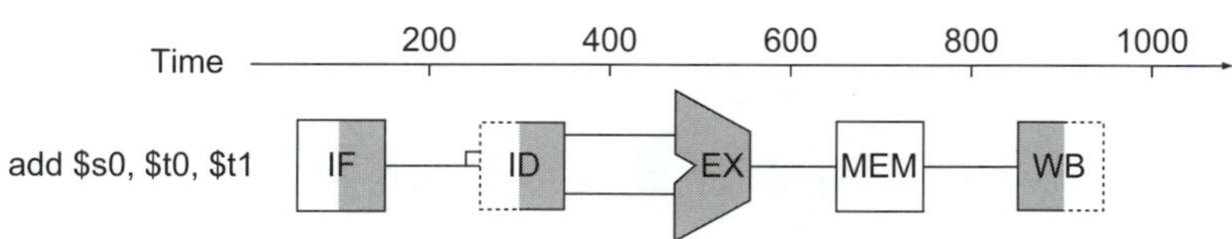

FIGURE 4.28 Graphical representation of the instruction pipeline, similar in spirit to the laundry pipeline in Figure 4.25. Here we use symbols representing the physical resources with the abbreviations for pipeline stages used throughout the chapter. The symbols for the five stages: *IF* for the instruction fetch stage, with the box representing instruction memory; *ID* for the instruction decode/register file read stage, with the drawing showing the register file being read; *EX* for the execution stage, with the drawing representing the ALU; *MEM* for the memory access stage, with the box representing data memory; and *WB* for the write-back stage, with the drawing showing the register file being written. The shading indicates the element is used by the instruction. Hence, MEM has a white background because add does not access the data memory. Shading on the right half of the register file or memory means the element is read in that stage, and shading of the left half means it is written in that stage. Hence the right half of ID is shaded in the second stage because the register file is read, and the left half of WB is shaded in the fifth stage because the register file is written.

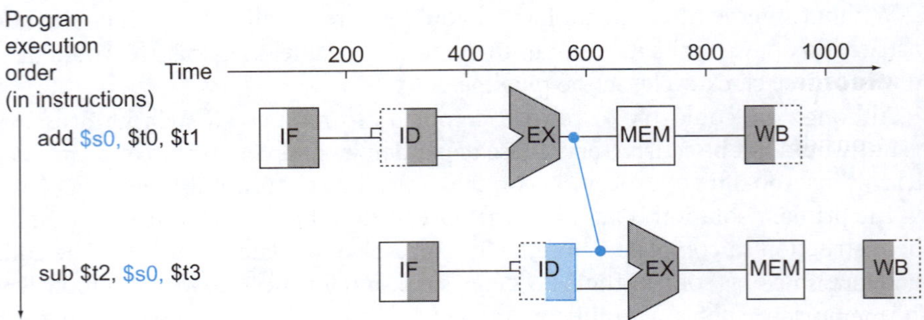

FIGURE 4.29 Graphical representation of forwarding. The connection shows the forwarding path from the output of the EX stage of add to the input of the EX stage for sub, replacing the value from register $s0 read in the second stage of sub.

instruction to the input of the execution stage of the following, since that would mean going backward in time.

Forwarding works very well and is described in detail in Section 4.8. It cannot prevent all pipeline stalls, however. For example, suppose the first instruction was a load of $s0 instead of an add. As we can imagine from looking at Figure 4.29, the desired data would be available only *after* the fourth stage of the first instruction in the dependence, which is too late for the *input* of the third stage of sub. Hence, even with forwarding, we would have to stall one stage for a **load-use data hazard**, as Figure 4.30 shows. This figure shows an important pipeline concept, officially called a **pipeline stall**, but often given the nickname **bubble**. We shall see stalls elsewhere in the pipeline. Section 4.8 shows how we can handle hard cases like these, using either hardware detection and stalls or software that reorders code to try to avoid load-use pipeline stalls, as this example illustrates.

load-use data hazard A specific form of data hazard in which the data being loaded by a load instruction has not yet become available when it is needed by another instruction.

pipeline stall Also called **bubble**. A stall initiated in order to resolve a hazard.

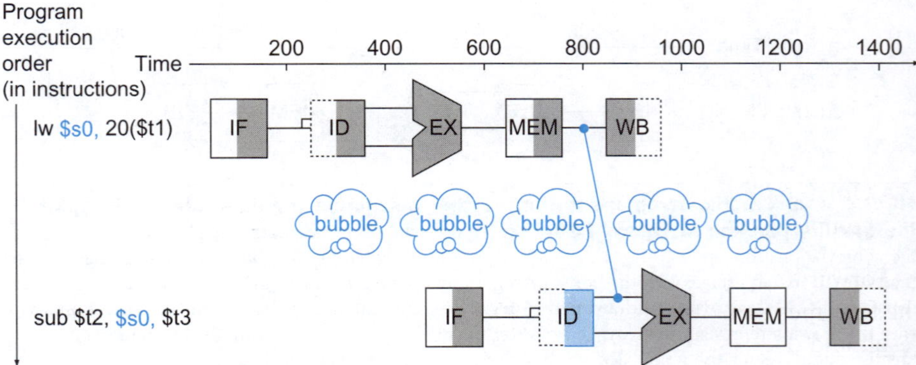

FIGURE 4.30 We need a stall even with forwarding when an R-format instruction following a load tries to use the data. Without the stall, the path from memory access stage output to execution stage input would be going backward in time, which is impossible. This figure is actually a simplification, since we cannot know until after the subtract instruction is fetched and decoded whether or not a stall will be necessary. Section 4.8 shows the details of what really happens in the case of a hazard.

Reordering Code to Avoid Pipeline Stalls

Consider the following code segment in C:

```
a = b + e;
c = b + f;
```

Here is the generated MIPS code for this segment, assuming all variables are in memory and are addressable as offsets from $t0:

```
lw      $t1, 0($t0)
lw      $t2, 4($t0)
add     $t3, $t1,$t2
sw      $t3, 12($t0)
lw      $t4, 8($t0)
add     $t5, $t1,$t4
sw      $t5, 16($t0)
```

Find the hazards in the preceding code segment and reorder the instructions to avoid any pipeline stalls.

EXAMPLE

Both add instructions have a hazard because of their respective dependence on the immediately preceding lw instruction. Notice that bypassing eliminates several other potential hazards, including the dependence of the first add on the first lw and any hazards for store instructions. Moving up the third lw instruction to become the third instruction eliminates both hazards:

ANSWER

```
lw      $t1, 0($t0)
lw      $t2, 4($t0)
lw      $t4, 8($t0)
add     $t3, $t1,$t2
sw      $t3, 12($t0)
add     $t5, $t1,$t4
sw      $t5, 16($t0)
```

On a pipelined processor with forwarding, the reordered sequence will complete in two fewer cycles than the original version.

Forwarding yields another insight into the MIPS architecture, in addition to the four mentioned on pages 289–290. Each MIPS instruction writes at most one result and does this in the last stage of the pipeline. Forwarding is harder if there are multiple results to forward per instruction or if there is a need to write a result early on in instruction execution.

Elaboration: The name "forwarding" comes from the idea that the result is passed forward from an earlier instruction to a later instruction. "Bypassing" comes from passing the result around the register file to the desired unit.

Control Hazards

control hazard Also called branch hazard. When the proper instruction cannot execute in the proper pipeline clock cycle because the instruction that was fetched is not the one that is needed; that is, the flow of instruction addresses is not what the pipeline expected.

The third type of hazard is called a control hazard, arising from the need to make a decision based on the results of one instruction while others are executing.

Suppose our laundry crew was given the happy task of cleaning the uniforms of a football team. Given how filthy the laundry is, we need to determine whether the detergent and water temperature setting we select is strong enough to get the uniforms clean but not so strong that the uniforms wear out sooner. In our laundry pipeline, we have to wait until the second stage to examine the dry uniform to see if we need to change the washer setup or not. What to do?

Here is the first of two solutions to control hazards in the laundry room and its computer equivalent.

Stall: Just operate sequentially until the first batch is dry and then repeat until you have the right formula.

This conservative option certainly works, but it is slow.

The equivalent decision task in a computer is the branch instruction. Notice that we must begin fetching the instruction following the branch on the very next clock cycle. Nevertheless, the pipeline cannot possibly know what the next instruction should be, since it *only just received* the branch instruction from memory! Just as with laundry, one possible solution is to stall immediately after we fetch a branch, waiting until the pipeline determines the outcome of the branch and knows what instruction address to fetch from.

Let's assume that we put in enough extra hardware so that we can test registers, calculate the branch address, and update the PC during the second stage of the pipeline (see Section 4.9 for details). Even with this extra hardware, the pipeline involving conditional branches would look like Figure 4.31. The lw instruction, executed if the branch fails, is stalled one extra 200 ps clock cycle before starting.

EXAMPLE

Performance of "Stall on Branch"

Estimate the impact on the *clock cycles per instruction* (CPI) of stalling on branches. Assume all other instructions have a CPI of 1.

ANSWER

Figure 3.28 in Chapter 3 shows that branches are 17% of the instructions executed in SPECint2006. Since the other instructions run have a CPI of 1, and branches took one extra clock cycle for the stall, then we would see a CPI of 1.17 and hence a slowdown of 1.17 versus the ideal case.

If we cannot resolve the branch in the second stage, as is often the case for longer pipelines, then we'd see an even larger slowdown if we stall on branches. The cost of this option is too high for most computers to use and motivates a second solution to the control hazard using one of our great ideas from Chapter 1:

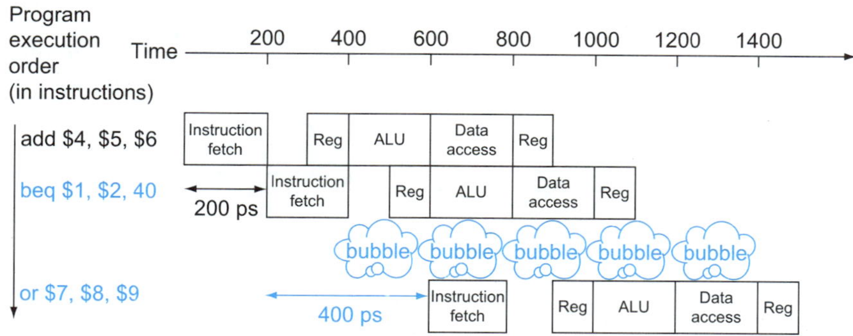

FIGURE 4.31 Pipeline showing stalling on every conditional branch as solution to control hazards. This example assumes the conditional branch is taken, and the instruction at the destination of the branch is the OR instruction. There is a one-stage pipeline stall, or bubble, after the branch. In reality, the process of creating a stall is slightly more complicated, as we will see in Section 4.9. The effect on performance, however, is the same as would occur if a bubble were inserted.

Predict: If you're pretty sure you have the right formula to wash uniforms, then just *predict* that it will work and wash the second load while waiting for the first load to dry.

This option does not slow down the pipeline when you are correct. When you are wrong, however, you need to redo the load that was washed while guessing the decision.

Computers do indeed use **prediction** to handle branches. One simple approach is to predict always that branches will be untaken. When you're right, the pipeline proceeds at full speed. Only when branches are taken does the pipeline stall. Figure 4.32 shows such an example.

A more sophisticated version of **branch prediction** would have some branches predicted as taken and some as untaken. In our analogy, the dark or home uniforms might take one formula while the light or road uniforms might take another. In the case of programming, at the bottom of loops are branches that jump back to the top of the loop. Since they are likely to be taken and they branch backward, we could always predict taken for branches that jump to an earlier address.

Such rigid approaches to branch prediction rely on stereotypical behavior and don't account for the individuality of a specific branch instruction. *Dynamic* hardware predictors, in stark contrast, make their guesses depending on the behavior of each branch and may change predictions for a branch over the life of a program. Following our analogy, in dynamic prediction a person would look at how dirty the uniform was and guess at the formula, adjusting the next **prediction** depending on the success of recent guesses.

One popular approach to dynamic prediction of branches is keeping a history for each branch as taken or untaken, and then using the recent past behavior to predict the future. As we will see later, the amount and type of history kept have become extensive, with the result being that dynamic branch predictors can correctly predict branches with more than 90% accuracy (see Section 4.9). When the guess is wrong, the pipeline control must ensure that the instructions following

branch prediction
A method of resolving a branch hazard that assumes a given outcome for the branch and proceeds from that assumption rather than waiting to ascertain the actual outcome.

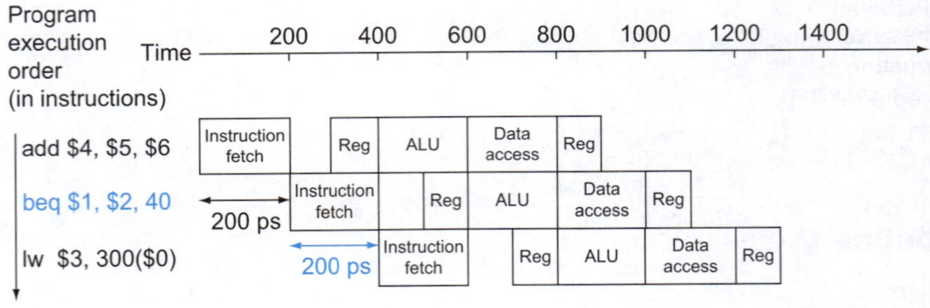

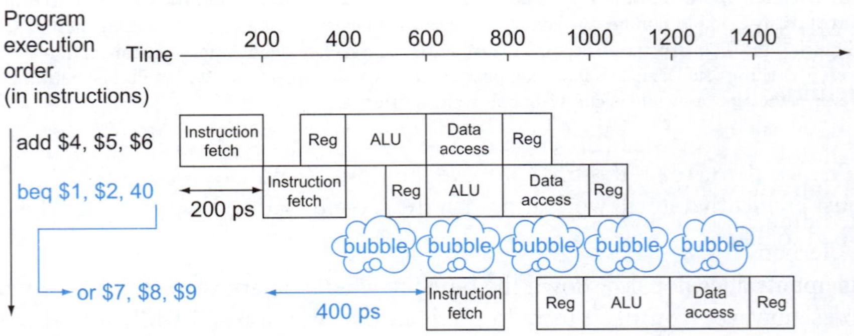

FIGURE 4.32 Predicting that branches are not taken as a solution to control hazard. The top drawing shows the pipeline when the branch is not taken. The bottom drawing shows the pipeline when the branch is taken. As we noted in Figure 4.31, the insertion of a bubble in this fashion simplifies what actually happens, at least during the first clock cycle immediately following the branch. Section 4.9 will reveal the details.

the wrongly guessed branch have no effect and must restart the pipeline from the proper branch address. In our laundry analogy, we must stop taking new loads so that we can restart the load that we incorrectly predicted.

As in the case of all other solutions to control hazards, longer pipelines exacerbate the problem, in this case by raising the cost of misprediction. Solutions to control hazards are described in more detail in Section 4.9.

Elaboration: There is a third approach to the control hazard, called *delayed decision*. In our analogy, whenever you are going to make such a decision about laundry, just place a load of nonfootball clothes in the washer while waiting for football uniforms to dry. As long as you have enough dirty clothes that are not affected by the test, this solution works fine.

Called the *delayed branch* in computers, and mentioned above, this is the solution actually used by the MIPS architecture. The delayed branch always executes the next sequential instruction, with the branch taking place *after* that one instruction delay. It is hidden from the MIPS assembly language programmer because the assembler can automatically arrange the instructions to get the branch behavior desired by the programmer. MIPS software will place an instruction immediately after the delayed branch instruction that is not affected by the branch, and a taken branch changes the address of the instruction that *follows* this safe instruction. In our example, the add instruction before the branch in Figure 4.31 does not affect the branch and can be moved after the branch to fully hide the branch delay. Since delayed branches are useful when the branches are short, no processor uses a delayed branch of more than one cycle. For longer branch delays, hardware-based branch prediction is usually used.

Pipeline Overview Summary

Pipelining is a technique that exploits **parallelism** among the instructions in a sequential instruction stream. It has the substantial advantage that, unlike programming a multiprocessor, it is fundamentally invisible to the programmer.

In the next few sections of this chapter, we cover the concept of pipelining using the MIPS instruction subset from the single-cycle implementation in Section 4.4 and show a simplified version of its pipeline. We then look at the problems that **pipelining** introduces and the performance attainable under typical situations.

If you wish to focus more on the software and the performance implications of pipelining, you now have sufficient background to skip to Section 4.11. Section 4.11 introduces advanced pipelining concepts, such as superscalar and dynamic scheduling, and Section 4.12 examines the pipelines of recent microprocessors.

Alternatively, if you are interested in understanding how pipelining is implemented and the challenges of dealing with hazards, you can proceed to examine the design of a pipelined datapath and the basic control, explained in Section 4.7. You can then use this understanding to explore the implementation of forwarding and stalls in Section 4.8. You can then read Section 4.9 to learn more about solutions to branch hazards, and then see how exceptions are handled in Section 4.10.

For each code sequence below, state whether it must stall, can avoid stalls using only forwarding, or can execute without stalling or forwarding.

Check Yourself

Sequence 1	Sequence 2	Sequence 3
lw $t0,0($t0)	add $t1,$t0,$t0	addi $t1,$t0,#1
add $t1,$t0,$t0	addi $t2,$t0,#5	addi $t2,$t0,#2
	addi $t4,$t1,#5	addi $t3,$t0,#2
		addi $t3,$t0,#4
		addi $t5,$t0,#5

Outside the memory system, the effective operation of the pipeline is usually the most important factor in determining the CPI of the processor and hence its performance. As we will see in Section 4.11, understanding the performance of a modern multiple-issue pipelined processor is complex and requires understanding more than just the issues that arise in a simple pipelined processor. Nonetheless, structural, data, and control hazards remain important in both simple pipelines and more sophisticated ones.

Understanding Program Performance

For modern pipelines, structural hazards usually revolve around the floating-point unit, which may not be fully pipelined, while control hazards are usually more of a problem in integer programs, which tend to have higher branch frequencies as well as less predictable branches. Data hazards can be performance bottlenecks in both integer and floating-point programs. Often it is easier to deal with data hazards in floating-point programs because the lower branch frequency and more regular memory access patterns allow the compiler to try to schedule instructions to avoid hazards. It is more difficult to perform such optimizations in integer programs that have less regular memory access, involving more use of pointers. As we will see in Section 4.11, there are more ambitious compiler and hardware techniques for reducing data dependences through scheduling.

The **BIG** Picture

latency (pipeline) The number of stages in a pipeline or the number of stages between two instructions during execution.

Pipelining increases the number of simultaneously executing instructions and the rate at which instructions are started and completed. Pipelining does not reduce the time it takes to complete an individual instruction, also called the **latency**. For example, the five-stage pipeline still takes 5 clock cycles for the instruction to complete. In the terms used in Chapter 1, pipelining improves instruction *throughput* rather than individual instruction *execution time* or *latency*.

Instruction sets can either simplify or make life harder for pipeline designers, who must already cope with structural, control, and data hazards. Branch **prediction** and forwarding help make a computer fast while still getting the right answers.

4.7   Pipelined Datapath and Control

Figure 4.33 shows the single-cycle datapath from Section 4.4 with the pipeline stages identified. The division of an instruction into five stages means a five-stage pipeline, which in turn means that up to five instructions will be in execution during any single clock cycle. Thus, we must separate the datapath into five pieces, with each piece named corresponding to a stage of instruction execution:

1. IF: Instruction fetch

2. ID: Instruction decode and register file read

3. EX: Execution or address calculation

4. MEM: Data memory access

5. WB: Write back

There is less in this than meets the eye.

Tallulah
Bankhead, remark
to Alexander
Woollcott, 1922

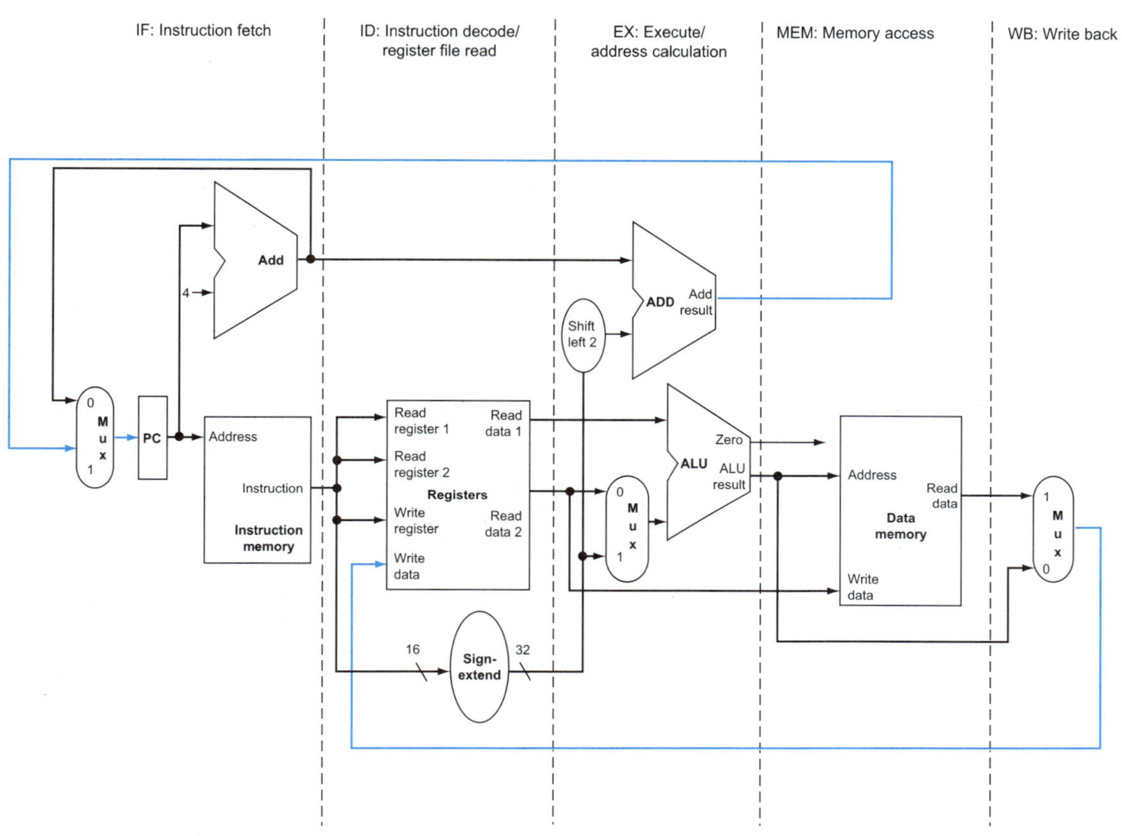

FIGURE 4.33 The single-cycle datapath from Section 4.4 (similar to Figure 4.17). Each step of the instruction can be mapped onto the datapath from left to right. The only exceptions are the update of the PC and the write-back step, shown in color, which sends either the ALU result or the data from memory to the left to be written into the register file. (Normally we use color lines for control, but these are data lines.)

In Figure 4.33, these five components correspond roughly to the way the datapath is drawn; instructions and data move generally from left to right through the five stages as they complete execution. Returning to our laundry analogy, clothes get cleaner, drier, and more organized as they move through the line, and they never move backward.

There are, however, two exceptions to this left-to-right flow of instructions:

- The write-back stage, which places the result back into the register file in the middle of the datapath

- The selection of the next value of the PC, choosing between the incremented PC and the branch address from the MEM stage

Data flowing from right to left does not affect the current instruction; these reverse data movements influence only later instructions in the pipeline. Note that the first right-to-left flow of data can lead to data hazards and the second leads to control hazards.

One way to show what happens in pipelined execution is to pretend that each instruction has its own datapath, and then to place these datapaths on a timeline to show their relationship. Figure 4.34 shows the execution of the instructions in Figure 4.27 by displaying their private datapaths on a common timeline. We use a stylized version of the datapath in Figure 4.33 to show the relationships in Figure 4.34.

Figure 4.34 seems to suggest that three instructions need three datapaths. Instead, we add registers to hold data so that portions of a single datapath can be shared during instruction execution.

For example, as Figure 4.34 shows, the instruction memory is used during only one of the five stages of an instruction, allowing it to be shared by following instructions during the other four stages. To retain the value of an individual instruction for its other four stages, the value read from instruction memory must be saved in a register. Similar arguments apply to every pipeline stage, so we must place registers wherever there are dividing lines between stages in Figure 4.33. Returning to our laundry analogy, we might have a basket between each pair of stages to hold the clothes for the next step.

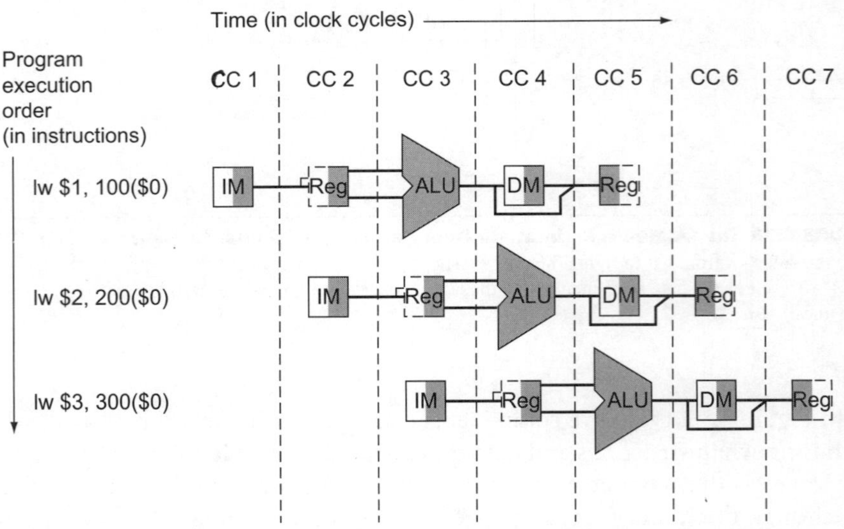

FIGURE 4.34 Instructions being executed using the single-cycle datapath in Figure 4.33, assuming pipelined execution. Similar to Figures 4.28 through 4.30, this figure pretends that each instruction has its own datapath, and shades each portion according to use. Unlike those figures, each stage is labeled by the physical resource used in that stage, corresponding to the portions of the datapath in Figure 4.33. *IM* represents the instruction memory and the PC in the instruction fetch stage, *Reg* stands for the register file and sign extender in the instruction decode/register file read stage (ID), and so on. To maintain proper time order, this stylized datapath breaks the register file into two logical parts: registers read during register fetch (ID) and registers written during write back (WB). This dual use is represented by drawing the unshaded left half of the register file using dashed lines in the ID stage, when it is not being written, and the unshaded right half in dashed lines in the WB stage, when it is not being read. As before, we assume the register file is written in the first half of the clock cycle and the register file is read during the second half.

Figure 4.35 shows the pipelined datapath with the pipeline registers highlighted. All instructions advance during each clock cycle from one pipeline register to the next. The registers are named for the two stages separated by that register. For example, the pipeline register between the IF and ID stages is called IF/ID.

Notice that there is no pipeline register at the end of the write-back stage. All instructions must update some state in the processor—the register file, memory, or the PC—so a separate pipeline register is redundant to the state that is updated. For example, a load instruction will place its result in 1 of the 32 registers, and any later instruction that needs that data will simply read the appropriate register.

Of course, every instruction updates the PC, whether by incrementing it or by setting it to a branch destination address. The PC can be thought of as a pipeline register: one that feeds the IF stage of the pipeline. Unlike the shaded pipeline registers in Figure 4.35, however, the PC is part of the visible architectural state; its contents must be saved when an exception occurs, while the contents of the pipeline registers can be discarded. In the laundry analogy, you could think of the PC as corresponding to the basket that holds the load of dirty clothes before the wash step.

To show how the pipelining works, throughout this chapter we show sequences of figures to demonstrate operation over time. These extra pages would seem to require much more time for you to understand. Fear not; the sequences take much

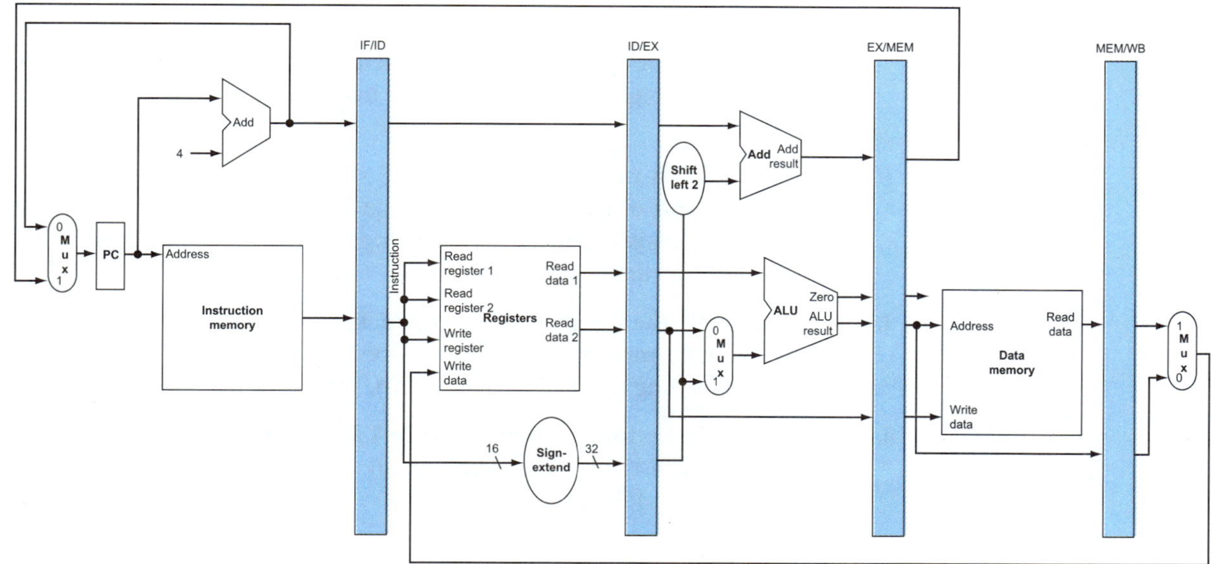

FIGURE 4.35 The pipelined version of the datapath in Figure 4.33. The pipeline registers, in color, separate each pipeline stage. They are labeled by the stages that they separate; for example, the first is labeled *IF/ID* because it separates the instruction fetch and instruction decode stages. The registers must be wide enough to store all the data corresponding to the lines that go through them. For example, the IF/ID register must be 64 bits wide, because it must hold both the 32-bit instruction fetched from memory and the incremented 32-bit PC address. We will expand these registers over the course of this chapter, but for now the other three pipeline registers contain 128, 97, and 64 bits, respectively.

less time than it might appear, because you can compare them to see what changes occur in each clock cycle. Section 4.8 describes what happens when there are data hazards between pipelined instructions; ignore them for now.

Figures 4.36 through 4.38, our first sequence, show the active portions of the datapath highlighted as a load instruction goes through the five stages of pipelined execution. We show a load first because it is active in all five stages. As in Figures 4.28 through 4.30, we highlight the *right half* of registers or memory when they are being *read* and highlight the *left half* when they are being *written*.

We show the instruction abbreviation `lw` with the name of the pipe stage that is active in each figure. The five stages are the following:

1. *Instruction fetch:* The top portion of Figure 4.36 shows the instruction being read from memory using the address in the PC and then being placed in the IF/ID pipeline register. The PC address is incremented by 4 and then written back into the PC to be ready for the next clock cycle. This incremented address is also saved in the IF/ID pipeline register in case it is needed later for an instruction, such as `beq`. The computer cannot know which type of instruction is being fetched, so it must prepare for any instruction, passing potentially needed information down the pipeline.

2. *Instruction decode and register file read:* The bottom portion of Figure 4.36 shows the instruction portion of the IF/ID pipeline register supplying the 16-bit immediate field, which is sign-extended to 32 bits, and the register numbers to read the two registers. All three values are stored in the ID/EX pipeline register, along with the incremented PC address. We again transfer everything that might be needed by any instruction during a later clock cycle.

3. *Execute or address calculation:* Figure 4.37 shows that the load instruction reads the contents of register 1 and the sign-extended immediate from the ID/EX pipeline register and adds them using the ALU. That sum is placed in the EX/MEM pipeline register.

4. *Memory access:* The top portion of Figure 4.38 shows the load instruction reading the data memory using the address from the EX/MEM pipeline register and loading the data into the MEM/WB pipeline register.

5. *Write-back:* The bottom portion of Figure 4.38 shows the final step: reading the data from the MEM/WB pipeline register and writing it into the register file in the middle of the figure.

This walk-through of the load instruction shows that any information needed in a later pipe stage must be passed to that stage via a pipeline register. Walking through a store instruction shows the similarity of instruction execution, as well as passing the information for later stages. Here are the five pipe stages of the store instruction:

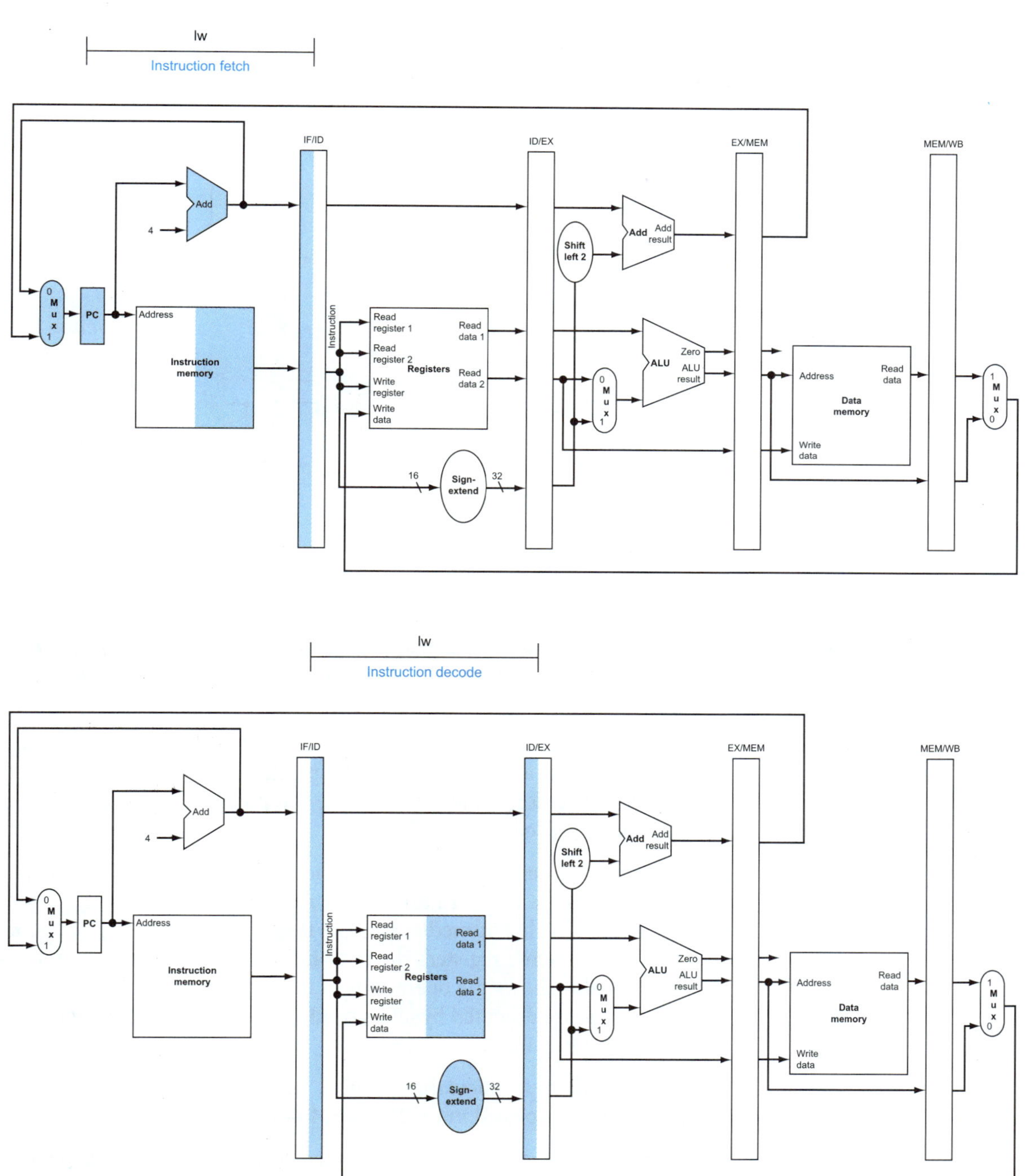

FIGURE 4.36 IF and ID: First and second pipe stages of an instruction, with the active portions of the datapath in Figure 4.35 highlighted. The highlighting convention is the same as that used in Figure 4.28. As in Section 4.2, there is no confusion when reading and writing registers, because the contents change only on the clock edge. Although the load needs only the top register in stage 2, the processor doesn't know what instruction is being decoded, so it sign-extends the 16-bit constant and reads both registers into the ID/EX pipeline register. We don't need all three operands, but it simplifies control to keep all three.

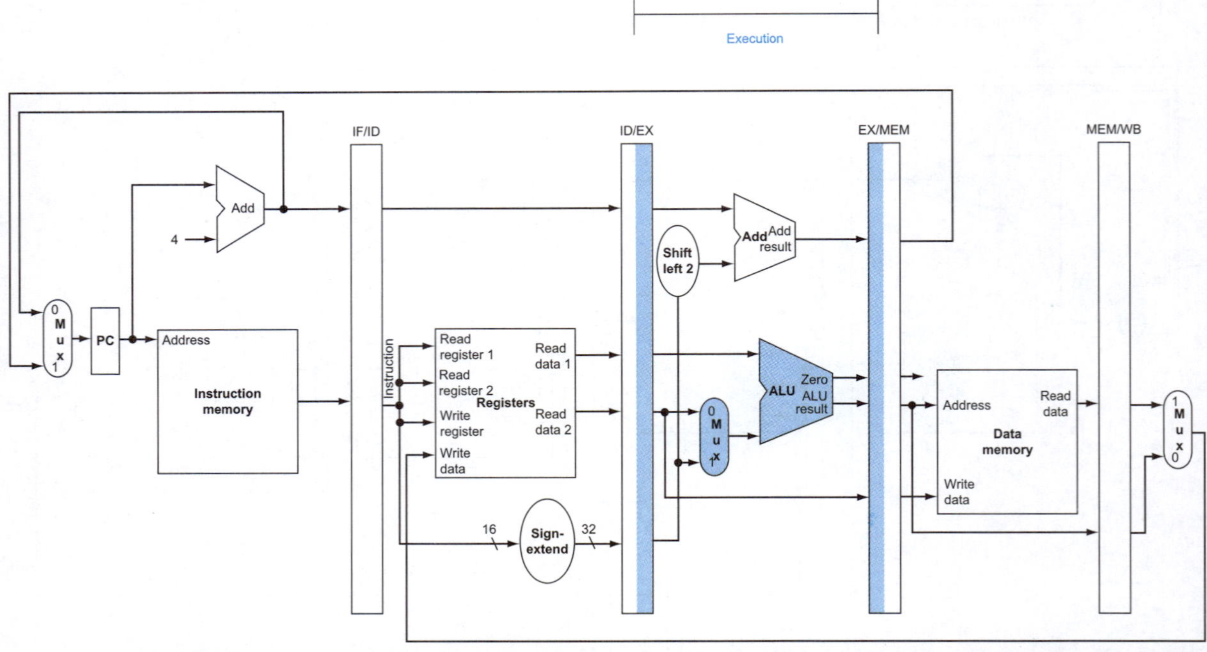

FIGURE 4.37 EX: The third pipe stage of a load instruction, highlighting the portions of the datapath in Figure 4.35 used in this pipe stage. The register is added to the sign-extended immediate, and the sum is placed in the EX/MEM pipeline register.

1. *Instruction fetch:* The instruction is read from memory using the address in the PC and then is placed in the IF/ID pipeline register. This stage occurs before the instruction is identified, so the top portion of Figure 4.36 works for store as well as load.

2. *Instruction decode and register file read:* The instruction in the IF/ID pipeline register supplies the register numbers for reading two registers and extends the sign of the 16-bit immediate. These three 32-bit values are all stored in the ID/EX pipeline register. The bottom portion of Figure 4.36 for load instructions also shows the operations of the second stage for stores. These first two stages are executed by all instructions, since it is too early to know the type of the instruction.

3. *Execute and address calculation:* Figure 4.39 shows the third step; the effective address is placed in the EX/MEM pipeline register.

4. *Memory access:* The top portion of Figure 4.40 shows the data being written to memory. Note that the register containing the data to be stored was read in an earlier stage and stored in ID/EX. The only way to make the data available during the MEM stage is to place the data into the EX/MEM pipeline register in the EX stage, just as we stored the effective address into EX/MEM.

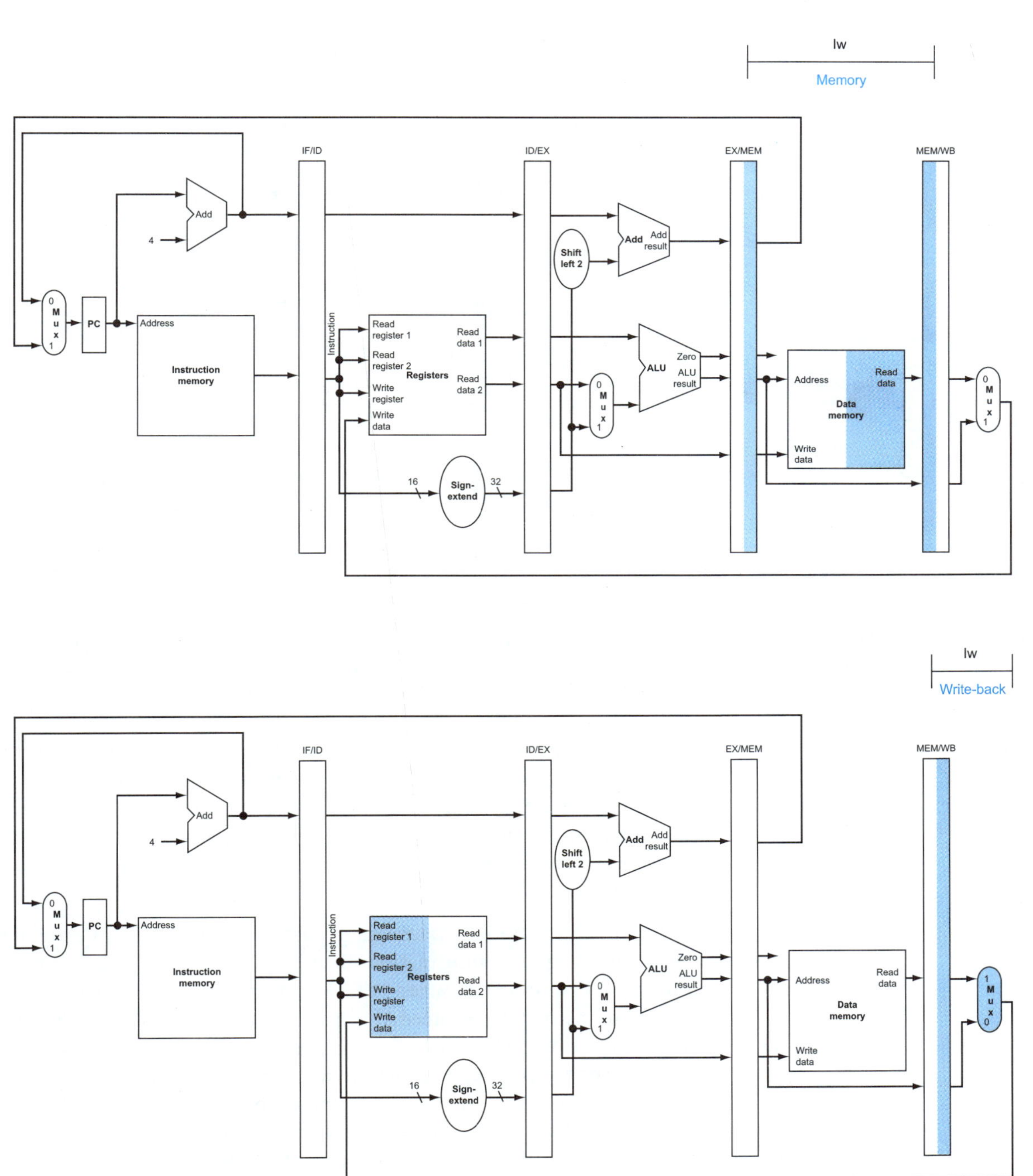

FIGURE 4.38 MEM and WB: The fourth and fifth pipe stages of a load instruction, highlighting the portions of the datapath in Figure 4.35 used in this pipe stage. Data memory is read using the address in the EX/MEM pipeline registers, and the data is placed in the MEM/WB pipeline register. Next, data is read from the MEM/WB pipeline register and written into the register file in the middle of the datapath. Note: there is a bug in this design that is repaired in Figure 4.41.

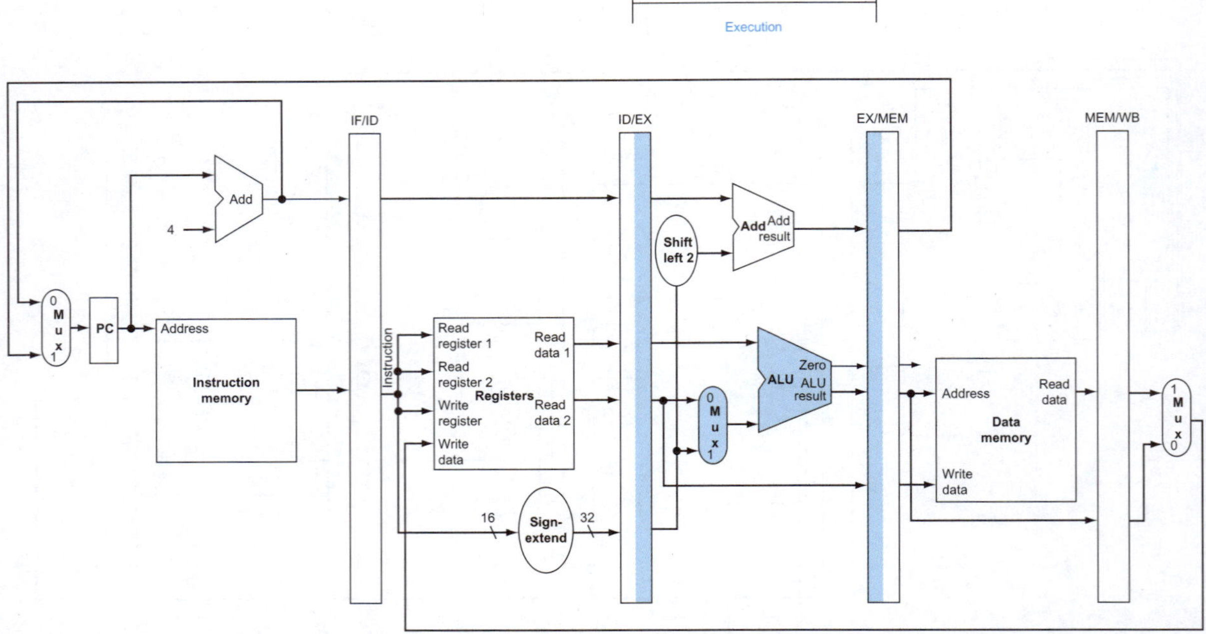

FIGURE 4.39 EX: The third pipe stage of a store instruction. Unlike the third stage of the load instruction in Figure 4.37, the second register value is loaded into the EX/MEM pipeline register to be used in the next stage. Although it wouldn't hurt to always write this second register into the EX/MEM pipeline register, we write the second register only on a store instruction to make the pipeline easier to understand.

5. *Write-back:* The bottom portion of Figure 4.40 shows the final step of the store. For this instruction, nothing happens in the write-back stage. Since every instruction behind the store is already in progress, we have no way to accelerate those instructions. Hence, an instruction passes through a stage even if there is nothing to do, because later instructions are already progressing at the maximum rate.

The store instruction again illustrates that to pass something from an early pipe stage to a later pipe stage, the information must be placed in a pipeline register; otherwise, the information is lost when the next instruction enters that pipeline stage. For the store instruction we needed to pass one of the registers read in the ID stage to the MEM stage, where it is stored in memory. The data was first placed in the ID/EX pipeline register and then passed to the EX/MEM pipeline register.

Load and store illustrate a second key point: each logical component of the datapath—such as instruction memory, register read ports, ALU, data memory, and register write port—can be used only within a *single* pipeline stage. Otherwise, we would have a *structural hazard* (see page 290). Hence these components, and their control, can be associated with a single pipeline stage.

Now we can uncover a bug in the design of the load instruction. Did you see it? Which register is changed in the final stage of the load? More specifically, which

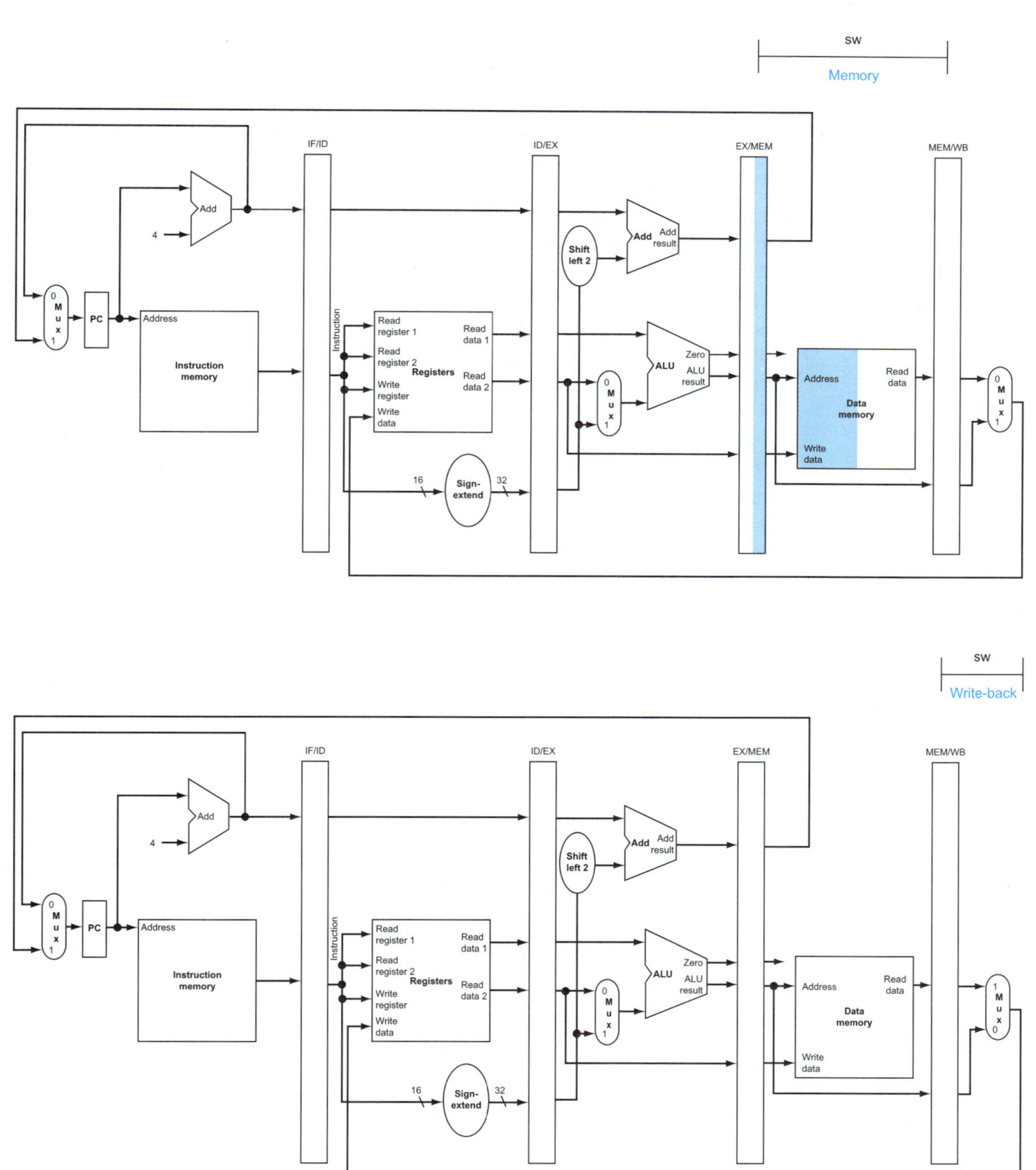

FIGURE 4.40 MEM and WB: The fourth and fifth pipe stages of a store instruction. In the fourth stage, the data is written into data memory for the store. Note that the data comes from the EX/MEM pipeline register and that nothing is changed in the MEM/WB pipeline register. Once the data is written in memory, there is nothing left for the store instruction to do, so nothing happens in stage 5.

instruction supplies the write register number? The instruction in the IF/ID pipeline register supplies the write register number, yet this instruction occurs considerably *after* the load instruction!

Hence, we need to preserve the destination register number in the load instruction. Just as store passed the register *contents* from the ID/EX to the EX/MEM pipeline registers for use in the MEM stage, load must pass the *register* number from the ID/EX through EX/MEM to the MEM/WB pipeline register for use in the WB stage. Another way to think about the passing of the register number is that to share the pipelined datapath, we need to preserve the instruction read during the IF stage, so each pipeline register contains a portion of the instruction needed for that stage and later stages.

Figure 4.41 shows the correct version of the datapath, passing the write register number first to the ID/EX register, then to the EX/MEM register, and finally to the MEM/WB register. The register number is used during the WB stage to specify the register to be written. Figure 4.42 is a single drawing of the corrected datapath, highlighting the hardware used in all five stages of the load word instruction in Figures 4.36 through 4.38. See Section 4.9 for an explanation of how to make the branch instruction work as expected.

Graphically Representing Pipelines

Pipelining can be difficult to understand, since many instructions are simultaneously executing in a single datapath in every clock cycle. To aid understanding, there are

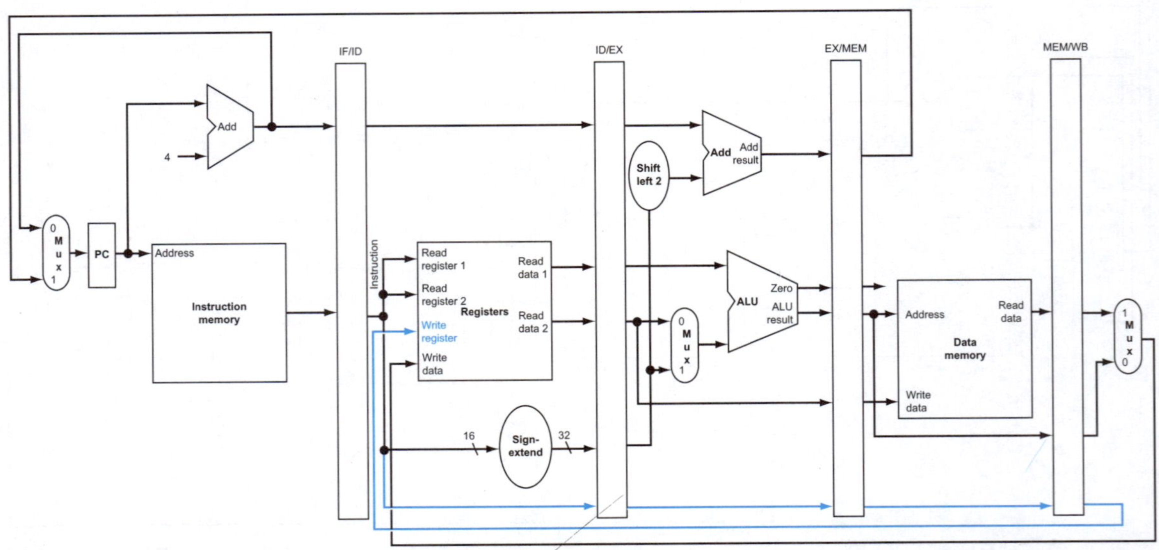

FIGURE 4.41 The corrected pipelined datapath to handle the load instruction properly. The write register number now comes from the MEM/WB pipeline register along with the data. The register number is passed from the ID pipe stage until it reaches the MEM/WB pipeline register, adding five more bits to the last three pipeline registers. This new path is shown in color.

two basic styles of pipeline figures: *multiple-clock-cycle pipeline diagrams*, such as Figure 4.34 on page 300, and *single-clock-cycle pipeline diagrams*, such as Figures 4.36 through 4.40. The multiple-clock-cycle diagrams are simpler but do not contain all the details. For example, consider the following five-instruction sequence:

```
lw      $10, 20($1)
sub     $11, $2, $3
add     $12, $3, $4
lw      $13, 24($1)
add     $14, $5, $6
```

Figure 4.43 shows the multiple-clock-cycle pipeline diagram for these instructions. Time advances from left to right across the page in these diagrams, and instructions advance from the top to the bottom of the page, similar to the laundry pipeline in Figure 4.25. A representation of the pipeline stages is placed in each portion along the instruction axis, occupying the proper clock cycles. These stylized datapaths represent the five stages of our pipeline graphically, but a rectangle naming each pipe stage works just as well. Figure 4.44 shows the more traditional version of the multiple-clock-cycle pipeline diagram. Note that Figure 4.43 shows the physical resources used at each stage, while Figure 4.44 uses the *name* of each stage.

Single-clock-cycle pipeline diagrams show the state of the entire datapath during a single clock cycle, and usually all five instructions in the pipeline are identified by labels above their respective pipeline stages. We use this type of figure to show the details of what is happening within the pipeline during each clock cycle; typically,

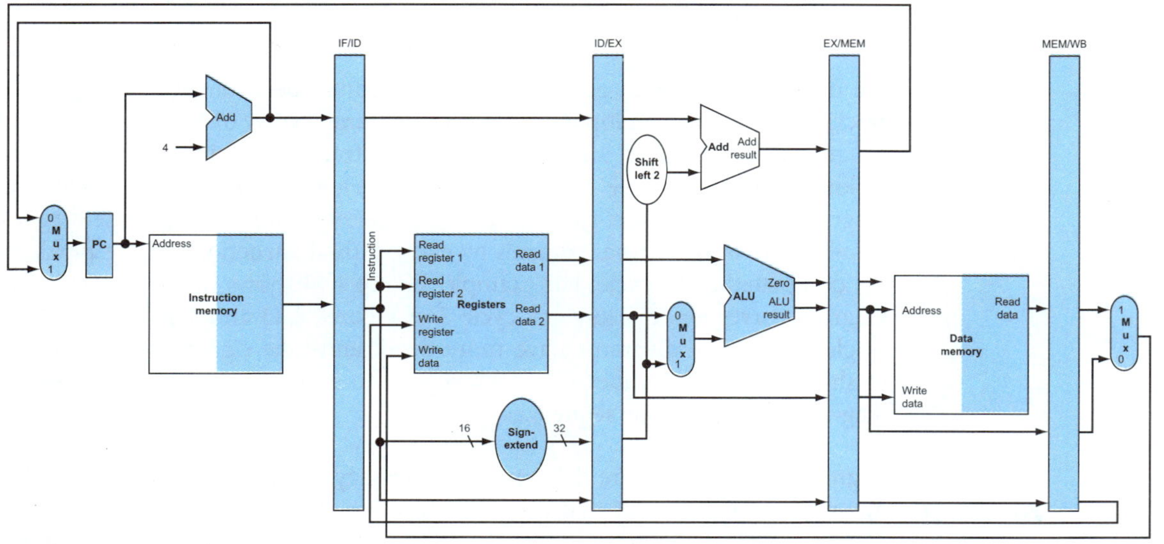

FIGURE 4.42 The portion of the datapath in Figure 4.41 that is used in all five stages of a load instruction.

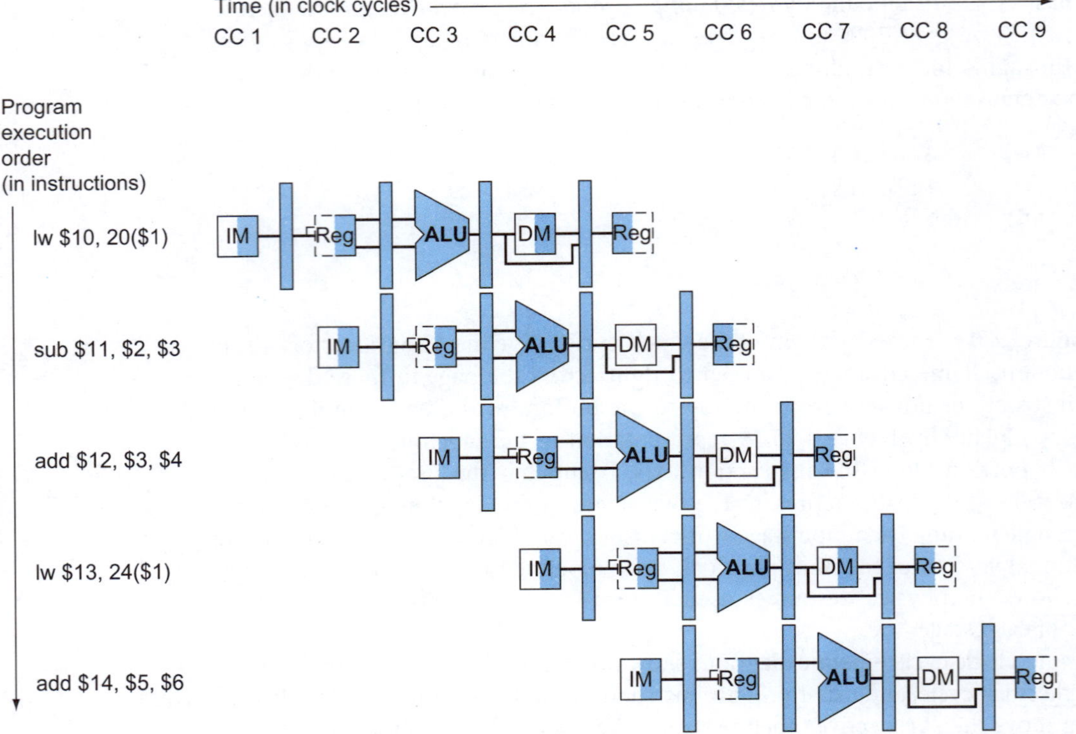

FIGURE 4.43 Multiple-clock-cycle pipeline diagram of five instructions. This style of pipeline representation shows the complete execution of instructions in a single figure. Instructions are listed in instruction execution order from top to bottom, and clock cycles move from left to right. Unlike Figure 4.28, here we show the pipeline registers between each stage. Figure 4.44 shows the traditional way to draw this diagram.

the drawings appear in groups to show pipeline operation over a sequence of clock cycles. We use multiple-clock-cycle diagrams to give overviews of pipelining situations. (⊕ Section 4.14 gives more illustrations of single-clock diagrams if you would like to see more details about Figure 4.43.) A single-clock-cycle diagram represents a vertical slice through a set of multiple-clock-cycle diagrams, showing the usage of the datapath by each of the instructions in the pipeline at the designated clock cycle. For example, Figure 4.45 shows the single-clock-cycle diagram corresponding to clock cycle 5 of Figures 4.43 and 4.44. Obviously, the single-clock-cycle diagrams have more detail and take significantly more space to show the same number of clock cycles. The exercises ask you to create such diagrams for other code sequences.

Check Yourself

A group of students were debating the efficiency of the five-stage pipeline when one student pointed out that not all instructions are active in every stage of the pipeline. After deciding to ignore the effects of hazards, they made the following four statements. Which ones are correct?

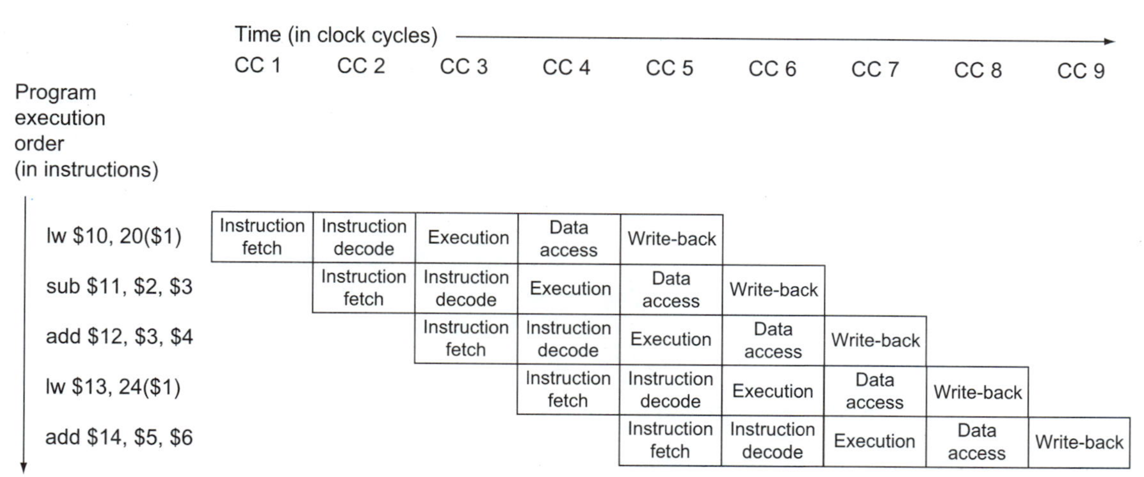

FIGURE 4.44 Traditional multiple-clock-cycle pipeline diagram of five instructions in Figure 4.43.

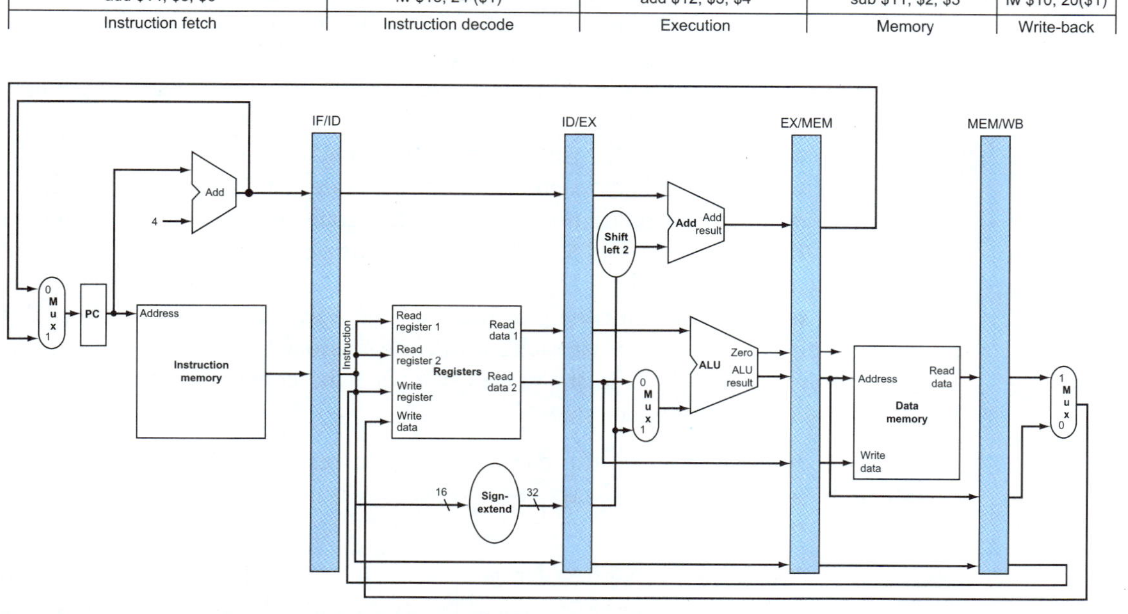

FIGURE 4.45 The single-clock-cycle diagram corresponding to clock cycle 5 of the pipeline in Figures 4.43 and 4.44. As you can see, a single-clock-cycle figure is a vertical slice through a multiple-clock-cycle diagram.

1. Allowing jumps, branches, and ALU instructions to take fewer stages than the five required by the load instruction will increase pipeline performance under all circumstances.

2. Trying to allow some instructions to take fewer cycles does not help, since the throughput is determined by the clock cycle; the number of pipe stages per instruction affects latency, not throughput.

3. You cannot make ALU instructions take fewer cycles because of the write-back of the result, but branches and jumps can take fewer cycles, so there is some opportunity for improvement.

4. Instead of trying to make instructions take fewer cycles, we should explore making the pipeline longer, so that instructions take more cycles, but the cycles are shorter. This could improve performance.

Pipelined Control

In the 6600 Computer, perhaps even more than in any previous computer, the control system is the difference.

James Thornton, *Design of a Computer: The Control Data 6600*, 1970

Just as we added control to the single-cycle datapath in Section 4.3, we now add control to the pipelined datapath. We start with a simple design that views the problem through rose-colored glasses.

The first step is to label the control lines on the existing datapath. Figure 4.46 shows those lines. We borrow as much as we can from the control for the simple datapath in Figure 4.17. In particular, we use the same ALU control logic, branch logic, destination-register-number multiplexor, and control lines. These functions are defined in Figures 4.12, 4.16, and 4.18. We reproduce the key information in Figures 4.47 through 4.49 in two pages in this section to make the following discussion easier to follow.

As was the case for the single-cycle implementation, we assume that the PC is written on each clock cycle, so there is no separate write signal for the PC. By the same argument, there are no separate write signals for the pipeline registers (IF/ID, ID/EX, EX/MEM, and MEM/WB), since the pipeline registers are also written during each clock cycle.

To specify control for the pipeline, we need only set the control values during each pipeline stage. Because each control line is associated with a component active in only a single pipeline stage, we can divide the control lines into five groups according to the pipeline stage.

1. *Instruction fetch*: The control signals to read instruction memory and to write the PC are always asserted, so there is nothing special to control in this pipeline stage.

2. *Instruction decode/register file read*: As in the previous stage, the same thing happens at every clock cycle, so there are no optional control lines to set.

3. *Execution/address calculation*: The signals to be set are RegDst, ALUOp, and ALUSrc (see Figures 4.47 and 4.48). The signals select the Result register, the ALU operation, and either Read data 2 or a sign-extended immediate for the ALU.

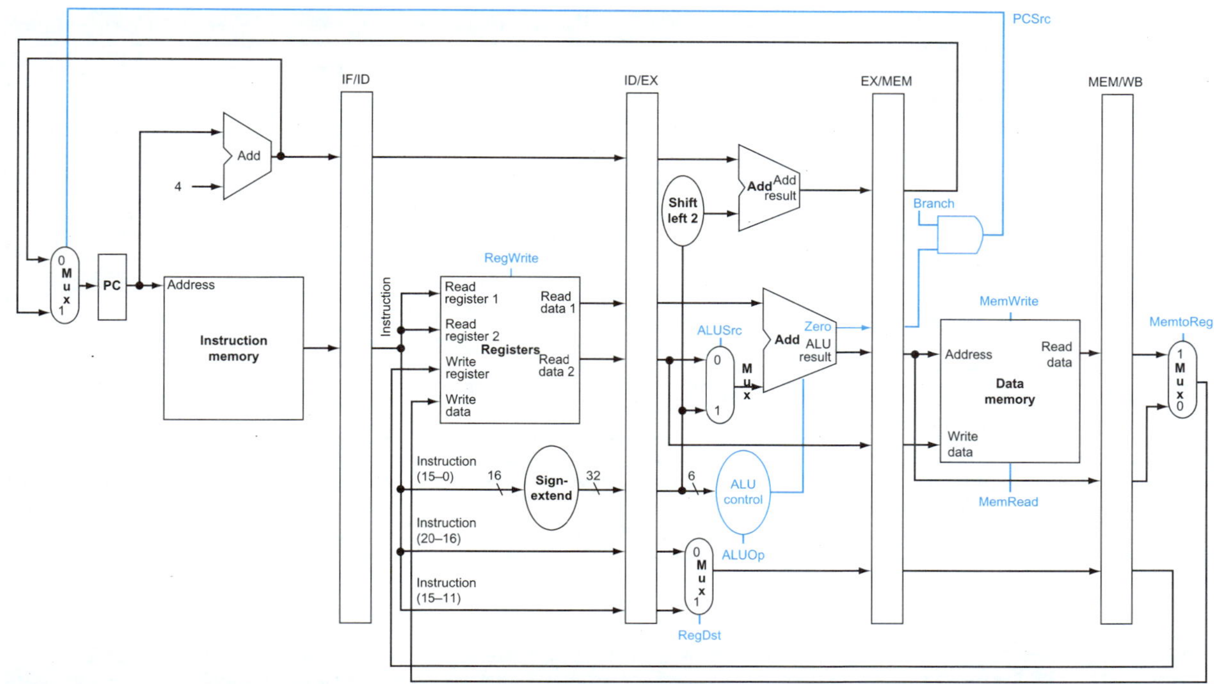

FIGURE 4.46 The pipelined datapath of Figure 4.41 with the control signals identified. This datapath borrows the control logic for PC source, register destination number, and ALU control from Section 4.4. Note that we now need the 6-bit funct field (function code) of the instruction in the EX stage as input to ALU control, so these bits must also be included in the ID/EX pipeline register. Recall that these 6 bits are also the 6 least significant bits of the immediate field in the instruction, so the ID/EX pipeline register can supply them from the immediate field since sign extension leaves these bits unchanged.

Instruction opcode	ALUOp	Instruction operation	Function code	Desired ALU action	ALU control input
LW	00	load word	XXXXXX	add	0010
SW	00	store word	XXXXXX	add	0010
Branch equal	01	branch equal	XXXXXX	subtract	0110
R-type	10	add	100000	add	0010
R-type	10	subtract	100010	subtract	0110
R-type	10	AND	100100	AND	0000
R-type	10	OR	100101	OR	0001
R-type	10	set on less than	101010	set on less than	0111

FIGURE 4.47 A copy of Figure 4.12. This figure shows how the ALU control bits are set depending on the ALUOp control bits and the different function codes for the R-type instruction.

Signal name	Effect when deasserted (0)	Effect when asserted (1)
RegDst	The register destination number for the Write register comes from the rt field (bits 20:16).	The register destination number for the Write register comes from the rd field (bits 15:11).
RegWrite	None.	The register on the Write register input is written with the value on the Write data input.
ALUSrc	The second ALU operand comes from the second register file output (Read data 2).	The second ALU operand is the sign-extended, lower 16 bits of the instruction.
PCSrc	The PC is replaced by the output of the adder that computes the value of PC + 4.	The PC is replaced by the output of the adder that computes the branch target.
MemRead	None.	Data memory contents designated by the address input are put on the Read data output.
MemWrite	None.	Data memory contents designated by the address input are replaced by the value on the Write data input.
MemtoReg	The value fed to the register Write data input comes from the ALU.	The value fed to the register Write data input comes from the data memory.

FIGURE 4.48 A copy of Figure 4.16. The function of each of seven control signals is defined. The ALU control lines (ALUOp) are defined in the second column of Figure 4.47. When a 1-bit control to a 2-way multiplexor is asserted, the multiplexor selects the input corresponding to 1. Otherwise, if the control is deasserted, the multiplexor selects the 0 input. Note that PCSrc is controlled by an AND gate in Figure 4.46. If the Branch signal and the ALU Zero signal are both set, then PCSrc is 1; otherwise, it is 0. Control sets the Branch signal only during a beq instruction; otherwise, PCSrc is set to 0.

Instruction	Execution/address calculation stage control lines				Memory access stage control lines			Write-back stage control lines	
	RegDst	ALUOp1	ALUOp0	ALUSrc	Branch	Mem-Read	Mem-Write	Reg-Write	Memto-Reg
R-format	1	1	0	0	0	0	0	1	0
lw	0	0	0	1	0	1	0	1	1
sw	X	0	0	1	0	0	1	0	X
beq	X	0	1	0	1	0	0	0	X

FIGURE 4.49 The values of the control lines are the same as in Figure 4.18, but they have been shuffled into three groups corresponding to the last three pipeline stages.

4. *Memory access:* The control lines set in this stage are Branch, MemRead, and MemWrite. The branch equal, load, and store instructions set these signals, respectively. Recall that PCSrc in Figure 4.48 selects the next sequential address unless control asserts Branch and the ALU result was 0.

5. *Write-back:* The two control lines are MemtoReg, which decides between sending the ALU result or the memory value to the register file, and RegWrite, which writes the chosen value.

Since pipelining the datapath leaves the meaning of the control lines unchanged, we can use the same control values. Figure 4.49 has the same values as in Section 4.4, but now the nine control lines are grouped by pipeline stage.

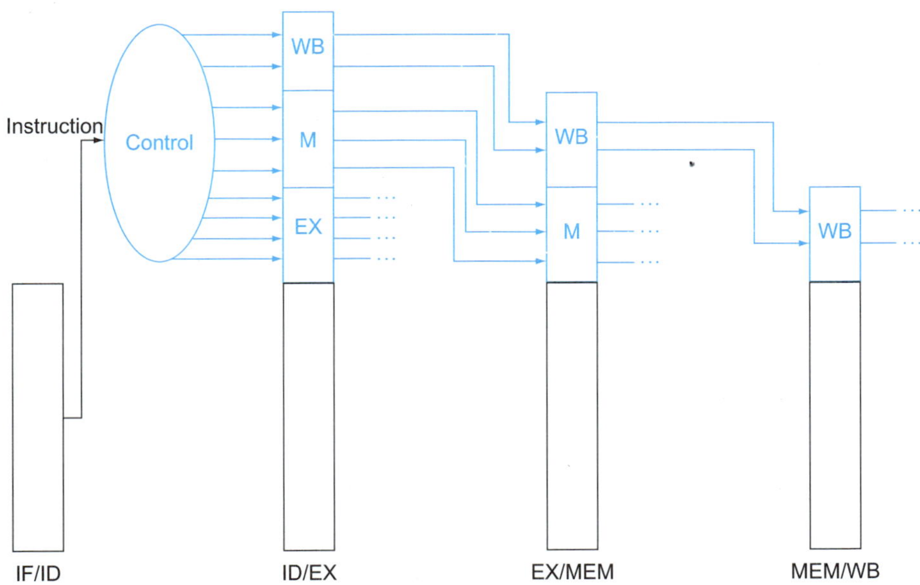

FIGURE 4.50 The control lines for the final three stages. Note that four of the nine control lines are used in the EX phase, with the remaining five control lines passed on to the EX/MEM pipeline register extended to hold the control lines; three are used during the MEM stage, and the last two are passed to MEM/WB for use in the WB stage.

Implementing control means setting the nine control lines to these values in each stage for each instruction. The simplest way to do this is to extend the pipeline registers to include control information.

Since the control lines start with the EX stage, we can create the control information during instruction decode. Figure 4.50 above shows that these control signals are then used in the appropriate pipeline stage as the instruction moves down the pipeline, just as the destination register number for loads moves down the pipeline in Figure 4.41. Figure 4.51 shows the full datapath with the extended pipeline registers and with the control lines connected to the proper stage. (⊕ **Section 4.14** gives more examples of MIPS code executing on pipelined hardware using single-clock diagrams, if you would like to see more details.)

4.8

Data Hazards: Forwarding versus Stalling

The examples in the previous section show the power of pipelined execution and how the hardware performs the task. It's now time to take off the rose-colored glasses and look at what happens with real programs. The instructions in Figures 4.43 through 4.45 were independent; none of them used the results calculated by any of the others. Yet in Section 4.6, we saw that data hazards are obstacles to pipelined execution.

What do you mean, why's it got to be built? It's a bypass. You've got to build bypasses.

Douglas Adams, *The Hitchhiker's Guide to the Galaxy,* 1979

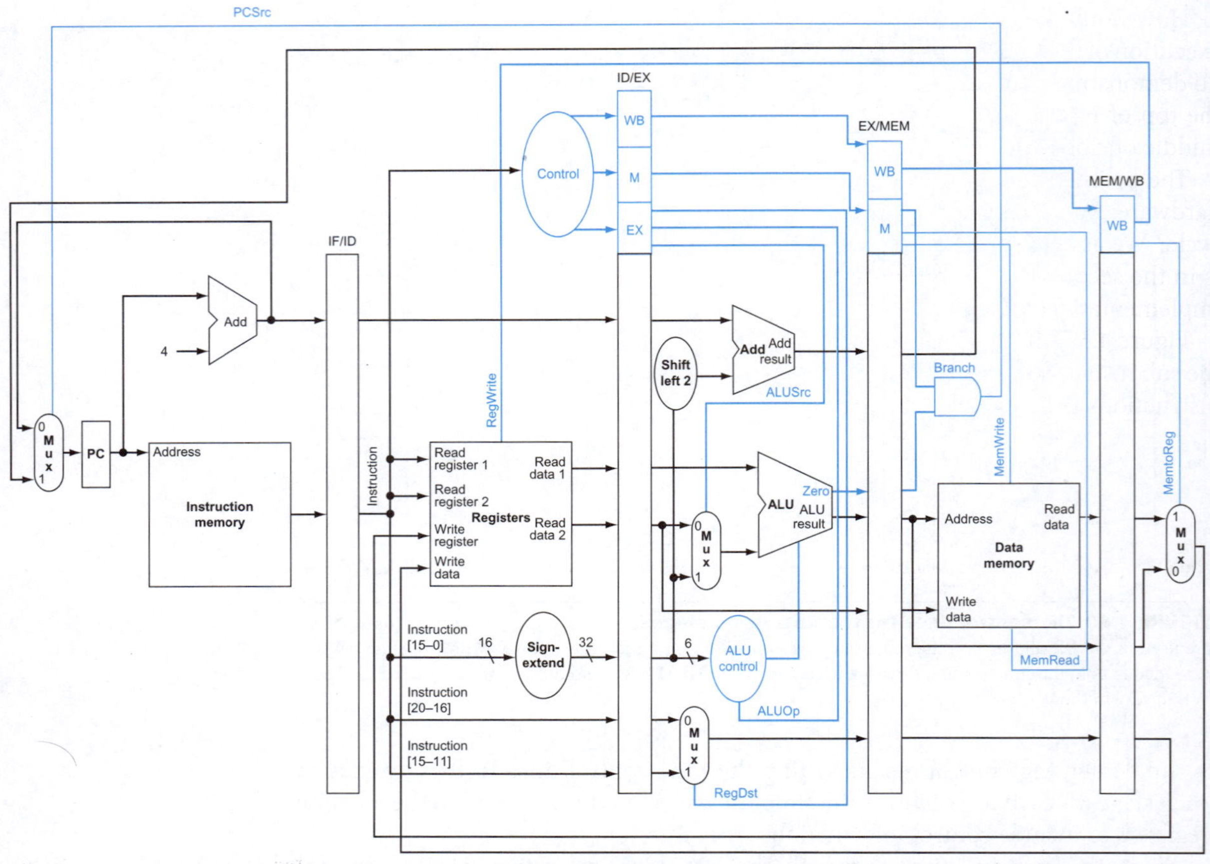

FIGURE 4.51 The pipelined datapath of Figure 4.46, with the control signals connected to the control portions of the pipeline registers. The control values for the last three stages are created during the instruction decode stage and then placed in the ID/EX pipeline register. The control lines for each pipe stage are used, and remaining control lines are then passed to the next pipeline stage.

Let's look at a sequence with many dependences, shown in color:

```
sub    $2, $1,$3      # Register $2 written by sub
and    $12,$2,$5      # 1st operand($2) depends on sub
or     $13,$6,$2      # 2nd operand($2) depends on sub
add    $14,$2,$2      # 1st($2) & 2nd($2) depend on sub
sw     $15,100($2)    # Base ($2) depends on sub
```

The last four instructions are all dependent on the result in register $2 of the first instruction. If register $2 had the value 10 before the subtract instruction and −20 afterwards, the programmer intends that −20 will be used in the following instructions that refer to register $2.

How would this sequence perform with our pipeline? Figure 4.52 illustrates the execution of these instructions using a multiple-clock-cycle pipeline representation. To demonstrate the execution of this instruction sequence in our current pipeline, the top of Figure 4.52 shows the value of register $2, which changes during the middle of clock cycle 5, when the sub instruction writes its result.

The potential hazard of add can be resolved by the design of the register file hardware: What happens when a register is read and written in the same clock cycle? We assume that the write is in the first half of the clock cycle and the read is in the second half, so the read delivers what is written. As is the case for many implementations of register files, we have no data hazard in this case.

Figure 4.52 shows that the values read for register $2 would *not* be the result of the sub instruction unless the read occurred during clock cycle 5 or later. Thus, the instructions that would get the correct value of −20 are add and sw; the AND and

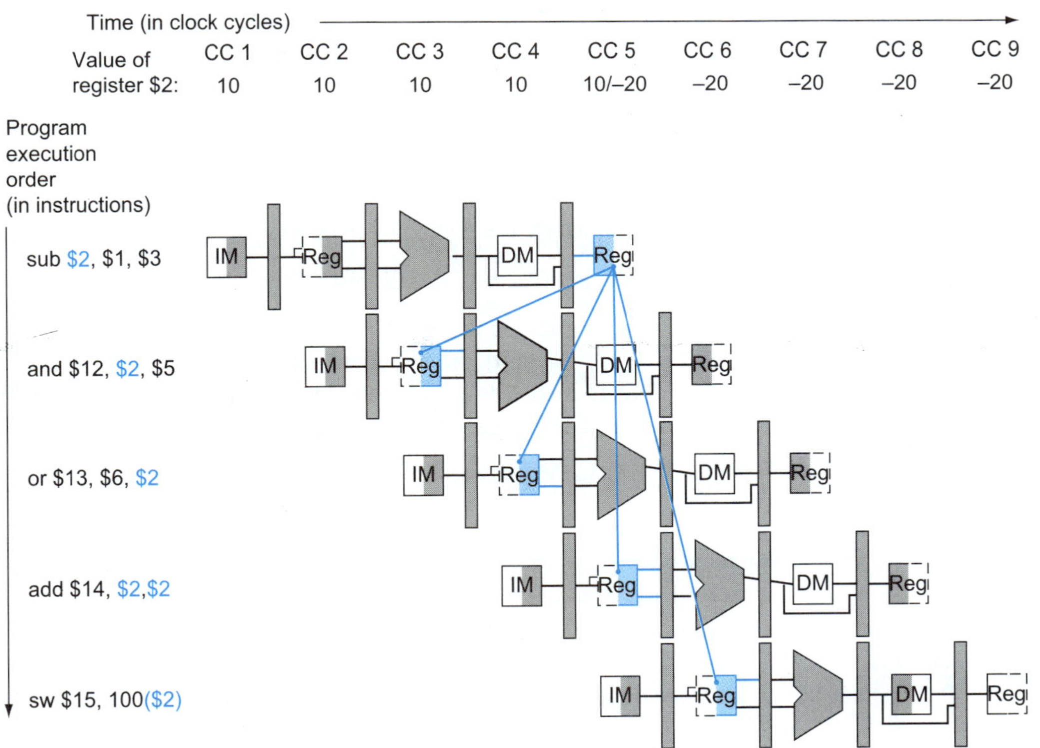

FIGURE 4.52 Pipelined dependences in a five-instruction sequence using simplified datapaths to show the dependences. All the dependent actions are shown in color, and "CC 1" at the top of the figure means clock cycle 1. The first instruction writes into $2, and all the following instructions read $2. This register is written in clock cycle 5, so the proper value is unavailable before clock cycle 5. (A read of a register during a clock cycle returns the value written at the end of the first half of the cycle, when such a write occurs.) The colored lines from the top datapath to the lower ones show the dependences. Those that must go backward in time are *pipeline data hazards*.

OR instructions would get the incorrect value 10! Using this style of drawing, such problems become apparent when a dependence line goes backward in time.

As mentioned in Section 4.6, the desired result is available at the end of the EX stage or clock cycle 3. When is the data actually needed by the AND and OR instructions? At the beginning of the EX stage, or clock cycles 4 and 5, respectively. Thus, we can execute this segment without stalls if we simply *forward* the data as soon as it is available to any units that need it before it is available to read from the register file.

How does forwarding work? For simplicity in the rest of this section, we consider only the challenge of forwarding to an operation in the EX stage, which may be either an ALU operation or an effective address calculation. This means that when an instruction tries to use a register in its EX stage that an earlier instruction intends to write in its WB stage, we actually need the values as inputs to the ALU.

A notation that names the fields of the pipeline registers allows for a more precise notation of dependences. For example, "ID/EX.RegisterRs" refers to the number of one register whose value is found in the pipeline register ID/EX; that is, the one from the first read port of the register file. The first part of the name, to the left of the period, is the name of the pipeline register; the second part is the name of the field in that register. Using this notation, the two pairs of hazard conditions are

1a. EX/MEM.RegisterRd = ID/EX.RegisterRs

1b. EX/MEM.RegisterRd = ID/EX.RegisterRt

2a. MEM/WB.RegisterRd = ID/EX.RegisterRs

2b. MEM/WB.RegisterRd = ID/EX.RegisterRt

The first hazard in the sequence on page 316 is on register $2, between the result of sub $2,$1,$3 and the first read operand of and $12,$2,$5. This hazard can be detected when the and instruction is in the EX stage and the prior instruction is in the MEM stage, so this is hazard 1a:

$$\text{EX/MEM.RegisterRd} = \text{ID/EX.RegisterRs} = \$2$$

EXAMPLE

Dependence Detection

Classify the dependences in this sequence from page 316:

```
sub $2,   $1, $3   # Register $2 set by sub
and $12,  $2, $5   # 1st operand($2) set by sub
or  $13,  $6, $2   # 2nd operand($2) set by sub
add $14,  $2, $2   # 1st($2) & 2nd($2) set by sub
sw  $15,  100($2)  # Index($2) set by sub
```

As mentioned above, the sub-and is a type 1a hazard. The remaining hazards are as follows:

- The sub-or is a type 2b hazard:

  $$\text{MEM/WB.RegisterRd} = \text{ID/EX.RegisterRt} = \$2$$

- The two dependences on sub-add are not hazards because the register file supplies the proper data during the ID stage of add.

- There is no data hazard between sub and sw because sw reads $2 the clock cycle *after* sub writes $2.

Because some instructions do not write registers, this policy is inaccurate; sometimes it would forward when it shouldn't. One solution is simply to check to see if the RegWrite signal will be active: examining the WB control field of the pipeline register during the EX and MEM stages determines whether RegWrite is asserted. Recall that MIPS requires that every use of $0 as an operand must yield an operand value of 0. In the event that an instruction in the pipeline has $0 as its destination (for example, sll $0, $1, 2), we want to avoid forwarding its possibly nonzero result value. Not forwarding results destined for $0 frees the assembly programmer and the compiler of any requirement to avoid using $0 as a destination. The conditions above thus work properly as long we add EX/MEM. RegisterRd $\neq$ 0 to the first hazard condition and MEM/WB.RegisterRd $\neq$ 0 to the second.

Now that we can detect hazards, half of the problem is resolved—but we must still forward the proper data.

Figure 4.53 shows the dependences between the pipeline registers and the inputs to the ALU for the same code sequence as in Figure 4.52. The change is that the dependence begins from a *pipeline* register, rather than waiting for the WB stage to write the register file. Thus, the required data exists in time for later instructions, with the pipeline registers holding the data to be forwarded.

If we can take the inputs to the ALU from *any* pipeline register rather than just ID/EX, then we can forward the proper data. By adding multiplexors to the input of the ALU, and with the proper controls, we can run the pipeline at full speed in the presence of these data dependences.

For now, we will assume the only instructions we need to forward are the four R-format instructions: add, sub, AND, and OR. Figure 4.54 shows a close-up of the ALU and pipeline register before and after adding forwarding. Figure 4.55 shows the values of the control lines for the ALU multiplexors that select either the register file values or one of the forwarded values.

This forwarding control will be in the EX stage, because the ALU forwarding multiplexors are found in that stage. Thus, we must pass the operand register numbers from the ID stage via the ID/EX pipeline register to determine whether to forward values. We already have the rt field (bits 20–16). Before forwarding, the ID/EX register had no need to include space to hold the rs field. Hence, rs (bits 25–21) is added to ID/EX.

Time (in clock cycles) →

	CC 1	CC 2	CC 3	CC 4	CC 5	CC 6	CC 7	CC 8	CC 9
Value of register $2:	10	10	10	10	10/–20	–20	–20	–20	–20
Value of EX/MEM:	X	X	X	–20	X	X	X	X	X
Value of MEM/WB:	X	X	X	X	–20	X	X	X	X

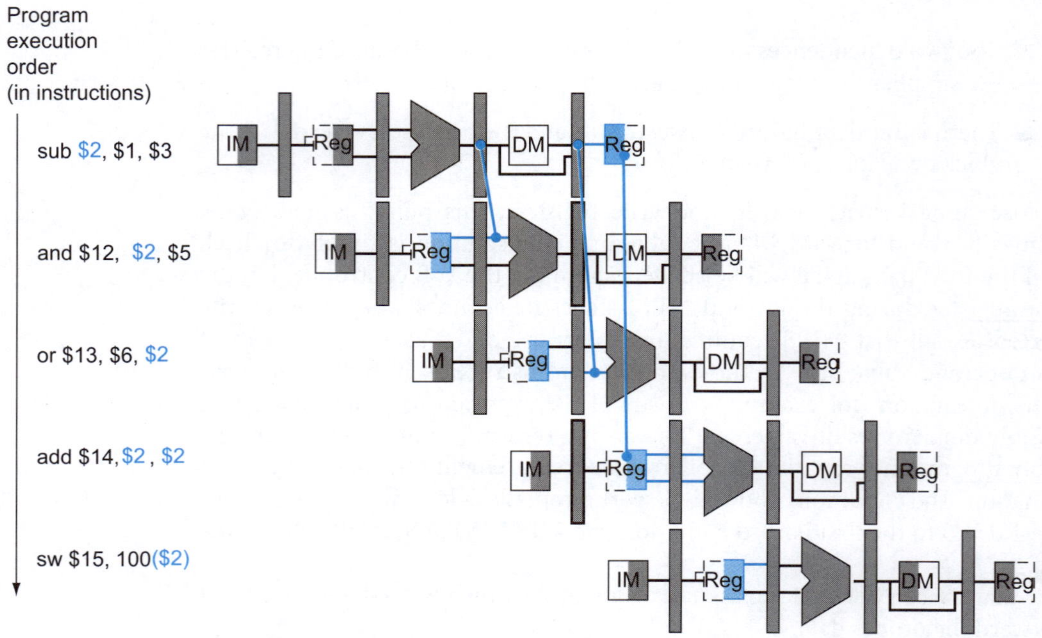

Program
execution
order
(in instructions)

FIGURE 4.53 The dependences between the pipeline registers move forward in time, so it is possible to supply the inputs to the ALU needed by the AND instruction and OR instruction by forwarding the results found in the pipeline registers. The values in the pipeline registers show that the desired value is available before it is written into the register file. We assume that the register file forwards values that are read and written during the same clock cycle, so the add does not stall, but the values come from the register file instead of a pipeline register. Register file "forwarding"—that is, the read gets the value of the write in that clock cycle—is why clock cycle 5 shows register $2 having the value 10 at the beginning and – 20 at the end of the clock cycle. As in the rest of this section, we handle all forwarding except for the value to be stored by a store instruction.

Let's now write both the conditions for detecting hazards and the control signals to resolve them:

1. *EX hazard:*

```
if (EX/MEM.RegWrite
and (EX/MEM.RegisterRd ≠ 0)
and (EX/MEM.RegisterRd = ID/EX.RegisterRs)) ForwardA = 10

if (EX/MEM.RegWrite
and (EX/MEM.RegisterRd ≠ 0)
and (EX/MEM.RegisterRd = ID/EX.RegisterRt)) ForwardB = 10
```

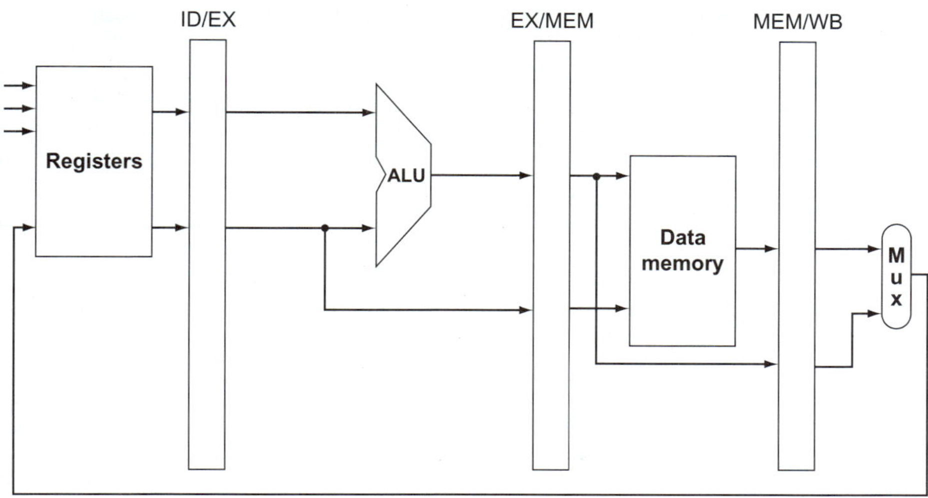

a. No forwarding

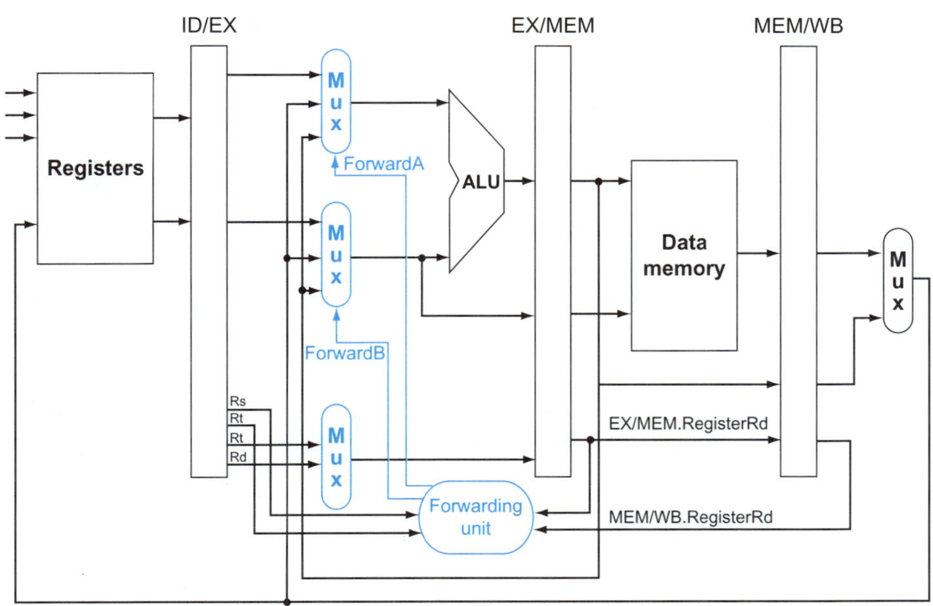

b. With forwarding

FIGURE 4.54 On the top are the ALU and pipeline registers before adding forwarding. On the bottom, the multiplexors have been expanded to add the forwarding paths, and we show the forwarding unit. The new hardware is shown in color. This figure is a stylized drawing, however, leaving out details from the full datapath such as the sign extension hardware. Note that the ID/EX.RegisterRt field is shown twice, once to connect to the Mux and once to the forwarding unit, but it is a single signal. As in the earlier discussion, this ignores forwarding of a store value to a store instruction. Also note that this mechanism works for slt instructions as well.

Mux control	Source	Explanation
ForwardA = 00	ID/EX	The first ALU operand comes from the register file.
ForwardA = 10	EX/MEM	The first ALU operand is forwarded from the prior ALU result.
ForwardA = 01	MEM/WB	The first ALU operand is forwarded from data memory or an earlier ALU result.
ForwardB = 00	ID/EX	The second ALU operand comes from the register file.
ForwardB = 10	EX/MEM	The second ALU operand is forwarded from the prior ALU result.
ForwardB = 01	MEM/WB	The second ALU operand is forwarded from data memory or an earlier ALU result.

FIGURE 4.55 The control values for the forwarding multiplexors in Figure 4.54. The signed immediate that is another input to the ALU is described in the *Elaboration* at the end of this section.

Note that the EX/MEM.RegisterRd field is the register destination for either an ALU instruction (which comes from the Rd field of the instruction) or a load (which comes from the Rt field).

This case forwards the result from the previous instruction to either input of the ALU. If the previous instruction is going to write to the register file, and the write register number matches the read register number of ALU inputs A or B, provided it is not register 0, then steer the multiplexor to pick the value instead from the pipeline register EX/MEM.

2. *MEM hazard:*

```
if (MEM/WB.RegWrite
and (MEM/WB.RegisterRd ≠  0)
and (MEM/WB.RegisterRd = ID/EX.RegisterRs)) ForwardA = 01

if (MEM/WB.RegWrite
and (MEM/WB.RegisterRd ≠  0)
and (MEM/WB.RegisterRd = ID/EX.RegisterRt)) ForwardB = 01
```

As mentioned above, there is no hazard in the WB stage, because we assume that the register file supplies the correct result if the instruction in the ID stage reads the same register written by the instruction in the WB stage. Such a register file performs another form of forwarding, but it occurs within the register file.

One complication is potential data hazards between the result of the instruction in the WB stage, the result of the instruction in the MEM stage, and the source operand of the instruction in the ALU stage. For example, when summing a vector of numbers in a single register, a sequence of instructions will all read and write to the same register:

```
add $1,$1,$2
add $1,$1,$3
add $1,$1,$4
 . . .
```

In this case, the result is forwarded from the MEM stage because the result in the MEM stage is the more recent result. Thus, the control for the MEM hazard would be (with the additions highlighted):

```
if (MEM/WB.RegWrite
and (MEM/WB.RegisterRd ≠ 0)
and not(EX/MEM.RegWrite and (EX/MEM.RegisterRd ≠ 0)
       and (EX/MEM.RegisterRd ≠ ID/EX.RegisterRs))
and (MEM/WB.RegisterRd = ID/EX.RegisterRs)) ForwardA = 01

if (MEM/WB.RegWrite
and (MEM/WB.RegisterRd ≠ 0)
and not(EX/MEM.RegWrite and (EX/MEM.RegisterRd ≠ 0)
       and (EX/MEM.RegisterRd ≠ ID/EX.RegisterRt))
and (MEM/WB.RegisterRd = ID/EX.RegisterRt)) ForwardB = 01
```

Figure 4.56 shows the hardware necessary to support forwarding for operations that use results during the EX stage. Note that the EX/MEM.RegisterRd field is the register destination for either an ALU instruction (which comes from the Rd field of the instruction) or a load (which comes from the Rt field).

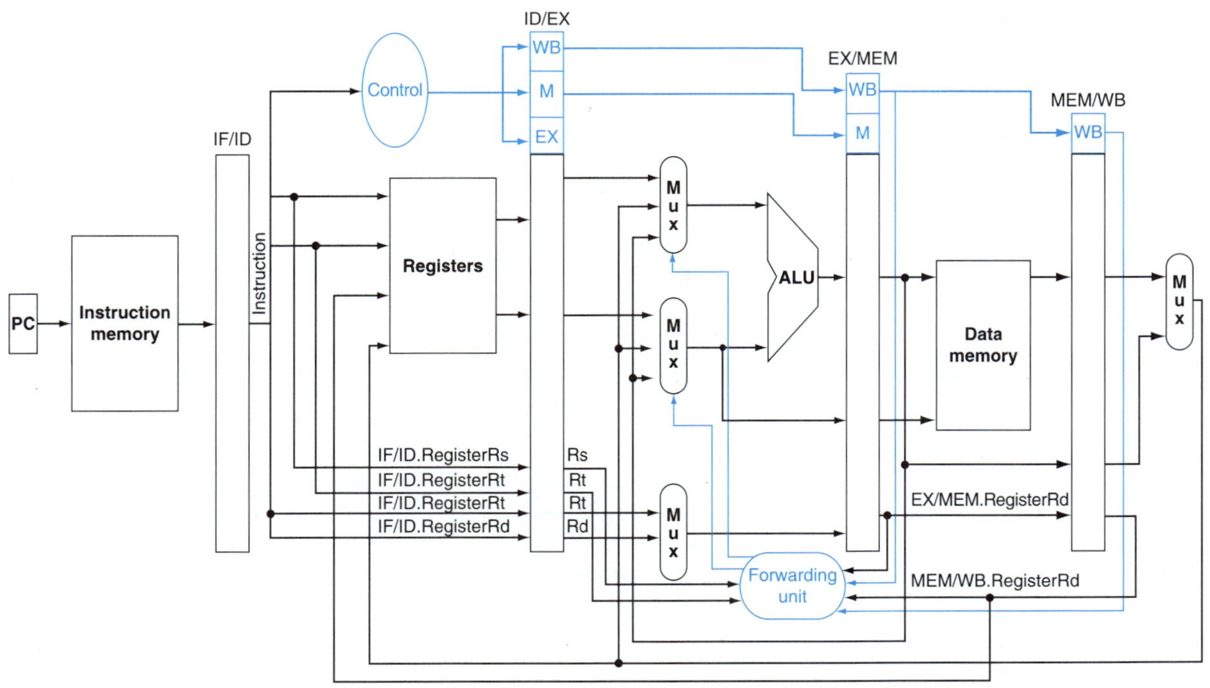

FIGURE 4.56 The datapath modified to resolve hazards via forwarding. Compared with the datapath in Figure 4.51, the additions are the multiplexors to the inputs to the ALU. This figure is a more stylized drawing, however, leaving out details from the full datapath, such as the branch hardware and the sign extension hardware.

⊕ **Section 4.14** shows two pieces of MIPS code with hazards that cause forwarding, if you would like to see more illustrated examples using single-cycle pipeline drawings.

Elaboration: Forwarding can also help with hazards when store instructions are dependent on other instructions. Since they use just one data value during the MEM stage, forwarding is easy. However, consider loads immediately followed by stores, useful when performing memory-to-memory copies in the MIPS architecture. Since copies are frequent, we need to add more forwarding hardware to make them run faster. If we were to redraw Figure 4.53, replacing the sub and AND instructions with lw and sw, we would see that it is possible to avoid a stall, since the data exists in the MEM/WB register of a load instruction in time for its use in the MEM stage of a store instruction. We would need to add forwarding into the memory access stage for this option. We leave this modification as an exercise to the reader.

In addition, the signed-immediate input to the ALU, needed by loads and stores, is missing from the datapath in Figure 4.56. Since central control decides between register and immediate, and since the forwarding unit chooses the pipeline register for a register

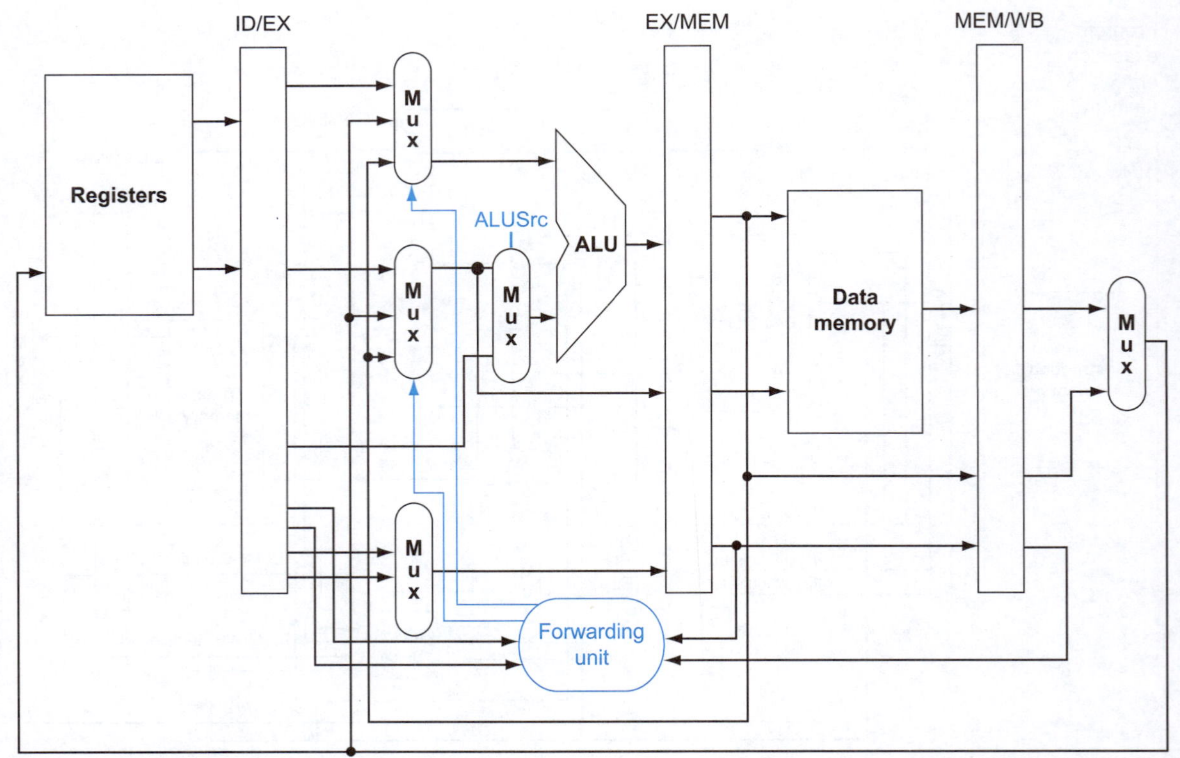

FIGURE 4.57 A close-up of the datapath in Figure 4.54 shows a 2:1 multiplexor, which has been added to select the signed immediate as an ALU input.

input to the ALU, the easiest solution is to add a 2:1 multiplexor that chooses between the ForwardB multiplexor output and the signed immediate. Figure 4.57 shows this addition.

Data Hazards and Stalls

As we said in Section 4.6, one case where forwarding cannot save the day is when an instruction tries to read a register following a load instruction that writes the same register. Figure 4.58 illustrates the problem. The data is still being read from memory in clock cycle 4 while the ALU is performing the operation for the following instruction. Something must stall the pipeline for the combination of load followed by an instruction that reads its result.

If at first you don't succeed, redefine success.

Anonymous

Hence, in addition to a forwarding unit, we need a *hazard detection unit*. It operates during the ID stage so that it can insert the stall between the load and its

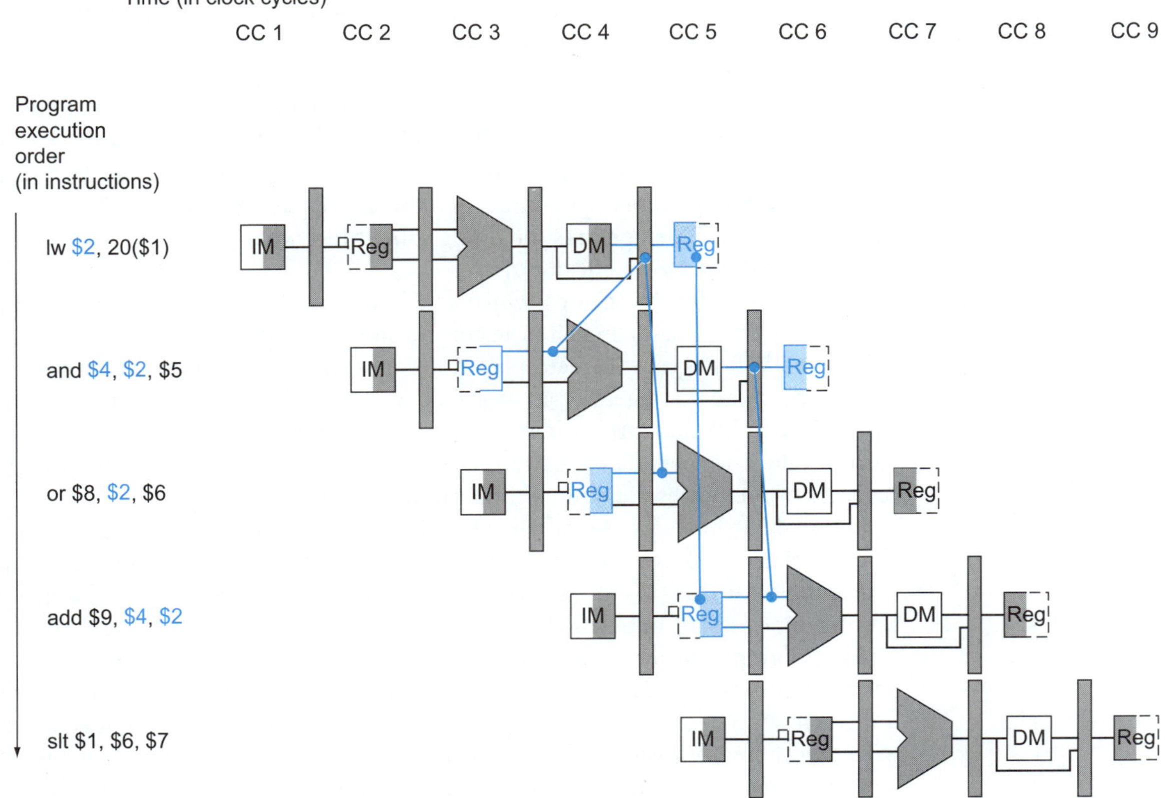

FIGURE 4.58 A pipelined sequence of instructions. Since the dependence between the load and the following instruction (and) goes backward in time, this hazard cannot be solved by forwarding. Hence, this combination must result in a stall by the hazard detection unit.

use. Checking for load instructions, the control for the hazard detection unit is this single condition:

```
if (ID/EX.MemRead and
   ((ID/EX.RegisterRt = IF/ID.RegisterRs) or
    (ID/EX.RegisterRt = IF/ID.RegisterRt)))
    stall the pipeline
```

The first line tests to see if the instruction is a load: the only instruction that reads data memory is a load. The next two lines check to see if the destination register field of the load in the EX stage matches either source register of the instruction in the ID stage. If the condition holds, the instruction stalls one clock cycle. After this 1-cycle stall, the forwarding logic can handle the dependence and execution proceeds. (If there were no forwarding, then the instructions in Figure 4.58 would need another stall cycle.)

If the instruction in the ID stage is stalled, then the instruction in the IF stage must also be stalled; otherwise, we would lose the fetched instruction. Preventing these two instructions from making progress is accomplished simply by preventing the PC register and the IF/ID pipeline register from changing. Provided these registers are preserved, the instruction in the IF stage will continue to be read using the same PC, and the registers in the ID stage will continue to be read using the same instruction fields in the IF/ID pipeline register. Returning to our favorite analogy, it's as if you restart the washer with the same clothes and let the dryer continue tumbling empty. Of course, like the dryer, the back half of the pipeline starting with the EX stage must be doing something; what it is doing is executing instructions that have no effect: **nops**.

nop An instruction that does no operation to change state.

How can we insert these nops, which act like bubbles, into the pipeline? In Figure 4.49, we see that deasserting all nine control signals (setting them to 0) in the EX, MEM, and WB stages will create a "do nothing" or nop instruction. By identifying the hazard in the ID stage, we can insert a bubble into the pipeline by changing the EX, MEM, and WB control fields of the ID/EX pipeline register to 0. These benign control values are percolated forward at each clock cycle with the proper effect: no registers or memories are written if the control values are all 0.

Figure 4.59 shows what really happens in the hardware: the pipeline execution slot associated with the AND instruction is turned into a nop and all instructions beginning with the AND instruction are delayed one cycle. Like an air bubble in a water pipe, a stall bubble delays everything behind it and proceeds down the instruction pipe one stage each cycle until it exits at the end. In this example, the hazard forces the AND and OR instructions to repeat in clock cycle 4 what they did in clock cycle 3: AND reads registers and decodes, and OR is refetched from instruction memory. Such repeated work is what a stall looks like, but its effect is to stretch the time of the AND and OR instructions and delay the fetch of the add instruction.

Figure 4.60 highlights the pipeline connections for both the hazard detection unit and the forwarding unit. As before, the forwarding unit controls the ALU

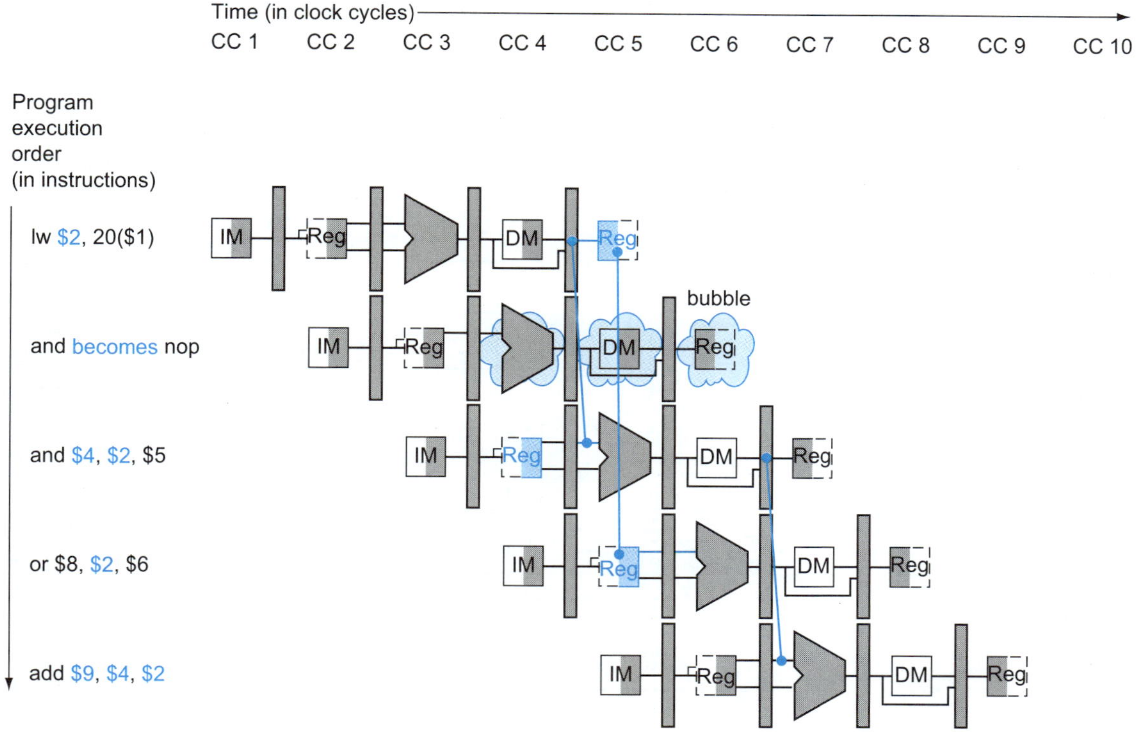

FIGURE 4.59 The way stalls are really inserted into the pipeline. A bubble is inserted beginning in clock cycle 4, by changing the `and` instruction to a nop. Note that the `and` instruction is really fetched and decoded in clock cycles 2 and 3, but its EX stage is delayed until clock cycle 5 (versus the unstalled position in clock cycle 4). Likewise the `OR` instruction is fetched in clock cycle 3, but its ID stage is delayed until clock cycle 5 (versus the unstalled clock cycle 4 position). After insertion of the bubble, all the dependences go forward in time and no further hazards occur.

multiplexors to replace the value from a general-purpose register with the value from the proper pipeline register. The hazard detection unit controls the writing of the PC and IF/ID registers plus the multiplexor that chooses between the real control values and all 0s. The hazard detection unit stalls and deasserts the control fields if the load-use hazard test above is true. Section 4.14 gives an example of MIPS code with hazards that causes stalling, illustrated using single-clock pipeline diagrams, if you would like to see more details.

Although the compiler generally relies upon the hardware to resolve hazards and thereby ensure correct execution, the compiler must understand the pipeline to achieve the best performance. Otherwise, unexpected stalls will reduce the performance of the compiled code.

The BIG Picture

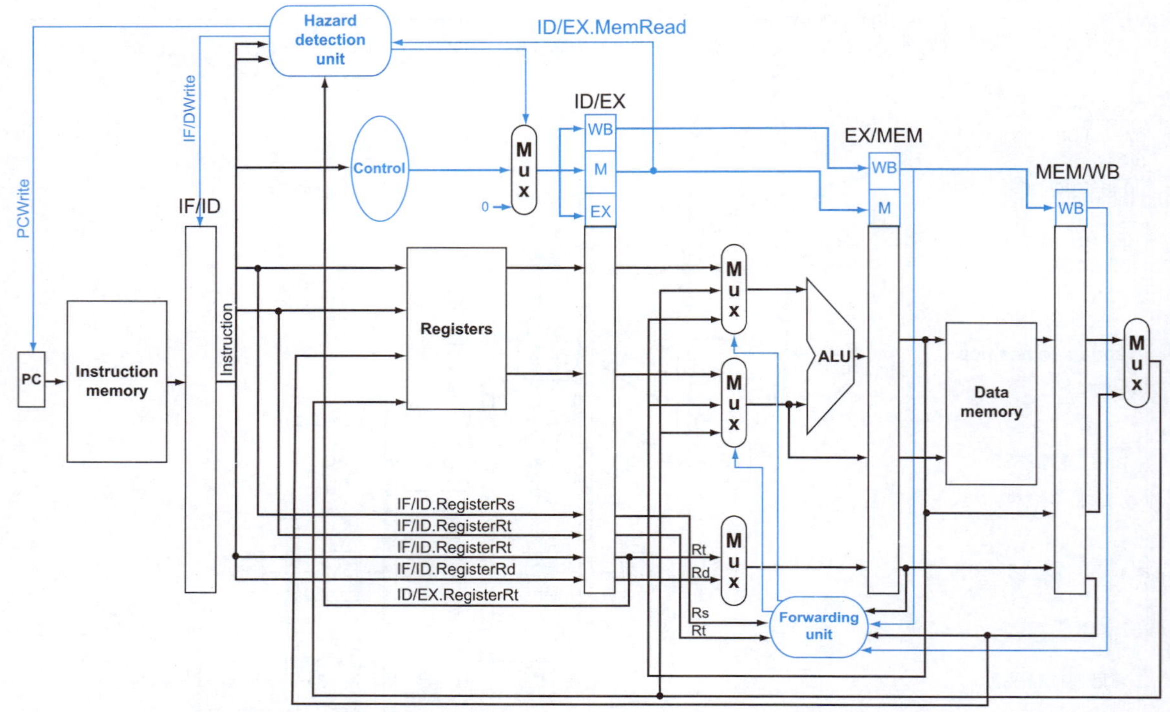

FIGURE 4.60 Pipelined control overview, showing the two multiplexors for forwarding, the hazard detection unit, and the forwarding unit. Although the ID and EX stages have been simplified—the sign-extended immediate and branch logic are missing—this drawing gives the essence of the forwarding hardware requirements.

Elaboration: Regarding the remark earlier about setting control lines to 0 to avoid writing registers or memory: only the signals RegWrite and MemWrite need be 0, while the other control signals can be don't cares.

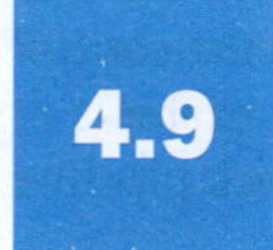

There are a thousand hacking at the branches of evil to one who is striking at the root.

Henry David Thoreau, *Walden*, 1854

4.9   Control Hazards

Thus far, we have limited our concern to hazards involving arithmetic operations and data transfers. However, as we saw in Section 4.6, there are also pipeline hazards involving branches. Figure 4.61 shows a sequence of instructions and indicates when the branch would occur in this pipeline. An instruction must be fetched at every clock cycle to sustain the pipeline, yet in our design the decision about whether to branch doesn't occur until the MEM pipeline stage. As mentioned in Section 4.6,

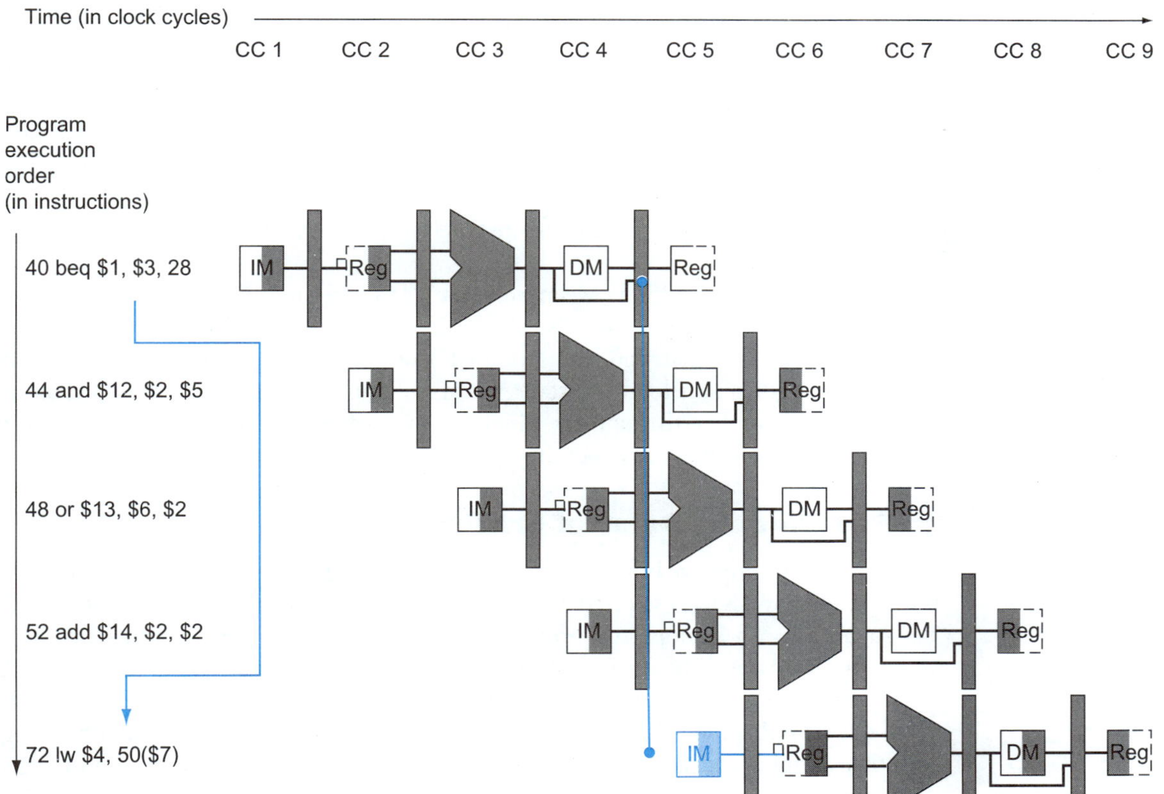

FIGURE 4.61 The impact of the pipeline on the branch instruction. The numbers to the left of the instruction (40, 44, ...) are the addresses of the instructions. Since the branch instruction decides whether to branch in the MEM stage—clock cycle 4 for the beq instruction above—the three sequential instructions that follow the branch will be fetched and begin execution. Without intervention, those three following instructions will begin execution before beq branches to lw at location 72. (Figure 4.31 assumed extra hardware to reduce the control hazard to one clock cycle; this figure uses the nonoptimized datapath.)

this delay in determining the proper instruction to fetch is called a *control hazard* or *branch hazard*, in contrast to the *data hazards* we have just examined.

This section on control hazards is shorter than the previous sections on data hazards. The reasons are that control hazards are relatively simple to understand, they occur less frequently than data hazards, and there is nothing as effective against control hazards as forwarding is against data hazards. Hence, we use simpler schemes. We look at two schemes for resolving control hazards and one optimization to improve these schemes.

flush To discard instructions in a pipeline, usually due to an unexpected event.

Assume Branch Not Taken

As we saw in Section 4.6, stalling until the branch is complete is too slow. One improvement over branch stalling is to **predict** that the branch will not be taken and thus continue execution down the sequential instruction stream. If the branch is taken, the instructions that are being fetched and decoded must be discarded. Execution continues at the branch target. If branches are untaken half the time, and if it costs little to discard the instructions, this optimization halves the cost of control hazards.

To discard instructions, we merely change the original control values to 0s, much as we did to stall for a load-use data hazard. The difference is that we must also change the three instructions in the IF, ID, and EX stages when the branch reaches the MEM stage; for load-use stalls, we just change control to 0 in the ID stage and let them percolate through the pipeline. Discarding instructions, then, means we must be able to **flush** instructions in the IF, ID, and EX stages of the pipeline.

Reducing the Delay of Branches

One way to improve branch performance is to reduce the cost of the taken branch. Thus far, we have assumed the next PC for a branch is selected in the MEM stage, but if we move the branch execution earlier in the pipeline, then fewer instructions need be flushed. The MIPS architecture was designed to support fast single-cycle branches that could be pipelined with a small branch penalty. The designers observed that many branches rely only on simple tests (equality or sign, for example) and that such tests do not require a full ALU operation but can be done with at most a few gates. When a more complex branch decision is required, a separate instruction that uses an ALU to perform a comparison is required—a situation that is similar to the use of condition codes for branches (see Chapter 2).

Moving the branch decision up requires two actions to occur earlier: computing the branch target address and evaluating the branch decision. The easy part of this change is to move up the branch address calculation. We already have the PC value and the immediate field in the IF/ID pipeline register, so we just move the branch adder from the EX stage to the ID stage; of course, the branch target address calculation will be performed for all instructions, but only used when needed.

The harder part is the branch decision itself. For branch equal, we would compare the two registers read during the ID stage to see if they are equal. Equality can be tested by first exclusive ORing their respective bits and then ORing all the results. (A zero output of the OR gate means the two registers are equal.) Moving the branch test to the ID stage implies additional forwarding and hazard detection hardware, since a branch dependent on a result still in the pipeline must still work properly with this optimization. For example, to implement branch on equal (and its inverse), we will need to forward results to the equality test logic that operates during ID. There are two complicating factors:

1. During ID, we must decode the instruction, decide whether a bypass to the equality unit is needed, and complete the equality comparison so that if the instruction is a branch, we can set the PC to the branch target address.

Forwarding for the operands of branches was formerly handled by the ALU forwarding logic, but the introduction of the equality test unit in ID will require new forwarding logic. Note that the bypassed source operands of a branch can come from either the ALU/MEM or MEM/WB pipeline latches.

2. Because the values in a branch comparison are needed during ID but may be produced later in time, it is possible that a data hazard can occur and a stall will be needed. For example, if an ALU instruction immediately preceding a branch produces one of the operands for the comparison in the branch, a stall will be required, since the EX stage for the ALU instruction will occur after the ID cycle of the branch. By extension, if a load is immediately followed by a conditional branch that is on the load result, two stall cycles will be needed, as the result from the load appears at the end of the MEM cycle but is needed at the beginning of ID for the branch.

Despite these difficulties, moving the branch execution to the ID stage is an improvement, because it reduces the penalty of a branch to only one instruction if the branch is taken, namely, the one currently being fetched. The exercises explore the details of implementing the forwarding path and detecting the hazard.

To flush instructions in the IF stage, we add a control line, called IF.Flush, that zeros the instruction field of the IF/ID pipeline register. Clearing the register transforms the fetched instruction into a `nop`, an instruction that has no action and changes no state.

EXAMPLE

Pipelined Branch

Show what happens when the branch is taken in this instruction sequence, assuming the pipeline is optimized for branches that are not taken and that we moved the branch execution to the ID stage:

```
36 sub $10, $4, $8
40 beq $1,  $3,  7 # PC-relative branch to 40+4+7*4=72
44 and $12, $2, $5
48 or  $13, $2, $6
52 add $14, $4, $2
56 slt $15, $6, $7
    . . .
72 lw $4, 50($7)
```

ANSWER

Figure 4.62 shows what happens when a branch is taken. Unlike Figure 4.61, there is only one pipeline bubble on a taken branch.

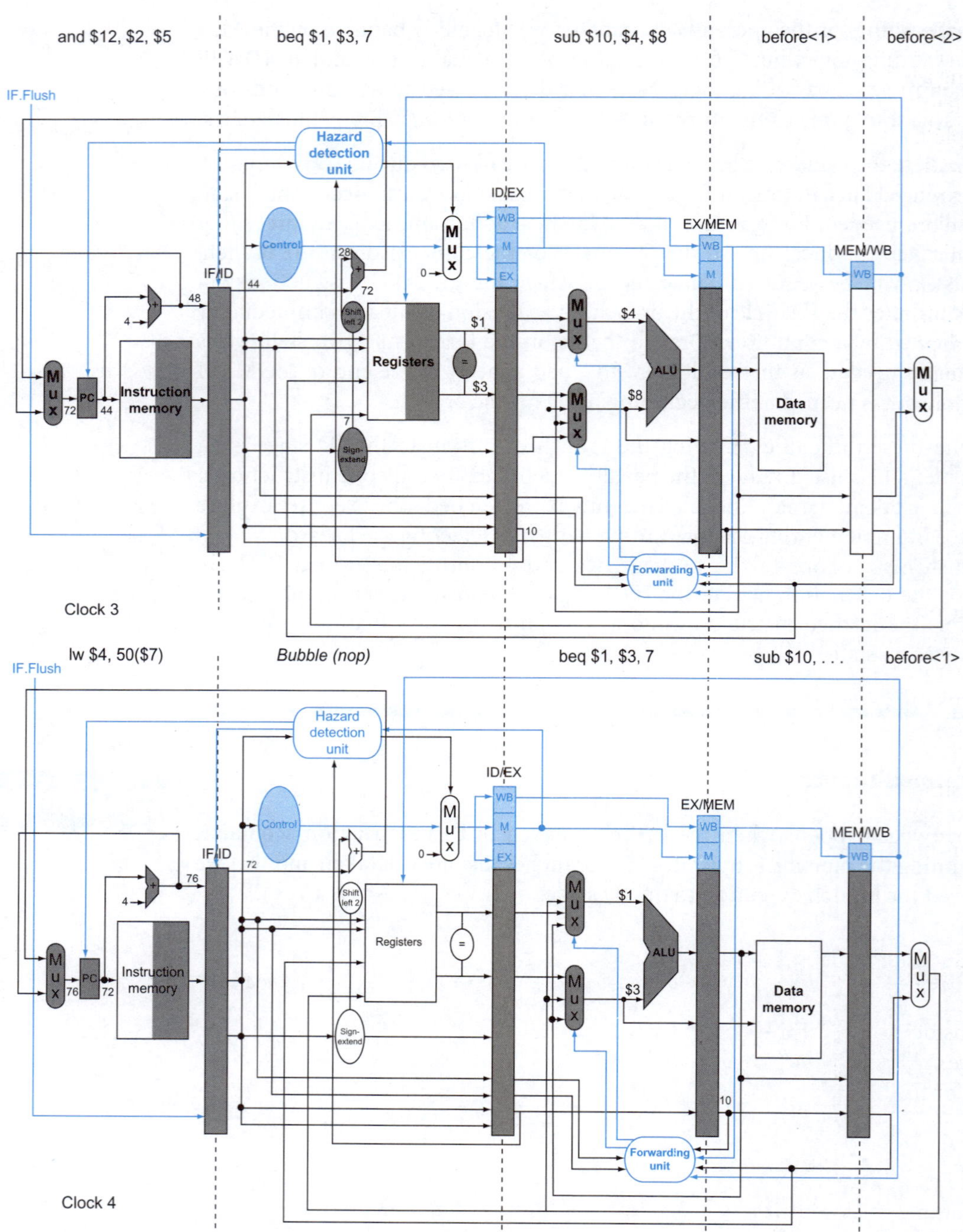

FIGURE 4.62 The ID stage of clock cycle 3 determines that a branch must be taken, so it selects 72 as the next PC address and zeros the instruction fetched for the next clock cycle. Clock cycle 4 shows the instruction at location 72 being fetched and the single bubble or nop instruction in the pipeline as a result of the taken branch. (Since the nop is really sll $0, $0, 0, it's arguable whether or not the ID stage in clock 4 should be highlighted.)

Dynamic Branch Prediction

Assuming a branch is not taken is one simple form of *branch prediction*. In that case, we predict that branches are untaken, flushing the pipeline when we are wrong. For the simple five-stage pipeline, such an approach, possibly coupled with compiler-based prediction, is probably adequate. With deeper pipelines, the branch penalty increases when measured in clock cycles. Similarly, with multiple issue (see Section 4.11), the branch penalty increases in terms of instructions lost. This combination means that in an aggressive pipeline, a simple static prediction scheme will probably waste too much performance. As we mentioned in Section 4.6, with more hardware it is possible to try to **predict** branch behavior during program execution.

One approach is to look up the address of the instruction to see if a branch was taken the last time this instruction was executed, and, if so, to begin fetching new instructions from the same place as the last time. This technique is called **dynamic branch prediction**.

One implementation of that approach is a **branch prediction buffer** or **branch history table**. A branch prediction buffer is a small memory indexed by the lower portion of the address of the branch instruction. The memory contains a bit that says whether the branch was recently taken or not.

This is the simplest sort of buffer; we don't know, in fact, if the prediction is the right one—it may have been put there by another branch that has the same low-order address bits. However, this doesn't affect correctness. Prediction is just a hint that we hope is accurate, so fetching begins in the predicted direction. If the hint turns out to be wrong, the incorrectly predicted instructions are deleted, the prediction bit is inverted and stored back, and the proper sequence is fetched and executed.

This simple 1-bit prediction scheme has a performance shortcoming: even if a branch is almost always taken, we can predict incorrectly twice, rather than once, when it is not taken. The following example shows this dilemma.

PREDICTION

dynamic branch prediction Prediction of branches at runtime using runtime information.

branch prediction buffer Also called **branch history table**. A small memory that is indexed by the lower portion of the address of the branch instruction and that contains one or more bits indicating whether the branch was recently taken or not.

Loops and Prediction

Consider a loop branch that branches nine times in a row, then is not taken once. What is the prediction accuracy for this branch, assuming the prediction bit for this branch remains in the prediction buffer?

EXAMPLE

The steady-state prediction behavior will mispredict on the first and last loop iterations. Mispredicting the last iteration is inevitable since the prediction bit will indicate taken, as the branch has been taken nine times in a row at that point. The misprediction on the first iteration happens because the bit is flipped on prior execution of the last iteration of the loop, since the branch was not taken on that exiting iteration. Thus, the prediction accuracy for this

ANSWER

branch that is taken 90% of the time is only 80% (two incorrect predictions and eight correct ones).

Ideally, the accuracy of the predictor would match the taken branch frequency for these highly regular branches. To remedy this weakness, we can use more prediction bits. In a 2-bit scheme, a prediction must be wrong twice before it is changed. Figure 4.63 shows the finite-state machine for a 2-bit prediction scheme.

A branch prediction buffer can be implemented as a small, special buffer accessed with the instruction address during the IF pipe stage. If the instruction is predicted as taken, fetching begins from the target as soon as the PC is known; as mentioned on page 330, it can be as early as the ID stage. Otherwise, sequential fetching and executing continue. If the prediction turns out to be wrong, the prediction bits are changed as Figure 4.63 shows.

branch delay slot: The slot directly after a delayed branch instruction, which in the MIPS architecture is filled by an instruction that does not affect the branch.

Elaboration: As we described in Section 4.6, in a five-stage pipeline we can make the control hazard a feature by redefining the branch. A delayed branch always executes the following instruction, but the second instruction following the branch will be affected by the branch.

Compilers and assemblers try to place an instruction that always executes after the branch in the **branch delay slot**. The job of the software is to make the successor instructions valid and useful. Figure 4.64 shows the three ways in which the branch delay slot can be scheduled.

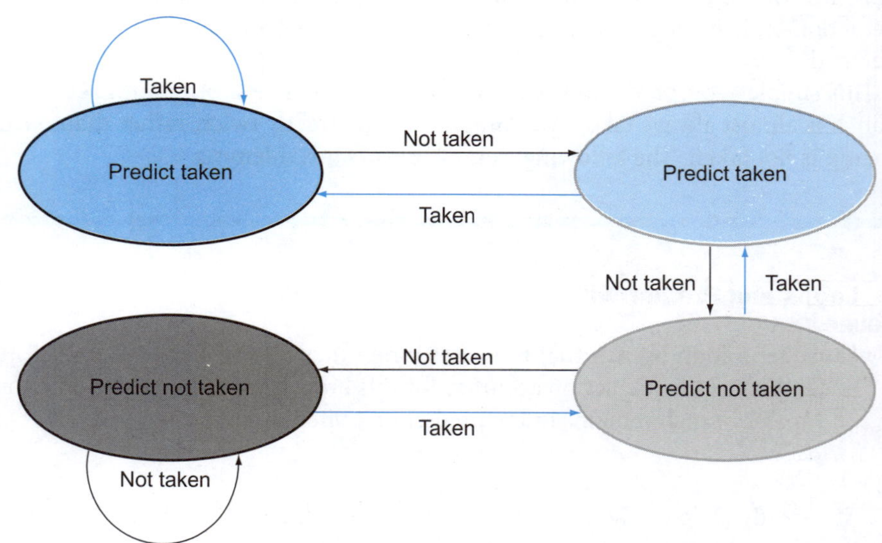

FIGURE 4.63 The states in a 2-bit prediction scheme. By using 2 bits rather than 1, a branch that strongly favors taken or not taken—as many branches do—will be mispredicted only once. The 2 bits are used to encode the four states in the system. The 2-bit scheme is a general instance of a counter-based predictor, which is incremented when the prediction is accurate and decremented otherwise, and uses the mid-point of its range as the division between taken and not taken.

The limitations on delayed branch scheduling arise from (1) the restrictions on the instructions that are scheduled into the delay slots and (2) our ability to predict at compile time whether a branch is likely to be taken or not.

Delayed branching was a simple and effective solution for a five-stage pipeline issuing one instruction each clock cycle. As processors go to both longer pipelines and issuing multiple instructions per clock cycle (see Section 4.11), the branch delay becomes longer, and a single delay slot is insufficient. Hence, delayed branching has lost popularity compared to more expensive but more flexible dynamic approaches. Simultaneously, the growth in available transistors per chip has due to Moore's Law made dynamic prediction relatively cheaper. There are more transistors in the branch predictor of modern microprocessors than there were in the whole first MIPS chips!

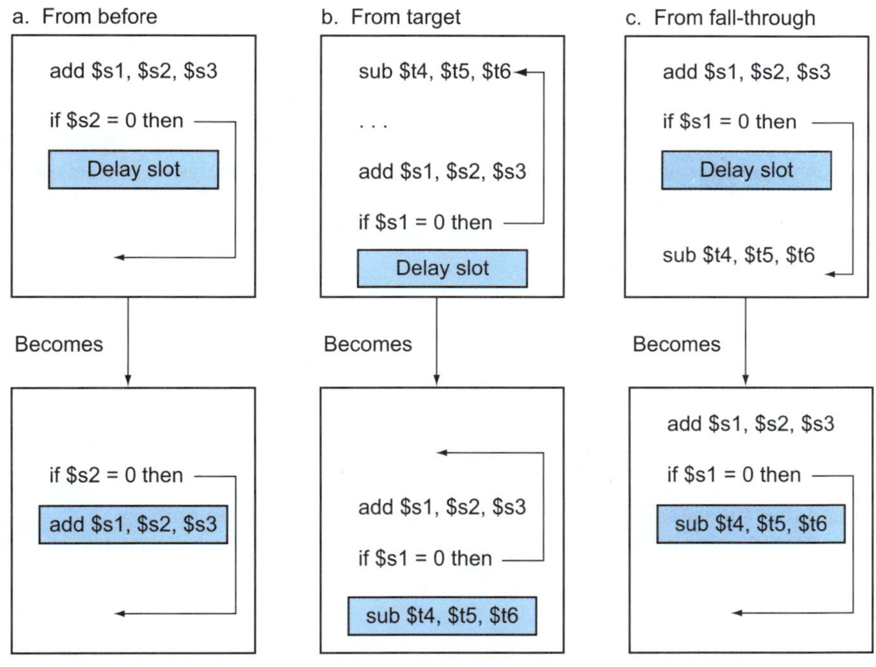

FIGURE 4.64 Scheduling the branch delay slot. The top box in each pair shows the code before scheduling; the bottom box shows the scheduled code. In (a), the delay slot is scheduled with an independent instruction from before the branch. This is the best choice. Strategies (b) and (c) are used when (a) is not possible. In the code sequences for (b) and (c), the use of $s1 in the branch condition prevents the add instruction (whose destination is $s1) from being moved into the branch delay slot. In (b) the branch delay slot is scheduled from the target of the branch; usually the target instruction will need to be copied because it can be reached by another path. Strategy (b) is preferred when the branch is taken with high probability, such as a loop branch. Finally, the branch may be scheduled from the not-taken fall-through as in (c). To make this optimization legal for (b) or (c), it must be OK to execute the sub instruction when the branch goes in the unexpected direction. By "OK" we mean that the work is wasted, but the program will still execute correctly. This is the case, for example, if $t4 were an unused temporary register when the branch goes in the unexpected direction.

branch target buffer:
A structure that caches
the destination PC or
destination instruction
for a branch. It is usually
organized as a cache with
tags, making it more
costly than a simple
prediction buffer.

correlating predictor:
A branch predictor that
combines local behavior
of a particular branch
and global information
about the behavior of
some recent number of
executed branches.

**tournament branch
predictor:** A branch
predictor with multiple
predictions for each
branch and a selection
mechanism that chooses
which predictor to enable
for a given branch.

Elaboration: A branch predictor tells us whether or not a branch is taken, but still requires the calculation of the branch target. In the five-stage pipeline, this calculation takes one cycle, meaning that taken branches will have a 1-cycle penalty. Delayed branches are one approach to eliminate that penalty. Another approach is to use a cache to hold the destination program counter or destination instruction using a **branch target buffer**.

The 2-bit dynamic prediction scheme uses only information about a particular branch. Researchers noticed that using information about both a local branch, and the global behavior of recently executed branches together yields greater prediction accuracy for the same number of prediction bits. Such predictors are called **correlating predictors**. A typical correlating predictor might have two 2-bit predictors for each branch, with the choice between predictors made based on whether the last executed branch was taken or not taken. Thus, the global branch behavior can be thought of as adding additional index bits for the prediction lookup.

A more recent innovation in branch prediction is the use of tournament predictors. A **tournament predictor** uses multiple predictors, tracking, for each branch, which predictor yields the best results. A typical tournament predictor might contain two predictions for each branch index: one based on local information and one based on global branch behavior. A selector would choose which predictor to use for any given prediction. The selector can operate similarly to a 1- or 2-bit predictor, favoring whichever of the two predictors has been more accurate. Some recent microprocessors use such elaborate predictors.

Elaboration: One way to reduce the number of conditional branches is to add *conditional move* instructions. Instead of changing the PC with a conditional branch, the instruction conditionally changes the destination register of the move. If the condition fails, the move acts as a `nop`. For example, one version of the MIPS instruction set architecture has two new instructions called `movn` (move if not zero) and `movz` (move if zero). Thus, `movn$8, $11, $4` copies the contents of register 11 into register 8, provided that the value in register 4 is nonzero; otherwise, it does nothing.

The ARMv7 instruction set has a condition field in most instructions. Hence, ARM programs could have fewer conditional branches than in MIPS programs.

Pipeline Summary

We started in the laundry room, showing principles of pipelining in an everyday setting. Using that analogy as a guide, we explained instruction pipelining step-by-step, starting with the single-cycle datapath and then adding pipeline registers, forwarding paths, data hazard detection, branch prediction, and flushing instructions on exceptions. Figure 4.65 shows the final evolved datapath and control. We now are ready for yet another control hazard: the sticky issue of exceptions.

**Check
Yourself**

Consider three branch prediction schemes: predict not taken, predict taken, and dynamic prediction. Assume that they all have zero penalty when they predict correctly and two cycles when they are wrong. Assume that the average predict

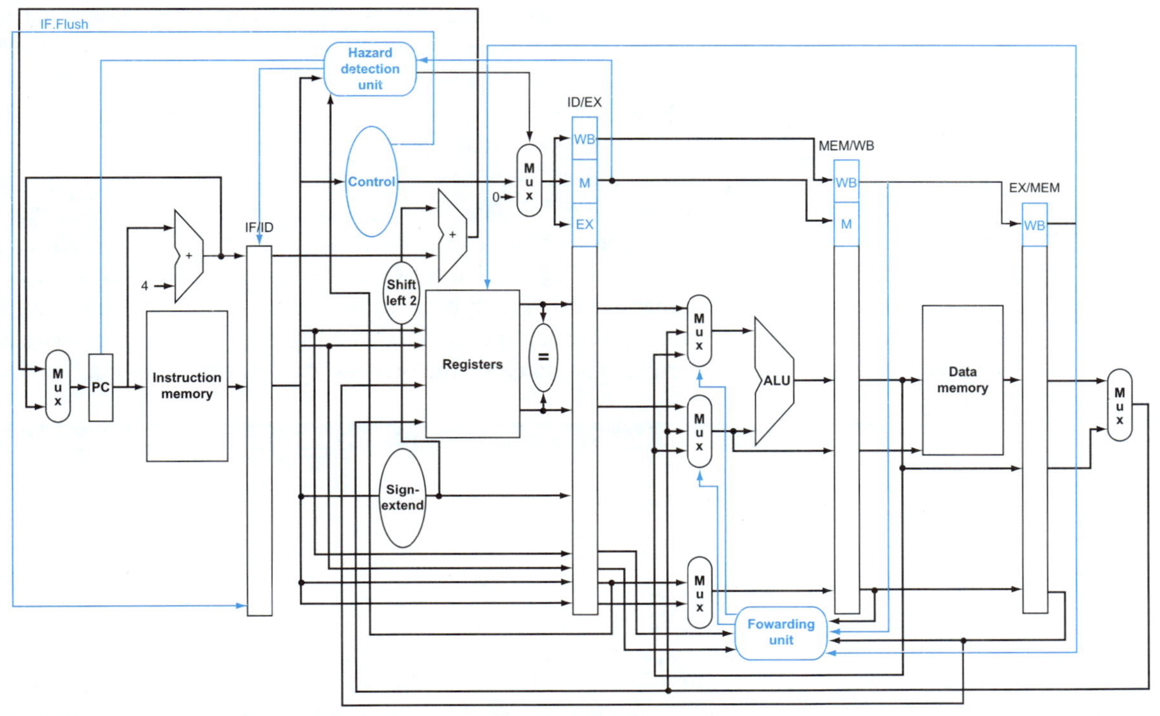

FIGURE 4.65 The final datapath and control for this chapter. Note that this is a stylized figure rather than a detailed datapath, so it's missing the ALUsrc Mux from Figure 4.57 and the multiplexor controls from Figure 4.51.

accuracy of the dynamic predictor is 90%. Which predictor is the best choice for the following branches?

1. A branch that is taken with 5% frequency

2. A branch that is taken with 95% frequency

3. A branch that is taken with 70% frequency

4.10 Exceptions

Control is the most challenging aspect of processor design: it is both the hardest part to get right and the hardest part to make fast. One of the hardest parts of

To make a computer with automatic program-interruption facilities behave [sequentially] was not an easy matter, because the number of instructions in various stages of processing when an interrupt signal occurs may be large.

Fred Brooks, Jr., *Planning a Computer System: Project Stretch,* 1962

exception Also called **interrupt**. An unscheduled event that disrupts program execution; used to detect overflow.

interrupt An exception that comes from outside of the processor. (Some architectures use the term *interrupt* for all exceptions.)

control is implementing **exceptions** and **interrupts**—events other than branches or jumps that change the normal flow of instruction execution. They were initially created to handle unexpected events from within the processor, like arithmetic overflow. The same basic mechanism was extended for I/O devices to communicate with the processor, as we will see in Chapter 5.

Many architectures and authors do not distinguish between interrupts and exceptions, often using the older name *interrupt* to refer to both types of events. For example, the Intel x86 uses interrupt. We follow the MIPS convention, using the term *exception* to refer to *any* unexpected change in control flow without distinguishing whether the cause is internal or external; we use the term *interrupt* only when the event is externally caused. Here are five examples showing whether the situation is internally generated by the processor or externally generated:

Type of event	From where?	MIPS terminology
I/O device request	External	Interrupt
Invoke the operating system from user program	Internal	Exception
Arithmetic overflow	Internal	Exception
Using an undefined instruction	Internal	Exception
Hardware malfunctions	Either	Exception or interrupt

Many of the requirements to support exceptions come from the specific situation that causes an exception to occur. Accordingly, we will return to this topic in Chapter 5, when we will better understand the motivation for additional capabilities in the exception mechanism. In this section, we deal with the control implementation for detecting two types of exceptions that arise from the portions of the instruction set and implementation that we have already discussed.

Detecting exceptional conditions and taking the appropriate action is often on the critical timing path of a processor, which determines the clock cycle time and thus performance. Without proper attention to exceptions during design of the control unit, attempts to add exceptions to a complicated implementation can significantly reduce performance, as well as complicate the task of getting the design correct.

How Exceptions Are Handled in the MIPS Architecture

The two types of exceptions that our current implementation can generate are execution of an undefined instruction and an arithmetic overflow. We'll use arithmetic overflow in the instruction add $1, $2, $1 as the example exception in the next few pages. The basic action that the processor must perform when an exception occurs is to save the address of the offending instruction in the *exception program counter* (EPC) and then transfer control to the operating system at some specified address.

The operating system can then take the appropriate action, which may involve providing some service to the user program, taking some predefined action in response to an overflow, or stopping the execution of the program and reporting an error. After performing whatever action is required because of the exception, the operating system can terminate the program or may continue its execution, using the EPC to determine where to restart the execution of the program. In Chapter 5, we will look more closely at the issue of restarting the execution.

For the operating system to handle the exception, it must know the reason for the exception, in addition to the instruction that caused it. There are two main methods used to communicate the reason for an exception. The method used in the MIPS architecture is to include a status register (called the *Cause register*), which holds a field that indicates the reason for the exception.

A second method, is to use **vectored interrupts**. In a vectored interrupt, the address to which control is transferred is determined by the cause of the exception. For example, to accommodate the two exception types listed above, we might define the following two exception vector addresses:

vectored interrupt An interrupt for which the address to which control is transferred is determined by the cause of the exception.

Exception type	Exception vector address (in hex)
Undefined instruction	$8000\ 0000_{hex}$
Arithmetic overflow	$8000\ 0180_{hex}$

The operating system knows the reason for the exception by the address at which it is initiated. The addresses are separated by 32 bytes or eight instructions, and the operating system must record the reason for the exception and may perform some limited processing in this sequence. When the exception is not vectored, a single entry point for all exceptions can be used, and the operating system decodes the status register to find the cause.

We can perform the processing required for exceptions by adding a few extra registers and control signals to our basic implementation and by slightly extending control. Let's assume that we are implementing the exception system used in the MIPS architecture, with the single entry point being the address $8000\ 0180_{hex}$. (Implementing vectored exceptions is no more difficult.) We will need to add two additional registers to our current MIPS implementation:

- *EPC:* A 32-bit register used to hold the address of the affected instruction. (Such a register is needed even when exceptions are vectored.)

- *Cause:* A register used to record the cause of the exception. In the MIPS architecture, this register is 32 bits, although some bits are currently unused. Assume there is a five-bit field that encodes the two possible exception sources mentioned above, with 10 representing an undefined instruction and 12 representing arithmetic overflow.

Exceptions in a Pipelined Implementation

A pipelined implementation treats exceptions as another form of control hazard. For example, suppose there is an arithmetic overflow in an add instruction. Just as we did for the taken branch in the previous section, we must flush the instructions that follow the add instruction from the pipeline and begin fetching instructions from the new address. We will use the same mechanism we used for taken branches, but this time the exception causes the deasserting of control lines.

When we dealt with branch mispredict, we saw how to flush the instruction in the IF stage by turning it into a nop. To flush instructions in the ID stage, we use the multiplexor already in the ID stage that zeros control signals for stalls. A new control signal, called ID.Flush, is ORed with the stall signal from the hazard detection unit to flush during ID. To flush the instruction in the EX phase, we use a new signal called EX.Flush to cause new multiplexors to zero the control lines. To start fetching instructions from location $8000\ 0180_{hex}$, which is the MIPS exception address, we simply add an additional input to the PC multiplexor that sends $8000\ 0180_{hex}$ to the PC. Figure 4.66 shows these changes.

This example points out a problem with exceptions: if we do not stop execution in the middle of the instruction, the programmer will not be able to see the original value of register $1 that helped cause the overflow because it will be clobbered as the Destination register of the add instruction. Because of careful planning, the overflow exception is detected during the EX stage; hence, we can use the EX.Flush signal to prevent the instruction in the EX stage from writing its result in the WB stage. Many exceptions require that we eventually complete the instruction that caused the exception as if it executed normally. The easiest way to do this is to flush the instruction and restart it from the beginning after the exception is handled.

The final step is to save the address of the offending instruction in the *exception program counter* (EPC). In reality, we save the address +4, so the exception handling routine must first subtract 4 from the saved value. Figure 4.66 shows a stylized version of the datapath, including the branch hardware and necessary accommodations to handle exceptions.

Exception in a Pipelined Computer

Given this instruction sequence,

```
40hex    sub $11, $2, $4
44hex    and $12, $2, $5
48hex    or  $13, $2, $6
4Chex    add $1, $2, $1
50hex    slt $15, $6, $7
54hex    lw  $16, 50($7)
         . . .
```

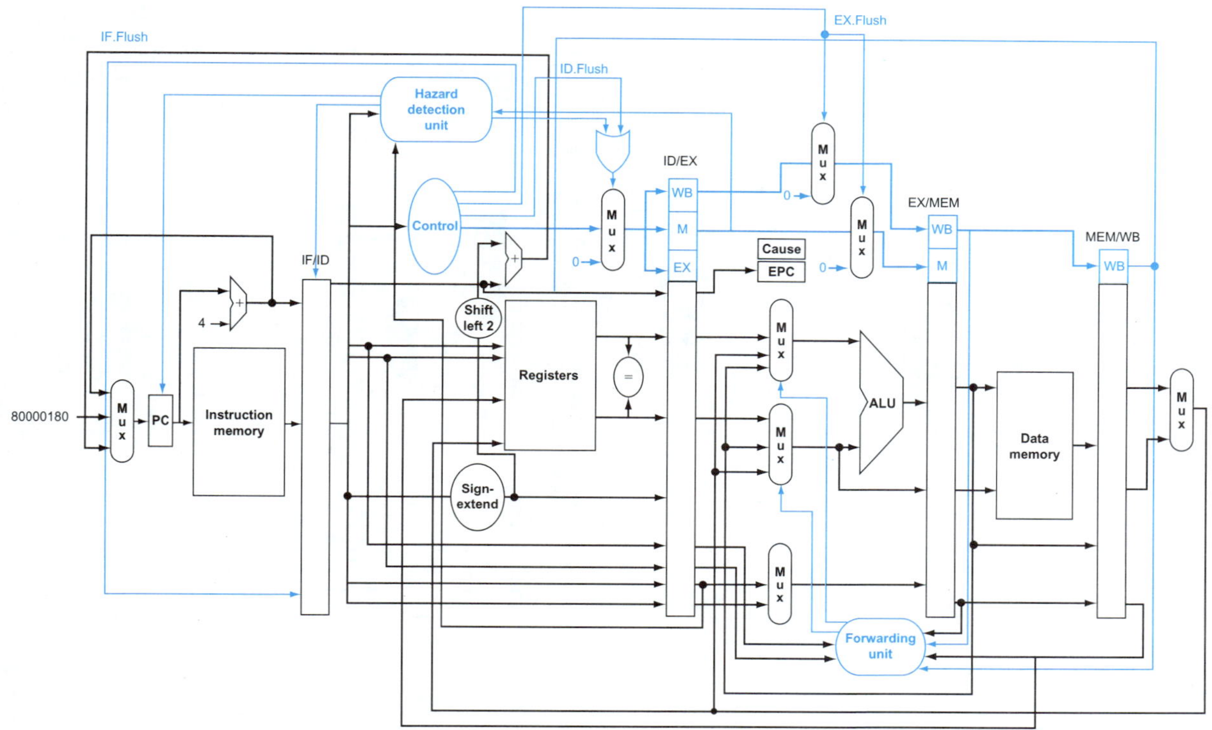

FIGURE 4.66 The datapath with controls to handle exceptions. The key additions include a new input with the value $8000\ 0180_{hex}$ in the multiplexor that supplies the new PC value; a Cause register to record the cause of the exception; and an Exception PC register to save the address of the instruction that caused the exception. The $8000\ 0180_{hex}$ input to the multiplexor is the initial address to begin fetching instructions in the event of an exception. Although not shown, the ALU overflow signal is an input to the control unit.

assume the instructions to be invoked on an exception begin like this:

```
80000180_hex   sw      $26, 1000($0)
80000184_hex   sw      $27, 1004($0)
. . .
```

Show what happens in the pipeline if an overflow exception occurs in the `add` instruction.

ANSWER

Figure 4.67 shows the events, starting with the `add` instruction in the EX stage. The overflow is detected during that phase, and $8000\ 0180_{hex}$ is forced into the PC. Clock cycle 7 shows that the `add` and following instructions are flushed, and the first instruction of the exception code is fetched. Note that the address of the instruction *following* the `add` is saved: $4C_{hex} + 4 = 50_{hex}$.

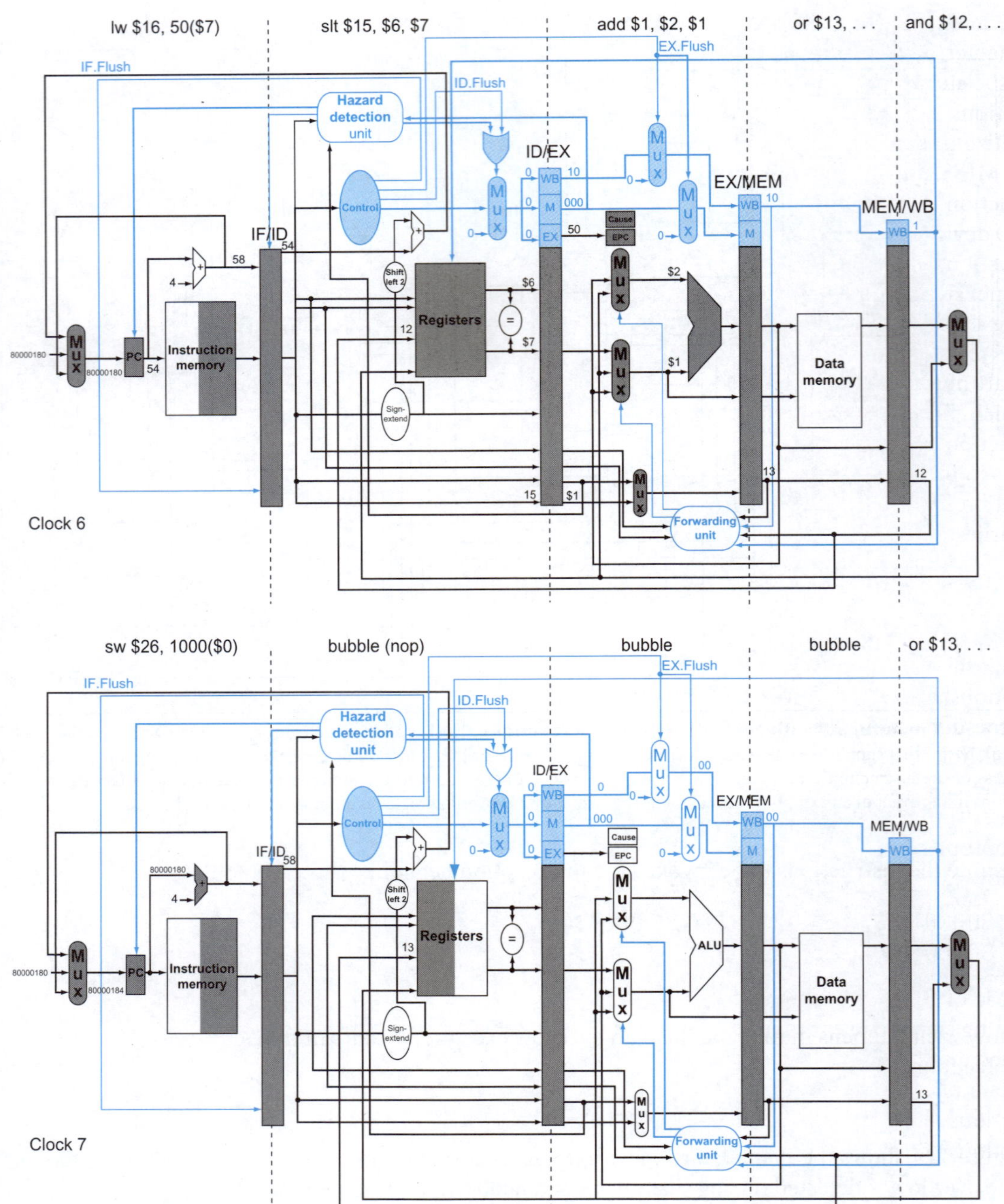

FIGURE 4.67 The result of an exception due to arithmetic overflow in the add instruction. The overflow is detected during the EX stage of clock 6, saving the address following the add in the EPC register ($4C + 4 = 50_{hex}$). Overflow causes all the Flush signals to be set near the end of this clock cycle, deasserting control values (setting them to 0) for the add. Clock cycle 7 shows the instructions converted to bubbles in the pipeline plus the fetching of the first instruction of the exception routine—sw $25,1000($0)—from instruction location $8000\ 0180_{hex}$. Note that the AND and OR instructions, which are prior to the add, still complete. Although not shown, the ALU overflow signal is an input to the control unit.

We mentioned five examples of exceptions on page 338, and we will see others in Chapter 5. With five instructions active in any clock cycle, the challenge is to associate an exception with the appropriate instruction. Moreover, multiple exceptions can occur simultaneously in a single clock cycle. The solution is to prioritize the exceptions so that it is easy to determine which is serviced first. In most MIPS implementations, the hardware sorts exceptions so that the earliest instruction is interrupted.

I/O device requests and hardware malfunctions are not associated with a specific instruction, so the implementation has some flexibility as to when to interrupt the pipeline. Hence, the mechanism used for other exceptions works just fine.

The EPC captures the address of the interrupted instructions, and the MIPS Cause register records all possible exceptions in a clock cycle, so the exception software must match the exception to the instruction. An important clue is knowing in which pipeline stage a type of exception can occur. For example, an undefined instruction is discovered in the ID stage, and invoking the operating system occurs in the EX stage. Exceptions are collected in the Cause register in a pending exception field so that the hardware can interrupt based on later exceptions, once the earliest one has been serviced.

Hardware/ Software Interface

The hardware and the operating system must work in conjunction so that exceptions behave as you would expect. The hardware contract is normally to stop the offending instruction in midstream, let all prior instructions complete, flush all following instructions, set a register to show the cause of the exception, save the address of the offending instruction, and then jump to a prearranged address. The operating system contract is to look at the cause of the exception and act appropriately. For an undefined instruction, hardware failure, or arithmetic overflow exception, the operating system normally kills the program and returns an indicator of the reason. For an I/O device request or an operating system service call, the operating system saves the state of the program, performs the desired task, and, at some point in the future, restores the program to continue execution. In the case of I/O device requests, we may often choose to run another task before resuming the task that requested the I/O, since that task may often not be able to proceed until the I/O is complete. Exceptions are why the ability to save and restore the state of any task is critical. One of the most important and frequent uses of exceptions is handling page faults and TLB exceptions; Chapter 5 describes these exceptions and their handling in more detail.

imprecise interrupt Also called **imprecise exception**. Interrupts or exceptions in pipelined computers that are not associated with the exact instruction that was the cause of the interrupt or exception.

Elaboration: The difficulty of always associating the correct exception with the correct instruction in pipelined computers has led some computer designers to relax this requirement in noncritical cases. Such processors are said to have **imprecise interrupts** or **imprecise exceptions**. In the example above, PC would normally have 58_{hex} at the start of the clock cycle after the exception is detected, even though the offending instruction

precise interrupt Also called **precise exception**. An interrupt or exception that is always associated with the correct instruction in pipelined computers.

is at address 4C$_{hex}$. A processor with imprecise exceptions might put 58$_{hex}$ into EPC and leave it up to the operating system to determine which instruction caused the problem. MIPS and the vast majority of computers today support **precise interrupts** or **precise exceptions**. (One reason is to support virtual memory, which we shall see in Chapter 5.)

Elaboration: Although MIPS uses the exception entry address 8000 0180$_{hex}$ for almost all exceptions, it uses the address 8000 0000$_{hex}$ to improve performance of the exception handler for TLB-miss exceptions (see Chapter 5).

Check Yourself

Which exception should be recognized first in this sequence?

```
1. add $1, $2, $1    # arithmetic overflow
2. XXX $1, $2, $1    # undefined instruction
3. sub $1, $2, $1    # hardware error
```

4.11   Parallelism via Instructions

Be forewarned: this section is a brief overview of fascinating but advanced topics. If you want to learn more details, you should consult our more advanced book, *Computer Architecture: A Quantitative Approach*, sixth edition, where the material covered in these 13 pages is expanded to almost 200 pages (including Appendices)!

Pipelining exploits the potential parallelism among instructions. This parallelism is called **instruction-level parallelism (ILP)**. There are two primary methods for increasing the potential amount of instruction-level parallelism. The first is increasing the depth of the pipeline to overlap more instructions. Using our laundry analogy and assuming that the washer cycle was longer than the others were, we could divide our washer into three machines that perform the wash, rinse, and spin steps of a traditional washer. We would then move from a four-stage to a six-stage pipeline. To get the full speed-up, we need to rebalance the remaining steps so they have the same duration, in processors or in laundry. The amount of parallelism being exploited is higher, since there are more operations being overlapped. Performance is potentially greater since the clock cycle can be shorter.

Another approach is to replicate the internal components of the computer so that it can launch multiple instructions in every pipeline stage. The general name for this technique is **multiple issue**. A multiple-issue laundry would replace our household washer and dryer with, say, three washers and three dryers. You would also have to recruit more assistants to fold and put away three times as much laundry in the same amount of time. The downside is the extra work to keep all the machines busy and transferring the loads to the next pipeline stage.

instruction-level parallelism The parallelism among instructions.

multiple issue A scheme whereby multiple instructions are launched in one clock cycle.

Launching multiple instructions per stage allows the instruction execution rate to exceed the clock rate or, stated alternatively, the CPI to be less than 1. As mentioned in Chapter 1, it is sometimes useful to flip the metric and use *IPC*, or *instructions per clock cycle*. Hence, a 4 GHz four-way multiple-issue microprocessor can execute a peak rate of 16 billion instructions per second and have a best-case CPI of 0.25, or an IPC of 4. Assuming a five-stage pipeline, such a processor would have 20 instructions in execution at any given time. Today's high-end microprocessors attempt to issue from three to six instructions in every clock cycle. Even moderate designs will aim at an IPC of 2. There are typically, however, many constraints on what types of instructions may be executed simultaneously, and what happens when dependences arise.

There are two major ways to implement a multiple-issue processor, with the major difference being the division of work between the compiler and the hardware. Because the division of work dictates whether decisions are being made statically (that is, at compile time) or dynamically (that is, during execution), the approaches are sometimes called **static multiple issue** and **dynamic multiple issue**. As we will see, both approaches have other, more commonly used names, which may be less precise or more restrictive.

There are two primary and distinct responsibilities that must be dealt with in a multiple-issue pipeline:

1. Packaging instructions into **issue slots**: how does the processor determine how many instructions and which instructions can be issued in a given clock cycle? In most static issue processors, this process is at least partially handled by the compiler; in dynamic issue designs, it is normally dealt with at runtime by the processor, although the compiler will often have already tried to help improve the issue rate by placing the instructions in a beneficial order.

2. Dealing with data and control hazards: in static issue processors, the compiler handles some or all of the consequences of data and control hazards statically. In contrast, most dynamic issue processors attempt to alleviate at least some classes of hazards using hardware techniques operating at execution time.

Although we describe these as distinct approaches, in reality one approach often borrows techniques from the other, and neither approach can claim to be perfectly pure.

The Concept of Speculation

One of the most important methods for finding and exploiting more ILP is speculation. Based on the great idea of **prediction**, **speculation** is an approach that allows the compiler or the processor to "guess" about the properties of an instruction, so as to enable execution to begin for other instructions that may depend on the speculated instruction. For example, we might speculate on the outcome of a branch, so that instructions after the branch could be executed earlier.

static multiple issue An approach to implementing a multiple-issue processor where many decisions are made by the compiler before execution.

dynamic multiple issue An approach to implementing a multiple-issue processor where many decisions are made during execution by the processor.

issue slots The positions from which instructions could issue in a given clock cycle; by analogy, these correspond to positions at the starting blocks for a sprint.

speculation An approach whereby the compiler or processor guesses the outcome of an instruction to remove it as a dependence in executing other instructions.

Another example is that we might speculate that a store that precedes a load does not refer to the same address, which would allow the load to be executed before the store. The difficulty with speculation is that it may be wrong. So, any speculation mechanism must include both a method to check if the guess was right and a method to unroll or back out the effects of the instructions that were executed speculatively. The implementation of this back-out capability adds complexity.

Speculation may be done in the compiler or by the hardware. For example, the compiler can use speculation to reorder instructions, moving an instruction across a branch or a load across a store. The processor hardware can perform the same transformation at runtime using techniques we discuss later in this section.

The recovery mechanisms used for incorrect speculation are rather different. In the case of speculation in software, the compiler usually inserts additional instructions that check the accuracy of the speculation and provide a fix-up routine to use when the speculation is incorrect. In hardware speculation, the processor usually buffers the speculative results until it knows they are no longer speculative. If the speculation is correct, the instructions are completed by allowing the contents of the buffers to be written to the registers or memory. If the speculation is incorrect, the hardware flushes the buffers and re-executes the correct instruction sequence.

Speculation introduces one other possible problem: speculating on certain instructions may introduce exceptions that were formerly not present. For example, suppose a load instruction is moved in a speculative manner, but the address it uses is not legal when the speculation is incorrect. The result would be an exception that should not have occurred. The problem is complicated by the fact that if the load instruction were not speculative, then the exception must occur! In compiler-based speculation, such problems are avoided by adding special speculation support that allows such exceptions to be ignored until it is clear that they really should occur. In hardware-based speculation, exceptions are simply buffered until it is clear that the instruction causing them is no longer speculative and is ready to complete; at that point the exception is raised, and normal exception handling proceeds.

Since speculation can improve performance when done properly and decrease performance when done carelessly, significant effort goes into deciding when it is appropriate to speculate. Later in this section, we will examine both static and dynamic techniques for speculation.

Static Multiple Issue

issue packet The set of instructions that issues together in one clock cycle; the packet may be determined statically by the compiler or dynamically by the processor.

Static multiple-issue processors all use the compiler to assist with packaging instructions and handling hazards. In a static issue processor, you can think of the set of instructions issued in a given clock cycle, which is called an **issue packet**, as one large instruction with multiple operations. This view is more than an analogy. Since a static multiple-issue processor usually restricts what mix of instructions can be initiated in a given clock cycle, it is useful to think of the issue packet as a single instruction allowing several operations in certain predefined fields. This view led to the original name for this approach: **Very Long Instruction Word (VLIW)**.

Most static issue processors also rely on the compiler to take on some responsibility for handling data and control hazards. The compiler's responsibilities may include static branch prediction and code scheduling to reduce or prevent all hazards. Let's look at a simple static issue version of a MIPS processor, before we describe the use of these techniques in more aggressive processors.

An Example: Static Multiple Issue with the MIPS ISA

To give a flavor of static multiple issue, we consider a simple two-issue MIPS processor, where one of the instructions can be an integer ALU operation or branch and the other can be a load or store. Such a design is like that used in some embedded MIPS processors. Issuing two instructions per cycle will require fetching and decoding 64 bits of instructions. In many static multiple-issue processors, and essentially all VLIW processors, the layout of simultaneously issuing instructions is restricted to simplify the decoding and instruction issue. Hence, we will require that the instructions be paired and aligned on a 64-bit boundary, with the ALU or branch portion appearing first. Furthermore, if one instruction of the pair cannot be used, we require that it be replaced with a nop. Thus, the instructions always issue in pairs, possibly with a nop in one slot. Figure 4.68 shows how the instructions look as they go into the pipeline in pairs.

Static multiple-issue processors vary in how they deal with potential data and control hazards. In some designs, the compiler takes full responsibility for removing *all* hazards, scheduling the code and inserting no-ops so that the code executes without any need for hazard detection or hardware-generated stalls. In others, the hardware detects data hazards and generates stalls between two issue packets, while requiring that the compiler avoid all dependences within an instruction pair. Even so, a hazard generally forces the entire issue packet containing the dependent

Very Long Instruction Word (VLIW)

A style of instruction set architecture that launches many operations that are defined to be independent in a single wide instruction, typically with many separate opcode fields.

Instruction type	Pipe stages							
ALU or branch instruction	IF	ID	EX	MEM	WB			
Load or store instruction	IF	ID	EX	MEM	WB			
ALU or branch instruction		IF	ID	EX	MEM	WB		
Load or store instruction		IF	ID	EX	MEM	WB		
ALU or branch instruction			IF	ID	EX	MEM	WB	
Load or store instruction			IF	ID	EX	MEM	WB	
ALU or branch instruction				IF	ID	EX	MEM	WB
Load or store instruction				IF	ID	EX	MEM	WB

FIGURE 4.68 Static two-issue pipeline in operation. The ALU and data transfer instructions are issued at the same time. Here we have assumed the same five-stage structure as used for the single-issue pipeline. Although this is not strictly necessary, it does have some advantages. In particular, keeping the register writes at the end of the pipeline simplifies the handling of exceptions and the maintenance of a precise exception model, which become more difficult in multiple-issue processors.

instruction to stall. Whether the software must handle all hazards or only try to reduce the fraction of hazards between separate issue packets, the appearance of having a large single instruction with multiple operations is reinforced. We will assume the second approach for this example.

To issue an ALU and a data transfer operation in parallel, the first need for additional hardware—beyond the usual hazard detection and stall logic—is extra ports in the register file (see Figure 4.69). In one clock cycle we may need to read two registers for the ALU operation and two more for a store, and also one write port for an ALU operation and one write port for a load. Since the ALU is tied up for the ALU operation, we also need a separate adder to calculate the effective address for data transfers. Without these extra resources, our two-issue pipeline would be hindered by structural hazards.

Clearly, this two-issue processor can improve performance by up to a factor of 2. Doing so, however, requires that twice as many instructions be overlapped in execution, and this additional overlap increases the relative performance loss from data and control hazards. For example, in our simple five-stage pipeline,

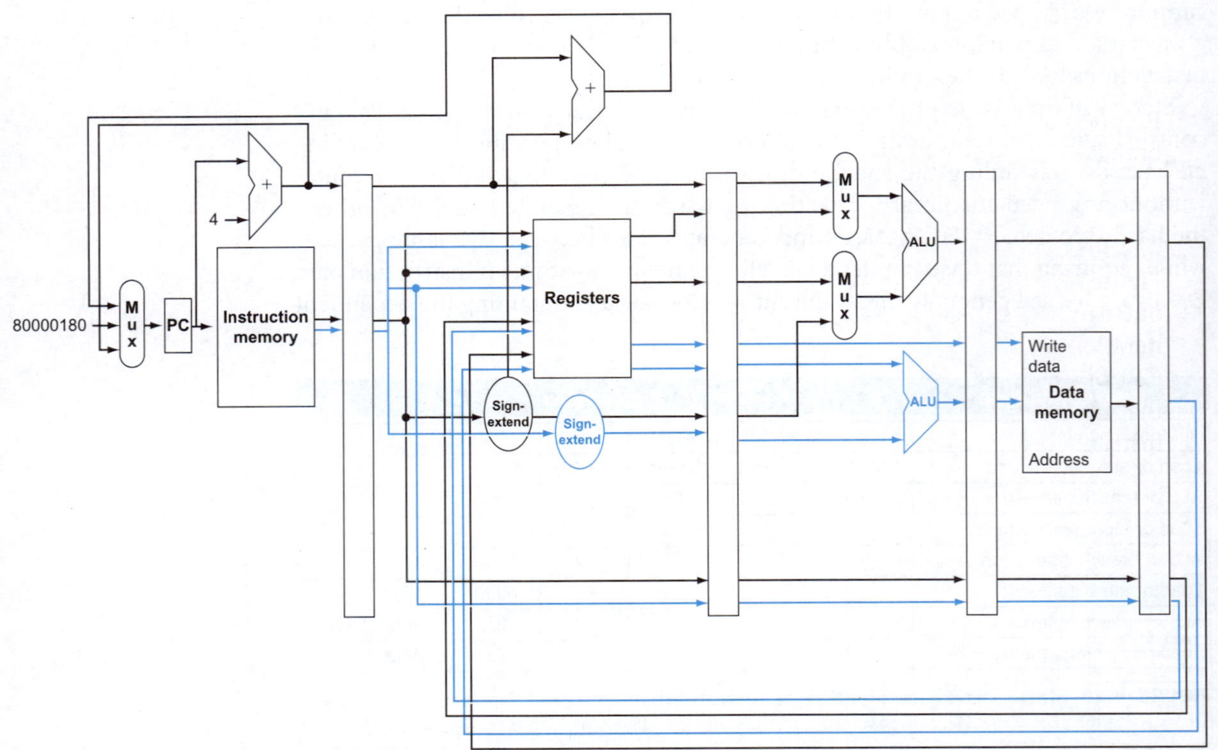

FIGURE 4.69 A static two-issue datapath. The additions needed for double issue are highlighted: another 32 bits from instruction memory, two more read ports and one more write port on the register file, and another ALU. Assume the bottom ALU handles address calculations for data transfers and the top ALU handles everything else.

loads have a **use latency** of one clock cycle, which prevents one instruction from using the result without stalling. In the two-issue, five-stage pipeline the result of a load instruction cannot be used on the next *clock cycle*. This means that the next *two* instructions cannot use the load result without stalling. Furthermore, ALU instructions that had no use latency in the simple five-stage pipeline now have a one-instruction use latency, since the results cannot be used in the paired load or store. To effectively exploit the parallelism available in a multiple-issue processor, more ambitious compiler or hardware scheduling techniques are needed, and static multiple issue requires that the compiler take on this role.

use latency Number of clock cycles between a load instruction and an instruction that can use the result of the load without stalling the pipeline.

Simple Multiple-Issue Code Scheduling

EXAMPLE

How would this loop be scheduled on a static two-issue pipeline for MIPS?

```
Loop: lw    $t0, 0($s1)    # $t0=array element
      addu  $t0,$t0,$s2    # add scalar in $s2
      sw    $t0, 0($s1)    # store result
      addi  $s1,$s1,-4     # decrement pointer
      bne   $s1,$zero,Loop # branch $s1!=0
```

Reorder the instructions to avoid as many pipeline stalls as possible. Assume branches are predicted, so that control hazards are handled by the hardware.

The first three instructions have data dependences, and so do the last two. Figure 4.70 shows the best schedule for these instructions. Notice that just one pair of instructions has both issue slots used. It takes four clocks per loop iteration; at four clocks to execute five instructions, we get the disappointing CPI of 0.8 versus the best case of 0.5., or an IPC of 1.25 versus 2.0. Notice that in computing CPI or IPC, we do not count any nops executed as useful instructions. Doing so would improve CPI, but not performance!

ANSWER

	ALU or branch instruction		Data transfer instruction		Clock cycle
Loop:			lw	$t0, 0($s1)	1
	addi	$s1,$s1,-4			2
	addu	$t0,$t0,$s2			3
	bne	$s1,$zero,Loop	sw	$t0, 4($s1)	4

FIGURE 4.70 The scheduled code as it would look on a two-issue MIPS pipeline. The empty slots are no-ops.

loop unrolling
A technique to get more performance from loops that access arrays, in which multiple copies of the loop body are made and instructions from different iterations are scheduled together.

An important compiler technique to get more performance from loops is **loop unrolling**, where multiple copies of the loop body are made. After unrolling, there is more ILP available by overlapping instructions from different iterations.

EXAMPLE

Loop Unrolling for Multiple-Issue Pipelines

See how well loop unrolling and scheduling work in the example above. For simplicity assume that the loop index is a multiple of four.

ANSWER

To significantly reduce the delays in the loop, we need to make four copies of the loop body. After unrolling and eliminating the unnecessary loop overhead instructions, the loop will contain four copies each of `lw`, `add`, and `sw`, plus one `addi` and one `bne`. Figure 4.71 shows the unrolled and scheduled code.

During the unrolling process, the compiler introduced additional registers (`$t1`, `$t2`, `$t3`). The goal of this process, called **register renaming**, is to eliminate dependences that are not true data dependences, but could either lead to potential hazards or prevent the compiler from flexibly scheduling the code. Consider how the unrolled code would look using only `$t0`. There would be repeated instances of `lw  $t0,0($$s1)`, addu `$t0,$t0,$s2` followed by `sw  t0,4($s1)`, but these sequences, despite using `$t0`, are actually completely independent—no data values flow between one set of these instructions and the next set. This case is what is called an **antidependence** or **name dependence**, which is an ordering forced purely by the reuse of a name, rather than a real data dependence that is also called a true dependence.

Renaming the registers during the unrolling process allows the compiler to move these independent instructions subsequently so as to better schedule

register renaming The renaming of registers by the compiler or hardware to remove antidependences.

antidependence Also called **name dependence**. An ordering forced by the reuse of a name, typically a register, rather than by a true dependence that carries a value between two instructions.

	ALU or branch instruction		Data transfer instruction		Clock cycle
Loop:	addi	$s1,$s1,-16	lw	$t0, 0($s1)	1
			lw	$t1,12($s1)	2
	addu	$t0,$t0,$s2	lw	$t2, 8($s1)	3
	addu	$t1,$t1,$s2	lw	$t3, 4($s1)	4
	addu	$t2,$t2,$s2	sw	$t0, 16($s1)	5
	addu	$t3,$t3,$s2	sw	$t1,12($s1)	6
			sw	$t2, 8($s1)	7
	bne	$s1,$zero,Loop	sw	$t3, 4($s1)	8

FIGURE 4.71 The unrolled and scheduled code of Figure 4.70 as it would look on a static two-issue MIPS pipeline. The empty slots are no-ops. Since the first instruction in the loop decrements $s1 by 16, the addresses loaded are the original value of $s1, then that address minus 4, minus 8, and minus 12.

the code. The renaming process eliminates the name dependences, while preserving the true dependences.

Notice now that 12 of the 14 instructions in the loop execute as pairs. It takes 8 clocks for 4 loop iterations, or 2 clocks per iteration, which yields a CPI of 8/14 = 0.57 and an IPC of 1.75. Loop unrolling and scheduling with dual issue gave us an improvement factor of almost 2, partly from reducing the loop control instructions and partly from dual issue execution. The cost of this performance improvement is using four temporary registers rather than one, as well as a significant increase in code size.

Dynamic Multiple-Issue Processors

Dynamic multiple-issue processors are also known as **superscalar** processors, or simply superscalars. In the simplest superscalar processors, instructions issue in order, and the processor decides whether zero, one, or more instructions can issue in a given clock cycle. Obviously, achieving good performance on such a processor still requires the compiler to try to schedule instructions to move dependences apart and thereby improve the instruction issue rate. Even with such compiler scheduling, there is an important difference between this simple superscalar and a VLIW processor: the code, whether scheduled or not, is guaranteed by the hardware to execute correctly. Furthermore, compiled code will always run correctly independent of the issue rate or pipeline structure of the processor. In some VLIW designs, this has not been the case, and recompilation was required when moving across different processor models; in other static issue processors, code would run correctly across different implementations, but often so poorly as to make compilation effectively required.

Many superscalars extend the basic framework of dynamic issue decisions to include **dynamic pipeline scheduling**. Dynamic pipeline scheduling chooses which instructions to execute in a given clock cycle while trying to avoid hazards and stalls. Let's start with a simple example of avoiding a data hazard. Consider the following code sequence:

```
lw      $t0, 20($s2)
addu    $t1, $t0, $t2
sub     $s4, $s4, $t3
slti    $t5, $s4, 20
```

superscalar An advanced pipelining technique that enables the processor to execute more than one instruction per clock cycle by selecting them during execution.

dynamic pipeline scheduling Hardware support for reordering the order of instruction execution so as to avoid stalls.

Even though the sub instruction is ready to execute, it must wait for the lw and addu to complete first, which might take many clock cycles if memory is slow. (Chapter 5 explains cache misses, the reason that memory accesses are sometimes very slow.) Dynamic **pipeline** scheduling allows such hazards to be avoided either fully or partially.

Dynamic Pipeline Scheduling

Dynamic pipeline scheduling chooses which instructions to execute next, possibly reordering them to avoid stalls. In such processors, the pipeline is divided into three major units: an instruction fetch and issue unit, multiple functional units

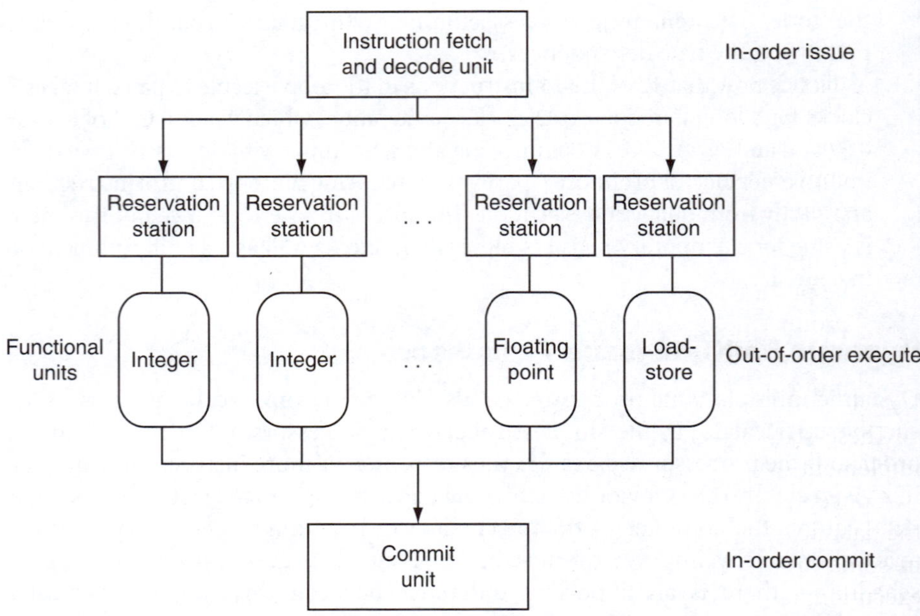

FIGURE 4.72 The three primary units of a dynamically scheduled pipeline. The final step of updating the state is also called retirement or graduation.

commit unit The unit in a dynamic or out-of-order execution pipeline that decides when it is safe to release the result of an operation to programmer-visible registers and memory.

reservation station A buffer within a functional unit that holds the operands and the operation.

reorder buffer The buffer that holds results in a dynamically scheduled processor until it is safe to store the results to memory or a register.

(a dozen or more in high-end designs in 2020), and a **commit unit**. Figure 4.72 shows the model. The first unit fetches instructions, decodes them, and sends each instruction to a corresponding functional unit for execution. Each functional unit has buffers, called **reservation stations**, which hold the operands and the operation. (In the next section, we will discusses an alternative to reservation stations used by many recent processors.) As soon as the buffer contains all its operands and the functional unit is ready to execute, the result is calculated. When the result is completed, it is sent to any reservation stations waiting for this particular result as well as to the commit unit, which buffers the result until it is safe to put the result into the register file or, for a store, into memory. The buffer in the commit unit, often called the **reorder buffer**, is also used to supply operands, in much the same way as forwarding logic does in a statically scheduled pipeline. Once a result is committed to the register file, it can be fetched directly from there, just as in a normal pipeline.

The combination of buffering operands in the reservation stations and results in the reorder buffer provides a form of register renaming, just like that used by the compiler in our earlier loop-unrolling example on page 350. To see how this conceptually works, consider the following steps:

1. When an instruction issues, it is copied to a reservation station for the appropriate functional unit. Any operands that are available in the register file or reorder buffer are also immediately copied into the reservation station. The instruction is buffered in the reservation station until all the operands and the functional unit are available. For the issuing instruction, the register copy of the operand is no longer required, and if a write to that register occurred, the value could be overwritten.

2. If an operand is not in the register file or reorder buffer, it must be waiting to be produced by a functional unit. The name of the functional unit that will produce the result is tracked. When that unit eventually produces the result, it is copied directly into the waiting reservation station from the functional unit bypassing the registers.

These steps effectively use the reorder buffer and the reservation stations to implement register renaming.

Conceptually, you can think of a dynamically scheduled pipeline as analyzing the data flow structure of a program. The processor then executes the instructions in some order that preserves the data flow order of the program. This style of execution is called an **out-of-order execution**, since the instructions can be executed in a different order than they were fetched.

To make programs behave as if they were running on a simple in-order pipeline, the instruction fetch and decode unit is required to issue instructions in order, which allows dependences to be tracked, and the commit unit is required to write results to registers and memory in program fetch order. This conservative mode is called **in-order commit**. Hence, if an exception occurs, the computer can point to the last instruction executed, and the only registers updated will be those written by instructions before the instruction causing the exception. Although the front end (fetch and issue) and the back end (commit) of the pipeline run in order, the functional units are free to initiate execution whenever the data they need is available. Today, all dynamically scheduled pipelines use in-order commit.

Dynamic scheduling is often extended by including hardware-based speculation, especially for branch outcomes. By predicting the direction of a branch, a dynamically scheduled processor can continue to fetch and execute instructions along the predicted path. Because the instructions are committed in order, we know whether or not the branch was correctly predicted before any instructions from the predicted path are committed. A speculative, dynamically scheduled pipeline can also support speculation on load addresses, allowing load-store reordering, and using the commit unit to avoid incorrect speculation. In the next section, we will look at the use of dynamic scheduling with speculation in the Intel Core i7 design.

out-of-order execution A situation in pipelined execution when an instruction blocked from executing does not cause the following instructions to wait.

in-order commit A commit in which the results of pipelined execution are written to the programmer visible state in the same order that instructions are fetched.

**Hardware/
Software
Interface**

Out-of-order execution creates new pipeline hazards that we did not see in the earlier pipelines. A *name dependence* occurs when two instructions use the same register or memory location, called a *name*, but there is no flow of data between the instructions associated with that name. There are two types of name dependences between an instruction i that precedes instruction j in program order:

1. An *antidependence* between instruction i and instruction j occurs when instruction j writes a register or memory location that instruction i reads. The original ordering must be preserved to ensure that i reads the correct value.

2. An *output dependence* occurs when instruction i and instruction j write the same register or memory location. The ordering between the instructions must be preserved to ensure that the value finally written corresponds to instruction j.

Our original pipeline hazard was the result of what is called a *true data dependence*.

For example, in this code below there is an antidependence between `swc1` and `addiu` on register x1 and a true data dependence between `lwc1` and `add.s` on register f0. While there are no output dependencies between instructions in a single loop, there are between different iterations of the loop, for example, between the `addiu` instructions of the first and second iterations.

```
Loop: lwc1 $f0,0(x1)     # f0=array element
      add.s $f4,$f0,$f2 # add scalar in f2
      swc1 $f4,0(x1)     # store result
      addiu x1,x1,4      # decrement pointer 8 bytes
      bne x1,x2,Loop     # branch if x1 != x2
```

A pipeline hazard exists whenever there is a name or data dependence between instructions, and they are close enough that the overlap during execution would change the order of access to the operand involved in the dependence. They lead to these more intuitive names of pipeline hazards:

1. An *antidependence* can lead to a Write-After-Read (WAR) hazard.

2. An *output dependence* can lead to a Write-After-Write (WAW) hazard.

3. A *true data dependence* or a Read-After-Write (RAW) hazard.

We do not have hazards for WAR or WAW hazards in our earlier pipelines because all instructions execute in order and the writes occur only in the last pipeline stage for register–register instructions and always in the same pipeline stage for data access in load and store instructions.

Given that compilers can also schedule code around data dependences, you might ask why a superscalar processor would use dynamic scheduling. There are three major reasons. First, not all stalls are predictable. In particular, cache misses (see Chapter 5) in the **memory hierarchy** cause unpredictable stalls. Dynamic scheduling allows the processor to hide some of those stalls by continuing to execute instructions while waiting for the stall to end.

Second, if the processor speculates on branch outcomes using dynamic branch **prediction**, it cannot know the exact order of instructions at compile time, since it depends on the predicted and actual behavior of branches. Incorporating dynamic speculation to exploit more *instruction-level parallelism* (ILP) without incorporating dynamic scheduling would significantly restrict the benefits of speculation.

Third, as the pipeline latency and issue width change from one implementation to another, the best way to compile a code sequence also changes. For example, how to schedule a sequence of dependent instructions is affected by both issue width and latency. The pipeline structure affects both the number of times a loop must be unrolled to avoid stalls as well as the process of compiler-based register renaming. Dynamic scheduling allows the hardware to hide most of these details. Thus, users and software distributors do not need to worry about having multiple versions of a program for different implementations of the same instruction set. Similarly, old legacy code will get much of the benefit of a new implementation without the need for recompilation.

Both **pipelining** and multiple-issue execution increase peak instruction throughput and attempt to exploit instruction-level **parallelism** (ILP). Data and control dependences in programs, however, offer an upper limit on sustained performance because the processor must sometimes wait for a dependence to be resolved. Software-centric approaches to exploiting ILP rely on the ability of the compiler to find and reduce the effects of such dependences, while hardware-centric approaches rely on extensions to the pipeline and issue mechanisms. Speculation, performed by the compiler or the hardware, can increase the amount of ILP that can be exploited via **prediction**, although care must be taken since speculating incorrectly is likely to reduce performance.

Hardware/ Software Interface

Modern, high-performance microprocessors are capable of issuing several instructions per clock; unfortunately, sustaining that issue rate is very difficult. For example, despite the existence of processors with four to six issues per clock, very few applications can sustain more than two instructions per clock. There are two primary reasons for this.

First, within the pipeline, the major performance bottlenecks arise from dependences that cannot be alleviated, thus reducing the parallelism among instructions and the sustained issue rate. Although little can be done about true data dependences, often the compiler or hardware does not know precisely whether a dependence exists or not, and so must conservatively assume the dependence exists. For example, code that makes use of pointers, particularly in ways that may lead to aliasing, will lead to more implied potential dependences. In contrast, the greater regularity of array accesses often allows a compiler to deduce that no dependences exist. Similarly, branches that cannot be accurately predicted whether at runtime or compile time will limit the ability to exploit ILP. Often, additional ILP is available, but the ability of the compiler or the hardware to find ILP that may be widely separated (sometimes by the execution of thousands of instructions) is limited.

Second, losses in the **memory hierarchy** (the topic of Chapter 5) also limit the ability to keep the pipeline full. Some memory system stalls can be hidden, but limited amounts of ILP also limit the extent to which such stalls can be hidden.

Energy Efficiency and Advanced Pipelining

The downside to the increasing exploitation of instruction-level parallelism via dynamic multiple issue and speculation is potential energy inefficiency. Each innovation was able to turn more transistors into performance, but they often did so very ineffectively. Now that we have hit the power wall, we are seeing designs with multiple processors per chip where the processors are not as deeply pipelined or as aggressively speculative as the predecessors.

The belief is that while the simpler processors are not as fast as their sophisticated brethren, they deliver better performance per joule, so that they can deliver more performance per chip when designs are constrained more by energy than they are by number of transistors.

Figure 4.73 shows the number of pipeline stages, the issue width, speculation level, clock rate, cores per chip, and power of several past and recent microprocessors. Note the drop in pipeline stages and power as companies switch to multicore designs.

Elaboration: A commit unit controls updates to the register file *and* memory. Some dynamically scheduled processors update the register file immediately during execution, using extra registers to implement the renaming function and preserving the older copy of a register until the instruction updating the register is no longer speculative. Other processors buffer the result, typically in a structure called a reorder buffer, and the actual update to the register file occurs later as part of the commit. Stores to memory must be buffered until commit time either in a *store buffer* (see Chapter 5) or in the reorder buffer. The commit unit allows the store to write to memory from the buffer when the buffer has a valid address and valid data, and when the store is no longer dependent on predicted branches.

Microprocessor	Year	Clock Rate	Pipeline Stages	Issue Width	Out-of-Order/ Speculation	Cores/ Chip	Power
Intel 486	1989	25 MHz	5	1	No	1	5W
Intel Pentium	1993	66 MHz	5	2	No	1	10W
Intel Pentium Pro	1997	200 MHz	10	3	Yes	1	29W
Intel Pentium 4 Willamette	2001	2000 MHz	22	3	Yes	1	75W
Intel Pentium 4 Prescott	2004	3600 MHz	31	3	Yes	1	103W
Intel Core	2006	3000 MHz	14	4	Yes	2	75W
Intel Core i7 Nehalem	2008	3600 MHz	14	4	Yes	2-4	87W
Intel Core Westmere	2010	3730 MHz	14	4	Yes	6	130W
Intel Core i7 Ivy Bridge	2012	3400 MHz	14	4	Yes	6	130W
Intel Core Broadwell	2014	3700 MHz	14	4	Yes	10	140W
Intel Core i9 Skylake	2016	3100 MHz	14	4	Yes	14	165W
Intel Ice Lake	2018	4200 MHz	14	4	Yes	16	185W

FIGURE 4.73 Record of Intel Microprocessors in terms of pipeline complexity, number of cores, and power. The Pentium 4 pipeline stages do not include the commit stages. If we included them, the Pentium 4 pipelines would be even deeper.

Elaboration: Memory accesses benefit from *nonblocking caches,* which continue servicing cache accesses during a cache miss (see Chapter 5). Out-of-order execution processors need the cache design to allow instructions to execute during a miss.

State whether the following techniques or components are associated primarily with a software- or hardware-based approach to exploiting ILP. In some cases, the answer may be both.

Check Yourself

1. Branch prediction

2. Multiple issue

3. VLIW

4. Superscalar

5. Dynamic scheduling

6. Out-of-order execution

7. Speculation

8. Reorder buffer

9. Register renaming

4.12 Putting It All Together: The Intel Core i7 6700 and ARM Cortex-A53

In this section, we explore the design of two multiple issue processors: the ARM Cortex-A53 core, which is used as the basis for several tablets and cell phones, and the Intel Core i7 6700, a high-end, dynamically scheduled, speculative processor intended for high-end desktops and server applications. We begin with the simpler processor. This section is based on Section 3.12 of *Computer Architecture: A Quantitative Approach*, sixth edition.

The ARM Cortex-A53

The A53 is a dual-issue, statically scheduled superscalar with dynamic issue detection, which allows the processor to issue two instructions per clock. Figure 4.74 shows the basic pipeline structure of the pipeline. For nonbranch, integer

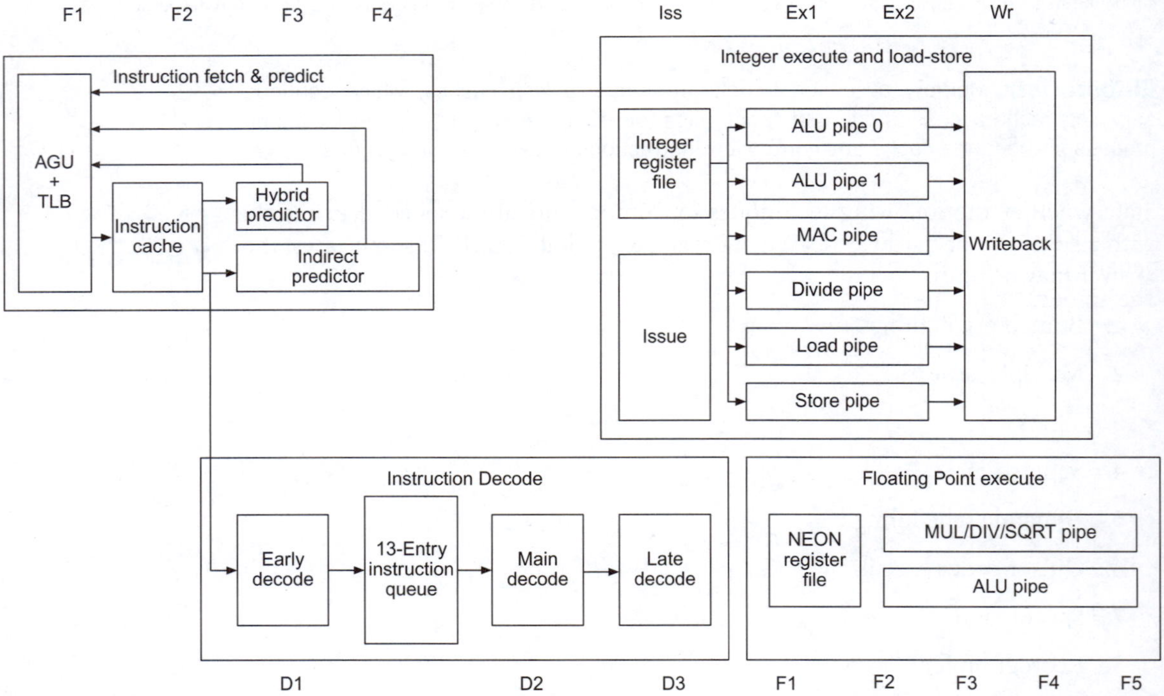

FIGURE 4.74 The basic structure of the A53 integer pipeline is eight stages: F1 and F2 fetch the instruction, D1 and D2 do the basic decoding, and D3 decodes some more complex instructions and is overlapped with the first stage of the execution pipeline (ISS). After ISS, the Ex1, EX2, and WB stages complete the integer pipeline. Branches use four different predictors, depending on the type. The floating-point execution pipeline is five cycles deep, in addition to the five cycles needed for fetch and decode, yielding 10 stages in total. AGU stands for *Address Generation Unit* and TLB for Transaction Lookaside Buffer (See Chapter 5). The NEON unit performs the ARM SIMD instructions of the same name. (From Hennessy JL, Patterson DA: *Computer architecture: A quantitative approach*, ed 6, Cambridge MA, 2018, Morgan Kaufmann.)

instructions, there are eight stages: F1, F2, D1, D2, D3/ISS, EX1, EX2, and WB, as described in the caption. The pipeline is in order, so an instruction can initiate execution only when its results are available and when proceeding instructions have initiated. Thus, if the next two instructions are dependent, both can proceed to the appropriate execution pipeline, but they will be serialized when they get to the beginning of that pipeline. When the pipeline issue logic indicates that the result from the first instruction is available, the second instruction can issue.

The four cycles of instruction fetch include an address generation unit that produces the next PC either by incrementing the last PC or from one of four predictors:

1. A single-entry branch target cache containing two instruction cache fetches (the next two instructions following the branch, assuming the prediction is correct). This target cache is checked during the first fetch cycle, if it hits; then the next two instructions are supplied from the target cache. In case of a hit and a correct prediction, the branch is executed with no delay cycles.

2. A 3072-entry hybrid predictor, used for all instructions that do not hit in the branch target cache, and operating during F3. Branches handled by this predictor incur a two-cycle delay.

3. A 256-entry indirect branch predictor that operates during F4; branches predicted by this predictor incur a three-cycle delay when predicted correctly.

4. An 8-deep return stack, operating during F4 and incurring a three-cycle delay.

Branch decisions are made in ALU pipe 0, resulting in a branch misprediction penalty of eight cycles. Figure 4.75 shows the misprediction rate for SPECint2006. The amount of work that is wasted depends on both the misprediction rate and the

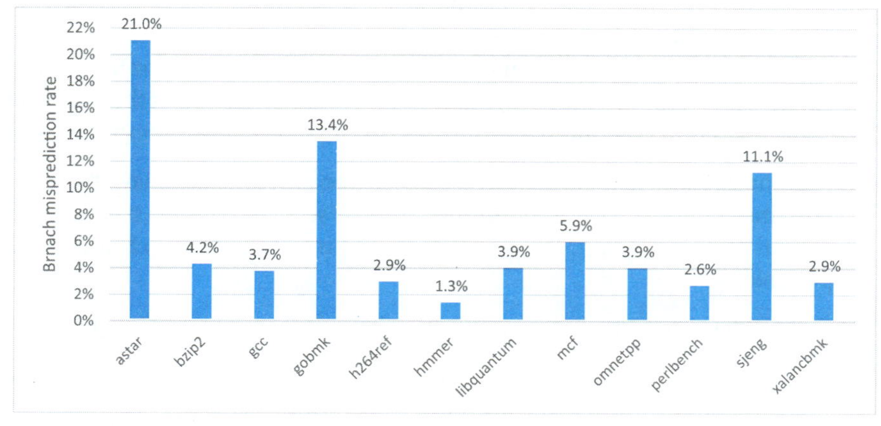

FIGURE 4.75 Misprediction rate of the A53 branch predictor for SPECint2006. (Adapted from Hennessy JL, Patterson DA: *Computer architecture: A quantitative approach*, ed 6, Cambridge MA, 2018, Morgan Kaufmann.)

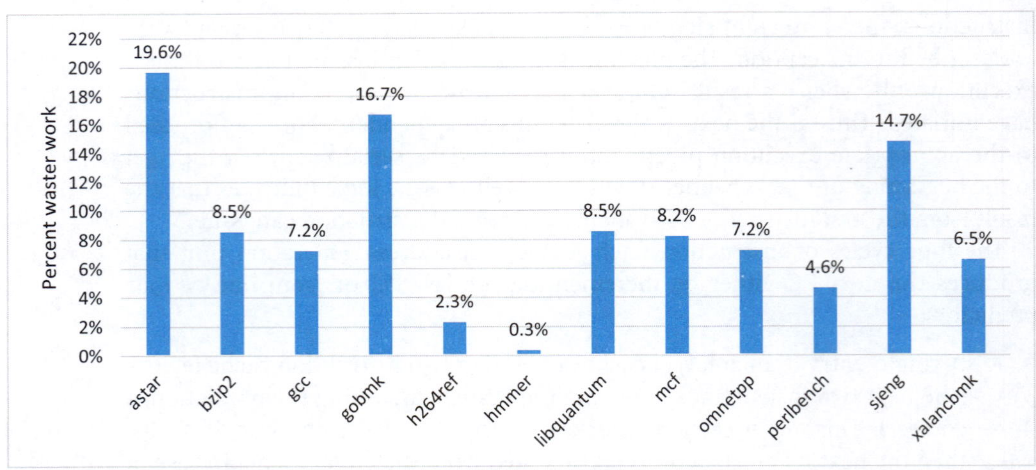

FIGURE 4.76 Wasted work due to branch misprediction on the A53. Because the A53 is an in-order machine, the amount of wasted work depends on a variety of factors, including data dependences and cache misses, both of which will cause a stall. (Adapted from Hennessy JL, Patterson DA: *Computer architecture: A quantitative approach*, ed 6, Cambridge MA, 2018, Morgan Kaufmann.)

issue rate sustained during the time that the mispredicted branch was followed. As Figure 4.76 shows, wasted work generally follows the misprediction rate, though it may be larger or occasionally shorter.

Performance of the A53 Pipeline

The A53 has an ideal CPI of 0.5 because of its dual-issue structure. Pipeline stalls can arise from three sources:

1. Functional hazards, which occur because two adjacent instructions selected for issue simultaneously, use the same functional pipeline. Because the A53 is statically scheduled, the compiler should try to avoid such conflicts. When such instructions appear sequentially, they will be serialized at the beginning of the execution pipeline, when only the first instruction will begin execution.

2. Data hazards, which are detected early in the pipeline and may stall either both instructions (if the first cannot issue, the second is always stalled) or the second of a pair. Again, the compiler should try to prevent such stalls when possible.

3. Control hazards, which arise only when branches are mispredicted.

Both TLB misses (Chapter 5) and cache misses also cause stalls. Figure 4.77 shows the CPI and the estimated contributions from various sources.

The A53 uses a shallow pipeline and a reasonably aggressive branch predictor, leading to modest pipeline losses, while allowing the processor to achieve high

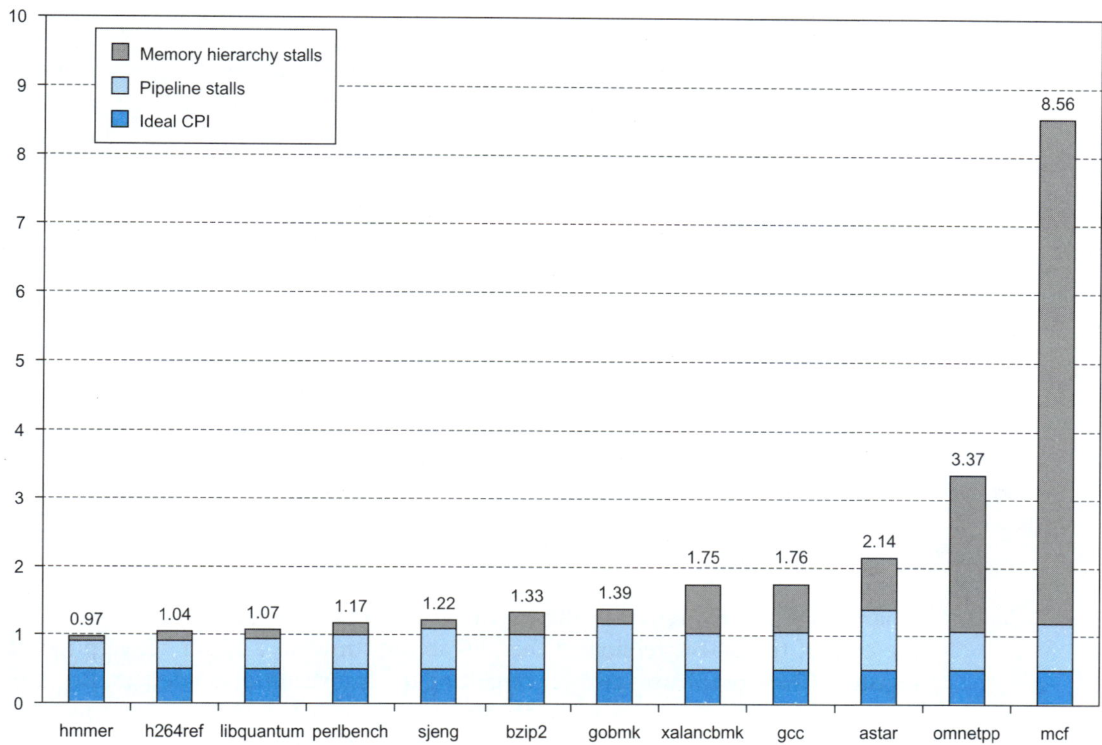

FIGURE 4.77 The estimated composition of the CPI on the ARM A53 shows that pipeline stalls are significant but are outweighed by cache misses in the poorest performing programs (Chapter 5). These are subtracted from the CPI measured by a detailed simulator to obtain the pipeline stalls. Pipeline stalls include all three hazards. (From Hennessy JL, Patterson DA: *Computer architecture: A quantitative approach*, ed 6, Cambridge MA, 2018, Morgan Kaufmann.)

clock rates at modest power consumption. In comparison with the i7, the A53 consumes approximately 1/200 the power for a quad core processor!

Elaboration: The Cortex-A53 is a configurable core that supports the ARMv8 instruction set architecture. It is delivered as an IP (*Intellectual Property*) *core*. IP cores are the dominant form of technology delivery in the embedded, personal mobile device, and related markets; billions of ARM and MIPS processors have been created from these IP cores.

Note that IP cores are different than the cores in the Intel i7 multicore computers. An IP core (which may itself be a multicore) is designed to be incorporated with other logic (hence it is the "core" of a chip), including application-specific processors (such as an encoder or decoder for video), I/O interfaces, and memory interfaces, and then fabricated to yield a processor optimized for a particular application. Although the processor core is almost identical, the resultant chips have many differences. One parameter is the size of the L2 cache, which can vary by a factor of 16.

The Intel Core i7 6700

x86 microprocessors employ sophisticated pipelining approaches, using both dynamic multiple issue and dynamic pipeline scheduling with out-of-order execution and speculation for its 14-stage pipeline. These processors, however, are still faced with the challenge of implementing the complex x86 instruction set, described in Chapter 2. Intel fetches x86 instructions and translates them into internal MIPS-like instructions, which Intel calls *micro-operations*. The micro-operations are then executed by a sophisticated, dynamically scheduled, speculative pipeline capable of sustaining an execution rate of up to six micro-operations per clock cycle. This section focuses on that micro-operation pipeline.

When we consider the design of sophisticated, dynamically scheduled processors, the design of the functional units, the cache and register file, instruction issue, and overall pipeline control becomes intermingled, making it difficult to separate the datapath from the pipeline. Because of this interdependence, many engineers and researchers use the term **microarchitecture** to refer to the detailed internal architecture of a processor.

The Intel Core i7 uses a scheme for resolving antidependences and incorrect speculation that uses a reorder buffer together with register renaming. Register renaming explicitly renames the **architectural registers** in a processor (16 in the case of the 64-bit version of the x86 architecture) to a larger set of physical registers. The Core i7 uses register renaming to remove antidependences. Register renaming requires the processor to maintain a map between the architectural registers and the physical registers, indicating which physical register is the most current copy of an architectural register. By keeping track of the renamings that have occurred, register renaming offers another approach to recovery in the event of incorrect speculation: simply undo the mappings that have occurred since the first incorrectly speculated instruction. This adjustment will cause the state of the processor to return to the last correctly executed instruction, keeping the correct mapping between the architectural and physical registers.

Figure 4.78 shows the overall structure of the i7 pipeline. We will examine the pipeline by starting with instruction fetch and continuing on to instruction commit, following eight steps labeled in the figure.

1. Instruction fetch—The processor uses a sophisticated multilevel branch predictor to achieve a balance between speed and prediction accuracy. There is also a return address stack to speed up function return. Mispredictions cause a penalty of about 17 cycles. Using the predicted address, the instruction fetch unit fetches 16 bytes from the instruction cache.

2. The 16 bytes are placed in the predecode instruction buffer—The predecode stage also breaks the 16 bytes into individual x86 instructions. This predecode is nontrivial because the length of an x86 instruction can be from 1 to 17 bytes and the predecoder must look through a number of bytes before it knows the instruction length. Individual x86 instructions are placed into the instruction queue.

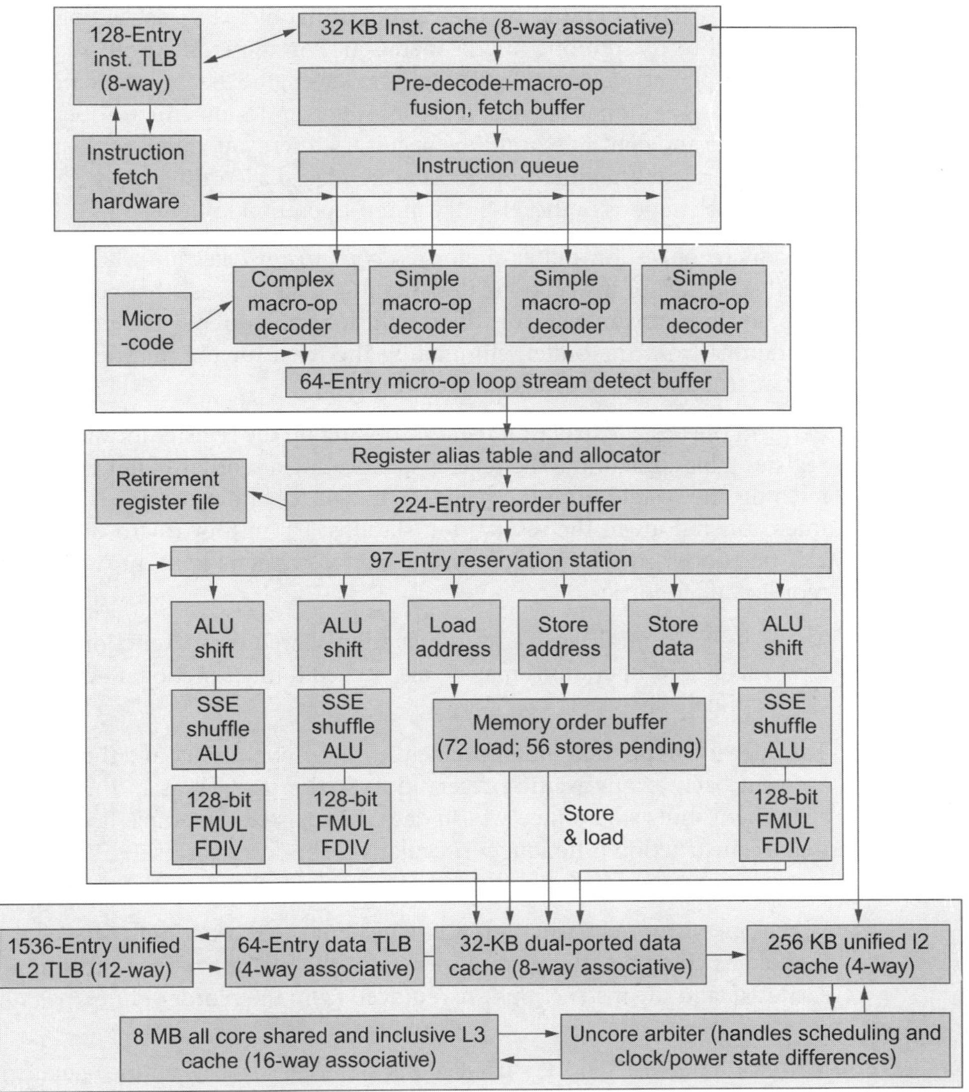

FIGURE 4.78 The Intel Core i7 pipeline structure shown with the memory system components. The total pipeline depth is 14 stages, with branch mispredictions typically costing 17 cycles, with the extra few cycles likely due to the time to reset the branch predictor. This design can buffer 72 loads and 56 stores. The six independent functional units can each begin execution of a ready micro-operation in the same cycle. Up to four micro-operations can be processed in the register renaming table. The first i7 processor was introduced in 2008; the i7 6700 is the sixth generation. The basic structure of the i7 is similar, but successive generations have enhanced performance by changing cache strategies (Chapter 5), increasing memory bandwidth, expanding the number of instructions in flight, enhancing branch prediction, and improving graphics support. (From Hennessy JL, Patterson DA: *Computer architecture: A quantitative approach*, ed 6, Cambridge MA, 2018, Morgan Kaufmann.)

3. Micro-op decode—Three of the decoders handle x86 instructions that translate directly into one micro-operation. For x86 instructions that have more complex semantics, there is a microcode engine that is used to produce the micro-operation sequence; it can produce up to four micro-operations every cycle and continues until the necessary micro-operation sequence has been generated. The micro-operations are placed according to the order of the x86 instructions in the 64-entry micro-operation buffer.

4. The micro-operation buffer preforms *loop stream detection*—If there is a small sequence of instructions (less than 64 instructions) that comprises a loop, the loop stream detector will find the loop and directly issue the micro-operations from the buffer, eliminating the need for the instruction fetch and instruction decode stages to be activated.

5. Perform the basic instruction issue—Looking up the register location in the register tables, renaming the registers, allocating a reorder buffer entry, and fetching any results from the registers or reorder buffer before sending the micro-operations to the reservation stations. Up to four micro-operations can be processed every clock cycle; they are assigned the next available reorder buffer entries.

6. The i7 uses a centralized reservation station shared by six functional units. Up to six micro-operations may be dispatched to the functional units every clock cycle.

7. The individual function units execute the micro-operations, and then results are sent back to any waiting reservation station as well as to the register retirement unit, where they will update the register state once it is known that the instruction is no longer speculative. The entry corresponding to the instruction in the reorder buffer is marked as complete.

8. When one or more instructions at the head of the reorder buffer have been marked as complete, the pending writes in the register retirement unit are executed, and the instructions are removed from the reorder buffer.

Elaboration: Hardware in the second and fourth steps can combine or *fuse* operations together to reduce the number of operations that must be performed. *Macro-op fusion* in the second step takes x86 instruction combinations, such as compare followed by a branch, and fuses them into a single operation. *Microfusion* in the fourth step combines micro-operation pairs such as load/ALU operation and ALU operation/store and issues them to a single reservation station (where they can still issue independently), thus increasing the usage of the buffer. In a study of the Intel Core architecture, which also incorporated microfusion and macrofusion, Bird et al. [2007] discovered that microfusion had little impact on performance, while macrofusion appears to have a modest positive impact on integer performance and little impact on floating-point performance.

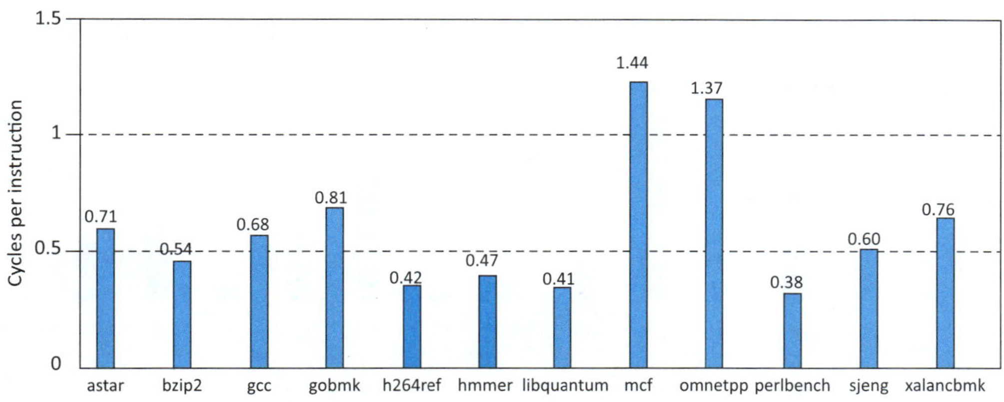

FIGURE 4.79 The CPI for the SPECCPUint2006 benchmarks on the i7 6700. The data in this section were collected by Professor Lu Peng and PhD student Qun Liu, both of Louisiana State University. (Adapted from Hennessy JL, Patterson DA: *Computer architecture: A quantitative approach*, ed 6, Cambridge MA, 2018, Morgan Kaufmann.)

Performance of the i7

Because of the presence of aggressive speculation, it is difficult to accurately attribute the gap between idealized performance and actual performance. The extensive queues and buffers on the 6700 reduce the probability of stalls because of a lack of reservation stations, renaming registers, or reorder buffers significantly.

Thus, most losses come either from branch mispredicts or cache misses. The cost of a branch mispredict is 17 cycles, whereas the cost of an L1 miss is about 10 cycles (Chapter 5). An L2 miss is slightly more than three times as costly as an L1 miss, and an L3 miss costs about 13 times what an L1 miss costs (130–135 cycles). Although the processor will attempt to find alternative instructions to execute during L2 and L3 misses, it is likely that some of the buffers will fill before a miss completes, causing the processor to stop issuing instructions.

Figure 4.79 shows the overall CPI for the 19 SPECCPUint2006 benchmarks. The average CPI on the i7 6700 is 0.71. Figure 4.80 shows the misprediction rate of the branch predictors of the Intel i7 6700. The misprediction rates are roughly half of those for the A53 in Figure 4.76—the median is 2.3% versus 3.9% for SPEC2006—and the CPI is less than half: the median is 0.64 versus 1.36 for the much more aggressive architecture. The clock rate is 3.4 GHz on the i7 versus up to 1.3 GHz for the A53, so the average instruction time is $0.64 \times 1/3.4\ \text{GHz} = 0.18$ ns versus $1.36 \times 1/1.3\ \text{GHz} = 1.05$ ns, or more than five times as fast. On the other hand, the i7 uses 200× as much power!

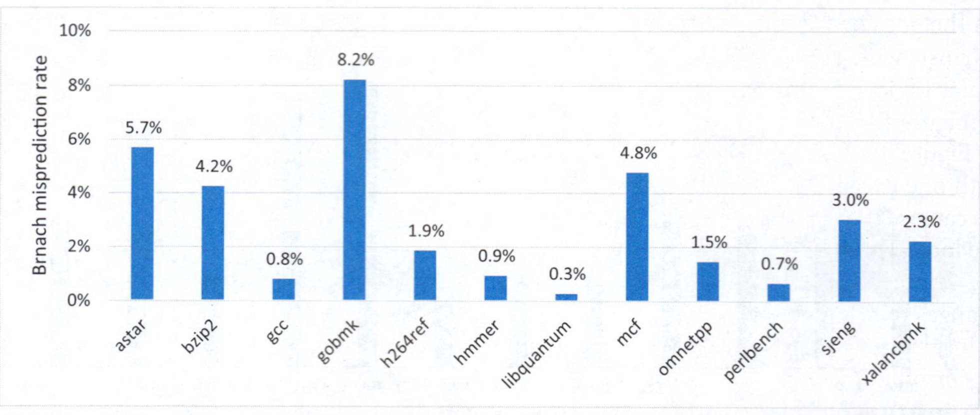

FIGURE 4.80 The misprediction rate for the integer SPECCPU2006 benchmarks on the Intel Core i7 6700. The misprediction rate is computed as the ratio of completed branches that are mispredicted versus all completed branches. (Adapted from Hennessy JL, Patterson DA: *Computer architecture: A quantitative approach*, ed 6, Cambridge MA, 2018, Morgan Kaufmann.)

The Intel Core i7 combines a 14-stage pipeline and aggressive multiple issue to achieve high performance. By keeping the latencies for back-to-back operations low, the impact of data dependences is reduced. What are the most serious potential performance bottlenecks for programs running on this processor? The following list includes some potential performance problems, the last three of which can apply in some form to any high-performance pipelined processor.

- The use of x86 instructions that do not map to a few simple micro-operations

- Branches that are diffi cult to predict, causing misprediction stalls and restarts when speculation fails

- Long dependences—typically caused by long-running instructions or the **memory hierarchy**—that lead to stalls

- Performance delays arising in accessing memory (see Chapter 5) that cause the processor to stall

4.13 Going Faster: Instruction-Level Parallelism and Matrix Multiply

Returning to the DGEMM example from Chapter 3, we can see the impact of instruction level parallelism by unrolling the loop so that the multiple issue, out-of-order execution processor has more instructions to work with. Figure 4.81 shows the unrolled version of Figure 3.21, which contains the C intrinsics to produce the AVX instructions.

Like the unrolling example in Figure 4.71 above, we are going to unroll the loop 4 times. (We use the constant `UNROLL` in the C code to control the amount of unrolling in case we want to try other values.) Rather than manually unrolling the loop in C by making 4 copies of each of the intrinsics in Figure 3.21, we can rely on the gcc compiler to do the unrolling at − O3 optimization. We surround each intrinsic with a simple *for* loop with 4 iterations (lines 9, 15, and 19) and replace the scalar C0 in Figure 3.22 with a 4-element array c[] (lines 8, 10, 16, and 20).

Figure 4.82 shows the assembly language output of the unrolled code. As expected, in Figure 4.82 there are 4 versions of each of the AVX instructions in Figure 3.22, with one exception. We only need 1 copy of the vbroadcastsd instruction, since we can use the eight copies of the B element in register %zmm0 repeatedly throughout the loop. Thus the 4 AVX instructions in Figure 3.22 become 13 in Figure 4.82, and the 7 integer instructions appear in both, although the constants and addressing changes to account for the unrolling. Hence, despite unrolling 4 times, the number of instructions in the body of the loop only doubles: from 11 to 20.

Unrolling nearly doubles performance. Optimizations for **subword parallelism** and **instruction level parallelism** result in an overall speedup of 4.4 versus the DGEMM in Figure 3.21. Compared to the Python version in Chapter 1, it is 4600 times as fast.

Elaboration: There are no pipeline stalls despite the reuse of register %zmm5 in lines 9 to 12 of Figure 4.82 because the Intel Core i7 pipeline renames the registers.

Are the following statements true or false?

1. The Intel Core i7 uses a multiple-issue pipeline to directly execute x86 instructions.

2. Both the A53 and the Core i7 use dynamic multiple issue.

```
1    #include <x86intrin.h>
2    #define UNROLL (4)
3
4    void dgemm (int n, double* A, double* B, double* C)
5    {
6      for (int i = 0; i < n; i+=UNROLL*8)
7        for (int j = 0; j < n; ++j){
8          __m512d c[UNROLL];
9          for (int r=0;r<UNROLL;r++)
10            c[r] = _mm512_load_pd(C+i+r*8+j*n); //[ UNROLL];
11
12         for( int k = 0; k < n; k++ )
13         {
14            __m512d bb = _mm512_broadcastsd_pd(_mm_load_sd(B+j*n+k));
15           for (int r=0;r<UNROLL;r++)
16             c[r] = _mm512_fmadd_pd(_mm512_load_pd(A+n*k+r*8+i), bb, c[r]);
17         }
18
19         for (int r=0;r<UNROLL;r++)
20           _mm512_store_pd(C+i+r*8+j*n, c[r]);
21       }
22    }
```

FIGURE 4.81 Optimized C version of DGEMM using C intrinsics to generate the AVX subword-parallel instructions for the x86 (Figure 3.21) and loop unrolling to create more opportunities for instruction-level parallelism. Figure 4.82 shows the assembly language produced by the compiler for the inner loop, which unrolls the three for-loop bodies to expose instruction level parallelism.

```
 1    vmovapd        (%r11),%zmm4                 # Load 8 elements of C into %zmm4
 2    mov            %rbx,%rcx                     # register %rcx = %rbx
 3    xor            %eax,%eax                     # register %eax = 0
 4    vmovapd        0x20(%r11),%zmm3              # Load 8 elements of C into %zmm3
 5    vmovapd        0x40(%r11),%zmm2              # Load 8 elements of C into %zmm2
 6    vmovapd        0x60(%r11),%zmm1              # Load 8 elements of C into %zmm1
 7    vbroadcastsd   (%rax,%r8,8),%zmm0            # Make 8 copies of B element in %zmm0
                                                   # register %rax = %rax + 8
 8    add            $0x8,%rax
 9    vfmadd231pd    (%rcx),%zmm0,%zmm4            # Parallel mul & add %zmm0, %zmm4
10    vfmadd231pd    0x20(%rcx),%zmm0,%zmm3        # Parallel mul & add %zmm0, %zmm3
11    vfmadd231pd    0x40(%rcx),%zmm0,%zmm2        # Parallel mul & add %zmm0, %zmm2
12    vfmadd231pd    0x60(%rcx),%zmm0,%zmm1        # Parallel mul & add %zmm0, %zmm1
13    add            %r9,%rcx                      # register %rcx = %rcx
14    cmp            %r10,%rax                     # compare %r10 to %rax
15    jne            50 <dgemm+0x50>               # jump if not %r10 != %rax
16    add            $0x1, %esi                    # register % esi = % esi + 1
17    vmovapd        %zmm4, (%r11)                 # Store %zmm4 into 8 C elements
18    vmovapd        %zmm3, 0x20(%r11)             # Store %zmm3 into 8 C elements
19    vmovapd        %zmm2, 0x40(%r11)             # Store %zmm2 into 8 C elements
20    vmovapd        %zmm1, 0x60(%r11)             # Store %zmm1 into 8 C elements
```

FIGURE 4.82 The x86 assembly language for the body of the nested loops generated by compiling the unrolled C code in Figure 4.81.

Check Yourself

3. The Core i7 microarchitecture has many more registers than x86 requires.

4. The Intel Core i7 uses less than half the pipeline stages of the earlier Intel Pentium 4 Prescott (see Figure 4.73).

4.14 Advanced Topic: an Introduction to Digital Design Using a Hardware Design Language to Describe and Model a Pipeline and More Pipelining Illustrations

Modern digital design is done using hardware description languages and modern computer-aided synthesis tools that can create detailed hardware designs from the descriptions using both libraries and logic synthesis. Entire books are written on such languages and their use in digital design. This section, which appears online, gives a brief introduction and shows how a hardware design language, Verilog in this case, can be used to describe the MIPS control both behaviorally and in a form suitable for hardware synthesis. It then provides a series of behavioral models in Verilog of the MIPS five-stage pipeline. The initial model ignores hazards, and additions to the model highlight the changes for forwarding, data hazards, and branch hazards.

We then provide about a dozen illustrations using the single-cycle graphical pipeline representation for readers who want to see more detail on how pipelines work for a few sequences of MIPS instructions.

4.15 Fallacies and Pitfalls

Fallacy: Pipelining is easy.

Our books testify to the subtlety of correct pipeline execution. Our advanced book had a pipeline bug in its first edition, despite its being reviewed by more than 100 people and being class-tested at 18 universities. The bug was uncovered only when someone tried to build the computer in that book. The fact that the Verilog to describe a pipeline like that in the Intel Core i7 will be many thousands of lines is an indication of the complexity. Beware!

Fallacy: Pipelining ideas can be implemented independent of technology.

When the number of transistors on-chip and the speed of transistors made a five-stage pipeline the best solution, then the delayed branch (see the first *Elaboration* on page 267) was a simple solution to control hazards. With longer pipelines, superscalar execution, and dynamic branch prediction, it is now redundant. In the early 1990s, dynamic pipeline scheduling took too many resources and was not required for high performance, but as transistor budgets continued to double due to Moore's Law logic became much faster than memory, then multiple functional units and dynamic pipelining made more sense. Today, concerns about power are leading to less aggressive designs.

Pitfall: Failure to consider instruction set design can adversely impact pipelining.

Many of the difficulties of pipelining arise because of instruction set complications. Here are some examples:

- Widely variable instruction lengths and running times can lead to imbalance among pipeline stages and severely complicate hazard detection in a design pipelined at the instruction set level. This problem was overcome, initially in the DEC VAX 8500 in the late 1980s, using the micro-operations and micropipelined scheme that the Intel Core i7 employs today. Of course, the overhead of translation and maintaining correspondence between the micro-operations and the actual instructions remains.

- Sophisticated addressing modes can lead to different sorts of problems. Addressing modes that update registers complicate hazard detection. Other addressing modes that require multiple memory accesses substantially complicate pipeline control and make it difficult to keep the pipeline flowing smoothly.

- Perhaps the best example is the DEC Alpha and the DEC NVAX. In comparable technology, the newer instruction set architecture of the Alpha allowed an implementation whose performance is more than twice as fast as NVAX. In another example, Bhandarkar and Clark [1991] compared the MIPS M/2000 and the DEC VAX 8700 by counting clock cycles of the SPEC benchmarks; they concluded that although the MIPS M/2000 executes more instructions, the VAX on average executes 2.7 times as many clock cycles, so the MIPS is faster.

Nine-tenths of wisdom consists of being wise in time.

American proverb

4.16   Concluding Remarks

As we have seen in this chapter, both the datapath and control for a processor can be designed starting with the instruction set architecture and an understanding of the basic characteristics of the technology. In Section 4.3, we saw how the datapath for a MIPS processor could be constructed based on the architecture and the decision to build a single-cycle implementation. Of course, the underlying technology also affects many design decisions by dictating what components can be used in the datapath, as well as whether a single-cycle implementation even makes sense.

instruction latency The inherent execution time for an instruction.

Pipelining improves throughput but not the inherent execution time, or **instruction latency**, of instructions; for some instructions, the latency is similar in length to the single-cycle approach. Multiple instruction issue adds additional datapath hardware to allow multiple instructions to begin every clock cycle, but at an increase in effective latency. Pipelining was presented as reducing the clock cycle time of the simple single-cycle datapath. Multiple instruction issue, in comparison, clearly focuses on reducing *clock cycles per instruction* (CPI).

Pipelining and multiple issue both attempt to exploit instruction-level parallelism. The presence of data and control dependences, which can become hazards, are the primary limitations on how much parallelism can be exploited. Scheduling and speculation via **prediction**, both in hardware and in software, are the primary techniques used to reduce the performance impact of dependences.

We showed that unrolling the DGEMM loop four times exposed more instructions that could take advantage of the out-of-order execution engine of the Core i7 to more than double performance.

The switch to longer pipelines, multiple instruction issue, and dynamic scheduling in the mid-1990s helped sustain the 60% per year processor performance increase that started in the early 1980s. As mentioned in Chapter 1, these microprocessors preserved the sequential programming model, but they eventually ran into the power wall. Thus, the industry was forced to switch to multiprocessors, which exploit parallelism at much coarser levels (the subject of Chapter 6). This trend has also caused designers to reassess the energy-performance implications of some of the inventions since the mid-1990s, resulting in a simplification of pipelines in the more recent versions of microarchitectures.

To sustain the advances in processing performance via parallel processors, Amdahl's law suggests that another part of the system will become the bottleneck. That bottleneck is the topic of the next chapter: the **memory hierarchy**.

4.17 Historical Perspective and Further Reading

This section, which appears online, discusses the history of the first pipelined processors, the earliest superscalars, and the development of out-of-order and speculative techniques, as well as important developments in the accompanying compiler technology.

4.18 Self Study

While higher performance processors have much longer pipelines than the five stages, some very low cost or low energy processors have shorter pipelines. Assume the same timing of the data path components as in Figures 4.26 and 4.27.

Three-Stage Pipe. How would you split the data path in stages if it was a three-stage pipeline instead of five?

Clock Rate. Ignoring an impact of pipeline registers or forwarding logic on the clock cycle time, what are the clock rates for the five-stage versus the three-stage pipelines? Assume the same timing of the data path components as in Figures 4.26 and 4.27.

Register Write/Read Data Hazards? Do you still have them in with three stages? If so, will forwarding fix them?

Load-Use Data Hazards? Do you still have them in with three stages? Do you need to stall the pipeline or can forwarding fix them?

Control Hazards? Do you still have them in with three stages? If so, how can you reduce their impact?

CPI. Will the clocks per instruction of the three-stage pipeline be higher or lower than the five-stage pipeline?

Self-Study Answers

Three-Stage Pipe. While there are multiple possible solutions, this one is a sensible split:

1. Instruction fetch, register read (300 ps)

2. ALU (200 ps)

3. Data access, register write (300 ps)

300	600	900	1200	1500

Instruction fetch & Register Read | ALU | Data access & Register Write
Instruction fetch & Register Read | ALU | Data access & Register Write
Instruction fetch & Register Read | ALU | Data access & Register Write

Clock Rate. Figure 4.27 shows the clock cycle time of the five-stage pipeline is 200 ps, so the clock rate is 1/200 ps or 5 GHz. The worst case stage for this three-stage pipeline is 300 ps, so the clock rate is 1/300 ps or 3.33 GHz.

Register Write/Read Data Hazards. As the pipeline drawing previously shows, there is still a write/read hazard. The first instruction does not write the data to register the third stage, but the next instruction needs the new value at the beginning of its second stage. The forwarding solution in Section 4.8 works fine for the three-stage pipeline, as the ALU result of the prior instruction is ready before the beginning of its second stage.

Load-Use Data Hazards. Even with three stages, we have to stall one clock cycle for a load use hazard as in Section 4.8. The data is not available until the third stage of the load instruction, but the following instruction needs the new data at the beginning of its second stage.

Control Hazards. This hazard is where the three stage pipeline shines. We can use the same optimization as in Section 4.9 to calculate the branch address and compare registers for equality before the ALU stage as we did in Figure 4.62. That calculation is performed before the instruction fetch of the following instruction, so early branch logic resolves the control hazard with no pipeline penalty.

CPI. The average clocks per instruction will shrink (get better) with a three-stage pipeline for a couple of reasons:

- Given the clock cycle is longer, it will take fewer clock cycles to access DRAM memory, which will affect the CPI when we have a miss in the cache (see Chapter 5).

- Branches will always execute in one clock cycle, whereas any software and hardware scheme to accelerate branches with five stages will fail some of the time, increasing the effective CPI.

- Our clock cycle time is longer for the ALU, which may allow some complex operations that might take more than one clock cycle in the five-stage pipeline. For example, integers that multiply or divide might need fewer of these longer clock cycles than does the five-stage pipeline.

4.19   Exercises

4.1 Consider the following instruction:

Instruction: `and rd, rs1, rs2`

Interpretation: `Reg[rd] = Reg[rs1] AND Reg[rs2]`

4.1.1 [5] <§4.3> What are the values of control signals generated by the control in Figure 4.10 for this instruction?

4.1.2 [5] <§4.3> Which resources (blocks) perform a useful function for this instruction?

4.1.3 [10] <§4.3> Which resources (blocks) produce no output for this instruction? Which resources produce output that is not used?

4.2 [10] <§4.4> Explain each of the "don't cares" in Figure 4.18.

4.3 Consider the following instruction mix:

R-type	I-type (non-lw)	Load	Store	Branch	Jump
24%	28%	25%	10%	11%	2%

4.3.1 [5] <§4.4> What fraction of all instructions use data memory?

4.3.2 [5] <§4.4> What fraction of all instructions use instruction memory?

4.3.3 [5] <§4.4> What fraction of all instructions use the sign extend?

4.3.4 [5] <§4.4> What is the sign extend doing during cycles in which its output is not needed?

4.4 When silicon chips are fabricated, defects in materials (e.g., silicon) and manufacturing errors can result in defective circuits. A very common defect is for one signal wire to get "broken" and always register a logical 0. This is often called a "stuck-at-0" fault.

4.4.1 [5] <§4.4> Which instructions fail to operate correctly if the `MemToReg` wire is stuck at 0?

4.4.2 [5] <§4.4> Which instructions fail to operate correctly if the `ALUSrc` wire is stuck at 0?

4.5 In this exercise, we examine in detail how an instruction is executed in a single-cycle datapath. Problems in this exercise refer to a clock cycle in which the processor fetches the following instruction word: `0x00c6ba23`.

4.5.1 [10] <§4.4> What are the values of the ALU control unit's inputs for this instruction?

4.5.2 [5] <§4.4> What is the new PC address after this instruction is executed? Highlight the path through which this value is determined.

4.5.3 [10] <§4.4> For each mux, show the values of its inputs and outputs during the execution of this instruction. List values that are register outputs at `Reg [xn]`.

4.5.4 [10] <§4.4> What are the input values for the ALU and the two add units?

4.5.5 [10] <§4.4> What are the values of all inputs for the registers unit?

4.6 Section 4.4 does not discuss I-type instructions like `addi` or `andi`.

4.6.1 [5] <§4.4> What additional logic blocks, if any, are needed to add I-type instructions to the CPU shown in Figure 4.21? Add any necessary logic blocks to Figure 4.21 and explain their purpose.

4.6.2 [10] <§4.4> List the values of the signals generated by the control unit for `addi`. Explain the reasoning for any "don't care" control signals.

4.7 Problems in this exercise assume that the logic blocks used to implement a processor's datapath have the following latencies:

I-Mem / D-Mem	Register File	Mux	ALU	Adder	Single gate	Register Read	Register Setup	Sign extend	Control
250ps	150ps	25ps	200ps	150ps	5ps	30ps	20ps	50ps	50ps

"Register read" is the time needed after the rising clock edge for the new register value to appear on the output. This value applies to the PC only. "Register setup" is the amount of time a register's data input must be stable before the rising edge of the clock. This value applies to both the PC and Register File.

4.7.1 [5] <§4.4> What is the latency of an R-type instruction (i.e., how long must the clock period be to ensure that this instruction works correctly)?

4.7.2 [10] <§4.4> What is the latency of `lw`? (Check your answer carefully. Many students place extra muxes on the critical path.)

4.7.3 [10] <§4.4> What is the latency of `sw`? (Check your answer carefully. Many students place extra muxes on the critical path.)

4.7.4 [5] <§4.4> What is the latency of `beq`?

4.7.5 [5] <§4.4> What is the latency of an arithmetic, logical, or shift I-type (non-load) instruction?

4.7.6 [5] <§4.4> What is the minimum clock period for this CPU?

4.8 [10] <§4.4> Suppose you could build a CPU where the clock cycle time was different for each instruction. What would the speedup of this new CPU be over the CPU presented in Figure 4.21 given the instruction mix below?

R-type/I-type (non-lw)	lw	sw	beq
52%	25%	11%	12%

4.9 Consider the addition of a multiplier to the CPU shown in Figure 4.21. This addition will add 300 ps to the latency of the ALU, but will reduce the number of instructions by 5% (because there will no longer be a need to emulate the multiply instruction).

4.9.1 [5] <§4.4> What is the clock cycle time with and without this improvement?

4.9.2 [10] <§4.4> What is the speedup achieved by adding this improvement?

4.9.3 [10] <§4.4> What is the slowest the new ALU can be and still result in improved performance?

4.10 When processor designers consider a possible improvement to the processor datapath, the decision usually depends on the cost/performance trade-off. In the following three problems, assume that we are beginning with the datapath from Figure 4.21, the latencies from Exercise 4.7, and the following costs:

I-Mem	Register File	Mux	ALU	Adder	D-Mem	Single Register	Sign extend	Sign gate	Control
1000	200	10	100	30	2000	5	100	1	500

Suppose doubling the number of general purpose registers from 32 to 64 would reduce the number of lw and sw instruction executed by 12%, but increase the latency of the register file from 150 ps to 160 ps and double the cost from 200 to 400. (Use the instruction mix from Exercise 4.8 and ignore the other effects on the ISA discussed in Exercise 2.18.)

4.10.1 [5] <§4.4> What is the speedup achieved by adding this improvement?

4.10.2 [10] <§4.4> Compare the change in performance to the change in cost.

4.10.3 [10] <§4.4> Given the cost/performance ratios you just calculated, describe a situation where it makes sense to add more registers and describe a situation where it doesn't make sense to add more registers.

4.11 Examine the difficulty of adding a proposed lwi.drd, rs1, rs2 ("Load With Increment") instruction to MIPS.

Interpretation: Reg[rd]=Mem[Reg[rs1]+Reg[rs2]]

4.11.1 [5] <§4.4> Which new functional blocks (if any) do we need for this instruction?

4.11.2 [5] <§4.4> Which existing functional blocks (if any) require modification?

4.11.3 [5] <§4.4> Which new data paths (if any) do we need for this instruction?

4.11.4 [5] <§4.4> What new signals do we need (if any) from the control unit to support this instruction?

4.12 Examine the difficulty of adding a proposed swap rs, rt instruction to MIPS.

Interpretation: Reg[rt]=Reg[rs]; Reg[rs]=Reg[rt]

4.12.1 [5] <§4.4> Which new functional blocks (if any) do we need for this instruction?

4.12.2 [10] <§4.4> Which existing functional blocks (if any) require modification?

4.12.3 [5] <§4.4> What new data paths do we need (if any) to support this instruction?

4.12.4 [5] <§4.4> What new signals do we need (if any) from the control unit to support this instruction?

4.12.5 [5] <§4.4> Modify Figure 4.21 to demonstrate an implementation of this new instruction.

4.13 Examine the difficulty of adding a proposed ss rt, rs, imm (Store Sum) instruction to MIPS.

Interpretation: Mem[Reg[rt]]=Reg[rs]+immediate

4.13.1 [10] <§4.4> Which new functional blocks (if any) do we need for this instruction?

4.13.2 [10] <§4.4> Which existing functional blocks (if any) require modification?

4.13.3 [5] <§4.4> What new data paths do we need (if any) to support this instruction?

4.13.4 [5] <§4.4> What new signals do we need (if any) from the control unit to support this instruction?

4.13.5 [5] <§4.4> Modify Figure 4.21 to demonstrate an implementation of this new instruction.

4.14 [5] <§4.4> For which instructions (if any) is the Imm Gen block on the critical path?

4.15 lw is the instruction with the longest latency on the CPU from Section 4.4. If we modified lw and sw so that there was no offset (i.e., the address to be loaded from/stored to must be calculated and placed in rs before calling lw/sw), then no instruction would use both the ALU and Data memory. This would allow us to reduce the clock cycle time. However, it would also increase the number of instructions, because many ld and sd instructions would need to be replaced with lw/add or sw/add combinations.

4.15.1 [5] <§4.4> What would the new clock cycle time be?

4.15.2 [10] <§4.4> Would a program with the instruction mix presented in Exercise 4.7 run faster or slower on this new CPU? By how much? (For simplicity, assume every lw and sw instruction is replaced with a sequence of two instructions.)

4.15.3 [5] <§4.4> What is the primary factor that influences whether a program will run faster or slower on the new CPU?

4.15.4 [5] <§4.4> Do you consider the original CPU (as shown in Figure 4.21) a better overall design; or do you consider the new CPU a better overall design? Why?

4.16 In this exercise, we examine how pipelining affects the clock cycle time of the processor. Problems in this exercise assume that individual stages of the datapath have the following latencies:

IF	ID	EX	MEM	WB
250ps	350ps	150ps	300ps	200ps

Also, assume that instructions executed by the processor are broken down as follows:

ALU/Logic	Jump/Branch	Load	Store
45%	20%	20%	15%

4.16.1 [5] <§4.6> What is the clock cycle time in a pipelined and non-pipelined processor?

4.16.2 [10] <§4.6> What is the total latency of an lw instruction in a pipelined and non-pipelined processor?

4.16.3 [10] <§4.6> If we can split one stage of the pipelined datapath into two new stages, each with half the latency of the original stage, which stage would you split and what is the new clock cycle time of the processor?

4.16.4 [10] <§4.6> Assuming there are no stalls or hazards, what is the utilization of the data memory?

4.16.5 [10] <§4.6> Assuming there are no stalls or hazards, what is the utilization of the write-register port of the "Registers" unit?

4.17 [10] <§4.6> What is the minimum number of cycles needed to completely execute n instructions on a CPU with a k stage pipeline? Justify your formula.

4.18 [5] <§4.6> Assume that $s0 is initialized to 11 and $s1 is initialized to 22. Suppose you executed the code below on a version of the pipeline from Section

4.6 that does not handle data hazards (i.e., the programmer is responsible for addressing data hazards by inserting NOP instructions where necessary). What would the final values of registers $s2 and $s3 be?

```
addi   $s0, $s1, 5
add    $s2, $s0, $s1
addi   $s3, $s0, 15
```

4.19 [10] <§4.6> Assume that $s0 is initialized to 11 and $s1 is initialized to 22. Suppose you executed the code below on a version of the pipeline from Section 4.6 that does not handle data hazards (i.e., the programmer is responsible for addressing data hazards by inserting NOP instructions where necessary). What would the final values of register $s4 be? Assume the register file is written at the beginning of the cycle and read at the end of a cycle. Therefore, an ID stage will return the results of a WB state occurring during the same cycle. See Section 4.8 and Figure 4.51 for details.

```
addi   $s0, $s1, 5
add    $s2, $s0, $s1
addi   $s3, $s0, 15
add    $s4, $s0, $s0
```

4.20 [5] <§4.6> Add NOP instructions to the code below so that it will run correctly on a pipeline that does not handle data hazards.

```
addi   $s0, $s1, 5
add    $s2, $s0, $s1
addi   $s3, $s0, 15
add    $s4, $s2, $s1
```

4.21 Consider a version of the pipeline from Section 4.6 that does not handle data hazards (i.e., the programmer is responsible for addressing data hazards by inserting NOP instructions where necessary). Suppose that (after optimization) a typical n-instruction program requires an additional 4*n NOP instructions to correctly handle data hazards.

4.21.1 [5] <§4.6> Suppose that the cycle time of this pipeline without forwarding is 250 ps. Suppose also that adding forwarding hardware will reduce the number of NOPs from .4*n to .05*n, but increase the cycle time to 300 ps. What is the speedup of this new pipeline compared to the one without forwarding?

4.21.2 [10] <§4.6> Different programs will require different amounts of NOPs. How many NOPs (as a percentage of code instructions) can remain in the typical program before that program runs slower on the pipeline with forwarding?

4.21.3 [10] <§4.6> Repeat 4.21.2; however, this time let x represent the number of NOP instructions relative to n. (In 4.21.2, x was equal to .4.) Your answer will be with respect to x.

4.21.4 [10] <§4.6> Can a program with only .075*n NOPs possibly run faster on the pipeline with forwarding? Explain why or why not.

4.21.5 [10] <§4.6> At minimum, how many NOPs (as a percentage of code instructions) must a program have before it can possibly run faster on the pipeline with forwarding?

4.22 [5] <§4.6> Consider the fragment of MIPS assembly below:

```
sd    $s5, 12($s3)
Id    $s5, 8($s3)
sub   $s4, $s2, $s1
beqz  $s4, label
add   $s2, $s0, $s1
sub   $s2, $s6, $s1
```

Suppose we modify the pipeline so that it has only one memory (that handles both instructions and data). In this case, there will be a structural hazard every time a program needs to fetch an instruction during the same cycle in which another instruction accesses data.

4.22.1 [5] <§4.6> Draw a pipeline diagram to show were the code above will stall.

4.22.2 [5] <§4.6> In general, is it possible to reduce the number of stalls/NOPs resulting from this structural hazard by reordering code?

4.22.3 [5] <§4.6> Must this structural hazard be handled in hardware? We have seen that data hazards can be eliminated by adding NOPs to the code. Can you do the same with this structural hazard? If so, explain how. If not, explain why not.

4.22.4 [5] <§4.6> Approximately how many stalls would you expect this structural hazard to generate in a typical program? (Use the instruction mix from Exercise 4.8.)

4.23 If we change load/store instructions to use a register (without an offset) as the address, these instructions no longer need to use the ALU. (See Exercise 4.15.)

As a result, the MEM and EX stages can be overlapped and the pipeline has only four stages.

4.23.1 [10] <§4.6> How will the reduction in pipeline depth affect the cycle time?

4.23.2 [5] <§4.6> How might this change improve the performance of the pipeline?

4.23.3 [5] <§4.6> How might this change degrade the performance of the pipeline?

4.24 [10] <§4.8> Which of the two pipeline diagrams below better describes the operation of the pipeline's hazard detection unit? Why?

Choice 1:

```
ld  x11, 0(x12):     IF ID EX ME WB
add x13, x11, X14:    IF ID EX..ME WB
or  x15, x16, X17:    IF ID..EX ME WB
```

Choice 2:

```
ld  x11, 0(x12):     IF ID EX ME WB
add x13, x11, x14:    IF ID..EX ME WB
or  x15, x16, x17:    IF..ID EX ME WB
```

4.25 Consider the following loop.

```
LOOP: ld   $s0, 0($s3)
      ld   $s1, 8($s3)
      add  $s2, $s0, $s1
      addi $s3, $s3, -16
      bnez $s2, LOOP
```

Assume that perfect branch prediction is used (no stalls due to control hazards), that there are no delay slots, that the pipeline has full forwarding support, and that branches are resolved in the EX (as opposed to the ID) stage.

4.25.1 [10] <§4.8> Show a pipeline execution diagram for the first two iterations of this loop.

4.25.2 [10] <§4.8> Mark pipeline stages that do not perform useful work. How often while the pipeline is full do we have a cycle in which all five pipeline stages are doing useful work? (Begin with the cycle during which the addi is in the IF stage. End with the cycle during which the bnez is in the IF stage.)

4.26 This exercise is intended to help you understand the cost/complexity/performance trade-offs of forwarding in a pipelined processor. Problems in this exercise refer to pipelined datapaths from Figure 4.53. These problems assume that, of all the instructions executed in a processor, the following fraction of these instructions has a particular type of RAW data dependence. The type of RAW data dependence is identified by the stage that produces the result (EX or MEM) and the next instruction that consumes the result (1st instruction that follows the one that produces the result, 2nd instruction that follows, or both). We assume that the register write is done in the first half of the clock cycle and that register reads are done in the second half of the cycle, so "EX to 3rd" and "MEM to 3rd" dependences are not counted because they cannot result in data hazards. We also assume that branches are resolved in the EX stage (as opposed to the ID stage), and that the CPI of the processor is 1 if there are no data hazards.

EX to 1st Only	MEM to 1st Only	EX to 2nd Only	MEM to 2nd Only	EX to 1st and EX to 2nd
5%	20%	5%	10%	10%

Assume the following latencies for individual pipeline stages. For the EX stage, latencies are given separately for a processor without forwarding and for a processor with different kinds of forwarding.

IF	ID	EX (no FW)	EX (full FW)	EX (FW from EX/ MEM only)	EX (FW from MEM/ WB only)	MEM	WB
120ps	100ps	110ps	130ps	120ps	120ps	120ps	100ps

4.26.1 [5] <§4.8> For each RAW dependency listed above, give a sequence of at least three assembly statements that exhibits that dependency.

4.26.2 [5] <§4.8> For each RAW dependency above, how many NOPs would need to be inserted to allow your code from 4.26.1 to run correctly on a pipeline with no forwarding or hazard detection? Show where the NOPs could be inserted.

4.26.3 [10] <§4.8> Analyzing each instruction independently will over-count the number of NOPsneeded to run a program on a pipeline with no forwarding or hazard detection. Write a sequence of three assembly instructions so that, when you consider each instruction in the sequence independently, the sum of the stalls is larger than the number of stalls the sequence actually needs to avoid data hazards.

4.26.4 [5] <§4.8> Assuming no other hazards, what is the CPI for the program described by the table above when run on a pipeline with no forwarding? What percent of cycles are stalls? (For simplicity, assume that all necessary cases are listed above and can be treated independently.)

4.26.5 [5] <§4.8> What is the CPI if we use full forwarding (forward all results that can be forwarded)? What percent of cycles are stalls?

4.26.6 [10] <§4.8> Let us assume that we cannot afford to have three-input multiplexors that are needed for full forwarding. We have to decide if it is better to forward only from the EX/MEM pipeline register (next-cycle forwarding) or only from the MEM/WB pipeline register (two-cycle forwarding). What is the CPI for each option?

4.26.7 [5] <§4.8> For the given hazard probabilities and pipeline stage latencies, what is the speedup achieved by each type of forwarding (EX/MEM, MEM/WB, for full) as compared to a pipeline that has no forwarding?

4.26.8 [5] <§4.8> What would be the additional speedup (relative to the fastest processor from 4.26.7) be if we added "time-travel" forwarding that eliminates all data hazards? Assume that the yet-to-be-invented time-travel circuitry adds 100 ps to the latency of the full-forwarding EX stage.

4.26.9 [5] <§4.8> The table of hazard types has separate entries for "EX to 1st" and "EX to 1st and EX to 2nd". Why is there no entry for "MEM to 1st and MEM to 2nd"?

4.27 Problems in this exercise refer to the following sequence of instructions, and assume that it is executed on a five-stage pipelined datapath:

```
add   $s3, $s1, $s0
lw    $s2, 4($s3)
lw    $s1, 0($s4)
or    $s2, $s3, $s2
sw    $s2, 0($s3)
```

4.27.1 [5] <§4.8> If there is no forwarding or hazard detection, insert NOPs to ensure correct execution.

4.27.2 [10] <§4.8> Now, change and/or rearrange the code to minimize the number of NOPs needed. You can assume register $t0 can be used to hold temporary values in your modified code.

4.27.3 [10] <§4> If the processor has forwarding, but we forgot to implement the hazard detection unit, what happens when the original code executes?

4.27.4 [20] <§4.8> If there is forwarding, for the first seven cycles during the execution of this code, specify which signals are asserted in each cycle by hazard detection and forwarding units in Figure 4.59.

4.27.5 [10] <§4.8> If there is no forwarding, what new input and output signals do we need for the hazard detection unit in Figure 4.59? Using this instruction sequence as an example, explain why each signal is needed.

4.27.6 [20] <§4.8> For the new hazard detection unit from 4.26.5, specify which output signals it asserts in each of the first five cycles during the execution of this code.

4.28 The importance of having a good branch predictor depends on how often conditional branches are executed. Together with branch predictor accuracy, this will determine how much time is spent stalling due to mispredicted branches. In this exercise, assume that the breakdown of dynamic instructions into various instruction categories is as follows:

R-type	beqz/bnez	jal	lw	sw
40%	25%	5%	25%	5%

Also, assume the following branch predictor accuracies:

Always-Taken	Always-Not-Taken	2-Bit
45%	55%	85%

4.28.1 [10] <§4.9> Stall cycles due to mispredicted branches increase the CPI. What is the extra CPI due to mispredicted branches with the always-taken predictor? Assume that branch outcomes are determined in the ID stage and applied in the EX stage that there are no data hazards, and that no delay slots are used.

4.28.2 [10] <§4.9> Repeat 4.28.1 for the "always-not-taken" predictor.

4.28.3 [10] <§4.9> Repeat 4.28.1 for the 2-bit predictor.

4.28.4 [10] <§4.9> With the 2-bit predictor, what speedup would be achieved if we could convert half of the branch instructions to some ALU instruction? Assume that correctly and incorrectly predicted instructions have the same chance of being replaced.

4.28.5 [10] <§4.9> With the 2-bit predictor, what speedup would be achieved if we could convert half of the branch instructions in a way that replaced each branch instruction with two ALU instructions? Assume that correctly and incorrectly predicted instructions have the same chance of being replaced.

4.28.6 [10] <§4.9> Some branch instructions are much more predictable than others. If we knowthat 80% of all executed branch instructions are easy-to-predict loop-back branches that are always predicted correctly, what is the accuracy of the 2-bit predictor on the remaining 20% of the branch instructions?

4.29 This exercise examines the accuracy of various branch predictors for the following repeating pattern (e.g., in a loop) of branch outcomes: T, NT, T, T, NT.

4.29.1 [5] <§4.9> What is the accuracy of always-taken and always-not-taken predictors for this sequence of branch outcomes?

4.29.2 [5] <§4.9> What is the accuracy of the 2-bit predictor for the first four branches in this pattern, assuming that the predictor starts off in the bottom left state from Figure 4.61 (predict not taken)?

4.29.3 [10] <§4.9> What is the accuracy of the 2-bit predictor if this pattern is repeated forever?

4.29.4 [30] <§4.9> Design a predictor that would achieve a perfect accuracy if this pattern is repeated forever. You predictor should be a sequential circuit with one output that provides a prediction (1 for taken, 0 for not taken) and no inputs other than the clock and the control signal that indicates that the instruction is a conditional branch.

4.29.5 [10] <§4.9> What is the accuracy of your predictor from 4.29.4 if it is given a repeating pattern that is the exact opposite of this one?

4.29.6 [20] <§4.9> Repeat 4.29.4, but now your predictor should be able to eventually (after a warm-up period during which it can make wrong predictions) start perfectly predicting both this pattern and its opposite. Your predictor should have an input that tells it what the real outcome was. Hint: this input lets your predictor determine which of the two repeating patterns it is given.

4.30 This exercise explores how exception handling affects pipeline design. The first three problems in this exercise refer to the following two instructions:

Instruction 1	Instruction 2
beqz $s0, LABEL	ld $s0, 0($s1)

4.30.1 [5] <§4.10> Which exceptions can each of these instructions trigger? For each of these exceptions, specify the pipeline stage in which it is detected.

4.30.2 [10] <§4.10> If there is a separate handler address for each exception, show how the pipeline organization must be changed to be able to handle this exception. You can assume that the addresses of these handlers are known when the processor is designed.

4.30.3 [10] <§4.10> If the second instruction is fetched immediately after the first instruction, describe what happens in the pipeline when the first instruction causes the first exception you listed in Exercise 4.30.1. Show the pipeline execution diagram from the time the first instruction is fetched until the time the first instruction of the exception handler is completed.

4.30.4 [20] <§4.10> In vectored exception handling, the table of exception handler addresses is in data memory at a known (fixed) address. Change the pipeline to implement this exception handling mechanism. Repeat Exercise 4.30.3 using this modified pipeline and vectored exception handling.

4.30.5 [15] <§4.10> We want to emulate vectored exception handling (described in Exercise 4.30.4) on a machine that has only one fixed handler address. Write the code that should be at that fixed address. Hint: this code should identify the exception, get the right address from the exception vector table, and transfer execution to that handler.

4.31 In this exercise we compare the performance of 1-issue and 2-issue processors, taking into account program transformations that can be made to optimize for 2-issue execution. Problems in this exercise refer to the following loop (written in C):

```
for(i=0;i!=j;i+=2)
    b[i]=a[i]-a[i+1];
```

A compiler doing little or no optimization might produce the following MIPS assembly code:

```
        li    $s0, 0
        jal   ENT
TOP:    sll   $t0, $s0, 3
        add   $t1, $s2, $t0
        lw    $t2, 0($t1)
        lw    $t3, 8($t1)
        sub   $t4, $t2, $t3
        add   $t5, $s3, $t0
        sw    $t4, 0($t5)
        addi  $s0, $s0, 2
ENT:    bne   $s0, $s1, TOP
```

The code above uses the following registers:

i	j	a	b	Temporary values
$s0	$s1	$s2	$s3	$t0-$t5

Assume the two-issue, statically scheduled processor for this exercise has the following properties:

1 One instruction must be a memory operation; the other must be an arithmetic/logic instruction or a branch.

2 The processor has all possible forwarding paths between stages (including paths to the ID stage for branch resolution).

3 The processor has perfect branch prediction.

4 Two instruction may not issue together in a packet if one depends on the other. (See page 336.)

5 If a stall is necessary, both instructions in the issue packet must stall. (See page 336.)

As you complete these exercises, notice how much effort goes into generating code that will produce a near-optimal speedup.

4.31.1 [30] <§4.11> Draw a pipeline diagram showing how MIPS code given above executes on the two-issue processor. Assume that the loop exits after two iterations.

4.31.2 [10] <§4.11> What is the speedup of going from a one-issue to a two-issue processor? (Assume the loop runs thousands of iterations.)

4.31.3 [10] <§4.11> Rearrange/rewrite the MIPS code given above to achieve better performance on the one-issue processor. Hint: Use the instruction "`beqz $s1,DONE`" to skip the loop entirely if j = 0.

4.31.4 [20] <§4.11> Rearrange/rewrite the MIPS code given above to achieve better performance on the two-issue processor. (Do not unroll the loop, however.)

4.31.5 [30] <§4.11> Repeat Exercise 4.31.1, but this time use your optimized code from Exercise 4.31.4.

4.31.6 [10] <§4.11> What is the speedup of going from a one-issue processor to a two-issue processor when running the optimized code from Exercises 4.31.3 and 4.31.4.

4.31.7 [10] <§4.11> Unroll the MIPS code from Exercise 4.31.3 so that each iteration of the unrolled loop handles two iterations of the original loop. Then, rearrange/rewrite your unrolled code to achieve better performance on the one-issue processor. You may assume that j is a multiple of 4.

4.31.8 [20] <§4.11> Unroll the MIPS code from Exercise 4.31.4 so that each iteration of the unrolled loop handles two iterations of the original loop. Then, rearrange/rewrite your unrolled code to achieve better performance on the two-issue processor. You may assume that j is a multiple of 4. (Hint: Re-organize the loop so that some calculations appear both outside the loop and at the end of the loop. You may assume that the values in temporary registers are not needed after the loop.)

4.31.9 [10] <§4.11> What is the speedup of going from a one-issue processor to a two-issue processor when running the unrolled, optimized code from Exercises 4.31.7 and 4.31.8?

4.31.10 [30] <§4.11> Repeat Exercises 4.31.8 and 4.31.9, but this time assume the two-issue processor can run two arithmetic/logic instructions together. (In other words, the first instruction in a packet can be any type of instruction, but the second must be an arithmetic or logic instruction. Two memory operations cannot be scheduled at the same time.)

4.32 This exercise explores energy efficiency and its relationship with performance. Problems in this exercise assume the following energy consumption for activity in

Instruction memory, Registers, and Data memory. You can assume that the other components of the datapath consume a negligible amount of energy. ("Register Read" and "Register Write" refer to the register file only.)

I-Mem	1 Register Read	Register Write	D-Mem Read	D-Mem Write
140pJ	70pJ	60pJ	140pJ	120pJ

Assume that components in the datapath have the following latencies. You can assume that the other components of the datapath have negligible latencies.

I-Mem	Control	Register Read or Write	ALU	D-Mem Read or Write
200ps	150ps	90ps	90ps	250ps

4.32.1 [5] <§§4.3, 4.7, 4.15> How much energy is spent to execute an add instruction in a single-cycle design and in the five-stage pipelined design?

4.32.2 [10] <§§4.7, 4.15> What is the worst-case MIPS instruction in terms of energy consumption? What is the energy spent to execute it?

4.32.3 [10] <§§4.7, 4.15> If energy reduction is paramount, how would you change the pipelined design? What is the percentage reduction in the energy spent by an `ld` instruction after this change?

4.32.4 [10] <§§4.7, 4.15> What other instructions can potentially benefit from the change discussed in Exercise 4.32.3?

4.32.5 [10] <§§4.7, 4.15> How do your changes from Exercise 4.32.3 affect the performance of a pipelined CPU?

4.32.6 [10] <§§4.7, 4.15> We can eliminate the `MemRead` control signal and have the data memory be readm every cycle, i.e., we can permanently have `MemRead=1`. Explain why the processor still functions correctly after this change. If 25% of instructions are loads, what is the effect of this change on clock frequency and energy consumption?

4.33 When silicon chips are fabricated, defects in materials (e.g., silicon) and manufacturing errors can result in defective circuits. A very common defect is for one wire to affect the signal in another. This is called a "cross-talk fault". A special class of cross-talk faults is when a signal is connected to a wire that has a constant logical value (e.g., a power supply wire). These faults, where the affected signal always has a logical value of either 0 or 1 are called "stuck-at-0" or "stuck- at-1" faults. The following problems refer to bit 0 of the Write Register input on the register file in Figure 4.21.

4.33.1 [10] <§§4.3, 4.4> Let us assume that processor testing is done by (1) filling the PC, registers, and data and instruction memories with some values (you can choose which values), (2) letting a single instruction execute, then (3) reading the PC, memories, and registers. These values are then examined to determine if a particular fault is present. Can you design a test (values for PC, memories, and registers) that would determine if there is a stuck-at-0 fault on this signal?

4.33.2 [10] <§§4.3, 4.4> Repeat Exercise 4.33.1 for a stuck-at-1 fault. Can you use a single test for both stuck-at-0 and stuck-at-1? If yes, explain how; if no, explain why not.

4.33.3 [10] <§§4.3, 4.4> If we know that the processor has a stuck-at-1 fault on this signal, is the processor still usable? To be usable, we must be able to convert any program that executes on a normal MIPS processor into a program that works on this processor. You can assume that there is enough free instruction memory and data memory to let you make the program longer and store additional data.

4.33.4 [10] <§§4.3, 4.4> Repeat Exercise 4.33.1; but now the fault to test for is whether the MemRead control signal becomes 0 if the branch control signal is 0, no fault otherwise.

4.33.5 [10] <§§4.3, 4.4> Repeat Exercise 4.33.1; but now the fault to test for is whether the MemRead control signal becomes 1 if RegRd control signal is 1, no fault otherwise. Hint: This problem requires knowledge of operating systems. Consider what causes segmentation faults.

Answers to
Check Yourself

§4.1, page 260: 3 of 5: Control, Datapath, Memory. Input and Output are missing.

§4.2, page 263: false. Edge-triggered state elements make simultaneous reading and writing both possible and unambiguous.

§4.3, page 269: I. a. II. c.

§4.4, page 284: Yes, Branch and ALUOp0 are identical. In addition, MemtoReg and RegDst are inverses of one another. You don't need an inverter; simply use the other signal and flip the order of the inputs to the multiplexor!

§4.5, page 4.5-22: 1. False. 2. Maybe; If the signal PCSource[0] is always set to zero when it is a don't care (which is most states), then it is identical to the PCWriteCond.

§4.6, page 297: 1. Stall on the lw result. 2. Bypass the first add result written into $t1. 3. No stall or bypass required.

§4.7, page 310: Statements 2 and 4 are correct; the rest are incorrect.

§4.9, page 336: 1. Predict not taken. 2. Predict taken. 3. Dynamic prediction.

§4.10, page 344: The first instruction, since it is logically executed before the others.

§4.11, page 357: 1. Both. 2. Both. 3. Software. 4. Hardware. 5. Hardware. 6. Hardware. 7. Both. 8. Hardware. 9. Both.

§4.13, page 368: First two are false and the last two are true.

Large and Fast: Exploiting Memory Hierarchy

The Five Classic Components of a Computer

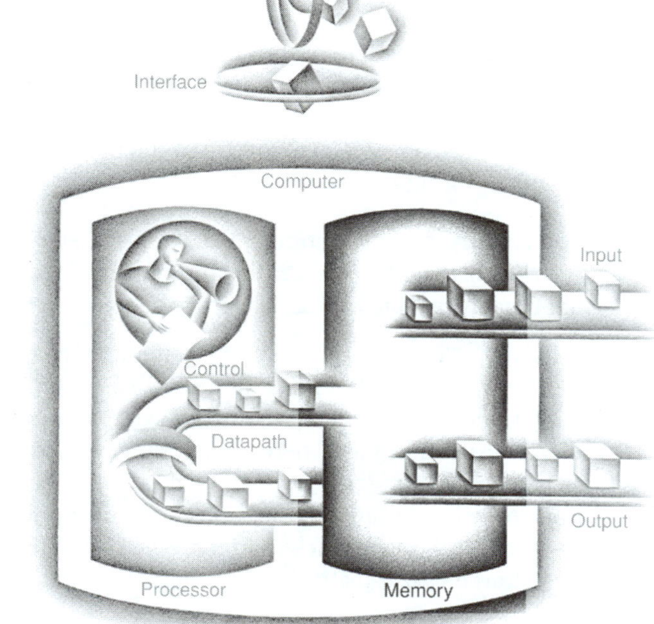

5.1   Introduction

From the earliest days of computing, programmers have wanted unlimited amounts of fast memory. The topics in this chapter aid programmers by creating that illusion. Before we look at creating the illusion, let's consider a simple analogy that illustrates the key principles and mechanisms that we use.

Suppose you were a student writing a term paper on important historical developments in computer hardware. You are sitting at a desk in a library with a collection of books that you have pulled from the shelves and are examining. You find that several of the important computers that you need to write about are described in the books you have, but there is nothing about the EDSAC. Therefore, you go back to the shelves and look for an additional book. You find a book on early British computers that covers the EDSAC. Once you have a good selection of books on the desk in front of you, there is a good probability that many of the topics you need can be found in them, and you may spend most of your time just using the books on the desk without going back to the shelves. Having several books on the desk in front of you saves time compared to having only one book there and constantly having to go back to the shelves to return it and take out another.

The same principle allows us to create the illusion of a large memory that we can access as fast as a very small memory. Just as you did not need to access all the books in the library at once with equal probability, a program does not access all of its code or data at once with equal probability. Otherwise, it would be impossible to make most memory accesses fast and still have large memory in computers, just as it would be impossible for you to fit all the library books on your desk and still find what you wanted quickly.

This *principle of locality* underlies both the way in which you did your work in the library and the way that programs operate. The principle of locality states that programs access a relatively small portion of their address space at any instant of time, just as you accessed a very small portion of the library's collection. There are two different types of locality:

temporal locality The principle stating that if a data location is referenced then it will tend to be referenced again soon.

spatial locality The locality principle stating that if a data location is referenced, data locations with nearby addresses will tend to be referenced soon.

- **Temporal locality** (locality in time): if an item is referenced, it will tend to be referenced again soon. If you recently brought a book to your desk to look at, you will probably need to look at it again soon.

- **Spatial locality** (locality in space): if an item is referenced, items whose addresses are close by will tend to be referenced soon. For example, when you brought out the book on early English computers to find out about the EDSAC, you also noticed that there was another book shelved next to it about early mechanical computers, so you also brought back that book and, later on, found something useful in that book. Libraries put books on the same topic together on the same shelves to increase spatial locality. We'll see how memory hierarchies use spatial locality a little later in this chapter.

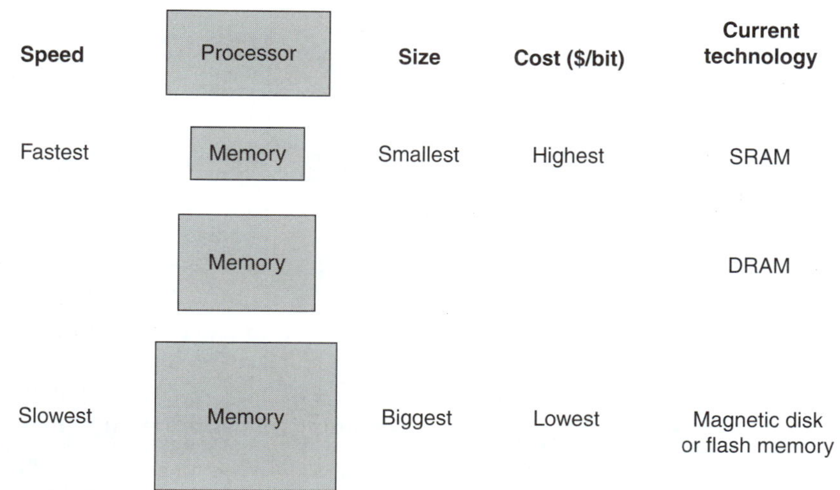

FIGURE 5.1 **The basic structure of a memory hierarchy.** By implementing the memory system as a hierarchy, the user has the illusion of a memory that is as large as the largest level of the hierarchy, but can be accessed as if it were all built from the fastest memory. Flash memory has replaced disks in many personal mobile devices, and may lead to a new level in the storage hierarchy for desktop and server computers; see Section 5.2.

Just as accesses to books on the desk naturally exhibit locality, locality in programs arises from simple and natural program structures. For example, most programs contain loops, so instructions and data are likely to be accessed repeatedly, showing high amounts of temporal locality. Since instructions are normally accessed sequentially, programs also show high spatial locality. Accesses to data also exhibit a natural spatial locality. For example, sequential accesses to elements of an array or a record will naturally have high degrees of spatial locality.

We take advantage of the principle of locality by implementing the memory of a computer as a **memory hierarchy**. A memory hierarchy consists of multiple levels of memory with different speeds and sizes. The faster memories are more expensive per bit than the slower memories and thus are smaller.

Figure 5.1 shows the faster memory is close to the processor and the slower, less expensive memory is below it. The goal is to present the user with as much memory as is available in the cheapest technology, while providing access at the speed offered by the fastest memory.

The data is similarly hierarchical: a level closer to the processor is generally a subset of any level further away, and all the data is stored at the lowest level. By analogy, the books on your desk form a subset of the library you are working in, which is in turn a subset of all the libraries on campus. Furthermore, as we move away from the processor, the levels take progressively longer to access, just as we might encounter in a hierarchy of campus libraries.

A memory hierarchy can consist of multiple levels, but data is copied between only two adjacent levels at a time, so we can focus our attention on just two levels.

memory hierarchy A structure that uses multiple levels of memories; as the distance from the processor increases, the size of the memories and the access time both increase while the cost per bit decreases.

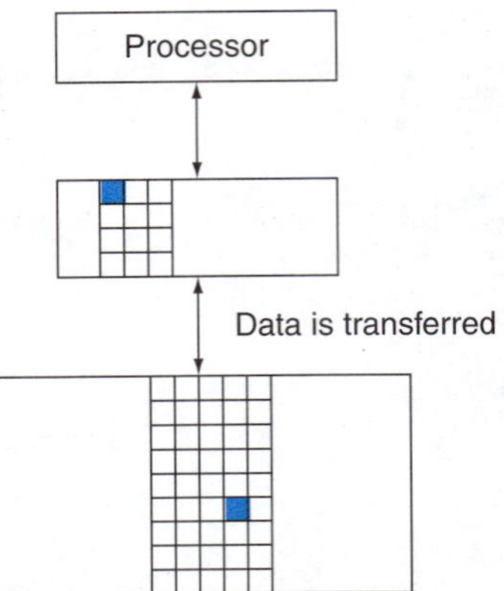

FIGURE 5.2   Every pair of levels in the memory hierarchy can be thought of as having an upper and lower level. Within each level, the unit of information that is present or not is called a *block* or a *line*. Usually we transfer an entire block when we copy something between levels.

block (or line) The minimum unit of information that can be either present or not present in a cache.

hit rate The fraction of memory accesses found in a level of the memory hierarchy.

miss rate The fraction of memory accesses not found in a level of the memory hierarchy.

hit time The time required to access a level of the memory hierarchy, including the time needed to determine whether the access is a hit or a miss.

miss penalty The time required to fetch a block into a level of the memory hierarchy from the lower level, including the time to access the block, transmit it from one level to the other, insert it in the level that experienced the miss, and then pass the block to the requestor.

The upper level—the one closer to the processor—is smaller and faster than the lower level, since the upper level uses technology that is more expensive. Figure 5.2 shows that the minimum unit of information that can be either present or not present in the two-level hierarchy is called a **block** or a **line**; in our library analogy, a block of information is one book.

If the data requested by the processor appears in some block in the upper level, this is called a *hit* (analogous to your finding the information in one of the books on your desk). If the data is not found in the upper level, the request is called a *miss*. The lower level in the hierarchy is then accessed to retrieve the block containing the requested data. (Continuing our analogy, you go from your desk to the shelves to find the desired book.) The **hit rate**, or *hit ratio*, is the fraction of memory accesses found in the upper level; it is often used as a measure of the performance of the memory hierarchy. The **miss rate** (1 − hit rate) is the fraction of memory accesses not found in the upper level.

Since performance is the major reason for having a memory hierarchy, the time to service hits and misses is important. **Hit time** is the time to access the upper level of the memory hierarchy, which includes the time needed to determine whether the access is a hit or a miss (that is, the time needed to look through the books on the desk). The **miss penalty** is the time to replace a block in the upper level with the corresponding block from the lower level, plus the time to deliver this block to the processor (or the time to get another book from the shelves and place it on the desk). Because the upper level is smaller and built using faster memory parts, the hit time will be much smaller than the time to access the next level in the hierarchy, which is the major component of the miss penalty. (The time to examine the books on the desk is much smaller than the time to get a new book from the shelves.)

As we will see in this chapter, the concepts used to build memory systems affect many other aspects of a computer, including how the operating system manages memory and I/O, how compilers generate code, and even how applications use the computer. Of course, because all programs spend much of their time accessing memory, the memory system is necessarily a major factor in determining performance. The reliance on memory hierarchies to achieve performance has meant that programmers, who are trained to think of memory as a flat, random access storage device, need to understand that memory is a hierarchy to get good performance. We show how important this understanding is in later examples, such as Figure 5.18 on page 426, and Section 5.14, which shows how to double matrix multiply performance.

Since memory systems are critical to performance, computer designers devote a great deal of attention to these systems and develop sophisticated mechanisms for improving the performance of the memory system. In this chapter, we discuss the major conceptual ideas, although we use many simplifications and abstractions to keep the material manageable in length and complexity.

Programs exhibit both temporal locality, the tendency to reuse recently accessed data items, and spatial locality, the tendency to reference data items that are close to other recently accessed items. Memory hierarchies take advantage of temporal locality by keeping more recently accessed data items closer to the processor. Memory hierarchies take advantage of spatial locality by moving blocks consisting of multiple contiguous words in memory to upper levels of the hierarchy.

Figure 5.3 shows that a memory hierarchy uses smaller and faster memory technologies close to the processor. Thus, accesses that hit in the highest level of the hierarchy can be processed quickly. Accesses that miss go to lower levels of the hierarchy, which are larger but slower. If the hit rate is high enough, the memory hierarchy has an effective access time close to that of the highest (and fastest) level and a size equal to that of the lowest (and largest) level.

In most systems, the memory is a true hierarchy, meaning that data cannot be present in level i unless it is also present in level $i+1$.

The BIG Picture

Which of the following statements are generally true?

1. Memory hierarchies take advantage of temporal locality.

2. On a read, the value returned depends on which blocks are in the cache.

3. Most of the cost of the memory hierarchy is at the highest level.

4. Most of the capacity of the memory hierarchy is at the lowest level.

Check Yourself

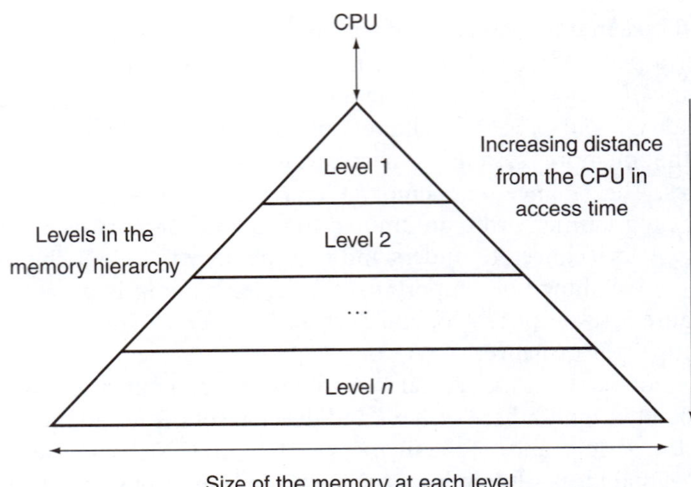

FIGURE 5.3   This diagram shows the structure of a memory hierarchy: as the distance from the processor increases, so does the size. This structure, with the appropriate operating mechanisms, allows the processor to have an access time that is determined primarily by level 1 of the hierarchy and yet have a memory as large as level *n*. Maintaining this illusion is the subject of this chapter. Although a local disk or flash memory is normally the bottom of the hierarchy, some systems use tape or a file server over a local area network as the next levels of the hierarchy.

5.2   Memory Technologies

There are four primary technologies used today in memory hierarchies. Main memory is implemented from DRAM (dynamic random access memory), while levels closer to the processor (caches) use SRAM (static random access memory). DRAM is less costly per bit than SRAM, although it is substantially slower. The price difference arises because DRAM uses significantly less area per bit of memory, and DRAMs thus have larger capacity for the same amount of silicon; the speed difference arises from several factors described in **Section B.9** of **Appendix B**. The third technology is flash memory. This nonvolatile memory is the secondary memory in Personal Mobile Devices. The fourth technology, used to implement the largest and slowest level in the hierarchy in servers, is magnetic disk. The access time and price per bit vary widely among these technologies, as the table below shows, using typical values for 2020:

Memory technology	Typical access time	$ per GiB in 2020
SRAM semiconductor memory	0.5–2.5 ns	$500–$1000
DRAM semiconductor memory	50–70 ns	$3–$6
Flash semiconductor memory	5,000–50,000 ns	$0.06–$0.12
Magnetic disk	5,000,000–20,000,000 ns	$0.01–$0.02

We describe each memory technology in the remainder of this section.

SRAM Technology

SRAMs are simply integrated circuits that are memory arrays with (usually) a single access port that can provide either a read or a write. SRAMs have a fixed access time to any datum, though the read and write access times may differ.

SRAMs don't need to refresh and so the access time is very close to the cycle time. The cycle time is the time between memory accesses. SRAMs typically use six to eight transistors per bit to prevent the information from being disturbed when read. SRAM needs only minimal power to retain the charge in standby mode.

In the past, most PCs and server systems used separate SRAM chips for either their primary, secondary, or even tertiary caches. Today, thanks to Moore's Law, all levels of caches are integrated onto the processor chip, so the market for separate SRAM chips has nearly evaporated.

DRAM Technology

In a SRAM, as long as power is applied, the value can be kept indefinitely. In a dynamic RAM (DRAM), the value kept in a cell is stored as a charge in a capacitor. A single transistor is then used to access this stored charge, either to read the value or to overwrite the charge stored there. Because DRAMs use only a single transistor per bit of storage, they are much denser and cheaper per bit than SRAM. As DRAMs store the charge on a capacitor, it cannot be kept indefinitely and must periodically be refreshed. Impersistence is why this memory structure is called dynamic, as opposed to the static storage in an SRAM cell.

To refresh the cell, we merely read its contents and write it back. The charge can be kept for several milliseconds. If every bit had to be read out of the DRAM and then written back individually, we would constantly be refreshing the DRAM, leaving no time for accessing it. Fortunately, DRAMs use a two-level decoding structure, and this allows us to refresh an entire *row* (which shares a word line) with a read cycle followed immediately by a write cycle.

Figure 5.4 shows the internal organization of a DRAM, and Figure 5.5 shows how the density, cost, and access time of DRAMs have changed over the years.

The row organization that helps with refresh also helps with performance. To improve performance, DRAMs buffer rows for repeated access. The buffer acts like an SRAM; by changing the address, random bits can be accessed in the buffer until the next row access. This capability improves the access time significantly, since the access time to bits in the row is much faster. Making the chip wider also improves the memory bandwidth of the chip. When the row is in the buffer, it can be transferred by successive addresses at whatever the width of the DRAM is (typically 4, 8, or 16 bits), or by specifying a block transfer and the starting address within the buffer.

To further improve the interface to processors, DRAMs added clocks and are properly called Synchronous DRAMs or SDRAMs. The advantage of SDRAMs is that the use of a clock eliminates the time for the memory and processor to synchronize. The speed advantage of synchronous DRAMs comes from the ability to transfer the bits in the burst without having to specify additional address bits.

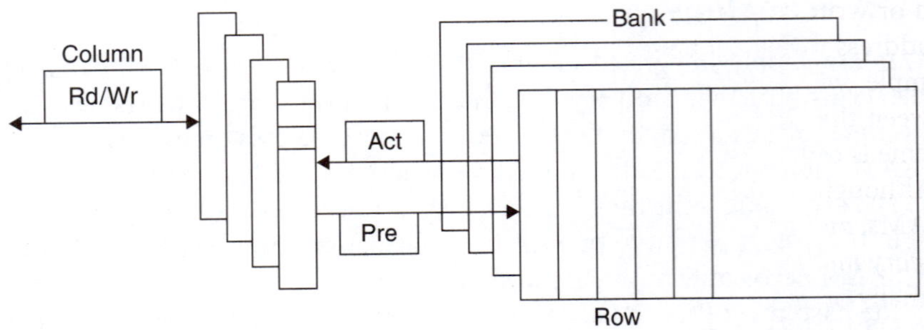

FIGURE 5.4   Internal organization of a DRAM. Modern DRAMs are organized in banks, typically four for DDR4. Each bank consists of a series of rows. Sending a PRE (precharge) command opens or closes a bank. A row address is sent with an Act (activate), which causes the row to transfer to a buffer. When the row is in the buffer, it can be transferred by successive column addresses at whatever the width of the DRAM is (typically 4, 8, or 16 bits in DDR4) or by specifying a block transfer and the starting address. Each command, as well as block transfers, is synchronized with a clock.

Year introduced	Chip size	$ per GiB	Total access time to a new row/column	Average column access time to existing row
1980	64 Kibibit	$6,480,000	250 ns	150 ns
1983	256 Kibibit	$1,980,000	185 ns	100 ns
1985	1 Mebibit	$720,000	135 ns	40 ns
1989	4 Mebibit	$128,000	110 ns	40 ns
1992	16 Mebibit	$30,000	90 ns	30 ns
1996	64 Mebibit	$9,000	60 ns	12 ns
1998	128 Mebibit	$900	60 ns	10 ns
2000	256 Mebibit	$840	55 ns	7 ns
2004	512 Mebibit	$150	50 ns	5 ns
2007	1 Gibibit	$40	45 ns	1.25 ns
2010	2 Gibibit	$13	40 ns	1 ns
2012	4 Gibibit	$5	35 ns	0.8 ns
2015	8 Gibibit	$7	30 ns	0.6 ns
2018	16 Gibibit	$6	25 ns	0.4 ns

FIGURE 5.5   DRAM size increased by multiples of four approximately once every three years until 1996, and thereafter considerably slower. The improvements in access time have been slower but continuous, and cost roughly tracks density improvements, although cost is often affected by other issues, such as availability and demand. The cost per gibibyte is not adjusted for inflation. Price source is https://jcmit.net/memoryprice.htm

Instead, the clock transfers the successive bits in a burst. It is called *Double Data Rate* (DDR) SDRAM. The name means data transfers on both the rising *and* falling edge of the clock, thereby getting twice as much bandwidth as you might expect based on the clock rate and the data width. The latest version of this technology is called DDR4. A DDR4-3200 DRAM can do 3200 million transfers per second, which means it has a 1600 MHz clock.

Sustaining that much bandwidth requires clever organization *inside* the DRAM. Instead of just one faster row buffer, the DRAM can be internally organized to read or write from multiple *banks*, with each having its own row buffer. Sending an address to several banks permits them all to read or write simultaneously. For example, with four banks, there is just one access time and then accesses rotate between the four banks to supply four times the bandwidth. This rotating access scheme is called *address interleaving*.

Although Personal Mobile Devices like the iPad (see Chapter 1) use individual DRAMs, memory for servers are commonly sold on small boards called *dual inline memory modules* (DIMMs). DIMMs typically contain 4–16 DRAMs, and they are normally organized to be 8 bytes wide for server systems. A DIMM using DDR4-3200 SDRAMs could transfer at $8 \times 3200 = 25{,}600$ megabytes per second. Such DIMMs are named after their bandwidth: PC25600. Since a DIMM can have so many DRAM chips that only a portion of them are used for a particular transfer, we need a term to refer to the subset of chips in a DIMM that share common address lines. To avoid confusion with the internal DRAM names of row and banks, we use the term *memory rank* for such a subset of chips in a DIMM.

Elaboration: One way to measure the performance of the memory system behind the caches is the Stream benchmark [McCalpin, 1995]. It measures the performance of long vector operations. They have no temporal locality and they access arrays that are larger than the cache of the computer being tested.

Flash Memory

Flash memory is a type of *electrically erasable programmable read-only memory* (EEPROM).

Unlike disks and DRAM, but like other EEPROM technologies, writes can wear out flash memory bits. To cope with such limits, most flash products include a controller to spread the writes by remapping blocks that have been written many times to less trodden blocks. This technique is called *wear leveling*. With wear leveling, personal mobile devices are very unlikely to exceed the write limits in the flash. Such wear leveling lowers the potential performance of flash, but it is needed unless higher-level software monitors block wear. Flash controllers that perform wear leveling can also improve yield by mapping out memory cells that were manufactured incorrectly.

Disk Memory

As Figure 5.6 shows, a magnetic hard disk consists of a collection of platters, which rotate on a spindle at 5400 to 15,000 revolutions per minute. The metal platters are covered with magnetic recording material on both sides, similar to the material found on a cassette or videotape. To read and write information on a hard disk, a movable *arm* containing a small electromagnetic coil called a *read-write head* is located just above each surface. The entire drive is permanently sealed to control the environment inside the drive, which, in turn, allows the disk heads to be much closer to the drive surface.

Each disk surface is divided into concentric circles, called tracks. There are typically tens of thousands of tracks per surface. Each track is in turn divided into

track One of thousands of concentric circles that makes up the surface of a magnetic disk.

sector One of the segments that make up a track on a magnetic disk; a sector is the smallest amount of information that is read or written on a disk.

sectors that contain the information; each track may have thousands of sectors. Sectors are typically 512 to 4096 bytes in size. The sequence recorded on the magnetic media is a sector number, a gap, the information for that sector including error correction code (see Section 5.5), a gap, the sector number of the next sector, and so on.

The disk heads for each surface are connected together and move in conjunction, so that every head is over the same track of every surface. The term *cylinder* is used to refer to all the tracks under the heads at a given point on all surfaces.

FIGURE 5.6 A disk showing 10 disk platters and the read/write heads. The diameter of today's disks is 2.5 or 3.5 inches, and there are typically one or two platters per drive today.

To access data, the operating system must direct the disk through a three-stage process. The first step is to position the head over the proper track. This operation is called a **seek**, and the time to move the head to the desired track is called the *seek time*.

seek The process of positioning a read/write head over the proper track on a disk.

Disk manufacturers report minimum seek time, maximum seek time, and average seek time in their manuals. The first two are easy to measure, but the average is open to wide interpretation because it depends on the seek distance. The industry calculates average seek time as the sum of the time for all possible seeks divided by the number of possible seeks. Average seek times are usually advertised as 3 ms to 13 ms, but, depending on the application and scheduling of disk requests, the actual average seek time may be only 25% to 33% of the advertised number because of locality of disk references. This locality arises both because of successive accesses to the same file and because the operating system tries to schedule such accesses together.

Once the head has reached the correct track, we must wait for the desired sector to rotate under the read/write head. This time is called the **rotational latency** or **rotational delay**. The average latency to the desired information is halfway around the disk. Disks rotate at 5400 RPM to 15,000 RPM. The average rotational latency at 5400 RPM is

$$\text{Average rotational latency} = \frac{0.5 \text{ rotation}}{5400 \text{ RPM}} = \frac{0.5 \text{ rotation}}{5400 \text{ RPM}/\left(60 \dfrac{\text{seconds}}{\text{minute}}\right)}$$

$$= 0.0056 \text{ seconds} = 5.6 \text{ ms}$$

The last component of a disk access, *transfer time*, is the time to transfer a block of bits. The transfer time is a function of the sector size, the rotation speed, and the recording density of a track. Transfer rates in 2020 were between 150 and 250 MB/sec.

One complication is that most disk controllers have a built-in cache that stores sectors as they are passed over; transfer rates from the cache are typically higher, and were up to 1500 MB/sec (12 Gbit/sec) in 2020.

Alas, where block are located is no longer intuitive. The assumptions of the sector-track-cylinder model above are that nearby blocks are on the same track, blocks in the same cylinder take less time to access since there is no seek time, and some tracks are closer than others. The reason for the change was the raising of the level of the disk interfaces. To speed-up sequential transfers, these higher-level interfaces organize disks more like tapes than like random access devices. The logical blocks are ordered in serpentine fashion across a single surface, trying to capture all the sectors that are recorded at the same bit density to try to get best performance. Hence, blocks with sequential addresses may be on different tracks.

In summary, the two primary differences between magnetic disks and semiconductor memory technologies are that disks have a slower access time because they are mechanical devices—flash latency is 1000 times as fast and DRAM is 100,000 times as fast—yet they are cheaper per bit because they have very high storage capacity at a modest cost—disk is 6 to 300 times cheaper. Magnetic disks are nonvolatile like flash, but unlike flash there is no write wear-out problem. However, flash is much more rugged and hence a better match to the jostling inherent in personal mobile devices.

5.3   The Basics of Caches

In our library example, the desk acted as a cache—a safe place to store things (books) that we needed to examine. *Cache* was the name chosen to represent the level of the memory hierarchy between the processor and main memory in the first commercial computer to have this extra level. The memories in the datapath in Chapter 4 are simply replaced by caches. Today, although this remains the dominant

rotational latency Also called **rotational delay**. The time required for the desired sector of a disk to rotate under the read/write head; usually assumed to be half the rotation time.

Cache: a safe place for hiding or storing things.

Webster's New World Dictionary of the American Language, Third College Edition, 1988

use of the word *cache*, the term is also used to refer to any storage managed to take advantage of locality of access. Caches first appeared in research computers in the early 1960s and in production computers later in that same decade; every general-purpose computer built today, from servers to low-power embedded processors, includes caches.

In this section, we begin by looking at a very simple cache in which the processor requests are each one word and the blocks also consist of a single word. (Readers already familiar with cache basics may want to skip to Section 5.4.) Figure 5.7 shows such a simple cache, before and after requesting a data item that is not initially in the cache. Before the request, the cache contains a collection of recent references X_1, X_2, ..., X_{n-1}, and the processor requests a word X_n that is not in the cache. This request results in a miss, and the word X_n is brought from memory into the cache.

In looking at the scenario in Figure 5.7, there are two questions to answer: How do we know if a data item is in the cache? Moreover, if it is, how do we find it? The answers are related. If each word can go in exactly one place in the cache, then it is straightforward to find the word if it is in the cache. The simplest way to assign a location in the cache for each word in memory is to assign the cache location based on the *address* of the word in memory. This cache structure is called **direct mapped**, since each memory location is mapped directly to exactly one location in the cache. The typical mapping between addresses and cache locations for a direct-mapped cache is usually simple. For example, almost all direct-mapped caches use this mapping to find a block:

> **direct-mapped cache** A cache structure in which each memory location is mapped to exactly one location in the cache.

(Block address) modulo (Number of blocks in the cache)

If the number of entries in the cache is a power of 2, then modulo can be computed simply by using the low-order $\log_2$ (cache size in blocks) bits of the address. Thus, an 8-block cache uses the three lowest bits ($8 = 2^3$) of the block address. For example, Figure 5.8 shows how the memory addresses between 1_{ten} (00001_{two}) and 29_{ten} (11101_{two}) map to locations 1_{ten} (001_{two}) and 5_{ten} (101_{two}) in a direct-mapped cache of eight words.

Because each cache location can contain the contents of a number of different memory locations, how do we know whether the data in the cache corresponds to a requested word? That is, how do we know whether a requested word is in the cache or not? We answer this question by adding a set of **tags** to the cache. The tags contain the address information required to identify whether a word in the cache corresponds to the requested word. The tag needs only to contain the upper portion of the address, corresponding to the bits that are not used as an index into the cache. For example, in Figure 5.8 we need only have the upper 2 of the 5 address bits in the tag, since the lower 3-bit index field of the address selects the block. Architects omit the index bits because they are redundant, since by definition the index field of any address of a cache block must be that block number.

> **tag** A field in a table used for a memory hierarchy that contains the address information required to identify whether the associated block in the hierarchy corresponds to a requested word.

We also need a way to recognize that a cache block does not have valid information. For instance, when a processor starts up, the cache does not have good data, and the tag fields will be meaningless. Even after executing many instructions,

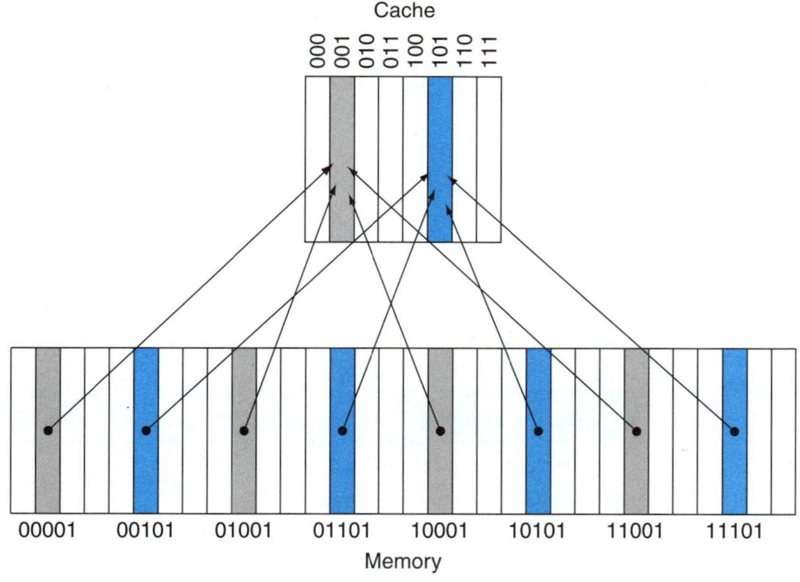

FIGURE 5.7 The cache just before and just after a reference to a word X$_n$ that is not initially in the cache. This reference causes a miss that forces the cache to fetch X$_n$ from memory and insert it into the cache.

FIGURE 5.8 A direct-mapped cache with eight entries showing the addresses of memory words between 0 and 31 that map to the same cache locations. Because there are eight words in the cache, an address X maps to the direct-mapped cache word X modulo 8. That is, the low-order $\log_2(8) = 3$ bits are used as the cache index. Thus, addresses 00001_{two}, 01001_{two}, 10001_{two}, and 11001_{two} all map to entry 001_{two} of the cache, while addresses 00101_{two}, 01101_{two}, 10101_{two}, and 11101_{two} all map to entry 101_{two} of the cache.

some of the cache entries may still be empty, as in Figure 5.7. Thus, we need to know that the tag should be ignored for such entries. The most common method is to add a **valid bit** to indicate whether an entry contains a valid address. If the bit is not set, there cannot be a match for this block.

For the rest of this section, we will focus on explaining how a cache deals with reads. In general, handling reads is a little simpler than handling writes, since reads do not have to change the contents of the cache. After seeing the basics of how reads work and how cache misses can be handled, we'll examine the cache designs for real computers and detail how these caches handle writes.

The BIG Picture

PREDICTION

Caching is perhaps the most important example of the big idea of **prediction**. It relies on the principle of locality to try to find the desired data in the higher levels of the memory hierarchy, and provides mechanisms to ensure that when the prediction is wrong it finds and uses the proper data from the lower levels of the memory hierarchy. The hit rates of the cache prediction on modern computers are often higher than 95% (see Figure 5.47).

Accessing a Cache

Below is a sequence of nine memory references to an empty eight-block cache, including the action for each reference. Figure 5.9 shows how the contents of the cache change on each miss. Since there are eight blocks in the cache, the low-order three bits of an address give the block number:

Decimal address of reference	Binary address of reference	Hit or miss in cache	Assigned cache block (where found or placed)
22	10110_{two}	miss (5.9b)	$(10110_{two}\ \mathrm{mod}\ 8) = 110_{two}$
26	11010_{two}	miss (5.9c)	$(11010_{two}\ \mathrm{mod}\ 8) = 010_{two}$
22	10110_{two}	hit	$(10110_{two}\ \mathrm{mod}\ 8) = 110_{two}$
26	11010_{two}	hit	$(11010_{two}\ \mathrm{mod}\ 8) = 010_{two}$
16	10000_{two}	miss (5.9d)	$(10000_{two}\ \mathrm{mod}\ 8) = 000_{two}$
3	00011_{two}	miss (5.9e)	$(00011_{two}\ \mathrm{mod}\ 8) = 011_{two}$
16	10000_{two}	hit	$(10000_{two}\ \mathrm{mod}\ 8) = 000_{two}$
18	10010_{two}	miss (5.9f)	$(10010_{two}\ \mathrm{mod}\ 8) = 010_{two}$
16	10000_{two}	hit	$(10000_{two}\ \mathrm{mod}\ 8) = 000_{two}$

Since the cache is empty, several of the first references are misses; the caption of Figure 5.9 describes the actions for each memory reference. On the eighth reference

Index	V	Tag	Data
000	N		
001	N		
010	N		
011	N		
100	N		
101	N		
110	N		
111	N		

a. The initial state of the cache after power-on

Index	V	Tag	Data
000	N		
001	N		
010	N		
011	N		
100	N		
101	N		
110	Y	10_{two}	Memory (10110_{two})
111	N		

b. After handling a miss of address (10110_{two})

Index	V	Tag	Data
000	N		
001	N		
010	Y	11_{two}	Memory (11010_{two})
011	N		
100	N		
101	N		
110	Y	10_{two}	Memory (10110_{two})
111	N		

c. After handling a miss of address (11010_{two})

Index	V	Tag	Data
000	Y	10_{two}	Memory (10000_{two})
001	N		
010	Y	11_{two}	Memory (11010_{two})
011	N		
100	N		
101	N		
110	Y	10_{two}	Memory (10110_{two})
111	N		

d. After handling a miss of address (10000_{two})

Index	V	Tag	Data
000	Y	10_{two}	Memory (10000_{two})
001	N		
010	Y	11_{two}	Memory (11010_{two})
011	Y	00_{two}	Memory (00011_{two})
100	N		
101	N		
110	Y	10_{two}	Memory (10110_{two})
111	N		

e. After handling a miss of address (00011_{two})

Index	V	Tag	Data
000	Y	10_{two}	Memory (10000_{two})
001	N		
010	Y	10_{two}	Memory (10010_{two})
011	Y	00_{two}	Memory (00011_{two})
100	N		
101	N		
110	Y	10_{two}	Memory (10110_{two})
111	N		

f. After handling a miss of address (10010_{two})

FIGURE 5.9 The cache contents are shown after each reference request that misses, with the index and tag fields shown in binary for the sequence of addresses on page 404. The cache is initially empty, with all valid bits (V entry in cache) turned off (N). The processor requests the following addresses: 10110_{two} (miss), 11010_{two} (miss), 10110_{two} (hit), 11010_{two} (hit), 10000_{two} (miss), 00011_{two} (miss), 10000_{two} (hit), 10010_{two} (miss), and 10000_{two} (hit). The figures show the cache contents after each miss in the sequence has been handled. When address 10010_{two} (18) is referenced, the entry for address 11010_{two} (26) must be replaced, and a reference to 11010_{two} will cause a subsequent miss. The tag field will contain only the upper portion of the address. The full address of a word contained in cache block i with tag field j for this cache is $j \times 8 + i$, or equivalently the concatenation of the tag field j and the index i. For example, in cache f above, index 010_{two} has tag 10_{two} and corresponds to address 10010_{two}.

we have conflicting demands for a block. The word at address 18 (10010_{two}) should be brought into cache block 2 (010_{two}). Hence, it must replace the word at address 26 (11010_{two}), which is already in cache block 2 (010_{two}). This behavior allows a cache to take advantage of temporal locality: recently referenced words replace less recently referenced words.

This situation is directly analogous to needing a book from the shelves and having no more space on your desk—some book already on your desk must be returned to the shelves. In a direct-mapped cache, there is only one place to put the newly requested item and hence only one choice of what to replace.

We know where to look in the cache for each possible address: the low-order bits of an address can be used to find the unique cache entry to which the address could map. Figure 5.10 shows how a referenced address is divided into

- A *tag field*, which is used to compare with the value of the tag field of the cache

- A *cache index*, which is used to select the block

The index of a cache block, together with the tag contents of that block, uniquely specifies the memory address of the word contained in the cache block. Because the index field is used as an address to reference the cache, and because an n-bit field has 2^n values, the total number of entries in a direct-mapped cache must be a power of 2. In the MIPS architecture, since words are aligned to multiples of four bytes, the least significant two bits of every address specify a byte within a word. Hence, the least significant two bits are ignored when selecting a word in the block.

The total number of bits needed for a cache is a function of the cache size and the address size, because the cache includes both the storage for the data and the tags. The size of the block above was one word, but normally it is several. For the following situation:

- 32-bit addresses

- A direct-mapped cache

- The cache size is 2^n blocks, so n bits are used for the index

- The block size is 2^m words (2^{m+2} bytes), so m bits are used for the word within the block, and two bits are used for the byte part of the address

the size of the tag field is

$$32 - (n + m + 2).$$

The total number of bits in a direct-mapped cache is

$$2^n \times (\text{block size} + \text{tag size} + \text{valid field size}).$$

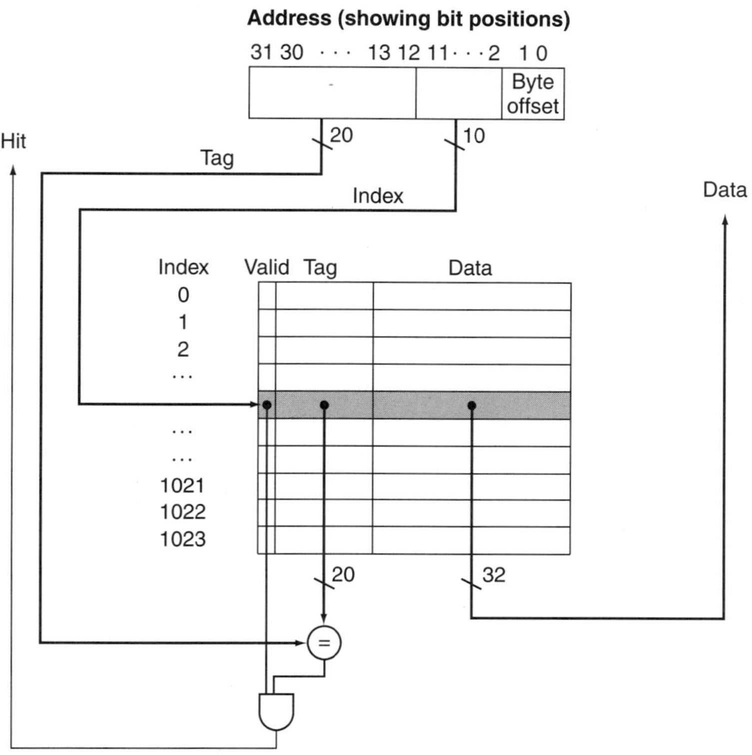

FIGURE 5.10 For this cache, the lower portion of the address is used to select a cache entry consisting of a data word and a tag. This cache holds 1024 words or 4 KiB. We assume 32-bit addresses in this chapter. The tag from the cache is compared against the upper portion of the address to determine whether the entry in the cache corresponds to the requested address. Because the cache has 2^{10} (or 1024) words and a block size of one word, 10 bits are used to index the cache, leaving $32 - 10 - 2 = 20$ bits to be compared against the tag. If the tag and upper 20 bits of the address are equal and the valid bit is on, then the request hits in the cache, and the word is supplied to the processor. Otherwise, a miss occurs.

Since the block size is 2^m words (2^{m+5} bits), and we need 1 bit for the valid field, the number of bits in such a cache is

$$2^n \times (2^m \times 32 + (32 - n - m - 2) + 1) = 2^n \times (2^m \times 32 + 31 - n - m).$$

Although this is the actual size in bits, the naming convention is to exclude the size of the tag and valid field and to count only the size of the data. Thus, the cache in Figure 5.10 is called a 4 KiB cache, even though it actually contains 1.375 KiB of tags and valid bits plus 4 KiB of data.

Bits in a Cache

EXAMPLE

How many total bits are required for a direct-mapped cache with 16 KiB of data and 4-word blocks, assuming a 32-bit address?

ANSWER

We know that 16 KiB is 4096 (2^{12}) words. With a block size of 4 words (2^{2}), there are 1024 (2^{10}) blocks. Each block has 4×32 or 128 bits of data plus a tag, which is $32 - 10 - 2 - 2$ bits, plus a valid bit. Thus, the total cache size is

$$2^{10} \times (4 \times 32 + (32 - 10 - 2 - 2) + 1) = 2^{10} \times 147 = 147\,\text{KiBibits}$$

or 18.4 KiB for a 16 KiB cache. For this cache, the total number of bits in the cache is about 1.15 times as many as needed just for the storage of the data.

Mapping an Address to a Multiword Cache Block

EXAMPLE

Consider a cache with 64 blocks and a block size of 16 bytes. To what block number does byte address 1200 map?

ANSWER

We saw the formula on page 402. The block is given by

$$(\text{Block address}) \text{ modulo } (\text{Number of blocks in the cache})$$

where the address of the block is

$$\frac{\text{Byte address}}{\text{Bytes per block}}$$

Notice that this block address is the block containing all addresses between

$$\left\lfloor \frac{\text{Byte address}}{\text{Bytes per block}} \right\rfloor \times \text{Bytes per block}$$

and

$$\left\lfloor \frac{\text{Byte address}}{\text{Bytes per block}} \right\rfloor \times \text{Bytes per block} + (\text{Bytes per block} - 1)$$

Thus, with 16 bytes per block, byte address 1200 is block address

$$\left\lfloor \frac{1200}{6} \right\rfloor = 75$$

which maps to cache block number (75 modulo 64) = 11. In fact, this block maps all addresses between 1200 and 1215.

Larger blocks exploit spatial locality to lower miss rates. As Figure 5.11 shows, increasing the block size usually decreases the miss rate. The miss rate may go up eventually if the block size becomes a significant fraction of the cache size, because the number of blocks that can be held in the cache will become small, and there will be a great deal of competition for those blocks. As a result, a block will be bumped out of the cache before many of its words are accessed. Stated alternatively, spatial locality among the words in a block decreases with a very large block; consequently, the benefits in the miss rate become smaller.

A more serious problem associated with just increasing the block size is that the cost of a miss increases. The miss penalty is determined by the time required to fetch

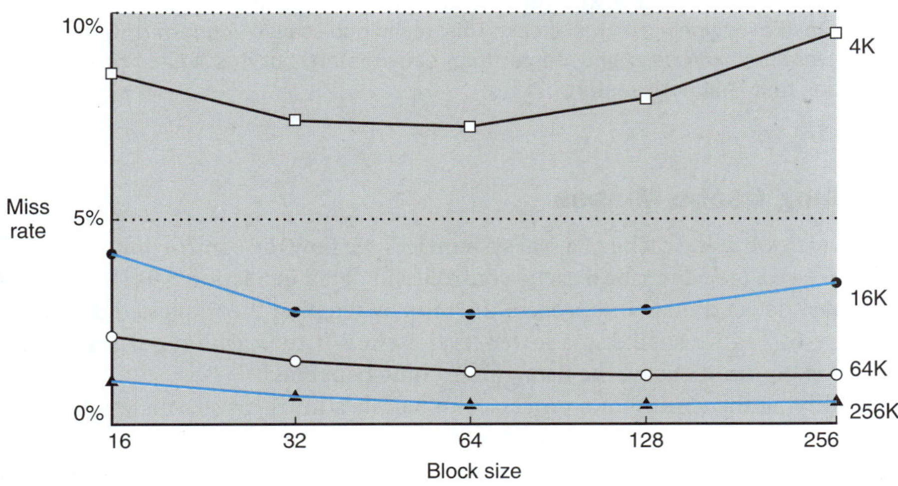

FIGURE 5.11   Miss rate versus block size. Note that the miss rate actually goes up if the block size is too large relative to the cache size. Each line represents a cache of different size. (This figure is independent of associativity, discussed soon.)

the block from the next lower level of the hierarchy and load it into the cache. The time to fetch the block has two parts: the latency to the first word and the transfer time for the rest of the block. Clearly, unless we change the memory system, the transfer time—and hence the miss penalty—will likely increase as the block size increases. Furthermore, the improvement in the miss rate starts to decrease as the blocks become larger. The result is that the increase in the miss penalty overwhelms the decrease in the miss rate for blocks that are too large, and cache performance thus decreases. Of course, if we design the memory to transfer larger blocks more efficiently, we can increase the block size and obtain further improvements in cache performance. We discuss this topic in the next section.

Elaboration: Although it is hard to do anything about the longer latency component of the miss penalty for large blocks, we may be able to hide some of the transfer time so that the miss penalty is effectively smaller. The simplest method for doing this, called *early restart*, is simply to resume execution as soon as the requested word of the block is returned, rather than wait for the entire block. Many processors use this technique for instruction access, where it works best. Instruction accesses are largely sequential, so if the memory system can deliver a word every clock cycle, the processor may be able to restart operation when the requested word is returned, with the memory system delivering new instruction words just in time. This technique is usually less effective for data caches because it is likely that the words will be requested from the block in a less predictable way, and the probability that the processor will need another word from a different cache block before the transfer completes is high. If the processor cannot access the data cache because a transfer is ongoing, then it must stall.

An even more sophisticated scheme is to organize the memory so that the requested word is transferred from the memory to the cache first. The remainder of the block is then transferred, starting with the address after the requested word and wrapping around to the beginning of the block. This technique, called *requested word first* or *critical word first*, can be slightly faster than early restart, but it is limited by the same properties that limit early restart.

Handling Cache Misses

Before we look at the cache of a real system, let's see how the control unit deals with **cache misses**. (We describe a cache controller in detail in Section 5.9). The control unit must detect a miss and process the miss by fetching the requested data from memory (or, as we shall see, a lower-level cache). If the cache reports a hit, the computer continues using the data as if nothing happened.

Modifying the control of a processor to handle a hit is trivial; misses, however, require some extra work. The cache miss handling is done in collaboration with the processor control unit and with a separate controller that initiates the memory access and refills the cache. The processing of a cache miss creates a pipeline stall (Chapter 4) as opposed to an interrupt, which would require saving the state of all registers. For a cache miss, we can stall the entire processor, essentially freezing the contents of the temporary and programmer-visible registers, while we wait

cache miss A request for data from the cache that cannot be filled because the data is not present in the cache.

for memory. More sophisticated out-of-order processors can allow execution of instructions while waiting for a cache miss, but we'll assume in-order processors that stall on cache misses in this section.

Let's look a little more closely at how instruction misses are handled; the same approach can be easily extended to handle data misses. If an instruction access results in a miss, then the content of the Instruction register is invalid. To get the proper instruction into the cache, we must be able to instruct the lower level in the memory hierarchy to perform a read. Since the program counter is incremented in the first clock cycle of execution, the address of the instruction that generates an instruction cache miss is equal to the value of the program counter minus 4. Once we have the address, we need to instruct the main memory to perform a read. We wait for the memory to respond (since the access will take multiple clock cycles), and then write the words containing the desired instruction into the cache.

We can now define the steps to be taken on an instruction cache miss:

1. Send the original PC value (current PC – 4) to the memory.

2. Instruct main memory to perform a read and wait for the memory to complete its access.

3. Write the cache entry, putting the data from memory in the data portion of the entry, writing the upper bits of the address (from the ALU) into the tag field, and turning the valid bit on if it was not on already.

4. Restart the instruction execution at the first step, which will refetch the instruction, this time finding it in the cache.

The control of the cache on a data access is essentially identical: on a miss, we simply stall the processor until the memory responds with the data.

Handling Writes

Writes work somewhat differently. Suppose on a store instruction, we wrote the data into only the data cache (without changing main memory); then, after the write into the cache, memory would have a different value from that in the cache. In such a case, the cache and memory are said to be *inconsistent*. The simplest way to keep the main memory and the cache consistent is always to write the data into both the memory and the cache. This scheme is called **write-through**.

The other key aspect of writes is what occurs on a write miss. We first fetch the words of the block from memory. After the block is fetched and placed into the cache, we can overwrite the word that caused the miss into the cache block. We also write the word to main memory using the full address.

Although this design handles writes very simply, it would not provide very good performance. With a write-through scheme, every write causes the data to be written to main memory. These writes will take a long time, likely at least 100 processor clock cycles, and could slow down the processor considerably. For example, suppose 10% of the instructions are stores. If the CPI without cache

write-through
A scheme in which writes always update both the cache and the next lower level of the memory hierarchy, ensuring that data is always consistent between the two.

misses was 1.0, spending 100 extra cycles on every write would lead to a CPI of $1.0 + 100 \times 10\% = 11$, reducing performance by more than a factor of 10!

One solution to this problem is to use a **write buffer**. A write buffer stores the data while it is waiting to be written to memory. After writing the data into the cache and into the write buffer, the processor can continue execution. When a write to main memory completes, the entry in the write buffer is freed. If the write buffer is full when the processor reaches a write, the processor must stall until there is an empty position in the write buffer. Of course, if the rate at which the memory can complete writes is less than the rate at which the processor is generating writes, no amount of buffering can help, because writes are being generated faster than the memory system can accept them.

The rate at which writes are generated may also be *less* than the rate at which the memory can accept them, and yet stalls may still occur. This can happen when the writes occur in bursts. To reduce the occurrence of such stalls, processors usually increase the depth of the write buffer beyond a single entry.

The alternative to a write-through scheme is a scheme called **write-back**. In a write-back scheme, when a write occurs, the new value is written only to the block in the cache. The modified block is written to the lower level of the hierarchy when it is replaced. Write-back schemes can improve performance, especially when processors can generate writes as fast or faster than the writes can be handled by main memory; a write-back scheme is, however, more complex to implement than write-through.

In the rest of this section, we describe caches from real processors, and we examine how they handle both reads and writes. In Section 5.8, we will describe the handling of writes in more detail.

write buffer A queue that holds data while the data is waiting to be written to memory.

write-back A scheme that handles writes by updating values only to the block in the cache, then writing the modified block to the lower level of the hierarchy when the block is replaced.

Elaboration: Writes introduce several complications into caches that are not present for reads. Here we discuss two of them: the policy on write misses and efficient implementation of writes in write-back caches.

Consider a miss in a write-through cache. The most common strategy is to allocate a block in the cache, called *write allocate*. The block is fetched from memory and then the appropriate portion of the block is overwritten. An alternative strategy is to update the portion of the block in memory but not put it in the cache, called *no write allocate*. The motivation is that sometimes programs write entire blocks of data, such as when the operating system zeros a page of memory. In such cases, the fetch associated with the initial write miss may be unnecessary. Some computers allow the write allocation policy to be changed on a per page basis.

Actually implementing stores efficiently in a cache that uses a write-back strategy is more complex than in a write-through cache. A write-through cache can write the data into the cache and read the tag; if the tag mismatches, then a miss occurs. Because the cache is write-through, the overwriting of the block in the cache is not catastrophic, since memory has the correct value. In a write-back cache, we must first write the block back to memory if the data in the cache is modified and we have a cache miss. If we simply overwrote the block on a store instruction before we knew whether the store had hit in the cache (as we could for a write-through cache), we would destroy the contents of the block, which is not backed up in the next lower level of the memory hierarchy.

In a write-back cache, because we cannot overwrite the block, stores either require two cycles (a cycle to check for a hit followed by a cycle to actually perform the write) or require a write buffer to hold that data—effectively allowing the store to take only one cycle by pipelining it. When a store buffer is used, the processor does the cache lookup and places the data in the store buffer during the normal cache access cycle. Assuming a cache hit, the new data is written from the store buffer into the cache on the next unused cache access cycle.

By comparison, in a write-through cache, writes can always be done in one cycle. We read the tag and write the data portion of the selected block. If the tag matches the address of the block being written, the processor can continue normally, since the correct block has been updated. If the tag does not match, the processor generates a write miss to fetch the rest of the block corresponding to that address.

Many write-back caches also include write buffers that are used to reduce the miss penalty when a miss replaces a modified block. In such a case, the modified block is moved to a write-back buffer associated with the cache while the requested block is read from memory. The write-back buffer is later written back to memory. Assuming another miss does not occur immediately, this technique halves the miss penalty when a dirty block must be replaced.

An Example Cache: The Intrinsity FastMATH Processor

The Intrinsity FastMATH is an embedded microprocessor that uses the MIPS architecture and a simple cache implementation. Near the end of the chapter, we will examine the more complex cache designs of ARM and Intel microprocessors, but we start with this simple, yet real, example for pedagogical reasons. Figure 5.12 shows the organization of the Intrinsity FastMATH data cache.

This processor has a 12-stage pipeline. When operating at peak speed, the processor can request both an instruction word and a data word on every clock. To satisfy the demands of the pipeline without stalling, separate instruction and data caches are used. Each cache is 16 KiB, or 4096 words, with 16-word blocks.

Read requests for the cache are straightforward. Because there are separate data and instruction caches, we need separate control signals to read and write each cache. (Remember that we need to update the instruction cache when a miss occurs.) Thus, the steps for a read request to either cache are as follows:

1. Send the address to the appropriate cache. The address comes either from the PC (for an instruction) or from the ALU (for data).

2. If the cache signals hit, the requested word is available on the data lines. Since there are 16 words in the desired block, we need to select the right one. A block index field is used to control the multiplexor (shown at the bottom of the figure), which selects the requested word from the 16 words in the indexed block.

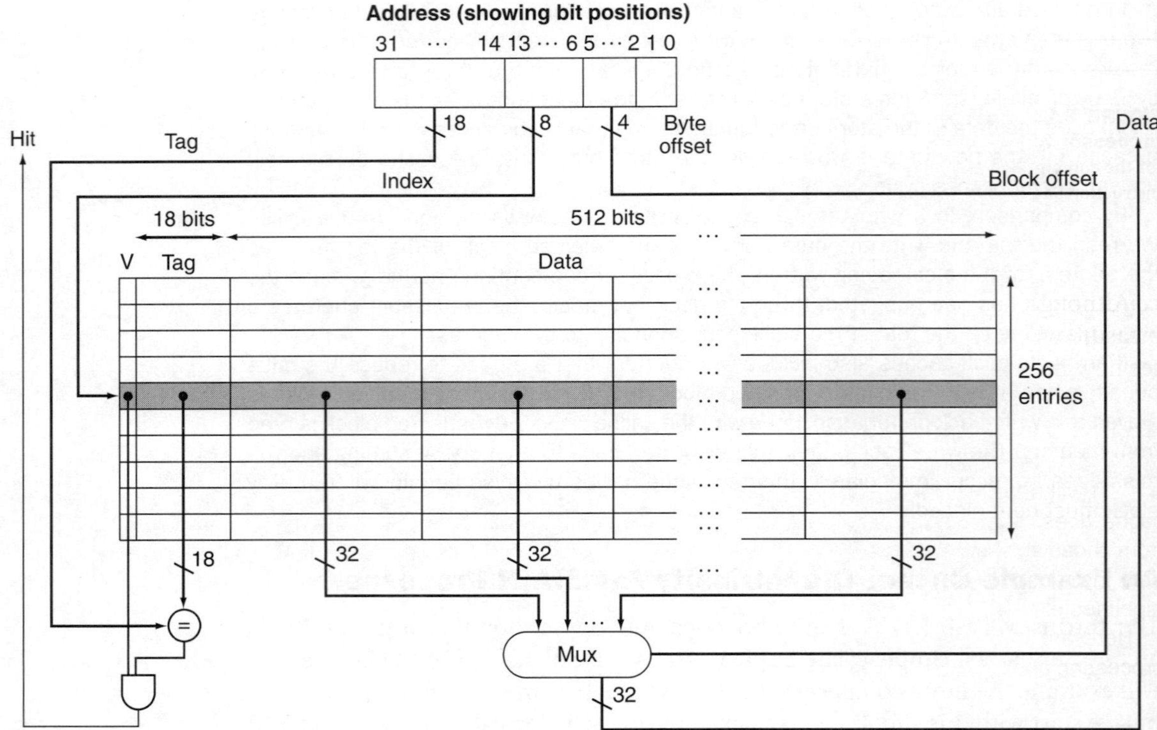

FIGURE 5.12   The 16 KiB caches in the Intrinsity FastMATH each contain 256 blocks with 16 words per block. The tag field is 18 bits wide and the index field is 8 bits wide, while a 4-bit field (bits 5–2) is used to index the block and select the word from the block using a 16-to-1 multiplexor. In practice, to eliminate the multiplexor, caches use a separate large RAM for the data and a smaller RAM for the tags, with the block offset supplying the extra address bits for the large data RAM. In this case, the large RAM is 32 bits wide and must have 16 times as many words as blocks in the cache.

3. If the cache signals miss, we send the address to the main memory. When the memory returns with the data, we write it into the cache and then read it to fulfill the request.

For writes, the Intrinsity FastMATH offers both write-through and write-back, leaving it up to the operating system to decide which strategy to use for an application. It has a one-entry write buffer.

What cache miss rates are attained with a cache structure like that used by the Intrinsity FastMATH? Figure 5.13 shows the miss rates for the instruction and data caches. The combined miss rate is the effective miss rate per reference for each program after accounting for the differing frequency of instruction and data accesses.

Instruction miss rate	Data miss rate	Effective combined miss rate
0.4%	11.4%	3.2%

FIGURE 5.13 Approximate instruction and data miss rates for the Intrinsity FastMATH processor for SPEC CPU2000 benchmarks. The combined miss rate is the effective miss rate seen for the combination of the 16 KiB instruction cache and 16 KiB data cache. It is obtained by weighting the instruction and data individual miss rates by the frequency of instruction and data references.

Although miss rate is an important characteristic of cache designs, the ultimate measure will be the effect of the memory system on program execution time; we'll see how miss rate and execution time are related shortly.

Elaboration: A combined cache with a total size equal to the sum of the two split caches will usually have a better hit rate. This higher rate occurs because the combined cache does not rigidly divide the number of entries that may be used by instructions from those that may be used by data. Nonetheless, almost all processors today use split instruction and data caches to increase cache *bandwidth* to match what modern pipelines expect. (There may also be fewer conflict misses; see Section 5.8.)

Here are miss rates for caches the size of those found in the Intrinsity FastMATH processor, and for a combined cache whose size is equal to the sum of the two caches:

split cache A scheme in which a level of the memory hierarchy is composed of two independent caches that operate in parallel with each other, with one handling instructions and one handling data.

- Total cache size: 32 KiB
- Split cache effective miss rate: 3.24%
- Combined cache miss rate: 3.18%

The miss rate of the split cache is only slightly worse.

The advantage of doubling the cache bandwidth, by supporting both an instruction and data access simultaneously, easily overcomes the disadvantage of a slightly increased miss rate. This observation cautions us that we cannot use miss rate as the sole measure of cache performance, as Section 5.4 shows.

Summary

We began the previous section by examining the simplest of caches: a direct-mapped cache with a one-word block. In such a cache, both hits and misses are simple, since a word can go in exactly one location and there is a separate tag for every word. To keep the cache and memory consistent, a write-through scheme can be used, so that every write into the cache also causes memory to be updated. The alternative to write-through is a write-back scheme that copies a block back to memory when it is replaced; we'll discuss this scheme further in upcoming sections.

To take advantage of spatial locality, a cache must have a block size larger than one word. The use of a larger block decreases the miss rate and improves the efficiency of the cache hardware by reducing the amount of tag storage relative to the amount of data storage in the cache. Although a larger block size decreases the miss rate, it can also increase the miss penalty. If the miss penalty increased linearly with the block size, larger blocks could easily lead to lower performance.

To avoid performance loss, the bandwidth of main memory is increased to transfer cache blocks more efficiently. Common methods for increasing bandwidth external to the DRAM are making the memory wider and interleaving. DRAM designers have steadily improved the interface between the processor and memory to increase the bandwidth of burst mode transfers to reduce the cost of larger cache block sizes.

Check Yourself

The speed of the memory system affects the designer's decision on the size of the cache block. Which of the following cache designer guidelines are generally valid?

1. The shorter the memory latency, the smaller the cache block
2. The shorter the memory latency, the larger the cache block
3. The higher the memory bandwidth, the smaller the cache block
4. The higher the memory bandwidth, the larger the cache block

5.4 Measuring and Improving Cache Performance

In this section, we begin by examining ways to measure and analyze cache performance. We then explore two different techniques for improving cache performance. One focuses on reducing the miss rate by reducing the probability that two different memory blocks will contend for the same cache location. The second technique reduces the miss penalty by adding an additional level to the hierarchy. This technique, called *multilevel caching*, first appeared in high-end computers selling for more than $100,000 in 1990; since then it has become common on personal mobile devices selling for a few hundred dollars!

CPU time can be divided into the clock cycles that the CPU spends executing the program and the clock cycles that the CPU spends waiting for the memory system. Normally, we assume that the costs of cache accesses that are hits are part of the normal CPU execution cycles. Thus,

$$\text{CPU time} = (\text{CPU execution clock cycles} + \text{Memory-stall clock cycles}) \times \text{Clock cycle time}$$

The memory-stall clock cycles come primarily from cache misses, and we make that assumption here. We also restrict the discussion to a simplified model of the memory system. In real processors, the stalls generated by reads and writes can be quite complex, and accurate performance prediction usually requires very detailed simulations of the processor and memory system.

Memory-stall clock cycles can be defined as the sum of the stall cycles coming from reads plus those coming from writes:

$$\text{Memory-stall clock cycles} = (\text{Read-stall cycles} + \text{Write-stall cycles})$$

The read-stall cycles can be defined in terms of the number of read accesses per program, the miss penalty in clock cycles for a read, and the read miss rate:

$$\text{Read-stall cycles} = \frac{\text{Reads}}{\text{Program}} \times \text{Read miss rate} \times \text{Read miss penalty}$$

Writes are more complicated. For a write-through scheme, we have two sources of stalls: write misses, which usually require that we fetch the block before continuing the write (see the *Elaboration* on page 412 for more details on dealing with writes), and write buffer stalls, which occur when the write buffer is full when a write occurs. Thus, the cycles stalled for writes equals the sum of these two:

$$\text{Write-stall cycles} = \left(\frac{\text{Writes}}{\text{Program}} \times \text{Write miss rate} \times \text{Write miss penalty} \right) + \text{Write buffer stalls}$$

Because the write buffer stalls depend on the proximity of writes, and not just the frequency, it is not possible to give a simple equation to compute such stalls. Fortunately, in systems with a reasonable write buffer depth (e.g., four or more words) and a memory capable of accepting writes at a rate that significantly exceeds the average write frequency in programs (e.g., by a factor of 2), the write buffer stalls will be small, and we can safely ignore them. If a system did not meet these criteria, it would not be well designed; instead, the designer should have used either a deeper write buffer or a write-back organization.

Write-back schemes also have potential additional stalls arising from the need to write a cache block back to memory when the block is replaced. We will discuss this more in Section 5.8.

In most write-through cache organizations, the read and write miss penalties are the same (the time to fetch the block from memory). If we assume that the write buffer stalls are negligible, we can combine the reads and writes by using a single miss rate and the miss penalty:

$$\text{Memory-stall clock cycles} = \frac{\text{Memory accesses}}{\text{Program}} \times \text{Miss rate} \times \text{Miss penalty}$$

We can also factor this as

$$\text{Memory-stall clock cycles} = \frac{\text{Instructions}}{\text{Program}} \times \frac{\text{Misses}}{\text{Instruction}} \times \text{Miss penalty}$$

Let's consider a simple example to help us understand the impact of cache performance on processor performance.

Calculating Cache Performance

EXAMPLE

Assume the miss rate of an instruction cache is 2% and the miss rate of the data cache is 4%. If a processor has a CPI of 2 without any memory stalls and the miss penalty is 100 cycles for all misses, determine how much faster a processor would run with a perfect cache that never missed. Assume the frequency of all loads and stores is 36%.

ANSWER

The number of memory miss cycles for instructions in terms of the Instruction count (I) is

$$\text{Instruction miss cycles} = \text{I} \times 2\% \times 100 = 2.00 \times \text{I}$$

As the frequency of all loads and stores is 36%, we can find the number of memory miss cycles for data references:

$$\text{Data miss cycles} = \text{I} \times 36\% \times 4\% \times 100 = 1.44 \times \text{I}$$

The total number of memory-stall cycles is 2.00 I + 1.44 I = 3.44 I. This is more than three cycles of memory stall per instruction. Accordingly, the total CPI including memory stalls is 2 + 3.44 = 5.44. Since there is no change in instruction count or clock rate, the ratio of the CPU execution times is

$$\frac{\text{CPU time with stalls}}{\text{CPU time with perfect cache}} = \frac{I \times \text{CPI}_{\text{stall}} \times \text{Clock cycle}}{I \times \text{CPI}_{\text{perfect}} \times \text{Clock cycle}}$$

$$= \frac{\text{CPI}_{\text{stall}}}{\text{CPI}_{\text{perfect}}} = \frac{5.44}{2}$$

The performance with the perfect cache is better by $\dfrac{5.44}{2} = 2.72$.

What happens if the processor is made faster, but the memory system is not? The amount of time spent on memory stalls will take up an increasing fraction of the execution time; Amdahl's Law, which we examined in Chapter 1, reminds us of this fact. A few simple examples show how serious this problem can be. Suppose we speed-up the computer in the previous example by reducing its CPI from 2 to 1 without changing the clock rate, which might be done with an improved pipeline. The system with cache misses would then have a CPI of 1 + 3.44 = 4.44, and the system with the perfect cache would be

$$\frac{4.44}{1} = 4.44 \text{ times as fast.}$$

The amount of execution time spent on memory stalls would have risen from

$$\frac{3.44}{5.44} = 63\%$$

to

$$\frac{3.44}{4.44} = 77\%$$

Similarly, increasing the clock rate without changing the memory system also increases the performance lost due to cache misses.

The previous examples and equations assume that the hit time is not a factor in determining cache performance. Clearly, if the hit time increases, the total time to access a word from the memory system will increase, possibly causing an increase in the processor cycle time. Although we will see additional examples of what can increase hit time shortly, one example is increasing the cache size. A larger cache could clearly have a longer access time, just as, if your desk in the library was very large (say, 3 square meters), it would take longer to locate a book on the desk. An increase in hit time likely adds another stage to the pipeline, since it may take multiple cycles for a cache hit. Although it is more complex to calculate the performance impact of a deeper pipeline, at some point the increase in hit time for a larger cache could dominate the improvement in hit rate, leading to a decrease in processor performance.

To capture the fact that the time to access data for both hits and misses affects performance, designers sometime use *average memory access time* (AMAT) as a way to examine alternative cache designs. Average memory access time is the average time to access memory considering both hits and misses and the frequency of different accesses; it is equal to the following:

$$AMAT = \text{Time for a hit} + \text{Miss rate} \times \text{Miss penalty}$$

Calculating Average Memory Access Time

EXAMPLE

Find the AMAT for a processor with a 1 ns clock cycle time, a miss penalty of 20 clock cycles, a miss rate of 0.05 misses per instruction, and a cache access time (including hit detection) of 1 clock cycle. Assume that the read and write miss penalties are the same and ignore other write stalls.

ANSWER

The average memory access time per instruction is

$$\begin{aligned} AMAT &= \text{Time for a hit} + \text{Miss rate} \times \text{Miss penalty} \\ &= 1 + 0.05 \times 20 \\ &= 2 \text{ clock cycles} \end{aligned}$$

or 2 ns.

The next subsection discusses alternative cache organizations that decrease miss rate but may sometimes increase hit time; additional examples appear in Section 5.15, Fallacies and Pitfalls.

Reducing Cache Misses by More Flexible Placement of Blocks

So far, when we place a block in the cache, we have used a simple placement scheme: A block can go in exactly one place in the cache. As mentioned earlier, it is called *direct mapped* because there is a direct mapping from any block address in memory to a single location in the upper level of the hierarchy. However, there is actually a whole range of schemes for placing blocks. Direct mapped, where a block can be placed in exactly one location, is at one extreme.

At the other extreme is a scheme where a block can be placed in *any* location in the cache. Such a scheme is called **fully associative**, because a block in memory may be associated with any entry in the cache. To find a given block in a fully associative cache, all the entries in the cache must be searched because a block can be placed in any one. To make the search practical, it is done in parallel with a comparator associated with each cache entry. These comparators significantly increase the hardware cost, effectively making fully associative placement practical only for caches with small numbers of blocks.

The middle range of designs between direct mapped and fully associative is called **set associative**. In a set-associative cache, there are a fixed number of locations where each block can be placed. A set-associative cache with *n* locations for a block is called an *n*-way set-associative cache. An *n*-way set-associative cache consists of a number of sets, each of which consists of *n* blocks. Each block in the memory maps to a unique *set* in the cache given by the index field, and a block can be placed in *any* element of that set. Thus, a set-associative placement combines direct-mapped placement and fully associative placement: a block is directly mapped into a set, and then all the blocks in the set are searched for a match. For example, Figure 5.14 shows where block 12 may be placed in a cache with eight blocks total, according to the three block placement policies.

Remember that in a direct-mapped cache, the position of a memory block is given by

$$\text{(Block number) modulo (Number of } \textit{blocks} \text{ in the cache)}$$

fully associative cache A cache structure in which a block can be placed in any location in the cache.

set-associative cache A cache that has a fixed number of locations (at least two) where each block can be placed.

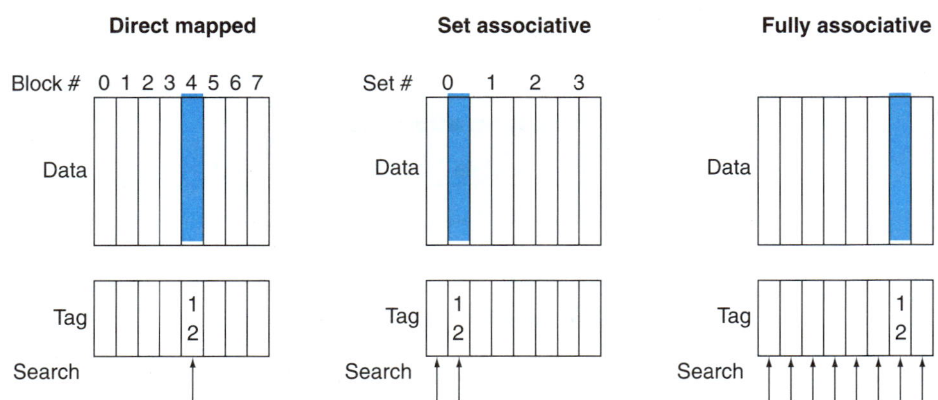

FIGURE 5.14 The location of a memory block whose address is 12 in a cache with eight blocks varies for direct-mapped, set-associative, and fully associative placement. In direct-mapped placement, there is only one cache block where memory block 12 can be found, and that block is given by (12 modulo 8) = 4. In a two-way set-associative cache, there would be four sets, and memory block 12 must be in set (12 mod 4) = 0; the memory block could be in either element of the set. In a fully associative placement, the memory block for block address 12 can appear in any of the eight cache blocks.

In a set-associative cache, the set containing a memory block is given by

(Block number) modulo (Number of *sets* in the cache)

Since the block may be placed in any element of the set, *all the tags of all the elements of the set* must be searched. In a fully associative cache, the block can go anywhere, and *all tags of all the blocks in the cache* must be searched.

We can also think of all block placement strategies as a variation on set associativity. Figure 5.15 shows the possible associativity structures for an eight-block cache. A direct-mapped cache is simply a one-way set-associative cache: each cache entry holds one block and each set has one element. A fully associative cache with *m* entries is simply an *m*-way set-associative cache; it has one set with *m* blocks, and an entry can reside in any block within that set.

The advantage of increasing the degree of associativity is that it usually decreases the miss rate, as the next example shows. The main disadvantage, which we discuss in more detail shortly, is a potential increase in the hit time.

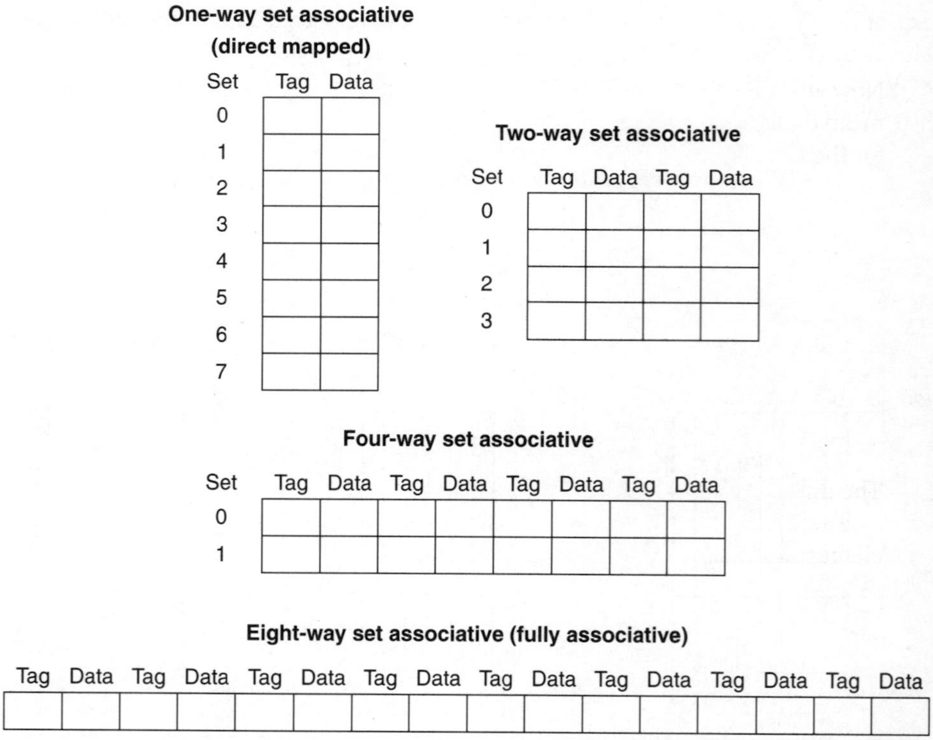

FIGURE 5.15   An eight-block cache configured as direct mapped, two-way set associative, four-way set associative, and fully associative. The total size of the cache in blocks is equal to the number of sets times the associativity. Thus, for a fixed cache size, increasing the associativity decreases the number of sets while increasing the number of elements per set. With eight blocks, an eight-way set-associative cache is the same as a fully associative cache.

Misses and Associativity in Caches

Assume there are three small caches, each consisting of four one-word blocks. One cache is fully associative, a second is two-way set-associative, and the third is direct-mapped. Find the number of misses for each cache organization given the following sequence of block addresses: 0, 8, 0, 6, and 8.

EXAMPLE

The direct-mapped case is easiest. First, let's determine to which cache block each block address maps:

ANSWER

Block address	Cache block
0	(0 modulo 4) = 0
6	(6 modulo 4) = 2
8	(8 modulo 4) = 0

Now we can fill in the cache contents after each reference, using a blank entry to mean that the block is invalid, colored text to show a new entry added to the cache for the associated reference, and plain text to show an old entry in the cache:

Address of memory block accessed	Hit or miss	Contents of cache blocks after reference			
		0	1	2	3
0	miss	Memory[0]			
8	miss	Memory[8]			
0	miss	Memory[0]			
6	miss	Memory[0]		Memory[6]	
8	miss	Memory[8]		Memory[6]	

The direct-mapped cache generates five misses for the five accesses.

The set-associative cache has two sets (with indices 0 and 1) with two elements per set. Let's first determine to which set each block address maps:

Block address	Cache set
0	(0 modulo 2) = 0
6	(6 modulo 2) = 0
8	(8 modulo 2) = 0

Because we have a choice of which entry in a set to replace on a miss, we need a replacement rule. Set-associative caches usually replace the *least recently used* block within a set; that is, the block that was used furthest in the past is replaced. (We will discuss other replacement rules in more detail shortly.) Using this replacement rule, the contents of the set-associative cache after each reference looks like this:

Address of memory block accessed	Hit or miss	Contents of cache blocks after reference			
		Set 0	Set 0	Set 1	Set 1
0	miss	Memory[0]			
8	miss	Memory[0]	Memory[8]		
0	hit	Memory[0]	Memory[8]		
6	miss	Memory[0]	Memory[6]		
8	miss	Memory[8]	Memory[6]		

Notice that when block 6 is referenced, it replaces block 8, since block 8 has been less recently referenced than block 0. The two-way set-associative cache has four misses, one less than the direct-mapped cache.

The fully associative cache has four cache blocks (in a single set); any memory block can be stored in any cache block. The fully associative cache has the best performance, with only three misses:

Address of memory block accessed	Hit or miss	Contents of cache blocks after reference			
		Block 0	Block 1	Block 2	Block 3
0	miss	Memory[0]			
8	miss	Memory[0]	Memory[8]		
0	hit	Memory[0]	Memory[8]		
6	miss	Memory[0]	Memory[8]	Memory[6]	
8	hit	Memory[0]	Memory[8]	Memory[6]	

For this series of references, three misses is the best we can do, because three unique block addresses are accessed. Notice that if we had eight blocks in the cache, there would be no replacements in the two-way set-associative cache (check this for yourself), and it would have the same number of misses as the fully associative cache. Similarly, if we had 16 blocks, all 3 caches would have the same number of misses. Even this trivial example shows that cache size and associativity are not independent in determining cache performance.

How much of a reduction in the miss rate is achieved by associativity? Figure 5.16 shows the improvement for a 64 KiB data cache with a 16-word block, and associativity ranging from direct mapped to eight-way. Going from one-way to two-way associativity decreases the miss rate by about 15%, but there is little further improvement in going to higher associativity.

Associativity	Data miss rate
1	10.3%
2	8.6%
4	8.3%
8	8.1%

FIGURE 5.16   The data cache miss rates for an organization like the Intrinsity FastMATH processor for SPEC CPU2000 benchmarks with associativity varying from one-way to eight-way. These results for 10 SPEC CPU2000 programs are from Hennessy and Patterson (2003).

Tag	Index	Block offset

FIGURE 5.17   The three portions of an address in a set-associative or direct-mapped cache. The index is used to select the set, then the tag is used to choose the block by comparison with the blocks in the selected set. The block offset is the address of the desired data within the block.

Locating a Block in the Cache

Now, let's consider the task of finding a block in a cache that is set associative. Just as in a direct-mapped cache, each block in a set-associative cache includes an address tag that gives the block address. The tag of every cache block within the appropriate set is checked to see if it matches the block address from the processor. Figure 5.17 decomposes the address. The index value is used to select the set containing the address of interest, and the tags of all the blocks in the set must be searched. Because speed is of the essence, all the tags in the selected set are searched in parallel. As in a fully associative cache, a sequential search would make the hit time of a set-associative cache too slow.

If the total cache size is kept the same, increasing the associativity increases the number of blocks per set, which is the number of simultaneous compares needed to perform the search in parallel: each increase by a factor of 2 in associativity doubles the number of blocks per set and halves the number of sets. Accordingly, each factor-of-2 increase in associativity decreases the size of the index by 1 bit and increases the size of the tag by 1 bit. In a fully associative cache, there is effectively only one set, and all the blocks must be checked in parallel. Thus, there is no index, and the entire address, excluding the block offset, is compared against the tag of every block. In other words, we search the entire cache without any indexing.

In a direct-mapped cache, only a single comparator is needed, because the entry can be in only one block, and we access the cache simply by indexing. Figure 5.18 shows that in a four-way set-associative cache, four comparators are needed, together with a 4-to-1 multiplexor to choose among the four potential members of the selected set. The cache access consists of indexing the appropriate set and then searching the tags of the set. The costs of an associative cache are the extra comparators and any delay imposed by having to do the compare and select from among the elements of the set.

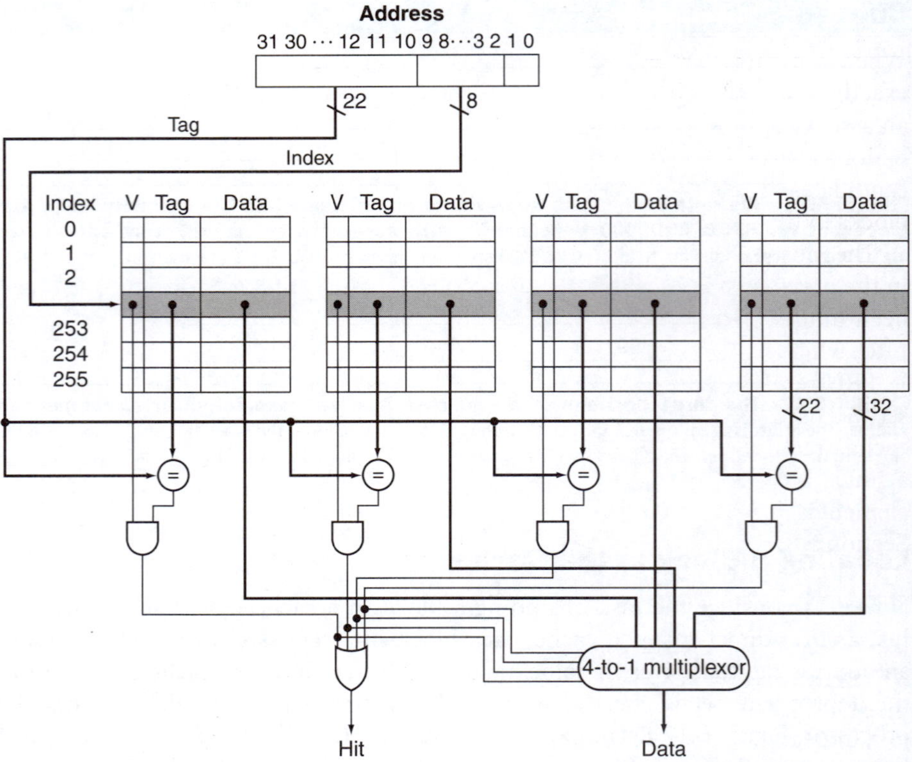

FIGURE 5.18 The implementation of a four-way set-associative cache requires four comparators and a 4-to-1 multiplexor. The comparators determine which element of the selected set (if any) matches the tag. The output of the comparators is used to select the data from one of the four blocks of the indexed set, using a multiplexor with a decoded select signal. In some implementations, the Output enable signals on the data portions of the cache RAMs can be used to select the entry in the set that drives the output. The Output enable signal comes from the comparators, causing the element that matches to drive the data outputs. This organization eliminates the need for the multiplexor.

The choice among direct-mapped, set-associative, or fully associative mapping in any memory hierarchy will depend on the cost of a miss versus the cost of implementing associativity, both in time and in extra hardware.

Elaboration: A *Content Addressable Memory* (CAM) is a circuit that combines comparison and storage in a single device. Instead of supplying an address and reading a word like a RAM, you supply the data and the CAM looks to see if it has a copy and returns the index of the matching row. CAMs mean that cache designers can afford to implement much higher set associativity than if they needed to build the hardware out of SRAMs and comparators. In 2020, the greater size and power of CAM generally leads to 2-way and 4-way set associativity being built from standard SRAMs and comparators, with 8-way and above built using CAMs.

Choosing Which Block to Replace

When a miss occurs in a direct-mapped cache, the requested block can go in exactly one position, and the block occupying that position must be replaced. In an associative cache, we have a choice of where to place the requested block, and hence a choice of which block to replace. In a fully associative cache, all blocks are candidates for replacement. In a set-associative cache, we must choose among the blocks in the selected set.

The most commonly used scheme is **least recently used (LRU)**, which we used in the previous example. In an LRU scheme, the block replaced is the one that has been unused for the longest time. The set associative example on page 423 uses LRU, which is why we replaced Memory(0) instead of Memory(6).

LRU replacement is implemented by keeping track of when each element in a set was used relative to the other elements in the set. For a two-way set-associative cache, tracking when the two elements were used can be implemented by keeping a single bit in each set and setting the bit to indicate an element whenever that element is referenced. As associativity increases, implementing LRU gets harder; in Section 5.8, we will see an alternative scheme for replacement.

least recently used (LRU) A replacement scheme in which the block replaced is the one that has been unused for the longest time.

Size of Tags versus Set Associativity

Increasing associativity requires more comparators and more tag bits per cache block. Assuming a cache of 4096 blocks, a 4-word block size, and a 32-bit address, find the total number of sets and the total number of tag bits for caches that are direct mapped, two-way and four-way set associative, and fully associative.

EXAMPLE

Since there are 16 ($= 2^4$) bytes per block, a 32-bit address yields $32 - 4 = 28$ bits to be used for index and tag. The direct-mapped cache has the same number of sets as blocks, and hence 12 bits of index, since $\log_2(4096) = 12$; hence, the total number is $(28 - 12) \times 4096 = 16 \times 4096 = 66\,K$ tag bits.

ANSWER

Each degree of associativity decreases the number of sets by a factor of 2 and thus decreases the number of bits used to index the cache by 1 and increases the number of bits in the tag by 1. Thus, for a two-way set-associative cache, there are 2048 sets, and the total number of tag bits is $(28 - 11) \times 2 \times 2048 = 34 \times 2048 = 70\,Kbits$. For a four-way set-associative cache, the total number of sets is 1024, and the total number is $(28 - 10) \times 4 \times 1024 = 72 \times 1024 = 74\,K$ tag bits.

For a fully associative cache, there is only one set with 4096 blocks, and the tag is 28 bits, leading to $28 \times 4096 \times 1 = 115\,K$ tag bits.

Reducing the Miss Penalty Using Multilevel Caches

All modern computers make use of caches. To close the gap further between the fast clock rates of modern processors and the increasingly long time required to access DRAMs, most microprocessors support an additional level of caching. This second-level cache is normally on the same chip and is accessed whenever a miss occurs in the primary cache. If the second-level cache contains the desired data, the miss penalty for the first-level cache will be essentially the access time of the second-level cache, which will be much less than the access time of main memory. If neither the primary nor the secondary cache contains the data, a main memory access is required, and a larger miss penalty is incurred.

How significant is the performance improvement from the use of a secondary cache? The next example shows us.

EXAMPLE

Performance of Multilevel Caches

Suppose we have a processor with a base CPI of 1.0, assuming all references hit in the primary cache, and a clock rate of 4 GHz. Assume a main memory access time of 100 ns, including all the miss handling. Suppose the miss rate per instruction at the primary cache is 2%. How much faster will the processor be if we add a secondary cache that has a 5 ns access time for either a hit or a miss and is large enough to reduce the miss rate to main memory to 0.5%?

ANSWER

The miss penalty to main memory is

$$\frac{100\,\text{ns}}{0.25\dfrac{\text{ns}}{\text{clock cycle}}} = 400 \text{ clock cycles}$$

The effective CPI with one level of caching is given by

$$\text{Total CPI} = \text{Base CPI} + \text{Memory-stall cycles per instruction}$$

For the processor with one level of caching,

$$\text{Total CPI} = 1.0 + \text{Memory-stall cycles per instruction} = 1.0 + 2\% \times 400 = 9$$

With two levels of caching, a miss in the primary (or first-level) cache can be satisfied either by the secondary cache or by main memory. The miss penalty for an access to the second-level cache is

$$\frac{5\,\text{ns}}{0.25\dfrac{\text{ns}}{\text{clock cycle}}} = 20 \text{ clock cycles}$$

If the miss is satisfied in the secondary cache, then this is the entire miss penalty. If the miss needs to go to main memory, then the total miss penalty is the sum of the secondary cache access time and the main memory access time.

Thus, for a two-level cache, total CPI is the sum of the stall cycles from both levels of cache and the base CPI:

Total CPI = 1 + Primary stalls per instruction + Secondary stalls per instruction
$$= 1 + 2\% \times 20 + 0.5\% \times 400 = 1 + 0.4 + 2.0 = 3.4$$

Thus, the processor with the secondary cache is faster by

$$\frac{9.0}{3.4} = 2.6$$

Alternatively, we could have computed the stall cycles by summing the stall cycles of those references that hit in the secondary cache $((2\% - 0.5\%) \times 20 = 0.3)$. Those references that go to main memory, which must include the cost to access the secondary cache as well as the main memory access time, are $(0.5\% \times (20 + 400) = 2.1)$. The sum, $1.0 + 0.3 + 2.1$, is again 3.4.

The design considerations for a primary and secondary cache are significantly different, because the presence of the other cache changes the best choice versus a single-level cache. In particular, a two-level cache structure allows the primary cache to focus on minimizing hit time to yield a shorter clock cycle or fewer pipeline stages, while allowing the secondary cache to focus on miss rate to reduce the penalty of long memory access times.

The effect of these changes on the two caches can be seen by comparing each cache to the optimal design for a single level of cache. In comparison to a single-level cache, the primary cache of a **multilevel cache** is often smaller. Furthermore, the primary cache may use a smaller block size, to go with the smaller cache size and also to reduce the miss penalty. In comparison, the secondary cache will be much larger than in a single-level cache, since the access time of the secondary cache is less critical. With a larger total size, the secondary cache may use a larger block size than appropriate with a single-level cache. It often uses higher associativity than the primary cache given the focus of reducing miss rates.

multilevel cache
A memory hierarchy with multiple levels of caches, rather than just a cache and main memory.

Sorting has been exhaustively analyzed to find better algorithms: Bubble Sort, Quicksort, Radix Sort, and so on. Figure 5.19(a) shows instructions executed by item searched for Radix Sort versus Quicksort. As expected, for large arrays, Radix Sort has an algorithmic advantage over Quicksort in terms of number of operations. Figure 5.19(b) shows time per key instead of instructions executed. We see that the

Understanding Program Performance

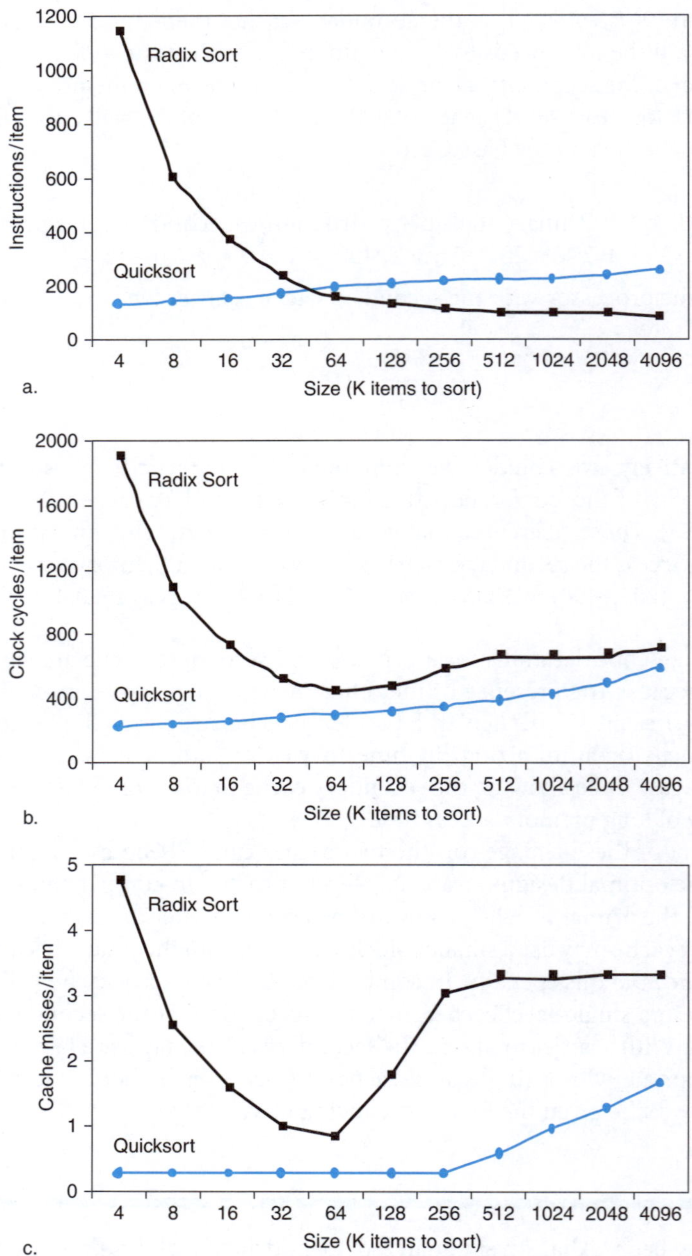

FIGURE 5.19 Comparing Quicksort and Radix Sort by (a) instructions executed per item sorted, (b) time per item sorted, and (c) cache misses per item sorted. This data is from a paper by LaMarca and Ladner [1996]. Due to such results, new versions of Radix Sort have been invented that take memory hierarchy into account, to regain its algorithmic advantages (see Section 5.15). The basic idea of cache optimizations is to use all the data in a block repeatedly before it is replaced on a miss.

lines start on the same trajectory as in Figure 5.19(a), but then the Radix Sort line diverges as the data to sort increases. What is going on? Figure 5.19(c) answers by looking at the cache misses per item sorted: Quicksort consistently has many fewer misses per item to be sorted.

Alas, standard algorithmic analysis often ignores the impact of the memory hierarchy. As faster clock rates and Moore's Law allowed architects to squeeze all of the performance out of a stream of instructions, using the memory hierarchy well is critical to high performance. As we said in the introduction, understanding the behavior of the memory hierarchy is critical to understanding the performance of programs on today's computers, as we'll see in Section 5.14.

Software Optimization via Blocking

Given the importance of the memory hierarchy to program performance, not surprisingly many software optimizations were invented that can dramatically improve performance by reusing data within the cache and hence lower miss rates due to improved temporal locality.

When dealing with arrays, we can get good performance from the memory system if we store the array in memory so that accesses to the array are sequential in memory. Suppose that we are dealing with multiple arrays, however, with some arrays accessed by rows and some by columns. Storing the arrays row-by-row (called *row major order*) or column-by-column (*column major order*) does not solve the problem because both rows and columns are used in every loop iteration.

Instead of operating on entire rows or columns of an array, *blocked* algorithms operate on submatrices or *blocks*. The goal is to maximize accesses to the data loaded into the cache before the data are replaced; that is, improve temporal locality to reduce cache misses.

For example, the inner loops of DGEMM (lines 4 through 9 of Figure 2.43 on page 166) are

```
for (int j = 0; j < n; ++j)
    {
    double cij = C[i+j*n]; /* cij = C[i][j] */
    for( int k = 0; k < n; k++ )
     cij += A[i+k*n] * B[k+j*n]; /* cij += A[i][k]*B[k][j] */
    C[i+j*n] = cij; /* C[i][j] = cij */
    }
}
```

It reads all N-by-N elements of B, reads the same N elements in what corresponds to one row of A repeatedly, and writes what corresponds to one row of N elements of C.

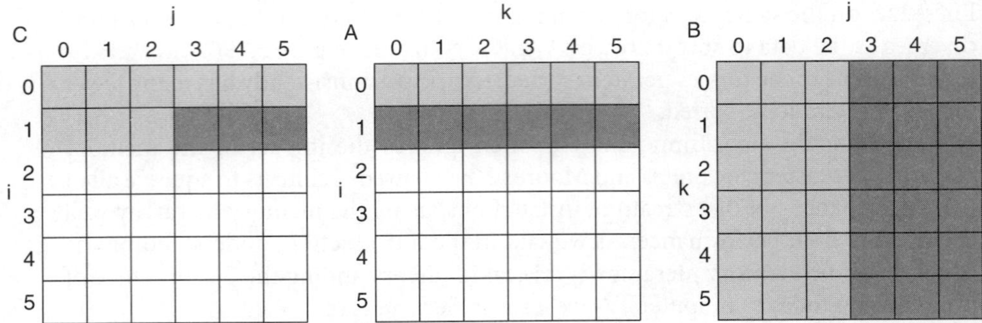

FIGURE 5.20 A snapshot of the three arrays C, A, **and** B **when** N=6 **and** i = 1. The age of accesses to the array elements is indicated by shade: white means not yet touched, light means older accesses, and dark means newer accesses. Compared to Figure 5.22, elements of A and B are read repeatedly to calculate new elements of C. The variables i, j, and k are shown along the rows or columns used to access the arrays.

(The comments make the rows and columns of the matrices easier to identify.) Figure 5.20 gives a snapshot of the accesses to the three arrays. A dark shade indicates a recent access, a light shade indicates an older access, and white means not yet accessed.

The number of capacity misses clearly depends on N and the size of the cache. If it can hold all three N-by-N matrices, then all is well, provided there are no cache conflicts. We purposely picked the matrix size of DGEMM for Chapters 3 and 4 so that this would be the case.

If the cache can hold one N-by-N matrix and one row of N, then at least the ith row of A and the array B may stay in the cache. Less than that and misses may occur for both B and C. In the worst case, there would be $2 N^3 + N^2$ memory words accessed for N^3 operations.

To ensure that the elements being accessed can fit in the cache, the original code is changed to compute on a submatrix. Hence, we essentially invoke the version of DGEMM from Figure 4.81 on page 367 repeatedly on matrices of size BLOCKSIZE by BLOCKSIZE. BLOCKSIZE is called the *blocking factor*.

Figure 5.21 shows the blocked version of DGEMM. The function do_block is DGEMM from Figure 2.43 with three new parameters si, sj, and sk to specify the starting position of each submatrix of of A, B, and C. The two inner loops of the do_block now compute in steps of size BLOCKSIZE rather than the full length of B and C. The gcc optimizer removes any function call overhead by "inlining" the function; that is, it inserts the code directly to avoid the conventional parameter passing and return address bookkeeping instructions.

Figure 5.22 illustrates the accesses to the three arrays using blocking. Looking only at capacity misses, the total number of memory words accessed is $2 N^3/\text{BLOCKSIZE} + N^2$. This total is an improvement by about a factor of BLOCKSIZE.

```
1   #define BLOCKSIZE 32
2   void do_block (int n, int si, int sj, int sk, double *A, double
3   *B, double *C)
4   {
5       for (int i = si; i < si+BLOCKSIZE; ++i)
6           for (int j = sj; j < sj+BLOCKSIZE; ++j)
7               {
8                   double cij = C[i+j*n];/* cij = C[i][j] */
9                   for( int k = sk; k < sk+BLOCKSIZE; k++ )
10                      cij += A[i+k*n] * B[k+j*n];/* cij+=A[i][k]*B[k][j] */
11                  C[i+j*n] = cij;/* C[i][j] = cij */
12              }
13  }
14  void dgemm (int n, double* A, double* B, double* C)
15  {
16      for ( int sj = 0; sj < n; sj += BLOCKSIZE )
17          for ( int si = 0; si < n; si += BLOCKSIZE )
18              for ( int sk = 0; sk < n; sk += BLOCKSIZE )
19                  do_block(n, si, sj, sk, A, B, C);
20  }
```

FIGURE 5.21 Cache blocked version of DGEMM in Figure 3.21. Assume C is initialized to zero. The do_block function is basically DGEMM from Chapter 2 with new parameters to specify the starting positions of the submatrices of BLOCKSIZE. The gcc optimizer can remove the function overhead instructions by inlining the do_block function.

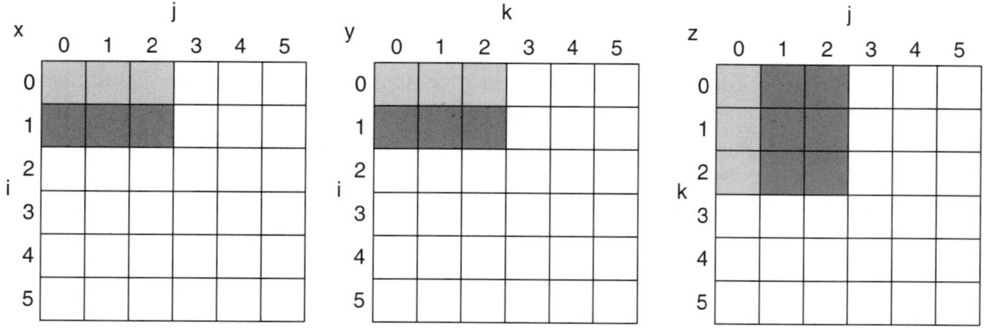

FIGURE 5.22 The age of accesses to the arrays C, A, **and** B **when** *BLOCKSIZE*=**3.** Note that, in contrast to Figure 5.20, a smaller number of elements is accessed.

Hence, blocking exploits a combination of spatial and temporal locality, since A benefits from spatial locality and B benefits from temporal locality. Depending on the computer and size of the matrices, blocking can improve performance by about a factor of 2 to more than a factor of 10 (see Section 5.14).

Although we have aimed at reducing cache misses, blocking can also be used to help register allocation. By taking a small blocking size such that the block can be held in registers, we can minimize the number of loads and stores in the program, which also improves performance.

Elaboration: Multilevel caches create several complications. First, there are now several different types of misses and corresponding miss rates. In the example on pages 428–429, we saw the primary cache miss rate and the global miss rate—the fraction of references that missed in all cache levels. There is also a miss rate for the secondary cache, which is the ratio of all misses in the secondary cache divided by the number of accesses to it. This miss rate is called the local miss rate of the secondary cache. Because the primary cache filters accesses, especially those with good spatial and temporal locality, the local miss rate of the secondary cache is much higher than the global miss rate. For the example on pages 428–429, we can compute the local miss rate of the secondary cache as 0.5%/2% = 25%! Luckily, the global miss rate dictates how often we must access the main memory.

global miss rate The fraction of references that miss in all levels of a multilevel cache.

local miss rate The fraction of references to one level of a cache that miss; used in multilevel hierarchies.

Elaboration: With out-of-order processors (see Chapter 4), performance is more complex, since they execute instructions during the miss penalty. Instead of instruction miss rates and data miss rates, we use misses per instruction, and this formula:

$$\frac{\text{Memory} - \text{stall cycles}}{\text{Instruction}} = \frac{\text{Misses}}{\text{Instruction}} \times (\text{Total miss latency} - \text{Overlapped miss latency})$$

There is no general way to calculate overlapped miss latency, so evaluations of memory hierarchies for out-of-order processors inevitably require simulation of the processor and the memory hierarchy. Only by seeing the execution of the processor during each miss can we see if the processor stalls waiting for data or simply finds other work to do. A guideline is that the processor often hides the miss penalty for an L1 cache miss that hits in the L2 cache, but it rarely hides a miss to both L1 and L2 caches.

Elaboration: The performance challenge for algorithms is that the memory hierarchy varies between different implementations of the same architecture in cache size, associativity, block size, and number of caches. To cope with such variability, some recent numerical libraries parameterize their algorithms and then search the parameter space at runtime to find the best combination for a particular computer. This approach is called *autotuning*.

Which of the following is generally true about a design with multiple levels of caches?   **Check Yourself**

1. First-level caches are more concerned about hit time, and second-level caches are more concerned about miss rate.

2. First-level caches are more concerned about miss rate, and second-level caches are more concerned about hit time.

Summary

In this section, we focused on four topics: cache performance, using associativity to reduce miss rates, the use of multilevel cache hierarchies to reduce miss penalties, and software optimizations to improve effectiveness of caches.

The memory system has a significant effect on program execution time. The number of memory-stall cycles depends on both the miss rate and the miss penalty. The challenge, as we will see in Section 5.8, is to reduce one of these factors without significantly affecting other critical factors in the memory hierarchy.

To reduce the miss rate, we examined the use of associative placement schemes. Such schemes can reduce the miss rate of a cache by allowing more flexible placement of blocks within the cache. Fully associative schemes allow blocks to be placed anywhere, but also require that every block in the cache be searched to satisfy a request. The higher costs make large fully associative caches impractical. Set-associative caches are a practical alternative, since we need only search among the elements of a unique set that is chosen by indexing. Set-associative caches have higher miss rates but are faster to access. The amount of associativity that yields the best performance depends on both the technology and the details of the implementation.

We looked at multilevel caches as a technique to reduce the miss penalty by allowing a larger secondary cache to handle misses to the primary cache. Second-level caches have become commonplace as designers find that limited silicon and the goals of high clock rates prevent primary caches from becoming large. The secondary cache, which is often ten or more times larger than the primary cache, handles many accesses that miss in the primary cache. In such cases, the miss penalty is that of the access time to the secondary cache (typically < 10 processor cycles) versus the access time to memory (typically > 100 processor cycles). As with associativity, the design tradeoffs between the size of the secondary cache and its access time depend on a number of aspects of the implementation.

Finally, given the importance of the memory hierarchy in performance, we looked at how to change algorithms to improve cache behavior, with blocking being an important technique when dealing with large arrays.

5.5   Dependable Memory Hierarchy

Implicit in all the prior discussion is that the memory hierarchy doesn't forget. Fast but undependable is not very attractive. As we learned in Chapter 1, the one great idea for **dependability** is redundancy. In this section we'll first go over the terms to define terms and measures associated with failure, and then show how redundancy can make nearly unforgettable memories .

Defining Failure

We start with an assumption that you have a specification of proper service. Users can then see a system alternating between two states of delivered service with respect to the service specification:

1. *Service accomplishment*, where the service is delivered as specified

2. *Service interruption*, where the delivered service is different from the specified service

Transitions from state 1 to state 2 are caused by *failures*, and transitions from state 2 to state 1 are called *restorations*. Failures can be permanent or intermittent. The latter is the more difficult case; it is harder to diagnose the problem when a system oscillates between the two states. Permanent failures are far easier to diagnose.

This definition leads to two related terms: reliability and availability.

Reliability is a measure of the continuous service accomplishment—or, equivalently, of the time to failure—from a reference point. Hence, *mean time to failure* (MTTF) is a reliability measure. A related term is *annual failure rate* (AFR), which is simply the percentage of devices that would be expected to fail in a year for a given MTTF. When MTTF gets large it can be misleading, while AFR leads to better intuition.

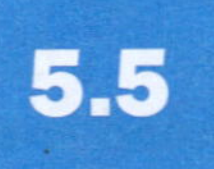

MTTF vs. AFR of Disks

Some disks today are quoted to have a 1,000,000-hour MTTF. As 1,000,000 hours is $1{,}000{,}000/(365 \times 24) = 114$ years, it would seem like they practically never fail. Warehouse scale computers (see Section 6.8) that run Internet services such as Search might have 50,000 servers. Assume each server has 2 disks. Use AFR to calculate how many disks we would expect to fail per year.

One year is $365 \times 24 = 8760$ hours. A 1,000,000-hour MTTF means an AFR of $8760/1,000,000 = 0.876\%$. With 100,000 disks, we would expect 876 disks to fail per year, or on average more than 2 disk failures per day!

Service interruption is measured as *mean time to repair* (MTTR). *Mean time between failures* (MTBF) is simply the sum of MTTF + MTTR. Although MTBF is widely used, MTTF is often the more appropriate term. *Availability* is then a measure of service accomplishment with respect to the alternation between the two states of accomplishment and interruption. Availability is statistically quantified as

$$\text{Availability} = \frac{\text{MTTF}}{(\text{MTTF} + \text{MTTR})}$$

Note that reliability and availability are actually quantifiable measures, rather than just synonyms for dependability. Shrinking MTTR can help availability as much as increasing MTTF. For example, tools for fault detection, diagnosis, and repair can help reduce the time to repair faults and thereby improve availability.

We want availability to be very high. One shorthand is to quote the number of "nines of availability" per year. For example, a very good Internet service today offers 4 or 5 nines of availability. Given 365 days per year, which is $365 \times 24 \times 60 = 526,000$ minutes, then the shorthand is decoded as follows:

One nine:	90%	=>	36.5 days of repair/year
Two nines:	99%	=>	3.65 days of repair/year
Three nines:	99.9%	=>	526 minutes of repair/year
Four nines:	99.99%	=>	52.6 minutes of repair/year
Five nines:	99.999%	=>	5.26 minutes of repair/year

and so on. (Five nines means 5 minutes of repair per year, which is a memory aid.)

To increase MTTF, you can improve the quality of the components or design systems to continue operation in the presence of components that have failed. Hence, failure needs to be defined with respect to a context, as failure of a component may not lead to a failure of the system. To make this distinction clear, the term *fault* is used to mean failure of a component. Here are three ways to improve MTTF:

1. *Fault avoidance:* Preventing fault occurrence by construction.

2. *Fault tolerance:* Using redundancy to allow the service to comply with the service specification despite faults occurring.

3. *Fault forecasting:* **Predicting** the presence and creation of faults, allowing the component to be replaced *before* it fails.

The Hamming Single Error Correcting, Double Error Detecting Code (SEC/DED)

Richard Hamming invented a popular redundancy scheme for memory, for which he received the Turing Award in 1968. To invent redundant codes, it is helpful to talk about how "close" correct bit patterns can be. What we call the *Hamming distance* is just the minimum number of bits that are different between any two correct bit patterns. For example, the distance between 011011 and 001111 is two. What happens if the minimum distance between members of a codes is two, and we get a one-bit error? It will turn a valid pattern in a code to an invalid one. Thus, if we can detect whether members of a code are valid or not, we can detect single bit errors, and can say we have a single bit **error detection code.**

Hamming used a *parity code* for error detection. In a parity code, the number of 1s in a word is counted; the word has odd parity if the number of 1s is odd and even otherwise. When a word is written into memory, the parity bit is also written (1 for odd, 0 for even). That is, the parity of the N + 1 bit word should always be even. Then, when the word is read out, the parity bit is read and checked. If the parity of the memory word and the stored parity bit do not match, an error has occurred.

error detection code A code that enables the detection of an error in data, but not the precise location and, hence, correction of the error.

> **EXAMPLE**
>
> Calculate the parity of a byte with the value 31_{ten} and show the pattern stored to memory. Assume the parity bit is on the right. Suppose the most significant bit was inverted in memory, and then you read it back. Did you detect the error? What happens if the two most significant bits are inverted?
>
> **ANSWER**
>
> 31_{ten} is 00011111_{two}, which has five 1s. To make parity even, we need to write a 1 in the parity bit, or 000111111_{two}. If the most significant bit is inverted when we read it back, we would see 100111111_{two} which has seven 1s. Since we expect even parity and calculated odd parity, we would signal an error. If the *two* most significant bits are inverted, we would see 110111111_{two} which has eight 1s or even parity and we would *not* signal an error.

If there are 2 bits of error, then a 1-bit parity scheme will not detect any errors, since the parity will match the data with two errors. (Actually, a 1-bit parity scheme can detect any odd number of errors; however, the probability of having 3 errors is much lower than the probability of having two, so, in practice, a 1-bit parity code is limited to detecting a single bit of error.)

Of course, a parity code cannot correct errors, which Hamming wanted to do as well as detect them. If we used a code that had a minimum distance of 3, then any single bit error would be closer to the correct pattern than to any other valid pattern. He came up with an easy to understand mapping of data into a distance 3 code that we call *Hamming Error Correction Code* (ECC) in his honor. We use extra parity bits to allow the position identification of a single error. Here are the steps to calculate Hamming ECC

1. Start numbering bits from 1 on the left, as opposed to the traditional numbering of the rightmost bit being 0.

2. Mark all bit positions that are powers of 2 as parity bits (positions 1, 2, 4, 8, 16, …) .

3. All other bit positions are used for data bits (positions 3, 5, 6, 7, 9, 10, 11, 12, 13, 14, 15, …).

4. The position of parity bit determines sequence of data bits that it checks (Figure 5.23 shows this coverage graphically) is:

   ■ Bit 1 (0001_{two}) checks bits (1,3,5,7,9,11,…), which are bits where rightmost bit of address is 1 (0001_{two}, 0011_{two}, 0101_{two}, 0111_{two}, 1001_{two}, 1011_{two},…).

   ■ Bit 2 (0010_{two}) checks bits (2,3,6,7,10,11,14,15,…), which are the bits where the second bit to the right in the address is 1.

   ■ Bit 4 (0100_{two}) checks bits (4–7, 12–15, 20–23,…) , which are the bits where the third bit to the right in the address is 1.

   ■ Bit 8 (1000_{two}) checks bits (8–15, 24–31, 40–47,…), which are the bits where the fourth bit to the right in the address is 1.

   Note that each data bit is covered by two or more parity bits.

5. Set parity bits to create even parity for each group.

Bit position	1	2	3	4	5	6	7	8	9	10	11	12
Encoded data bits	p1	p2	d1	p4	d2	d3	d4	p8	d5	d6	d7	d8
Parity bit coverage — p1	X		X		X		X		X		X	
Parity bit coverage — p2		X	X			X	X			X	X	
Parity bit coverage — p4				X	X	X	X					X
Parity bit coverage — p8								X	X	X	X	X

FIGURE 5.23 Parity bits, data bits, and field coverage in a Hamming ECC code for eight data bits.

In what seems like a magic trick, you can then determine whether bits are incorrect by looking at the parity bits. Using the 12 bit code in Figure 5.23, if the value of the four parity calculations (p8,p4,p2,p1) was 0000, then there was no error. However, if the pattern was, say, 1010, which is 10_{ten}, then Hamming ECC tells us that bit 10 (d6) is an error. Since the number is binary, we can correct the error just by inverting the value of bit 10.

EXAMPLE

Assume one byte data value is 10011010$_{two}$. First show the Hamming ECC code for that byte, and then invert bit 10 and show that the ECC code finds and corrects the single bit error.

ANSWER

Leaving spaces for the parity bits, the 12 bit pattern is_ _ 1_ 0 0 1_ 1 0 1 0.
Position 1 checks bits 1,3,5,7,9, and 11, which we highlight: __ **1**_ **0** 0 **1**_ **1** 0 **1** 0. To make the group even parity, we should set bit 1 to 0.
Position 2 checks bits 2,3,6,7,10,11, which is 0 _ **1**_ **0** 0 **1**_ **1 0 1** 0 or odd parity, so we set position 2 to a 1.
Position 4 checks bits 4,5,6,7,12, which is 0 1 1 _ **0 0 1**_ 1 0 **1**, so we set it to a 1.
Position 8 checks bits 8,9,10,11,12, which is 0 1 1 1 0 0 1 _ **1 0 1 0**, so we set it to a 0.
The final code word is **011100101010**. Inverting bit 10 changes it to 011100101110.
Parity bit 1 is 0 (**0**1**1**1**0**0**1**0**1**1**1**0 is four 1s, so even parity; this group is OK).
Parity bit 2 is 1 (0**11**1**00**1**01**1**1**0 is five 1s, so odd parity; there is an error somewhere).
Parity bit 4 is 1 (011**100**101**1**10 is two 1s, so even parity; this group is OK).
Parity bit 8 is 1 (0111001**01110** is three 1s, so odd parity; there is an error somewhere).
Parity bits 2 and 8 are incorrect. As 2 + 8 = 10, bit 10 must be wrong. Hence, we can correct the error by inverting bit 10: 011100101**0**10. Voila!

Hamming did not stop at single bit error correction code. At the cost of one more bit, we can make the minimum Hamming distance in a code be 4. This means we can correct single bit errors *and detect double bit errors*. The idea is to add a parity bit that is calculated over the whole word. Let's use a four-bit data word as an example, which would only need 7 bits for single bit error detection. Hamming parity bits H (p1 p2 p3) are computed (even parity as usual) plus the even parity over the entire word, p4:

$$1 \quad 2 \quad 3 \quad 4 \quad 5 \quad 6 \quad 7 \quad \underline{\textbf{8}}$$
$$p_1 \quad p_2 \quad d_1 \quad p_3 \quad d_2 \quad d_3 \quad d_4 \quad \underline{\textbf{p}_4}$$

Then the algorithm to correct one error and detect two is just to calculate parity over the ECC groups (H) as before plus one more over the whole group (p_4). There are four cases:

1. H is even and p_4 is even, so no error occurred.

2. H is odd and p_4 is odd, so a correctable single error occurred. (p_4 should calculate odd parity if one error occurred.)

3. H is even and p_4 is odd, a single error occurred in p_4 bit, not in the rest of the word, so correct the p_4 bit.

4. H is odd and p_4 is even, a double error occurred. (p_4 should calculate even parity if two errors occurred.)

Single Error Correcting / Double Error Detecting (SEC/DED) is common in memory for servers today. Conveniently, eight byte data blocks can get SEC/DED with just one more byte, which is why many DIMMs are 72 bits wide.

Elaboration: To calculate how many bits are needed for SEC, let p be total number of parity bits and d number of data bits in $p + d$ bit word. If p error correction bits are to point to error bit ($p + d$ cases) plus one case to indicate that no error exists, we need:

$$2^p \geq p + d + 1 \text{ bits, and thus } p \geq \log(p + d + 1).$$

For example, for 8 bits data means $d = 8$ and $2^p \geq p + 8 + 1$, so $p = 4$. Similarly, $p = 5$ for 16 bits of data, 6 for 32 bits, 7 for 64 bits, and so on.

Elaboration: In very large systems, the possibility of multiple errors as well as complete failure of a single wide memory chip becomes significant. IBM introduced *chipkill* to solve this problem, and many very large systems use this technology. (Intel calls their version SDDC.) Similar in nature to the RAID approach used for disks (see Section 5.11), Chipkill distributes the data and ECC information, so that the complete failure of a single memory chip can be handled by supporting the reconstruction of the missing data from the remaining memory chips. Assuming a 10,000-processor cluster with 4 GiB per processor, IBM calculated the following rates of *unrecoverable* memory errors in three years of operation:

■ Parity only—about 90,000, or one unrecoverable (or undetected) failure every 17 minutes.

■ SEC/DED only—about 3500, or about one undetected or unrecoverable failure every 7.5 hours.

■ Chipkill—6, or about one undetected or unrecoverable failure every 2 months.

Hence, Chipkill is a requirement for warehouse-scale computers (see Section 6.8).

Elaboration: While single or double bit errors are typical for memory systems, networks can have bursts of bit errors. One solution is called *Cyclic Redundancy Check*. For a block of k bits, a transmitter generates an $n\text{-}k$ bit frame check sequence. It transmits n bits exactly divisible by some number. The receiver divides frame by that number. If there is no remainder, it assumes there is no error. If there is, the receiver rejects the message, and asks the transmitter to send again. As you might guess from Chapter 3, it is easy to calculate division for some binary numbers with a shift register, which made CRC codes popular even when hardware was more precious. Going even further, Reed-Solomon codes use Galois fields to *correct* multibit transmission errors, but now data is considered coefficients of a polynomials and the code space is values of a polynomial. The Reed-Solomon calculation is considerably more complicated than binary division!

5.6   Virtual Machines

Virtual Machines (VM) were first developed in the mid-1960s, and they have remained an important part of mainframe computing over the years. Although largely ignored in the single user PC era in the 1980s and 1990s, they have recently gained popularity due to

- The increasing importance of isolation and security in modern systems

- The failures in security and reliability of standard operating systems

- The sharing of a single computer among many unrelated users, in particular for cloud computing

- The dramatic increases in raw speed of processors over the decades, which made the overhead of VMs more acceptable

The broadest definition of VMs includes basically all emulation methods that provide a standard software interface, such as the Java VM. In this section, we are interested in VMs that provide a complete system-level environment at the binary *instruction set architecture* (ISA) level. Although some VMs run different ISAs in the VM from the native hardware, we assume they always match the hardware. Such VMs are called (Operating) *System Virtual Machines*. IBM VM/370, VirtualBox, VMware ESX Server, and Xen are examples.

System virtual machines present the illusion that the users have an entire computer to themselves, including a copy of the operating system. A single computer runs multiple VMs and can support a number of different *operating systems* (OSes). On a conventional platform, a single OS "owns" all the hardware resources, but with a VM, multiple OSes all share the hardware resources.

The software that supports VMs is called a *virtual machine monitor* (VMM) or *hypervisor*; the VMM is the heart of virtual machine technology. The underlying hardware platform is called the *host*, and its resources are shared among the *guest* VMs. The VMM determines how to map virtual resources to physical resources: a physical resource may be time-shared, partitioned, or even emulated in software. The VMM is much smaller than a traditional OS; the isolation portion of a VMM is perhaps only 10,000 lines of code.

Although our interest here is in VMs for improving protection, VMs provide two other benefits that are commercially significant:

1. *Managing software.* VMs provide an abstraction that can run the complete software stack, even including old operating systems like DOS. A typical deployment might be some VMs running legacy OSes, many running the current stable OS release, and a few testing the next OS release.

2. *Managing hardware.* One reason for multiple servers is to have each application running with the compatible version of the operating system on separate computers, as this separation can improve dependability. VMs

allow these separate software stacks to run independently yet share hardware, thereby consolidating the number of servers. Another example is that some VMMs support migration of a running VM to a different computer, either to balance load or to evacuate from failing hardware.

Amazon Web Services (AWS) uses the virtual machines in its cloud computing offering EC2 for five reasons:

Hardware/ Software Interface

1. It allows AWS to protect users from each other while sharing the same server.

2. It simplifies software distribution within a warehouse scale computer. A customer installs a virtual machine image configured with the appropriate software, and AWS distributes it to all the instances a customer wants to use.

3. Customers (and AWS) can reliably "kill" a VM to control resource usage when customers complete their work.

4. Virtual machines hide the identity of the hardware on which the customer is running, which means AWS can keep using old servers *and* introduce new, more efficient servers. The customer expects performance for instances to match their ratings in "EC2 Compute Units," which AWS defines: to "provide the equivalent CPU capacity of a 1.0–1.2 GHz 2007 AMD Opteron or 2007 Intel Xeon processor." Newer servers usually offer more EC2 Compute Units than older ones, but AWS can keep renting old servers as long as they are economical.

5. Virtual Machine Monitors can control the rate that a VM uses the processor, the network, and disk space, which allows AWS to offer many price points of instances of different types running on the same underlying servers. For example, in 2020 AWS offered more than 200 instance types, from less than half a cent per hour (t3a.nano at $0.0047) to more than $25 (memory optimized x1e.32xlarge at $26.69), a price range of over 5000:1.

In general, the cost of processor virtualization depends on the workload. User-level processor-bound programs have zero virtualization overhead, because the OS is rarely invoked, so everything runs at native speeds. I/O-intensive workloads are generally also OS-intensive, executing many system calls and privileged instructions that can result in high virtualization overhead. On the other hand, if the I/O-intensive workload is also *I/O-bound*, the cost of processor virtualization can be completely hidden, since the processor is often idle waiting for I/O.

The overhead is determined by both the number of instructions that must be emulated by the VMM and by how much time each takes to emulate them. Hence, when the guest VMs run the same ISA as the host, as we assume here, the goal of the architecture and the VMM is to run almost all instructions directly on the native hardware.

Requirements of a Virtual Machine Monitor

What must a VM monitor do? It presents a software interface to guest software, it must isolate the state of guests from each other, and it must protect itself from guest software (including guest OSes). The qualitative requirements are:

- Guest software should behave on a VM exactly as if it were running on the native hardware, except for performance-related behavior or limitations of fixed resources shared by multiple VMs.

- Guest software should not be able to change allocation of real system resources directly.

To "virtualize" the processor, the VMM must control just about everything—access to privileged state, I/O, exceptions, and interrupts—even though the guest VM and OS currently running are temporarily using them.

For example, in the case of a timer interrupt, the VMM would suspend the currently running guest VM, save its state, handle the interrupt, determine which guest VM to run next, and then load its state. Guest VMs that rely on a timer interrupt are provided with a virtual timer and an emulated timer interrupt by the VMM.

To be in charge, the VMM must be at a higher privilege level than the guest VM, which generally runs in user mode; this also ensures that the execution of any privileged instruction will be handled by the VMM. The basic requirements of system virtual:

- At least two processor modes, system and user.

- A privileged subset of instructions that is available only in system mode, resulting in a trap if executed in user mode; all system resources must be controllable only via these instructions.

(Lack of) Instruction Set Architecture Support for Virtual Machines

If VMs are planned for during the design of the ISA, it's relatively easy to reduce both the number of instructions that must be executed by a VMM and improve their emulation speed. An architecture that allows the VM to execute directly on the hardware earns the title *virtualizable*, and the IBM 370 architecture proudly bears that label.

Alas, since VMs have been considered for PC and server applications only fairly recently, most instruction sets were created without virtualization in mind. These culprits include x86 and most RISC architectures, including ARMv7 and MIPS.

Because the VMM must ensure that the guest system only interacts with virtual resources, a conventional guest OS runs as a user mode program on top of the

VMM. Then, if a guest OS attempts to access or modify information related to hardware resources via a privileged instruction—for example, reading or writing a status bit that enables interrupts—it will trap to the VMM. The VMM can then effect the appropriate changes to corresponding real resources.

Hence, if any instruction that tries to read or write such sensitive information traps when executed in user mode, the VMM can intercept it and support a virtual version of the sensitive information, as the guest OS expects.

In the absence of such support, other measures must be taken. A VMM must take special precautions to locate all problematic instructions and ensure that they behave correctly when executed by a guest OS, thereby increasing the complexity of the VMM and reducing the performance of running the VM.

Protection and Instruction Set Architecture

Protection is a joint effort of architecture and operating systems, but architects had to modify some awkward details of existing instruction set architectures when virtual memory became popular.

For example, the x86 instruction POPF loads the flag registers from the top of the stack in memory. One of the flags is the *Interrupt Enable* (IE) flag. If you run the POPF instruction in user mode, rather than trap it, it simply changes all the flags except IE. In system mode, it does change the IE. Since a guest OS runs in user mode inside a VM, this is a problem, as it expects to see a changed IE.

Historically, IBM mainframe hardware and VMM took three steps to improve performance of virtual machines:

1. Reduce the cost of processor virtualization.

2. Reduce interrupt overhead cost due to the virtualization.

3. Reduce interrupt cost by steering interrupts to the proper VM without invoking VMM.

AMD and Intel tried to address the first point in 2006 by reducing the cost of processor virtualization. It will be interesting to see how many generations of architecture and VMM modifications it will take to address all three points, and how long before virtual machines of the 21st century will be as efficient as the IBM mainframes and VMMs of the 1970s.

Elaboration: The final portion of the architecture to virtualize is I/O. This is by far the most difficult part of system virtualization because of the increasing number of I/O devices attached to the computer *and* the increasing diversity of I/O device types. Another difficulty is the sharing of a real device among multiple VMs, and yet another comes from supporting the myriad of device drivers that are required, especially if different guest OSes are supported on the same VM system. The VM illusion can be maintained by giving each VM generic versions of each type of I/O device driver, and then leaving it to the VMM to handle real I/O.

5.7   Virtual Memory

... a system has been devised to make the core drum combination appear to the programmer as a single level store, the requisite transfers taking place automatically.

Kilburn et al., *One-level storage system*, 1962

virtual memory
A technique that uses main memory as a "cache" for secondary storage.

physical address
An address in main memory.

protection A set of mechanisms for ensuring that multiple processes sharing the processor, memory, or I/O devices cannot interfere, intentionally or unintentionally, with one another by reading or writing each other's data. These mechanisms also isolate the operating system from a user process.

In earlier sections, we saw how caches provided fast access to recently used portions of a program's code and data. Similarly, the main memory can act as a "cache" for the secondary storage, usually implemented with magnetic disks. This technique is called **virtual memory**. Historically, there were two major motivations for virtual memory: to allow efficient and safe sharing of memory among multiple programs, such as for the memory needed by multiple virtual machines for cloud computing, and to remove the programming burdens of a small, limited amount of main memory. Five decades after its invention, it's the former reason that reigns today.

Of course, to allow multiple virtual machines to share the same memory, we must be able to protect the virtual machines from each other, ensuring that a program can only read and write the portions of main memory that have been assigned to it. Main memory need contain only the active portions of the many virtual machines, just as a cache contains only the active portion of one program. Thus, the principle of locality enables virtual memory as well as caches, and virtual memory allows us to efficiently share the processor as well as the main memory.

We cannot know which virtual machines will share the memory with other virtual machines when we compile them. In fact, the virtual machines sharing the memory change dynamically while the virtual machines are running. Because of this dynamic interaction, we would like to compile each program into its own *address space*—a separate range of memory locations accessible only to this program. Virtual memory implements the translation of a program's address space to **physical addresses**. This translation process enforces **protection** of a program's address space from other virtual machines.

The second motivation for virtual memory is to allow a single user program to exceed the size of primary memory. Formerly, if a program became too large for memory, it was up to the programmer to make it fit. Programmers divided programs into pieces and then identified the pieces that were mutually exclusive. These *overlays* were loaded or unloaded under user program control during execution, with the programmer ensuring that the program never tried to access an overlay that was not loaded and that the overlays loaded never exceeded the total size of the memory. Overlays were traditionally organized as modules, each containing both code and data. Calls between procedures in different modules would lead to overlaying of one module with another.

As you can well imagine, this responsibility was a substantial burden on programmers. Virtual memory, which was invented to relieve programmers of this difficulty, automatically manages the two levels of the memory hierarchy represented by main memory (sometimes called *physical memory* to distinguish it from virtual memory) and secondary storage.

Although the concepts at work in virtual memory and in caches are the same, their differing historical roots have led to the use of different terminology. A virtual memory block is called a *page*, and a virtual memory miss is called a **page fault**. With virtual memory, the processor produces a **virtual address**, which is translated by a combination of hardware and software to a *physical address*, which in turn can be used to access main memory. Figure 5.24 shows the virtually addressed memory with pages mapped to main memory. This process is called *address mapping* or **address translation**. Today, the two memory hierarchy levels controlled by virtual memory are usually DRAMs and flash memory in personal mobile devices and DRAMs and magnetic disks in servers (see Section 5.2). If we return to our library analogy, we can think of a virtual address as the title of a book and a physical address as the location of that book in the library, such as might be given by the Library of Congress call number.

Virtual memory also simplifies loading the program for execution by providing *relocation*. Relocation maps the virtual addresses used by a program to different physical addresses before the addresses are used to access memory. This relocation allows us to load the program anywhere in main memory. Furthermore, all virtual memory systems in use today relocate the program as a set of fixed-size blocks (pages), thereby eliminating the need to find a contiguous block of memory to allocate to a program; instead, the operating system need only find a sufficient number of free pages in main memory.

In virtual memory, the address is broken into a *virtual page number* and a *page offset*. Figure 5.25 shows the translation of the virtual page number to a *physical page number*. The physical page number constitutes the upper portion of the physical address, while the page offset, which is not changed, constitutes the lower portion. The number of bits in the page offset field determines the page size. The

page fault An event that occurs when an accessed page is not present in main memory.

virtual address An address that corresponds to a location in virtual space and is translated by address mapping to a physical address when memory is accessed.

address translation Also called **address mapping**. The process by which a virtual address is mapped to an address used to access memory.

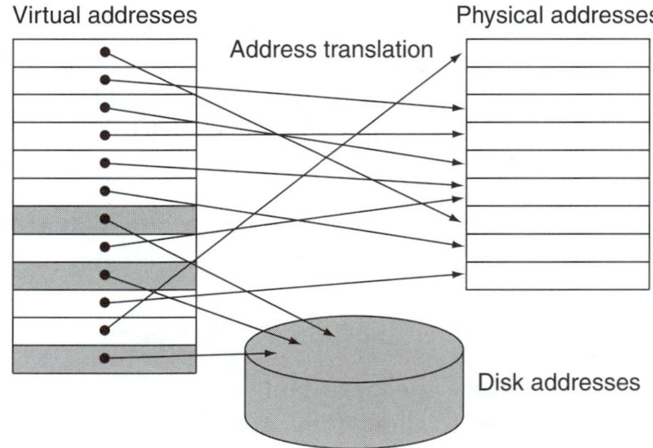

FIGURE 5.24 In virtual memory, blocks of memory (called *pages*) are mapped from one set of addresses (called *virtual addresses*) to another set (called *physical addresses*). The processor generates virtual addresses while the memory is accessed using physical addresses. Both the virtual memory and the physical memory are broken into pages, so that a virtual page is mapped to a physical page. Of course, it is also possible for a virtual page to be absent from main memory and not be mapped to a physical address; in that case, the page resides on disk. Physical pages can be shared by having two virtual addresses point to the same physical address. This capability is used to allow two different programs to share data or code.

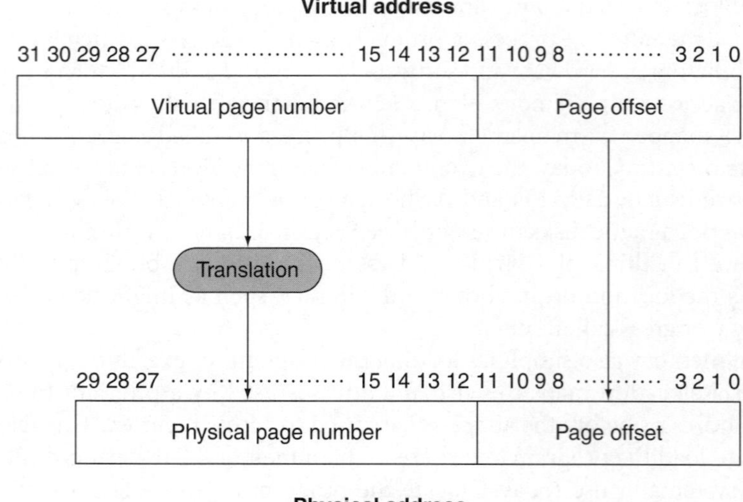

FIGURE 5.25 Mapping from a virtual to a physical address. The page size is $2^{12} = 4$ KiB. The number of physical pages allowed in memory is 2^{18}, since the physical page number has 18 bits in it. Thus, main memory can have at most 1 GiB (2^{30}), while the virtual address space is 4 GiB (2^{30}).

number of pages addressable with the virtual address need not match the number of pages addressable with the physical address. Having a larger number of virtual pages than physical pages is the basis for the illusion of an essentially unbounded amount of virtual memory.

Many design choices in virtual memory systems are motivated by the high cost of a page fault. A page fault to disk will take millions of clock cycles to process. (The table on page 396 shows that main memory latency is about 100,000 times quicker than disk.) This enormous miss penalty, dominated by the time to get the first word for typical page sizes, leads to several key decisions in designing virtual memory systems:

- Pages should be large enough to try to amortize the high access time. Sizes from 4 KiB to 16 KiB are typical today. New desktop and server systems are being developed to support 32 KiB and 64 KiB pages, but new embedded systems are going in the other direction, to 1 KiB pages.

- Organizations that reduce the page fault rate are attractive. The primary technique used here is to allow fully associative placement of pages in memory.

- Page faults can be handled in software because the overhead will be small compared to the disk access time. In addition, software can afford to use clever algorithms for choosing how to place pages because even small reductions in the miss rate will pay for the cost of such algorithms.

- Write-through will not work for virtual memory, since writes take too long. Instead, virtual memory systems use write-back.

The next few subsections address these factors in virtual memory design.

Elaboration: We present the motivation for virtual memory as many virtual machines sharing the same memory, but virtual memory was originally invented so that many programs could share a computer as part of a timesharing system. Since many readers today have no experience with time-sharing systems, we use virtual machines to motivate this section.

Elaboration: For servers and PCs, 32-bit address processors are problematic. Although we normally think of virtual addresses as much larger than physical addresses, the opposite can occur when the processor address size is small relative to the state of the memory technology. No single program or virtual machine can benefit, but a collection of programs or virtual machines running at the same time can benefit from not having to be swapped to memory or by running on parallel processors.

Elaboration: The discussion of virtual memory in this book focuses on paging, which uses fixed-size blocks. There is also a variable-size block scheme called **segmentation**. In segmentation, an address consists of two parts: a segment number and a segment offset. The segment number is mapped to a physical address, and the offset is *added* to find the actual physical address. Because the segment can vary in size, a bounds check is also needed to make sure that the offset is within the segment. The major use of segmentation is to support more powerful methods of protection and sharing in an address space. Most operating system textbooks contain extensive discussions of segmentation compared to paging and of the use of segmentation to logically share the address space. The major disadvantage of segmentation is that it splits the address space into logically separate pieces that must be manipulated as a two-part address: the segment number and the offset. Paging, in contrast, makes the boundary between page number and offset invisible to programmers and compilers.

Segments have also been used as a method to extend the address space without changing the word size of the computer. Such attempts have been unsuccessful because of the awkwardness and performance penalties inherent in a two-part address, of which programmers and compilers must be aware.

Many architectures divide the address space into large fixed-size blocks that simplify protection between the operating system and user programs and increase the efficiency of implementing paging. Although these divisions are often called "segments," this mechanism is much simpler than variable block size segmentation and is not visible to user programs; we discuss it in more detail shortly.

> **segmentation**
> A variable-size address mapping scheme in which an address consists of two parts: a segment number, which is mapped to a physical address, and a segment offset.

Placing a Page and Finding it Again

Because of the incredibly high penalty for a page fault, designers reduce page fault frequency by optimizing page placement. If we allow a virtual page to be mapped to any physical page, the operating system can then choose to replace any page it wants when a page fault occurs. For example, the operating system can use a

page table The table containing the virtual to physical address translations in a virtual memory system. The table, which is stored in memory, is typically indexed by the virtual page number; each entry in the table contains the physical page number for that virtual page if the page is currently in memory.

sophisticated algorithm and complex data structures that track page usage to try to choose a page that will not be needed for a long time. The ability to use a clever and flexible replacement scheme reduces the page fault rate and simplifies the use of fully associative placement of pages.

As mentioned in Section 5.4, the difficulty in using fully associative placement is in locating an entry, since it can be anywhere in the upper level of the hierarchy. A full search is impractical. In virtual memory systems, we locate pages by using a table that indexes the memory; this structure is called a **page table**, and it resides in memory. A page table is indexed with the page number from the virtual address to discover the corresponding physical page number. Each program has its own page table, which maps the virtual address space of that program to main memory. In our library analogy, the page table corresponds to a mapping between book titles and library locations. Just as the card catalog may contain entries for books in another library on campus rather than the local branch library, we will see that the page table may contain entries for pages not present in memory. To indicate the location of the page table in memory, the hardware includes a register that points to the start of the page table; we call this the *page table register*. Assume for now that the page table is in a fixed and contiguous area of memory.

Hardware/ Software Interface

The page table, together with the program counter and the registers, specifies the *state* of a virtual machine. If we want to allow another virtual machine to use the processor, we must save this state. Later, after restoring this state, the virtual machine can continue execution. We often refer to this state as a *process*. The process is considered *active* when it is in possession of the processor; otherwise, it is considered *inactive*. The operating system can make a process active by loading the process's state, including the program counter, which will initiate execution at the value of the saved program counter.

The process's address space, and hence all the data it can access in memory, is defined by its page table, which resides in memory. Rather than save the entire page table, the operating system simply loads the page table register to point to the page table of the process it wants to make active. Each process has its own page table, since different processes use the same virtual addresses. The operating system is responsible for allocating the physical memory and updating the page tables, so that the virtual address spaces of different processes do not collide. As we will see shortly, the use of separate page tables also provides protection of one process from another.

Figure 5.26 uses the page table register, the virtual address, and the indicated page table to show how the hardware can form a physical address. A valid bit is used in each page table entry, just as we did in a cache. If the bit is off, the page is not present in main memory and a page fault occurs. If the bit is on, the page is in memory and the entry contains the physical page number.

Because the page table contains a mapping for every possible virtual page, no tags are required. In cache terminology, the index that is used to access the page table consists of the full block address, which is the virtual page number.

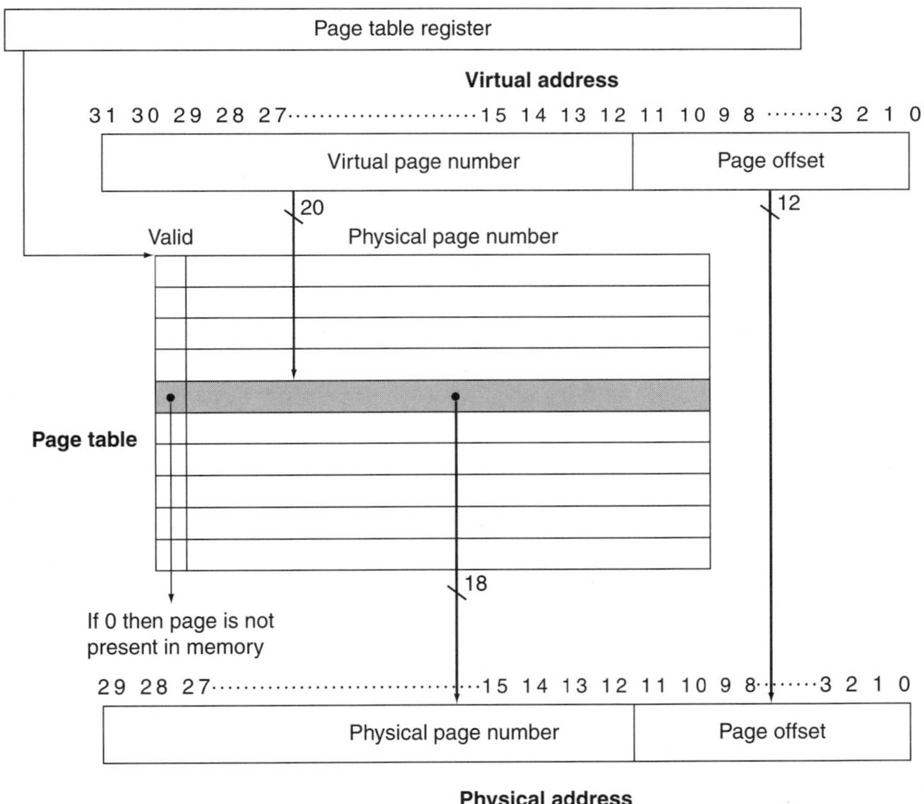

FIGURE 5.26 The page table is indexed with the virtual page number to obtain the corresponding portion of the physical address. We assume a 32-bit address. The page table pointer gives the starting address of the page table. In this figure, the page size is 2^{12} bytes, or 4 KiB. The virtual address space is 2^{32} bytes, or 4 GiB, and the physical address space is 2^{30} bytes, which allows main memory of up to 1 GiB. The number of entries in the page table is 2^{20}, or 1 million entries. The valid bit for each entry indicates whether the mapping is legitimate. If it is off, then the page is not present in memory. Although the page table entry shown here need only be 19 bits wide, it would typically be rounded up to 32 bits for ease of indexing. The extra bits would be used to store additional information that needs to be kept on a per-page basis, such as protection.

Page Faults

If the valid bit for a virtual page is off, a page fault occurs. The operating system must be given control. This transfer is done with the exception mechanism, which we saw in Chapter 4 and will discuss again later in this section. Once the operating system gets control, it must find the page in the next level of the hierarchy (usually flash memory or magnetic disk) and decide where to place the requested page in main memory.

The virtual address alone does not immediately tell us where the page is on disk. Returning to our library analogy, we cannot find the location of a library book on the shelves just by knowing its title. Instead, we go to the catalog and look up the book, obtaining an address for the location on the shelves, such as the Library of Congress call number. Likewise, in a virtual memory system, we must keep track of the location on disk of each page in virtual address space.

swap space The space on the disk reserved for the full virtual memory space of a process.

Because we do not know ahead of time when a page in memory will be replaced, the operating system usually creates the space on flash memory or disk for all the pages of a process when it creates the process. This space is called the **swap space**. At that time, it also creates a data structure to record where each virtual page is stored on disk. This data structure may be part of the page table or may be an auxiliary data structure indexed in the same way as the page table. Figure 5.27 shows the organization when a single table holds either the physical page number or the disk address.

The operating system also creates a data structure that tracks which processes and which virtual addresses use each physical page. When a page fault occurs, if all the pages in main memory are in use, the operating system must choose a page to replace. Because we want to minimize the number of page faults, most operating systems try to choose a page that they hypothesize will not be needed in the near future. Using the past to predict the future, operating systems follow the least recently used (LRU) replacement scheme, which we mentioned in Section 5.4. The operating system searches for the least recently used page, assuming that a page that has not been used in a long time is less likely to be needed than a more recently accessed page. The replaced pages are written to swap space on the disk. In case you are wondering, the operating system is just another process, and these tables controlling memory are in memory; the details of this seeming contradiction will be explained shortly.

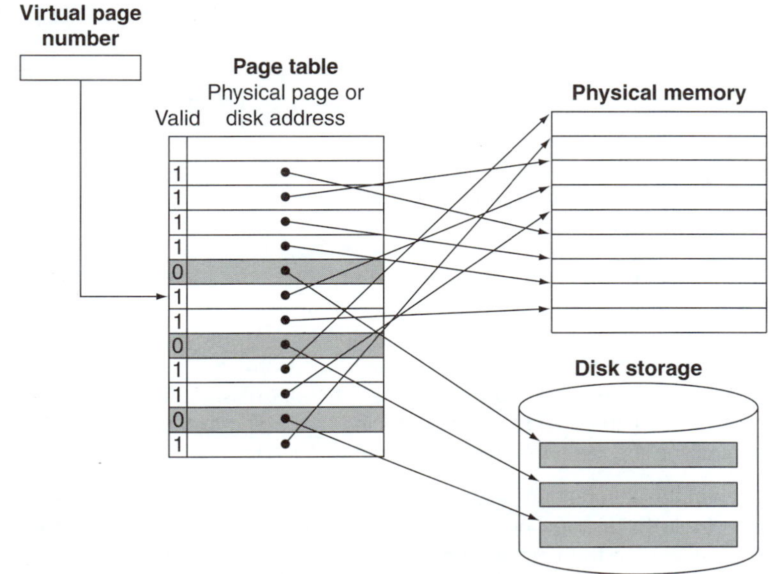

FIGURE 5.27 The page table maps each page in virtual memory to either a page in main memory or a page stored on disk, which is the next level in the hierarchy. The virtual page number is used to index the page table. If the valid bit is on, the page table supplies the physical page number (i.e., the starting address of the page in memory) corresponding to the virtual page. If the valid bit is off, the page currently resides only on disk, at a specified disk address. In many systems, the table of physical page addresses and disk page addresses, while logically one table, is stored in two separate data structures. Dual tables are justified in part because we must keep the disk addresses of all the pages, even if they are currently in main memory. Remember that the pages in main memory and the pages on disk are the same size.

Hardware/ Software Interface

Implementing a completely accurate LRU scheme is too expensive, since it requires updating a data structure on *every* memory reference. Instead, most operating systems approximate LRU by keeping track of which pages have and which pages have not been recently used. To help the operating system estimate the LRU pages, some computers provide a **reference bit** or **use bit**, which is set whenever a page is accessed. The operating system periodically clears the reference bits and later records them so it can determine which pages were touched during a particular time period. With this usage information, the operating system can select a page that is among the least recently referenced (detected by having its reference bit off). If this bit is not provided by the hardware, the operating system must find another way to estimate which pages have been accessed.

reference bit Also called **use bit**. A field that is set whenever a page is accessed and that is used to implement LRU or other replacement schemes.

Elaboration: With a 32-bit virtual address, 4 KiB pages, and 4 bytes per page table entry, we can compute the total page table size:

$$\text{Number of page table entries} = \frac{2^{32}}{2^{12}} = 2^{20}$$

$$\text{Size of page table} = 2^{20} \text{ page table entries} \times 2^2 \frac{\text{bytes}}{\text{page table entry}} = 4\,\text{MiB}$$

That is, we would need to use 4 MiB of memory for each program in execution at any time. This amount is not so bad for a single process. What if there are hundreds of processes running, each with their own page table? And how should we handle 64-bit addresses, which by this calculation would need 2^{52} words?

A range of techniques is used to reduce the amount of storage required for the page table. The five techniques below aim at reducing the total maximum storage required as well as minimizing the main memory dedicated to page tables:

1. The simplest technique is to keep a limit register that restricts the size of the page table for a given process. If the virtual page number becomes larger than the contents of the limit register, entries must be added to the page table. This technique allows the page table to grow as a process consumes more space. Thus, the page table will only be large if the process is using many pages of virtual address space. This technique requires that the address space expand in only one direction.

2. Allowing growth in only one direction is not sufficient, since most languages require two areas whose size is expandable: one area holds the stack and the other area holds the heap. Because of this duality, it is convenient to divide the page table and let it grow from the highest address down, as well as from the lowest address up. This means that there will be two separate page tables and two separate limits. The use of two page tables breaks the address space into two segments. The high-order bit of an address usually determines which segment and thus which page table to use for that address. Since the high-order address bit specifies the segment, each segment can be as large as one-half of the address space. A limit register for each segment specifies the current size of the segment, which grows in units of pages. This type of segmentation is used by many architectures, including MIPS. Unlike the type of segmentation discussed in the second *Elaboration* on page 449, this form of segmentation is invisible to the application program, although not to the operating system. The major disadvantage of this scheme is that it does not work well when the address space is used in a sparse fashion rather than as a contiguous set of virtual addresses.

3. Another approach to reducing the page table size is to apply a hashing function to the virtual address so that the page table need be only the size of the number of *physical* pages in main memory. Such a structure is called an *inverted page table*. Of course, the lookup process is slightly more complex with an inverted page table, because we can no longer just index the page table.

4. Multiple levels of page tables can also be used to reduce the total amount of page table storage. The first level maps large fixed-size blocks of virtual address space, perhaps 64 to 256 pages in total. These large blocks are sometimes called segments, and this first-level mapping table is sometimes called a

segment table, though the segments are again invisible to the user. Each entry in the segment table indicates whether any pages in that segment are allocated and, if so, points to a page table for that segment. Address translation happens by first looking in the segment table, using the highest-order bits of the address. If the segment address is valid, the next set of high-order bits is used to index the page table indicated by the segment table entry. This scheme allows the address space to be used in a sparse fashion (multiple noncontiguous segments can be active) without having to allocate the entire page table. Such schemes are particularly useful with very large address spaces and in software systems that require noncontiguous allocation. The primary disadvantage of this two-level mapping is the more complex process for address translation.

5. To reduce the actual main memory tied up in page tables, most modern systems also allow the page tables to be paged. Although this sounds tricky, it works by using the same basic ideas of virtual memory and simply allowing the page tables to reside in the virtual address space. In addition, there are some small but critical problems, such as a never-ending series of page faults, which must be avoided. How these problems are overcome is both very detailed and typically highly processor specific. In brief, these problems are avoided by placing all the page tables in the address space of the operating system and placing at least some of the page tables for the operating system in a portion of main memory that is physically addressed and is always present and thus never on disk.

What about Writes?

The difference between the access time to the cache and main memory is tens to hundreds of cycles, and write-through schemes can be used, although we need a write buffer to hide the latency of the write from the processor. In a virtual memory system, writes to the next level of the hierarchy (disk) can take millions of processor clock cycles; therefore, building a write buffer to allow the system to write-through to disk would be completely impractical. Instead, virtual memory systems must use write-back, performing the individual writes into the page in memory, and copying the page back to disk when it is replaced in the memory.

A write-back scheme has another major advantage in a virtual memory system. Because the disk transfer time is small compared with its access time, copying back an entire page is much more efficient than writing individual words back to the disk. A write-back operation, although more efficient than transferring individual words, is still costly. Thus, we would like to know whether a page *needs* to be copied back when we choose to replace it. To track whether a page has been written since it was read into the memory, a *dirty bit* is added to the page table. The dirty bit is set when any word in a page is written. If the operating system chooses to replace the page, the dirty bit indicates whether the page needs to be written out before its location in memory can be given to another page. Hence, a modified page is often called a *dirty* page.

**Hardware/
Software
Interface**

Making Address Translation Fast: the TLB

Since the page tables are stored in main memory, every memory access by a program can take at least twice as long: one memory access to obtain the physical address and a second access to get the data. The key to improving access performance is to rely on locality of reference to the page table. When a translation for a virtual page number is used, it will probably be needed again in the near future, because the references to the words on that page have both temporal and spatial locality.

Accordingly, modern processors include a special cache that keeps track of recently used translations. This special address translation cache is traditionally referred to as a **translation-lookaside buffer (TLB)**, although it would be more accurate to call it a translation cache. The TLB corresponds to that little piece of paper we typically use to record the location of a set of books we look up in the card catalog; rather than continually searching the entire catalog, we record the location of several books and use the scrap of paper as a cache of Library of Congress call numbers.

Figure 5.28 shows that each tag entry in the TLB holds a portion of the virtual page number, and each data entry of the TLB holds a physical page number.

translation-lookaside buffer (TLB) A cache that keeps track of recently used address mappings to try to avoid an access to the page table.

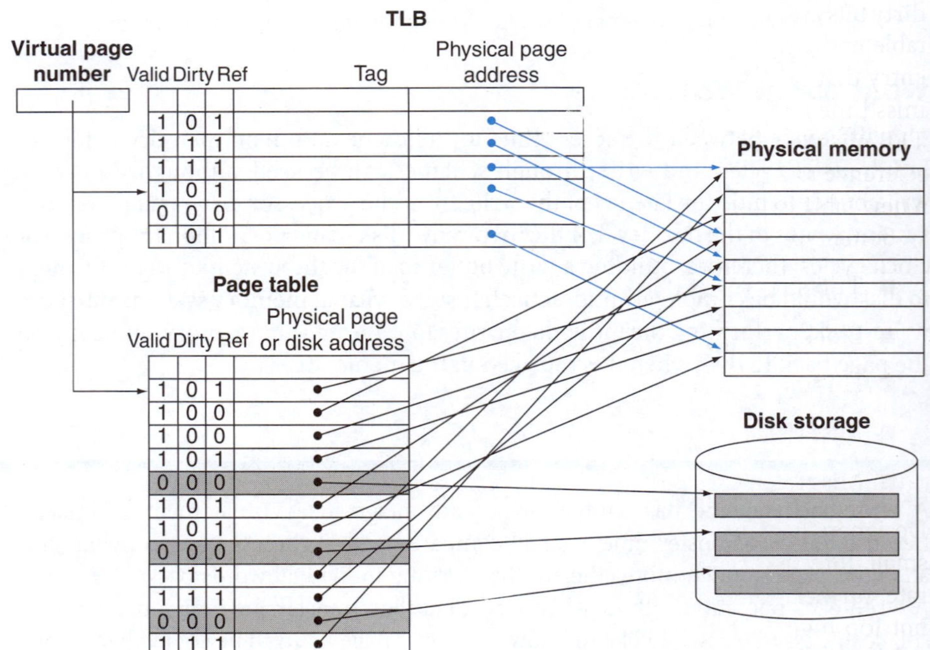

FIGURE 5.28 The TLB acts as a cache of the page table for the entries that map to physical pages only. The TLB contains a subset of the virtual-to-physical page mappings that are in the page table. The TLB mappings are shown in color. Because the TLB is a cache, it must have a tag field. If there is no matching entry in the TLB for a page, the page table must be examined. The page table either supplies a physical page number for the page (which can then be used to build a TLB entry) or indicates that the page resides on disk, in which case a page fault occurs. Since the page table has an entry for every virtual page, no tag field is needed; in other words, unlike a TLB, a page table is *not* a cache.

Because we access the TLB instead of the page table on every reference, the TLB will need to include other status bits, such as the dirty and the reference bits.

On every reference, we look up the virtual page number in the TLB. If we get a hit, the physical page number is used to form the address, and the corresponding reference bit is turned on. If the processor is performing a write, the dirty bit is also turned on. If a miss in the TLB occurs, we must determine whether it is a page fault or merely a TLB miss. If the page exists in memory, then the TLB miss indicates only that the translation is missing. In such cases, the processor can handle the TLB miss by loading the translation from the page table into the TLB and then trying the reference again. If the page is not present in memory, then the TLB miss indicates a true page fault. In this case, the processor invokes the operating system using an exception. Because the TLB has many fewer entries than the number of pages in main memory, TLB misses will be much more frequent than true page faults.

TLB misses can be handled either in hardware or in software. In practice, with care there can be little performance difference between the two approaches, because the basic operations are the same in either case.

After a TLB miss occurs and the missing translation has been retrieved from the page table, we will need to select a TLB entry to replace. Because the reference and dirty bits are contained in the TLB entry, we need to copy these bits back to the page table entry when we replace an entry. These bits are the only portion of the TLB entry that can be changed. Using write-back—that is, copying these entries back at miss time rather than when they are written—is very efficient, since we expect the TLB miss rate to be small. Some systems use other techniques to approximate the reference and dirty bits, eliminating the need to write into the TLB except to load a new table entry on a miss.

Some typical values for a TLB might be

- TLB size: 16–512 entries

- Block size: 1–2 page table entries (typically 4–8 bytes each)

- Hit time: 0.5–1 clock cycle

- Miss penalty: 10–100 clock cycles

- Miss rate: 0.01%–1%

Designers have used a wide variety of associativities in TLBs. Some systems use small, fully associative TLBs because a fully associative mapping has a lower miss rate; furthermore, since the TLB is small, the cost of a fully associative mapping is not too high. Other systems use large TLBs, often with small associativity. With a fully associative mapping, choosing the entry to replace becomes tricky since implementing a hardware LRU scheme is too expensive. Furthermore, since TLB misses are much more frequent than page faults and thus must be handled more cheaply, we cannot afford an expensive software algorithm, as we can for page faults. As a result, many systems provide some support for randomly choosing an entry to replace. We'll examine replacement schemes in a little more detail in Section 5.8.

The Intrinsity FastMATH TLB

To see these ideas in a real processor, let's take a closer look at the TLB of the Intrinsity FastMATH. The memory system uses 4 KiB pages and a 32-bit address space; thus, the virtual page number is 20 bits long, as in the top of Figure 5.29. The physical address is the same size as the virtual address. The TLB contains 16 entries, it is fully associative, and it is shared between the instruction and data references. Each entry is 64 bits wide and contains a 20-bit tag (which is the virtual page number for that TLB entry), the corresponding physical page number (also 20 bits), a valid bit, a dirty bit, and other bookkeeping bits. Like most MIPS systems, it uses software to handle TLB misses.

Figure 5.29 shows the TLB and one of the caches, while Figure 5.30 shows the steps in processing a read or write request. When a TLB miss occurs, the MIPS hardware saves the page number of the reference in a special register and generates an exception. The exception invokes the operating system, which handles the miss in software. To find the physical address for the missing page, the TLB miss routine indexes the page table using the page number of the virtual address and the page table register, which indicates the starting address of the active process page table. Using a special set of system instructions that can update the TLB, the operating system places the physical address from the page table into the TLB. A TLB miss takes about 13 clock cycles, assuming the code and the page table entry are in the instruction cache and data cache, respectively. (We will see the MIPS TLB code on page 467.) A true page fault occurs if the page table entry does not have a valid physical address. The hardware maintains an index that indicates the recommended entry to replace; the recommended entry is chosen randomly.

There is an extra complication for write requests: namely, the write access bit in the TLB must be checked. This bit prevents the program from writing into pages for which it has only read access. If the program attempts a write and the write access bit is off, an exception is generated. The write access bit forms part of the protection mechanism, which we will discuss shortly.

Integrating Virtual Memory, TLBs, and Caches

Our virtual memory and cache systems work together as a hierarchy, so that data cannot be in the cache unless it is present in main memory. The operating system helps maintain this hierarchy by flushing the contents of any page from the cache when it decides to migrate that page to disk. At the same time, the OS modifies the page tables and TLB, so that an attempt to access any data on the migrated page will generate a page fault.

Under the best of circumstances, a virtual address is translated by the TLB and sent to the cache where the appropriate data is found, retrieved, and sent back to the processor. In the worst case, a reference can miss in all three components of the memory hierarchy: the TLB, the page table, and the cache. The following example illustrates these interactions in more detail.

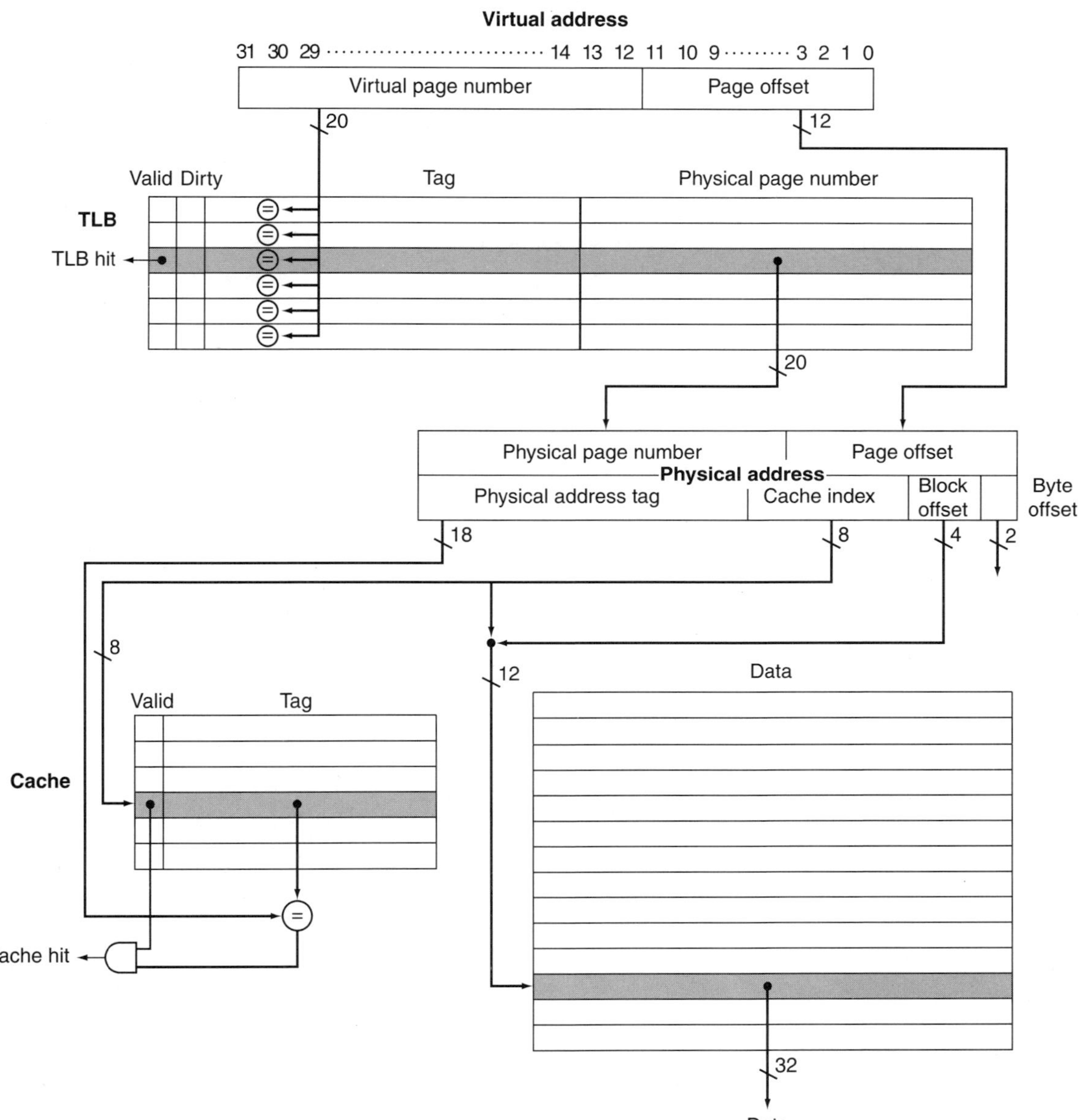

FIGURE 5.29 The TLB and cache implement the process of going from a virtual address to a data item in the Intrinsity FastMATH. This figure shows the organization of the TLB and the data cache, assuming a 4 KiB page size. This diagram focuses on a read; Figure 5.30 describes how to handle writes. Note that unlike Figure 5.12, the tag and data RAMs are split. By addressing the long but narrow data RAM with the cache index concatenated with the block offset, we select the desired word in the block without a 16:1 multiplexor. While the cache is direct mapped, the TLB is fully associative. Implementing a fully associative TLB requires that every TLB tag be compared against the virtual page number, since the entry of interest can be anywhere in the TLB. (See content addressable memories in the *Elaboration* on page 426.) If the valid bit of the matching entry is on, the access is a TLB hit, and bits from the physical page number together with bits from the page offset form the index that is used to access the cache.

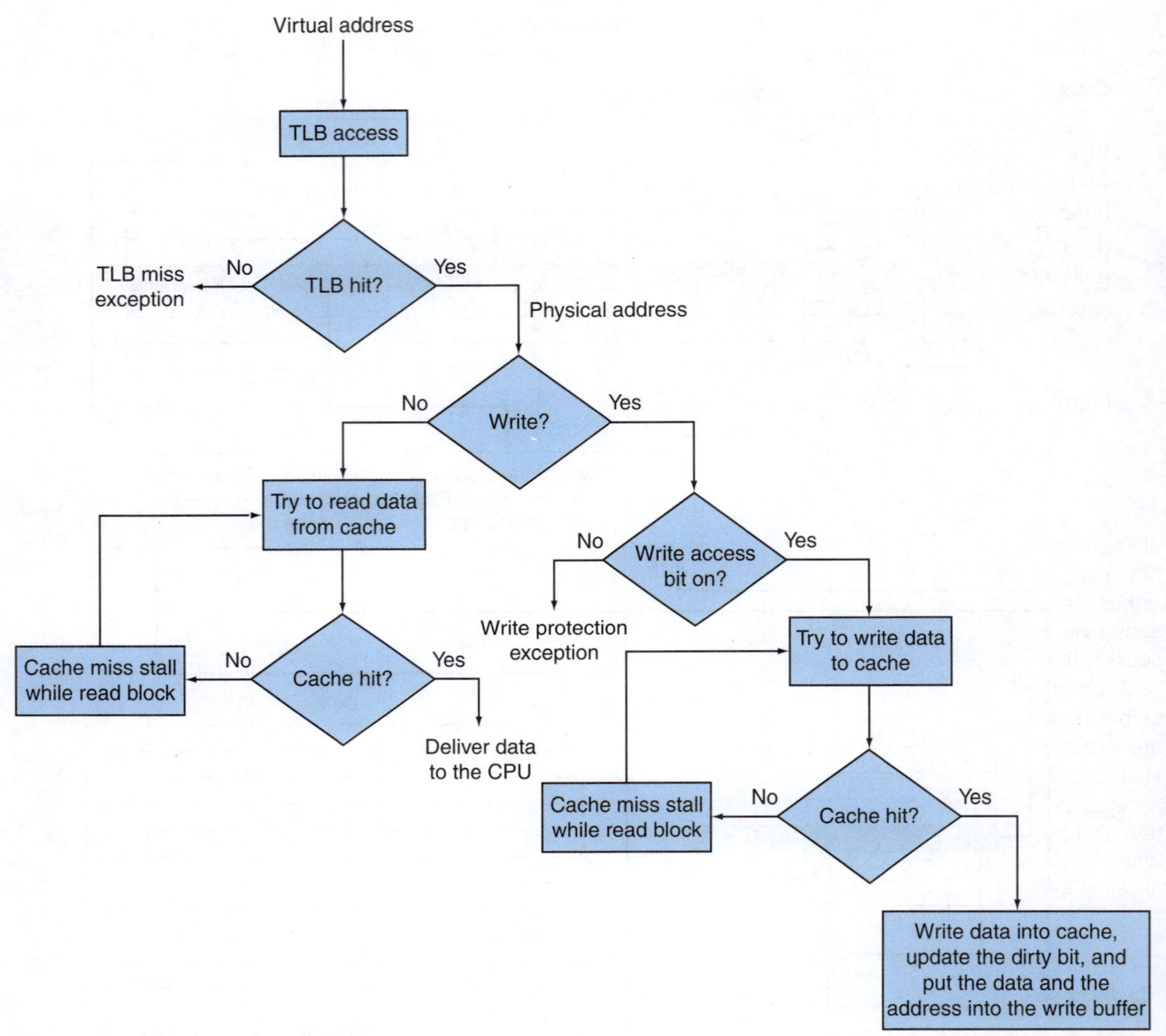

FIGURE 5.30 Processing a read or a write-through in the Intrinsity FastMATH TLB and cache. If the TLB generates a hit, the cache can be accessed with the resulting physical address. For a read, the cache generates a hit or miss and supplies the data or causes a stall while the data is brought from memory. If the operation is a write, a portion of the cache entry is overwritten for a hit and the data is sent to the write buffer if we assume write-through. A write miss is just like a read miss except that the block is modified after it is read from memory. Write-back requires writes to set a dirty bit for the cache block, and a write buffer is loaded with the whole block only on a read miss or write miss if the block to be replaced is dirty. Notice that a TLB hit and a cache hit are independent events, but a cache hit can only occur after a TLB hit occurs, which means that the data must be present in memory. The relationship between TLB misses and cache misses is examined further in the following example and the exercises at the end of this chapter.

Overall Operation of a Memory Hierarchy

In a memory hierarchy like that of Figure 5.29, which includes a TLB and a cache organized as shown, a memory reference can encounter three different types of misses: a TLB miss, a page fault, and a cache miss. Consider all the combinations of these three events with one or more occurring (seven possibilities). For each possibility, state whether this event can actually occur and under what circumstances.

Figure 5.31 shows all combinations and whether each is possible in practice.

PIPELINING

virtually addressed cache A cache that is accessed with a virtual address rather than a physical address.

Elaboration: Figure 5.31 assumes that all memory addresses are translated to physical addresses before the cache is accessed. In this organization, the cache is *physically indexed* and *physically tagged* (both the cache index and tag are physical, rather than virtual, addresses). In such a system, the amount of time to access memory, assuming a cache hit, must accommodate both a TLB access and a cache access; of course, these accesses can be **pipelined**.

Alternatively, the processor can index the cache with an address that is completely or partially virtual. This is called a virtually addressed cache, and it uses tags that are virtual addresses; hence, such a cache is *virtually indexed* and *virtually tagged*. In such caches, the address translation hardware (TLB) is unused during the normal cache access, since the cache is accessed with a virtual address that has not been translated to a physical address. This takes the TLB out of the critical path, reducing cache latency. When a cache miss occurs, however, the processor needs to translate the address to a physical address so that it can fetch the cache block from main memory.

TLB	Page table	Cache	Possible? If so, under what circumstance?
Hit	Hit	Miss	Possible, although the page table is never really checked if TLB hits.
Miss	Hit	Hit	TLB misses, but entry found in page table; after retry, data is found in cache.
Miss	Hit	Miss	TLB misses, but entry found in page table; after retry, data misses in cache.
Miss	Miss	Miss	TLB misses and is followed by a page fault; after retry, data must miss in cache.
Hit	Miss	Miss	Impossible: cannot have a translation in TLB if page is not present in memory.
Hit	Miss	Hit	Impossible: cannot have a translation in TLB if page is not present in memory.
Miss	Miss	Hit	Impossible: data cannot be allowed in cache if the page is not in memory.

FIGURE 5.31 The possible combinations of events in the TLB, virtual memory system, and cache. Three of these combinations are impossible, and one is possible (TLB hit, virtual memory hit, cache miss) but never detected.

aliasing A situation in which two addresses access the same object; it can occur in virtual memory when there are two virtual addresses for the same physical page.

When the cache is accessed with a virtual address and pages are shared between processes (which may access them with different virtual addresses), there is the possibility of **aliasing**. Aliasing occurs when the same object has two names—in this case, two virtual addresses for the same page. This ambiguity creates a problem, because a word on such a page may be cached in two different locations, each corresponding to different virtual addresses. This ambiguity would allow one program to write the data without the other program being aware that the data had changed. Completely virtually addressed caches either introduce design limitations on the cache and TLB to reduce aliases or require the operating system, and possibly the user, to take steps to ensure that aliases do not occur.

A common compromise between these two design points is caches that are virtually indexed—sometimes using just the page-offset portion of the address, which is really a physical address since it is not translated—but use physical tags. These designs, which are *virtually indexed but physically tagged*, attempt to achieve the performance advantages of virtually indexed caches with the architecturally simpler advantages of a **physically addressed cache**. For example, there is no alias problem in this case. Figure 5.29 assumed a 4 KiB page size, but it's really 16 KiB, so the Intrinsity FastMATH can use this trick. To pull it off, there must be careful coordination between the minimum page size, the cache size, and associativity.

physically addressed cache A cache that is addressed by a physical address.

Implementing Protection with Virtual Memory

Perhaps the most important function of virtual memory today is to allow sharing of a single main memory by multiple processes, while providing memory protection among these processes and the operating system. The protection mechanism must ensure that although multiple processes are sharing the same main memory, one renegade process cannot write into the address space of another user process or into the operating system either intentionally or unintentionally. The write access bit in the TLB can protect a page from being written. Without this level of protection, computer viruses would be even more widespread.

Hardware/ Software Interface

To enable the operating system to implement protection in the virtual memory system, the hardware must provide at least the three basic capabilities summarized below. Note that the first two are the same requirements as needed for virtual machines (Section 5.6).

supervisor mode Also called **kernel mode**. A mode indicating that a running process is an operating system process.

1. Support at least two modes that indicate whether the running process is a user process or an operating system process, variously called a **supervisor** process, a **kernel** process, or an *executive* process.

2. Provide a portion of the processor state that a user process can read but not write. This includes the user/supervisor mode bit, which dictates whether the processor is in user or supervisor mode, the page table pointer, and the

TLB. To write these elements, the operating system uses special instructions that are only available in supervisor mode.

3. Provide mechanisms whereby the processor can go from user mode to supervisor mode and vice versa. The first direction is typically accomplished by a system call exception, implemented as a special instruction (*syscall* in the MIPS instruction set) that transfers control to a dedicated location in supervisor code space. As with any other exception, the program counter from the point of the system call is saved in the exception PC (EPC), and the processor is placed in supervisor mode. To return to user mode from the exception, use the *return from exception* (ERET) instruction, which resets to user mode and jumps to the address in EPC.

By using these mechanisms and storing the page tables in the operating system's address space, the operating system can change the page tables while preventing a user process from changing them, ensuring that a user process can access only the storage provided to it by the operating system.

We also want to prevent a process from reading the data of another process. For example, we wouldn't want a student program to read an upcoming exam if it was in the processor's memory. Once we begin sharing main memory, we must provide the ability for a process to protect its data from both reading and writing by another process; otherwise, sharing the main memory will be a mixed blessing!

Remember that each process has its own virtual address space. Thus, if the operating system keeps the page tables organized so that the independent virtual pages map to disjoint physical pages, one process will not be able to access another's data. Of course, this also requires that a user process be unable to change the page table mapping. The operating system can assure safety if it prevents the user process from modifying its own page tables. However, the operating system must be able to modify the page tables. Placing the page tables in the protected address space of the operating system satisfies both requirements.

When processes want to share information in a limited way, the operating system must assist them, since accessing the information of another process requires changing the page table of the accessing process. The write access bit can be used to restrict the sharing to just read sharing, and, like the rest of the page table, this bit can be changed only by the operating system. To allow another process, say, P1, to read a page owned by process P2, P2 would ask the operating system to create a page table entry for a virtual page in P1's address space that points to the same physical page that P2 wants to share. The operating system could use the write protection bit to prevent P1 from writing the data, if that was P2's wish. Any bits that determine the access rights for a page must be included in both the page table and the TLB, because the page table is accessed only on a TLB miss.

> **system call** A special instruction that transfers control from user mode to a dedicated location in supervisor code space, invoking the exception mechanism in the process.

context switch

A changing of the internal state of the processor to allow a different process to use the processor that includes saving the state needed to return to the currently executing process.

Elaboration: When the operating system decides to change from running process P1 to running process P2 (called a **context switch** or *process switch*), it must ensure that P2 cannot get access to the page tables of P1 because that would compromise protection. If there is no TLB, it suffices to change the page table register to point to P2's page table (rather than to P1's); with a TLB, we must clear the TLB entries that belong to P1—both to protect the data of P1 and to force the TLB to load the entries for P2. If the process switch rate were high, this could be quite inefficient. For example, P2 might load only a few TLB entries before the operating system switched back to P1. Unfortunately, P1 would then find that all its TLB entries were gone and would have to pay TLB misses to reload them. This problem arises because the virtual addresses used by P1 and P2 can be the same, and we must clear out the TLB to avoid confusing these addresses.

A common alternative is to extend the virtual address space by adding a *process identifier* or *task identifier*. The Intrinsity FastMATH has an 8-bit address space ID (ASID) field for this purpose. This small field identifies the currently running process; it is kept in a register loaded by the operating system when it switches processes. The process identifier is concatenated to the tag portion of the TLB, so that a TLB hit occurs only if both the page number *and* the process identifier match. This combination eliminates the need to clear the TLB, except on rare occasions, such as recycling an ASID.

Similar problems can occur for a cache, since on a process switch the cache will contain data from the running process. These problems arise in different ways for physically addressed and virtually addressed caches, and a variety of different solutions, such as process identifiers, are used to ensure that a process gets its own data.

Handling TLB Misses and Page Faults

Although the translation of virtual to physical addresses with a TLB is straightforward when we get a TLB hit, as we saw earlier, handling TLB misses and page faults is more complex. A TLB miss occurs when no entry in the TLB matches a virtual address. Recall that a TLB miss can indicate one of two possibilities:

1. The page is present in memory, and we need only create the missing TLB entry.

2. The page is not present in memory, and we need to transfer control to the operating system to deal with a page fault.

MIPS traditionally handles a TLB miss in software. It brings in the page table entry from memory and then re-executes the instruction that caused the TLB miss. Upon re-executing, it will get a TLB hit. If the page table entry indicates the page is not in memory, this time it will get a page fault exception.

Handling a TLB miss or a page fault requires using the exception mechanism to interrupt the active process, transferring control to the operating system, and later resuming execution of the interrupted process. A page fault will be recognized sometime during the clock cycle used to access memory. To restart the instruction after the page fault is handled, the program counter of the instruction that caused the page fault must be saved. Just as in Chapter 4, the *exception program counter* (EPC) is used to hold this value.

Moreover, a TLB miss or page fault exception must be asserted by the end of the same clock cycle that the memory access occurs, so that the next clock cycle will begin exception processing rather than continue normal instruction execution. If the page fault was not recognized in this clock cycle, a load instruction could overwrite a register, and this could be disastrous when we try to restart the instruction. For example, consider the instruction `lw  $1,0($1)`: the computer must be able to prevent the write pipeline stage from occurring; otherwise, it could not properly restart the instruction, since the contents of `$1` would have been destroyed. A similar complication arises on stores. We must prevent the write into memory from actually completing when there is a page fault; this is usually done by deasserting the write control line to the memory.

Hardware/ Software Interface

Between the time we begin executing the exception handler in the operating system and the time that the operating system has saved all the state of the process, the operating system is particularly vulnerable. For example, if another exception occurred when we were processing the first exception in the operating system, the control unit would overwrite the exception program counter, making it impossible to return to the instruction that caused the page fault! We can avoid this disaster by providing the ability to **disable** and **enable exceptions**. When an exception first occurs, the processor sets a bit that disables all other exceptions; this could happen at the same time the processor sets the supervisor mode bit. The operating system will then save just enough state to allow it to recover if another exception occurs— namely, the *exception program counter* (EPC) and Cause registers. EPC and Cause are two of the special control registers that help with exceptions, TLB misses, and page faults; Figure 5.32 shows the rest. The operating system can then re-enable exceptions. These steps make sure that exceptions will not cause the processor to lose any state and thereby be unable to restart execution of the interrupting instruction.

exception enable Also called interrupt enable. A signal or action that controls whether the process responds to an exception or not; necessary for preventing the occurrence of exceptions during intervals before the processor has safely saved the state needed to restart.

Once the operating system knows the virtual address that caused the page fault, it must complete three steps:

1. Look up the page table entry using the virtual address and find the location of the referenced page on disk.

2. Choose a physical page to replace; if the chosen page is dirty, it must be written out to disk before we can bring a new virtual page into this physical page.

3. Start a read to bring the referenced page from disk into the chosen physical page.

Register	CP0 register number	Description
EPC	14	Where to restart after exception
Cause	13	Cause of exception
BadVAddr	8	Address that caused exception
Index	0	Location in TLB to be read or written
Random	1	Pseudorandom location in TLB
EntryLo	2	Physical page address and flags
EntryHi	10	Virtual page address
Context	4	Page table address and page number

FIGURE 5.32 MIPS control registers. These are considered to be in coprocessor 0, and hence are read using `mfc0` and written using `mtc0`.

Of course, this last step will take millions of processor clock cycles (so will the second if the replaced page is dirty); accordingly, the operating system will usually select another process to execute in the processor until the disk access completes. Because the operating system has saved the state of the process, it can freely give control of the processor to another process.

When the read of the page from disk is complete, the operating system can restore the state of the process that originally caused the page fault and execute the instruction that returns from the exception. This instruction will reset the processor from kernel to user mode, as well as restore the program counter. The user process then re-executes the instruction that faulted, accesses the requested page successfully, and continues execution.

Page fault exceptions for data accesses are difficult to implement properly in a processor because of a combination of three characteristics:

1. They occur in the middle of instructions, unlike instruction page faults.

2. The instruction cannot be completed before handling the exception.

3. After handling the exception, the instruction must be restarted as if nothing had occurred.

restartable instruction An instruction that can resume execution after an exception is resolved without the exception's affecting the result of the instruction.

Making instructions **restartable**, so that the exception can be handled and the instruction later continued, is relatively easy in an architecture like the MIPS. Because each instruction writes only one data item and this write occurs at the end of the instruction cycle, we can simply prevent the instruction from completing (by not writing) and restart the instruction at the beginning.

Let's look in more detail at MIPS. When a TLB miss occurs, the MIPS hardware saves the page number of the reference in a special register called BadVAddr (see Figure 5.33) and generates an exception.

The exception invokes the operating system, which handles the miss in software. Control is transferred to address 8000 0000$_{hex}$, the location of the TLB miss **handler**. To find the physical address for the missing page, the TLB miss routine indexes the page table using the page number of the virtual address and the page table register, which indicates the starting address of the active process page table. To make this indexing fast, MIPS hardware places everything you need in the special `Context` register (Figure 5.33): the upper 12 bits have the address of the base of the page table, and the next 18 bits have the virtual address of the missing page. Each page table entry is one word, so the last 2 bits are 0. Thus, the first two instructions copy the Context register into the kernel temporary register `$k1` and then load the page table entry from that address into `$k1`. Recall that `$k0` and `$k1` are reserved for the operating system to use without saving; a major reason for this convention is to make the TLB miss handler fast. Below is the MIPS code for a typical TLB miss handler:

handler Name of a software routine invoked to "handle" an exception or interrupt.

```
TLBmiss:
    mfc0    $k1,Context     # copy address of PTE into temp $k1
    lw      $k1,0($k1)      # put PTE into temp $k1
    mtc0    $k1,EntryLo     # put PTE into special register EntryLo
    tlbwr                   # put EntryLo into TLB entry at Random
    eret                    # return from TLB miss exception
```

As shown above, MIPS has a special set of system instructions to update the TLB. The instruction `tlbwr` copies from control register `EntryLo` into the TLB entry selected by the control register `Random` (Figure 5.33). Random implements random replacement, so it is basically a free-running counter. A TLB miss takes about a dozen clock cycles.

Note that the TLB miss handler does not check to see if the page table entry is valid. Because the exception for TLB entry missing is much more frequent than a page fault, the operating system loads the TLB from the page table without examining the entry and restarts the instruction. If the entry is invalid, another and different exception occurs, and the operating system recognizes the page fault. This method makes the frequent case of a TLB miss fast, at a slight performance penalty for the infrequent case of a page fault.

Once the process that generated the page fault has been interrupted, it transfers control to 8000 0180$_{hex}$, a different address than the TLB miss handler. This location is the general address for exceptions; TLB miss has a special entry point to lower the penalty for a TLB miss. The operating system uses the exception Cause register to diagnose the cause of the exception. Because the exception is a page fault, the operating system knows that extensive processing will be required. Thus, unlike a TLB miss, it saves the entire state of the active process. This state includes all the general-purpose and floating-point registers, the page table address register, the EPC, and the exception Cause register. Since most exception handlers do not usually use the floating-point registers, the general entry point does not save them, leaving that to the few handlers that need them.

Figure 5.35 sketches the MIPS code of an exception handler. Note that we save and restore the state in MIPS code, taking care when we enable and disable exceptions, but we invoke C code to handle the particular exception.

The virtual address that caused the fault depends on whether the fault was an instruction or data fault. The address of the instruction that generated the fault is in the EPC. If it was an instruction page fault, the EPC contains the virtual address of the faulting page; otherwise, the faulting virtual address can be computed by examining the instruction (whose address is in the EPC) to find the base register and offset field.

unmapped A portion of the address space that cannot have page faults.

Elaboration: This simplified version assumes that the *stack pointer* (sp) is valid. To avoid the problem of a page fault during this low-level exception code, MIPS sets aside a portion of its address space that cannot have page faults, called unmapped. The operating system places the exception entry point code and the exception stack in unmapped memory. MIPS hardware translates virtual addresses 8000 0000$_{hex}$ to BFFF FFFF$_{hex}$ to physical addresses simply by ignoring the upper bits of the virtual address, thereby placing these addresses in the low part of physical memory. Thus, the operating system places exception entry points and exception stacks in unmapped memory.

Elaboration: The code in Figure 5.35 shows the MIPS-32 exception return sequence. The older MIPS-I architecture uses `rfe` and `jr` instead of `eret`.

Elaboration: For processors with more complex instructions that can touch many memory locations and write many data items, making instructions restartable is much harder. Processing one instruction may generate a number of page faults in the middle of the instruction. For example, x86 processors have block move instructions that touch thousands of data words. In such processors, instructions often cannot be restarted from the beginning, as we do for MIPS instructions. Instead, the instruction must be interrupted and later continued midstream in its execution. Resuming an instruction in the middle of its execution usually requires saving some special state, processing the exception, and restoring that special state. Making this work properly requires careful and detailed coordination between the exception-handling code in the operating system and the hardware.

Elaboration: Rather than pay an extra level of indirection on every memory access, in virtual machines the VMM maintains a *shadow page table* that maps directly from the guest virtual address space to the physical address space of the hardware. By detecting all modifications to the guest's page table, the VMM can ensure the shadow page table entries being used by the hardware for translations correspond to those of the guest OS environment, with the exception of the correct physical pages substituted for the real pages in the guest tables. Hence, the VMM must trap any attempt by the guest OS to change its page table or to access the page table pointer. This oversight is commonly done by write protecting the guest page tables and trapping any access to the page table pointer by a guest OS. As noted above, the latter happens naturally if accessing the page table pointer is a privileged operation.

Save state			
Save GPR	addi	$k1,$sp, -XCPSIZE	# save space on stack for state
	sw	$sp, XCT_SP($k1)	# save $sp on stack
	sw	$v0, XCT_V0($k1)	# save $v0 on stack
	...		# save $v1, $ai, $si, $ti,... on stack
	sw	$ra, XCT_RA($k1)	# save $ra on stack
Save hi, lo	mfhi	$v0	# copy Hi
	mflo	$v1	# copy Lo
	sw	$v0, XCT_HI($k1)	# save Hi value on stack
	sw	$v1, XCT_LO($k1)	# save Lo value on stack
Save exception registers	mfc0	$a0, $cr	# copy cause register
	sw	$a0, XCT_CR($k1)	# save $cr value on stack
	...		# save $v1,....
	mfc0	$a3, $sr	# copy status register
	sw	$a3, XCT_SR($k1)	# save $sr on stack
Set sp	move	$sp, $k1	# sp = sp - XCPSIZE
Enable nested exceptions			
	andi	$v0, $a3, MASK1	# $v0 = $sr & MASK1, enable exceptions
	mtc0	$v0, $sr	# $sr = value that enables exceptions
Call C exception handler			
Set $gp	move	$gp, GPINIT	# set $gp to point to heap area
Call C code	move	$a0, $sp	# arg1 = pointer to exception stack
	jal	xcpt_deliver	# call C code to handle exception
Restoring state			
Restore most GPR, hi, lo	move	$at, $sp	# temporary value of $sp
	lw	$ra, XCT_RA($at)	# restore $ra from stack
	...		# restore $t0,....., $a1
	lw	$a0, XCT_A0($k1)	# restore $a0 from stack
Restore status register	lw	$v0, XCT_SR($at)	# load old $sr from stack
	li	$v1, MASK2	# mask to disable exceptions
	and	$v0, $v0, $v1	# $v0 = $sr & MASK2, disable exceptions
	mtc0	$v0, $sr	# set status register
Exception return			
Restore $sp and rest of GPR used as temporary registers	lw	$sp, XCT_SP($at)	# restore $sp from stack
	lw	$v0, XCT_V0($at)	# restore $v0 from stack
	lw	$v1, XCT_V1($at)	# restore $v1 from stack
	lw	$k1, XCT_EPC($at)	# copy old $epc from stack
	lw	$at, XCT_AT($at)	# restore $at from stack
Restore ERC and return	mtc0	$k1, $epc	# restore $epc
	eret	$ra	# return to interrupted instruction

FIGURE 5.33 MIPS code to save and restore state on an exception.

Elaboration: In addition to virtualizing the instruction set for a virtual machine, another challenge is virtualization of virtual memory, as each guest OS in every virtual machine manages its own set of page tables. To make this work, the VMM separates the notions of *real* and *physical memory* (which are often treated synonymously), and makes real memory a separate, intermediate level between virtual memory and physical memory. (Some use the terms *virtual memory, physical memory*, and *machine memory* to name the same three levels.) The guest OS maps virtual memory to real memory via its page tables, and the VMM page tables map the guest's real memory to physical memory. The virtual memory architecture is specified either via page tables, as in IBM VM/370 and the x86, or via the TLB structure, as in MIPS.

Summary

Virtual memory is the name for the level of memory hierarchy that manages caching between the main memory and secondary memory. Virtual memory allows a single program to expand its address space beyond the limits of main memory. More importantly, virtual memory supports sharing of the main memory among multiple, simultaneously active processes, in a protected manner.

Managing the memory hierarchy between main memory and disk is challenging because of the high cost of page faults. Several techniques are used to reduce the miss rate:

1. Pages are made large to take advantage of spatial locality and to reduce the miss rate.

2. The mapping between virtual addresses and physical addresses, which is implemented with a page table, is made fully associative so that a virtual page can be placed anywhere in main memory.

3. The operating system uses techniques, such as LRU and a reference bit, to choose which pages to replace.

Writes to secondary memory are expensive, so virtual memory uses a write-back scheme and also tracks whether a page is unchanged (using a dirty bit) to avoid writing unchanged pages.

The virtual memory mechanism provides address translation from a virtual address used by the program to the physical address space used for accessing memory. This address translation allows protected sharing of the main memory and provides several additional benefits, such as simplifying memory allocation. Ensuring that processes are protected from each other requires that only the operating system can change the address translations, which is implemented by preventing user programs from changing the page tables. Controlled sharing of pages among processes can be implemented with the help of the operating system and access bits in the page table that indicate whether the user program has read or write access to a page.

If a processor had to access a page table resident in memory to translate every access, virtual memory would be too expensive, as caches would be pointless! Instead, a TLB acts as a cache for translations from the page table. Addresses are then translated from virtual to physical using the translations in the TLB.

Caches, virtual memory, and TLBs all rely on a common set of principles and policies. The next section discusses this common framework.

Understanding Program Performance

Although virtual memory was invented to enable a small memory to act as a large one, the performance difference between secondary memory and main memory means that if a program routinely accesses more virtual memory than it has physical memory, it will run very slowly. Such a program would be continuously swapping pages between memory and disk, called *thrashing*. Thrashing is a disaster if it occurs, but it is rare. If your program thrashes, the easiest solution is to run it on a computer with more memory or buy more memory for your computer. A more complex choice is to re-examine your algorithm and data structures to see if you can change the locality and thereby reduce the number of pages that your program uses simultaneously. This set of popular pages is informally called the *working set*.

A more common performance problem is TLB misses. Since a TLB might handle only 32–64 page entries at a time, a program could easily see a high TLB miss rate, as the processor may access less than a quarter mebibyte directly: 64 × 4 KiB = 0.25 MiB. For example, TLB misses are often a challenge for Radix Sort. To try to alleviate this problem, most computer architectures now support variable page sizes. For example, in addition to the standard 4 KiB page, MIPS hardware supports 16 KiB, 64 KiB, 256 KiB, 1 MiB, 4 MiB, 16 MiB, 64 MiB, and 256 MiB pages. Hence, if a program uses large page sizes, it can access more memory directly without TLB misses.

The practical challenge is getting the operating system to allow programs to select these larger page sizes. Once again, the more complex solution to reducing TLB misses is to re-examine the algorithm and data structures to reduce the working set of pages; given the importance of memory accesses to performance and the frequency of TLB misses, some programs with large working sets have been redesigned with that goal.

Match the definitions in the right column to the terms in the left column.

1. L1 cache
2. L2 cache
3. Main memory
4. TLB

a. A cache for a cache
b. A cache for disks
c. A cache for a main memory
d. A cache for page table entries

5.8 A Common Framework for Memory Hierarchy

By now, you've recognized that the different types of memory hierarchies have a great deal in common. Although many of the aspects of memory hierarchies differ quantitatively, many of the policies and features that determine how a hierarchy functions are similar qualitatively. Figure 5.34 shows how some of the quantitative characteristics of memory hierarchies can differ. In the rest of this section, we will discuss the common operational alternatives for memory hierarchies, and how these determine their behavior. We will examine these policies as a series of four questions that apply between any two levels of a memory hierarchy, although for simplicity we will primarily use terminology for caches.

Question 1: Where Can a Block Be Placed?

We have seen that block placement in the upper level of the hierarchy can use a range of schemes, from direct mapped to set associative to fully associative. As mentioned above, this entire range of schemes can be thought of as variations on a set-associative scheme where the number of sets and the number of blocks per set varies:

Feature	Typical values for L1 caches	Typical values for L2 caches	Typical values for paged memory	Typical values for a TLB
Total size in blocks	250–2000	2500–25,000	16,000–250,000	40–1024
Total size in kilobytes	16–64	125–2000	1,000,000–1,000,000,000	0.25–16
Block size in bytes	16–64	64–128	4000–64,000	4–32
Miss penalty in clocks	10–25	100–1000	10,000,000–100,000,000	10–1000
Miss rates (global for L2)	2%–5%	0.1%–2%	0.00001%–0.0001%	0.01%–2%

FIGURE 5.34 The key quantitative design parameters that characterize the major elements of memory hierarchy in a computer. These are typical values for these levels as of 2020. Although the range of values is wide, this is partially because many of the values that have shifted over time are related; for example, as caches become larger to overcome larger miss penalties, block sizes also grow. While not shown, server microprocessors today also have L3 caches, which can be 4 to 50 MiB and contain many more blocks than L2 caches. L3 caches lower the L2 miss penalty to 30 to 40 clock cycles.

Scheme name	Number of sets	Blocks per set
Direct mapped	Number of blocks in cache	1
Set associative	$\dfrac{\text{Number of blocks in cache}}{\text{Associativity}}$	Associativity (typically 2–16)
Fully associative	1	Number of blocks in the cache

The advantage of increasing the degree of associativity is that it usually decreases the miss rate. The improvement in miss rate comes from reducing misses that compete for the same location. We will examine these in more detail shortly. First, let's look at how much improvement is gained. Figure 5.35 shows the miss rates for several cache sizes as associativity varies from direct mapped to eight-way set associative. The largest gains are obtained in going from direct mapped to two-way set associative, which yields between a 20% and 30% reduction in the miss rate. As cache sizes grow, the relative improvement from associativity increases only slightly; since the overall miss rate of a larger cache is lower, the opportunity for improving the miss rate decreases and the absolute improvement in the miss rate from associativity shrinks significantly. The potential disadvantages of associativity, as we mentioned earlier, are increased cost and slower access time.

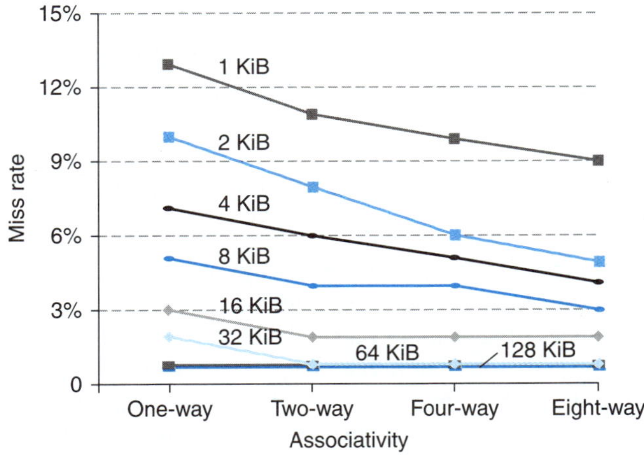

FIGURE 5.35 The data cache miss rates for each of eight cache sizes improve as the associativity increases. While the benefit of going from one-way (direct mapped) to two-way set associative is significant, the benefits of further associativity are smaller (e.g., 1%–10% improvement going from two-way to four-way versus 20%–30% improvement going from one-way to two-way). There is even less improvement in going from four-way to eight-way set associative, which, in turn, comes very close to the miss rates of a fully associative cache. Smaller caches obtain a significantly larger absolute benefit from associativity because the base miss rate of a small cache is larger. Figure 5.16 explains how this data was collected.

Question 2: How is a Block Found?

The choice of how we locate a block depends on the block placement scheme, since that dictates the number of possible locations. We can summarize the schemes as follows:

Associativity	Location method	Comparisons required
Direct mapped	Index	1
Set associative	Index the set, search among elements	Degree of associativity
Full	Search all cache entries	Size of the cache
	Separate lookup table	0

The choice among direct-mapped, set-associative, or fully associative mapping in any memory hierarchy will depend on the cost of a miss versus the cost of implementing associativity, both in time and in extra hardware. Including the L2 cache on the chip enables much higher associativity, because the hit times are not as critical and the designer does not have to rely on standard SRAM chips as the building blocks. Fully associative caches are prohibitive except for small sizes, where the cost of the comparators is not overwhelming and where the absolute miss rate improvements are greatest.

In virtual memory systems, a separate mapping table—the page table—is kept to index the memory. In addition to the storage required for the table, using an index table requires an extra memory access. The choice of full associativity for page placement and the extra table is motivated by these facts:

1. Full associativity is worthwhile, since misses are very expensive.

2. Full associativity allows software to use sophisticated replacement schemes that are designed to reduce the miss rate.

3. The full map can be easily indexed with no extra hardware and no searching required.

Therefore, virtual memory systems almost always use fully associative placement.

Set-associative placement is often used for caches and TLBs, where the access combines indexing and the search of a small set. A few systems have used direct-mapped caches because of their advantage in access time and simplicity. The advantage in access time occurs because finding the requested block does not depend on a comparison. Such design choices depend on many details of the implementation, such as the technology used for implementing the cache and the critical role of cache access time in determining the processor cycle time.

Question 3: Which Block Should Be Replaced on a Cache Miss?

When a miss occurs in an associative cache, we must decide which block to replace. In a fully associative cache, all blocks are candidates for replacement. If the cache is set associative, we must choose among the blocks in the set. Of course, replacement is easy in a direct-mapped cache because there is only one candidate.

There are the two primary strategies for replacement in set-associative or fully associative caches:

- *Random:* Candidate blocks are randomly selected, possibly using some hardware assistance. For example, MIPS supports random replacement for TLB misses.

- *Least recently used* (LRU): The block replaced is the one that has been unused for the longest time.

In practice, LRU is too costly to implement for hierarchies with more than a small degree of associativity (two to four, typically), since tracking the usage information is costly. Even for four-way set associativity, LRU is often approximated—for example, by keeping track of which pair of blocks is LRU (which requires 1 bit), and then tracking which block in each pair is LRU (which requires 1 bit per pair).

For larger associativity, either LRU is approximated or random replacement is used. In caches, the replacement algorithm is in hardware, which means that the scheme should be easy to implement. Random replacement is simple to build in hardware, and for a two-way set-associative cache, random replacement has a miss rate about 1.1 times higher than LRU replacement. As the caches become larger, the miss rate for both replacement strategies falls, and the absolute difference becomes small. In fact, random replacement can sometimes be better than the simple LRU approximations that are easily implemented in hardware.

In virtual memory, some form of LRU is always approximated, since even a tiny reduction in the miss rate can be important when the cost of a miss is enormous. Reference bits or equivalent functionality are often provided to make it easier for the operating system to track a set of less recently used pages. Because misses are so expensive and relatively infrequent, approximating this information primarily in software is acceptable.

Question 4: What Happens on a Write?

A key characteristic of any memory hierarchy is how it deals with writes. We have already seen the two basic options:

- *Write-through:* The information is written to both the block in the cache and the block in the lower level of the memory hierarchy (main memory for a cache). The caches in Section 5.3 used this scheme.

- *Write-back:* The information is written only to the block in the cache. The modified block is written to the lower level of the hierarchy only when it is replaced. Virtual memory systems always use write-back, for the reasons discussed in Section 5.7.

Both write-back and write-through have their advantages. The key advantages of write-back are the following:

- Individual words can be written by the processor at the rate that the cache, rather than the memory, can accept them.

- Multiple writes within a block require only one write to the lower level in the hierarchy.

- When blocks are written back, the system can make effective use of a high-bandwidth transfer, since the entire block is written.

Write-through has these advantages:

- Misses are simpler and cheaper because they never require a block to be written back to the lower level.

- Write-through is easier to implement than write-back, although to be practical, a write-through cache will still need to use a write buffer.

The BIG Picture

Caches, TLBs, and virtual memory may initially look very different, but they rely on the same two principles of locality, and they can be understood by their answers to four questions:

Question 1: Where can a block be placed?
Answer: One place (direct mapped), a few places (set associative), or any place (fully associative).

Question 2: How is a block found?
Answer: There are four methods: indexing (as in a direct-mapped cache), limited search (as in a set-associative cache), full search (as in a fully associative cache), and a separate lookup table (as in a page table).

Question 3: What block is replaced on a miss?
Answer: Typically, either the least recently used or a random block.

Question 4: How are writes handled?
Answer: Each level in the hierarchy can use either write-through or write-back.

In virtual memory systems, only a write-back policy is practical because of the long latency of a write to the lower level of the hierarchy. The rate at which writes are generated by a processor generally exceeds the rate at which the memory system can process them, even allowing for physically and logically wider memories and burst modes for DRAM. Consequently, today lowest-level caches typically use write-back.

The Three Cs: An Intuitive Model for Understanding the Behavior of Memory Hierarchies

In this subsection, we look at a model that provides insight into the sources of misses in a memory hierarchy and how the misses will be affected by changes in the hierarchy. We will explain the ideas in terms of caches, although the ideas carry over directly to any other level in the hierarchy. In this model, all misses are classified into one of three categories (the **three Cs**):

- **Compulsory misses**: These are cache misses caused by the first access to a block that has never been in the cache. These are also called **cold-start misses**.

- **Capacity misses**: These are cache misses caused when the cache cannot contain all the blocks needed during execution of a program. Capacity misses occur when blocks are replaced and then later retrieved.

- **Conflict misses**: These are cache misses that occur in set-associative or direct-mapped caches when multiple blocks compete for the same set. Conflict misses are those misses that are eliminated in a fully associative cache of the same size. These cache misses are also called **collision misses**.

Figure 5.36 shows how the miss rate divides into the three sources. These sources of misses can be directly attacked by changing some aspect of the cache design. Since conflict misses arise directly from contention for the same cache block, increasing associativity reduces conflict misses. Associativity, however, may slow access time, leading to lower overall performance.

Capacity misses can easily be reduced by enlarging the cache; indeed, second-level caches have been growing steadily larger for many years. Of course, when we make the cache larger, we must also be careful about increasing the access time, which could lead to lower overall performance. Thus, first-level caches have been growing slowly, if at all.

Because compulsory misses are generated by the first reference to a block, the primary way for the cache system to reduce the number of compulsory misses is to increase the block size. This expansion will reduce the number of references required to touch each block of the program once, because the program will consist

three Cs model A cache model in which all cache misses are classified into one of three categories: compulsory misses, capacity misses, and conflict misses.

compulsory miss Also called **cold-start miss**. A cache miss caused by the first access to a block that has never been in the cache.

capacity miss A cache miss that occurs because the cache, even with full associativity, cannot contain all the blocks needed to satisfy the request.

conflict miss Also called **collision miss**. A cache miss that occurs in a set-associative or direct-mapped cache when multiple blocks compete for the same set and that are eliminated in a fully associative cache of the same size.

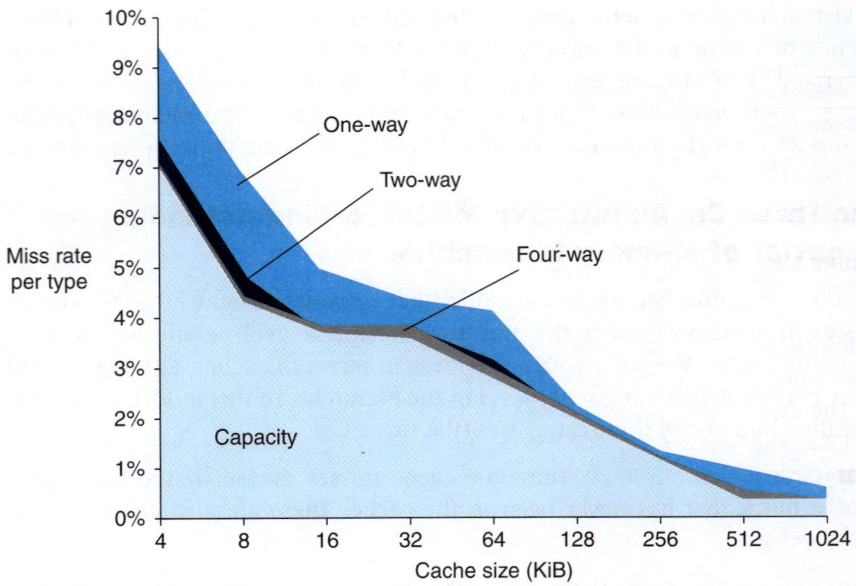

FIGURE 5.36 The miss rate can be broken into three sources of misses. This graph shows the total miss rate and its components for a range of cache sizes. This data is for the SPEC CPU2000 integer and floating-point benchmarks and is from the same source as the data in Figure 5.36 The compulsory miss component is 0.006% and cannot be seen in this graph. The next component is the capacity miss rate, which depends on cache size. The conflict portion, which depends both on associativity and on cache size, is shown for a range of associativities from one-way to eight-way. In each case, the labeled section corresponds to the increase in the miss rate that occurs when the associativity is changed from the next higher degree to the labeled degree of associativity. For example, the section labeled *two-way* indicates the additional misses arising when the cache has associativity of two rather than four. Thus, the difference in the miss rate incurred by a direct-mapped cache versus a fully associative cache of the same size is given by the sum of the sections marked *four-way*, *two-way*, and *one-way*. The difference between eight-way and four-way is so small that it is difficult to see on this graph.

The challenge in designing memory hierarchies is that every change that potentially improves the miss rate can also negatively affect overall performance, as Figure 5.37 summarizes. This combination of positive and negative effects is what makes the design of a memory hierarchy interesting.

Design change	Effect on miss rate	Possible negative performance effect
Increases cache size	Decreases capacity misses	May increase access time
Increases associativity	Decreases miss rate due to conflict misses	May increase access time
Increases block size	Decreases miss rate for a wide range of block sizes due to spatial locality	Increases miss penalty. Very large blocks could increase miss rate

FIGURE 5.37 Memory hierarchy design challenges.

of fewer cache blocks. As mentioned above, increasing the block size too much can have a negative effect on performance because of the increase in the miss penalty.

The decomposition of misses into the three Cs is a useful qualitative model. In real cache designs, many of the design choices interact, and changing one cache characteristic will often affect several components of the miss rate. Despite such shortcomings, this model is a useful way to gain insight into the performance of cache designs.

Which of the following statements (if any) are generally true?

1. There is no way to reduce compulsory misses.

2. Fully associative caches have no conflict misses.

3. In reducing misses, associativity is more important than capacity.

5.9   Using a Finite-State Machine to Control a Simple Cache

We can now implement control for a cache, just as we implemented control for the single-cycle and pipelined datapaths in Chapter 4. This section starts with a definition of a simple cache and then a description of *finite-state machines* (FSMs). It finishes with the FSM of a controller for this simple cache.  Section 5.12 goes into more depth, showing the cache and controller in a new hardware description language.

A Simple Cache

We're going to design a controller for a simple cache. Here are the key characteristics of the cache:

■ Direct-mapped cache

■ Write-back using write allocate

- Block size is 4 words (16 bytes or 128 bits)
- Cache size is 16 KiB, so it holds 1024 blocks
- 32-bit addresses
- The cache includes a valid bit and dirty bit per block

From Section 5.3, we can now calculate the fields of an address for the cache:

- Cache index is 10 bits
- Block offset is 4 bits
- Tag size is $32 - (10 + 4)$ or 18 bits

The signals between the processor to the cache are

- 1-bit Read or Write signal
- 1-bit Valid signal, saying whether there is a cache operation or not
- 32-bit address
- 32-bit data from processor to cache
- 32-bit data from cache to processor
- 1-bit Ready signal, saying the cache operation is complete

The interface between the memory and the cache has the same fields as between the processor and the cache, except that the data fields are now 128 bits wide. The extra memory width is generally found in microprocessors today, which deal with either 32-bit or 64-bit words in the processor while the DRAM controller is often 128 bits. Making the cache block match the width of the DRAM simplified the design. Here are the signals:

- 1-bit Read or Write signal
- 1-bit Valid signal, saying whether there is a memory operation or not
- 32-bit address
- 128-bit data from cache to memory
- 128-bit data from memory to cache
- 1-bit Ready signal, saying the memory operation is complete

Note that the interface to memory is not a fixed number of cycles. We assume a memory controller that will notify the cache via the Ready signal when the memory read or write is finished.

Before describing the cache controller, we need to review finite-state machines, which allow us to control an operation that can take multiple clock cycles.

Finite-State Machines

To design the control unit for the single-cycle datapath, we used a set of truth tables that specified the setting of the control signals based on the instruction class. For a cache, the control is more complex because the operation can be a series of steps. The control for a cache must specify both the signals to be set in any step and the next step in the sequence.

The most common multistep control method is based on **finite-state machines**, which are usually represented graphically. A finite-state machine consists of a set of states and directions on how to change states. The directions are defined by a **next-state function**, which maps the current state and the inputs to a new state. When we use a finite-state machine for control, each state also specifies a set of outputs that are asserted when the machine is in that state. The implementation of a finite-state machine usually assumes that all outputs that are not explicitly asserted are deasserted. Similarly, the correct operation of the datapath depends on the fact that a signal that is not explicitly asserted is deasserted, rather than acting as a don't care.

Multiplexor controls are slightly different, since they select one of the inputs whether they are 0 or 1. Thus, in the finite-state machine, we always specify the setting of all the multiplexor controls that we care about. When we implement the finite-state machine with logic, setting a control to 0 may be the default and thus may not require any gates. A simple example of a finite-state machine appears in Appendix B, and if you are unfamiliar with the concept of a finite-state machine, you may want to examine Appendix B before proceeding.

A finite-state machine can be implemented with a temporary register that holds the current state and a block of combinational logic that determines both the data-path signals to be asserted and the next state. Figure 5.38 shows how such an implementation might look. 🌐 **Appendix D** describes in detail how the finite-state machine is implemented using this structure. In Section B.3, the combinational control logic for a finite-state machine is implemented both with either a ROM (*read-only memory*) and a PLA (*programmable logic array*). (Also see Appendix B for a description of these logic elements.)

finite-state machine
A sequential logic function consisting of a set of inputs and outputs, a next-state function that maps the current state and the inputs to a new state, and an output function that maps the current state and possibly the inputs to a set of asserted outputs.

next-state function
A combinational function that, given the inputs and the current state, determines the next state of a finite-state machine.

Elaboration: Note that this simple design is called a *blocking* cache, in that the processor must wait until the cache has finished the request. 🌐 **Section 5.12** describes the alternative, which is called a *nonblocking* cache.

Elaboration: The style of finite-state machine in this book is called a Moore machine, after Edward Moore. Its identifying characteristic is that the output depends only on the current state. For a Moore machine, the box labeled combinational control logic can be split into two pieces. One piece has the control output and only the state input, while the other has only the next-state output.

An alternative style of machine is a Mealy machine, named after George Mealy. The Mealy machine allows both the input and the current state to be used to determine the output. Moore machines have potential implementation advantages in speed and size of the control unit. The speed advantages arise because the control outputs, which are

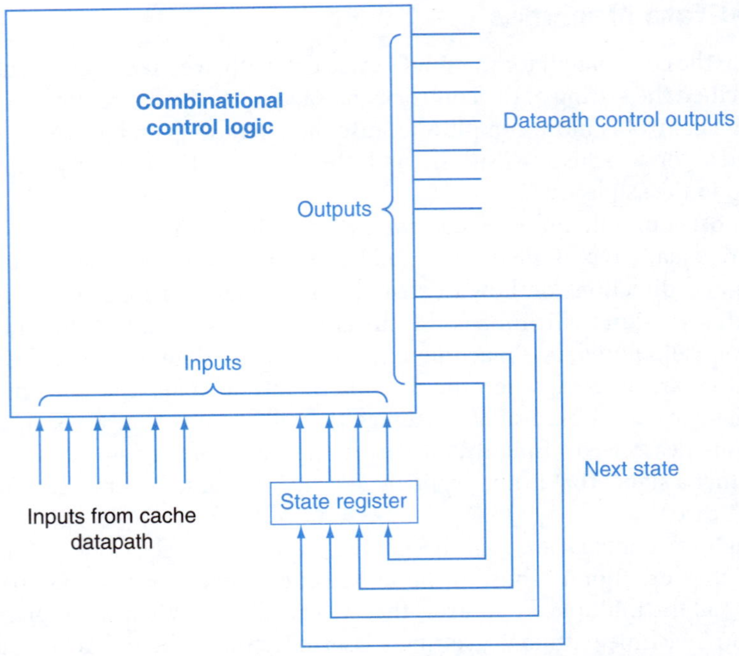

FIGURE 5.38 Finite-state machine controllers are typically implemented using a block of combinational logic and a register to hold the current state. The outputs of the combinational logic are the next-state number and the control signals to be asserted for the current state. The inputs to the combinational logic are the current state and any inputs used to determine the next state. Notice that in the finite-state machine used in this chapter, the outputs depend only on the current state, not on the inputs. The *Elaboration* explains this in more detail.

needed early in the clock cycle, do not depend on the inputs, but only on the current state. In Appendix B, when the implementation of this finite-state machine is taken down to logic gates, the size advantage can be clearly seen. The potential disadvantage of a Moore machine is that it may require additional states. For example, in situations where there is a one-state difference between two sequences of states, the Mealy machine may unify the states by making the outputs depend on the inputs.

FSM for a Simple Cache Controller

Figure 5.39 shows the four states of our simple cache controller:

- *Idle:* This state waits for a valid read or write request from the processor, which moves the FSM to the Compare Tag state.

- *Compare Tag:* As the name suggests, this state tests to see if the requested read or write is a hit or a miss. The index portion of the address selects the tag to be compared. If the data in the cache block referred to by the index portion of the address is valid, and the tag portion of the address matches the tag, then it is a hit. Either the data is read from the selected word if it is a load or written to the selected word if it is a store. The Cache Ready signal is then

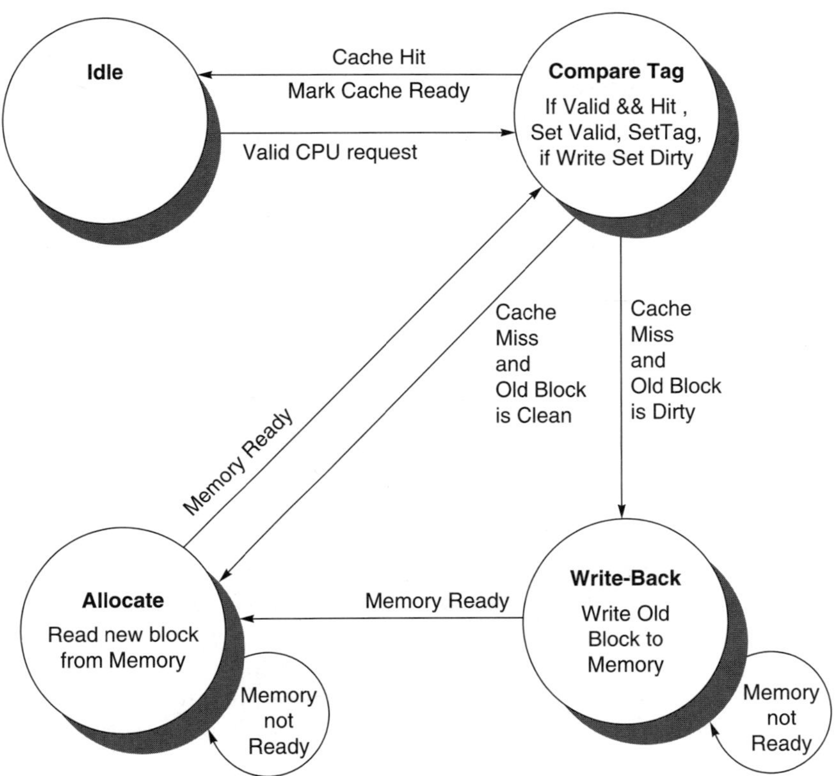

FIGURE 5.39 Four states of the simple controller.

set. If it is a write, the dirty bit is set to 1. Note that a write hit also sets the valid bit and the tag field; while it seems unnecessary, it is included because the tag is a single memory, so to change the dirty bit we also need to change the valid and tag fields. If it is a hit and the block is valid, the FSM returns to the idle state. A miss first updates the cache tag and then goes either to the Write-Back state, if the block at this location has dirty bit value of 1, or to the Allocate state if it is 0.

- *Write-Back:* This state writes the 128-bit block to memory using the address composed from the tag and cache index. We remain in this state waiting for the Ready signal from memory. When the memory write is complete, the FSM goes to the Allocate state.

- *Allocate:* The new block is fetched from memory. We remain in this state waiting for the Ready signal from memory. When the memory read is complete, the FSM goes to the Compare Tag state. Although we could have gone to a new state to complete the operation instead of reusing the Compare Tag state, there is a good deal of overlap, including the update of the appropriate word in the block if the access was a write.

This simple model could easily be extended with more states to try to improve performance. For example, the Compare Tag state does both the compare and the read or write of the cache data in a single clock cycle. Often the compare and cache access are done in separate states to try to improve the clock cycle time. Another optimization would be to add a write buffer so that we could save the dirty block and then read the new block first so that the processor doesn't have to wait for two memory accesses on a dirty miss. The cache would then write the dirty block from the write buffer while the processor is operating on the requested data.

Section 5.12 goes into more detail about the FSM, showing the full controller in a hardware description language and a block diagram of this simple cache.

5.10 Parallelism and Memory Hierarchy: Cache Coherence

Given that a multicore multiprocessor means multiple processors on a single chip, these processors very likely share a common physical address space. Caching shared data introduces a new problem, because the view of memory held by two different processors is through their individual caches, which, without any additional precautions, could end up seeing two different values. Figure 5.40 illustrates the problem and shows how two different processors can have two different values for the same location. This difficulty is generally referred to as the *cache coherence problem*.

Informally, we could say that a memory system is coherent if any read of a data item returns the most recently written value of that data item. This definition, although intuitively appealing, is vague and simplistic; the reality is much more complex. This simple definition contains two different aspects of memory system behavior, both of which are critical to writing correct shared memory programs. The first aspect, called *coherence*, defines *what values* can be returned by a read. The second aspect, called *consistency*, determines *when* a written value will be returned by a read.

Let's look at coherence first. A memory system is coherent if

1. A read by a processor P to a location X that follows a write by P to X, with no writes of X by another processor occurring between the write and the read by P, always returns the value written by P. Thus, in Figure 5.40, if CPU A were to read X after time step 3, it should see the value 1.

2. A read by a processor to location X that follows a write by another processor to X returns the written value if the read and write are sufficiently separated in time and no other writes to X occur between the two accesses. Thus, in Figure 5.40, we need a mechanism so that the value 0 in the cache of CPU B is replaced by the value 1 after CPU A stores 1 into memory at address X in time step 3.

3. Writes to the same location are *serialized*; that is, two writes to the same location by any two processors are seen in the same order by all processors. For example, if CPU B stores 2 into memory at address X after time step 3, processors can never read the value at location X as 2 and then later read it as 1.

The first property simply preserves program order—we certainly expect this property to be true in uniprocessors, for example. The second property defines the notion of what it means to have a coherent view of memory: if a processor could continuously read an old data value, we would clearly say that memory was incoherent.

The need for *write serialization* is more subtle, but equally important. Suppose we did not serialize writes, and processor P1 writes location X followed by P2 writing location X. Serializing the writes ensures that every processor will see the write done by P2 at some point. If we did not serialize the writes, it might be the case that some processor could see the write of P2 first and then see the write of P1, maintaining the value written by P1 indefinitely. The simplest way to avoid such difficulties is to ensure that all writes to the same location are seen in the same order, which we call *write serialization*.

Basic Schemes for Enforcing Coherence

In a cache coherent multiprocessor, the caches provide both *migration* and *replication* of shared data items:

- *Migration:* A data item can be moved to a local cache and used there in a transparent fashion. Migration reduces both the latency to access a shared data item that is allocated remotely and the bandwidth demand on the shared memory.

Time step	Event	Cache contents for CPU A	Cache contents for CPU B	Memory contents for location X
0				0
1	CPU A reads X	0		0
2	CPU B reads X	0	0	0
3	CPU A stores 1 into X	1	0	1

FIGURE 5.40 The cache coherence problem for a single memory location (X), read and written by two processors (A and B). We initially assume that neither cache contains the variable and that X has the value 0. We also assume a write-through cache; a write-back cache adds some additional but similar complications. After the value of X has been written by A, A's cache and the memory both contain the new value, but B's cache does not, and if B reads the value of X, it will receive 0!

■ *Replication:* When shared data are being simultaneously read, the caches make a copy of the data item in the local cache. Replication reduces both latency of access and contention for a read shared data item.

Supporting migration and replication is critical to performance in accessing shared data, so many multiprocessors introduce a hardware protocol to maintain coherent caches. The protocols to maintain coherence for multiple processors are called *cache coherence protocols*. Key to implementing a cache coherence protocol is tracking the state of any sharing of a data block.

The most popular cache coherence protocol is *snooping*. Every cache that has a copy of the data from a block of physical memory also has a copy of the sharing status of the block, but no centralized state is kept. The caches are all accessible via some broadcast medium (a bus or network), and all cache controllers monitor or *snoop* on the medium to determine whether or not they have a copy of a block that is requested on a bus or switch access.

In the following section we explain snooping-based cache coherence as implemented with a shared bus, but any communication medium that broadcasts cache misses to all processors can be used to implement a snooping-based coherence scheme. This broadcasting to all caches makes snooping protocols simple to implement but also limits their scalability.

Snooping Protocols

One method of enforcing coherence is to ensure that a processor has exclusive access to a data item before it writes that item. This style of protocol is called a *write invalidate protocol* because it invalidates copies in other caches on a write. Exclusive access ensures that no other readable or writable copies of an item exist when the write occurs: all other cached copies of the item are invalidated.

Figure 5.41 shows how an invalidation protocol for a snooping bus with write-back caches works. To see how this protocol ensures coherence, consider a write followed by a read by another processor: since the write requires exclusive access, any copy held by the reading processor must be invalidated (hence the protocol name). Thus, when the read occurs, it misses in the cache, and the cache is forced to fetch a new copy of the data. For a write, we require that the writing processor have exclusive access, preventing any other processor from being able to write simultaneously. If two processors do attempt to write the same data simultaneously, one of them wins the race, causing the other processor's copy to be invalidated. For the other processor to complete its write, it must obtain a new copy of the data, which must now contain the updated value. Therefore, this protocol also enforces write serialization.

Processor activity	Bus activity	Contents of CPU A's cache	Contents of CPU B's cache	Contents of memory location X
				0
CPU A reads X	Cache miss for X	0		0
CPU B reads X	Cache miss for X	0	0	0
CPU A writes a 1 to X	Invalidation for X	1		0
CPU B reads X	Cache miss for X	1	1	1

FIGURE 5.41 An example of an invalidation protocol working on a snooping bus for a single cache block (X) with write-back caches. We assume that neither cache initially holds X and that the value of X in memory is 0. The CPU and memory contents show the value after the processor and bus activity have both completed. A blank indicates no activity or no copy cached. When the second miss by B occurs, CPU A responds with the value canceling the response from memory. In addition, both the contents of B's cache and the memory contents of X are updated. This update of memory, which occurs when a block becomes shared, simplifies the protocol, but it is possible to track the ownership and force the write-back only if the block is replaced. This optimization requires the introduction of an additional state called "owner," which indicates that a block may be shared, but the owning processor is responsible for updating any other processors and memory when it changes the block or replaces it.

One insight is that block size plays an important role in cache coherency. For example, take the case of snooping on a cache with a block size of eight words, with a single word alternatively written and read by two processors. Most protocols exchange full blocks between processors, thereby increasing coherency bandwidth demands.

Large blocks can also cause what is called **false sharing**: when two unrelated shared variables are located in the same cache block, the full block is exchanged between processors even though the processors are accessing different variables. Programmers and compilers should lay out data carefully to avoid false sharing.

Hardware/ Software Interface

false sharing When two unrelated shared variables are located in the same cache block and the full block is exchanged between processors even though the processors are accessing different variables.

Elaboration: Although the three properties on pages 484 and 485 are sufficient to ensure coherence, the question of when a written value will be seen is also important. To see why, observe that we cannot require that a read of X in Figure 5.40 instantaneously sees the value written for X by some other processor. If, for example, a write of X on one processor precedes a read of X on another processor very shortly beforehand, it may be impossible to ensure that the read returns the value of the data written, since the written data may not even have left the processor at that point. The issue of exactly *when* a written value must be seen by a reader is defined by a *memory consistency model*.

We make the following two assumptions. First, a write does not complete (and allow the next write to occur) until all processors have seen the effect of that write. Second, the processor does not change the order of any write with respect to any other memory access. These two conditions mean that if a processor writes location X followed by location Y, any processor that sees the new value of Y must also see the new value of X. These restrictions allow the processor to reorder reads, but forces the processor to finish a write in program order.

Elaboration: Since input can change memory behind the caches and since output could need the latest value in a write back cache, there is also a cache coherency problem for I/O with the caches of a single processor as well as just between caches of multiple processors. The cache coherence problem for multiprocessors and I/O (see Chapter 6), although similar in origin, has different characteristics that affect the appropriate solution. Unlike I/O, where multiple data copies are a rare event—one to be avoided whenever possible—a program running on multiple processors will normally have copies of the same data in several caches.

Elaboration: In addition to the snooping cache coherence protocol where the status of shared blocks is distributed, a *directory-based* cache coherence protocol keeps the sharing status of a block of physical memory in just one location, called the *directory*. Directory-based coherence has slightly higher implementation overhead than snooping, but it can reduce traffic between caches and thus scale to larger processor counts.

5.11 Parallelism and Memory Hierarchy: Redundant Arrays of Inexpensive Disks

This online section describes how using many disks in conjunction can offer much higher throughput, which was the orginal inspiration of *Redundant Arrays of Inexpensive Disks* (RAID). The real popularlity of RAID, however, was due more to the much greater dependability offered by including a modest number of redundant disks. The section explains the differences in performance, cost, and **dependability** between the different RAID levels .

5.12 Advanced Material: Implementing Cache Controllers

This online section shows how to implement control for a cache, just as we implemented control for the single-cycle and pipelined datapaths in Chapter 4. This section starts with a description of finite-state machines and the implemention of a cache controller for a simple data cache, including a description of the cache controller in a hardware description language. It then goes into details of an example cache coherence protocol and the difficulties in implementing such a protocol.

 5.13   Real Stuff: The ARM Cortex-A8 and Intel Core i7 Memory Hierarchies

In this section, we will look at the memory hierarchy of the same two microprocessors described in the previous chapter: the ARM Cortex-A8 and Intel Core i7. This section is based on Section 2.6 of *Computer Architecture: A Quantitative Approach*, 6th edition.

The Cortex-A53 is a configurable core that supports the ARMv8A instruction set architecture, which includes both 32-bit and 64-bit modes. The Cortex-A53 is delivered as an IP (intellectual property) core. The Cortex-A53 IP core is used in a variety of tablets and smart phones; it is designed to be highly energy-efficient, a key criterion in battery-based PMDs. The A53 core is capable of being configured with multiple cores per chip for use in high-end PMDs; our discussion here focuses on a single core. The Cortex-A53 can issue two instructions per clock at clock rates up to 1.3 GHz.

The i7 supports the x86-64 instruction set architecture, a 64-bit extension of the x86 architecture. The i7 is an out-of-order execution processor that includes four cores. We focus here on the memory system design and performance from the viewpoint of a single core. Each core in an i7 can execute up to four x86 instructions per clock cycle, using a multiple-issue, dynamically scheduled, 16-stage pipeline, which we describe in detail in Chapter 4. The i7 can support up to three memory channels, each consisting of a separate set of DIMMs, and each of which can transfer in parallel. Using DDR3-1066, the i7 has a peak memory bandwidth of just over 25 GB/s.

Figure 5.42 summarizes the address sizes and TLBs of the two processors. The A53 has three TLBs with a 32-bit virtual address space and a 32-bit physical address space. The Core i7 has three TLBs with a 48-bit virtual address and a 36-bit physical address. Although the 64-bit registers of the Core i7 could hold a larger virtual address, there was no software need for such a large space, and 48-bit virtual addresses shrinks both the page table memory footprint and the TLB hardware.

Figure 5.43 shows their caches. Each has an L1 instruction cache and L1 data cache per core with 64 byte blocks, but each is two-way set associative for the A53 and eight-way for the i7. The i7 L1 data caches are 32 KiB, but they are configurable from 8 to 64 KiB for the A53. Both have identically organized 32 KiB, four-way set associative, L1 instruction caches (per core). Both use a unified L2 cache (per core) with 64 byte blocks, although the A53 size varies from 128 KiB to 1 MiB, while the Core i7 is fixed at 256 KiB. Since it is used for servers, the i7 also has a 16-way set associative unified L3 cache, whose size is 2 MiB per core and shared by all the cores on the chip.

Characteristic	ARM Cortex-A53	Intel Core i7
Virtual address	48 bits	48 bits
Physical address	40 bits	36 bits
Page size	Variable: 4, 16, 64 KiB, 1, 2 MiB, 1 GiB	Variable: 4 KiB, 2/4 MiB
TLB organizatio n	1 TLB for instructions and 1 TLB for data Both L1 TLBs are fully associative, with 10 entries, round robin replacement Unified L2 TLB with 512 entries, 4-way set associate TLB misses handled in hardware	1 TLB for instructions and 1 TLB for data per core Both L1 TLBs are four-way set associative, LRU replacement L1 I-TLB has 128 entries for small pages, 7 per thread for large pages L1 D-TLB has 64 entries for small pages, 32 for large pages The L2 TLB is four-way set associative, LRU replacement The L2 TLB has 512 entries TLB misses handled in hardware

FIGURE 5.42 Address translation and TLB hardware for the ARM Cortex-A8 and Intel Core i7 920. Both processors provide support for large pages, which are used for things like the operating system or mapping a frame buffer. The large-page scheme avoids using a large number of entries to map a single object that is always present.

Characteristic	ARM Cortex-A53	Intel Core i7
L1 cache organization	Split instruction and data caches	Split instruction and data caches
L1 cache size	8-64 KiB each for instructions/data	32 KiB each for instructions/data per core
L1 cache associativity	2-way (I), 2-way (D) set associative	8-way (I), 8-way (D) set associative
L1 replacement	Random	Approximated LRU
L1 block size	64 bytes	64 bytes
L1 write policy	Write-back, Write-allocate(?)	Write-back, No-write-allocate
L1 hit time (load-use)	1 clock cycle	4 clock cycles, pipelined
L2 cache organization	Unified (instruction and data)	Unified (instruction and data) per core
L2 cache size	128 KiB to 2 MiB	256 KiB (0.25 MiB)
L2 cache associativity	8-way set associative	4-way set associative
L2 replacement	Approximated LRU	Approximated LRU
L2 block size	64 bytes	64 bytes
L2 write policy	Write-back, Write-allocate	Write-back, Write-allocate
L2 hit time	11 clock cycles	12 clock cycles
L3 cache organization	–	Unified (instruction and data)
L3 cache size	–	2 MiB/core, shared
L3 cache associativity	–	16-way set associative
L3 replacement	–	Approximated LRU
L3 block size	–	64 bytes
L3 write policy	–	Write-back, Write-allocate
L3 hit time	–	44 clock cycles

FIGURE 5.43 Caches in the ARM Cortex-A53 and Intel Core i7 6700. The miss penalty on the A53 is 13 clock cycles for the L1 cache and 124 for the L2 cache.

The Core i7 has additional optimizations to reduce the miss penalty. The first of these is the return of the requested word first on a miss. It also continues to execute instructions that access the data cache during a cache miss. Designers who are attempting to hide the cache miss latency commonly use this technique, called a **nonblocking cache**, when building out-of-order processors. They implement two flavors of nonblocking. *Hit-under-miss* allows additional cache hits during a miss, while *miss-under-miss* allows multiple outstanding cache misses. The aim of the first of these two is hiding some miss latency with other work, while the aim of the second is overlapping the latency of two different misses.

Overlapping a large fraction of miss times for multiple outstanding misses requires a high-bandwidth memory system capable of handling multiple misses in parallel. In a personal mobile device, the memory may only be able to take limited advantage of this capability, but large servers often have memory systems capable of handling more than one outstanding miss in parallel.

The Core i7 has a prefetch mechanism for data accesses. It looks at a pattern of data misses and uses this information to try to **predict** the next address to start fetching the data before the miss occurs. Such techniques generally work best when accessing arrays in loops. In most cases, the prefetched line is simply the next block in the cache.

The sophisticated memory hierarchies of these chips and the large fraction of the dies dedicated to caches and TLBs shows the significant design effort expended to try to close the gap between processor cycle times and memory latency.

nonblocking cache
A cache that allows the processor to make references to the cache while the cache is handling an earlier miss.

Performance of the Cortex-A53 and Core i7 Memory Hierarchies

The memory hierarchy of the Cortex-A8 was measured with 32 KiB primary caches and a 1 MiB L2 cache running the SPECInt2006 benchmarks. The instruction cache miss rates for these SPECInt2006 are very small even for just the L1: close to zero for most and under 1% for all of them. This low rate probably results from the computationally intensive nature of the SPECCPU programs and the two-way set associative cache that eliminates most conflict misses.

Figure 5.44 shows the data cache results, which have significant L1 and L2 miss rates. The L1 rate varies by a factor of 75, from 0.5% to 37.2% with a median miss rate of 2.4%. The global L2 miss rate varies by a factor of 180, from 0.05% to 9.0% with a median of 0.3%. The MCF benchmark, which is known as a cache buster, sets the upper bound and significantly affects the mean. Remember that the L2 global miss rate is significantly lower than the L2 local miss rate, for example, the median L2 stand-alone miss rate is 15.1% versus the global miss rate of 0.3%.

Using these miss penalties in Figure 5.43, Figure 5.45 shows the average penalty per data access. Although the L1 miss rates are about 7 times higher than the L2 miss rate, the L2 penalty is 9.5 times as high, leading to L2 misses slightly dominating for the benchmarks that stress the memory system.

The i7's instruction fetch unit attempts to fetch 16 bytes every cycle, which complicates comparing instruction cache miss rates because multiple instructions

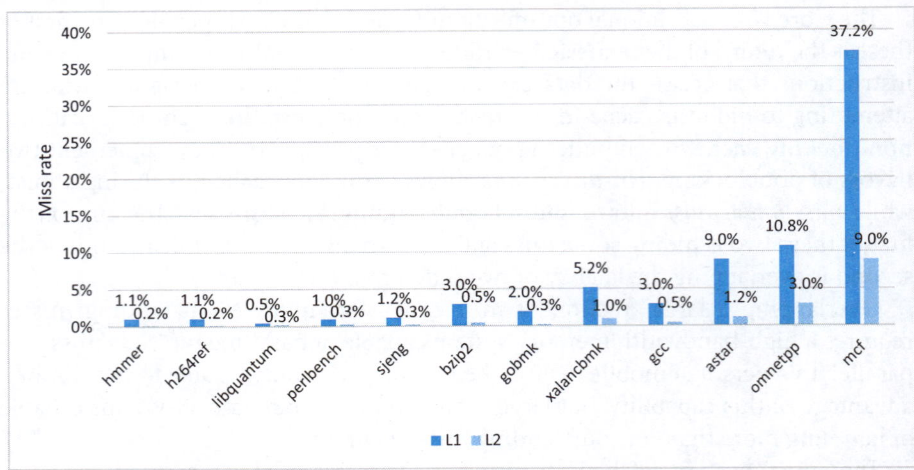

FIGURE 5.44 The data miss rate for ARM with a 32 KiB L1 and the global data miss rate for a 1 MiB L2 using the SPECInt2006 benchmarks are significantly affected by the applications. Applications with larger memory footprints tend to have higher miss rates in both L1 and L2. Note that the L2 rate is the global miss rate that is counting all references, including those that hit in L1. The mcf benchmark is known as a cache buster.

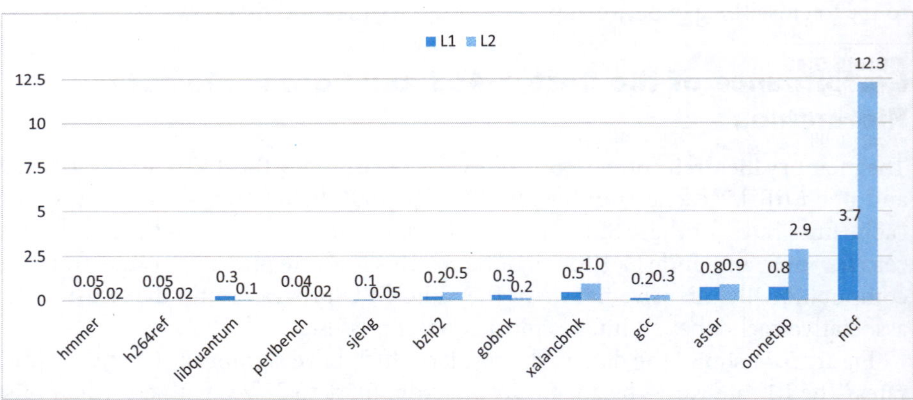

FIGURE 5.45 The average memory access penalty per data memory reference coming from L1 and L2 is shown for the A53 processor when running SPECInt2006. Although the miss rates for L1 are significantly higher, the L2 miss penalty, which is more than five times higher, means that the L2 misses can contribute significantly.

are fetched every cycle (roughly 4.5 on average). The 32 KiB, eight-way set associative instruction cache leads to a very low instruction miss rate for the SPECint2006 programs; the instruction miss rates are typically under 1%. The frequency at which the instruction fetch unit is stalled waiting for the I-cache misses is similarly small.

Figures 5.46 and 5.47 show the miss rates of the L1 and L2 caches for demand accesses, both versus the number of L1 references (reads and writes). Because the cost for a miss to memory is over 100, L3 is obviously critical. The average L3 data

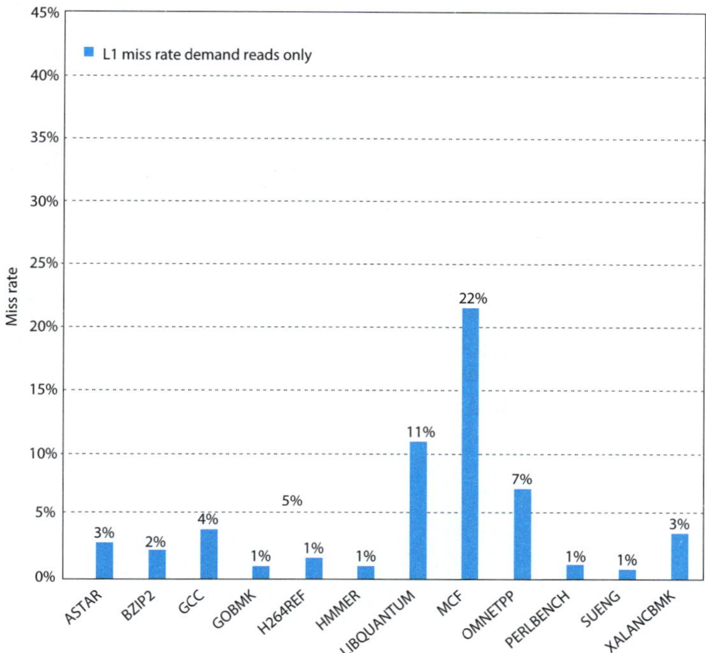

FIGURE 5.46 The L1 data cache miss rate for the SPECint2006 benchmarks is shown in two ways relative to the demand L1 reads for demand accesses (excluding prefetched). These data, like the rest in this section, were collected by Professor Lu Peng and PhD student Qun Liu, both of Louisiana State University (see Peng *et al.*, [2008]).

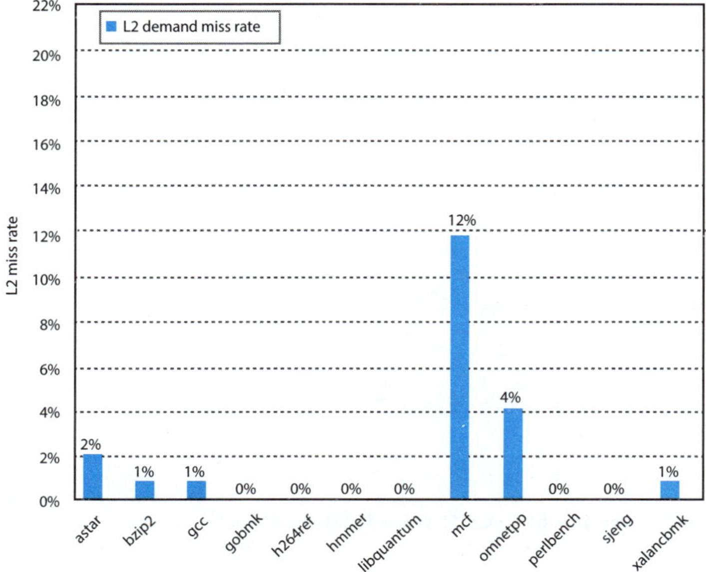

FIGURE 5.47 The L2 miss rate shown relative to L1 references to L1.

miss rate of 0.5%, which is still significant, is less than one-third of the L2 demand miss rate and 10 times less than the L1 demand miss rate.

5.14   Going Faster: Cache Blocking and Matrix Multiply

Our next step in the continuing saga of improving performance of DGEMM by tailoring it to the underlying hardware is to add cache blocking to the subword parallelism and instruction level parallelism optimizations of Chapters 3 and 4. Figure 5.48 shows the blocked version of DGEMM from Figure 4.80. The changes

```
1    #include <x86intrin.h>
2    #define UNROLL (4)
3    #define BLOCKSIZE 32
4    void do_block (int n, int si, int sj, int sk,
5                      double *A, double *B, double *C)
6    {
7      for ( int i = si; i < si+BLOCKSIZE; i+=UNROLL*8 )
8        for ( int j = sj; j < sj+BLOCKSIZE; j++ ) {
9           __m512d c[UNROLL];
10          for (int r=0;r<UNROLL;r++)
11            c[r] = _mm512_load_pd(C+i+r*8+j*n); //[ UNROLL];
12
13          for( int k = sk; k < sk+BLOCKSIZE; k++ )
14          {
15             __m512d bb = _mm512_broadcastsd_pd(_mm_load_sd(B+j*n+k));
16            for (int r=0;r<UNROLL;r++)
17              c[r] = _mm512_fmadd_pd(_mm512_load_pd(A+n*k+r*8+i), bb, c[r]);
18          }
19
20          for (int r=0;r<UNROLL;r++)
21            _mm512_store_pd(C+i+r*8+j*n, c[r]);
22        }
23    }
24
25   void dgemm (int n, double* A, double* B, double* C)
26   {
27     for ( int sj = 0; sj < n; sj += BLOCKSIZE )
28       for ( int si = 0; si < n; si += BLOCKSIZE )
29         for ( int sk = 0; sk < n; sk += BLOCKSIZE )
30           do_block(n, si, sj, sk, A, B, C);
31   }
```

FIGURE 5.48 Optimized C version of DGEMM from Figure 4.80 using cache blocking. These changes are the same ones found in Figure 5.21. The assembly language produced by the compiler for the do_block function is nearly identical to Figure 4.81. Once again, there is no overhead to call the do_block because the compiler inlines the function call.

are the same as was made earlier in going from unoptimized DGEMM in Figure 2.43 to blocked DGEMM in Figure 5.21 above. This time we taking the unrolled version of DGEMM from Chapter 4 and invoke it many times on the submatrices of A, B, and C. Indeed, lines 25–31 and lines 7–8 in Figure 5.48 are identical to lines 14–20 and lines 5–6 in Figure 5.21, with the exception of incrementing the for loop in line 7 by the amount unrolled.

The benefit of blocking increases with the size of the matrix. Since the number of floating-point operations per matrix element is the same independent of the size of the matrix, we can fairly measure performance by the number of floating-point operations computed per second. Figure 5.49 compares performance in GFLOPS/second of the original C version to optimizations for subword parallelism, instruction-level parallelism, and caches. Blocking improves performance over unrolled AVX code by factors of 1.5–1.7 for the intermediate-sized matrices and a factor of 10 for the largest matrix. The smallest matrix fits in the L1 cache, and so blocking makes almost no difference. When we compare unoptimized code to the code with all three optimizations, the performance improvement is factors of 14–41, with the largest improvement for the largest matrix.

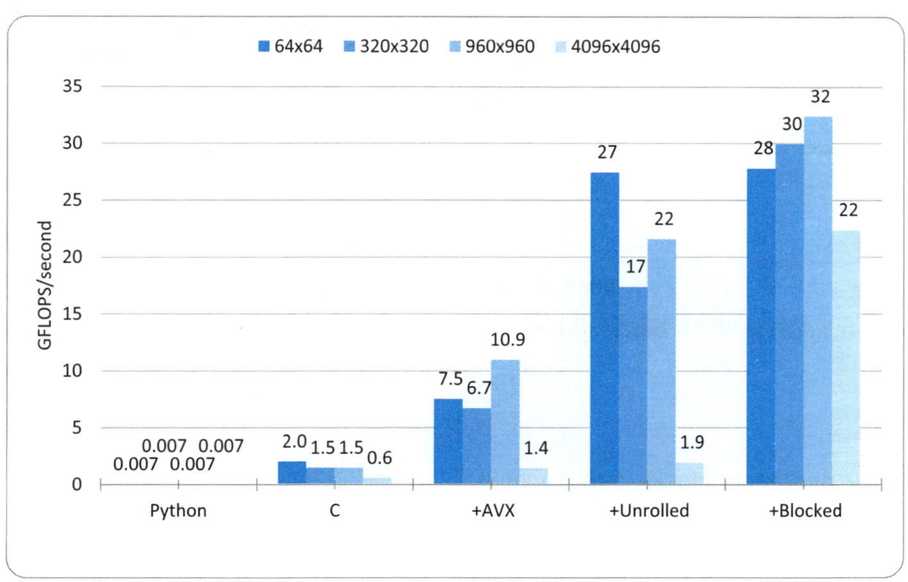

FIGURE 5.49 Performance of multiple versions of DGEMM as change matrix size measured in billion floating point operations per second (GFLOPS/second). The fully optimized code is 14–32 times as fast as the C version in Chapter 2. Python runs at 0.007 GFLOPS/second for all matrix sizes. The Intel i7 hardware speculates by prefetching from the L3 cache to the L1 and L2 caches, which is why the benefits of blocking are not as high as on some microprocessors.

5.15   Fallacies and Pitfalls

As one of the most naturally quantitative aspects of computer architecture, the memory hierarchy would seem to be less vulnerable to fallacies and pitfalls. Not only have there been many fallacies propagated and pitfalls encountered, but some have led to major negative outcomes. We start with a pitfall that often traps students in exercises and exams.

Pitfall: Forgetting to account for byte addressing or the cache block size in simulating a cache.

When simulating a cache (by hand or by computer), we need to make sure we account for the effect of byte addressing and multiword blocks in determining into which cache block a given address maps. For example, if we have a 32-byte direct-mapped cache with a block size of 4 bytes, the byte address 36 maps into block 1 of the cache, since byte address 36 is block address 9 and (9 modulo 8) = 1. On the other hand, if address 36 is a word address, then it maps into block (36 mod 8) = 4. Make sure the problem clearly states the base of the address.

In like fashion, we must account for the block size. Suppose we have a cache with 256 bytes and a block size of 32 bytes. Into which block does the byte address 300 fall? If we break the address 300 into fields, we can see the answer:

31	30	29	... ...	11	10	9	8	7	6	5	4	3	2	1	0
0	0	0	... ...	0	0	0	1	0	0	1	0	1	1	0	0

Cache block number (bits 5–7)   Block offset (bits 0–4)

Block address

Byte address 300 is block address

$$\left\lfloor \frac{300}{32} \right\rfloor = 9$$

The number of blocks in the cache is

$$\left\lfloor \frac{256}{32} \right\rfloor = 8$$

Block number 9 falls into cache block number (9 modulo 8) = 1.

This mistake catches many people, including the authors (in earlier drafts) and instructors who forget whether they intended the addresses to be in words, bytes, or block numbers. Remember this pitfall when you tackle the exercises.

Pitfall: Ignoring memory system behavior when writing programs or when generating code in a compiler.

This could easily be rewritten as a fallacy: "Programmers can ignore memory hierarchies in writing code." The evaluation of sort in Figure 5.19 and of cache blocking in Section 5.14 demonstrate that programmers can easily double performance if they factor the behavior of the memory system into the design of their algorithms.

Pitfall: Having less set associativity for a shared cache than the number of cores or threads (Chapter 6) sharing that cache.

Without extra care, a **parallel** program running on 2^n processors or threads can easily allocate data structures to addresses that would map to the same set of a shared L2 cache. If the cache is at least 2^n-way associative, then these accidental conflicts are hidden by the hardware from the program. If not, programmers could face apparently mysterious performance bugs—actually due to L2 conflict misses—when migrating from, say, a 16-core design to 32-core design if both use 16-way associative L2 caches.

Pitfall: Using average memory access time to evaluate the memory hierarchy of an out-of-order processor.

If a processor stalls during a cache miss, then you can separately calculate the memory-stall time and the processor execution time, and hence evaluate the memory hierarchy independently using average memory access time (see page 417).

If the processor continues to execute instructions, and may even sustain more cache misses during a cache miss, then the only accurate assessment of the memory hierarchy is to simulate the out-of-order processor along with the memory hierarchy.

Pitfall: Extending an address space by adding segments on top of an unsegmented address space.

During the 1970s, many programs grew so large that not all the code and data could be addressed with just a 16-bit address. Computers were then revised to offer 32-bit addresses, either through an unsegmented 32-bit address space (also called a *flat address space*) or by adding 16 bits of segment to the existing 16-bit address. From a marketing point of view, adding segments that were programmer-visible and that forced the programmer and compiler to decompose programs into segments could solve the addressing problem. Unfortunately, there is trouble any time a programming language wants an address that is larger than one segment, such as indices for large arrays, unrestricted pointers, or reference parameters. Moreover, adding segments can turn every address into two words—one for the segment number and one for the segment offset—causing problems in the use of addresses in registers.

Fallacy: Disk failure rates in the field match their specifications.

Two studies evaluated large collections of disks to check the relationship between results in the field compared to specifications. One study was of almost 100,000 disks that had quoted MTTF of 1,000,000 to 1,500,000 hours, or AFR of 0.6% to 0.8%. They found AFRs of 2% to 4% to be common, often three to five times higher than the specified rates [Schroeder and Gibson, 2007]. A second study of more than 100,000 disks at Google, which had a quoted AFR of about 1.5%, saw failure rates of 1.7% for drives in their first year rise to 8.6% for drives in their third year, or about five to six times the specified rate [Pinheiro, Weber, and Barroso, 2007].

Fallacy: Operating systems are the best place to schedule disk accesses.

As mentioned in Section 5.2, higher-level disk interfaces offer logical block addresses to the host operating system. Given this high-level abstraction, the best an OS can do to try to help performance is to sort the logical block addresses into increasing order. However, since the disk knows the actual mapping of the logical addresses onto the physical geometry of sectors, tracks, and surfaces, it can reduce the rotational and seek latencies by rescheduling.

For example, suppose the workload is four reads [Anderson, 2003]:

Operation	Starting LBA	Length
Read	724	8
Read	100	16
Read	9987	1
Read	26	128

The host might reorder the four reads into logical block order:

Operation	Starting LBA	Length
Read	26	128
Read	100	16
Read	724	8
Read	9987	1

Depending on the relative location of the data on the disk, reordering could make it worse, as Figure 5.50 shows. The disk-scheduled reads complete in three-quarters of a disk revolution, but the OS-scheduled reads take three revolutions.

Pitfall: Implementing a virtual machine monitor on an instruction set architecture that wasn't designed to be virtualizable.

Many architects in the 1970s and 1980s weren't careful to make privileged all instructions that read or wrote information related to hardware resource information. This *laissez-faire* attitude causes problems for VMMs for all of these architectures, including the x86, which we use here as an example.

Figure 5.51 describes the 18 instructions that cause problems for virtualization [Robin and Irvine, 2000]. The two broad classes are instructions that

- Read control registers in user mode that reveals that the guest operating system is running in a virtual machine (such as POPF, mentioned earlier), or

- Check protection as required by the segmented architecture but assume that the operating system is running at the highest privilege level.

To simplify implementations of VMMs on the x86, both AMD and Intel have proposed extensions to the architecture via a new mode. Intel's VT-x provides a new execution mode for running VMs, an architected definition of the VM state, instructions to swap VMs rapidly, and a large set of parameters to select the

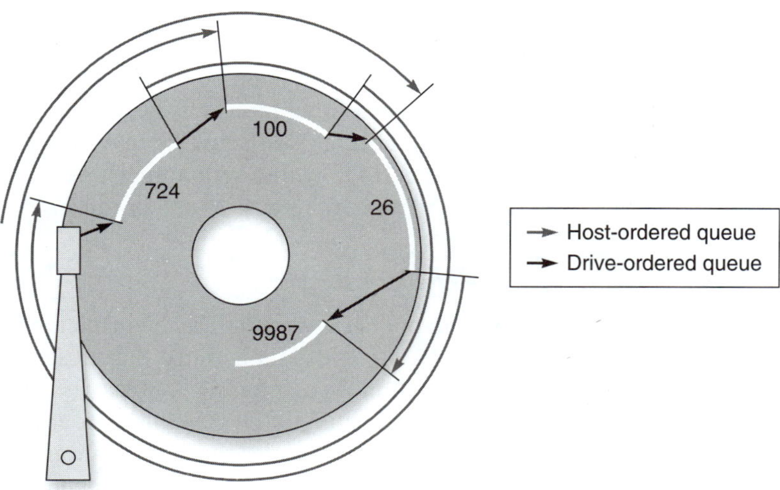

FIGURE 5.50 Example showing OS versus disk schedule accesses, labeled host-ordered versus drive-ordered. The former takes three revolutions to complete the four reads, while the latter completes them in just three-fourths of a revolution (from Anderson [2003]).

Problem category	Problem x86 instructions
Access sensitive registers without trapping when running in user mode	Store global descriptor table register (SGDT) Store local descriptor table register (SLDT) Store interrupt descriptor table register (SIDT) Store machine status word (SMSW) Push flags (PUSHF, PUSHFD) Pop flags (POPF, POPFD)
When accessing virtual memory mechanisms in user mode, instructions fail the x86 protection checks	Load access rights from segment descriptor (LAR) Load segment limit from segment descriptor (LSL) Verify if segment descriptor is readable (VERR) Verify if segment descriptor is writable (VERW) Pop to segment register (POP CS, POP SS, . . .) Push segment register (PUSH CS, PUSH SS, . . .) Far call to different privilege level (CALL) Far return to different privilege level (RET) Far jump to different privilege level (JMP) Software interrupt (INT) Store segment selector register (STR) Move to/from segment registers (MOVE)

FIGURE 5.51 Summary of 18 x86 instructions that cause problems for virtualization [Robin and Irvine, 2000]. The first five instructions in the top group allow a program in user mode to read a control register, such as descriptor table registers, without causing a trap. The pop flags instruction modifies a control register with sensitive information but fails silently when in user mode. The protection checking of the segmented architecture of the x86 is the downfall of the bottom group, as each of these instructions checks the privilege level implicitly as part of instruction execution when reading a control register. The checking assumes that the OS must be at the highest privilege level, which is not the case for guest VMs. Only the Move to segment register tries to modify control state, and protection checking foils it as well.

circumstances where a VMM must be invoked. Altogether, VT-x adds 11 new instructions for the x86. AMD's Pacifica makes similar proposals.

An alternative to modifying the hardware is to make small modifications to the operating system to avoid using the troublesome pieces of the architecture. This technique is called *paravirtualization*, and the open source Xen VMM is a good example. The Xen VMM provides a guest OS with a virtual machine abstraction that uses only the easy-to-virtualize parts of the physical x86 hardware on which the VMM runs.

Pitfall: Hardware attacks can compromise security

While the numerous software bugs in operating systems are the primary vehicle of attackers of computer systems, in 2015, Google demonstrated that a user program could subvert virtual memory protection by exploiting a weakness in DDR3 DRAM chips. Given the two-dimensional nature of DRAM internals and the very small memory cells of DDR3 DRAMs, researchers observed that "hammering" one row of a DDR3 DRAM by writing it repeatedly could cause disturbance errors in an adjacent row, which would flip bits in the victim row. A clever attacker could use the "row hammer" technique to change the protection bits of page table entries, and thereby grant the program access to memory regions that the operating system is trying to protect. Later microprocessors and DRAMs include mechanisms to detect row hammer attacks so as to defeat them.

The attack stunned many security researchers who up until then had thought hardware was not invulnerable to security issues. As we shall see in the Fallacies and Pitfalls section of Chapter 6, row hammer was just the opening volley of this new attack vector.

5.16 Concluding Remarks

The difficulty of building a memory system to keep pace with faster processors is underscored by the fact that the raw material for main memory, DRAMs, is essentially the same in the fastest computers as it is in the slowest and cheapest.

It is the principle of locality that gives us a chance to overcome the long latency of memory access—and the soundness of this strategy is demonstrated at all levels of the **memory hierarchy**. Although these levels of the hierarchy look quite different in quantitative terms, they follow similar strategies in their operation and exploit the same properties of locality.

Multilevel caches make it possible to use more cache optimizations more easily for two reasons. First, the design parameters of a lower-level cache are different from a first-level cache. For example, because a lower-level cache will be much larger, it is possible to use larger block sizes. Second, a lower-level cache is not constantly being used by the processor, as a first-level cache is. This split allows us to consider having the lower-level cache do something when it is idle that may be useful in preventing future misses.

Another trend is to seek software help. Efficiently managing the memory hierarchy using a variety of program transformations and hardware facilities is a major focus of compiler enhancements. Two different ideas are being explored. One idea is to reorganize the program to enhance its spatial and temporal locality. This approach focuses on loop-oriented programs that use large arrays as the major data structure; large linear algebra problems are a typical example, such as DGEMM. By restructuring the loops that access the arrays, substantially improved locality—and, therefore, cache performance—can be obtained.

Another approach is **prefetching**. In prefetching, a block of data is brought into the cache before it is actually referenced. Many microprocessors use hardware prefetching to try to *predict* accesses that may be difficult for software to notice.

A third approach is special cache-aware instructions that optimize memory transfer. For example, the microprocessors in Section 6.11 in Chapter 6 use an optimization that does not fetch the contents of a block from memory on a write miss because the program is going to write the full block. This optimization significantly reduces memory traffic for one kernel.

As we will see in Chapter 6, memory systems are a central design issue for parallel processors. The growing importance of the memory hierarchy in determining system performance means that this important area will continue to be a focus for both designers and researchers for some years to come.

prefetching A technique in which data blocks needed in the future are brought into the cache early by the use of special instructions that specify the address of the block.

5.17 Historical Perspective and Further Reading

This section, which appears online, gives an overview of memory technologies, from mercury delay lines to DRAM, the invention of the memory hierarchy, protection mechanisms, and virtual machines, and concludes with a brief history of operating systems, including CTSS, MULTICS, UNIX, BSD UNIX, MS-DOS, Windows, and Linux.

5.18 Self-Study

The more, the merrier? Figure 5.9 on page 405 shows the state of a small direct mapped cache after nine addresses, ending with address 16. Suppose the next five memory references are from a loop that accesses every other address: 18, 20, 22, 24, and 26. How many are hits? What does the cache look like afterwards?

Is associativity merry? Suppose instead of direct mapped, the cache in Figure 5.9 was two-way set associative. Would that turn the misses in the memory references 18, 20, 22, 24 into hits? Why or why not? Use the Three Cs model to explain your answer.

Frozen Analogy. From the library to the laundry, we rely on analogies to explain computer concepts in this book. This time we will let you try to explain how the memory hierarchy is like cold storage of food. Which levels and concepts of a memory hierarchy are analogous to these cold food storage mechanisms and events?

1. The refrigerator in the kitchen

2. Integrated freezer (usually packaged with the refrigerator on top and the freezer on the bottom as one unit)

3. Standalone freezer unit in the garage or basement

4. Frozen food freezers at a grocery store

5. Suppliers of frozen food in the grocery store

6. Getting food from the refrigerator to cook

7. Time it takes to get food from the refrigerator

8. Putting cooked food into the refrigerator

9. Moving frozen food from the integrated freezer to the refrigerator to thaw before cooking

10. Time it takes to thaw food from the integrated freezer

11. Moving frozen food from the refrigerator to the integrated freezer to preserve to eat later

12. Moving food between the standalone freezer and the integrated freezer

13. Getting new food from the grocery store to put in the integrated freezer

Frozen Framework. Section 5.8 gives a common framework for a memory hierarchy. Which framework ideas do and do not translate to cold food?

Frozen Cs. Section 5.8 also explains the intuitive Three Cs model to understand cache misses. Which apply here? Given an analogy for each one that works and explain why not if it does not apply.

Frozen failures. List at least three examples in which this analogy fails to be close to a computer memory hierarchy.

Hammering Virtual Machines. Why might hardware vulnerabilities of insecurity (such as Row Hammer in Section 5.18) be especially worrisome for cloud computing companies such as Amazon Web Services?

Self-Study Answers

The more, the merrier?

Here are the next five addresses and outcomes:

Decimal address of reference	Binary address of reference	Hit or miss in cache	Assigned cache block (where found or placed)
18	10010	hit	(10010two mod 8) = 010two
20	10100	miss	(10100two mod 8) = 110two
22	10110	hit	(10110two mod 8) = 110two
24	11000	miss	(11000two mod 8) = 000two
26	11010	miss	(11010two mod 8) = 010two

2 hits and 3 misses from 5 addresses.

Here is what the cache looks like after address 26.

Index	v	Tag	Data
000	Y	10two	Memory (11000two)
001	N		
010	Y	10two	Memory (11010two)
011	Y	00two	Memory (00011two)
100	Y	10two	Memory (10100two)
101	N		
110	Y	10two	Memory (10110two)
111	N		

Is associativity merry?

The misses for blocks 20 and 24 are the first accesses, so they are compulsory misses in the Three Cs model, and associativity cannot help.

Block 26 was fetched originally in the second memory reference in Section 5.3 and placed in cache block 2. It was replaced by block for address 18 in the eighth step due to a conflict miss in the direct mapped cache, as it also maps to block 2. A two-way set associate cache could avoid that conflict miss, giving one more hit out of these five addresses.

To really figure out all the hits and misses, we would have to reevaluate all the nine original addresses and these five extra addresses with a two-way associative organization to see which set each address would fall into to see the full impact, as the address mapping changes with associativity. We will leave that as an exercise to the reader, and depart with the simple observation about the opportunity of avoiding the conflict miss on block 26.

Frozen Analogy

There are two plausible interpretations of the hierarchy, depending if you think the standalone freezer is a third-level cache or main memory. We will go with the former in this answer.

1. First-level cache: The refrigerator in the kitchen

2. Second-level cache: Integrated freezer

3. Third-level cache: Standalone freezer unit in the garage or basement

4. Main memory: Frozen food freezers at a grocery store

5. Secondary memory: Suppliers of frozen food in the grocery store

6. First-level cache read: Getting food from the refrigerator to cook

7. First-level cache read hit time: Time it takes to get food from the refrigerator

8. First-level cache write: Putting cooked food into the refrigerator

9. Miss in first-level cache to second-level cache: Moving frozen food from the integrated freezer to the refrigerator to thaw before cooking

10. Second-level cache read hit time: Time it takes to thaw food from the integrated freezer

11. Traffic between first-level cache and second-level cache, such as on a first-level cache miss or a write-back: Moving frozen food from the refrigerator to the integrated freezer to preserve to eat later

12. Traffic between second-level cache and third-level cache, such as on a first-level cache miss or a write-back: Moving food between the standalone freezer and the integrated freezer

13. Read miss from third-level cache to main memory: Getting new food from the grocery store to put in the integrated freezer

Frozen Framework

- *Where Can a Block Be Placed?* There are no restrictions on placement of food at any level in our frozen analogy, so the closest equivalent is fully associative placement at all levels. The one exception is the grocery store, which groups frozen foods by types, and there is an index in the store of which freezer has which food type.

- *How Is a Block Found?* Given fully associative placement, we search the whole cold storage unit (except for the grocery store).

- *Which Block Should Be Replaced on a Cache Miss?* Plausibly we would use an informal version of least recently purchased, using the expiration date on the package.

- *What Happens on a Write?* While the memory hierarchy is generally copying data rather than moving data, we do not have that option with physical objects, so the closest option is write-back.

Frozen Cs

The three Cs are:

1. Compulsory misses

2. Capacity misses

3. Conflict misses

A (very sad) compulsory miss is that you want a dish of chocolate ice cream, but there is none in the refrigerator, integrated freezer, or standalone freezer, so you have to go to the grocery store to get some. While chocolate ice cream could be unavailable at the grocery store too—getting a frozen page fault!—chances are they have some, and you can satisfy your wish, but much more slowly than you hoped originally.

Capacity misses also make sense, where the desired item is not at the level you want because there was not enough room to include it, so you need to fetch it again from the next lower level.

Just as the case with real caches, with fully associative placement, there are no conflict misses.

Frozen Failures

Here are cases where the analogy does not work.

1. *Fixed block size.* Food comes in all kinds of shapes and size, so there is no equivalent of a block. The closest would be the military's Meals Ready to Eat (MRE), which fortunately is not what most people eat.

2. *Spatial locality.* Since we do not have a block size, it is hard to figure out the analogy to spatial locality. The exception is the grocery store, where many copies of the desired item are physically adjacent, thereby exhibiting spatial locality.

3. *Third-level cache write back.* It is unlikely your grocery store would let you return food from your standalone freezer by explaining, "I haven't used this item in a long time, and I need to keep something else in my standalone freezer, so would you store this item for me until I need it?"

4. *First-level cache misses and data integrity.* While the analogy works pretty well between freezers, most foods cannot be repeatedly thawed and refrozen without spoiling, so there is a problem in the analogy for first-level caches misses. The computer equivalent would be that the data is destroyed after some number of cache misses, which would be so catastrophic if it were true that caches would have never been used.

5. *Inclusivity across levels.* The most popular cache policy of inclusivity means that every data item at one level of the cache is also at the next lowest level, as it is easy to make copies of data. (Write-back and other situations can lead to inconsistent values, but some version of the data is at the lower levels.) We cannot instantly make copies of physical objects for lower levels, so we are following an exclusivity policy where the data exists at only one level.

Hammering Virtual Machines

Companies like Amazon Web Services can offer low cloud prices by having many virtual machines sharing a single server. The argument is that the protection provided by virtual memory and virtual machines make it safe for competitors to run at the same time on the same hardware, since they cannot access each other's sensitive data as long as AWS ensures there are no security bugs in these mechanisms. A hardware attack like row hammer means even if the software is perfect, adversaries could still take over the server and learn sensitive data from competitors.

As a result of such potential weaknesses, AWS offers customers the option of ensuring that only tasks from your organization run at the servers you are using, although this guarantee has a 5% higher hourly price in 2020.

5.19   Exercises

5.1 In this exercise we look at memory locality properties of matrix computation. The following code is written in C, where elements within the same row are stored contiguously. Assume each word is a 32-bit integer.

```
for (I=0; I<8; I++)
  for (J=0; J<8000; J++)
    A[I][J]=B[I][0]+A[J][I];
```

5.1.1 [5] <§5.1> How many 32-bit integers can be stored in a 16-byte cache block?

5.1.2 [5] <§5.1> Which variable references exhibit temporal locality?

5.1.3 [5] <§5.1> Which variable references exhibit spatial locality?

Locality is affected by both the reference order and data layout. The same computation can also be written below in Matlab, which differs from C by storing matrix elements within the same column contiguously in memory.

```
for I=1:8
  for J=1:8000
    A(I,J)=B(I,0)+A(J,I);
  end
end
```

5.1.4 [10] <§5.1> How many 16-byte cache blocks are needed to store all 32-bit matrix elements being referenced?

5.1.5 [5] <§5.1> Which variable references exhibit temporal locality?

5.1.6 [5] <§5.1> Which variable references exhibit spatial locality?

5.2 Caches are important to providing a high-performance memory hierarchy to processors. Below is a list of 32-bit memory address references, given as word addresses.

```
0x03, 0xb4, 0x2b, 0x02, 0xbf, 0x58, 0xbe, 0x0e, 0xb5, 0x2c,
0xba, 0xfd
```

5.2.1 [10] <§5.3> For each of these references, identify the binary address, the tag, and the index given a direct-mapped cache with 16 one-word blocks. Also list if each reference is a hit or a miss, assuming the cache is initially empty.

5.2.2 [10] <§5.3> For each of these references, identify the binary address, the tag, and the index given a direct-mapped cache with two-word blocks and a total size of 8 blocks. Also list if each reference is a hit or a miss, assuming the cache is initially empty.

5.2.3 [20] <§§5.3, 5.4> You are asked to optimize a cache design for the given references. There are three direct-mapped cache designs possible, all with a total of 8 words of data:

- C1 has 1-word blocks,

- C2 has 2-word blocks, and

- C3 has 4-word blocks.

5.3 By convention, a cache is named according to the amount of data it contains (i.e., a 4 KiB cache can hold 4 KiB of data); however, caches also require SRAM to store metadata such as tags and valid bits. For this exercise, you will examine how a cache's configuration affects the total amount of SRAM needed to implement it, as well as the performance of the cache. For all parts, assume that the caches are byte addressable, and that addresses and words are 64 bits.

5.3.1. [10] < §5.3> Calculate the total number of bits required to implement a 32 KiB cache with two-word blocks.

5.3.2. [10] < §5.3> Calculate the total number of bits required to implement a 64 KiB cache with 16-word blocks. How much bigger is this cache than the 32 KiB cache described in Exercise 5.3.1? (Notice that, by changing the block size, we doubled the amount of data without doubling the total size of the cache.)

5.3.3. [5] < §5.3> Explain why this 64 KiB cache, despite its larger data size, might provide slower performance than the first cache.

5.3.4. [10] < §§5.3, 5.4> Generate a series of read requests that have a lower miss rate on a 32 KiB two-way set associative cache than on the cache described in Exercise 5.3.1.

5.4 [15] < §5.3> Section 5.3 shows the typical method to index a direct-mapped cache, specifically (block address) modulo (number of blocks in the cache). Assuming a 64-bit address and 1024 blocks in the cache, consider a different indexing function, specifically (Block address [63:54] XOR Block address [53:44]). Is it possible to use this to index a direct-mapped cache? If so, explain why and discuss any changes that might need to be made to the cache. If it is not possible, explain why.

5.5 For a direct-mapped cache design with a 32-bit address, the following bits of the address are used to access the cache.

Tag	Index	Offset
31–10	9–5	4–0

5.5.1 [5] <§5.3> What is the cache block size (in words)?

5.5.2 [5] <§5.3> How many entries does the cache have?

5.5.3 [5] <§5.3> What is the ratio between total bits required for such a cache implementation over the data storage bits?

Beginning from power on, the following byte-addressed cache references are recorded.

Address											
Hex	00	04	10	84	E8	A0	400	1E	8C	C1C	B4	884
Dec	0	4	16	132	232	160	1024	30	140	3100	180	2180

5.5.4 [20] <§5.3> For each reference, list (1) its tag, index, and offset, (2) whether it is a hit or a miss, and (3) which bytes were replaced (if any).

5.5.5 [10] <§5.3> What is the hit ratio?

5.5.6 [20] <§5.3> List the final state of the cache, with each valid entry represented as a record of <index, tag, data>.

5.6 Recall that we have two write policies and write allocation policies, and their combinations can be implemented either in L1 or L2 cache. Assume the following choices for L1 and L2 caches:

L1	L2
Write through, non-write allocate	Write back, write allocate

5.6.1 [5] <§§5.3, 5.8> Buffers are employed between different levels of memory hierarchy to reduce access latency. For this given configuration, list the possible buffers needed between L1 and L2 caches, as well as L2 cache and memory.

5.6.2 [20] <§§5.3, 5.8> Describe the procedure of handling an L1 write-miss, considering the component involved and the possibility of replacing a dirty block.

5.6.3 [20] <§§5.3, 5.8> For a multilevel exclusive cache (a block can only reside in one of the L1 and L2 caches), configuration, describe the procedure of handling an L1 write-miss, considering the component involved and the possibility of replacing a dirty block.

5.7 Consider the following program and cache behaviors.

Data Reads per 1000 Instructions	Data Writes per 1000 Instructions	Instruction Cache Miss Rate	Data Cache Miss Rate	Block Size (byte)
250	100	0.30%	2%	64

5.7.1 [10] <§§5.3, 5.8> Suppose a CPU with a write-through, write-allocate cache achieves a CPI of 2. What are the read and write bandwidths (measured by bytes per cycle) between RAM and the cache? (Assume each miss generates a request for one block.)

5.7.2 [5] <§§5.3, 5.8> For a write-back, write-allocate cache, assuming 30% of replaced data cache blocks are dirty, what are the minimal read and write bandwidths needed for a CPI of 2?

5.8 Media applications that play audio or video files are part of a class of workloads called "streaming" workloads (i.e., they bring in large amounts of data but do not reuse much of it). Consider a video streaming workload that accesses a 512 KiB working set sequentially with the following address stream:

```
0, 1, 2, 3, 4, 5, 6, 7, 8, 9 ...
```

5.8.1 [10] <§§5.4, 5.8> Assume a 64 KiB direct-mapped cache with a 32-byte block. What is the miss rate for the address stream above? How is this miss rate sensitive to the size of the cache or the working set? How would you categorize the misses this workload is experiencing, based on the 3C model?

5.8.2 [5] <§§5.1, 5.8> Re-compute the miss rate when the cache block size is 16 bytes, 64 bytes, and 128 bytes. What kind of locality is this workload exploiting?

5.8.3 [10] <§5.13 > "Prefetching" is a technique that leverages predictable address patterns to speculatively bring in additional cache blocks when a particular cache block is accessed. One example of prefetching is a stream buffer that prefetches sequentially adjacent cache blocks into a separate buffer when a particular cache block is brought in. If the data is found in the prefetch buffer, it is considered as a hit and moved into the cache and the next cache block is prefetched. Assume a two-entry stream buffer and assume that the cache latency is such that a cache block can be loaded before the computation on the previous cache block is completed. What is the miss rate for the address stream above?

5.9 Cache block size (B) can affect both miss rate and miss latency. Assuming a 1-CPI machine with an average of 1.35 references (both instruction and data) per instruction, help find the optimal block size given the following miss rates for various block sizes.

8: 4%	16: 3%	32: 2%	64: 1.5%	128: 1%

5.9.1 [10] <§5.3> What is the optimal block size for a miss latency of $20 \times B$ cycles?

5.9.2 [10] <§5.3> What is the optimal block size for a miss latency of $24 + B$ cycles?

5.9.3 [10] <§5.3> For constant miss latency, what is the optimal block size?

5.10 In this exercise, we will look at the different ways capacity affects overall performance. In general, cache access time is proportional to capacity. Assume that main memory accesses take 70 ns and that memory accesses are 36% of all instructions. The following table shows data for L1 caches attached to each of two processors, P1 and P2.

	L1 Size	L1 Miss Rate	L1 Hit Time
P1	2 KB	8.0%	0.66 ns
P2	4 KB	6.0%	0.90 ns

5.10.1 [5] <§5.4> Assuming that the L1 hit time determines the cycle times for P1 and P2, what are their respective clock rates?

5.10.2 [5] <§5.4> What is the Average Memory Access Time for P1 and P2?

5.10.3 [5] <§5.4> Assuming a base CPI of 1.0 without any memory stalls, what is the total CPI for P1 and P2? Which processor is faster? (When we say a "base CPI of 1.0", we mean that instructions complete in one cycle, unless either the instruction access or the data access causes a cache miss.)

For the next three problems, we will consider the addition of an L2 cache to P1 to presumably make up for its limited L1 cache capacity. Use the L1 cache capacities and hit times from the previous table when solving these problems. The L2 miss rate indicated is its local miss rate.

L2 Size	L2 Miss Rate	L2 Hit Time
1 MB	95%	5.62 ns

5.10.4 [10] <§5.4> What is the AMAT for P1 with the addition of an L2 cache? Is the AMAT better or worse with the L2 cache?

5.10.5 [5] <§5.4> Assuming a base CPI of 1.0 without any memory stalls, what is the total CPI for P1 with the addition of an L2 cache?

5.10.6 [10] <§5.4> What would the L2 miss rate need to be in order for P1 with an L2 cache to be faster than P1 without an L2 cache?

5.10.7 [15] <§5.4> What would the L2 miss rate need to be in order for P1 with an L2 cache to be faster than P2 without an L2 cache?

5.11 This exercise examines the effect of different cache designs, specifically comparing associative caches to the direct-mapped caches from Section 5.4. For these exercises, refer to the sequence of word address shown below.

```
0x03, 0xb4, 0x2b, 0x02, 0xbe, 0x58, 0xbf, 0x0e, 0x1f, 0xb5,
0xbf, 0xba, 0x2e, 0xce
```

5.11.1 [10] < §5.4> Sketch the organization of a three-way set associative cache with two-word blocks and a total size of 48 words. Your sketch should have a style similar to Figure 5.18 but clearly show the width of the tag and data fields.

5.11.2 [10] < §5.4> Trace the behavior of the cache from Exercise 5.11.1. Assume a true LRU replacement policy. For each reference, identify

- the binary word address,
- the tag,
- the index,
- the offset,
- whether the reference is a hit or a miss, and
- which tags are in each way of the cache after the reference has been handled.

5.11.3 [5] < §5.4> Sketch the organization of a fully associative cache with one-word blocks and a total size of eight words. Your sketch should have a style similar to Figure 5.18 but clearly show the width of the tag and data fields.

5.11.4 [10] < §5.4> Trace the behavior of the cache from Exercise 5.11.3. Assume a true LRU replacement policy. For each reference, identify

- the binary word address,
- the tag,
- the index,
- the offset,
- whether the reference is a hit or a miss, and
- the contents of the cache after each reference has been handled.

5.11.5 [5] < §5.4> Sketch the organization of a fully associative cache with two-word blocks and a total size of eight words. Your sketch should have a style similar to Figure 5.18 but clearly show the width of the tag and data fields.

5.11.6 [10] < §5.4> Trace the behavior of the cache from Exercise 5.11.5. Assume an LRU replacement policy. For each reference, identify

- the binary word address,
- the tag,
- the index,
- the offset,
- whether the reference is a hit or a miss, and
- the contents of the cache after each reference has been handled.

5.11.7 [10] < §5.4> Repeat Exercise 5.11.6 using MRU (most recently used) replacement.

5.11.8 [15] < §5.4> Repeat Exercise 5.11.6 using the optimal replacement policy (i.e., the one that gives the lowest miss rate).

5.12 Multilevel caching is an important technique to overcome the limited amount of space that a first level cache can provide while still maintaining its speed. Consider a processor with the following parameters:

Base CPI, No Memory Stalls	Processor Speed	Main Memory Access Time	First Level Cache MissRate per Instruction	Second Level Cache, Direct-Mapped Speed	Global Miss Rate with Second Level Cache, Direct-Mapped	Second Level Cache, Eight-Way Set Associative Speed	Global Miss Rate with Second Level Cache, Eight-Way Set Associative
1.5	2 GHz	100 ns	7%	12 cycles	3.5%	28 cycles	1.5%

**First Level Cache miss rate is per instruction. Assume the total number of L1 cache misses (instruction and data combined) is equal to 7% of the number of instructions.

5.12.1 [10] <§5.4> Calculate the CPI for the processor in the table using: 1) only a first level cache, 2) a second level direct-mapped cache, and 3) a second level eight-way set associative cache. How do these numbers change if main memory access time is doubled? (Give each change as both an absolute CPI and a percent change.) Notice the extent to which an L2 cache can hide the effects of a slow memory.

5.12.2 [10] <§5.4> It is possible to have an even greater cache hierarchy than two levels. Given the processor above with a second level, direct-mapped cache, a designer wants to add a third level cache that takes 50 cycles to access and will have a 13% miss rate. Would this provide better performance? In general, what are the advantages and disadvantages of adding a third level cache?

5.12.3 [20] <§5.4> In older processors such as the Intel Pentium or Alpha 21264, the second level of cache was external (located on a different chip) from the main processor and the first level cache. While this allowed for large second level caches, the latency to access the cache was much higher, and the bandwidth was typically lower because the second level cache ran at a lower frequency. Assume a 512 KB off-chip second level cache has a global miss rate of 4%. If each additional 512 KB of cache lowered global miss rates by 0.7%, and the cache had a total access time of 50 cycles, how big would the cache have to be to match the performance of the second level direct-mapped cache listed above?

5.13 Mean Time Between Failures (MTBF), Mean Time To Replacement (MTTR), and Mean Time To Failure (MTTF) are useful metrics for evaluating the reliability and availability of a storage resource. Explore these concepts by answering the questions about devices with the following metrics.

MTTF	MTTR
3 Years	1 Day

5.13.1 [5] <§5.5> Calculate the MTBF for each of the devices in the table.

5.13.2 [5] <§5.5> Calculate the availability for each of the devices in the table.

5.13.3 [5] <§5.5> What happens to availability as the MTTR approaches 0? Is this a realistic situation?

5.13.4 [5] <§5.5> What happens to availability as the MTTR gets very high, i.e., a device is difficult to repair? Does this imply the device has low availability?

5.14 The exercise examines the single error correcting, double error detecting (SEC/DED) Hamming code.

5.14.1 [5] <§5.5> What is the minimum number of parity bits required to protect a 128-bit word using the SEC/DED code?

5.14.2 [5] <§5.5> Section 5.5 states that modern server memory modules (DIMMs) employ SEC/DED ECC to protect each 64 bits with 8 parity bits. Compute the cost/performance ratio of this code to the code from Exercise 5.14.1. In this case, cost is the relative number of parity bits needed while performance is the relative number of errors that can be corrected. Which is better?

5.14.3 [5] <§5.5> Consider a SEC code that protects 8 bit words with 4 parity bits. If we read the value 0 × 375, is there an error? If so, correct the error.

5.15 For a high-performance system such as a B-tree index for a database, the page size is determined mainly by the data size and disk performance. Assume that on average a B-tree index page is 70% full with fix-sized entries. The utility of a page is its B-tree depth, calculated as $\log_2$(entries). The following table shows that for 16-byte entries, and a 10-year-old disk with a 10 ms latency and 10 MB/s transfer rate, the optimal page size is 16 K.

Page Size (KB)	Page Utility or B-Tree Depth (Number of Disk Accesses Saved)	Index Page Access Cost (ms)	Utility/Cost
2	6.49 (or $\log_2(2048/16 \times 0.7)$)	10.2	0.64
4	7.49	10.4	0.72
8	8.49	10.8	0.79
16	9.49	11.6	0.82
32	10.49	13.2	0.79
64	11.49	16.4	0.70
128	12.49	22.8	0.55
256	13.49	35.6	0.38

5.15.1 [10] <§5.7> What is the best page size if entries now become 128 bytes?

5.15.2 [10] < §5.7> Based on 5.15.1, what is the best page size if pages are half full?

5.15.3 [20] <§5.7> Based on 5.15.2, what is the best page size if using a modern disk with a 3 ms latency and 100 MB/s transfer rate? Explain why future servers are likely to have larger pages.

Keeping "frequently used" (or "hot") pages in DRAM can save disk accesses, but how do we determine the exact meaning of "frequently used" for a given system? Data engineers use the cost ratio between DRAM and disk access to quantify the reuse time threshold for hot pages. The cost of a disk access is $Disk/accesses_per_sec, while the cost to keep a page in DRAM is $DRAM_MB/page_size. The typical DRAM and disk costs and typical database page sizes at several time points are listed below:

Year	DRAM Cost ($/MB)	Page Size (KB)	Disk Cost ($/disk)	Disk Access Rate (access/sec)
1987	5000	1	15,000	15
1997	15	8	2000	64
2007	0.05	64	80	83

5.15.4 [20] <§5.7> What other factors can be changed to keep using the same page size (thus avoiding software rewrite)? Discuss their likeliness with current technology and cost trends.

5.16 As described in Section 5.7, virtual memory uses a page table to track the mapping of virtual addresses to physical addresses. This exercise shows how this table must be updated as addresses are accessed. The following data constitutes a stream of virtual addresses as seen on a system. Assume 4 KiB pages, a 4-entry fully associative TLB, and true LRU replacement. If pages must be brought in from disk, increment the next largest page number.

Address							
Decimal	4669	2227	13916	34587	48870	12608	49225
hex	0x123d	0x08b3	0x365c	0x871b	0xbee6	0x3140	0xc049

TLB

Valid	Tag	Physical Page Number	Time Since Last Access
1	11	12	4
1	7	4	1
1	3	6	3
0	4	9	7

Page table

Index	Valid	Physical Page or in Disk
0	1	5
1	0	Disk
2	0	Disk
3	1	6
4	1	9
5	1	11
6	0	Disk
7	1	4
8	0	Disk
9	0	Disk
a	1	3
b	1	12

5.16.1 [10] <§5.7> For each access shown above, list

- whether the access is a hit or miss in the TLB,
- whether the access is a hit or miss in the page table,
- whether the access is a page fault,
- the updated state of the TLB.

5.16.2 [15] <§5.7> Repeat 5.16.1, but this time use 16 KiB pages instead of 4 KiB pages. What would be some of the advantages of having a larger page size? What are some of the disadvantages?

5.16.3 [15] <§5.7> Repeat Exercise 5.16.1, but this time use 4 KiB pages and a two-way set associative TLB.

5.16.4 [15] <§5.7> Repeat Exercise 5.16.1, but this time use 4 KiB pages and a direct mapped TLB.

5.16.5 [10] <§§5.4, 5.7> Discuss why a CPU must have a TLB for high performance. How would virtual memory accesses be handled if there were no TLB?

5.17 There are several parameters that impact the overall size of the page table. Listed below are key page table parameters.

Virtual Address Size	Page Size	Page Table Entry Size
32 bits	8 KB	4 bytes

5.17.1 [5] <§5.7> Given the parameters shown above, calculate the total page table size for a system running 5 applications that utilize half of the memory available.

5.17.2 [10] <§5.7> Given the parameters shown above, calculate the total page table size for a system running 5 applications that utilize half of the virtual memory available, given a two level page table approach with up to 256 entries at the first level. Assume each entry of the main page table is 6 bytes. Calculate the minimum and maximum amount of memory required for this page table.

5.17.3 [10] <§5.7> A cache designer wants to increase the size of a 4 KiB virtually indexed, physically tagged cache. Given the page size shown above, is it possible to make a 16 KiB direct-mapped cache, assuming 2 64-bit words per block? How would the designer increase the data size of the cache?

5.18 In this exercise, we will examine space/time optimizations for page tables. The following list provides parameters of a virtual memory system.

Virtual Address (bits)	Physical DRAM Installed	Page Size	PTE Size (byte)
43	16 GB	4 KB	4

5.18.1 [10] <§5.7> For a single-level page table, how many page table entries (PTEs) are needed? How much physical memory is needed for storing the page table?

5.18.2 [10] <§5.7> Using a multilevel page table can reduce the physical memory consumption of page tables, by only keeping active PTEs in physical memory. How many levels of page tables will be needed if the segment tables (the upper-level page tables) are allowed to be of unlimited size? And how many memory references are needed for address translation if missing in TLB?

5.18.3 [10] <§5.7> Suppose the segments are limited to the 4 KiB page size (so that they can be paged). Is 4 bytes large enough for all page table entries (including those in the segment tables?

5.18.4 [10] <§5.7> How many levels of page tables are needed if the segments are limited to the 4 KiB page size?

5.18.5 [15] <§5.7> An inverted page table can be used to further optimize space and time. How many PTEs are needed to store the page table? Assuming a hash table implementation, what are the common case and worst case numbers of memory references needed for servicing a TLB miss?

5.19 The following table shows the contents of a 4-entry TLB.

Entry-ID	Valid	VA Page	Modified	Protection	PA Page
1	1	140	1	RW	30
2	0	40	0	RX	34
3	1	200	1	RO	32
4	1	280	0	RW	31

5.19.1 [5] <§5.7> Under what scenarios would entry 2's valid bit be set to zero?

5.19.2 [5] <§5.7> What happens when an instruction writes to VA page 30? When would a software managed TLB be faster than a hardware managed TLB?

5.19.3 [5] <§5.7> What happens when an instruction writes to VA page 200?

5.20 In this exercise, we will examine how replacement policies impact miss rate. Assume a 2-way set associative cache with 4 one word blocks. Consider the following word address sequence: 0, 1, 2, 3, 4, 2, 3, 4, 5, 6, 7, 0, 1, 2, 3, 4, 5, 6, 7, 0.

5.20.1 [5] <§5.4, 5.8> Assuming an LRU replacement policy, which accesses are hits?

5.20.2 [5] <§5.4, 5.8> Assuming an MRU (most recently used) replacement policy, which accesses are hits?

5.20.3 [5] <§5.4, 5.8> Simulate a random replacement policy by flipping a coin. For example, "heads" means to evict the first block in a set and "tails" means to evict the second block in a set. How many hits does this address sequence exhibit?

5.20.4 [10] <§5.4, 5.8> Describe an optimal replacement policy for this sequence. Which accesses are hits using this policy?

5.20.5 [10] <§5.4, 5.8> Describe why it is difficult to implement a cache replacement policy that is optimal for all address sequences.

5.20.6 [10] <§5.4, 5.8> Assume you could make a decision upon each memory reference whether or not you want the requested address to be cached. What impact could this have on miss rate?

5.21 One of the biggest impediments to widespread use of virtual machines is the performance overhead incurred by running a virtual machine. Listed below are various performance parameters and application behavior.

Base CPI	Priviliged O/S Accesses per 10,000 Instructions	Performance Impact to Trap to the Guest O/S	Performance Impact to Trap to VMM	I/O Access per 10,000 Instructions	I/O Access Time (Includes Time to Trap to Guest O/S)
1.5	120	15 cycles	175 cycles	30	1100 cycles

5.21.1 [10] <§5.6> Calculate the CPI for the system listed above assuming that there are no accesses to I/O. What is the CPI if the VMM performance impact doubles? If it is cut in half? If a virtual machine software company wishes to limit the performance degradation to 10%, what is the longest possible penalty to trap to the VMM?

5.21.2 [15] <§5.6> I/O accesses often have a large impact on overall system performance. Calculate the CPI of a machine using the performance characteristics above, assuming a non-virtualized system. Calculate the CPI again, this time using a virtualized system. How do these CPIs change if the system has half the I/O accesses?

5.22 [31] <§5.6, 5.7> Compare and contrast the ideas of virtual memory and virtual machines. How do the goals of each compare? What are the pros and cons of each? List a few cases where virtual memory is desired, and a few cases where virtual machines are desired.

5.23 [10] <§5.6> Section 5.6 discusses virtualization under the assumption that the virtualized system is running the same ISA as the underlying hardware. However, one possible use of virtualization is to emulate non-native ISAs. An example of this is QEMU, which emulates a variety of ISAs such as MIPS, SPARC, and PowerPC. What are some of the difficulties involved in this kind of virtualization? Is it possible for an emulated system to run faster than on its native ISA?

5.24 In this exercise, we will explore the control unit for a cache controller for a processor with a write buffer. Use the finite state machine found in Figure 5.39 as a starting point for designing your own finite state machines. Assume that the cache controller is for the simple direct-mapped cache described on page 483 (Figure 5.39 in Section 5.9), but you will add a write buffer with a capacity of one block.

Recall that the purpose of a write buffer is to serve as temporary storage so that the processor doesn't have to wait for two memory accesses on a dirty miss. Rather than writing back the dirty block before reading the new block, it buffers the dirty block and immediately begins reading the new block. The dirty block can then be written to main memory while the processor is working.

5.24.1 [10] <§5.8, 5.9> What should happen if the processor issues a request that *hits* in the cache while a block is being written back to main memory from the write buffer?

5.24.2 [10] <§5.8, 5.9> What should happen if the processor issues a request that *misses* in the cache while a block is being written back to main memory from the write buffer?

5.24.3 [30] <§5.8, 5.9> Design a finite state machine to enable the use of a write buffer.

5.25 Cache coherence concerns the views of multiple processors on a given cache block. The following data shows two processors and their read/write operations on two different words of a cache block X (initially X[0] = X[1] = 0). Assume the size of integers is 32 bits.

P1	P2
`X[0] ++ ; X[1] = 3;`	`X[0] = 5; X[1] + = 2;`

5.25.1 [15] <§5.10> List the possible values of the given cache block for a correct cache coherence protocol implementation. List at least one more possible value of the block if the protocol doesn't ensure cache coherency.

5.25.2 [15] <§5.10> For a snooping protocol, list a valid operation sequence on each processor/cache to finish the above read/write operations.

5.25.3 [10] <§5.10> What are the best-case and worst-case numbers of cache misses needed to execute the listed read/write instructions?

Memory consistency concerns the views of multiple data items. The following data shows two processors and their read/write operations on different cache blocks (A and B initially 0).

P1	P2
`A = 1; B = 2; A+=2; B++;`	`C = B; D = A;`

5.25.4 [15] <§5.10> List the possible values of C and D for an implementation that ensures both consistency assumptions on page 488.

5.25.5 [15] <§5.10> List at least one more possible pair of values for C and D if such assumptions are not maintained.

5.25.6 [15] <§§5.3, 5.10> For various combinations of write policies and write allocation policies, which combinations make the protocol implementation simpler?

5.26 Chip multiprocessors (CMPs) have multiple cores and their caches on a single chip. CMP on-chip L2 cache design has interesting trade-offs. The following table shows the miss rates and hit latencies for two benchmarks with private vs. shared L2 cache designs. Assume L1 cache has a 3% miss rate and a 1-cycle access time.

	Private	Shared
Benchmark A misses-per-instruction	10%	4%
Benchmark B misses-per-instruction	2%	1%

Assume the following hit latencies:

Private Cache	Shared Cache	Memory
5	20	180

5.26.1 [15] <§5.13> Which cache design is better for each of these benchmarks? Use data to support your conclusion.

5.26.2 [15] <§5.13> Off-chip bandwidth becomes the bottleneck as the number of CMP cores increases. How does this bottleneck affect private and shared cache systems differently? Choose the best design if the latency of the first off-chip link doubles.

5.26.3 [10] <§5.13> Discuss the pros and cons of shared vs. private L2 caches for both single-threaded, multi-threaded, and multiprogrammed workloads, and reconsider them if having on-chip L3 caches.

5.26.4 [15] <§5.13> Would a non-blocking L2 cache produce more improvement on a CMP with a shared L2 cache or with a private L2 cache? Why?

5.26.5 [10] <§5.13> Assume new generations of processors double the number of cores every 18 months. To maintain the same level of per-core performance, how much more off-chip memory bandwidth is needed for a processor released in three years?

5.26.6 [15] <§5.13> Consider the entire memory hierarchy. What kinds of optimizations can improve the number of concurrent misses?

5.27 In this exercise we show the definition of a web server log and examine code optimizations to improve log processing speed. The data structure for the log is defined as follows:

```
struct entry {
  int srcIP;    // remote IP address
  char URL[128]; // request URL (e.g., "GET index.html")
  long long refTime; // reference time
  int status;   // connection status
  char browser[64]; // client browser name
} log [NUM_ENTRIES];
```

Assume the following processing function for the log:

```
topK_sourceIP (int hour);
```

This function determines the most frequently observed source IPs during the given hour.

5.27.1 [5] <§5.15> Which fields in a log entry will be accessed for the given log processing function? Assuming 64-byte cache blocks and no prefetching, how many cache misses per entry does the given function incur on average?

5.27.2 [5] <§5.15> How can you reorganize the data structure to improve cache utilization and access locality?

5.27.3 [10] <§5.15> Give an example of another log processing function that would prefer a different data structure layout. If both functions are important, how would you rewrite the program to improve the overall performance? Supplement the discussion with code snippet and data.

5.28 For the problems below, use data from "Cache Performance for SPEC CPU2000 Benchmarks" (http://www.cs.wisc.edu/multifacet/misc/spec2000cache-data/) for the pairs of benchmarks shown in the following table.

a.	`Mesa/gcc`
b.	`mcf/swim`

5.28.1 [10] <§5.15> For 64 KiB data caches with varying set associativities, what are the miss rates broken down by miss types (cold, capacity, and conflict misses) for each benchmark?

5.28.2 [10] <§5.15> Select the set associativity to be used by a 64 KiB L1 data cache shared by both benchmarks. If the L1 cache has to be directly mapped, select the set associativity for the 1 MiB L2 cache.

5.28.3 [20] <§5.15> Give an example in the miss rate table where higher set associativity actually increases miss rate. Construct a cache configuration and reference stream to demonstrate this.

5.29 To support multiple virtual machines, two levels of memory virtualization are needed. Each virtual machine still controls the mapping of virtual address (VA) to physical address (PA), while the hypervisor maps the PA of each virtual machine to the actual machine address (MA). To accelerate such mappings, a software approach called "shadow paging" duplicates each virtual machine's page tables in the hypervisor, and intercepts VA to PA mapping changes to keep both copies consistent. To remove the complexity of shadow page tables, a hardware approach called *nested page table (NPT)* explicitly supports two classes of page tables (VA⇒PA and PA⇒MA) and can walk such tables purely in hardware.

Consider the following sequence of operations: (1) create process; (2) TLB miss; (3) page fault; (4) context switch.

5.29.1 [10] <§§5.6, 5.7> What would happen for the given operation sequence for shadow page table and nested page table, respectively?

5.29.2 [10] <§§5.6, 5.7> Assuming an x86-based four-level page table in both guest and nested page table, how many memory references are needed to service a TLB miss for native versus nested page table?

5.29.3 [15] <§§5.6, 5.7> Among TLB miss rate, TLB miss latency, page fault rate, and page fault handler latency, which metrics are more important for shadow page table? What are important for nested page table?

Assume the following parameters for a shadow paging system.

TLB misses per 1000 instructions	NPT TLB miss latency	Page faults per 1000 instructions	Shadowing page fault overhead
0.2	200 cycles	0.001	30,000 cycle

5.29.4 [10] <§5.6> For a benchmark with native execution CPI of 1, what are the CPI numbers if using shadow page tables versus NPT (assuming only page table virtualization overhead)?

5.29.5 [10] <§5.6> What techniques can be used to reduce page table shadowing induced overhead?

5.29.6 [10] <§5.6> What techniques can be used to reduce NPT-induced overhead?

Answers to Check Yourself

§5.1, page 395: 1 and 4. (3 is false because the cost of the memory hierarchy varies per computer, but in 2013 the highest cost is usually the DRAM.)
§5.3, page 416: 1 and 4: A lower miss penalty can enable smaller blocks, since you don't have that much latency to amortize, yet higher memory bandwidth usually leads to larger blocks, since the miss penalty is only slightly larger.
§5.4, page 435: 1.
§5.7, page 472: 1-a, 2-c, 3-b, 4-d.
§5.8, page 479: 2. (Both large block sizes and prefetching may reduce compulsory misses, so 1 is false.)

Parallel Processors from Client to Cloud

"I swing big, with everything I've got. I hit big or I miss big. I like to live as big as I can."

Babe Ruth
American baseball player

Multiprocessor or Cluster Organization

multiprocessor A computer system with at least two processors. This computer is in contrast to a uniprocessor, which has one, and is increasingly hard to find today.

task-level parallelism or **process-level parallelism** Utilizing multiple processors by running independent programs simultaneously.

parallel processing program A single program that runs on multiple processors simultaneously.

cluster A set of computers connected over a local area network that function as a single large multiprocessor.

6.1 Introduction

Computer architects have long sought the "The City of Gold" (El Dorado) of computer design: to create powerful computers simply by connecting many existing smaller ones. This golden vision is the fountainhead of **multiprocessors**. Ideally, customers order as many processors as they can afford and receive a commensurate amount of performance. Thus, multiprocessor software must be designed to work with a variable number of processors. As mentioned in Chapter 1, energy has become the overriding issue for both microprocessors and datacenters. Replacing large inefficient processors with many smaller, efficient processors can deliver better performance per Joule both in the large and in the small, if software can efficiently use them. Thus, improved energy efficiency joins scalable performance in the case for multiprocessors .

Since multiprocessor software should scale, some designs support operation in the presence of broken hardware; that is, if a single processor fails in a multiprocessor with n processors, these system would continue to provide service with $n-1$ processors. Hence, multiprocessors can also improve availability (see Chapter 5).

High performance can mean high throughput for independent tasks, called **task-level parallelism** or **process-level parallelism**. These tasks are independent single-threaded applications, and they are an important and popular use of multiple processors. This approach is in contrast to running a single job on multiple processors. We use the term **parallel processing program** to refer to a single program that runs on multiple processors simultaneously.

There have long been scientific problems that have needed much faster computers, and this class of problems has been used to justify many novel parallel computers over the decades. Some of these problems can be handled simply today, using a **cluster** composed of microprocessors housed in many independent servers (see Section 6.8). In addition, clusters can serve equally demanding applications outside the sciences, such as search engines, Web servers, email servers, and databases.

As described in Chapter 1, multiprocessors have been shoved into the spotlight because the energy problem means that future increases in performance must come from some place other than much higher clock rates or vastly improved CPI. As we said in Chapter 1, they are called

multicore microprocessors instead of multiprocessor microprocessors, presumably to avoid redundancy in naming. Hence, processors are often called *cores* in a multicore chip. The number of cores is expected to increase with improved hardware technology. These multicores are almost always **Shared Memory Processors (SMPs)**, as they usually share a single physical address space. We'll see SMPs more in Section 6.5.

The state of technology today means that programmers who care about performance must become parallel programmers (see Section 6.12).

The tall challenge facing the industry is to create hardware and software that will make it easy to write correct parallel processing programs that will execute efficiently in performance and energy as the number of cores per chip scales.

This abrupt shift in microprocessor design caught many off guard, so there is a great deal of confusion about the terminology and what it means. Figure 6.1 tries to clarify the terms serial, parallel, sequential, and concurrent. The columns of this figure represent the software, which is either inherently sequential or concurrent. The rows of the figure represent the hardware, which is either serial or parallel. For example, the programmers of compilers think of them as sequential programs: the steps include parsing, code generation, optimization, and so on. In contrast, the programmers of operating systems normally think of them as concurrent programs: cooperating processes handling I/O events due to independent jobs running on a computer.

The point of these two axes of Figure 6.1 is that concurrent software can run on serial hardware, such as operating systems for the Intel Pentium 4 uniprocessor, or on parallel hardware, such as an OS on the more recent Intel Core i7. The same is true for sequential software. For example, the MATLAB programmer writes a matrix multiply thinking about it sequentially, but it could run serially on the Pentium 4 or in parallel on the Intel Core i7.

You might guess that the only challenge of the parallel revolution is figuring out how to make naturally sequential software have high performance on parallel hardware, but it is also to make concurrent programs have high performance on multiprocessors as the number of processors increases. With this distinction made, in the rest of this chapter we will use *parallel processing program* or *parallel software* to mean either sequential or concurrent software running on parallel hardware. The next section of this chapter describes why it is hard to create efficient parallel processing programs.

multicore microprocessor A microprocessor containing multiple processors ("cores") in a single integrated circuit. Virtually all microprocessors today in desktops and servers are multicore.

shared memory multiprocessor (SMP) A parallel processor with a single physical address space.

		Software	
		Sequential	**Concurrent**
Hardware	Serial	Matrix Multiply written in MatLab running on an Intel Pentium 4	Windows Vista Operating System running on an Intel Pentium 4
	Parallel	Matrix Multiply written in MATLAB running on an Intel Core i7	Windows Vista Operating System running on an Intel Core i7

FIGURE 6.1 Hardware/software categorization and examples of application perspective on concurrency versus hardware perspective on parallelism.

Before proceeding further down the path to parallelism, don't forget our initial incursions from the earlier chapters:

- Chapter 2, Section 2.11: Parallelism and Instructions: Synchronization

- Chapter 3, Section 3.6: Parallelism and Computer Arithmetic: Subword Parallelism

- Chapter 4, Section 4.11: Parallelism via Instructions

- Chapter 5, Section 5.10: Parallelism and Memory Hierarchy: Cache Coherence

Check Yourself

True or false: To benefit from a multiprocessor, an application must be concurrent.

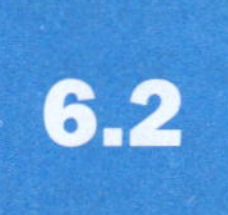 6.2 The Difficulty of Creating Parallel Processing Programs

The challenge with parallelism is not the hardware; it is that too few important application programs have been rewritten to complete tasks sooner on multiprocessors. It is difficult to write software that uses multiple processors to complete one task faster, and the problem gets worse as the number of processors increases.

Why has this been so? Why have parallel processing programs been so much harder to develop than sequential programs?

The first reason is that you *must* get better performance or better energy efficiency from a parallel processing program on a multiprocessor; otherwise, you would just use a sequential program on a uniprocessor, as sequential programming is simpler. In fact, uniprocessor design techniques such as superscalar and out-of-order execution take advantage of instruction-level parallelism (see Chapter 4), normally without the involvement of the programmer. Such innovations reduced the demand for rewriting programs for multiprocessors, since programmers could do nothing and yet their sequential programs would run faster on new computers.

Why is it difficult to write parallel processing programs that are fast, especially as the number of processors increases? In Chapter 1, we used the analogy of eight reporters trying to write a single story in hopes of doing the work eight times faster. To succeed, the task must be broken into eight equal-sized pieces, because otherwise some reporters would be idle while waiting for the ones with larger pieces to finish. Another speed-up obstacle could be that the reporters would spend too much time communicating with each other instead of writing their pieces of the story. For both this analogy and parallel programming, the challenges include scheduling, partitioning the work into parallel pieces, balancing the load evenly between the workers, time to synchronize, and overhead for communication between the parties. The challenge is stiffer with the more reporters for a newspaper story and with the more processors for parallel programming.

Our discussion in Chapter 1 reveals another obstacle, namely Amdahl's Law. It reminds us that even small parts of a program must be parallelized if the program is to make good use of many cores.

Speed-up Challenge

EXAMPLE

Suppose you want to achieve a speed-up of 90 times faster with 100 processors. What percentage of the original computation can be sequential?

ANSWER

Amdahl's Law (Chapter 1) says

$$\text{Execution time after improvement} = \frac{\text{Execution time affected by improvement}}{\text{Amount of improvement}} + \text{Execution time unaffected}$$

We can reformulate Amdahl's Law in terms of speed-up versus the original execution time:

$$\text{Speed-up} = \frac{\text{Execution time before}}{(\text{Execution time before} - \text{Execution time affected}) + \dfrac{\text{Execution time affected}}{\text{Amount of improvement}}}$$

This formula is usually rewritten assuming that the execution time before is 1 for some unit of time, and the execution time affected by improvement is considered the fraction of the original execution time:

$$\text{Speed-up} = \frac{1}{(1 - \text{Fraction time affected}) + \dfrac{\text{Fraction time affected}}{\text{Amount of improvement}}}$$

Substituting 90 for speed-up and 100 for amount of improvement into the formula above:

$$90 = \frac{1}{(1 - \text{Fraction time affected}) + \dfrac{\text{Fraction time affected}}{100}}$$

Then simplifying the formula and solving for fraction time affected:

$$90 \times (1 - 0.99 \times \text{Fraction time affected}) = 1$$
$$90 - (90 \times 0.99 \times \text{Fraction time affected}) = 1$$
$$90 - 1 = 90 \times 0.99 \times \text{Fraction time affected}$$
$$\text{Fraction time affected} = 89/89.1 = 0.999$$

Thus, to achieve a speed-up of 90 from 100 processors, the sequential percentage can only be 0.1%.

Yet, there are applications with plenty of parallelism, as we shall see next.

EXAMPLE

Speed-up Challenge: Bigger Problem

Suppose you want to perform two sums: one is a sum of 10 scalar variables, and one is a matrix sum of a pair of two-dimensional arrays, with dimensions 10 by 10. For now let's assume only the matrix sum is parallelizable; we'll see soon how to parallelize scalar sums. What speed-up do you get with 10 versus 40 processors? Next, calculate the speed-ups assuming the matrices grow to 20 by 20.

ANSWER

If we assume performance is a function of the time for an addition, t, then there are 10 additions that do not benefit from parallel processors and 100 additions that do. If the time for a single processor is 110 t, the execution time for 10 processors is

$$\text{Execution time after improvement} = \frac{\text{Execution time affected by improvement}}{\text{Amount of improvement}} + \text{Execution time unaffected}$$

$$\text{Execution time after improvement} = \frac{100t}{10} + 10t = 20t$$

so the speed-up with 10 processors is $110t/20t = 5.5$. The execution time for 40 processors is

$$\text{Execution time after improvement} = \frac{100t}{40} + 10t = 12.5t$$

so the speed-up with 40 processors is $110t/12.5t = 8.8$. Thus, for this problem size, we get about 55% of the potential speed-up with 10 processors, but only 22% with 40.

Look what happens when we increase the matrix. The sequential program now takes $10t + 400t = 410t$. The execution time for 10 processors is

$$\text{Execution time after improvement} = \frac{400t}{10} + 10t = 50t$$

so the speed-up with 10 processors is $410t/50t = 8.2$. The execution time for 40 processors is

$$\text{Execution time after improvement} = \frac{400t}{40} + 10t = 20t$$

so the speed-up with 40 processors is $410t/20t = 20.5$. Thus, for this larger problem size, we get 82% of the potential speed-up with 10 processors and 51% with 40.

These examples show that getting good speed-up on a multiprocessor while keeping the problem size fixed is harder than getting good speed-up by increasing the size of the problem. This insight allows us to introduce two terms that describe ways to scale up.

Strong scaling means measuring speed-up while keeping the problem size fixed. **Weak scaling** means that the problem size grows proportionally to the increase in the number of processors. Let's assume that the size of the problem, M, is the working set in main memory, and we have P processors. Then the memory per processor for strong scaling is approximately M/P, and for weak scaling, it is approximately M.

Note that the **memory hierarchy** can interfere with the conventional wisdom about weak scaling being easier than strong scaling. For example, if the weakly scaled dataset no longer fits in the last level cache of a multicore microprocessor, the resulting performance could be much worse than by using strong scaling .

Depending on the application, you can argue for either scaling approach. For example, the TPC-C debit-credit database benchmark requires that you scale up the number of customer accounts in proportion to the higher transactions per minute. The argument is that it's nonsensical to think that a given customer base is suddenly going to start using ATMs 100 times a day just because the bank gets a faster computer. Instead, if you're going to demonstrate a system that can perform 100 times the numbers of transactions per minute, you should run the experiment with 100 times as many customers. Bigger problems often need more data, which is an argument for weak scaling.

This final example shows the importance of load balancing.

Speed-up Challenge: Balancing Load

To achieve the speed-up of 20.5 on the previous larger problem with 40 processors, we assumed the load was perfectly balanced. That is, each of the 40 processors had 2.5% of the work to do. Instead, show the impact on speed-up if one processor's load is higher than all the rest. Calculate at twice the load (5%) and five times the load (12.5%) for that hardest working processor. How well utilized are the rest of the processors?

ANSWER

If one processor has 5% of the parallel load, then it must do 5% × 400 or 20 additions, and the other 39 will share the remaining 380. Since they are operating simultaneously, we can just calculate the execution time as a maximum

$$\text{Execution time after improvement} = \text{Max}\left(\frac{380t}{39}, \frac{20t}{1}\right) + 10t = 30t$$

The speed-up drops from 20.5 to $410t/30t = 14$. The remaining 39 processors are utilized less than half the time: while waiting 20t for hardest working processor to finish, they only compute for $380t/39 = 9.7t$.

If one processor has 12.5% of the load, it must perform 50 additions. The formula is:

$$\text{Execution time after improvement} = \text{Max}\left(\frac{350t}{39}, \frac{50t}{1}\right) + 10t = 60t$$

The speed-up drops even further to $410t/60t = 7$. The rest of the processors are utilized less than 20% of the time ($9t/50t$). This example demonstrates the importance of balancing load, for just a single processor with twice the load of the others cuts speed-up by a third, and five times the load on just one processor reduces speed-up by almost a factor of three.

Now that we better understand the goals and challenges of parallel processing, we give an overview of the rest of the chapter. The next section (6.3) describes a much older classification scheme than in Figure 6.1. In addition, it describes two styles of instruction set architectures that support running of sequential applications on parallel hardware, namely *SIMD* and *vector*. Section 6.4 then describes *multithreading*, a term often confused with multiprocessing, in part because it relies upon similar concurrency in programs. Section 6.5 describes the first the two alternatives of a fundamental parallel hardware characteristic, which is whether or not all the processors in the systems rely upon a single physical address space. As mentioned above, the two popular versions of these alternatives are called *shared memory multiprocessors* (SMPs) and *clusters*, and this section covers the former. Section 6.6 describes a relatively new style of computer from the graphics hardware community, called a *graphics-processing unit* (GPU) that also assumes a single physical address. (⊕ **Appendix C** describes GPUs in even more detail.) Section 6.7 introduces domain specific architectures (DSA), where the processors are customized to perform well in one domain but need not run all programs well. Section 6.8 describes clusters, a popular example of a computer with multiple physical address spaces. Section 6.9 shows typical topologies used to connect many processors together, either server nodes in a cluster or cores in a microprocessor. ⊕ **Section 6.10** describes the hardware and software for communicating between nodes in a cluster using Ethernet. It shows how to optimize its performance using custom software and hardware. We next discuss the difficulty of finding parallel benchmarks in Section 6.11. This section also includes a simple, yet insightful performance model that helps in the design of applications as well as architectures. We use this model as well as parallel benchmarks in Section 6.12 to compare a DSA to a GPU. Section 6.13 divulges the final and largest step in our journey of accelerating matrix multiply. Parallel processing uses 48 cores to improve performance by a factor of 12 to 17 if we increase matrix size (weak scaling). We close with fallacies and pitfalls and our conclusions for parallelism.

In the next section, we introduce acronyms that you probably have already seen to identify different types of parallel computers.

True or false: Strong scaling is not bound by Amdahl's Law.

6.3 SISD, MIMD, SIMD, SPMD, and Vector

One categorization of parallel hardware proposed in the 1960s is still used today. It was based on the number of instruction streams and the number of data streams. Figure 6.2 shows the categories. Thus, a conventional uniprocessor has a single instruction stream and single data stream, and a conventional multiprocessor has multiple instruction streams and multiple data streams. These two categories are abbreviated **SISD** and **MIMD**, respectively.

While it is possible to write separate programs that run on different processors on a MIMD computer and yet work together for a grander, coordinated goal, programmers normally write a single program that runs on all processors of an **MIMD** computer, relying on conditional statements when different processors should execute different sections of code. This style is called **Single Program Multiple Data (SPMD)**, but it is just the normal way to program a MIMD computer.

The closest we can come to multiple instruction streams and single data stream (**MISD**) processor might be a "stream processor" that would perform a series of computations on a single data stream in a pipelined fashion: parse the input from the network, decrypt the data, decompress it, search for match, and so on. The

SISD or Single Instruction stream, Single Data stream. A uniprocessor.

MIMD or Multiple Instruction streams, Multiple Data streams. A multiprocessor.

SPMD Single Program, Multiple Data streams. The conventional MIMD programming model, where a single program runs across all processors.

SIMD or Single Instruction stream, Multiple Data streams. The same instruction is applied to many data streams, as in a vector processor.

| | | Data Streams | |
		Single	Multiple
Instruction Streams	Single	SISD: Intel Pentium 4	SIMD: SSE instructions of x86
	Multiple	MISD: No examples today	MIMD: Intel Core i7

FIGURE 6.2 Hardware categorization and examples based on number of instruction streams and data streams: SISD, SIMD, MISD, and MIMD.

inverse of MISD is much more popular. SIMD computers operate on vectors of data. For example, a single SIMD instruction might add 64 numbers by sending 64 data streams to 64 ALUs to form 64 sums within a single clock cycle. The subword parallel instructions that we saw in Sections 3.6 and 3.7 are another example of SIMD; indeed, the middle letter of Intel's SSE acronym stands for SIMD.

The virtues of SIMD are that all the parallel execution units are synchronized and they all respond to a single instruction that emanates from a single *program counter* (PC). From a programmer's perspective, this is close to the already familiar SISD. Although every unit will be executing the same instruction, each execution unit has its own address registers, and so each unit can have different data addresses. Thus, in terms of Figure 6.1, a sequential application might be compiled to run on serial hardware organized as a SISD or in parallel hardware that was organized as a SIMD.

The original motivation behind SIMD was to amortize the cost of the control unit over dozens of execution units. Another advantage is the reduced instruction bandwidth and space—SIMD needs only one copy of the code that is being simultaneously executed, while message-passing MIMDs may need a copy in every processor, and shared memory MIMD will need multiple instruction caches.

SIMD works best when dealing with arrays in `for` loops. Hence, for parallelism to work in SIMD, there must be a great deal of identically structured data, which is called **data-level parallelism**. SIMD is at its weakest in `case` or `switch` statements, where each execution unit must perform a different operation on its data, depending on what data it has. Execution units with the wrong data must be disabled so that units with proper data may continue. If there are n cases, in these situations SIMD processors essentially run at $1/n$th of peak performance.

The so-called array processors that inspired the SIMD category lost popularity until recently (see Section 6.7 and 🌐 Section 6.16 online), but two current interpretations of SIMD have been active for decades.

data-level parallelism Parallelism achieved by performing the same operation on independent data.

SIMD in x86: Multimedia Extensions

As described in Chapter 3, subword parallelism for narrow integer data was the original inspiration of the Multimedia Extension (MMX) instructions of the x86 in 1996. As Moore's Law continued, more instructions were added, leading first to *Streaming SIMD Extensions* (SSE) and now *Advanced Vector Extensions* (AVX). AVX supports the simultaneous execution of eight 64-bit floating-point numbers. The width of the operation and the registers is encoded in the opcode of these multimedia instructions. As the data width of the registers and operations grew, the number of opcodes for multimedia instructions exploded, and now there are hundreds of SSE and AVX instructions (see Chapter 3).

Vector

An older and, as we shall see, more elegant interpretation of SIMD is called a *vector architecture*, which has been closely identified with computers designed by Seymour Cray starting in the 1970s. It is also a great match to problems with lots of data-level parallelism. Rather than having 64 ALUs perform 64 additions simultaneously, like the old array processors, the vector architectures pipelined the ALU to get good performance at lower cost. The basic philosophy of vector architecture is to collect data elements from memory, put them in order into a large set of registers, operate on them sequentially in registers using **pipelined execution units**, and then write the results back to memory. A key feature of vector architectures is then a set of vector registers. Thus, a vector architecture might have 32 vector registers, each with 64 64-bit elements .

Comparing Vector to Conventional Code

Suppose we extend the MIPS instruction set architecture with vector instructions and vector registers. Vector operations use the same names as MIPS operations, but with the letter "V" appended. For example, `addv.d` adds two double-precision vectors. The vector instructions take as their input either a pair of vector registers (`addv.d`) or a vector register and a scalar register (`addvs.d`). In the latter case, the value in the scalar register is used as the input for all operations—the operation `addvs.d` will add the contents of a scalar register to each element in a vector register. The names `lv` and `sv` denote vector load and vector store, and they load or store an entire vector of double-precision data. One operand is the vector register to be loaded or stored; the other operand, which is a MIPS general-purpose register, is the starting address of the vector in memory. Given this short description, show the conventional MIPS code versus the vector MIPS code for

$$Y = a \times X + Y$$

where X and Y are vectors of 64 double precision floating-point numbers, initially resident in memory, and a is a scalar double precision variable. (This example is the so-called *DAXPY* loop that forms the inner loop of the Linpack benchmark; DAXPY stands for double precision $a \times X$ plus Y.). Assume that the starting addresses of X and Y are in $s0 and $s1, respectively.

Here is the conventional (scalar) MIPS code for DAXPY:

```
       l.d      $f0,a($sp)      #load scalar a
       addiu    $t0,$s0,#512    #upper bound of what to load
loop:  l.d      $f2,0($s0)      #load x(i)
       mul.d    $f2,$f2,$f0     #a x x(i)
       l.d      $f4,0($s1)      #load y(i)
       add.d    $f4,$f4,$f2     #a x x(i) + y(i)
       s.d      $f4,0($s1)      #store into y(i)
       addiu    $s0,$s0,#8      #increment index to x
       addiu    $s1,$s1,#8      #increment index to y
       subu     $t1,$t0,$s0     #compute bound
       bne      $t1,$zero,loop  #check if done
```

Here is the vector MIPS code for DAXPY:

```
l.d       $f0,a($sp)        #load scalar a
lv        $v1,0($s0)        #load vector x
mulvs.d   $v2,$v1,$f0       #vector-scalar multiply
lv        $v3,0($s1)        #load vector y
addv.d    $v4,$v2,$v3       #add y to product
sv        $v4,0($s1)        #store the result
```

There are some interesting comparisons between the two code segments in this example. The most dramatic is that the vector processor greatly reduces the dynamic instruction bandwidth, executing only 6 instructions versus almost 600 for the traditional MIPS architecture. This reduction occurs both because the vector operations work on 64 elements at a time and because the overhead instructions that constitute nearly half the loop on MIPS are not present in the vector code. As you might expect, this reduction in instructions fetched and executed saves energy.

Another important difference is the frequency of **pipeline** hazards (Chapter 4). In the straightforward MIPS code, every `add.d` must wait for a `mul.d`, every `s.d` must wait for the `add.d` and every `add.d` *and* `mul.d` must wait on `l.d`. On the vector processor, each vector instruction will only stall for the first element in each vector, and then subsequent elements will flow smoothly down the pipeline. Thus, pipeline stalls are required only once per vector *operation*, rather than once per vector *element*. In this example, the pipeline stall frequency on MIPS will be about 64 times higher than it is on the vector version of MIPS. The pipeline stalls can be reduced on MIPS by using loop unrolling (see Chapter 4). However, the large difference in instruction bandwidth cannot be reduced .

Since the vector elements are independent, they can be operated on in parallel, much like subword parallelism for AVX instructions. All modern vector computers have vector functional units with multiple parallel pipelines (called *vector lanes*; see Figures 6.2 and 6.3) that can produce two or more results per clock cycle.

Elaboration: The loop in the example above exactly matched the vector length. When loops are shorter, vector architectures use a register that reduces the length of vector operations. When loops are larger, we add bookkeeping code to iterate full-length vector operations and to handle the leftovers. This latter process is called *strip mining*.

Vector versus Scalar

Vector instructions have several important properties compared to conventional instruction set architectures, which are called *scalar architectures* in this context:

- A single vector instruction specifies a great deal of work—it is equivalent to executing an entire loop. The instruction fetch and decode bandwidth needed is dramatically reduced.

- By using a vector instruction, the compiler or programmer indicates that the computation of each result in the vector is independent of the computation of other results in the same vector, so hardware does not have to check for data hazards within a vector instruction.

- Vector architectures and compilers have a reputation of making it much easier than when using MIMD multiprocessors to write efficient applications when they contain data-level parallelism.

- Hardware need only check for data hazards between two vector instructions once per vector operand, not once for every element within the vectors. Reduced checking can save energy as well as time.

- Vector instructions that access memory have a known access pattern. If the vector's elements are all adjacent, then fetching the vector from a set of heavily interleaved memory banks works very well. Thus, the cost of the latency to main memory is seen only once for the entire vector, rather than once for each word of the vector.

- Because an entire loop is replaced by a vector instruction whose behavior is predetermined, control hazards that would normally arise from the loop branch are nonexistent.

- The savings in instruction bandwidth and hazard checking plus the efficient use of memory bandwidth give vector architectures advantages in power and energy versus scalar architectures.

For these reasons, vector operations can be made faster than a sequence of scalar operations on the same number of data items, and designers are motivated to include vector units if the application domain can often use them.

Vector versus Multimedia Extensions

Like multimedia extensions found in the x86 AVX instructions, a vector instruction specifies multiple operations. However, multimedia extensions typically specify a few operations while vector specifies dozens of operations. Unlike multimedia extensions, the number of elements in a vector operation is not in the opcode but in a separate register. This distinction means different versions of the vector architecture can be implemented with a different number of elements just by changing the contents of that register and hence retain binary compatibility. In contrast, a new large set of opcodes is added each time the "vector" length changes in the multimedia extension architecture of the x86: MMX, SSE, SSE2, AVX, AVX2, … .

Also unlike multimedia extensions, the data transfers need not be contiguous. Vectors support both strided accesses, where the hardware loads every nth data element in memory, and indexed accesses, where hardware finds the addresses of the items to be loaded in a vector register. Indexed accesses are also called *gather-scatter*, in that indexed loads gather elements from main memory into contiguous vector elements and indexed stores scatter vector elements across main memory.

Like multimedia extensions, vector architectures easily capture the flexibility in data widths, so it is easy to make a vector operation work on 32 64-bit data elements or 64 32-bit data elements or 128 16-bit data elements or 256 8-bit data elements. The parallel semantics of a vector instruction allows an implementation to execute these operations using a deeply **pipelined** functional unit, an array of parallel functional units, or a combination of parallel and pipelined functional units. Figure 6.3 illustrates how to improve vector performance by using parallel pipelines to execute a vector add instruction .

Vector arithmetic instructions usually only allow element N of one vector register to take part in operations with element N from other vector registers. This

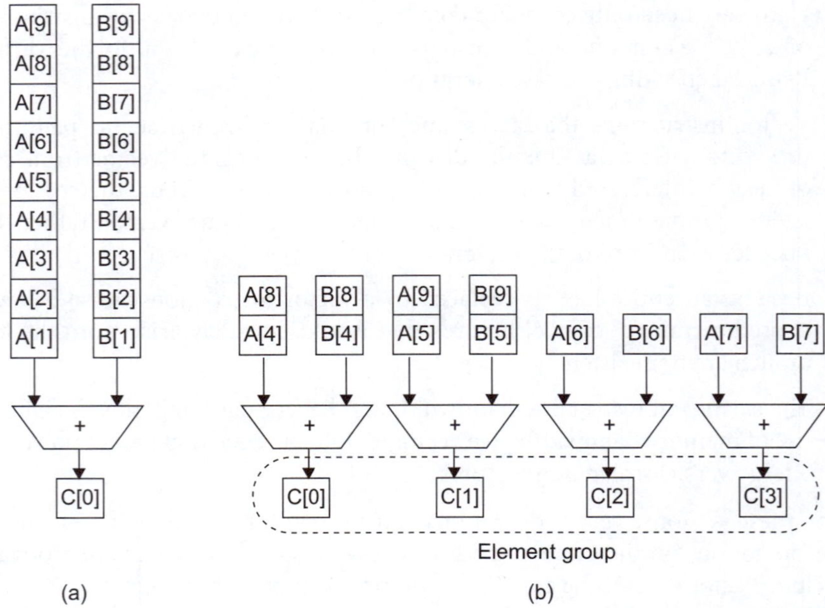

FIGURE 6.3 Using multiple functional units to improve the performance of a single vector add instruction, C = A + B. The vector processor (a) on the left has a single add pipeline and can complete one addition per cycle. The vector processor (b) on the right has four add pipelines or lanes and can complete four additions per cycle. The elements within a single vector add instruction are interleaved across the four lanes.

vector lane One or more vector functional units and a portion of the vector register file. Inspired by lanes on highways that increase traffic speed, multiple lanes execute vector operations simultaneously.

PARALLELISM

dramatically simplifies the construction of a highly parallel vector unit, which can be structured as multiple parallel **vector lanes**. As with a traffic highway, we can increase the peak throughput of a vector unit by adding more lanes. Figure 6.4 shows the structure of a four-lane vector unit. Thus, going to four lanes from one lane reduces the number of clocks per vector instruction by roughly a factor of four. For multiple lanes to be advantageous, both the applications and the architecture must support long vectors. Otherwise, they will execute so quickly that you'll run out of instructions, requiring instruction level **parallel** techniques like those in Chapter 4 to supply enough vector instructions.

Generally, vector architectures are a very efficient way to execute data parallel processing programs; they are better matches to compiler technology than multimedia extensions; and they are easier to evolve over time than the multimedia extensions to the x86 architecture.

Given these classic categories, we next see how to exploit parallel streams of instructions to improve the performance of a *single* processor, which we will reuse with multiple processors.

Check Yourself

True or false: As exemplified in the x86, multimedia extensions can be thought of as a vector architecture with short vectors that supports only contiguous vector data transfers.

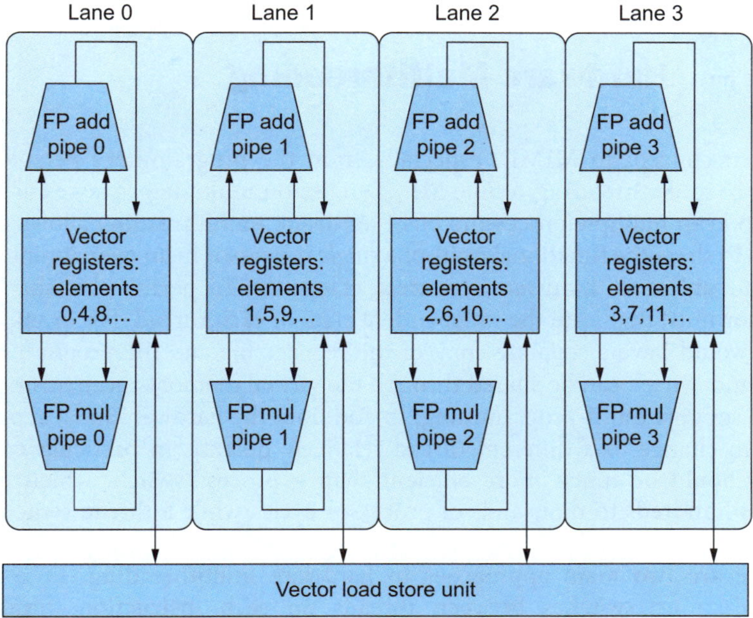

FIGURE 6.4 Structure of a vector unit containing four lanes. The vector-register storage is divided across the lanes, with each lane holding every fourth element of each vector register. The figure shows three vector functional units: an FP add, an FP multiply, and a load-store unit. Each of the vector arithmetic units contains four execution pipelines, one per lane, which acts in concert to complete a single vector instruction. Note how each section of the vector-register file only needs to provide enough read and write ports (see Chapter 4) for functional units local to its lane.

Elaboration: Given the advantages of vector, why aren't they more popular outside high-performance computing? There were concerns about the larger state for vector registers increasing context switch time and the difficulty of handling page faults in vector loads and stores, and SIMD instructions achieved some of the benefits of vector instructions. In addition, as long as advances in instruction level parallelism could deliver on the performance promise of Moore's Law, there was little reason to take the chance of changing architecture styles.

Elaboration: Another advantage of vector and multimedia extensions is that it is relatively easy to extend a scalar instruction set architecture with these instructions to improve performance of data parallel operations.

Elaboration: The Haswell-generation x86 processors from Intel support AVX2, which has a gather operation but not a scatter operation. Skylake and later-generation processors support AVX512, which adds a scatter operation.

hardware multithreading Increasing utilization of a processor by switching to another thread when one thread is stalled.

thread A thread includes the program counter, the register state, and the stack. It is a lightweight process; whereas threads commonly share a single address space, processes don't.

process A process includes one or more threads, the address space, and the operating system state. Hence, a process switch usually invokes the operating system, but not a thread switch.

fine-grained multithreading A version of hardware multithreading that implies switching between threads after every instruction.

coarse-grained multithreading A version of hardware multithreading that implies switching between threads only after significant events, such as a last-level cache miss.

6.4 Hardware Multithreading

A related concept to MIMD, especially from the programmer's perspective, is **hardware multithreading**. While MIMD relies on multiple **processes** or **threads** to try to keep multiple processors busy, hardware multithreading allows multiple threads to share the functional units of a *single* processor in an overlapping fashion to try to utilize its hardware resources efficiently. To permit this sharing, the processor must duplicate the independent state of each thread. For example, each thread would have a separate copy of the register file and the program counter. The memory itself can be shared through the virtual memory mechanisms, which already support multi-programming. In addition, the hardware must support the ability to change to a different thread relatively quickly. In particular, a thread switch should be much more efficient than a process switch, which typically requires hundreds to thousands of processor cycles while a thread switch can be instantaneous.

There are two main approaches to hardware multithreading. **Fine-grained multithreading** switches between threads on each instruction, resulting in interleaved execution of multiple threads. This interleaving is often done in a round-robin fashion, skipping any threads that are stalled at that clock cycle. To make fine-grained multithreading practical, the processor must be able to switch threads on every clock cycle. One advantage of fine-grained multithreading is that it can hide the throughput losses that arise from both short and long stalls, since instructions from other threads can be executed when one thread stalls. The primary disadvantage of fine-grained multithreading is that it slows down the execution of the individual threads, since a thread that is ready to execute without stalls will be delayed by instructions from other threads.

Coarse-grained multithreading was invented as an alternative to fine-grained multithreading. Coarse-grained multithreading switches threads only on costly stalls, such as last-level cache misses. This change relieves the need to have thread switching be extremely fast and is much less likely to slow down the execution of an individual thread, since instructions from other threads will only be issued when a thread encounters a costly stall. Coarse-grained multithreading suffers, however, from a major drawback: it is limited in its ability to overcome throughput losses, especially from shorter stalls. This limitation arises from the **pipeline** start-up costs of coarse-grained multithreading. Because a processor with coarse-grained multithreading issues instructions from a single thread, when a stall occurs, the pipeline must be emptied or frozen. The new thread that begins executing after the stall must fill the pipeline before instructions will be able to complete. Due to this start-up overhead, coarse-grained multithreading is much more useful for reducing the penalty of high-cost stalls, where pipeline refill is negligible compared to the stall time.

Simultaneous multithreading (SMT) is a variation on hardware multithreading that uses the resources of a multiple-issue, dynamically scheduled **pipelined** processor to exploit thread-level parallelism at the same time it exploits instruction-level parallelism (see Chapter 4). The key insight that motivates SMT is that multiple-issue processors often have more functional unit parallelism available than most single threads can effectively use. Furthermore, with register renaming and dynamic scheduling (see Chapter 4), multiple instructions from independent threads can be issued without regard to the dependences among them; the resolution of the dependences can be handled by the dynamic scheduling capability.

Since SMT relies on the existing dynamic mechanisms, it does not switch resources every cycle. Instead, SMT is *always* executing instructions from multiple threads, leaving it up to the hardware to associate instruction slots and renamed registers with their proper threads.

Figure 6.5 conceptually illustrates the differences in a processor's ability to exploit superscalar resources for the following processor configurations. The top portion shows

simultaneous multithreading (SMT) A version of multithreading that lowers the cost of multithreading by utilizing the resources needed for multiple issue, dynamically scheduled microarchitecture.

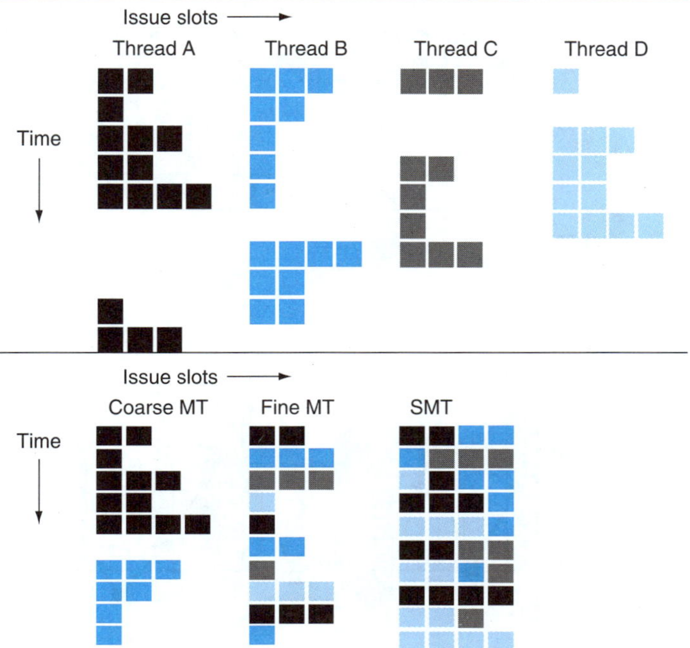

FIGURE 6.5   How four threads use the issue slots of a superscalar processor in different approaches. The four threads at the top show how each would execute running alone on a standard superscalar processor without multithreading support. The three examples at the bottom show how they would execute running together in three multithreading options. The horizontal dimension represents the instruction issue capability in each clock cycle. The vertical dimension represents a sequence of clock cycles. An empty (white) box indicates that the corresponding issue slot is unused in that clock cycle. The shades of gray and color correspond to four different threads in the multithreading processors. The additional pipeline start-up effects for coarse multithreading, which are not illustrated in this figure, would lead to further loss in throughput for coarse multithreading.

how four threads would execute independently on a superscalar with no multithreading support. The bottom portion shows how the four threads could be combined to execute on the processor more efficiently using three multithreading options:

- A superscalar with coarse-grained multithreading
- A superscalar with fine-grained multithreading
- A superscalar with simultaneous multithreading

In the superscalar without hardware multithreading support, the use of issue slots is limited by a lack of **instruction-level parallelism**. In addition, a major stall, such as an instruction cache miss, can leave the entire processor idle.

In the coarse-grained multithreaded superscalar, the long stalls are partially hidden by switching to another thread that uses the resources of the processor. Although this reduces the number of completely idle clock cycles, the pipeline start-up overhead still leads to idle cycles, and limitations to ILP means all issue slots will not be used. In the fine-grained case, the interleaving of threads mostly eliminates idle clock cycles. Because only a single thread issues instructions in a given clock cycle, however, limitations in instruction-level parallelism still lead to idle slots within some clock cycles.

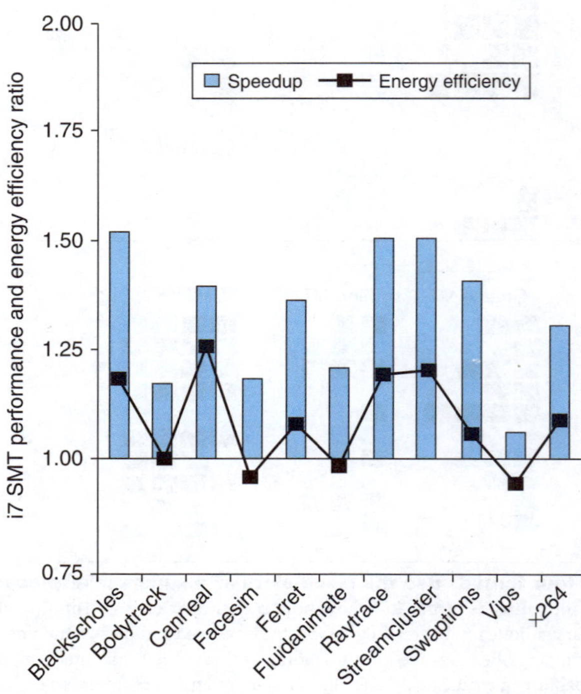

FIGURE 6.6 The speed-up from using multithreading on one core on an i7 processor averages 1.31 for the PARSEC benchmarks (see ⊕ Section 6.10) and the energy efficiency improvement is 1.07. This data was collected and analyzed by Esmaeilzadeh et. al. [2011].

In the SMT case, thread-level parallelism and instruction-level parallelism are both exploited, with multiple threads using the issue slots in a single clock cycle. Ideally, the issue slot usage is limited by imbalances in the resource needs and resource availability over multiple threads. In practice, other factors can restrict how many slots are used. Although Figure 6.5 greatly simplifies the real operation of these processors, it does illustrate the potential performance advantages of multithreading in general and SMT in particular.

Figure 6.6 plots the performance and energy benefits of multithreading on a single processors of the Intel Core i7 960, which has hardware support for two threads, as does the more recent i7 6700. The changes between the i7 920 and the 6700 are relatively small and are unlikely to significantly change the results in this figure. The average speed-up is 1.31, which is not bad given the modest extra resources for hardware multithreading. The average improvement in energy efficiency is 1.07, which is excellent. In general, you'd be happy with a performance speed-up being energy neutral.

Now that we have seen how multiple threads can utilize the resources of a single processor more effectively, we next show how to use them to exploit multiple processors.

1. True or false: Both multithreading and multicore rely on parallelism to get more efficiency from a chip.

2. True or false: *Simultaneous multithreading* (SMT) uses threads to improve resource utilization of a dynamically scheduled, out-of-order processor.

Check Yourself

6.5   Multicore and Other Shared Memory Multiprocessors

While hardware multithreading improved the efficiency of processors at modest cost, a big challenge has been to deliver on the traditional performance gain of Moore's Law by efficiently programming the increasing number of processors per chip.

Given the difficulty of rewriting old programs to run well on parallel hardware, a natural question is: what can computer designers do to simplify the task? One answer was to provide a single physical address space that all processors can share, so that programs need not concern themselves with where their data is, merely that programs may be executed in parallel. In this approach, all variables of a program can be made available at any time to any processor. The alternative is to have a separate address space per processor that requires that sharing must be explicit; we'll describe this option in the Section 6.8. When the physical address space is common then the hardware typically provides cache coherence to give a consistent view of the shared memory (see Section 5.8).

As mentioned above, a *shared memory multiprocessor* (SMP) is one that offers the programmer a *single physical address space* across all processors—which is

uniform memory access (UMA) A multiprocessor in which latency to any word in main memory is about the same no matter which processor requests the access.

nonuniform memory access (NUMA) A type of single address space multiprocessor in which some memory accesses are much faster than others depending on which processor asks for which word.

synchronization The process of coordinating the behavior of two or more processes, which may be running on different processors.

lock A synchronization device that allows access to data to only one processor at a time.

nearly always the case for multicore chips—although a more accurate term would have been shared-*address* multiprocessor. Processors communicate through shared variables in memory, with all processors capable of accessing any memory location via loads and stores. Figure 6.7 shows the classic organization of an SMP. Note that such systems can still run independent jobs in their own virtual address spaces, even if they all share a physical address space.

Single address space multiprocessors come in two styles. In the first style, the latency to a word in memory does not depend on which processor asks for it. Such machines are called **uniform memory access (UMA)** multiprocessors. In the second style, some memory accesses are much faster than others, depending on which processor asks for which word, typically because main memory is divided and attached to different processors or to different memory controllers on the same chip. Such machines are called **nonuniform memory access (NUMA)** multiprocessors. As you might expect, the programming challenges are harder for a NUMA multiprocessor than for a UMA multiprocessor, but NUMA machines can scale to larger sizes and NUMAs can have lower latency to nearby memory.

As processors operating in parallel will normally share data, they also need to coordinate when operating on shared data; otherwise, one processor could start working on data before another is finished with it. This coordination is called **synchronization**, which we saw in Chapter 2. When sharing is supported with a single address space, there must be a separate mechanism for synchronization. One approach uses a **lock** for a shared variable. Only one processor at a time can acquire the lock, and other processors interested in shared data must wait until the original processor unlocks the variable. Section 2.11 of Chapter 2 describes the instructions for locking in the MIPS instruction set.

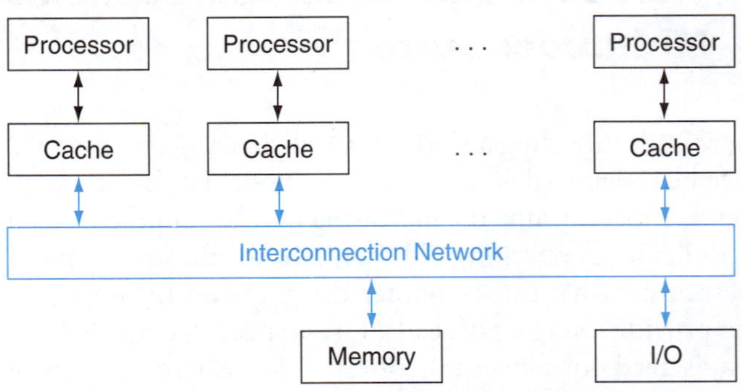

FIGURE 6.7 Classic organization of a shared memory multiprocessor.

A Simple Parallel Processing Program for a Shared Address Space

Suppose we want to sum 64,000 numbers on a shared memory multiprocessor computer with uniform memory access time. Let's assume we have 64 processors.

The first step is to ensure a balanced load per processor, so we split the set of numbers into subsets of the same size. We do not allocate the subsets to a different memory space, since there is a single memory space for this machine; we just give different starting addresses to each processor. Pn is the number that identifies the processor, between 0 and 63. All processors start the program by running a loop that sums their subset of numbers:

```
sum[Pn] = 0;
for (i = 1000*Pn; i < 1000*(Pn + 1); i += 1)
  sum[Pn] += A[i]; /*sum the assigned areas*/
```

(Note the C code i += 1 is just a shorter way to say i = i + 1.)

The next step is to add these 64 partial sums. This step is called a **reduction**, where we divide to conquer. Half of the processors add pairs of partial sums, and then a quarter add pairs of the new partial sums, and so on until we have the single, final sum. Figure 6.8 illustrates the hierarchical nature of this reduction.

reduction A function that processes a data structure and returns a single value.

In this example, the two processors must synchronize before the "consumer" processor tries to read the result from the memory location written by the "producer" processor; otherwise, the consumer may read the old value of

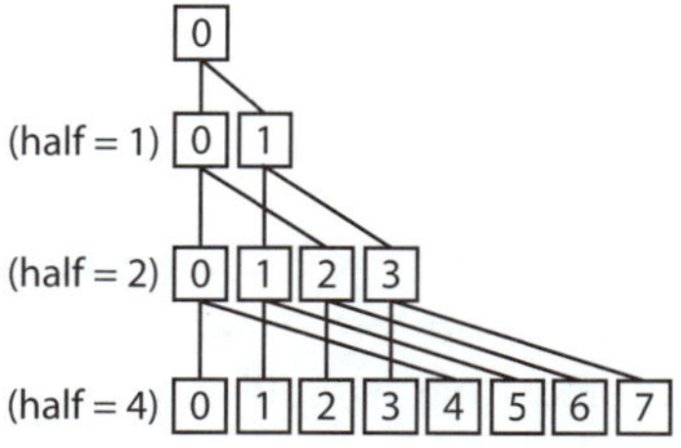

FIGURE 6.8 The last four levels of a reduction that sums results from each processor, from bottom to top. For all processors whose number i is less than half, add the sum produced by processor number (i + half) to its sum.

the data. We want each processor to have its own version of the loop counter variable i, so we must indicate that it is a "private" variable. Here is the code (half is private also):

```
half = 64; /*64 processors in multiprocessor*/
do
    synch(); /*wait for partial sum completion*/
    if (half%2 != 0 && Pn == 0)
        sum[0] += sum[half-1];
        /*Conditional sum needed when half is
        odd; Processor0 gets missing element */
        half = half/2; /*dividing line on who sums */
        if (Pn < half) sum[Pn] += sum[Pn+half];
while (half > 1); /*exit with final sum in Sum[0] */
```

Hardware/ Software Interface

OpenMP An API for shared memory multiprocessing in C, C++, or Fortran that runs on UNIX and Microsoft platforms. It includes compiler directives, a library, and runtime directives.

Given the long-term interest in parallel programming, there have been hundreds of attempts to build parallel programming systems. A limited but popular example is **OpenMP**. It is just an *Application Programmer Interface* (API) along with a set of compiler directives, environment variables, and runtime library routines that can extend standard programming languages. It offers a portable, scalable, and simple programming model for shared memory multiprocessors. Its primary goal is to parallelize loops and to perform reductions.

Most C compilers already have support for OpenMP. The command to uses the OpenMP API with the UNIX C compiler is just:

```
cc -fopenmp foo.c
```

OpenMP extends C using *pragmas*, which are just commands to the C macro preprocessor like #define and #include. To set the number of processors we want to use to be 64, as we wanted in the example above, we just use the command

```
#define P 64 /* define a constant that we'll use a few times */
#pragma omp parallel num_threads(P)
```

That is, the runtime libraries should use 64 parallel threads.

To turn the sequential for loop into a parallel for loop that divides the work equally between all the threads that we told it to use, we just write (assuming sum is initialized to 0)

```
#pragma omp parallel for
for (Pn = 0; Pn < P; Pn += 1)
    for (i = 0; 1000*Pn; i < 1000*(Pn+1); i += 1)
        sum[Pn] += A[i]; /*sum the assigned areas*/
```

To perform the reduction, we can use another command that tells OpenMP what the reduction operator is and what variable you need to use to place the result of the reduction.

```
#pragma omp parallel for reduction(+ : FinalSum)
for (i = 0; i < P; i += 1)
    FinalSum += sum[i]; /* Reduce to a single number */
```

Note that it is now up to the OpenMP library to find efficient code to sum 64 numbers efficiently using 64 processors.

While OpenMP makes it easy to write simple parallel code, it is not very helpful with debugging, so many parallel programmers use more sophisticated parallel programming systems than OpenMP, just as many programmers today use more productive languages than C.

Given this tour of classic MIMD hardware and software, our next step is a more exotic tour of a type of MIMD architecture with a different heritage and thus a very different perspective on the parallel programming challenge.

True or false: Shared memory multiprocessors cannot take advantage of task-level parallelism.

Check Yourself

Elaboration: Some writers repurposed the acronym SMP to mean *symmetric multiprocessor*, to indicate that the latency from processor to memory was about the same for all processors. This shift was done to contrast them from large-scale NUMA multiprocessors, as both classes used a single address space. As clusters proved much more popular than large-scale NUMA multiprocessors, in this book we restore SMP to its original meaning, and use it to contrast against that use multiple address spaces, such as clusters.

Elaboration: An alternative to sharing the physical address space would be to have separate physical address spaces but share a common virtual address space, leaving it up to the operating system to handle communication. This approach has been tried, but it has too high an overhead to offer a practical shared memory abstraction to the performance-oriented programmer.

6.6 Introduction to Graphics Processing Units

The original justification for adding SIMD instructions to existing architectures was that many microprocessors were connected to graphics displays in PCs and workstations, so an increasing fraction of processing time was used for graphics. As Moore's Law increased the number of transistors available to microprocessors, it therefore made sense to improve graphics processing.

A major driving force for improving graphics processing was the computer game industry, both on PCs and in dedicated game consoles such as the Sony PlayStation. The rapidly growing game market encouraged many companies to make increasing investments in developing faster graphics hardware, and this positive feedback loop led graphics processing to improve at a faster rate than general-purpose processing in mainstream microprocessors.

Given that the graphics and game community had different goals than the microprocessor development community, it evolved its own style of processing and terminology. As the graphics processors increased in power, they earned the name *Graphics Processing Units* or *GPUs* to distinguish themselves from CPUs.

For a few hundred dollars, anyone can buy a GPU today with hundreds of parallel floating-point units, which makes high-performance computing more accessible. The interest in GPU computing blossomed when this potential was combined with a programming language that made GPUs easier to program. Hence, many programmers of scientific and multimedia applications today are pondering whether to use GPUs or CPUs.

(This section concentrates on using GPUs for computing. To see how GPU computing combines with the traditional role of graphics acceleration, see **Appendix C**.)

Here are some of the key characteristics as to how GPUs vary from CPUs:

- GPUs are accelerators that supplement a CPU, so they do not need be able to perform all the tasks of a CPU. This role allows them to dedicate all their resources to graphics. It's fine for GPUs to perform some tasks poorly or not at all, given that in a system with both a CPU and a GPU, the CPU can do them if needed.

- The GPU problems sizes are typically hundreds of megabytes to gigabytes, but not hundreds of gigabytes to terabytes.

These differences led to different styles of architecture:

- Perhaps the biggest difference is that GPUs do not rely on multilevel caches to overcome the long latency to memory, as do CPUs. Instead, GPUs rely on hardware multithreading (Section 6.4) to hide the latency to memory. That is, between the time of a memory request and the time that data arrives, the GPU executes hundreds or thousands of threads that are independent of that request.

- The GPU memory is thus oriented toward bandwidth rather than latency. There are even special graphics DRAM chips for GPUs that are wider and have higher bandwidth than DRAM chips for CPUs. In addition, GPU memories have traditionally had smaller main memories than conventional microprocessors. In 2020, GPUs typically have 4 to 16 GiB or less, while CPUs have 64–512 GiB or more. Finally, keep in mind that for general-purpose computation, you must include the time to transfer the data between CPU memory and GPU memory, since the GPU is a coprocessor.

- Given the reliance on many threads to deliver good memory bandwidth, GPUs can accommodate many parallel processors (MIMD) as well as many threads. Hence, each GPU processor is more highly multithreaded than a typical CPU, plus they have more processors.

Hardware/ Software Interface

Although GPUs were designed for a narrower set of applications, some programmers wondered if they could specify their applications in a form that would let them tap the high potential performance of GPUs. After tiring of trying to specify their problems using the graphics APIs and languages, they developed C-inspired programming languages to allow them to write programs directly for the GPUs. An example is NVIDIA's CUDA (Compute Unified Device Architecture), which enables the programmer to write C programs to execute on GPUs, albeit with some restrictions. Appendix C gives examples of CUDA code. (OpenCL is a multi-company initiative to develop a portable programming language that provides many of the benefits of CUDA.)

NVIDIA decided that the unifying theme of all these forms of parallelism is the *CUDA Thread*. Using this lowest level of parallelism as the programming primitive, the compiler and the hardware can gang thousands of CUDA Threads together to utilize the various styles of parallelism within a GPU: multithreading, MIMD, SIMD, and instruction-level parallelism. These threads are blocked together and executed in groups of 32 at a time. A multithreaded processor inside a GPU executes these blocks of threads, and a GPU consists of 8 to 128 of these multithreaded processors.

An Introduction to the NVIDIA GPU Architecture

We use NVIDIA systems as our example as they are representative of GPU architectures. Specifically, we follow the terminology of the CUDA parallel programming language and use the Fermi architecture as the example.

Like vector architectures, GPUs work well only with data-level parallel problems. Both styles have gather-scatter data transfers, and GPU processors have even more registers than do vector processors. Unlike most vector architectures, GPUs also rely on hardware multithreading within a single multi-threaded SIMD processor to hide memory latency (see Section 6.4).

A multithreaded SIMD processor is similar to a Vector Processor, but the former has many parallel functional units instead of just a few that are deeply pipelined, as does the latter.

As mentioned above, a GPU contains a collection of multithreaded SIMD processors; that is, a GPU is a MIMD composed of multithreaded SIMD processors. For example, in 2020, NVIDIA has four implementations of the Tesla at different price points with 15, 24, 56, or 80 multithreaded SIMD processors. To provide transparent scalability across models of GPUs with differing number of multithreaded SIMD processors, the Thread Block Scheduler hardware assigns blocks of threads to multithreaded SIMD processors. Figure 6.9 shows a simplified block diagram of a multithreaded SIMD processor.

Dropping down one more level of detail, the machine object that the hardware creates, manages, schedules, and executes is a *thread of SIMD instructions*, which we will also call a *SIMD thread*. It is a traditional thread, but it contains exclusively SIMD instructions. These SIMD threads have their own program counters and they run on a multithreaded SIMD processor. The *SIMD Thread Scheduler* includes a controller that lets it know which threads of SIMD instructions are ready to run, and then it sends them off to a dispatch unit to be run on the multithreaded

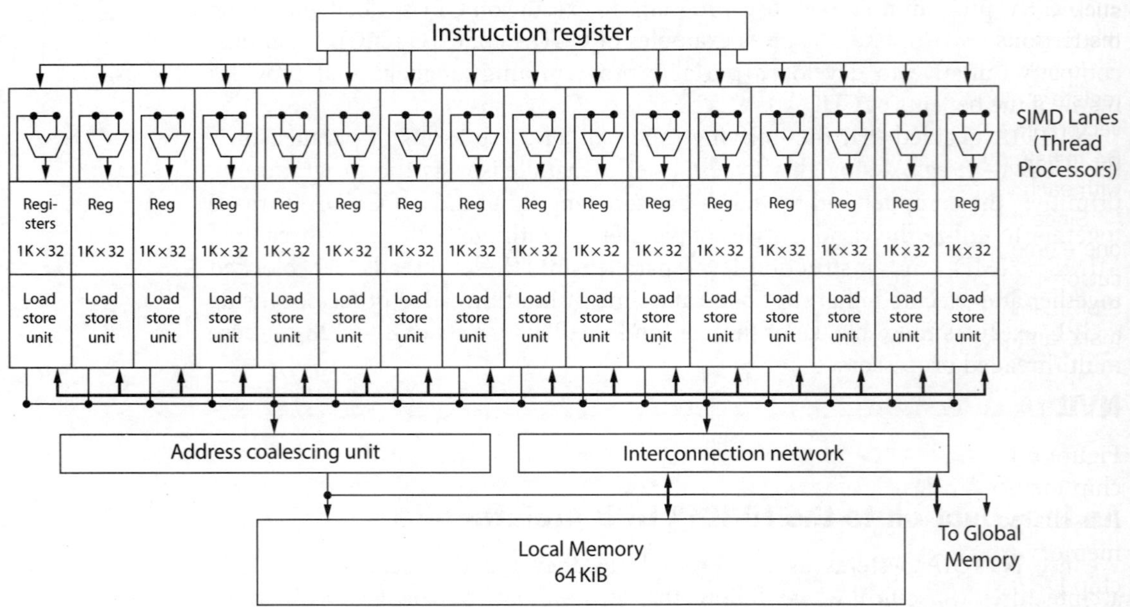

FIGURE 6.9 Simplified block diagram of the datapath of a multithreaded SIMD Processor. It has 16 SIMD lanes. The SIMD Thread Scheduler has many independent SIMD threads that it chooses from to run on this processor.

SIMD processor. It is identical to a hardware thread scheduler in a traditional multithreaded processor (see Section 6.4), except that it is scheduling threads of SIMD instructions. Thus, GPU hardware has two levels of hardware schedulers:

1. The *Thread Block Scheduler* that assigns blocks of threads to multithreaded SIMD processors, and

2. the SIMD Thread Scheduler within a SIMD processor, which schedules when SIMD threads should run.

The SIMD instructions of these threads are 32 wide, so each thread of SIMD instructions would compute 32 of the elements of the computation. Since the thread consists of SIMD instructions, the SIMD processor must have parallel functional units to perform the operation. We call them *SIMD Lanes*, and they are quite similar to the Vector Lanes in Section 6.3.

Elaboration: Each 32-wide thread of SIMD instructions is mapped to 16 SIMD Lanes, so each SIMD instruction in a thread of SIMD instructions takes two clock cycles to complete. Each thread of SIMD instructions is executed in lock step. Staying with the analogy of a SIMD processor as a vector processor, you could say that it has 16 lanes, and the vector length would be 32. This wide but shallow nature is why we use the term SIMD processor instead of vector processor, as it is more intuitive.

Since by definition the threads of SIMD instructions are independent, the SIMD Thread Scheduler can pick whatever thread of SIMD instructions is ready, and need not stick with the next SIMD instruction in the sequence within a single thread. Thus, using the terminology of Section 6.4, it uses fine-grained multithreading.

To hold these memory elements, a SIMD processor has an impressive 32,768 32-bit registers. Just like a vector processor, these registers are divided logically across the vector lanes or, in this case, SIMD Lanes. Each SIMD Thread is limited to no more than 64 registers, so you might think of a SIMD Thread as having up to 64 vector registers, with each vector register having 32 elements and each element being 32 bits wide.

Since it has 16 SIMD Lanes, each contains 2048 registers. Each CUDA Thread gets one element of each of the vector registers. Note that a CUDA thread is just a vertical cut of a thread of SIMD instructions, corresponding to one element executed by one SIMD Lane. Beware that CUDA Threads are very different from POSIX threads; you can't make arbitrary system calls or synchronize arbitrarily in a CUDA Thread.

NVIDIA GPU Memory Structures

Figure 6.10 shows the memory structures of an NVIDIA GPU. We call the on-chip memory that is local to each multithreaded SIMD processor *Local Memory*. It is shared by the SIMD Lanes within a multithreaded SIMD processor, but this memory is not shared between multithreaded SIMD processors. We call the off-chip DRAM shared by the whole GPU and all thread blocks *GPU Memory*.

Rather than rely on large caches to contain the whole working sets of an application, GPUs traditionally use smaller streaming caches and rely on extensive multithreading of threads of SIMD instructions to hide the long latency to DRAM,

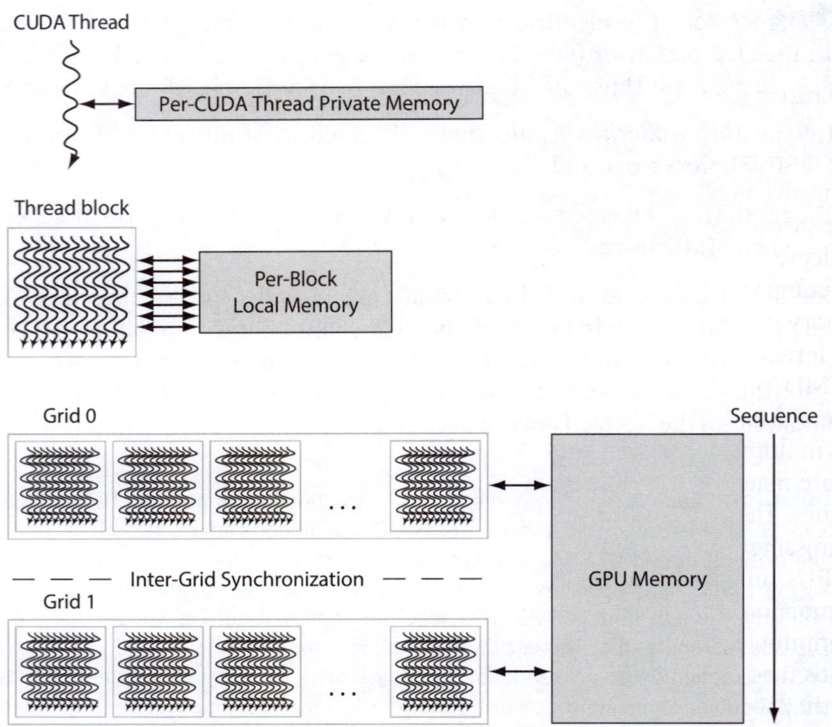

FIGURE 6.10 GPU Memory structures. GPU Memory is shared by the vectorized loops. All threads of SIMD instructions within a thread block share Local Memory.

since their working sets can be hundreds of megabytes. Thus, they will not fit in the last level cache of a multicore microprocessor. Given the use of hardware multithreading to hide DRAM latency, the chip area used for caches in system processors is spent instead on computing resources and on the large number of registers to hold the state of the many threads of SIMD instructions.

Elaboration: While hiding memory latency is the underlying philosophy, note that the latest GPUs and vector processors have added caches. They are thought of as either bandwidth filters to reduce demands on GPU Memory or as accelerators for the few variables whose latency cannot be hidden by multithreading. Local memory for stack frames, function calls, and register spilling is a good match to caches, since latency matters when calling a function. Caches can also save energy, since on-chip cache accesses take much less energy than accesses to multiple, external DRAM chips.

Putting GPUs into Perspective

At a high level, multicore computers with SIMD instruction extensions do share similarities with GPUs. Figure 6.11 summarizes the similarities and differences. Both are MIMDs whose processors use multiple SIMD lanes, although GPUs have more processors and many more lanes. Both use hardware multithreading to improve processor utilization, although GPUs have hardware support for many more threads. Both use caches, although GPUs use smaller streaming caches and multicore computers use large multilevel caches that try to contain whole working sets completely. Both use a 64-bit address space, although the physical main memory is much smaller in GPUs. While GPUs support memory protection at the page level, they do not yet support demand paging.

SIMD processors are also similar to vector processors. The multiple SIMD processors in GPUs act as independent MIMD cores, just as many vector computers have multiple vector processors. This view would consider the Volta V100 as an 80-core machine with hardware support for multithreading, where each core has 16 lanes. The biggest difference is multithreading, which is fundamental to GPUs and missing from most vector processors.

GPUs and CPUs do not go back in computer architecture genealogy to a common ancestor; there is no Missing Link that explains both. As a result of this uncommon heritage, GPUs have not used the terms common in the computer architecture community, which has led to confusion about what GPUs are and how they work. To help resolve the confusion, Figure 6.12 (from left to right) lists the more descriptive term used in this section, the closest term from mainstream computing, the official NVIDIA GPU term in case you are interested, and then a short description of the term. This "GPU Rosetta Stone" may help relate this section and ideas to more conventional GPU descriptions, such as those found in Appendix C.

While GPUs are moving toward mainstream computing, they can't abandon their responsibility to continue to excel at graphics. Thus, the design of GPUs may

Feature	Multicore with SIMD	GPU
SIMD processors	8 to 32	15 to 128
SIMD lanes/processor	2 to 4	8 to 16
Multithreading hardware support for SIMD threads	2 to 4	16 to 32
Largest cache size	48 MiB	6 MiB
Size of memory address	64-bit	64-bit
Size of main memory	64 GiB to 1024 GiB	4 GiB to 16 GiB
Memory protection at level of page	Yes	Yes
Demand paging	Yes	No
Cache coherent	Yes	No

FIGURE 6.11 Similarities and differences between multicore with Multimedia SIMD extensions and recent GPUs.

Type	More descriptive name	Closest old term outside of GPUs	Official CUDA/ NVIDIA GPU term	Book definition
Program abstractions	Vectorizable Loop	Vectorizable Loop	Grid	A vectorizable loop, executed on the GPU, made up of one or more Thread Blocks (bodies of vectorized loop) that can execute in parallel.
	Body of Vectorized Loop	Body of a (Strip-Mined) Vectorized Loop	Thread Block	A vectorized loop executed on a multithreaded SIMD Processor, made up of one or more threads of SIMD instructions. They can communicate via Local Memory.
	Sequence of SIMD Lane Operations	One iteration of a Scalar Loop	CUDA Thread	A vertical cut of a thread of SIMD instructions corresponding to one element executed by one SIMD Lane. Result is stored depending on mask and predicate register.
Machine object	A Thread of SIMD Instructions	Thread of Vector Instructions	Warp	A traditional thread, but it contains just SIMD instructions that are executed on a multithreaded SIMD Processor. Results stored depending on a per-element mask.
	SIMD Instruction	Vector Instruction	PTX Instruction	A single SIMD instruction executed across SIMD Lanes.
Processing hardware	Multithreaded SIMD Processor	(Multithreaded) Vector Processor	Streaming Multiprocessor	A multithreaded SIMD Processor executes threads of SIMD instructions, independent of other SIMD Processors.
	Thread Block Scheduler	Scalar Processor	Giga Thread Engine	Assigns multiple Thread Blocks (bodies of vectorized loop) to multithreaded SIMD Processors.
	SIMD Thread Scheduler	Thread scheduler in a Multithreaded CPU	Warp Scheduler	Hardware unit that schedules and issues threads of SIMD instructions when they are ready to execute; includes a scoreboard to track SIMD Thread execution.
	SIMD Lane	Vector lane	Thread Processor	A SIMD Lane executes the operations in a thread of SIMD instructions on a single element. Results stored depending on mask.
Memory hardware	GPU Memory	Main Memory	Global Memory	DRAM memory accessible by all multithreaded SIMD Processors in a GPU.
	Local Memory	Local Memory	Shared Memory	Fast local SRAM for one multithreaded SIMD Processor, unavailable to other SIMD Processors.
	SIMD Lane Registers	Vector Lane Registers	Thread Processor Registers	Registers in a single SIMD Lane allocated across a full thread block (body of vectorized loop).

FIGURE 6.12 Quick guide to GPU terms. We use the first column for hardware terms. Four groups cluster these 12 terms. From top to bottom: Program Abstractions, Machine Objects, Processing Hardware, and Memory Hardware.

make more sense when architects ask, given the hardware invested to do graphics well, how can we supplement it to improve the performance of a wider range of applications?

GPUs are the first example of accelerators justified by improving the performance of a single domain, in this case computer graphics. The next section gives more examples, with the domain of machine learning (ML) getting the most attention.

True or false: GPUs rely on graphics DRAM chips to reduce memory latency and thereby increase performance on graphics applications.

6.7   Domain Specific Architectures

The combination of the slowing of Moore's Law, the end of Dennard scaling, and the practical limits to multicore performance due to Amdahl's Law moved the prevailing wisdom that the only path left to improved performance and energy efficiency is **domain specific architectures (DSAs)**. Like GPUs, DSAs do only a narrow range of tasks, but they do them extremely well. Thus, just as the field switched from uniprocessors to multiprocessors in the past decade out of necessity, desperation is the reason architects are now working on DSAs.

domain specific architecture A special purpose computer tailored to an application domain, in contrast to a general-purpose computer

The new normal is that a computer will consist of standard processors to run conventional large programs such as operating systems along with domain-specific processors. We expect that computers will be much more heterogeneous than the homogeneous multicore chips of the past. This section, new to this book, is based on a new 80-page chapter on DSAs in *Computer Architecture: A Quantitative Approach*, 6th edition, if you are interested in going into greater depth.

DSAs follow five principles:

1. *Use dedicated memories to minimize the distance over which data is moved.* The many levels of caches in general-purpose microprocessors use a great deal of area and energy trying to move data optimally for a program. For example, a two-way set associative cache uses 2.5 times as much energy as an equivalent software-controlled scratchpad memory. By definition, the compiler writers and programmers of DSAs understand their domain, so there is no need for the hardware to try to move data for them. Instead, data movement is reduced with software-controlled memories that are dedicated to and tailored for specific functions within the domain.

2. *Invest the resources saved from dropping advanced microarchitectural optimizations into more arithmetic units or bigger memories.* Architects turned the bounty from Moore's Law into the resource-intensive optimizations for CPUs and GPUs: out-of-order execution, speculation, multithreading, multiprocessing, prefetching, multilevel caches, and so on. Given the superior understanding of program execution in these narrower domains, these resources are much better spent on more processing units or larger on-chip memories.

3. *Use the easiest form of parallelism that matches the domain.* Target domains for DSAs almost always have inherent parallelism. A key decision for a DSA is how to take advantage of that parallelism and how to expose it to software. The goal is to design the DSA around the natural granularity of the parallelism of the domain and expose that parallelism simply in the programming model. For example, with respect to data-level parallelism, if

SIMD works in the domain, it is certainly easier for the programmer and the compiler writer than MIMD. Similarly, if VLIW can express the instruction-level parallelism for the domain, the design can be smaller and more energy-efficient than out-of-order execution.

4. *Reduce data size and type to the simplest needed for the domain.* Applications in many domains are memory-bound, so you can increase the effective memory bandwidth and on-chip memory utilization by using narrower data types. Narrower and simpler data also lets you pack more arithmetic units into the same chip area or in the same energy budget.

5. *Use a domain-specific programming language to port code to the DSA.* A classic challenge for special-purpose architectures is getting applications to run on your novel architecture. Fortunately, domain-specific programming languages became popular even before architects were forced to switch their attention to DSAs, such as Halide for vision processing and TensorFlow for ML. Raising the level of programming abstraction makes porting applications to a DSA much more feasible.

Examples of domains that have been accelerated beyond graphics include bioinformatics, image processing, and simulation, but the most popular by far has been *artificial intelligence (AI)*. Instead of building AI as a large set of logical rules, in the past decade the focus switched to ML from example data as the most promising path to AI. The amount of data and computation needed to learn was much greater than thought. The warehouse-scale computers (WSCs) of this century, which harvest and store peta-bytes of information found on the Internet from the billions of users and their smart phones, supply the ample data. We also underestimated the amount of computation needed to learn from the massive data, but GPUs—which have excellent single-precision floating-point cost-performance—embedded in the thousands of servers of WSCs deliver sufficient computing.

One part of ML, called *deep neural networks* (DNNs), has been the ML star since 2012. There seems to be a new breakthrough enabled by DNNs publicized almost every month, such as in object recognition, language translation, and enabling a computer program for the first time to beat a human champion at Go.

A prominent example of a DNN DSA is Google's Tensor Processing Unit (TPUv1). Starting as far back as 2006, Google engineers had discussions about deploying GPUs, FPGAs, or custom chips in their data centers. They concluded that the few applications that could run on special hardware could be done virtually for free using the excess capacity of the large data centers, and it is hard to improve on free. The conversation changed in 2013 when it was projected that if people used voice search for 3 minutes a day using speech recognition DNNs, it would have required Google's data centers to double in order to meet computation demands. That would be very expensive and time-consuming to satisfy with conventional CPUs. Google started a high-priority project to quickly produce a custom chip for DNNs. The goal was to improve cost-performance 10-fold over CPUs or GPUs. Given this urgent mandate, the TPU was designed, verified, built, and deployed in data centers in only 15 months. If you use Google applications, you have been using TPUv1s, as they have been deployed since 2015.

Figure 6.13 shows the block diagram of the TPUv1. The internal blocks are typically connected together by 256-byte-wide paths. Starting in the upper right corner, the Matrix Multiply Unit is the heart of the TPU. It follows the DSA guideline of investing the resources saved from dropping CPU features into more arithmetic units, as it contains an array of 256 × 256 ALUs. That is 250 times as many ALUs as a contemporary server CPU and 25 times as many as a contemporary GPU. Using SIMD parallelism for the 65,536 ALUs follows the guideline of using the simplest form of parallelism to fit the domain. Moreover, TPUv1 reduces the data size and type to 8-bit and 16-bit integers from 32-bit floating-point type used in the contemporary GPU, which is sufficient for this DNN domain. Following the guideline utilizing dedicated memories, the matrix unit products are collected in the 4 MiB of Accumulators and the intermediate results are held in the 24 MiB Unified Buffer, which can serve as inputs to the Matrix Multiply Unit. TPUv1 has almost four times the on-chip memory of the equivalent GPU. Finally, it is programmed using TensorFlow, which simplifies porting DNN applications to this DSA.

The TPUv1 clock rate is 700 MHz, which despite the modest clock rate gives 65,536 ALUs yield a peak performance of 90 Tera-operations per second. The die

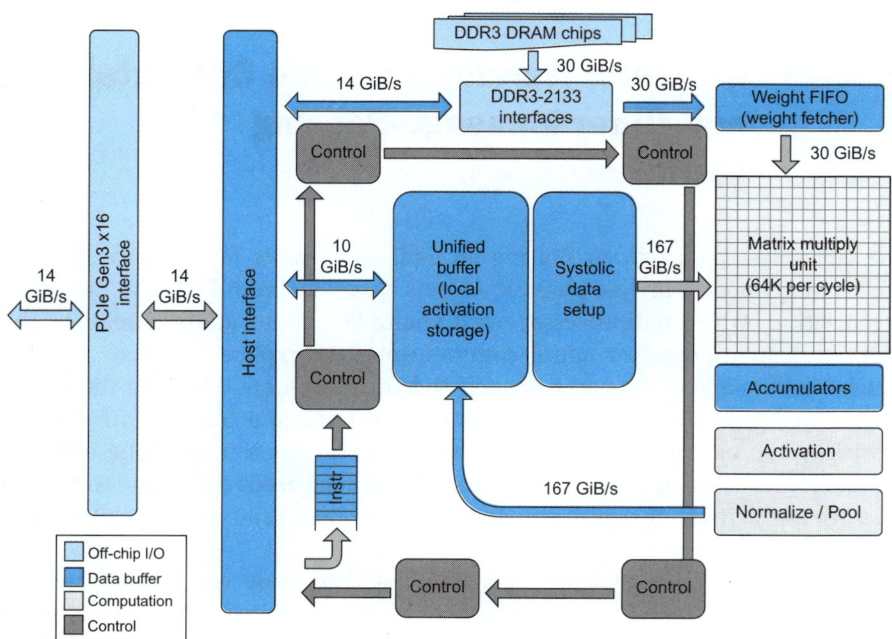

FIGURE 6.13 TPUv1 Block Diagram. The main computation part is the Matrix Multiply Unit in the upper right corner. Its inputs are the Weight FIFO and the Unified Buffer, and its output is the Accumulators. The 24 MiB Unified Buffer is almost a third of the TPUv1 die, and the Matrix Multiply Unit with 65,536 multiple-accumulate ALUs is a quarter, so the datapath is nearly two-thirds of the TPUv1 die. For CPUs, multilevel caches are often two-thirds of the die.

area is less than half the size of a contemporary CPU or GPU, and at 75 W, it is less than half their power.

Using the average of six production DNN applications, TPUv1 is 29.2 times as fast as a contemporary CPU and 15.3 times as fast as a contemporary GPU. In a datacenter, we care about cost-performance as well as performance. The best measure of datacenter cost is total cost of ownership (TCO): the cost of purchase plus the cost of operation over several years for power, cooling, and space. Indeed, the original goal for TPUv1 was 10 times the performance per TCO dollar of CPUs or GPUs. Alas, TCO numbers are closely guarded secrets and so unavailable for comparisons. The good news is that TCO is correlated with power, which is available. TPUv1 has 29 times the performance per Watt of the contemporary GPUs and 83 times the performance per Watt of contemporary CPUs, thereby overshooting its original target.

We return to more traditional architectures in the next section, introducing parallel processors where each processor has its own private address space, which makes it much easier to build much larger systems. The Internet services that you use every day depend on these large-scale systems, and Google does indeed use these large-scale systems to deploy its TPUv1s.

 True or False: DSAs are more effective than CPUs or GPUs in their domains primarily because you can justify using a much larger die for a domain.

6.8

Clusters, Warehouse Scale Computers, and Other Message-Passing Multiprocessors

message passing
Communicating between multiple processors by explicitly sending and receiving information.

send message routine
A routine used by a processor in machines with private memories to pass a message to another processor.

receive message routine
A routine used by a processor in machines with private memories to accept a message from another processor.

The alternative approach to sharing an address space is for the processors to each have their own private physical address space. Figure 6.14 shows the classic organization of a multiprocessor with multiple private address spaces. This alternative multiprocessor must communicate via explicit **message passing**, which traditionally is the name of such style of computers. Provided the system has routines to **send** and **receive messages**, coordination is built in with message passing, since one processor knows when a message is sent, and the receiving processor knows when a message arrives. If the sender needs confirmation that the message has arrived, the receiving processor can then send an acknowledgment message back to the sender.

There have been several attempts to build large-scale computers based on high-performance message-passing networks, and they do offer better absolute communication performance than clusters built using local area networks. Indeed, many supercomputers today use custom networks. The problem is that they are usually much more expensive than local area networks like Ethernet. Few applications today outside of high performance computing can justify the higher communication performance, given that costs are usually much higher.

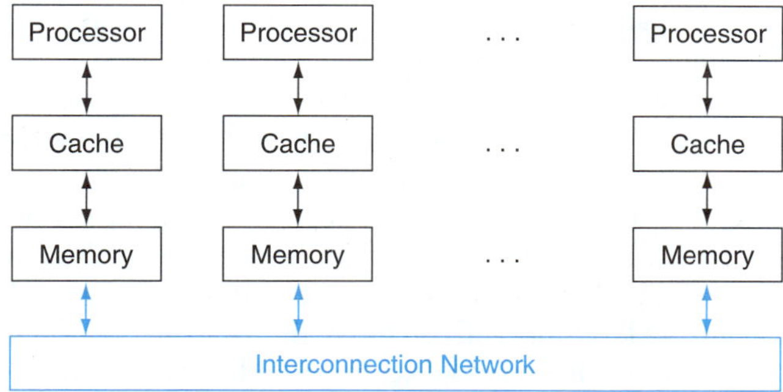

FIGURE 6.14 Classic organization of a multiprocessor with multiple private address spaces, traditionally called a message-passing multiprocessor. Note that unlike the SMP in Figure 6.7, the interconnection network is not between the caches and memory but is instead between processor-memory nodes.

Hardware/ Software Interface

Computers that rely on message passing for communication rather than cache coherent shared memory are much easier for hardware designers to build (see Section 5.8). There is an advantage for programmers as well, in that communication is explicit, which means there are fewer performance surprises than with the implicit communication in cache-coherent shared memory computers. The downside for programmers is that it's harder to port a sequential program to a message-passing computer, since every communication must be identified in advance or the program doesn't work. Cache-coherent shared memory allows the hardware to figure out what data needs to be communicated, which makes porting easier. There are differences of opinion as to which is the shortest path to high performance, given the pros and cons of implicit communication, but there is no confusion in the marketplace today. Multicore microprocessors use shared physical memory and nodes of a cluster communicate with each other using message passing.

Some concurrent applications run well on parallel hardware, independent of whether it offers shared addresses or message passing. In particular, task-level parallelism and applications with little communication—like Web search, mail servers, and file servers—do not require shared addressing to run well. As a result, **clusters** have become the most widespread example today of the message-passing parallel computer. Given the separate memories, each node of a cluster runs a distinct copy of the operating system. In contrast, the cores inside a microprocessor are connected using a high-speed network inside the chip, using a single operating system, and a multichip shared-memory system uses the memory interconnect for communication. The memory interconnect has higher bandwidth and lower latency, allowing much better communication performance for shared memory multiprocessors.

clusters Collections of computers connected via I/O over standard network switches to form a message-passing multiprocessor.

The weakness of separate memories for user memory from a parallel programming perspective turns into a strength in system dependability (see Section 5.5). Since a cluster consists of independent computers connected through a local area network, it is much easier to replace a computer without bringing down the system in a cluster than in an shared memory multiprocessor. Fundamentally, the shared address means that it is difficult to isolate a processor and replace it without heroic work by the operating system and in the physical design of the server. It is also easy for clusters to scale down gracefully when a server fails, thereby improving **dependability**. Since the cluster software is a layer that runs on top of the local operating systems running on each computer, it is much easier to disconnect and replace a broken computer.

Given that clusters are constructed from whole computers and independent, scalable networks, this isolation also makes it easier to expand the system without bringing down the application that runs on top of the cluster.

Their lower cost, higher availability, and rapid, incremental expandability make clusters attractive to service Internet providers, despite their poorer communication performance when compared to large-scale shared memory multiprocessors. The search engines that hundreds of millions of us use every day depend upon this technology. Amazon, Facebook, Google, Microsoft, and others all have multiple datacenters each with clusters of tens of thousands of servers. Clearly, the use of multiple processors in Internet service companies has been hugely successful.

Warehouse-Scale Computers

Anyone can build a fast CPU. The trick is to build a fast system.

Seymour Cray, considered the father of the supercomputer.

Internet services, such as those described above, necessitated the construction of new buildings to house, power, and cool 50,000 servers. Although they may be classified as just large clusters, their architecture and operation are more sophisticated. They act as one giant computer and cost on the order of $150M for the building, the electrical and cooling infrastructure, the servers, and the networking equipment that connects and houses 50,000 servers. We consider them a new class of computer, called Warehouse-Scale Computers (WSC).

Hardware/ Software Interface

The most popular framework for batch processing in a WSC is MapReduce [Dean, 2008] and its open-source twin Hadoop. Inspired by the Lisp functions of the same name, Map first applies a programmer-supplied function to each logical input record. Map runs on thousands of servers to produce an intermediate result of key-value pairs. Reduce collects the output of those distributed tasks and collapses them using another programmer-defined function. With appropriate software support, both are highly parallel yet easy to understand and to use. Within 30 minutes, a novice programmer can run a MapReduce task on thousands of servers.

For example, one MapReduce program calculates the number of occurrences of every English word in a large collection of documents. Below is a simplified version of that program, which shows just the inner loop and assumes just one occurrence of all English words found in a document:

```
map(String key, String value):
    // key: document name
    // value: document contents
    for each word w in value:
    EmitIntermediate(w, "1"); // Produce list of all words
    reduce(String key, Iterator values):
// key: a word
// values: a list of counts
    int result = 0;
    for each v in values:
    result += ParseInt(v); // get integer from key-value pair
    Emit(AsString(result));
```

The function `EmitIntermediate` used in the Map function emits each word in the document and the value one. Then the Reduce function sums all the values per word for each document using `ParseInt()` to get the number of occurrences per word in all documents. The MapReduce runtime environment schedules map tasks and reduce tasks to the servers of a WSC.

At this extreme scale, which requires innovation in power distribution, cooling, monitoring, and operations, the WSC is a modern descendant of the 1970s supercomputers—making Seymour Cray the godfather of today's WSC architects. His extreme computers handled computations that could be done nowhere else, but were so expensive that only a few companies could afford them. This time the target is providing information technology for the world instead of high performance computing for scientists and engineers. Hence, WSCs surely play a more important societal role today than Cray's supercomputers did in the past.

While they share some common goals with servers, WSCs have three major distinctions:

1. *Ample, easy parallelism*: A concern for a server architect is whether the applications in the targeted marketplace have enough parallelism to justify the amount of parallel hardware and whether the cost is too high for sufficient communication hardware to exploit this parallelism. A WSC architect has no such concern. First, batch applications like MapReduce benefit from the large number of independent data sets that need independent processing, such as billions of Web pages from a Web crawl. Second, interactive Internet service applications, also known as **Software as a Service (SaaS)**, can benefit from millions of independent users of interactive Internet services. Reads and writes are rarely dependent in SaaS, so SaaS rarely needs to synchronize. For example, search uses a read-only index and email is normally reading and writing independent information. We call this type of easy parallelism *Request-Level Parallelism*, as many independent efforts can proceed in parallel naturally with little need for communication or synchronization.

software as a service (SaaS) Rather than selling software that is installed and run on customers' own computers, software is run at a remote site and made available over the Internet typically via a Web interface to customers. SaaS customers are charged based on use versus on ownership.

2. *Operational Costs Count*: Traditionally, server architects design their systems for peak performance within a cost budget and worry about energy only to make sure they don't exceed the cooling capacity of their enclosure. They usually ignored operational costs of a server, assuming that they pale in comparison to purchase costs. WSC have longer lifetimes—the building and electrical and cooling infrastructure are often amortized over 10 or 20 years—so the operational costs add up: energy, power distribution, and cooling represent more than 30% of the costs of a WSC over 10 years.

3. *Scale and the Opportunities/Problems Associated with Scale*: To construct a single WSC, you must purchase 50,000 servers along with the supporting infrastructure, which means volume discounts. Hence, WSCs are so massive internally that you get economy of scale even if there are not many WSCs. These economies of scale led to *cloud computing*, as the lower per unit costs of a WSC meant that cloud companies could rent servers at a profitable rate and still be below what it costs outsiders to do it themselves. The flip side of the economic opportunity of scale is the need to cope with the failure frequency of scale. Even if a server had a Mean Time To Failure of an amazing 25 years (200,000 hours), the WSC architect would need to design for 5 server failures every day. Section 5.15 mentioned annualized disk failure rate (AFR) was measured at Google at 2% to 4%. If there were 4 disks per server and their annual failure rate was 4%, the WSC architect should expect to see one disk fail every *hour*. Thus, fault tolerance is even more important for the WSC architect than the server architect .

The economies of scale uncovered by WSC have realized the long dreamed of goal of computing as a utility. Cloud computing means anyone anywhere with good ideas, a business model, and a credit card can tap thousands of servers to deliver their vision almost instantly around the world.

To put the growth rate of cloud computing into perspective, in 2012 Amazon Web Services (AWS) announced that it adds enough new server capacity *every day* to support all of Amazon's global infrastructure as of 2003, when Amazon was a $5.2Bn annual revenue enterprise with 6000 employees. In 2020, the majority of the profits of Amazon come from cloud computing despite it representing only 10% of Amazon's revenues. AWS is growing at 40% annually.

Now that we understand the importance of message-passing multiprocessors, especially for cloud computing, we next cover ways to connect the nodes of a WSC together. Thanks to the increasing number of cores per chip, we now need networks inside a chip as well, so these topologies are important in the small as well as in the large.

Elaboration: The MapReduce framework shuffles and sorts the key-value pairs at the end of the Map phase to produce groups that all share the same key. These groups are then passed to the Reduce phase.

Elaboration: Another form of large scale computing is *grid computing*, where the computers are spread across large areas, and then the programs that run across them must communicate via long haul networks. The most popular and unique form of grid computing was pioneered by the SETI@home project. As millions of PCs are idle at any one time doing nothing useful, they could be harvested and put to good uses if someone developed software that could run on those computers and then gave each PC an independent piece of the problem to work on. The first example was the Search for *ExtraTerrestrial Intelligence* (SETI), which was launched at UC Berkeley in 1999. Over 5 million computer users in more than 200 countries have signed up for SETI@home, with more than 50% outside the US. In June 2013, the average performance of the SETI@home grid was 668 PetaFLOPS, 50 times faster than the best supercomputer of 2013.

1. True or false: Like SMPs, message-passing computers rely on locks for synchronization.

2. True or false: Clusters have separate memories and thus need many copies of the operating system.

Check Yourself

<table><tr><td>**6.9**</td><td># Introduction to Multiprocessor Network Topologies</td></tr></table>

Multicore chips require on-chip networks to connect cores together, and clusters require local area networks to connect servers together. This section reviews the pros and cons of different interconnection network topologies.

Network costs include the number of switches, the number of links on a switch to connect to the network, the width (number of bits) per link, and length of the links when the network is mapped into silicon. For example, some cores or servers may be adjacent and others may be on the other side of the chip or the other side of the datacenter. Network performance is multifaceted as well. It includes the latency on an unloaded network to send and receive a message, the throughput in terms of the maximum number of messages that can be transmitted in a given time period, delays caused by contention for a portion of the network, and variable performance depending on the pattern of communication. Another obligation of the network may be fault tolerance, since systems may be required to operate in the presence of broken components. Finally, in this era of energy-limited systems, the energy efficiency of different organizations may trump other concerns.

Networks are normally drawn as graphs, with each edge of the graph representing a link of the communication network. In the figures in this section, the processor-memory node is shown as a black square and the switch is shown as a colored circle. We assume here that all links are *bidirectional*; that is, information can flow in either direction. All networks consist of *switches* whose links go to processor-memory nodes and to other switches. The first network connects a sequence of nodes together:

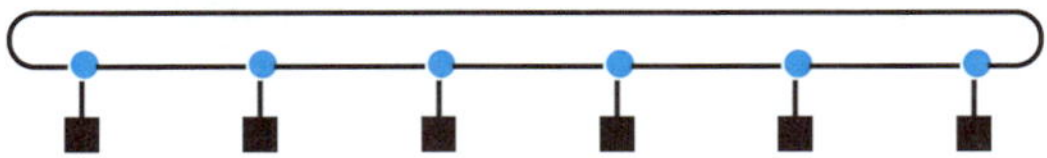

This topology is called a *ring*. Since some nodes are not directly connected, some messages will have to hop along intermediate nodes until they arrive at the *final* destination.

Unlike a bus—a shared set of wires that allows broadcasting to all connected devices—a ring is capable of many simultaneous transfers.

Because there are numerous topologies to choose from, performance metrics are needed to distinguish these designs. Two are popular. The first is *total* **network bandwidth**, which is the bandwidth of each link multiplied by the number of links. This represents the peak bandwidth. For the ring network above, with P processors, the total network bandwidth would be P times the bandwidth of one link; the total network bandwidth of a bus is just the bandwidth of that bus.

To balance this best bandwidth case, we include another metric that is closer to the worst case: the **bisection bandwidth**. This metric is calculated by dividing the machine into two halves. Then you sum the bandwidth of the links that cross that imaginary dividing line. The bisection bandwidth of a ring is two times the link bandwidth. It is one times the link bandwidth for the bus. If a single link is as fast as the bus, the ring is only twice as fast as a bus in the worst case, but it is P times faster in the best case.

Since some network topologies are not symmetric, the question arises of where to draw the imaginary line when bisecting the machine. Bisection bandwidth is a worst-case metric, so the answer is to choose the division that yields the most pessimistic network performance. Stated alternatively, calculate all possible bisection bandwidths and pick the smallest. We take this pessimistic view because parallel programs are often limited by the weakest link in the communication chain.

At the other extreme from a ring is a **fully connected network**, where every processor has a bidirectional link to every other processor. For fully connected networks, the total network bandwidth is $P \times (P-1)/2$, and the bisection bandwidth is $(P/2)^2$.

The tremendous improvement in performance of fully connected networks is offset by the tremendous increase in cost. This consequence inspires engineers to invent new topologies that are between the cost of rings and the performance of fully connected networks. The evaluation of success depends in large part on the nature of the communication in the workload of parallel programs run on the computer.

The number of different topologies that have been discussed in publications would be difficult to count, but only a few have been used in commercial parallel processors. Figure 6.15 illustrates two of the popular topologies.

An alternative to placing a processor at every node in a network is to leave only the switch at some of these nodes. The switches are smaller than processor-memory-switch nodes, and thus may be packed more densely, thereby lessening distance and increasing performance. Such networks are frequently called **multistage networks** to reflect the multiple steps that a message may travel. Types of multistage networks are as numerous as single-stage networks; Figure 6.16 illustrates two of the popular multistage organizations. A **fully connected** or **crossbar network** allows any node to communicate with any other node in one pass through the network. An

---

network bandwidth　Informally, the peak transfer rate of a network; can refer to the speed of a single link or the collective transfer rate of all links in the network.

bisection bandwidth　The bandwidth between two equal parts of a multiprocessor. This measure is for a worst case split of the multiprocessor.

fully connected network　A network that connects processor-memory nodes by supplying a dedicated communication link between every node.

multistage network　A network that supplies a small switch at each node.

crossbar network　A network that allows any node to communicate with any other node in one pass through the network.

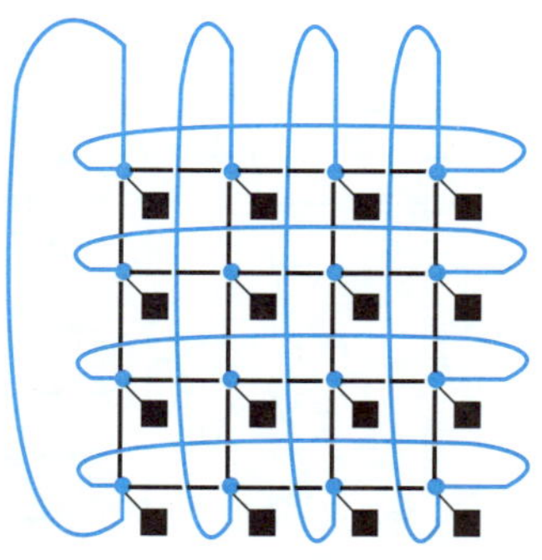
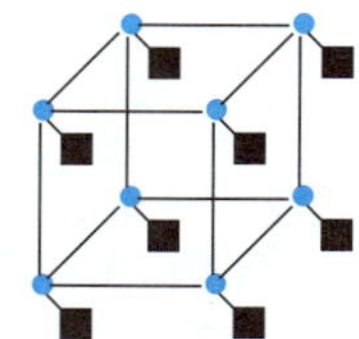

a. 2-D grid or torus of 16 nodes   b. *n*-cube tree of 8 nodes (8 = 2^3 so $n = 3$)

FIGURE 6.15 Network topologies that have appeared in commercial parallel processors. The colored circles represent switches and the black squares represent processor-memory nodes. Even though a switch has many links, generally only one goes to the processor. The Boolean n-cube topology is an n-dimensional interconnect with 2^n nodes, requiring n links per switch (plus one for the processor) and thus n nearest-neighbor nodes. Frequently, these basic topologies have been supplemented with extra arcs to improve performance and reliability.

Omega network uses less hardware than the crossbar network ($2n \log_2 n$ versus n^2 switches), but contention can occur between messages, depending on the pattern of communication. For example, the Omega network in Figure 6.16 cannot send a message from P_0 to P_6 at the same time that it sends a message from P_1 to P_4.

Implementing Network Topologies

This simple analysis of all the networks in this section ignores important practical considerations in the construction of a network. The distance of each link affects the cost of communicating at a high clock rate—generally, the longer the distance, the more expensive it is to run at a high clock rate. Shorter distances also make it easier to assign more wires to the link, as the power to drive many wires is less if the wires are short. Shorter wires are also cheaper than longer wires. Another practical limitation is that the three-dimensional drawings must be mapped onto chips that are essentially two-dimensional media. The final concern is energy. Energy concerns may force multicore chips to rely on simple grid topologies, for example. The bottom line is that topologies that appear elegant when sketched on paper may be impractical when constructed in silicon or in a datacenter.

Now that we understand the importance of clusters and have seen topologies that we can follow to connect them together, we next look at the hardware and software of the interface of the network to the processor.

True or false: For a ring with P nodes, the ratio of the total network bandwidth to the bisection bandwidth is P/2.

Check Yourself

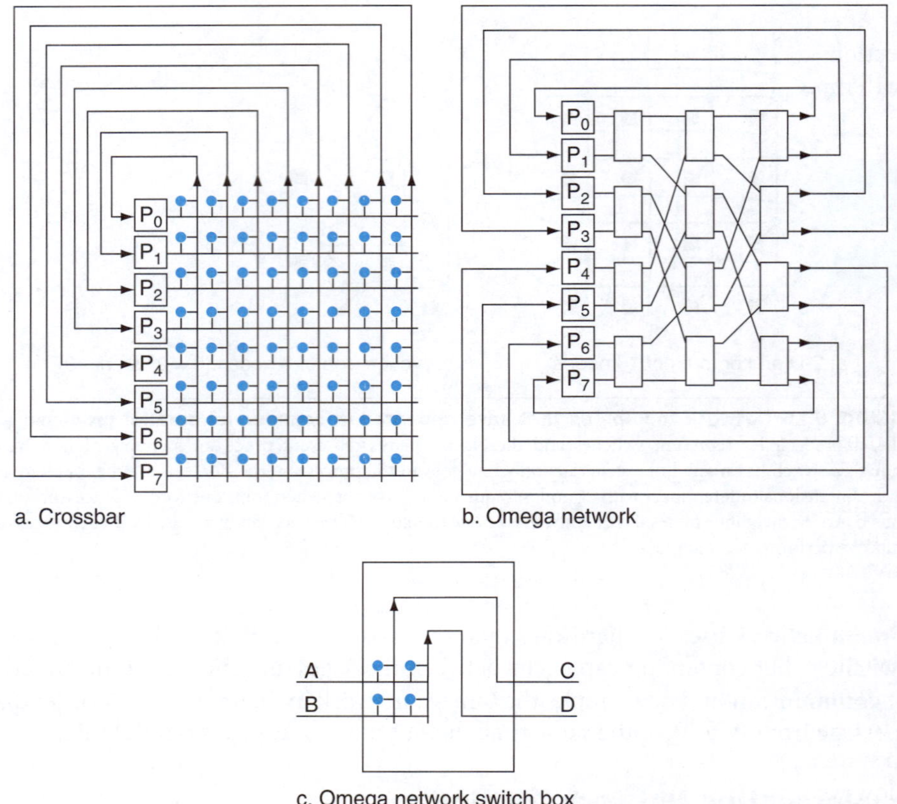

FIGURE 6.16 Popular multistage network topologies for eight nodes. The switches in these drawings are simpler than in earlier drawings because the links are unidirectional; data comes in at the left and exits out the right link. The switch box in c can pass A to C and B to D or B to C and A to D. The crossbar uses n² switches, where n is the number of processors, while the Omega network uses 2n log₂n of the large switch boxes, each of which is logically composed of four of the smaller switches. In this case, the crossbar uses 64 switches versus 12 switch boxes, or 48 switches, in the Omega network. The crossbar, however, can support any combination of messages between processors, while the Omega network cannot.

6.10   Communicating to the Outside World: Cluster Networking

This online section describes the networking hardware and software used to connect the nodes of a cluster together. The example is 10 gigabit/second Ethernet connected to the computer using *Peripheral Component Interconnect Express* (PCIe). It shows both software and hardware optimizations how to improve network performance, including zero copy messaging, user space communication, using polling instead of I/O interrupts, and hardware calculation of checksums. While the example is networking, the techniques in this section apply to storage controllers and other I/O devices as well.

After covering the performance of network at a low level of detail in this online section, the next section shows how to benchmark multiprocessors of all kinds with much higher-level programs.

6.11 Multiprocessor Benchmarks and Performance Models

As we saw in Chapter 1, benchmarking systems is always a sensitive topic, because it is a highly visible way to try to determine which system is better. The results affect not only the sales of commercial systems, but also the reputation of the designers of those systems. Hence, all participants want to win the competition, but they also want to be sure that if someone else wins, they deserve to win because they have a genuinely better system. This desire leads to rules to ensure that the benchmark results are not simply engineering tricks for that benchmark, but are instead advances that improve performance of real applications.

To avoid possible tricks, a typical rule is that you can't change the benchmark. The source code and data sets are fixed, and there is a single proper answer. Any deviation from those rules makes the results invalid.

Many multiprocessor benchmarks follow these traditions. A common exception is to be able to increase the size of the problem so that you can run the benchmark on systems with a widely different number of processors. That is, many benchmarks allow weak scaling rather than require strong scaling, even though you must take care when comparing results for programs running different problem sizes.

Figure 6.17 gives a summary of several parallel benchmarks, also described below:

- *Linpack* is a collection of linear algebra routines, and the routines for performing Gaussian elimination constitute what is known as the Linpack benchmark. The DGEMM routine in the example on page 225 represents a small fraction of the source code of the Linpack benchmark, but it accounts for most of the execution time for the benchmark. It allows weak scaling, letting the user pick any size problem. Moreover, it allows the user to rewrite Linpack in almost any form and in any language, as long as it computes the proper result and performs the same number of floating point operations for a given problem size. Twice a year, the 500 computers with the fastest Linpack performance are published at www.top500.org. The first on this list is considered by the press to be the world's fastest computer. Given the importance of energy efficiency today, the same organization also publishes a Green500 list, where they resort the Top500 list based on performance per Watt running Linpack to celebrate the most efficient supercomputer.

- *SPECrate* is a throughput metric based on the SPEC CPU benchmarks, such as SPEC CPU 2017 (see Chapter 1). Rather than report performance of the individual programs, SPECrate runs many copies of the program simultaneously. Thus, it measures task-level parallelism, as there is no

Benchmark	Scaling?	Reprogram?	Description
Linpack	Weak	Yes	Dense matrix linear algebra [Dongarra, 1979]
SPECrate	Weak	No	Independent job parallelism [Henning, 2007]
Stanford Parallel Applications for Shared Memory SPLASH 2 [Woo et al., 1995]	Strong (although offers two problem sizes)	No	Complex 1D FFT Blocked LU Decomposition Blocked Sparse Cholesky Factorization Integer Radix Sort Barnes-Hut Adaptive Fast Multipole Ocean Simulation Hierarchical Radiosity Ray Tracer Volume Renderer Water Simulation with Spatial Data Structure Water Simulation without Spatial Data Structure
NAS Parallel Benchmarks [Bailey et al., 1991]	Weak	Yes (C or Fortran only)	EP: embarrassingly parallel MG: simplified multigrid CG: unstructured grid for a conjugate gradient method FT: 3-D partial differential equation solution using FFTs IS: large integer sort
PARSEC Benchmark Suite [Bienia et al., 2008]	Weak	No	Blackscholes—Option pricing with Black-Scholes PDE Bodytrack—Body tracking of a person Canneal—Simulated cache-aware annealing to optimize routing Dedup—Next-generation compression with data deduplication Facesim—Simulates the motions of a human face Ferret—Content similarity search server Fluidanimate—Fluid dynamics for animation with SPH method Freqmine—Frequent itemset mining Streamcluster—Online clustering of an input stream Swaptions—Pricing of a portfolio of swaptions Vips—Image processing x264—H.264 video encoding
Berkeley Design Patterns [Asanovic et al., 2006]	Strong or Weak	Yes	Finite-State Machine Combinational Logic Graph Traversal Structured Grid Dense Matrix Sparse Matrix Spectral Methods (FFT) Dynamic Programming N-Body MapReduce Backtrack/Branch and Bound Graphical Model Inference Unstructured Grid

FIGURE 6.17 Examples of parallel benchmarks.

communication between the tasks. You can run as many copies of the programs as you want, so this is again a form of weak scaling.

- *SPLASH* and *SPLASH 2* (Stanford Parallel Applications for Shared Memory) were efforts by researchers at Stanford University in the 1990s to put together a parallel benchmark suite similar in goals to the SPEC CPU benchmark suite. It includes both kernels and applications, including many from the high-performance computing community. This benchmark requires strong scaling, although it comes with two data sets.

- The *NAS (NASA Advanced Supercomputing) parallel benchmarks* were another attempt from the 1990s to benchmark multiprocessors. Taken from computational fluid dynamics, they consist of five kernels. They allow weak scaling by defining a few data sets. Like Linpack, these benchmarks can be rewritten, but the rules require that the programming language can only be C or Fortran.

- The *PARSEC (Princeton Application Repository for Shared Memory Computers) benchmark suite* consists of multithreaded programs that use **Pthreads** (POSIX threads) and OpenMP (Open MultiProcessing; see Section 6.5). They focus on emerging computational domains and consist of nine applications and three kernels. Eight rely on data parallelism, three rely on pipelined parallelism, and one on unstructured parallelism.

- On the cloud front, the goal of the *Yahoo! Cloud Serving Benchmark* (YCSB) is to compare performance of cloud data services. It offers a framework that makes it easy for a client to benchmark new data services, using Cassandra and HBase as representative examples. [Cooper, 2010]

Pthreads A UNIX API for creating and manipulating threads. It is structured as a library.

The downside of such traditional restrictions to benchmarks is that innovation is chiefly limited to the architecture and compiler. Better data structures, algorithms, programming languages, and so on often cannot be used, since that would give a misleading result. The system could win because of, say, the algorithm, and not because of the hardware or the compiler.

While these guidelines are understandable when the foundations of computing are relatively stable—as they were in the 1990s and the first half of this decade— they are undesirable during a programming revolution. For this revolution to succeed, we need to encourage innovation at all levels.

Researchers at the University of California at Berkeley have advocated one approach. They identified 13 design patterns that they claim will be part of applications of the future. Frameworks or kernels implement these design patterns. Examples are sparse matrices, structured grids, finite-state machines, map reduce, and graph traversal. By keeping the definitions at a high level, they hope to encourage innovations at any level of the system. Thus, the system with the fastest sparse matrix solver is welcome to use any data structure, algorithm, and programming language, in addition to novel architectures and compilers.

While not primarily a parallel computing benchmark, MLPerf is a recent benchmark for ML that usually runs on parallel computers. It includes programs, data sets, and ground rules. New versions of the MLPerf benchmarks occur every 3 months to keep up with the rapid advances in ML. To normalize for different-sized computers, MLPerf includes the power to run the benchmarks. A novel benchmarking feature is to offer both closed and open divisions of the benchmarks. The closed division has tightly controlled rules for submission to try to ensure fair comparisons between systems. The open division encourages innovation, including better data structures, algorithms, programming systems, and so on. Open division submissions just need to perform the same task using the same data sets. We use MLPerf to evaluate DSAs in the next section.

Performance Models

A topic related to benchmarks is performance models. As we have seen with the increasing architectural diversity in this chapter—multithreading, SIMD,

GPUs, TPUs—it would be especially helpful if we had a simple model that offered insights into the performance of different architectures. It need not be perfect, just insightful.

The 3Cs for cache performance from Chapter 5 is an example performance model. It is not a perfect performance model, since it ignores potentially important factors like block size, block allocation policy, and block replacement policy. Moreover, it has quirks. For example, a miss can be ascribed due to capacity in one design and to a conflict miss in another cache of the same size. Yet 3Cs model has been popular for 30 years, because it offers insight into the behavior of programs, helping both architects and programmers improve their creations based on insights from that model.

To find such a model for parallel computers, let's start with small kernels, like those from the 13 Berkeley design patterns in Figure 6.17. While there are versions with different data types for these kernels, floating point is popular in several implementations. Hence, peak floating-point performance is a limit on the speed of such kernels on a given computer. For multicore chips, peak floating-point performance is the collective peak performance of all the cores on the chip. If there were multiple microprocessors in the system, you would multiply the peak per chip by the total number of chips.

The demands on the memory system can be estimated by dividing this peak floating-point performance by the average number of floating-point operations per byte accessed:

$$\frac{\text{Floating-Point Operations/Sec}}{\text{Floating-Point Operations/Byte}} = \text{Bytes/Sec}$$

arithmetic intensity
The ratio of floating-point operations in a program to the number of data bytes accessed by a program from main memory.

The ratio of floating-point operations per byte of memory accessed is called the **arithmetic intensity**. It can be calculated by taking the total number of floating-point operations for a program divided by the total number of data bytes transferred to main memory during program execution. Figure 6.18 shows the arithmetic intensity of several of the Berkeley design patterns from Figure 6.17.

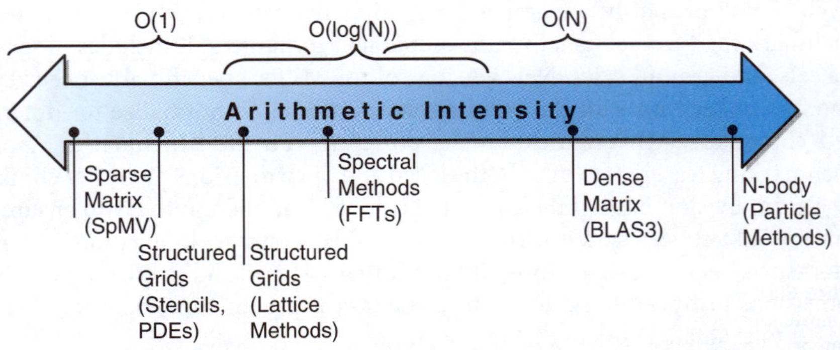

FIGURE 6.18 Arithmetic intensity, specified as the number of float-point operations to run the program divided by the number of bytes accessed in main memory [Williams, Waterman, and Patterson, 2009]. Some kernels have an arithmetic intensity that scales with problem size, such as Dense Matrix, but there are many kernels with arithmetic intensities independent of problem size. For kernels in this former case, weak scaling can lead to different results, since it puts much less demand on the memory system.

The Roofline Model

This simple model ties floating-point performance, arithmetic intensity, and memory performance together in a two-dimensional graph [Williams, Waterman, and Patterson, 2009]. Peak floating-point performance can be found using the hardware specifications mentioned above. The working sets of the kernels we consider here do not fit in on-chip caches, so peak memory performance may be defined by the memory system behind the caches. One way to find the peak memory performance is the Stream benchmark. (See the *Elaboration* on page 399 in Chapter 5).

Figure 6.19 shows the model, which is done once for a computer, not for each kernel. The vertical Y-axis is achievable floating-point performance from 0.5 to 64.0 GFLOPs/second. The horizontal X-axis is arithmetic intensity, varying from 1/8 FLOPs/DRAM byte accessed to 16 FLOPs/DRAM byte accessed. Note that the graph is a log-log scale.

For a given kernel, we can find a point on the X-axis based on its arithmetic intensity. If we draw a vertical line through that point, the performance of the kernel on that computer must lie somewhere along that line. We can plot a horizontal line showing peak floating-point performance of the computer. Obviously, the actual floating-point performance can be no higher than the horizontal line, since that is a hardware limit.

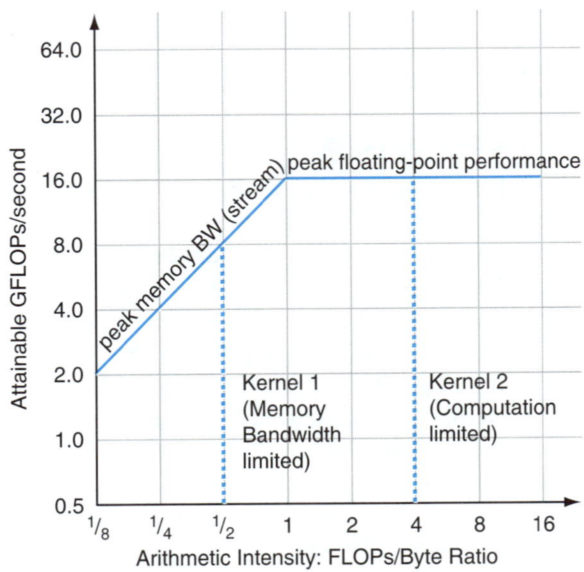

FIGURE 6.19 Roofline Model [Williams, Waterman, and Patterson, 2009]. This example has a peak floating-point performance of 16 GFLOPS/sec and a peak memory bandwidth of 16 GB/sec from the Stream benchmark. (Since Stream is actually four measurements, this line is the average of the four.) The dotted vertical line in color on the left represents Kernel 1, which has an arithmetic intensity of 0.5 FLOPs/ byte. It is limited by memory bandwidth to no more than 8 GFLOPS/sec on this Opteron X2. The dotted vertical line to the right represents Kernel 2, which has an arithmetic intensity of 4 FLOPs/byte. It is limited only computationally to 16 GFLOPS/s. This data is based on the AMD Opteron X2 (Revision F) using dual cores running at 2 GHz in a dual socket system.

How could we plot the peak memory performance, which is measured in bytes/second? Since the X-axis is FLOPs/byte and the Y-axis FLOPs/second, bytes/second is just a diagonal line in this figure. Hence, we can plot a third line that gives the maximum floating-point performance that the memory system of that computer can support for a given arithmetic intensity. We can express the limits as a formula to plot the line in the graph in Figure 6.19:

$$\text{Atainable GELOPs/sec} = \text{Min (Peak Memory BW} \times \text{Arithmetic Intensity, Peak Floating-Point Performance)}$$

The horizontal and diagonal lines give this simple model its name and indicate its value. The "roofline" sets an upper bound on performance of a kernel depending on its arithmetic intensity. Given a roofline of a computer, you can apply it repeatedly, since it doesn't vary by kernel.

If we think of arithmetic intensity as a pole that hits the roof, either it hits the slanted part of the roof, which means performance is ultimately limited by memory bandwidth, or it hits the flat part of the roof, which means performance is computationally limited. In Figure 6.19, kernel 1 is an example of the former, and kernel 2 is an example of the latter.

Note that the "ridge point," where the diagonal and horizontal roofs meet, offers an interesting insight into the computer. If it is far to the right, then only kernels with very high arithmetic intensity can achieve the maximum performance of that computer. If it is far to the left, then almost any kernel can potentially hit the maximum performance.

Comparing Two Generations of Opterons

The AMD Opteron X4 (Barcelona) with four cores is the successor to the Opteron X2 with two cores. To simplify board design, they use the same socket. Hence, they have the same DRAM channels and thus the same peak memory bandwidth. In addition to doubling the number of cores, the Opteron X4 also has twice the peak floating-point performance per core: Opteron X4 cores can issue two floating-point SSE2 instructions per clock cycle, while Opteron X2 cores issue at most one. As the two systems we're comparing have similar clock rates—2.2 GHz for Opteron X2 versus 2.3 GHz for Opteron X4—the Opteron X4 has about four times the peak floating-point performance of the Opteron X2 with the same DRAM bandwidth. The Opteron X4 also has a 2MB L3 cache, which is not found in the Opteron X2.

In Figure 6.20 the roofline models for both systems are compared. As we would expect, the ridge point moves to the right, from 1 in the Opteron X2 to 5 in the Opteron X4. Hence, to see a performance gain in the next generation, kernels need an arithmetic intensity higher than 1, or their working sets must fit in the caches of the Opteron X4.

The roofline model gives an upper bound to performance. Suppose your program is far below that bound. What optimizations should you perform, and in what order?

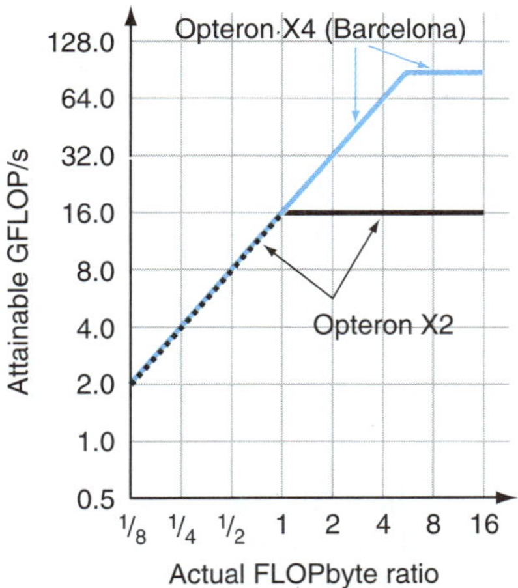

FIGURE 6.20 Roofline models of two generations of Opterons. The Opteron X2 roofline, which is the same as in Figure 6.19, is in black, and the Opteron X4 roofline is in color. The bigger ridge point of Opteron X4 means that kernels that were computationally bound on the Opteron X2 could be memory-performance bound on the Opteron X4.

To reduce computational bottlenecks, the following two optimizations can help almost any kernel:

1. *Floating-point operation mix.* Peak floating-point performance for a computer typically requires an equal number of nearly simultaneous additions and multiplications. That balance is necessary either because the computer supports a fused multiply-add instruction (see the *Elaboration* on page 230 in Chapter 3) or because the floating-point unit has an equal number of floating-point adders and floating-point multipliers. The best performance also requires that a significant fraction of the instruction mix is floating-point operations and not integer instructions.

2. *Improve* **instruction-level parallelism** *and* *apply SIMD.* For modern architectures, the highest performance comes when fetching, executing, and committing three to four instructions per clock cycle (see Section 4.11). The goal for this step is to improve the code from the compiler to increase ILP. One way is by unrolling loops, as we saw in Section 4.13. For the x86 architectures, a single AVX instruction can operate on eight double precision operands, so they should be used whenever possible (see Sections 3.7 and 3.8).

To reduce memory bottlenecks, the following two optimizations can help:

1. *Software prefetching.* Usually the highest performance requires keeping many memory operations in flight, which is easier to do by performing **predicting** accesses via software prefetch instructions rather than waiting until the data is required by the computation.

2. *Memory affinity.* Microprocessors today include a memory controller on the same chip with the microprocessor, which improves performance of the **memory hierarchy**. If the system has multiple chips, this means that some addresses go to the DRAM that is local to one chip, and the rest require accesses over the chip interconnect to access the DRAM that is local to another chip. This split results in non-uniform memory accesses, described in Section 6.5. Accessing memory through another chip lowers performance. This second optimization tries to allocate data and the threads tasked to operate on that data to the same memory-processor pair, so that the processors rarely have to access the memory of the other chips.

The roofline model can help decide which of these optimizations to perform and the order in which to perform them. We can think of each of these optimizations as a "ceiling" below the appropriate roofline, meaning that you cannot break through a ceiling without performing the associated optimization.

The computational roofline can be found from the manuals, and the memory roofline can be found from running the Stream benchmark. The computational ceilings, such as floating-point balance, can also come from the manuals for that computer. A memory ceiling, such as memory affinity, requires running experiments on each computer to determine the gap between them. The good news is that this process only need be done once per computer, for once someone characterizes a computer's ceilings, everyone can use the results to prioritize their optimizations for that computer.

Figure 6.21 adds ceilings to the roofline model in Figure 6.19, showing the computational ceilings in the top graph and the memory bandwidth ceilings on the bottom graph. Although the higher ceilings are not labeled with both optimizations, they are implied in this figure; to break through the highest ceiling, you need to have already broken through all the ones below.

The width of the gap between the ceiling and the next higher limit is the reward for trying that optimization. Thus, Figure 6.21 suggests that optimization 2, which improves ILP, has a large benefit for improving computation on that computer, and optimization 4, which improves memory affinity, has a large benefit for improving memory bandwidth on that computer.

Figure 6.22 combines the ceilings of Figure 6.21 into a single graph. The arithmetic intensity of a kernel determines the optimization region, which in turn suggests which optimizations to try. Note that the computational optimizations and the memory bandwidth optimizations overlap for much of the arithmetic intensity. Three regions are shaded differently in Figure 6.22 to indicate the different optimization strategies. For example, Kernel 2 falls in the blue trapezoid on the right, which suggests working only on the computational optimizations. Kernel 1 falls in the blue-gray parallelogram in the middle, which suggests trying both types of optimizations. Moreover, it suggests starting with optimizations 2 and 4. Note that the Kernel 1 vertical lines fall below the floating-point imbalance optimization, so optimization 1 may be unnecessary. If a kernel fell in the gray triangle on the lower left, it would suggest trying just memory optimizations.

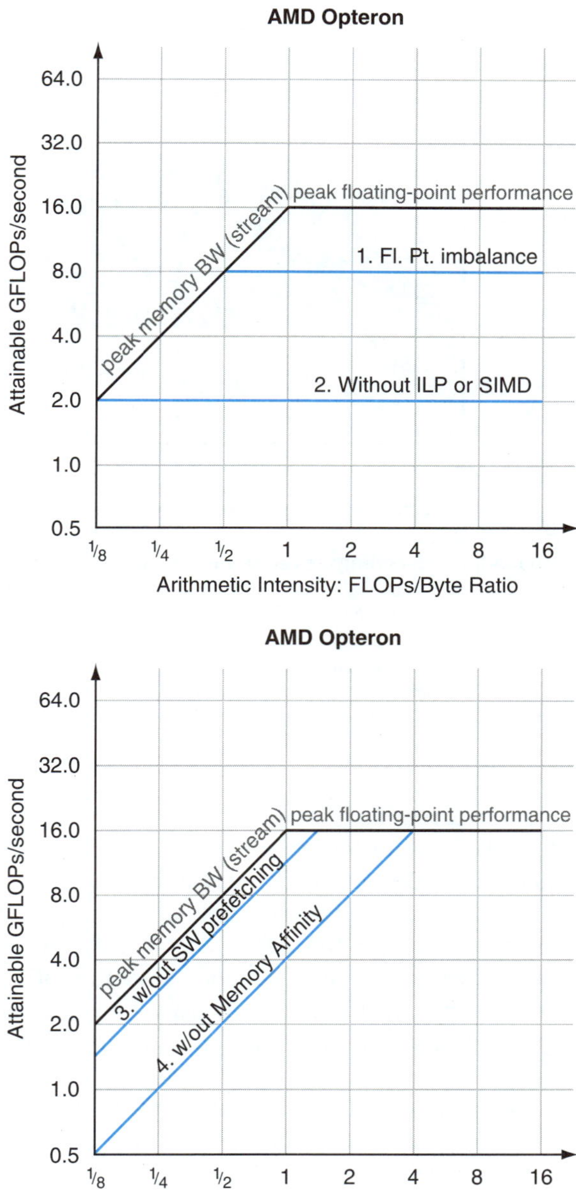

FIGURE 6.21 Roofline model with ceilings. The top graph shows the computational "ceilings" of 8 GFLOPs/sec if the floating-point operation mix is imbalanced and 2 GFLOPs/sec if the optimizations to increase ILP and SIMD are also missing. The bottom graph shows the memory bandwidth ceilings of 11 GB/sec without software prefetching and 4.8 GB/sec if memory affinity optimizations are also missing.

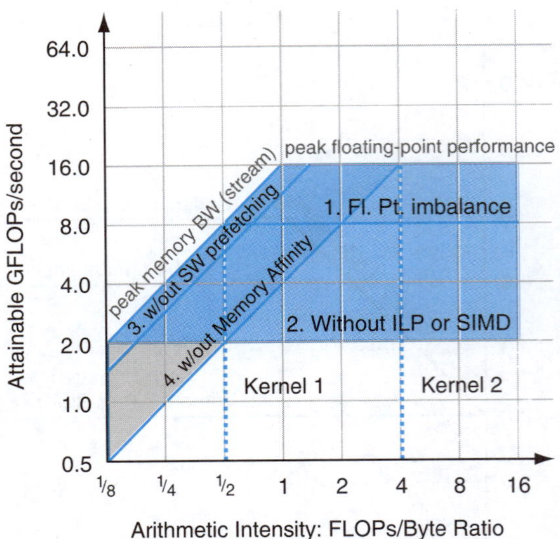

FIGURE 6.22 Roofline model with ceilings, overlapping areas shaded, and the two kernels from Figure 6.19. Kernels whose arithmetic intensity land in the blue trapezoid on the right should focus on computation optimizations, and kernels whose arithmetic intensity land in the gray triangle in the lower left should focus on memory bandwidth optimizations. Those that land in the blue-gray parallelogram in the middle need to worry about both. As Kernel 1 falls in the parallelogram in the middle, try optimizing ILP and SIMD, memory affinity, and software prefetching. Kernel 2 falls in the trapezoid on the right, so try optimizing ILP and SIMD and the balance of floating-point operations.

Thus far, we have been assuming that the arithmetic intensity is fixed, but that is not really the case. First, there are kernels where the arithmetic intensity increases with problem size, such as for Dense Matrix and N-body problems (see Figure 6.18). Indeed, this can be a reason that programmers have more success with weak scaling than with strong scaling. Second, the effectiveness of the **memory hierarchy** affects the number of accesses that go to memory, so optimizations that improve cache performance also improve arithmetic intensity. One example is improving temporal locality by unrolling loops and then grouping together statements with similar addresses. Many computers have special cache instructions that allocate data in a cache but do not first fill the data from memory at that address, since it will soon be over-written. Both these optimizations reduce memory traffic, thereby moving the arithmetic intensity pole to the right by a factor of, say, 1.5. This shift right could put the kernel in a different optimization region .

While the examples above show how to help programmers improve performance, architects can also use the model to decide where they should optimize hardware to improve performance of the kernels that they think will be important.

The next section includes the roofline model to compare the performance difference between a DSA and a GPU and to see whether these differences reflect performance of real programs.

Elaboration: The ceilings are ordered so that lower ceilings are easier to optimize. Clearly, a programmer can optimize in any order, but following this sequence reduces the chances of wasting effort on an optimization that has no benefit due to other constraints. Like the 3Cs model, as long as the roofline model delivers on insights, a model can have assumptions that may prove optimistic. For example, roofline assumes the load is balanced between all processors.

Elaboration: An alternative to the Stream benchmark is to use the raw DRAM bandwidth as the roofline. While the raw bandwidth definitely is a hard upper bound, actual memory performance is often so far from that boundary that it's not that useful. That is, no program can go close to that bound. The downside to using Stream is that very careful programming may exceed the Stream results, so the memory roofline may not be as hard a limit as the computational roofline. We stick with Stream because few programmers will be able to deliver more memory bandwidth than Stream discovers.

Elaboration: Although the roofline model shown is for multicore processors, it clearly would work for a uniprocessor as well.

True or false: The main drawback with conventional approaches to benchmarks for parallel computers is that the rules that ensure fairness also slow software innovation.

Check Yourself

6.12 Real Stuff: Benchmarking the Google TPUv3 Supercomputer and an NVIDIA Volta GPU Cluster

DNNs, introduced in Section 6.7, have two phases: *training*, which constructs accurate models, and *inference*, which serves those models. Training can take days or weeks to compute, while inference often runs in milliseconds. TPUv1 was designed for inference. This section explores how Google built a production DSA for the much harder training problem. It is based on the paper, "A Domain-Specific Supercomputer for Training Deep Neural Networks," *Communications of the ACM*, 2020 by N. P. Jouppi, D. Yoon, G. Kurian, S. Li, N. Patil, J. Laudon, C. Young, and D. A. Patterson.

DNN Training versus Inference

Let us quickly review of DNNs. Training starts with a huge training data set of known-correct (`input, result`) pairs. Pairs might be an image and what it depicts. It also starts with a neural network *model*, which transforms the input into the result through an intensive calculation of *weights*; the weights are random initially. Models are typically defined as a graph of layers, where a layer contains a linear algebra part (often a matrix multiplication or convolution using the weights) followed by a nonlinear *activation function* (often a scalar function, applied element wise; we call the results *activations*). Training "learns" weights that raise the likelihood of correctly mapping from input to result.

How do we get from random initial weights to trained weights? Current best practices use variants of *stochastic gradient descent* (*SGD*). SGD consists of much iteration of three steps: forward propagation, back-propagation, and weight update.

1. *Forward propagation* takes a randomly chosen training example, applies its inputs to the model, and runs the calculation through the layers to produce a result (which, with the random initial weights, is garbage the first time). Forward propagation is functionally similar to DNN inference, and if we were building an inference accelerator, we could stop there. For training, this is less than a third of the story. SGD next measures the difference or error between the model's result and the known good result from the training set using a *loss function*.

2. Then *back-propagation* runs the model in reverse, layer-by-layer, to produce a set of error/loss values for each layer's output. These losses measure the deviation from the desired output.

3. Last, *weight update* combines the input of each layer with the loss value to calculate a set of deltas—changes to weights—which, when added to the weights, would have resulted in nearly zero loss. Updates can have small magnitude.

Each SGD step makes a tiny adjustment to the weights that improve the model with respect to a single (`input, result`) pair. SGD gradually transforms the random initial weights into a trained model, sometimes capable of superhuman accuracy that results in articles in newspapers.

DSA Supercomputer Network

The DNN training computation appetite is essentially unlimited, thus Google chose to build a DSA supercomputer instead of clustering CPU hosts with DSA chips as was done for TPUv1. The first reason is that training time is huge. One TPUv3 chip would take *months* to train a single Google production application, so a typical application might want to use hundreds of chips. Second, DNN wisdom is that bigger data sets plus bigger machines lead to bigger breakthroughs.

The critical architectural feature of a modern supercomputer is how its chips communicate: what is the speed of a link; what is the interconnect topology; does it have centralized versus distributed switches; and so on. This choice is much easier for a DSA supercomputer, as the communication patterns are limited and known. For training, most traffic is an all-reduce over weight updates from all nodes of the machine. It turns out that all reduce can be mapped efficiently onto a 2D torus topology (see Figure 6.15a). An on-chip switch routes messages. To enable a 2D torus, the TPUv3 chip has four custom *Inter-Core Interconnect (ICI)* links, each running at 656 Gbits/s each direction. ICI enables direct connections between chips to form a supercomputer using only a small fraction of each chip.

The TPUv3 supercomputer uses a 32 × 32 2D torus (1024 chips), which is 64 links × 656 Gbits/s = 42.3 Terabits/s of bisection bandwidth. As a comparison, a separate Infiniband switch (used in CPU clusters) that connected 64 hosts (each with 16 DSA chips) has 64 ports using "only" 100 Gbit/s links and a bisection bandwidth of at most 6.4 Terabits/s. The TPUv3 supercomputer provides 6.6× the bisection bandwidth over conventional cluster switches while skipping the cost of the Infiniband network cards, Infiniband switch, and the communication delays of going through the CPU hosts of clusters.

DSA Supercomputer Node

The node of the TPUv3 supercomputer followed the main ideas of TPUv1: a large two-dimensional matrix multiply unit (MXU) plus large, software-controlled on-chip memories instead of caches. Unlike TPUv1, TPUv3 uses two cores per chip. Global wires on a chip do not scale with shrinking feature size, so their relative delay increases. Given that training can use many processors, two smaller *TensorCores* per chip prevented the excessive latencies of a single large full-chip core. Google stopped at two because it is easier to efficiently generate programs for two "brawny" cores per chip than numerous "wimpy" cores.

Figure 6.23 shows the six major blocks of a TensorCore:

1. *Inter-Core Interconnect (ICI)*, which is explained previously.

2. *High Bandwidth Memory* (*HBM*). TPUv1 was memory bound for most of its applications [Jouppi, 2018]. Google solved the memory bottleneck of TPUv1 by using High Bandwidth Memory (HBM) DRAM. It offers 25 times the bandwidth of TPUv1 DRAMs by using an interposer substrate that connects the TPUv3 chip via 64 64-bit buses to four short stacks of DRAM chips. Conventional CPU servers support many more DRAM chips, but at much lower bandwidth of at most eight 64-bit busses.

3. The *Core Sequencer* executes *VLIW* instructions from the core's on-chip, software-managed Instruction Memory (*Imem*), executes scalar operations using a 4K 32-bit scalar data memory (*Smem*) and 32 32-bit scalar registers (*Sregs*), and forwards vector instructions to the VPU. The 322-bit VLIW instruction can launch eight operations: two scalar ALU, two vector ALU, vector load and store, and a pair of slots that queue data to and from the matrix multiply and transpose units.

4. The *Vector Processing Unit* (VPU) performs vector operations using a large on-chip vector memory (Vmem) with 32K 128 × 32-bit elements (16 MiB) and 32 2D vector registers (Vregs) that each contain 128 × 8 32-bit elements (4 KiB). The VPU collects and distributes data to Vmem via data-level

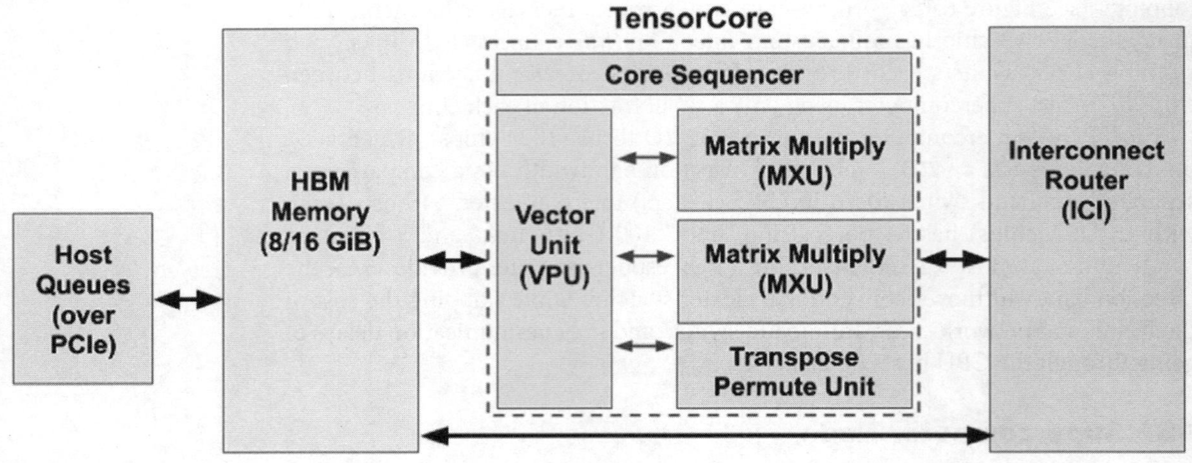

FIGURE 6.23 Block diagram of a TPUv3 TensorCore.

parallelism (2D matrix and vector functional units) and instruction-level parallelism (eight operations per instruction).

5. The MXU produces 32-bit FP products from 16-bit FP inputs that accumulate in 32 bits. All other computations are in 32-bit FP except for results going directly to an MXU input, which are converted to 16-bit FP. TPUv3 has two MXUs per TensorCore.

6. The Transpose Reduction Permute Unit does 128×128 matrix transposes, reductions, and permutations of the VPU lanes.

Figure 6.24 shows the TPUv3 supercomputer and the TPUv3 node board, and Figure 6.25 lists the specification of TPUv1, TPUv3, and NVIDIA Volta GPU that we will use for comparisons. Figure 6.26 shows the rooflines, which are quite similar. The memory bandwidths are the same (900 Gbytes/second), the 16-bit floating point rooflines are nearly indistinguishable for TPUv3 and Volta (123 versus 125 TeraFLOPS/second), and there is a small difference in 32-bit floating point (14 versus 16 TeraFLOPS/second). Note the large performance difference between 16- and 32-bit floating point arithmetic for both chips.

DSA Arithmetic

Peak performance is 8× higher when using 16-bit floating point instead of 32-bit floating point for matrix multiply (see Figure 6.23), so it is vital to use 16-bit to get the highest performance. While Google could have built an MXU using standard IEEE half (fp16) and single (fp32) floating-point formats (see Figure 3.27), they first checked the accuracy of 16-bit floating-point operations for DNNs. They found that:

FIGURE 6.24 A TPUv3 supercomputer consisting of up to 1024 chips (left). It is about 6 ft tall and 40 ft long. A TPUv3 board (right) has four chips and uses liquid cooling.

- Matrix multiplication outputs and internal sums must remain in fp32.

- The 5-bit exponent of fp16 matrix multiplication inputs leads to failure of computations that go outside its narrow range, which the 8-bit exponent of fp32 avoids.

- Reducing the matrix multiplication input mantissa size from fp32's 23 bits to 7 bits did not hurt accuracy.

The resulting *Brain floating format* (*bf16*) keeps the same 8-bit exponent as fp32 but chops the mantissa to 7 bits. Given the same exponent size, there is no danger in losing the small update values due to floating point underflow of a smaller exponent, so all programs in this section used bf16 on TPUv3 without much difficulty. However, fp16 requires adjustments to training software to deliver convergence and efficiency. Micikevicius *et al.* used *loss scaling* on GPUs, which preserves the effect from small gradients by scaling losses to fit the smaller exponents of fp16 [Micikevicius *et al.*, 2017; Kalamkar *et al.*, 2019].

Feature	TPUv1	TPUv3	Volta
Peak TeraFLOPS / Chip	92 (8b int)	123 (16b), 14 (32b)	125 (16b),16 (32b)
Network links x Gbits/s / Chip	--	4 x 656	6 x 200
Max chips / supercomputer	--	1024	Varies
Clock Rate (MHz)	700	940	1530
TDP (Watts) / Chip	75	450	450
Die Size (mm^2)	<310	<685	815
Chip Technology	28 nm	>12 nm	12 nm
Memory size (on-/off-chip)	28 MiB / 8 GiB	32 MiB /32 GiB	36 MiB / 32 GiB
Memory GB/s/Chip	34	900	900
MXUs / Core, MXU Size	1 256x256	2 128x128	8 4x4
Cores / Chip	1	2	80
Chips / CPU Host	4	8	8 or 16

FIGURE 6.25 Key processor features of TPUv1, TPUv3, and NVIDIA Volta GPU.

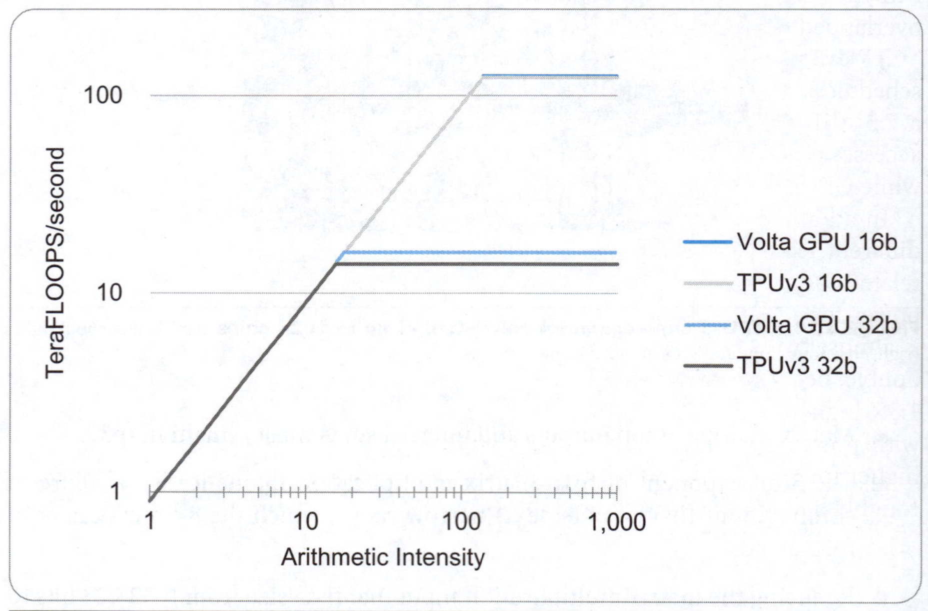

FIGURE 6.26 Rooflines of TPUv3 and Volta.

As the size of an FP multiplier scales with the square of the *mantissa* width, the bf16 multiplier is half the size and energy of an fp16 multiplier. Bf16 delivers a rare combination: reducing hardware and energy while simplifying software by making loss scaling unnecessary.

TPUv3 DSA versus Volta GPU

Let us compare TPUv3 and Volta GPU architectures before we compare performance.

Multichip parallelization is built into TPUv3 through ICI and supported through all-reduce operations supported by the TPUv3 compiler. Similar-sized multichip GPU systems use a tiered networking approach, with NVIDIA's NVLink inside a chassis and host-controlled InfiniBand networks and switches to tie multiple chassis together.

TPUv3 offers 16-bit brain floating point arithmetic designed for DNNs inside 128×128 arrays that halves the hardware and energy versus IEEE fp16 multipliers. Volta GPUs have also embraced arrays, with a finer granularity—4×4 or 16×16 depending on hardware or software descriptions—while using fp16 rather than bf16, so they may require software to perform loss scaling plus extra die area and energy.

TPUv3 is a dual-core, in-order machine, where the compiler overlaps computation, memory, and network activities. Volta GPUs are latency-tolerant 80-core machines, where each core has many threads and thus very large (20 MiB) register files. Threading hardware plus CUDA coding conventions support overlapped operations.

TPUv3 use a software-controlled 32 MiB scratchpad memory that the compiler schedules, while Volta hardware manages a 6 MiB cache and software manages a 7.5 MiB scratchpad memory. The TPUv3 compiler directs sequential DRAM accesses typical of DNNs via direct memory access (DMA) controllers on TPUv3s while GPUs use multithreading plus coalescing hardware for them.

In addition to the contrasting architectural choices, TPU and GPU chips use different technologies, die areas, clock rates, and power. Figure 6.27 gives three related cost measures of these systems: approximate die size adjusted for technology, power for a 16-chip system, and cloud price per chip. The GPU adjusted die size is almost twice that of the TPUs, which suggests the capital costs of the chips is double, because there would be twice as many TPU dies per wafer. GPU power is 1.3× higher, which suggests higher operating expenses, as the TCO is correlated with power. Finally, the hourly rental prices on Google Cloud Engine are 1.6x higher for the GPU. These three different measures consistently suggest TPUv3 is roughly half to three-fourths as expensive as the Volta GPU.

	Die size	Adjusted die size	TDP (kw)	Cloud price
Volta	815	815	12.0	$3.24
TPUv3	<685	<438	9.3	$2.00

FIGURE 6.27 Adjusted comparison of GPU and TPUv3. Die sizes are adjusted by the square of the technology, as the semiconductor technology for TPUs is similar but larger and older than that of the GPU. Google picked 15 nm for TPUs based on the information in Figure 6.25. Thermal Design Power (TDP) is for 16-chip systems.

Performance

Before showing performance of TPUv3 supercomputers, let us establish the virtues of a single chip, for a 1024× speedup from 1024 wimpy chips is uninteresting. Figure 6.28 shows the performance of TPUv3 relative to the Volta GPU chips for two sets of programs. The first set is five programs that Google and NVIDIA both submitted to MLPerf 0.6, and both use 16-bit arithmetic with NVIDIA software performing loss scaling. The TPUv3 geometric mean of these programs versus Volta is 0.95, so they are about the same speed. Google also wanted to measure performance of its production workloads, similar to what they used for TPUv1 in Section 6.7. The TPUv3 geometric mean speedup of the production applications over Volta was 4.8 for TPUv3, primarily because they use 8× slower fp32 on GPUs instead of fp16 (Figure 6.26). These are large production applications that are continuously improved, and not simple benchmarks, so it is a lot of work to get them to run at all, and more to run well. Applications programmers focus on TPUv3, since they are in everyday use, so there is little enthusiasm to include loss scaling needed for fp16.

Alas, only ResNet-50 from MLPerf 0.6 can scale beyond 1000 TPUs and GPUs. Figure 6.29 shows ResNet-50 results for MLPerf 0.6; NVIDIA ran ResNet-50 on a cluster of 96 DGX-2H each with 16 Voltas connected via Infiniband switches at 41% of linear scale-up for 1536 chips. MLPerf 0.6 benchmarks are much smaller than the production applications; the time to train them is orders-of-magnitude less than production training runs. Thus, Google included production applications

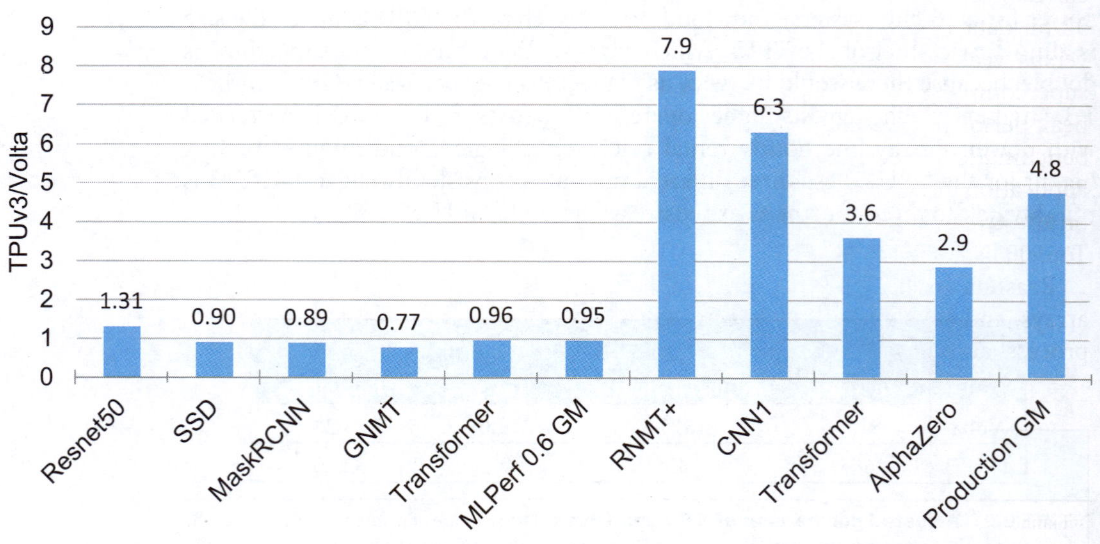

FIGURE 6.28 Performance per chip of TPUv3 relative to Volta for five MLPerf 0.6 benchmarks and four production applications.

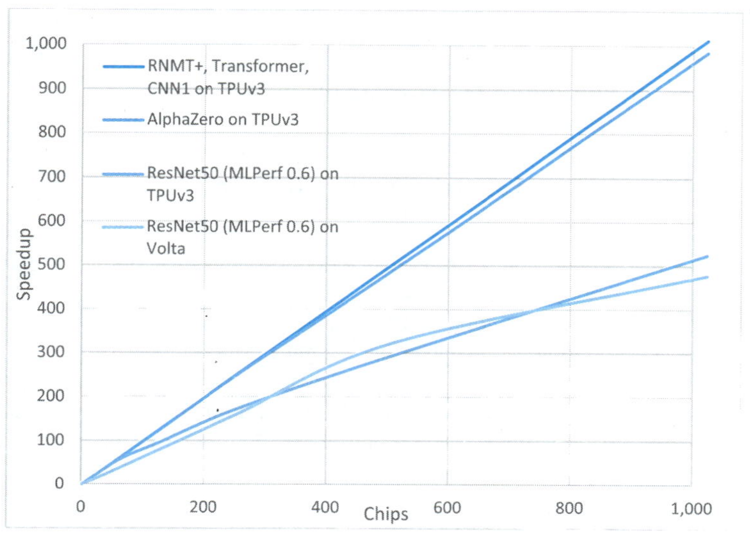

FIGURE 6.29 Supercomputer scaling: TPUv3 and Volta.

largely to show substantial programs that can scale to supercomputer size. One runs at 96% and three run at 99% of perfect linear scale-up for 1024 chips!

Figure 6.30 shows where PetaFLOPs/second and FLOPs/Watt of AlphaZero on TPUv3 would rank in the Top500 and Green500 lists. This comparison is imperfect: conventional supercomputers crunch 32- and 64-bit data rather than the 16- and 32-bit data of TPUs. However, TPUs are running a real application on real data versus weakly scaled Linpack benchmark on synthetic data. Remarkably, a TPUv3 supercomputer runs a production application using real world data at 70% of peak performance, higher than general-purpose supercomputers run the Linpack benchmark. Moreover, TPUv3 supercomputers with chips running a production application have 10× performance/Watt of the #1 traditional supercomputer on the Green500 list running Linpack and 44× of the #4 supercomputer on the Top500 list.

Reasons for TPUv3's success include the built-in ICI network, large multiplier arrays, and bf16 arithmetic. TPUv3 has a smaller die in an older semiconductor process and lower cloud prices despite being less mature at many levels of

Name	Cores	Benchmark	Peta Flop/s	% of Peak	Megawatts	GFlops/ Watt	Top500	Green500
Tianhe	4865k	Linpack	61.4	61%	18.48	3.3	4	57
SaturnV	22k	Linpack	1.1	59%	0.97	15.1	469	1
TPUv3	2k	AlphaZero	86.9	70%	0.59	146.3	4	1

FIGURE 6.30 Traditional versus TPUv3 supercomputer Top500 and Green500 rank (June 2019) for Linpack and AlphaZero.

hardware/software system stack than CPUs and GPUs. These good results despite technological disadvantages suggest the TPU DSA approach is cost-effective and can deliver high architectural efficiency into the future.

Now that we have seen a wide range of results of benchmarking different architectures, let us return to our DGEMM example to see in detail how much we have to change the C code to exploit multiple processors.

Elaboration: The original TPUv3 paper included two more production applications, MLP0 and MLP1. They rely on embeddings. An embedding at the start of a DNN model transforms from sparse representations into a dense representation suitable for linear algebra; embeddings also contain weights. Embeddings might use vectors where features can be represented by notions of distance between vectors. Embeddings involve table lookups, link traversal, and variable-length data fields, so they are irregular and memory intensive. TensorFlow kernels for embeddings had not been developed for GPUs, so Google excluded MLPs. On TPUv3, their speedups at 1024 chips are 14% and 40%, limited by the embeddings.

6.13   Going Faster: Multiple Processors and Matrix Multiply

This section is the final and largest step in our incremental performance journey of adapting DGEMM to the underlying hardware of the Intel Core i7 (Skylake). Each Core i7 has 24 cores, and the computer we have been using has two Core i7s. Thus, we have 48 cores on which to run DGEMM.

Figure 6.31 shows the OpenMP version of DGEMM that utilizes those cores. Note that line 27 is the *single* line added to Figure 5.48 to make this code run on multiple processors: an OpenMP pragma that tells the compiler to use multiple threads in the outermost for loop. It tells the computer to spread the work of the outermost loop across all the threads.

Figure 6.32 plots a classic multiprocessor speedup graph, showing the performance improvement versus a single thread as the number of threads increase. This graph makes it easy to see the challenges of strong scaling versus weak scaling. When everything fits in the first level data cache, as is the case for 64×64 matrices, adding threads actually hurts performance. The 48-threaded version of DGEMM is almost half as fast as the single-threaded version in this case. In contrast, the two largest matrices get a $17 \times$ speedup from 48 threads, and hence the classic two "up and to the right" lines in Figure 6.32.

Figure 6.33 shows the absolute performance increase as we increase the number of threads from 1 to 48. DGEMM now operates at 308 GLOPS for 960×960 matrices. As our original C version of DGEMM in Figure 2.43 ran this code at

```c
1   #include <x86intrin.h>
2   #define UNROLL (4)
3   #define BLOCKSIZE 32
4   void do_block (int n, int si, int sj, int sk,
5                        double *A, double *B, double *C)
6   {
7     for ( int i = si; i < si+BLOCKSIZE; i+=UNROLL*8 )
8       for ( int j = sj; j < sj+BLOCKSIZE; j++ ) {
9           __m512d c[UNROLL];
10          for (int r=0;r<UNROLL;r++)
11            c[r] = _mm512_load_pd(C+i+r*8+j*n); //[ UNROLL];
12
13          for( int k = sk; k < sk+BLOCKSIZE; k++ )
14          {
15            __m512d bb = _mm512_broadcastsd_pd(_mm_load_sd(B+j*n+k));
16            for (int r=0;r<UNROLL;r++)
17              c[r] = _mm512_fmadd_pd(_mm512_load_pd(A+n*k+r*8+i), bb, c[r]);
18          }
19
20        for (int r=0;r<UNROLL;r++)
21          _mm512_store_pd(C+i+r*8+j*n, c[r]);
22        }
23    }
24
25  void dgemm (int n, double* A, double* B, double* C)
26  {
27  #pragma omp parallel for
28    for ( int sj = 0; sj < n; sj += BLOCKSIZE )
29      for ( int si = 0; si < n; si += BLOCKSIZE )
30        for ( int sk = 0; sk < n; sk += BLOCKSIZE )
31          do_block(n, si, sj, sk, A, B, C);
32  }
```

FIGURE 6.31 OpenMP version of DGEMM from Figure 5.48. Line 27 is the only OpenMP code, making the outermost for loop operate in parallel. This line is the only difference from Figure 5.48.

just 2 GFLOPS, the optimizations in Chapters 3 to 6 that tailor the code to the underlying hardware result in a speedup of 150 times! If we start with the Python version, the speedup is nearly 50,000 for a C version of DGEMM optimized for data-level parallelism, instruction-level parallelism, the memory hierarchy, and thread level parallelism.

Next up is our warnings of the fallacies and pitfalls of multiprocessing. The computer architecture graveyard is filled with parallel processing projects that have ignored them.

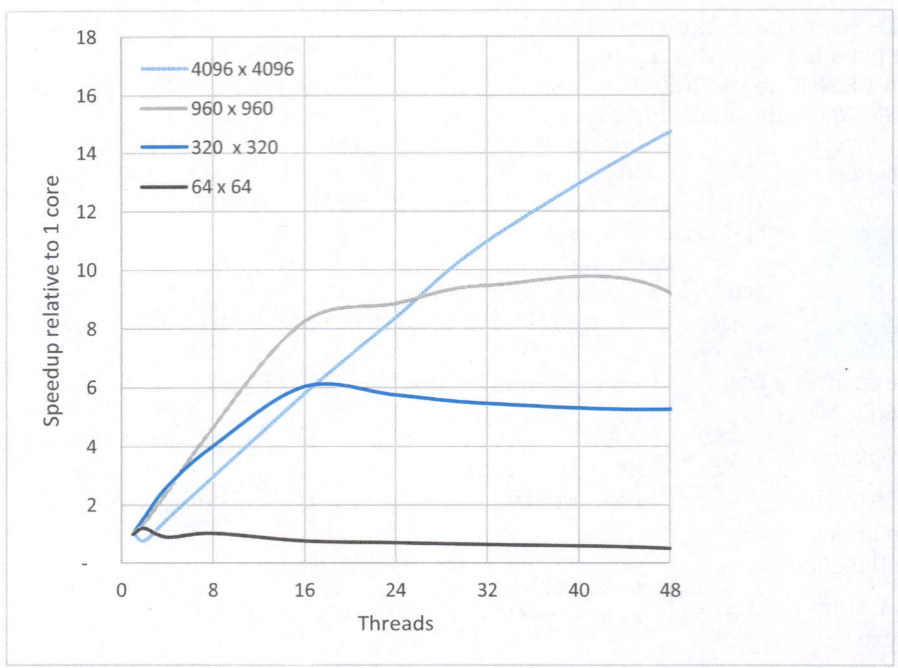

FIGURE 6.32 Performance improvements relative to a single thread as the number of threads increase. The most honest way to present such graphs is to make performance relative to the best version of a single processor program, which we did. This plot is relative to the performance of the code in Figure 5.48 *without* including OpenMP pragmas.

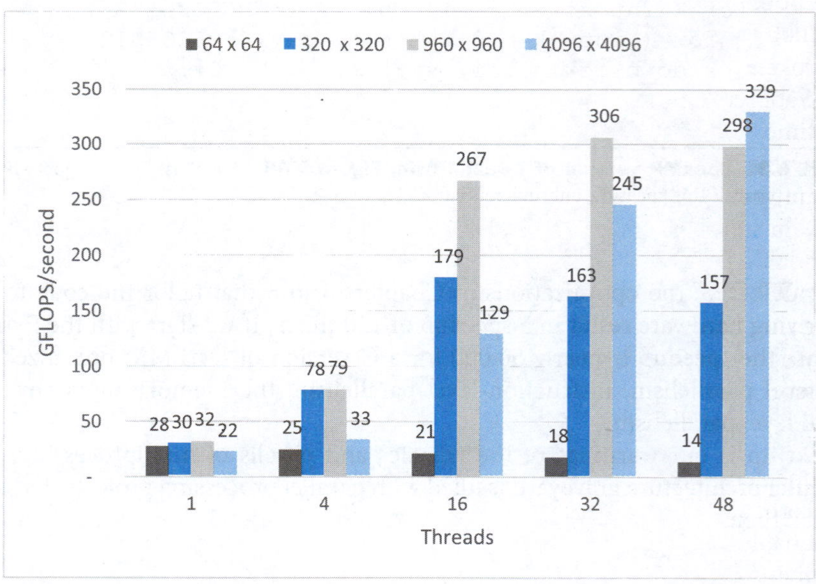

FIGURE 6.33 DGEMM performance versus the number of threads for four matrix sizes. The performance improvement compared to the original C code in Figure 2.43 for the 960 × 960 matrix with 32 threads is an astounding 150 times faster!

Elaboration: Although the Skyelake supports two hardware threads per core, we get more performance from 96 threads only for the 4096 x 4096 matrix: the peak is 364 GFLOPS at 64 threads, which drops to 344 at 96 threads. The reason is that a single AVX hardware is shared between the two threads multiplexed onto one core, so assigning two threads per core can hurt performance due to the multiplexing overhead if there is not enough data to keep all the threads busy.

6.14 Fallacies and Pitfalls

The many assaults on parallel processing have uncovered numerous fallacies and pitfalls. We cover four here.

Fallacy: Amdahl's Law doesn't apply to parallel computers.

In 1987, the head of a research organization claimed that a multiprocessor machine had broken Amdahl's Law. To try to understand the basis of the media reports, let's see the quote that gave us Amdahl's Law [1967, p. 483]:

> *A fairly obvious conclusion which can be drawn at this point is that the effort expended on achieving high parallel processing rates is wasted unless it is accompanied by achievements in sequential processing rates of very nearly the same magnitude.*

This statement must still be true; the neglected portion of the program must limit performance. One interpretation of the law leads to the following lemma: portions of every program must be sequential, so there must be an economic upper bound to the number of processors—say, 100. By showing linear speed-up with 1000 processors, this lemma is disproved; hence the claim that Amdahl's Law was broken.

The approach of the researchers was just to use weak scaling: rather than going 1000 times faster on the same data set, they computed 1000 times more work in comparable time. For their algorithm, the sequential portion of the program was constant, independent of the size of the input, and the rest was fully parallel—hence, linear speed-up with 1000 processors.

Amdahl's Law obviously applies to parallel processors. What this research does point out is that one of the main uses of faster computers is to run larger problems. Just be sure that users really care about those problems versus being a justification to buying an expensive computer by finding a problem that just keeps lots of processors busy.

Fallacy: Peak performance tracks observed performance.

The supercomputer industry once used this metric in marketing, and the fallacy is exacerbated with parallel machines. Not only are marketers using the nearly unattainable peak performance of a uniprocessor node, but also they are then multiplying it by the total number of processors, assuming perfect speed-up! Sadly, we've seen some of the same claims recently by developers of DSAs for

> *What I was really frustrated about was the fact, with Iliac IV, programming the machine was very difficult and the architecture probably was not very well suited to some of the applications we were trying to run.*
>
> David Kuck, the sole software architect of the Illiac IV SIMD computer, circa 1975.

neural networks. Amdahl's Law suggests how difficult it is to reach either peak; multiplying the two together multiplies the sins. The roofline model helps put peak performance in perspective.

Pitfall: Not developing the software to take advantage of, or optimize for, a novel architecture.

There is a long history of parallel software lagging behind on parallel hardware, possibly because the software problems are much harder. There are many examples we could choose!

One frequently encountered problem occurs when software designed for a uniprocessor is adapted to a multiprocessor environment. For example, the Silicon Graphics operating system originally protected the page table with a single lock, assuming that page allocation is infrequent. In a uniprocessor, this does not represent a performance problem. In a multiprocessor, it can become a major performance bottleneck for some programs. Consider a program that uses a large number of pages that are initialized at start-up, which UNIX does for statically allocated pages. Suppose the program is parallelized so that multiple processes allocate the pages. Because page allocation requires the use of the page table, which is locked whenever it is in use, even an OS kernel that allows multiple threads in the OS will be serialized if the processes all try to allocate their pages at once (which is exactly what we might expect at initialization time!).

This page table serialization eliminates parallelism in initialization and has significant impact on overall parallel performance. This performance bottleneck persists even for task-level parallelism. For example, suppose we split the parallel processing program apart into separate jobs and run them, one job per processor, so that there is no sharing between the jobs. (This is exactly what one user did, since he reasonably believed that the performance problem was due to unintended sharing or interference in his application.) Unfortunately, the lock still serializes all the jobs—so even the independent job performance is poor.

This pitfall indicates the kind of subtle but significant performance bugs that can arise when software runs on multiprocessors. Like many other key software components, the OS algorithms and data structures must be rethought in a multiprocessor context. Placing locks on smaller portions of the page table effectively eliminated the problem.

A more recent example of this pitfall comes from DSAs for DNNs. More than 100 companies are developing them in 2020, and the MLPerf benchmark is determining their relative success. A common failure mode has been to develop novel hardware without a software stack that shows that hardware in its best light, which has already led to start-up companies going out of business a few years after they were founded.

Fallacy: You can get good vector performance without providing memory bandwidth.

As we saw with the Roofline model, memory bandwidth is quite important to all architectures. DAXPY requires 1.5 memory references per floating-point operation, and this ratio is typical of many scientific codes. Even if the floating-point operations took no time, a Cray-1 could not increase the DAXPY performance of the vector sequence used, since it was memory limited. The Cray-1 performance on Linpack jumped when the compiler used blocking to change the computation so that values could be kept in the vector registers. This approach lowered the number of memory references per FLOP and improved the performance by nearly a factor of two! Thus, the memory bandwidth on the Cray-1 became sufficient for a loop that formerly required more bandwidth, which is just what the Roofline model would predict.

Pitfall: Assuming the instruction set architecture (ISA) completely hides all physical implementation properties

Timing channels have been known as a vulnerability since at least the 1980s, but most architects incorrectly considered them practically unimportant.[1] However, implementation properties, such as timing, can affect function. This pitfall was prominently exhibited by the 2018 exposure of Spectre that used microarchitecture speculation to leak private information to user-level attacker code from user-level sandboxes, the kernel, or the hypervisor. Spectre exploited these three microarchitecture techniques:

1. **Instruction speculation:** A processor core seeks to execute dozens of instructions concurrently by speculating past branches, committing ISA changes if speculation is correct, and rolling them back when speculation is wrong. Perversely, Spectre speculatively executes instructions whose ISA changes it knows will be rolled back. Its subtle goal is to leave microarchitectural "breadcrumbs" of what the programmer thinks are hidden secrets.

2. **Caching:** Caches are invisible to an ISA. In particular, according to conventional computer architecture wisdom, which block is least recently used in a set associative cache did not matter for proper execution, so its status need not be restored on misspeculation. Spectre exploits this surprising vulnerability to place and later find "breadcrumbs" that reveal a secret. It thus uses the contents of a cache as a "side channel" to transmit a (secret) data value.

3. **Hardware multithreading:** It is much easier to notice such subtle timing changes if the attacking program can run in close proximity to the target program. Hardware multithreading, where instructions from one program can intermix with others, simplifies this task. Hardware attacks are worrisome enough that cloud providers now offer the option to prevent sharing your server with programs of other customers. For example, AWS offers "Dedicated Instances," which cost about 5% more than the traditional shared instances.

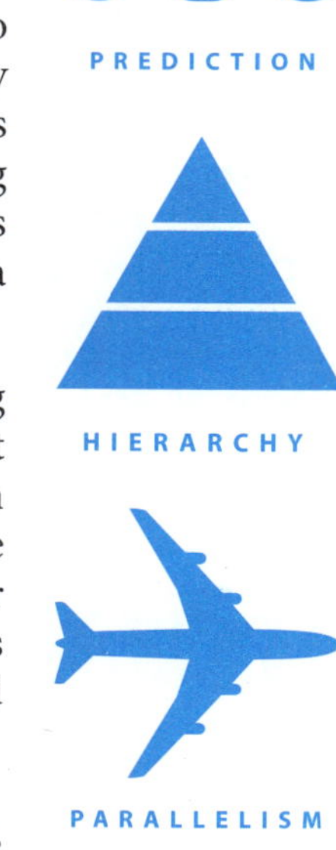

[1]This pitfall is derived from Mark Hill's perspective in *Communications of the ACM*, 2020, "Why 'Correct' Computers Can Leak Your Information," and was written with his help.

6.15 Concluding Remarks

The dream of building computers by simply aggregating processors has been around since the earliest days of computing. Progress in building and using effective and efficient parallel processors, however, has been slow. This rate of progress has been limited by difficult software problems as well as by a long process of evolving the architecture of multiprocessors to enhance usability and improve efficiency. We have discussed many of the software challenges in this chapter, including the difficulty of writing programs that obtain good speed-up due to Amdahl's Law. The wide variety of different architectural approaches and the limited success and short life of many of the parallel architectures of the past have compounded the software difficulties. We discuss the history of the development of these multiprocessors in online 🌐 **Section 6.16**. To go into even greater depth on topics in this chapter, see Chapter 4 of *Computer Architecture: A Quantitative Approach, Sixth Edition* for more on GPUs and comparisons between GPUs and CPUs and Chapter 6 for more on WSCs and Chapter 7 for more on DSAs.

As we said in Chapter 1, despite this long and checkered past, the information technology industry has now tied to parallel computing. Here are some reasons it's different now than in the past:

- Clearly, *software as a service* (SaaS) is growing in importance, and clusters have proven to be a very successful way to deliver such services. By providing redundancy at a higher-level, including geographically distributed datacenters, such services have delivered 24 × 7 × 365 availability for customers around the world.

- Warehouse-Scale Computer WSCs are changing the goals and principles of server design, just as the needs of mobile clients are changing the goals and principles of microprocessor design. Both are revolutionizing the software industry as well. Performance per dollar and performance per Joule drive both mobile client hardware and the WSC hardware, and parallelism is the key to delivering on those sets of goals.

- SIMD and vector operations are a good match to multimedia applications, which are playing a larger role in the PostPC Era. They share the advantage of being easier for the programmer than classic parallel MIMD programming and being more energy efficient than MIMD.

- The rapidly rising popularity of machine learning is changing the nature of applications, and the neural network models that drive machine learning are naturally parallel. Moreover, the domain specific software platforms like PyTorch and TensorFlow operate on arrays, making it much easier to express and exploit data level parallelism than programs written in C++.

- All desktop and server microprocessor manufacturers are building multiprocessors to achieve higher performance, so, unlike in the past, there is no easy path to higher performance for sequential applications.

- In the past, microprocessors and multiprocessors were subject to different definitions of success. When scaling uniprocessor performance, microprocessor architects were happy if single thread performance went up by the square root of the increased silicon area. Thus, they were happy with sublinear performance in terms of resources. Multiprocessor success used to be defined as *linear* speed-up as a function of the number of processors, assuming that the cost of purchase or cost of administration of n processors was n times as much as one processor. Now that parallelism is happening on-chip via multicore, we can use the traditional microprocessor metric of being successful with sublinear performance improvement.

- Unlike in the past, the open source movement has become a critical portion of the software industry. This movement is a meritocracy, where better engineering solutions can win the mind share of the developers over legacy concerns. It also embraces innovation, inviting change to old software and welcoming new languages and software products. Such an open culture could be extremely helpful in this time of change.

To motivate readers to embrace this revolution, we demonstrated the potential of parallelism concretely for matrix multiply on the Intel Core i7 (Skyelake) in the Going Faster sections of Chapters 3 to 6:

- Data-level parallelism in Chapter 3 improved performance by a factor of 7.8 by executing eight 64-bit floating-point operations in parallel using the 512-bit operands of the AVX instructions, demonstrating the value of SIMD.

- Instruction-level parallelism in Chapter 4 pushed performance up by another factor of 1.8 by unrolling loops four times to give the out-of-order execution hardware more instructions to schedule.

- Cache optimizations in Chapter 5 improved performance of matrices that didn't fit into the L1 data cache by another factor of 1.5 by using cache blocking to reduce cache misses.

- Thread-level parallelism in this chapter improved performance of matrices that don't fit into a single L1 data cache by another factor of 12 to 17 by utilizing all 48 cores of our multicore chips, demonstrating the value of MIMD. We did this by adding a single line using an OpenMP pragma.

Using the ideas in this book and tailoring the software to this computer added 21 lines of code to DGEMM. The overall performance speedup from these ideas realized in those two-dozen lines of code is over a factor of 150!

In an era without Dennard scaling, a reduced Moore's Law, and Amdahl's Law in full effect will see improvements in performance of general-purpose cores of only a few percent per year. Just as the industry spent a decade starting in about 2005 to try to exploit the opportunity of parallel processing, we project the challenge of the next decade will be to develop and program DSAs.

This sea change will provide many new research and business prospects inside and outside the IT field, and the companies that dominate the DSA era may not be the same ones that dominate it today. After understanding the underlying hardware trends and how to adapt software to them that you gained from this book, perhaps you will be one of the innovators who will seize the opportunities that are certain to appear in the uncertain times ahead. We look forward to benefiting from your inventions!

Historical Perspective and Further Reading

This section online gives the rich and often disastrous history of multiprocessors over the last 50 years.

6.17   Self-Study

DSAs are leading to more computing options and a greater need to compare the costs of alternatives. For example, how do we compare the cost of running a program on a general-purpose CPU, a GPU, or an FPGA? Costs are traditionally difficult to measure, as the list price may not be what customers really have to pay, especially if they are buying a large number of computers.

Cloudy Prices. One marketplace where the prices are fixed and public for everyone is the cloud. Go to a favorite cloud provider and find the current hourly cost to rent a CPU, an FPGA, and a GPU. What are the rental prices of the FPGA and GPU relative to CPU from Amazon Web Services (AWS)?

- CPU: r5.2xlarge

- FPGA: f1.2xlarge

- GPU: p3.2xlarge

Enhanced Genomes. One estimate is that the total number of people whose genomes have been sequenced is about 1 million as of 2020. The dropping cost of genome sequencing could lead to large demand to analyze the raw sequencing data. A paper by Wu *et al.* [2019] used a DSA implemented in an FPGA to accelerate a critical piece of genomic analysis from 42 hours on a CPU to 31 minutes on an FPGA. Although Wu *et al.* were skeptical that the program would run faster on GPUs due to load imbalances between threads, for the sake of argument, let us suppose it runs three times as fast on a GPU as on a CPU. Using your answer to Cloudy Prices, what are the costs to sequence a genome on each platform? What are the costs of the FPGA and GPU relative to CPU?

Really Enhanced Genomes. A rough rule of thumb is that a custom chip is at least 10 times as fast as the equivalent design in an FPGA. The issue is that a custom chip has a much higher development cost ("Non-Recurring Costs" or NRE) than an

FPGA. Michael Taylor and his students did some novel investigations to establish these costs [Magaki *et al.*, 2016; Khazraee *et al.*, 2017]. The ASIC NRE must include the cost of making the masks, and they are a substantial part of the overall costs, as this table shows, for some example, designs as of 2017 [Khazraee *et al.*, 2017]. The authors point out that ASICs are so much faster than the alternative, that the main question is how to pay for the NRE.

Technology (nm)	40	28	16
Mask cost ($)	1,250,000	$2,250,000	$5,700,000
Percentage of overall NRE	38	52	66
Total NRE ($)	3,259,000	4,301,000	8,616,000

How many genomes do you need to sequence to recover the NRE for each ASIC design? The wet lab cost of genome sequencing in 2020 is about $700 per genome. Would you use FPGAs or custom ASICs for data processing?

Answers to Self-Study

Cloudy Prices for AWS US East in 2020.

- CPU r5.2× large: $0.504 per hour

- GPU p3.2× large: $3.06 per hour. It costs 6.1 times as much as the CPU.

- FPGA f1.2× large: $1.65 per hour. It costs 3.3 times as much as the CPU.

Enhanced Genomes.

- 42 hours × $0.504 per hour = $21.17 to sequence one genome on CPUs.

- 31 minutes/60 minute per hour × $1.65 per hour = $0.85. FPGAs cost 0.04 times as much as CPUs (1/25th)

- 42/3 hours × $3.06 per hour = $21.17 = $42.84. GPUs cost 2.0 times as much as CPUs

Really Enhanced Genomes.

Technology (nm)	40	28	16
Total NRE ($)	3,259,000	4,301,000	8,616,000
Cost per genome on FPGA ($)	0.85	0.85	0.85
Number of genomes to recover NRE	3,834,118	5,060,000	10,136,471

Given these assumptions, the data-processing cost per genome is already so cheap compared to the wet lab cost that it will be hard to justify ASICs until the demand for sequencing per year per site is for tens of millions of genomes.

6.18   Exercises

6.1 First, write down a list of your daily activities that you typically do on a weekday. For instance, you might get out of bed, take a shower, get dressed, eat breakfast, dry your hair, brush your teeth. Make sure to break down your list so you have a minimum of 10 activities.

6.1.1 [5] <§6.2> Now consider which of these activities is already exploiting some form of parallelism (e.g., brushing multiple teeth at the same time, versus one at a time, carrying one book at a time to school, versus loading them all into your backpack and then carry them "in parallel"). For each of your activities, discuss if they are already working in parallel, but if not, why they are not.

6.1.2 [5] <§6.2> Next, consider which of the activities could be carried out concurrently (e.g., eating breakfast and listening to the news). For each of your activities, describe which other activity could be paired with this activity.

6.1.3 [5] <§6.2> For 6.1.2, what could we change about current systems (e.g., showers, clothes, TVs, cars) so that we could perform more tasks in parallel?

6.1.4 [5] <§6.2> Estimate how much shorter time it would take to carry out these activities if you tried to carry out as many tasks in parallel as possible.

6.2 You are trying to bake 3 blueberry pound cakes. Cake ingredients are as follows:

1 cup butter, softened
1 cup sugar
4 large eggs
1 teaspoon vanilla extract
1/2 teaspoon salt
1/4 teaspoon nutmeg
1 1/2 cups flour
1 cup blueberries

The recipe for a single cake is as follows:

Step 1: Preheat oven to 325°F (160°C). Grease and flour your cake pan.

Step 2: In large bowl, beat together with a mixer butter and sugar at medium speed until light and fluffy. Add eggs, vanilla, salt and nutmeg. Beat until thoroughly blended. Reduce mixer speed to low and add flour, 1/2 cup at a time, beating just until blended.

Step 3: Gently fold in blueberries. Spread evenly in prepared baking pan. Bake for 60 minutes.

6.2.1 [5] <§6.2> Your job is to cook 3 cakes as efficiently as possible. Assuming that you only have one oven large enough to hold one cake, one large bowl, one cake pan, and one mixer, come up with a schedule to make three cakes as quickly as possible. Identify the bottlenecks in completing this task.

6.2.2 [5] <§6.2> Assume now that you have three bowls, 3 cake pans and 3 mixers. How much faster is the process now that you have additional resources?

6.2.3 [5] <§6.2> Assume now that you have two friends that will help you cook, and that you have a large oven that can accommodate all three cakes. How will this change the schedule you arrived at in Exercise 6.2.1 above?

6.2.4 [5] <§6.2> Compare the cake-making task to computing 3 iterations of a loop on a parallel computer. Identify data-level parallelism and task-level parallelism in the cake-making loop.

6.3 Many computer applications involve searching through a set of data and sorting the data. A number of efficient searching and sorting algorithms have been devised in order to reduce the runtime of these tedious tasks. In this problem we will consider how best to parallelize these tasks.

6.3.1 [10] <§6.2> Consider the following binary search algorithm (a classic divide and conquer algorithm) that searches for a value X in an sorted N-element array A and returns the index of matched entry:

```
BinarySearch(A[0..N−1], X) {
    low = 0
    high = N −1
    while (low <= high) {
        mid = (low + high) / 2
        if (A[mid] >X)
            high = mid −1
        else if (A[mid] <X)
            low = mid + 1
        else
            return mid // found
    }
    return −1 // not found
}
```

Assume that you have Y cores on a multi-core processor to run BinarySearch. Assuming that Y is much smaller than N, express the speedup factor you might expect to obtain for values of Y and N. Plot these on a graph.

6.3.2 [5] <§6.2> Next, assume that Y is equal to N. How would this affect your conclusions in your previous answer? If you were tasked with obtaining the best speedup factor possible (i.e., strong scaling), explain how you might change this code to obtain it.

6.4 Consider the following piece of C code:

```
for (j = 2;j<1000;j++)
   D[j] = D[j − 1]+D[j − 2];
```

The MIPS code corresponding to the above fragment is:

```
         li      $s0,  8000
         add     $s1,  $a0, $s0
         addi    $s2,  $a0, 16
loop:    l.d     $f0,  −16($s2)
         l.d     $f2,  −8($s2)
         add.d   $f4,  $f0, $f2
         s.d     $f4,  0($s2)
         addi    $s2,  $s2, 8
         bne     $s2,  $s1, loop
```

Instructions have the following associated latencies (in cycles):

add.d	l.d	s.d	addiu
4	6	1	2

6.4.1 [10] <§6.2> How many cycles does it take to execute this code?

6.4.2 [10] <§6.2> Reorder the code to reduce stalls. Now, how many cycles does it take to execute this code? (Hint: You can remove additional stalls by changing the offset on the fsd instruction.)

6.4.3 [10] <§6.2> When an instruction in a later iteration of a loop depends upon a data value produced in an earlier iteration of the same loop, we say that there is a *loop carried dependence* between iterations of the loop. Identify the loop-carried dependences in the above code. Identify the dependent program variable and assembly-level registers. You can ignore the loop induction variable j.

6.4.4 [15] <§6.2> Rewrite the code by using registers to carry the data between iterations of the loop (as opposed to storing and reloading the data from main memory). Show where this code stalls, and calculate the number of cycles required to execute. Note that for this problem you will need to use the assembler pseudoinstruction "mov.d rd, rs", which writes the value of floating-point register rs1 into floating-point register rd. Assume that mov,d executes in a single cycle.

6.4.5 [10] <§6.2> Loop unrolling was described in Chapter 4. Unroll and optimize the loop above so that each unrolled loop handles three iterations of the original loop. Show where this code stalls and calculate the number of cycles required to execute.

6.4.6 [10] <§6.2> The unrolling from Exercise 6.4.5. works nicely because we happen to want a multiple of three iterations. What happens if the number of iterations is not known at compile time? How can we efficiently handle a number of iterations that is not a multiple of the number of iterations per unrolled loop?

6.4.7 [15] <§6.2> Consider running this code on a two-node distributed memory message passing system. Assume that we are going to use message passing as described in Section 6.7, where we introduce a new operation send (x, y) that sends to node x the value y, and an operation receive( ) that waits for the value being sent to it. Assume that send operations take one cycle to issue (i.e., later instructions on the same node can proceed on the next cycle) but take several cycles to be received on the receiving node. Receive instructions stall execution on the node where they are executed until they receive a message. Can you use such a system to speedup the code for this exercise? If so, what is the maximum latency for receiving information that can be tolerated? If not, why not?

6.5 Consider the following recursive mergesort algorithm (another classic divide and conquer algorithm). Mergesort was first described by John Von Neumann in 1945. The basic idea is to divide an unsorted list x of m elements into two sublists of about half the size of the original list. Repeat this operation on each sublist, and continue until we have lists of size 1 in length. Then starting with sublists of length 1, "merge" the two sublists into a single sorted list.

```
Mergesort(m)
    var list left, right, result
    if length(m) ≤ 1
        return m
    else
        var middle = length(m) / 2
        for each x in m up to middle
            add x to left
        for each x in m after middle
            add x to right
        left = Mergesort(left)
        right = Mergesort(right)
        result = Merge(left, right)
        return result
```

The merge step is carried out by the following code:

```
Merge(left,right)
  var list result
  while length(left) >0 and length(right) > 0
    if first(left) ≤ first(right)
      append first(left) to result
      left = rest(left)
    else
      append first(right) to result
      right = rest(right)
    if length(left) >0
      append rest(left) to result
    if length(right) >0
      append rest(right) to result
  return result
```

6.5.1 [10] <§6.2> Assume that you have Y cores on a multicore processor to run Mergesort. Assuming that Y is much smaller than length(m), express the speedup factor you might expect to obtain for values of Y and length(m). Plot these on a graph.

6.5.2 [10] <§6.2> Next, assume that Y is equal to length (m). How would this affect your conclusions your previous answer? If you were tasked with obtaining the best speedup factor possible (i.e., strong scaling), explain how you might change this code to obtain it.

6.6 Matrix multiplication plays an important role in a number of applications. Two matrices can only be multiplied if the number of columns of the first matrix is equal to the number of rows in the second.

Let's assume we have an $m \times n$ matrix A and we want to multiply it by an $n \times p$ matrix B. We can express their product as an $m \times p$ matrix denoted by AB (or $A \cdot B$). If we assign $C = AB$, and $c_{i,j}$ denotes the entry in C at position (i, j), then for each element i and j with $1 \leq i \leq m$ and $1 \leq j \leq p c_{i,j} = \sum_{k=1}^{n} a_{i,k} = b_{k,j}$. Now we want to see if we can parallelize the computation of C. Assume that matrices are laid out in memory sequentially as follows: $a_{1,1}, a_{2,1}, a_{3,1}, a_{4,1}, \ldots$, etc.

6.6.1 [10] <§6.5> Assume that we are going to compute C on both a single core shared memory machine and a 4-core shared-memory machine. Compute the speedup we would expect to obtain on the 4-core machine, ignoring any memory issues.

6.6.2 [10] <§6.5> Repeat Exercise 6.6.1, assuming that updates to C incur a cache miss due to false sharing when consecutive elements are in a row (i.e., index i) are updated.

6.6.3 [10] <§6.5> How would you fix the false sharing issue that can occur?

6.7 Consider the following portions of two different programs running at the same time on four processors in a symmetric multicore processor (SMP). Assume that before this code is run, both x and y are 0.

Core 1: x = 2;

Core 2: y = 2;

Core 3: w = x + y + 1;

Core 4: z = x + y;

6.7.1 [10] <§6.5> What are all the possible resulting values of w, x, y, and z? For each possible outcome, explain how we might arrive at those values. You will need to examine all possible interleavings of instructions.

6.7.2 [5] <§6.5> How could you make the execution more deterministic so that only one set of values is possible?

6.8 The dining philosopher's problem is a classic problem of synchronization and concurrency. The general problem is stated as philosophers sitting at a round table doing one of two things: eating or thinking. When they are eating, they are not thinking, and when they are thinking, they are not eating. There is a bowl of pasta in the center. A fork is placed in between each philosopher. The result is that each philosopher has one fork to her left and one fork to her right. Given the nature of eating pasta, the philosopher needs two forks to eat, and can only use the forks on her immediate left and right. The philosophers do not speak to one another.

6.8.1 [10] <§6.8> Describe the scenario where none of philosophers ever eats (i.e., starvation). What is the sequence of events that happen that lead up to this problem?

6.8.2 [10] <§6.8> Describe how we can solve this problem by introducing the concept of a priority? But can we guarantee that we will treat all the philosophers fairly? Explain.

Now assume we hire a waiter who is in charge of assigning forks to philosophers. Nobody can pick up a fork until the waiter says they can. The waiter has global knowledge of all forks. Further, if we impose the policy that philosophers will always request to pick up their left fork before requesting to pick up their right fork, then we can guarantee to avoid deadlock.

6.8.3 [10] <§6.8> We can implement requests to the waiter as either a queue of requests or as a periodic retry of a request. With a queue, requests are handled in the order they are received. The problem with using the queue is that we may not always be able to service the philosopher whose request is at the head of the queue (due to the unavailability of resources). Describe a scenario with 5 philosophers where a queue is provided, but service is not granted even though there are forks available for another philosopher (whose request is deeper in the queue) to eat.

6.8.4 [10] <§6.8> If we implement requests to the waiter by periodically repeating our request until the resources become available, will this solve the problem described in Exercise 6.8.3? Explain.

6.9 Consider the following three CPU organizations:

CPU SS: A 2-core superscalar microprocessor that provides out-of-order issue capabilities on 2 function units (FUs). Only a single thread can run on each core at a time.

CPU MT: A fine-grained multithreaded processor that allows instructions from 2 threads to be run concurrently (i.e., there are two functional units), though only instructions from a single thread can be issued on any cycle.

CPU SMT: An SMT processor that allows instructions from 2 threads to be run concurrently (i.e., there are two functional units), and instructions from either or both threads can be issued to run on any cycle.

Assume we have two threads X and Y to run on these CPUs that include the following operations:

Thread X	Thread Y
A1 – takes 3 cycles to execute	B1 – take 2 cycles to execute
A2 – no dependences	B2 – conflicts for a functional unit with B1
A3 – conflicts for a functional unit with A1	B3 – depends on the result of B2
A4 – depends on the result of A3	B4 – no dependences and takes 2 cycles to execute

Assume all instructions take a single cycle to execute unless noted otherwise or they encounter a hazard.

6.9.1 [10] <§6.4> Assume that you have 1 SS CPU. How many cycles will it take to execute these two threads? How many issue slots are wasted due to hazards?

6.9.2 [10] <§6.4> Now assume you have 2 SS CPUs. How many cycles will it take to execute these two threads? How many issue slots are wasted due to hazards?

6.9.3 [10] <§6.4> Assume that you have 1 MT CPU. How many cycles will it take to execute these two threads? How many issue slots are wasted due to hazards?

6.9.4 [10] <§6.4> Assume you have 1 SMT CPU. How many cycles will it take to execute the two threads? How many issue slots are wasted due to hazards?

6.10 Virtualization software is being aggressively deployed to reduce the costs of managing today's high performance servers. Companies like VMWare, Microsoft and IBM have all developed a range of virtualization products. The general concept, described in Chapter 5, is that a hypervisor layer can be introduced between the hardware and the operating system to allow multiple operating systems to share the same physical hardware. The hypervisor layer is then responsible for allocating CPU and memory resources, as well as handling services typically handled by the operating system (e.g., I/O).

Virtualization provides an abstract view of the underlying hardware to the hosted operating system and application software. This will require us to rethink how multi-core and multiprocessor systems will be designed in the future to support the sharing of CPUs and memories by a number of operating systems concurrently.

6.10.1 [30] <§6.4> Select two hypervisors on the market today, and compare and contrast how they virtualize and manage the underlying hardware (CPUs and memory).

6.10.2 [15] <§6.4> Discuss what changes may be necessary in future multi-core CPU platforms in order to better match the resource demands placed on these systems. For instance, can multithreading play an effective role in alleviating the competition for computing resources?

6.11 We would like to execute the loop below as efficiently as possible. We have two different machines, a MIMD machine and a SIMD machine.

```
for (i = 0; i < 2000; i+ + )
   for (j = 0; j < 3000; j+ + )

       X_array[i][j] = Y_array[j][i] + 200;
```

6.11.1 [10] <§6.3> For a 4 CPU MIMD machine, show the sequence of MIPS instructions that you would execute on each CPU. What is the speedup for this MIMD machine?

6.11.2 [20] <§6.3> For an 8-wide SIMD machine (i.e., 8 parallel SIMD functional units), write an assembly program in using your own SIMD extensions to MIPS to execute the loop. Compare the number of instructions executed on the SIMD machine to the MIMD machine.

6.12 A systolic array is an example of an MISD machine. A systolic array is a pipeline network or "wavefront" of data processing elements. Each of these elements does not need a program counter since execution is triggered by the arrival of data. Clocked systolic arrays compute in "lock-step" with each processor undertaking alternate compute and communication phases.

6.12.1 [10] <§6.3> Consider proposed implementations of a systolic array (you can find these in on the Internet or in technical publications). Then attempt to program the loop provided in Exercise 6.11 using this MISD model. Discuss any difficulties you encounter.

6.12.2 [10] <§6.3> Discuss the similarities and differences between an MISD and SIMD machine. Answer this question in terms of data-level parallelism.

6.13 Assume we want to execute the DAXPY loop show on page 535 in MIPS assembly on the NVIDIA 8800 GTX GPU described in this chapter. In this problem, we will assume that all math operations are performed on single-precision floating-point numbers (we will rename the loop SAXPY). Assume that instructions take the following number of cycles to execute.

Loads	Stores	Add.S	Mult.S
5	2	3	4

6.13.1 [20] <§6.6> Describe how you will constructs warps for the SAXP loop to exploit the 8 cores provided in a single multiprocessor.

6.14 Download the CUDA Toolkit and SDK from https://developer.nvidia.com/cuda-downloads. Make sure to use the "emurelease" (Emulation Mode) version of the code (you will not need actual NVIDIA hardware for this assignment). Build the example programs provided in the SDK, and confirm that they run on the emulator.

6.14.1 [90] <§6.6> Using the "template" SDK sample as a starting point, write a CUDA program to perform the following vector operations:

1) $a - b$ (vector-vector subtraction)

2) a · b (vector dot product)

The dot product of two vectors $a = [a_1, a_2, \ldots, a_n]$ and $b = [b_1, b_2, \ldots, b_n]$ is defined as:

$$a \cdot b = \sum_{i=1}^{n} a_i b_i = a_1 b_1 + a_2 b_2 + \ldots + a_n b_n$$

Submit code for each program that demonstrates each operation and verifies the correctness of the results.

6.14.2 [90] <§6.6> If you have GPU hardware available, complete a performance analysis on your program, examining the computation time for the GPU and a CPU version of your program for a range of vector sizes. Explain any results you see.

6.15 AMD has recently announced that they will be integrating a graphics processing unit with their X86 cores in a single package, though with different clocks for each of the cores. This is an example of a heterogeneous multiprocessor system which we expect to see produced commericially in the near future. One of the key design points will be to allow for fast data communication between the CPU and the GPU. Presently communications must be performed between discrete CPU and GPU chips. But this is changing in AMDs Fusion architecture.

Presently the plan is to use multiple (at least 16) PCI express channels for facilitate intercommunication.

6.15.1 [25] <§6.6> Compare the bandwidth and latency associated with these two interconnect technologies.

6.16 Refer to Figure 6.15b, which shows an n-cube interconnect topology of order 3 that interconnects 8 nodes. One attractive feature of an n-cube interconnection network topology is its ability to sustain broken links and still provide connectivity.

6.16.1 [10] <§6.9> Develop an equation that computes how many links in the n-cube (where n is the order of the cube) can fail and we can still guarantee an unbroken link will exist to connect any node in the n-cube.

6.16.2 [10] <§6.9> Compare the resiliency to failure of n-cube to a fully-connected interconnection network. Plot a comparison of reliability as a function of the added number of links for the two topologies.

6.17 Benchmarking is field of study that involves identifying representative workloads to run on specific computing platforms in order to be able to objectively compare performance of one system to another. In this exercise we will compare two classes of benchmarks: the Whetstone CPU benchmark and the PARSEC Benchmark suite. Select one program from PARSEC. All programs should be freely available on the Internet. Consider running multiple copies of Whetstone versus running the PARSEC Benchmark on any of systems described in Section 6.11.

6.17.1 [60] <§6.11> What is inherently different between these two classes of workload when run on these multi-core systems?

6.17.2 [60] <§6.11> In terms of the Roofline Model, how dependent will the results you obtain when running these benchmarks be on the amount of sharing and synchronization present in the workload used?

6.18 When performing computations on sparse matrices, latency in the memory hierarchy becomes much more of a factor. Sparse matrices lack the spatial locality in the data stream typically found in matrix operations. As a result, new matrix representations have been proposed.

One of the earliest sparse matrix representations is the Yale Sparse Matrix Format. It stores an initial sparse $m \times n$ matrix, M in row form using three one-dimensional arrays. Let R be the number of nonzero entries in M. We construct an array A of length R that contains all nonzero entries of M (in left-to-right top-to-bottom order). We also construct a second array IA of length

$m + 1$ (i.e., one entry per row, plus one). $IA(i)$ contains the index in A of the first nonzero element of row i. Row i of the original matrix extends from $A(IA(i))$ to $A(IA(i+1)-1)$. The third array, JA, contains the column index of each element of A, so it also is of length R.

6.18.1 [15] <§6.11> Consider the sparse matrix X below and write C code that would store this code in Yale Sparse Matrix Format.

```
Row 1 [1, 2, 0, 0, 0, 0]
Row 2 [0, 0, 1, 1, 0, 0]
Row 3 [0, 0, 0, 0, 9, 0]
Row 4 [2, 0, 0, 0, 0, 2]
Row 5 [0, 0, 3, 3, 0, 7]
Row 6 [1, 3, 0, 0, 0, 1]
```

6.18.2 [10] <§6.11> In terms of storage space, assuming that each element in matrix X is single precision floating point, compute the amount of storage used to store the Matrix above in Yale Sparse Matrix Format.

6.18.3 [15] <§6.11> Perform matrix multiplication of Matrix X by Matrix Y shown below.

```
[2, 4, 1, 99, 7, 2]
```

Put this computation in a loop, and time its execution. Make sure to increase the number of times this loop is executed to get good resolution in your timing measurement. Compare the runtime of using a naïve representation of the matrix, and the Yale Sparse Matrix Format.

6.18.4 [15] <§6.11> Can you find a more efficient sparse matrix representation (in terms of space and computational overhead)?

6.19 In future systems, we expect to see heterogeneous computing platforms constructed out of heterogeneous CPUs. We have begun to see some appear in the embedded processing market in systems that contain both floating point DSPs and a microcontroller CPUs in a multichip module package.

Assume that you have three classes of CPU:

CPU A—A moderate speed multi-core CPU (with a floating point unit) that can execute multiple instructions per cycle.

CPU B—A fast single-core integer CPU (i.e., no floating point unit) that can execute a single instruction per cycle.

CPU C—A slow vector CPU (with floating point capability) that can execute multiple copies of the same instruction per cycle.

Assume that our processors run at the following frequencies:

CPU A	CPU B	CPU C
1 GHz	3 GHz	250 MHz

CPU A can execute 2 instructions per cycle, CPU B can execute 1 instruction per cycle, and CPU C can execute 8 instructions (though the same instruction) per cycle. Assume all operations can complete execution in a single cycle of latency without any hazards.

All three CPUs have the ability to perform integer arithmetic, though CPU B cannot perform floating point arithmetic. CPU A and B have an instruction set similar to a MIPS processor. CPU C can only perform floating point add and subtract operations, as well as memory loads and stores. Assume all CPUs have access to shared memory and that synchronization has zero cost.

The task at hand is to compare two matrices X and Y that each contain 1024×1024 floating point elements. The output should be a count of the number indices where the value in X was larger or equal to the value in Y.

6.19.1 [10] <§6.12> Describe how you would partition the problem on the 3 different CPUs to obtain the best performance.

6.19.2 [10] <§6.12> What kind of instruction would you add to the vector CPU C to obtain better performance?

6.20 This question looks at the amount of queuing that is occurring in the system given a maximum transaction processing rate, and the latency observed on average for a transaction. The latency includes both the service time (which is computed by the maximum rate) and the queue time. Assume a quad-core computer system can process database queries at a steady state rate of requests per second. Also assume that each transaction takes, on average, a fixed amount of time to process. The following table shows pairs of transaction latency and processing rate.

Average Transaction Latency	Maximum transaction processing rate
1 ms	5000/sec
2 ms	5000/sec
1 ms	10,000/sec
2 ms	10,000/sec

For each of the pairs in the table, answer the following questions:

6.20.1 [10] <§6.12> On average, how many requests are being processed at any given instant?

6.20.2 [10] <§6.12> If move to an 8-core system, ideally, what will happen to the system throughput (i.e., how many queries/second will the computer process)?

6.20.3 [10] <§6.12> Discuss why we rarely obtain this kind of speedup by simply increasing the number of cores.

§6.1, page 528: False. Task-level parallelism can help sequential applications and sequential applications can be made to run on parallel hardware, although it is more challenging.

§6.2, page 533: False. *Weak* scaling can compensate for a serial portion of the program that would otherwise limit scalability, but not so for strong scaling.

§6.3, page 538: True, but they are missing useful vector features like gather-scatter and vector length registers that improve the efficiency of vector architectures. (As an *Elaboration* in this section mentions, the AVX2 SIMD extensions offers indexed loads via a gather operation but *not* scatter for indexed stores. The Haswell generation x86 microprocessor is the first to support AVX2.)

§6.4, page 543: 1. True. 2. True.

§6.5, page 547: False. Since the shared address is a *physical* address, multiple tasks each in their own *virtual* address spaces can run well on a shared memory multiprocessor.

§6.6, page 555: False. Graphics DRAM chips are prized for their higher bandwidth.

§6.7, page 558: False. GPUs and CPUs include redundant features to increase die yield, which, combined with their large volumes, makes large dies affordable, unlike the case for DSAs. The DSA advantages include leaving out features of CPUs and GPUs not needed by the domain, and reusing those resources for more arithmetic units and large memory on chip, both tailored to the problem domain.

§6.8, page 563: 1. False. Sending and receiving a message is an implicit synchronization, as well as a way to share data. 2. True.

§6.9, page 565: True.

§6.11, page 577: True. We likely need innovation at all levels of the hardware and software stack for parallel computing to succeed.

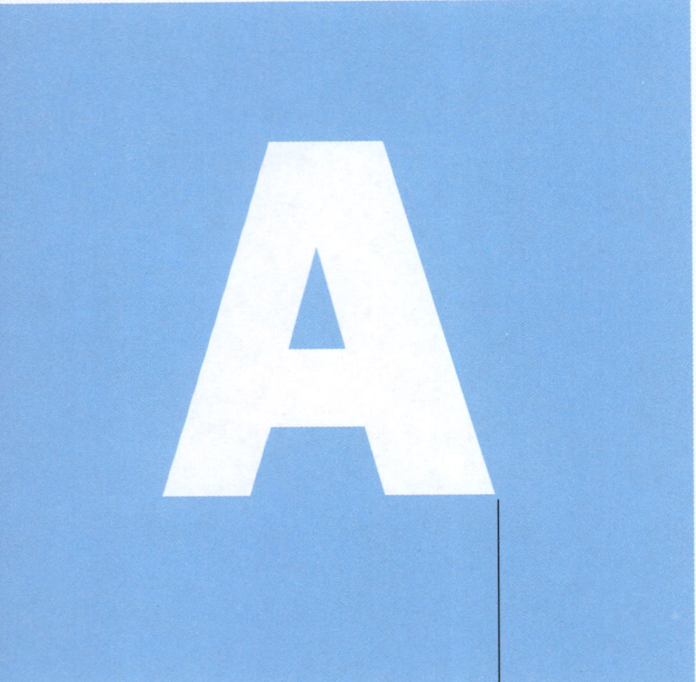

Assemblers, Linkers, and the SPIM Simulator

*Fear of serious injury
cannot alone justify
suppression of free
speech and assembly.*

Louis Brandeis
Whitney v. California, 1927

James R. Larus
Microsoft Research, Microsoft

A.1   Introduction

Encoding instructions as binary numbers is natural and efficient for computers. Humans, however, have a great deal of difficulty understanding and manipulating these numbers. People read and write symbols (words) much better than long sequences of digits. Chapter 2 showed that we need not choose between numbers and words, because computer instructions can be represented in many ways. Humans can write and read symbols, and computers can execute the equivalent binary numbers. This appendix describes the process by which a human-readable program is translated into a form that a computer can execute, provides a few hints about writing assembly programs, and explains how to run these programs on SPIM, a simulator that executes MIPS programs. UNIX, Windows, and Mac OS X versions of the SPIM simulator are available on the CD.

Assembly language is the symbolic representation of a computer's binary encoding—the **machine language**. Assembly language is more readable than machine lan guage, because it uses symbols instead of bits. The symbols in assembly language name commonly occurring bit patterns, such as opcodes and register specifiers, so people can read and remember them. In addition, assembly language

machine language
Binary representation used for communication within a computer system.

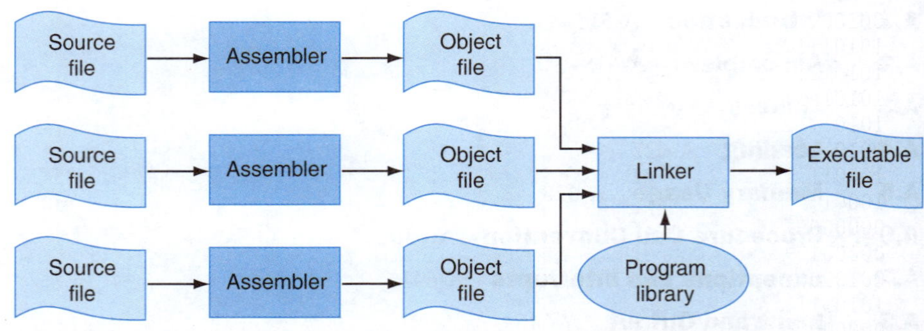

FIGURE A.1.1 The process that produces an executable file. An assembler translates a file of assembly language into an object file, which is linked with other files and libraries into an executable file.

assembler A program that translates a symbolic version of instruction into the binary version.

macro A pattern-matching and replacement facility that pro vides a simple mechanism to name a frequently used sequence of instructions.

unresolved reference A reference that requires more information from an outside source to be complete.

linker Also called **link editor**. A systems program that com bines independently assembled machine language programs and resolves all undefined labels into an executable file.

permits programmers to use *labels* to identify and name particular memory words that hold instructions or data.

A tool called an **assembler** translates assembly language into binary instructions. Assemblers provide a friendlier representation than a computer's 0s and 1s, which simplifies writing and reading programs. Symbolic names for operations and locations are one facet of this representation. Another facet is programming facilities that increase a program's clarity. For example, **macros**, discussed in **Section A.2**, enable a programmer to extend the assembly language by defining new operations.

An assembler reads a single assembly language *source file* and produces an *object file* containing machine instructions and bookkeeping information that helps combine several object files into a program. Figure A.1.1 illustrates how a program is built. Most programs consist of several files—also called *modules*— that are written, compiled, and assembled independently. A program may also use prewritten routines supplied in a *program library*. A module typically contains *references* to subroutines and data defined in other modules and in libraries. The code in a module cannot be executed when it contains **unresolved references** to labels in other object files or libraries. Another tool, called a **linker**, combines a collection of object and library files into an *executable file*, which a computer can run.

To see the advantage of assembly language, consider the following sequence of figures, all of which contain a short subroutine that computes and prints the sum of the squares of integers from 0 to 100. Figure A.1.2 shows the machine language that a MIPS computer executes. With considerable effort, you could use the opcode and instruction format tables in Chapter 2 to translate the instructions into a symbolic program similar to that shown in Figure A.1.3. This form of the routine is much

```
00100111101111011111111111100000
10101111101111110000000000010100
10101111101001000000000000100000
10101111101001010000000000100100
10101111101000000000000000011000
10101111101000000000000000011100
10001111101011100000000000011100
10001111101110000000000000011000
00000001110011100000000000011001
00100101110010000000000000000001
00101001000000010000000001100101
10101111101010000000000000011100
00000000000000001111000001001 0
00000011000011111100100000100001
00010100001000001111111111110111
10101111101110010000000000011000
00111100000001000001000000000000
10001111101001010000000000011000
00001100000100000000000011101100
00100100100001000000010000110000
10001111101111110000000000010100
00100111101111010000000000100000
00000011111000000000000000001000
00000000000000000001000000100001
```

FIGURE A.1.2 MIPS machine language code for a routine to compute and print the sum of the squares of integers between 0 and 100.

easier to read, because operations and operands are written with symbols rather than with bit patterns. However, this assembly language is still difficult to follow, because memory locations are named by their address rather than by a symbolic label.

Figure A.1.4 shows assembly language that labels memory addresses with mnemonic names. Most programmers prefer to read and write this form. Names that begin with a period, for example .data and .globl, are **assembler directives** that tell the assembler how to translate a program but do not produce machine instructions. Names followed by a colon, such as str: or main:, are labels that name the next memory location. This program is as readable as most assembly language programs (except for a glaring lack of comments), but it is still difficult to follow, because many simple operations are required to accomplish simple tasks and because assembly language's lack of control flow constructs provides few hints about the program's operation.

By contrast, the C routine in Figure A.1.5 is both shorter and clearer, since variables have mnemonic names and the loop is explicit rather than constructed with branches. In fact, the C routine is the only one that we wrote. The other forms of the program were produced by a C compiler and assembler.

In general, assembly language plays two roles (see Figure A.1.6). The first role is the output language of compilers. A *compiler* translates a program written in a

assembler directive An opera tion that tells the assembler how to translate a program but does not produce machine instructions; always begins with a period.

```
addiu      $29, $29, -32
sw         $31, 20($29)
sw         $4, 32($29)
sw         $5, 36($29)
sw         $0, 24($29)
sw         $0, 28($29)
lw         $14, 28($29)
lw         $24, 24($29)
multu      $14, $14
addiu      $8, $14, 1
slti       $1, $8, 101
sw $8,     28($29)
mflo       $15
addu       $25, $24, $15
bne        $1, $0, -9
sw         $25, 24($29)
lui        $4, 4096
lw         $5, 24($29)
jal        1048812
addiu      $4, $4, 1072
lw         $31, 20($29)
addiu      $29, $29, 32
jr         $31
move       $2, $0
```

FIGURE A.1.3 The same routine written in assembly language. However, the code for the routine does not label registers or memory locations nor include comments.

source language The
high-level language in
which a pro gram is
originally written.

high-level language (such as C or Pascal) into an equivalent program in machine or assembly language. The high-level language is called the **source language**, and the compiler's output is its *target language*.

Assembly language's other role is as a language in which to write programs. This role used to be the dominant one. Today, however, because of larger main memories and better compilers, most programmers write in a high-level language and rarely, if ever, see the instructions that a computer executes. Nevertheless, assembly language is still important to write programs in which speed or size is critical or to exploit hardware features that have no analogues in high-level languages.

Although this appendix focuses on MIPS assembly language, assembly programming on most other machines is very similar. The additional instructions and address modes in CISC machines, such as the VAX, can make assembly programs shorter but do not change the process of assembling a program or provide assembly language with the advantages of high-level languages, such as type-checking and structured control flow.

```
        .text
        .align  2
        .globl  main
main:
        subu    $sp, $sp, 32
        sw      $ra, 20($sp)
        sd      $a0, 32($sp)
        sw      $0,  24($sp)
        sw      $0,  28($sp)
loop:
        lw      $t6, 28($sp)
        mul     $t7, $t6, $t6
        lw      $t8, 24($sp)
        addu    $t9, $t8, $t7
        sw      $t9, 24($sp)
        addu    $t0, $t6, 1
        sw      $t0, 28($sp)
        ble     $t0, 100, loop
        la      $a0, str
        lw      $a1, 24($sp)
        jal     printf
        move    $v0, $0
        lw      $ra, 20($sp)
        addu    $sp, $sp, 32
        jr      $ra

        .data
        .align  0
str:
        .asciiz "The sum from 0 .. 100 is %d\n"
```

FIGURE A.1.4 The same routine written in assembly language with labels, but no comments.
The commands that start with periods are assembler directives (see pages A-47–49). .text indicates that
succeeding lines contain instructions. .data indicates that they contain data. .align n indicates that
the items on the succeeding lines should be aligned on a 2^n byte boundary. Hence, .align 2 means the
next item should be on a word boundary. .globl main declares that main is a global symbol that
should be visible to code stored in other files. Finally, .asciiz stores a null-terminated string in memory

When to Use Assembly Language

The primary reason to program in assembly language, as opposed to an available
high-level language, is because the speed or size of a program is critically important.
For example, consider a computer that controls a piece of machinery, such as a car's
brakes. A computer that is incorporated in another device, such as a car, is called an
embedded computer. This type of computer needs to respond rapidly and predictably
to events in the outside world. Because a compiler introduces uncertainty about the

```c
    #include <stdio.h>
int
main (int argc, char *argv[])
{
    int i;
    int sum = 0;
    for (i = 0; i <= 100; i = i + 1) sum = sum + i * i;
    printf ("The sum from 0 .. 100 is %d\n", sum);
}
```

FIGURE A.1.5 The routine written in the C programming language.

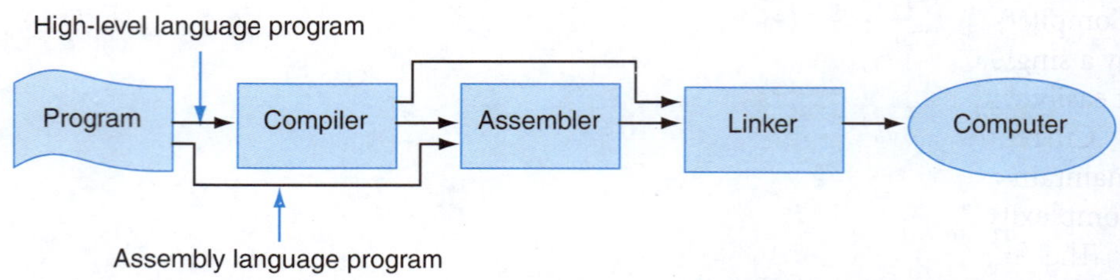

FIGURE A.1.6 Assembly language either is written by a programmer or is the output of a compiler.

time cost of operations, programmers may find it difficult to ensure that a high-level language program responds within a definite time interval—say, 1 millisecond after a sensor detects that a tire is skidding. An assembly language programmer, on the other hand, has tight control over which instructions execute. In addition, in embedded applications, reducing a program's size, so that it fits in fewer memory chips, reduces the cost of the embedded computer.

A hybrid approach, in which most of a program is written in a high-level language and time-critical sections are written in assembly language, builds on the strengths of both languages. Programs typically spend most of their time executing a small fraction of the program's source code. This observation is just the principle of locality that underlies caches (see Section 5.1 in Chapter 5).

Program profiling measures where a program spends its time and can find the time-critical parts of a program. In many cases, this portion of the program can be made faster with better data structures or algorithms. Sometimes, however, significant performance improvements only come from recoding a critical portion of a program in assembly language.

This improvement is not necessarily an indication that the high-level language's compiler has failed. Compilers typically are better than programmers at producing uniformly high-quality machine code across an entire program. Programmers, however, understand a program's algorithms and behavior at a deeper level than a compiler and can expend considerable effort and ingenuity improving small sections of the program. In particular, programmers often consider several procedures simultaneously while writing their code. Compilers typically compile each procedure in isolation and must follow strict conventions governing the use of registers at procedure boundaries. By retaining commonly used values in registers, even across procedure boundaries, programmers can make a program run faster.

Another major advantage of assembly language is the ability to exploit specialized instructions—for example, string copy or pattern-matching instructions. Compilers, in most cases, cannot determine that a program loop can be replaced by a single instruction. However, the programmer who wrote the loop can replace it easily with a single instruction.

Currently, a programmer's advantage over a compiler has become difficult to maintain as compilation techniques improve and machines' pipelines increase in complexity (Chapter 4).

The final reason to use assembly language is that no high-level language is available on a particular computer. Many older or specialized computers do not have a compiler, so a programmer's only alternative is assembly language.

Drawbacks of Assembly Language

Assembly language has many disadvantages that strongly argue against its widespread use. Perhaps its major disadvantage is that programs written in assembly language are inherently machine-specific and must be totally rewritten to run on another computer architecture. The rapid evolution of computers discussed in Chapter 1 means that architectures become obsolete. An assembly language program remains tightly bound to its original architecture, even after the computer is eclipsed by new, faster, and more cost-effective machines.

Another disadvantage is that assembly language programs are longer than the equivalent programs written in a high-level language. For example, the C program in Figure A.1.5 is 11 lines long, while the assembly program in Figure A.1.4 is 31 lines long. In more complex programs, the ratio of assembly to high-level language (its *expansion factor*) can be much larger than the factor of three in this example. Unfortunately, empirical studies have shown that programmers write roughly the same number of lines of code per day in assembly as in high-level languages. This means that programmers are roughly x times more productive in a high-level language, where x is the assembly language expansion factor.

To compound the problem, longer programs are more difficult to read and understand, and they contain more bugs. Assembly language exacerbates the problem because of its complete lack of structure. Common programming idioms, such as *if-then* statements and loops, must be built from branches and jumps. The resulting programs are hard to read, because the reader must reconstruct every higher-level construct from its pieces and each instance of a statement may be slightly different. For example, look at Figure A.1.4 and answer these questions: What type of loop is used? What are its lower and upper bounds?

Elaboration: Compilers can produce machine language directly instead of relying on an assembler. These compilers typically execute much faster than those that invoke an assembler as part of compilation. However, a compiler that generates machine language must perform many tasks that an assembler normally handles, such as resolving addresses and encoding instructions as binary numbers. The tradeoff is between compilation speed and compiler simplicity.

Elaboration: Despite these considerations, some embedded applications are writ ten in a high-level language. Many of these applications are large and complex programs that must be extremely reliable. Assembly language programs are longer and more difficult to write and read than high-level language programs. This greatly increases the cost of writing an assembly language program and makes it extremely difficult to verify the correctness of this type of program. In fact, these considerations led the Department of Defense, which pays for many complex embedded systems, to develop Ada, a new high-level language for writing embedded systems.

A.2   Assemblers

An assembler translates a file of assembly language statements into a file of binary machine instructions and binary data. The translation process has two major parts. The first step is to find memory locations with labels so that the relationship between symbolic names and addresses is known when instructions are translated. The second step is to translate each assembly statement by combining the numeric equivalents of opcodes, register specifiers, and labels into a legal instruction. As shown in Figure A.1.1, the assembler produces an output file, called an *object file*, which contains the machine instructions, data, and bookkeeping information.

An object file typically cannot be executed, because it references procedures or data in other files. A **label** is **external** (also called **global**) if the labeled object can

external label Also called **global label**. A label referring to an object that can be referenced from files other than the one in which it is defined.

be referenced from files other than the one in which it is defined. A label is *local* if the object can be used only within the file in which it is defined. In most assemblers, labels are local by default and must be explicitly declared global. Subroutines and global variables require external labels since they are referenced from many files in a program. **Local labels** hide names that should not be visible to other modules— for example, static functions in C, which can only be called by other functions in the same file. In addition, compiler-generated names—for example, a name for the instruction at the beginning of a loop—are local so that the compiler need not produce unique names in every file.

local label A label referring to an object that can be used only within the file in which it is defined.

Local and Global Labels

Consider the program in Figure A.1.4. The subroutine has an external (global) label main. It also contains two local labels—loop and str—that are only visible with this assembly language file. Finally, the routine also contains an unresolved reference to an external label printf, which is the library routine that prints values. Which labels in Figure A.1.4 could be referenced from another file?

EXAMPLE

Only global labels are visible outside a file, so the only label that could be referenced from another file is main.

ANSWER

Since the assembler processes each file in a program individually and in isolation, it only knows the addresses of local labels. The assembler depends on another tool, the linker, to combine a collection of object files and libraries into an executable file by resolving external labels. The assembler assists the linker by providing lists of labels and unresolved references.

However, even local labels present an interesting challenge to an assembler. Unlike names in most high-level languages, assembly labels may be used before they are defined. In the example, in Figure A.1.4, the label str is used by the la instruction before it is defined. The possibility of a **forward reference**, like this one, forces an assembler to translate a program in two steps: first fnd all labels and then produce instructions. In the example, when the assembler sees the la instruction, it does not know where the word labeled str is located or even whether str labels an instruction or datum.

forward reference A label that is used before it is defined.

An assembler's first pass reads each line of an assembly file and breaks it into its component pieces. These pieces, which are called *lexemes*, are individual words, numbers, and punctuation characters. For example, the line

```
ble $t0, 100, loop
```

contains six lexemes: the opcode `ble`, the register specifer `$t0`, a comma, the number 100, a comma, and the symbol `loop`.

symbol table A table that matches names of labels to the addresses of the memory words that instructions occupy.

If a line begins with a label, the assembler records in its **symbol table** the name of the label and the address of the memory word that the instruction occupies. The assembler then calculates how many words of memory the instruction on the current line will occupy. By keeping track of the instructions' sizes, the assembler can determine where the next instruction goes. To compute the size of a variable-length instruction, like those on the VAX, an assembler has to examine it in detail. However, fixed-length instructions, like those on MIPS, require only a cursory examination. The assembler performs a similar calculation to compute the space required for data statements. When the assembler reaches the end of an assembly file, the symbol table records the location of each label defined in the file.

The assembler uses the information in the symbol table during a second pass over the file, which actually produces machine code. The assembler again examines each line in the file. If the line contains an instruction, the assembler combines the binary representations of its opcode and operands (register specifiers or memory address) into a legal instruction. The process is similar to the one used in Section 2.5 in Chapter 2. Instructions and data words that reference an external symbol defined in another file cannot be completely assembled (they are unresolved), since the symbol's address is not in the symbol table. An assembler does not complain about unresolved references, since the corresponding label is likely to be defined in another file.

The BIG Picture

Assembly language is a programming language. Its principal difference from high-level languages such as BASIC, Java, and C is that assembly language provides only a few, simple types of data and control flow. Assembly language programs do not specify the type of value held in a variable. Instead, a programmer must apply the appropriate operations (e.g., integer or floating-point addition) to a value. In addition, in assembly language, programs must implement all control flow with *go tos*. Both factors make assembly language programming for any machine—MIPS or x86—more difficult and error-prone than writing in a high-level language.

Elaboration: If an assembler's speed is important, this two-step process can be done in one pass over the assembly file with a technique known as **backpatching**. In its pass over the file, the assembler builds a (possibly incomplete) binary representation of every instruction. If the instruction references a label that has not yet been defined, the assembler records the label and instruction in a table. When a label is defined, the assembler consults this table to find all instructions that contain a forward reference to the label. The assembler goes back and corrects their binary representation to incorporate the address of the label. Backpatching speeds assembly because the assembler only reads its input once. However, it requires an assembler to hold the entire binary representation of a program in memory so instructions can be backpatched. This requirement can limit the size of programs that can be assembled. The process is complicated by machines with several types of branches that span different ranges of instructions. When the assembler first sees an unresolved label in a branch instruction, it must either use the largest possible branch or risk having to go back and readjust many instructions to make room for a larger branch.

Object File Format

Assemblers produce object files. An object file on UNIX contains six distinct sections (see Figure A.2.1):

- The *object file header* describes the size and position of the other pieces of the file.

- The **text segment** contains the machine language code for routines in the source file. These routines may be unexecutable because of unresolved references.

- The **data segment** contains a binary representation of the data in the source file. The data also may be incomplete because of unresolved references to labels in other files.

- The **relocation information** identifes instructions and data words that depend on **absolute addresses**. These references must change if portions of the program are moved in memory.

- The *symbol table* associates addresses with external labels in the source file and lists unresolved references.

- The *debugging information* contains a concise description of the way the program was compiled, so a debugger can find which instruction addresses correspond to lines in a source file and print the data structures in readable form.

The assembler produces an object file that contains a binary representation of the program and data and additional information to help link pieces of a program. This

backpatching: A method for translating from assembly language to machine instructions in which the assembler builds a (possibly incomplete) binary representation of every instruction in one pass over a program and then returns to fill in previously undefined labels.

text segment The segment of a UNIX object file that contains the machine language code for routines in the source file.

data segment The segment of a UNIX object or executable file that contains a binary representation of the initialized data used by the program.

relocation information The segment of a UNIX object file that identifies instructions and data words that depend on absolute addresses.

absolute address A variable's or routine's actual address in memory.

Object file header	Text segment	Data segment	Relocation information	Symbol table	Debugging information

FIGURE A.2.1 Object file. A UNIX assembler produces an object file with six distinct sections.

relocation information is necessary because the assembler does not know which memory locations a procedure or piece of data will occupy after it is linked with the rest of the program. Procedures and data from a file are stored in a contiguous piece of memory, but the assembler does not know where this memory will be located. The assembler also passes some symbol table entries to the linker. In particular, the assembler must record which external symbols are defined in a file and what unresolved references occur in a file.

Elaboration: For convenience, assemblers assume each file starts at the same address (for example, location 0) with the expectation that the linker will *relocate* the code and data when they are assigned locations in memory. The assembler produces *relocation information*, which contains an entry describing each instruction or data word in the file that references an absolute address. On MIPS, only the subroutine call, load, and store instructions reference absolute addresses. Instructions that use PC- relative addressing, such as branches, need not be relocated.

Additional Facilities

Assemblers provide a variety of convenience features that help make assembler programs shorter and easier to write, but do not fundamentally change assembly language. For example, *data layout directives* allow a programmer to describe data in a more concise and natural manner than its binary representation. In Figure A.1.4, the directive

```
.asciiz "The sum from 0 .. 100 is %d\n"
```

stores characters from the string in memory. Contrast this line with the alternative of writing each character as its ASCII value (Figure 2.15 in Chapter 2 describes the ASCII encoding for characters):

```
.byte 84, 104, 101, 32, 115, 117, 109, 32
.byte 102, 114, 111, 109, 32, 48, 32, 46
.byte 46, 32, 49, 48, 48, 32, 105, 115
.byte 32, 37, 100, 10, 0
```

The .asciiz directive is easier to read because it represents characters as letters, not binary numbers. An assembler can translate characters to their binary representation much faster and more accurately than a human can. Data layout directives specify data in a human-readable form that the assembler translates to binary. Other layout directives are described in Section A.10.

String Directive

Define the sequence of bytes produced by this directive:

EXAMPLE

```
.asciiz "The quick brown fox jumps over the lazy dog"
```

ANSWER

```
.byte 84,   104,  101,  32,   113,  117,  105,  99
.byte 107,  32,   98,   114,  111,  119,  110,  32
.byte 102,  111,  120,  32,   106,  117,  109,  112
.byte 115,  32,   111,  118,  101,  114,  32,   116
.byte 104,  101,  32,   108,  97,   122,  121,  32
.byte 100,  111,  103,  0
```

Macro is a pattern-matching and replacement facility that provides a simple mechanism to name a frequently used sequence of instructions. Instead of repeatedly typing the same instructions every time they are used, a programmer invokes the macro and the assembler replaces the macro call with the corresponding sequence of instructions. Macros, like subroutines, permit a programmer to create and name a new abstraction for a common operation. Unlike subroutines, however, macros do not cause a subroutine call and return when the program runs, since a macro call is replaced by the macro's body when the program is assembled. After this replacement, the resulting assembly is indistinguishable from the equivalent program written without macros.

Macros

As an example, suppose that a programmer needs to print many numbers. The library routine `printf` accepts a format string and one or more values to print as its arguments. A programmer could print the integer in register $7 with the following instructions:

EXAMPLE

```
          .data
int_str:  .asciiz"%d"
          .text
          la      $a0, int_str  # Load string address #
                                # into first arg
          mov     $a1, $7       # Load value into
                                # second arg
          jal         printf    # Call the printf routine
```

The .data directive tells the assembler to store the string in the program's data segment, and the .text directive tells the assembler to store the instructions in its text segment.

However, printing many numbers in this fashion is tedious and produces a verbose program that is difficult to understand. An alternative is to introduce a macro, print_int, to print an integer:

```
        .data
int_str:.asciiz "%d"
        .text
        .macro print_int($arg)
        la $a0, int_str     # Load string address into
                # first arg
        mov $a1, $arg  # Load macro's parameter
                # ($arg) into second arg
        jal printf      # Call the printf routine
        .end_macro
print_int($7)
```

formal parameter
A variable that is the argument to a procedure or macro; replaced by that argument once the macro is expanded.

The macro has a **formal parameter**, $arg, that names the argument to the macro. When the macro is expanded, the argument from a call is substituted for the formal parameter throughout the macro's body. Then the assembler replaces the call with the macro's newly expanded body. In the first call on print_int, the argument is $7, so the macro expands to the code

```
la $a0, int_str
mov $a1, $7
jal printf
```

In a second call on print_int, say, print_int($t0), the argument is $t0, so the macro expands to

```
la $a0, int_str
mov $a1, $t0
jal printf
```

What does the call print_int($a0) expand to?

```
la $a0, int_str
mov $a1, $a0
jal printf
```


This example illustrates a drawback of macros. A programmer who uses this macro must be aware that `print_int` uses register $a0 and so cannot correctly print the value in that register.

Hardware/ Software Interface

Some assemblers also implement *pseudoinstructions*, which are instructions provided by an assembler but not implemented in hardware. Chapter 2 contains many examples of how the MIPS assembler synthesizes pseudoinstructions and addressing modes from the spartan MIPS hardware instruction set. For example, Section 2.7 in Chapter 2 describes how the assembler synthesizes the `blt` instruc tion from two other instructions: `slt` and `bne`. By extending the instruction set, the MIPS assembler makes assembly language programming easier without complicating the hardware. Many pseudoinstructions could also be simulated with macros, but the MIPS assembler can generate better code for these instructions because it can use a dedicated register ($at) and is able to optimize the generated code.

Elaboration: Assemblers *conditionally assemble* pieces of code, which permits a programmer to include or exclude groups of instructions when a program is assembled. This feature is particularly useful when several versions of a program differ by a small amount. Rather than keep these programs in separate files—which greatly complicates fixing bugs in the common code—programmers typically merge the versions into a single file. Code particular to one version is conditionally assembled, so it can be excluded when other versions of the program are assembled.

If macros and conditional assembly are useful, why do assemblers for UNIX systems rarely, if ever, provide them? One reason is that most programmers on these systems write programs in higher-level languages like C. Most of the assembly code is produced by compilers, which find it more convenient to repeat code rather than define macros. Another reason is that other tools on UNIX—such as cpp, the C preprocessor, or m4, a general macro processor—can provide macros and conditional assembly for assembly language programs.

A.3 Linkers

Separate compilation permits a program to be split into pieces that are stored in different files. Each file contains a logically related collection of subroutines and data structures that form a *module* in a larger program. A file can be compiled and assembled independently of other files, so changes to one module do not require recompiling the entire program. As we discussed above, separate compilation necessitates the additional step of linking to combine object files from separate modules and fx their unresolved references.

The tool that merges these files is the *linker* (see Figure A.3.1). It performs three tasks:

- Searches the program libraries to fnd library routines used by the program

- Determines the memory locations that code from each module will occupy and relocates its instructions by adjusting absolute references

- Resolves references among files

A linker's first task is to ensure that a program contains no undefined labels. The linker matches the external symbols and unresolved references from a program's files. An external symbol in one file resolves a reference from another file if both refer to a label with the same name. Unmatched references mean a symbol was used but not defined anywhere in the program.

Unresolved references at this stage in the linking process do not necessarily mean a programmer made a mistake. The program could have referenced a library routine whose code was not in the object files passed to the linker. After matching symbols in the program, the linker searches the system's program libraries to find predefined subroutines and data structures that the program references. The basic libraries contain routines that read and write data, allocate and deallocate memory, and perform numeric operations. Other libraries contain routines to access a database or manipulate terminal windows. A program that references an unresolved symbol that is not in any library is erroneous and cannot be linked. When the program uses a library routine, the linker extracts the routine's code from the library and incorporates it into the program text segment. This new routine, in turn, may depend on other library routines, so the linker continues to fetch other library routines until no external references are unresolved or a routine cannot be found.

If all external references are resolved, the linker next determines the memory locations that each module will occupy. Since the files were assembled in isolation,

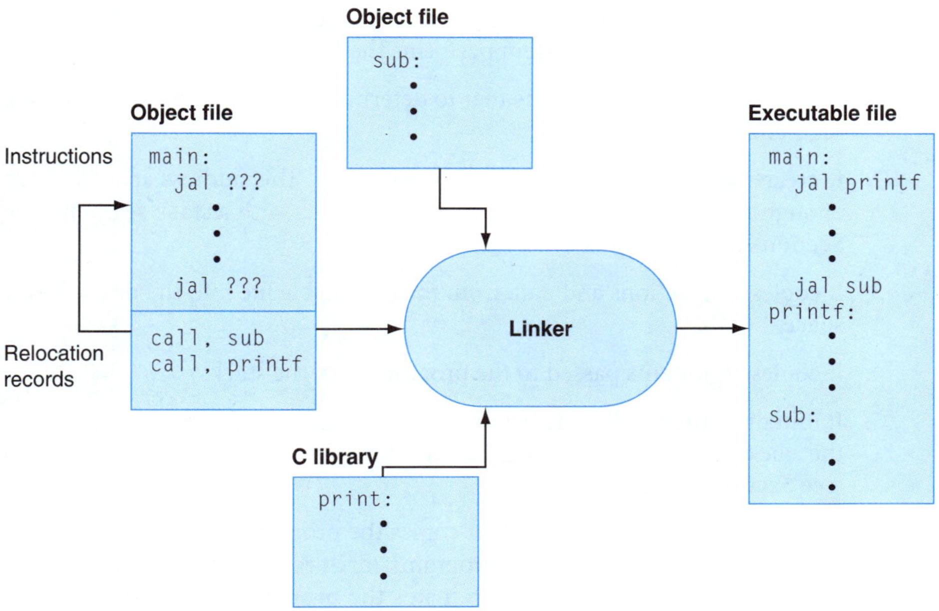

FIGURE A.3.1 The linker searches a collection of object files and program libraries to find nonlocal routines used in a program, combines them into a single executable file, and resolves references between routines in different files.

the assembler could not know where a module's instructions or data would be placed relative to other modules. When the linker places a module in memory, all absolute references must be *relocated* to reflect its true location. Since the linker has relocation information that identifies all relocatable references, it can efficiently find and backpatch these references.

The linker produces an executable file that can run on a computer. Typically, this file has the same format as an object file, except that it contains no unresolved references or relocation information.

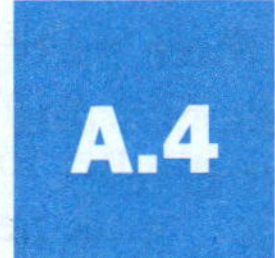

A.4   Loading

A program that links without an error can be run. Before being run, the program resides in a file on secondary storage, such as a disk. On UNIX systems, the operating system kernel brings a program into memory and starts it running. To start a program, the operating system performs the following steps:

1. It reads the executable file's header to determine the size of the text and data segments.

2. It creates a new address space for the program. This address space is large enough to hold the text and data segments, along with a stack segment (see Section A.5).

3. It copies instructions and data from the executable file into the new address space.

4. It copies arguments passed to the program onto the stack.

5. It initializes the machine registers. In general, most registers are cleared, but the stack pointer must be assigned the address of the first free stack location (see Section A.5).

6. It jumps to a start-up routine that copies the program's arguments from the stack to registers and calls the program's main routine. If the main routine returns, the start-up routine terminates the program with the exit system call.

A.5   Memory Usage

The next few sections elaborate the description of the MIPS architecture presented earlier in the book. Earlier chapters focused primarily on hardware and its relationship with low-level software. These sections focus primarily on how assembly language programmers use MIPS hardware. These sections describe a set of conventions followed on many MIPS systems. For the most part, the hardware does not impose these conventions. Instead, they represent an agreement among programmers to follow the same set of rules so that software written by different people can work together and make effective use of MIPS hardware.

Systems based on MIPS processors typically divide memory into three parts (see Figure A.5.1). The first part, near the bottom of the address space (starting at address 400000_{hex}), is the *text segment*, which holds the program's instructions.

The second part, above the text segment, is the *data segment*, which is further divided into two parts. **Static data** (starting at address 10000000_{hex}) contains objects whose size is known to the compiler and whose lifetime—the interval during which a program can access them—is the program's entire execution. For example, in C, global variables are statically allocated, since they can be referenced anytime

static data The portion of memory that contains data whose size is known to the compiler and whose lifetime is the program's entire execution.

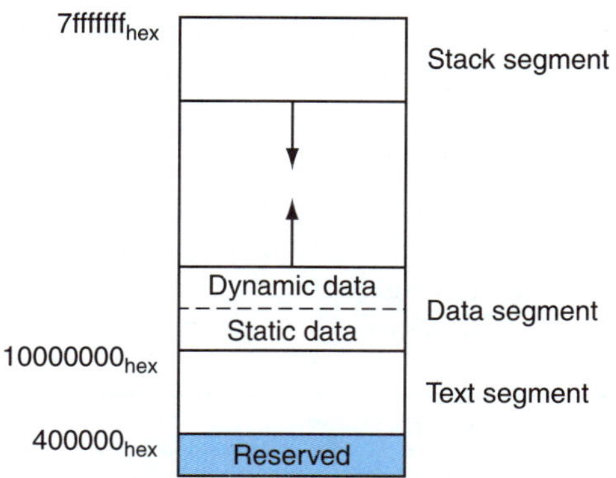

FIGURE A.5.1 Layout of memory.

during a program's execution. The linker both assigns static objects to locations in the data segment and resolves references to these objects.

Immediately above static data is *dynamic data*. This data, as its name implies, is allocated by the program as it executes. In C programs, the `malloc` library routine finds and returns a new block of memory. Since a compiler cannot predict how much memory a program will allocate, the operating system expands the dynamic data area to meet demand. As the upward arrow in the figure indicates, `malloc` expands the dynamic area with the `sbrk` system call, which causes the operating system to add more pages to the program's virtual address space (see Section 5.4 in Chapter 5) immediately above the dynamic data segment.

Hardware/ Software Interface

Because the data segment begins far above the program at address 10000000_{hex}, load and store instructions cannot directly reference data objects with their 16-bit offset fields (see Section 2.5 in Chapter 2). For example, to load the word in the data segment at address 10010020_{hex} into register $\$v0$ requires two instructions:

```
lui $s0, 0x1001 # 0x1001 means 1001 base 16
lw $v0, 0x0020($s0) # 0x10010000 + 0x0020 = 0x10010020
```

(The *0x* before a number means that it is a hexadecimal value. For example, $0x8000$ is 8000_{hex} or $32,768_{ten}$.)

To avoid repeating the `lui` instruction at every load and store, MIPS systems typically dedicate a register ($\$gp$) as *a global pointer to* the static data segment. This register contains address 10008000_{hex}, so load and store instructions can use their signed 16-bit offset fields to access the first 64 KB of the static data segment. With this global pointer, we can rewrite the example as a single instruction:

```
lw $v0, 0x8020($gp)
```

Of course, a global pointer register makes addressing locations 10000000_{hex}–10010000_{hex} faster than other heap locations. The MIPS compiler usually stores *global variables* in this area, because these variables have fxed locations and ft better than other global data, such as arrays.

stack segment The portion of memory used by a program to hold procedure call frames.

The third part, the program **stack segment**, resides at the top of the virtual address space (starting at address $7fffffff_{hex}$). Like dynamic data, the maximum size of a program's stack is not known in advance. As the program pushes values on to the stack, the operating system expands the stack segment down toward the data segment.

This three-part division of memory is not the only possible one. However, it has two important characteristics: the two dynamically expandable segments are as far apart as possible, and they can grow to use a program's entire address space.

A.6   Procedure Call Convention

Conventions governing the use of registers are necessary when procedures in a program are compiled separately. To compile a particular procedure, a compiler must know which registers it may use and which registers are reserved for other procedures. Rules for using registers are called **register use** or **procedure call conventions**. As the name implies, these rules are, for the most part, conventions followed by software rather than rules enforced by hardware. However, most compilers and programmers try very hard to follow these conventions because violating them causes insidious bugs.

register use convention Also called **procedure call convention**. A software protocol governing the use of registers by procedures.

The calling convention described in this section is the one used by the gcc compiler. The native MIPS compiler uses a more complex convention that is slightly faster.

The MIPS CPU contains 32 general-purpose registers that are numbered 0–31. Register $0 always contains the hardwired value 0.

- Registers $at (1), $k0 (26), and $k1 (27) are reserved for the assembler and operating system and should not be used by user programs or compilers.

- Registers $a0-$a3 (4–7) are used to pass the first four arguments to routines (remaining arguments are passed on the stack). Registers $v0 and $v1 (2, 3) are used to return values from functions.

- Registers $t0-$t9 (8–15, 24, 25) are **caller-saved registers** that are used to hold temporary quantities that need not be preserved across calls (see Section 2.8 in Chapter 2).

- Registers $s0-$s7 (16–23) are **callee-saved registers** that hold long-lived values that should be preserved across calls.

- Register $gp (28) is a global pointer that points to the middle of a 64K block of memory in the static data segment.

- Register $sp (29) is the stack pointer, which points to the last location on the stack. Register $fp (30) is the frame pointer. The jal instruction writes register $ra (31), the return address from a procedure call. These two registers are explained in the next section.

The two-letter abbreviations and names for these registers—for example $sp for the stack pointer—reflect the registers' intended uses in the procedure call convention. In describing this convention, we will use the names instead of register numbers. Figure A.6.1 lists the registers and describes their intended uses.

Procedure Calls

This section describes the steps that occur when one procedure (the *caller*) invokes another procedure (the *callee*). Programmers who write in a high-level language (like C or Pascal) never see the details of how one procedure calls another, because the compiler takes care of this low-level bookkeeping. However, assembly language programmers must explicitly implement every procedure call and return.

Most of the bookkeeping associated with a call is centered around a block of memory called a **procedure call frame**. This memory is used for a variety of purposes:

- To hold values passed to a procedure as arguments

- To save registers that a procedure may modify, but which the procedure's caller does not want changed

- To provide space for variables local to a procedure

In most programming languages, procedure calls and returns follow a strict last-in, first-out (LIFO) order, so this memory can be allocated and deallocated on a stack, which is why these blocks of memory are sometimes called stack frames.

Figure A.6.2 shows a typical stack frame. The frame consists of the memory between the frame pointer ($fp), which points to the first word of the frame, and the stack pointer ($sp), which points to the last word of the frame. The stack grows down from higher memory addresses, so the frame pointer points above the stack

caller-saved register
A register saved by the routine being called.

callee-saved register
A register saved by the routine making a procedure call.

procedure call frame
A block of memory that is used to hold values passed to a procedure as arguments, to save registers that a procedure may modify but that the procedure's caller does not want changed, and to provide space for variables local to a procedure.

Register name	Number	Usage
$zero	0	constant 0
$at	1	reserved for assembler
$v0	2	expression evaluation and results of a function
$v1	3	expression evaluation and results of a function
$a0	4	argument 1
$a1	5	argument 2
$a2	6	argument 3
$a3	7	argument 4
$t0	8	temporary (not preserved across call)
$t1	9	temporary (not preserved across call)
$t2	10	temporary (not preserved across call)
$t3	11	temporary (not preserved across call)
$t4	12	temporary (not preserved across call)
$t5	13	temporary (not preserved across call)
$t6	14	temporary (not preserved across call)
$t7	15	temporary (not preserved across call)
$s0	16	saved temporary (preserved across call)
$s1	17	saved temporary (preserved across call)
$s2	18	saved temporary (preserved across call)
$s3	19	saved temporary (preserved across call)
$s4	20	saved temporary (preserved across call)
$s5	21	saved temporary (preserved across call)
$s6	22	saved temporary (preserved across call)
$s7	23	saved temporary (preserved across call)
$t8	24	temporary (not preserved across call)
$t9	25	temporary (not preserved across call)
$k0	26	reserved for OS kernel
$k1	27	reserved for OS kernel
$gp	28	pointer to global area
$sp	29	stack pointer
$fp	30	frame pointer
$ra	31	return address (used by function call)

FIGURE A.6.1 MIPS registers and usage convention.

pointer. The executing procedure uses the frame pointer to quickly access values in its stack frame. For example, an argument in the stack frame can be loaded into register $v0 with the instruction

```
lw $v0, 0($fp)
```

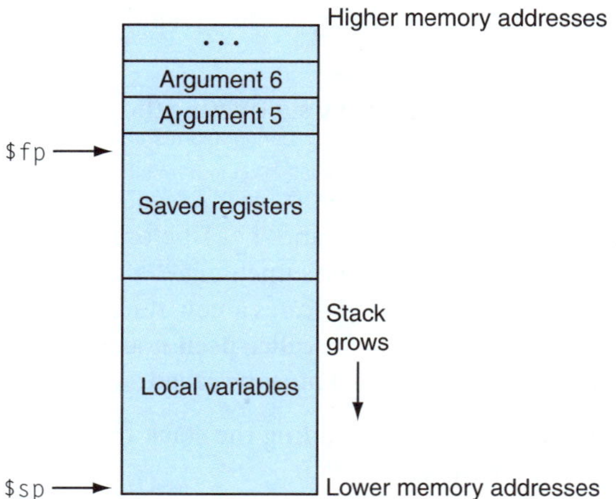

FIGURE A.6.2 Layout of a stack frame. The frame pointer ($fp) points to the first word in the currently executing procedure's stack frame. The stack pointer ($sp) points to the last word of the frame. The first four arguments are passed in registers, so the fifth argument is the first one stored on the stack.

A stack frame may be built in many different ways; however, the caller and callee must agree on the sequence of steps. The steps below describe the calling convention used on most MIPS machines. This convention comes into play at three points during a procedure call: immediately before the caller invokes the callee, just as the callee starts executing, and immediately before the callee returns to the caller. In the first part, the caller puts the procedure call arguments in standard places and invokes the callee to do the following:

1. Pass arguments. By convention, the first four arguments are passed in registers $a0-$a3. Any remaining arguments are pushed on the stack and appear at the beginning of the called procedure's stack frame.

2. Save caller-saved registers. The called procedure can use these registers ($a0-$a3 and $t0-$t9) without first saving their value. If the caller expects to use one of these registers after a call, it must save its value before the call.

3. Execute a `jal` instruction (see Section 2.8 of Chapter 2), which jumps to the callee's first instruction and saves the return address in register $ra.

Before a called routine starts running, it must take the following steps to set up its stack frame:

1. Allocate memory for the frame by subtracting the frame's size from the stack pointer.

2. Save callee-saved registers in the frame. A callee must save the values in these registers ($s0-$s7, $fp, and $ra) before altering them, since the caller expects to fnd these registers unchanged after the call. Register $fp is saved by every procedure that allocates a new stack frame. However, register $ra only needs to be saved if the callee itself makes a call. The other callee-saved registers that are used also must be saved.

3. Establish the frame pointer by adding the stack frame's size minus 4 to $sp and storing the sum in register $fp.

Hardware/ Software Interface

The MIPS register use convention provides callee- and caller-saved registers, because both types of registers are advantageous in different circumstances. Callee-saved registers are better used to hold long-lived values, such as variables from a user's program. These registers are only saved during a procedure call if the callee expects to use the register. On the other hand, caller-saved registers are better used to hold short-lived quantities that do not persist across a call, such as immediate values in an address calculation. During a call, the callee can also use these registers for short-lived temporaries.

Finally, the callee returns to the caller by executing the following steps:

1. If the callee is a function that returns a value, place the returned value in register $v0.

2. Restore all callee-saved registers that were saved upon procedure entry.

3. Pop the stack frame by adding the frame size to $sp.

4. Return by jumping to the address in register $ra.

recursive procedures Procedures that call themselves either directly or indirectly through a chain of calls.

Elaboration: A programming language that does not permit **recursive procedures**— procedures that call themselves either directly or indirectly through a chain of calls— need not allocate frames on a stack. In a nonrecursive language, each procedure's frame may be statically allocated, since only one invocation of a procedure can be active at a time. Older versions of Fortran prohibited recursion, because statically allocated frames produced faster code on some older machines. However, on load store architectures like MIPS, stack frames may be just as fast, because a frame pointer register points directly to the active stack frame, which permits a single load or store instruction to access values in the frame. In addition, recursion is a valuable programming technique.

Procedure Call Example

As an example, consider the C routine

```
main ()
{
    printf ("The factorial of 10 is %d\n", fact (10));
}
int fact (int n)
{
    if (n < 1)
        return (1);
    else
        return (n * fact (n - 1));
}
```

which computes and prints 10! (the factorial of 10, 10! = $10 \times 9 \times \ldots \times 1$). fact is a recursive routine that computes $n!$ by multiplying n times $(n - 1)!$. The assembly code for this routine illustrates how programs manipulate stack frames.

Upon entry, the routine main creates its stack frame and saves the two callee-saved registers it will modify: $fp and $ra. The frame is larger than required for these two register because the calling convention requires the minimum size of a stack frame to be 24 bytes. This minimum frame can hold four argument registers ($a0-$a3) and the return address $ra, padded to a double-word boundary (24 bytes). Since main also needs to save $fp, its stack frame must be two words larger (remember: the stack pointer is kept doubleword aligned).

```
        .text
        .globl main
main:
        subu    $sp,$sp,32      # Stack frame is 32 bytes long
        sw      $ra,20($sp)     # Save return address
        sw      $fp,16($sp)     # Save old frame pointer
        addiu   $fp,$sp,28      # Set up frame pointer
```

The routine main then calls the factorial routine and passes it the single argument 10. After fact returns, main calls the library routine printf and passes it both a format string and the result returned from fact:

```
li      $a0,10       # Put argument (10) in $a0
jal     fact         # Call factorial function

la      $a0,$LC      # Put format string in $a0
move    $a1,$v0      # Move fact result to $a1
jal     printf       # Call the print function
```

Finally, after printing the factorial, main returns. But first, it must restore the
registers it saved and pop its stack frame:

```
lw      $ra,20($sp)      # Restore return address
lw      $fp,16($sp)      # Restore frame pointer
addiu   $sp,$sp,32       # Pop stack frame
jr      $ra              # Return to caller

        .rdata
$LC:
.ascii  "The factorial of 10 is %d\n\000"
```

The factorial routine is similar in structure to main. First, it creates a stack frame
and saves the callee-saved registers it will use. In addition to saving $ra and $fp,
fact also saves its argument ($a0), which it will use for the recursive call:

```
        .text
fact:
        subu    $sp,$sp,32       # Stack frame is 32 bytes long
        sw      $ra,20($sp)      # Save return address
        sw      $fp,16($sp)      # Save frame pointer
        addiu   $fp,$sp,28       # Set up frame pointer
        sw      $a0,0($fp)       # Save argument (n)
```

The heart of the fact routine performs the computation from the C program.
It tests whether the argument is greater than 0. If not, the routine returns the value
1. If the argument is greater than 0, the routine recursively calls itself to compute
fact(n-1) and multiplies that value times *n*:

```
        lw      $v0,0($fp)   # Load n
        bgtz    $v0,$L2      # Branch if n > 0
        li      $v0,1        # Return 1
        jr      $L1          # Jump to code to return
$L2:
        lw      $v1,0($fp)   # Load n
        subu    $v0,$v1,1    # Compute n - 1
        move    $a0,$v0      # Move value to $a0
```

```
lw   $v1 ,0($fp)   # Load n
mul  $v0,$v0,$v1   # Compute fact(n-1) * n
```

Finally, the factorial routine restores the callee-saved registers and returns the value in register $v0:

```
$L1:                              # Result is in $v0
        lw        $ra, 20($sp)    # Restore $ra
        lw        $fp, 16($sp)    # Restore $fp
        addiu     $sp, $sp, 32    # Pop stack
        jr        $ra             # Return to caller
```

Stack in Recursive Procedure

Figure A.6.3 shows the stack at the call `fact(7)`. `main` runs first, so its frame is deepest on the stack. main calls `fact(10)`, whose stack frame is next on the stack. Each invocation recursively invokes fact to compute the next-lowest factorial. The stack frames parallel the LIFO order of these calls. What does the stack look like when the call to `fact(10)` returns?

EXAMPLE

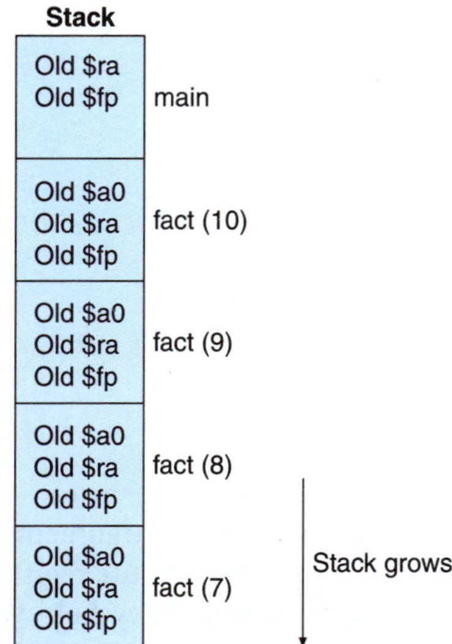

FIGURE A.6.3 Stack frames during the call of `fact(7)`.

ANSWER

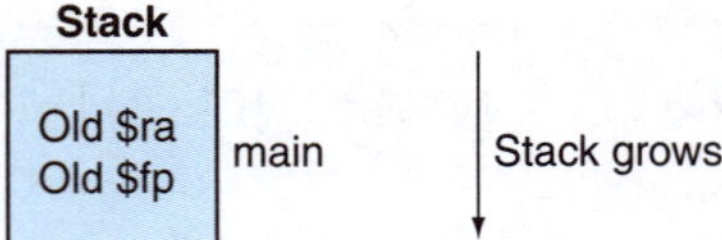

Elaboration: The difference between the MIPS compiler and the gcc compiler is that the MIPS compiler usually does not use a frame pointer, so this register is available as another callee-saved register, $s8. This change saves a couple of instructions in the procedure call and return sequence. However, it complicates code generation, because a procedure must access its stack frame with $sp, whose value can change during a procedure's execution if values are pushed on the stack.

Another Procedure Call Example

As another example, consider the following routine that computes the tak function, which is a widely used benchmark created by Ikuo Takeuchi. This function does not compute anything useful, but is a heavily recursive program that illustrates the MIPS calling convention.

```
int tak (int x, int y, int z)
{
    if (y < x)
        return 1+ tak (tak (x - 1, y, z),
            tak (y - 1, z, x),
            tak (z - 1, x, y));
    else
        return z;
}
int main ()
{
    tak(18, 12, 6);
}
```

The assembly code for this program is shown below. The tak function first saves its return address in its stack frame and its arguments in callee-saved regis ters, since the routine may make calls that need to use registers $a0-$a2 and $ra. The function uses callee-saved registers, since they hold values that persist over the lifetime of the function, which includes several calls that could potentially modify registers.

```
        .text
        .globl  tak

tak:
    subu        $sp, $sp, 40
    sw          $ra, 32($sp)

    sw          $s0, 16($sp)        # x
    move        $s0, $a0
    sw          $s1, 20($sp)        # y
    move        $s1, $a1
    sw          $s2, 24($sp)        # z
    move        $s2, $a2
    sw          $s3, 28($sp)        # temporary
```

The routine then begins execution by testing if y < x. If not, it branches to label L1, which is shown below.

```
    bge         $s1, $s0, L1        # if (y < x)
```

If y < x, then it executes the body of the routine, which contains four recursive calls. The first call uses almost the same arguments as its parent:

```
    addiu       $a0, $s0, -1
    move        $a1, $s1
    move        $a2, $s2
    jal         tak                 # tak (x - 1, y, z)
    move        $s3, $v0
```

Note that the result from the first recursive call is saved in register $s3, so that it can be used later.

The function now prepares arguments for the second recursive call.

```
    addiu       $a0, $s1, -1
    move        $a1, $s2
    move        $a2, $s0
    jal         tak                 # tak (y - 1, z, x)
```

In the instructions below, the result from this recursive call is saved in register $s0. But first we need to read, for the last time, the saved value of the first argument from this register.

```
addiu     $a0, $s2, -1
move      $a1, $s0
move      $a2, $s1
move      $s0, $v0
jal       tak              # tak (z - 1, x, y)
```

After the three inner recursive calls, we are ready for the final recursive call. After the call, the function's result is in $v0 and control jumps to the function's epilogue.

```
move      $a0, $s3
move      $a1, $s0
move      $a2, $v0
jal       tak              # tak (tak(...), tak(...),
          tak(...))
addiu     $v0, $v0, 1
j         L2
```

This code at label L1 is the consequent of the if-then-else statement. It just moves the value of argument z into the return register and falls into the function epilogue.

```
L1:
          move           $v0, $s2
```

The code below is the function epilogue, which restores the saved registers and returns the function's result to its caller.

```
L2:
          lw             $ra, 32($sp)
          lw             $s0, 16($sp)
          lw             $s1, 20($sp)
          lw             $s2, 24($sp)
          lw             $s3, 28($sp)
          addiu          $sp, $sp, 40
          jr             $ra
```

The main routine calls the tak function with its initial arguments, then takes the computed result (7) and prints it using SPIM's system call for printing integers.

```
.globl    main
main:
subu      $sp, $sp, 24
sw        $ra, 16($sp)

li        $a0, 18
```

```
        .globl      main
        main:
        subu        $sp, $sp, 24
        sw          $ra, 16($sp)

        li          $a0, 18
        li          $a1, 12

        li          $a2, 6
        jal         tak                 # tak(18, 12, 6)

        move        $a0, $v0
        li          $v0, 1              # print_int syscall
        syscall


        lw          $ra, 16($sp)
        addiu       $sp, $sp, 24
        jr          $ra
```

A.7   Exceptions and Interrupts

Section 4.9 of Chapter 4 describes the MIPS exception facility, which responds both to exceptions caused by errors during an instruction's execution and to external interrupts caused by I/O devices. This section describes exception and **interrupt handling** in more detail.[1] In MIPS processors, a part of the CPU called *coprocessor 0* records the information the software needs to handle excep tions and interrupts. The MIPS simulator SPIM does not implement all of copro cessor 0's registers, since many are not useful in a simulator or are part of the memory system, which SPIM does not implement. However, SPIM does provide the following coprocessor 0 registers:

interrupt handler
A piece of code that is run as a result of an exception or an interrupt.

Register name	Register number	Usage
BadVAddr	8	memory address at which an offending memory reference occurred
Count	9	timer
Compare	11	value compared against timer that causes interrupt when they match
Status	12	interrupt mask and enable bits
Cause	13	exception type and pending interrupt bits
EPC	14	address of instruction that caused exception
Confg	16	confguration of machine

[1]This section discusses exceptions in the MIPS-32 architecture, which is what SPIM implements in Version 7.0 and later. Earlier versions of SPIM implemented the MIPS-1 architecture, which handled exceptions slightly differently. Converting programs from these versions to run on MIPS-32 should not be diffcult, as the changes are limited to the Status and Cause register fields and the replacement of the `rfe` instruction by the `eret` instruction.

These seven registers are part of coprocessor 0's register set. They are accessed by the `mfc0` and `mtc0` instructions. After an exception, register EPC contains the address of the instruction that was executing when the exception occurred. If the exception was caused by an external interrupt, then the instruction will not have started executing. All other exceptions are caused by the execution of the instruction at EPC, except when the offending instruction is in the delay slot of a branch or jump. In that case, EPC points to the branch or jump instruction and the BD bit is set in the Cause register. When that bit is set, the exception handler must look at EPC + 4 for the offending instruction. However, in either case, an exception handler properly resumes the program by returning to the instruction at EPC.

If the instruction that caused the exception made a memory access, register BadVAddr contains the referenced memory location's address.

The Count register is a timer that increments at a fxed rate (by default, every 10 milliseconds) while SPIM is running. When the value in the Count register equals the value in the Compare register, a hardware interrupt at priority level 5 occurs.

Figure A.7.1 shows the subset of the Status register fields implemented by the MIPS simulator SPIM. The `interrupt mask` field contains a bit for each of the six hardware and two software interrupt levels. A mask bit that is 1 allows interrupts at that level to interrupt the processor. A mask bit that is 0 disables interrupts at that level. When an interrupt arrives, it sets its interrupt pending bit in the Cause register, even if the mask bit is disabled. When an interrupt is pending, it will interrupt the processor when its mask bit is subsequently enabled.

The user mode bit is 0 if the processor is running in kernel mode and 1 if it is running in user mode. On SPIM, this bit is fxed at 1, since the SPIM processor does not implement kernel mode. The exception level bit is normally 0, but is set to 1 after an exception occurs. When this bit is 1, interrupts are disabled and the EPC is not updated if another exception occurs. This bit prevents an exception handler from being disturbed by an interrupt or exception, but it should be reset when the handler fnishes. If the `interrupt enable` bit is 1, interrupts are allowed. If it is 0, they are disabled.

Figure A.7.2 shows the subset of Cause register fields that SPIM implements. The branch delay bit is 1 if the last exception occurred in an instruction executed in the delay slot of a branch. The interrupt pending bits become 1 when an interrupt is raised at a given hardware or software level. The exception code register describes the cause of an exception through the following codes:

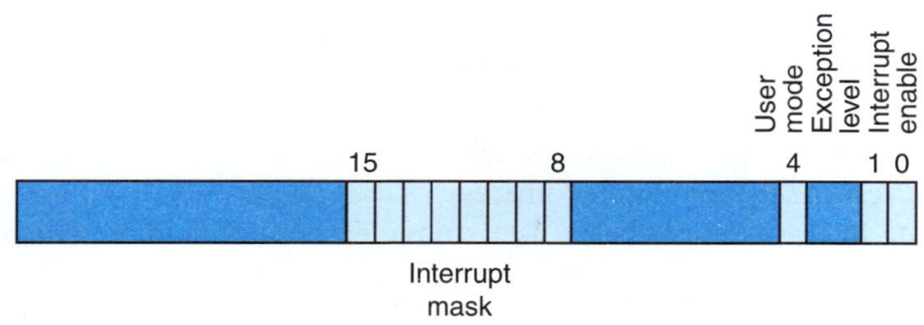

FIGURE A.7.1 The Status register.

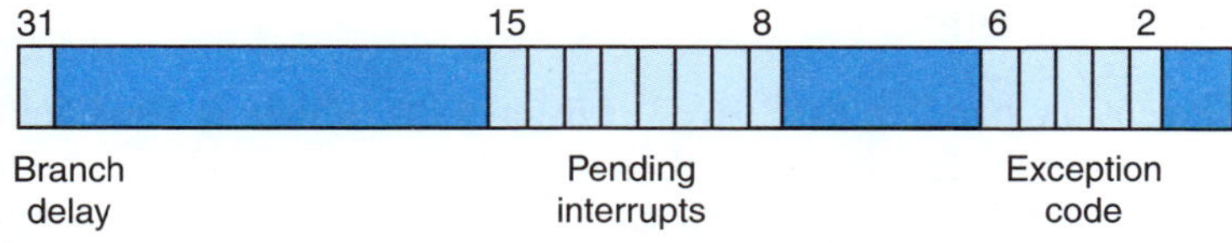

FIGURE A.7.2 The Cause register.

Number	Name	Cause of exception
0	Int	interrupt (hardware)
4	AdEL	address error exception (load or instruction fetch)
5	AdES	address error exception (store)
6	BE	bus error on instruction fetch
7	DBE	bus error on data load or store
8	Sys	syscall exception
9	Bp	breakpoint exception
10	RI	reserved instruction exception
11	CpU	coprocessor unimplemented
12	Ov	arithmetic overflow exception
13	Tr	trap
15	FPE	floating point

Exceptions and interrupts cause a MIPS processor to jump to a piece of code, at address 80000180_{hex} (in the kernel, not user address space), called an *exception handler*. This code examines the exception's cause and jumps to an appropriate point in the operating system. The operating system responds to an exception either by terminating the process that caused the exception or by performing some action. A process that causes an error, such as executing an unimplemented instruction, is killed by the operating system. On the other hand, other exceptions such as page faults are requests from a process to the operating system to perform a service, such as bringing in a page from disk. The operating system processes these requests and resumes the process. The final type of exceptions are interrupts from external devices. These generally cause the operating system to move data to or from an I/O device and resume the interrupted process.

The code in the example below is a simple exception handler, which invokes a routine to print a message at each exception (but not interrupts). This code is similar to the exception handler (exceptions.s) used by the SPIM simulator.

EXAMPLE

Exception Handler

The exception handler first saves register $at, which is used in pseudo-instructions in the handler code, then saves $a0 and $a1, which it later uses to pass arguments. The exception handler cannot store the old values from these registers on the stack, as would an ordinary routine, because the cause of the exception might have been a memory reference that used a bad value (such as 0) in the stack pointer. Instead, the exception handler stores these registers in an exception handler register ($k1, since it can't access memory without using $at) and two memory locations (save0 and save1). If the exception routine itself could be interrupted, two locations would not be enough since the second exception would overwrite values saved during the first exception. However, this simple exception handler fnishes running before it enables interrupts, so the problem does not arise.

```
.ktext 0x80000180
mov $k1, $at    # Save $at register
sw $a0, save0   # Handler is not re-entrant and can't use
sw $a1, save1   # stack to save $a0, $a1
                # Don't need to save $k0/$k1
```

The exception handler then moves the Cause and EPC registers into CPU registers. The Cause and EPC registers are not part of the CPU register set. In stead, they are registers in coprocessor 0, which is the part of the CPU that handles exceptions. The instruction mfc0 $k0, $13 moves coprocessor 0's register 13 (the Cause register) into CPU register $k0. Note that the exception handler need not save registers $k0 and $k1, because user programs are not supposed to use these registers. The exception handler uses the value from the Cause reg ister to test whether the exception was caused by an interrupt (see the preceding ta ble). If so, the exception is ignored. If the exception was not an interrupt, the handler calls print_excp to print a message.

```
mfc0   $k0, $13          # Move Cause into $k0

srl    $a0, $k0, 2       # Extract ExcCode field
andi   $a0, $a0, 0xf

bgtz   $a0, done         # Branch if ExcCode is Int (0)

mov    $a0, $k0          # Move Cause into $a0
mfco   $a1, $14          Move EPC into $a1
jal    print_excp        # Print exception error message
```

Before returning, the exception handler clears the Cause register; resets the Status register to enable interrupts and clear the EXL bit, which allows subse quent exceptions to change the EPC register; and restores registers $a0, $a1, and $at. It then executes the eret (exception return) instruction, which returns to the instruction pointed to by EPC. This exception handler returns to the instruction following the one that caused the exception, so as to not re-execute the faulting instruction and cause the same exception again.

```
done:  mfc0   $k0, $14      # Bump EPC
       addiu  $k0, $k0, 4 # Do not re-execute
                          # faulting instruction
       mtc0   $k0, $14      # EPC

       mtc0   $0, $13       # Clear Cause register

       mfc0   $k0, $12      # Fix Status register
       andi   $k0, 0xfffd # Clear EXL bit
       ori    $k0, 0x1    # Enable interrupts
       mtc0   $k0, $12

       lw     $a0, save0  # Restore registers
       lw     $a1, save1
       mov    $at, $k1

       eret                 # Return to EPC

       .kdata
save0: .word 0
save1: .word 0
```

Elaboration: On real MIPS processors, the return from an exception handler is more complex. The exception handler cannot always jump to the instruction following EPC. For example, if the instruction that caused the exception was in a branch instruction's delay slot (see Chapter 4), the next instruction to execute may not be the following instruction in memory.

A.8   Input and Output

SPIM simulates one I/O device: a memory-mapped console on which a program can read and write characters. When a program is running, SPIM connects its own terminal (or a separate console window in the X-window version xspim or the Windows version PCSpim) to the processor. A MIPS program running on SPIM can read the characters that you type. In addition, if the MIPS program writes characters to the terminal, they appear on SPIM's terminal or console window. One exception to this rule is control-C: this character is not passed to the program, but instead causes SPIM to stop and return to command mode. When the program stops running (for example, because you typed control-C or because the program hit a breakpoint), the terminal is reconnected to SPIM so you can type SPIM commands.

To use memory-mapped I/O (see below), spim or xspim must be started with the -mapped_io flag. PCSpim can enable memory-mapped I/O through a command line flag or the "Settings" dialog.

The terminal device consists of two independent units: a *receiver* and a *transmitter*. The receiver reads characters from the keyboard. The transmitter displays characters on the console. The two units are completely independent. This means, for example, that characters typed at the keyboard are not automatically echoed on the display. Instead, a program echoes a character by reading it from the receiver and writing it to the transmitter.

A program controls the terminal with four memory-mapped device registers, as shown in Figure A.8.1. "Memory-mapped" means that each register appears as a special memory location. The *Receiver Control register* is at location $\text{ffff0000}_{\text{hex}}$. Only two of its bits are actually used. Bit 0 is called "ready": if it is 1, it means that a character has arrived from the keyboard but has not yet been read from the Receiver Data register. The ready bit is read-only: writes to it are ignored. The ready bit changes from 0 to 1 when a character is typed at the keyboard, and it changes from 1 to 0 when the character is read from the Receiver Data register.

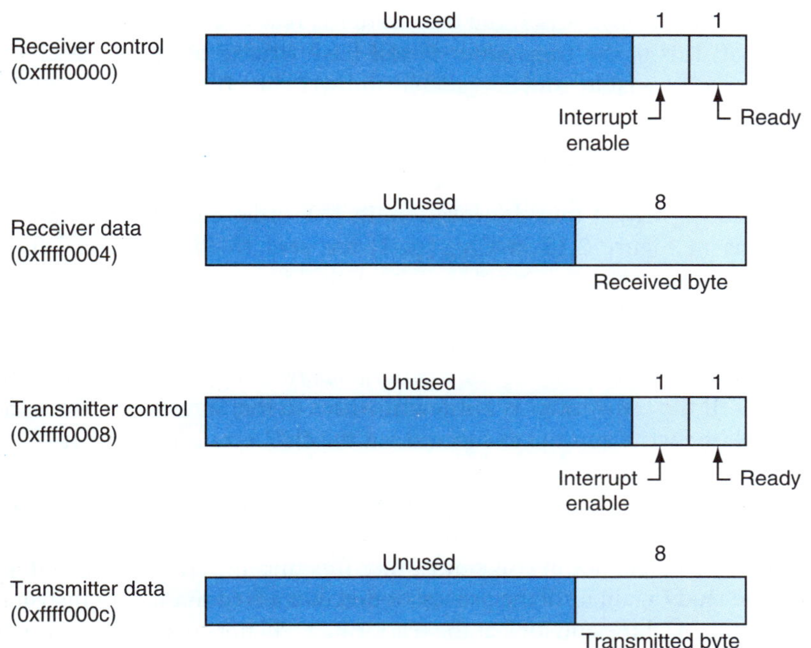

FIGURE A.8.1 The terminal is controlled by four device registers, each of which appears as a memory location at the given address. Only a few bits of these registers are actually used. The others always read as 0s and are ignored on writes.

Bit 1 of the Receiver Control register is the keyboard "interrupt enable." This bit may be both read and written by a program. The interrupt enable is initially 0. If it is set to 1 by a program, the terminal requests an interrupt at hardware level 1 whenever a character is typed, and the ready bit becomes 1. However, for the interrupt to affect the processor, interrupts must also be enabled in the Status register (see **Section A.7**). All other bits of the Receiver Control register are unused.

The second terminal device register is the *Receiver Data register* (at address $ffff0004_{hex}$). The low-order eight bits of this register contain the last character typed at the keyboard. All other bits contain 0s. This register is read-only and changes only when a new character is typed at the keyboard. Reading the Receiver Data register resets the ready bit in the Receiver Control register to 0. The value in this register is undefined if the Receiver Control register is 0.

The third terminal device register is the *Transmitter Control register* (at address $ffff0008_{hex}$). Only the low-order two bits of this register are used. They behave much like the corresponding bits of the Receiver Control register. Bit 0 is called "ready" and is read-only. If this bit is 1, the transmitter is ready to accept a new character for output. If it is 0, the transmitter is still busy writing the previous character. Bit 1 is "interrupt enable" and is readable and writable. If this bit is set to 1, then the terminal requests an interrupt at hardware level 0 whenever the transmitter is ready for a new character, and the ready bit becomes 1.

The final device register is the *Transmitter Data register* (at address ffff000c$_{hex}$). When a value is written into this location, its low-order eight bits (i.e., an ASCII character as in Figure 2.15 in Chapter 2) are sent to the console. When the Transmitter Data register is written, the ready bit in the Transmitter Control register is reset to 0. This bit stays 0 until enough time has elapsed to transmit the character to the terminal; then the ready bit becomes 1 again. The Trans mitter Data register should only be written when the ready bit of the Transmitter Control register is 1. If the transmitter is not ready, writes to the Transmitter Data register are ignored (the write appears to succeed but the character is not output).

Real computers require time to send characters to a console or terminal. These time lags are simulated by SPIM. For example, after the transmitter starts to write a character, the transmitter's ready bit becomes 0 for a while. SPIM measures time in instructions executed, not in real clock time. This means that the transmitter does not become ready again until the processor executes a fxed number of instructions. If you stop the machine and look at the ready bit, it will not change. However, if you let the machine run, the bit eventually changes back to 1.

A.9 SPIM

SPIM is a software simulator that runs assembly language programs written for processors that implement the MIPS-32 architecture, specifcally Release 1 of this architecture with a fxed memory mapping, no caches, and only coprocessors 0 and 1.[2] SPIM's name is just MIPS spelled backwards. SPIM can read and immediately execute assembly language files. SPIM is a self-contained system for running MIPS

---

[2]Earlier versions of SPIM (before 7.0) implemented the MIPS-1 architecture used in the original MIPS R2000 processors. This architecture is almost a proper subset of the MIPS-32 architecture, with the difference being the manner in which exceptions are handled. MIPS-32 also introduced approximately 60 new instructions, which are supported by SPIM. Programs that ran on the earlier versions of SPIM and did not use exceptions should run unmodifed on newer versions of SPIM. Programs that used exceptions will require minor changes.

programs. It contains a debugger and provides a few operating system–like services. SPIM is much slower than a real computer (100 or more times). How ever, its low cost and wide availability cannot be matched by real hardware!

An obvious question is, "Why use a simulator when most people have PCs that contain processors that run signifcantly faster than SPIM?" One reason is that the processor in PCs are Intel 80x86s, whose architecture is far less regular and far more complex to understand and program than MIPS processors. The MIPS architecture may be the epitome of a simple, clean RISC machine.

In addition, simulators can provide a better environment for assembly programming than an actual machine because they can detect more errors and provide a better interface than an actual computer.

Finally, simulators are useful tools in studying computers and the programs that run on them. Because they are implemented in software, not silicon, simulators can be examined and easily modifed to add new instructions, build new systems such as multiprocessors, or simply collect data.

Simulation of a Virtual Machine

The basic MIPS architecture is diffcult to program directly because of delayed branches, delayed loads, and restricted address modes. This diffculty is tolerable since these computers were designed to be programmed in high-level languages and present an interface designed for compilers rather than assembly language programmers. A good part of the programming complexity results from delayed instructions. A *delayed branch* requires two cycles to execute (see the *Elaborations* on pages 267 and 296 of Chapter 4). In the second cycle, the instruction immediately following the branch executes. This instruction can perform useful work that normally would have been done before the branch. It can also be a nop (no operation) that does nothing. Similarly, *delayed loads* require two cycles to bring a value from memory, so the instruction immediately following a load cannot use the value (see Section 4.2 of Chapter 4).

MIPS wisely chose to hide this complexity by having its assembler implement a **virtual machine**. This virtual computer appears to have nondelayed branches and loads and a richer instruction set than the actual hardware. The assembler *reorganizes* (rearranges) instructions to fll the delay slots. The virtual computer also provides *pseudoinstructions*, which appear as real instructions in assembly lan guage programs. The hardware, however, knows nothing about pseudoinstructions, so the assembler must translate them into equivalent sequences of actual machine instructions. For example, the MIPS hardware only provides instructions to branch when a register is equal to or not equal to 0. Other conditional branches, such as one that branches when one register is greater than another, are synthesized by comparing the two registers and branching when the result of the comparison is true (nonzero).

virtual machine
A virtual computer that appears to have nondelayed branches and loads and a richer instruction set than the actual hardware.

By default, SPIM simulates the richer virtual machine, since this is the machine that most programmers will find useful. However, SPIM can also simulate the delayed branches and loads in the actual hardware. Below, we describe the virtual machine and only mention in passing features that do not belong to the actual hardware. In doing so, we follow the convention of MIPS assembly language programmers (and compilers), who routinely use the extended machine as if it was implemented in silicon.

Getting Started with SPIM

The rest of this appendix introduces SPIM and the MIPS R2000 Assembly language. Many details should never concern you; however, the sheer volume of information can sometimes obscure the fact that SPIM is a simple, easy-to-use program. This section starts with a quick tutorial on using SPIM, which should enable you to load, debug, and run simple MIPS programs.

SPIM comes in different versions for different types of computer systems. The one constant is the simplest version, called `spim`, which is a command-line-driven program that runs in a console window. It operates like most programs of this type: you type a line of text, hit the `return` key, and `spim` executes your command. Despite its lack of a fancy interface, `spim` can do everything that its fancy cousins can do.

There are two fancy cousins to `spim`. The version that runs in the X-windows environment of a UNIX or Linux system is called `xspim`. `xspim` is an easier program to learn and use than `spim`, because its commands are always visible on the screen and because it continually displays the machine's registers and memory. The other fancy version is called `PCspim` and runs on Microsoft Windows. The UNIX and Windows versions of **SPIM** 🌐 are on the CD (click on Tutorials). Tutorials on `xspim`, `pcSpim`, `spim`, and **SPIM command-line options** 🌐 are on the CD (click on Software).

If you are going to run SPIM on a PC running Microsoft Windows, you should first look at the tutorial on **PCSpim** 🌐 on the CD. If you are going to run SPIM on a computer running UNIX or Linux, you should read the tutorial on **xspim** 🌐 (click on Tutorials).

Surprising Features

Although SPIM faithfully simulates the MIPS computer, SPIM is a simulator, and certain things are not identical to an actual computer. The most obvious differences are that instruction timing and the memory systems are not identical. SPIM does not simulate caches or memory latency, nor does it accurately refect floating-point operation or multiply and divide instruction delays. In addition, the floating-point instructions do not detect many error conditions, which would cause exceptions on a real machine.

Another surprise (which occurs on the real machine as well) is that a pseudo-instruction expands to several machine instructions. When you single-step or examine memory, the instructions that you see are different from the source program. The correspondence between the two sets of instructions is fairly simple, since SPIM does not reorganize instructions to fll delay slots.

Byte Order

Processors can number bytes within a word so the byte with the lowest number is either the leftmost or rightmost one. The convention used by a machine is called its *byte order*. MIPS processors can operate with either *big-endian* or *little-endian* byte order. For example, in a big-endian machine, the directive `.byte 0, 1, 2, 3` would result in a memory word containing

Byte #			
0	1	2	3

while in a little-endian machine, the word would contain

Byte #			
3	2	1	0

SPIM operates with both byte orders. SPIM's byte order is the same as the byte order of the underlying machine that runs the simulator. For example, on an Intel 80 × 86, SPIM is little-endian, while on a Macintosh or Sun SPARC, SPIM is big-endian.

System Calls

SPIM provides a small set of operating system-like services through the system call (`syscall`) instruction. To request a service, a program loads the system call code (see Figure A.9.1) into register $v0 and arguments into registers $a0-$a3 (or $f12 for floating-point values). System calls that return values put their results in register $v0 (or $f0 for floating-point results). For example, the follow ing code prints "the answer = 5":

```
        .data
str:
        .asciiz "the answer = "
        .text
```

Service	System call code	Arguments	Result
print_int	1	$a0 = integer	
print_float	2	$f12 = float	
print_double	3	$f12 = double	
print_string	4	$a0 = string	
read_int	5		integer (in $v0)
read_float	6		float (in $f0)
read_double	7		double (in $f0)
read_string	8	$a0 = buffer, $a1 = length	
sbrk	9	$a0 = amount	address (in $v0)
exit	10		
print_char	11	$a0 = char	
read_char	12		char (in $v0)
open	13	$a0 = filename (string), $a1 = flags, $a2 = mode	file descriptor (in $a0)
read	14	$a0 = file descriptor, $a1 = buffer, $a2 = length	num chars read (in $a0)
write	15	$a0 = file descriptor, $a1 = buffer, $a2 = length	num chars written (in $a0)
close	16	$a0 = file descriptor	
exit2	17	$a0 = result	

FIGURE A.9.1 System services.

```
li       $v0, 4      # system call code for print_str
la       $a0, str    # address of string to print
syscall              # print the string

li       $v0, 1      # system call code for print_int
li       $a0, 5      # integer to print
syscall              # print it
```

The print_int system call is passed an integer and prints it on the console. print_float prints a single floating-point number; print_double prints a double precision number; and print_string is passed a pointer to a null-terminated string, which it writes to the console.

The system calls read_int, read_float, and read_double to read an entire line of input up to and including the newline. Characters following the number are ignored. read_string has the same semantics as the UNIX library routine fgets. It reads up to $n - 1$ characters into a buffer and terminates the string with a null byte. If fewer than $n - 1$ characters are on the current line, read_string reads up to and including the newline and again null-terminates the string. *Warning*:

Programs that use these syscalls to read from the terminal should not use memory-mapped I/O (see Section A.8).

`sbrk` returns a pointer to a block of memory containing n additional bytes. `exit` stops the program SPIM is running. `exit2` terminates the SPIM program, and the argument to `exit2` becomes the value returned when the SPIM simulator itself terminates.

`print_char` and `read_char` write and read a single character. `open`, `read`, `write`, and `close` are the standard UNIX library calls.

A.10　MIPS R2000 Assembly Language

A MIPS processor consists of an integer processing unit (the CPU) and a collection of coprocessors that perform ancillary tasks or operate on other types of data, such as floating-point numbers (see Figure A.10.1). SPIM simulates two coproces sors. Coprocessor 0 handles exceptions and interrupts. Coprocessor 1 is the floating-point unit. SPIM simulates most aspects of this unit.

Addressing Modes

MIPS is a load store architecture, which means that only load and store instruc tions access memory. Computation instructions operate only on values in registers. The bare machine provides only one memory-addressing mode: `c(rx)`, which uses the sum of the immediate c and register `rx` as the address. The virtual machine provides the following addressing modes for load and store instructions:

Format	Address computation
(register)	contents of register
imm	immediate
imm (register)	immediate + contents of register
label	address of label
label ± imm	address of label + or − immediate
label ± imm (register)	address of label + or − (immediate + contents of register)

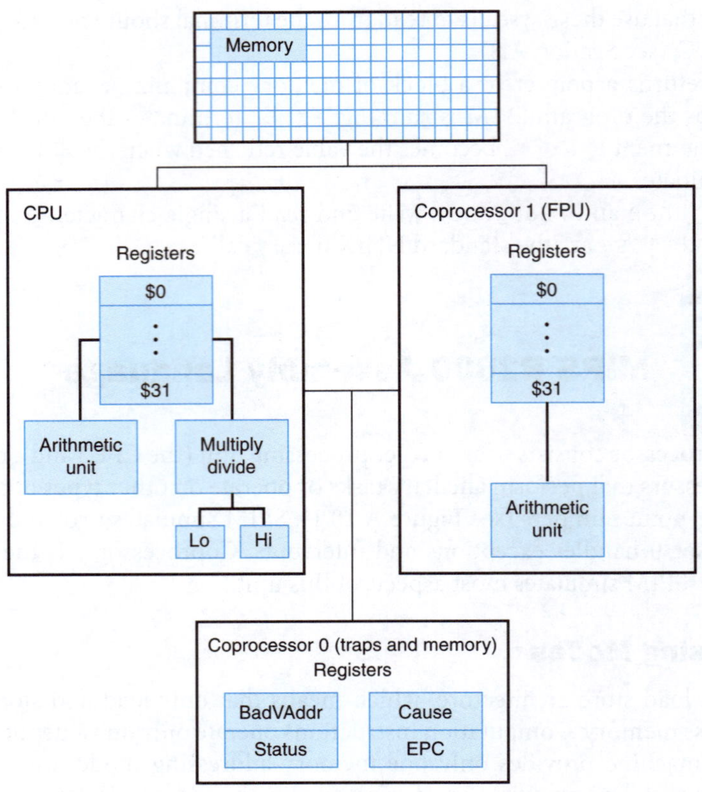

FIGURE A.10.1 MIPS R2000 CPU and FPU.

Most load and store instructions operate only on aligned data. A quantity is *aligned* if its memory address is a multiple of its size in bytes. Therefore, a half word object must be stored at even addresses, and a full word object must be stored at addresses that are a multiple of four. However, MIPS provides some instructions to manipulate unaligned data (`lwl`, `lwr`, `swl`, and `swr`).

Elaboration: The MIPS assembler (and SPIM) synthesizes the more complex addressing modes by producing one or more instructions before the load or store to compute a complex address. For example, suppose that the label `table` referred to memory location 0x10000004 and a program contained the instruction

```
ld $a0, table + 4($a1)
```

The assembler would translate this instruction into the instructions

```
lui $at, 4096
addu $at, $at, $a1
lw $a0, 8($at)
```

The first instruction loads the upper bits of the label's address into register $at, which is the register that the assembler reserves for its own use. The second instruction adds the contents of register $a1 to the label's partial address. Finally, the load instruction uses the hardware address mode to add the sum of the lower bits of the label's address and the offset from the original instruction to the value in register $at.

Assembler Syntax

Comments in assembler files begin with a sharp sign (#). Everything from the sharp sign to the end of the line is ignored.

Identifers are a sequence of alphanumeric characters, underbars (_), and dots (.) that do not begin with a number. Instruction opcodes are reserved words that *cannot* be used as identifers. Labels are declared by putting them at the beginning of a line followed by a colon, for example:

```
          .data
item:     .word 1
          .text
          .globl main    # Must be global
main:     lw           $t0, item
```

Numbers are base 10 by default. If they are preceded by *0x*, they are interpreted as hexadecimal. Hence, 256 and 0x100 denote the same value.

Strings are enclosed in double quotes ("). Special characters in strings follow the C convention:

- newline   \n

- tab   \t

- quote   \"

SPIM supports a subset of the MIPS assembler directives:

`.align n`	Align the next datum on a *2n* byte boundary. For example, `.align 2` aligns the next value on a word boundary. `.align 0` turns off automatic alignment of `.half`, `.word`, `.float`, and `.double` directives until the next `.data` or `.kdata` directive.

`.ascii str`	Store the string *str* in memory, but do not null-terminate it.
`.asciiz str`	Store the string *str* in memory and null-terminate it.
`.byte b1,..., bn`	Store the *n* values in successive bytes of memory.
`.data <addr>`	Subsequent items are stored in the data segment. If the optional argument *addr* is present, subsequent items are stored starting at address *addr*.
`.double d1,..., dn`	Store the *n* floating-point double precision numbers in successive memory locations.
`.extern sym size`	Declare that the datum stored at *sym* is *size* bytes large and is a global label. This directive enables the assembler to store the datum in a portion of the data segment that is effciently accessed via register $gp.
`.float f1,..., fn`	Store the *n* floating-point single precision numbers in successive memory locations.
`.globl sym`	Declare that label *sym* is global and can be referenced from other files.
`.half h1,..., hn`	Store the *n* 16-bit quantities in successive memory halfwords.
`.kdata <addr>`	Subsequent data items are stored in the kernel data segment. If the optional argument *addr* is present, subsequent items are stored starting at address *addr*.
`.ktext <addr>`	Subsequent items are put in the kernel text segment. In SPIM, these items may only be instructions or words (see the `.word` directive below). If the optional argument *addr* is present, subse quent items are stored starting at address *addr*.
`.set noat and .set at`	The first directive prevents SPIM from complaining about subsequent instructions that use register $at. The second directive re-enables the warning. Since pseudoinstructions expand into code that uses register $at, programmers must be very careful about leaving values in this register.
`.space n`	Allocates *n* bytes of space in the current segment (which must be the data segment in SPIM).

`.text <addr>`	Subsequent items are put in the user text segment. In SPIM, these items may only be instruc tions or words (see the `.word` directive below). If the optional argument *addr* is present, subse quent items are stored starting at address *addr*.
`.word w1,..., wn`	Store the *n* 32-bit quantities in successive memory words.

SPIM does not distinguish various parts of the data segment (`.data`, `.rdata`, and `.sdata`).

Encoding MIPS Instructions

Figure A.10.2 explains how a MIPS instruction is encoded in a binary number. Each column contains instruction encodings for a field (a contiguous group of bits) from an instruction. The numbers at the left margin are values for a field. For example, the j opcode has a value of 2 in the opcode field. The text at the top of a column names a field and specifes which bits it occupies in an instruction. For example, the op field is contained in bits 26–31 of an instruction. This field encodes most instructions. However, some groups of instructions use additional fields to distinguish related instructions. For example, the different floating-point instructions are specifed by bits 0–5. The arrows from the first column show which opcodes use these additional fields.

Instruction Format

The rest of this appendix describes both the instructions implemented by actual MIPS hardware and the pseudoinstructions provided by the MIPS assembler. The two types of instructions are easily distinguished. Actual instructions depict the fields in their binary representation. For example, in

Addition (with overflow)

`add rd, rs, rt`

0	rs	rt	rd	0	0x20
6	5	5	5	5	6

the add instruction consists of six fields. Each field's size in bits is the small num ber below the field. This instruction begins with six bits of 0s. Register specifers begin with an *r*, so the next field is a 5-bit register specifer called `rs`. This is the same register that is the second argument in the symbolic assembly at the left of this line. Another common field is $\texttt{imm}_{16}$, which is a 16-bit immediate number.

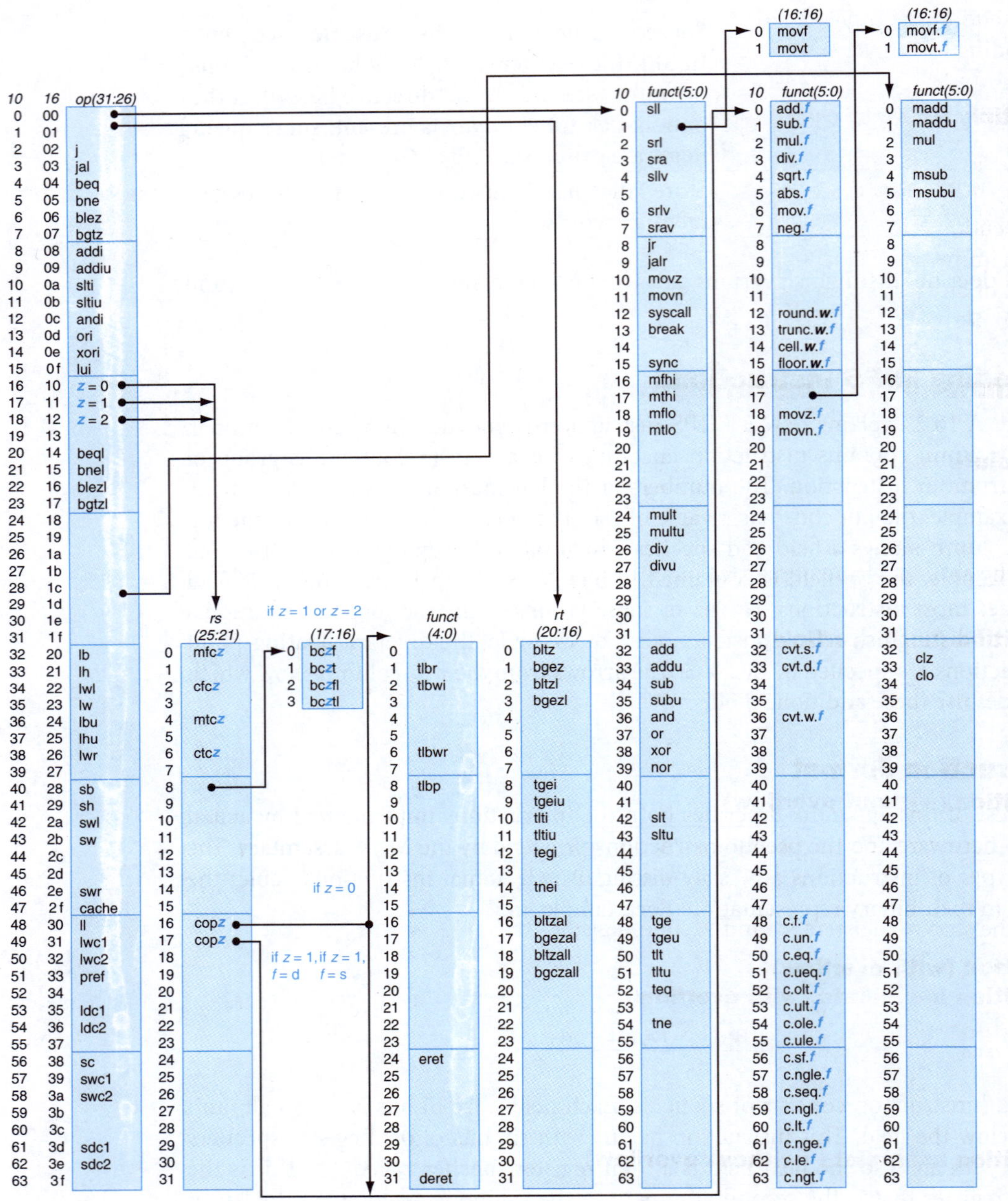

FIGURE A.10.2 MIPS opcode map. The values of each field are shown to its left. The first column shows the values in base 10, and the second shows base 16 for the op field (bits 31 to 26) in the third column. This op field completely specifies the MIPS operation except for six op values: 0, 1, 16, 17, 18, and 19. These operations are determined by other fields, identified by pointers. The last field (funct) uses "*f*" to mean "s" if rs = 16 and op = 17 or "d" if rs = 17 and op = 17. The second field (rs) uses "*z*" to mean "0", "1", "2", or "3" if op = 16, 17, 18, or 19, respectively. If rs = 16, the operation is specified elsewhere: if *z* = 0, the operations are specified in the fourth field (bits 4 to 0); if *z* = 1, then the operations are in the last field with *f* = s. If rs = 17 and *z* = 1, then the operations are in the last field with *f* = d.

Pseudoinstructions follow roughly the same conventions, but omit instruction encoding information. For example:

Multiply (without overflow)

```
mill rdest, rsrc1, src2      pseudoinstruction
```

In pseudoinstructions, rdest and rsrc1 are registers and src2 is either a register or an immediate value. In general, the assembler and SPIM translate a more general form of an instruction (e.g., add $v1, $a0, 0x55) to a specialized form (e.g., addi $v1, $a0, 0x55).

Arithmetic and Logical Instructions

Absolute value

```
abs rdest, rsrc        pseudoinstruction
```

Put the absolute value of register rsrc in register rdest.

Addition (with overflow)

```
add rd, rs, rt
```

0	rs	rt	rd	0	0x20
6	5	5	5	5	6

Addition (without overflow)

```
add rd, rs, rt
```

0	rs	rt	rd	0	0x21
6	5	5	5	5	6

Put the sum of registers rs and rt into register rd.

Addition immediate (with overflow)

```
addi rt, rs, imm
```

8	rs	rt	imm
6	5	5	16

Addition immediate (without overflow)

```
addiu rt, rs, immr
```

9	rs	rt	imm
6	5	5	16

Put the sum of register rs and the sign-extended immediate into register rt.

AND

and rd, rs, rt

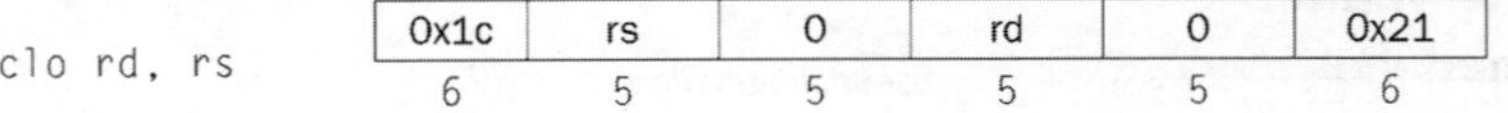

Put the logical AND of registers rs and rt into register rd.

AND immediate

addi rt, rs, immr

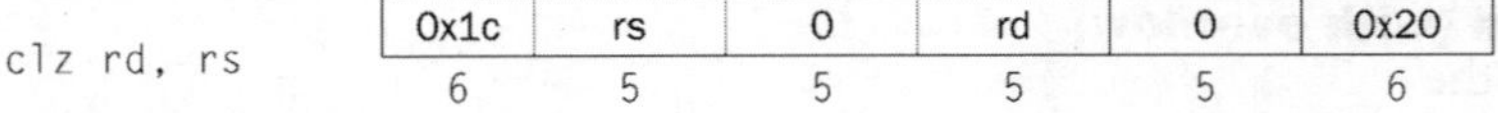

Put the logical AND of register rs and the zero-extended immediate into register rt.

Count leading ones

clo rd, rs

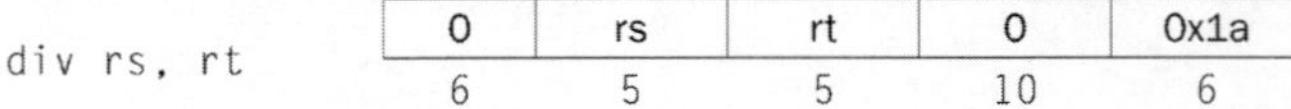

Count leading zeros

clz rd, rs

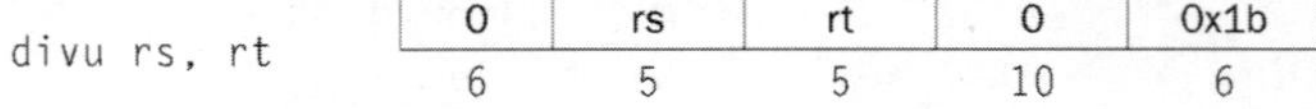

Count the number of leading ones (zeros) in the word in register rs and put the result into register rd. If a word is all ones (zeros), the result is 32.

Divide (with overflow)

div rs, rt

Divide (without overflow)

divu rs, rt

Divide register rs by register rt. Leave the quotient in register lo and the remainder in register hi. Note that if an operand is negative, the remainder is unspecifed by the MIPS architecture and depends on the convention of the machine on which SPIM is run.

Divide (with overflow)

```
div rdest, rsrc1, src2          pseudoinstruction
```

Divide (without overflow)

```
divu rdest, rsrc1, src2         pseudoinstruction
```

Put the quotient of register `rsrc1` and `src2` into register `rdest`.

Multiply

`mult rs, rt`

0	rs	rt	0	0x18
6	5	5	10	6

Unsigned multiply

`multu rs, rt`

0	rs	rt	0	0x19
6	5	5	10	6

Multiply registers `rs` and `rt`. Leave the low-order word of the product in register `lo` and the high-order word in register `hi`.

Multiply (without overflow)

`mul rd, rs, rt`

0x1c	rs	rt	rd	0	2
6	5	5	5	5	6

Put the low-order 32 bits of the product of `rs` and `rt` into register `rd`.

Multiply (with overflow)

```
mulo rdest, rsrc1, src2         pseudoinstruction
```

Unsigned multiply (with overflow)

```
mulou rdest, rsrc1, src2        pseudoinstruction
```

Put the low-order 32 bits of the product of register `rsrc1` and `src2` into register `rdest`.

Multiply add

`madd rs, rt`	0x1c	rs	rt	0	0
	6	5	5	10	6

Unsigned multiply add

`maddu rs, rt`	0x1c	rs	rt	0	1
	6	5	5	10	6

Multiply registers `rs` and `rt` and add the resulting 64-bit product to the 64-bit value in the concatenated registers `lo` and `hi`.

Multiply subtract

`msub rs, rt`	0x1c	rs	rt	0	4
	6	5	5	10	6

Unsigned multiply subtract

`msub rs, rt`	0x1c	rs	rt	0	5
	6	5	5	10	6

Multiply registers `rs` and `rt` and subtract the resulting 64-bit product from the 64-bit value in the concatenated registers `lo` and `hi`.

Negate value (with overflow)

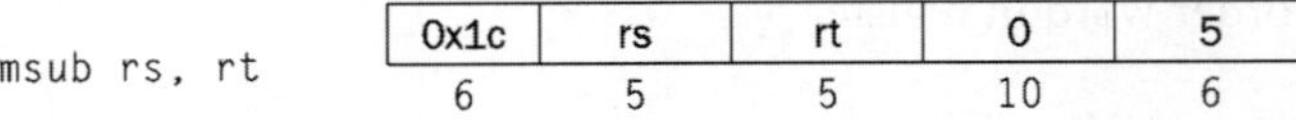

Negate value (without overflow)

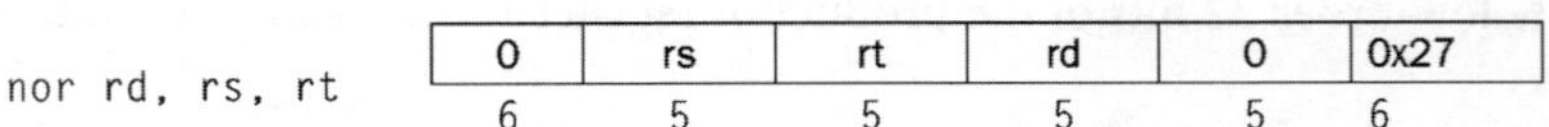

Put the negative of register `rsrc` into register `rdest`.

NOR

`nor rd, rs, rt`	0	rs	rt	rd	0	0x27
	6	5	5	5	5	6

Put the logical NOR of registers `rs` and `rt` into register `rd`.

NOT

not rdest, rsrc	pseudoinstruction

Put the bitwise logical negation of register rsrc into register rdest.

OR

or rd, rs, rt

0	rs	rt	rd	0	0x25
6	5	5	5	5	6

Put the logical OR of registers rs and rt into register rd.

OR immediate

ori rt, rs, imm

0xd	rs	rt	imm
6	5	5	16

Put the logical OR of register rs and the zero-extended immediate into register rt.

Remainder

rem rdest, rsrc1, rsrc2	pseudoinstruction

Unsigned remainder

remu rdest, rsrc1, rsrc2	pseudoinstruction

Put the remainder of register rsrc1 divided by register rsrc2 into register rdest. Note that if an operand is negative, the remainder is unspecifed by the MIPS architecture and depends on the convention of the machine on which SPIM is run.

Shift left logical

sll rd, rt, shamt

0	rs	rt	rd	shamt	0
6	5	5	5	5	6

Shift left logical variable

sllv rd, rt, rs

0	rs	rt	rd	0	4
6	5	5	5	5	6

Shift right arithmetic

```
sra rd, rt, shamt
```

0	rs	rt	rd	shamt	3
6	5	5	5	5	6

Shift right arithmetic variable

```
srav rd, rt, rs
```

0	rs	rt	rd	0	7
6	5	5	5	5	6

Shift right logical

```
srl rd, rt, shamt
```

0	rs	rt	rd	shamt	2
6	5	5	5	5	6

Shift right logical variable

```
srlv rd, rt, rs
```

0	rs	rt	rd	0	6
6	5	5	5	5	6

Shift register rt left (right) by the distance indicated by immediate shamt or the register rs and put the result in register rd. Note that argument rs is ignored for sll, sra, and srl.

Rotate left

```
rol rdest, rsrc1, rsrc2
```
pseudoinstruction

Rotate right

```
ror rdest, rsrc1, rsrc2
```
pseudoinstruction

Rotate register rsrc1 left (right) by the distance indicated by rsrc2 and put the result in register rdest.

Subtract (with overflow)

```
sub rd, rs, rt
```

0	rs	rt	rd	0	0x22
6	5	5	5	5	6

Subtract (without overflow)

```
subu rd, rs, rt
```

0	rs	rt	rd	0	0x23
6	5	5	5	5	6

Put the difference of registers rs and rt into register rd.

Exclusive OR

```
xor rd, rs, rt
```

0	rs	rt	rd	0	0x26
6	5	5	5	5	6

Put the logical XOR of registers rs and rt into register rd.

XOR immediate

```
xori rt, rs, imm
```

0xe	rs	rt	Imm
6	5	5	16

Put the logical XOR of register rs and the zero-extended immediate into register rt.

Constant-Manipulating Instructions

Load upper immediate

```
lui rt, imm
```

0xf	0	rt	imm
6	5	5	16

Load the lower halfword of the immediate imm into the upper halfword of register rt. The lower bits of the register are set to 0.

Load immediate

Move the immediate imm into register rdest.

Comparison Instructions

Set less than

```
slt rd, rs, rt
```

0	rs	rt	rd	0	0x2a
6	5	5	5	5	6

Set less than unsigned

```
sltu rd, rs, rt
```

0	rs	rt	rd	0	0x2b
6	5	5	5	5	6

Set register rd to 1 if register rs is less than rt, and to 0 otherwise.

Set less than immediate

```
slti rt, rs, imm
```

0xa	rs	rt	imm
6	5	5	16

Set less than unsigned immediate

```
sltiu rt, rs, imm
```

0xb	rs	rt	imm
6	5	5	16

Set register rt to 1 if register rs is less than the sign-extended immediate, and to 0 otherwise.

Set equal

seq rdest, rsrc1, rsrc2	*pseudoinstruction*

Set register rdest to 1 if register rsrc1 equals rsrc2, and to 0 otherwise.

Set greater than equal

sge rdest, rsrc1, rsrc2	*pseudoinstruction*

Set greater than equal unsigned

sgeu rdest, rsrc1, rsrc2	*pseudoinstruction*

Set register rdest to 1 if register rsrc1 is greater than or equal to rsrc2, and to 0 otherwise.

Set greater than

sgt rdest, rsrc1, rsrc2	*pseudoinstruction*

Set greater than unsigned

```
sgtu rdest, rsrc1, rsrc2          pseudoinstruction
```

Set register `rdest` to 1 if register `rsrc1` is greater than `rsrc2`, and to 0 otherwise.

Set less than equal

```
sle rdest, rsrc1, rsrc2           pseudoinstruction
```

Set less than equal unsigned

```
sleu rdest, rsrc1, rsrc2          pseudoinstruction
```

Set register `rdest` to 1 if register `rsrc1` is less than or equal to `rsrc2`, and to 0 otherwise.

Set not equal

```
sne rdest, rsrc1, rsrc2           pseudoinstruction
```

Set register `rdest` to 1 if register `rsrc1` is not equal to `rsrc2`, and to 0 otherwise.

Branch Instructions

Branch instructions use a signed 16-bit instruction *offset* field; hence, they can jump $2^{15} - 1$ *instructions* (not bytes) forward or 2^{15} instructions backward. The *jump* instruction contains a 26-bit address field. In actual MIPS processors, branch instructions are delayed branches, which do not transfer control until the instruction following the branch (its "delay slot") has executed (see Chapter 4). Delayed branches affect the offset calculation, since it must be computed relative to the address of the delay slot instruction (PC + 4), which is when the branch occurs. SPIM does not simulate this delay slot, unless the `-bare` or `-delayed_branch` flags are specifed.

In assembly code, offsets are not usually specifed as numbers. Instead, an instructions branch to a label, and the assembler computes the distance between the branch and the target instructions.

In MIPS-32, all actual (not pseudo) conditional branch instructions have a "likely" variant (for example, `beq`'s likely variant is `beql`), which does *not* execute the instruction in the branch's delay slot if the branch is not taken. Do not use these instructions; they may be removed in subsequent versions of the architecture. SPIM implements these instructions, but they are not described further.

Branch instruction

Unconditionally branch to the instruction at the label.

Branch coprocessor false

bclf cc label
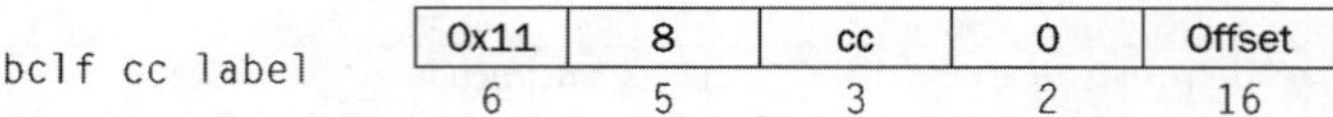

Branch coprocessor true

bclt cc label
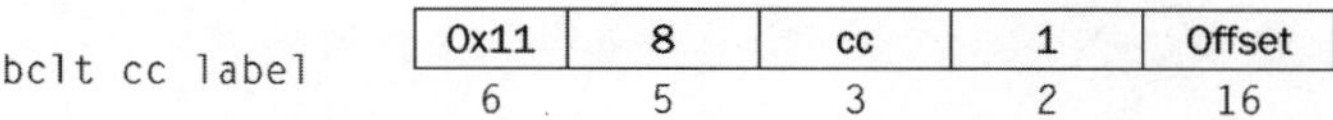

Conditionally branch the number of instructions specifed by the offset if the floating-point coprocessor's condition flag numbered *cc* is false (true). If *cc* is omitted from the instruction, condition code flag 0 is assumed.

Branch on equal

beq rs, rt, label
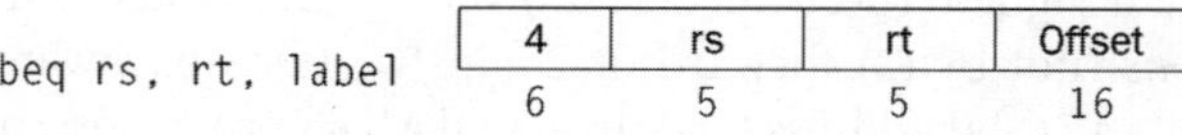

Conditionally branch the number of instructions specifed by the offset if register rs equals rt.

Branch on greater than equal zero

bgez rs, label
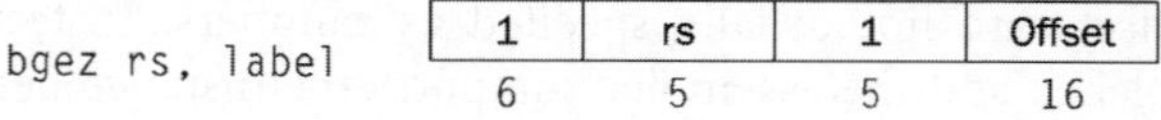

Conditionally branch the number of instructions specifed by the offset if register rs is greater than or equal to 0.

Branch on greater than equal zero and link

```
bgezal rs, label
```

1	rs	0x11	Offset
6	5	5	16

Conditionally branch the number of instructions specifed by the offset if register rs is greater than or equal to 0. Save the address of the next instruction in register 31.

Branch on greater than zero

```
bgtz rs, label
```

7	rs	0	Offset
6	5	5	16

Conditionally branch the number of instructions specifed by the offset if register rs is greater than 0.

Branch on less than equal zero

```
blez rs, label
```

6	rs	0	Offset
6	5	5	16

Conditionally branch the number of instructions specifed by the offset if register rs is less than or equal to 0.

Branch on less than and link

```
bltzal rs, label
```

1	rs	0x10	Offset
6	5	5	16

Conditionally branch the number of instructions specifed by the offset if register rs is less than 0. Save the address of the next instruction in register 31.

Branch on less than zero

```
bltz rs, label
```

1	rs	0	Offset
6	5	5	16

Conditionally branch the number of instructions specifed by the offset if register rs is less than 0.

Branch on not equal

bne rs, rt, label

5	rs	rt	Offset
6	5	5	16

Conditionally branch the number of instructions specifed by the offset if register rs is not equal to rt.

Branch on equal zero

beqz rsrc, label	*pseudoinstruction*

Conditionally branch to the instruction at the label if rsrc equals 0.

Branch on greater than equal

bge rsrc1, rsrc2, label	*pseudoinstruction*

Branch on greater than equal unsigned

bgeu rsrc1, rsrc2, label	*pseudoinstruction*

Conditionally branch to the instruction at the label if register rsrc1 is greater than or equal to rsrc2.

Branch on greater than

bgt rsrc1, src2, label	*pseudoinstruction*

Branch on greater than unsigned

bgtu rsrc1, src2, label	*pseudoinstruction*

Conditionally branch to the instruction at the label if register rsrc1 is greater than src2.

Branch on less than equal

ble rsrc1, src2, label	*pseudoinstruction*

Branch on less than equal unsigned

| `bleu rsrc1, src2, label` | *pseudoinstruction* |

Conditionally branch to the instruction at the label if register `rsrc1` is less than or equal to `src2`.

Branch on less than

| `blt rsrc1, rsrc2, label` | *pseudoinstruction* |

Branch on less than unsigned

| `bltu rsrc1, rsrc2, label` | *pseudoinstruction* |

Conditionally branch to the instruction at the label if register `rsrc1` is less than `rsrc2`.

Branch on not equal zero

| `bnez rsrc, label` | *pseudoinstruction* |

Conditionally branch to the instruction at the label if register `rsrc` is not equal to 0.

Jump Instructions

Jump

`j target`

2	target
6	26

Unconditionally jump to the instruction at target.

Jump and link

`jal target`

3	target
6	26

Unconditionally jump to the instruction at target. Save the address of the next instruction in register `$ra`.

Jump and link register

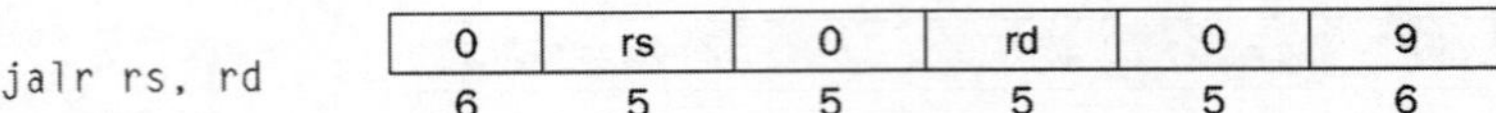

`jalr rs, rd`

Unconditionally jump to the instruction whose address is in register `rs`. Save the address of the next instruction in register `rd` (which defaults to 31).

Jump register

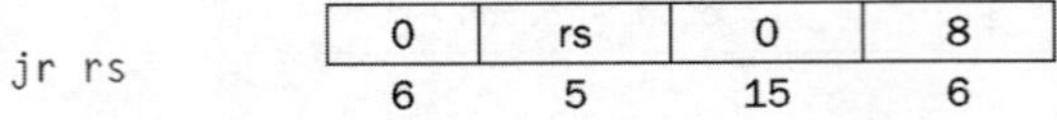

`jr rs`

Unconditionally jump to the instruction whose address is in register `rs`.

Trap Instructions

Trap if equal

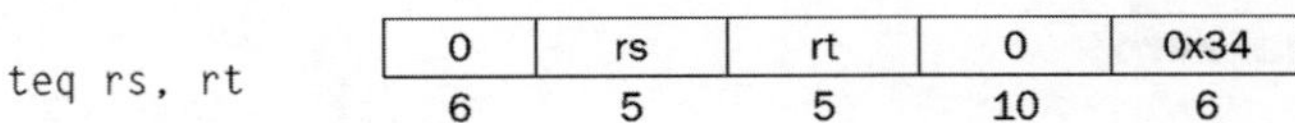

`teq rs, rt`

If register `rs` is equal to register `rt`, raise a Trap exception.

Trap if equal immediate

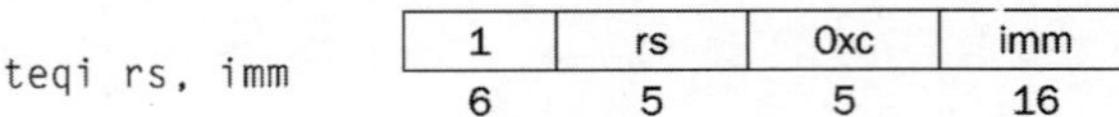

`teqi rs, imm`

If register `rs` is equal to the sign-extended value `imm`, raise a Trap exception.

Trap if not equal

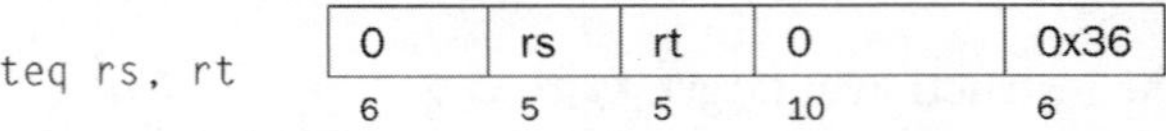

`teq rs, rt`

If register `rs` is not equal to register `rt`, raise a Trap exception.

Trap if not equal immediate

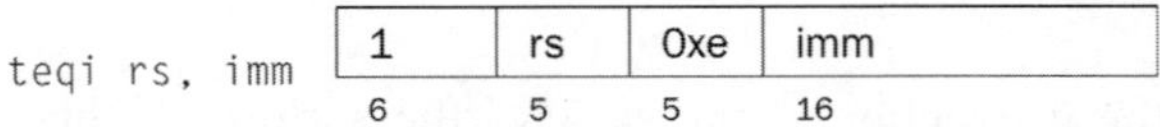

`teqi rs, imm`

If register `rs` is not equal to the sign-extended value `imm`, raise a Trap exception.

Trap if greater equal

`tge rs, rt`

0	rs	rt	0	0x30
6	5	5	10	6

Unsigned trap if greater equal

`tgeu rs, rt`

0	rs	rt	0	0x31
6	5	5	10	6

If register rs is greater than or equal to register rt, raise a Trap exception.

Trap if greater equal immediate

`tgei rs, imm`

1	rs	8	imm
6	5	5	16

Unsigned trap if greater equal immediate

`teqi rs, imm`

1	rs	9	imm
6	5	5	16

If register rs is greater than or equal to the sign-extended value imm, raise a Trap exception.

Trap if less than

`tlt rs, rt`

0	rs	rt	0	0x32
6	5	5	10	6

Unsigned trap if less than

`tltu rs, rt`

0	rs	rt	0	0x33
6	5	5	10	6

If register rs is less than register rt, raise a Trap exception.

Trap if less than immediate

`tlti rs, imm`

1	rs	a	imm
6	5	5	16

Unsigned trap if less than immediate

```
tltiu rs, imm
```

1	rs	b	imm
6	5	5	16

If register `rs` is less than the sign-extended value `imm`, raise a Trap exception.

Load Instructions

Load address

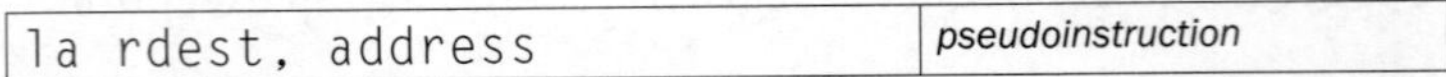

`la rdest, address`	*pseudoinstruction*

Load computed *address*—not the contents of the location—into register `rdest`.

Load byte

```
lb rt, address
```

0x20	rs	rt	Offset
6	5	5	16

Load unsigned byte

```
lbu rt, address
```

0x24	rs	rt	Offset
6	5	5	16

Load the byte at *address* into register `rt`. The byte is sign-extended by `lb`, but not by `lbu`.

Load halfword

```
lh rt, address
```

0x21	rs	rt	Offset
6	5	5	16

Load unsigned halfword

```
lhu rt, address
```

0x25	rs	rt	Offset
6	5	5	16

Load the 16-bit quantity (halfword) at *address* into register `rt`. The halfword is sign-extended by `lh`, but not by `lhu`.

Load word

```
lw rt, address
```

0x23	rs	rt	Offset
6	5	5	16

Load the 32-bit quantity (word) at *address* into register rt.

Load word coprocessor 1

```
lwc1 ft, address
```

0x31	rs	rt	Offset
6	5	5	16

Load the word at *address* into register ft in the floating-point unit.

Load word left

```
lwl rt, address
```

0x22	rs	rt	Offset
6	5	5	16

Load word right

```
lwr rt, address
```

0x26	rs	rt	Offset
6	5	5	16

Load the left (right) bytes from the word at the possibly unaligned *address* into register rt.

Load doubleword

ld rdest, address	*pseudoinstruction*

Load the 64-bit quantity at *address* into registers rdest and rdest + 1.

Unaligned load halfword

ulh rdest, address	*pseudoinstruction*

Unaligned load halfword unsigned

ulhu rdest, address	*pseudoinstruction*

Load the 16-bit quantity (halfword) at the possibly unaligned *address* into register rdest. The halfword is sign-extended by ulh, but not ulhu.

Unaligned load word

ulw rdest, address	*pseudoinstruction*

Load the 32-bit quantity (word) at the possibly unaligned *address* into register rdest.

Load linked

ll rt, address

0x30	rs	rt	Offset
6	5	5	16

Load the 32-bit quantity (word) at *address* into register rt and start an atomic read-modify-write operation. This operation is completed by a store conditional (sc) instruction, which will fail if another processor writes into the block containing the loaded word. Since SPIM does not simulate multiple processors, the store conditional operation always succeeds.

Store Instructions

Store byte

sb rt, address

0x28	rs	rt	Offset
6	5	5	16

Store the low byte from register rt at *address*.

Store halfword

sh rt, address

0x29	rs	rt	Offset
6	5	5	16

Store the low halfword from register rt at *address*.

Store word

```
sw rt, address
```

0x2b	rs	rt	Offset
6	5	5	16

Store the word from register rt at *address*.

Store word coprocessor 1

```
swc1 ft, address
```

0x31	rs	rt	Offset
6	5	5	16

Store the floating-point value in register ft of floating-point coprocessor at *address*.

Store double coprocessor 1

```
sdc1 ft, address
```

0x3d	rs	rt	Offset
6	5	5	16

Store the doubleword floating-point value in registers ft and ft + 1 of floating-point coprocessor at *address*. Register ft must be even numbered.

Store word left

```
swl rt, address
```

0x2a	rs	rt	Offset
6	5	5	16

Store word right

```
swr rt, address
```

0x2e	rs	rt	Offset
6	5	5	16

Store the left (right) bytes from register rt at the possibly unaligned *address*.

Store doubleword

sd rsrc, address	*pseudoinstruction*

Store the 64-bit quantity in registers rsrc and rsrc + 1 at *address*.

Unaligned store halfword

`ush rsrc, address`	*pseudoinstruction*

Store the low halfword from register `rsrc` at the possibly unaligned *address*.

Unaligned store word

`usw rsrc, address`	*pseudoinstruction*

Store the word from register `rsrc` at the possibly unaligned *address*.

Store conditional

`sc rt, address`

0x38	rs	rt	Offset
6	5	5	16

Store the 32-bit quantity (word) in register `rt` into memory at *address* and com
plete an atomic read-modify-write operation. If this atomic operation is success
ful, the memory word is modifed and register `rt` is set to 1. If the atomic operation
fails because another processor wrote to a location in the block contain ing the
addressed word, this instruction does not modify memory and writes 0 into
register `rt`. Since SPIM does not simulate multiple processors, the instruc tion
always succeeds.

Data Movement Instructions

Move

`move rdest, rsrc`	*pseudoinstruction*

Move register `rsrc` to `rdest`.

Move from hi

`mfhi rd`

0	0	rd	0	0x10
6	10	5	5	6

Move from lo

`mflo rd`
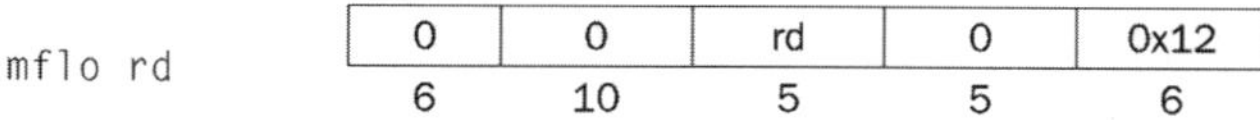

The multiply and divide unit produces its result in two additional registers, `hi` and `lo`. These instructions move values to and from these registers. The multiply, divide, and remainder pseudoinstructions that make this unit appear to operate on the general registers move the result after the computation fnishes.
Move the `hi` (`lo`) register to register `rd`.

Move to hi

`mthi rs`
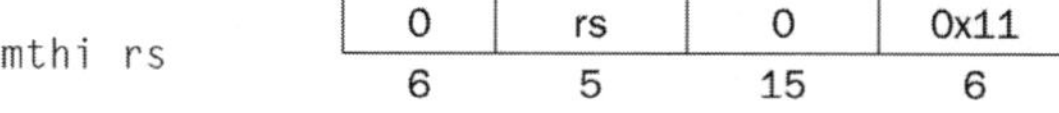

Move to lo

`mtlo rs`
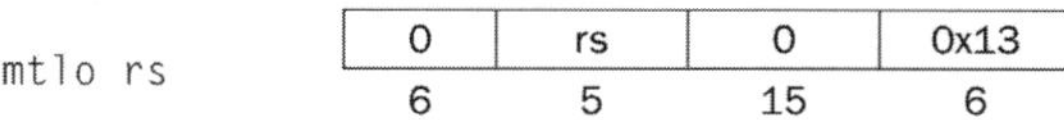

Move register `rs` to the `hi` (`lo`) register.

Move from coprocessor 0

`mfc0 rt, rd`
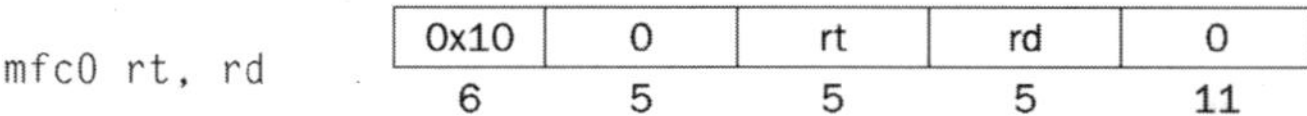

Move from coprocessor 1

`mfc1 rt, fs`
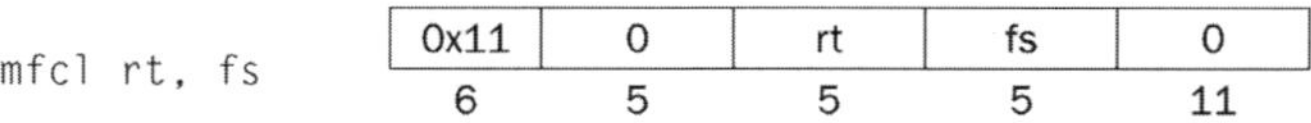

Coprocessors have their own register sets. These instructions move values between these registers and the CPU's registers.
Move register `rd` in a coprocessor (register `fs` in the FPU) to CPU register `rt`. The floating-point unit is coprocessor 1.

Move double from coprocessor 1

`mfc1.d rdest, frsrc1`	*pseudoinstruction*

Move floating-point registers `frsrc1` and `frsrc1 + 1` to CPU registers `rdest` and `rdest + 1`.

Move to coprocessor 0

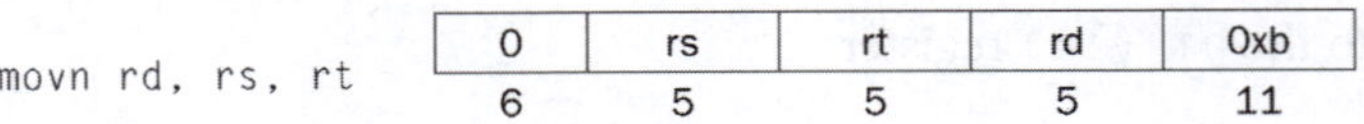

`mtc0 rd, rt`

0x10	4	rt	rd	0
6	5	5	5	11

Move to coprocessor 1

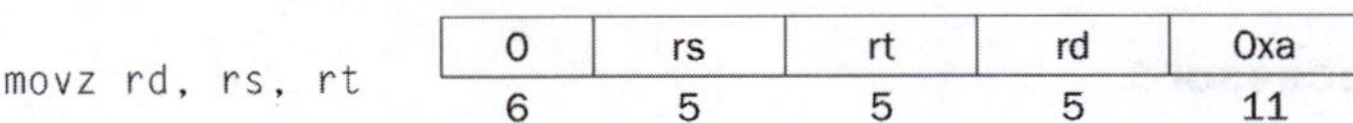

`mtc1 rd, fs`

0x11	4	rt	fs	0
6	5	5	5	11

Move CPU register `rt` to register `rd` in a coprocessor (register `fs` in the FPU).

Move conditional not zero

`movn rd, rs, rt`

0	rs	rt	rd	0xb
6	5	5	5	11

Move register `rs` to register `rd` if register `rt` is not 0.

Move conditional zero

`movz rd, rs, rt`

0	rs	rt	rd	0xa
6	5	5	5	11

Move register `rs` to register `rd` if register `rt` is 0.

Move conditional on FP false

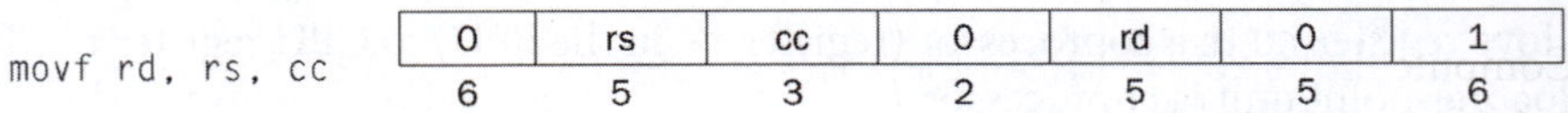

`movf rd, rs, cc`

0	rs	cc	0	rd	0	1
6	5	3	2	5	5	6

Move CPU register `rs` to register `rd` if FPU condition code flag number *cc* is 0. If *cc* is omitted from the instruction, condition code flag 0 is assumed.

Move conditional on FP true

0	rs	cc	1	rd	0	1
6	5	3	2	5	5	6

`movt rd, rs, cc`

Move CPU register `rs` to register `rd` if FPU condition code flag number cc is 1. If cc is omitted from the instruction, condition code bit 0 is assumed.

Floating-Point Instructions

The MIPS has a floating-point coprocessor (numbered 1) that operates on single precision (32-bit) and double precision (64-bit) floating-point numbers. This coprocessor has its own registers, which are numbered `$f0-$f31`. Because these registers are only 32 bits wide, two of them are required to hold doubles, so only floating-point registers with even numbers can hold double precision values. The floating-point coprocessor also has eight condition code (cc) flags, numbered 0–7, which are set by compare instructions and tested by branch (`bc1f` or `bc1t`) and conditional move instructions.

Values are moved in or out of these registers one word (32 bits) at a time by `lwc1`, `swc1`, `mtc1`, and `mfc1` instructions or one double (64 bits) at a time by `ldc1` and `sdc1`, described above, or by the `l.s`, `l.d`, `s.s`, and `s.d` pseudoinstructions described below.

In the actual instructions below, bits 21–26 are 0 for single precision and 1 for double precision. In the pseudoinstructions below, `fdest` is a floating-point register (e.g., `$f2`).

Floating-point absolute value double

0x11	1	0	fs	fd	5
6	5	5	5	5	6

`abs.d fd, fs`

Floating-point absolute value single

0x11	0	0	fs	fd	5
6	5	5	5	5	6

`abs.s fd, fs`

Compute the absolute value of the floating-point double (single) in register `fs` and put it in register `fd`.

Floating-point addition double

0x11	0x11	ft	fs	fd	0
6	5	5	5	5	6

`add.d fd, fs, ft`

Floating-point addition single

`add.s fd, fs, ft`

0x11	0x10	ft	fs	fd	0
6	5	5	5	5	6

Compute the sum of the floating-point doubles (singles) in registers `fs` and `ft` and put it in register `fd`.

Floating-point ceiling to word

`ceil.w.d fd, fs`

0x11	0x10	0	fs	fd	0xe
6	5	5	5	5	6

`ceil.w.s fd, fs`

0x11	0x10	0	fs	fd	0xe

Compute the ceiling of the floating-point double (single) in register `fs`, convert to a 32-bit fxed-point value, and put the resulting word in register `fd`.

Compare equal double

`c.eq.d cc fs, ft`

0x11	0x11	ft	fs	cc	0	FC	2
6	5	5	5	3	2	2	4

Compare equal single

`c.eq.s cc fs, ft`

0x11	0x11	ft	fs	cc	0	FC	2
6	5	5	5	3	2	2	4

Compare the floating-point double (single) in register `fs` against the one in `ft` and set the floating-point condition flag cc to 1 if they are equal. If cc is omitted, condition code flag 0 is assumed.

Compare less than equal double

`c.le.d cc fs, ft`

0x11	0x11	ft	fs	cc	0	FC	0xe
6	5	5	5	3	2	2	4

Compare less than equal single

`c.le.s cc fs, ft`

0x11	0x10	ft	fs	cc	0	FC	0xe
6	5	5	5	3	2	2	4

Compare the floating-point double (single) in register ƒs against the one in ƒt and set the floating-point condition flag *cc* to 1 if the first is less than or equal to the second. If *cc* is omitted, condition code flag 0 is assumed.

Compare less than double

`c.lt.d cc fs, ft`

0x11	0x11	ft	fs	cc	0	FC	0xc
6	5	5	5	3	2	2	4

Compare less than single

`c.lt.s cc fs, ft`

0x11	0x10	ft	fs	cc	0	FC	0xc
6	5	5	5	3	2	2	4

Compare the floating-point double (single) in register ƒs against the one in ƒt and set the condition flag *cc* to 1 if the first is less than the second. If *cc* is omitted, condition code flag 0 is assumed.

Convert single to double

`cvt.d.s fd, fs`

0x11	0x10	0	fs	fd	0x21
6	5	5	5	5	6

Convert integer to double

`cvt.d.w fd, fs`

0x11	0x14	0	fs	fd	0x21
6	5	5	5	5	6

Convert the single precision floating-point number or integer in register ƒs to a double (single) precision number and put it in register ƒd.

Convert double to single

`cvt.s.d fd, fs`

0x11	0x11	0	fs	fd	0x20
6	5	5	5	5	6

Convert integer to single

`cvt.s.w fd, fs`

0x11	0x14	0	fs	fd	0x20
6	5	5	5	5	6

Convert the double precision floating-point number or integer in register ƒs to a single precision number and put it in register ƒd.

Convert double to integer

```
cvt.w.s fd, fs
```

0x11	0x11	0	fs	fd	0x24
6	5	5	5	5	6

Convert single to integer

```
cvt.w.s fd, fs
```

0x11	0x10	0	fs	fd	0x24
6	5	5	5	5	6

Convert the double or single precision floating-point number in register fs to an integer and put it in register fd.

Floating-point divide double

```
div.d fd, fs, ft
```

0x11	0x11	ft	fs	fd	3
6	5	5	5	5	6

Floating-point divide single

```
div.s fd, fs, ft
```

0x11	0x10	ft	fs	fd	3
6	5	5	5	5	6

Compute the quotient of the floating-point doubles (singles) in registers fs and ft and put it in register fd.

Floating-point floor to word

```
floor.w.d fd, fs
```

0x11	0x11	0	fs	fd	0xf
6	5	5	5	5	6

```
floor.w.s fd, fs
```

0x11	0x10	0	fs	fd	0xf

Compute the foor of the floating-point double (single) in register fs and put the resulting word in register fd.

Load floating-point double

```
l.d fdest, address
```
	pseudoinstruction

Load floating-point single

`l.s fdest, address`	*pseudoinstruction*

Load the floating-point double (single) at address into register fdest.

Move floating-point double

`mov.d fd, fs`

0x11	0x11	0	fs	fd	6
6	5	5	5	5	6

Move floating-point single

`mov.s fd, fs`

0x11	0x10	0	fs	fd	6
6	5	5	5	5	6

Move the floating-point double (single) from register fs to register fd.

Move conditional floating-point double false

`movf.d fd, fs, cc`

0x11	0x11	cc	0	fs	fd	0x11
6	5	3	2	5	5	6

Move conditional floating-point single false

`movf.s fd, fs, cc`

0x11	0x10	cc	0	fs	fd	0x11
6	5	3	2	5	5	6

Move the floating-point double (single) from register fs to register fd if condition code flag *cc* is 0. If *cc* is omitted, condition code flag 0 is assumed.

Move conditional floating-point double true

`movt.d fd, fs, cc`

0x11	0x11	cc	1	fs	fd	0x11
6	5	3	2	5	5	6

Move conditional floating-point single true

`movt.s fd, fs, cc`

0x11	0x10	cc	0	fs	fd	0x11
6	5	3	2	5	5	6

Move the floating-point double (single) from register fs to register fd if condition code flag cc is 1. If cc is omitted, condition code flag 0 is assumed.

Move conditional floating-point double not zero

```
movn.d fd, fs, rt
```

0x11	0x11	rt	fs	fd	0x13
6	5	5	5	5	6

Move conditional floating-point single not zero

```
movn.s fd, fs, rt
```

0x11	0x10	rt	fs	fd	0x13
6	5	5	5	5	6

Move the floating-point double (single) from register fs to register fd if processor register rt is not 0.

Move conditional floating-point double zero

```
movz.d fd, fs, rt
```

0x11	0x11	rt	fs	fd	0x12
6	5	5	5	5	6

Move conditional floating-point single zero

```
movz.s fd, fs, rt
```

0x11	0x10	rt	fs	fd	0x12
6	5	5	5	5	6

Move the floating-point double (single) from register fs to register fd if processor register rt is 0.

Floating-point multiply double

```
mul.d fd, fs, ft
```

0x11	0x11	ft	fs	fd	2
6	5	5	5	5	6

Floating-point multiply single

```
mul.s fd, fs, ft
```

0x11	0x10	ft	fs	fd	2
6	5	5	5	5	6

Compute the product of the floating-point doubles (singles) in registers fs and ft and put it in register fd.

Negate double

```
neg.d fd, fs
```

0x11	0x11	0	fs	fd	7
6	5	5	5	5	6

Negate single

`neg.s fd, fs`

0x11	0x10	0	fs	fd	7
6	5	5	5	5	6

Negate the floating-point double (single) in register `fs` and put it in register `fd`.

Floating-point round to word

`round.w.d fd, fs`

0x11	0x11	0	fs	fd	0xc
6	5	5	5	5	6

`round.w.s fd, fs`

0x11	0x10	0	fs	fd	0xc
6	5	5	5	5	6

Round the floating-point double (single) value in register `fs`, convert to a 32-bit fxed-point value, and put the resulting word in register `fd`.

Square root double

`sqrt.d fd, fs`

0x11	0x11	0	fs	fd	4
6	5	5	5	5	6

Square root single

`sqrt.s fd, fs`

0x11	0x10	0	fs	fd	4
6	5	5	5	5	6

Compute the square root of the floating-point double (single) in register `fs` and put it in register `fd`.

Store floating-point double

`s.d fdest, address`	*pseudoinstruction*

Store floating-point single

`s.s fdest, address`	*pseudoinstruction*

Store the floating-point double (single) in register `fdest` at *address*.

Floating-point subtract double

`sub.d fd, fs, ft`

0x11	0x11	ft	fs	fd	1
6	5	5	5	5	6

Floating-point subtract single

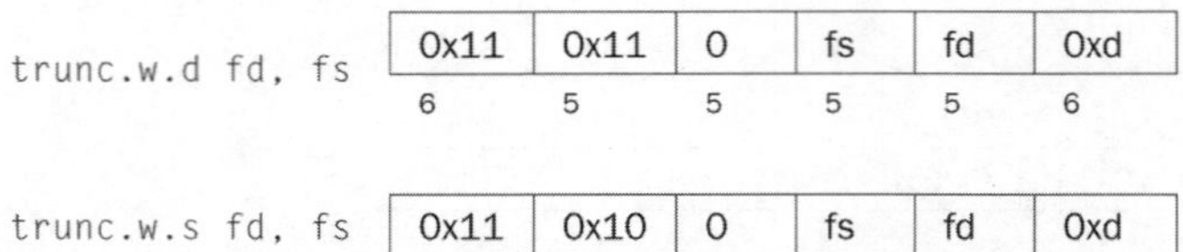

Compute the difference of the floating-point doubles (singles) in registers fs and ft and put it in register fd.

Floating-point truncate to word

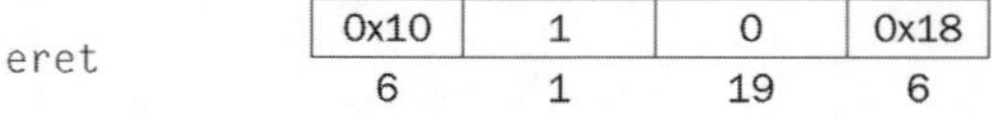

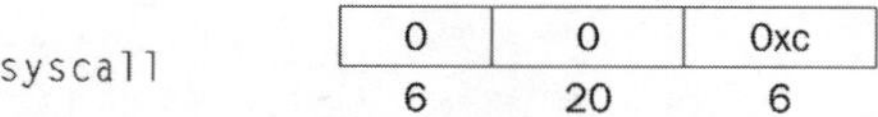

Truncate the floating-point double (single) value in register fs, convert to a 32-bit fixed-point value, and put the resulting word in register fd.

Exception and Interrupt Instructions

Exception return

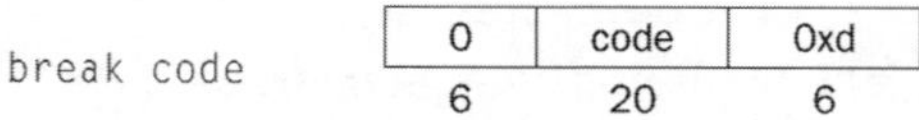

Set the EXL bit in coprocessor 0's Status register to 0 and return to the instruction pointed to by coprocessor 0's EPC register.

System call

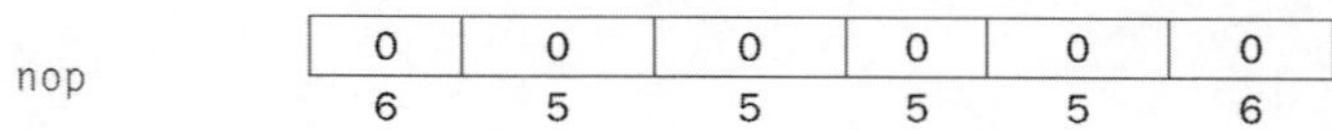

Register $v0 contains the number of the system call (see Figure A.9.1) provided by SPIM.

Break

break code

Cause exception *code*. Exception 1 is reserved for the debugger.

No operation

nop

Do nothing.

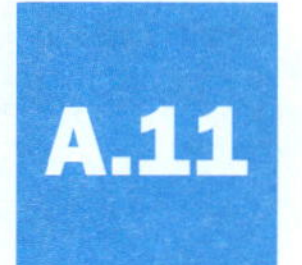

A.11 Concluding Remarks

Programming in assembly language requires a programmer to trade helpful features of high-level languages—such as data structures, type checking, and control constructs—for complete control over the instructions that a computer executes. External constraints on some applications, such as response time or program size, require a programmer to pay close attention to every instruction. However, the cost of this level of attention is assembly language programs that are longer, more time-consuming to write, and more difficult to maintain than high-level language programs.

Moreover, three trends are reducing the need to write programs in assembly language. The first trend is toward the improvement of compilers. Modern com pilers produce code that is typically comparable to the best handwritten code—and is sometimes better. The second trend is the introduction of new processors that are not only faster, but in the case of processors that execute multiple instructions simultaneously, also more difficult to program by hand. In addition, the rapid evolution of the modern computer favors high-level language programs that are not tied to a single architecture. Finally, we witness a trend toward increasingly complex applications, characterized by complex graphic interfaces and many more features than their predecessors. Large applications are written by teams of programmers and require the modularity and semantic checking features provided by high-level languages.

Further Reading

Aho, A., Sethi, R., & Ullman, J. (1985). *Compilers: Principles, Techniques, and Tools.* Reading, MA: Addison-Wesley.*Slightly dated and lacking in coverage of modern architectures, but still the standard reference on compilers.*

Sweetman, D. (1999). *See MIPS Run.* San Francisco, CA: Morgan Kaufmann Publishers.*A complete, detailed, and engaging introduction to the MIPS instruction set and assembly language program ming on these machines.*

Detailed documentation on the MIPS-32 architecture is available on the Web:

MIPS32™ Architecture for Programmers Volume I: Introduction to the MIPS32™ Architecture   *(http://mips.com/content/Documentation/MIPSDocumentation/ ProcessorArchitecture/ArchitectureProgrammingPublicationsforMIPS32/MD00082-2B-MIPS32INT-AFP-02.00.pdf/getDownload)*

MIPS32™ Architecture for Programmers Volume II: The MIPS32™ Instruction Set   *(http://mips.com/content/Documentation/MIPSDocumentation/ ProcessorArchitecture/ArchitectureProgrammingPublicationsforMIPS32/MD00086-2B-MIPS32BIS-AFP-02.00.pdf/getDownload)*

MIPS32™ Architecture for Programmers Volume III: The MIPS32™ Privileged Resource Architecture   *(http://mips.com/content/Documentation/MIPSDocumentation/ ProcessorArchitecture/ArchitectureProgrammingPublicationsforMIPS32/MD00090-2B-MIPS32PRA-AFP-02.00.pdf/getDownload)*

A.12   Exercises

A.I [5] <§A.5> Section A.5 described how memory is partitioned on most MIPS systems. Propose another way of dividing memory that meets the same goals.

A.2 [20] <§A.6> Rewrite the code for `fact` to use fewer instructions.

A.3 [5] <§A.7> Is it ever safe for a user program to use registers $k0 or $k1?

A.4 [25] <§A.7> Section A.7 contains code for a very simple exception handler. One serious problem with this handler is that it disables interrupts for a long time. This means that interrupts from a fast I/O device may be lost. Write a better exception handler that is interruptable and enables interrupts as quickly as possible.

A.5 [15] <§A.7> The simple exception handler always jumps back to the instruction following the exception. This works fne unless the instruction that causes the exception is in the delay slot of a branch. In that case, the next instruction is the target of the branch. Write a better handler that uses the EPC register to determine which instruction should be executed after the exception.

A.6 [5] <§A.9> Using SPIM, write and test an adding machine program that repeatedly reads in integers and adds them into a running sum. The program should stop when it gets an input that is 0, printing out the sum at that point. Use the SPIM system calls described on pages A-43 and A-45.

A.7 [5] <§A.9> Using SPIM, write and test a program that reads in three integers and prints out the sum of the largest two of the three. Use the SPIM system calls described on pages A-43 and A-45. You can break ties arbitrarily.

A.8 [5] <§A.9> Using SPIM, write and test a program that reads in a positive integer using the SPIM system calls. If the integer is not positive, the program should terminate with the message "Invalid Entry"; otherwise the program should print out the names of the digits of the integers, delimited by exactly one space. For example, if the user entered "728," the output would be "Seven Two Eight."

A.9 [25] <§A.9> Write and test a MIPS assembly language program to compute and print the first 100 prime numbers. A number n is prime if no numbers except 1 and n divide it evenly. You should implement two routines:

- `test_prime (n)` Return 1 if n is prime and 0 if n is not prime.

- `main ( )` Iterate over the integers, testing if each is prime. Print the first 100 numbers that are prime.

Test your programs by running them on SPIM.

A.10 [10] <§§A.6, A.9> Using SPIM, write and test a recursive program for solv ing the classic mathematical recreation, the Towers of Hanoi puzzle. (This will require the use of stack frames to support recursion.) The puzzle consists of three pegs (1, 2, and 3) and n disks (the number n can vary; typical values might be in the range from 1 to 8). Disk 1 is smaller than disk 2, which is in turn smaller than disk 3, and so forth, with disk n being the largest. Initially, all the disks are on peg 1, starting with disk n on the bottom, disk $n - 1$ on top of that, and so forth, up to disk 1 on the top. The goal is to move all the disks to peg 2. You may only move one disk at a time, that is, the top disk from any of the three pegs onto the top of either of the other two pegs. Moreover, there is a constraint: You must not place a larger disk on top of a smaller disk.

The C program below can be used to help write your assembly language program.

```c
/*  move n smallest disks from start to finish using
extra */

void hanoi(int n, int start, int finish, int extra){
     if(n != 0){
             hanoi(n-1, start, extra, finish);
             print_string("Move disk");
             print_int(n);
             print_string("from peg");
             print_int(start);
             print_string("to peg");
             print_int(finish);
             print_string(".\n");
             hanoi(n-1, extra, finish, start);
     }
}
main(){
     int n;
     print_string("Enter number of disks>");
     n = read_int();
     hanoi(n, 1, 2, 3);
     return 0;
}
```

I always loved that word, Boolean.

Claude Shannon
IEEE Spectrum, April 1992
(Shannon's master's thesis showed
that the algebra invented by George
Boole in the 1800s could represent the
workings of electrical switches.)

B.1   Introduction

This appendix provides a brief discussion of the basics of logic design. It does not replace a course in logic design, nor will it enable you to design significant working logic systems. If you have little or no exposure to logic design, however, this appendix will provide sufficient background to understand all the material in this book. In addition, if you are looking to understand some of the motivation behind how computers are implemented, this material will serve as a useful introduction. If your curiosity is aroused but not sated by this appendix, the references at the end provide several additional sources of information.

Section B.2 introduces the basic building blocks of logic, namely, *gates*. Section B.3 uses these building blocks to construct simple *combinational* logic systems, which contain no memory. If you have had some exposure to logic or digital systems, you will probably be familiar with the material in these first two sections. Section B.5 shows how to use the concepts of Sections B.2 and B.3 to design an ALU for the MIPS processor. Section B.6 shows how to make a fast adder, and may be safely skipped if you are not interested in this topic. Section B.7 is a short introduction to the topic of clocking, which is necessary to discuss how memory elements work. Section B.8 introduces memory elements, and Section B.9 extends it to focus on random access memories; it describes both the characteristics that are important to understanding how they are used, as discussed in Chapter 4, and the background that motivates many of the aspects of memory hierarchy design discussed Chapter 5. Section B.10 describes the design and use of finite-state machines, which are sequential logic blocks. If you intend to read 🌐 **Appendix D**, you should thoroughly understand the material in Sections B.2 through B.10. If you intend to read only the material on control in Chapter 4, you can skim the appendices; however, you should have some familiarity with all the material except Section B.11. Section B.11 is intended for those who want a deeper understanding of clocking methodologies and timing. It explains the basics of how edge-triggered clocking works, introduces another clocking scheme, and briefly describes the problem of synchronizing asynchronous inputs.

Throughout this appendix, where it is appropriate, we also include segments to demonstrate how logic can be represented in Verilog, which we introduce in Section B.4. A more extensive and complete Verilog tutorial is available online on the Companion Site for this book.

B.2   Gates, Truth Tables, and Logic Equations

The electronics inside a modern computer are *digital*. Digital electronics operate with only two voltage levels of interest: a high voltage and a low voltage. All other voltage values are temporary and occur while transitioning between the values. (As we discuss later in this section, a possible pitfall in digital design is sampling a signal when it not clearly either high or low.) The fact that computers are digital is also a key reason they use binary numbers, since a binary system matches the underlying abstraction inherent in the electronics. In various logic families, the values and relationships between the two voltage values differ. Thus, rather than refer to the voltage levels, we talk about signals that are (logically) true, or 1, or are **asserted**; or signals that are (logically) false, or 0, or are **deasserted**. The values 0 and 1 are called *complements* or *inverses* of one another.

Logic blocks are categorized as one of two types, depending on whether they contain memory. Blocks without memory are called *combinational*; the output of a combinational block depends only on the current input. In blocks with memory, the outputs can depend on both the inputs and the value stored in memory, which is called the *state* of the logic block. In this section and the next, we will focus

asserted signal A signal that is (logically) true, or 1.

deasserted signal A signal that is (logically) false, or 0.

only on **combinational logic**. After introducing different memory elements in Section B.8, we will describe how **sequential logic**, which is logic including state, is designed.

Truth Tables

Because a combinational logic block contains no memory, it can be completely specified by defining the values of the outputs for each possible set of input values. Such a description is normally given as a *truth table*. For a logic block with n inputs, there are $2n$ entries in the truth table, since there are that many possible combinations of input values. Each entry specifies the value of all the outputs for that particular input combination.

combinational logic
A logic system whose blocks do not contain memory and hence compute the same output given the same input.

sequential logic
A group of logic elements that contain memory and hence whose value depends on the inputs as well as the current contents of the memory.

EXAMPLE

Truth Tables

Consider a logic function with three inputs, A, B, and C, and three outputs, D, E, and F. The function is defined as follows: D is true if at least one input is true, E is true if exactly two inputs are true, and F is true only if all three inputs are true. Show the truth table for this function.

ANSWER

The truth table will contain $2^3 = 8$ entries. Here it is:

Input			Outputs		
A	B	C	D	E	F
0	0	0	0	0	0
0	0	1	1	0	0
0	1	0	1	0	0
0	1	1	1	1	0
1	0	0	1	0	0
1	0	1	1	1	0
1	1	0	1	1	0
1	1	1	1	0	1

Truth tables can completely describe any combinational logic function; however, they grow in size quickly and may not be easy to understand. Sometimes we want to construct a logic function that will be 0 for many input combinations, and we use a shorthand of specifying only the truth table entries for the nonzero outputs. This approach is used in Chapter 4 and ⊕ **Appendix D**.

Boolean Algebra

Another approach is to express the logic function with logic equations. This is done with the use of *Boolean algebra* (named after Boole, a 19th-century mathematician). In Boolean algebra, all the variables have the values 0 or 1 and, in typical formulations, there are three operators:

- The OR operator is written as +, as in $A + B$. The result of an OR operator is 1 if either of the variables is 1. The OR operation is also called a *logical sum*, since its result is 1 if either operand is 1.

- The AND operator is written as ·, as in $A \cdot B$. The result of an AND operator is 1 only if both inputs are 1. The AND operator is also called *logical product*, since its result is 1 only if both operands are 1.

- The unary operator NOT is written as $\overline{A}$. The result of a NOT operator is 1 only if the input is 0. Applying the operator NOT to a logical value results in an inversion or negation of the value (i.e., if the input is 0 the output is 1, and vice versa).

There are several laws of Boolean algebra that are helpful in manipulating logic equations.

- Identity law: $A + 0 = A$ and $A \cdot 1 = A$.
- Zero and One laws: $A + 1 = 1$ and $A \cdot 0 = 0$.
- Inverse laws: $A + \overline{A} = 1$ and $A \cdot \overline{A} = 0$.
- Commutative laws: $A + B = B + A$ and $A \cdot B = B \cdot A$.
- Associative laws: $A + (B + C) = (A + B) + C$ and $A \cdot (B \cdot C) = (A \cdot B) \cdot C$.
- Distributive laws: $A \cdot (B + C) = (A \cdot B) + (A \cdot C)$ and $A + (B \cdot C) = (A + B) \cdot (A + C)$.

In addition, there are two other useful theorems, called DeMorgan's laws, that are discussed in more depth in the exercises.

Any set of logic functions can be written as a series of equations with an output on the left-hand side of each equation and a formula consisting of variables and the three operators above on the right-hand side.

Logic Equations

Show the logic equations for the logic functions, D, E, and F, described in the previous example.

EXAMPLE

Here's the equation for D:

$$D = A + B + C$$

ANSWER

F is equally simple:

$$F = A \cdot B \cdot C$$

E is a little tricky. Think of it in two parts: what must be true for E to be true (two of the three inputs must be true), and what cannot be true (all three cannot be true). Thus we can write E as

$$E = ((A \cdot B) + (A \cdot C) + (B \cdot C)) \cdot (\overline{A \cdot B \cdot C})$$

We can also derive E by realizing that E is true only if exactly two of the inputs are true. Then we can write E as an OR of the three possible terms that have two true inputs and one false input:

$$E = (A \cdot B \cdot \overline{C}) + (A \cdot C \cdot \overline{B}) + (B \cdot C \cdot \overline{A})$$

Proving that these two expressions are equivalent is explored in the exercises.

In Verilog, we describe combinational logic whenever possible using the assign statement, which is described beginning on page B-23. We can write a definition for E using the Verilog exclusive-OR operator as `assign E = (A ^ B ^ C) * (A + B + C) * (A * B * C)`, which is yet another way to describe this function. D and F have even simpler representations, which are just like the corresponding C code: `D = A | B | C` and `F = A & B & C`.

Gates

gate A device that implements basic logic functions, such as AND or OR.

Logic blocks are built from **gates** that implement basic logic functions. For example, an AND gate implements the AND function, and an OR gate implements the OR function. Since both AND and OR are commutative and associative, an AND or an OR gate can have multiple inputs, with the output equal to the AND or OR of all the inputs. The logical function NOT is implemented with an inverter that always has a single input. The standard representation of these three logic building blocks is shown in Figure B.2.1.

Rather than draw inverters explicitly, a common practice is to add "bubbles" to the inputs or outputs of a gate to cause the logic value on that input line or output line to be inverted. For example, Figure B.2.2 shows the logic diagram for the function $\overline{A} + B$, using explicit inverters on the left and bubbled inputs and outputs on the right.

Any logical function can be constructed using AND gates, OR gates, and inversion; several of the exercises give you the opportunity to try implementing some common logic functions with gates. In the next section, we'll see how an implementation of any logic function can be constructed using this knowledge.

NOR gate An inverted OR gate.

NAND gate An inverted AND gate.

In fact, all logic functions can be constructed with only a single gate type, if that gate is inverting. The two common inverting gates are called **NOR** and **NAND** and correspond to inverted OR and AND gates, respectively. NOR and NAND gates are called *universal*, since any logic function can be built using this one gate type. The exercises explore this concept further.

Are the following two logical expressions equivalent? If not, find a setting of the variables to show they are not:

- $(A \cdot B \cdot \overline{C}) + (A \cdot C \cdot \overline{B}) + (B \cdot C \cdot \overline{A})$
- $B \cdot (A \cdot \overline{C} + C \cdot \overline{A})$

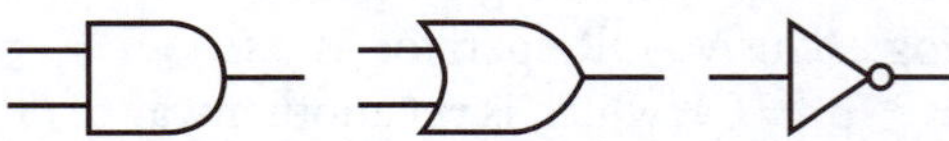

FIGURE B.2.1   Standard drawing for an AND gate, OR gate, and an inverter, shown from left to right. The signals to the left of each symbol are the inputs, while the output appears on the right. The AND and OR gates both have two inputs. Inverters have a single input.

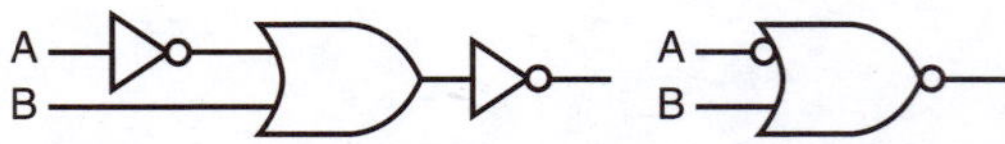

FIGURE B.2.2   Logic gate implementation of $\overline{A} + B$ using explicit inverts on the left and bubbled inputs and outputs on the right. This logic function can be simplified to $A \cdot \overline{B}$ or in Verilog, A & ~ B.

B.3 Combinational Logic

In this section, we look at a couple of larger logic building blocks that we use heavily, and we discuss the design of structured logic that can be automatically implemented from a logic equation or truth table by a translation program. Last, we discuss the notion of an array of logic blocks.

Decoders

One logic block that we will use in building larger components is a **decoder**. The most common type of decoder has an n-bit input and $2n$ outputs, where only one output is asserted for each input combination. This decoder translates the n-bit input into a signal that corresponds to the binary value of the n-bit input. The outputs are thus usually numbered, say, Out0, Out1, …, Out$2n$ − 1. If the value of the input is i, then Out$i$ will be true and all other outputs will be false. Figure B.3.1 shows a 3-bit decoder and the truth table. This decoder is called a *3-to-8 decoder* since there are 3 inputs and 8 (2^3) outputs. There is also a logic element called an *encoder* that performs the inverse function of a decoder, taking $2n$ inputs and producing an n-bit output.

decoder A logic block that has an n-bit input and $2n$ out puts, where only one output is asserted for each input combination.

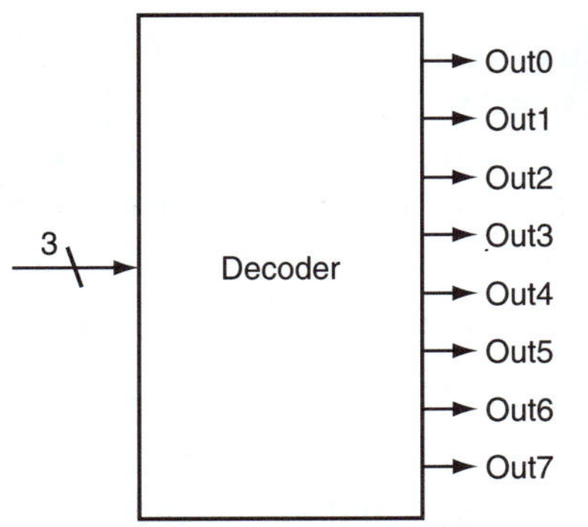

a. A 3-bit decoder

Inputs			Outputs							
12	11	10	Out7	Out6	Out5	Out4	Out3	Out2	Out1	Out0
0	0	0	0	0	0	0	0	0	0	1
0	0	1	0	0	0	0	0	0	1	0
0	1	0	0	0	0	0	0	1	0	0
0	1	1	0	0	0	0	1	0	0	0
1	0	0	0	0	0	1	0	0	0	0
1	0	1	0	0	1	0	0	0	0	0
1	1	0	0	1	0	0	0	0	0	0
1	1	1	1	0	0	0	0	0	0	0

b. The truth table for a 3-bit decoder

FIGURE B.3.1 A 3-bit decoder has 3 inputs, called 12, 11, and 10, and 2^3 = 8 outputs, called Out0 to Out7. Only the output corresponding to the binary value of the input is true, as shown in the truth table. The label 3 on the input to the decoder says that the input signal is 3 bits wide.

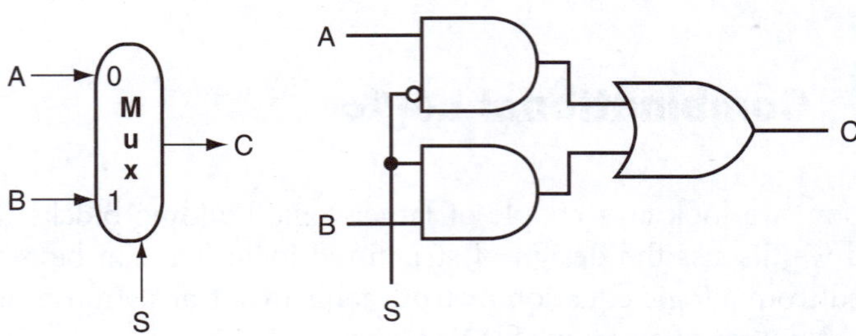

FIGURE B.3.2   A two-input multiplexor on the left and its implementation with gates on the right. The multiplexor has two data inputs (*A* and *B*), which are labeled *0* and *1*, and one selector input (*S*), as well as an output *C*. Implementing multiplexors in Verilog requires a little more work, especially when they are wider than two inputs. We show how to do this beginning on page B-23.

Multiplexors

One basic logic function that we use quite often in Chapter 4 is the *multiplexor*. A multiplexor might more properly be called a *selector*, since its output is one of the inputs that is selected by a control. Consider the two-input multiplexor. The left side of Figure B.3.2 shows this multiplexor has three inputs: two data values and a **selector** (or **control**) **value**. The selector value determines which of the inputs becomes the output. We can represent the logic function computed by a two-input multiplexor, shown in gate form on the right side of Figure B.3.2, as $C = (A \cdot \overline{S}) + (B \cdot S)$.

selector value Also called **control value**. The control signal that is used to select one of the input values of a multiplexor as the output of the multiplexor.

Multiplexors can be created with an arbitrary number of data inputs. When there are only two inputs, the selector is a single signal that selects one of the inputs if it is true (1) and the other if it is false (0). If there are *n* data inputs, there will need to be $\lceil \log_2 n \rceil$ selector inputs. In this case, the multiplexor basically consists of three parts:

1. A decoder that generates *n* signals, each indicating a different input value

2. An array of *n* AND gates, each combining one of the inputs with a signal from the decoder

3. A single large OR gate that incorporates the outputs of the AND gates

To associate the inputs with selector values, we often label the data inputs numerically (i.e., 0, 1, 2, 3, …, *n* − 1) and interpret the data selector inputs as a binary number. Sometimes, we make use of a multiplexor with undecoded selector signals.

Multiplexors are easily represented combinationally in Verilog by using *if* expressions. For larger multiplexors, *case* statements are more convenient, but care must be taken to synthesize combinational logic.

Two-Level Logic and PLAs

As pointed out in the previous section, any logic function can be implemented with only AND, OR, and NOT functions. In fact, a much stronger result is true. Any logic function can be written in a canonical form, where every input is either a true or complemented variable and there are only two levels of gates—one being AND and the other OR—with a possible inversion on the final output. Such a representation is called a *two-level representation*, and there are two forms, called **sum of products** and *product of sums*. A sum-of-products representation is a logical sum (OR) of products (terms using the AND operator); a product of sums is just the opposite. In our earlier example, we had two equations for the output E:

$$E = ((A \cdot B) + (A \cdot C) + (B \cdot C)) \cdot (\overline{A \cdot B \cdot C})$$

and

$$E = (A \cdot B \cdot \overline{C}) + (A \cdot C \cdot \overline{B}) \cdot (B \cdot C \cdot \overline{A})$$

This second equation is in a sum-of-products form: it has two levels of logic and the only inversions are on individual variables. The first equation has three levels of logic.

Elaboration: We can also write E as a product of sums:

$$E = \overline{(\overline{A} + \overline{B} + C) \cdot (\overline{A} + \overline{C} + B) \cdot (\overline{B} + C + A)}$$

To derive this form, you need to use *DeMorgan's theorems*, which are discussed in the exercises.

In this text, we use the sum-of-products form. It is easy to see that any logic function can be represented as a sum of products by constructing such a representation from the truth table for the function. Each truth table entry for which the function is true corresponds to a product term. The product term consists of a logical product of all the inputs or the complements of the inputs, depending on whether the entry in the truth table has a 0 or 1 corresponding to this variable. The logic function is the logical sum of the product terms where the function is true. This is more easily seen with an example.

sum of products A form of logical representation that employs a logical sum (OR) of products (terms joined using the AND operator).

Sum of Products

Show the sum-of-products representation for the following truth table for D.

Inputs			Output
A	B	C	D
0	0	0	0
0	0	1	1
0	1	0	1
0	1	1	0
1	0	0	1
1	0	1	0
1	1	0	0
1	1	1	1

There are four product terms, since the function is true (1) for four different input combinations. These are:

$$\overline{A} \cdot \overline{B} \cdot C$$
$$\overline{A} \cdot B \cdot C$$
$$A \cdot \overline{B} \cdot \overline{C}$$
$$A \cdot B \cdot C$$

Thus, we can write the function for D as the sum of these terms:

$$D = (\overline{A} \cdot \overline{B} \cdot C)(\overline{A} \cdot B \cdot \overline{C})(A \cdot \overline{B} \cdot \overline{C})(A \cdot B \cdot C)$$

Note that only those truth table entries for which the function is true generate terms in the equation.

programmable logic array (PLA)
A structured-logic element composed of a set of inputs and corresponding input complements and two stages of logic: the first generating product terms of the inputs and input complements, and the second generating sum terms of the product terms. Hence, PLAs implement logic functions as a sum of products.

minterms Also called **product terms**. A set of logic inputs joined by conjunction (AND operations); the product terms form the first logic stage of the *programmable logic array* (PLA).

We can use this relationship between a truth table and a two-level representation to generate a gate-level implementation of any set of logic functions. A set of logic functions corresponds to a truth table with multiple output columns, as we saw in the example on page B-5. Each output column represents a different logic function, which may be directly constructed from the truth table.

The sum-of-products representation corresponds to a common structured-logic implementation called a **programmable logic array (PLA)**. A PLA has a set of inputs and corresponding input complements (which can be implemented with a set of inverters), and two stages of logic. The first stage is an array of AND gates that form a set of **product terms** (sometimes called **minterms**); each prod uct term can consist of any of the inputs or their complements. The second stage is an array of OR gates, each of which forms a logical sum of any number of the product terms. Figure B.3.3 shows the basic form of a PLA.

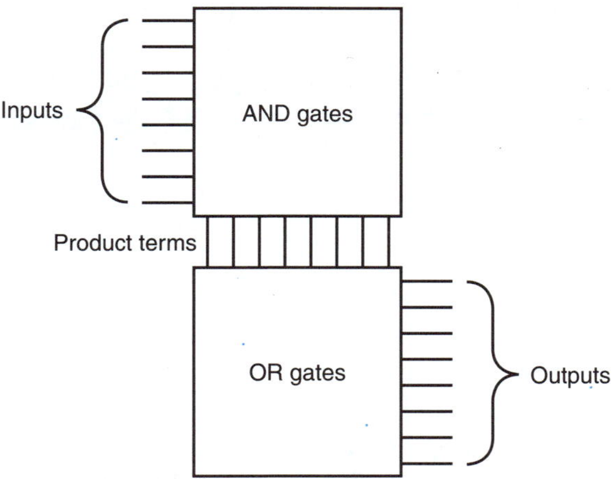

FIGURE B.3.3   The basic form of a PLA consists of an array of AND gates followed by an array of OR gates. Each entry in the AND gate array is a product term consisting of any number of inputs or inverted inputs. Each entry in the OR gate array is a sum term consisting of any number of these product terms.

A PLA can directly implement the truth table of a set of logic functions with multiple inputs and outputs. Since each entry where the output is true requires a product term, there will be a corresponding row in the PLA. Each output corresponds to a potential row of OR gates in the second stage. The number of OR gates corresponds to the number of truth table entries for which the output is true. The total size of a PLA, such as that shown in Figure B.3.3, is equal to the sum of the size of the AND gate array (called the *AND plane*) and the size of the OR gate array (called the *OR plane*). Looking at Figure B.3.3, we can see that the size of the AND gate array is equal to the number of inputs times the number of different product terms, and the size of the OR gate array is the number of outputs times the number of product terms.

A PLA has two characteristics that help make it an efficient way to implement a set of logic functions. First, only the truth table entries that produce a true value for at least one output have any logic gates associated with them. Second, each different product term will have only one entry in the PLA, even if the product term is used in multiple outputs. Let's look at an example.

PLAs

Consider the set of logic functions defined in the example on page B-5. Show a PLA implementation of this example for D, E, and F.

EXAMPLE

Here is the truth table we constructed earlier:

Input			Outputs		
A	B	C	D	E	F
0	0	0	0	0	0
0	0	1	1	0	0
0	1	0	1	0	0
0	1	1	1	1	0
1	0	0	1	0	0
1	0	1	1	1	0
1	1	0	1	1	0
1	1	1	1	0	1

Since there are seven unique product terms with at least one true value in the output section, there will be seven columns in the AND plane. The number of rows in the AND plane is three (since there are three inputs), and there are also three rows in the OR plane (since there are three outputs). Figure B.3.4 shows the resulting PLA, with the product terms corresponding to the truth table entries from top to bottom.

Rather than drawing all the gates, as we do in Figure B.3.4, designers often show just the position of AND gates and OR gates. Dots are used on the intersection of a product term signal line and an input line or an output line when a corresponding AND gate or OR gate is required. Figure B.3.5 shows how the PLA of Figure B.3.4 would look when drawn in this way. The contents of a PLA are fixed when the PLA is created, although there are also forms of PLA-like structures, called *PALs*, that can be programmed electronically when a designer is ready to use them.

ROMs

Another form of structured logic that can be used to implement a set of logic functions is a **read-only memory (ROM)**. A ROM is called a memory because it has a set of locations that can be read; however, the contents of these locations are fixed, usually at the time the ROM is manufactured. There are also **programmable ROMs (PROMs)** that can be programmed electronically, when a designer knows their contents. There are also erasable PROMs; these devices require a slow erasure process using ultraviolet light, and thus are used as read-only memories, except during the design and debugging process.

A ROM has a set of input address lines and a set of outputs. The number of addressable entries in the ROM determines the number of address lines: if the

read-only memory (ROM) A memory whose contents are designated at creation time, after which the contents can only be read. ROM is used as structured logic to implement a set of logic functions by using the terms in the logic functions as address inputs and the out puts as bits in each word of the memory.

programmable ROM (PROM) A form of read-only memory that can be programmed when a designer knows its contents.

ROM contains $2m$ addressable entries, called the *height*, then there are m input lines. The number of bits in each addressable entry is equal to the number of output bits and is sometimes called the *width* of the ROM. The total number of bits in the ROM is equal to the height times the width. The height and width are sometimes collectively referred to as the *shape* of the ROM.

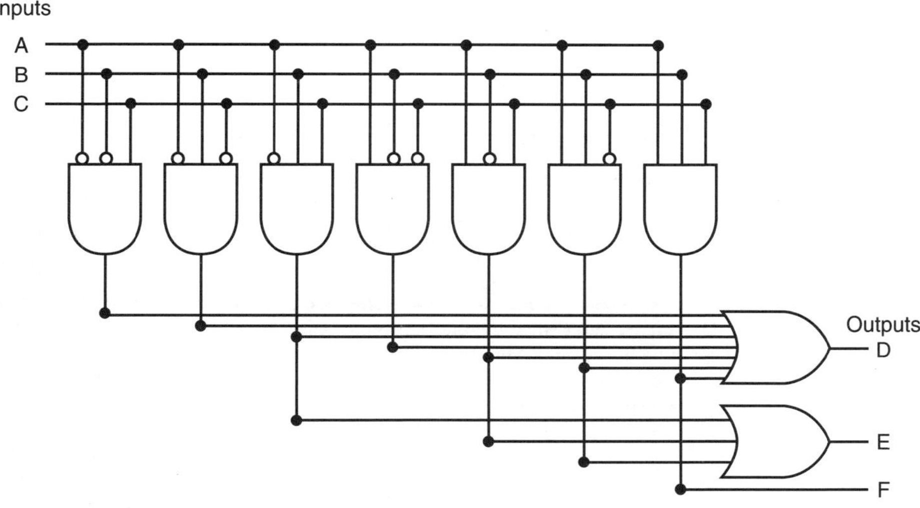

FIGURE B.3.4   The PLA for implementing the logic function described in the example.

A ROM can encode a collection of logic functions directly from the truth table. For example, if there are n functions with m inputs, we need a ROM with m address lines (and $2m$ entries), with each entry being n bits wide. The entries in the input portion of the truth table represent the addresses of the entries in the ROM, while the contents of the output portion of the truth table constitute the contents of the ROM. If the truth table is organized so that the sequence of entries in the input portion constitutes a sequence of binary numbers (as have all the truth tables we have shown so far), then the output portion gives the ROM contents in order as well. In the example starting on page B-13, there were three inputs and three outputs. This leads to a ROM with $2^3 = 8$ entries, each 3 bits wide. The contents of those entries in increasing order by address are directly given by the output portion of the truth table that appears on page B-14.

ROMs and PLAs are closely related. A ROM is fully decoded: it contains a full output word for every possible input combination. A PLA is only partially decoded. This means that a ROM will always contain more entries. For the earlier truth table on page B-14, the ROM contains entries for all eight possible inputs, whereas the PLA contains only the seven active product terms. As the number of inputs grows,

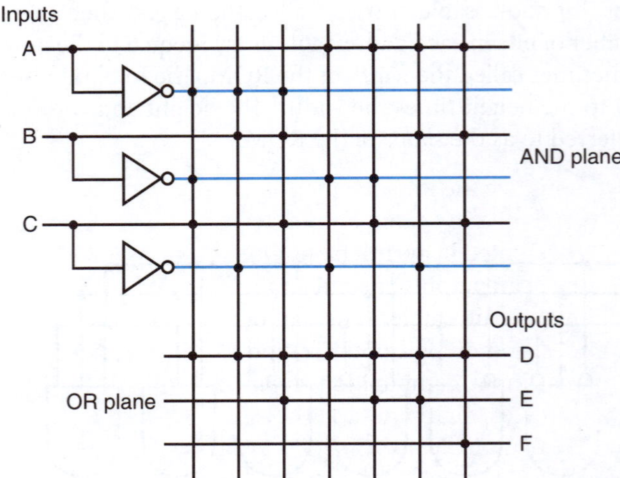

FIGURE B.3.5   A PLA drawn using dots to indicate the components of the product terms and sum terms in the array. Rather than use inverters on the gates, usually all the inputs are run the width of the AND plane in both true and complement forms. A dot in the AND plane indicates that the input, or its inverse, occurs in the product term. A dot in the OR plane indicates that the corresponding product term appears in the corresponding output.

the number of entries in the ROM grows exponentially. In contrast, for most real logic functions, the number of product terms grows much more slowly (see the examples in 🌐 **Appendix D**). This difference makes PLAs generally more efficient for implementing combinational logic functions. ROMs have the advantage of being able to implement any logic function with the matching number of inputs and outputs. This advantage makes it easier to change the ROM contents if the logic function changes, since the size of the ROM need not change.

In addition to ROMs and PLAs, modern logic synthesis systems will also translate small blocks of combinational logic into a collection of gates that can be placed and wired automatically. Although some small collections of gates are usually not area efficient, for small logic functions they have less overhead than the rigid structure of a ROM and PLA and so are preferred.

For designing logic outside of a custom or semicustom integrated circuit, a common choice is a field programming device; we describe these devices in Section B.12.

Don't Cares

Often in implementing some combinational logic, there are situations where we do not care what the value of some output is, either because another output is true or because a subset of the input combinations determines the values of the outputs. Such situations are referred to as *don't cares*. Don't cares are important because they make it easier to optimize the implementation of a logic function.

There are two types of don't cares: output don't cares and input don't cares, both of which can be represented in a truth table. *Output don't cares* arise when we don't care about the value of an output for some input combination. They appear as Xs in the output portion of a truth table. When an output is a don't care for some input combination, the designer or logic optimization program is free to make the output true or false for that input combination. *Input don't cares* arise when an output depends on only some of the inputs, and they are also shown as Xs, though in the input portion of the truth table.

Don't Cares

Consider a logic function with inputs A, B, and C defined as follows:

- If A or C is true, then output D is true, whatever the value of B.

- If A or B is true, then output E is true, whatever the value of C.

- Output F is true if exactly one of the inputs is true, although we don't care about the value of F, whenever D and E are both true.

Show the full truth table for this function and the truth table using don't cares. How many product terms are required in a PLA for each of these?

EXAMPLE

Here's the full truth table, without don't cares:

ANSWER

Inputs			Outputs		
A	B	C	D	E	F
0	0	0	0	0	0
0	0	1	1	0	1
0	1	0	0	1	1
0	1	1	1	1	0
1	0	0	1	1	1
1	0	1	1	1	0
1	1	0	1	1	0
1	1	1	1	1	0

This requires seven product terms without optimization. The truth table written with output don't cares looks like this:

Inputs			Outputs		
A	B	C	D	E	F
0	0	0	0	0	0
0	0	1	1	0	1
0	1	0	0	1	1
0	1	1	1	1	X
1	0	0	1	1	X
1	0	1	1	1	X
1	1	0	1	1	X
1	1	1	1	1	X

If we also use the input don't cares, this truth table can be further simplified to yield the following:

Inputs			Outputs		
A	B	C	D	E	F
0	0	0	0	0	0
0	0	1	1	0	1
0	1	0	0	1	1
X	1	1	1	1	X
1	X	X	1	1	X

This simplified truth table requires a PLA with four minterms, or it can be implemented in discrete gates with one two-input AND gate and three OR gates (two with three inputs and one with two inputs). This compares to the original truth table that had seven minterms and would have required four AND gates.

Logic minimization is critical to achieving efficient implementations. One tool useful for hand minimization of random logic is *Karnaugh maps*. Karnaugh maps represent the truth table graphically, so that product terms that may be combined are easily seen. Nevertheless, hand optimization of significant logic functions using Karnaugh maps is impractical, both because of the size of the maps and their complexity. Fortunately, the process of logic minimization is highly mechanical and can be performed by design tools. In the process of minimization, the tools take advantage of the don't cares, so specifying them is important. The text book references at the end of this Appendix provide further discussion on logic minimization, Karnaugh maps, and the theory behind such minimization algorithms.

Arrays of Logic Elements

Many of the combinational operations to be performed on data have to be done to an entire word (32 bits) of data. Thus we often want to build an array of logic elements, which we can represent simply by showing that a given operation will happen to an entire collection of inputs. Inside a machine, much of the time we want to select between a pair of *buses*. A **bus** is a collection of data lines that is treated together as a single logical signal. (The term *bus* is also used to indicate a shared collection of lines with multiple sources and uses.)

For example, in the MIPS instruction set, the result of an instruction that is written into a register can come from one of two sources. A multiplexor is used to choose which of the two buses (each 32 bits wide) will be written into the Result register. The 1-bit multiplexor, which we showed earlier, will need to be replicated 32 times.

We indicate that a signal is a bus rather than a single 1-bit line by showing it with a thicker line in a figure. Most buses are 32 bits wide; those that are not are explicitly labeled with their width. When we show a logic unit whose inputs and outputs are buses, this means that the unit must be replicated a sufficient number of times to accommodate the width of the input. Figure B.3.6 shows how we draw a multiplexor that selects between a pair of 32-bit buses and how this expands in terms of 1-bit-wide multiplexors. Sometimes we need to construct an array of logic elements where the inputs for some elements in the array are outputs from earlier elements. For example, this is how a multibit-wide ALU is constructed. In such cases, we must explicitly show how to create wider arrays, since the individual elements of the array are no longer independent, as they are in the case of a 32-bit-wide multiplexor.

bus In logic design, a collection of data lines that is treated together as a single logical signal; also, a shared collection of lines with multiple sources and uses.

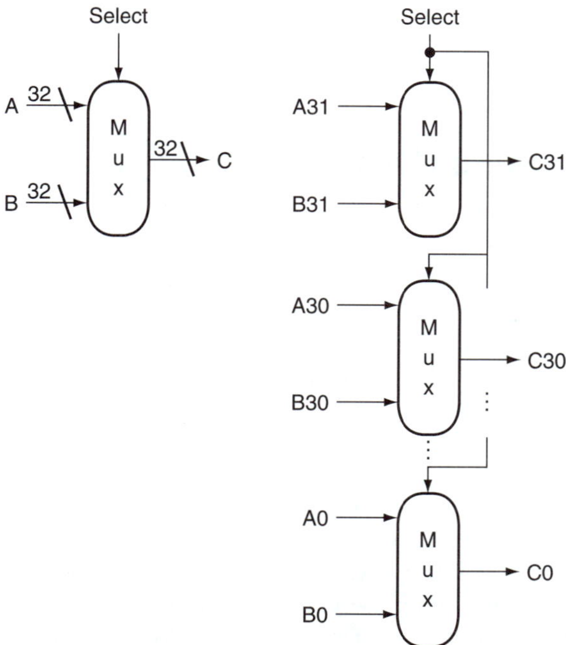

FIGURE B.3.6   A multiplexor is arrayed 32 times to perform a selection between two 32-bit inputs. Note that there is still only one data selection signal used for all 32 1-bit multiplexors.

Check Yourself

Parity is a function in which the output depends on the number of 1s in the input. For an even parity function, the output is 1 if the input has an even number of ones. Suppose a ROM is used to implement an even parity function with a 4-bit input. Which of A, B, C, or D represents the contents of the ROM?

Address	A	B	C	D
0	0	1	0	1
1	0	1	1	0
2	0	1	0	1
3	0	1	1	0
4	0	1	0	1
5	0	1	1	0
6	0	1	0	1
7	0	1	1	0
8	1	0	0	1
9	1	0	1	0
10	1	0	0	1
11	1	0	1	0
12	1	0	0	1
13	1	0	1	0
14	1	0	0	1
15	1	0	1	0

B.4   Using a Hardware Description Language

Today most digital design of processors and related hardware systems is done using a **hardware description language**. Such a language serves two purposes. First, it provides an abstract description of the hardware to simulate and debug the design. Second, with the use of logic synthesis and hardware compilation tools, this description can be compiled into the hardware implementation.

In this section, we introduce the hardware description language Verilog and show how it can be used for combinational design. In the rest of the appendix, we expand the use of Verilog to include design of sequential logic. In the optional sections of Chapter 4 that appear on the CD, we use Verilog to describe processor implementations. In the optional section from Chapter 5 that appears online, we use system Verilog to describe cache controller implementations. System Verilog adds structures and some other useful features to Verilog.

Verilog is one of the two primary hardware description languages; the other is **VHDL**. Verilog is somewhat more heavily used in industry and is based on C, as opposed to VHDL, which is based on Ada. The reader generally familiar with C will find the basics of Verilog, which we use in this appendix, easy to follow.

hardware description language A programming lan guage for describing hardware, used for generating simulations of a hardware design and also as input to synthesis tools that can generate actual hardware.

Verilog One of the two most common hardware description languages.

VHDL One of the two most common hardware description languages.

Readers already familiar with VHDL should find the concepts simple, provided they have been exposed to the syntax of C.

Verilog can specify both a behavioral and a structural definition of a digital system. A **behavioral specification** describes how a digital system functionally operates. A **structural specification** describes the detailed organization of a digital system, usually using a hierarchical description. A structural specification can be used to describe a hardware system in terms of a hierarchy of basic elements such as gates and switches. Thus, we could use Verilog to describe the exact contents of the truth tables and datapath of the last section.

With the arrival of **hardware synthesis** tools, most designers now use Verilog or VHDL to structurally describe only the datapath, relying on logic synthesis to generate the control from a behavioral description. In addition, most CAD systems provide extensive libraries of standardized parts, such as ALUs, multiplexors, register files, memories, and programmable logic blocks, as well as basic gates.

Obtaining an acceptable result using libraries and logic synthesis requires that the specification be written with an eye toward the eventual synthesis and the desired outcome. For our simple designs, this primarily means making clear what we expect to be implemented in combinational logic and what we expect to require sequential logic. In most of the examples we use in this section and the remainder of this appendix, we have written the Verilog with the eventual synthesis in mind.

Datatypes and Operators in Verilog

There are two primary datatypes in Verilog:

1. A **wire** specifies a combinational signal.

2. A **reg** (register) holds a value, which can vary with time. A reg need not necessarily correspond to an actual register in an implementation, although it often will.

A register or wire, named X, that is 32 bits wide is declared as an array: `reg [31:0] X` or `wire [31:0] X`, which also sets the index of 0 to designate the least significant bit of the register. Because we often want to access a subfield of a register or wire, we can refer to a contiguous set of bits of a register or wire with the notation `[starting bit: ending bit]`, where both indices must be constant values.

An array of registers is used for a structure like a register file or memory. Thus, the declaration

```
reg [31:0] registerfile[0:31]
```

specifies a variable registerfile that is equivalent to a MIPS registerfile, where register 0 is the first. When accessing an array, we can refer to a single element, as in C, using the notation `registerfile[regnum]`.

behavioral specification Describes how a digital system operates functionally.

structural specification Describes how a digital system is organized in terms of a hierarchical connection of elements.

hardware synthesis tools Computer-aided design software that can generate a gate-level design based on behavioral descriptions of a digital system.

wire In Verilog, specifies a combinational signal.

reg In Verilog, a register.

The possible values for a register or wire in Verilog are

- 0 or 1, representing logical false or true

- X, representing unknown, the initial value given to all registers and to any wire not connected to something

- Z, representing the high-impedance state for tristate gates, which we will not discuss in this appendix

Constant values can be specified as decimal numbers as well as binary, octal, or hexadecimal. We often want to say exactly how large a constant field is in bits. This is done by prefixing the value with a decimal number specifying its size in bits. For example:

- `4'b0100` specifies a 4-bit binary constant with the value 4, as does `4'd4`.

- `- 8 'h4` specifies an 8-bit constant with the value −4 (in two's complement representation)

Values can also be concatenated by placing them within { } separated by commas. The notation `{x {bit field}}` replicates `bit field` x times. For example:

- `{16{2'b01}}` creates a 32-bit value with the pattern 0101 … 01.

- `{A[31:16],B[15:0]}` creates a value whose upper 16 bits come from A and whose lower 16 bits come from B.

Verilog provides the full set of unary and binary operators from C, including the arithmetic operators (+, −, *. /), the logical operators (&, |, ~), the comparison operators (= =, !=, >, <, < =, > =), the shift operators (<<, >>), and C's conditional operator (?, which is used in the form `condition ? expr1 :expr2` and returns `expr1` if the condition is true and `expr2` if it is false). Verilog adds a set of unary logic reduction operators (&, |, ^) that yield a single bit by applying the logical operator to all the bits of an operand. For example, &A returns the value obtained by ANDing all the bits of A together, and ^A returns the reduction obtained by using exclusive OR on all the bits of A.

Check Yourself

Which of the following define exactly the same value?

```
1.  8'bimoooo
2.  8'hF0
3.  8'd240
4.  {{4{1'b1}},{4{1'b0}}}
5.  {4'b1,4'b0)
```

Structure of a Verilog Program

A Verilog program is structured as a set of modules, which may represent anything from a collection of logic gates to a complete system. Modules are similar to classes in C++, although not nearly as powerful. A module specifies its input and output ports, which describe the incoming and outgoing connections of a module. A module may also declare additional variables. The body of a module consists of:

- `initial` constructs, which can initialize `reg` variables

- Continuous assignments, which define only combinational logic

- `always` constructs, which can define either sequential or combinational logic

- Instances of other modules, which are used to implement the module being defined

Representing Complex Combinational Logic in Verilog

A continuous assignment, which is indicated with the keyword `assign`, acts like a combinational logic function: the output is continuously assigned the value, and a change in the input values is reflected immediately in the output value. Wires may only be assigned values with continuous assignments. Using continuous assignments, we can define a module that implements a half-adder, as Figure B.4.1 shows.

Assign statements are one sure way to write Verilog that generates combinational logic. For more complex structures, however, assign statements may be awkward or tedious to use. It is also possible to use the `always` block of a module to describe a combinational logic element, although care must be taken. Using an `always` block allows the inclusion of Verilog control constructs, such as *if-then–else, case* statements, *for* statements, and *repeat* statements, to be used. These state ments are similar to those in C with small changes.

An `always` block specifies an optional list of signals on which the block is sensitive (in a list starting with @). The `always` block is re-evaluated if any of the

```
module half_adder (A,B,Sum,Carry);
   input A,B; //two 1-bit inputs
   output Sum, Carry; //two 1-bit outputs
   assign Sum = A ^ B; //sum is A xor B
   assign Carry = A & B; //Carry is A and B
endmodule
```

FIGURE B.4.1 A Verilog module that defines a half-adder using continuous assignments.

listed signals changes value; if the list is omitted, the `always` block is constantly re-evaluated. When an `always` block is specifying combinational logic, the **sensitivity list** should include all the input signals. If there are multiple Verilog statements to be executed in an `always` block, they are surrounded by the keywords `begin` and `end`, which take the place of the { and } in C. An `always` block thus looks like this:

```
always @(list of signals that cause reevaluation) begin
    Verilog statements including assignments and other
control statements end
```

`Reg` variables may only be assigned inside an `always` block, using a procedural assignment statement (as distinguished from continuous assignment we saw earlier). There are, however, two different types of procedural assignments. The assignment operator = executes as it does in C; the right-hand side is evaluated, and the left-hand side is assigned the value. Furthermore, it executes like the normal C assignment statement: that is, it is completed before the next statement is executed. Hence, the assignment operator = has the name **blocking assignment**. This blocking can be useful in the generation of sequential logic, and we will return to it shortly. The other form of assignment (**nonblocking**) is indicated by <=. In nonblocking assignment, all right-hand sides of the assignments in an `always` group are evaluated and the assignments are done simultaneously. As a first example of combinational logic implemented using an `always` block, Figure B.4.2 shows the implementation of a 4-to-1 multiplexor, which uses a case construct to make it easy to write. The `case` construct looks like a C `switch` statement. Figure B.4.3 shows a definition of a MIPS ALU, which also uses a case statement.

Since only reg variables may be assigned inside `always` blocks, when we want to describe combinational logic using an `always` block, care must be taken to ensure that the reg does not synthesize into a register. A variety of pitfalls are described in the *Elaboration* below.

Elaboration: Continuous assignment statements always yield combinational logic, but other Verilog structures, even when in `always` blocks, can yield unexpected results during logic synthesis. The most common problem is creating sequential logic by implying the existence of a latch or register, which results in an implementation that is both slower and more costly than perhaps intended. To ensure that the logic that you intend to be combinational is synthesized that way, make sure you do the following:

1. Place all combinational logic in a continuous assignment or an `always` block.

2. Make sure that all the signals used as inputs appear in the sensitivity list of an `always` block.

3. Ensure that every path through an `always` block assigns a value to the exact same set of bits.

The last of these is the easiest to overlook; read through the example in Figure B.5.15 to convince yourself that this property is adhered to.

```
module Mult4to1 (In1,In2,In3,In4,Sel,Out);
   input [31:0] In1, In2, In3, In4; /four 32-bit inputs
   input [1:0] Sel; //selector signal
   output reg [31:0] Out;// 32-bit output
   always @(In1, In2, In3, In4, Sel)
   case (Sel) //a 4->1 multiplexor
      0: Out <= In1;
      1: Out <= In2;
      2: Out <= In3;
      default: Out <= In4;
   endcase
endmodule
```

FIGURE B.4.2 A Verilog definition of a 4-to-1 multiplexor with 32-bit inputs, using a case
statement. The case statement acts like a C switch statement, except that in Verilog only the code
associated with the selected case is executed (as if each case state had a break at the end) and there is no fall-
through to the next statement.

```
module MIPSALU (ALUctl, A, B, ALUOut, Zero);
   input [3:0] ALUctl;
   input [31:0] A,B;
   output reg [31:0] ALUOut;
   output Zero;
   assign Zero = (ALUOut==0); //Zero is true if ALUOut is 0; goes anywhere
   always @(ALUctl, A, B) //reevaluate if these change
      case (ALUctl)
         0: ALUOut <= A & B;
         1: ALUOut <= A | B;
         2: ALUOut <= A + B;
         6: ALUOut <= A - B;
         7: ALUOut <= A < B ? 1:0;
         12: ALUOut <= ~(A | B); // result is nor
         default: ALUOut <= 0; //default to 0, should not happen;
      endcase
endmodule
```

FIGURE B.4.3 A Verilog behavioral definition of a MIPS ALU. This could be synthesized using a module library containing basic
arithmetic and logical operations.

Assuming all values are initially zero, what are the values of A and B after executing this Verilog code inside an `always` block?

```
C=1;
A <= C;
B = C;
```

B.5 Constructing a Basic Arithmetic Logic Unit

ALU n. [Arthritic Logic Unit or (rare) Arithmetic Logic Unit] A random-number generator supplied as standard with all computer systems.

Stan Kelly-Bootle, *The Devil's DP Dictionary*, 1981

The **arithmetic logic unit (ALU)** is the brawn of the computer, the device that performs the arithmetic operations like addition and subtraction or logical operations like AND and OR. This section constructs an ALU from four hardware building blocks (AND and OR gates, inverters, and multiplexors) and illustrates how combinational logic works. In the next section, we will see how addition can be sped up through more clever designs.

Because the MIPS word is 32 bits wide, we need a 32-bit-wide ALU. Let's assume that we will connect 32 1-bit ALUs to create the desired ALU. We'll therefore start by constructing a 1-bit ALU.

A 1-Bit ALU

The logical operations are easiest, because they map directly onto the hardware components in Figure B.2.1.

The 1-bit logical unit for AND and OR looks like Figure B.5.1. The multiplexor on the right then selects *a* AND *b* or *a* OR *b*, depending on whether the value of *Operation* is 0 or 1. The line that controls the multiplexor is shown in color to distinguish it from the lines containing data. Notice that we have renamed the control and output lines of the multiplexor to give them names that reflect the function of the ALU.

The next function to include is addition. An adder must have two inputs for the operands and a single-bit output for the sum. There must be a second output to pass on the carry, called *CarryOut*. Since the CarryOut from the neighbor adder must be included as an input, we need a third input. This input is called *CarryIn*. Figure B.5.2 shows the inputs and the outputs of a 1-bit adder. Since we know what addition is supposed to do, we can specify the outputs of this "black box" based on its inputs, as Figure B.5.3 demonstrates.

We can express the output functions Carry Out and Sum as logical equations, and these equations can in turn be implemented with logic gates. Let's do CarryOut. Figure B.5.4 shows the values of the inputs when CarryOut is a 1.

We can turn this truth table into a logical equation:

$$CarryOut = (b \cdot CarryIn) + (a \cdot CarryIn) + (a \cdot b) + (a \cdot b \cdot CarryIn)$$

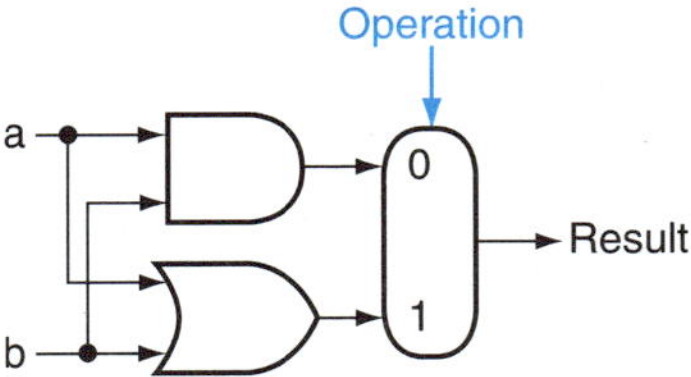

FIGURE B.5.1 The 1-bit logical unit for AND and OR.

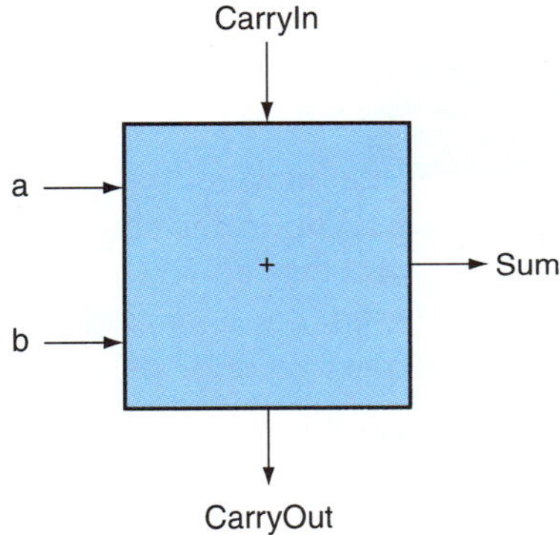

FIGURE B.5.2 A 1-bit adder. This adder is called a full adder; it is also called a (3,2) adder because it has 3 inputs and 2 outputs. An adder with only the a and b inputs is called a (2,2) adder or half-adder

Inputs			Outputs		
a	**b**	**CarryIn**	**CarryOut**	**Sum**	**Comments**
0	0	0	0	0	$0 + 0 + 0 = 00_{two}$
0	0	1	0	1	$0 + 0 + 1 = 01_{two}$
0	1	0	0	1	$0 + 1 + 0 = 01_{two}$
0	1	1	1	0	$0 + 1 + 1 = 10_{two}$
1	0	0	0	1	$1 + 0 + 0 = 01_{two}$
1	0	1	1	0	$1 + 0 + 1 = 10_{two}$
1	1	0	1	0	$1 + 1 + 0 = 10_{two}$
1	1	1	1	1	$1 + 1 + 1 = 11_{two}$

FIGURE B.5.3 Input and output specification for a 1-bit adder.

If $a \cdot b \cdot CarryIn$ is true, then all of the other three terms must also be true, so we can leave out this last term corresponding to the fourth line of the table. We can thus simplify the equation to

$$CarryOut = (b \cdot CarryIn) + (a \cdot CarryIn) + (a \cdot b)$$

Figure B.5.5 shows that the hardware within the adder black box for CarryOut consists of three AND gates and one OR gate. The three AND gates correspond exactly to the three parenthesized terms of the formula above for CarryOut, and the OR gate sums the three terms.

Inputs		
a	**b**	**CarryIn**
0	1	1
1	0	1
1	1	0
1	1	1

FIGURE B.5.4   Values of the inputs when CarryOut is a 1.

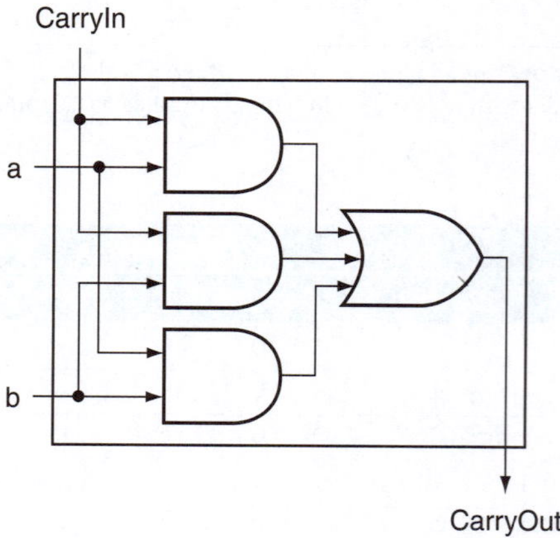

FIGURE B.5.5   Adder hardware for the CarryOut signal. The rest of the adder hardware is the logic for the Sum output given in the equation on this page.

The Sum bit is set when exactly one input is 1 or when all three inputs are 1. The Sum results in a complex Boolean equation (recall that $\overline{a}$ means NOT a):

$$Sum = (a \cdot \overline{b} \cdot \overline{CarryIn}) + (\overline{a} \cdot b \cdot \overline{CarryIn}) + (\overline{a} \cdot \overline{b} \cdot CarryIn) + (a \cdot b \cdot CarryIn)$$

The drawing of the logic for the Sum bit in the adder black box is left as an exercise for the reader.

Figure B.5.6 shows a 1-bit ALU derived by combining the adder with the earlier components. Sometimes designers also want the ALU to perform a few more simple operations, such as generating 0. The easiest way to add an operation is to expand the multiplexor controlled by the Operation line and, for this example, to connect 0 directly to the new input of that expanded multiplexor.

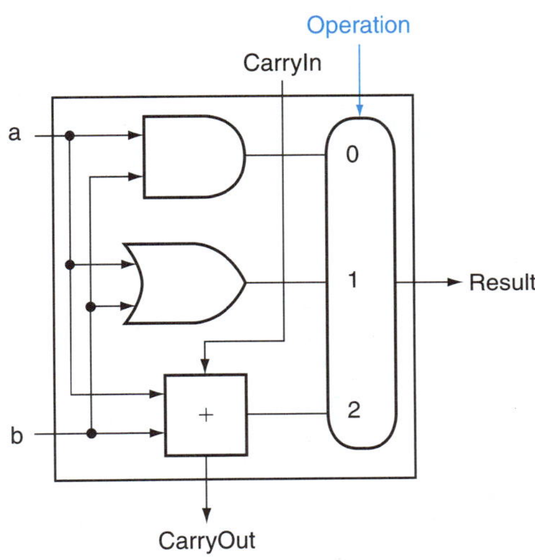

FIGURE B.5.6   A 1-bit ALU that performs AND, OR, and addition (see Figure B.5.5).

A 32-Bit ALU

Now that we have completed the 1-bit ALU, the full 32-bit ALU is created by connecting adjacent "black boxes." Using xi to mean the ith bit of x, Figure B.5.7 shows a 32-bit ALU. Just as a single stone can cause ripples to radiate to the shores of a quiet lake, a single carry out of the least significant bit (Result0) can ripple all the way through the adder, causing a carry out of the most significant bit (Result31). Hence, the adder created by directly linking the carries of 1-bit adders is called a *ripple carry* adder. We'll see a faster way to connect the 1-bit adders starting on page B-38.

Subtraction is the same as adding the negative version of an operand, and this is how adders perform subtraction. Recall that the shortcut for negating a two's complement number is to invert each bit (sometimes called the *one's complement*) and then add 1. To invert each bit, we simply add a 2:1 multiplexor that chooses between b and $\bar{b}$, as Figure B.5.8 shows.

Suppose we connect 32 of these 1-bit ALUs, as we did in Figure B.5.7. The added multiplexor gives the option of b or its inverted value, depending on Binvert, but

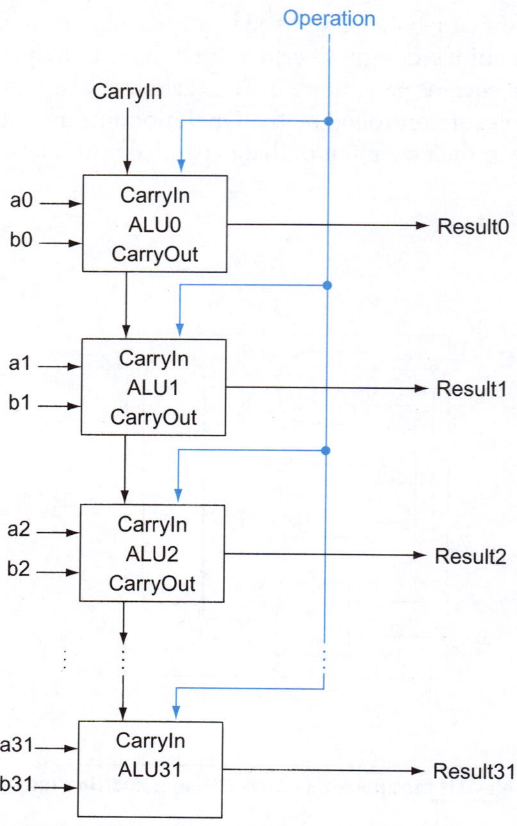

FIGURE B.5.7   A 32-bit ALU constructed from 32 1-bit ALUs. CarryOut of the less significant bit is connected to the CarryIn of the more significant bit. This organization is called ripple carry.

this is only one step in negating a two's complement number. Notice that the least significant bit still has a CarryIn signal, even though it's unnecessary for addition. What happens if we set this CarryIn to 1 instead of 0? The adder will then calculate $a + b + 1$. By selecting the inverted version of b, we get exactly what we want:

$$a + \overline{b} + 1 = a + (\overline{b} + 1) = a + (-b) = a - b$$

The simplicity of the hardware design of a two's complement adder helps explain why two's complement representation has become the universal standard for integer computer arithmetic.

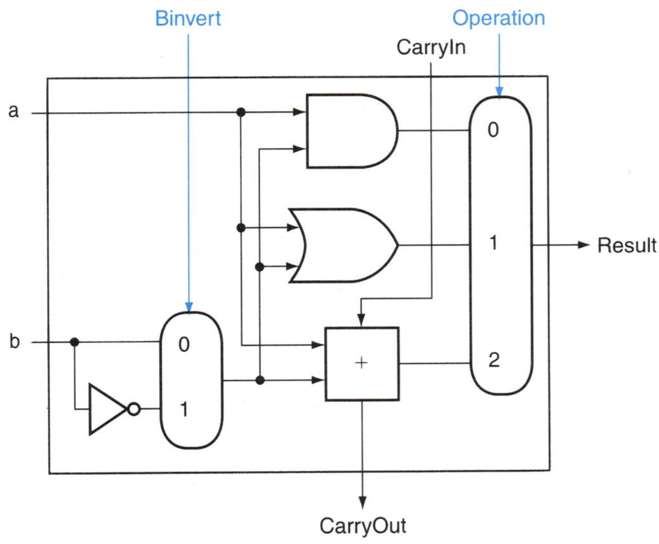

FIGURE B.5.8 A 1-bit ALU that performs AND, OR, and addition on a and b or a and $\overline{b}$. By selecting $\overline{b}$ (Binvert = 1) and setting CarryIn to 1 in the least significant bit of the ALU, we get two's complement subtraction of b from a instead of addition of b to a.

A MIPS ALU also needs a NOR function. Instead of adding a separate gate for NOR, we can reuse much of the hardware already in the ALU, like we did for subtract. The insight comes from the following truth about NOR:

$$\overline{(a + b)} = \overline{a} \cdot \overline{b}$$

That is, NOT (a OR b) is equivalent to NOT a AND NOT b. This fact is called DeMorgan's theorem and is explored in the exercises in more depth.

Since we have AND and NOT b, we only need to add NOT a to the ALU. Figure B.5.9 shows that change.

Tailoring the 32-Bit ALU to MIPS

These four operations—add, subtract, AND, OR—are found in the ALU of almost every computer, and the operations of most MIPS instructions can be performed by this ALU. But the design of the ALU is incomplete.

One instruction that still needs support is the set on less than instruction (slt). Recall that the operation produces 1 if rs , rt, and 0 otherwise. Consequently, slt will set all but the least significant bit to 0, with the least significant bit set according to the comparison. For the ALU to perform slt, we first need to expand the three-input

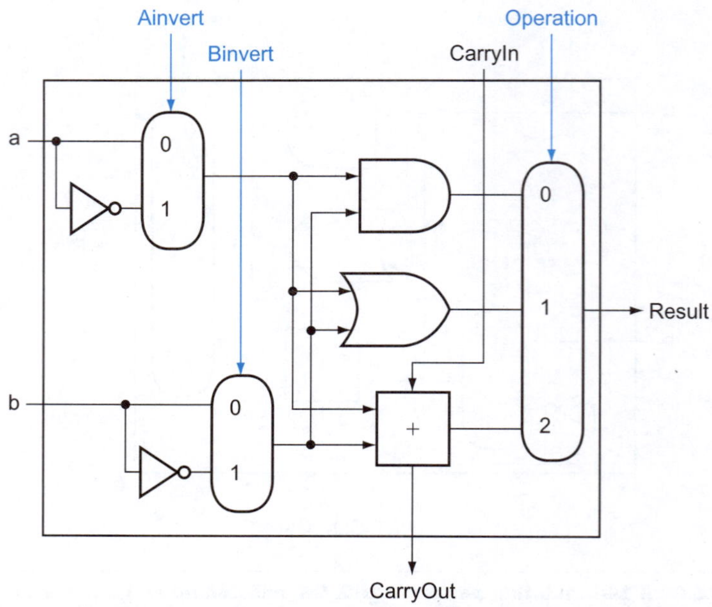

FIGURE B.5.9   A 1-bit ALU that performs AND, OR, and addition on a and b or $\bar{a}$ and $\bar{b}$. By selecting $\bar{a}$ (Ainvert = 1) and $\bar{b}$ (Binvert = 1), we get a NOR b instead of a AND b.

multiplexor in Figure B.5.8 to add an input for the slt result. We call that new input *Less* and use it only for slt.

The top drawing of Figure B.5.10 shows the new 1-bit ALU with the expanded multiplexor. From the description of slt above, we must connect 0 to the Less input for the upper 31 bits of the ALU, since those bits are always set to 0. What remains to consider is how to compare and set the *least significant bit* for set on less than instructions.

What happens if we subtract b from a? If the difference is negative, then a < b since

$$(a - b) < 0 \Rightarrow ((a - b) + b) < (0 + b)$$
$$\Rightarrow a < b$$

We want the least significant bit of a set on less than operation to be a 1 if a < b; that is, a 1 if a − b is negative and a 0 if it's positive. This desired result corresponds exactly to the sign bit values: 1 means negative and 0 means positive. Following this line of argument, we need only connect the sign bit from the adder output to the least significant bit to get set on less than.

Unfortunately, the Result output from the most significant ALU bit in the top of Figure B.5.10 for the slt operation is *not* the output of the adder; the ALU output for the slt operation is obviously the input value Less.

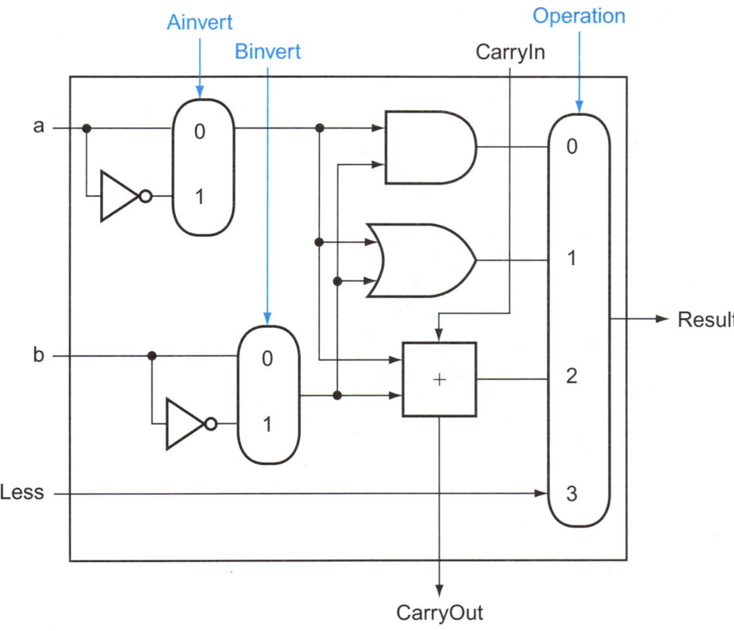

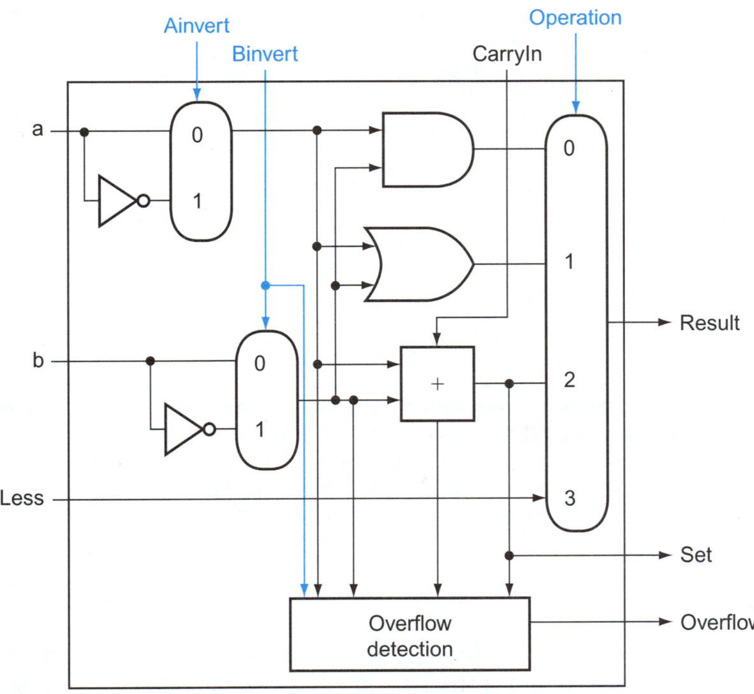

FIGURE B.5.10 **(Top) A 1-bit ALU that performs AND, OR, and addition on a and b or $\overline{b}$, and (bottom) a 1-bit ALU for the most significant bit.** The top drawing includes a direct input that is connected to perform the set on less than operation (see Figure B.5.11); the bottom has a direct output from the adder for the less than comparison called Set. (See Exercise B.24 at the end of this appendix to see how to calculate overflow with fewer inputs.)

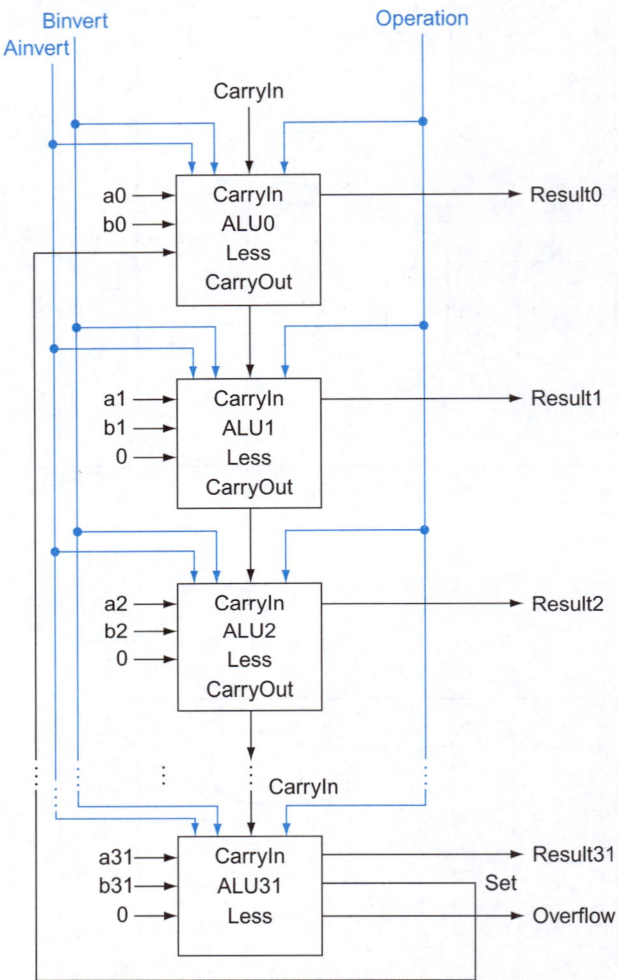

FIGURE B.5.11   A 32-bit ALU constructed from the 31 copies of the 1-bit ALU in the top of Figure B.5.10 and one 1-bit ALU in the bottom of that figure. The Less inputs are connected to 0 except for the least significant bit, which is connected to the Set output of the most significant bit. If the ALU performs a − b and we select the input 3 in the multiplexor in Figure B.5.10, then Result = 0 … 001 if a < b, and Result = 0 … 000 otherwise.

Thus, we need a new 1-bit ALU for the most significant bit that has an extra output bit: the adder output. The bottom drawing of Figure B.5.10 shows the design, with this new adder output line called *Set*, and used only for `slt`. As long as we need a special ALU for the most significant bit, we added the overflow detection logic since it is also associated with that bit.

Alas, the test of less than is a little more complicated than just described because of overflow, as we explore in the exercises. Figure B.5.11 shows the 32-bit ALU.

Notice that every time we want the ALU to subtract, we set both CarryIn and Binvert to 1. For adds or logical operations, we want both control lines to be 0. We can therefore simplify control of the ALU by combining the CarryIn and Binvert to a single control line called *Bnegate*.

To further tailor the ALU to the MIPS instruction set, we must support conditional branch instructions. These instructions branch either if two registers are equal or if they are unequal. The easiest way to test equality with the ALU is to subtract b from a and then test to see if the result is 0, since

$$(a - b = 0) \Rightarrow a = b$$

Thus, if we add hardware to test if the result is 0, we can test for equality. The simplest way is to OR all the outputs together and then send that signal through an inverter:

$$Zero = \overline{(Result31 + Result30 + \ldots + Result2 + Result1 + Result0)}$$

Figure B.5.12 shows the revised 32-bit ALU. We can think of the combination of the 1-bit Ainvert line, the 1-bit Binvert line, and the 2-bit Operation lines as 4-bit control lines for the ALU, telling it to perform add, subtract, AND, OR, or set on less than. Figure B.5.13 shows the ALU control lines and the corresponding ALU operation.

Finally, now that we have seen what is inside a 32-bit ALU, we will use the universal symbol for a complete ALU, as shown in Figure B.5.14.

Defining the MIPS ALU in Verilog

Figure B.5.15 shows how a combinational MIPS ALU might be specified in Verilog; such a specification would probably be compiled using a standard parts library that provided an adder, which could be instantiated. For completeness, we show the ALU control for MIPS in Figure B.5.16, which is used in Chapter 4, where we build a Verilog version of the MIPS datapath.

The next question is, "How quickly can this ALU add two 32-bit operands?" We can determine the a and b inputs, but the CarryIn input depends on the operation in the adjacent 1-bit adder. If we trace all the way through the chain of dependencies, we connect the most significant bit to the least significant bit, so the most significant bit of the sum must wait for the *sequential* evaluation of all 32 1-bit adders. This sequential chain reaction is too slow to be used in time-critical hardware. The next section explores how to speed-up addition. This topic is not crucial to understanding the rest of the appendix and may be skipped.

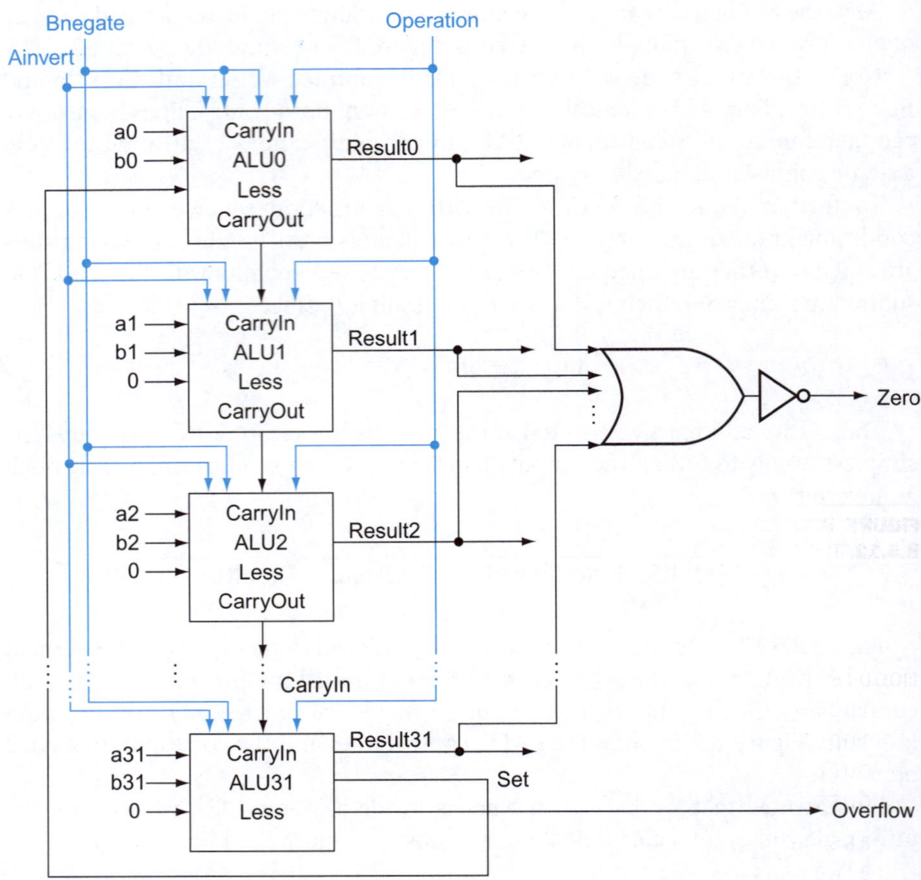

FIGURE B.5.12   The final 32-bit ALU. This adds a Zero detector to Figure B.5.11.

ALU control lines	Function
0000	AND
0001	OR
0010	add
0110	subtract
0111	set on less than
1100	NOR

FIGURE B.5.13   The values of the three ALU control lines, Bnegate, and Operation, and the corresponding ALU operations.

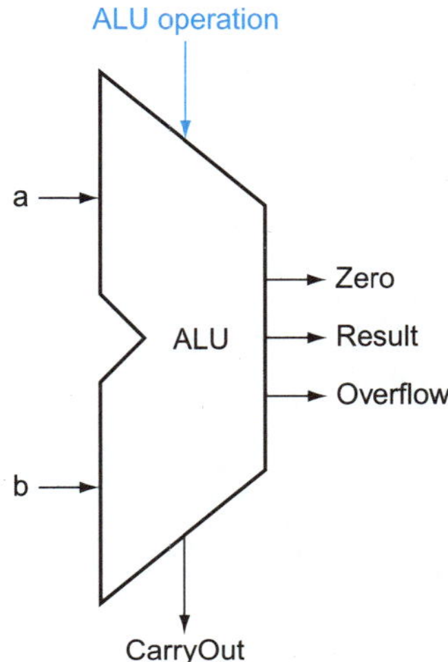

FIGURE B.5.14 The symbol commonly used to represent an ALU, as shown in Figure B.5.12. This symbol is also used to represent an adder, so it is normally labeled either with ALU or Adder.

```
module MIPSALU (ALUctl, A, B, ALUOut, Zero);
   input [3:0] ALUctl;
   input [31:0] A,B;
   output reg [31:0] ALUOut;
   output Zero;

   assign Zero = (ALUOut==0); //Zero is true if ALUOut is 0
   always @(ALUctl, A, B) begin //reevaluate if these change
     case (ALUctl)
        0: ALUOut <= A & B;
        1: ALUOut <= A | B;
        2: ALUOut <= A + B;
        6: ALUOut <= A - B;
        7: ALUOut <= A < B ? 1 : 0;
        12: ALUOut <= ~(A | B); // result is nor
        default: ALUOut <= 0;
     endcase
   end
endmodule
```

FIGURE B.5.15 A Verilog behavioral definition of a MIPS ALU.

```verilog
module ALUControl (ALUOp, FuncCode, ALUCtl);
   input [1:0] ALUOp;
   input [5:0] FuncCode;
   output [3:0] reg ALUCtl;

   always case (FuncCode)
   32: ALUOp<=2; // add
   34: ALUOp<=6; //subtract
   36: ALUOP<=0; // and
   37: ALUOp<=1; // or
   39: ALUOp<=12; // nor
   42: ALUOp<=7; // slt
   default: ALUOp<=15; // should not happen
   endcase
endmodule
```

FIGURE B.5.16   The MIPS ALU control: a simple piece of combinational control logic.

Check Yourself

Suppose you wanted to add the operation NOT (a AND b), called NAND. How could the ALU change to support it?

1. No change. You can calculate NAND quickly using the current ALU since $\overline{(a \cdot b)} = \overline{a} + \overline{b}$ and we already have NOT a, NOT b, and OR.

2. You must expand the big multiplexor to add another input, and then add new logic to calculate NAND.

B.6   Faster Addition: Carry Lookahead

The key to speeding up addition is determining the carry in to the high-order bits sooner. There are a variety of schemes to anticipate the carry so that the worst-case scenario is a function of the $\log_2$ of the number of bits in the adder. These anticipatory signals are faster because they go through fewer gates in sequence, but it takes many more gates to anticipate the proper carry.

A key to understanding fast-carry schemes is to remember that, unlike software, hardware executes in parallel whenever inputs change.

Fast Carry Using "Infinite" Hardware

As we mentioned earlier, any equation can be represented in two levels of logic. Since the only external inputs are the two operands and the CarryIn to the least significant bit of the adder, in theory we could calculate the CarryIn values to all the remaining bits of the adder in just two levels of logic.

For example, the CarryIn for bit 2 of the adder is exactly the CarryOut of bit 1, so the formula is

$$CarryIn2 = (b1 \cdot CarryIn1) + (a1 \cdot CarryIn1) + (a1 \cdot b1)$$

Similarly, CarryIn1 is defined as

$$CarryIn1 = (b0 \cdot CarryIn0) + (a0 \cdot CarryIn0) + (a0 \cdot b0)$$

Using the shorter and more traditional abbreviation of ci for CarryIni, we can rewrite the formulas as

$$c2 = (b1 \cdot c1) + (a1 \cdot c1) + (a1 \cdot b1)$$
$$c1 = (b0 \cdot c0) + (a0 \cdot c0) + (a0 \cdot b0)$$

Substituting the definition of c1 for the first equation results in this formula:

$$c2 = (a1 \cdot a0 \cdot b0) + (a1 \cdot a0 \cdot c0) \cdot (a1 \cdot b0 \cdot c0)$$
$$+ (b1 \cdot a0 \cdot b0) + (b1 \cdot a0 \cdot c0) + (b1 \cdot b0 \cdot c0) + (a1 \cdot b1)$$

You can imagine how the equation expands as we get to higher bits in the adder; it grows rapidly with the number of bits. This complexity is reflected in the cost of the hardware for fast carry, making this simple scheme prohibitively expensive for wide adders.

Fast Carry Using the First Level of Abstraction: Propagate and Generate

Most fast-carry schemes limit the complexity of the equations to simplify the hardware, while still making substantial speed improvements over ripple carry. One such scheme is a *carry-lookahead adder*. In Chapter 1, we said computer systems cope with complexity by using levels of abstraction. A carry-lookahead adder relies on levels of abstraction in its implementation.

Let's factor our original equation as a first step:

$$ci + 1 = (bi \cdot ci) + (ai \cdot ci) + (ai \cdot bi)$$
$$= (ai \cdot bi) + (ai + bi) \cdot ci$$

If we were to rewrite the equation for c2 using this formula, we would see some repeated patterns:

$$c2 = (a1 \cdot b1) + (a1 \cdot b1) \cdot ((a0 \cdot b0) + (a0 + b0) \cdot c0)$$

Note the repeated appearance of $(ai \cdot bi)$ and $(ai + bi)$ in the formula above. These two important factors are traditionally called *generate* (gi) and *propagate* (pi):

$$g_i = a_i \cdot b_i$$
$$p_i = a_i + b_i$$

Using them to define c_{i+1}, we get

$$c_{i+1} = g_i + p_i \cdot c_i$$

To see where the signals get their names, suppose g_i is 1. Then

$$c_{i+1} = g_i + p_i \cdot c_i = 1 + p_i \cdot c_i = 1$$

That is, the adder *generates* a CarryOut (c_{i+1}) independent of the value of CarryIn (c_i). Now suppose that g_i is 0 and p_i is 1. Then

$$c_{i+1} = g_i + p_i \cdot c_i = 0 + 1 \cdot c_i = c_i$$

That is, the adder *propagates* CarryIn to a CarryOut. Putting the two together, CarryIn$_{i+1}$ is a 1 if either g_i is 1 or both p_i is 1 and CarryIn$_i$ is 1.

As an analogy, imagine a row of dominoes set on edge. The end domino can be tipped over by pushing one far away, provided there are no gaps between the two. Similarly, a carry out can be made true by a generate far away, provided all the propagates between them are true.

Relying on the definitions of propagate and generate as our first level of abstraction, we can express the CarryIn signals more economically. Let's show it for 4 bits:

$$c_1 = g_0 + (p_0 \cdot c_0)$$
$$c_2 = g_1 + (p_1 \cdot g_0) + (p_1 \cdot p_0 \cdot c_0)$$
$$c_3 = g_2 + (p_2 \cdot g_1) + (p_2 \cdot p_1 \cdot g_0) + (p_2 \cdot p_1 \cdot p_0 \cdot c_0)$$
$$c_4 = g_3 + (p_3 \cdot g_2) + (p_3 \cdot p_2 \cdot g_1) + (p_3 \cdot p_2 \cdot p_1 \cdot g_0)$$
$$+ (p_3 \cdot p_2 \cdot p_1 \cdot p_0 \cdot c_0)$$

These equations just represent common sense: CarryIn$_i$ is a 1 if some earlier adder generates a carry and all intermediary adders propagate a carry. Figure B.6.1 uses plumbing to try to explain carry lookahead.

Even this simplified form leads to large equations and, hence, considerable logic even for a 16-bit adder. Let's try moving to two levels of abstraction.

Fast Carry Using the Second Level of Abstraction

First, we consider this 4-bit adder with its carry-lookahead logic as a single building block. If we connect them in ripple carry fashion to form a 16-bit adder, the add will be faster than the original with a little more hardware.

To go faster, we'll need carry lookahead at a higher level. To perform carry look ahead for 4-bit adders, we need to propagate and generate signals at this higher level. Here they are for the four 4-bit adder blocks:

$$P0 = p3 \cdot p2 \cdot p1 \cdot p0$$
$$P1 = p7 \cdot p6 \cdot p5 \cdot p4$$
$$P2 = p11 \cdot p10 \cdot p9 \cdot p8$$
$$P3 = p15 \cdot p14 \cdot p13 \cdot p12$$

That is, the "super" propagate signal for the 4-bit abstraction (Pi) is true only if each of the bits in the group will propagate a carry.

For the "super" generate signal (Gi), we care only if there is a carry out of the most significant bit of the 4-bit group. This obviously occurs if generate is true for that most significant bit; it also occurs if an earlier generate is true *and* all the intermediate propagates, including that of the most significant bit, are also true:

$$G0 = g3 + (p3 \cdot g2) + (p3 \cdot p2 \cdot g1) + (p3 \cdot p2 \cdot p1 \cdot g0)$$
$$G1 = g7 + (p7 \cdot g6) + (p7 \cdot p6 \cdot g5) + (p7 \cdot p6 \cdot p5 \cdot g4)$$
$$G2 = g11 + (p11 \cdot g10) + (p11 \cdot p10 \cdot g9) + (p11 \cdot p10 \cdot p9 \cdot g8)$$
$$G3 = g15 + (p15 \cdot g14) + (p15 \cdot p14 \cdot g13) + (p15 \cdot p14 \cdot p13 \cdot g12)$$

Figure B.6.2 updates our plumbing analogy to show P0 and G0.

Then the equations at this higher level of abstraction for the carry in for each 4-bit group of the 16-bit adder (C1, C2, C3, C4 in Figure B.6.3) are very similar to the carry out equations for each bit of the 4-bit adder (c1, c2, c3, c4) on page B-40:

$$C1 = G0 + (P0 \cdot c0)$$
$$C2 = G1 + (P1 \cdot G0) + (P1 \cdot P0 \cdot c0)$$
$$C3 = G2 + (P2 \cdot G1) + (P2 \cdot P1 \cdot G0) + (P2 \cdot P1 \cdot P0 \cdot c0)$$
$$C4 = G3 + (P3 \cdot G2) + (P3 \cdot P2 \cdot G1) + (P3 \cdot P2 \cdot P1 \cdot G0)$$
$$+ (P3 \cdot P2 \cdot P1 \cdot P0 \cdot c0)$$

Figure B.6.3 shows 4-bit adders connected with such a carry-lookahead unit. The exercises explore the speed differences between these carry schemes, different notations for multibit propagate and generate signals, and the design of a 64-bit adder.

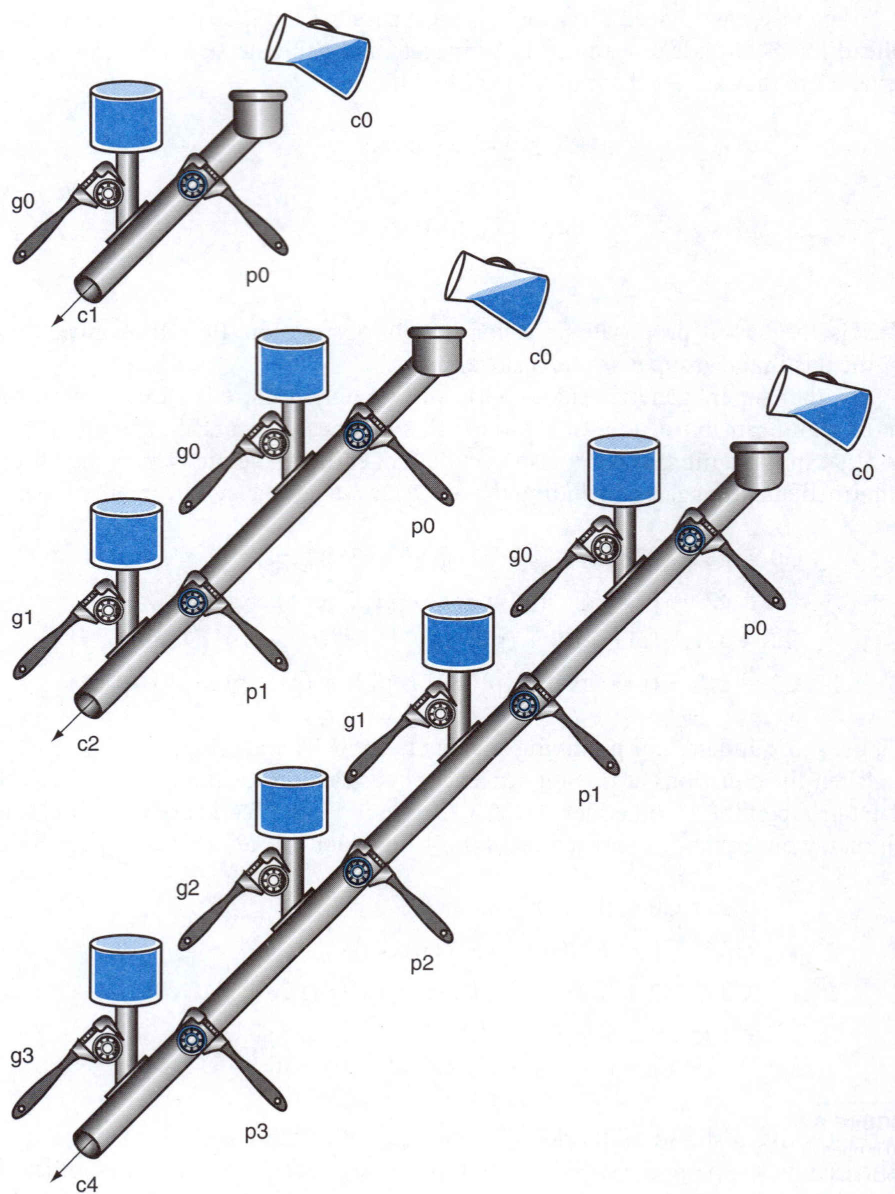

FIGURE B.6.1   A plumbing analogy for carry lookahead for 1 bit, 2 bits, and 4 bits using water pipes and valves. The wrenches are turned to open and close valves. Water is shown in color. The output of the pipe ($c_{i} + 1$) will be full if either the nearest generate value (g_i) is turned on or if the i propagate value (p_i) is on and there is water further upstream, either from an earlier generate or a propagate with water behind it. CarryIn (c_0) can result in a carry out without the help of any generates, but with the help of *all* propagates.

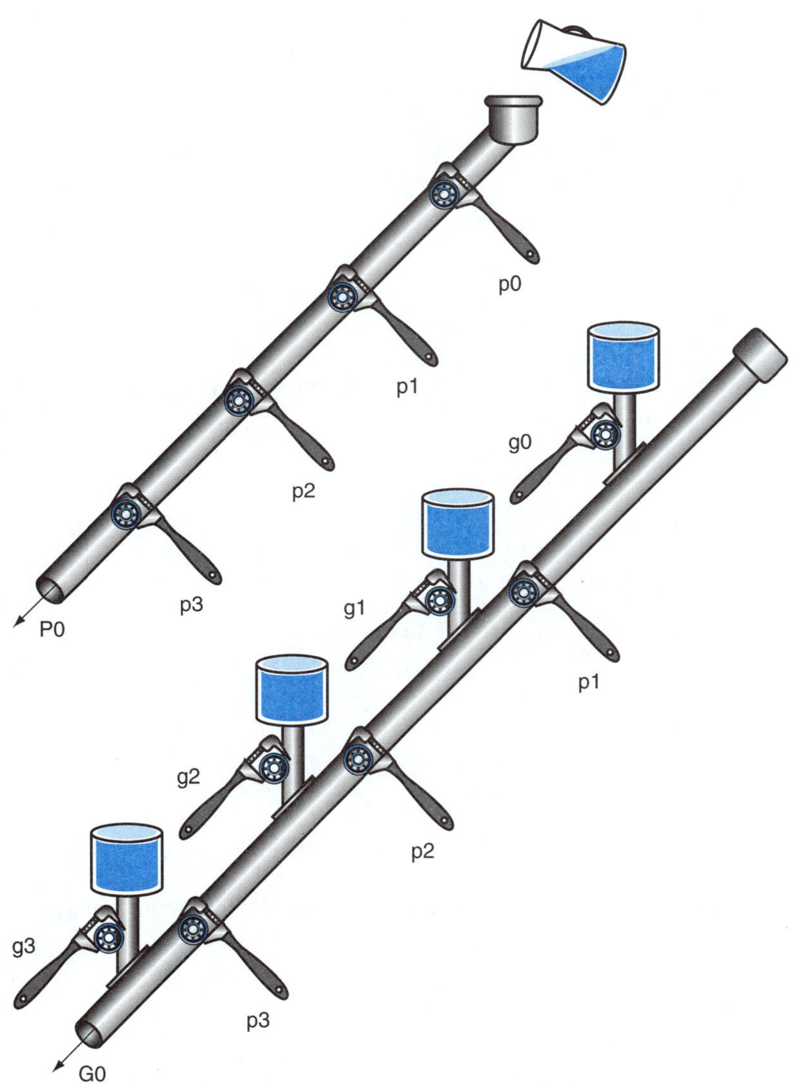

FIGURE B.6.2   A plumbing analogy for the next-level carry-lookahead signals P0 and G0.
P0 is open only if all four propagates (pi) are open, while water flows in G0 only if at least one generate (gi) is open and all the propagates downstream from that generate are open.

Both Levels of the Propagate and Generate

EXAMPLE

Determine the g_i, p_i, P_i, and G_i values of these two 16-bit numbers:

$$a: \quad 0001 \quad 1010 \quad 0011 \quad 0011_{two}$$
$$b: \quad 1110 \quad 0101 \quad 1110 \quad 1011_{two}$$

Also, what is CarryOut15 (C4)?

ANSWER

Aligning the bits makes it easy to see the values of generate g_i ($a_i \cdot b_i$) and propagate p_i ($a_i + b_i$):

$$
\begin{array}{llllll}
a: & 0001 & 1010 & 0011 & 0011 \\
b: & 1110 & 0101 & 1110 & 1011 \\
g_i: & 0000 & 0000 & 0010 & 0011 \\
p_i: & 1111 & 1111 & 1111 & 1011 \\
\end{array}
$$

where the bits are numbered 15 to 0 from left to right. Next, the "super" propagates (P3, P2, P1, P0) are simply the AND of the lower-level propagates:

$$P3 = 1 \cdot 1 \cdot 1 \cdot 1 = 1$$
$$P2 = 1 \cdot 1 \cdot 1 \cdot 1 = 1$$
$$P1 = 1 \cdot 1 \cdot 1 \cdot 1 = 1$$
$$P0 = 1 \cdot 0 \cdot 1 \cdot 1 = 0$$

The "super" generates are more complex, so use the following equations:

$$
\begin{aligned}
G0 &= g3 + (p3 \cdot g2) + (p3 \cdot p2 \cdot g1) + (p3 \cdot p2 \cdot p1 \cdot g0) \\
&= 0 + (1 \cdot 0) + (1 \cdot 0 \cdot 1) + (1 \cdot 0 \cdot 1 \cdot 1) = 0 + 0 + 0 + 0 = 0 \\
G1 &= g7 + (p7 \cdot g6) + (p7 \cdot p6 \cdot g5) + (p7 \cdot p6 \cdot p5 \cdot g4) \\
&= 0 + (1 \cdot 0) + (1 \cdot 1 \cdot 1) + (1 \cdot 1 \cdot 1 \cdot 0) = 0 + 0 + 1 + 0 = 1 \\
G2 &= g11 + (p11 \cdot g10) + (p11 \cdot p10 \cdot g9) + (p11 \cdot p10 \cdot p9 \cdot g8) \\
&= 0 + (1 \cdot 0) + (1 \cdot 1 \cdot 0) + (1 \cdot 1 \cdot 1 \cdot 0) = 0 + 0 + 0 + 0 = 0 \\
G3 &= g15 + (p15 \cdot g14) + (p15 \cdot p14 \cdot g13) + (p15 \cdot p14 \cdot p13 \cdot g12) \\
&= 0 + (1 \cdot 0) + (1 \cdot 1 \cdot 0) + (1 \cdot 1 \cdot 1 \cdot 0) = 0 + 0 + 0 + 0 = 0 \\
\end{aligned}
$$

Finally, CarryOut15 is

$$
\begin{aligned}
C4 &= G3 + (P3 \cdot G2) + (P3 \cdot P2 \cdot G1) + (P3 \cdot P2 \cdot P1 \cdot G0) \\
&\quad + (P3 \cdot P2 \cdot P1 \cdot P0 \cdot c0) \\
&= 0 + (1 \cdot 0) + (1 \cdot 1 \cdot 1) + (1 \cdot 1 \cdot 1 \cdot 0) + (1 \cdot 1 \cdot 1 \cdot 0 \cdot 0) \\
&= 0 + 0 + 1 + 0 + 0 = 1 \\
\end{aligned}
$$

Hence, there *is* a carry out when adding these two 16-bit numbers.

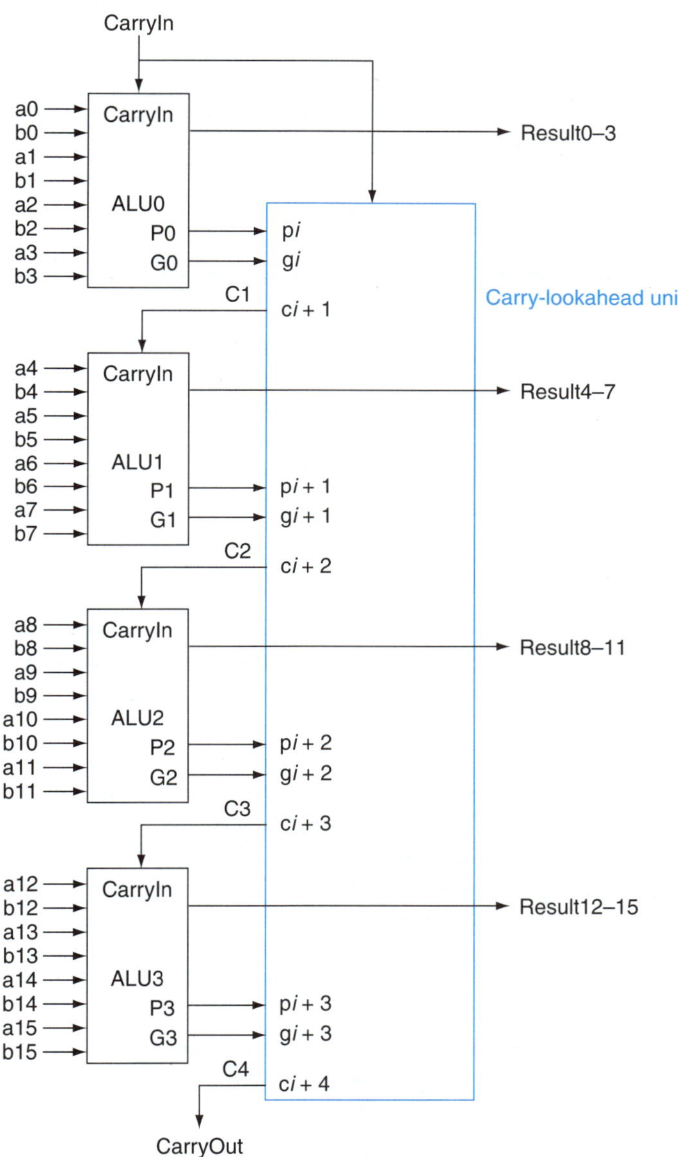

FIGURE B.6.3   Four 4-bit ALUs using carry lookahead to form a 16-bit adder. Note that the carries come from the carry-lookahead unit, not from the 4-bit ALUs.

The reason carry lookahead can make carries faster is that all logic begins evaluating the moment the clock cycle begins, and the result will not change once the output of each gate stops changing. By taking the shortcut of going through fewer gates to send the carry in signal, the output of the gates will stop changing sooner, and hence the time for the adder can be less.

To appreciate the importance of carry lookahead, we need to calculate the relative performance between it and ripple carry adders.

EXAMPLE

Speed of Ripple Carry versus Carry Lookahead

One simple way to model time for logic is to assume each AND or OR gate takes the same time for a signal to pass through it. Time is estimated by simply counting the number of gates along the path through a piece of logic. Compare the number of *gate delays* for paths of two 16-bit adders, one using ripple carry and one using two-level carry lookahead.

ANSWER

Figure B.5.5 on page B-28 shows that the carry out signal takes two gate delays per bit. Then the number of gate delays between a carry in to the least significant bit and the carry out of the most significant is $16 \times 2 = 32$.

For carry lookahead, the carry out of the most significant bit is just C4, defined in the example. It takes two levels of logic to specify C4 in terms of P_i and G_i (the OR of several AND terms). P_i is specified in one level of logic (AND) using p_i, and G_i is specified in two levels using p_i and g_i, so the worst case for this next level of abstraction is two levels of logic. p_i and g_i are each one level of logic, defined in terms of a_i and b_i. If we assume one gate delay for each level of logic in these equations, the worst case is $2 + 2 + 1 = 5$ gate delays.

Hence, for the path from carry in to carry out, the 16-bit addition by a carry-lookahead adder is six times faster, using this very simple estimate of hardware speed.

Summary

Carry lookahead offers a faster path than waiting for the carries to ripple through all 32 1-bit adders. This faster path is paved by two signals, generate and propagate.

The former creates a carry regardless of the carry input, and the latter passes a carry along. Carry lookahead also gives another example of how abstraction is important in computer design to cope with complexity.

Using the simple estimate of hardware speed above with gate delays, what is the relative performance of a ripple carry 8-bit add versus a 64-bit add using carry-lookahead logic?

Check Yourself

1. A 64-bit carry-lookahead adder is three times faster: 8-bit adds are 16 gate delays and 64-bit adds are 7 gate delays.

2. They are about the same speed, since 64-bit adds need more levels of logic in the 16-bit adder.

3. 8-bit adds are faster than 64 bits, even with carry lookahead.

Elaboration: We have now accounted for all but one of the arithmetic and logical operations for the core MIPS instruction set: the ALU in Figure B.5.14 omits support of shift instructions. It would be possible to widen the ALU multiplexor to include a left shift by 1 bit or a right shift by 1 bit. But hardware designers have created a circuit called a *barrel shifter,* which can shift from 1 to 31 bits in no more time than it takes to add two 32-bit numbers, so shifting is normally done outside the ALU.

Elaboration: The logic equation for the Sum output of the full adder on page B-28 can be expressed more simply by using a more powerful gate than AND and OR. An *exclusive OR* gate is true if the two operands disagree; that is,

$$x \neq y \Rightarrow 1 \text{ and } x == y \Rightarrow 0$$

In some technologies, exclusive OR is more efficient than two levels of AND and OR gates. Using the symbol $\oplus$ to represent exclusive OR, here is the new equation:

$$\text{Sum} = a \oplus b \oplus \text{CarryIn}$$

Also, we have drawn the ALU the traditional way, using gates. Computers are designed today in CMOS transistors, which are basically switches. CMOS ALU and bar rel shifters take advantage of these switches and have many fewer multiplexors than shown in our designs, but the design principles are similar.

Elaboration: Using lowercase and uppercase to distinguish the hierarchy of generate and propagate symbols breaks down when you have more than two levels. An alternate notation that scales is $g_{i..j}$ and $p_{i..j}$ for the generate and propagate signals for bits i to j. Thus, $g_{1..1}$ is generated for bit 1, $g_{4..1}$ is for bits 4 to 1, and $g_{16..1}$ is for bits 16 to 1.

B.7 Clocks

Before we discuss memory elements and sequential logic, it is useful to discuss briefly the topic of clocks. This short section introduces the topic and is similar to the discussion found in Section 4.2. More details on clocking and timing methodologies are presented in Section B.11.

Clocks are needed in sequential logic to decide when an element that contains state should be updated. A clock is simply a free-running signal with a fixed *cycle time*; the *clock frequency* is simply the inverse of the cycle time. As shown in Figure B.7.1, the *clock cycle time* or *clock period* is divided into two portions: when the clock is high and when the clock is low. In this text, we use only **edge-triggered clocking**. This means that all state changes occur on a clock edge. We use an edge-triggered methodology because it is simpler to explain. Depending on the technology, it may or may not be the best choice for a **clocking methodology**.

edge-triggered clocking A clocking scheme in which all state changes occur on a clock edge.

clocking methodology The approach used to determine when data is valid and stable relative to the clock.

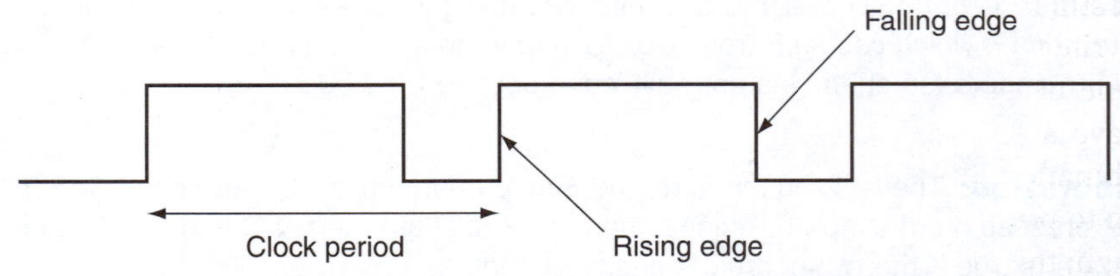

FIGURE B.7.1   A clock signal oscillates between high and low values. The clock period is the time for one full cycle. In an edge-triggered design, either the rising or falling edge of the clock is active and causes state to be changed.

In an edge-triggered methodology, either the rising edge or the falling edge of the clock is *active* and causes state changes to occur. As we will see in the next section, the **state elements** in an edge-triggered design are implemented so that the contents of the state elements only change on the active clock edge. The choice of which edge is active is influenced by the implementation technology and does not affect the concepts involved in designing the logic.

The clock edge acts as a sampling signal, causing the value of the data input to a state element to be sampled and stored in the state element. Using an edge trigger means that the sampling process is essentially instantaneous, eliminating problems that could occur if signals were sampled at slightly different times.

The major constraint in a clocked system, also called a **synchronous system**, is that the signals that are written into state elements must be *valid* when the active

state element A memory element.

synchronous system A memory system that employs clocks and where data signals are read only when the clock indicates that the signal values are stable.

clock edge occurs. A signal is valid if it is stable (i.e., not changing), and the value will not change again until the inputs change. Since combinational circuits cannot have feedback, if the inputs to a combinational logic unit are not changed, the outputs will eventually become valid.

Figure B.7.2 shows the relationship among the state elements and the combinational logic blocks in a synchronous, sequential logic design. The state elements, whose outputs change only after the clock edge, provide valid inputs to the combinational logic block. To ensure that the values written into the state elements on the active clock edge are valid, the clock must have a long enough period so that all the signals in the combinational logic block stabilize, then the clock edge samples those values for storage in the state elements. This constraint sets a lower bound on the length of the clock period, which must be long enough for all state element inputs to be valid.

In the rest of this appendix, as well as in Chapter 4, we usually omit the clock signal, since we are assuming that all state elements are updated on the same clock edge. Some state elements will be written on every clock edge, while others will be written only under certain conditions (such as a register being updated). In such cases, we will have an explicit write signal for that state element. The write signal must still be gated with the clock so that the update occurs only on the clock edge if the write signal is active. We will see how this is done and used in the next section.

One other advantage of an edge-triggered methodology is that it is possible to have a state element that is used as both an input and output to the same combinational logic block, as shown in Figure B.7.3. In practice, care must be taken to prevent races in such situations and to ensure that the clock period is long enough; this topic is discussed further in Section B.11.

Now that we have discussed how clocking is used to update state elements, we can discuss how to construct the state elements.

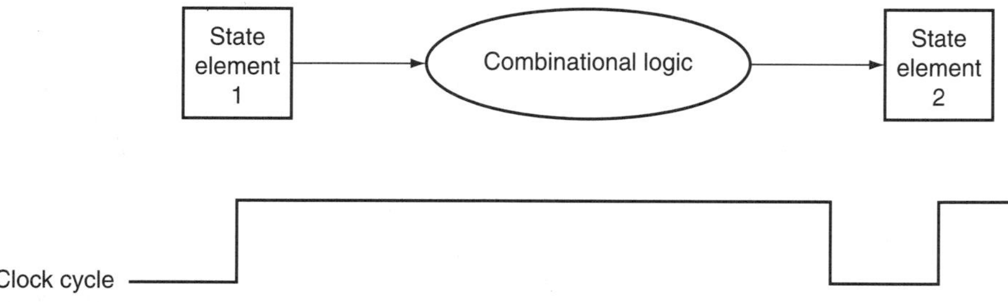

FIGURE B.7.2 The inputs to a combinational logic block come from a state element, and the outputs are written into a state element. The clock edge determines when the contents of the state elements are updated.

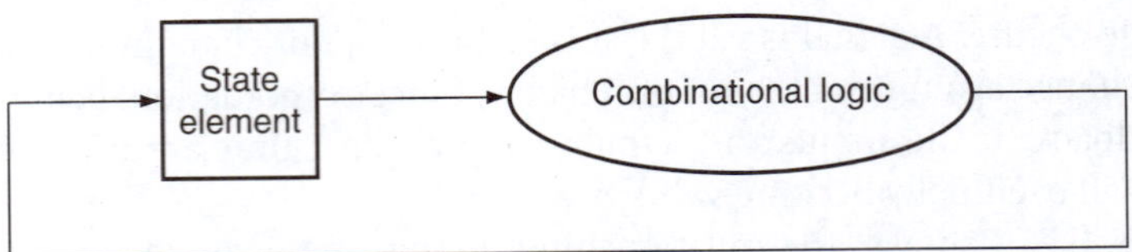

FIGURE B.7.3 An edge-triggered methodology allows a state element to be read and written in the same clock cycle without creating a race that could lead to undetermined data values. Of course, the clock cycle must still be long enough so that the input values are stable when the active clock edge occurs.

Elaboration: Occasionally, designers find it useful to have a small number of state elements that change on the opposite clock edge from the majority of the state elements. Doing so requires extreme care, because such an approach has effects on both the inputs and the outputs of the state element. Why then would designers ever do this? Consider the case where the amount of combinational logic before and after a state element is small enough so that each could operate in one-half clock cycle, rather than the more usual full clock cycle. Then the state element can be written on the clock edge corresponding to a half clock cycle, since the inputs and outputs will both be usable after one-half clock cycle. One common place where this technique is used is in **register files**, where simply reading or writing the register file can often be done in half the normal clock cycle. Chapter 4 makes use of this idea to reduce the pipelining over head.

register file: A state element that consists of a set of registers that can be read and written by supplying a register number to be accessed.

B.8　Memory Elements: Flip-Flops, Latches, and Registers

In this section and the next, we discuss the basic principles behind memory elements, starting with flip-flops and latches, moving on to register files, and finishing with memories. All memory elements store state: the output from any memory element depends both on the inputs and on the value that has been stored inside the memory element. Thus all logic blocks containing a memory element contain state and are sequential.

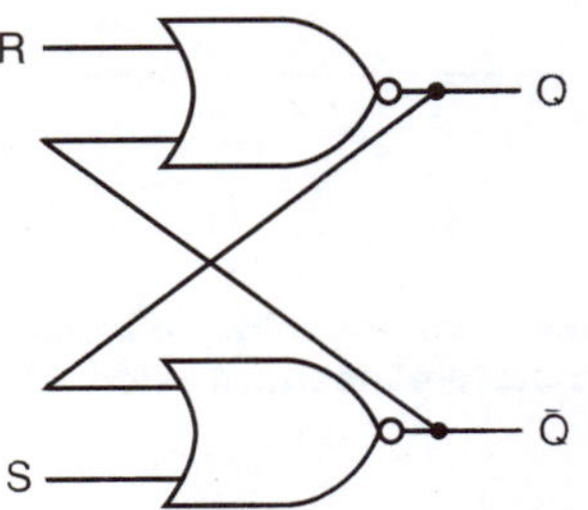

FIGURE B.8.1 A pair of cross-coupled NOR gates can store an internal value. The value stored on the output Q is recycled by inverting it to obtain Q̄ and then inverting Q̄ to obtain Q. If either R or is asserted, Q will be deasserted and vice versa.

The simplest type of memory elements are *unclocked*; that is, they do not have any clock input. Although we only use clocked memory elements in this text, an unclocked latch is the simplest memory element, so let's look at this circuit first. Figure B.8.1 shows an *S-R latch* (set-reset latch), built from a pair of NOR gates (OR gates with inverted outputs). The outputs Q and $\overline{Q}$ represent the value of the stored state and its complement. When neither S nor R are asserted, the cross-coupled NOR gates act as inverters and store the previous values of Q and $\overline{Q}$.

For example, if the output, Q, is true, then the bottom inverter produces a false output (which is $\overline{Q}$), which becomes the input to the top inverter, which produces a true output, which is Q, and so on. If S is asserted, then the output Q will be asserted and $\overline{Q}$ will be deasserted, while if R is asserted, then the output $\overline{Q}$ will be asserted and Q will be deasserted. When S and R are both deasserted, the last values of Q and $\overline{Q}$ will continue to be stored in the cross-coupled structure. Asserting S and R simultaneously can lead to incorrect operation: depending on how S and R are deasserted, the latch may oscillate or become metastable (this is described in more detail in Section B.11).

This cross-coupled structure is the basis for more complex memory elements that allow us to store data signals. These elements contain additional gates used to store signal values and to cause the state to be updated only in conjunction with a clock. The next section shows how these elements are built.

Flip-Flops and Latches

Flip-flops and **latches** are the simplest memory elements. In both flip-flops and latches, the output is equal to the value of the stored state inside the element. Furthermore, unlike the S-R latch described above, all the latches and flip-flops we will use from this point on are clocked, which means that they have a clock input and the change of state is triggered by that clock. The difference between a flip-flop and a latch is the point at which the clock causes the state to actually change. In a clocked latch, the state is changed whenever the appropriate inputs change and the clock is asserted, whereas in a flip-flop, the state is changed only on a clock edge. Since throughout this text we use an edge-triggered timing methodology where state is only updated on clock edges, we need only use flip-flops. Flip-flops are often built from latches, so we start by describing the operation of a simple clocked latch and then discuss the operation of a flip-flop constructed from that latch.

For computer applications, the function of both flip-flops and latches is to store a signal. A *D latch* or **D flip-flop** stores the value of its data input signal in the internal memory. Although there are many other types of latches and flip-flop, the D type is the only basic building block that we will need. A D latch has two inputs and two outputs. The inputs are the data value to be stored (called D) and a clock signal (called C) that indicates when the latch should read the value on the D input and store it. The outputs are simply the value of the internal state (Q)

flip-flop A memory element for which the output is equal to the value of the stored state inside the element and for which the internal state is changed only on a clock edge.

latch A memory element in which the output is equal to the value of the stored state inside the element and the state is changed whenever the appropriate inputs change and the clock is asserted.

D flip-flop A flip-flop with one data input that stores the value of that input signal in the internal memory when the clock edge occurs.

and its complement ($\overline{Q}$). When the clock input C is asserted, the latch is said to be *open*, and the value of the output (Q) becomes the value of the input D. When the clock input C is deasserted, the latch is said to be *closed*, and the value of the out put (Q) is whatever value was stored the last time the latch was open.

Figure B.8.2 shows how a D latch can be implemented with two additional gates added to the cross-coupled NOR gates. Since when the latch is open the value of Q changes as D changes, this structure is sometimes called a *transparent latch*. Figure B.8.3 shows how this D latch works, assuming that the output Q is initially false and that D changes first.

As mentioned earlier, we use flip-flops as the basic building block, rather than latches. Flip-flops are not transparent: their outputs change *only* on the clock edge. A flip-flop can be built so that it triggers on either the rising (positive) or falling (negative) clock edge; for our designs we can use either type. Figure B.8.4 shows how a falling-edge D flip-flop is constructed from a pair of D latches. In a D flip-flop, the output is stored when the clock edge occurs. Figure B.8.5 shows how this flip-flop operates.

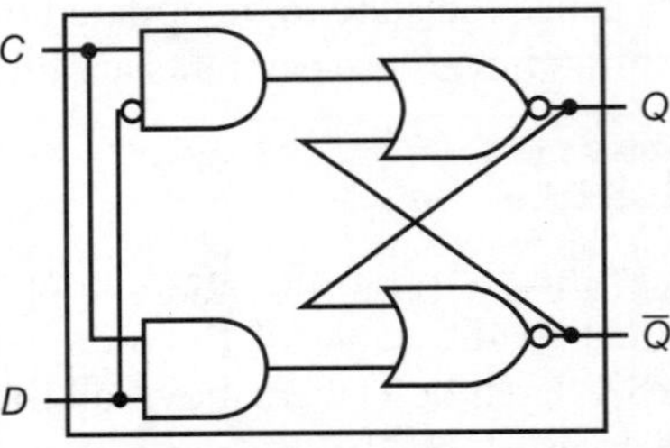

FIGURE B.8.2   A D latch implemented with NOR gates. A NOR gate acts as an inverter if the other input is 0. Thus, the cross-coupled pair of NOR gates acts to store the state value unless the clock input, C, is asserted, in which case the value of input D replaces the value of Q and is stored. The value of input D must be stable when the clock signal C changes from asserted to deasserted.

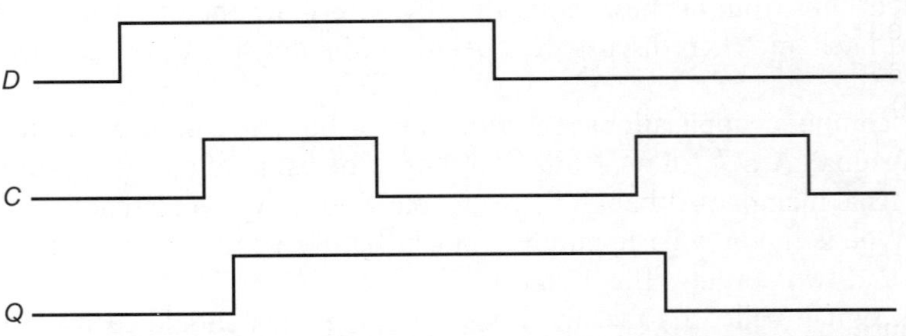

FIGURE B.8.3   Operation of a D latch, assuming the output is initially deasserted. When the clock, C, is asserted, the latch is open and the Q output immediately assumes the value of the D input.

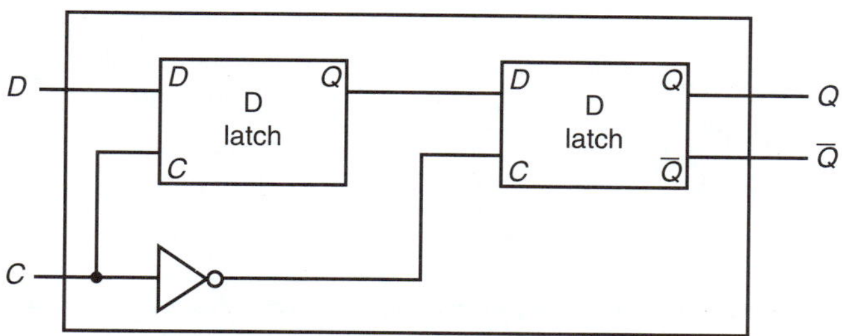

FIGURE B.8.4 A D flip-flop with a falling-edge trigger. The first latch, called the master, is open and follows the input D when the clock input, C, is asserted. When the clock input, C, falls, the first latch is closed, but the second latch, called the slave, is open and gets its input from the output of the master latch.

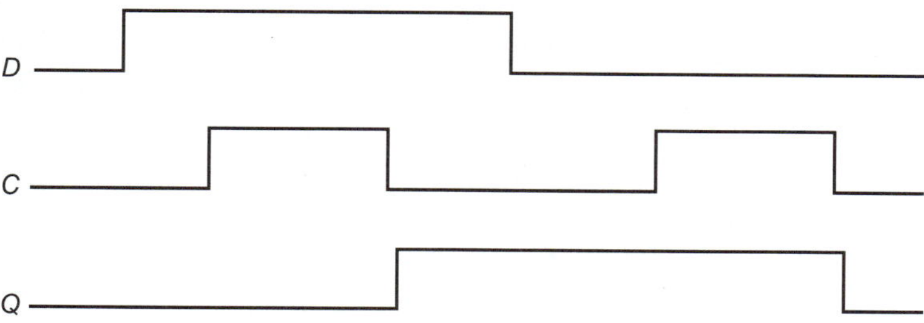

FIGURE B.8.5 Operation of a D flip-flop with a falling-edge trigger, assuming the output is initially deasserted. When the clock input (C) changes from asserted to deasserted, the Q output stores the value of the D input. Compare this behavior to that of the clocked D latch shown in Figure B.8.3. In a clocked latch, the stored value and the output, Q, both change whenever C is high, as opposed to only when C transitions.

Here is a Verilog description of a module for a rising-edge D flip-flop, assuming that C is the clock input and D is the data input:

```
module DFF(clock,D,Q,Qbar);
    input clock, D;
    output reg Q; // Q is a reg since it is assigned in an
always block
    output Qbar;
    assign Qbar = ~ Q; // Qbar is always just the inverse
of Q
    always @(posedge clock) // perform actions whenever the
clock rises
    Q = D;
endmodule
```

Because the D input is sampled on the clock edge, it must be valid for a period of time immediately before and immediately after the clock edge. The minimum time that the input must be valid before the clock edge is called the **setup time**; the

setup time The minimum time that the input to a memory device must be valid before the clock edge.

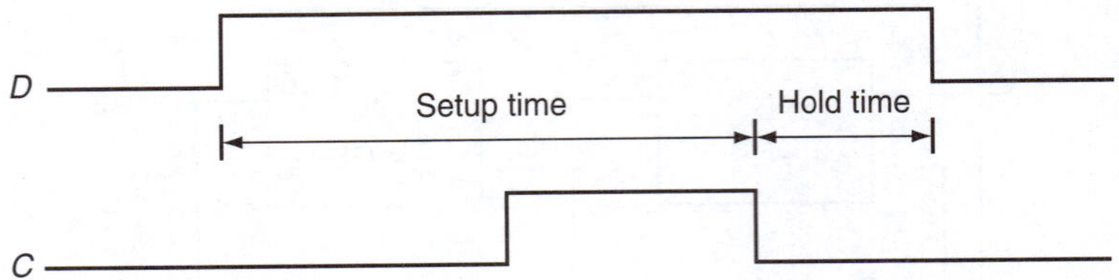

FIGURE B.8.6   Setup and hold time requirements for a D flip-flop with a falling-edge trigger. The input must be stable for a period of time before the clock edge, as well as after the clock edge. The minimum time the signal must be stable before the clock edge is called the setup time, while the minimum time the signal must be stable after the clock edge is called the hold time. Failure to meet these minimum require ments can result in a situation where the output of the flip-flop may not be predictable, as described in Section B.11. Hold times are usually either 0 or very small and thus not a cause of worry.

hold time The minimum time during which the input must be valid after the clock edge.

minimum time during which it must be valid after the clock edge is called the **hold time**. Thus the inputs to any flip-flop (or anything built using flip-flops) must be valid during a window that begins at time t_{setup} before the clock edge and ends at t_{hold} after the clock edge, as shown in Figure B.8.6. Section B.11 talks about clocking and timing constraints, including the propagation delay through a flip-flop, in more detail.

We can use an array of D flip-flops to build a register that can hold a multibit datum, such as a byte or word. We used registers throughout our datapaths in Chapter 4.

Register Files

One structure that is central to our datapath is a *register file*. A register file consists of a set of registers that can be read and written by supplying a register number to be accessed. A register file can be implemented with a decoder for each read or write port and an array of registers built from D flip-flops. Because reading a register does not change any state, we need only supply a register number as an input, and the only output will be the data contained in that register. For writing a register we will need three inputs: a register number, the data to write, and a clock that controls the writing into the register. In Chapter 4, we used a register file that has two read ports and one write port. This register file is drawn as shown in Figure B.8.7. The read ports can be implemented with a pair of multiplexors, each of which is as wide as the number of bits in each register of the register file. Figure B.8.8 shows the implementation of two register read ports for a 32-bit-wide register file.

Implementing the write port is slightly more complex, since we can only change the contents of the designated register. We can do this by using a decoder to generate a signal that can be used to determine which register to write. Figure B.8.9 shows how to implement the write port for a register file. It is important to remember that the flip-flop changes state only on the clock edge. In Chapter 4, we hooked up write signals for the register file explicitly and assumed the clock shown in Figure B.8.9 is attached implicitly.

What happens if the same register is read and written during a clock cycle? Because the write of the register file occurs on the clock edge, the register will be

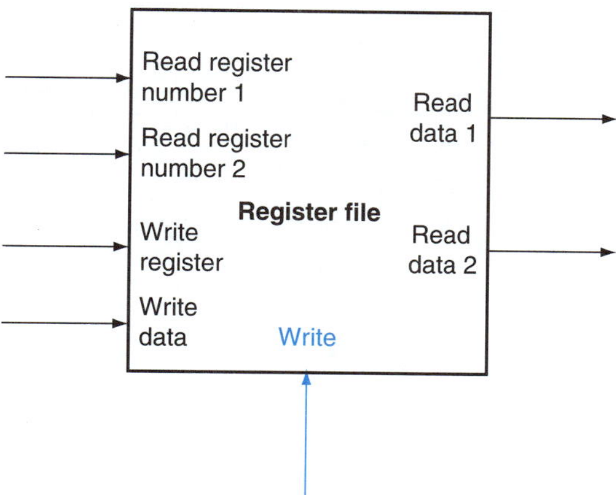

FIGURE B.8.7   A register file with two read ports and one write port has five inputs and two outputs. The control input Write is shown in color.

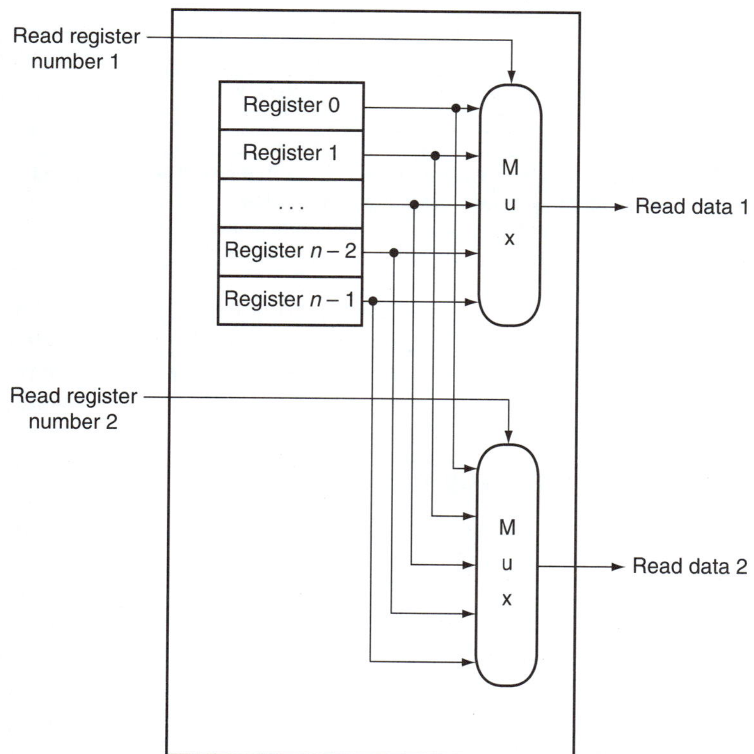

FIGURE B.8.8   The implementation of two read ports for a register file with *n* registers can be done with a pair of n-to-1 multiplexors, each 32 bits wide. The register read number signal is used as the multiplexor selector signal. Figure B.8.9 shows how the write port is implemented.

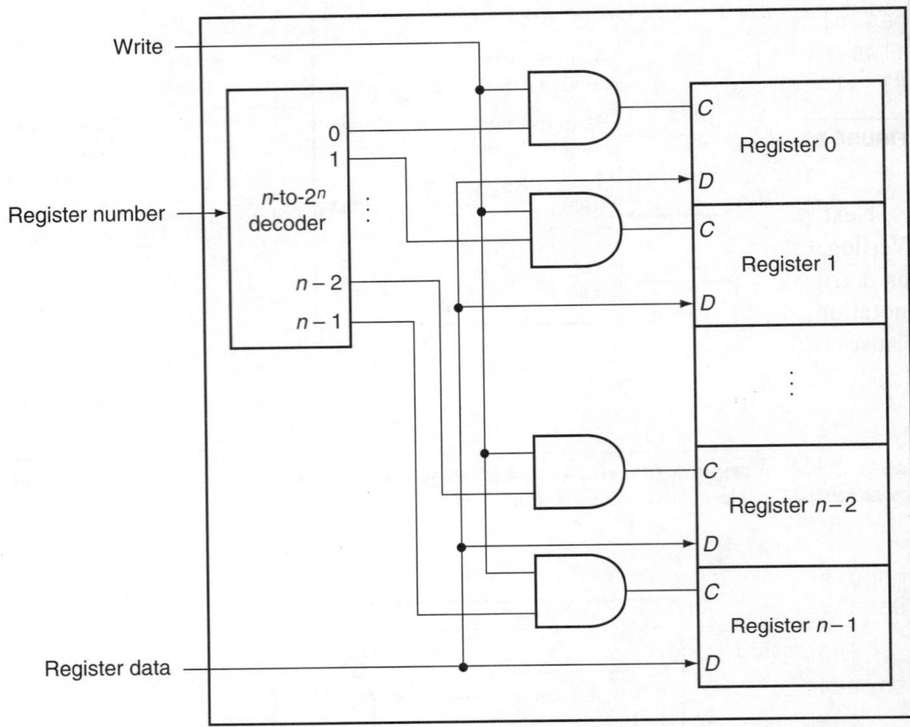

FIGURE B.8.9   The write port for a register file is implemented with a decoder that is used with the write signal to generate the C input to the registers. All three inputs (the register number, the data, and the write signal) will have setup and hold-time constraints that ensure that the correct data is written into the register file.

valid during the time it is read, as we saw earlier in Figure B.7.2. The value returned will be the value written in an earlier clock cycle. If we want a read to return the value currently being written, additional logic in the register file or outside of it is needed. Chapter 4 makes extensive use of such logic.

Specifying Sequential Logic in Verilog

To specify sequential logic in Verilog, we must understand how to generate a clock, how to describe when a value is written into a register, and how to specify sequential control. Let us start by specifying a clock. A clock is not a predefined object in Verilog; instead, we generate a clock by using the Verilog notation #n before a statement; this causes a delay of n simulation time steps before the execution of the statement. In most Verilog simulators, it is also possible to generate a clock as an external input, allowing the user to specify at simulation time the number of clock cycles during which to run a simulation.

The code in Figure B.8.10 implements a simple clock that is high or low for one simulation unit and then switches state. We use the delay capability and blocking assignment to implement the clock.

```
reg clock; // clock is a register
always
#1 clock = 1; #1 clock = 0;
```

FIGURE B.8.10   A specification of a clock.

Next, we must be able to specify the operation of an edge-triggered register. In Verilog, this is done by using the sensitivity list on an always block and specifying as a trigger either the positive or negative edge of a binary variable with the notation posedge or negedge, respectively. Hence, the following Verilog code causes register A to be written with the value b at the positive edge clock:

```
    reg [31:0] A;
    wire [31:0] b;

    always @(posedge clock) A <= b;
module registerfile (Read1,Read2,WriteReg,WriteData,RegWrite,
Data1,Data2,clock);
    input [5:0] Read1,Read2,WriteReg; // the register numbers
to read or write
    input [31:0] WriteData; // data to write
    input RegWrite, // the write control
      clock; // the clock to trigger write
    output [31:0] Data1, Data2; // the register values read
    reg [31:0] RF [31:0]; // 32 registers each 32 bits long

    assign Data1 = RF[Read1];
    assign Data2 = RF[Read2];

    always begin
      // write the register with new value if Regwrite is
high
      @(posedge clock) if (RegWrite) RF[WriteReg] <=
WriteData;
    end
endmodule
```

FIGURE B.8.11   A MIPS register file written in behavioral Verilog. This register file writes on the rising clock edge.

Throughout this chapter and the Verilog sections of Chapter 4, we will assume a positive edge-triggered design. Figure B.8.11 shows a Verilog specification of a MIPS register file that assumes two reads and one write, with only the write being clocked.

**Check
Yourself**
In the Verilog for the register file in Figure B.8.11, the output ports corresponding to the registers being read are assigned using a continuous assignment, but the register being written is assigned in an `always` block. Which of the following is the reason?

a.   There is no special reason. It was simply convenient.

b.   Because Data1 and Data2 are output ports and WriteData is an input port.

c.   Because reading is a combinational event, while writing is a sequential event.

B.9   Memory Elements: SRAMs and DRAMs

static random access memory (SRAM) A memory where data is stored statically (as in flip-flops) rather than dynamically (as in DRAM). SRAMs are faster than DRAMs, but less dense and more expensive per bit.

Registers and register files provide the basic building blocks for small memories, but larger amounts of memory are built using either **SRAMs (static random access memories)** or *DRAMs* (dynamic random access memories). We first discuss SRAMs, which are somewhat simpler, and then turn to DRAMs.

SRAMs

SRAMs are simply integrated circuits that are memory arrays with (usually) a single access port that can provide either a read or a write. SRAMs have a fixed access time to any datum, though the read and write access characteristics often differ. An SRAM chip has a specific configuration in terms of the number of addressable locations, as well as the width of each addressable location. For example, a 4M × 8 SRAM provides 4M entries, each of which is 8 bits wide. Thus it will have 22 address lines (since $4M = 2^{22}$), an 8-bit data output line, and an 8-bit single data input line. As with ROMs, the number of addressable locations is often called the *height*, with the number of bits per unit called the *width*. For a variety of technical reasons, the newest and fastest SRAMs are typically available in narrow configurations: × 1 and × 4. Figure B.9.1 shows the input and output signals for a 2M × 16 SRAM.

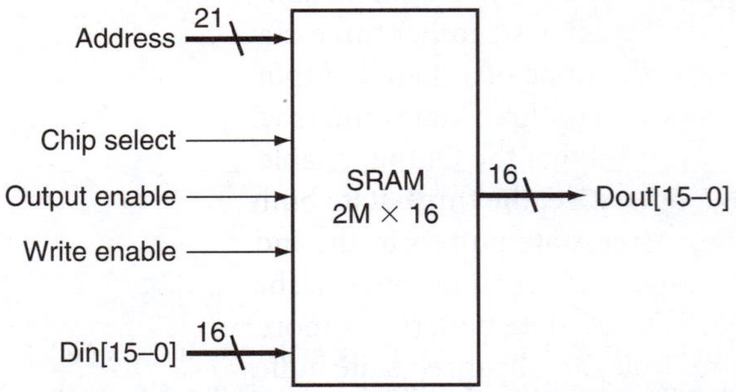

FIGURE B.9.1   A 32K × 8 SRAM showing the 21 address lines (32K = 2^{15}) and 16 data inputs, the 3 control lines, and the 16 data outputs.

To initiate a read or write access, the Chip select signal must be made active. For reads, we must also activate the Output enable signal that controls whether or not the datum selected by the address is actually driven on the pins. The Output enable is useful for connecting multiple memories to a single-output bus and using Output enable to determine which memory drives the bus. The SRAM read access time is usually specified as the delay from the time that Output enable is true and the address lines are valid until the time that the data is on the output lines. Typical read access times for SRAMs in 2004 varied from about 2–4 ns for the fastest CMOS parts, which tend to be somewhat smaller and narrower, to 8–20 ns for the typical largest parts, which in 2004 had more than 32 million bits of data. The demand for low-power SRAMs for consumer products and digital appliances has grown greatly in the past five years; these SRAMs have much lower stand-by and access power, but usually are 5–10 times slower. Most recently, synchronous SRAMs—similar to the synchronous DRAMs, which we discuss in the next section—have also been developed.

For writes, we must supply the data to be written and the address, as well as signals to cause the write to occur. When both the Write enable and Chip select are true, the data on the data input lines is written into the cell specified by the address. There are setup-time and hold-time requirements for the address and data lines, just as there were for D flip-flops and latches. In addition, the Write enable signal is not a clock edge but a pulse with a minimum width requirement. The time to complete a write is specified by the combination of the setup times, the hold times, and the Write enable pulse width.

Large SRAMs cannot be built in the same way we build a register file because, unlike a register file where a 32-to-1 multiplexor might be practical, the 64K-to-1 multiplexor that would be needed for a 64K × 1 SRAM is totally impractical. Rather than use a giant multiplexor, large memories are implemented with a shared output line, called a *bit line*, which multiple memory cells in the memory array can assert. To allow multiple sources to drive a single line, a *three-state buffer* (or *tristate buffer*) is used. A three-state buffer has two inputs—a data signal and an Output enable—and a single output, which is in one of three states: asserted, deasserted, or high impedance. The output of a tristate buffer is equal to the data input signal, either asserted or deasserted, if the Output enable is asserted, and is otherwise in a *high-impedance state* that allows another three-state buffer whose Output enable is asserted to determine the value of a shared output.

Figure B.9.2 shows a set of three-state buffers wired to form a multiplexor with a decoded input. It is critical that the Output enable of at most one of the three-state buffers be asserted; otherwise, the three-state buffers may try to set the output line differently. By using three-state buffers in the individual cells of the SRAM, each cell that corresponds to a particular output can share the same out put line. The use of a set of distributed three-state buffers is a more efficient implementation than a large centralized multiplexor. The three-state buffers are incorporated into the flip-flops that form the basic cells of the SRAM. Figure B.9.3 shows how a small 4 × 2 SRAM might be built, using D latches with an input called Enable that controls the three-state output.

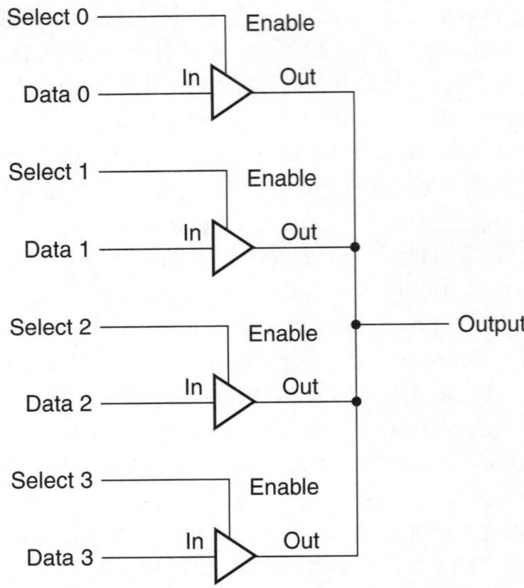

FIGURE B.9.2   Four three-state buffers are used to form a multiplexor. Only one of the four Select inputs can be asserted. A three-state buffer with a deasserted Output enable has a high-impedance output that allows a three-state buffer whose Output enable is asserted to drive the shared output line.

The design in Figure B.9.3 eliminates the need for an enormous multiplexor; however, it still requires a very large decoder and a correspondingly large number of word lines. For example, in a 4M × 8 SRAM, we would need a 22-to-4M decoder and 4M word lines (which are the lines used to enable the individual flip-flops)! To circumvent this problem, large memories are organized as rectangular arrays and use a two-step decoding process. Figure B.9.4 shows how a 4M × 8 SRAM might be organized internally using a two-step decode. As we will see, the two-level decoding process is quite important in understanding how DRAMs operate.

Recently we have seen the development of both synchronous SRAMs (SSRAMs) and synchronous DRAMs (SDRAMs). The key capability provided by synchronous RAMs is the ability to transfer a *burst* of data from a series of sequential addresses within an array or row. The burst is defined by a starting address, supplied in the usual fashion, and a burst length. The speed advantage of synchronous RAMs comes from the ability to transfer the bits in the burst without having to specify additional address bits. Instead, a clock is used to transfer the successive bits in the burst. The elimination of the need to specify the address for the transfers within the burst significantly improves the rate for transferring the block of data. Because of this capability, synchronous SRAMs and DRAMs are rapidly becoming the RAMs of choice for building memory systems in computers. We discuss the use of synchronous DRAMs in a memory system in more detail in the next section and in Chapter 5.

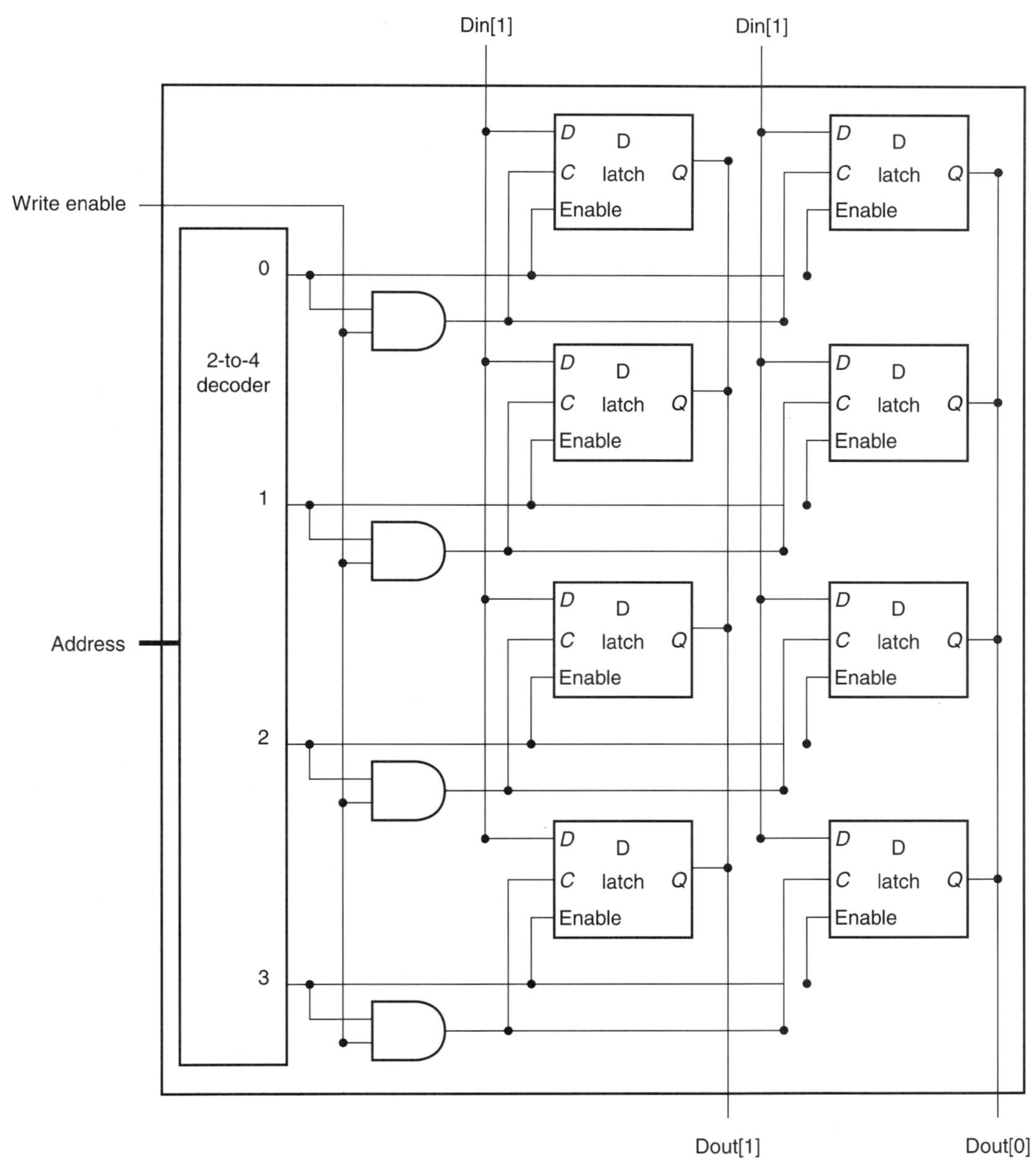

FIGURE B.9.3   The basic structure of a 4 × 2 SRAM consists of a decoder that selects which pair of cells to activate. The activated cells use a three-state output connected to the vertical bit lines that supply the requested data. The address that selects the cell is sent on one of a set of horizontal address lines, called word lines. For simplicity, the Output enable and Chip select signals have been omitted, but they could easily be added with a few AND gates.

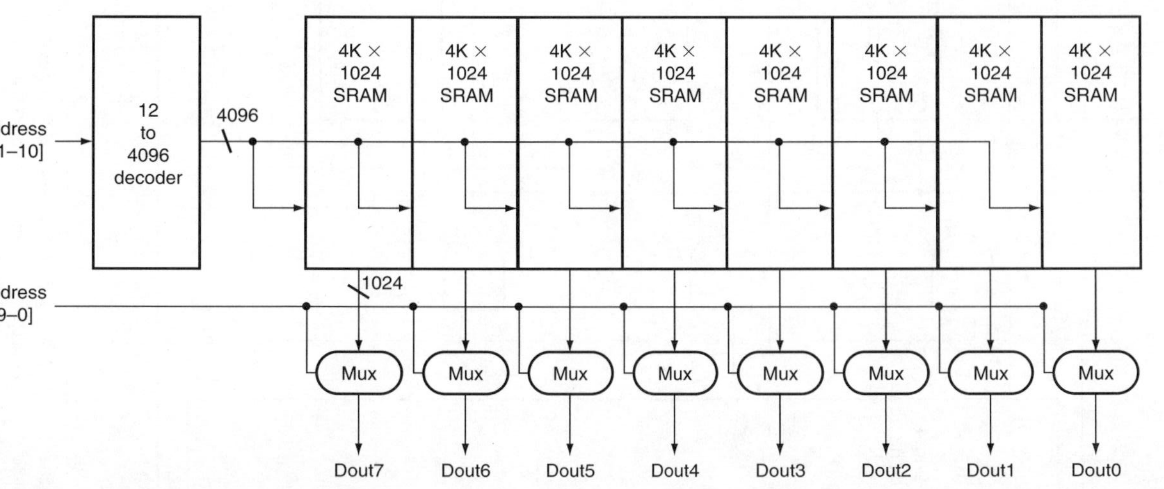

FIGURE B.9.4 Typical organization of a 4M × 8 SRAM as an array of 4K × 1024 arrays. The first decoder generates the addresses for eight 4K × 1024 arrays; then a set of multiplexors is used to select 1 bit from each 1024-bit-wide array. This is a much easier design than a single-level decode that would need either an enormous decoder or a gigantic multiplexor. In practice, a modern SRAM of this size would probably use an even larger number of blocks, each somewhat smaller.

DRAMs

In a static RAM (SRAM), the value stored in a cell is kept on a pair of inverting gates, and as long as power is applied, the value can be kept indefinitely. In a dynamic RAM (DRAM), the value kept in a cell is stored as a charge in a capacitor. A single transistor is then used to access this stored charge, either to read the value or to overwrite the charge stored there. Because DRAMs use only a single transistor per bit of storage, they are much denser and cheaper per bit. By comparison, SRAMs require four to six transistors per bit. Because DRAMs store the charge on a capacitor, it cannot be kept indefinitely and must periodically be *refreshed*. That is why this memory structure is called *dynamic*, as opposed to the static storage in a SRAM cell.

To refresh the cell, we merely read its contents and write it back. The charge can be kept for several milliseconds, which might correspond to close to a million clock cycles. Today, single-chip memory controllers often handle the refresh function independently of the processor. If every bit had to be read out of the DRAM and then written back individually, with large DRAMs containing multiple megabytes, we would constantly be refreshing the DRAM, leaving no time for accessing it. Fortunately, DRAMs also use a two-level decoding structure, and this allows us to refresh an entire row (which shares a word line) with a read cycle followed immediately by a write cycle. Typically, refresh operations consume 1% to 2% of the active cycles of the DRAM, leaving the remaining 98% to 99% of the cycles available for reading and writing data.

Elaboration: How does a DRAM read and write the signal stored in a cell? The transistor inside the cell is a switch, called a *pass transistor*, that allows the value stored on the capacitor to be accessed for either reading or writing. Figure B.9.5 shows how the single-transistor cell looks. The pass transistor acts like a switch: when the signal on the word line is asserted, the switch is closed, connecting the capacitor to the bit line. If the operation is a write, then the value to be written is placed on the bit line. If the value is a 1, the capacitor will be charged. If the value is a 0, then the capacitor will be discharged. Reading is slightly more complex, since the DRAM must detect a very small charge stored in the capacitor. Before activating the word line for a read, the bit line is charged to the voltage that is halfway between the low and high voltage. Then, by activating the word line, the charge on the capacitor is read out onto the bit line. This causes the bit line to move slightly toward the high or low direction, and this change is detected with a sense amplifier, which can detect small changes in voltage.

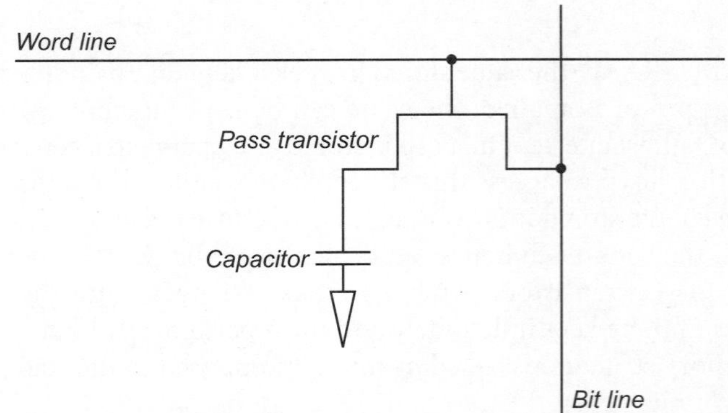

FIGURE B.9.5   A single-transistor DRAM cell contains a capacitor that stores the cell contents and a transistor used to access the cell.

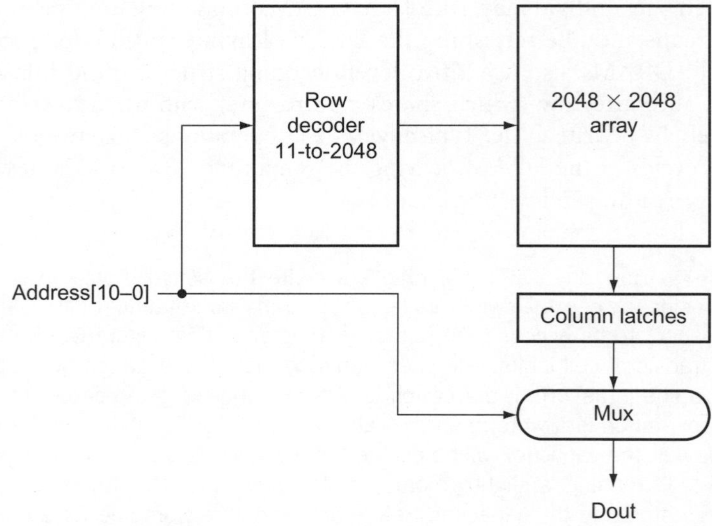

FIGURE B.9.6   A 4M × 1 DRAM is built with a 2048 × 2048 array. The row access uses 11 bits to select a row, which is then latched in 2048 1-bit latches. A multiplexor chooses the output bit from these 2048 latches. The RAS and CAS signals control whether the address lines are sent to the row decoder or column multiplexor.

DRAMs use a two-level decoder consisting of a *row access* followed by a *column access*, as shown in Figure B.9.6. The row access chooses one of a number of rows and activates the corresponding word line. The contents of all the columns in the active row are then stored in a set of latches. The column access then selects the data from the column latches. To save pins and reduce the package cost, the same address lines are used for both the row and column address; a pair of signals called RAS (Row Access Strobe) and CAS (Column Access Strobe) are used to signal the DRAM that either a row or column address is being supplied. Refresh is performed by simply reading the columns into the column latches and then writing the same values back. Thus, an entire row is refreshed in one cycle. The two-level addressing scheme, combined with the internal circuitry, make DRAM access times much longer (by a factor of 5–10) than SRAM access times. In 2004, typical DRAM access times ranged from 45 to 65 ns; 256 Mbit DRAMs are in full production, and the first customer samples of 1 GB DRAMs became available in the first quarter of 2004. The much lower cost per bit makes DRAM the choice for main memory, while the faster access time makes SRAM the choice for caches.

You might observe that a 64M × 4 DRAM actually accesses 8K bits on every row access and then throws away all but 4 of those during a column access. DRAM designers have used the internal structure of the DRAM as a way to provide higher bandwidth out of a DRAM. This is done by allowing the column address to change without changing the row address, resulting in an access to other bits in the column latches. To make this process faster and more precise, the address inputs were clocked, leading to the dominant form of DRAM in use today: synchronous DRAM or SDRAM.

Since about 1999, SDRAMs have been the memory chip of choice for most cache-based main memory systems. SDRAMs provide fast access to a series of bits within a row by sequentially transferring all the bits in a burst under the control of a clock signal. In 2004, DDRRAMs (Double Data Rate RAMs), which are called double data rate because they transfer data on both the rising and falling edge of an externally supplied clock, were the most heavily used form of SDRAMs. As we discuss in Chapter 5, these high-speed transfers can be used to boost the bandwidth available out of main memory to match the needs of the processor and caches.

Error Correction

Because of the potential for data corruption in large memories, most computer systems use some sort of error-checking code to detect possible corruption of data. One simple code that is heavily used is a *parity code*. In a parity code the number of 1s in a word is counted; the word has odd parity if the number of 1s is odd and even otherwise. When a word is written into memory, the parity bit is also written (1 for odd, 0 for even). Then, when the word is read out, the parity bit is read and checked. If the parity of the memory word and the stored parity bit do not match, an error has occurred.

A 1-bit parity scheme can detect at most 1 bit of error in a data item; if there are 2 bits of error, then a 1-bit parity scheme will not detect any errors, since the parity will match the data with two errors. (Actually, a 1-bit parity scheme can detect any odd number of errors; however, the probability of having three errors is much lower than the probability of having two, so, in practice, a 1-bit parity code is limited to detecting a single bit of error.) Of course, a parity code cannot tell which bit in a data item is in error.

error detection code
A code that enables the detection of an error in data, but not the precise location and, hence, correction of the error.

A 1-bit parity scheme is an **error detection code**; there are also *error correction codes* (ECC) that will detect and allow correction of an error. For large main memories, many systems use a code that allows the detection of up to 2 bits of error and the correction of a single bit of error. These codes work by using more bits to encode the data; for example, the typical codes used for main memories require 7 or 8 bits for every 128 bits of data.

Elaboration: A 1-bit parity code is a *distance-2 code*, which means that if we look at the data plus the parity bit, no 1-bit change is sufficient to generate another legal combination of the data plus parity. For example, if we change a bit in the data, the parity will be wrong, and vice versa. Of course, if we change 2 bits (any 2 data bits or 1 data bit and the parity bit), the parity will match the data and the error cannot be detected. Hence, there is a distance of two between legal combinations of parity and data.

To detect more than one error or correct an error, we need a *distance-3 code*, which has the property that any legal combination of the bits in the error correction code and the data has at least 3 bits differing from any other combination. Suppose we have such a code and we have one error in the data. In that case, the code plus data will be one bit away from a legal combination, and we can correct the data to that legal combination. If we have two errors, we can recognize that there is an error, but we cannot correct the errors. Let's look at an example. Here are the data words and a distance-3 error correction code for a 4-bit data item.

Data Word	Code bits	Data	Code bits
0000	000	1000	111
0001	011	1001	100
0010	101	1010	010
0011	110	1011	001
0100	110	1100	001
0101	101	1101	010
0110	011	1110	100
0111	000	1111	111

To see how this works, let's choose a data word, say, 0110, whose error correction code is 011. Here are the four 1-bit error possibilities for this data: 1110, 0010, 0100, and 0111. Now look at the data item with the same code (011), which is the entry with the value 0001. If the error correction decoder received one of the four pos sible data words with an error, it would have to choose between correcting to 0110 or 0001. While these four words with error have only one bit changed from the correct pat tern of 0110, they each have two bits that are different from the alternate correction of 0001. Hence, the error correction mechanism can easily choose to correct to 0110, since a single error is a much higher probability. To see that two errors can be detected, simply notice that all the combinations with two bits changed have a different code. The one reuse of the same code is with three bits different, but if we correct a 2-bit error, we will correct to the wrong value, since the decoder will assume that only a single error has occurred. If we want to correct 1-bit errors and detect, but not erroneously correct, 2-bit errors, we need a distance-4 code.

Although we distinguished between the code and data in our explanation, in truth, an error correction code treats the combination of code and data as a single word in a larger code (7 bits in this example). Thus, it deals with errors in the code bits in the same fashion as errors in the data bits.

While the above example requires $n - 1$ bits for n bits of data, the number of bits required grows slowly, so that for a distance-3 code, a 64-bit word needs 7 bits and a 128-bit word needs 8. This type of code is called a *Hamming code*, after R. Hamming, who described a method for creating such codes.

B.10 Finite-State Machines

As we saw earlier, digital logic systems can be classified as combinational or sequential. Sequential systems contain state stored in memory elements internal to the system. Their behavior depends both on the set of inputs supplied and on the contents of the internal memory, or state of the system. Thus, a sequential sys tem cannot be described with a truth table. Instead, a sequential system is described as a **finite-state machine** (or often just *state machine*). A finite-state machine has a set of states and two functions, called the **next-state function** and the *output function*. The set of states corresponds to all the possible values of the internal storage. Thus, if there are n bits of storage, there are $2n$ states. The next-state function is a combinational function that, given the inputs and the current state, determines the next state of the system. The output function produces a set of outputs from the current state and the inputs. Figure B.10.1 shows this dia grammatically.

The state machines we discuss here and in Chapter 4 are *synchronous*. This means that the state changes together with the clock cycle, and a new state is computed once every clock. Thus, the state elements are updated only on the clock edge. We use this methodology in this section and throughout Chapter 4, and we do not

finite-state machine A sequential logic function consisting of a set of inputs and out puts, a next-state function that maps the current state and the inputs to a new state, and an output function that maps the current state and possibly the inputs to a set of asserted outputs.

next-state function A combinational function that, given the inputs and the current state, determines the next state of a finite-state machine.

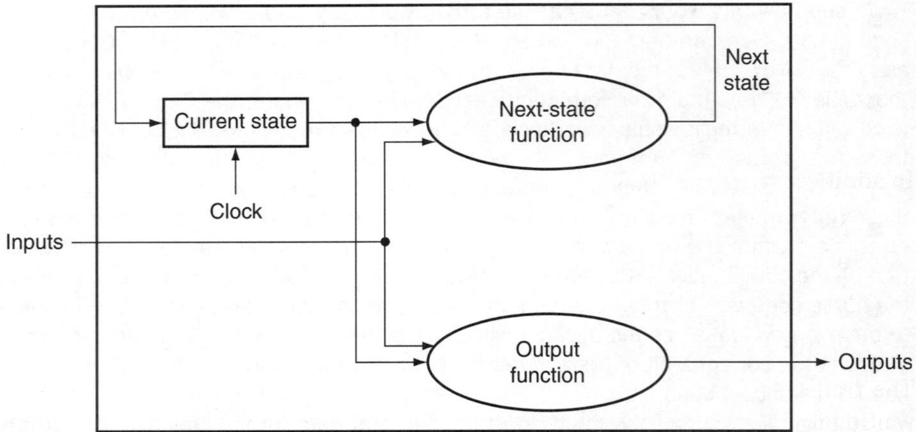

FIGURE B.10.1   A state machine consists of internal storage that contains the state and two combinational functions: the next-state function and the output function. Often, the output function is restricted to take only the current state as its input; this does not change the capability of a sequential machine, but does affect its internals.

usually show the clock explicitly. We use state machines throughout Chapter 4 to control the execution of the processor and the actions of the datapath.

To illustrate how a finite-state machine operates and is designed, let's look at a simple and classic example: controlling a traffic light. (Chapters 4 and 5 contain more detailed examples of using finite-state machines to control processor execution.) When a finite-state machine is used as a controller, the output function is often restricted to depend on just the current state. Such a finite-state machine is called a *Moore machine*. This is the type of finite-state machine we use throughout this book. If the output function can depend on both the current state and the current input, the machine is called a *Mealy machine*. These two machines are equivalent in their capabilities, and one can be turned into the other mechanically. The basic advantage of a Moore machine is that it can be faster, while a Mealy machine may be smaller, since it may need fewer states than a Moore machine. In Chapter 5, we discuss the differences in more detail and show a Verilog version of finite-state control using a Mealy machine.

Our example concerns the control of a traffic light at an intersection of a north-south route and an east-west route. For simplicity, we will consider only the green and red lights; adding the yellow light is left for an exercise. We want the lights to cycle no faster than 30 seconds in each direction, so we will use a 0.033 Hz clock so that the machine cycles between states at no faster than once every 30 seconds. There are two output signals:

- *NSlite:* When this signal is asserted, the light on the north-south road is green; when this signal is deasserted, the light on the north-south road is red.

- *EWlite:* When this signal is asserted, the light on the east-west road is green; when this signal is deasserted, the light on the east-west road is red.

In addition, there are two inputs:

- *NScar:* Indicates that a car is over the detector placed in the roadbed in front of the light on the north-south road (going north or south).

- *EWcar:* Indicates that a car is over the detector placed in the roadbed in front of the light on the east-west road (going east or west).

The traffic light should change from one direction to the other only if a car is waiting to go in the other direction; otherwise, the light should continue to show green in the same direction as the last car that crossed the intersection.

To implement this simple traffic light we need two states:

- *NSgreen:* The traffic light is green in the north-south direction.

- *EWgreen:* The traffic light is green in the east-west direction.

We also need to create the next-state function, which can be specified with a table:

	Inputs		
	NScar	EWcar	Next state
NSgreen	0	0	NSgreen
NSgreen	0	1	EWgreen
NSgreen	1	0	NSgreen
NSgreen	1	1	EWgreen
EWgreen	0	0	EWgreen
EWgreen	0	1	EWgreen
EWgreen	1	0	NSgreen
EWgreen	1	1	NSgreen

Notice that we didn't specify in the algorithm what happens when a car approaches from both directions. In this case, the next-state function given above changes the state to ensure that a steady stream of cars from one direction cannot lock out a car in the other direction.

The finite-state machine is completed by specifying the output function.

Before we examine how to implement this finite-state machine, let's look at a graphical representation, which is often used for finite-state machines. In this representation, nodes are used to indicate states. Inside the node we place a list of the outputs that are active for that state. Directed arcs are used to show the next-state

	Outputs	
	NSlite	**EWlite**
NSgreen	1	0
EWgreen	0	1

function, with labels on the arcs specifying the input condition as logic functions. Figure B.10.2 shows the graphical representation for this finite-state machine.

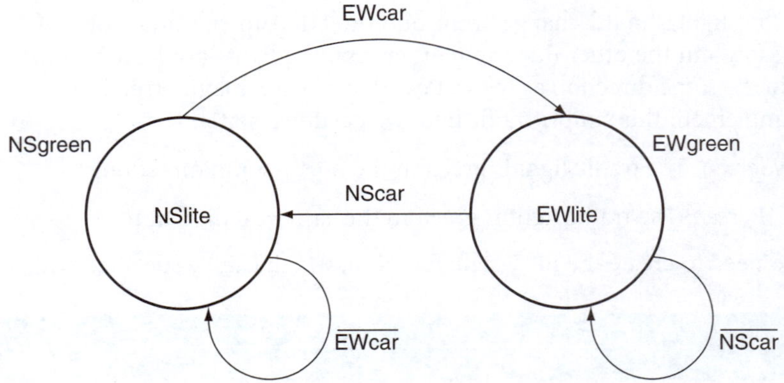

FIGURE B.10.2   The graphical representation of the two-state traffic light controller. We simplified the logic functions on the state transitions. For example, the transition from NSgreen to EWgreen in the next-state table is $(\overline{\text{NScar}} \cdot \text{EWcar}) + (\text{NScar} \cdot \text{EWcar})$, which is equivalent to EWcar.

A finite-state machine can be implemented with a register to hold the current state and a block of combinational logic that computes the next-state function and the output function. Figure B.10.3 shows how a finite-state machine with 4 bits of state, and thus up to 16 states, might look. To implement the finite-state machine in this way, we must first assign state numbers to the states. This process is called *state assignment*. For example, we could assign NSgreen to state 0 and EWgreen to state 1. The state register would contain a single bit. The next-state function would be given as

$$\text{NextState} = (\overline{\text{CurrentState} \cdot \text{EWcar}}) + (\text{CurrentState} \cdot \overline{\text{NScar}})$$

where Current State is the contents of the state register (0 or 1) and NextState is the output of the next-state function that will be written into the state register at the end of the clock cycle. The output function is also simple:

$$\text{NSlite} = \overline{\text{CurrentState}}$$
$$\text{EWlite} = \text{CurrentState}$$

The combinational logic block is often implemented using structured logic, such as a PLA. A PLA can be constructed automatically from the next-state and output function tables. In fact, there are computer-aided design (CAD) programs

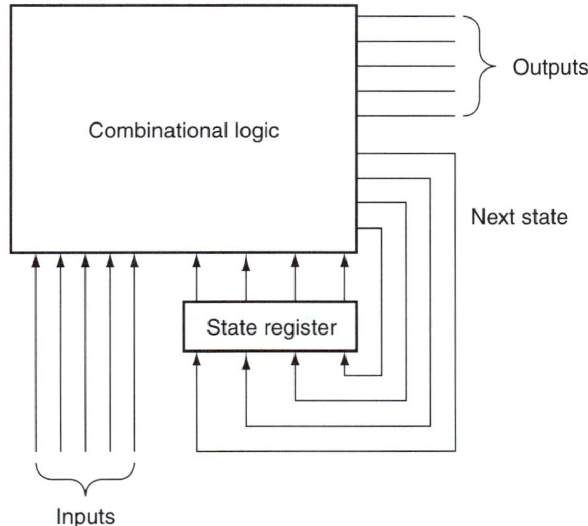

FIGURE B.10.3 A finite-state machine is implemented with a state register that holds the current state and a combinational logic block to compute the next state and output functions. The latter two functions are often split apart and implemented with two separate blocks of logic, which may require fewer gates.

that take either a graphical or textual representation of a finite-state machine and produce an optimized implementation automatically. In Chapters 4 and 5, finite-state machines were used to control processor execution. ⊕ **Appendix D** discusses the detailed implementation of these controllers with both PLAs and ROMs.

To show how we might write the control in Verilog, Figure B.10.4 shows a Verilog version designed for synthesis. Note that for this simple control function, a Mealy machine is not useful, but this style of specification is used in Chapter 5 to implement a control function that is a Mealy machine and has fewer states than the Moore machine controller.

```verilog
module TrafficLite (EWCar,NSCar,EWLite,NSLite,clock);

   input EWCar, NSCar,clock;
output EWLite,NSLite;

reg state;

initial state=0;  //set initial state

//following two assignments set the output, which is based
only on the state variable
assign NSLite = ~ state; //NSLite on if state = 0;
assign EWLite = state; //EWLite on if state = 1

always @(posedge clock) // all state updates on a positive
clock edge
   case (state)
      0: state = EWCar; //change state only if EWCar

      1: state = NSCar; //change state only if NSCar

   endcase
endmodule
```

FIGURE B.10.4   A Verilog version of the traffic light controller.

Check
Yourself

What is the smallest number of states in a Moore machine for which a Mealy machine could have fewer states?

   a. Two, since there could be a one-state Mealy machine that might do the same thing.

   b. Three, since there could be a simple Moore machine that went to one of two different states and always returned to the original state after that. For such a simple machine, a two-state Mealy machine is possible.

   c. You need at least four states to exploit the advantages of a Mealy machine over a Moore machine.

B.11   Timing Methodologies

Throughout this appendix and in the rest of the text, we use an edge-triggered timing methodology. This timing methodology has an advantage in that it is simpler to explain and understand than a level-triggered methodology. In this section, we explain this timing methodology in a little more detail and also introduce level-sensitive clocking. We conclude this section by briefly discussing the issue of asynchronous signals and synchronizers, an important problem for digital designers.

The purpose of this section is to introduce the major concepts in clocking methodology. The section makes some important simplifying assumptions; if you are interested in understanding timing methodology in more detail, consult one of the references listed at the end of this appendix.

We use an edge-triggered timing methodology because it is simpler to explain and has fewer rules required for correctness. In particular, if we assume that all clocks arrive at the same time, we are guaranteed that a system with edge- triggered registers between blocks of combinational logic can operate correctly without races if we simply make the clock long enough. A *race* occurs when the contents of a state element depend on the relative speed of different logic elements. In an edge-triggered design, the clock cycle must be long enough to accommodate the path from one flip-flop through the combinational logic to another flip-flop where it must satisfy the setup-time requirement. Figure B.11.1 shows this requirement for a system using rising edge-triggered flip-flops. In such a system the clock period (or cycle time) must be at least as large as

$$t_{\text{prop}} + t_{\text{combinational}} + t_{\text{setup}}$$

for the worst-case values of these three delays, which are defined as follows:

- t_{prop} is the time for a signal to propagate through a flip-flop; it is also sometimes called clock-to-Q.

- $t_{\text{combinational}}$ is the longest delay for any combinational logic (which by definition is surrounded by two flip-flops).

- t_{setup} is the time before the rising clock edge that the input to a flip-flop must be valid.

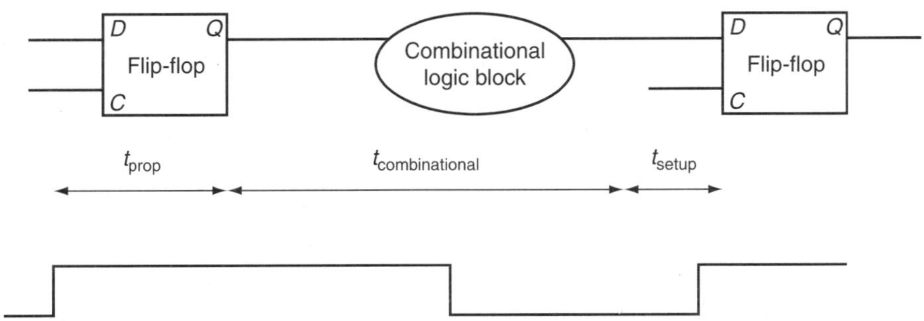

FIGURE B.11.1 In an edge-triggered design, the clock must be long enough to allow signals to be valid for the required setup time before the next clock edge. The time for a flip-flop input to propagate to the flip-flip outputs is t_{prop}; the signal then takes $t_{\text{combinational}}$ to travel through the combinational logic and must be valid t_{setup} before the next clock edge.

clock skew The difference in absolute time between the times when two state elements see a clock edge.

We make one simplifying assumption: the hold-time requirements are satisfied, which is almost never an issue with modern logic.

One additional complication that must be considered in edge-triggered designs is **clock skew**. Clock skew is the difference in absolute time between when two state elements see a clock edge. Clock skew arises because the clock signal will often use two different paths, with slightly different delays, to reach two different state elements. If the clock skew is large enough, it may be possible for a state element to change and cause the input to another flip-flop to change before the clock edge is seen by the second flip-flop.

Figure B.11.2 illustrates this problem, ignoring setup time and flip-flop propagation delay. To avoid incorrect operation, the clock period is increased to allow for the maximum clock skew. Thus, the clock period must be longer than

$$t_{prop} + t_{combinational} + t_{setup} + t_{skew}$$

With this constraint on the clock period, the two clocks can also arrive in the opposite order, with the second clock arriving t_{skew} earlier, and the circuit will work

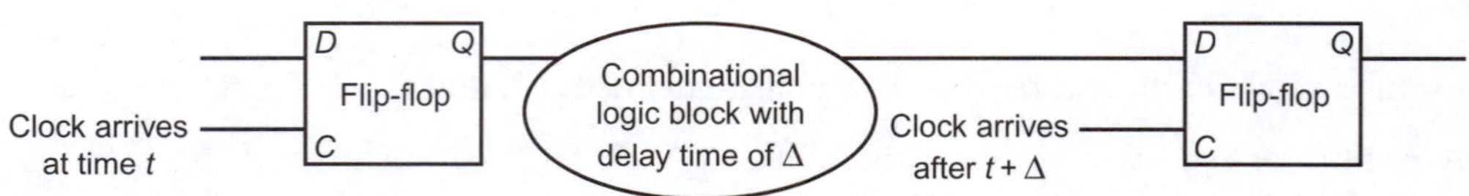

FIGURE B.11.2   Illustration of how clock skew can cause a race, leading to incorrect operation. Because of the difference in when the two flip-flops see the clock, the signal that is stored into the first flip-flop can race forward and change the input to the second flip-flop before the clock arrives at the second flip-flop.

level-sensitive clocking A timing methodology in which state changes occur at either high or low clock levels but are not instantaneous, as such changes are in edge-triggered designs.

correctly. Designers reduce clock-skew problems by carefully routing the clock signal to minimize the difference in arrival times. In addition, smart designers also provide some margin by making the clock a little longer than the minimum; this allows for variation in components as well as in the power supply. Since clock skew can also affect the hold-time requirements, minimizing the size of the clock skew is important.

Edge-triggered designs have two drawbacks: they require extra logic and they may sometimes be slower. Just looking at the D flip-flop versus the level-sensitive latch that we used to construct the flip-flop shows that edge- triggered design requires more logic. An alternative is to use **level-sensitive clocking**. Because state changes in a level-sensitive methodology are not instantaneous, a level-sensitive scheme is slightly more complex and requires additional care to make it operate correctly.

Level-Sensitive Timing

In level-sensitive timing, the state changes occur at either high or low levels, but they are not instantaneous as they are in an edge-triggered methodology. Because of the noninstantaneous change in state, races can easily occur. To ensure that a level-sensitive design will also work correctly if the clock is slow enough, designers use *two-phase clocking*. Two-phase clocking is a scheme that makes use of two nonoverlapping clock signals. Since the two clocks, typically called Φ_1 and Φ_2, are nonoverlapping, at most one of the clock signals is high at any given time, as Figure B.11.3 shows. We can use these two clocks to build a system that contains level-sensitive latches but is free from any race conditions, just as the edge-triggered designs were.

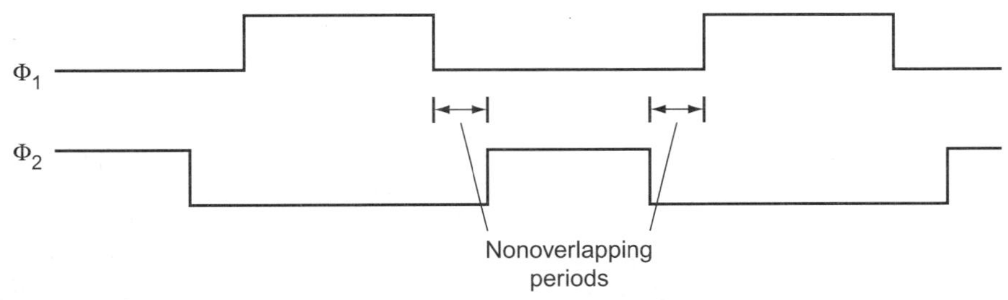

FIGURE B.11.3   A two-phase clocking scheme showing the cycle of each clock and the nonoverlapping periods.

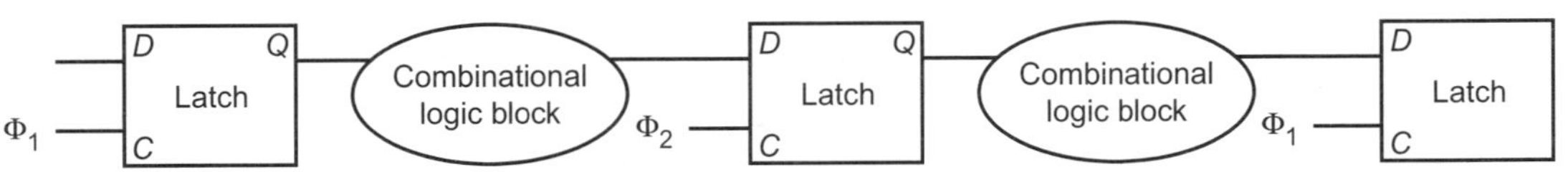

FIGURE B.11.4   A two-phase timing scheme with alternating latches showing how the system operates on both clock phases. The output of a latch is stable on the opposite phase from its C input. Thus, the first block of combinational inputs has a stable input during ϕ_2, and its output is latched by ϕ_2. The second (rightmost) combinational block operates in just the opposite fashion, with stable inputs during ϕ_1. Thus, the delays through the combinational blocks determine the minimum time that the respective clocks must be asserted. The size of the nonoverlapping period is determined by the maximum clock skew and the minimum delay of any logic block.

One simple way to design such a system is to alternate the use of latches that are open on Φ_1 with latches that are open on Φ_2. Because both clocks are not asserted at the same time, a race cannot occur. If the input to a combinational block is a Φ_1 clock, then its output is latched by a Φ_2 clock, which is open only during Φ_2 when the input latch is closed and hence has a valid output. Figure B.11.4 shows how a system with two-phase timing and alternating latches operates. As in an edge-triggered design, we must pay attention to clock skew, particularly between the two clock phases. By increasing the amount of nonoverlap between the two phases, we can reduce the potential margin of error. Thus, the system is guaranteed to operate correctly if each phase is long enough and if there is large enough nonoverlap between the phases.

Asynchronous Inputs and Synchronizers

By using a single clock or a two-phase clock, we can eliminate race conditions if clock-skew problems are avoided. Unfortunately, it is impractical to make an entire system function with a single clock and still keep the clock skew small. While the CPU may use a single clock, I/O devices will probably have their own clock. An asynchronous device may communicate with the CPU through a series of handshaking steps. To translate the asynchronous input to a synchronous signal that can be used to change the state of a system, we need to use a *synchronizer*, whose inputs are the asynchronous signal and a clock and whose output is a signal synchronous with the input clock.

Our first attempt to build a synchronizer uses an edge-triggered D flip-flop, whose *D* input is the asynchronous signal, as Figure B.11.5 shows. Because we communicate with a handshaking protocol, it does not matter whether we detect the asserted state of the asynchronous signal on one clock or the next, since the signal will be held asserted until it is acknowledged. Thus, you might think that this simple structure is enough to sample the signal accurately, which would be the case except for one small problem.

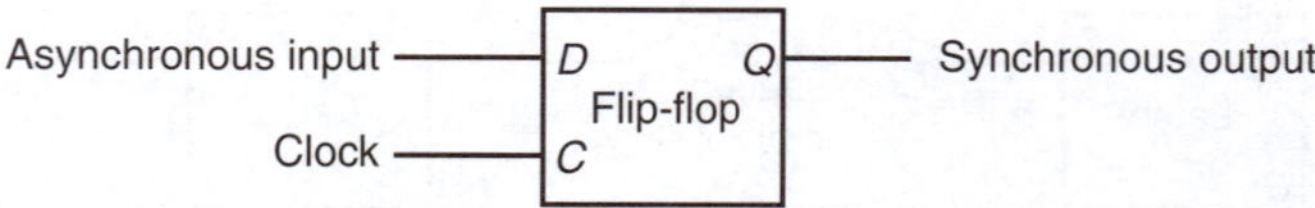

FIGURE B.11.5   A synchronizer built from a D flip-flop is used to sample an asynchronous signal to produce an output that is synchronous with the clock. This "synchronizer" will *not* work properly!

metastability

A situation that occurs if a signal is sampled when it is not stable for the required setup and hold times, possibly causing the sampled value to fall in the indeterminate region between a high and low value

The problem is a situation called **metastability**. Suppose the asynchronous signal is transitioning between high and low when the clock edge arrives. Clearly, it is not possible to know whether the signal will be latched as high or low. That problem we could live with. Unfortunately, the situation is worse: when the signal that is sampled is not stable for the required setup and hold times, the flip-flop may go into a *metastable* state. In such a state, the output will not have a legitimate high or low value, but will be in the indeterminate region between them. Furthermore, the flip-flop is not guaranteed to exit this state in any bounded amount of time. Some logic blocks that look at the output of the flip-flop may see its output as 0, while others may see it as 1. This situation is called a **synchronizer failure**.

In a purely synchronous system, synchronizer failure can be avoided by ensuring that the setup and hold times for a flip-flop or latch are always met, but this is impossible when the input is asynchronous. Instead, the only solution possible is to wait long enough before looking at the output of the flip-flop to ensure that its output is stable, and that it has exited the metastable state, if it ever entered it. How long is long enough? Well, the probability that the flip-flop will stay in the metastable state decreases exponentially, so after a very short time the probability that the flip-flop is in the metastable state is very low; however, the probability never reaches 0! So designers wait long enough that the probability of a synchronizer failure is very low, and the time between such failures will be years or even thousands of years.

For most flip-flop designs, waiting for a period that is several times longer than the setup time makes the probability of synchronization failure very low. If the clock rate is longer than the potential metastability period (which is likely), then a safe synchronizer can be built with two D flip-flops, as Figure B.11.6 shows. If you are interested in reading more about these problems, look into the references.

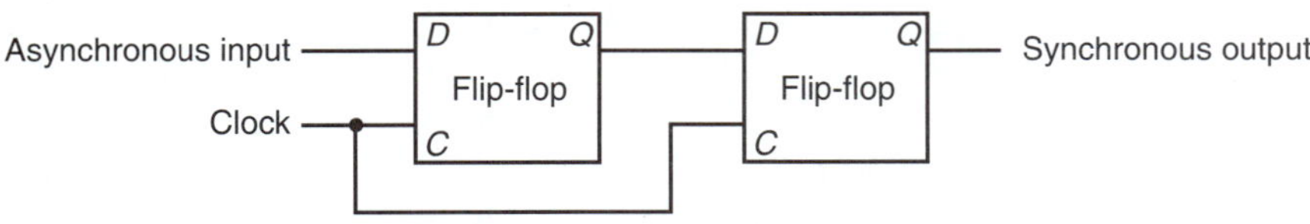

FIGURE B.11.6 This synchronizer will work correctly if the period of metastability that we wish to guard against is less than the clock period. Although the output of the first flip-flop may be metastable, it will not be seen by any other logic element until the second clock, when the second D flip-flop samples the signal, which by that time should no longer be in a metastable state.

Check Yourself

Suppose we have a design with very large clock skew—longer than the register **propagation time**. Is it always possible for such a design to slow the clock down enough to guarantee that the logic operates properly?

a. Yes, if the clock is slow enough the signals can always propagate and the design will work, even if the skew is very large.

b. No, since it is possible that two registers see the same clock edge far enough apart that a register is triggered, and its outputs propagated and seen by a second register with the same clock edge.

synchronizer failure A situation in which a flip-flop enters a metastable state and where some logic blocks reading the output of the flip-flop see a 0 while others see a 1.

propagation time The time required for an input to a flip-flop to propagate to the outputs of the flip-flop.

B.12   Field Programmable Devices

Within a custom or semicustom chip, designers can make use of the flexibility of the underlying structure to easily implement combinational or sequential logic. How can a designer who does not want to use a custom or semicustom IC implement a complex piece of logic taking advantage of the very high levels of integration available? The most popular component used for sequential and combinational logic design outside of a custom or semicustom IC is a **field programmable device (FPD)**. An FPD is an integrated circuit containing combinational logic, and possibly memory devices, that are configurable by the end user.

FPDs generally fall into two camps: **programmable logic devices (PLDs)**, which are purely combinational, and **field programmable gate arrays (FPGAs)**, which provide both combinational logic and flip-flops. PLDs consist of two forms: **simple PLDs (SPLDs)**, which are usually either a PLA or a **programmable array logic (PAL)**, and complex PLDs, which allow more than one logic block as well as configurable interconnections among blocks. When we speak of a PLA in a PLD, we mean a PLA with user programmable and-plane and or-plane. A PAL is like a PLA, except that the or-plane is fixed.

Before we discuss FPGAs, it is useful to talk about how FPDs are configured. Configuration is essentially a question of where to make or break connections. Gate and register structures are static, but the connections can be configured. Notice that by configuring the connections, a user determines what logic functions are implemented. Consider a configurable PLA: by determining where the connections are in the and-plane and the or-plane, the user dictates what logical functions are computed in the PLA. Connections in FPDs are either permanent or reconfigurable. Permanent connections involve the creation or destruction of a connection between two wires. Current FPLDs all use an **antifuse** technology, which allows a connection to be built at programming time that is then permanent. The other way to configure CMOS FPLDs is through an SRAM. The SRAM is downloaded at power-on, and the contents control the setting of switches, which in turn determines which metal lines are connected. The use of SRAM control has the advantage in that the FPD can be reconfigured by changing the contents of the SRAM. The disadvantages of the SRAM-based control are two fold: the configuration is volatile and must be reloaded on power-on, and the use of active transistors for switches slightly increases the resistance of such connections.

FPGAs include both logic and memory devices, usually structured in a two-dimensional array with the corridors dividing the rows and columns used for global interconnect between the cells of the array. Each cell is a combination of gates and flip-flops that can be programmed to perform some specific function. Because they are basically small, programmable RAMs, they are also called **lookup tables (LUTs)**. Newer FPGAs contain more sophisticated building blocks such as pieces of adders and RAM blocks that can be used to build register files. A few large FPGAs even contain 32-bit RISC cores!

In addition to programming each cell to perform a specific function, the interconnections between cells are also programmable, allowing modern FPGAs with hundreds of blocks and hundreds of thousands of gates to be used for complex logic functions. Interconnect is a major challenge in custom chips, and this is even more true for FPGAs, because cells do not represent natural units of decomposition for structured design. In many FPGAs, 90% of the area is reserved for interconnect and only 10% is for logic and memory blocks.

Just as you cannot design a custom or semicustom chip without CAD tools, you also need them for FPDs. Logic synthesis tools have been developed that target FPGAs, allowing the generation of a system using FPGAs from structural and behavioral Verilog.

> **lookup tables (LUTs)**
> In a field programmable device, the name given to the cells because they consist of a small amount of logic and RAM.

B.13 Concluding Remarks

This appendix introduces the basics of logic design. If you have digested the material in this appendix, you are ready to tackle the material in Chapters 4 and 5, both of which use the concepts discussed in this appendix extensively.

Further Reading

There are a number of good texts on logic design. Here are some you might like to look into.

Ciletti, M. D. (2002). *Advanced Digital Design with the Verilog HDL*. Englewood Cliffs, NJ: Prentice Hall. *A thorough book on logic design using Verilog.*

Katz, R. H. (2004). *Modern Logic Design* (2nd ed.). Reading, MA: Addison-Wesley. *A general text on logic design.*

Wakerly, J. F. (2000). *Digital Design: Principles and Practices* (3rd ed.). Englewood Cliffs, NJ: Prentice Hall. *A general text on logic design.*

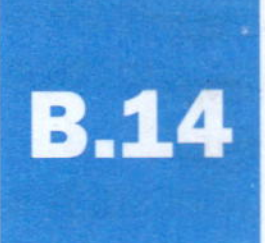

B.14   Exercises

B.1 [10] <§B.2> In addition to the basic laws we discussed in this section, there are two important theorems, called DeMorgan's theorems:

$$\overline{A + B} = \overline{A} \cdot \overline{B} \text{ and } \overline{A \cdot B} = \overline{A} + \overline{B}$$

Prove DeMorgan's theorems with a truth table of the form

A	B	$\overline{A}$	$\overline{B}$	$\overline{A + B}$	$\overline{A} \cdot \overline{B}$	$\overline{A \cdot B}$	$\overline{A} + \overline{B}$
0	0	1	1	1	1	1	1
0	1	1	0	0	0	1	1
1	0	0	1	0	0	1	1
1	1	0	0	0	0	0	0

B.2 [15] <§B.2> Prove that the two equations for E in the example starting on page B-7 are equivalent by using DeMorgan's theorems and the axioms shown on page B-7.

B.3 [10] <§B.2> Show that there are $2n$ entries in a truth table for a function with n inputs.

B.4 [10] <§B.2> One logic function that is used for a variety of purposes (including within adders and to compute parity) is *exclusive OR*. The output of a two-input exclusive OR function is true only if exactly one of the inputs is true. Show the truth table for a two-input exclusive OR function and implement this function using AND gates, OR gates, and inverters.

B.5 [15] <§B.2> Prove that the NOR gate is universal by showing how to build the AND, OR, and NOT functions using a two-input NOR gate.

B.6 [15] <§B.2> Prove that the NAND gate is universal by showing how to build the AND, OR, and NOT functions using a two-input NAND gate.

B.7 [10] <§§B.2, B.3> Construct the truth table for a four-input odd-parity function (see page B-65 for a description of parity).

B.8 [10] <§§B.2, B.3> Implement the four-input odd-parity function with AND and OR gates using bubbled inputs and outputs.

B.9 [10] <§§B.2, B.3> Implement the four-input odd-parity function with a PLA.

B.10 [15] <§§B.2, B.3> Prove that a two-input multiplexor is also universal by showing how to build the NAND (or NOR) gate using a multiplexor.

B.11 [5] <§§4.2, B.2, B.3> Assume that X consists of 3 bits, x2 x1 x0. Write four logic functions that are true if and only if

- X contains only one 0

- X contains an even number of 0s

- X when interpreted as an unsigned binary number is less than 4

- X when interpreted as a signed (two's complement) number is negative

B.12 [5] <§§4.2, B.2, B.3> Implement the four functions described in Exercise B.11 using a PLA.

B.13 [5] <§§4.2, B.2, B.3> Assume that X consists of 3 bits, x2 x1 x0, and Y consists of 3 bits, y2 y1 y0. Write logic functions that are true if and only if

- X < Y, where X and Y are thought of as unsigned binary numbers

- X < Y, where X and Y are thought of as signed (two's complement) numbers

- X = Y

Use a hierarchical approach that can be extended to larger numbers of bits. Show how can you extend it to 6-bit comparison.

B.14 [5] <§§B.2, B.3> Implement a switching network that has two data inputs (A and B), two data outputs (C and D), and a control input (S). If S equals 1, the network is in pass-through mode, and C should equal A, and D should equal B. If S equals 0, the network is in crossing mode, and C should equal B, and D should equal A.

B.15 [15] <§§B.2, B.3> Derive the product-of-sums representation for E shown on page B-11 starting with the sum-of-products representation. You will need to use DeMorgan's theorems.

B.16 [30] <§§B.2, B.3> Give an algorithm for constructing the sum-of- products representation for an arbitrary logic equation consisting of AND, OR, and NOT. The algorithm should be recursive and should not construct the truth table in the process.

B.17 [5] <§§B.2, B.3> Show a truth table for a multiplexor (inputs A, B, and S; output C), using don't cares to simplify the table where possible.

B.18 [5] <§B.3> What is the function implemented by the following Verilog modules:

```
module FUNC1 (I0, I1, S, out);
      input I0, I1;
      input S;
      output out;
      out = S? I1: I0;
endmodule

module FUNC2 (out,ctl,clk,reset);
      output [7:0] out;
      input ctl, clk, reset;
      reg [7:0] out;
      always @(posedge clk)

      if (reset) begin
                  out <= 8'b0 ;
      end
      else if (ctl) begin
                  out <= out + 1;
      end
      else begin
                  out <= out - 1;
      end
endmodule
```

B.19 [5] <§B.4> The Verilog code on page B-53 is for a D flip-flop. Show the Verilog code for a D latch.

B.20 [10] <§§ B.3, B.4> Write down a Verilog module implementation of a 2-to-4 decoder (and/or encoder).

B.21 [10] <§§B.3, B.4> Given the following logic diagram for an accumulator, write down the Verilog module implementation of it. Assume a positive edge-triggered register and asynchronous Rst.

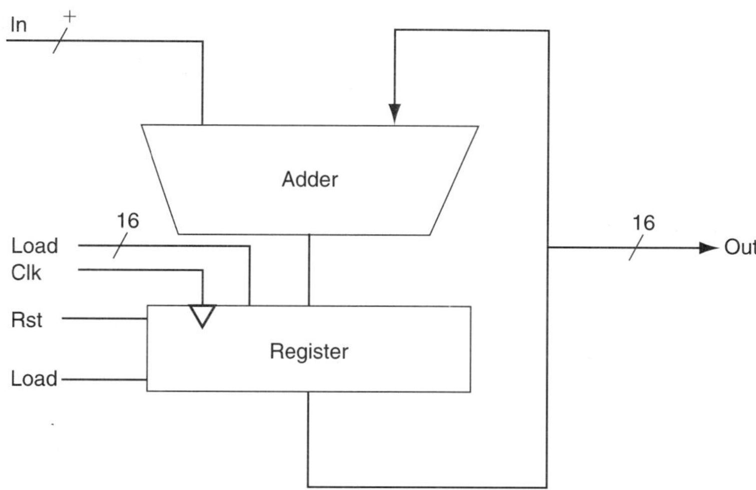

B.22 [20] <§§C3, B.4, B.5> Section 3.3 presents basic operation and possible implementations of multipliers. A basic unit of such implementations is a shift-and-add unit. Show a Verilog implementation for this unit. Show how can you use this unit to build a 32-bit multiplier.

B.23 [20] <§§C3, B.4, B.5> Repeat Exercise B.22, but for an unsigned divider rather than a multiplier.

B.24 [15] <§B.5> The ALU supported set on less than (slt) using just the sign bit of the adder. Let's try a set on less than operation using the values -7_{ten} and 6_{ten}. To make it simpler to follow the example, let's limit the binary representations to 4 bits: 1001_{two} and 0110_{two}.

$$1001_{two} - 0110_{two} = 1001_{two} + 1010_{two} = 0011_{two}$$

This result would suggest that $-7 > 6$, which is clearly wrong. Hence, we must factor in overflow in the decision. Modify the 1-bit ALU in Figure B.5.10 on page B-33 to handle slt correctly. Make your changes on a photocopy of this figure to save time.

B.25 [20] <§B.6> A simple check for overflow during addition is to see if the CarryIn to the most significant bit is not the same as the CarryOut of the most significant bit. Prove that this check is the same as in Figure 3.2.

B.26 [5] <§B.6> Rewrite the equations on page B-44 for a carry-lookahead logic for a 16-bit adder using a new notation. First, use the names for the CarryIn signals of the individual bits of the adder. That is, use c4, c8, c12, ... instead of C1, C2, C3, ... In addition, let Pi,j; mean a propagate signal for bits i to j, and Gi,j; mean a generate signal for bits i to j. For example, the equation

$$C2 = G1 + (P1 \cdot G0) + (P1 \cdot P0 \cdot c0)$$

can be rewritten as

$$c8 = G_{7,4} + (P_{7,4} \cdot G_{3,0}) + (P_{7,4} \cdot P_{3,0} \cdot c0)$$

This more general notation is useful in creating wider adders.

B.27 [15] <§B.6> Write the equations for the carry-lookahead logic for a 64-bit adder using the new notation from Exercise B.26 and using 16-bit adders as building blocks. Include a drawing similar to Figure B.6.3 in your solution.

B.28 [10] <§B.6> Now calculate the relative performance of adders. Assume that hardware corresponding to any equation containing only OR or AND terms, such as the equations for pi and gi on page B-40, takes one time unit T. Equations that consist of the OR of several AND terms, such as the equations for $c1$, $c2$, $c3$, and $c4$ on page B-40, would thus take two time units, 2T. The reason is it would take T to produce the AND terms and then an additional T to produce the result of the OR. Calculate the numbers and performance ratio for 4-bit adders for both ripple carry and carry lookahead. If the terms in equations are further defined by other equations, then add the appropriate delays for those intermediate equations, and continue recursively until the actual input bits of the adder are used in an equation. Include a drawing of each adder labeled with the calculated delays and the path of the worst-case delay highlighted.

B.29 [15] <§B.6> This exercise is similar to Exercise B.28, but this time calculate the relative speeds of a 16-bit adder using ripple carry only, ripple carry of 4-bit groups that use carry lookahead, and the carry-lookahead scheme on page B-39.

B.30 [15] <§B.6> This exercise is similar to Exercises B.28 and B.29, but this time calculate the relative speeds of a 64-bit adder using ripple carry only, ripple carry of 4-bit groups that use carry lookahead, ripple carry of 16-bit groups that use carry lookahead, and the carry-lookahead scheme from Exercise B.27.

B.31 [10] <§B.6> Instead of thinking of an adder as a device that adds two numbers and then links the carries together, we can think of the adder as a hardware device that can add three inputs together (ai, bi, ci) and produce two outputs (s, $ci + 1$). When adding two numbers together, there is little we can do with this observation. When we are adding more than two operands, it is possible to reduce the cost of the carry. The idea is to form two independent sums, called S′ (sum bits) and C′ (carry bits). At the end of the process, we need to add C′ and S′ together using a normal adder. This technique of delaying carry propagation until the end of a sum of numbers is called *carry save addition*. The block drawing on the lower right of Figure B.14.1 (see below) shows the organization, with two levels of carry save adders connected by a single normal adder.

Calculate the delays to add four 16-bit numbers using full carry-lookahead adders versus carry save with a carry-lookahead adder forming the final sum. (The time unit T in Exercise B.28 is the same.)

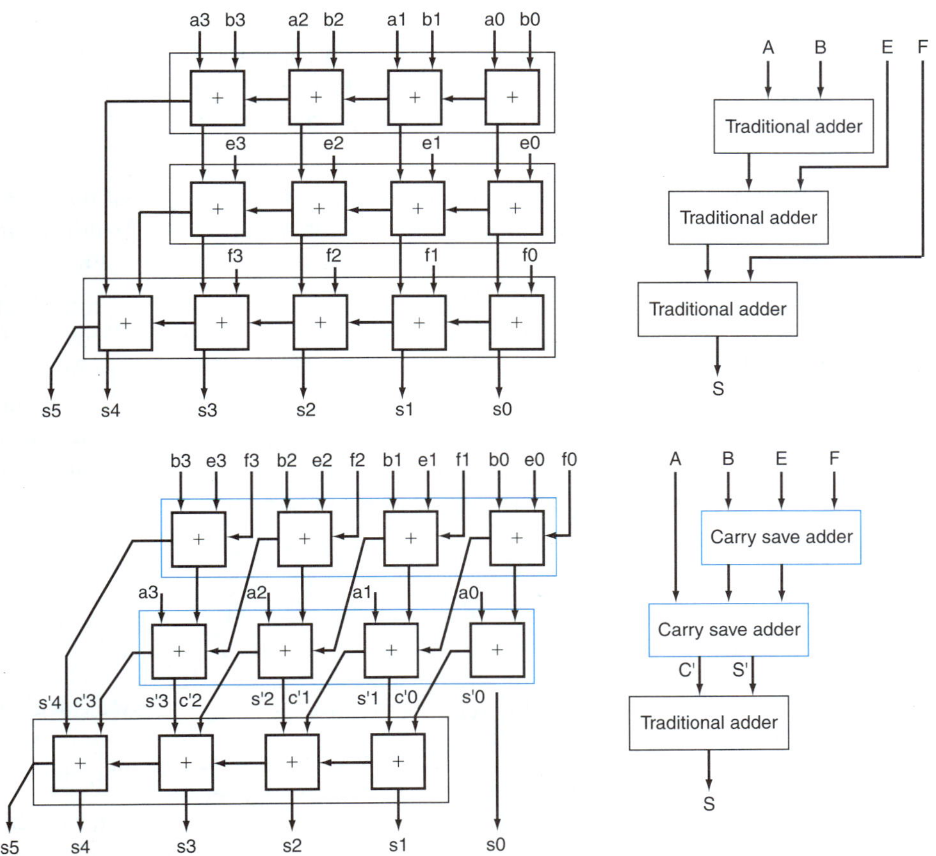

FIGURE B.14.1 Traditional ripple carry and carry save addition of four 4-bit numbers. The details are shown on the left, with the individual signals in lowercase, and the corresponding higher-level blocks are on the right, with collective signals in upper case. Note that the sum of four n-bit numbers can take $n + 2$ bits.

B.32 [20] <§B.6> Perhaps the most likely case of adding many numbers at once in a computer would be when trying to multiply more quickly by using many adders to add many numbers in a single clock cycle. Compared to the multiply algorithm in Chapter 3, a carry save scheme with many adders could multiply more than 10 times faster. This exercise estimates the cost and speed of a combinational multiplier to multiply two positive 16-bit numbers. Assume that you have 16 intermediate terms M15, M14, …, M0, called *partial products*, that contain the multiplicand ANDed with multiplier bits m15, m14, …, m0. The idea is to use carry save adders to reduce the n operands into $2n/3$ in parallel groups of three, and do this repeatedly until you get two large numbers to add together with a traditional adder.

First, show the block organization of the 16-bit carry save adders to add these 16 terms, as shown on the right in Figure B.14.1. Then calculate the delays to add these 16 numbers. Compare this time to the iterative multiplication scheme in Chapter 3 but only assume 16 iterations using a 16-bit adder that has full carry lookahead whose speed was calculated in Exercise B.29.

B.33 [10] <§B.6> There are times when we want to add a collection of numbers together. Suppose you wanted to add four 4-bit numbers (A, B, E, F) using 1-bit full adders. Let's ignore carry lookahead for now. You would likely connect the 1-bit adders in the organization at the top of Figure B.14.1. Below the traditional organization is a novel organization of full adders. Try adding four numbers using both organizations to convince yourself that you get the same answer.

B.34 [5] <§B.6> First, show the block organization of the 16-bit carry save adders to add these 16 terms, as shown in Figure B.14.1. Assume that the time delay through each 1-bit adder is 2T. Calculate the time of adding four 4-bit numbers to the organization at the top versus the organization at the bottom of Figure B.14.1.

B.35 [5] <§B.8> Quite often, you would expect that given a timing diagram containing a description of changes that take place on a data input D and a clock input C (as in Figures B.8.3 and B.8.6 on pages B-52 and B-54, respectively), there would be differences between the output waveforms (Q) for a D latch and a D flip-flop. In a sentence or two, describe the circumstances (e.g., the nature of the inputs) for which there would not be any difference between the two output waveforms.

B.36 [5] <§B.8> Figure B.8.8 on page B-55 illustrates the implementation of the register file for the MIPS datapath. Pretend that a new register file is to be built, but that there are only two registers and only one read port, and that each register has only 2 bits of data. Redraw Figure B.8.8 so that every wire in your diagram corresponds to only 1 bit of data (unlike the diagram in Figure B.8.8, in which some wires are 5 bits and some wires are 32 bits). Redraw the registers using D flip-flops. You do not need to show how to implement a D flip-flop or a multiplexor.

B.37 [10] <§B.10> A friend would like you to build an "electronic eye" for use as a fake security device. The device consists of three lights lined up in a row, controlled by the outputs Left, Middle, and Right, which, if asserted, indicate that a light should be on. Only one light is on at a time, and the light "moves" from left to right and then from right to left, thus scaring away thieves who believe that the device is monitoring their activity. Draw the graphical representation for the finite-state machine used to specify the electronic eye. Note that the rate of the eye's movement will be controlled by the clock speed (which should not be too great) and that there are essentially no inputs.

B.38 [10] <§B.10> Assign state numbers to the states of the finite-state machine you constructed for Exercise B.37 and write a set of logic equations for each of the outputs, including the next-state bits.

B.39 [15] <§§B.2, B.8, B.10> Construct a 3-bit counter using three D flip-flops and a selection of gates. The inputs should consist of a signal that resets the counter to 0, called *reset*, and a signal to increment the counter, called *inc*. The outputs should be the value of the counter. When the counter has value 7 and is incremented, it should wrap around and become 0.

B.40 [20] <§B.10> A *Gray code* is a sequence of binary numbers with the property that no more than 1 bit changes in going from one element of the sequence to another. For example, here is a 3-bit binary Gray code: 000, 001, 011, 010, 110, 111, 101, and 100. Using three D flip-flops and a PLA, construct a 3-bit Gray code counter that has two inputs: *reset*, which sets the counter to 000, and *inc*, which makes the counter go to the next value in the sequence. Note that the code is cyclic, so that the value after 100 in the sequence is 000.

B.41 [25] <§B.10> We wish to add a yellow light to our traffic light example on page B-68. We will do this by changing the clock to run at 0.25 Hz (a 4-second clock cycle time), which is the duration of a yellow light. To prevent the green and red lights from cycling too fast, we add a 30-second timer. The timer has a single input, called *TimerReset*, which restarts the timer, and a single output, called *TimerSignal*, which indicates that the 30-second period has expired. Also, we must redefine the traffic signals to include yellow. We do this by defining two out put signals for each light: green and yellow. If the output NS green is asserted, the green light is on; if the output NSyellow is asserted, the yellow light is on. If both signals are off, the red light is on. Do *not* assert both the green and yellow signals at the same time, since American drivers will certainly be confused, even if European drivers understand what this means! Draw the graphical representation for the finite-state machine for this improved controller. Choose names for the states that are *different* from the names of the outputs.

B.42 [15] <§B.10> Write down the next-state and output-function tables for the traffic light controller described in Exercise B.41.

B.43 [15] <§§B.2, B.10> Assign state numbers to the states in the traf-fic light example of Exercise B.41 and use the tables of Exercise B.42 to write a set of logic equations for each of the outputs, including the next-state outputs.

B.44 [15] <§§B.3, B.10> Implement the logic equations of Exercise B.43 as a PLA.

§B.2, page B-8: No. If $A = 1$, $C = 1$, $B = 0$, the first is true, but the second is false.
§B.3, page B-20: C.
§B.4, page B-22: They are all exactly the same.
§B.4, page B-26: $A = 0$, $B = 1$.
§B.5, page B-38: 2.
§B.6, page B-47: 1.
§B.8, page B-58: c.
§B.10, page B-72: b.
§B.11, page B-77: b.

**Answers to
Check Yourself**

Index

F